Current Biography Yearbook 2020

H. W. Wilson

A Division of EBSCO Information Services, Inc.

Ipswich, Massachusetts

GREY HOUSE PUBLISHING

EIGHTY-FIRST ANNUAL CUMULATION—2020

International Standard Serial No. 0084-9499

International Standard Book No. 978-1-68217-709-9

Library of Congress Catalog Card No. 40-27432

Current Biography Yearbook, 2020, published by Grey House Publishing, Inc., Amenia, NY, under exclusive license from EBSCO Information Services, Inc.

PRINTED IN CANADA

CONTENTS

LIST OF BIOGRAPHICAL SKETCHES

List of Biographical Sketches

List of Biographical Sketches

List of Biographical Sketches

LIST OF OBITUARIES

List of Obituaries

Current Biography Yearbook 2020

Jennifer Aaker

Born: January 15,1967
Occupation: Social psychologist and professor

Jennifer Aaker is an expert in a variety of socially relevant topics, including the ways in which time and money can contribute to enduring happiness, how individuals can make choices that lend their lives purpose and meaning, how emotion affects physical well-being, the importance of storytelling, the power of humor, and how technology can beneficially impact society. In addition to having taught such popular courses as Designing for AI: Cultivating Human Well-Being and Humor: Serious Business at Stanford Graduate School of Business, Aaker has served as a successful brand consultant to major technology firms like Facebook, Adobe, and AOL. She advises them to be authentic and to leverage the concept of happiness to both attract customers and raise the productivity of employees. "The idea of brands enabling happiness and providing greater meaning in the world is powerful," she explained to Nancy Cook for *Fast Company* (28 Feb. 2011). "People have an aversion to anything that feels overly manufactured."

Aaker's work has appeared in the *Washington Post*, the *Economist*, the *New York Times*, and *Forbes*, among other high-profile outlets, as well as in scholarly journals. Additionally, she has coauthored books aimed at the public, including *The Dragonfly Effect* (2010), a primer on driving societal change through social media. Recognized by the Society for Consumer Psychology (SCP) with its 2013 Distinguished Scientific Contribution Award, she was also named the MBA Professor of the Year 2018 by *Poets & Quants*.

EARLY LIFE AND EDUCATION

Born on January 15, 1967, Jennifer Aaker was raised with her two sisters in California. Her father, David, was a professor of marketing strategy at the Haas School of Business, part of the University of California, Berkeley, until his retirement in 2000. He authored several seminal books—including *Building Strong Brands* (1996), *Brand Portfolio Strategy: Creating Relevance, Differentiation, Energy, Leverage, and Clarity* (2004), and *Aaker on Branding: 20*

Photo by JSFarman via Wikimedia Commons

Principles That Drive Success (2014)—and is often referred to as the "father of modern branding." Her mother, Kay, was an elementary school teacher who also volunteered extensively with hospice patients. "I was lucky to grow up with two remarkable parents and role models," Aaker told John A. Byrne for *Poets & Quants* (1 Jan. 2019). "It was my desire to have an impact in the world, serving others and having impact on the lives of others."

While interviewers have often highlighted the influence that her father must have had on her future career path and focus, Aaker has also pointed out how her mother's work and philosophies shaped her own thinking. "I grew up hearing stories around the dinner table of people dying," she recalled in an essay she wrote for *Brilliant Minds* (31 Jan. 2020). She explained that because of her mother's volunteer work, "Over the years, we heard stories of love, meaning and purpose. But [we] also heard stories of regret—what people wish for when they are on their deathbed." Later, she would incorporate that experience into hundreds of studies about the relationship between meaning and happiness and the differences between the two.

EARLY LIFE AND EDUCATION

In 1989 Aaker earned an undergraduate degree in psychology from Berkeley, where she was a member of the Psi Chi honor society. Her choice of major had come as something of a surprise to her family. "I thought about what I was disproportionately good at," she told Byrne. "I was always strong at math and science so becoming a social scientist and using social science in ways that I could positively impact others didn't come early."

Aaker went on to enroll in Stanford Graduate School of Business. She left in 1995 after receiving her doctoral degree in marketing, with a minor in psychology. During her doctoral studies, she was named a Jaedicke Scholar, an award honoring longtime professor and dean Robert K. Jaedicke. Her dissertation was also a finalist for the American Marketing Association Doctoral Dissertation Award. In it, she delved into brand personality, the human characteristics attributed to a brand in an effort to appeal to consumers. She posited that sincerity, excitement, competence, sophistication, and ruggedness form a framework with which to describe and measure the symbolic impact of product brands. In 1997 she published the framework in the *Journal of Marketing Research* (*JMR*), and that paper, "Dimensions of Brand Personality" continues to be cited for its insight into how brands communicate their values and intentions.

BEGINNING A CAREER IN ACADEMIA

Upon graduating, Aaker became an assistant professor at the University of California, Los Angeles (UCLA) Anderson School of Management. There she taught courses in marketing management as well as consumer behavior and regularly won teaching awards. Despite her prowess in the classroom and the satisfaction she got from learning alongside her students, she considered herself a relative introvert. She particularly relished conducting research. During her tenure at UCLA, she received multiple grants aimed at furthering her work, including an Academic Senate Grant and a CIBER (Centers for International Business Education and Research) Grant.

In 1999, Aaker accepted an assistant professorship at her alma mater Stanford. There she steadily climbed the academic ladder, being promoted to associate professor in 2001, full professor in 2004, and General Atlantic Professor of Marketing in 2005. From 2006 to 2008 she was also affiliated with Berkeley's Haas School of Business, where her classes focused on creativity and innovation in marketing and where she held the titles of Thomas W. Tusher Professor and Xerox Distinguished Professor of Knowledge.

Some of Aaker's popular course offerings at Stanford included How to Tell a Story, which stressed to her MBA students the importance of creating a compelling narrative when developing businesses and brands. "Research shows our brains are not hard-wired to understand logic or retain facts for very long. Our brains are wired to understand and retain stories," she told Brianne Carlon Rush for the *Guardian* (28 Aug. 2014). "A story is a journey that moves the listener, and when the listener goes on that journey they feel different and the result is persuasion and sometimes action."

THINKING ABOUT HAPPINESS AND MEANING

By the mid-2000s Aaker had begun focusing some of her research on the topic of happiness, Through considering how both money and time factor into happiness, she discovered the importance of being intentional in how and with whom time, a rather scant and valuable resource, is spent to potentially maximize happiness. Additionally, she found that the definition of happiness shifts with age: young people feel happiest when they are excited, and older people equate happiness with peace and contentment. In 2010, she began teaching Designing (for) Happiness at Stanford to help students to develop stronger businesses and brands by exploring and better understanding the concept of happiness. Cook wrote the following year, "Offering a happiness class to future masters of the universe at one of the country's leading business schools does sound a bit touchy-feely. Yet, last fall, 80 of these type-A students signed up for Aaker's graduate-level course . . . with another 100 clamoring to get in."

Motivated by her work on the link between happiness and meaning derived from impactful acts and happiness, Aaker wanted to provide a guide to help others achieve such goals. Consequently, she cowrote *The Dragonfly Effect: Quick, Effective, and Powerful Ways to Use Social Media to Drive Social Change* (2010) with her husband, the venture capitalist Andy Smith. The title is derived from dragonflies' ability to use four wings in concert to propel themselves in a desired direction—a metaphor, the authors felt, for how small, integrated acts can lead to transformative action and positive impact. In the book, Aaker and Smith outline four essential components of the "Dragonfly effect": having a specific, measurable goal; creating authentic, memorable content that will attract attention; encouraging engagement through appeals to higher emotions like empathy and compassion; and empowering people to act. A companion volume, *Dragonfly Effect Workbook: The Power of Stories* (2013), cowritten with Smith and Barbara McCarthy, provides hands-on exercises and further psychological insight.

Further advocating the potential positive power of social media and networking, Aaker put those principles to work in cofounding 100K

Cheeks. The Stanford initiative was launched with the aim of registering one hundred thousand donors, particularly of South Asian descent, in the national bone marrow registry.

SHARING INSIGHTS ON HUMOR AND MORE

Aaker instructed on topics such as building innovative brands and rethinking purpose between 2010 and 2017 and received the SCP's Distinguished Scientific Contribution Award in 2013. Joining with Naomi Bagdonas, she began offering another popular course at Stanford called Humor: Serious Business in 2017. "By the end of the class, [students] experience a profound shift—and report having much more laughter in their lives," Aaker wrote for *Brilliant Minds*. "They simply noticed opportunities for humor that would have otherwise passed them by."

Having become increasingly interested in making a social science impact through technology as well as business, she also started coteaching Designing for AI: Cultivating Human Well-Being with a Stanford computer science professor in 2019. "To harness technology to help us, we have to understand how to push the next generation of AI [artificial intelligence] systems away from addictive-yet-empty activities and towards meaningful pursuits," she wrote for *Brilliant Minds*. In recognition of her years of innovative work in education, *Poets & Quants* named her its 2018 MBA Professor of the Year in 2019.

Aaker, aware of her own misperceptions about the possibilities of humor in different aspects of life, reteamed with Bagdonas to write a book about humor, specifically in the workplace. Titled *Humor, Seriously: Why Humor Is a Secret Weapon in Business and Life*, it was prepared for publication in 2020. "People hold the false belief that humor is the opposite of serious," she explained in her *Brilliant Minds* essay. "In fact, when people use humor at work, they are perceived as higher in status, more competent, and more confident."

PERSONAL LIFE

Aaker and Smith have three children: twin sons, Cooper and Devon, and daughter, Tea Sloane. They live in Northern California. While she has garnered a number of laurels for her work, she has claimed that she considers coming out on top in a dance competition in the early 1980s as one of her most poignant achievements.

Despite her professional focus on happiness, Aaker has said she does not always prioritize her own joy, realizing that sometimes day-to-day activities and occurrences will interfere. "The knowledge that happiness shifts doesn't allow you to put a great premium on it," she asserted to Cook.

SUGGESTED READING

Aaker, Jennifer. "Redefining Purpose." *Brilliant Minds*, 31 Jan. 2020, brilliantminds.co/brilliant-voices/a-new-story-redefining-purpose. Accessed 2 July 2020.

Byrne, John A. "MBA Prof of the Year: Stanford's Jennifer Aaker." *Poets & Quants*, 1 Jan. 2019, poetsandquants.com/2019/01/01/mba-prof-of-the-year-stanfords-jennifer-aaker. Accessed 2 July 2020.

Cook, Nancy. "The Corporate Pursuit of Happiness." *Fast Company*, 28 Feb. 2011, www.fastcompany.com/1722637/corporate-pursuit-happiness. Accessed 2 July 2020.

David, Avril. "Names You Need to Know: The Dragonfly Effect." *Forbes*, 17 May 2011, www.forbes.com/sites/avrildavid/2011/05/17/names-you-need-to-know-the-dragonfly-effect/#6952f1a26a09. Accessed 2 July 2020.

"Jennifer Aaker." *Stanford Graduate School of Business*, www.gsb.stanford.edu/faculty-research/faculty/jennifer-lynn-aaker. Accessed 10 July 2020.

Rush, Brianne Carlon. "Science of Storytelling: Why and How to Use It in Your Marketing." *The Guardian*, 28 Aug. 2014, www.theguardian.com/media-network/media-network-blog/2014/aug/28/science-storytelling-digital-marketing. Accessed 2 July 2020.

—*Mari Rich*

Abiy Ahmed Ali

Date of birth: August 15, 1976
Occupation: Politician

When Abiy Ahmed Ali was named prime minister of Ethiopia, Africa's second-most populous country in 2018, he became the country's first Oromo prime minister (the marginalized Oromos, the largest ethnic group in the country, constitute just over one-third of Ethiopia's population). Abiy, then forty-two, also became the youngest leader in Africa. Upon taking office, Abiy implemented a number of liberal-minded changes aimed at soothing the unrest that had plagued the country since 2015. He freed sixty thousand political prisoners including journalists, initiated dialogue with political opposition parties, and appointed women to half of the positions in his cabinet. In 2019, he received the Nobel Peace Prize for his reforms, chief among them ending a bloody twenty-year conflict with neighboring Eritrea.

Abiy's politics are rooted in a philosophy he calls *medemer*, an Amharic word that means "coming together" or "adding up." In Ethiopia, coming together is easier said than done given a long history of strife among the country's

Photo by Aron Simeneh via Wikimedia Commons

many ethnic groups. That history was codified in Ethiopia's 1995 constitution, which created ethnically based states. "Over the years [this system] has infused politics with a kind of sectarian fervor," Tobias Hagmann and Kjetil Tronvoll wrote for the *New York Times* (17 Oct. 2019). Abiy published a book on the subject, *Medemer* (2012; English translation, 2019), and, as prime minister, aimed to use the philosophy to unify Ethiopia's disparate factions. "Closing the door is the worst approach," he told Somini Sengupta for the *New York Times* (17 Sept. 2018). However, his liberal-minded reforms appeared to have the unintended consequence of reigniting divisions; sectarian violence in Ethiopia displaced more than 2.1 million people by the end of 2018 and another half million in the first half of 2019, according to the Internal Displacement Monitoring Centre.

EARLY LIFE AND EDUCATION

Abiy Ahmed Ali was born on August 15, 1976, and grew up in the village of Beshasha in central Ethiopia. His father, Ahmed Ali, was a Muslim Oromo who had thirteen children by four wives. His mother, Tezeta Wolde, was an Amhara who converted from Orthodox Christianity to Islam when she married. Their youngest child, Abiy was called Abiyot, a common nickname meaning "revolution," because he was born in the wake of the 1974 revolution in which the monarchy was overthrown.

Abiy began his studies at Beshasha Primary School. His mother voiced her dreams for him early. When he was seven, he recalled to Sengupta, she whispered in his ear before school: "You're unique, my son. You will end up in the palace. So when you go to school, bear in mind that one day you'll be someone [who] will serve the nation." After the sixth grade, Abiy attended school in nearby Agaro. "Abiy was different from most of the children of his age," his eldest sister, Tiruye Ahmed, recalled to Dawit Endeshaw for the Addis Ababa *Reporter Ethiopia* (31 Mar. 2018). "They wanted to become rich coffee traders, but Abiy was quite different."

Abiy became politically conscious as a young teen, just before the fall of the Derg, the military junta that had ruled Ethiopia since the socialist revolution, in 1991. Around that time, his father and brother Kedir Ahmed were jailed for their political affiliation; Kedir was later killed, presumably for his politics. Kedir's death had a profound effect on Abiy, who joined the armed struggle with the Oromo People's Democratic Organization (OPDO) by his mid-teens. "Losing his brother at that age was a turning point in Abiy's life," Abiy's childhood friend Miftah Hudin Aba Jebel told Dawit Endeshaw. "I mean we were young and I remember one night Abiy asking me to join the struggle. To be honest, it was difficult for me to understand what he was saying." In 1991 a coalition of political parties—including the OPDO—took power under the umbrella of the Ethiopian People's Revolutionary Democratic Front (EPRDF).

MILITARY CAREER AND CYBERSECURITY

Abiy joined the new Ethiopian National Defense Forces in the early 1990s and soon went to Rwanda as a United Nations (UN) peacekeeper in the wake of that country's genocide. When he returned, he served as a radio operator in the Ethiopian-Eritrean War, which began in 1998 over a border dispute between Ethiopia and Eritrea, then newly independent from Ethiopia. Despite the war ostensibly concluding in 2000, hostilities remained between the two countries.

While still in the military, Abiy studied computer engineering at MicroLink Information Technology College in Addis Ababa, the Ethiopian capital. He left the military in 2007, having achieved the rank of lieutenant colonel, and cofounded the government cybersecurity firm Information Network Security Agency (INSA) in 2008. During that time, he also served on the boards of the state-run Ethio Telecom and Ethiopian TV.

Abiy left INSA in 2010 and in 2011 received a master's degree in transformational leadership and change from the University of Greenwich through their partner school, the International Leadership Institute (ILI) in Addis Ababa. He completed a doctorate through the Institute for Peace and Security Studies at Addis Ababa University in 2017. His dissertation was titled "Social Capital and Its Role in Traditional Conflict Resolution in Ethiopia: The Case of Inter-Religious Conflict in Jimma

Zone State." It was inspired by another important moment in Abiy's life when, in 2010, he was asked by the federal government to resolve tensions between Muslims and Christians in his hometown of Beshasha.

EARLY POLITICAL CAREER

In 2010, Abiy won a seat in parliament. During his tenure he oversaw the construction of a new high school and a hospital in Agaro. In 2013, he became the director general of the new Science and Technology Information Center (STIC). In 2015, he joined the executive ranks of the OPDO and was named the science and technology minister. He only served the position for one year, forfeiting the job in the melee following the 2015 elections in which the ruling coalition won every parliamentary seat. (Despite the liberal democratic principles outlined in the 1995 constitution, the EPRDF ran the country with an authoritarian grip, outlawing opposition parties and reportedly rigging elections.) Ethiopians in the state of Oromia, led by frustrated Oromo youth, rose up in protest. The EPRDF issued a brutal crackdown, and between 2016 and 2018 a thousand protesters were killed and over twenty thousand were imprisoned. In 2016, Abiy directed the Oromia Urban Development and Housing Office and then headed the ODPO secretariat, as protests continued to grow.

In hopes of relieving tensions, Ethiopian Prime Minister Hailemariam Desalegn agreed to release thousands of political prisoners and resigned from his post and party leadership in February 2018. After about six weeks of political negotiations among coalition parties, Abiy was named prime minister in late March. Among the possible candidates, Abiy was likely the most popular, notable for his ability to gain support among protesters while maintaining his role as a government insider. "The short term significance of this choice is that it will calm things down," Mekonnen Mengesha, a political analyst and Wolkite University lecturer, told Hadra Ahmed and Jina Moore for the *New York Times* (28 Mar. 2018). "But in the long run the main question is, is this move just shuffling leaders, or is it a systematic change from the administration?"

After taking office on April 2, 2018, Abiy issued a series of liberal reforms and decrees that surprised many onlookers. He narrowly survived an assassination attempt that June. Then, in July he and Eritrean President Isaias Afwerki declared peace, ending a twenty-year conflict in which at least eighty thousand people had died. The peace agreement reopened the border between the two countries, allowing Ethiopia access to a vital Eritrean port on the Red Sea, and restored diplomatic relations. Abiy also released thousands of political prisoners, reversed the ban on opposition groups, allowed political

exiles to return home, and cracked down on government and military corruption. In October Abiy appointed women to half of the positions in his cabinet—including the newly formed Ministry of Peace—and to the presidency and the chief justice of the Supreme Court, both historic firsts. He also moved to privatize certain state-run enterprises and strengthen the economy.

NOBEL PEACE PRIZE

In 2019 Abiy exported his brand of medemer, helping to broker a power-sharing agreement in Sudan that August, but unrest was simmering in Ethiopia. In June there was an attempted coup in the Amhara region. Meanwhile, the Committee to Protect Journalists (CPJ) reported that the Ethiopian government was blocking internet access and arresting journalists in an area of Sidama separatism. In October Abiy won the Nobel Peace Prize for his reforms in Ethiopia and for ending Ethiopia's war with Eritrea. Weeks after the announcement, however, protests broke out in Addis Ababa and Oromia, in which an estimated eighty-six people were killed and hundreds injured. The protests were led by influential media owner Jawar Mohammed, a critic of Abiy who claimed the security forces were plotting to arrest or kill him. Abiy, who was in Russia at the time, drew criticism for his lack of response to the protests. This criticism grew louder when he received the Nobel Peace Prize in Oslo, Norway, that December and conspicuously avoided any interaction with the press. In his Nobel lecture, Abiy warned of the perils of social media being used to sow discord. Some interpreted this theme to be a reference to Mohammed, who had a large online following.

Around the same time, Abiy disbanded the ethnic coalition EPRDF in favor of a new national unity party called the Prosperity Party. However, observers feared that rather than heal divisions, the move threatened to worsen tensions over ethnic federalism. In January 2020 one of the four EPRDF parties refused to join.

Sectarian violence continued to escalate into 2020, particularly on college campuses. In December 2019 armed men kidnapped dozens of students, many of them of Amharas, from Dembi Dollo University in Oromia. With twenty-one students rescued and at least twelve missing, thousands of Ethiopians took to the streets in late January 2020 to demand action from Abiy and the Ethiopian government, which had released scant details about the abductions.

These events were particularly troubling given the national election scheduled for August 2020, postponed from its original May date. One of Abiy's first decrees was a promise of multiparty elections. The 2020 election would be the first truly competitive election in Ethiopia. "I'm not a king," Abiy told Sengupta. "My ultimate objective is to see democratic elections in Ethiopia. If that happened, I'll feel I fulfilled my objective."

PERSONAL LIFE

Abiy and his wife, Zinash Tayachew Bere, met in the National Defense Forces. They have three daughters together, Deborah, Rakeb, and Amen, and adopted a son, Million. Bere and their daughters lived for a time in Colorado before Abiy's appointment to the premiership. Abiy is a convert to Protestantism.

SUGGESTED READING

Ahmed, Hadra, and Jina Moore. "Ethiopia Seeks Calm with a New Leader." *The New York Times*, 28 Mar. 2018, www.nytimes.com/2018/03/28/world/africa/ethiopia-prime-minister-oromo.html. Accessed 10 Feb. 2020.

Endeshaw, Dawit. "The Rise of Abiy 'Abiyot' Ahmed." *The Reporter Ethiopia*, 31 Mar. 2018, www.thereporterethiopia.com/article/rise-abiy-abiyot-ahmed. Accessed 8 Feb. 2020.

Hagmann, Tobias, and Kjetil Tronvoll. "Abiy Ahmed Won the Nobel Peace Prize. Now He Needs to Earn It." *The New York Times*, 17 Oct. 2019, www.nytimes.com/2019/10/17/opinion/abiy-ahmed-nobel-peace-prize.html. Accessed 10 Feb. 2020.

Sengupta, Somini. "Can Ethiopia's New Leader, a Political Insider, Change It from the Inside Out?" *The New York Times*, 17 Sept. 2018, www.nytimes.com/2018/09/17/world/africa/ethiopia-abiy-ahmed.html. Accessed 8 Feb. 2020.

Van Eyssen, Benita. "Does Ethiopian Nobel Laureate Abiy Ahmed Have New Enemies?" *DW*, 10 Dec. 2019, www.dw.com/en/does-ethiopian-nobel-laureate-abiy-ahmed-have-new-enemies/a-51612010. Accessed 19 Feb. 2020.

—*Molly Hagan*

Ronald Acuña Jr.

Born: December 18, 1997
Occupation: Baseball player

Throughout the history of Major League Baseball (MLB), scouts and coaches have always yearned to discover the rare five-tool player—one who is able to hit for both average and power, possesses fielding and arm strength, and runs the bases with speed. Venezuelan outfielder Ronald Acuña Jr., who broke into the big leagues in 2018 with the Atlanta Braves, not only lived up to his billing as true five-tool phenom but also rapidly

established himself as "one of the premier players" in the game, as Matt Ehalt noted for *Yahoo! Sports* (17 Aug. 2019). Signed by the Braves as a teenager in 2014, Acuña spent just three seasons in the team's minor-league system before making his major league debut. He went on to win the 2018 National League (NL) Rookie of the Year Award after leading the Braves and all league rookies with 26 home runs.

Acuña had an even stronger sophomore campaign in 2019, which saw him earn his first career All-Star selection and enter the prestigious 30-30 club—so-named for a player who has hit at least 30 home runs and stolen at least 30 bases in a season. Along the way he set several "youngest-ever" MLB and Braves franchise records. This early success led many baseball analysts and fans to dub Acuña the heir apparent to Los Angeles Angels superstar Mike Trout as baseball's best player. "He's blessed with talent," the Braves' third base coach Ron Washington told Ehalt. "He works at it. He's a special kid. Every day he does something that leaves you saying, 'Jesus, that's unbelievable.'"

EARLY LIFE

Ronald José Acuña Blanco Jr., the oldest of four sons, was born on December 18, 1997, in La Guaira, Venezuela. He was raised in La Sabana, a small coastal town located roughly sixty-five miles east of the Venezuelan capital of Caracas. His family had deep baseball roots. His grandfather, Romualdo "Romo" Blanco, was a pitcher in the Houston Astros organization, and his father, Ronald Acuña Sr., played in the minor leagues for eight years (1999–2006) as

Photo by Ian D'Andrea on Flickr

an outfielder for the New York Mets, Toronto Blue Jays, and Milwaukee Brewers organizations. Meanwhile, his cousins Kelvim Escobar, Alcides Escobar, Edwin Escobar, and José Escobar all played in the major leagues, with Kelvim and Alcides enjoying notable success; Kelvim won 101 career games over a twelve-year pitching career with the Blue Jays and Angels, and Alcides was an All-Star shortstop who was part of the Kansas City Royals' 2015 World Series–winning team.

Growing up in La Sabana, which has its own rich baseball tradition, Acuña naturally developed a love for the sport at an early age. He started playing organized baseball at around the age of five, aspiring to follow in the footsteps of his cousins. Kelvim and Alcides both took him under their wings; Kelvim once brought him to Yankee Stadium in New York City, and on another occasion, Alcides invited him to MLB spring training in Arizona. During the MLB off-season many of Acuña's cousins played in the Venezuelan Winter League, and he would seize any opportunity to attend their games. "I loved watching them play," he recalled to Ehalt. "I was constantly pleading with them to go along and watch them."

The biggest influence on Acuña's baseball development, however, was his father, who instilled in him the importance of hard work, discipline, and humility. Acuña Sr.—who, despite showing promise as a player, never progressed past double-A ball—warned his son that natural skills would not compensate for a lack of hustle or a bad attitude. Acuña heeded that advice as a youth when his slim frame initially prevented him from standing out among his peers. He began weightlifting to develop his power, and by age fourteen he was a top local prospect. In an article for *La Vida Baseball* (25 Apr. 2018), Acuña Sr. told César Augusto Márquez that his son "was born with talent. But the little things that you do to polish that talent, he learned from all of us."

ROAD TO THE MAJORS

Acuña's budding talent caught the attention of several MLB organizations. However, as a teen he was still relatively undersized, which discouraged some scouts. In July 2014, he signed as an international free agent with the Atlanta Braves for a relatively modest $100,000 signing bonus. He entered the Braves' minor league system with a humble, workmanlike mindset. "The truth is, the bonus doesn't make the player—and it doesn't matter what a team gives you, you work hard and that's what they want," Acuña explained to Jesse Sanchez for *MLB.com* (June 30, 2018). "You have to work hard every day."

In 2015, at age seventeen, Acuña made his professional debut with the Braves' rookie-level affiliate, the Gulf Coast Braves. Later that season he was promoted to the team's advanced rookie-level squad, the Danville Braves. Appearing in a combined 55 games, he batted .269 with 22 extra-base hits, 18 runs batted in (RBIs), and 16 stolen bases. He began to show more flashes of his five-tool potential during the 2016 season, when, despite spending two separate stints on the injured list, he hit .311 with 4 home runs and 18 RBIs in 40 games with the single-A Rome Braves.

Acuña emerged as one of the top prospects in all of baseball in 2017, when he hit .325 with 21 home runs, 82 RBIs, and 44 stolen bases across three different minor league levels. At the conclusion of that season, the Braves assigned him to the Peoria Javelinas in the Arizona Fall League, which is often referred to as a "finishing school" for top baseball prospects. With the Javelinas, Acuña continued to impress, posting a 1.053 on-base plus slugging percentage (OPS) in 23 games en route to helping the team win the league championship. He was named the league's Most Valuable Player (MVP) after leading all players in runs (22), home runs (7), extra-base hits (12), and total bases (53). At nineteen years old, he became the youngest player ever to earn that honor.

After being named minor league player of the year by both *Baseball America* and *USA Today*, Acuña entered the 2018 season ranked by many as the top MLB prospect. He was invited to participate in the Braves' annual spring training, where he only bolstered his case for a promotion to the team's big-league squad: in 16 games, he hit a scorching .432 with 4 home runs and 11 RBIs. Despite that performance, the Braves reassigned Acuña to the triple-A Gwinnett Stripers one week before the 2018 season. The move was criticized by some observers as a manipulation of MLB service time rules, as by waiting to promote a prospect, a team could earn an extra year on that player's rookie contract.

MLB DEBUT AND ROOKIE OF THE YEAR

Undaunted by his relegation back to the minors Acuña kept his sights on becoming the best player he could be. He continued to be hyped by sportswriters and fans, with his all-around abilities earning him comparisons to Braves legend and Hall-of-Famer Hank Aaron. For his part, Acuña noted his desire to match a more contemporary baseball superstar, one almost universally recognized as the best then playing, and perhaps of all time. "I want to be like Mike Trout," he told Eddie Matz for *ESPN.com* (23 Apr. 2018). "I want to be at that level. I want to be great. I want to get to the big leagues, stay in the big leagues and play for a lot of years."

After appearing in 23 games with the Stripers, Acuña was called up to the Braves on April 25, 2018. That day he made his major-league debut against the Cincinnati Reds, collecting one hit in five at-bats and scoring the game-tying run in a 5–4 Braves win. At the time of his promotion, Acuña, at twenty years old, became the youngest player in the majors (a distinction he would relinquish to the Washington Nationals' Juan Soto just a month later). He proceeded to post modest numbers during the first half of the 2018 season, hitting .249 with seven homers and a .742 OPS over 184 plate appearances.

However, after improving his plate discipline, making several mechanical adjustments to his swing, and moving to the leadoff spot in the batting order, Acuña transformed into a bona fide five-tool star. Following the 2018 All-Star break, he hit .322 with 19 home runs and a 1.028 OPS in 68 games. That August he made history by becoming the youngest MLB player ever to hit a home run in five consecutive games, which also tied a Braves franchise record for most consecutive games with a homer. He recorded 11 home runs in total that month, to go along with a .336 batting average, 25 runs scored, and 38 hits, which helped him claim his first NL Player of the Month honor. During Acuña's record run, teammate Ender Inciarte declared to Matthew Leach for *MLB.com* (17 Aug. 2018), "He's the best leadoff hitter I've ever seen. He's the best player I've ever seen. He's just unbelievable."

Acuña's historic performance helped galvanize a youthful Braves team that unexpectedly won the NL East Division with a 90–72 record. (The Braves ultimately lost to the Los Angeles Dodgers in the NL Division play-off series.) Acuña finished his first major-league season with a .293 batting average, 64 RBIs, a .917 OPS, and a team- and rookie-best 26 home runs in 111 games. For much of the season he had been considered in a close race with Soto for NL Rookie of the Year honors, but Acuña ended up earning the award by a wide margin, with twenty-seven of a possible thirty first-place votes. He became the eighth Braves player to win Rookie of the Year and the first Braves position player to do so since Rafael Furcal in 2000.

2019 SEASON

Prior to the 2019 season Acuña signed an eight-year, $100 million contract extension with the Braves. The deal, running through the 2026 season and with team options for two more years, was unusual for coming so early in his career. It was also the richest ever for a player with only one season of experience and made him the youngest player to sign for $100 million or more. Still, some observers noted the contract would be a bargain if Acuña lived up to his potential. "No one can see the future," he told Jeff Passan for *ESPN* (2 Apr. 2019). "No one knows what's going to happen tomorrow, so I'm extremely

happy with the decision we've all made and I'm just excited to be here."

Acuña dispelled fears of a sophomore slump in 2019, rewarding the Braves' faith in him with his first All-Star selection. Across the entire season his batting average dropped slightly, to a still-solid .280, but more importantly he hit a team-best 41 home runs and led the NL with 37 stolen bases. The feat made him just the fortieth player in MLB history to enter the prestigious 30-30 club. At twenty-one years old, he was also the second-youngest player to join the club, after Trout in 2012.

During the 2019 season Acuña also led the NL in runs scored (127) while finishing tied for fifth in the league in home runs and seventh in hits (175). Those numbers helped him earn his first Silver Slugger Award, given each year to the best hitter at each position in each league. He equally impressed baseball observers with his stellar defensive play in the outfield. Anchored by Acuña's all-around play, the Braves secured a second straight NL East Division title with a 97–65 record. However, they were again eliminated from the postseason in the division series, losing to the St. Louis Cardinals. Still, the season was largely considered a success for the team and especially its budding superstar, who came in fifth in NL MVP voting. Braves manager Brian Snitker was among those deeply impressed by Acuña's rapid development and strong work ethic. "He has so much talent, it's almost mind-boggling, but none of it has gone to his head. That's what makes him special," Snitker told Bob Klapisch for *Bleacher Report* (30 Aug. 2019).

Acuña entered the 2020 season poised to solidify his status as one of the game's best players. The season, however, was postponed indefinitely in March 2020 due to the coronavirus pandemic. Acuña, who typically spent a good portion of the MLB offseason with his family in Venezuela, sought to remain appreciative. "Every day I give thanks for the opportunity I've been given," he told Klapisch. "I thank God, I thank my family, my teammates. I try to honor the people who've helped me get there."

SUGGESTED READING

Ehalt, Matt. "Baseball Is a Family Affair for Braves Phenom Ronald Acuña Jr." *Yahoo! Sports*, 17 Aug. 2019, sports.yahoo.com/for-ronald-acuna-jr-baseball-is-a-family-affair-130007865.html. Accessed 23 Apr. 2020.

Klapisch, Bob. "'The Beast' Is Born: 21-Year-Old Ronald Acuna Jr. Is the New King of the ATL." *Bleacher Report*, 30 Aug. 2019, bleacherreport.com/articles/2851545-the-beast-is-born-21-year-old-ronald-acuna-jr-is-the-new-king-of-the-atl. Accessed 23 Apr. 2020.

Leach, Matthew. "Here's Why the Acuna-Soto ROTY Chase is Historic." *MLB.com*,

17 Aug. 2018, www.mlb.com/news/ronald-acuna-juan-soto-chasing-historic-years-c290719054. Accessed 23 Apr. 2020.

Márquez, César Augusto. "Ronald Acuña: Avoiding the Sins of the Father." *La Vida Baseball*, 25 Apr. 2018, www.lavidabaseball.com/ronald-acuna-atlanta-braves-father/. Accessed 23 Apr. 2020.

Matz, Eddie. "Introducing Ronald Acuna, MLB's Next Superstar." *ESPN*, 23 Apr. 2018, www.espn.com/mlb/story/_/id/23245463/introducing-ronald-acuna-mlb-next-superstar. Accessed 23 Apr. 2020.

Passan, Jeff. "Braves, Acuna Agree to Historic $100M Extension." *ESPN*, 2 Apr. 2019, www.espn.com/mlb/story/_/id/26423778/braves-acuna-agree-historic-100m-extension. Accessed 23

Sanchez, Jesse. "How Atlanta Got Acuna When Everyone Else Missed." *MLB.com*, 30 June 2018, wap.mlb.com/atl/news/article/20180630283634544/. Accessed 8 Apr. 2020.

—Chris Cullen

Mike Adenuga

Born: April 29, 1953
Occupation: Businessman

Despite rising to become the second-wealthiest individual in Nigeria and one of the top three hundred wealthiest people in the world, businessman Mike Adenuga focused less on his own financial standing than on the services and opportunities he could make available in his home country. "I am not interested in being the richest man in the world," he said in one of his rare interviews, as quoted by *Ventures Africa* (5 May 2012). "If I can be seen as adding value to Nigerians and Africans, it is more fulfilling." From the mid-1970s Adenuga worked to do just that, launching businesses in industries such as imports, construction, and banking. During the early 1990s his company Consolidated Oil began drilling operations in Nigeria's Niger Delta, becoming one of few locally owned oil companies at work in the region.

Perhaps the most significant of Adenuga's contributions, however, were those within the telecommunications sector, and specifically in the field of mobile technology. As head of the telecommunications company Globacom, Adenuga oversaw the founding of Glo Mobile, a popular mobile telephone service provider that would come to serve nearly fifty million Nigerians by mid-2019. In addition to winning over customers with services such as mobile internet

and practices such as per-second billing, Globacom was especially dedicated to improving Nigeria's telecommunications infrastructure, and in 2010 inaugurated the company's Glo 1 project, a fiber-optic cable that extended between Nigeria and the United Kingdom. Yet while Adenuga himself was the focus of much of the publicity surrounding Globacom's work, he often emphasized the extent to which the company's success was a team effort. "Like anybody else I have two hands, two eyes," he told Bisi Olatilo in an interview for the *Bisi Olatilo Show* (uploaded to *YouTube* 3 Aug. 2014). "But what we've been lucky about is that we put a lot of premium on making sure that when we go out there to resource a company, we look for the very, very best, and I think we've been very lucky in that area. We have very competent, highly competent people."

EARLY LIFE AND EDUCATION

Michael Agbolade Adenuga Jr. was born in Oyo State, in southwestern Nigeria, on April 29, 1953. His father, Michael Agbolade Adenuga, was a teacher, while his mother, Juliana Oyindamola Adenuga, was engaged in business. His family also owned a small sawmill. Adenuga's mother was of royal ancestry, from a Yoruba people called the Ijebu, and Adenuga himself would later hold a royal title among the Ijebu people. As a child, Adenuga lived with his family in Ibadan, the capital of Oyo. Although as an adult he would live primarily in the Nigerian metropolis of Lagos, he stayed connected to Ibadan and recalled his time there fondly in his interview with Olatilo. "I've always identified with Ibadan. I have a home in Ibadan; I have offices in Ibadan. I'm always in Ibadan," he said. Adenuga completed his secondary education at Comprehensive High School in Aiyetoro, in neighboring Ogun State.

After high school, Adenuga traveled to the United States to study business. He earned a bachelor's degree from Northwestern Oklahoma State University and went on to pursue graduate studies at Pace University in New York, from which he received a master's in business administration. Adenuga worked a variety of jobs to support himself during his time as a student, serving at times as a taxi driver and a security guard. He would later receive an honorary doctorate from Ogun State University in Nigeria after establishing himself as a major business leader in the country.

EARLY BUSINESS CAREER

Upon his return to Nigeria during the mid-1970s, Adenuga entered the world of business, taking over the sawmill operation that belonged to his family. He also sought out new business opportunities and soon began working in imports, bringing products such as textiles and beverages into the country. Perhaps his greatest success during that period, however, centered on the importation of automotive accessories. "You had a lot of vehicles coming into the country without the air conditioning, without stereo, so there were opportunities in those areas," he recalled to Olatilo. To meet the needs of Nigerian drivers, Adenuga imported numerous car stereos and particularly specialized in removable models, which drivers could take with them when they parked, to reduce the risk of theft. According to the *Ventures Africa* profile, Adenuga made his first million dollars by age twenty-six.

Over the next decades, Adenuga established himself as an entrepreneur with diverse business interests, entering industries such as construction and finance. In 1989 he founded Devcom Bank, which would later merge with Equatorial Trust Bank, another Adenuga venture. Among Adenuga's most significant businesses during the 1990s was Consolidated Oil, later known as Conoil, an oil and gas company that began commercial drilling operations in the Niger Delta region around 1991. In addition to further solidifying Adenuga's reputation as a business owner, Consolidated Oil was particularly significant due to its status as a locally owned oil company, a rarity in Nigeria at the time. One of several companies owned simultaneously by Adenuga, Consolidated Oil would come to be included alongside several banking, real estate, and communication ventures under the umbrella of the Mike Adenuga Group.

GLOBACOM
While Adenuga made significant contributions to the Nigerian business landscape over the rise of his career, a particularly key moment came in 2003, when his newly founded telecommunications company, Globacom, succeeded in obtaining a Second National Operator telecommunications license from the Nigerian government. This was a major win, allowing Globacom to operate as a national telecommunications carrier and to serve as an international telecommunications gateway in the country. That move marked Adenuga's second attempt to obtain a telecommunications license, as a prior attempt had failed when Adenuga was unable to raise the necessary funds by the government's deadline. "Big business doesn't fight government, they work with government, and that's what we tried to do," he told Olatilo of the experience.

For Adenuga, the newly founded Globacom represented an opportunity to provide telecommunications services suitable for Nigeria's population. "Globacom is Nigerian. The brand itself is Nigerian. The aspiration of the brand itself is to meet the needs of Nigerians, and that's the focus. That's the driving force," he told Olatilo. In addition to offering landline telephone services and broadband internet service over the course of its first decades of existence, Globacom became particularly known as a provider of mobile telephone and internet services. Operating under the brand name Glo Mobile, the mobile branch of the company's operations offered benefits such as per-second billing, a practice that Adenuga cited as particularly important to Nigerian customers. "You talk for five seconds, you are billed for five seconds," he explained to Olatilo, distinguishing Glo Mobile's approach from the common practice of per-minute billing. Thanks in part to such selling points, Glo Mobile became the second-largest mobile network operator in Nigeria by late 2019, providing services to more than 49 million customers in September of that year.

TELECOMMUNICATIONS INFRASTRUCTURE
In addition to providing mobile- and landline-based telecommunications services within Nigeria, Adenuga and Globacom focused heavily on developing the infrastructure necessary to bring higher-quality telecommunications technologies to both Nigeria and other countries in western Africa. Alongside providing faster and more robust services, such infrastructure projects had the goal of enabling Nigerians to "start to compete with the rest of the world on an equal footing," Adenuga explained in a video statement posted to *YouTube* in November of 2011. To that end, Globacom in 2005 began work on Glo 1, a submarine fiber-optic cable between Nigeria and the United Kingdom. Developed in conjunction with the French telecommunications manufacturer Alcatel-Lucent, the cable was set to span more than six thousand miles (nearly ten thousand kilometers) and make high-speed internet access available to Nigeria and other nations along the path of the cable.

After several years of development, the Glo 1 cable reached Lagos in late 2009 and was inaugurated the following year. The milestone was a particularly meaningful one for Adenuga, who considered the fiber-optic cable a key addition to Globacom's technological capabilities. "I promise you things are never going to be the same again," he said in his 2011 video statement following Glo 1's inauguration. "We can provide our country with clearer lines as well as high-quality internet bandwidth to any global destination at really affordable prices. I promise you no one else can do this because no one else has a submarine cable to Europe, and on to America, connected to his own massive national network." Seeking to expand its infrastructure and services further, Globacom in 2018 announced plans to build a second submarine cable, known as Glo 2, in partnership with the Chinese technology giant Huawei.

PHILANTHROPY AND RECOGNITION

Adenuga's business interests became well-known for supporting a variety of cultural and athletic events in Nigeria through corporate sponsorships. Adenuga also contributed to numerous charitable causes through his Mike Adenuga Foundation, which sought to address economic and social issues in Nigeria as well as elsewhere in Africa. The foundation also became active in public-health initiatives; for example, in March 2020 it donated 1.5 billion Nigerian naira (nearly $4 million) to support efforts to fight the ongoing COVID-19 pandemic within Nigeria.

Adenuga has also been recognized for his contributions to French-Nigerian cultural exchange through the construction of the Mike Adenuga Centre in Lagos, the home to that city's branch of the French cultural organization Alliance Français. For that work he was awarded the title of commander of the French Legion of Honor by French president Emmanuel Macron in 2018. He was also widely honored in the business world for his many accomplishments. By April 2020 Adenuga was the second-richest person in Nigeria, with a reported net worth of $5.9 billion. He was listed third on the *Forbes* magazine's 2020 list of African billionaires, after fellow Nigerian Aliko Dangote and Egyptian businessman Nassef Sawiris, and claimed the 286th spot on *Forbes*'s 2020 global billionaires list.

PERSONAL LIFE

Adenuga lived primarily in Lagos, Nigeria. He met his wife, Titi, at Devcom Bank. Adenuga has seven children, several of whom followed him into business. His daughter Bella Disu serves as executive vice chair of Globacom.

SUGGESTED READING

Adebola, Bolatito. "Globacom Boss' Wife, Titi Adenuga, Glows Again." *Independent* [Nigeria], 3 Nov. 2018, www.independent.ng/globacom-boss-wife-titi-adenuga-glows-again/. Accessed 12 Apr. 2020.

Adenuga, Mike. "Mike Adenuga Interview." Interview with Bisi Olatilo. *YouTube*, uploaded by theBOSofficial, 3 Aug. 2014, www.youtube.com/watch?v=vCdJjdLP2ZQ.

———. "Mike Adenuga Speaks Glo 1 Submarine Cable." *YouTube*, uploaded by TechnologyTimesiTV, 13 Nov. 2011, www.youtube.com/watch?v=NaDOmOHldMk.

Ajiboye, Kayode. "Mike Adenuga: 66 Cheers to a Media Guru." *Independent* [Nigeria], 29 Apr. 2019, www.independent.ng/mike-adenuga-66-cheers-to-a-media-guru/. Accessed 12 Apr. 2020.

"Glo Topples Airtel as Second-Largest Network Operator." *PM News Nigeria*, 6 Nov. 2019, www.pmnewsnigeria.com/2019/11/06/glo-topples-airtel-as-second-largest-network-operator/. Accessed 12 Apr. 2020.

Olawoyin, Oladeinde. "In Major Investments, Globacom Moves to Shape Africa's Digital Fortune, Future." *Premium Times* [Nigeria], 1 Apr. 2020, www.premiumtimesng.com/business/business-interviews/317351-in-major-investments-globacom-moves-to-shape-africas-digital-fortune-future.html. Accessed 12 Apr. 2020.

"Spotlight on Mike Adenuga: Why Is He Called 'The Bull'?" *Ventures Africa*, 5 May 2012, venturesafrica.com/spotlight-on-mike-adenuga-why-is-he-called-the-bull/. Accessed 12 Apr. 2020.

—Joy Crelin

Adut Akech

Date of birth: December 25, 1999
Occupation: Model

Supermodel Adut Akech became a rising star in the international fashion industry after walking the runway in 2016 at Saint Laurent's spring/summer 2017 show during one of the most significant events in the industry: Paris Fashion Week. In 2018, she was chosen by the late Karl Lagerfeld to conclude the Chanel Haute Couture show as its "bride," one of the most coveted roles in fashion. Named Model of the Year by the British Fashion Council in 2019 as she continued modeling for top brands and designers, she also appeared on the *TIME* 100 Next list in part for her advocacy work with refugees through the United Nations. Akech spent her early childhood in a refugee camp in Kenya before moving to Australia around the age of seven. She takes pride in her story and has used her platform to raise awareness of the stories of other refugees and address pervasive societal problems such as racism and poverty. Additionally, she has spoken candidly about her struggles with anxiety and depression. In an article for the Australian edition of *Vogue* (20 Dec. 2019), which featured her on the cover for the January 2020 issue, an introduction described her flourishing career and continued potential: "With a maturity that transcends her age, she faces the future with the kind of nous that is enlivening and contagious."

EARLY LIFE IN KENYA

Adut Akech Bior was born on December 25, 1999. Her mother, Mary, gave birth to her en route to the Kakuma refugee camp in Kenya, after her family had left Sudan (having lived in what would become independent South Sudan in 2011) to escape the violent and debilitating civil war that had enveloped the country for years. "I feel like my life could be a movie," Akech told Gina Way for *Marie Claire* (26 Sept. 2019) when asked to describe her development. She spent her first five years at Kakuma. Later recalling being able to sense the fear of the adults around her and how hard her mother had to work to provide for the family, she has also shared that many of her memories of that period are pleasant ones. "I obviously didn't own a lot of things, but I had food to eat and somewhere to sleep," she told Way. "I didn't have a lot of clothes, but I still had something to wear. I just remember waking up every day, playing with my cousins and my friends, and being a child."

When Akech was five, she and her mother and siblings left Kakuma and settled in, among other locations in Kenya, Nairobi, while they waited for visas. (Akech's father is deceased; as of late 2018, she has five siblings.) Though fondly remembering the smell of incense made at home and her mother's cooking, she later recalled being upset that her mother could not afford to send her to school as other children were able to do. Meanwhile, her older sister had been helping her learn to write. She often brought her cousin lunch, just so she could peek through the gates of the local school and see the other children playing on the playground.

GROWING UP IN ADELAIDE

When Akech was about seven or eight years old, she and her family joined her aunt and older sister in Adelaide, the capital of the state of South Australia. Her mother eventually worked as a laundry supervisor, while her aunt, who had done some modeling and had designed clothes, ran a small boutique. As she did not really know the English language, Akech's first formal education began at an institution at which she and other international children were taught how to speak English. While the transition to her life in a new country was exciting but not without challenges, she was comforted in this school setting by knowing that she and the others attending were having the same types of experiences. That changed when she began attending public school, where she went by the name Mary—her mother's name—because her teachers found her given name difficult to pronounce. (She reclaimed the name when she became a model.) Akech was teased about her height and her teeth, traits that made her insecure at the time but that she embraced and would become defining features of her career. While she began increasingly nurturing an interest in fashion and came to idolize Alek Wek, a model from present-day South Sudan who found fame in the 1990s, she was not as familiar with the modeling side of the industry.

When Akech was thirteen, her aunt asked her to appear in a small-scale, local fashion show for her boutique. "I knew I wanted to be a model the first time I walked down a runway," she told Way. Others saw her potential from early on as well. "I've actually been scouted at airports three separate times!" she told Isabelle Hellyer for *i-D* magazine (19 July 2017). But at that point in her life, she felt she was too young to be making any potential career commitments.

DEBUT WITH SAINT LAURENT

Feeling more prepared, in April 2016 Akech signed with Australia's Chadwick Models. She found work with surprising speed. Following her appearance in shows at the Melbourne Fashion Week not long after, she was on the phone with her agent who was telling her that Saint Laurent representatives wanted her to fly to Paris. She had only a day to procure a suitcase, and as her mother was in Africa, she made the trip by herself. She recalled the harrowing experience for Jane Rocca for the *Sydney Morning Herald* (4 Aug. 2019): "Nobody told me to wear compression stockings on the flight, so I slept the entire trip and woke with a humongous foot and couldn't wear any shoes." While she was laid up in a hospital for eight hours, doctors found a piece of glass lodged in her foot that resulted in an infection. Later, at rehearsal, she crumpled in pain, crying. "The casting director ran up to me and picked me up off the floor," she recounted to Rocca. "I told him I couldn't walk in any of the shoes they wanted me to wear. I thought I had blown my chances." She appeared in Saint Laurent's spring/summer 2017 show in September 2016, her European runway and Paris Fashion Week debut, wearing a pair of men's tuxedo shoes with her gold lamé dress.

Akech went on to take part in the shooting of the French label's spring/summer 2017 campaign, which was helmed by photographer Collier Schorr. In 2017, in addition to walking in and closing Saint Laurent's autumn/winter 2017 show and posing for more of the fashion house's photographed campaigns, she joined rapper Sean "Diddy" Combs, actor Whoopi Goldberg, and supermodel Naomi Campbell, among others, for the shooting in London of the 2018 Pirelli Calendar. The themed calendar, which featured only black figures for that iteration, was shot by British photographer Tim Walker and styled by Edward Enninful, the editor in chief of British *Vogue*. That specific shoot also proved fortuitous because it introduced Akech to Campbell, who took her under her wing.

That same year, Akech experienced her first brush with racism as a public figure. She appeared in the spring/summer campaign for David Jones, an Australian department store, on the cover of their beauty catalog. After a white woman expressed her displeasure with seeing Akech as the face of the retailer on Facebook, David Jones came under fire for its tepid response. Initially Akech chose not to weigh in, though she wrote an Instagram post expressing her pride for appearing on the cover. "I really took the time to think about it—am I going to overreact, or am I just not going to let this thing get to me?" she told Alexandra Spring for the *Guardian* (27 Sept. 2017). "I chose not to let it get to me because that was the first time I had a stupid racist comment made about me." Although the company apologized to her and she maintained praise for their efforts at inclusion, commentators noted that the incident brought the Australian fashion industry's traditional lack of diversity to the fore.

BREAKOUT SEASON

Despite her busy 2017 schedule, which included closing out Saint Laurent's particularly high-profile spring/summer 2018 show at Paris Fashion Week in September, Akech managed to graduate from high school at Adelaide's St. Columba College by the end of the year, a personal achievement. "There's nothing more important to me than making my mum proud, and education was one of the biggest reasons she took us to Australia," she told Australian *Vogue*. The following year, 2018, with her exclusivity contract with Saint Laurent having ended, only saw her more in demand as she appeared on the cover of *i-D* magazine twice, as well as on the covers of British *Vogue*, Korean *Vogue*, Italian *Vogue*, and Australian *Vogue*, the latter of which published an editorial that featured her alongside members of her family. She also walked in shows for Prada, Givenchy, Tom Ford, Alexander McQueen, Miu, and Versace, among others. Upon meeting Pierpaolo Piccioli of Valentino, she "basically immediately fell in love with him," as she told Stephanie Eckardt for *W* magazine (10 July 2019), and became his muse. After opening Valentino's autumn/winter 2018 show, she even went to New York's Met Gala as Piccioli's guest in 2018 and 2019. In 2019, she was brought in to serve as one of the faces of the campaign for Valentino's Born in Roma fragrance.

Akech felt a similar connection with Chanel's Lagerfeld, whom she met during Milan Fashion Week in February 2018. She explained to Rocca that when Lagerfeld complimented her, she fought to keep up a professional appearance while wishing she could just call her mother to tell her about it. "Then he started asking why no one had brought me to him before: 'Why haven't I seen her at Chanel?' The room went silent. It was awkward." The late designer chose her to don an unconventional skirt-suit in a shade of green to appear as the Chanel couture "bride" in that year's fall haute couture show in July. Media

coverage of the event often noted that this made her the second black model in the house's history to close the show in that traditional, coveted position. (The first was Alek Wek.) In interviews following Lagerfeld's death in 2019, she emphasized that collaborating with him and having such a close relationship with him would always be among her most cherished memories.

MODEL OF THE YEAR

Of 2018, Akech told Grace O'Neill for *Harper's Bazaar* (23 Oct. 2018), "Everything that's happened this year has happened so fast, I really haven't had the chance to let anything sink in yet." The next year would only serve to solidify her success as she remained a notable model at 2019's major shows. Selected by Meghan Markle, the Duchess of Sussex, Akech was one of fifteen women to appear in British *Vogue's* September "Forces for Change" issue. Markle chose Akech for her advocacy work with the UN Refugee Agency, which she had begun in earnest around 2018 to increase awareness as to the harsh realities many refugees face. Meanwhile, she had also begun to speak more openly about issues such as racism and diversity, particularly related to the world of fashion. In December, she was named Model of the Year at the British Fashion Awards by the British Fashion Council. Although she was able to start off 2020 walking the runways at some of the major world shows to model autumn/winter collections, the end of the season was partly shrouded in public health concerns due to the worldwide outbreak of the novel coronavirus 2019 (COVID-19), and the future of the rest of the year's shows was brought into question.

PERSONAL LIFE

Though her work in the fashion industry has meant that she has had to travel frequently, including stints living in New York, Akech still considers Adelaide her true home.

SUGGESTED READING

Akech, Adut. "Adut Akech on Achieving Your Dreams." Interview by Gina Way. *Marie Claire*, 26 Sept. 2019, www.marieclaire.com/beauty/a28900617/adut-akech/. Accessed 11 June 2020.

———. "For Valentino Muse Adut Akech, the Best Makeup Is No Makeup." Interview by Stephanie Eckardt. *W*, 10 July 2019, www.wmagazine.com/story/adut-akech-valentino-campaign-beauty-notes/. Accessed 11 June 2020.

———. "From South Sudan to Saint Laurent, via Adelaide." Interview by Jane Rocca. *The Sydney Morning Herald*, 4 Aug. 2019, www.smh.com.au/lifestyle/fashion/

from-south-sudan-to-saint-laurent-via-ade-laide-20190802-p52dag.html. Accessed 11 June 2020.

———. "Model Adut Akech Stars on the Cover of Vogue Australia's January 2020 Issue." *Vogue Australia*, 20 Dec. 2019, www.vogue.com.au/fashion/news/model-adut-akech-stars-on-the-cover-of-vogue-australias-january-2020-issue/news-story/0c80fefc5e6cd8dfeec6b1fcd544e474. Accessed 11 June 2020.

Hellyer, Isabelle. "Adut Akech Isn't a Star on the Rise, She's a Supernova." *i-D*, Vice, 19 July 2017, i-d.vice.com/en_uk/article/pap5kz/adut-akech-isnt-a-star-on-the-rise-shes-a-supernova. Accessed 11 June 2020.

O'Neill, Grace. "Meet Adut Akech: The Next Australian Supermodel." *Harper's Bazaar*, 23 Oct. 2018, www.harpersbazaar.com.au/fashion/adut-akech-australian-supermodel-17539. Accessed 11 June 2020.

Spring, Alexandra. "Adut's Triumph: The Australian Refugee Taking On the Fashion World." *The Guardian*, 27 Sept. 2017, www.theguardian.com/lifeandstyle/2017/sep/27/aduts-triumph-the-australian-refugee-taking-on-the-fashion-world. Accessed 11 June 2020.

—*Molly Hagan*

Vikky Alexander

Born: January 30, 1959
Occupation: Artist

Vikky Alexander is a Canadian artist whose disciplines have included photography and photoconceptualism, collage, and installation. Alexander was a young member of the Pictures Generation, a postmodern arts movement in New York City in the 1970s and 1980s, and later, a prominent artist in the Vancouver school of photoconceptualism. Her work explores the commodification of nature, sex, and desire. Her early work, typified by *Obsession* (1983), a series of ten images of the model Christie Brinkley, appropriated and recontextualized images from fashion advertisements. In the late 1980s and 1990s, Alexander returned to an earlier interest in architecture and artifice. Photographic works like the series *West Edmonton Mall* (1988) explore the relationship between architecture and consumerism, another concept that has driven much of Alexander's work.

Other recurring themes have included the tension between the natural and the artificial. Alexander has often used reflection to illustrate her ideas. She described her work this way: "It's always about the architecture, how things are framed to project an ideal," she told Becky Rynor for the *National Gallery of Canada* magazine (19

Dec. 2018). "Sort of the way storefronts are arranged to promote sales, to make you want what is in that window. I'm interested in that, as well as making the viewer be self-aware—as in, 'I'm looking in the store window and I'm seeing that handbag, but because there is glass I'm also seeing it reflected, so how does it look in my hand?'"

EARLY LIFE AND EDUCATION

Vikky Alexander was born in Victoria, British Columbia, on January 30, 1959. She was raised in Ottawa and studied art at the Nova Scotia College of Art and Design (NSCAD). Inspired by Dan Graham, an American conceptual artist who served as one of her instructors, Alexander took an interest in architecture, and she enrolled in an experimental architecture course at the Technical University of Nova Scotia. A 1972 book called *Learning from Las Vegas*, by Robert Venturi and Denise Scott Brown, became a foundational inspiration in her work. The authors describe a concept they call the "Architecture of Persuasion," Alexander recalled in an interview with the Vancouver magazine *Here and Elsewhere* (15 May 2012). "I'm interested in the areas of architecture where there is a relationship between the physical structures and spaces of wealth and consumerism—malls, property developments, casinos, furniture showrooms, Crystal Palaces—and the dream world of fantasy and desire they perpetuate," she said.

Alexander earned her BFA degree in 1979 and moved to New York City, where she fell in with the so-called Pictures Generation.

PICTURES GENERATION

The Pictures Generation encompassed a cohort of artists who used mass media imagery to interrogate advertising and consumerism. "'The Pictures Generation' has become a ubiquitous, awkward catchall term, probably abrasive to the artists themselves, for something that was less an organized movement than a heterogeneous expression of a zeitgeist," Gary Indiana wrote for the *New York Times Style Magazine* (13 Feb. 2017). "Their art was connected by an interest in examining power and identity in a media-saturated, politically uncertain age." The movement was typified by artists like Richard Prince, best known for appropriating the images of others. (At one point, Prince mounted a show featuring framed screenshots of other people's Instagram pages.) Another Pictures Generation artist, Sherrie Levine, is known for re-photographing a 1936 Walker Evans portrait of a woman named Allie Mae Burroughs in 1981, "reframing" it in a feminist, postmodern context. Barbara Kruger, meanwhile, combined images of women with subversive text, like, "Your body is a battlefield."

In a similar vein, Alexander, who was younger and less well known than the other Pictures Generation artists, began re-photographing images from fashion advertisements in the early 1980s. "I don't want to speak for all women, but I think many of us have a love/hate relationship with fashion," she told Isabella Smith for *An-Other* magazine (24 May 2016). "You can try, but you will never attain the idealized glamour of an editorial. There's an ambivalent push-pull effect; one knows the unattainability of media images, but desire can make you blind to reality." (In this context, an editorial is a type of fashion photography.) Alexander sought to convey this idea by manipulating the photographs and presenting them in a new context. An early series, including works like *The Four Seasons* (1980) and *St. Sebastian* (1982), utilizes diptych and triptych formats, recalling the panels of altar paintings.

Alexander's diptych *Pietà* (1981) features a man holding a woman, a reversal of the famous sculpture by Michelangelo of the Virgin Mary holding the body of Christ in her arms. "Alexander's women become less passive objects awaiting visual consumption in the space of an editorial," Smith wrote, "and more protagonists, existing in a rich historical lineage." Similarly, Alexander's triptych *Ecstasy* (1982), which uses photographs from an advertisement featuring model Isabella Rossellini, references the *Ecstasy of Saint Teresa*, a seventeenth-century sculpture by Gian Lorenzo Bernini.

Alexander's *Obsession* (1983–2016) features ten images of model Christie Brinkley, who was ubiquitous in advertisements in the early 1980s. "Almost every magazine had images of her: the smoking Christie Brinkley, the photographer, the girl-next-door, the swimsuit model, the gambler in Las Vegas," Alexander recalled to Rynor. "As I collected these images, I started seeing how she had all these different personas, so I couldn't use one image to show who she is." The piece, Alexander explained, "is kind of an infinite description of her."

Her early work, Alexander told Alison Sinkewicz for *BOMB* magazine (13 Apr. 2020), was interested in the "commodification of sex." "Sex is the thing that sells the luxury good. From that, I moved on to combining figure and landscape. I started to think about the commodification of nature: 'the view' is a big part of architecture and what makes a place sell." Her installation *Lake in the Woods* (1986) is fitted into a narrow hallway. One wall features an image of an alpine lake in a forest. The other wall features wood paneling and a mirror that reflects the viewer into the landscape on the opposite wall.

VANCOUVER SCHOOL

Alexander moved to Vancouver in 1992, where she became a part of a movement known as the Vancouver school of photoconceptualism. Guided by her interest in architecture, Alexander produced three series: *West Edmonton Mall* (1988),

Disneyland (1992), and *Las Vegas* (1995). She chose these locations for their artificial and constructed elements. "I photographed places like the West Edmonton Mall where nature is incorporated to make it more of a pleasant environment," she explained to Sinkewicz. Photos of the West Edmonton Mall focus on mirrored surfaces, an artificial lagoon, and tanks of exotic fish. *Disneyland* focuses on manipulated natural landscapes, like hedges trimmed in the shape of animals, or flowers planted in mosaic-like patterns. Meanwhile, in *Las Vegas*, photographs like *Las Vegas, Royal White Tigers #2* and *Las Vegas, Bathroom at Caesar's*, capture interiors that evoke a generalized idea of opulence. Alexander explored similar themes in her *Model Suites* series in 2005. The photographs were taken at a condominium showroom in Vancouver. "I was quite interested in how the views from the fake windows were all backlit images as if the condo was on the 40th or the 50th floor," she told Rynor. "None of the views made any sense together: one of the views was dark, the one in the bedroom was quite bright." The confusion with regard to space and time offers insight into the confusion of desire.

THE TROUBLESOME WINDOW

In 1998, Alexander made an installation called *Vaux-le-Vicomte-Panorama*. It features projected images of the garden at the seventeenth-century French château and eight mirrored columns. The columns distort and reflect the garden in a manner that emphasizes the artificiality of the image. The columns recall those captured in Alexander's photographs of the West Edmonton Mall. She compared the two works in her interview with *Here and Elsewhere*. "I thought of [the mall] as a contemporary 19th Century World's Fair where exotic phenomena of nature were featured as specimens behind glass." As with *Vaux-le-Vicomte-Panorama*, which incorporates images of a garden designed by André Le Nôtre in 1661, she added, "The two centuries seemed to collide for me."

Reflection has been an important element of Alexander's work. She often uses, or makes reference to, glass or mirrored surfaces, suggesting their distorting and reflective properties. "A lot of my work uses mirrors . . . so you are always projecting yourself into this idealized space," she told Sinkewicz. While the earlier *Lake in the Woods* literally projected the viewer into an alluring landscape, Alexander's collages perform the same feat metaphorically. Pieces like *Aqua Bedroom* (2000), *Wave Diver's Den* (2003), and *High Tide* (2004) incorporate photographed images, textures, and ink. *Snowy Boardroom* (2000), depicting an office interior with panoramic views of a desolate arctic landscape, juxtaposes the natural and the artificial. Later collages, like *Cheetah* and Pavilion at Sans Souci (2013), Moose Cows at Fontainebleau (2014), and Giraffe at Olana (2014), combine postcards of historic places with cutouts of animals. Alexander's 2010 black-and-white Island photo series, taken at the Palm House at the Royal Botanic Gardens in England, engages with a similar theme. The photographs—including Collision (2010), Canopy (2010), and Tower (2010)—depict a wild profusion of tropical plants, with the cold steel of their greenhouse confines visible in the background. The series, Alexander told Here and Elsewhere, expresses the tension between nature and culture, which she describes as "a critical element" in her work. "There is a utopian desire in being as close to nature as possible without necessarily realizing that nature is chaotic and not necessarily benign," she said.

In 2015, Alexander mounted an exhibition at TrépanierBaer Gallery in Calgary called The Troublesome Window, featuring photographs taken through showroom windows. Pieces like Paris Showrooms, Cream Sectional (2009), Istanbul Showrooms, White and Gold Greyhounds (2013), and Tokyo Showrooms, Prada Couple (2014) illustrate the objects on display within the showroom, as well as reflections from the street outside, emphasizing the interplay between real and artificial. Art critic Donald Brackett wrote of the series for the website Critics at Large (7 Sept. 2019), "Of uniquely impactful power for me were Alexander's series of large scale photographs of shiny retail store windows, filled with an array of products but also highly reflective glass which absorbed passersby on the street and turned them into a big part of the commercial display."

Alexander enjoyed her first career retrospective, called Extreme Beauty, at the Vancouver Art Gallery from July 2019 to January 2020. She started teaching in the visual arts department at the University of Victoria in 1992 and eventually became a professor emeritus there.

PERSONAL LIFE

Vikky Alexander lives in Montreal.

SUGGESTED READING

Alexander, Vikky. "Framed Reflections: An Interview with Vikky Alexander." Interview by Becky Rynor. National Gallery of Canada, 19 Dec. 2018, www.gallery.ca/magazine/artists/interviews/framed-reflections-an-interview-with-vikky-alexander. Accessed 14 May 2020.

———. "An Interview with Vikky Alexander." Here and Elsewhere [Vancouver], 15 May 2012, hereelsewhere.com/see/vikky-alexander/. Accessed 14 May 2020.

———. "Reflections of Desire: Vikky Alexander Interviewed by Alison Sinkewicz." BOMB, 13 Apr. 2020, bombmagazine.org/articles/reflections-of-desire-vikky-alexander-interviewed/. Accessed 13 May 2020.

Brackett, Donald. "Eye of the Beholder: The Extremity of Vikky Alexander." Critics at Large, 7 Sept. 2019, www.criticsatlarge.ca/2019/09/eye-of-beholder-extremity-of-vikky.html. Accessed 15 May 2020.

Indiana, Gary. "These '80s Artists Are More Important Than Ever." The New York Times Style Magazine, 13 Feb. 2017, www.nytimes.com/2017/02/13/t-magazine/pictures-generation-new-york-artists-cindy-sherman-robert-longo.html. Accessed 13 May 2020.

Smith, Isabella. "Rewriting the Language of Fashion Photography." AnOther, 24 May 2016, www.anothermag.com/art-photography/8717/rewriting-the-language-of-fashion-photography. Accessed 13 May 2020.

SELECTED WORKS

Obsession, 1983; Lake in the Woods, 1986; West Edmonton Mall, 1990; Vaux-le-Vicomte-Panorama, 1998; Island, 2010

—Molly Hagan

Kimia Alizadeh

Born: July 10, 1998
Occupation: Athlete

Kimia Alizadeh made history at the 2016 Summer Olympics in Rio de Janeiro when she took home a bronze medal in the 57 kg women's taekwondo event. With that win, she became the first-ever female Olympic medalist from Iran, a country whose repressive regime has imposed severe restrictions on how women are permitted to act and dress when in public. Her achievement caused a major buzz in Iran, as well as in the Western world. "The historic bronze that she won at Rio Olympics did not weigh any less than a gold in the eyes of Iranian nation," Marjohn Sheikhi wrote for the Tehran-based Mehr News Agency (28 Aug. 2016). "In fact, many called her medal 'the goldest bronze in the history of Iran's sports.'" As Najmeh Bozorgmehr, writing for the Financial Times (11 Oct. 2017), pointed out, "Alizadeh has fought hard to become a sporting champion in a country that does not win many plaudits for its record on women's rights, and has been struggling with the clash between tradition and modernity for more than a century."

Despite the esteem in which many of her fellow Iranians held her, Alizadeh chafed against what she called, as quoted by Megan Specia in the New York Times (14 Jan. 2020), the "hypocrisy, lies, injustice and flattery" that characterized

Photo by Mohammad Hassanzadeh/Tasnim News Agency via Wikimedia Commons

being an athlete in that country, and in early 2020, she defected to Germany, asserting in a widely quoted Instagram announcement, "I have no other wish except for taekwondo, security and a happy and healthy life."

EARLY LIFE AND EDUCATION

Kimia Alizadeh Zonouzi was born on July 10, 1998, in the large Iranian city of Karaj, not far from Tehran. Her last name is sometimes reported to be Zenoorin. Her family is of Iranian Azerbaijani descent and moved from Iran's northeastern province of Azeri in the 1970s. Alizadeh's mother ran the home, while her father, Keyvan, launched a business producing embroidered tablecloths. By the time of her birth, it had grown enough to provide the family with a middle-class income. His embroidery has adorned her taekwondo belts as well.

Although neither of her parents were particularly interested in sports, when Alizadeh was about seven years old, her mother, seeking a healthy activity for her to do after school, enrolled her in the closest sports facility for girls and women. It happened to be a taekwondo club.

Taekwondo is a traditional Korean martial art that stresses not just physical fighting skills, but discipline and mindfulness. Alizadeh, a good math and science student who dreamed of one day becoming an astronaut, was initially unenthusiastic about the sport. The coach, Mahroo Komrani, convinced her to continue, however, based in part on her impressive height. By age

twelve, she had grown taller than her father, and at age fourteen, she stood almost six feet tall.

The Taekwondo Federation of the Islamic Republic of Iran, established in 2001, had deemed it permissible for women to train, provided they covered their hair and neck and avoided wearing Lycra or other tight-fitting materials when competing in public, so as to adhere to traditional standards of modesty. Alizadeh counted herself lucky; some sports were totally closed to female athletes because of the impossibility of competing while wearing the hijab—the hair and neck covering that has been compulsory for women since the Iranian Revolution in 1979. Additionally, her parents supported her in her endeavors—rare in a country in which most families were reluctant to allow their daughters to pursue sports seriously.

It quickly became apparent that Alizadeh possessed formidable natural ability. Even after the family moved to a town a two-hour bus ride from her training facility, she continued to work with Komrani. Irani education officials agreed to exempt her from taking in-person high school classes as long as she passed all exams. "When I was in the second grade of high school, I had only fourteen days to study for the exams and slept perhaps only six hours altogether those days," she recalled to Bozorgmehr.

THE INTERNATIONAL SPORTS WORLD

In 2014, when Alizadeh was fifteen years old, she garnered her first international gold medal, at that year's World Junior Taekwondo Championships, held in Taipei under the auspices of World Taekwondo (WT), the federation that governs the sport on a global level. In that match, she trounced Rhonda Nat of Germany, 9–1, in the junior female 52 kg weight category. Later that year, she served as Iran's flag bearer during the opening ceremonies of the Youth Olympic Games (YOG) in Nanjing. There, she triumphed over Cameroon's Ornella Elsa Ngassa Sokeng, 23–0, in the first round; beat Amber Pannemans from Belgium, 15–2, in the quarterfinals; and guaranteed herself a spot in the finals by besting Debbie Natalia Yopasa Gomez of Columbia, 12–2. She ultimately took home her second international gold of the year after defeating Russian Yulia Turutina, 10–7, in the final game.

At the 2015 World Taekwondo Championships in Chelyabinsk, Russia, Alizadeh stunned spectators by narrowly beating favored two-time Welsh Olympic gold medalist Jade Jones in the quarterfinals, and she ended the event with a bronze. The same year, in Moscow, she took part in the World Taekwondo Grand Prix, an event series that had been launched by the World Federation in 2013 to provide a consistent standard for Olympic qualification. There, she once again faced Jones, beating the older competitor in a so-called golden-point round. (A taekwondo match consists of three two-minute rounds; it goes into a golden-point round if the score is tied at the end of three rounds, and the first fighter to score after that wins. Points are won by landing kicks to an opponent's body or head, as counted electronically by special socks with sensors.)

Even after winning a gold at the high-profile event, Alizadeh, then just sixteen, did not think of herself as a role model for other Iranian girls. However, she still recognized the importance of her successes, telling Bozorgmehr, "My medals have helped kids believe in themselves, and families are more supportive [of girls playing sports] now." In addition, her growing collection of medals gave her enough pull with the Iranian Taekwondo Federation to ask that Komrani be appointed head coach of the National Women's Taekwondo Team.

THE OLYMPIC GAMES AND BEYOND

Alizadeh clinched a spot at the 2016 Olympic Games with a gold medal–winning performance at the Asian Olympic Qualification Tournament, held in Manila, in April. Alizadeh, considered to be the Iranian female contender most likely to medal, arrived in Rio carrying the hopes of her nation. She won her first Olympic match, against Croatian athlete Ana Zaninović, and advanced to the quarterfinals.

Unbeknownst to observers, she was suffering from a seriously injured ligament; in severe pain, she lost her next match, 7–8, to Eva Calvo Gómez of Spain. Even worse than the physical pain, she told interviewers, was the weight of the expectations that had been placed upon her. "I put a towel on my face and told God that I do not want to play anymore. I could not bear more pressure," she admitted to Bozorgmehr. "But then I told myself that today is a new day." Alizadeh later rallied, defeating Hedaya Malak Washba of Egypt, Phannapa Harnsujin of Thailand, and Nikita Glasnović of Sweden to win the Olympic bronze.

Olympic taekwondo matches are fought in direct elimination brackets, with the winners of each bracket vying for the gold. All participants who lose to one of the finalists at any stage of the competition engage in a repechage bracket, and, ultimately, two bronze medals are awarded; Alizadeh's fellow bronze medalist turned out to be Malak, and the podium thus featured two women in hijab.

Alizadeh's bronze was the first Olympic medal ever won by an Iranian woman; at just eighteen, she also had the distinction of being the youngest Iranian athlete, male or female, to medal at the Games. The win was especially important to the country because, as Sheikhi wrote, "This was a great moment in history for Iranian women, athletes or otherwise, for whom Kimia's victory touched every corner of their hearts and rekindled the flames of hope for triumph in the face of limitations and hardship."

Government officials weighed in to congratulate or acknowledge her, with Iranian president Hassan Rouhani writing on Twitter, "My dear girl Kimia, you have brought happiness to all the Iranians, and particularly to the women," as reported by Sheikhi. Ayatollah Khamenei, Iran's Supreme Leader, while not referring to Alizadeh by name or mentioning her medal, praised the country's female athletes overall for displaying "an honorable form of hijab as an Iranian code for all."

Following the Olympics, Alizadeh took a break for several months but seemed well enough to participate in the 2017 World Taekwondo Championships in Muju, South Korea. Suffering from swollen knees and pain in her other joints, however, she forced herself to compete and became the first Iranian female to reach the finals of that competition.

Komrani warned her that fighting the final match, against the Ivory Coast's Ruth Gbagbi, might result in permanent injuries, but, as Alizadeh recalled to Bozorgmehr, "I thought, if I were to fail, it should happen during the game but not by withdrawal. . . . Emotionally, I would have been more hurt if I had given up without trying."

By all accounts, Alizadeh fought valiantly against the aggressive Gbagbi, whose kicks landed percussively. The match ended with her opponent in the lead, 19–9. Alizadeh, returning to Iran with the silver medal, spent weeks in the hospital recuperating.

DEFECTION

Although Alizadeh sometimes missed major matches due to her ongoing injuries, she continued to fare well in competition, winning a bronze at the 2018 Asian Taekwondo Championships, for example. Iranian officials and fans were thus shocked on January 11, 2020, to read an Instagram post in which she stated, as quoted by Thomas Kika in the *International Business Times* (12 Jan. 2020), "Let me start with a greeting, a farewell or condolences. I am one of the millions of oppressed women in Iran who they have been playing with for years. They took me wherever they wanted. I wore whatever they said. Every sentence they ordered me to say, I repeated. Whenever they saw fit, they exploited me." She went on to say that while she still hoped to compete in the future, she would no longer be representing her native country. She did not disclose her location, but it was later reported that she had spent time in the Netherlands before making her way to Germany, where she applied for asylum.

PERSONAL LIFE

In 2018, Alizadeh married pro volleyball player Hamed Madanchi, who defected with her. She has said that when she can no longer compete, she may try to earn a college degree in physiotherapy or sports pathology.

SUGGESTED READING

Anonymous Citizen Journalist. "Meet Iran's Taekwondo Genius." *IranWire*, 4 July 2017, iran-wire.com/en/features/4692. Accessed 20 Apr. 2020.

Bozorgmehr, Najmeh. "Kimia Alizadeh, the Iranian Olympic Medalist Fighting Inequality." *Financial Times*, 11 Oct. 2017, www.ft.com/content/cf502dd6-7c26-11e7-ab01-a13271d-1ee9c. Accessed 20 Apr. 2020.

Kika, Thomas. "Who Is Kimia Alizadeh? What to Know about the Female Iranian Athlete Who Defected." *International Business Times*, 12 Jan. 2020, www.ibtimes.com/who-kimia-alizadeh-what-know-about-female-iranian-athlete-who-defected-2900996. Accessed 20 Apr. 2020.

"Kimia Alizadeh: The YOG Star Flying the Flag for Female Athletes in Iran." *Olympic*, 26 Aug. 2016, www.olympic.org/news/kimia-alizadeh-the-yog-star-flying-the-flag-for-female-athletes-in-iran. Accessed 20 Apr. 2020.

Nestler, Stefan. "Kimia Alizadeh and Co.: Why Iranian Athletes Are Turning Their Backs on Tehran." *Deutsche Welle*, 23 Jan. 2020, www.dw.com/en/kimia-alizadeh-and-co-why-iranian-athletes-are-turning-their-backs-on-tehran/a-52125589. Accessed 20 Apr. 2020.

Sheikhi, Marjohn. "Kimia's Bronze Shines Golden in Iranian Women's Eyes." *Mehr News Agency*, 28 Aug. 2016, en.mehrnews.com/news/119212/Kimia-s-bronze-shines-golden-in-Iranian-women-s-eyes. Accessed 20 Apr. 2020.

Specia, Megan. "Iran's Only Female Olympic Medalist Defects Over 'Lies' and 'Injustice.'" *The New York Times*, 13 Jan. 2020, www.nytimes.com/2020/01/13/world/middleeast/kimia-alizadeh-iran-defection.html. Accessed 20 Apr. 2020.

—*Mari Rich*

Ted Allen

Date of birth: May 20, 1965
Occupation: Author and television personality

Introduced to nationwide audiences as the resident food and wine expert for the reality show *Queer Eye for the Straight Guy* in 2003, Ted Allen has sought to broaden viewers' culinary

Photo by Ben Hider/Getty Images for City Harvest

knowledge and become an award-winning television personality in the process. "*Queer Eye* was often about trying to make a more sophisticated, well-rounded, grown-up man," he explained in an interview for the blog *The New Potato* (10 Sept. 2012). "Knowledge of food and wine is a big part of that." After *Queer Eye* was canceled in 2007, Allen continued his mission largely by hosting Food Network programs and making frequent guest-judge appearances on many of the channel's competitive cooking programs.

Allen is perhaps best known, however, as the host of the long-running Food Network show *Chopped*, a competitive program that pits talented cooks against both each other and each round's challenging basket of mystery ingredients. For Allen, shows like *Chopped* and the spin-off *Chopped Junior* play a key role in spreading the knowledge of food and cooking due to their blend of education and entertainment. "A good competitive show like ours makes more sense in prime-time than say a stand-and-stir show," he told Helen Rosner and Greg Morabito for *Eater* (22 Aug. 2016). "As much as I love cooking shows and always have, it's just a much broader audience and people who don't ever cook can appreciate it." Having broadcast more than five hundred episodes over a decade, *Chopped*—and Allen himself—became the focus of widespread appreciation, and in 2012, both the show and its host received prestigious James Beard Awards for their contributions to the culinary landscape.

EARLY LIFE AND EDUCATION

Edward "Ted" Allen was born to Donna and Lowell Allen on May 20, 1965, in Columbus, Ohio. He has a younger sister named Lisa. In 1973 the family settled in the city of Carmel, Indiana. Allen spent the remainder of his childhood there and attended local schools. As a teenager, he played several musical instruments and aspired to be a rock musician.

Allen graduated from Carmel High School in 1983 and was later inducted into the school's alumni hall of fame in 2011. After graduation he enrolled in Purdue University, where he studied psychology and completed his bachelor's degree in that subject in 1987.

Following his undergraduate years, Allen decided to pursue graduate studies as well but was unsure of his preferred path. "I ridiculously dabbled in an MBA for about five seconds and realized that I hated that," he told Emily Heil for the *Washington Post* (4 Feb. 2019). "But my teachers had always told me that I was good at writing and I thought, 'OK I'll go into journalism and I'll take the lousy pay.'" Allen went on to enroll in the graduate program in journalism at New York University (NYU). He received his master's degree from NYU's Graduate School of Arts and Sciences in 1990.

WRITING CAREER

Allen began his journalism career in Indiana, first working for the Lafayette *Journal & Courier* copydesk. After completing his graduate program at NYU, he moved to Chicago, Illinois, where he found work as a journalist with Lerner Newspapers, which published a variety of community papers. He joined the monthly magazine *Chicago* in 1993 and went on to serve as a senior editor, overseeing a broad range of content. However, Allen's work with *Chicago* was especially key in developing his love of food and cooking, which became an increasingly major focus of his writing. "I wrote feature stories about anything, not just food. But I found myself getting sent out to interview chefs and include chefs in my section and getting invited to, you know, seasonal menu tastings at restaurants, and I just fell in love with it," he recalled to Rosner and Morabito. In addition to handling his regular responsibilities, Allen tried out for and ultimately won a position as junior food critic for the magazine, working under acclaimed dining editor Penny Pollack. Although he lacked formal cooking experience or training, Allen was a dedicated home cook and developed a substantial knowledge of food trends and culinary practices through his work as a journalist.

During the late 1990s Allen began writing for the magazine *Esquire*, contributing articles related to food as well as numerous other topics. A contributing editor for the magazine, he was also credited with cowriting a handful of books relevant to the publication's audience, including *Esquire's Things Men Should Know about Style* (1999) and *Esquire's Things a Man Should Know about Handshakes, White Lies, and Which Fork Goes Where: Easy Business Etiquette for Complicated Times* (2001). Allen would continue to contribute to *Esquire* after beginning his television career and also publish articles in magazines such as *Popular Science* and *Popular Mechanics*.

The author of numerous recipes, Allen published the cookbook *The Food You Want to Eat: 100 Smart, Simple Recipes* in 2005. His second cookbook, *In My Kitchen: 100 Recipes and Discoveries for Passionate Cooks*, came out in 2012.

Queer Eye

A turning point in Allen's career came around 2002, when a friend told him about a casting notice for the Bravo television show *Queer Eye for the Straight Guy*, a makeover program in which a group of gay men would work to improve the lives of unfashionable and uncultured straight men. Based in New York, the show was casting a group of hosts and was seeking men who had expertise in areas such as style, interior design, and dining. Convinced that he would not be chosen to star in the show, Allen decided to audition anyway. "I had a contract with *Esquire* magazine, so had been coming to New York City regularly and thought I'd catch a cheap flight, crash on a friend's sofa and do this hilarious audition that I had no chance of winning," he told Jen Murphy for *Food & Wine* magazine (31 Mar. 2015). The *Queer Eye for the Straight Guy* casting team, however, was impressed by Allen's culinary knowledge and his work for *Esquire*, and Allen became one of the first two hosts selected for the program, alongside fashion expert Carson Kressley. Due to his background in food journalism and his love of cooking, Allen was specifically cast as the show's food and wine expert and was responsible for instructing the episodes' guests in relevant topics, teaching them to cook a variety of dishes and at times introducing them to prominent chefs.

As casting progressed, Allen and Kressley were joined by three additional hosts: Kyan Douglas, Thom Filicia, and Jai Rodriguez. Known as the Fab Five, the group became the center of widespread media attention following the premiere of *Queer Eye for the Straight Guy* in July 2003. Popular among Bravo viewers, the show quickly became a much-discussed fixture in US popular culture and in 2004 received the Emmy Award for Outstanding Reality Program. In 2005, the title of the show was shortened simply to *Queer Eye*, a move intended to broaden the program's focus. *Queer Eye* ultimately aired for a total of five seasons, the last of which concluded in October 2007; the show was later rebooted by Netflix in 2018, with a new cast including Allen's protégé Antoni Porowski.

FOOD TELEVISION
Alongside his previous experience in culinary journalism, Allen's role on *Queer Eye* raised his profile as a member of the food media and opened up new opportunities. During his tenure there, Allen also appeared as a judge for the Food Network cooking competition *Iron Chef America: Battle of the Masters* (2004) and became a recurring judge for its successor, *Iron Chef America: The Series*. In addition, he joined *Top Chef*, a cooking program aired on Bravo, as a guest judge during the show's 2006 debut season and continued as a guest judge and later a regular judge for the subsequent seasons. "I got really lucky the way it worked out," Allen told Rosner and Morabito about his experience working for both Food Network and Bravo. He added, "Neither network cared that I was doing those things simultaneously because I was just a judge and it wasn't a role. They didn't see me as a host, or a real family member." He went on to note that his judging appearances "kept [him] visible on two very visible food shows," which he explained to Rosner and Morabito was essential to his continuing success following *Queer Eye*'s cancellation in 2007. He ultimately left *Top Chef* in 2008 to work primarily with Food Network, for which he hosted the program *Food Detectives* from 2008 to 2009.

Over more than a decade, Allen established himself as a key member of Food Network's stable of culinary talent, appearing in *America's Best Cook*, *All-Star Academy*, *The Best Thing I Ever Ate*, and *Beat Bobby Flay*, among other shows. Despite often working in a judging capacity, Allen also had the opportunity to cook himself and to serve in a more informational role, transmitting his own culinary knowledge and love of cooking to viewers. "What I do differently from a lot of TV chefs is that I break down barriers and make fine food more accessible to the regular person, who might be intimidated. I try hard, particularly with wine, to make it not intimidating," he explained to Murphy about his approach. "It's sort of a teaching job."

Chopped
Of all his food-centered roles, Allen is best known for his work as the host of *Chopped*, a cooking contest that debuted on Food Network in 2009. Each episode features four chefs who compete to win prize money and the title of champion through three timed rounds of cooking. Each round, the chefs receive a basket of four often-incongruous mystery ingredients that they must incorporate into their dishes. At the

end of each round, judges assess each dish and eliminate, or "chop," the contestant with the weakest offering. As the host, Allen introduces the contestants, explains the rules, and discusses the contestants' performance with the judges. In addition to hosting, he has appeared as a contestant in various special episodes, including a Mother's Day episode with his mother.

Popular among Food Network viewers, *Chopped* likewise received acclaim from critics and in 2012 won a James Beard Award for best television program. Allen himself was similarly honored, receiving that year's award for best media personality or host. Due to the ever-changing nature of the mystery ingredients and the constant stream of cooks seeking to test their skills in competition, *Chopped* became one of Food Network's most enduring programs, airing more than five hundred episodes between 2009 and 2019. Allen has noted that by around year seven, he had brief misgivings about his ongoing involvement with the show but quickly dismissed the notion. He remarked to Maura Rhodes for *TV Insider* (8 July 2019), "*Chopped* is a place of passion, discovery, talent. Even though it's tightly formatted, there's no end to the ways it surprises and shocks and even makes you shed a tear." In addition to episodes that followed the standard format in terms of competition and contestants, the series encompassed a variety of special events, including specials starring established Food Network personalities, all-star tournaments, and competitions featuring teenage cooks.

A spin-off program featuring children, *Chopped Junior*, debuted in 2015, with Allen as host. He has noted in interviews that *Chopped Junior* features a high level of talent and commitment to the culinary arts but differs from the main series in certain respects; for instance, the younger contestants are often more experimental and uninhibited than their older counterparts. "One funny thing is they'll call basically every sauce a reduction, which is wrong, of course," he told Rhodes of the *Chopped Junior* contestants. "A hollandaise is not a reduction!"

PERSONAL LIFE
Allen is active in several charities. These have included the educational organization Reach Higher and the food-related initiatives Dining Out for Life and the James Beard Foundation. He and his spouse, interior designer Barry Rice, live in Brooklyn, New York.

SUGGESTED READING
Allen, Ted. "5 Minutes with 'Chopped' Host Ted Allen: 'We Are Never Going to Get a Second Ice Cream Machine.'" Interview by Emily Heil. *The Washington Post*, 4 Feb. 2019, www.washingtonpost.com/

arts-entertainment/2019/02/04/minutes-with-chopped-host-ted-allen-we-are-never-going-get-second-ice-cream-machine. Accessed 13 Dec. 2019.

———. Interview. *Parade*, 29 Feb. 2008, parade.com/27487/parade/interview-with-ted-allen. Accessed 13 Dec. 2019.

———. "An Interview with Ted Allen." By John Linn. *Miami New Times*, 15 Dec. 2008, www.miaminewtimes.com/restaurants/an-interview-with-ted-allen-6606214. Accessed 13 Dec. 2019.

———. "Interview with TV Chef Ted Allen." Interview by Jen Murphy. *Food & Wine*, 31 Mar. 2015, www.foodandwine.com/articles/tv-chef-interview-ted-allen. Accessed 13 Dec. 2019.

———. "Tastemakers: Ted Allen Reflects on 10 Years with 'Chopped.'" Interview by Maura Rhodes. *TV Insider*, 8 July 2019, www.tvinsider.com/790607/tastemakers-ted-allen-chopped-chopped-junior-food-network. Accessed 13 Dec. 2019.

———. "Ted Allen Explains the Hoax That Is His Career." Interview by Helen Rosner and Greg Morabito. *Eater*, 22 Aug. 2016, www.eater.com/platform/amp/2016/8/22/12538242/ted-allen-interview-eater-upsell. Accessed 13 Dec. 2019.

SELECTED WORKS

Queer Eye, 2003–7; *Iron Chef America: The Series*, 2005–13; *Top Chef*, 2006–8; *Food Detectives*, 2008–10; *Chopped*, 2009– ; *America's Best Cook*, 2014; *All-Star Academy*, 2015; *Chopped Junior*, 2015–

—Joy Crelin

Photo by Amy Sussman/Getty Images

Stephen Amell

Date of birth: May 8, 1981
Occupation: Actor

Canadian actor Stephen Amell began starring as billionaire Oliver Queen, also known as the Green Arrow, in the CW hit television series *Arrow* in 2012. His character, based on the DC Comics superhero, mastered archery to survive after he was shipwrecked on a desert island. Upon Queen's return to the corrupt Starling City, he becomes the Green Arrow, a Robin Hood–like vigilante fighting crime to better society. The CW version of the story begins after Queen's five-year island sojourn. The show was a hit with critics and audiences when it premiered in 2012, but Amell told Chancellor Agard for *Entertainment Weekly* (14 Oct. 2019) that he did not realize how big the show had become

until 2017, when he met a fan on a tiny Italian island off the coast of Sicily. "People think that the height of the show is when it's premiering, when my torso is 90 ft. tall on Sunset Boulevard," Amell told Agard. "That's not it. It actually compounds over the years, and people become really, really big fans because of the amount of content that you're pushing up." The popularity of the show spawned the Arrowverse, a franchise of shows featuring characters, including Amell's Oliver Queen/Green Arrow, and plot elements from *Arrow*. The Arrowverse includes television shows like *The Flash*, *Supergirl*, *Legends of Tomorrow*, and *Superwoman*, as well as the web series *Vixen*. In addition to his appearances on those shows, Amell appeared in the 2016 film *Teenage Mutant Ninja Turtles: Out of the Shadows*. In 2019, he starred alongside his cousin, Robbie Amell, in the science-fiction thriller *Code 8*. It was also announced in 2019 that *Arrow* would come to an end in 2020 after its eighth season.

EARLY LIFE AND EDUCATION
Amell was born to Sandra and Thomas Amell on May 8, 1981, in Toronto, Ontario. He attended St. Andrew's College, a prestigious boy's prep school in Aurora, Ontario, where he played football and rugby, and swam and skied. He also became interested in acting and played the role of Tony, the male lead in the musical *West Side Story*, and Lysander, the male lead in Shakespeare's *A Midsummer Night's Dream*. He graduated in 2000 and moved to California to pursue acting training at the American Academy of Dramatic

Arts in Los Angeles. He was not happy there, and soon he returned to Toronto, where he got a job in the insurance industry while he continued to audition. "Honestly, the sensible decision would have been a Canadian university where I could earn a degree and maybe play some football," he recalled to the *Andrean*, a publication of St. Andrew's College, in 2007. In 2004, Amell began to land bit parts on shows like *Queer as Folk* and *Degrassi: The Next Generation*. In 2005, he appeared in several episodes of a show called *Beautiful People*, as well as two episodes of the soap opera *Dante's Cove*. In 2006, he landed his first major film role in a period drama, directed by Richard Attenborough, called *Closing the Ring*. Amell, who played a World War II pilot, appeared alongside actor Mischa Barton, and Academy Award winners Shirley MacLaine and Christopher Plummer. The film was poorly reviewed when it premiered at the Toronto International Film Festival in 2007, but Amell won an agent on the strength of his performance.

In 2007, Amell won a Gemini Award—analogous to the Emmy Awards in the United States—for his guest role on the Canadian television series *ReGenesis*. During the same period, Amell appeared on other Canadian shows including the comedy *Rent-a-Goalie* (for which he earned a Gemini nomination) from 2006 to 2008, *'Da Kink in My Hair* from 2007 to 2009, and *Heartland* from 2007 to 2010. In 2009, Amell experienced "a little personal, professional upheaval," as he told Michelle Singerman for *TRNTO* magazine (24 Oct. 2012). "I asked myself an honest question, which was, 'What is it in my life that makes me happy?' And my friends make me happy, and my family makes me happy, and acting really made me happy," he recalled. "I just decided that I was 28 and it was just time to go to L.A. and give it a proper try."

EARLY CAREER IN LOS ANGELES

With a $15,000 loan from his grandfather, Amell moved to Los Angeles in early 2010. He told Singerman, "I was very comfortable in my own skin. And I think that that's 95 per cent of the battle when it comes to embodying someone else on the television screen or the movie screen." He was booking jobs by the end of the year. A rite of passage for many actors, he first booked guest roles on procedurals like *CSI: Miami*, *NCIS: Los Angeles*, and *CSI: Crime Scene Investigation*. In 2011, Amell landed a guest-starring role on the third season of the HBO comedy *Hung*, about a high school teacher-turned-gigolo. Amell, according to Shinan Govani for Canada's *National Post* (23 Nov. 2011), played a "younger, hotter, possibly more dexterous" rival to the main character. The role required a fair share of nudity, but Govani praised Amell for his acting performance. "Playing a busboy-gone-pro, he has the

right light touch in the performance—a kind of winning oafish-ness," Govani wrote. *Hung* was canceled in 2011. In 2012, Amell played a paramedic on the drama series *Private Practice*.

ARROW

Amell landed his most famous role up to that point, Oliver Queen, a.k.a. the Green Arrow, on the action television series *Arrow*, in 2012. In an interview with Larry King for *Larry King Now* (16 Dec. 2019), Amell's first cousin, Robbie Amell, recalled reading the script for *Arrow*. (Robbie is also an actor; he played Firestorm on the hit CW series *The Flash* from 2014 to 2017.) "My agent sent [the script] to me and I read it, and you always picture yourself when you're reading something [but] I pictured Steve," Robbie recalled. Executive producer Greg Berlanti was similarly convinced that Amell should play the role. "He was the first guy we auditioned," Berlanti told Rob Salem for the *Toronto Star* (30 July 2012). "Every step of the way, it was Stephen, Stephen, Stephen."

Amell won the role a week after he auditioned and began a serious training program that included martial arts, gymnastics, structure-jumping parkour, and archery. Amell had never shot an arrow before. "The first thing was getting the form," Amell told Salem. "If you think comic book fans are aggressive and interested, archery fans and enthusiasts are just as much so. So you want to please them as much as you want to please comic book fans." By the time Amell landed *Arrow*, he had appeared on a number of television shows, but carrying a show proved to be a challenge. "The first season was very, very difficult for me," he recalled to Agard. The positive reaction to *Arrow* initially intensified Amell's stress. He contracted walking pneumonia, and was sick into the shooting of the show's second season. In his review of *Arrow* for the *New York Times* (9 Oct. 2012), Neil Genzlinger praised Amell's performance. "Stephen Amell is a good fit for Oliver: muscular, handsome and just inscrutable enough to pull off the transition from the playboy he was before the shipwreck to the avenging, bow-wielding Green Arrow he becomes on his return to civilization," he wrote.

Amell told Agard that he felt a sense of ownership over his character by the show's second season, which Amell declared the show's strongest. By then, he said, "*Arrow* was the most important thing in my entire life by a wide margin." Despite his love for the show, Amell told Berlanti that he wanted *Arrow* to end after season seven. The CW opted to make one more season; it was announced in 2019 that the show's eighth season would be its last. "I think *Arrow* as you know it effectively ended [in season 7]," Amell told Agard. "It's a different show in season 8. It's like we're playing our greatest hits."

TEENAGE MUTANT NINJA TURTLES AND OTHER WORK

In 2016, Amell appeared alongside Megan Fox, Laura Linney, Will Arnett, and Tyler Perry in the action film *Teenage Mutant Ninja Turtles: Out of the Shadows*. He played Casey Jones, an aspiring detective and hockey stick–wielding vigilante. Amell told Brian Truitt for *USA Today* (6 June 2016) that he was excited to play a character that was a little less stoic than Oliver Queen. "Oliver, you can count the number of smiles he's cracked over the past two seasons on two hands," he joked. In 2019, Arnell and his cousin Robbie teamed up to produce and star in a sci-ence-fiction film called *Code 8*. The film takes place in a futuristic universe in which people with supernatural psychic powers are a sup-pressed minority. Amell plays the head of a ne-farious crime ring, who employs the electrically endowed to commit robberies. Reviewers were positive, if reserved in their praise. Dennis Har-vey wrote for *Variety* (12 Dec. 2019) that *Code 8* "is a well-crafted mix of crime melodrama and fantasy," despite its limitations. "The performers are generally strong, even if their roles don't give them a lot of room for depth or invention."

Amell is also the cofounder of a wine club called Nocking Point. The idea for the business was hatched in 2012, when Amell's friend and cofounder Andrew Harding took Amell to visit a winery for the first time. The pair oversee col-laborations with local wineries to create specific blends.

PERSONAL LIFE

Amell married Carolyn Lawrence in Toronto in 2007, but the two divorced in 2010. He married actor, model, and former reality show contes-tant Cassandra Jean in 2012. They have a young daughter, born in 2013, named Mavi Alexandra Jean Arnell. They live in Los Angeles.

SUGGESTED READING

Amell, Stephen. "Stephen Amell Reflects on His *Arrow* Journey: 'I F——ing Care a Lot about It.'" Interview by Chancellor Agard. *Entertainment Weekly*, 14 Oct. 2019, ew.com/tv/2019/10/14/arrow-stephen-amell-season-8-interview/. Accessed 18 Dec. 2019.

Genzlinger, Neil. "Castaways Gain New Leases on Lives of Promise." Review of *Arrow*, cre-ated by Greg Berlanti, et al., and *Beauty & the Beast*, created by Sherri Cooper-Landsman, et al. *The New York Times*, 9 Oct. 2012, www.ny-times.com/2012/10/10/arts/television/arrow-and-beauty-the-beast-on-the-cw-network.html. Accessed 18 Dec. 2019.

Govani, Shinan. "Shinan: Stephen Amell Hangs Up His Wardrobe." *National Post*, 23 Nov. 2011, nationalpost.com/scene/shinan-stephen-amell-hangs-up-his-ward-robe. Accessed 18 Dec. 2019.

Harvey, Dennis. "'Code 8': Film Review." Review of *Code 8*, directed by Jeff Chan. *Variety*, 12 Dec. 2019, variety.com/2019/film/reviews/code-8-review-1203430757/. Accessed 18 Dec. 2019.

Salem, Rob. "Stephen Amell Hits Bull's Eye with *Arrow*." *The Star*, 30 July 2012, www.thestar.com/entertainment/television/2012/07/30/stephen_amell_hits_bulls_eye_with_arrow.html. Accessed 18 Dec. 2019.

Singerman, Michelle. "Stephen Amell's Career Takes Off." *TRNTO*, Post City Magazines, 24 Oct. 2012, trnto.com/stephen-amells-career-takes-off/. Accessed 18 Dec. 2019.

"Stephen Amell: Realizing His Dream." *The An-drean*, Spring 2007, issuu.com/standrewscol-lege/docs/andrean-spring-2007/21. Accessed 18 Dec. 2019.

SELECTED WORKS

Arrow, 2012–20; *Teenage Mutant Ninja Turtles: Out of the Shadows*, 2016; *Code 8*, 2019

—*Molly Hagan*

Bianca Andreescu

Date of birth: June 16, 2000
Occupation: Tennis player

According to former tennis great and *ESPN* com-mentator John McEnroe, the future of profes-sional tennis belongs to Canadian player Bianca Andreescu. McEnroe told Simon Briggs for the UK *Telegraph* (27 Aug. 2019): "She's one of the best young competitors I've seen in 10 years." At nineteen years old, Andreescu came seemingly out of nowhere during the 2019 tennis season, winning both the Rogers Cup (Canadian Open) and the US Open, after defeating American ten-nis veteran Serena Williams for both titles. Af-ter not playing any Women's Tennis Association (WTA) matches in the 2018 season, in 2019 she became the highest-ranked Canadian player to date in the WTA, the first Canadian to claim a Grand Slam singles title, and the first teenaged Grand Slam singles titleholder in more than a dozen years. She completed the season ranked fifth in the world.

Andreescu plays the game with an energy and an enthusiasm that has earned her numer-ous fans, who concur that she is a fast-rising star who could be the future of the game. In an interview with Julia Elbaba for the *US Open* website (23 Aug. 2019), Andreescu noted: "I am very dedicated to the sport. I did always believe I could do big things. I am so grateful for what's

Photo by Tim Clayton/Corbis via Getty Images

happening right now in my life, and I'm gaining more and more experience playing these top players and being on big stages."

EARLY LIFE

Bianca Vanessa Andreescu was born in Mississauga, Ontario, outside Toronto, on June 16, 2000. Her parents, Nicu and Maria, had emigrated from Romania to the Toronto area in the mid-1990s with degrees in mechanical engineering and financial management, respectively, but little money. Grigore Andreescu, her paternal grandfather, recalled in an interview with Colin Freeze for the *Globe and Mail* (9 Sept. 2019), "All they had was one bag and a frying pan. That's all they could take with them."

In Canada, the Andreescu's father found work at an automotive company, and her mother started working at a bank. When Andreescu turned six, she moved to Romania so her mother could start a business and began her schooling there. After her mother's business closed, she returned to Canada, where her mother became the chief compliance officer at a financial services company.

Andreescu's time in Romania was beneficial for her development as an athlete. It was there she began participating in gymnastics, skating, soccer, swimming, and especially tennis. Picking up tennis at age seven, she showed considerable talent at an early age. Her first coach was Gabriel Hristache. When she returned to Canada in 2009, more serious coaching seemed necessary. She began playing her father often, and eventually she proved a far better player. "I was

10 when I first beat him," she recalled to Briggs. "We were both very competitive and he had to do sprints on the court as a forfeit."

That same year she joined first the Ontario Racquet Club and then the Tennis Canada Regional Training Centre in Toronto. Later she continued her training at the National Training Centre in Montreal, Quebec.

JUNIOR TENNIS CAREER

Andreescu's junior tennis career began in earnest in 2012. From 2011 to 2015 she won eighty-five individual Tennis Canada events as well as twenty-two junior doubles tournaments.

In early 2014, she won the youth tournament Les Petits As in Tarbes, France. That same year she followed that victory with a string of International Tennis Federation (ITF) World Tennis Tour Juniors tournament victories, including at the Copa Horizontes de la Amistad in Cuba, the Ace Tennis Under-18 Canadian World Ranking Event, and South Carolina ITF.

In 2015 Andreescu continued to dominate ITF junior events, winning the Condor De Plata in Bolivia in February, the Canadian Open Junior Championships in September, and the Metropolia Orange Bowl International Tennis Championship in Florida in December. That summer, she had also made her Wimbledon debut but was eliminated in the first round of girls' singles competition and the second round of girls' doubles. Wimbledon, the Australian Open, the French Open (also called Roland-Garros), and the US Open—known collectively as the Grand Slams—are the most prestigious events in elite tennis. Tennis Canada named her the Outstanding Junior Female Player of the Year 2015 in recognition of her international under-16 and under-18 championship wins in 2014 and 2015, respectively. Around this time, Andreescu also entered her first women's professional tournament, the ITF Gatineau National Bank Challenger in Quebec, where she made the finals.

The 2016 season proved mixed for Andreescu. She made it to the quarterfinals at the Australian Open junior doubles but missed the first half of the season due to leg and foot injuries. Upon her return to play, she began having success at ITF events across Canada and played two qualifying rounds in the Rogers Cup. That August, she won her first professional title at the Challenger Banque Nationale de Gatineau tournament in Quebec, by beating American player Elizabeth Halbauer. She also progressed to the finals of another ITF event in Saguenay, Quebec. By the end of the year, she was once again named Tennis Canada's Junior Female Player of the Year and was designated its most improved player.

GOING PRO

In 2017 Andreescu transitioned from the junior circuit to the professional one. At the 2017 Australian Open and French Open, she and tennis partner Carson Branstine won the junior girls' doubles tournament, and she reached the semifinals in the Australian Open singles. She then won a couple ITF tournaments, in California in February and Italy in April. Andreescu qualified for the women's division at Wimbledon for the first time in July 2017 but lost to Kirstina Kučová of Slovakia in the round of 128. She ultimately ranked 182nd worldwide for that season. Despite that, Andreescu received her third consecutive Tennis Canada Junior Female Player of the Year title as well as its female player and singles player honors. The lack of steady progress frustrated her, however. "I would get very negative thoughts going through my mind. I would smash racquets," she recalled to Cathal Kelly for the *Globe and Mail* (8 Sept. 2019).

Andreescu entered the 2018 season at the Australian Open qualifiers but failed to make it past the first round. She did a little better at the French Open and Wimbledon, where she got to the third qualifying round, but faced immediate elimination in the US Open qualifiers in August. Andreescu, plagued by injury, primarily competed at ITF events. Through fits and starts, she reached the finals in four ITF tournaments, the quarterfinals at the Midland Tennis Classic, and the semifinals of the Challenger Banque Nationale de Granby, from which she withdrew due to a back injury. Unable to qualify for the Grand Slams, she ended the season ranked 178th.

ROGERS CUP

In the offseason, with the help of her coaches, family, and friends, she worked more on her creative visualization and meditation, which she had been practicing from the age of twelve. Through it, she imagines the best positive outcomes of events and, in combination with her tennis training and yoga, makes those imagined outcomes a reality. Her practice began to pay dividends in the 2019 tennis season. Early on that year she progressed to the finals in the ASB Classic in Auckland, New Zealand, where she defeated Dane Caroline Wozniacki and American Venus Williams before losing to Julia Goerges of Germany.

More successes followed. She made it to the round of 64 at the Australian Open, then won the Oracle Challenger Series in Newport Beach, California. After advancing to the semifinals in Acapulco, Mexico, she landed a wild-card spot at and won the Indian Wells, California, tournament in March, beating Angelique Kerber of Germany in the finals. Up to then, no Canadian had ever won a WTA Premier Mandatory tournament.

Injuries came back to haunt Andreescu, however, after the Miami Open in late March. Sidelined for over two months because of a shoulder problem, she returned to play at the French Open, where she made it to the round of 64. Andreesu staged her comeback at the 2019 Rogers Cup (formerly the Canadian Open) in Toronto in early August. There, she won a memorable first-round match against fellow Canadian Eugenie Bouchard, then collected five more wins to become the first Canadian in a half-century to reach—and win—the finals of the Rogers Cup. Among her defeated opponents were three top-ten players: Kiki Bertens of the Netherlands, Karolina Plíšková of the Czech Republic, and Serena Williams, who withdrew from the finals with upper back spasms.

HISTORIC US OPEN

Heading into the 2019 US Open, Andreescu was ranked fifteenth in the world, with a win-loss record of 25–4 and having faced seven top-ten players. When asked about the pressure she might feel facing such formidable opponents, she said to Elbaba: "There's always pressure—external pressure or the pressure you put on yourself. I try to embrace it as much as I can, and I think I play better when there is some pressure, especially when the pressure is from myself, because I always want to do well. . . . If I go out there and give my best, that's all that matters to me."

If Andreescu's potential as a champion was hinted at throughout the 2019 season, it was fully on display at the US Open, in which she beat a slew of tough and talented competitors before becoming the third Canadian to advance to the finals at a Grand Slam event. Here, she again faced the veteran Serena Williams, but bested her in straight sets. In doing so, she became the first teen to win a Grand Slam since 2006, when Russian player Maria Sharapova won the US Open. She was also the first Canadian to secure a Grand Slam singles victory. An estimated 3.4 million Canadian television viewers, or roughly 10 percent of the total population of Canada, and 3.2 million Americans watched her historic win. Andreescu also earned a considerable amount of prize money: more than $6.5 million within just that calendar year.

Andreescu went on to lose in her China Open quarterfinal match against Japanese star player Naomi Osaka mere weeks after her historic US Open victory. That October, at the highly selective WTA Finals in Shenzhen, China, she suffered two more losses and another injury ended her season prematurely.

Sports reporters saw this year as just the beginning for the Canadian, as long as she could stay injury-free. "The one thing I worry about is her injuries," Chris Evert, a former tennis great and EPSN analyst, told Peter Bodo for *ESPN* (4 Dec. 2019). "But I love her game. She plays in-your-face tennis. I love that aggressiveness." Others agreed, leading to her being awarded the Lou Marsh Trophy for Canadian athlete of the year.

PERSONAL LIFE

Andreescu has been seen as more outgoing than other tennis stars of comparable age. She enjoys hip-hop music and animals. When not touring for tennis, she lives in Thornhill, Ontario.

SUGGESTED READING

Andreescu, Bianca. "2019 US Open Interview: Bianca Andreescu." Interview by Julia Elbaba. *US Open*, 23 Aug. 2019, www.usopen.org/en_US/news/articles/2019-08-23/2019_us_open_interview_bianca_andreescu.html. Accessed 3 Dec. 2019.

Bodo, Peter. "Rafael Nadal, Bianca Andreescu and the Best Tennis in 2019." *ESPN*, 4 Dec. 2019, www.espn.com/tennis/story/_/id/28210826/rafael-nadal-bianca-andreescu-best-tennis-2019. Accessed 5 Dec. 2019.

Briggs, Simon. "Bianca Andreescu Exclusive Interview: 'I Want to Be Social, but Love Means Nothing in This Sport.'" *Telegraph*, 27 Aug. 2019, www.telegraph.co.uk/tennis/2019/08/27/bianca-andreescu-exclusive-interview-want-social-love-means. Accessed 4 Dec. 2019.

Freeborn, Jeremy. "Bianca Andreescu." *The Canadian Encyclopedia*, 23 Oct. 2019, the-canadianencyclopedia.ca/en/article/bianca-andreescu. Accessed 4 Dec. 2019.

Freeze, Colin. "Bianca Andreescu's Cool, Hard-Working Demeanour Comes from the Example Set by Her Romanian Parents." *The Globe and Mail*, 9 Sept. 2019, www.theglo-beandmail.com/sports/article-from-romania-to-ontario-ambition-has-always-driven-the-andreescu/. Accessed 4 Dec. 2019.

Kelly, Cathal. "There's Just One Explanation for Bianca Andreescu's Success: She's a Born Winner." *The Globe and Mail*, 8 Sept. 2019, www.theglobeandmail.com/sports/article-theres-just-one-explanation-for-bianca-an-dreescus-success-shes-a/. Accessed 3 Dec. 2019.

Rush, Curtis. "Bianca Andreescu's Historic US Open Win Attracts Record 3.4 Million Canadian Viewers." *Forbes*, 10 Sept. 2019, www.forbes.com/sites/curtisrush/2019/09/10/bianca-andreescus-historic-us-open-win-attracts-record-34-million-canadian-viewers/#14bc20a8610e. Accessed 3 Dec. 2019.

—Christopher Mari

Yalitza Aparicio

Date of birth: December 11, 1993
Occupation: Actor

Yalitza Aparicio came to the attention of moviegoers in 2018, when she made her on-screen debut in director Alfonso Cuarón's critically acclaimed *Roma*. The semiautobiographical film is based upon the auteur's childhood in Mexico City and focuses on two women who had a deep impact on him: his mother, played in the picture by Marina de Tavira, and his nanny, played by Aparicio.

Aparicio's performance earned her an Academy Award nomination for best actress, and although she lost out to Olivia Colman, star of the costume drama *The Favourite*, her nomination alone was considered groundbreaking, as she was the first indigenous woman ever to be nominated in the best-actress category. She went on to break other ground as well, appearing on the cover of such glossy magazines as *Vanity Fair* and *Vogue*.

Roma—and Aparicio herself—were widely credited with starting "a national conversation about inequality, the treatment of domestic workers and who is welcome on the red carpet in a country where indigenous women are rarely seen in magazines, much less at Hollywood awards shows," as Laura Tillman wrote for the *New York Times* (17 Jan. 2019).

"I am showing my people that they also can reach something like this, that just because you don't have blonde hair and green eyes, it doesn't

Photo by Stefanie Keenan/Getty Images for FIJI Water

mean you can't be a part of it," Aparicio told a reporter for Agence France-Presse, as published on the *Voice of America* website (11 Dec. 2018). "There are certain things that will change little by little in our culture and let's hope that with this picture, something is learned."

In recognition of her commitment to challenging racism and stereotyping, the editors of *Time* magazine included her on their 2019 list of the 100 most influential people in the world, and, leveraging her newfound visibility to do even more, in October 2019 Aparicio accepted a post as a UNESCO (United Nations Educational, Scientific and Cultural Organization) Goodwill Ambassador for Indigenous Peoples. Praising his star in a tribute for *Time* (17 Apr. 2019), Cuarón wrote, "She's incredibly grounded in her truth and not easily swept away by the glitz and glamour of Hollywood. She focuses on being a force of change and empowerment for indigenous women, embracing the symbolic value of what she has done and carrying that responsibility with dignity and grace."

EARLY LIFE AND EDUCATION

Yalitza Aparicio Martínez was born on December 11, 1993, in Tlaxiaco, an agricultural town in the southern Mexican state of Oaxaca. She is of mixed indigenous heritage. Her father, a street vendor, is Mixtec, and her mother, a domestic worker, is Triqui. When interviewers ask about the derivation of her unusual first name, Aparicio has no ready answer. When her parents attempted to register her name at birth, administrators were initially resistant to doing so, suggesting it was not a real name.

Her father adamantly refused to teach Aparicio and her three siblings the Mixtec language, fearing that speaking it would expose them to the same prejudices that he had experienced throughout his life. "When people heard him speak his native language they would dismiss him," she explained to Carlos Aguilar for *Flood Magazine* (6 Dec. 2018). She had to learn it, however, for her role in *Roma* and has expressed hope that the movie will lead to greater appreciation for Mexico's rich linguistic traditions.

As a child, Aparicio loved to draw and read, and she was known for being exceptionally shy. She had no evident interest in performing, and when asked one year to carry the flag into school assemblies, she was reluctant and had to be talked into it.

Although she harbors some fond memories of her father—they occasionally watched action movies together, with Arnold Schwarzenegger films being a favorite—he left home when she was in her teens and her two youngest siblings were still toddlers. Her mother supported the family on her own by working as a maid; Aparicio has recalled to interviewers that she sometimes pitched in with the cleaning so that her mother could get home earlier.

Aparicio, who had always loved children, set her sights on becoming a teacher, despite discouragement from those who thought she should not aspire to a profession. "People would tell me, 'Why do you study?'" she recalled to Carolina A. Miranda for the *Los Angeles Times* (7 Feb. 2019). "One, you are a woman. Two, you don't have the right color. Three, your economic station doesn't help. You'll end up getting married and becoming a servant." Despite those naysayers, in 2016 she earned her teaching degree from Escuela Normal Experimental Presidente Lázaro Cárdenas, a teacher's college in the Oaxaca town of Putla.

ACTING CAREER

Shortly after Aparicio graduated, and before she found a teaching job, her older sister, Edith, asked her to come along to an audition she had heard about from a local community leader. The famed director Alfonso Cuarón—celebrated for such films as *Y Tu Mamá También* [And Your Mother Too] (2001), *Harry Potter and the Prisoner of Azkaban* (2004), and *Gravity* (2013)—was casting his newest project and was intent upon finding actors who could not only emote on the big screen but who bore a strong resemblance to the women on whom their characters were based: Mexican domestic workers, like Aparicio's mother.

Aparicio, who had never even heard of Cuarón, seemed an unlikely candidate for a film role, as she had never been particularly interested in film or television. The Mexican film industry was known for casting mainly light-skinned actors, and when indigenous people did appear, they were often portrayed stereotypically. "I never found a [film] representation that seemed similar to me or that touched on the ways I was raised," she told Miranda. Still, she went to the audition to meet with Cuarón's scouts, who had been combing Mexico for almost a year and had auditioned more than three thousand actors by then.

Cuarón has said that from the moment he set eyes on Aparicio, who bore a striking resemblance to his childhood nanny, Libo, he knew she was right for the role of Cleodegaria, also known as Cleo, a domestic worker from an indigenous tribe living with an upper-middle-class family in Mexico City during the 1970s.

It was not an optimal hiring period for teachers in Mexico, so Aparicio accepted the role, telling the highly regarded director in an oft-reported remark that she had "nothing better to do." "So many things were going through my head," she told Miranda of the moment Cuarón extended his offer. "I didn't have work, I had just graduated, I had to pay back the loans I took to get my degree. I thought, my mother will be proud and I can use this to pay for my expenses."

Cuarón introduced the fledgling actor to the elderly Libo before filming started so that the two could confer, and he built a close replica of the house in which he had grown up. He did not give his cast the entire script at once, doling out only small portions at a time and encouraging them to improvise. The result was a naturalistic and poignant tour de force that was met with almost universally rapturous reviews. "Cuarón uses one household on one street to open up a world, working on a panoramic scale often reserved for war stories, but with the sensibility of a personal diarist," Manohla Dargis wrote for the *New York Times* (20 Nov. 2018). "It's an expansive, emotional portrait of life buffeted by violent forces, and a masterpiece."

In addition to Aparicio's Oscar nomination, the film garnered her a slew of other prestigious best-actress nods—including those from the Chicago Film Critics Association, the Critics' Choice Movie Awards, the Gotham Awards, the San Francisco Film Critics Circle, and the Women Film Critics Circle—and she won a number of regional awards, including the New Hollywood Award at the Hollywood Film Awards and the best actress award at both the Platino Awards for Iberoamerican Cinema and the Premios ACE, given by the Association of Latin Entertainment Critics. Marina de Tavira, the actor who portrayed the mother in the film, was nominated at the Academy Awards ceremony as best supporting actress, and Cuarón took home statuettes for best director, best cinematography, and best foreign language film.

Unfortunately, Aparicio received not only accolades and adulation. She also became a target for racist online trolls, particularly after she appeared in early 2019 on the covers of *Vanity Fair*'s annual "Hollywood" issue and *Vogue México*. (The *Vogue* cover featured a Mixtec-language headline, "*In tiu'n ntav'i*," which translates to "A Star Is Born.") She appeared admirably capable of ignoring the vitriol. "Despite the many years between the period depicted in the movie and our present time," she told Aguilar, "I have experienced the same discrimination as Cleo because of the color of my skin, because of my indigenous roots, and because of my social class."

ADVOCACY

Roma's release precipitated a new wave of awareness about the plight of Mexico's indigenous people—more than 70 percent of whom live in poverty and face rampant discrimination. The film has also highlighted conditions for Mexico's 2 million domestic workers, and at premieres in that country, Cuarón invited workers' rights advocates to speak.

In October 2019, the United Nations' cultural agency UNESCO appointed Aparicio as a goodwill ambassador, charging her with helping to preserve indigenous culture and advocate for equal access to education.

Although she has not confirmed her next film project, Aparicio has expressed a willingness to continue acting. "In the end, this isn't so different from [the teaching] I wanted to do," she told Tillman. "I realized that film can educate people of all ages, in a far-reaching way."

SUGGESTED READING
Aguilar, Carlos. "Children of Women: Yalitza Aparicio and Marina de Tavira's Trip to 'Roma.'" *Flood Magazine*, 6 Dec. 2018, floodmagazine.com/55434/children-of-women-yalitza-aparicio-and-marina-de-taviras-trip-to-roma/. Accessed 10 Nov. 2019.

Chi, Paul. "No Matter What Happens at the Oscars, Yalitza Aparicio Is Having the Time of Her Life." *Vanity Fair*, 23 Feb. 2019, www.vanityfair.com/hollywood/2019/02/yalitza-aparicio-oscars-roma-best-actress. Accessed 10 Nov. 2019.

Cuarón, Alfonso. "Time 100: Yalitza Aparicio." *Time*, 17 Apr. 2019, time.com/collection/100-most-influential-people-2019/5567863/yalitza-aparicio/. Accessed 10 Nov. 2019.

Dargis, Manohla. "Alfonso Cuarón's Masterpiece of Memory." Review of *Roma*, directed by Alphonso Cuarón. *The New York Times*, 20 Nov. 2018, www.nytimes.com/2018/11/20/movies/roma-review.html. Accessed 10 Nov. 2019.

Miranda, Carolina A. "*Roma* Star Yalitza Aparicio Is So Much More Than Her Oscar Fairy Tale." *Los Angeles Times*, 7 Feb. 2019, www.latimes.com/entertainment/arts/miranda/la-et-cam-yalitza-aparicio-roma-oscars-20190128-story.html. Accessed 10 Nov. 2019.

Tillman, Laura. "Yalitza Aparicio of 'Roma' and the Politics of Stardom in Mexico." *The New York Times*, 17 Jan. 2019, www.nytimes.com/2019/01/17/movies/yalitza-aparicio-roma.html. Accessed 10 Nov. 2019.

"Yalitza Aparicio: An Indigenous Mexican Woman Captivates Hollywood." *Voice of America*, 11 Dec. 2018, www.voanews.com/arts-culture/yalitza-aparicio-indigenous-mexican-woman-captivates-hollywood. Accessed 10 Nov. 2019.

—*Mari Rich*

Awkwafina

Born: June 2, 1988
Occupation: Actor and rapper

Awkwafina is the alter ego Nora Lum concocted for her rap persona when she was around fifteen. More than fifteen years later, the rapper turned actor has steadily forged her path in the film and television industries, where the moniker became a representation of her duality. "Awkwafina is big and brash," she told Jiayang Fan for the *New Yorker* (13 Aug. 2018). "She's the person who says whatever's on her mind. But she also hasn't grown up or thought about consequences. Nora is the person who is neurotic and overthinks."

It was this impromptu, unapologetic side of her personality that led Awkwafina to release a 2012 rap video whose raw, unfiltered lyrics made it viral, amassing millions of views on YouTube. While this song gave her an entry into the music industry—following it with the hip-hop album *Yellow Ranger* in 2014—it also earned her enough notoriety to be cast on television series, such as MTV's *Girl Code* (2014–15), and in films, such as *Neighbors 2: Sorority Rising* (2016). As Awkwafina continued to take on acting roles, she released a new EP, *In Fina We Trust*, and appeared in two commercially successful ensemble features in 2018: *Ocean's 8* and *Crazy Rich Asians*. However, it was her leading performance as Billi in the comedy-drama *The Farewell* (2019) that earned her a Golden Globe Award for Best Performance by an Actress in a Motion Picture—Musical or Comedy, catapulting her to stardom.

Although Lum's road to fame was an unconventional one—given that she had no initial intention of pursuing a career in the entertainment industry—she became increasingly convinced that acting was her destined vocation. As she told Allison Glock for *Marie Claire* (11 Sept. 2019), "This career really, truly feels like what I'm supposed to be doing."

EARLY LIFE AND EDUCATION

Awkwafina was born Nora Lum on June 2, 1988, in New York City, New York, to Wally and Tia Lum. Her father, who works in the information technology field, is Chinese American while her mother, a painter, had immigrated from South Korea. When she was four years old, her mother died from pulmonary hypertension—and the future rapper and actor was raised by her father along with her grandmother. Following this event, loss shaped her childhood as she grew up in the Forest Hills neighborhood of the Queens borough.

Aside from finding solace in the close bond she shared with her grandmother, Powah, Lum also found another ally: comedy. "I

Photo by Casi Moss via Wikimedia Commons

started watching *Saturday Night Live* and *Mad TV* at maybe six or seven. I remember going into school making my teachers crack up. I was really into audacious comedy," she explained to Glock. Her fondness for unfiltered, cheeky humor followed her to Fiorello H. LaGuardia High School of Music and Art and Performing Arts, where she studied music, specifically the trumpet, and read the verses of poet Charles Bukowski. It was also during this time that she, jokingly, came up with the stage name of Awkwafina for her rap persona—a hobby she had taken up when she was thirteen—and began producing music using a program on her MacBook.

Following her high school graduation in 2006, Lum moved to Beijing, China, for two years to study Mandarin at the Beijing Language and Culture University. "I was growing up my whole life with people telling me to go back to this place, on the street or whatever," she explained to Rachel Aroesti for the *Guardian* (7 Sept. 2019) of this period that she viewed as a challenging one, characterized by culture shock and a sense of not belonging. "And you go back, and you genuinely feel like you don't belong there—you don't speak the language and you were never taught it, you feel like a failure in that way. It's ironic." When she returned to the United States, she enrolled at the State University of New York at Albany, where she majored in journalism and women's studies, completing her degree in 2011.

RELEASING AUDACIOUS RAP

After graduating from college, having spent time working at a video store in her late teens, Lum worked at a publishing company as a publicity assistant—that is, until she uploaded the 2012 Awkwafina music video on YouTube, a comeback to a 2006 track by rapper Mickey Avalon. Although the song caused her to lose her publishing job and any likelihood of securing another such position in a professional office setting, it also made her a viral sensation, garnering hundreds of thousands of views in a short time and receiving attention from well-known publications, such as *New York* magazine. After releasing her 2012 song, she worked several jobs to make a living, including at a Japanese restaurant and a vegan bodega, before becoming aware that she was really onto something with Awkwafina. "When I realized Awkwafina was bigger than I thought, I didn't work [those jobs] anymore," she told Momo Chang in an interview for the Center for Asian American Media (CAMM) (23 Feb. 2015).

Propelled by the unexpected momentum her music had gained, Awkwafina continued to write and produce songs, releasing a hip-hop album titled *Yellow Ranger* in 2014. Composed of eleven tracks, this album helped solidify her unique style; that of a comic persona who is not afraid to be sassy or bawdy while remorselessly singing about controversial topics. Soon, this unapologetic approach to her craft won her a legion of fans.

It was also around this time that Awkwafina broke into acting and began to appear both on television and in films. In 2014, she appeared in several episodes of MTV's *Girl Code*, a series in which female figures in comedy, music, and acting discuss topics and issues relevant to all women, and, the following year, served as cohost on the spin-off, *Girl Code Live*. Also that year, she brought an offbeat twist to the late-night talk show format with the beginning of her new series *Tawk*, housed on Verizon's free video service, in which she hosted a wide range of guests at various locations, over the course of several seasons. After her videos had caught the attention of high-profile figures in the industry, including actor Seth Rogen, her film debut came with her portrayal of an energetic Kappa Nu sister named Christine in the comedy *Neighbors 2: Sorority Rising* (2016), a film starring Zac Efron, Rogen, and Rose Byrne. Furthermore, in the computer-animated family film *Storks*, released in 2016, she lent her voice to Quail, a minor character that nonetheless introduced her to voice acting.

MAKING A NAME FOR HERSELF IN FILM

The year 2018 was a particularly triumphant one for the rapper-turned-actor. In June, Awkwafina was seen in theaters as part of the cast of *Ocean's 8*, an all-female spin-off—and continuation—of the Ocean's trilogy. Directed by Gary Ross and featuring the likes of Sandra Bullock, Cate Blanchett, and Anne Hathaway, the film follows Debbie Ocean (portrayed by Bullock) as she recruits a crew to attempt a jewelry heist. Playing the part of Constance, a loudmouthed pickpocket, Awkwafina more than proved her talent and capabilities against a cast of veterans, demonstrating her comedic timing to a broader audience in a film that went on to become a summer box-office success. Around that same time, she also released a new EP, *In Fina We Trust*.

However, *Ocean's 8* was not the only commercially successful film in which Awkwafina appeared that year—or that summer. In August, audiences could watch her in *Crazy Rich Asians*, a film based on the 2013 best-selling novel of the same name by Kevin Kwan. Directed by Jon M. Chu and starring a cast predominantly of Asian descent, *Crazy Rich Asians* tells the story of Rachel Chu (played by Constance Wu), a Chinese American economics professor who travels to Singapore to meet her boyfriend's family only to discover they are among the wealthiest people there. In the film, Awkwafina played Rachel's college best friend, Goh Peik Lin, with whom the protagonist reunites during her stay in Singapore. Delivering a string of scene-stealing moments, Awkwafina was praised for portraying a character who was boisterous and witty—qualities that are part of her real-life nature. As she told Aroesti, "My grandma watched *Crazy Rich Asians* and was like: 'So what? You're not even doing anything!'"

Awkwafina did demonstrate true versatility in acting when she appeared in the 2019 dramedy *The Farewell*, written and directed by Lulu Wang. In the film Awkwafina played the lead role of Billi, a young Chinese American woman who travels to China to visit her grandmother who has been diagnosed with cancer and has only a few months to live. Keeping this information from her grandmother about her illness, Billi and her family choose not to divulge that the real purpose of the trip is to say their goodbyes to her, pretending they are there solely for a wedding. The overall seriousness of the role pushed Awkwafina out of her comedic comfort zone, which, as she explained to Yohana Desta for *Vanity Fair* (12 July 2019), was challenging at times: "From a very young age, I wanted to make people laugh to defer from the heavy stuff." Nevertheless, she did not disappoint. Her performance, which critics noted effectively exuded vulnerability and pain, received glowing reviews and earned her a 2020 Golden Globe Award for Best Performance by an Actress in a Motion Picture—Musical or Comedy.

STARRING IN *AWKWAFINA IS NORA FROM QUEENS*

The success of *The Farewell* was only the beginning of 2019 for the actor. In August of that year, she, once again, lent her voice to an animated production, this one titled *The Angry Birds Movie 2*. In this sequel—which continues the adventures of the flightless birds and green pigs living on Bird Island and Pig Island, respectively—Awkwafina portrayed a pig named Courtney. She then also made an impression with her turn as a patient at an island rehabilitation center for women in the dystopian fantasy-thriller *Paradise Hills*. When *Jumanji: The Next Level* premiered in December, the actor was seen in the role of Ming Fleetfoot, a new avatar inside the video game of *Jumanji*, whose other characters include Dr. Xander "Smolder" Bravestone (played by Dwayne Johnson) and Professor Sheldon "Shelly" Oberon (portrayed by Jack Black).

In January 2020, Awkwafina effortlessly transitioned from the silver screen to television when *Awkwafina Is Nora from Queens* premiered to especially good ratings on Comedy Central. An exaggerated, fictionalized account of her upbringing in Queens, the series stars Awkwafina as Nora, an often lazy, unmotivated, and insecure young woman who lives in her childhood home with her father, Wally, and her stubborn but clever grandmother. As season one progresses, Nora grapples with adulthood and its challenges while, at the same time, stumbling into a search for herself.

Even before its premiere, Comedy Central greenlighted the production of the second season of *Awkwafina Is Nora from Queens*, anticipating its success. A follow-up season, however, was only one of several upcoming projects for the star at that point. It had been announced in 2019 that she would voice a lead character in a new Disney animated film *Raya and the Last Dragon*. Although satisfied with where her career has taken her, she remains relentless in her quest for more roles: "I don't think I'll ever be satisfied to the point of not being hungry," she said to Glock. "I worry this is all a dream, that I won't know what to do to keep it going. This career is always going to be a risk. It's always going to be a ride."

PERSONAL LIFE

Before moving to Los Angeles, California, in 2018 and purchasing a condo there in 2019, Awkwafina lived in a railroad apartment in the Brooklyn borough of New York City for several years.

SUGGESTED READING

Awkwafina. "Nora Lum on Awkwafina." Interview by Momo Chang. *Center for Asian American Media*, 23 Feb. 2015, caamedia. org/blog/2015/02/23/awkwafina/. Accessed 6 Aug. 2020.

———. "Awkwafina on Race and Hollywood: 'Growing Up, I Latched On to Strong Asian-American Idols.'" Interview by Rachel Aroesti. *The Guardian*, 7 Sept. 2019, www.theguardian.com/film/2019/sep/07/awkwafina-farewell-crazy-rich-asians-oceans-8-nora-lum. Accessed 25 July 2020.

———. "Awkwafina Never Thought She'd End Up Here." Interview by Allison Glock. *Marie Claire*, 11 Sept. 2019, www.marieclaire.com/celebrity/a28943785/awkwafina-interview-2019. Accessed 25 July 2020.

Desta, Yohana. "Awkwafina Finds Herself in *The Farewell*." *Vanity Fair*, 12 July 2019, www.vanityfair.com/hollywood/2019/07/awkwafina-the-farewell-interview. Accessed 25 July 2020.

Fan, Jiayang. "Awkwafina Comes Home." *The New Yorker*, Condé Nast. 13 Aug. 2018, www.newyorker.com/magazine/2018/08/20/awkwafina-comes-home. Accessed 25 July 2020.

SELECTED WORKS

Neighbors 2: Sorority Rising, 2016; *Ocean's 8*, 2018; *Crazy Rich Asians*, 2018; *The Farewell*, 2019; *Jumanji: The Next Level*, 2019; *Awkwafina Is Nora from Queens*, 2020–

—*Maria del Pilar Guzman*

Javier Báez

Date of birth: December 1, 1992
Occupation: Baseball player

Javier Báez, a versatile and skilled professional baseball player who has filled nearly every defensive position available, is perhaps best known for the energetic and playful approach that he brings to his sport. "I like to run around and have fun out there, obviously to play hard, but at the same time to have fun," he told Danny Knobler for *Bleacher Report* (2 Oct. 2018). His expressive style of play has drawn younger fans' attention and been heralded by some as the future of the sport.

Since 2014 Báez has demonstrated his talents largely as an infielder for the Chicago Cubs, the major-league team that drafted him straight out of high school in 2011. With the Cubs, he has not only developed into a key, award-winning contributor to the franchise but also assisted in some of the team's most memorable victories to date, including the 2016 World Series win that ended more than a century of disappointment for Cubs fans. Although he has acknowledged in interviews that his career might one day take

Photo by Arturo Pardavila III via Wikimedia Commons

grandmother died unexpectedly within days of one another. "I went from being a child who saw his father every day to never seeing him again," he told Rivera for *ESPN* (26 Sept. 2016). "It was very difficult." Not long afterward, the family moved to the mainland United States, first to North Carolina and then Florida.

Báez spent most of his teen years in Jacksonville, Florida, where he attended the private Arlington Country Day School and learned English. On the varsity baseball team, the ambidextrous player rotated through several positions but focused particularly on those of third base and shortstop. A successful player throughout his high school career, Báez earned the title of the team's Player of the Year in 2010 and 2011 and was also named to high school All-American teams. His skills on the field and impressive statistics—including a batting average of .771 and fifty-two runs batted-in (RBI) during his senior season—captured the attention of scouts from both colleges and professional baseball franchises. He graduated from Arlington Country Day School in 2011.

MINOR LEAGUES
Báez had accepted admission to Jacksonville University to play baseball for the institution but was also eligible to be drafted during the MLB Draft, the annual event in which professional baseball organizations select and attempt to sign new players. On June 6, 2011, the Chicago Cubs selected him as the ninth overall draft pick in the first round of the draft. Following a period of negotiations, he signed with the organization in August of that year and subsequently began to play for the franchise's minor-league developmental teams, also known as "farm teams." Báez began his career in the minor leagues with the rookie-league Arizona League (AZL) Cubs before moving on to the Class A short-season Boise Hawks, playing in only a handful of games during that period.

The following season proved a more active one for Báez, who played for fifty-seven games for the Class A Peoria Chiefs and twenty-three for the Class A Advanced Daytona Cubs. During the fall, he also played for the Mesa Solar Sox, a team that competes in the Arizona Fall League.

After a 2013 season split between Daytona and the Class AA Tennessee Smokies, Báez played for the Leones de Ponce (Ponce Lions) in the Puerto Rican Winter League. That period of training improved his running significantly, and he was designated the 2013 Cubs Minor League Player of the Year.

Báez went on to join the Class AAA Iowa Cubs in the spring of 2014. Although a sprained ankle early in his time with Iowa proved challenging for him, he experienced significant success with the team, playing in more than one

him elsewhere, Báez has noted that remaining with the Cubs throughout his career would be especially meaningful. "It's a blessing when a player can wear the same uniform their whole life," he told Marly Rivera for *ESPN* (6 May 2020). He added, "For me, it's about loyalty. This is the team that has seen me grow up."

EARLY LIFE AND EDUCATION
Often referred to by fans and colleagues as Javy, Ednel Javier Báez was born on December 1, 1992, in Bayamón, Puerto Rico. He was the third of four children and the youngest son born to Nelida "Nelly" and Angel Luis Báez. As a small child he had difficulty walking and underwent orthopedic treatment.

Báez was raised in a family heavily immersed in the sport of baseball: both his paternal grandfather and his father had pitched for the Puerto Rican baseball leagues. In keeping with that legacy, Báez and his older brothers, Rolando and Gadiel, learned to play the sport as children, coached by their father. "It's what I grew up doing, and it's what I know how to do," he recalled to Gordon Wittenmyer for the *Chicago Sun Times* (6 July 2019) about his sport. "I couldn't stop." Initially alternating between catcher and centerfielder for his teams, Báez played in local youth baseball organizations and at times represented Puerto Rico in tournaments abroad. His lifelong love of baseball fueled his desire to play professionally one day, and he would go on to get a tattoo of the Major League Baseball (MLB) logo at the age of sixteen.

In 2004, when Báez was eleven, he survived a mugging. Some weeks later his father and his hundred games that season and demonstrating his growth as a player to Cubs franchise leadership.

MAJOR-LEAGUE DEBUT

In August 2014, the Cubs called Báez up from Iowa. He made his MLB debut with the team on August 5, in a game against the Colorado Rockies that went into extra innings. The Cubs won that game thanks in large part to Báez, who hit the tie-breaking home run. Following his debut, he remained with the Cubs for the rest of the year, appearing in fifty-two games during the regular season. Though a milestone season for Báez, the 2014 season was a disappointing one for the Cubs, which finished last in the National League (NL) Central division with a 73–89 win-loss record. He went on to play for Puerto Rico's Cangrejeros de Santurce that October.

Despite finishing the previous season in the MLB, Báez returned to the minor leagues for the start of 2015, again playing for the Iowa Cubs. Although long devoted to baseball, he seriously considered leaving the sport in April of that year following the death of his younger sister, Noely, from complications related to spina bifida, a congenital medical condition. "I didn't have purpose to play anymore," he told Wittenmyer. Following a three-week leave of absence from the Iowa Cubs, however, Báez decided to return to the team and resume playing in honor of his sister, a baseball fan who had been a fixture at his games. "My sister would want me to keep playing, obviously," he explained to Wittenmyer. "I decided to get better at it, and to have fun."

After several months with Iowa, Báez was again called up to the Chicago Cubs, rejoining the team in September 2015. He appeared in twenty-eight games during the regular season and went on to compete with the Cubs in the postseason after the team secured a wild card berth. Following the Cubs' defeat of the Pittsburgh Pirates in the NL Wild Card Game, the team went on to beat the St. Louis Cardinals in the National League Division Series (NLDS) before experiencing a decisive loss to the New York Mets in the National League Championship Series (NLCS).

GAME-CHANGING SEASON

Báez again spent the first several games of 2016 with the Iowa Cubs on a rehabilitation assignment but rejoined Chicago in mid-April and remained in the major leagues for the remainder of the season. The season proved successful for the Cubs, who finished the regular season ranked first in the NL Central division. In the postseason, the Cubs defeated the San Francisco Giants in the NLDS, with Báez hitting the first run of the series, and went on to beat the Los Angeles Dodgers, four games to two, in the NLCS. Báez and Cubs pitcher Jon Lester shared the title of NLCS Most Valuable Player (MVP) in recognition of their contributions during the series—including Báez's three runs scored in Game 5 and five RBIs as well as his high-quality defensive work.

Following the NLCS, the Cubs faced off against Cleveland in the World Series, the first world series for the franchise in seventy-one years. Although motivated by his earlier success, Báez initially found the experience of playing in the World Series daunting. "All the noise, the motivation, the feelings you get on that field—and the whole world is watching you," he told Rivera for *ESPN* (20 June 2017). "That got to me. When I went out to Game 1 in Cleveland, there was so much noise, I really felt smaller." Despite such challenges, and the weight of loyal Cubs fans' expectations, Báez and his teammates prevailed during the seven-game series, beating Cleveland by a single game to claim the Cubs' first World Series title since 1908.

ALL-STAR PLAYER

Báez remained with the Cubs for the next several seasons, consistently appearing in most of each season's games. After finishing first in the NL Central division for a second season in 2017, the Cubs beat the Washington Nationals in the NLDS before being defeated by the Dodgers in the NLCS. The 2018 regular season was also a successful one for Báez, who led the NL in RBIs and also scored the second-most triples, third-most bases, and seventh-most home runs in the league. His contributions to the team earned him a NL Silver Slugger Award and the title of NL Player of the Week in July, and Báez was likewise selected for his first MLB All-Star Game during the season. He was also short-listed for the Hank Aaron Award and Rawlings NL Gold Glove Award. The Cubs appeared briefly in the postseason competition that fall but were eliminated from the tournament after losing the NL Wild Card Game to the Colorado Rockies. The 2019 season—though less successful than its predecessors for the Cubs, who placed only third in the NL Central division despite an 84–78 win-loss record—was another strong one for Báez, who was selected for his second consecutive All-Star Game.

Although prepared to begin the season in March 2020, the MLB postponed the start of the baseball season due to concerns about the coronavirus 2019 (COVID-19) pandemic, which prompted event cancellations and shutdowns throughout the United States during the first half of that year. By late May, the MLB had proposed an abbreviated season that would start in July, with protective measures and prorated salaries; however, a conclusive season opening date had not yet been announced by the start of June.

In addition to postponing the start of play, the pandemic postponed talks between Báez and Cubs leadership regarding a potential contract extension, which would take effect following the expiration of his existing contract in 2021. "Obviously, we want to reach an agreement, but right now everything is on hiatus. Just like it happened with baseball, we decided to leave it there," Báez said, as reported by Rivera for *ESPN* (6 May 2020). Although he expressed a desire to remain with the team, he noted that such negotiations and their results were ultimately "business."

PERSONAL LIFE

Báez and his wife, Irmarie Márquez, met as children and later reconnected as adults. They had a son, Adrián, in 2018 and married in Puerto Rico in early 2019. When not playing baseball elsewhere, Báez splits his time between Greater Chicago and Puerto Rico, where he owns a ranch.

Long involved with charities dedicated to people with spina bifida, he has also participated in local philanthropic projects, including youth baseball programs, in Puerto Rico and Chicago.

SUGGESTED READING

Báez, Javier. "Javier Baez on the Art of the Tag." Interview by Marly Rivera. *ESPN*, 20 June 2017, www.espn.com/mlb/story/_/page/body-javierbaez/chicago-cubs-infielder-javier-baez-world-series-win art-tag-body-issue-2017. Accessed 6 June 2020.

Frenette, Gene. "Former Arlington Country Day Standout Javier Baez's Star Keeps Rising for Chicago Cubs." *Jacksonville.com*, 25 Oct. 2016, www.jacksonville.com/sports/2016-10-25/former-arlington-country-day-standout-javier-baez-s-star-keeps-rising-chicago-cubs. Accessed 6 June 2020.

Knobler, Danny. "Cubs Swag King Javier Baez Can Be MLB's Best Weapon to Win Back Young Fans." *Bleacher Report*, 2 Oct. 2018, bleacherreport.com/articles/2797369-cubs-swag-king-javier-baez-can-be-mlbs-best-weapon-to-win-back-young-fans. Accessed 6 June 2020.

Niesen, Joan. "Tag, You're It: Javier Baez Breaks Out as Cubs' Unexpected Star in October." *Sports Illustrated*, 26 Oct. 2016, www.si.com/mlb/2016/10/26/javier-baez-chicago-cubs-world-series. Accessed 6 June 2020.

Rivera, Marly. "Coronavirus Pandemic Slows Contract Talks between Javier Baez and Chicago Cubs." *ESPN*, 6 May 2020, www.espn.com/mlb/story/_/id/29142921/coronavirus-pandemic-slows-contract-talks-javier-baez-chicago-cubs. Accessed 6 June 2020.

———. "Javier Baez's Tattoos Tell His Story." *ESPN*, 26 Sept. 2016, www.espn.com/mlb/story/_/id/17628444/chicago-cubs-infielder-javier-baez-life-story-inked-body. Accessed 6 June 2020.

Wittenmyer, Gordon. "How Close the Cubs Came to Losing Javy Baez and Why He Plays the Game the Way He Does." *Chicago Sun Times*, 6 July 2019, chicago.suntimes.com/cubs/2019/7/6/20684135/how close-the-cubs-came-to-losing-javy-baez-and-why-he-plays-the-game-the-way-he-does. Accessed 6 June 2020.

—Joy Crelin

Adrienne Bailon

Date of birth: October 24, 1983
Occupation: Singer and talk show host

In April 2018, the hosts of the syndicated talk show *The Real* received a perhaps unexpected honor: the daytime Emmy Award for Outstanding Entertainment Talk Show Host. Although a relatively new talk show in comparison to some of its competitors—*The Real* had existed only since 2013—the personalities of the hosts and the show's cultivation of a dedicated viewer base made the program a force to be reckoned with. "We thought it wasn't possible for a little show like ours so early on," Adrienne Bailon, one of the show's hosts since its inception, told Susan Cheng for *O: The Oprah Magazine* (5 Oct. 2018) about winning the Emmy. "Now I don't doubt that we can do anything." For Bailon—also known as Adrienne Houghton following her marriage in 2016—the key to both the success of *The Real* and her own success has been authenticity. "I believe the right doors will open for you if you remain true to yourself and that authenticity is key in realizing your destiny," she explained to Vivian Nunez for *Forbes* (24 Oct. 2019). "Viewers and consumers are attracted to what is real and authentic and I think my candidness and authenticity has been a driving force in my success." As a show known for discussing a wide variety of topics, *The Real* has proven instrumental in enabling Bailon to showcase her authentic voice and reclaim her identity as a singer, an identity the former member of the singing groups 3LW and the Cheetah Girls had long avoided.

EARLY LIFE AND EDUCATION

Adrienne Eliza Bailon was born on October 24, 1983, in New York City, New York. Her mother, Nilda, is Puerto Rican, and her father, Freddie, moved to the United States from Ecuador in

Photo by RumorFix via Wikimedia Commons

1969. She grew up bilingual on the New York's Lower East Side, where she lived with her parents and sister, Claudette. Her parents divorced when she was thirteen, and she was raised by her separated parents and her mother's new husband, Joe Felix. Bailon was very close with her family during her early years and attributed her successful evolution from child star to well-rounded adult in large part to their influence. "I have to credit my family for being a great foundation. My upbringing and humble beginnings made me appreciate the opportunities I have received, and I never wanted to do anything that would ruin that," she explained to Dontaira Terrell for *New You* (19 May 2016).

In addition to establishing her close family relationships, Bailon's childhood gave her a deep love of music and performance. "We always were dancing, there was always music on, and it was just a part of my life," she told Hannah Rae for the *Jim Brickman Show* (31 May 2018). Bailon performed in plays and sang with performing groups such as church choirs during her childhood. Although she initially wanted to pursue a career in medicine, her aspirations shifted significantly in the late 1990s, when she and a group of other choir singers were selected to sing backup for the singer Ricky Martin. The opportunity helped her capture the attention of a music producer, who offered her a spot in the newly formed singing group 3LW.

3LW AND THE CHEETAH GIRLS

Formed in 1999, 3LW consisted of Bailon and fellow teenage singers Kiely Williams and Naturi Naughton. Their debut album, *3LW*, was released in 2000 and subsequently produced the hit singles "No More (Baby I'ma Do Right)" and "Playas Gon' Play," both of which tapped into the popularity of pop and R&B music at the time. The group released a second album, *A Girl Can Mack*, in 2002 and later that year released the Christmas album *Naughty or Nice*. Naughton left the group prior to the release of *A Girl Can Mack*, and singer Jessica Benson subsequently joined 3LW in 2003. Although 3LW continued to perform together for a time and was scheduled to release an additional album, the album was never released, and the group eventually disbanded in the mid-2000s.

While still a member of 3LW, Bailon costarred in the 2003 Disney Channel original film *The Cheetah Girls*, a work based on a series of novels by writer Deborah Gregory. Also starring 3LW colleague Williams, as well as actors and singers Raven-Symoné and Sabrina Bryan, the film follows the adventures of a group of teenagers as they attempt to establish themselves as a singing group. The film proved popular among the Disney Channel's young audience, and Bailon and her costars reprised their roles in the 2006 sequel, *The Cheetah Girls 2*. Although Raven-Symoné later left the franchise, the remaining stars again reunited for *The Cheetah Girls: One World* in 2008. Bailon enjoyed the process of filming the *Cheetah Girls* sequels, which took the group to countries such as Spain and India. "We're best friends and we get to travel," she told *OK!* (7 Nov. 2007). "I think for a lot of kids who may never be able to go to these places, we get to bring a whole new world into their living rooms." In addition to starring in the *Cheetah Girls* films, Bailon and her costars performed songs from the films on tour and released several albums, including multiple film soundtracks, the Christmas album *Cheetah-licious Christmas* (2005), and the album *TCG* (2007), which consisted of new material.

FILM AND TELEVISION PERSONALITY

During her time with the Cheetah Girls, Bailon also appeared in a variety of additional Disney Channel programs, including a documentary series about the Cheetah Girls' tours. She made guest appearances on scripted Disney series such as *That's So Raven* and *The Suite Life of Zack & Cody*, and in 2005, she played a supporting role in the Disney Channel original film *Buffalo Dreams*. In addition to Disney projects, Bailon acted in the theatrical films *Coach Carter* (2005) and *The Sisterhood of the Traveling Pants 2* (2008). Alongside her work in scripted television and film, Bailon made various appearances on the reality show *Keeping Up with the Kardashians* between 2008 and 2011, during the period in which she was dating cast member Rob Kardashian. In 2012 she starred in the reality series *Empire Girls: Julissa & Adrienne* alongside Julissa Bermúdez, a friend and aspiring performer.

In 2013, Bailon appeared in the television film *Lovestruck: The Musical*, and costarred in the independent Christian drama *I'm in Love with a Church Girl*. The latter follows a former drug dealer, played by the rapper and actor Ja Rule, who turns his life around after falling in love with a religious woman, played by Bailon. "It's a true testimony that your past does not determine your future, and I think it's got an incredibly great message," she told Elle Breezy for *Singersroom* (17 Oct. 2013) about the film.

THE REAL
A key point in Bailon's career came in July 2013, when the new daytime talk show *The Real* premiered on television. A panel talk show in the tradition of earlier shows such as *The View*, *The Real* launched with a five-host panel that included Bailon, actor Tamera Mowry-Housley, comedian Loni Love, singer Tamar Braxton, and fashion expert Jeannie Mai. Much like similar programs, the syndicated talk show features discussions of a wide range of topics as well as interviews with celebrities and public figures of interest to the program's target audience. Following Braxton's departure from the show, *The Real* continued with four hosts until 2020, when comedian and actor Amanda Seales joined the group.

For Bailon, joining the cast of *The Real* changed her life dramatically, enabling her to introduce audiences to her true self rather than her Cheetah Girl or reality-television personas. "*The Real* has had a profound impact on my career and I'm immensely proud to be on the show," she told Nunez. "It's allowed us into people's homes five days a week. Our audience has gotten to know a sillier, crazier, and more opinionated side of me." Popular among viewers and on social media, *The Real* was nominated for several daytime Emmy Awards between 2016 and 2019; Bailon and her cohosts won the 2018 Emmy Award for Outstanding Entertainment Talk Show Host.

RETURN TO MUSIC AND OTHER VENTURES
In addition to working in film and television, Bailon kept active in music following her time in the Cheetah Girls. In 2009, she announced that she had signed a solo deal with the record company Island Def Jam. Over the next several years, Bailon spoke about an upcoming record in interviews, referencing artists and producers with whom she hoped to work, but her solo album never materialized. She later explained that she did not release new music because of her fear of failure. "To step out on my own and let my voice be heard, I'm scared," she explained in a 2015 episode of *The Real*, as reported by Bruna

Nessif for *E! News* (28 Jan. 2015). "Like what if people don't like it? . . . What if it's not successful? Like I almost have been saying I would rather it not come out and just say, 'Well it just never came out,' [than] for it come out and be wack."

Bailon returned to music in 2017 with the Christmas album *New Tradiciones*. She then collaborated with her husband, Christian music singer Israel Houghton, on two songs from his 2018 album *The Road to DeMaskUs*. Bailon and Houghton were nominated for the 2019 daytime Emmy Award for Outstanding Musical Performance in a Daytime Program for their performance of the song "Secrets" from the album, which was aired on *The Real* in September 2018. She received further publicity for her singing in December 2019, when she was revealed to have been one of the contestants of the television show *The Masked Singer*, a singing competition in which contestants perform while wearing costumes that disguise their identities. Known during the competition as the Flamingo, Bailon impressed the show's judges with her vocal talents and placed third in the competition.

In late 2018, Bailon launched the first collection for her Christian-themed jewelry business, XIXI. "It's been a huge learning experience all around," Bailon told Nunez about her jewelry business, which launched several additional collections following the success of the first. "I design everything myself; I sketch out designs to send to our manufacturers who then make multiple samples. . . . It's a long process but it's worth it." Bailon also began to star in the YouTube series *All Things Adrienne* in 2018.

PERSONAL LIFE
Bailon was engaged to music executive Lenny Santiago in 2015, but the couple ended their engagement. She began dating Israel Houghton, a longtime friend who served as executive producer of her film *I'm in Love with a Church Girl* and contributed songs to the film's soundtrack, in early 2016. The couple married at the Hôtel Plaza Athénée Paris in November of that year. Following their marriage, Bailon began using the names Adrienne Bailon-Houghton or Adrienne Houghton. She has four stepchildren from Houghton's previous marriage.

SUGGESTED READING
Bailon, Adrienne. "Adrienne Bailon's Many Shades of Success." Interview by Dontaira Terrell. *New You*, 19 May 2016, www.newyou. com/archive/adrienne-bailons-many-shades-of-success/. Accessed 8 Mar. 2020.
——. "Adrienne Bailon Talks 'Church Girl' Message, 'The Real' Experience, Fall Fashion, New Music Dish, More." Interview by Elle Breezy. *Singersroom*, 17 Oct. 2013, singersroom.com/content/2013-10-17/

adrienne-bailon-talks-church-girl-message-the-real-experience-fall-fashion-new-music-dish-more/. Accessed 8 Mar. 2020.

——. Interview by Hannah Rae. *Jim Brick-man*, 31 May 2018, www.jimbrickman.com/adrienne-bailon-houghton/. Accessed 8 Mar. 2020.

Cheng, Susan. "The Co-Hosts of *The Real* Changed Television for Women of Color." *O: The Oprah Magazine*, 5 Oct. 2018, www.oprahmag.com/entertainment/tv-movies/a23309571/the-real-hosts-women-of-color-history. Accessed 8 Mar. 2020.

Nessif, Bruna. "Adrienne Bailon Breaks Down When Asked about Her Singing Career." *E! News*, 28 Jan. 2015, www.eonline.com/news/619620/adrienne-bailon-breaks-down-when-asked-about-her-singing-career-watch-the-emotional-clip. Accessed 8 Mar. 2020.

Nunez, Vivian. "Adrienne Bailon-Houghton Shares How Her Latinidad Inspired Her Latest Business Venture, XIXI." *Forbes*, 24 Oct. 2019, www.forbes.com/sites/vivian-nunez/2019/10/24/adrienne-bailon-shares-how-her-latinidad-inspired-her-latest-business-venture-xixi/#1005746d3b1b. Accessed 8 Mar. 2020.

"OK! Interview: The Cheetah Girls." *OK!*, 7 Nov. 2007, okmagazine.com/news/ok-interview-cheetah-girls/. Accessed 8 Mar. 2020.

SELECTED WORKS
The Cheetah Girls, 2003; *The Cheetah Girls 2*, 2006; *The Cheetah Girls: One World*, 2008; *Empire Girls: Julissa & Adrienne*, 2012; *I'm in Love with a Church Girl*, 2013; *The Real*, 2013– ; *All Things Adrienne*, 2018– ; *The Masked Singer*, 2019

—Joy Crelin

Abhijit Banerjee

Date of birth: February 21, 1961
Occupation: Economist

On October 14, 2019, the winners of the annual Nobel Prize in Economics were announced; the three economists, among them Massachusetts Institute of Technology (MIT) professor Abhijit Banerjee, would be sharing the award of nine million Swedish krona (approximately $945,000) "for their experimental approach to alleviating global poverty," as the official press release stated.

The release asserted that "one of humanity's most urgent issues is the reduction of global poverty, in all its forms," pointing out that more than 700 million people around the world subsist on

Photo by Financial Times via Wikimedia Commons

extremely low incomes and that each year some five million children under age five die of diseases that could have been prevented or cured by inexpensive treatments. According to the release, the trio (which also includes Harvard economist Michael Kremer and Esther Duflo—Banerjee's wife and MIT colleague) "have introduced a new approach to obtaining reliable answers about the best ways to fight global poverty" and "have dramatically improved our ability to fight poverty in practice."

It was the practical aspects of Banerjee, Duflo, and Kremer's approach that set it apart from most of the economics work that had previously won the Nobel. Although previous winners have been honored largely for theoretical research, by contrast, the 2019 laureates' fieldwork—which involves identifying specific, discrete problems that contribute to poverty and determining the best solutions through carefully designed experiments—has led to public policy changes (such as increased public spending on preventative healthcare and tutoring programs) and a widespread shift in the field of development economics, where their methods have now become standard.

Banerjee is perplexed that more of the world's problems are not addressed by those methods, which have been likened to the clinical trials methodically conducted by medical researchers. "I come from fairly pure theory and mathematical theories—so my background is very much that of someone who is trained to pose and solve puzzles," he explained to Decca Aitkenhead for the *Guardian* (22 Apr. 2012). "It's not that I don't want the poor to have better lives—quite the contrary. But it would be dishonest to say that that's where [my research] came out of, rather than out of a sense that I know all this economics, so why isn't it helping me understand stuff that I see next to me?"

In addition to the Nobel, Banerjee has garnered numerous other honors, including an Alfred P. Sloan Research Fellowship, multiple National Science Foundation (NSF) grants, an Econometric Society Fellowship, a Guggenheim Fellowship, an American Academy of Arts and Sciences Fellowship, and inclusion on *Foreign Policy* magazine's 2011 Top 100 Global Thinkers list.

EARLY LIFE AND EDUCATION

Abhijit Vinayak Banerjee was born on February 21, 1961, in Mumbai (then known as Bombay), the capital of the Indian state of Maharashtra. His parents were both economists: his mother, the former Nirmala Patankar, was of Marathi descent, the main ethnic group of Maharashtra; his father, Dipak Banerjee, hailed from a Bengali family of some academic renown.

When Banerjee was young his parents moved to Kolkata, when his father accepted a teaching post at Presidency College, a public institution whose founding dates to the early nineteenth century. Banerjee's father eventually chaired what was widely acknowledged as among the finest economics departments in the world, and he was considered something of a legend in India's academic circles. His mother also taught, securing a post at Kolkata's Centre for Studies in Social Sciences.

The Banerjee family home was on the upscale Ballygunge Circular Road, in southern Kolkata; despite that, it was not far from one of the city's many slums, and Banerjee has recalled that he sometimes envied his impoverished neighbors' freedom to play outdoors constantly while he was obligated to study.

Throughout his time as a student, Banerjee was recognized for his intelligence and mathematical ability, as well as his easy-going personality, eclectic taste in music, and well-honed sense of humor. In the late 1970s, after completing secondary school at South Point, an exclusive private institution popular with the Ballygunge area's educated elite, Banerjee entered Presidency College, then a top constituent school of the University of Calcutta. (It has since been named a university.) There he studied economics under, among other instructors, his father, who delighted in calling on him to explain complex mathematical concepts. Upon earning a Bachelor of Science degree in economics in 1981, Banerjee embarked upon graduate studies at Jawaharlal Nehru University, obtaining a master's degree in 1983 with an almost unbroken string of A-plus and A grades to his credit. Banerjee's academic path next took him to Cambridge, Massachusetts, where he earned a PhD in economics in 1988 from Harvard, with a thesis titled "Essays in Information Economics."

CAREER AS AN ECONOMIST

Banerjee remained in the United States after finishing his doctorate, teaching economics at Princeton University from 1988 to 1992. After a brief stint back at Harvard to teach during the 1992–93 academic year, he joined the faculty of MIT as an associate professor of economics. At MIT, he steadily took on positions of increasing prestige, being named full professor in 1996 and Ford Foundation International Professor of Economics in 2003.

In 2003 he also established MIT's Abdul Latif Jameel Poverty Action Lab (J-PAL), a research center that encourages scientifically informed policy-making in response to global poverty. Among his cofounders was Duflo, who had been Banerjee's graduate student at MIT and who had subsequently become one of the youngest MIT faculty members ever to be granted tenure.

While most economists seeking to make a difference in the developing world were then emphasizing theory and macroeconomic questions, members of J-PAL took a more granular approach—breaking those large questions into precise, testable pieces; pinpointing effective (and often inexpensive) interventions; and partnering with local authorities or nongovernmental organizations to carry them out. At first, "people thought this is kind of a loony agenda," Banerjee recalled to Jeanna Smialek for the *New York Times* (14 Oct. 2019). "People often told us: That's not how you learn about anything, because it's too small, too local." Gradually, however, their use of randomized control trials gained acceptance, as other researchers realized they provided a way to objectively test the real-world efficacy of poverty interventions.

The Nobel committee cited as an example an early set of Kremer's field experiments in Africa in the 1990s. He found at that time that giving schoolchildren access to extra textbooks or more nutritious breakfasts did not improve their test scores as expected; the problem was thus not a simple lack of common resources. Building upon that work, Banerjee and Duflo traveled to India to test the hypothesis that student learning is hampered instead by insufficiently personalized or rigorous teaching methods—and that outcomes could be improved by providing remedial tutoring and computer-assisted study programs. Proven correct, they later found that class size did not matter, but that preventing teacher absenteeism did, among other findings. They also turned their attention to issues of public health, discovering, for example, that deploying mobile clinics boosted vaccination rates significantly. They also found, somewhat counterintuitively, that microcredit programs, which give small loans to local business owners, did not significantly increase investment in or profitability of the recipients' small businesses.

In 2012, Banerjee and Duflo cowrote *Poor Economics: A Radical Rethinking of the Way to Fight Global Poverty*, whose jacket copy asked: "Why would a man in Morocco who doesn't have enough to eat buy a television?" and, "Why do the poorest people in the Indian state of Maharashtra spend 7 percent of their food budget on sugar?"

"On first impressions, you probably wouldn't take Abhijit Banerjee for the author of a gripping international bestseller," Aitkenhead wrote. "Then again, a page-turner about the microeconomics of aid policy might not sound too probable either. But that's what the mild-mannered Indian economist and his French coauthor, Esther Duflo, have written, and it is a truly remarkable book, best described as *Freakonomics* for the billion people on earth who live on less than a dollar a day."

THE NOBEL PRIZE AND ITS AFTERMATH

The book helped cement the couple's reputation as practical visionaries with solid, implementable ideas for alleviating poverty, but they were still surprised when, in the early morning hours of October 14, 2019, they were awakened by a call from Stockholm, informing them that they and Kremer, whom they considered a close colleague and mentor, would be sharing a 2019 Nobel Prize. (Mindful of the impending media onslaught and ever practical, Banerjee returned to bed to sleep for another hour after the call.)

The two are the sixth married couple in history to become Nobel laureates, and Duflo herself is the youngest person, at age forty-six, ever to win in the category of economics. Additionally, she is the second female economist (after Elinor Ostrom in 2009) to win the award. Banerjee is the second economist from India to win a Nobel, following in the footsteps of Amartya Sen, who won in 1998.

Although Banerjee's father died in 2007, before his son gained international fame, his mother, Nirmala, spoke to several journalists in the wake of the Nobel announcement, expressing pride in his accomplishments and admitting that although she too is an economist, his scholarly publications are too heavily grounded in mathematics to be understandable to her.

Just a month after they were awarded the prize, Banerjee and Duflo published a second book together, *Good Economics for Hard Times: Better Answers to Our Biggest Problems*. "The book's authors," Yanis Varoufakis wrote in his review for the *Guardian* (11 Nov. 2019), "write beautifully and are in full command of their subject. They examine the most crucial issues humanity faces (migration, trade wars, the scourge of inequality, climate catastrophe) with a combination of humility over what economics cannot tell us and pride over its contributions to our limited understanding." Varoufakis, a former finance minister of Greece, continued, "Their own conception of what economists should be doing is disarmingly down to earth. They see themselves as society's 'plumbers: we solve problems with a combination of intuition grounded in science, some guesswork aided by experience and a bunch of pure trial and error.'"

PERSONAL LIFE

Banerjee's first marriage, to Arundhati Tuli Banerjee—whom he had met as a teen back at the South Point School and who now teaches international literature at MIT—ended in divorce. They had one son, Kabir, who died in 2016, while still in his twenties. Banerjee has established a memorial scholarship fund in Kabir's name at a school in Jogiwala, India. Banerjee and Duflo married in 2015. The couple have two children, who were seven and five years old at the time the Nobel was announced.

SUGGESTED READING

"Abhijit Banerjee, Esther Duflo and Michael Kremer Win Nobel in Economics." *Economic Times*, 15 Oct. 2019, economictimes.indiatimes.com/news/politics-and-nation/abhijit-banerjee-esther-duflo-and-michael-kremer-win-nobel-in-economics/articleshow/71580136.cms. Accessed 16 Jan. 2020.

Aitkenhead, Decca. "Abhijit Banerjee: 'The Poor, Probably Rightly, See That Their Chances of Getting Somewhere Different Are Minimal.'" *The Guardian*, 22 Apr. 2012, www.theguardian.com/books/2012/apr/22/abhijit-banerjee-poor-chances-minimal. Accessed 16 Jan. 2020.

Banerjee, Rabi. "AB Positive." *The Week*, 19 Oct. 2019, www.theweek.in/theweek/cover/2019/10/18/ab-positive.html. Accessed 16 Jan. 2020.

Biswas, Soutik. "Abhijit Banerjee and Esther Duflo: The Nobel Couple Fighting Poverty." *BBC News*, 15 Oct. 2019, www.bbc.com/news/world-asia-india-50048519. Accessed 16 Jan. 2020.

Matthews, Dylan. "2 Nobel-Winning Economists Speak Out on Our Big Economic Problem: Not Enough Immigration." *Vox*, 6 Dec. 2019, www.vox.com/future-perfect/2019/12/6/20992071/abhijit-banerjee-esther-duflo-good-economics-hard-times-interview. Accessed 16 Jan. 2020.

Smialek, Jeanna. "Nobel Economics Prize Goes to Pioneers in Reducing Poverty." *The New York Times*, 14 Oct. 2019, www.nytimes.

com/2019/10/14/business/nobel-economics.
html. Accessed 16 Jan. 2020.

Varoufakis, Yanis. "Methodical Deconstruction
of Fake Facts." *The Guardian*, 11 Nov. 2019,
www.theguardian.com/books/2019/nov/11/
good-economics-for-hard-times-abhijit-ba-
nerjee-esther-duflo-review. Accessed 16 Jan.
2020.

—*Mari Rich*

Elizabeth Banks

Date of birth: February 10, 1974
Occupation: Actor

Elizabeth Banks is an American actor, comedian,
producer, and director best known for the *Hunger Games* and *Pitch Perfect* films.

EARLY LIFE AND EDUCATION
Elizabeth Banks was born Elizabeth Maresal
Mitchell in Pittsfield, Massachusetts, on February 10, 1974. The oldest of four children, Banks
was raised in the working-class neighborhood of
a factory town where her father worked for General Electric and her mother worked as a bank
clerk. She recalls her upbringing as one filled
with sports and community events.

She was bullied in middle school for being small but later became popular through her
athletic skills. Banks attended Pittsfield High
School, where she was a successful student
and a member of the Latin club and the school
council. Banks played basketball, tennis, and
baseball, but when she broke her leg sliding into
third base during a baseball game, she diverted
her attention to acting rather than sports.

Banks attended the University of Pennsylvania, where she graduated magna cum laude and
earned a degree in communications. She considered several jobs in journalism but took a friend's
advice to follow her dream of starting a career
in acting. Banks moved to San Francisco and
attended the American Conservatory Theater,
where she earned a master of fine arts degree in
1996. Upon graduating, Banks moved to New
York, where she landed several television roles
that helped to launch her acting career.

ACTOR AND DIRECTOR
Banks made her film debut in 1998 in *Surren-
der Dorothy*, an independent drama. She then
appeared in episodes of the popular television
shows *All My Children* and *Third Watch* before
appearing in her first major comedy film, *Wet
Hot American Summer*, in 2001. The film solidified Banks as a regular in the work of director
David Wain and was the first of five films she

Photo by Gage Skidmore via Wikimedia Commons

has made with actor Paul Rudd. The film was
also the first in which she was credited as Elizabeth Banks, a stage name she adopted because
the Screen Actors Guild (SAG) already had an
Elizabeth Mitchell registered.

Over the next several years, Banks moved
to Los Angeles and became a rising star as she
acted in a string of major Hollywood films, including *Spider-Man* (2002), *Catch Me If You
Can* (2002), and *Seabiscuit* (2003).

Her next major comedy film, *The 40-Year-
Old Virgin* (2005), provided Banks with an
experience she would later draw on as a filmmaker. The directorial debut of Judd Apatow,
The 40-Year Old Virgin employed an improvisation filming technique called cross coverage,
which Banks later used when directing *Pitch
Perfect 2*. Banks has spoken in interviews about
the importance of comedy improvisation in her
work and the technical skill required in filming
improvisation.

Banks had recurring roles on the television
series *Scrubs* between 2006 and 2009, *30 Rock*
between 2010 and 2012, and *Modern Family* between 2009 and 2015. During this period, she
appeared in a series of action movies, including
the Spider-Man sequels; independent dramas
such as *Lovely, Still* (2008); horror films such as
Slither (2006) and *The Uninvited* (2009); romantic comedies such as *Definitely, Maybe* (2008);
and comedies *Role Models* (2008) and *Our Idiot
Brother* (2011). Banks had a leading role in the
comedy *Zack and Miri Make a Porno* (2008) and
starred as former first lady Laura Bush in Oliver
Stone's *W.* (2008).

In 2009 Banks launched the production company Brownstone with her husband, writer and producer Max Handelman. Banks produced *Surrogates* the same year and later produced the comedy *Pitch Perfect* (2012), a major critical and commercial success. Banks was cast to play the supporting role of Effie Trinket in *The Hunger Games* (2012), which she reprised in the film's three sequels. Grossing nearly $3 billion in worldwide box office sales, the Hunger Games films elevated Banks to broad stardom. Making her directorial debut, Banks produced and directed *Pitch Perfect* 2 in 2015. The film grossed more than $287 million internationally.

IMPACT

Banks has appeared in more than seventy films. She was nominated for an Emmy Award twice, in 2011 and 2012, for her role on *30 Rock* and once, in 2015, for her role on *Modern Family*. Although originally known as an alternative comedy actor, Banks has established herself as a major Hollywood actor, appearing in films directed by Steven Spielberg, Oliver Stone, and Sam Raimi.

Upon its release, *Pitch Perfect* 2 won a People's Choice Award for favorite comedic movie as well as several Teen Choice Awards.

PERSONAL LIFE

Though she was raised Catholic, Banks later converted to Judaism. Banks and Handelman met at the University of Pennsylvania and were married in 2003. They have two sons; Felix was born in 2011 and Magnus was born in 2012. Banks and Handelman are both avid sports fans and enjoy playing fantasy football.

SUGGESTED READING

Abramovitch, Seth. "Elizabeth Banks' $200 Million Path to Directing 'Pitch Perfect 2.'" *Hollywood Reporter*. 29 Apr. 2015. www.hollywoodreporter.com/news/elizabeth-banks-200-million-path-791855. Accessed 1 May 2020..

Banks, Elizabeth. "Episode 352–Elizabeth Banks, " 14 Jan. 2013. Interview by Marc Maron. *WTF with Marc Maron*, www.wtfpod.com/podcast/tag/Elizabeth+Banks. Accessed 1 May 2020.

———Interview by Rory Evans. *Women's Health*. Hearst Magazine Media, 28 Aug. 2008. Web. 16 Jan. 2016.

———. "Q&A With *Walk of Shame*'s Elizabeth Banks: 'I Think We Left Some Raunch on the Table.'" Interview by R. Kurt Osenlund. *Details*. Condé Nast, 2014. Web. 17 Jan. 2016.

Walden, Celia. "Elizabeth Banks: 'They Said I Wouldn't Get the Job Unless I Showed My Body.'" *Telegraph*. Telegraph Media Group, 12 May 2015, www.telegraph.co.uk/film/pitch-perfect-2/elizabeth-banks-interview/. Accessed 1 May 2020.

SELECTED WORKS

Wet Hot American Summer, 2001; *Spider-Man*, 2002; *Seabiscuit*, 2003; *The 40-Year-Old Virgin*, 2005; *Scrubs*, 2006–9; *W.*, 2008; *30 Rock*, 2010–12; *The Hunger Games*, 2012; *Pitch Perfect*, 2012; *Pitch Perfect 2*, 2015

—*Richard Means*

Saquon Barkley

Born: February 9, 1997
Occupation: Football player

Saquon Barkley rose rapidly to National Football League (NFL) stardom, earning recognition as one of the most talented running backs in football. After three outstanding years of college football at Penn State, he became the second overall pick in the 2018 NFL Draft and signed with the New York Giants. In his first NFL season in 2018 he set several Giants rookie records, including for rushing yards (1,307) and total touchdowns (15). He also set or tied several NFL records and was named to the Pro Bowl, among other honors. Although Barkley's 2019 season was marred by a slow-healing ankle injury that forced him to miss three regular season games and impaired his playing for the rest of the season, he still put up relatively good numbers, rushing for 1,003 yards. This made him the

Photo by AtlantaFX via YouTube and Wikimedia Commons

first player in Giants history to rush for at least a thousand yards in their first two seasons.

Barkley's athleticism and competitive drive helped make him extremely popular with fans even as the Giants struggled to find success. His superstar status also helped him land lucrative sponsorships, including one of the biggest such deals ever for a football player: a $25 million four-year contract signed in 2019 with apparel company Nike. Indeed, in many ways his ambition extended beyond football as he marketed himself as a media icon and sought to be an inspiration to young fans in particular. Yet, Barkley remains aware of the fleeting nature of football careers and the need for constant hard work. "I'm a person that didn't come from much financially, but I worked my a** off to get where I want to be," Barkley told Ryan Dunleavy for the *New York Post* (14 July 2020). "I'm going to continue to do that."

EARLY LIFE AND EDUCATION

Saquon Barkley was born on February 9, 1997, in the Bronx borough of New York City, to Alibay Barkley and Tonya Johnson. In 2001, his mother moved the family to Pennsylvania to escape the poor social conditions of their Bronx neighborhood. They first lived in Bethlehem, then Allentown before settling in Coplay. Barkley's family had a history of athletic talent; his great-uncle was a world-champion boxer, his father also boxed, and one of his brothers would become a star high school baseball player. Barkley became a fan of the New York Jets football team, especially admiring the star running back Curtis Martin. He began to prove his own football talent early, starring on his youth team at the age of eight.

Barkley attended Whitehall High School in Whitehall Township, Pennsylvania, where he excelled in several sports, including basketball and track and field. However, it was football in which he demonstrated the kind of prowess that gained the attention of college scouts and recruiters. He agreed to a scholarship offer from Rutgers University in New Jersey, but then was heavily recruited by the Pennsylvania State University (Penn State) football program. In February 2014, he decided to break his commitment to Rutgers. "It was one of the hardest things I had to do, because I felt like I was going against my word," he told Mark Wogenrich for the *Morning Call* (17 Dec. 2016). "But we had to look at the bigger picture. . . . I felt like Penn State presented more opportunities for me for the rest of my life. Sometimes you have to grow up and make decisions that impact your life."

COLLEGE FOOTBALL

As a freshman in 2015, Barkley immediately made an impact with the Penn State Nittany Lions, competing in the Big Ten Conference of the National Collegiate Athletic Association (NCAA) Division I. He rushed for 1,076 yards and 7 touchdowns while adding 161 yards and another touchdown as a receiver, setting a school freshman record for total yards. Wowing many spectators with his all-around athleticism, he was named freshman of the year by the Big Ten Network. In his sophomore year he posted even better statistics, with 1,496 rushing yards and a Big Ten–leading 18 rushing touchdowns as well as 28 pass receptions for 402 yards and 4 touchdowns. He earned numerous honors, including Big Ten Offensive Player of the Year, and he helped Penn State win the 2016 Big Ten Championship Game. He also had a strong showing in the 2017 Rose Bowl, scoring three touchdowns, though his team ultimately lost.

Barkley was again an offensive force in his junior year. As a rusher he amassed 1,271 rushing yards and 18 touchdowns, while as a receiver he had 54 catches for 632 yards and 3 touchdowns. He was again named Big Ten Offensive Player of the Year, and he also earned Consensus All-American honors, among many other recognitions. After helping Penn State win the 2017 Fiesta Bowl, he announced he would enter the 2018 NFL Draft. He finished his college career as Penn State's all-time leader in all-purpose yards (5,538), total touchdowns (53), and rushing touchdowns (43).

JOINING THE GIANTS

Many analysts projected Barkley to be a top draft pick, and after he impressed at the NFL Combine player showcase, he was seen as an even more desirable prospect. When the draft was held in April 2018, he was selected second overall by the New York Giants. A few months later the team announced it had officially signed Barkley to a rookie contract worth a reported $31.2 million fully guaranteed over four years, plus a $20.8 million signing bonus.

Barkley made his presence known right away for the Giants, developing one of the greatest rookie seasons in franchise history in 2018. In his first game he recorded his first touchdown, and in his second he made fourteen catches—setting a Giants record and tying the NFL record for a rookie. Over the course of the regular season he appeared in all sixteen games, rushing for 1,307 yards and 11 touchdowns and adding 721 receiving yards and 4 receiving touchdowns. Along the way he set or matched several other franchise and league records, and his 2,028 yards from scrimmage led the league. However, his dominance was not enough to make the Giants a Super Bowl contender, as the team finished 5–11 and missed the playoffs.

Barkley's outstanding play secured him the 2018 NFL Offensive Rookie of the Year Award, making him just the second Giant (after Odell Beckham Jr. in 2014) to earn that honor. He was also named to the NFL All-Rookie Team and selected for the Pro Bowl. Unofficially, he was named the Pepsi NFL Rookie of the Year by fan vote and earned the NFL FedEx Ground NFL Player of the Year Award. During the off-season he was ranked sixteenth on the NFL Top 100 list of best players for the upcoming season, as voted by fellow players.

Entering the 2019 season as an emergent superstar, Barkley was named one of the Giants' captains, a move that recognized his leadership skills rather than his celebrity status. He started the season off strong, surpassing 100 rushing yards in each of the first two games. However, he injured his ankle in the third game and was projected to miss up to eight weeks. Although he ultimately sat out just three games, the lingering injury prevented him from being as effective as the previous season. He still managed to surpass the 1,000-yard mark over thirteen games, with 6 rushing touchdowns and 2 receiving touchdowns, but overall, his statistics declined in most areas.

Meanwhile the Giants continued to struggle, going just 4–12 in 2019. Barkley acknowledged that all he could do was work to lead the way to improvement. "You have to try to improve on every year, try to be a better version of yourself, try to improve your game," he told Michael Eisen for the *Giants'* website (17 Aug. 2020). "The way I feel I can be a better Saquon Barkley, I guess you could say, is by coming here every single day, coming to work and trying to continue to earn the respect of my teammates. Continuing to try to push myself and push my teammates. At the end of the day, it's all about the team."

LOOKING TO THE FUTURE

Even as his football career was still getting underway, Barkley showed foresight in planning for beyond his playing days. "I keep the main thing the main thing—football and trying to be the best I can be to bring a championship to this city," he told Dunleavy. "But the same way I'm trying to learn to be a better player, I'm trying to learn to become a better businessman. This game is going to be taken away. For me, it could be at 30, 32, 33. It's a short time I have with football, and I'm going to take advantage of it."

For Barkley, taking advantage included leveraging his superstar status into some of the most lucrative sponsorships in sports. Notably, although he had already signed an endorsement with Nike, he and his management team renegotiated the deal in October 2019. The new contract was worth a reported guaranteed $25 million over four years, making it the second largest ever given to a football player. (Odell Beckham Jr.'s 2017 contract was $29 million

over five years.) The terms of the deal included Barkley's full ownership of intellectual property; the right to collaborate rights with all other Nike designers; the right to work with other companies on non-Nike products; and a five percent merchandise royalty rate—twice the standard for the industry. Nike also promised regular financial and creative support for various charity and community efforts, and Barkley retained the right to sell his branded merchandise to support his own charitable foundation. Many industry analysts considered the deal a game changer for the high-end endorsement market.

The Nike Saquon Barkley apparel collection, featuring a distinctive "S" logo, officially debuted in November 2019. Within minutes the entire line sold out. Barkley noted that in addition to securing his future, one of his key goals with his self-promotion was to inspire young people. "No matter your circumstances, if you have the right mindset and are passionate, anything is possible," he told Dunleavy, but he added that kids should not strive simply to emulate him but rather completely explore their own strengths. "If I strive to be the next Barry Sanders or Bo Jackson, I'm putting a cap on my potential. Why not try to be better? Never try to be the next Saquon Barkley. Be the best version of yourself."

MORE SETBACKS

Like other sports leagues, the NFL was disrupted by the global COVID-19 pandemic that caused widespread social and economic shutdowns in 2020. Barkley and other players were unable to participate in many of the usual training regimens, including extended team practice camps and official preseason games. However, the NFL planned to begin regular season play in early September as usual. Entering the 2020 season Barkley faced heavy expectations, with the Giants organization and countless fans counting on him to return to the remarkable production of his rookie year. "We want to involve this guy in every facet of the game," Giants running backs coach Burton Burns said, as quoted by Zack Rosenblatt for *NJ.com* (26 Aug. 2020). "We're just going to let the flow of the offense happen and get him involved when we can."

Indications from limited preseason workouts were that Barkley had put his 2019 injury behind him. "It feels good to get out there, get the feel and get some work with the defense and get each other better," he said after one practice, as quoted by Tom Rock for *Newsday* (17 Aug. 2020). "I want to be great and I want to be great for this team." Unfortunately, things did not go as he and the Giants hoped. Barkley had one of the worst games of his career in the 2020 season opener, struggling to produce behind a weak offensive line. Then, in the second game of the year, he tore the anterior cruciate ligament (ACL) in his right knee, a serious injury with a typical recovery time of around one year. The news made waves throughout the football world, as commentators discussed the impact on the Giants' season and on Barkley's future in the sport.

PERSONAL LIFE

Saquon Barkley became a father in 2018 when he welcomed a daughter, Jada Clare, with his girlfriend Anna Congdon. In interviews and other media appearances he often stressed the importance of family in his life, including it as a motivator for realizing his full potential.

SUGGESTED READING

Dunleavy, Ryan. "Saquon Barkley Entering New Stratosphere with Bar-Raising Nike Line." *New York Post*, 14 July 2020, nypost. com/2020/07/14/saquon-barkley-entering-new-stratosphere-with-bar-raising-nike-line/. Accessed 8 Sept. 2020.

Eisen, Michael. "RB Saquon Barkley Still Eager to Be Coached." *NY Giants*, 17 Aug. 2020, www.giants.com/news/saquon-barkley-training-camp-2020-joe-judge-sterling-shepard-corey-coleman. Accessed 8 Sept. 2020.

Rock, Tom. "Saquon Barkley Aims to Improve This Year, and Every Year." *Newsday*, 17 Aug. 2020, www.newsday.com/sports/football/giants/saquon-barkley-healthy-1.48225787. Accessed 18 Aug. 2020.

Rosenblatt, Zack. "Expect Giants' Saquon Barkley to Play a Bigger Role in the Passing Game in 2020; Here's Why." *NJ.com*, 26 Aug. 2020, www.nj.com/giants/2020/08/expect-giants-saquon-barkley-to-play-a-bigger-role-in-the-passing-game-in-2020-heres-why.html. Accessed 8 Sept. 2020.

"Saquon Barkley." *NY Giants*, 2020, www.giants. com/team/players-roster/saquon-barkley/ Accessed 8 Sept. 2020.

Taddeo, Frankie. "How Many Yards Will Saquon Barkley Rush for in 2020?" *Sports Illustrated*, 19 May 2020, www.si.com/gambling/2020/05/19/saquon-barkley-rushing-yards-2020-giants. Accessed 8 Sept. 2020.

Wogenrich, Mark. "Born to Run: Saquon Barkley's Journey from the Bronx to Pennsylvania to Penn State to Pasadena." *The Morning Call*, 17 Dec. 2016, www.mcall.com/sports/penn-state/mc-penn-state-football-saquon-barkley-father-20161217-story.html. Accessed 8 Sept. 2020.

—*Christopher Mari*

Ashleigh Barty

Date of birth: April 24, 1996
Occupation: Tennis player

In September 2014, professional tennis player Ashleigh Barty made the decision to step away from the sport to which she had devoted her time, energy, and focus since around the age of five. Stunning some within the tennis community, though not those aware of the strain that years of international touring and separation from her family had placed on the young player, Barty returned home to Queensland, Australia, where she took time to recharge and also took up a new role as a professional cricketer. Tennis, however, continued to call to Barty, whose early career had seen her develop an array of valuable skills and win high-profile tournaments such as the girls' junior singles competition at Wimbledon in 2011. "I was really enjoying my time, but deep down I knew that tennis was my sport. It's a sport that I've loved since I was five years old," she explained to Kevin Mitchell for the *Guardian* (28 June 2019). "I just needed to get that passion and that drive back." As Barty's performance on the court following her return to tennis in early 2016 demonstrated, her passion and drive came back in abundance. After raising her international singles tennis ranking from unranked to fifteenth in the world between 2016 and 2018, Barty solidified her status as a major competitor further in 2019, when she claimed her first Grand Slam women's singles victory at the French Open and went on to become the top-ranked women's singles player in the world.

Photo by Rob Keating via Wikimedia Commons

EARLY LIFE AND JUNIOR CAREER

Ashleigh "Ash" Barty was born on April 24, 1996, in Ipswich, Queensland, Australia. She grew up in Springfield, a suburb of Ipswich, alongside two older sisters. Her father, Robert, was a government worker, and her mother, Josie, worked as a radiographer. Athletic pursuits were of importance in Barty's family: her father had played golf competitively earlier in life, and her sisters both played netball.

Although Barty did follow in her father's footsteps by learning to play golf, she focused on the sport of tennis at the age of four or five and soon demonstrated a talent for it. Introduced to the sport by local junior tennis coach Jim Joyce, she went on to train with him at the West Brisbane Tennis Centre. She focused more on training than on competing during her first years as a tennis player, developing the range of skills that would serve her well on the court. Following her entrance into competitive tennis, she began to win numerous tournaments on the junior level and at one point was ranked second in the world among female junior singles players.

Barty began playing on the adult-level International Tennis Federation (ITF) circuit in 2010. A series of international tennis competitions that encompasses both singles and doubles play, the ITF circuit is considered a developmental circuit through which players hone their skills before qualifying to compete on the highest level of competition, which for women is the Women's Tennis Association (WTA) Tour. A competitor in both singles and doubles matches, Barty competed primarily within Australia but at times traveled abroad to compete or to learn from established tennis professionals. "I was 13, 14, playing against other WTA players. It was an eye-opening experience," she recalled to Mitchell. "Any time you get to rub shoulders with legends, it's incredible. To be able to speak with them—albeit very briefly—made memories that I will never forget." Barty began playing in WTA events in 2011 and that year competed in a qualifying round for the prestigious US Open. Remaining active at the junior level, she competed in and ultimately won the 2011 junior singles championship at Wimbledon. The event distinguished her as a young competitor to watch but also brought a stress-inducing level of media attention.

WTA TOUR

With the start of the 2012 professional tennis season, Barty began to establish herself as a serious competitor on the adult level, competing in both ITF and WTA events. She won her first ITF singles title in February 2012, at an event in Sydney, Australia, and went on to win three more singles titles over the course of the year. That year also saw Barty compete more extensively in the Grand Slam events, a set of four competitions on the WTA Tour that are considered to be the most prestigious tournaments in professional tennis: the Australian Open, the French Open (also known as Roland-Garros), Wimbledon, and the US Open. She made her true adult-level Grand Slam debut in January 2012, competing in the first round of the Australian Open as a wild card but ultimately losing to Georgian player Anna Tatishvili. She went on to play in the first rounds of the French Open and Wimbledon.

Barty continued to compete in the Grand Slam tournaments over the next couple of years, progressing to the round of sixty-four at both the French Open and the US Open in 2013. She was most successful in doubles competitions in 2013, competing in the doubles finals at the Australian Open, Wimbledon, and the US Open alongside her doubles partner, fellow Australian Casey Dellacqua. The duo also claimed the women's doubles title at the Internationaux de Strasbourg in France in 2014. Despite such successes—or perhaps because of them—Barty struggled in 2014, dealing with levels of stress and isolation that had troubled her since she first began competing on the international level. "It was terrible. It was all just too much," she recalled to Konrad Marshall for *Good Weekend* (2017) about her early experiences on an international tour. "I was younger than the other girls on tour, so I knew them but not well. I just felt lonely and strange." Experiencing burnout and wanting to return to Australia, she decided to step away from the sport of tennis following the 2014 US Open. At the time, her break had no defined ending date.

BREAK FROM TENNIS

Following her return to Australia, Barty took her time adjusting to life outside of competitive tennis. Although she continued to play the game to a limited extent and trained other players, she devoted much of her time to other pursuits, including fishing, spending time with family members whom she had seen little of due to her busy touring schedule, and undergoing treatment for mental health concerns that had gone largely untreated during her time on tour. Barty would later credit her hiatus from tennis with giving her time to "mentally refresh and restart," as she explained in an interview with Paul Newman for the *Independent* (12 Jan. 2018). "It was a really, really good 18 months of my life. I was able to relax and just enjoy."

In addition to engaging in personal growth, Barty took her hiatus from tennis as an opportunity to explore new athletic pursuits, namely the sport of cricket. Drawn to the concept of competing with a group of teammates rather than as a solitary athlete, she began her involvement with the sport by training with the Queensland

Fire before joining the Western Suburbs District Cricket Club, which competed in the relatively short-form Twenty20 cricket competitions. She also signed with the team the Brisbane Heat, which played in the Women's Big Bash League Twenty20 league, in 2015.

Although Barty thoroughly enjoyed her time playing cricket, she made it clear in interviews that she had no intention of playing the sport on the international level. "I didn't think I was good enough, if I'm being honest," she told Mitchell. "The standard of women's cricket in Australia is so high, there are a lot of girls a lot better than me." Nevertheless, she received significant attention during her brief tenure as a cricketer, during which she put the skills she had accumulated as a tennis player to use in a very different but ultimately complementary sport.

RETURN TO TENNIS

Barty made her return to professional tennis in February 2016, beginning with an Australia-based ITF doubles event. In May of that year, she took to the court as a singles player once more in an ITF event in Eastbourne, England, during which she progressed to the semifinals. She also competed in two singles qualifying rounds at Wimbledon and reached the first round of competition in doubles. As Barty had been absent from competition for more than a year, she had lost her international tour ranking, one of the measures by which professional tennis leadership determines which players will be selected to compete in high-level tournaments. To regain her standing among professional tennis players, she competed in a variety of lower-level events, amassing enough victories and strong finishes to earn her the rank of 325 by the end of 2016.

Demonstrating that Barty had truly returned to her sport, the year 2017 saw the resurgent athlete compete in singles in all four Grand Slam events and reach the round of thirty-two, a new high, in the Australian Open and the US Open. She also reached the doubles finals at the French Open, but she and Dellacqua were defeated by American player Bethanie Mattek-Sands and Czech player Lucie Šafářová. In addition to those finishes, Barty won a WTA singles title in Kuala Lumpur, Malaysia, and claimed three doubles titles, wins that helped propel her to seventeenth place in the WTA's singles rankings. "Coming back, I feel like I've worked for every single ranking spot, and haven't had to rely on wildcards," she told Marshall of her approach. "I'm a big believer that your ranking reflects who you are. I feel like I've earned my spot." The subsequent year was likewise a strong one for Barty, who won two WTA singles titles and four doubles titles, including claiming a Grand Slam doubles crown after she and her partner, US player CoCo Vandeweghe, emerged victorious in

the final round of the US Open, before finishing the year with a singles rank of fifteen.

WOMEN'S SINGLES GRAND SLAM VICTORY

The 2019 tennis season started off strong for Barty, who competed in the Australian Open and progressed to the quarterfinals before being eliminated. She went on to win the Miami Open in March of that year. In late May and early June, she took to the court for the French Open, where she defeated all opponents in the early rounds of competition before beating US player Amanda Anisimova in the semifinals. She advanced to the final round, where she overcame Czech player Markéta Vondroušová to claim her first professional-level women's singles Grand Slam victory.

Over the remainder of the year, Barty continued to put forth a strong performance. She won singles titles at the Nature Valley Classic Birmingham and the Shiseido WTA Finals Shenzhen as well as a doubles title at Internazionali BNL d'Italia, all while rising to the top of the WTA's singles rankings. As Barty and her team had aspired only to break into the top ten during 2019, her win at the French Open and subsequent ascent to the number-one spot by the end of the year prompted her to further revise her plans for the future. "Once we did that," she explained to Ben Rothenberg for the *New York Times* (1 July 2019) of making it into the top ten, "we automatically set new goals, we kept working, to try and get better every single day in every facet of my tennis: physically, mentally, technically."

Moving on into 2020, Barty started off the year with a singles victory at the Adelaide International in January. At the Australian Open that year she progressed to the singles semifinals.

PERSONAL LIFE

Despite the extensive international travel required by her career, Barty has described herself as more of a homebody. When not playing tennis, Barty, who is of Indigenous Australian descent, has worked to promote the sport of tennis among Indigenous Australian peoples and particularly among Indigenous Australian children. She was named Tennis Australia's National Indigenous Tennis Ambassador in 2018.

SUGGESTED READING

Chenery, Susan. "'I Thought That Was It': Why Ash Barty Almost Gave Up Tennis for Good." *The Guardian*, 22 June 2019, www.theguardian.com/sport/2019/jun/23/i-thought-that-was-it-why-ash-barty-almost-gave-up-tennis-for-good. Accessed 9 Feb. 2020.

Marshall, Konrad. "Second Serve." *Good Weekend*, 2017. *The Sydney Morning Herald*, 2017, www.smh.com.au/interactive/2017/second-serve/. Accessed 9 Feb. 2020.

Mitchell, Kevin. "Ashleigh Barty: 'I've Learned to Embrace Fame, but It's Impossible to Please Everyone.'" *The Guardian*, 28 June 2019, www.theguardian.com/sport/2019/jun/28/ashleigh-barty-interview-wimbledon-tennis. Accessed 9 Feb. 2020.

Newman, Paul. "Australian Open 2018: Home Hope Ashleigh Barty Thriving under the Pressure ahead of Season Opening Slam." *Independent*, 12 Jan. 2018, www.independent.co.uk/sport/tennis/ashleigh-barty-interview-australian-open-sydney-international-samstosur-a8155921.html. Accessed 11 Feb. 2020.

Rothenberg, Ben. "As Wimbledon Begins, Ashleigh Barty Is on Top of the World." *The New York Times*, 1 July 2019, www.nytimes.com/2019/07/01/sports/ashleigh-barty-wimbledon.html. Accessed 9 Feb. 2020.

——. "Ash Barty, a Rising Tennis Star, Hits Pause." *The New York Times*, 18 Jan. 2016, www.nytimes.com/2016/01/19/sports/tennis/ash-barty-left-pro-tennis-for-cricket-will-she-ever-return.html. Accessed 11 Feb. 2020.

—*Joy Crelin*

Photo by Monica King via Wikimedia Commons

David Bellavia

Date of birth: November 10, 1975
Occupation: US Army veteran

The Medal of Honor, the United States' highest military distinction, immediately conjures the image of a soldier engaging in epic feats of valor and heroism, ones that repeatedly put his or her life at risk to save others. Awarded to service members across every branch of the military, the prestigious medal recognizes those whose actions have conspicuously gone above and beyond the call of duty and that have proved to be exceptions to the norm—like a nineteen-year-old Audie Murphy standing against and repelling an entire company of German infantrymen on his own during World War II. For that reason, only around 3,500 service members have received the medal between when it was first awarded in 1863 and early 2020.

David Bellavia, a western New York native and US Army veteran, joined this exclusive group in June 2019, when he was awarded the Medal of Honor for actions in the Iraq War, which lasted from 2003 to 2011. The first living Iraq War veteran to receive the honor, Bellavia was credited with saving the lives of his squad members during a brutal house-to-house mission in Fallujah, Iraq, on November 10, 2004. He left the army with the rank of staff sergeant in 2005 but later spent further time in Iraq as an embedded reporter. In 2007, he published the highly acclaimed war memoir *House to House*. He later became involved in Republican politics in western New York, making a close but unsuccessful run for New York's Twenty-Seventh Congressional District in 2012, and served as a conservative talk radio host in Buffalo.

A cofounder of the advocacy organization Vets for Freedom, Bellavia recommitted himself to the army after receiving the medal in an effort to bring people together, irrespective of politics. "All throughout our history, we have had people that have dissented, that have disagreed," he explained, as quoted by Corey Dickstein in *Stars and Stripes* (25 June 2019), "and we've found ways to put everything aside and focus on what's best for this nation, what's best for mission success."

EARLY LIFE AND EDUCATION

The youngest in a family that included three brothers, David Gregory Bellavia was born on November 10, 1975, in Buffalo, New York. He was raised in a devout religious family in Lyndonville, a village in New York's Orleans County located approximately an hour's drive north of Buffalo. Bellavia has said that growing up in rural Orleans County helped him develop a strong sense of individuality without worrying about outside criticism or rejection. "They said be different, go out and try something different," he recalled of his local community to John Anderson for the Batavia, New York, *Daily News* (12 June 2019). "But you wouldn't get thrown aside."

From an early age, Bellavia learned the importance of duty to one's country through his grandfather, Joseph Brunacini, a Bronze Star–winning US Army veteran who would regale him with stories of his experiences fighting in World War II during the Normandy campaign. However, it was his father, Bill, who instilled in him the value of hard work and of cultivating a single-minded purpose in life. According to Bellavia, his father, whom he has called his hero, progressed from community college to dental school, working his way up from nothing to establish a successful dental practice.

Bellavia attended Houghton Academy and Lyndonville Central School District's high school, where he played sports and was active in the arts and the theater. After graduating from Lyndonville in 1994, he enrolled at Franklin Pierce University in Rindge, New Hampshire. He eventually transferred to the University at Buffalo, where he studied biology and theater. Through the latter discipline, he enjoyed the invaluable benefits of being part of a team. "I'm really motivated by being part of that dynamic. I love that camaraderie," he told Robert J. McCarthy for the *Buffalo News* (11 June 2019).

MAKINGS OF A SOLDIER

Ironically, it was Bellavia's involvement in the theater that partly led to his entry into the US Army. Bellavia, who did not graduate from college, idolized the American composer and lyricist Stephen Sondheim, and after starting his own theater company in Buffalo, he created and produced musicals that paid homage to Sondheim's work. An original production that took creative liberties with Sondheim's 1990 Off-Broadway musical *Assassins*, which portrays a group of real-life US presidential assassins, nonetheless resulted in the composer pursuing legal action against Bellavia, who was forced to stop the show and pay a thousand-dollar fine. "Next thing I know I'm field-dressing machine guns," Bellavia recounts in *House to House* (2007), which he cowrote with the military and aviation historian John R. Bruning.

Another crystallizing moment occurred for Bellavia shortly after his twenty-third birthday, when he was unable to thwart a robbery at his family's home. By his own admission, Bellavia was too afraid and unprepared to confront the assailants, who pillaged the house as his parents sequestered themselves in their bedroom. In *House to House*, he explains that it was the reaction on his father's face, "a mixture of disgust and pity," that ultimately prompted him to join the US Army in 1999. "I needed to understand courage," he writes in the memoir. "I needed to become a man."

Following his completion of One Station Unit Training at Fort Benning in Georgia, Bellavia was assigned to the US Army recruiting battalion in Syracuse, New York. He remained there for two and a half years, during which his son, who was born with birth defects, received appropriate medical care. After the terrorist attacks of September 11, 2001, Bellavia opted to remain in the infantry and spent the next three years in Germany on an unaccompanied tour, also known as an "All Others Tour," in which soldiers are permanently stationed overseas without their families. In 2003, he participated in his first military campaign, serving nine months in Kosovo before being deployed to Iraq as part of Operation Iraqi Freedom.

HEROISM IN A HOUSE OF HORRORS

Bellavia had risen to the rank of staff sergeant when, on November 10, 2004, his twenty-ninth birthday, he embarked on a mission that would forever change the course of his life. Fighting in support of Operation Phantom Fury in the insurgent stronghold of Fallujah, Bellavia was charged with leading his squadron—officially, Third Platoon, Alpha Company, Second Battalion, Second Infantry Regiment, Third Brigade Combat Team of the army's storied First Infantry Division—through a sweep of twelve buildings, mainly to support other soldiers who were fighting elsewhere in the city. "We were well-prepared for close-quarter combat," he noted, as quoted by Jerry Zremski in the *Buffalo News* (6 Nov. 2019). "You're opening the doors to the OK Corral, and it's psychologically debilitating."

Bellavia and his squad cleared the first nine buildings without incident, but upon entering the tenth, they were ambushed by a group of insurgents. While his squad was trapped in a vortex of bullets, Bellavia used an M249 machine gun to provide cover fire so he and his comrades could exit the three-story building. After briefly catching his breath, Bellavia then reentered the building, this time only being trailed by Michael Ware, a journalist who was embedded with his squad. Bellavia subsequently "fought with gun, grenades, and knife in a dark house with sewage flooding the floor and broken mirrors glinting on the bullet-marked walls," as James Kitfield wrote for *Breaking Defense* (26 June 2019).

By the end of the battle, Bellavia had killed four insurgents and severely injured a fifth, essentially single-handedly saving his entire squad and eliminating an enemy hot zone. Not long afterward, he was nominated for the Medal of Honor by his company commander, Captain Douglas Walter. "This was different than anything I had seen," Walter, who later became a colonel, said of his decision to Dickstein. "It stood out. The more I went through it, the more I was convinced that he had saved the lives of a squad." Bellavia received the Silver Star, the nation's third-highest military honor for valor, for his actions.

MEDAL OF HONOR RECIPIENT

Upon leaving the army in the summer of 2005, Bellavia returned to Western New York and co-founded Vets for Freedom, an advocacy organization composed of Iraq and Afghanistan war veterans. He returned to Iraq on two separate occasions, in 2006 and 2008, respectively, while serving as an embedded reporter. In that role, he covered significant battles fought in the cities of Fallujah and Ramadi and in the province of Diyala. During that time, he published his memoir *House to House* (2007), which offers a chilling chronicle of his courageous actions in Iraq. The book received widespread praise from critics and came to be regarded as one of the best firsthand accounts of the Iraq war ever written. Concurrently with his journalism work, Bellavia became involved in local Republican politics. In 2012, he led a strong campaign for New York's Twenty-Seventh Congressional District but lost the Republican primary to Chris Collins, who had served as the executive of Erie County. That same year he started working for the Buffalo radio station WBEN as a conservative talk radio host and contributor, and by 2016 he had joined Tom Bauerle to host an afternoon program.

In 2018 and early 2019, Bellavia emerged as a leading candidate to replace Collins in the Twenty-Seventh Congressional District after the Republican politician was charged with insider trading in August 2018. Any potential political plans, however, were put on indefinite hold in the summer of 2019, when Bellavia was informed by US President Donald Trump that his Silver Star would be upgraded to the Medal of Honor. The upgraded distinction came as a result of a sweeping 2016 Pentagon review of post–September 11 valor awards.

On June 25, 2019, Bellavia was officially awarded the Medal of Honor in a ceremony held at the White House. In the process, he became the first living recipient of the honor from the Iraq War; he was just the sixth overall recipient of the honor from that armed conflict. Accepting the medal in the presence of not only his family but also living members of his task force, Bellavia said, as quoted by Dickstein, "I never thought I would see love on a battlefield." He added, "It's horrible, it's ghastly, and it's ghoulish. But you see people doing these things for each other that they would never, ever do in any other circumstance—it's a sight to see."

In the wake of his Medal of Honor win, Bellavia founded a charitable organization, the Deuce Deuce Relief Fund (DDRF), which assists soldiers of his former task force in Iraq. Following Collins's resignation in late September, Bellavia officially announced that he would not be running for Congress as he had renewed his full-time commitment to the US Army, using his newfound status to espouse the military branch's life-changing benefits at guest speaking engagements all over the country.

PERSONAL LIFE

Bellavia resides in Batavia, a city in western New York, with his wife, Deanna King, with whom he has three children. Some of his other honors have included the Bronze Star, New York State's Conspicuous Service Cross, three Army Commendation medals, and two Army Achievement medals. In 2005, he was inducted into the New York State Senate Veterans' Hall of Fame.

SUGGESTED READING

Anderson, John. "Medal of Honor Recipient David Bellavia Talks about the Importance of His Father, Growing Up in the Region." *The Daily News*, 12 June 2019, www.thedailynewsonline.com/bdn01/medal-of-honor-recipient-david-bellavia-talks-about-the-importance-of-his-father-growing-up-in-the-region-20190612. Accessed 27 Feb. 2020.

Bellavia, David, and John R. Bruning. *House to House: An Epic Memoir of War*. Free Press, 2007.

Dickstein, Corey. "David Bellavia Receives the Medal of Honor for His Actions in a 'House of Nightmares.'" *Stars and Stripes*, 25 June 2019, www.stripes.com/news/us/david-bellavia-receives-the-medal-of-honor-for-his-actions-in-a-house-of-nightmares-1.587428. Accessed 27 Feb. 2020.

Kitfield, James. "Sgt. Bellavia: Knife Fight in the House of Broken Mirrors." *Breaking Defense*, 26 June 2019, breakingdefense.com/2019/06/sergeant-david-bellavia-knife-fight-in-the-house-of-broken-mirrors/. Accessed 27 Feb. 2020.

McCarthy, Robert J. "David Bellavia Prepares for a Life Changed Forever by Medal of Honor." *The Buffalo News*, 11 June 2019, buffalonews.com/2019/06/11/bellavia-prepares-for-a-life-changed-forever-by-medal-of-honor/. Accessed 27 Feb. 2020.

"Staff Sergeant David G. Bellavia: Medal of Honor; Operation Iraqi Freedom." *U.S. Army*, www.army.mil/medalofhonor/bellavia/?from=features. Accessed 17 Mar. 2020.

Zremski, Jerry. "United by Blood and Battle: David Bellavia on the Makings of a War Hero." *The Buffalo News*, 6 Nov. 2019, buffalonews.com/2019/11/06/united-by-blood-and-battle-david-bellavia-demystifies-the-making-of-a-war-hero/. Accessed 27 Feb. 2020.

—*Chris Cullen*

Perry Bellegarde

Born: August 29, 1962
Occupation: Politician and advocate

"Meaningful change," Canadian politician and advocate Perry Bellegarde told Nicole McCormick for the Toronto, Ontario, *CityNews* (21 June 2020), "requires daily action on your vision, followed by perseverance—lots of perseverance. . . . Persistence in the face of adversity is your best friend." Indeed, as national chief of the Assembly of First Nations (AFN), Bellegarde—a member of the Little Black Bear First Nation—has needed to demonstrate a great deal of persistence in his efforts to combat the centuries of systemic racism and oppression that have made First Nations some of the poorest and most marginalized populations in Canada. Since being elected national chief for the first time in 2014, he has overseen a host of initiatives designed to close the gap between Canada's Indigenous and non-Indigenous population and to bring an end to discriminatory practices and long-standing injustice. Yet, despite the strides made by organizations such as the AFN under Bellegarde's leadership, he remains adamant that much more must be done to improve the lives of First Nations people throughout Canada. "Progress doesn't mean parity," he explained to Amy Smart for the *Canadian Press* (23 Oct. 2019). "There's opportunity to maintain momentum and keep pushing and opening up doors."

Photo by Monica King via Wikimedia Commons

EARLY LIFE AND EDUCATION

Perry Bellegarde was born on August 29, 1962, in Fort Qu'Appelle, Saskatchewan, Canada. He was one of six sons born to members of the Little Black Bear First Nation, a Cree and Assiniboine band in southern Saskatchewan. Bellegarde grew up on a reserve with limited resources. "There was no running water, we chopped wood, hunted, fished and trapped to survive," he told Chloe E. Girvan for *iPolitics* (16 Mar. 2018). "We were poor but I never knew it."

Bellegarde began his education in the nearby village of Goodeve, to which he was bussed. He attended high school in the town of Balcarres and was active in sports such as hockey; due to the distance between his home and school, he stayed in the home of a local woman. As an adult, he credited his experiences as the only Indigenous person in his classes with offering him early instruction in advocacy and alliance building. Bellegarde graduated from high school in 1980.

After high school, Bellegarde enrolled in Saskatchewan Indian Federated College (SIFC), a college affiliated with the University of Regina and now known as the First Nations University of Canada. During his time there, he learned a great deal about First Nations cultures and traditional ceremonies from Elders affiliated with the institution, whom he credited with helping him build a deeper connection with his heritage. "They were really instrumental in giving you your identity," he recalled to Deborah Sproat for the *Third Degree*, the alumni magazine of the University of Regina (Spring 2003). "A lot of times, because of the system that's there, you don't really have pride or dignity in who you are as a First Nations person. You don't get it from TV, you don't get it from the curriculum, you don't get it from society as a whole."

Bellegarde ultimately transferred to the University of Regina's Faculty of Administration, where he pursued studies in business. He earned his bachelor's degree from the university in 1984.

EARLY CAREER

Bellegarde began his career with the Saskatchewan Indian Institute of Technologies in Saskatoon, the provincial capital. Within a couple years, however, he had shifted his focus to politics, with the goal of improving the lives of First Nations people, who had long faced inequitable treatment due to long-standing biases in Canadian society, the official policies of the Canadian government, and the federal government's inconsistent adherence to the terms of the Numbered Treaties signed by Canadian officials and First Nations leaders during the late nineteenth and early twentieth centuries. "First Nations people just want the same quality of life as everyone else," Bellegarde later told Girvan. He added, "This country was founded on peaceful coexistence and mutual respect and we were to jointly benefit from sharing the land and resource wealth but that is not what we see."

At the behest of friends and elders, Bellegarde began his political career in 1986, when he became an assistant tribal representative and vice president for the File Hills Qu'Appelle (FHQ) Tribal Council. He became a full representative and president of that council in 1988. Bellegarde would remain active in the role until 1998, when he was elected to be grand chief of the Federation of Saskatchewan Indian Nations (FSIN; now the Federation of Sovereign Indigenous Nations).

FSIN GRAND CHIEF

As grand chief of the FSIN, Bellegarde was responsible for representing the interests of the First Nations bands of Saskatchewan and advocating for policies and legislation that would benefit the Indigenous residents of the province. He focused on calling attention to violations of the rights set forth in the Numbered Treaties and the systemic inequity faced by First Nations populations under existing policies. "If our treaty is nation-to-nation, why aren't we at the United Nations?" he asked Sproat. "Why aren't we telling the world that they (the Government of Canada) are not fulfilling obligations, they are not implementing these nation-to-nation agreements? . . . And if they are, why are we still the poorest of the poor people?"

In addition to speaking out about treaty rights, Bellegarde secured government benefits for First Nations veterans and their spouses and developed a gaming agreement that would contribute to the economies of the First Nations of Saskatchewan. Legal bills mounted, however, as Bellegarde took on the federal government over various policy issues.

Bellegarde's position as grand chief of the FSIN also made him a regional chief in the Assembly of First Nations (AFN). An advocacy organization that seeks to represent the interests of First Nations people throughout Canada, the AFN is led by an elected national chief, a group of regional chiefs, and representatives from elder, youth, and women's councils. Bellegarde held both positions until 2003, when voters gravitated to the pragmatic Alphonse Bird. Bellegarde went on to serve as FHQ Tribal Council member and chief before gaining reelection as grand chief of the FSIN in 2012.

NATIONAL CHIEF

Bellegarde, having become established as a key figure in Saskatchewan First Nations leadership, ran for national chief of the AFN in July 2009. Although he was narrowly defeated on the eighth ballot, he experienced far greater success on his second attempt in December 2014. He won the election with 63 percent of the delegates in a single vote.

During his first term as national chief, Bellegarde focused on systemic inequity First Nations people face in areas including widespread poverty, a lack of physical and mental health resources, and unequal treatment under the criminal justice system in Canada. "There's 40,000 children living in foster care, and there's 132 First Nations communities on boiled water advisories," he told *Maclean's* writer Evan Solomon in an interview for the satellite radio show *Everything Is Political* (3 Oct. 2015). "We're 4.3 per cent of the population; 25 per cent of the jails are filled with our people. And our youth suicide numbers are five to seven times higher than the national average . . . there's 1,200 missing murdered indigenous women and girls." To address such problems, Bellegarde and the AFN engaged in federal lobbying and advocacy in addition to providing support to specific First Nations as needed.

As national chief, Bellegarde also led the AFN through a period in which First Nations opposed the Canadian government and various corporations over efforts to build oil and natural gas pipelines across, mine in, or otherwise extract natural resources from First Nations lands. In addition to the environmental ramifications of such efforts, they raised concerns about First Nations sovereignty and the Canadian government's adherence to long-established treaties, a familiar topic for Bellegarde. He asserts the resource development rights were never ceded and that non-Indigenous entities unjustly amassed wealth from them. "If our lands and resources are to be developed, it will be done only with our fair share of the royalties, with our ownership of the resources and jobs for our people. It will be done on our terms and our timeline," he said in a speech following his election, as quoted by Chinta Puxley for the *Canadian Press* in an article published in the *Global News* (10 Dec. 2014). "Canada is Indian land. This is my truth and this is the truth of our peoples."

In addition to seeking to effect change as leader of the AFN, Bellegarde also worked to mobilize voters in the period leading up to the 2015 Canadian federal election, hoping to increase First Nations turnout and participation in the political process.

REELECTION

After several years as national chief of the AFN, Bellegarde was reelected in July 2018, winning 63 percent of the final vote. Following his reelection, he continued to focus on the AFN's longstanding goal of closing the gap in standards of living between Indigenous and non-Indigenous

Canadians, particularly the wide gap that is evident when comparing those populations based on the United Nations' Human Development Index. He also oversaw the AFN's negotiations with the Canadian government to attain First Nations control over child and family services pertaining to First Nations populations.

Bellegarde remained an outspoken advocate for First Nations interests throughout 2019 and 2020. In the run-up to the 2019 federal election he and the AFN outlined priorities for relations with any incoming administration. The following June, Bellegarde demanded answers in the police killings of Chantel Moore (Tla-o-qui-aht First Nation) and Rodney Levi (Metepenagiag First Nation) and called for systemic police reforms such as zero tolerance of excessive force, greater community policing, and increased civilian oversight. He was likewise active in efforts to raise funds to fight the COVID-19 pandemic and to promote preventive measures, such as self-isolation and the wearing of masks, among First Nations.

Though Bellegarde has often called attention to the continuing hardships and injustice faced by many First Nations people throughout Canada, he remained optimistic that continued efforts on the part of the AFN and other organizations could bring about substantial systemic change in the future. "One of our elders' biggest teachings is to always try to leave more hope in a room than when you walked in, because there may be no hope," he explained to Girvan. "You want to leave people with hope that things can get better and can get fixed with persistence and tenacity. That we will provide a better future for our children and those yet unborn."

PERSONAL LIFE

Perry Bellegarde is married to Valerie Galley, a Nipissing First Nation policy analyst and writer who has collaborated with him in the FSIN and AFN. They have two sons. When not traveling, they reside in Ottawa, Ontario, where the AFN headquarters is located.

Bellegarde has been the recipient of numerous honors, including a Confederation Medal in 1992, Queen's Jubilee Medals in 2002 and 2012, and the Saskatchewan Order of Merit in 2020.

SUGGESTED READING

Bellegarde, Perry. "'We Have to Have Change': Q&A with Perry Bellegarde." Interview by Evan Solomon. *Everything Is Political*, 3 Oct. 2015. *Maclean's*, www.macleans.ca/politics/ottawa/we-have-to-have-change-qa-with-perry-bellegarde. Accessed 8 Sept. 2020.

Girvan, Chloe E. "With Persistence and Tenacity: A Conversation with National Chief Perry Bellegarde." *iPolitics*, 16 Mar. 2018, ipolitics.ca/article/with-persistence-and-tenacity-a-conversation-with-national-chief-perry-bellegarde. Accessed 8 Sept. 2020.

McCormick, Nicole. "Words of Wisdom from National Chief Perry Bellegarde on National Indigenous Peoples Day." *CityNews*, 22 June 2020, toronto.citynews.ca/2020/06/21/words-of-wisdom-from-national-chief-perry-bellegarde-on-national-indigenous-peoples-day. Accessed 8 Sept. 2020.

"Perry Bellegarde, New AFN Chief, Has Known Triumphs and Disappointment." *CBC News*, 10 Dec. 2014, www.cbc.ca/news/canada/saskatoon/perry-bellegarde-new-afn-chief-has-known-triumphs-and-disappointment-1.2869064. Accessed 8 Sept. 2020.

Puxley, Chinta. "New National Chief Perry Bellegarde: 'Canada Is Indian Land.'" 10 Dec. 2014, *Global News*, 7 June 2015, globalnews.ca/news/1719790/new-national-chief-perry-bellegarde-canada-is-indian-land. Accessed 8 Sept. 2020.

Smart, Amy. "AFN Chief Bellegarde Calls on Liberals to 'Maintain Momentum' on Indigenous Issues." *The Canadian Press*, 23 Oct. 2019. *EBSCOhost*, search.ebscohost.com/login.aspx?direct=true&db=p3h&AN=MYO386727501919&lang=en-ca&site=pov-can. Accessed 8 Sept. 2020.

Sproat, Deborah. "Born to Lead." *The Third Degree: University of Regina Alumni Magazine*, Spring 2003, pp. 10–12, ourspace.uregina.ca/bitstream/handle/10294/3062/Third_Degree_2003-Spring.pdf?sequence=1&isAllowed=y. Accessed 8 Sept. 2020.

—*Joy Crelin*

Kiki Bertens

Born: December 10, 1991
Occupation: Tennis player

In late 2017, Kiki Bertens seriously considered leaving tennis—the sport to which she had dedicated her life for two decades. A tennis player from the age of six, Bertens had played on the developmental-level International Tennis Federation (ITF) Women's Circuit throughout her late teens and debuted on the Women's Tennis Association (WTA) Tour, the highest level of competition in women's professional tennis, in 2011. The title-winning competitor known for her aggressive style had nevertheless long struggled with her confidence, with the pressure of fan expectations, and with the strain of constant travel, and by the end of 2017, the stress had become nearly unmanageable. "I was really close to quitting," Bertens told Charlie Eccleshare for the *Telegraph* (30 June 2019). "It was the end

Photo by Steven Pisano and Vinkje83 via Wikimedia Commons

of the year so I was exhausted. I just needed a break from everything."

Ultimately, however, Bertens chose not to quit, but instead, returned to her sport with a new mindset and approach to competition. Her new mentality proved to be successful: Over the next two seasons, she won singles titles at events such as the St. Petersburg Ladies Trophy and the Mutua Madrid Open, earned recognition as the WTA's Most Improved Player (MIP) of 2018, and ranked within the top ten women's singles players in the world. "Every tournament I go in and I have the feeling that I can win it," she told Ben Rothenberg for the *New York Times* (24 May 2019) about her newfound confidence. "I know I can do it, and that's a change." By early 2020 she had amassed ten WTA career titles.

EARLY LIFE AND CAREER
Kiki Bertens was born to Rob and Doré Bertens on December 10, 1991, in Wateringen, the Netherlands. The second of three children, she has two sisters, Joyce and Daisy. Bertens began playing tennis at her aunt and uncle's Rotterdam area tennis club when she was six years old and quickly displayed a talent for the sport. Increasingly devoted to tennis as she grew older, she admired the Belgian player Kim Clijsters, who notably won four Grand Slam singles titles between 2005 and 2011.

Bertens began competing in senior-level tennis as a teenager, and in August 2006, the fourteen-year-old debuted on the ITF Women's Circuit, a developmental tour of professional tennis competitions. At her first ITF Women's Circuit event, the Vlaardingen tournament in

the Netherlands, she beat Ukrainian player Irina Buryachok in two sets in the first round before losing to fellow Dutch player Claire Lablans in three sets in the second.

Throughout her early years in professional tennis, Bertens not only developed the skills to compete at a high level but also became acutely aware of the variable nature of her chosen sport. "I can lose against anyone," she later explained to Rothenberg. "That's how tennis is sometimes: You can have good days, you can have bad days, your opponents can play really well. I know all the other girls can play really well; everyone's working really hard to get here. . . . I'm just trying to do my best, and we'll see if it's enough or not."

Over the years following her professional debut, Bertens remained an active competitor on the ITF Women's Circuit and won her first singles tournament on that tour, the Netherlands' Almere tournament, in September 2009. She went on to win a second singles tournament in Turkey the following month and found success in doubles matches with various partners, winning five doubles competitions during the 2009 season. Bertens would continue to compete in ITF singles and doubles events intermittently through 2015.

WTA TOUR DEBUT
Bertens began playing in WTA Tour tournaments in the 2011 season. She competed in the qualifying rounds of several WTA Tour tournaments and as part of the main draw in the 's-Hertogenbosch tournament in the Netherlands. That season also saw Bertens compete in the singles qualifying rounds of the French Open (or Roland Garros) and the US Open, two of four high-level Grand Slam tournaments, which also include the Australian Open and Wimbledon. Although Bertens would go on to make regular appearances in Grand Slam events, she would long express discomfort with the level of publicity and scrutiny she received as a player in such major competitions. "I don't like the big stage, I don't like to be on there," she later told Eccleshare. "If a couple of people are watching I feel better than in a full stadium." Nevertheless, Bertens remained committed to professional tennis as well as to representing the Netherlands on the international level, including at the 2011 Fed Cup.

Active in both the ITF and the WTA circuits during the 2012 season, Bertens reached a major milestone in April of that year, when she won her first WTA Tour title in Fés, Morocco. She also qualified for three Grand Slam events. Thanks to her strong performance in Morocco and throughout the season, she reached the ranking of ninety-second among all WTA singles players, her highest to that point and first top-hundred WTA ranking. She first entered the top fifty the following season, during which she reached the first round at all four Grand Slams and reached the quarterfinals in several other tournaments.

TOURNAMENT SUCCESS

Despite her years of experience and demonstrated skill on the court, Bertens continued to struggle with confidence in the years after joining the WTA Tour, particularly when it came time to play in major events like the Grand Slam tournaments. "Maybe I didn't know, still, that I was kind of good," she told Rothenberg about that period. "I felt everyone else was so much better than I was, and I didn't really feel like I belonged there." Despite such doubts, Bertens progressed to the fourth round, or round of sixteen, at the French Open in 2014, her best Grand Slam singles finish to that point.

The 2014 season also saw the beginning of a string of successful doubles outings with Swedish athlete Johanna Larsson, with whom Bertens would claim ten doubles titles between 2014 and late 2017 and place second at the 2017 WTA Finals. Bertens credited their success not only to their strong partnership and friendship but also their compatible approaches to the sport. "We just go on court, have fun in the doubles and of course we want to win, but it's also about the fun and I think that's the most important thing," she explained to John Lupo for *Vavel* (20 Oct. 2016).

TURNING POINT

Bertens's performance in the Grand Slams continued to improve over the next several seasons. In June 2016 she reached the semifinals of the French Open after beating Swiss player Timea Bacsinszky but ultimately lost to veteran American player Serena Williams. Bertens and Larsson also reached the quarterfinals in doubles at that tournament. That year likewise brought Bertens's debut appearance in the Olympic Games, held in Rio de Janeiro, Brazil, but she fell to Italy's Sara Errani during the first round of singles competition.

Bertens had a strong 2017 season, winning two WTA Tour singles titles and breaking the WTA's top-twenty rankings for the first time. Despite that, she seriously considered quitting tennis late in the year. The constant travel and stress of competition had become difficult for her to manage. "I was thinking if I need to carry on my career like this then it's not a good thing," she told Eccleshare. "It doesn't make me happy, so something needs to change." Rather than leave competitive tennis, Bertens ultimately chose to prioritize her own well-being, rather than the expectations of tennis fans or the media, and began regular yoga practice, which she later identified as beneficial both to her mental health and to her movement on the court. She also began to set goals for herself and strove to learn from games that went poorly.

Her efforts proved fruitful. At Wimbledon the following spring, she progressed to the quarterfinals before losing to German player Julia Görges, and she won titles in Seoul, South Korea; Charleston, North Carolina; and Cincinnati, Ohio. During the 2018 season, Bertens reached ninth in the WTA, her first top-ten WTA singles ranking. She was also awarded the title of WTA MIP of the Year, largely due to her improved performance on court surfaces other than the clay on which she had long been most comfortable.

BREAKTHROUGH SEASON

The 2019 season proved to be a breakthrough for Bertens, who, that February, progressed through the rounds of competition at the St. Petersburg Ladies Trophy in Russia and defeated Croatian player Donna Vekić in a well-fought, two-set final. Then, at Spain's Mutua Madrid Open in May, she bested top-ten players Petra Kvitová and Sloane Stephens and beat Simona Halep, then the latest French Open champion and top-three player, in the final to claim that Premier Mandatory title. Speaking of the event, she told Courtney Nguyen for the *WTA Insider Podcast* (12 May 2019), "I played some really good tennis, really solid." Bertens's performance in Madrid raised her ranking to fourth, the highest ranking she had achieved to that point. It also made her the highest-ranked woman of Dutch nationality in the sport to date.

Bertens continued to reach high levels of competition throughout the season, including competing in three additional tournament finals and the semifinals at the China Open. Despite ending the season ranked ninth, not within the top five, she remained pleased with her performance that season. "My confidence grew a lot I would say after the last year," she said, as quoted on the *WTA*'s website (2 Dec. 2019). "I'm really proud I'm still in the top 10, which was a goal in the beginning of the season. I knew it was going to be really tough. But I'm still here, so really proud of that."

Bertens had a strong start to her 2020 season, including a finals appearance in Brisbane with partner Ashleigh Barty and a fourth-round singles finish at the Australian Open in late January. She won her first tournament of the year in February, defending her St. Petersburg Ladies Trophy title against Kazakh Elena Rybakina shortly before the COVID-19 pandemic put most tennis competitions on hold for much of 2020. Bertens also defended her Madrid title in a virtual contest that May.

Though Bertens had planned to compete in the US Open in late August and early September, she decided to withdraw after learning that she would be required to quarantine for two weeks after arriving home, as the Netherlands had identified the United States as a high-risk country during the pandemic. "Of course we respect that as a team, but this would hinder the preparation for my beloved clay court tournaments in Rome and Paris," she explained about her decision, as quoted by Agence France-Presse (AFP) reporter Olga Maltseva on *Yahoo! Sports* (7 Aug. 2020). Though she opted to sit out the US Open, Bertens expressed interest in competing in major events held elsewhere, including the French Open, which had been rescheduled from May to late September.

PERSONAL LIFE

Kiki Bertens married Remko de Rijke, a Dutch physiotherapist and fitness coach who has worked as part of her team, on November 30, 2019. Her sister Joyce has also served as her business manager. When not competing abroad, Bertens lives in the Netherlands.

In 2020, Bertens and writer René van Hattum published the book *Tennis met Kiki* (Tennis with Kiki), the proceeds of which were to benefit the Youth Fund for Sports and Culture.

SUGGESTED READING

Bertens, Kiki. "Champions Corner: Bertens from the Brink of Retirement to World No. 4—'I Came a Long Way.'" Interview by Courtney Nguyen. *WTA Insider Podcast*, 12 May 2019, www.wtatennis.com/news/1448375/champions-corner-bertens-from-the-brink-of-retirement-to-world-no4-i-came-a-long-way. Accessed 8 Sept. 2020.

———. "Kiki Bertens Interview: 'I'd Rather Only 10 People Watched Me Play on Centre Court.'" Interview by Charlie Eccleshare. *The Telegraph*, 30 June 2019, www.telegraph.co.uk/tennis/2019/06/30/kiki-bertens-interview-rather-10-people-watched-play-centre. Accessed 8 Sept. 2020.

———. "VAVEL Exclusive Interview with Kiki Bertens: 'It Was Amazing' to Reach the French Open Semi-Finals." Interview by John Lupo. *Vavel*, 20 Oct. 2016, www.vavel.com/en/more-sport/2016/10/20/tennis/710245-vavel-exclusive-interview-with-kiki-bertens.html. Accessed 8 Sept. 2020.

Maltseva, Olga. "Kiki Bertens Withdraws from US Open over Virus Fears." *Yahoo! Sports*, 7 Aug. 2020, sports.yahoo.com/kiki-bertens-withdraws-us-open-131330824.html. Accessed 8 Sept. 2020.

Rothenberg, Ben. "Kiki Bertens Tries to Get Used to a New Label: French Open Contender." *The New York Times*, 24 May 2019, www.nytimes.com/2019/05/24/sports/tennis/kiki-bertens-french-open.html. Accessed 8 Sept. 2020.

"What a Day!'—Wedding Bells Ring for Kiki Bertens." *WTA*, 2 Dec. 2019, www.wtatennis.com/news/1513139/-what-a-day-wedding-bells-ring-for-kiki-bertens. Accessed 8 Sept. 2020.

—Joy Crelin

Xavier Bettel

Date of birth: March 3, 1973
Occupation: Prime minister of Luxembourg

Xavier Bettel is the leader of the center-right Democratic Party (DP). Once the youngest member of Luxembourg's Parliament, he became Luxembourg's prime minister in December 2013, marking the first time since 1979 that Luxembourg has had a party other than the Christian Social People's Party (CSV) in power.

EARLY LIFE AND EDUCATION

Xavier Bettel was born on March 3, 1973, in Luxembourg City, Luxembourg, to a wine merchant and former flight attendant. His mother was the grandniece of the Russian composer Sergei Rachmaninoff. Bettel grew up in Bonnevoie and attended local schools.

When Bettel was fifteen, his father died, and his mother took over running the family's wine business. Bettel joined the Democratic Party in 1989, becoming the vice president of its youth group two years later. He later became its president.

Bettel attended the University of Nancy in France, receiving a master's degree in public and European law and a diploma of advanced studies (DEA, Diplôme d'études approfondies) in political sciences and public law. He also attended Aristotle University in Greece, where he studied maritime and ecclesiastical law.

POLITICAL CAREER

Bettel entered politics in 1999, successfully standing for the Democratic Party for a seat in Parliament representing Centre. The next year, he entered local government, becoming a municipal councillor of Luxembourg City. He worked as a barrister in Luxembourg City from 2001 to 2013.

Winning re-election to Parliament in the elections of 2004, 2009, and 2013, Bettel took on leadership roles, serving as vice-chair of the Legal Affairs Committee from 2004 to 2013 and vice-chair of the Committee of Enquiry into the State Intelligence Service from 2012 to 2013. He was chair of the DP parliamentary group from 2009 to 2011. In 2013, he became the chair of the DP.

In 2005, Bettel became an alderman of Luxembourg City. Six years later, he became the city's mayor, a position he held until he became prime minister.

Following the October 2013 elections, Luxembourg Grand Duke Henri appointed Bettel the prime minister in a coalition government of the DP, Green Party, and Luxembourg Socialist Workers Party. He also was appointed the minister of state, minister for religious affairs, and minister for communications and media. Bettel was sworn in on December 4, 2013.

Bettel's appointment as prime minister disrupted the political status quo of Luxembourg. His predecessor, Jean-Claude Juncker, had been the head of government for eighteen years, and Juncker's party, the Christian Social People's Party, had been in power for all but five years since the end of World War II.

Shortly after taking office, Bettel pledged to cut spending on public expenditures to preserve Luxembourg's triple-A credit rating. He implemented a public savings program, and Luxembourg retained its coveted triple-A rating—one of only two eurozone countries to do so.

In 2014, Bettel's government formally recognized the Palestinian Authority as the state of Palestine. The following year Bettel and several ministers signed a declaration apologizing to the Jewish community of Luxembourg for injustices inflicted on it during World War II and for the actions of Luxembourg authorities who had cooperated with the Nazis during their occupation of Luxembourg.

Not all Bettel's actions have met with his constituents' approval. In Luxembourg, almost half of the residents are foreign nationals, and Bettel proposed giving noncitizen residents the right to vote. The proposal was put to a referendum in May 2015, but was overwhelmingly rejected.

In July 2015, Bettel began a six-month rotating presidency of the Council of the European Union (EU). At the time the EU was facing several challenges, including an economic crisis in Greece and a migration crisis with thousands of Syrian, Iranian, and Afghan refugees fleeing to Europe. Bettel announced human rights would be a cornerstone of his EU presidency, as well as a priority of Luxembourg. During his EU presidency, he helped to resolve the Greek crisis and worked to find solutions to the migration crisis. He promoted sustainable development and employment growth, helped to establish the foundations for a free trade agreement between the EU and Japan, worked to gain consensus on climate change for the 2015 Paris Climate Change Conference, and promoted a ceasefire and reopening dialogue between Russia and the Ukraine. He also met with the leaders of both countries, giving support to the Ukraine and its integration into Europe while striving to improve relations between Russia and the EU.

Bettel has integrated many of the EU priorities with those of Luxembourg. While acknowledging Luxembourg's constraints in taking in additional refugees due to exceeded capacity in existing shelters, Bettel planned to create container accommodations and promoted an initiative to house refugees with local families.

In December 2015, Luxembourg hosted a seminar on EU–Russia relations. In a speech to the attendees, Bettel emphasized the interdependence of Russia and the EU and challenges testing their relationship. He called for increased communication and cooperation and made an impassioned plea for countries to de-escalate conflicts and work together to solve problems such as terrorism, border disputes, migration, unemployment, sustainable development, and economic problems.

IMPACT

In his leadership of both Luxembourg and the Council of the EU, Bettel has demonstrated his intent to make meaningful changes and to promote bilateral relations with other countries. He has worked toward solving many of the most pressing problems facing Europe in the 2010s, including climate change, the Greek economic crisis, the Syrian refugee crisis, and the conflict between Russia and Ukraine.

PERSONAL LIFE

Bettel married Gauthier Destenay, an architect, in May 2015, just four months after the legalization of same-sex marriages in Luxembourg took effect. Bettel and Destenay have been in a civil partnership since 2010.

SUGGESTED READING

Bettel, Xavier. "Luxembourg PM: European Union, Russia Not Rivals, Require One Another as Partners—Speech." *Eurasia Review*, 10 Dec. 2015, www.eurasiareview.com/10122015-luxembourg-pm-european-union-russia-not-rivals-require-one-another-as-partners-oped/. Accessed 24 June 2020.

Chu, Henry. "Luxembourg Premier Joins Vanguard of Gay Leaders." *The Los Angeles Times*. Los Angeles Times Media Group, 20 Aug. 2014, www.latimes.com/world/europe/la-fg-c1-0820-europe-gay-leaders-pictures-photogallery.html.

"Wedding on Friday: Xavier Bettel—Husband to Be." *Luxemburger Wort*, 14 May 2015, contactoapp.wort.lu/articles/mywort/5554993d0c88b46a8ce593f4. Accessed 25 June 2020.

"Xavier Bettel Biography." *Gouvernement.lu*. Government of Luxembourg, Dec. 2015, gouvernement.lu/en/gouvernement/xavier-bettel/CV.html. Accessed 25 June 2020.

"Xavier Bettel Presented the European Parliament at a Plenary Session with the Priorities for the Luxembourg Presidency of the Council of the European Union." *Grand Duchy of Luxembourg and Presidency of the Council of the European Union.* Government of Luxembourg, 7 Aug. 2015, www.eu2015lu.eu/en/actualites/articles-actualite/2015/07/pe-bettel-priorites/. Accessed 25 June 2020.

"Xavier Bettel Presents Priorities of the Luxembourg EU Presidency." *Alliance of Liberals and Democrats for Europe Party.* ALDE, 7 Aug. 2015.. .

—*Barb Lightner*

Sangeeta N. Bhatia

Born: June 24, 1968
Occupation: Biological engineer

When biological engineer Sangeeta N. Bhatia was a child, her family's answering machine stopped working. The young Bhatia took the machine apart, diagnosed and fixed the problem, and put the machine back together. Though that incident may have originally formed the basis of merely an entertaining anecdote about an inquisitive child, it ultimately came to serve as an early example of the curiosity, dedication, and focus on addressing complex problems that characterized Bhatia's career in research. Throughout her years as a professor and researcher, first at the University of California, San Diego starting in the late 1990s and, beginning in 2005, at the Massachusetts Institute of Technology (MIT), Bhatia worked to develop technological means of tackling persistent medical problems, including the diagnosis of diseases and the testing of treatments. "We're engineers working in a science environment, thinking about human health," she told *NBC News* (9 Sept. 2014) about her laboratory's approach to their field. "What engineers like to do is tinker, so we encourage that spirit of tinkering in the lab."

Though Bhatia won numerous awards and other honors over the course of her career, including the 2014 Lemelson-MIT Prize, she preferred to focus on the results of her research rather than the accolades she received for them. "It's really not, for me, about the awards and the academies. I think those are wonderful and important parts of science and engineering. But for me, I really care about touching patients," she explained in an undated interview for the *MIT Infinite History.* "I want to make inventions that have a clinical impact or have a technological impact." By 2019, widely recognized for her efforts behind the creation of what was considered the first human "microliver," and having founded two companies building upon and integrating such innovations and research, she had been elected to the National Academy of Sciences, the National Academy of Engineering, and the National Academy of Medicine.

EARLY LIFE

Sangeeta N. Bhatia was born in Boston, Massachusetts, on June 24, 1968. She was one of two daughters born to Narain, an engineer and entrepreneur, and Vidya, one of the first women in India to earn a master's degree in business administration. As a child growing up in the Boston suburb of Lexington, Bhatia was drawn to science and technology. She particularly enjoyed projects that involved building and other hands-on activities, including taking household machines apart and putting them back together. "My mom said I was very busy with my hands," she told the *Guardian* (31 Jan. 2017). "I was always fidgeting, always crafting. I really loved to build things." Her parents valued education highly and encouraged their daughter's curiosity in ways that she would later characterize as essential to her development as a researcher and entrepreneur.

As a teenager, Bhatia developed an interest in biology while taking a class in that subject at her high school. She likewise became fascinated with medical science, and with the innovations that would be needed to provide improved medical care throughout the world, during her family's summer visits with family in India. "An aunt [who] was a physician would take me to the clinic, and I would see what medical care is like in a low-resource setting," she recalled to Meir Rinde for the Science History Institute website *Distillations* (9 July 2019). "That stuck with me in the back of my head." In addition to learning about biology and medicine, the teenage Bhatia also had the opportunity to visit the mechanical engineering department at the Massachusetts Institute of Technology (MIT) in Cambridge, Massachusetts, where she was able to learn about the groundbreaking research taking place there.

EDUCATION
After graduating from Lexington High School in 1986, Bhatia enrolled at Brown University. An engineering student with a long-standing interest in biology and medicine, she found herself drawn to the specific field of biomedical engineering and chose Brown largely because of its strength in that area. Although Bhatia explored a variety of areas related to her chosen field through summer jobs, including a stint with a biotechnology company, a particularly key moment in her undergraduate career came during her senior year, when she asked for and secured a summer position in what was then known as the university's Artificial Organs Laboratory. "I was interested in the idea that you could engineer organs," she recalled for *India Abroad* (9 July 2008). "I told them, 'I'm small, I won't take up much room!'" In addition to expanding her understanding of the capabilities of bioengineering, specifically regarding tissue engineering, Bhatia's time as an undergraduate sparked what would be a long-lasting scientific interest in the liver, an organ to which she would later devote a great deal of study. She earned her bachelor's degree from Brown in 1990.

Following a brief period of employment in the pharmaceutical industry, Bhatia enrolled in MIT to pursue graduate studies beginning in 1991. As she was initially rejected from her preferred program, a health sciences and technology program that MIT operated jointly with Harvard University, she began her studies at MIT within the field of mechanical engineering and went on to earn a master's degree in that field in 1993. She ultimately transferred into the joint MIT-Harvard program, during which she pursued a doctorate in biomedical engineering at MIT as well as a medical doctorate (MD) at Harvard. In addition to focusing on her studies and performing laboratory work at Massachusetts General Hospital (MGH), Bhatia cofounded the organization Keys to Empowering Youth and worked to promote science among young people, particularly girls, by arranging visits to MIT for preteens and young teenagers. Foundationally, it was also during this period that she initiated,

through a collaboration with the MIT facility manufacturing computer chips, what would become a lengthy focus on using this technology (microfabrication) to grow, sustain, and organize functioning liver cells outside of the body. After completing her PhD in biomedical engineering in 1997, she went on to earn her MD from Harvard Medical School (HMS) in 1999.

CAREER IN ACADEMIA
Continuing to push herself early on, Bhatia began her career in academia in California, accepting an assistant professorship at the University of California (UC), San Diego while she was still completing medical school. Not long after her arrival, she became a member of the 1999 class of fellows of the David and Lucile Packard Foundation, an organization that provides financial support to science professors in the early stages of their career. Bhatia was promoted from assistant professor to associate professor of bioengineering and medicine in 2002 and succeeded in attaining a tenured position at the university prior to her departure from the institution in 2005.

Although Bhatia's time at UC San Diego was productive, including further liver studies, she found herself missing the characteristic intellectual environment of MIT in which she had been immersed throughout her graduate studies. "You see these maps sometimes where they show that Cambridge is the center of the universe," she explained in her interview for *MIT Infinite History*. "And I think intellectually, if you train [in] this environment, that is actually how you see the world. And I absolutely felt that way." After leaving California in 2005, Bhatia returned to MIT, where she would eventually hold the title of John J. and Dorothy Wilson Professor at the Department of Electrical Engineering and Computer Science and the Institute for Medical Engineering and Science. In addition to that role, she started serving as an intramural member of the Koch Institute for Integrative Cancer Research at MIT in 2007, an investigator of the Howard Hughes Medical Institute (HHMI) in 2009, and the director of the Marble Center for Cancer Nanomedicine within the Koch Institute in 2016.

RESEARCH INTERESTS
As head of MIT's Laboratory for Multiscale Regenerative Technologies, Bhatia conducted and oversaw research in a number of different areas, most inhabiting the intersection of engineering and medicine. Long interested in diseases of the liver and the detection and treatment of such conditions, she continued to devote substantial attention to the development and refining of what she and her colleagues refer to as human "microlivers," small models of livers created from carefully arranged cells that can be used to study

diseases or study the results of drugs. For Bhatia, discovering new means of developing and testing treatments for liver diseases was particularly essential because, except for transplants, means of addressing serious liver conditions remained largely nonexistent. "For most other organs we have some sort of stopgap measure," she explained to Josh Seftel for *NOVA Science-NOW* (Mar. 2009). "If your heart is failing, and you can't yet get a transplant, we have a pump. And if your kidney is failing, and you can't get a transplant, we have a filter. In the case of the liver, there's nothing." Through experimentation that by the mid-2010s had included the development of a liver tissue scaffold that could be implanted into mice and the implementation of 3-D printing, Bhatia maintained hope that scientists would one day be able to grow entire new livers for transplantation purposes.

In addition to their work with microlivers, Bhatia and her colleagues built on research she had started spearheading at UC San Diego, working to develop means of using nanotechnology for medical purposes, including for the purpose of detecting diseases. In one such application, medical professionals could make use of diagnostic nanoparticles that function as synthetic biomarkers. "We make [the nanoparticles] responsive to certain enzymes that are disease associated. When the particle finds the enzyme that it's been designed for, there's a chemical reaction and they emit a little reporter, a little synthetic signal, which is a chemical molecule that's not found in your body," she told Rinde. "If you find these signals in the urine, then you could diagnose this disease." She has further noted in interviews that such forms of diagnostic technology could prove particularly useful in low-resource medical environments in which advanced imaging equipment, for example, is not available.

In recognition of her work toward advancing medical science, Bhatia received numerous honors. Among her most notable awards were the 2014 Lemelson-MIT Prize and the 2019 Othmer Gold Medal of the Science History Institute.

INNOVATION AND ENTREPRENEURSHIP

While much of the research conducted in Bhatia's laboratory centered on the lab's specific areas of interest, Bhatia, a believer in independent research and innovation, encouraged students to pursue other work as well. To that end, students working in the lab typically were tasked with devoting 20 percent of their time to work that may or may not prove fruitful. "My goal always is to create independent thinkers," she told Rinde. "I tell all my students, by the time that you graduate, the perfect trajectory is that now you know

more than I do, and you go off and you create your own world."

In addition to conducting and overseeing research, Bhatia played an active role in the founding of multiple companies formed to work on commercial applications for the technologies developed in the lab. Around 2008 she cofounded the company Hepregen to produce microlivers for drug-testing purposes. She also helped found the biotechnology company Glympse Bio, which formed in 2015 to develop biosensors for detecting and assessing diseases based on the work conducted at MIT. "The start-up has oncology and nononcology programs in its pipeline. They are beginning first-in-human studies with a multiplex protease panel for [the liver disease] non-alcoholic steatohepatitis," Bhatia told Prashant Nair for *PNAS* (21 Jan. 2020) about Glympse Bio. "I'm excited to see how this plays out in patients; you can do all of the experiments you want in animal models, but you're not going to really learn about both the power and limitations of a technology until you enter clinical trials."

Additionally, Bhatia became a member of the board of directors for the firm Vertex Pharmaceuticals in 2015. She was also elected to the distinguished National Academy of Sciences, the National Academy of Engineering, and the National Academy of Medicine.

PERSONAL LIFE

Sangeeta N. Bhatia met her husband, Jagesh Shah, while they were both attending graduate school. Shah later became a professor affiliated with Harvard Medical School and Brigham and Women's Hospital. They have two daughters.

SUGGESTED READING

Bhatia, Sangeeta N. "Interview: Sangeeta Bhatia." Interview by Meir Rinde. *Distillations*, 9 July 2019, www.sciencehistory.org/distillations/interview-sangeeta-bhatia. Accessed 8 Sept. 2020.

———. "The Many Sides of Sangeeta Bhatia." Interview by Josh Seftel. *NOVA Science-NOW*, Mar. 2009, www.pbs.org/wgbh/nova/sciencenow/0404/04-bhat-nf.html. Accessed 8 Sept. 2020.

———. "QnAs with Sangeeta N. Bhatia." Interview by Prashant Nair. *PNAS*, 21 Jan. 2020, www.pnas.org/content/117/3/1243. Accessed 8 Sept. 2020.

———. "Sangeeta N. Bhatia SM '93, PhD '97." *MIT Infinite History*, infinitehistory.mit.edu/video/sangeeta-n-bhatia-sm-93-phd-97. Transcript. Accessed 8 Sept. 2020.

"Cancer-Fighting Inventor Sangeeta Bhatia Wins $500,000 Prize." *NBC News*, 9 Sept. 2014, www.nbcnews.com/science/science-news/cancer-fighting-inventor-sangeeta-bhatia-wins-500-000-prize-n198841. Accessed 8 Sept. 2020.

"Indian Chosen for Prestigious Scientists' Body." *India Abroad*, 9 July 2008, www.rediff.com/news/2008/jul/09doc.htm. Accessed 8 Sept. 2020.

"Sangeeta Bhatia: The Biotech Entrepreneur Advocating for Gender Equity in STEM Fields." *The Guardian*, 31 Jan. 2017, www.theguardian.com/personal-investments/ng-interactive/2017/jan/31/sangeeta-bhatia-stem-engineer-mit-biotech-gender. Accessed 8 Sept. 2020.

—*Joy Crelin*

Sophie Blackall

Date of birth: July 2, 1970
Occupation: Author and illustrator

Each year, the American Library Association (ALA) awards one writer and/or illustrator the Randolph Caldecott Medal for the "most distinguished American picture book for children." Kate Murphy, who interviewed acclaimed author and illustrator Sophie Blackall for the *New York Times* in 2016, compared winning the Caldecott Medal to winning "an Oscar in the children's book world." As with the Oscars, winning the Caldecott more than once is a rare honor, and Blackall is one of only nine illustrators to do so since the award was established in 1938. Her first, in 2016, was for illustrating *Finding Winnie: The True Story of the World's Most Famous Bear* (2015). Written by Lindsay Mattick, *Finding Winnie* tells the story of how A. A. Milne was inspired by a real bear to write the Winnie-the-Pooh series. Blackall received her second Caldecott in 2019 for writing and illustrating *Hello Lighthouse*. Her other honors include an Ezra Jack Keats New Illustrator Award, a Blue Ribbon Picture Book Award, and a Founders Award from the Society of Illustrators. Two books that she illustrated, *Big Red Lollipop* (2012), written by Rukhsana Khan, and *The Baby Tree* (2014), written by Blackall, were selected as the New York Times Best Illustrated Children's Books.

Blackall is the author and/or illustrator of more than forty books. As John Rocco, who shared workspace with her, told Josh Greenhut for *Horn Book* (July–Aug. 2019), "She works like her pants are on fire, just constantly working on something new. And when she's not working on books, she's making some sort of art. She is the type of person that has to be creating constantly."

Blackall's work has also ignited controversy in addition to winning praise and honors, however. In 2015, she and author Emily Jenkins

published *A Fine Dessert: Four Families, Four Centuries, One Delicious Treat*, a picture book for readers four to eight years of age. The book which won the Texas Bluebonnet Award for 2016–17, tells the story of four families from different historical eras who make the same dessert, blackberry fool. Jenkins and Blackall were criticized for a story sequence about an enslaved mother and daughter making the dessert and then hiding in a closet to lick the bowl. Critics said that while Jenkins and Blackall had good intentions, their depiction of the mother and daughter as happy slaves was racially insensitive.

CHILDHOOD AND EDUCATION

Sophie Blackall was born in Melbourne, Victoria, in Australia on July 2, 1970. Growing up in Adelaide, South Australia, she and her brother read paperback books while sitting in neighboring trees. They devised a basket, rope, and pulley system to exchange books. Blackall's childhood also included a very tame pet goat named Josephine. She credits her mother with teaching her the value of kindness.

Blackall's parents divorced in 1977. That was also the year she decided to be an illustrator of children's books, after seeing the art Ernst Howell Shepard created for A. A. Milne's Winnie-the-Pooh books. She began drawing with sticks on the beach and requested paper to draw on from the local butcher. In a 2019 talk at the University of Richmond, Blackall recalled several other books that influenced her, including DuBose Heyward's *The Country Bunny and the Little Gold Shoes*, Maira Kalman's *The Principles*

Photo by Steven Pis Photo by JSFarman via Wikimedia Commons ano and Vinkje83 via Wikimedia Commons

of Uncertainty, and Herman Melville's classic novel, *Moby Dick*.

Blackall attended the Walford Anglican School in Hyde Park, South Australia, graduating from its senior school in 1987. In 1992 she earned a bachelor's degree in design, with honors, from the University of Technology in Sydney, New South Wales.

EARLY CAREER

After graduating, Blackall exhibited her paintings in galleries in Sydney and Melbourne. She also took on odd jobs. She provided the hands doing the work for a televised do-it-yourself show and painted robotic figures for amusement parks. She also wrote a column of household hints.

In 1997 she published her first book, *20 Party Tricks to Amuse and Amaze Your Friends*, which she wrote and illustrated. The sixty-page picture book for adults gives instructions for performing tricks that vary in difficulty, ranging from "Putting Your Head through a Business Card" to "The Broken Arm" and "Flying Amaretti." In her introduction, Blackall notes that all the tricks have been tested by the author but that "we take no responsibility for your fame or your misfortune."

In 2000 Blackall left Australia to move to an apartment in the Cobble Hill neighborhood of Brooklyn, New York, prompted by little more than a note of encouragement from the *New Yorker*. Her return ticket was for six months later, but she cashed it in to pay the rent. She caught her first break when the *New York Times* assigned her to create nine illustrations of caviar for a food series over several weeks. The *Times* assignment led to her first book-length assignment in 2002 as an illustrator for Shirin Yim Bridges's children's book *Ruby's Wish*. For her work, Blackall won the Ezra Jack Keats New Illustrator Award the following year.

ILLUSTRATING AND WRITING CHILDREN'S BOOKS

In the mid-2000s, Blackall started illustrating Annie Barrows's best-selling Ivy and Bean chapter book series. It details the adventures of two girls who become unlikely best friends. Between 2006, when the titular first book was published, and 2018, Barrows and Blackall published twelve volumes in the series.

Living and working in Brooklyn, Blackhall developed friendships with other children's book illustrators and authors in the area. In the early 2010s she joined with four of them to rent a shared workspace in an old factory in Brooklyn's Gowanus neighborhood. As Edward Hemingway told Greenhut, "Sophie occupied the corner position, right where the two lines of the L meet. It makes sense to have Sophie in the center, because I would say she is the beating heart of

the studio." Over the years, sharing space has sparked collaborations between Blackall and her studio mates. For example, she collaborated with writer John Bemelmans Marciano, grandson of author-illustrator Ludwig Bemelmans of Madeline picture-book series fame, on *The 9 Lives of Alexander Baddenfield* (2013) and on their Witches of Benevento series (2016–).

Blackall illustrated award-winning author Jacqueline Woodson's *Pecan Pie Baby* (2010). The book, for ages three to six, tells the story of Gia, a big-sister-to-be who has conflicted feelings about the impending arrival of a new sibling. Woodson and Blackall received the 2011 Boston Globe–Horn Book Picture Book Honor for their work.

In addition to collaborations, Blackall has illustrated children's books that she has written. In 2011 she published *Are You Awake?*, a picture book about a young boy named Edward who asks his mom a series of questions at four o'clock in the morning before he finally falls asleep. Another of her solo works is *The Baby Tree* (2014), a sex-education picture book that shows a boy attempting to answer the question "Where do babies come from?" for himself after he is told that he will become a big brother. Blackall was inspired to write the book in response to a 2010 *New Yorker* article by Jill Lepore, who lamented the lack of relevant and progressive age-appropriate sex-education books for young readers. Lepore had pleaded, "Sophie Blackall, will you please attempt a funny, sensible, beautiful book on this subject?" Blackall researched the best information and vocabulary to use for three- to six-year-olds, as she explained to Kitty Flynn for *Horn Book* (9 May 2014), "I spoke to pediatricians and elementary teachers and other parents, and the one thing that seemed really clear is that children will absorb as much information as is appropriate for them at any given age; the rest will just spill over."

CALDECOTT AWARDS

In 2016 Blackall won the Caldecott Medal for Lindsay Mattick's book *Finding Winnie*, which she illustrated at the request of Susan Rich, an editor at the publisher Little, Brown Books for Young Readers. In response to Rich's invitation, Blackall told the editor that she had first wanted to become an illustrator because of E. H. Shepard's work for A. A. Milne's *Winnie-the-Pooh*. Milne began the series after he and his son Christopher had seen a real bear named Winnie—named for Winnipeg, the hometown of the soldier who adopted the bear—at a London Zoo.

Blackall told Natasha Gilmore for *Publishers Weekly* (12 Jan. 2016), "I was obsessed with Winnie the Pooh as a child," she said. "It was the first book I bought with my own money. I read it over and over again. My friends and I would play

'Hundred Acre Woods' in the garden. I lived and breathed it for most of my childhood." Blackall later worked with Mattick on a 2018 sequel, *Winnie's Great War*.

Blackall won a second Caldecott for *Hello Lighthouse*, published in 2019. Due in part to reading *Moby Dick*, she had long been interested in lighthouses and whales. A print she purchased at a flea market of the Eddystone Lighthouse in England was the catalyst for her book. She stayed in a lighthouse for several days and visited others to get the details right. She deliberately structured the book so that one spread was of the lighthouse, always in the same place on each spread, with changing seasons and weather around it. She was influenced in that decision by the work of Barbara Cooney and Virginia Burton, whose illustrated children's books are among her favorites. Those spreads alternated with depictions of the life going on inside the lighthouse, where a family lived and grew.

MISSED CONNECTIONS AND ART IN TRANSIT
In addition to children's books, Blackall has also taken on projects for adult readers and viewers of all ages. In 2009 Blackall started her Missed Connections project, for which she illustrated the Missed Connections entries on Craigslist. As Blackall told Jenna Wortham for the *New York Times* (29 Sept. 2009), the project was a fortunate accident. "I lost about two hours of my life reading [the Missed Connections entries] and thought this is just an extraordinary mine of material, ranging from the lyrical, poetic to unintentionally hilarious. Many of them threw out ideas for images to me right away." Blackall used watercolor and Chinese ink to manifest those ideas. She expanded her search to random online postings and the *Village Voice*, a Greenwich Village newspaper.

Blackall's project, which focused only on listings in New York, grew into a blog and then into an Etsy shop, where she sold prints. Finally, she published *Missed Connections: Love Lost and Found*, a collection of the prints, in 2011. As she explained the charm of them to Wortham, she said, "These illustrations have recurring themes of love, loss, regret and hope. Even the most grim postings have this little kernel of unflagging hope which is just so lovely and optimistic."

In 2012, Blackall created a poster for the Arts for Transit project of the New York City subway. The poster showed a cross-section of people who regularly rode the subway, and copies were placed in many subway cars. Several people contacted Blackall to claim they were a person in the drawing—which came entirely from Blackall's imagination.

VOLUNTEER WORK AND PERSONAL LIFE
In 2012 Blackall traveled to Democratic Republic of the Congo (DRC) on behalf of the Measles and Rubella Initiative (MRI), a collaboration among world health organizations to vaccinate all children. During the trip, Blackall kept a blog that formed the basis of *Let Every Child Have a Name: The Road to a World Without Measles* (2012), which she wrote and illustrated. She visited India for the MRI in 2013 and later went to Bhutan and Rwanda for Save the Children's literacy initiative.

Blackall owns Milkwood Farm, a twenty-one-acre retreat center for writers and artists that she established on an abandoned nineteenth-century farm in upstate New York. Blackall has two children, Olive, who identifies as non-binary, and a son, Edward. She also has a stepdaughter from her second marriage. The family took refuge at the farm when the 2020 coronavirus pandemic began.

SUGGESTED READING
Blackall, Sophie. "Sophie Blackall Is in the (Light)house! An INTERVIEW!!!!! Yay!!!!" Interview by Jennifer Black Reinhardt. *Picture Book Builders*, 12 June 2018, picturebookbuilders.com/2018/06/sophie-blackall-is-in-the-lighthouse-an-interview-yay/. Accessed 22 July 2020.

Gilmore, Natasha. "'Celebrating with Champagne and Donuts': Sophie Blackall on Her 2016 Caldecott." *Publishers Weekly*, 12 Jan. 2016, www.publishersweekly.com/pw/by-topic/childrens/childrens-authors/article/69123-celebrating-with-champagne-and-donuts-sophie-blackall-on-her-2016-caldecott.html. Accessed 22 July 2020.

Rich, Susan. "The Audacious Choice of Sophie Blackall." *The Horn Book Magazine*, vol. 92, no. 4, July 2016, pp. 51–55. *Literary Reference Center Plus*, search.ebscohost.com/login.aspx?direct=true&db=lkh&AN=116502244&site=lrc-plus. Accessed 22 July 2020.

Ruzzier, Sergio, et al. "Hello Studio: A Profile of Sophie Blackall." *The Horn Book Magazine*, vol. 95, no. 4, July 2019, pp. 57–61. *Literary Reference Center Plus*, search.ebscohost.com/login.aspx?direct=true&db=lkh&AN=136901868&site=lrc-plus. Accessed 22 July 2020.

Wortham, Jenna. "Craigslist's Missed Connections as Art." *The New York Times*, 29 Sept. 2009, bits.blogs.nytimes.com/2009/09/29/craigslists-missed-connections-as-art/. Accessed 17 June 2020.

SELECTED WORKS
Ivy and Bean series, 2006–; *Pecan Pie Baby*, 2010; *Missed Connections*, 2011; *Are You Awake?*, 2011; *Let Every Child Have a Name*,

2012; *The Baby Tree*, 2014; *Finding Winnie*, 2016; *Hello Lighthouse*, 2019

—*Judy Johnson*

Alex Blumberg
Date of birth: ca. 1967
Occupation: Entrepreneur and producer

Award-winning radio journalist Alex Blumberg cofounded the podcasting company Gimlet Media in 2014 with business partner Matt Leiber. In February 2019, the pair made headlines when they sold the venture to the music streaming service Spotify for approximately $230 million. Even before that lucrative sale, Blumberg had earned a reputation as a savvy entrepreneur thanks to his company's success as the podcast market boomed. Gimlet was launched the same year as *Serial*, a blockbuster true-crime podcast that introduced legions of new listeners to the medium. With on-demand streaming media rapidly growing in popularity, the production company was perfectly positioned for, as Blumberg put it to Dan Schawbel for *Forbes* (24 Jan. 2017), "the dawn of a new golden age in audio."

Blumberg had previously made his name in an older audio format: radio. He worked as a freelance reporter and then as producer on the popular public radio program *This American Life* from 1999 to 2014. That experience made him highly familiar with the kind of intimate, narrator-driven storytelling that would become commonplace in the podcast format. Blumberg also co-developed the National Public Radio (NPR) podcast *Planet Money*, which first aired in 2008 and became a hit. These successes helped inspire him to take on the challenge of starting his own company. "I love the idea of building new stuff," Blumberg noted in a 2015 profile for CNN. "Every new podcast we launch is a chance to do something new, or do something old in a new way. I love that feeling."

EARLY LIFE AND EDUCATION
Alex Blumberg was raised in Cincinnati, Ohio, along with his sister, Kate. His father, Richard, was the cofounder of a major advertising agency in the city. As Blumberg explained in a 2014 story for *This American Life*, his father also regularly smoked marijuana, keeping the extent of his habit a secret for years. In the program Blumberg admitted that his father's desire to smoke, even during happy times with family, occasionally made him feel inadequate and ultimately affected their relationship.

Some other details of Blumberg's early life were revealed in another episode of *This*

Photo by Roy Rochlin/Getty Images

American Life, aired in 2001, in which he tracked down and interviewed his former babysitter. She remembered him as an unusually bookish and serious child. Blumberg worked as a cashier for a grocery store as a teenager and graduated from Walnut Hills High School. He was a good student and enjoyed reading, especially narrative nonfiction. Some of his early influences were authors such as Joseph Mitchell and E. B. White as well as magazines such as the *New Yorker* and *Harper's*. However, he had no conception of pursuing writing or any other media career. "Somehow it never occurred to me that I could actually do that for a living," he told Tim Ferriss for the *Tim Ferriss Show* business podcast (29 Jan. 2015). "I just somehow thought that people who did that were some sort of different world of people."

Blumberg went on to attend Oberlin College in northeast Ohio, graduating with a bachelor's degree in 1989. After college he taught eighth grade science in Chicago for four years. In Chicago he began to develop a more cosmopolitan outlook and realized that working in media might be possible. A difficult breakup in his late twenties ultimately inspired Blumberg to pursue his interest in nonfiction writing and reporting. He made attempts at freelancing and landed a summer internship at *Harper's* while still a teacher. The connections he made there helped him land a job as an administrative assistant with *This American Life* in 1997.

THIS AMERICAN LIFE
A public radio program broadcast out of WBEZ Chicago, *This American Life* had begun airing in 1995 (originally under the title *Your Radio*

Playhouse). When Blumberg joined the team, the show had only four other employees: host Ira Glass and three producers. The entire team was still figuring out how to make the show work, especially as they were aiming for a documentary style and quality unlike anything before. "I learned a lot on the job," Blumberg told Ferriss, noting that his early duties included routine office tasks like answering the mail and running errands. "It was all hands on deck. And so occasionally I would get to produce stuff or help with the editorial side of things."

After helping produce a major story about Harold Washington, the first black mayor of Chicago, Blumberg expected Glass to make him a full-time producer. However, Glass told him that there was no open position or budget to create a new one. Blumberg asked whether he would be hired if a position did open and was bluntly told that he did not have enough experience for the role. He promptly quit to build experience as a freelance writer. With the help of a loan from his parents, he dedicated himself to writing. He soon found reasonable success selling pieces to magazines and other radio programs. After about a year and a half a producer position at *This American Life* finally opened; Blumberg applied and was hired in 1999. Meanwhile, the program was steadily growing in popularity. It would become a public radio staple and eventually be credited with pioneering an intimate style of narrative nonfiction that later paved the way for the podcast boom.

Even though Blumberg had already worked at *This American Life*, he had a steep learning curve as a producer. "The first couple of years, I was just trying to get my head above water and figure out how this stuff worked," he told Ferriss. As the show grew and evolved, so did his job description. After the terrorist attacks of September 11, 2001, the *This American Life* team became more serious about journalism in many ways, reporting about the attacks and the wars in Afghanistan and Iraq that followed. Blumberg also branched out into other media, most notably serving as an executive producer for a *This American Life* television series that ran on the Showtime network from 2007 to 2009. He later recalled that experience as a particularly difficult one, due to the challenge of translating radio-style storytelling to the screen. "You can't watch people telling a story about something that happened a long time ago. Something about it just does not work," he recalled to Ferriss of the television show. "You just need so much more visual information than just watching people talk." Still, the show won multiple Emmy Awards, including for Outstanding Nonfiction Series.

PLANET MONEY

In May 2008 Blumberg and journalist Adam Davidson teamed up to produce an hour-long story for *This American Life* called "The Giant Pool of Money," about the housing crisis then unfolding. "We were both interested in what was going on in the housing market: Adam was the expert reporter, and I had become sort of an interested dilettante, trolling on the internet," Blumberg told Karen Everhart for *Current* (11 May 2009). Though the creators were initially unsure there would be an audience for the subject, the program became one of *This American Life*'s most popular episodes and generated an unprecedented amount of listener feedback. It earned Blumberg and Davidson a George Polk Award for radio reporting, a duPont-Columbia Award, and a Peabody Award. In 2010, New York University's (NYU) Arthur L. Carter Journalism Institute named "A Giant Pool of Money" one of the decade's top ten works of journalism.

Sensing a public appetite for further explanations of complex economic subjects, Blumberg and Davidson planned a follow up. Several months after the story aired, just as the global economy crashed, they launched *Planet Money*, a podcast and blog for NPR that aimed to demystify money and global economics. It quickly proved successful with listeners. The program's multimedia approach also earned attention and critical praise. As the production grew, Blumberg focused on bringing in "good storytellers and people who have a strong narrative ability to tell a story in a fun way," as Blumberg explained to Everhart. "People who find the unexpected moments and follow them and pursue them—that's what we're looking for. Curiosity is the most important tool."

In 2013 *Planet Money* launched an innovative series demonstrating the reach of the global economy. The show followed the process of making a *Planet Money* T-shirt—featuring an image of a squirrel holding a martini—from the cotton farms where the material was grown to the factories where it was manufactured and beyond. Blumberg and his team created a crowdfunding campaign to raise money for their experiment. Listeners were surprisingly enthusiastic, and *Planet Money* ultimately raised more than half a million dollars. The success of the T-shirt campaign inspired Blumberg to consider ways to profit from the show's growing audience.

GIMLET MEDIA

With the growing success of *Planet Money* and other podcasts, Blumberg realized a new media frontier was emerging. "I didn't have a great idea for a podcast of my own, but I knew other people with great ideas for podcasts," he told Eilene Zimmerman for the *New York Times* (9 Dec. 2014). "And I also knew I had the skills to make those podcasts better. At 'Planet Money,' my one true skill was editing, so basically, I wanted to start a company that would let me edit." In 2014, he decided to leave his public radio career behind to found, with Matt Leiber, a podcast production company.

Originally called the American Podcasting Corporation, the company's first project was a podcast called *StartUp*, a real-time chronicle of the company's creation and Blumberg's misadventures as a budding entrepreneur. Over the course of the program's first season, Blumberg hones his elevator pitch for investors and hires a marketing firm to give his company a better name—Gimlet Media. Among his missteps was forgetting to register a handle for Gimlet Media on the social media platform *Twitter*, something he realized right after posting the episode about naming the company. Sure enough, he found that someone had already taken the name. A stroke of luck came, however, when he reached out to the owner, who turned out to be a fan of the show who, upon hearing the latest episode, had sought out Gimlet Media on *Twitter* and, finding the account did not exist, created one specifically to give to the fledgling company. The interaction is demonstrative of the unusually integrated relationship Blumberg managed to create between himself and his listeners, and ultimately Gimlet and its customers. Over the course of Gimlet's first year, it raised over $1 million from investors, including $200,000 from *StartUp* listeners.

The shrewd decision to begin his company by documenting its earliest days and his own stumbles was born from Blumberg's experience on *This American Life*, where journalists often exhibit vulnerability, even naiveté, regarding their subjects. It is a narrative technique that draws the listener deeper into the story by creating empathy for the storyteller. *StartUp* was a significant success, and even spawned a short-lived sitcom starring Zach Braff, called *Alex, Inc.*, in 2018.

Gimlet soon released many more podcasts, including the popular *Reply All*, about internet culture, which began in 2018. By that year the company reported its productions had over twelve million downloads per month by listeners in nearly two hundred countries worldwide. Gimlet attracted considerable venture capital investment, but Blumberg and Davidson ultimately agreed to sell to Spotify in early 2019. As Blumberg explained to Peter Kafka for *Recode* (7 Feb. 2019), "To me, the driving factor was, will this be better for the work we're trying to do?"

PERSONAL LIFE
Blumberg married Nazanin Rafsanjani in 2007. A fellow producer, Rafsanjani worked for *The Rachel Maddow Show* and then became a creative director at Gimlet Media. The couple has two children together.

SUGGESTED READING
Blumberg, Alex. "Alex Blumberg: Lessons from His Transition from Traditional to New Media." Interview by Dan Schawbel. *Forbes*, 24 Jan. 2017, www.forbes.com/sites/danschawbel/2017/01/24/alex-blumberg-lessons-from-his-transition-from-traditional-to-new-media/#17fdb42f8ec2. Accessed 12 Nov. 2019.

———. "Cincinnati Kid: Alex Blumberg." Interview by Alyssa Brandt. *Cincinnati Magazine*, 28 Jan. 2016, www.cincinnatimagazine.com/citywiseblog/cincinnati-kid-alex-blumberg/. Accessed 13 Nov. 2019.

———. "15 Questions with . . . Alex Blumberg." *CNN*, 2015, money.cnn.com/interactive/technology/15-questions-with-alex-blumberg/index.html. Accessed 13 Nov. 2019.

———. "How to Create a Blockbuster Podcast." Interview by Tim Ferriss. *Tim Ferriss Show*, episode 58, 29 Jan. 2015, tim.blog/2015/01/29/alex-blumberg/. Accessed 12 Nov. 2019.

Blumberg, Alex, and Adam Davidson. "Planet Money Grew 'Organically' from 'A Giant Pool of Money.'" Interview by Karen Everhart. *Current*, 11 May 2009, current.org/2009/05/planet-money-grew-organically-from-a-giant-pool-of-money/. Accessed 12 Nov. 2019.

Blumberg, Alex, and Matt Lieber. "Full Q&A: Alex Blumberg and Matt Lieber Explain Why They Sold Gimlet to Spotify." Interview by Peter Kafka. *Recode*, Vox, 7 Feb. 2019, www.vox.com/2019/2/7/18214941/alex-blumberg-matt-lieber-gimlet-spotify-deal-acquisition-peter-kafka-media-podcast-audio-interview. Accessed 13 Nov. 2019.

Zimmerman, Eilene. "Documenting the Journey from Public Radio to Start-Up Owner." *The New York Times*, 9 Dec. 2014, boss.blogs.nytimes.com/2014/12/09/documenting-the-journey-from-public-radio-to-start-up-owner/. Accessed 12 Nov. 2019.

—*Molly Hagan*

Keisha Lance Bottoms

Born: January 18, 1970
Occupation: Politician

In January 2018 Keisha Lance Bottoms took office as the sixtieth mayor of Atlanta, Georgia, the largest city in the state and one of the most economically dynamic cities in all the American South. She was the only Atlanta mayor at that point to have served in all three branches of government: in the judiciary as a judge, in the city's legislature as a councilmember, and in the executive branch as mayor. A member of the Democratic Party, Bottoms sought to put forward a progressive agenda that was welcoming to both documented and undocumented immigrants, supportive of the poor, and attentive to the needs of businesses, her police department, and average citizens. During her time in office she signed an executive order declaring that the city jails would not house undocumented immigrants for the US Immigrations and Customs Enforcement (ICE) agency; got the city council to approve a redevelopment project in downtown Atlanta that would include affordable housing; and secured pay increases for the city's police officers and firefighters. In June 2019, she became one of the first mayors in the country to endorse former vice president Joe Biden during the presidential primaries, and she was on a shortlist to become his running mate after Biden secured the Democratic nomination, though she was not ultimately chosen.

In 2020, Bottoms came to national attention for her leadership in major crises. She challenged the federal and state governments' responses to the COVID-19 pandemic by mandating that the citizens of Atlanta wear facemasks in public and stay at home except for basic necessities. During the riots that spread throughout the country following the death of unarmed Black man George Floyd in police custody, she expressed solidarity with peaceful protestors but condemned violent ones who were clashing with police and destroying public and private property. She also forcefully and publicly condemned President Donald Trump for both his handling of the pandemic and his stoking of racial tensions in the United States.

EARLY LIFE

Keisha Lance Bottoms was born Keisha Lance in Atlanta, Georgia, on January 18, 1970. Her family is able to trace their history in Atlanta back some five generations to Shepherd Peek, a formerly enslaved man who possibly served in the state legislature during Reconstruction. Bottoms's parents were Sylvia Robinson and Major Lance. Her father, a rhythm and blues singer and songwriter, had a number of hit songs during the 1960s and toured with the Beatles. Unfortunately, when his career fell on hard times, he took to selling drugs. When she was eight, she came home from school to find her father being arrested for possessing and selling cocaine. "I learned very early on that good people sometimes make bad decisions," she recalled, as quoted on *AJC*, the website of the *Atlanta Journal-Constitution* (30 May 2020).

The Lance family went on to lose their home. They moved often, usually to visit her

father while he was in prison for the next three years. Her parents eventually divorced, and her mother took the best jobs she could find to make ends meet. Bottoms had reconciled with her father by the time he died in 1994 at age fifty-five.

EDUCATION AND EARLY CAREER

The difficulties of Bottoms's childhood made her focus her attention on helping others. At Frederick Douglass High School, she became active in student government, and was sworn in by Congressman David Scott of the Georgia State Legislature. She then attended Florida A&M University, a historically Black college, where she earned her undergraduate degree in broadcast journalism. She then received her law degree at Georgia State University College of Law in 1994.

Once out of law school, Bottoms began working as an attorney. She recalled to Susan Percy for *Georgia Trend* (31 Dec. 2019): "My experience with formalized public service actually began when I practiced law. I represented children in juvenile court and served as a prosecutor for a while in the city of Atlanta."

At the time, however, politics was far from Bottoms's mind. It was not until 2008 that she began to consider running for public office. While serving as a part-time magistrate judge in Fulton Superior Court, she decided to run against another judge who she felt was doing an inadequate job. Although she lost that election decisively, she did not lose her interest in serving Atlanta. In 2009 she ran for a seat on the Atlanta City Council, representing District Eleven, after learning that the district's representative was retiring. She won the election and began serving in 2010. She was then reelected in 2013, continuing to serve the southwest Atlanta district. She remained a councilmember until 2017.

During her time on the council, Bottoms was also the executive director of the Atlanta Fulton County Recreation Authority (AFCRA). Her appointment to this position in 2015 led to questions regarding a conflict of interest, as AFCRA oversaw maintaining some of the city's public facilities, including the Philips Arena, Zoo Atlanta, and the Olympic cauldron. As executive director, she oversaw a deal that allowed Georgia State University and Carter, a private development group, to buy the Turner Field baseball stadium and its parking lots for $30 million. To avoid any perception of a conflict of interest, Bottoms recused herself from Atlanta City Council votes pertaining to AFCRA.

ATLANTA'S MAYOR

Bottoms announced her run for mayor in 2017, among a field of twelve candidates. During the election she faced questions about lump payments that were given to her campaign staff by an Atlanta city engineering contractor whose office was raided by the Federal Bureau of Investigation (FBI); Bottoms voluntarily returned a portion of the money. The issue did not appear to damage her campaign considerably. On Election Day, she earned a plurality of the vote—26 percent—and then bested Mary Norwood, an Independent candidate and fellow councilmember, in a runoff election. Bottoms was sworn into office in January 2018.

Bottoms faced several challenges during her first year in office, including a ransomware attack that damaged the city's computer network and a City Hall corruption scandal investigation that began during the administration of her predecessor, Kasim Reed, who had endorsed her candidacy. But that year also brought considerable accomplishments as well. She secured a redevelopment project for the downtown area known as the Gulch that included a $28 million trust fund for affordable housing, and she ended the city's involvement with the detaining of undocumented immigrants for ICE. In *Georgia Trend*, she told Susan Percy: "There's a huge learning curve to being mayor. It sounds a bit simple, but every new mayor is a new mayor. Once I realized that, I became much more forgiving of myself just in terms of uncertainty and anxiety."

In 2019, Bottoms secured a 30 percent pay increase for police officers and a 20 percent increase for firefighters. The city also hosted Super Bowl LIII, which helped to bring a $2.4 million renovation of the John F. Kennedy Park, the planting of 20,000 trees, and close coordination among forty public safety agencies from all levels of government. Bottoms also came out as an early supporter of former vice president Joe Biden in a crowded field of Democrats running in the 2020 presidential election. Of her early support for Biden, who clinched the Democratic nomination, she told Jonathan Capehart, as quoted by Eugene Scott of the *Washington Post* (20 Aug. 2020): "We know Joe, and Joe knows us. He's known working people all his life. He's a blue-collar guy that never forgot where he came from. He knows the importance of a job is more than just wages. It's about dignity and it's about respect, and Joe actually understands that."

FACING THE COVID-19 PANDEMIC AND POLICE REFORM

One of the greatest challenges Bottoms faced during her mayoralty was the COVID-19 pandemic, which began in China toward the end of 2019 and spread across the world in the early months of 2020. In March, as outbreaks of the virus in the United States increased, federal, state, and local officials began outlining ways to prevent people from getting ill. Debates emerged across the political spectrum about how stringently everyday activities should be curtailed to

prevent infection. On March 23, Bottoms signed a fourteen-day stay-at-home order for all Atlanta residents, which would keep them from going out except to perform essential tasks. Other orders followed, including a mandate to wear masks in public and for schools to be closed for the duration.

Although Atlanta and other municipalities kept residents under strict public gathering restrictions, Georgia governor Brian Kemp began easing restrictions in mid-summer and later sued Bottoms over Atlanta's mask mandate in July. The lawsuit was eventually withdrawn by the governor, but not before Bottoms publicly criticized him for opening Georgia up too early and advocating a return to normality, including a return to school. "It's too soon for schools to reopen," she said, as quoted by Sanya Mansoor of *Time* (13 Aug. 2020). "Parents and teachers and staff need to have an option on whether or not they will engage in virtual learning or send kids back into the classroom. It's simply too soon."

Despite Bottoms's efforts to keep the virus's spread to a minimum, both she and her husband tested positive for COVID-19, after she noticed that her husband was sleeping more than usual. Both, however, were spared the more serious effects of the virus, complaining of symptoms not dissimilar to ones common for people with seasonal allergies. Of her diagnosis, she said to Justin Carissimo for *CBS News* (7 July 2020): "It leaves me for a loss of words because I think it really speaks to how contagious this virus is. We've taken all the precautions that you can possibly take. I have no idea when and where we were exposed."

Alongside the pandemic challenge, Bottoms also had to contend with protests of police brutality that sparked across her city following the death of George Floyd, an African American man who died in police custody in Minnesota. As an African American parent, she expressed grave concern that young African American men like her son were often more often targeted by police during investigations and may be shot or killed by police officers. As mayor, she expressed support for peaceful protesters, but excoriated violent ones. "What I see happening on the streets of Atlanta is not Atlanta. This is not a protest. This is not in the spirit of Martin Luther King, Jr.," Bottoms said at a news conference, as quoted by Gregory Krieg and Paul LeBlanc for *CNN* (1 June 2020). "This is chaos." In an op-ed she wrote for the *New York Times* shortly thereafter, she urged those who wanted to bring about police reform to vote in the November presidential elections.

PERSONAL LIFE

Keisha Lance Bottoms married Derek W. Bottoms, an attorney and vice president for the

Home Depot, in October 1994. The couple met while they were first-year students at Georgia State University College of Law and married at Ben Hill United Methodist Church in Atlanta. They adopted four children: Lance, Langston, Lennox, and Lincoln. The family lives in Southwest Atlanta.

SUGGESTED READING

Bottoms, Keisha Lance. "The Police Report to Me, but I Knew I Couldn't Protect My Son." *The New York Times*, 3 June 2020, www.nytimes.com/2020/06/03/opinion/police-protests-atlanta-keisha-bottoms.html. Accessed 15 Sept. 2020.

Carissimo, Justin. "Atlanta Mayor Keisha Lance Bottoms Tests Positive for Coronavirus." *CBS News*, 7 July 2020, www.cbsnews.com/news/atlanta-mayor-keisha-lance-bottoms-test-positive-coronavirus/. Accessed 15 Sept. 2020.

Mansoor, Sanya. "'We Opened Up Too Soon.' Atlanta Mayor Keisha Lance Bottoms Wants Georgia to Roll Back Reopening." *Time*, 13 Aug. 2020, time.com/5879027/keisha-lance-bottoms-time-100-coronavirus/. Accessed 15 Sept. 2020.

"Meet the Mayor." *Atlantaga.gov*, www.atlantaga.gov/government/mayor-s-office/meet-the-mayor. Accessed 15 Sept. 2020.

Percy, Susan. "2020 Georgian of the Year: Keisha Lance Bottoms." *Georgia Trend Daily*, 31 Dec. 2019, www.georgiatrend.com/2019/12/31/2020-georgian-of-the-year-keisha-lance-bottoms/. Accessed 15 Sept. 2020.

Scott, Eugene. "Keisha Lance Bottoms, the Biden Endorser When Many Mayors Backed Others." *The Washington Post*, 20 Aug. 2020, www.washingtonpost.com/politics/2020/08/20/keisha-lance-bottoms-biden-endorser-when-many-mayors-backed-others/. Accessed 15 Sept. 2020.

"Who Is Atlanta Mayor Keisha Lance Bottoms?" *AJC. The Atlanta Journal Constitution*, 30 May 2020, www.ajc.com/lifestyles/who-atlanta-mayor-keisha-lance-bottoms/ffQ2hCT-1lUYkse7lrJ1WxI/. Accessed 15 Sept. 2020.

—*Christopher Mari*

Grayson Boucher

Born: June 10, 1984
Occupation: Streetball player and actor

An aspiring basketball player who had struggled to make a name for himself on the court in both high school and college, in 2003, Grayson Boucher attended a game played as part of the AND1 Mixtape Tour, a professional athletic organization that specialized in the form of basketball known as streetball. His attendance, and subsequent contract with the organization, changed his life overnight. "Streetball," Boucher explained to Mike Patton for *Sports Awakening* (13 Apr. 2011), "is more improvised, less-structured and is more fast-paced" than the traditional basketball played in the National Basketball Association (NBA). Whereas NBA players focus on winning games and championships, he continued, streetball players "use our skills to wow the crowd," impressing audiences with tricky moves not often seen in traditional basketball competitions. "Both games have a different focus but we have a common goal: entertainment," he told Patton.

A longtime fan of AND1 Tour–style streetball, Boucher decided to participate in an open tryout. His performance won him a spot in an ongoing competition with the organization. By the end of the competition, he had secured himself a spot on the team. Over the next decade, Boucher—known to fans and fellow athletes as the Professor—established himself as one of the United States' preeminent streetball players, touring widely with the AND1 Mixtape Tour and, later, with the streetball organization Ball Up. Although his time with both organizations eventually drew to a close around the mid-2010s, he reinvented himself as a social media star, earning millions of views for YouTube videos in which he showed off his streetball skills, sometimes while costumed as the superhero Spider-Man.

Photo by Paul Mounce/Corbis via Getty Images

EARLY LIFE AND EDUCATION

Grayson Scott Boucher was born on June 10, 1984, in Keizer, Oregon. He spent his childhood and teen years living in Keizer with his family, which included his parents, Steve and Molly, and a younger brother, Landon. Boucher began playing basketball as a toddler, having been introduced to the game by his father. The owner of a jewelry store, Steve Boucher was an avid supporter of the Portland Trail Blazers NBA team and played the sport in local leagues. "He didn't play in college or anything, but he lived and breathed basketball," Boucher recalled to Jemele Hill for *ESPN* (15 Aug. 2007) about his father.

Having played the sport at various points throughout his early childhood, Boucher began playing basketball on a regular basis while in elementary school and continued to do so into high school. He attended McNary High School in Keizer, where he played for the junior varsity team. Although he loved basketball and aspired to play in the NBA, he struggled to distinguish himself on his team and was considered to be at a particular disadvantage due to his height; Boucher measured five feet six as a teenager and five feet ten as an adult, significantly shorter than most successful basketball players. In addition to playing for McNary High, Boucher played within an Amateur Athletic Union (AAU) team, but was cut from his team as a teenager. He experienced greater success as a player in informal games at local parks, where he was able to display skills that in some cases were frowned upon on the high school court. Often preferring the streetball style of basketball, he was an avid fan of the videos released by the AND1 Mixtape Tour, a professional basketball organization that held streetball games throughout the United States.

Following his junior year of high school, Boucher transferred to Salem Academy, a private school in Salem, Oregon. Although he was more successful on the court at Salem Academy than he had been at McNary High, he was unable to attract the attention of college recruiters and did not receive a single offer to play for a college basketball team. After graduating from high school, he enrolled in Chemeketa Community College and joined the school's basketball team as a walk-on. Although he had limited opportunities to play in games, he dedicated himself to improving his physical fitness and basketball skills during that period, working out extensively at a local gym and playing against players from higher-ranked college basketball programs whenever possible.

AND1 MIXTAPE TOUR

In 2003, the AND1 Mixtape Tour's streetball team traveled to Portland, Oregon, to play an exhibit game and to host what was referred to as an open run—effectively open tryouts for a spot in an upcoming competition in which aspiring players competed for a contract with the team. Attending the game with his brother, Boucher decided to participate in the tryouts and impressed the organization with his strong grasp of streetball's moves and signature style of basketball. Selected to compete for a spot on the team, he went on to prove his skills against established players with the goal of progressing successfully through the competition. "I was just hoping to make the final game," he told Ben Cramer for *ESPN* (28 Feb. 2005). "I didn't know anything about a contract." Eventually winning a contract with the organization, Boucher joined the team and soon gained the nickname the Professor in recognition of his supposedly nerdy appearance and ability to "school" players on the court.

Over the next several years, Boucher played regularly on the AND1 Mixtape Tour and became one of the tour's most popular players. Although he questioned his decision to join the organization occasionally, he found that it was a good fit for his skills and enabled him to explore the form of basketball in which he was most confident. "I remember a couple times thinking, 'Man I hope this is for me—I skipped out on college for this,'" he recalled to Paul Eide for the *I80 Sports Blog*. "But I just kept working and never stopped having confidence. There may have been doubt, but I never lost confidence." After about five successful years, Boucher's time playing for the tour on a regular basis came to an end in 2008, after the sports-focused ESPN family of television channels ended its relationship with AND1. While Boucher continued to play in occasional professional streetball games over the next years, he played his final game with the AND1 organization in 2010.

BALL UP

Following the end of his time with the AND1 Mixtape Tour, Boucher "went completely broke," as he told Alex Shultz for *Bleacher Report* (26 Jan. 2018), but managed to support himself for a time by selling off his old AND1 jerseys. "I unintentionally kept like 50 to 100 AND1 jerseys, and I sold them all firsthand on eBay and lived off that for a good year," he explained to Shultz. His fortunes changed around 2011, when Boucher joined the streetball organization Ball Up. Like the AND1 team, the Ball Up team was a group of streetball players that toured in the United States as well as around the world, playing against local teams in various destinations.

For Boucher, joining Ball Up represented an opportunity not only to continue his career but also "to bring streetball to the forefront . . . and really be a good example to the kids," as he told Ethan Norof for *Bleacher Report* (28 Aug. 2013). Over the course of his years with Ball Up,

Boucher appeared in a variety of recorded content produced by the organization, including a 2012 documentary series about the tour called *Life on the Road*. As a group with an international focus, the team toured extensively both in the United States and abroad, a practice Boucher enjoyed but also at times found draining. "People might not realize we tour all year," he told Norof. "Some months might be a couple of weeks out of the month, other months it might be the whole month. The travel can definitely be a grind."

YOUTUBE STAR

From early on in his career, Boucher was no stranger to the camera, having appeared in television and video programming for the AND1 Mixtape Tour. He made his debut as an actor in 2008, appearing in a small role as a basketball player in the Will Ferrell sports comedy *Semi-Pro* after winning his role through an open tryout. "They were picking the top thirty-six players to be in this movie and play against Will Ferrell's team," he recalled to Hill. "So I went down there and tried out for an afternoon. I kept making it back to the second cut and the third cut. I made the final cut and got a role. I don't have any speaking lines. I just play ball." The year 2008 also saw the film festival debut of *Ball Don't Lie*, a sports drama based on the 2005 novel of the same name by Matt de la Peña. Boucher starred in the lead role of Sticky, a teenager from a troubled background who excels at basketball, and later described the process of making the film as "one of the greatest experiences of my life," as he told Evan Bleier for *Bleacher Report* (21 Nov. 2012).

Despite Boucher's experience on camera, the success of his shift to social media personality during and after his time with Ball Up was in some ways a surprise. Having created the channel ProfessorLive on the video-sharing website YouTube in 2009, he experienced relatively limited success with the videos he created until 2013, when he posted a video titled "Spiderman Basketball Episode 1." The first installment in what would become known as his *Spider-Man Basketball* series of videos, his 2013 upload sparked a string of videos in which Boucher, dressed in full costume as the Marvel Comics superhero Spider-Man, engages unsuspecting strangers in games of basketball. The original video went viral, calling extensive online attention to Boucher's streetball skills and talents as an entertainer, and remained one of the most popular videos on his channel, amassing nearly forty-two million views by May 2020.

Following the debut of the *Spider-Man Basketball* series, Boucher expanded his YouTube and social media presence significantly, establishing himself as an online influencer. In addition to his Spider-Man videos, his YouTube channel encompasses video blogs, recordings of his workouts and training sessions, and videos of Boucher playing basketball against various individuals. Although he initially launched his channel as a one-person operation and was unable to hire a video editor or other staff members, the rapid expansion and profitability of ProfessorLive enabled Boucher to hire several employees by 2018. He likewise sought to expand his brand through sponsorships and brand partnerships and sold a variety of apparel through his brand Global Hooper.

PERSONAL LIFE

Boucher lives near Los Angeles, California.

SUGGESTED READING

Bleier, Evan. "Grayson 'The Professor' Boucher Teaches on and off the Court." *Bleacher Report*, 21 Nov. 2012, bleacherreport.com/articles/1417017-the-professors-master-class-grayson-boucher-can-teach-on-and-off-the-court. Accessed 10 May 2020.

Boucher, Grayson. "Ball Up Streetball Tour—The Professor SPEAKS." Interview by Paul Eide. *I80 Sports Blog*, 2015, i80sportsblog.com/ball-up-streetball-tour-the-professor-speaks. Accessed 10 May 2020.

———. "Interview with Grayson 'The Professor' Boucher." Interview by Mike Patton. *Sports Awakening*, 13 Apr. 2011, www.sportsawakening.com/interviews/interview-with-grayson-the-professor-boucher. Accessed 10 May 2020.

———. "Riding with . . . Grayson Boucher." Interview by Jemele Hill. *ESPN*, 15 Aug. 2007, www.espn.com/espn/page2/story?page=hill/070815. Accessed 10 May 2020.

Cramer, Ben. "Street Smart." *ESPN*, 28 Feb. 2005, www.espn.com/espnmag/story?id=3775982. Accessed 10 May 2020.

Norof, Ethan. "An Exclusive Interview with Streetball Legend 'The Professor.'" *Bleacher Report*, 28 Aug. 2013, bleacherreport.com/articles/1739725-an-exclusive-interview-with-streetball-legend-the-professor. Accessed 10 May 2020.

Shultz, Alex. "Streetball Legend the Professor Still Making Moves." *Bleacher Report*, 26 Jan. 2018, bleacherreport.com/articles/2755958-streetball-legend-the-professor-still-making-moves. Accessed 10 May 2020.

SELECTED WORKS

Semi-Pro, 2008; *Ball Don't Lie*, 2008; *Life on the Road*, 2012; *Spider-Man Basketball*, 2013–

—Joy Crelin

Jericho Brown

Date of birth: April 14, 1976
Occupation: Poet

Jericho Brown is an award-winning poet and an associate professor and director of the creative writing program at Emory University in Atlanta. He published his American Book Award–winning debut poetry collection, *Please*, in 2008, and subsequently won a 2011 National Endowment for the Arts literature fellowship for poetry. After publishing his second collection, *The New Testament* (2014), Brown won a prestigious Guggenheim Fellowship in 2016. His next collection, *The Tradition* (2019), was a finalist for the National Book Award for Poetry and the National Book Critics Circle Award. In it, he introduces a new poetic form that he created, the duplex.

As a poet, Brown has said that he values both vulnerability and surprise. He is willing to plumb the depths of childhood abuse, sexual assault, and racial violence, but his work aspires to a kind of spiritual transcendence. Raised in the Baptist church, he compares a poem to a church service. "You don't know who is going to shout or why they are going to shout or how loudly or if they are going to be sitting next to you and knock your glasses halfway across the room," he once told a class of seminary students, as quoted by Jeremy Redmon for the *Atlanta Journal-Constitution* (22 May 2016). "You know you are going to have a good time. As we enter the space of a poem, you enter the space understanding, 'Oh, this is going to change me.'"

EARLY LIFE AND EDUCATION

Jericho Brown was born Nelson Demery III on April 14, 1976. He and his younger sister, Nequella Demery, grew up in Shreveport, Louisiana. His father, Nelson Demery Jr., owned a dry-cleaning and landscaping business. His mother, Neomia Demery, worked a variety of jobs, teaching school, cleaning houses, and working for the family's business. Brown says his father was physically abusive growing up. In one of his earliest memories, he told Redmon, he ran from the family's house with his mother and sister to escape his father. It was one such night among many. To Brown and his sister's anguish, his mother always returned. "I felt like 'Oh, wow. There is nothing we can do. There really is no way out of this situation—I can't just fix it,'" he recalled to Redmon. "And I wanted to just fix it."

Brown grew up singing in the choir at Shreveport's Mount Canaan Baptist Church. He also spent a lot of time at the local library, discovering poets like Nikki Giovanni, Langston Hughes, Emily Dickinson, and Walt Whitman. By the time he was ten, he had already read a

Photo by Brian Cornelius via Wikimedia Commons

handful of John Updike novels. He saw writing and literature in terms of his involvement in the Baptist church. He loved the "pomp and circumstance and drama and theater," of worship, he told Kimber Williams for Emory University's *Emory Report* (13 Mar. 2013). "I became interested in writing as a space where you could put things you couldn't necessarily talk about in the grocery store line, but that you knew existed."

Though Brown's relationship with his parents remains fraught, he credits them with pushing him academically. He attended C. E. Byrd High School, where at sixteen, he was assigned to write a research paper about confessional poets, including Anne Sexton, Sylvia Plath, and Robert Lowell. By design, the project took an entire year. Spending so long engaging with the poets and criticism of their work inspired Brown to think seriously about becoming a poet himself. He graduated high school in 1994 and attended Dillard University, a historically black college in New Orleans, where he met an early mentor, poet Mona Lisa Savoy. He graduated magna cum laude from Dillard with a BA in English in 1998.

BIRTH OF JERICHO BROWN

Brown went on to earn his Master of Fine Arts degree from the University of New Orleans while working as a speechwriter for New Orleans Mayor Marc Morial, who served from 1994 to 2002. Brown also wrote press releases and opinion pieces for newspapers. It was good training for writing on a deadline, but he was not passionate about the work. "Poetry became an escape from that kind of writing," Brown told Williams. "I think the big difference was whenever you write a speech you know what will happen, but when you write a poem you don't know."

During this time, Brown had a prophetic dream in 2002, in which he was sitting in a sterile waiting room surrounded by other black men. The white receptionist would call a name, and a man would stand up and walk through the door behind her. She called the name Jericho. When no one responded, Brown claimed it for himself. Brown woke up, and unable to return to sleep, went out for a drink at a gay bar. An older man at the bar asked for his name. Without thinking, Brown responded, "Jericho." The man told him that the name, a Biblical city, meant "straightly shut up" but also "defense" and "good-smelling." Brown took it as a sign, choosing to adopt the name alongside the surname Brown.

As Brown tells it, his decision to adopt a new name freed him from the legacy of his father. It also allowed him to write candidly about his childhood and his sexuality—topics that his parents would not want to see associated with the family name.

PLEASE AND THE NEW TESTAMENT
Brown earned his PhD in literature and creative writing from the University of Houston and joined the writing faculty at the University of San Diego in 2007. He published his debut poetry collection, *Please*, through the small press New Issues Poetry & Prose at Western Michigan University in 2008. He was shocked by the enthusiasm that greeted the book. It won the 2009 American Book Award and earned him a 2009 Whiting Award. He was named a Bunting Fellow at Harvard University's Radcliffe Institute for Advanced Study the same year and received a National Endowment for the Arts poetry fellowship in 2011.

Brown joined the faculty at Emory University in Atlanta in 2012 and published his second book of poems, *The New Testament*, in 2014. The book's title was inspired by Brown's return to faith after contracting HIV in 2010. "I had spent so much time, as a child, talking with God and felt he was speaking to me. When I got sick, I wondered what he would say about this devastating thing," he told Kate Kellaway for the *Guardian* (28 July 2018). "I wondered if God could comfort me in the ways I had once been taught to comfort myself."

In *The New Testament*, Brown uses passages from and language inspired by the Bible to explore themes of racism and violence—in "Langston's Blues," Brown invokes the twentieth-century African American writer Langston Hughes to explore the legacy of African slavery, mass incarceration, and exploitation—as well as sexuality. In the poem "Psalm 150," Brown inverts the passage of the title, which exhorts readers to loudly "praise the Lord." He writes about finding

solace in the give-and-take of intimate love. "We learned to make love for each other / Rather than doing it to each other. As for praise / And worship, I prefer the latter," he writes. "No gay poet has made such subtle and subversive use of the Bible since D. A. Powell's masterful *Cocktails*" in 2004, poet Craig Moran Teicher wrote in his review for *NPR* (18 Oct. 2014). Brown "rewrites bits of the Gospels throughout the book and invokes 'Him' like someone making fun of thunder." *The New Testament* won the Anisfield-Wolf Book Award and was named one of the best poetry books of the year by the *Library Journal*.

THE TRADITION (2019) AND THE DUPLEX
In March 2016, Brown published a poem called "Bullet Points" on *BuzzFeed News*. The poem was inspired by a slew of highly publicized murders of black people at the hands of police officers. In it, he invokes the deaths of Sandra Bland, who was taken into custody after a traffic stop and mysteriously died of asphyxiation in a jail cell. He also invokes Mike Brown, the Ferguson teenager who was shot and killed in 2014. Police officers left his dead body in the street for hours before covering it with a sheet. "I promise that if you hear / Of me dead anywhere near / A cop, then that cop killed me," Brown writes. The explosive poem appears in his third book, *The Tradition*.

The Tradition builds on the themes of Brown's previous works but also forges new territory. In it, he challenges poetic "tradition" by subverting classical imagery—including flowers and Greek mythology—and inventing a new form called the duplex. The duplex, described by poet Maya Phillips for the *New York Times* (2 Apr. 2019) is a fourteen-line poem comprised of "staggered couplets that's part pantoum, part sonnet and part ghazal." Brown explained to Candace Williams of the *Rumpus* (1 Apr. 2019), that the form arose from his desire to "gut the sonnet." Brown's explanation for how a duplex works is technical, but his need to create it is straightforward. "I feel completely in love with and oppressed by the sonnet," Brown told Williams. "It's been pushed down my throat the entirety of my life. There is something in me that doesn't like that, and doesn't trust that, because I'm a rebellious human being. I need to be a rebellious human being because I'm black and gay in this nation and in this world which has not been good to me or anybody like me."

The collection's opening poem, "Ganymede," sets the thematic tone. In it, Brown begins to retell a Greek myth in which Zeus kidnaps a beautiful boy named Ganymede. Over the course of a few lines, Brown contorts the myth to explore sexual subjugation and slavery. It begins: "A man trades his son for horses. / That's the version I prefer. I like / The safety of it, no one at fault, / Everyone rewarded." The title poem, a sonnet, offers a similar lens. It begins by naming flowers—"*Aster. Nasturtium. Delphinium*"—and goes on to collide the "traditions" of natural science and human slavery. It ends by naming John Crawford, Eric Garner, and Mike Brown—three African American men killed by police. "His poems delight in their own swerves, some discreetly steered toward like a bend in a road and others making a sudden about-face," Phillips wrote. Other poems, such as "Duplex," are more confessional, describing his family, sexual assault, and living with HIV.

SUGGESTED READING

Brown, Jericho. "Gutting the Sonnet: A Conversation with Jericho Brown." Interview by Candace Williams. *The Rumpus*, 1 Apr. 2019, therumpus.net/2019/04/the-rumpus-interview-with-jericho-brown/. Accessed 11 Feb. 2020.

——. "Jericho Brown: 'Poetry Is a Veil in Front of a Heart Beating at a Fast Pace.'" Interview by Kate Kellaway. *The Guardian*, 28 July 2018, www.theguardian.com/books/2018/jul/28/jericho-brown-book-interview-q-and-a-new-testament-poetry. Accessed 11 Feb. 2020.

——. "Jericho Brown: The Pulse of the Poem." Interview by Kimber Williams. *Emory News Center*, 13 Mar. 2013, news.emory.edu/stories/2013/03/er_profile_jericho_brown/campus.html. Accessed 11 Feb. 2020.

Phillips, Maya. "A Poetic Body of Work Grapples with the Physical Body at Risk." Review of *The Tradition*, by Jericho Brown. *The New York Times*, 2 Apr. 2019, www.nytimes.com/2019/04/02/books/review/jericho-brown-tradition-poems.html. Accessed 11 Feb. 2020.

Redmon, Jeremy. "Becoming Jericho Brown." *Atlanta Journal-Constitution*, 22 May 2016, specials.myajc.com/jericho/. Accessed 11 Feb. 2020.

Teicher, Craig Morgan. "A Collection of Poems That Offers an Unlikely Kind of Hope." Review of *The New Testament*, by Jericho Brown. *NPR*, 18 Oct. 2014, www.npr.org/2014/09/02/345290779/a-collection-of-poems-that-offers-an-unlikely-kind-of-hope. Accessed 11 Feb. 2020.

SELECTED WORKS

Please, 2008; *The New Testament* 2014; *The Tradition* 2019

—*Molly Hagan*

Kate Brown

Date of birth: June 21, 1960
Occupation: Politician

Democrat Kate Brown served as an Oregon state representative between 1991 and 1997, and then as a state senator from 1997 to 2007. She served as state senate majority leader and as Oregon's twenty-fourth secretary of state before being appointed Oregon's thirty-eighth governor in February 2015.

EARLY LIFE AND EDUCATION

Kate Brown was born in Madrid, Spain, on June 21, 1960, while her father was stationed there with the US Air Force. She was raised in Minnesota, where she lived until she went to college. She attended the University of Colorado Boulder, earning an undergraduate degree in environmental studies in 1981.

After graduating, Brown attended law school at Lewis & Clark College in Portland, Oregon, where she earned a law degree and a certificate in environmental law in 1985. She then taught at Portland State University and worked with the Juvenile Rights Project and Oregon Women's Health and Wellness Alliance. Before entering politics, Brown worked as a family and juvenile attorney for several years, during which time she advocated for the nation's first family-leave law. The law passed in Oregon in 1991.

STATE LAWMAKER

Brown got her start in the Oregon state legislature in November 1991, when she was appointed to fill a vacancy left by Representative Judy Bauman, who had resigned to accept another appointment. In 1997, Brown was elected to the Oregon State Senate, where she represented one of Portland's urban districts. She was elected Democratic senate leader in 1998.

While in the state senate, Brown focused much of her legislative work on civil rights and economic issues, presenting her platform as beneficial to Oregon's working families. Viewed as a liberal and noted for her promotion of women's rights, Brown became Oregon's first female senate majority leader in 2004. As senate majority leader, Brown helped pass an ethics reform bill protecting gay, lesbian, bisexual, and transgender Oregonians from discrimination in housing and employment.

OREGON SECRETARY OF STATE

Brown left the state senate and was elected Oregon secretary of state in 2008. While serving as secretary of state, she received criticism for her handling of the state's 2012 labor commissioner election. The *Oregonian* suggested that Brown had intentionally delayed the election by six months to disadvantage Bruce Starr, the Republican contender for the nonpartisan office. Although both candidates were frustrated by the unexpected delay of the election, Starr filed an unsuccessful lawsuit in response, which the *Oregonian* said hurt his chances of defeating Democrat Brad Avakian, who ultimately won.

Brown's most enduring legislation passed while serving as secretary of state concerned voter participation. In 2013, she proposed automatic voter registration for all citizens with a valid driver's license. The bill was signed into law in 2015, making Oregon the first state to enact automatic voter registration.

In January 2015, the *Verge* alleged that Brown had endorsed Comcast's attempted merger with Time Warner Cable in the form of a letter ghostwritten by Comcast. The *Verge* said that Brown had accepted campaign funds from Comcast in her bids for the office of secretary of state but disclosed neither the funding nor the letter to the public. The report, which named several other prominent politicians, did not significantly affect Brown's popularity.

GOVERNOR

Brown became governor following the resignation of incumbent John Kitzhaber on February 18, 2015, amid a controversy surrounding his relationship with his fiancé, an energy consultant to the state of Oregon. Oregon has no lieutenant governor, which made Brown, then secretary of state, Kitzhaber's immediate successor. Brown's appointment as governor expires in January 2017.

Although Brown's appointment came under somewhat unusual circumstances, her long record of public service led to early bipartisan support from Oregon's legislature. The controversy surrounding the 2012 labor commissioner election proved inconsequential to Brown's early success as governor. Four months after she assumed the office, her approval rating surpassed 55 percent. State Republicans publicly commented that Brown's early work as governor was positive.

IMPACT

Brown's legislative activities have included bills to improve women's rights in areas such as economics and health care, bills to ensure domestic partnership laws, and ethics laws to promote transparency in campaign contributions. Her bill to register voters using Division of Motor Vehicles (DMV) data increased Oregon's voter rolls by nearly 14 percent—an estimated three hundred thousand people.

Brown received national media attention as the country's first openly bisexual state governor. Her appointment was met with celebration from LGBTQ rights organizations.

PERSONAL LIFE

Brown practices yoga and enjoys cycling. She married Dan Little in 1997 and helped raise Little's two children from his previous marriage. The couple live in the official governor's residence, Mahonia Hall, in Salem.

SUGGESTED READING

Esteve, Harry. "Oregon Labor Commissioner Election in November, Not May—as Candidates Thought." *OregonLive*. Advance, 19 Mar. 2012, www.oregonlive.com/politics/2012/03/surprise_oregon_labor_commissi.html. Accessed 23 Dec. 2019.

"Governor Kate Brown." *Oregon Blue Book*. Oregon Secretary of State, 2015, sos.oregon.gov/blue-book/Pages/state/executive/governor-bio.aspx. Accessed 23 Dec. 2019.

Johnson, Kirk. "Kate Brown, New Governor in Oregon, Seeks Public's Trust." *The New York Times*. 18 Feb. 2015, www.nytimes.com/2015/02/19/us/kate-brown-replacing-john-kitzhaber-as-oregon-governor.html. Accessed 23 Dec. 2019.

Rappeport, Alan. "Who Is Kate Brown, Oregon's Next Governor?" *The New York Times*. 13 Feb. 2015, www.nytimes.com/politics/first-draft/2015/02/13/who-is-kate-brown-oregons-next-governor.html. Accessed 23 Dec. 2019.

Theriault, Denis C. "Poll: Kate Brown's Approval Rating Hits 55 Percent." *OregonLive*. Advance, 3 June 2015, www.oregonlive.com/politics/2015/06/poll_kate_browns_approval_rati.html. Accessed 23 Dec. 2019.

———. "'We Traded Up': Kate Brown Wins Over Lawmakers—but What about Voters?" *OregonLive*. Advance, 10 July 2015, www.oregonlive.com/politics/2015/07/kate_brown_charm_politics.html. Accessed 23 Dec. 2019.

Woodman, Spencer. "Exclusive: Politicians Are Supporting Comcast's TWC Merger with Letters Ghostwritten by Comcast." *Verge*. Vox Media, 26 Jan. 2015, www.theverge.com/2015/1/26/7878239/comcast-twc-fcc-merger-letters-politicians-ghostwritten. Accessed 23 Dec. 2019.

—*Richard Means*

Samantha Brown

Born: March 31, 1970
Occupation: Television host

As the host of several popular series, television personality Samantha Brown has been all over the world, but she has maintained that her favorite part has not been the luxurious hotels or

Photo by Nehrams2020 via Wikimedia Commons

exotic locales. "I really love that I get to spend time in somebody else's life," she explained to Emily Co for *PopSugar* (23 Sept. 2010). "I get to see life through the perspective of a different person in a different part of the world. It's enlightening, it's humbling. . . . I have the best job in the world for reasons I think people don't even see on camera."

Brown, who formerly appeared on such Travel Channel shows as *Girl Meets Hawaii* (2000–01), *Passport to Europe* (2005), and *Samantha Brown: Passport to China* (2008), broke ranks with the channel in 2017 to join PBS, where she began hosting the Emmy Award–winning *Samantha Brown's Places to Love*. "Travel does not have to be bucket list big to count," she told Eric Bowman for *Travel Pulse* (11 Mar. 2020), explaining why many of the locales she has chosen for her shoots have been relatively low-key places that do not tend to attract hordes of tourists. (One episode of *Places to Love* featured Lake Winnipesaukee, in her home state of New Hampshire, for example.) Nonetheless, she has estimated that she has been to more than 250 cities in sixty-two countries around the globe.

Brown's goal, she has told interviewers, is to convey her genuine love of travel to viewers and encourage them to explore as well. "People have seen me travel, they see me in the world," she told Rachel Tepper Paley for *Condé Nast Traveler* (30 Aug. 2017). "All of a sudden it makes it possible."

EARLY LIFE AND EDUCATION
Samantha Brown was born on March 31, 1970, in Dallas, Texas, to Christopher D. and Elsie Mae Brown. She is of Scottish and German descent,

as she has discussed on episodes involving those countries. When Brown was a child, the family moved to New Castle, New Hampshire, a town on an island near Portsmouth. They did not regularly take elaborate vacations. Although they once drove to Quebec when she was in junior high, most trips involved loading up their station wagon with snacks and driving to Pennsylvania to visit relatives.

Brown was a gifted singer and took voice lessons throughout her youth. She attended Pinkerton Academy, which is among the largest independent high schools in the United States. The school, located in Derry, New Hampshire, is home to a thriving arts program, in which Brown was deeply involved, and she also served as the captain of Pinkerton's cheerleading team. She graduated from Pinkerton in 1988.

Although she began her college career at Chapman University, in California, Brown transferred to Syracuse University, in Upstate New York. There, she studied in the drama department of the university's College of Visual and Performing Arts. Immediately upon graduating with a degree in fine arts in 1992, she settled in New York City hoping to forge a career in musical theater.

EARLY CAREER
Like many aspiring performers, Brown waited on tables while going to as many auditions as she could. She landed an occasional part, including one in an Off-Broadway production of *Brutality of Fact* (1997), but most of her acting jobs involved commercials. She landed spots for Cedar Point, an Ohio amusement park; ECCO Shoes; HP Pavilion computers; and Century Cable, for which she played a recurring character named Wendy Wire.

Brown received what she has characterized as her big break in 1999, when a Travel Channel producer saw one of her commercials and invited her to audition in Florida for a new show called *Great Vacation Homes*. Brown missed her connecting flight to Florida, but an understanding casting agent allowed her to reschedule the audition for the following week. She met with scheduling mishaps on that second attempt as well: her initial flight was so delayed that she had only minutes to sprint to the gate to catch her connecting flight. The fifty-seat plane was sitting on the tarmac preparing for takeoff when a tearful Brown positioned herself under its nose to plead with the pilot to allow her to board. He relented, and she arrived in Florida in time to try out.

Brown's wholesome appearance, approachability, and polish won over Travel Channel executives, and in 1999 she began hosting the show, giving viewers a voyeuristic look at properties ranging from rustic cabins to beachfront showplaces. A string of other series followed, including *Girl Meets Hawaii*, which aired for a fourteen-episode season beginning in 2000 and followed Brown as she feasted at luaus, found the most picturesque beaches, and met the legendary singer Don Ho.

Among her most-viewed series were *Samantha Brown: Passport to Europe* (2005), *Samantha Brown: Passport to Latin America* (2007), and *Samantha Brown: Passport to China* (2008), the last of which was timed to air during the Summer Olympics in Beijing. Asked by Emily Co to name the "craziest" thing that ever happened while filming, Brown recalled filming with pandas in China. Advised by the panda handler to keep moving, she asked why and was told, "'They're bears.' . . . If you stop and the panda locks eye with you, he will see that as a challenge." Brown, realizing that the cameras were already set up and that having permission to be in the bear pen was hard to get, kept filming and kept moving until her director, who was unaware of the dangers of standing still in the pen, asked her to do so and to move closer to the panda. "Sure enough when I stop, the panda locked eyes with me and started charging at me like a rottweiler in an attack mode." The handler threw himself in front of her, and the two ran out of the pen, seconds before the rampaging panda slammed against the door. "Of course, what we showed on camera was me having a great time," she concluded.

In addition to the series, Brown filmed several specials, such as *Great Cruises: Freedom of the Seas* (2006), which featured what was then the largest passenger ship in the world; *Disney Holiday Magic with Samantha Brown* (2007); *Holidays in New York* (2009); and *Samantha Brown's Greek Islands* (2010).

By 2010 Brown was enough of a fixture on the network that it aired a special series in her honor, *Samantha Brown's Tenth Anniversary Specials*. The series consisted of four hour-long specials that aired in February 2010: *Samantha Brown's Vancouver*, focusing on the 2010 Winter Olympics host city's winter activities and culture; *Samantha Brown: Inside the Suitcase*, featuring Brown's travel secrets and favorite moments from her travels; *Samantha Brown Fan-a-thon*, a celebration held at Walt Disney World Resort in Orlando, Florida, with fans; and *Samantha Brown's World of Sports*, a compilation of Brown's sports-related moments on her Travel Channel shows. She was recognized by such a large segment of the television viewing audience that she was invited to make a guest appearance that April on the iconic game show *The Price Is Right*, where she presented a travel-themed showcase of prizes.

BREAKING WITH THE TRAVEL CHANNEL

Although Brown continued to work with the Travel Channel for several years, filming a steady succession of series and specials, she gradually grew discontented. She attributed some of her dissatisfaction to sexism on the part of the industry. "If I'm not getting the ratings they want, I'm pulled right away," she told Paley. "But a male host is allowed to spend more time getting more ratings. . . . I feel there's more confidence in a male traveler than a female traveler." At times she also felt pressure to be more like the channel's edgier personalities. "Anthony Bourdain was everything," she told Nina Ruggiero for *Travel+Leisure* (4 Jan. 2018), referencing the late chef and adventurer whose show *No Reservations* aired for more than seven seasons beginning in 2005. "Everyone wanted the next Bourdain, and they wanted me to be the next, kind of, off the cuff, too cool for school [host]." She continued, "I love Anthony Bourdain, but we're very different. And the reason why Anthony Bourdain is amazing is because he is who he is. He's very authentic. And so everyone asked me, can you be more like him? I just said I can't."

In 2017, she cut ties with the Travel Channel and joined forces with PBS to create *Samantha Brown's Places to Love*, which premiered in January 2018. The following year it received three Daytime Emmy nominations and won two: outstanding travel/adventure program and outstanding host in a lifestyle program. After it began airing, *Places to Love* featured Brown in locales from New Zealand to Maine.

"I draw upon what I really love about travel, which is simply getting to know the people on a more personal basis," she told Ruggiero. "Really understanding their effort that goes into creating the experiences that we as travelers get to be a part of, whether it's the effort to create a meal that you eat at a restaurant, a piece of music you hear at a concert, a piece of art." Brown further explained that the purpose of *Places to Love* is to promote the idea that travelers can be part of these efforts as well. In addition to hosting, Brown contributed to writing, editing, and raising funding for the program.

PERSONAL LIFE

Brown married Kevin O'Leary, who worked as an information technology manager at the time of their wedding and became a producer for *Places to Love*, on October 28, 2006. They are the parents of twins, Elizabeth Mae and Ellis James, born in 2013, who have traveled with them since infancy. When they are not on the road filming, the family lives in Brooklyn, New York.

Brown has lent her name to a line of luggage available on the Home Shopping Network (HSN). She has also appeared regularly as a resident travel expert on cruises and rail trips.

SUGGESTED READING

Bowman, Eric. "Samantha Brown Talks Travel Agents, Coronavirus, 'Places to Love' and More." *Travel Pulse*, 11 Mar. 2020, www.travelpulse.com/news/features/samantha-brown-talks-travel-agents-coronavirus-places-to-love-and-more.html. Accessed 8 May 2020.

Chaffin, Sean. "Travel Star." *Syracuse University Magazine*, Spring 2015, www.syracuse.edu/wp-content/uploads/sumagazine-2015-spring.pdf. Accessed 8 May 2020.

Co, Emily. "In Her Shoes: Samantha Brown, Travel Channel Host." *PopSugar*, 23 Sept. 2010, www.popsugar.com/smart-living/Samantha-Brown-Travel-Channel-Interview-11158641. Accessed 8 May 2020.

Fitzsimmons, Annie. "Travel Goddess' Samantha Brown: 'I Am Nesting.'" *CNN Travel*, 14 Dec. 2012, www.cnn.com/travel/article/samantha-brown-q-and-a/index.html. Accessed 8 May 2020.

Paley, Rachel Tepper. "Travel TV Embarrassingly Lacks Female Hosts." *Condé Nast Traveler*, 30 Aug. 2017, www.cntraveler.com/story/travel-tv-embarrassingly-lacks-female-hosts. Accessed 8 May 2020.

Rhodes, Elizabeth. "Samantha Brown's Encouraging Message for Travel after COVID-19: 'Travel Comes Back.'" *Travel+Leisure*, 2 Apr. 2020, www.travelandleisure.com/travel-news/samantha-brown-on-travel-after-covid-19. Accessed 8 May 2020.

Ruggiero, Nina. "Samantha Brown Is Still Traveling the World—and She's Finally Doing It Her Way." *Travel+Leisure*, 4 Jan. 2018, www.travelandleisure.com/travel-news/samantha-brown-places-to-love. Accessed 8 May 2020.

SELECTED WORKS

Great Vacation Homes, 1999; *Girl Meets Hawaii*, 2000–01; *Samantha Brown: Passport to Europe*, 2005; *Samantha Brown: Passport to Latin America*, 2007; *Samantha Brown: Passport to China*, 2008; *Samantha Brown's Greek Islands*, 2010; *Samantha Brown's Places to Love*, 2018–

—*Mari Rich*

Mitchie Brusco

Date of birth: February 20, 1997
Occupation: Skateboarder

Skateboarding prodigy Mitchie Brusco earned the nickname "Little Tricky" for his ability to push the boundaries of the sport from a very young age. He began skating when he was just three years old, surprising his parents with the depth of his devotion and his undeniable talent.

He soon became a celebrity at local skate parks and won numerous youth competitions, earning an unprecedented trip to the Gravity Games and securing an agent when he was just five. A slew of sponsorships brought him national attention. Brusco made his official X Games debut in 2011, the same year he briefly became the youngest skater ever to land a 900—a two-and-a-half-revolution aerial spin. He continued to make history, in 2013 becoming the third person to officially land a 1080 (three revolutions) and in 2019 landing the first-ever 1260 (three-and-a-half revolutions). "I'm competitive in my blood," he told Michelle Bruton for *OZY* (30 July 2019). "I always want people to be on the edge of their seats."

Competing in both the Big Air and Vert disciplines (which differ in the size of the ramp used), Brusco won several X Games medals over the years. These included a gold medal in 2018, when he landed the first 1080 in official X Games competition. He also took up skydiving, both as a competitive sport in its own right and as a way to hone his aerial tricks in skating. His achievements placed him at the very forefront of the skateboarding community. "Mitchie is the driver as far as what's possible," X Games commentator Brandon Graham told Bruton. "The highest risk in competitive skateboarding is what you can do off that quarter-pipe in big air. I don't know that anybody is pushing that further than Mitchie Brusco."

EARLY LIFE

Mitchell "Mitchie" Brusco was born on February 20, 1997. The fourth of five children, he grew up in Kirkland, a suburb of Seattle. His father,

Photo by Sean M. Haffey/Getty Images

Mick, a roof truss salesman, had played college baseball at Lewis-Clark State College in Idaho and tried out for the Seattle Mariners major league team. His mother, Jennifer, was also an athlete; she played college basketball at the University of Nevada.

Brusco asked his parents for a skateboard when he was three years old. His mother bought him one from a department store for $10. She was surprised by her son's enthusiasm for skating. "I thought it was because of the Tasmanian Devil," Jennifer Brusco told Brenda Blevins for the Longview, Washington *Daily News* (9 May 2009), referring to the cartoon character featured on that first skateboard, which was little more than a toy. However, she soon came to realize there was more to it than that. After his older siblings left for school, she recalled, "He would stand there, doing little tricks that I didn't know were tricks. He would stand on the skateboard all day."

After Brusco put a hole in the kitchen floor with his constant skating, his mother decided to take him to a skatepark, though finding protective gear to fit a toddler was a challenge. There he practiced with kids twice his age, quickly surpassing most of them in skill. By the time Brusco was four, he was a local celebrity. People came to the park to watch him skate and get his autograph—even before he knew how to write. (Brusco's older sister helped him devise a special signature: the letter "M" with a skateboard drawn underneath.) When another skater warned Brusco's mother that the toy skateboard was dangerous as Brusco's tricks grew more sophisticated, she took him to a skate shop where he found a more durable board his own size. After seeing Brusco practice with it, the shop asked him to join their sponsored team. The employees and regulars at the shop soon dubbed him "Little Tricky."

EARLY COMPETITIONS AND SPONSORSHIPS

As Brusco's reputation as a skateboarding prodigy grew, he began to enter youth competitions. Often, he beat out older competitors. In 2002, at the age of five, he won a regional eight-and-under skateboarding title, which earned him a trip to the Gravity Games in Cleveland, Ohio. His fame preceded him. As Gravity Games spokeswoman Joanie McCaw told Nick Perry for the *Seattle Times* (1 Aug. 2002), "It is pretty unusual. Most kids at that age are just starting to push a board on a flat surface." Brusco became the youngest competitor in Gravity Games history, participating in an amateur showcase alongside skaters in their teens.

The attention landed him an agent and a slew of sponsorships. An early sponsor, Triple 8 Safety Gear, began manufacturing a line of "Little Tricky" safety gear for skaters 70 pounds

or lighter. Brusco was also featured in the safety video accompanying the products. "A lot of times parents will come up and tell me, my kid would not put a helmet on until they saw Mitch. He makes it cool. He makes it his," Jennifer Brusco told Blevins. Sponsorships from DC Shoes, Jones Soda, and the clothing manufacturer ZeroXposur followed.

For some sponsors and observers Brusco's youth was a novelty, but others recognized him as a budding star with notable talent regardless of his age. Before he turned eight, he had appeared on several television programs, including the *Today Show*, and been featured in publications such as *Sports Illustrated* magazine. He also went on a tour providing entertainment to children living on a US military base. Although many of these experiences were positive, at times the attention was overwhelming. When Brusco was in kindergarten, he reportedly told his classmates that the famous skateboarder known as Mitchie Brusco was actually his twin brother. Later, Brusco began to be homeschooled to accommodate his hectic practice and competition schedule.

X GAMES DEBUT AND 900

When he was thirteen Brusco moved to Southern California, a hotbed of extreme sports home to skateboarding legends such as Tony Hawk and Bob Burnquist. Brusco trained with both those stars and continued to develop his skills, pushing to master some of the hardest moves in the sport. "Landing a new trick has always been my main motivation to skate," he told Don Shelton for the *Seattle Times* (18 Sept. 2014).

In 2011, at the MegaRamp Championship series in São Paulo, Brazil, Brusco landed one of the most impressive tricks in skateboarding: a 900. When asked about it later, Brusco told Colin Bane of *ESPN* (28 July 2011), "I just kind of threw one in practice without any intention of landing it, and once I started trying it, I ended up getting it. I didn't really think about it a lot before I did it, and I think that actually helped me." He became one of just a handful of people to accomplish the move, and for a short time was the youngest to do so, solidifying his position as a true talent. Even Hawk— the first person to land a 900 and arguably the most famous skateboarder of all time—was impressed, congratulating Brusco on the social media platform *Twitter* for pulling off "the cleanest 900 to date."

Later in 2011, fourteen-year-old Brusco made his official X Games debut (he had appeared in an amateur's competition at the X Games in 2010). There he landed another 900 in practice. Though he failed his attempt at the trick in competition, he still placed fifth in the Big Air event. At the 2012 X Games, fresh out of an eight-week recovery period for a broken wrist,

Brusco became the first person to land a 900 in competition on an X Games MegaRamp. Despite the historic nature of the feat, he placed second in the Big Air event that year as his friend and rival Tom Schaar (who was twelve at the time) later pulled off two 900s in consecutive runs. Along with his silver medal, Brusco also placed ninth in the Vert competition at the games.

1080 AND SKY-DIVING

Brusco became a fixture of X Games competition, continuing to push both his own boundaries and those of his sport. In 2013, he landed a 1080 at the X Games in Barcelona, Spain. While Schaar had pioneered the trick the year before, Brusco was just the third person to complete it and the first to land it on a MegaRamp. The crowd, and fellow competitors including Burnquist, were euphoric to witness the achievement. "We're definitely all trying to beat each other and going for gold," Brusco told Bane for the X Games website (17 May 2013). "But when we get up there, if someone lands something amazing, everyone's just as hyped as they are." Once again, however, Brusco was edged out of first place and took home a silver medal.

While Brusco continued to focus on skateboarding, he also explored other extreme sports, often simply for fun. Notably, he went skydiving for the first time for his eighteenth birthday in 2015 and quickly became hooked. He would go on to participate in nearly one thousand jumps over the next few years, moving from hobbyist to serious competitor and signing with a sponsored team for the skydiving sport known as bodyflight. The experience also influenced his approach to the aerial tricks in skateboarding. "My spatial awareness and overall awareness has been challenged so much," he told Bruton of skydiving. "Getting on a mega ramp or spinning a different way on a vert ramp—those things just started to make sense. . . . You just get comfortable. You don't touch the ground for five minutes at a time. You live in the air."

X GAMES GOLD AND HISTORIC 1260

Although Brusco's reputation as a top skater continued to grow, the top prize at the illustrious X Games remained elusive. He earned bronze medals in 2014 and 2017, both in Vert, but otherwise struggled to reach the podium. However, this changed in 2018, when Brusco pulled off another 1080 in the Big Air event to win his first X Games gold medal. He also claimed the bronze medal that year in the Vert competition, his fifth overall.

Brusco then set his sights on a new trick. In June 2019 he attempted a 1260 at the X Games in Shanghai, though he failed to land it. Even just trying such a difficult trick—which no one had ever managed to land—was so unprecedented

the announcers initially failed to realize what he had done. The attempt generated much hype for Brusco's next X Games appearance, in Minneapolis, Minnesota, in August 2019. There he cleanly landed a 1260, holding his focus as the crowd erupted. Fellow skaters leapt to hug him, but Brusco remained stoic in the face of his historic accomplishment. To the dismay of many fans, the first-ever 1260 was ultimately not enough to secure the gold medal, and Brusco settled for his fourth X Games silver.

Brusco's ability to maintain the laid-back attitude common in the skating community while performing at an elite level earned respect from many fellow athletes. "I don't even really know how to fathom the adrenaline or whatever he must be feeling prior to trying [a 1260]," Brusco's friends and fellow pro skater Clay Kreiner told Bruton. "But he's super calculated. He trusts himself so much." Others noted his careful preparation, valuing precision and safety to reach new heights.

PERSONAL LIFE

Around 2016 Brusco moved into a house owned by fellow skater Alex Perelson in Southern California. Five other pro skaters—Kreiner, Sam Beckett, C. J. Titus, Josh Stafford, and Mats Hatlem—joined them, drawing media attention for the sheer amount of youthful talent under one roof. Yet, as Bruton revealed in an article about the house for Fansided (22 July 2018), it is less a place for parties than for mutual support and the rare moment of relaxation. Brusco has earned a reputation as the messiest housemate, however. "Mitchie lives in another reality than all of us," Perelson said. "But he's a genius, so we tolerate it and we just watch him do his thing."

SUGGESTED READING

Bane, Colin. "Mitchie Brusco Lands 900 in Practice." ESPN, 28 July 2011, www.espn.co.uk/action/xgames/summer/2011/news/story?id=6813207. Accessed 15 Dec. 2019.

———. "Mitchie Brusco Lands 1080, Silver Medal." X Games, 17 May 2013, www.xgames.com/events/2013/barcelona/article/9287498/x-games-barcelona-2013-mitchie-brusco-lands-1080-en-route-skateboard-big-air-silver. Accessed 16 Dec. 2019.

Bruton, Michelle. "Animal House: 7 Pro Skaters Living under One Roof." Fansided, 22 July 2018, fansided.com/2018/07/22/skateboarders-live-together-mitchie-brusco-perelson-kreiner/. Accessed 16 Dec. 2019.

———. "This Innovative Skateboarder's Secret Weapon: Skydiving." OZY, 30 July 2019, www.ozy.com/the-huddle/this-innovative-skateboarders-secret-weapon-skydiving/95814/. Accessed 16 Dec. 2019.

McCorkle, Brenda Blevins. "'Little Tricky' Already Making His Mark in the World of Skateboarding." *TDN.com*, 9 May 2009, tdn.com/lifestyles/little-tricky-already-making-his-mark-in-world-of-skateboarding/article_ce2fdbe6-96ce-5062-890d-a36a6821e484.html. Accessed 15 Dec. 2019.

Perry, Nick. "Young Skateboarder Soars into the Limelight." *The Seattle Times*, 1 Aug. 2002, community.seattletimes.nwsource.com/archive/?date=20020801&slug=skateboard01e. Accessed 15 Dec. 2019.

Shelton, Don. "Skateboarder Mitchie Brusco on His Love for the Sport." *The Seattle Times*, 18 Sept. 2014, www.seattletimes.com/sports/skateboarder-mitchie-brusco-on-his-love-for-the-sport/. Accessed 15 Dec. 2019.

—*Molly Hagan*

Pete Buttigieg

Date of birth: January 19, 1982
Occupation: Politician

In April 2019, when Democrat Pete Buttigieg officially threw his hat in the ring for the 2020 presidential campaign, his website touted him as a member of "the generation that came of age with school shootings, the generation that provided the majority of the troops in the conflicts after 9/11, the generation that is on the business end of climate change, and the generation that—unless we take action—stands to be the first to be worse off economically than their parents."

In a crowded Democratic primary field that also included seventy-year-old Massachusetts Senator Elizabeth Warren, seventy-seven-year-old former Vice President Joe Biden, and seventy-eight-year-old Vermont Senator Bernie Sanders, it did not take a campaign website to point out that the thirty-seven-year-old Buttigieg came from an entirely different generation. Indeed, had he been elected, Buttigieg would have been the youngest US president ever to serve.

Other factors made him an unusual candidate. The former mayor of South Bend, Indiana, Buttigieg had never, unlike most contenders, been a member of Congress, governor, or vice-president. Additionally, he was the first openly gay person to run for the Democratic Presidential nomination.

Buttigieg performed remarkably well as a candidate early on: out of an initial field of well over twenty Democratic presidential hopefuls, he proved a durable, engaging, and articulate moderate, and when it came to the first contest,

Photo by Gage Skidmore via Wikimedia Commons

the Iowa caucuses of February 2020, Buttigieg pulled off a stunning win, narrowly edging out Sanders, a progressive who was seen as one of the top candidates. It was to be Buttigieg's only win, however, as he ultimately failed to inspire the needed groundswell of support and pulled out of the primaries shortly before Super Tuesday in March. Nonetheless, many insiders feel his political future is bright. Some expressed hope that he would appear on the ticket as the vice presidential candidate in 2020, and others pointed out that Indiana's two Republican freshman senators each won with barely a majority of the vote, making them vulnerable to defeat in their respective reelection races in 2022 and 2024—particularly against an ambitious candidate like Buttigieg, who possesses Midwestern pragmatism and obvious intelligence. At minimum, his most ardent supporters fervently hope he will run for president again—if not in 2024, should the 2020 Democratic nominee not win, then in 2028, when Buttigieg will still only be forty-six.

EARLY LIFE AND EDUCATION

Peter Paul Montgomery Buttigieg (pronounced "boot-edge-edge" according to his campaign ads) was born on January 19, 1982. An only child, he was raised in South Bend, Indiana, a small city that had once been a thriving hub of manufacturing but had declined precipitously by the time of his birth.

His father, Joseph Buttigieg, was a first-generation immigrant from Malta; his mother, the former Jennifer Anne Montgomery, had deep roots in Indiana. Joseph had studied to be a Jesuit priest before immigrating to the United

States but later decided to become a professor of literature; he and Buttigieg's mother, a linguist, met while both were teaching at New Mexico State University. They married in 1980, and that year they accepted positions at the University of Notre Dame, in South Bend, where they remained on the faculty for decades.

Buttigieg was a star student at St. Joseph's Catholic High School in South Bend. Of the well-rounded education he received there, he once wrote, as quoted by Daniel Burke for CNN (17 Aug. 2019): "At St. Joe, we were brought up not only to learn Church doctrine on matters like sexuality and abortion, but also to understand the history of the Church as a voice for the oppressed and downtrodden."

His senior year he won first prize in the John F. Kennedy Presidential Library and Museum's Profiles in Courage essay contest, writing about his admiration for future rival and then US Representative Bernie Sanders of Vermont. Buttigieg graduated in 2000 as class valedictorian and next entered Harvard, where he majored in history and literature, became head of the Student Advisory Committee of the Harvard Institute of Politics, and wrote occasional liberal-leaning op-eds for the *Harvard Crimson*. He also served as an intern at an NBC news affiliate and volunteered for Democrat Jill Long Thompson when she ran unsuccessfully for Congress in 2002.

In 2004 Buttigieg graduated from Harvard magna cum laude and was elected a member of the academic honor society Phi Beta Kappa. That year he also worked as a policy and research specialist on John Kerry's unsuccessful 2004 presidential campaign. Offered a Rhodes Scholarship, Buttigieg next traveled to England to study philosophy, politics, and economics at Oxford University.

FORGING A PRIVATE-SECTOR CAREER

In 2007 Buttigieg became a consultant at the Chicago office of the global consulting firm McKinsey & Company, where his clients included Blue Cross Blue Shield of Michigan, Canadian supermarket chain Loblaws, the Natural Resources Defense Council, the US Department of Energy, the US Postal Service, and the US Department of Defense. That career move became a source of some contention during his political bids. "What was Buttigieg doing at McKinsey for two and a half years? How many people had lost their jobs because of him? How shady was the work conveniently hidden behind a standard McKinsey nondisclosure agreement?" Edward-Isaac Dovere asked in an article for the *Atlantic* (10 Dec. 2019).

"I never worked or was asked to work on things that I had a problem with, but it's a place that I think, like any other law firm or firms that deal with companies, just thinks about client

work and doesn't always think about the bigger implications," Buttigieg admitted to Dovere. "I was looking for a place where I could learn as much as I could by working on interesting problems and challenges in the private sector, the public sector, in the nonprofit sector," he said. "And that's what I got to do."

ENTERING POLITICS

Buttigieg left McKinsey in 2010 to run for state treasurer in Indiana, hoping that he could play some small part in defending President Obama's economic policy against right-wing candidates. Few were surprised when the young and unknown Buttigieg lost the general election to Tea Party Republican Richard Mourdock by nearly 25 points. The year before, in 2009, Buttigieg had joined the US Navy Reserve as an ensign in naval intelligence, and he was later dogged by accusations that he had signed up with a future political career in mind. He has refuted those charges for years, telling Olivia Nuzzi for *New York Magazine* (14 Apr. 2019), "Something like serving in the military—especially the extent to which it has a real price, and I don't just mean the risk of coming into harm but the moral cost of becoming involved even peripherally in killing—means it's not something you do lightly."

MAYORALTY

In 2011 Buttigieg, undaunted by his loss in the treasurer's race, ran for mayor of South Bend. Leading the pack in fundraising and promising to transform the city's economy, he won almost three-quarters of the nearly 15,000 votes cast, making him, at age twenty-eight, the youngest serving mayor of a US city with at least 100,000 residents. He made missteps during his first term—most notably being accused of not doing enough for South Bend's minority communities and poorly handling a disciplinary matter involving the city's first black police chief—but he was popular and coasted to a second term in 2015 with over 80 percent of the vote.

In 2014 Buttigieg took a leave of absence from the mayor's office and deployed to Afghanistan for seven months as a Navy lieutenant, assigned to a unit charged with disrupting terrorist financial networks. He garnered the Joint Service Commendation Medal and in 2017 resigned his commission.

While mayor, Buttigieg publicly announced he was gay via an op-ed in the *South Bend Tribune* (16 June 2015). In it, he wrote, "Putting something this personal on the pages of a newspaper does not come easy. We Midwesterners are instinctively private to begin with, and I'm not used to viewing this as anyone else's business. But it's clear to me that at a moment like this, being more open about it could do some good. For a local student struggling with her sexuality, it might be helpful for an openly gay mayor to send the message that her community will always have a place for her. And for a conservative resident from a different generation, whose unease with social change is partly rooted in the impression that he doesn't know anyone gay, perhaps a familiar face can be a reminder that we're all in this together as a community."

PRESIDENTIAL CAMPAIGN

After the 2016 election of Donald Trump, Buttigieg had written a blog post on Medium titled "A Letter from Flyover Country," outlining his vision for the Democratic Party. Soon after that, he vied to become chair of the Democratic National Committee (DNC). Although he suffered a stinging defeat, he raised his political profile, and soon he was being mentioned in such outlets as the *New York Times* and *New Yorker* as a rising talent in the Democratic Party.

Opting against seeking a third mayoral term, Buttigieg announced in late January 2019 that he was exploring a run for the presidency, positioning himself as a progressive yet traditional option. He officially launched his campaign on April 14 of that year, with a platform that included making Medicare available to all who wanted it; offering a national service option to young people; and something he called the Douglass Plan, named after civil rights activist Frederick Douglass. The plan offered more access to credit for black entrepreneurs and businesses, greater reinvestment in education and healthcare, and criminal justice reform, but it did little to earn the support of minority voters, particularly after it was discovered that his campaign staff had used a stock photograph from Kenya to illustrate the plan online and had claimed endorsements from a handful of black politicians who had not clearly agreed to having their names used.

Still, despite lacking the name recognition and campaign war chests of other leading Democratic candidates, he was soon trailing only Biden, Sanders, and Warren in the crowded field. In early February 2020 he made an impressive showing in the Iowa Democratic caucuses, coming in first with fourteen delegates to Sanders's twelve. Shortly thereafter, he finished second only to Sanders in the New Hampshire Democratic primary.

Despite those successes, he lost momentum in the ensuing races in Nevada and South Carolina, where he came in third and fourth, respectively. He dropped out of the race on March 1, telling an emotional crowd of supporters in South Bend, "Our goal has always been to unify Americans to defeat Donald Trump and to win the era for our values. So we must recognize that at this point in the race the best way to keep faith with those goals and ideals is to step aside

and to help bring our party and our country together." The next day he endorsed Biden.

PERSONAL LIFE

Buttigieg married his husband, Chasten (Glezman) Buttigieg, a junior high school teacher, on June 16, 2018, at the Cathedral of St. James in South Bend, the Episcopal church where they are congregants.

The author of a 2019 memoir, *Shortest Way Home: One Mayor's Challenge and a Model for America's Future*, Buttigieg speaks various levels of Italian, Maltese, Spanish, Dari Persian, Arabic, French, and Norwegian. He also plays the piano and guitar.

SUGGESTED READING

Bruni, Frank. "The Case for Pete Buttigieg." *The New York Times*, 27 Feb. 2020, www.nytimes.com/2020/02/27/opinion/sunday/pete-buttigieg-2020.html. Accessed 3 Mar. 2020.

Burke, Daniel. "How Pete Buttigieg Found God." *CNN*, 17 Aug. 2019, www.cnn.com/2019/08/16/politics/pete-buttigieg-religious-journey/index.html. Accessed 3 Mar. 2020.

Buttigieg, Pete. "South Bend Mayor: Why Coming Out Matters." *South Bend Tribune*, 16 June 2015, www.southbendtribune.com/news/local/south-bend-mayor-why-coming-out-matters/article_4dce0d12-1415-11e5-83c0-739eebd623ee.html. Accessed 3 Mar. 2020.

Dovere, Edward-Isaac. "What Pete Buttigieg Says He Did at McKinsey." *The Atlantic*, 10 Dec. 2019, www.theatlantic.com/politics/archive/2019/12/pete-buttigieg-mckinsey/603421/. Accessed 3 Mar. 2020.

Fuller, Jaime. "The Most Interesting Mayor You've Never Heard Of." *The Washington Post*, 10 Mar. 2014, www.washingtonpost.com/news/the-fix/wp/2014/03/10/the-most-interesting-mayor-youve-never-heard-of/. Accessed 3 Mar. 2020.

Nuzzi, Olivia. "Wonder Boy." *New York Magazine*, 14 Apr. 2019, nymag.com/intelligencer/2019/04/pete-buttigieg-2020-presidential-campaign.html. Accessed 3 Mar. 2020.

"Pete Buttigieg: Former Mayor of South Bend, Ind." *The New York Times*, 16 Jan. 2020, www.nytimes.com/interactive/2020/01/16/opinion/pete-buttigieg-nytimes-interview.html. Accessed 3 Mar. 2020.

—*Mari Rich*

William C. Campbell
Date of birth: June 28, 1930
Occupation: Biologist

William C. Campbell, a parasitologist and biologist, was instrumental in discovering new ways to treat infections caused by roundworms. He is the second Irish citizen to win a Nobel Prize.

EARLY LIFE AND EDUCATION
William C. Campbell was born on June 28, 1930, in Ramelton, Ireland, which is a small town in northeastern County Donegal. Campbell has stated in interviews that the agrarian culture and natural beauty of Ramelton greatly influenced his formative years. His father, R. J. Campbell, owned a farm-supplies shop that provided Ramelton citizens with electricity during the 1930s. As both his parents placed a high value on education, Campbell began working with a tutor when he was six years old. Later, he and his two brothers, Lexi and Bert, were sent to Campbell College, a boarding school in Belfast.

After graduating from secondary school, Campbell attended Trinity College in Dublin to study zoology. It was there that he met his mentor, Professor J. Desmond Smyth. Smyth changed the trajectory of Campbell's career by developing the young scientist's interest in field-parasitic worms. After graduating from Trinity College with honors in 1952, Campbell went to the United States to do graduate work. There, Campbell attended the University of Wisconsin–Madison on a Fulbright travel scholarship, earning a master's degree in veterinary science in 1954 and a PhD in zoology by 1957. His doctorate work focused on the liver fluke, a parasite often found in sheep.

CAREER
In 1957, Campbell began working for the Merck Institute for Therapeutic Research, a New Jersey–based pharmaceutical company. One of his first major discoveries was the veterinary application of the compound Thiabendazole (also known as Tiabendazole or TBZ). By conducting a series of studies on mice and dogs throughout the 1960s and early 1970s, Campbell determined that Thiabendazole was an antiparasitic capable of killing roundworms and hookworms in mammals. In further studies that used pigs and humans as test subjects, Campbell discovered that Thiabendazole could also be used to cure trichinosis. He was also able to prove that Thiabendazole was a fungicide that could prevent fruits and vegetables from developing blight.

In the mid-1970s, Campbell began developing what would become his most famous scientific achievement: avermectin, the discovery of

Photo by Bengt Nyman via Wikimedia Commons

which was the result of an intercontinental collaboration between Campbell and Japanese microbiologist Dr. Satoshi Ōmura. In 1974, Ōmura isolated and cultured a unique bacterium from Japanese soil and sent a sample to Campbell at the Merck laboratories. After running several tests, Campbell discovered that Ōmura's cultures could produce avermectin, a potent anthelmintic substance with antiparasitic properties. He then determined that avermectin and its modified derivative ivermectin could successfully be used to treat animals afflicted with roundworm, hookworm, and lungworm. This discovery would go on to save livestock farmers billions of dollars a year.

Campbell posited that ivermectin also had the potential to treat humans afflicted with onchocerciasis, commonly known as river blindness. Campbell and his research team conducted clinical trials in 1981 on the effects of ivermectin on patients in Senegal and Paris who were suffering from river blindness. After achieving promising results, the Merck Institute teamed up with the World Health Organization (WHO) in 1987 to provide the drug Mectizan, to developing nations for little to no cost. Campbell was instrumental in the Mectizan Donation Program and was the first to propose ivermectin be made free. As a result, tens of millions of people living in subtropical Africa and South America have been cured of river blindness.

During the mid-1980s, Campbell also began testing the effects of ivermectin on lymphatic filariasis, a disfiguring and debilitating disease commonly known as elephantiasis, which once threatened the health of over 1 billion people worldwide. By conducting clinical and field trials with the Special Programme for Research and Training in Tropical Diseases (TDR), Campbell's research team determined that a single dose of ivermectin was effective in treating the disease.

Campbell became a senior scientist and the director of research and development at the Merck Institute in 1984. After ending his thirty-three-year career at the Merck Institute in 1990, he became a scientist and research fellow at New Jersey's Drew University's Research Institute for Scientists Emeriti (RISE) program. In October 2015, Campbell received word that he and former colleague Satoshi Ōmura would be sharing half of the 2015 Nobel Prize in Physiology or Medicine for their discovery of avermectin. The other half was awarded to Dr. Youyou Tu, a Chinese scientist responsible for developing artemisinin as a malaria treatment. During the ceremony, which took place on December 10, 2015, the Nobel Committee stated that all three scientists were being honored for transforming the way parasitic diseases were treated.

IMPACT

By developing avermectin and ivermectin and ensuring that they are available at a low cost to people in need, Campbell has improved the quality of life for hundreds of millions of people worldwide. Furthermore, Campbell's work has led to the near eradication of river blindness and elephantiasis.

PERSONAL LIFE

Campbell has been married to Mary Mastin Campbell since 1962. He is a poet, painter, and an avid ping-pong player. He and his wife reside in North Andover, Massachusetts.

SUGGESTED READING

Altman, Lawrence K. "Nobel Prize in Medicine Awarded to 3 Scientists for Parasite-Fighting Therapies." *New York Times*, 5 Oct. 2015, www.nytimes.com/2015/10/06/science/william-c-campbell-satoshi-omura-youyou-tu-nobel-prize-physiology-medicine.html. Accessed 24 June 2020.

Crump, Andy, and Satoshi Ōmura. "Ivermectin, 'Wonder Drug' from Japan: The Human Perspective." *Proceedings of the Japan Academy. Series B, Physical and Biological Sciences,* vol. 87, no. 2 (2011), pp. 13–28. doi:10.2183/pjab.87.13. Accessed 24 June 2020.

"Londonderry Scientist Receives Nobel Prize for Medicine." *BBC*, 11 Dec. 2015, www.bbc.com/news/uk-northern-ireland-foyle-west-35069409. Accessed 24 June 2020.

Murphy, Darragh. "Meet Ireland's New Nobel Laureate, William C. Campbell." *Irish Times*. Irish Times, 9 Oct. 2015, www.irishtimes.com/life-and-style/people/meet-ireland-s-new-nobel-laureate-william-c-campbell-1.2385532.

Winslow, Ron, and Anna Molin. "Nobel in Medicine Awarded to Three for Advances against Tropical Diseases." *WSJ*. Dow Jones, 5 Oct. 2015, www.wsj.com/articles/nobel-prize-in-physiology-or-medicine-awarded-to-william-c-campbell-satoshi-omura-youyou-tu-1444038938.

—*Emily Turner*

Lewis Capaldi

Born: October 7, 1996
Occupation: Singer-songwriter

Following the release of his full-length debut album, 2019's *Divinely Uninspired to a Hellish Extent*, Lewis Capaldi, whose powerful, soulful voice has drawn comparisons to British vocalist Adele, became a global phenomenon. His meteoric rise has largely been fueled by the breakout hit ballad "Someone You Loved," an ode to his late grandmother that became the biggest-selling single of 2019 in the United Kingdom, after spending an unprecedented seven consecutive weeks at the top of the Official Singles Chart Top 40.

"Someone You Loved" performed equally well in the United States, achieving platinum status and reaching the top spot on the Billboard Hot 100 after twenty-four weeks on the chart. With this milestone, Capaldi became the first artist from Scotland to notch a number-one solo

Photo by Justin Higuchi via Wikimedia Commons

hit since Sheena Easton's 1981 hit "Morning Train (Nine to Five)." Capaldi's song has managed to strike a chord with audiences, although the self-deprecating singer-songwriter does not fit the traditional mold of a pop superstar. "It's his complete transparency that breaks through," Ryan Walter, Capaldi's manager, explained to James Hanley for *Music Week* (3 May 2019). "His accessibility and relatability [are] resonating with people because they see a bit of themselves in him." Even Capaldi has seemed pleasantly baffled by his mainstream success. "I'm not going to question it," he told Josh Glicksman for *Billboard* (8 July 2019). "I'm just going to hold on for dear life."

EARLY YEARS AS A MUSICIAN

Lewis Marc Capaldi was born to Carol and Mark Capaldi on October 7, 1996, in Glasgow, Scotland's largest city. He grew up with his mother, a nurse, and his fishmonger father, along with his three older siblings, Aidan, Warren, and Danielle, in the quiet town of Whitburn, West Lothian, located outside of Glasgow. Capaldi's parents exposed him to music early, often listening to Elvis Presley, Fleetwood Mac, Genesis, and Adam Ant on repeat during long holiday road trips to France. Capaldi was first bitten by the music bug at age three or four, after a cabaret band's performance turned into an impromptu open mic night. Capaldi was obsessed with Queen at the time, having gotten a free CD of "We Will Rock You" and "We Are the Champions" from a newspaper. "The cabaret people asked us if anyone wanted to come up and sing. . . . I got up and I sang 'We Will Rock You,'" he told Ruth Kinane for *Entertainment Weekly* (10 Sept. 2019). "Before I even knew what music really was, or being a musician was, I remember just really enjoying the feeling of being up [on stage] and singing in front of everyone."

Following closely in the footsteps of his singer-songwriter brother Warren, Capaldi honed his musical skills, picking up his first guitar and learning to write songs when he was nine. School also proved instrumental in further reinforcing Capaldi's passion for music. By age eleven, he had joined the after school guitar club at St. Joseph's Primary School in Whitburn, where he met future bandmate Aidan Beattie. Capaldi left a lasting impression at the school talent show, belting the winning Oasis tune "Live Forever," alongside Beattie. "Everybody loved it. The two boys sat in front of the stage and just played away. And it was actually quite emotional, quite overwhelming," Mrs. Mooney, one of Capaldi's teachers, recalled to Joe Kasper for *The Sun* (23 Mar. 2010). The music department at St. Kentigern's Academy in Blackburn also inspired Capaldi to continue nurturing his musical passion.

Despite being introduced by Warren to heavy metal artists such as Slipknot, Capaldi's musical tastes gravitated toward a wide array of pop-rock artists, ranging from English duo Oasis and boy band Busted to the American groups Foo Fighters and Blink-182, as well as Scottish singer-songwriter Paolo Nutini, his idol. At age twelve, Capaldi cut his teeth by performing at local pubs around Glasgow and Edinburgh, often hiding in restrooms before the show and leaving immediately after his set. The following year he auditioned—unsuccessfully—for *Britain's Got Talent* before joining an indie rock group at age fourteen. In addition to performing covers of the Scottish band the View, he also began experimenting with his vocal style, mimicking blues singer Joe Cocker's raspy voice, after watching Cocker belt out a Beatles cover during a BBC special.

"BRUISES" *BLOOM* AND "FADE"

By his late teens, Capaldi was still performing local pub gigs, alongside St. Kentigern's Academy classmate Adam Warrington. He also continued posting YouTube covers and uploading original songs to SoundCloud, which he had been doing since age eleven. Upon completing secondary school, the eighteen-year-old enrolled in a two-year music course at New College Lanarkshire (NCL) to further develop his songwriting and live performance skills. Capaldi's persistence paid off in 2015, when talent manager Ryan Walter came across one of his SoundCloud recordings. "Within 10 seconds, I knew I had to get in touch," Walter told Glicksman. "It was an equal combination of two things: his vocal, which was absolutely flawless, and the level of depth to his songwriting. It's such a rare thing to ever witness both."

Over the next six months, Capaldi would travel back-and-forth to London—at Walter's expense—to take part in songwriting sessions. By early 2017 he had recorded and self-released the first track from his upcoming disc, with impressive results. "Bruises" quickly amassed more than twenty-five million plays on the music streaming service Spotify, making Capaldi the fastest unsigned artist to achieve this feat while also earning him a recording contract with Virgin Records (part of Universal Music Group). For his four-song EP *Bloom*, released in October 2017, Capaldi collaborated with Malay, a Grammy-winning producer, on the song "Fade," which reached number thirty-three on the Scottish Singles Chart and was certified silver by the British Phonographic Industry (BPI).

To promote his debut album, Capaldi served as the opening act for British singer-songwriter Rag'n'Bone Man on his European fall tour before headlining his own sold-out UK headline tour in November and December 2017. He closed out the year with a bang, winning the Breakthrough Artist Award at the SSE Scottish Music Awards, as well as appearing on the 2018 Vevo DSCVR Artists to Watch list and BBC Music's Sound of 2018 long-list.

DANCING WITH "GRACE"

After starting the new year as the opener for German folk group Milky Chance's North American leg, Capaldi embarked on a European tour in February 2018. It was not long before he had attracted the attention of former One Direction member Niall Horan, who contacted Capaldi via Instagram and offered him an opening slot on the Glasgow dates of the 2018 Flicker World Tour, on March 18 and 19. Capaldi subsequently scored another coveted supporting slot, this time on the UK and European legs of Sam Smith's The Thrill of It All tour, from late March until late May. He also became a highly sought-after commodity on the summer music festival circuit, performing at Lollapalooza, Bonnaroo, Firefly, and TRNSMT, among others. That fall he released his sophomore EP, *Breach*, whose first hit was the uplifting second single "Grace," which was certified platinum by BPI and reached the top ten of the Official Scottish Singles Top 100 and the UK Top 40 Singles Chart. Capaldi's sense of humor was on full display in the "Grace" video, which takes place at a gentleman's club and features Capaldi performing a pole-dancing routine backed by a male revue, after agreeing to fill in for his female friend, an exotic dancer.

BREAKS THROUGH WITH "SOMEONE YOU LOVED"

In November 2018, after embarking on yet another sold-out UK and European headlining tour, Capaldi achieved a career breakthrough with the digital-download release of his third song, "Someone You Loved," which entered the UK Singles Chart in January 2019—the same month he was voted winner of the MTV UK PUSH Ones to Watch prize. The first version of the "Someone You Loved" music video was released to raise awareness of organ donation and starred *Dr. Who* actor Peter Capaldi—Capaldi's second cousin once removed—as a grieving widower who meets face-to-face with the woman who received his wife's heart. By March, the heart-wrenching, piano-heavy ballad had reached the top spot, becoming Capaldi's first-ever number-one single in the United Kingdom. He achieved another milestone in April, when his eight-date 2020 UK arena tour, representing almost one hundred thousand seats, sold out in ten minutes, making him the first-ever artist to achieve this feat before the release of a full-length disc, *Divinely Uninspired to a Hellish Extent*, which features three previously released tracks: "Grace," "Hold Me While You Wait," and "Someone You Loved."

Divinely Uninspired was released in May 2019, topping the UK album chart in its opening week and becoming the year's fastest-selling record to date—just as "Someone You Loved" was entering the Billboard Hot 100 in the United States. Over the next two months, Capaldi headlined several sold-out US summer shows and made his debut on the US talk-show circuit, performing his breakout hit on NBC's *Today* show, as well as CBS's *The Late Show with Stephen Colbert* and *The Late Late Show with James Corden*.

In August 2019, Capaldi unveiled a second version of the "Someone You Loved" music video (featuring a brief cameo by his brother Warren) and opened for Ed Sheeran on his UK tour dates in Ipswich and Leeds. That fall he set out on the road again, on a second North American tour of his own. At the time, he had also released an extended version of his full-length record, which includes the ballad "Before You Go," a song inspired by his aunt's suicide. It would become Capaldi's second number-one on the UK Singles Chart. He capped off his banner year with a first-time Grammy Award nomination in the Song of the Year category for "Someone You Loved." Despite losing out to Billie Eilish's "Bad Guy," Capaldi still managed to make headlines at the January 2020 event, when he was mistaken for a seat filler, someone who sits in an attendee's seat to save it if they have to take a break. Capaldi had better luck at the Brit Awards, where he scooped up four nominations and won two awards, for Best New Artist and Song of the Year. The singer, who seemed inebriated, raised eyebrows for swearing during one acceptance speech and thanking his late grandmother— the inspiration for "Someone You Loved"—for passing away in another. Capaldi followed that up with a sold-out UK and Ireland arena tour, which wrapped up in mid-March 2020. He was criticized after deciding against canceling his final show, held in Aberdeen on March 15 for an audience of some eleven thousand people, in the midst of the coronavirus pandemic. Capaldi's spokesperson responded to critics by saying that the organizers and venue were compliant with an advisory on mass gatherings issued by the Scottish government the afternoon of the show.

Upcoming plans for Capaldi included a joint tour with Horan, which was originally scheduled to kick off in April 2020 but was postponed indefinitely due to the pandemic. While in isolation, Capaldi was collaborating on new material with Horan via Zoom, an online videoconferencing service.

PERSONAL LIFE

Capaldi's offbeat sense of humor has also won over legions of fans on social media, where he boasted more than five million Instagram followers by May 2020. The singer split from Paige Turley, a fellow NCL graduate and British reality television contestant, in 2016. He lives with his parents at their family home in Bathgate.

SUGGESTED READING

Glicksman, Josh. "Chartbreaker: Lewis Capaldi on Not Wanting to Write Another Breakup Song Landing His Biggest Hit Yet." *Billboard*, 8 July 2019, www.billboard.com/articles/columns/pop/8518207/lewis-capaldi-someone-you-loved-chartbreaker-interview. Accessed 10 May 2020.

Kasper, Joe. "Lost on Lew: Lewis Capaldi Reveals He Was a Mistake as His Dad Was Supposed to Get a Vasectomy." *The Sun*, 23 Mar. 2010, www.thesun.co.uk/tvandshowbiz/11238562/lewis-capaldi-mistake-dad-vasectomy/. Accessed 10 May 2020.

Kinane, Ruth. "Lewis Has 'No F——ing Clue' Why You Love His Song 'Someone You Loved' So Much." *Entertainment Weekly*, 10 Sept. 2019, ew.com/music/2019/09/10/lewis-capaldi-someone-you-loved-success/. Accessed 10 May 2020.

Walter, Ryan. "'This Is Already Wildest Dream Territory': Q&A with Lewis Capaldi's Manager Ryan Walter." Interview by James Hanley. *Music Week*, 3 May 2019, www.musicweek.com/management/read/this-is-already-wildest-dream-territory-q-a-with-lewis-capaldi-s-manager-ryan-walter/076086. Accessed 12 May 2020.

SELECTED WORKS

Bloom, 2017; *Breach*, 2018; *Divinely Uninspired to a Hellish Extent*, 2019

—*Bertha Muteba*

Zuzana Čaputová

Date of birth: June 21, 1973
Occupation: Politician

On March 30, 2019, Zuzana Čaputová was elected president of Slovakia, a small Central European nation located just south of Poland that became independent in 1993, after splitting with the Czech Republic. Reporting on her victory for the *New York Times* (30 Mar. 2019), Marc Santora and Miroslava Germanova called it a "stunning rebuke of Slovakia's populist governing party" and wrote: "Riding a wave of popular discontent over widespread corruption but refusing to engage in personal attacks on her opponents, [Čaputová] vowed to return a sense of decency to Slovakia's often toxic political climate. Her sweeping victory in a runoff election gave hope to opposition parties across the region that the tide might be turning against the ethnic nationalist and populist movements that have swept to power in recent years."

Čaputová won with 58 percent of the vote, triumphing over longtime diplomat Maroš Šefčovič, who had been backed by Smer-SD (Direction–Social Democracy), the country's governing party. In the first round of voting, earlier in March, she had fended off more than a dozen other candidates, including some extremists who campaigned on anti-immigrant, anti-gay, and anti-Semitic platforms. By contrast, as Santora and Germanova wrote, Čaputová "managed to express outrage without rage, calmly calling for transparency, decency and fairness in politics and in public life."

At a rally celebrating her election, she addressed a fervent crowd, asserting, "Maybe we thought that justice and fairness in politics were signs of weakness, [but] today, we see that they are actually our strengths."

EARLY LIFE AND EDUCATION

Zuzana Čaputová was born into what she has described as a working-class family on June 21, 1973, in the town of Pezinok, outside the capital city of Bratislava and near the low mountain range known as the Little Carpathians.

As a teen, Čaputová came across a book about the benefits of Zen meditation and adopted the practice; she has remained a proponent

Photo by VLADIMIR SIMICEK / AFP via Getty Images

as an adult. She came of age under a repressive Communist regime. "I remember how schizophrenic it felt," she recalled to Santora for the *New York Times* (15 June 2019). "To be talking with your friends honestly one moment and then having to hide your opinions with other groups."

In 1989, following a wave of mass protests across Eastern Europe, the Communist regime fell. In the wake of what became known in Slovakia as the Velvet Revolution, Čaputová and her family could travel for the first time without a permit, and they spent the Christmas season in Vienna that year. She has told journalists that to this day she remembers the dazzling holiday lights and the impression they made on her.

Čaputová knew that she wanted to forge a career in which she could help people, and she was deeply interested in history, psychology, and law: she ultimately decided to study law. In 1996—three years after Czechoslovakia split into the Czech and Slovak Republics—she graduated with a law degree from Bratislava's Comenius University, the largest institution of higher education in Slovakia. While still a student she began working as a legal assistant in the mayor's office in Pezinok, volunteering to take on work involving neglected or abused children.

In 1998 Čaputová left the mayoral administration, completed training courses in management and mediation, and got involved with the Open Society Foundation, a group dedicated to supporting freedom of expression, accountable government, justice, and equality. (The organization's founder, George Soros, a Holocaust survivor and pro-democracy advocate, is often portrayed by the far right as a left-wing puppet master, and political opponents of Čaputová would later criticize her association with the foundation.)

In the early 2000s Čaputová, by then a member of the public-interest law firm Via Iuris, became enmeshed in a case that would thrust her into the public eye for the first time.

PEZINOK LANDFILL

For hundreds of years, Pezinok was known for its tourist-worthy Gothic castle and its picturesque vineyards. In the 1960s, however, neighboring towns, and even other countries, began trucking their waste to a dumping ground built with no permits or oversight just 500 feet from a residential area. When that dump began to reach critical capacity in the early 2000s, a wealthy developer with close ties to local politicians made plans to build a second such facility—even though an ordinance had been enacted in 2002 that prohibited landfills within city limits.

Meanwhile, residents of the town were subject to high rates of respiratory disease and cancer; those who lived in Pezinok were eight times more likely to suffer one particular form of

leukemia than the national average. With people afraid to even open their windows and an uncle and friend diagnosed with cancer in a single week, Čaputová engaged in a tireless campaign of environmental activism.

She and her colleagues distributed leaflets and petitions throughout Pezinok, working in concert with a citizen's initiative called "Dumps Don't Belong in Towns," supported by Greenpeace, church leaders, and the area's many wine producers, whose livelihoods were being severely affected by the pollution.

In addition to those successful grassroots efforts—one early petition to the European Parliament garnered 8,000 signatures—Čaputová used her legal training to mount a series of challenges through the Slovakian and European Union judiciaries.

Finally, in 2013 the Slovakian Supreme Court ruled that the newly proposed landfill was illegal and withdrew permission for its operation; it also ordered the older dumpsite to shut down.

Čaputová, who continued to fight for stricter construction laws and better public access to environmental information, was awarded the prestigious Goldman Environmental Prize in 2016. "The victory in Pezinok—the largest mobilization of Slovak citizens since the 1989 Velvet Revolution—sets an important precedent for civic engagement in Slovakia, and is inspiring citizens in the country to stand up for their rights to a clean and safe environment," the *Goldman Environmental Prize* website states. Many observers began referring to Čaputová as "the Erin Brockovich of Slovakia," a reference to the American activist who spearheaded a case against the Pacific Gas and Electric Company (PG&E) of California in 1993 and who was played by the actor Julia Roberts in a Hollywood film about Brockovich's efforts.

POLITICAL CAREER

On February 26, 2018, journalist Ján Kuciak and his fiancé, Martina Kušnirová, were shot dead in their home by an assassin hired to stop his investigation of government corruption and ties to organized crime. (Later, several people would be charged, including the gunman and the businessman who ordered the hit.) In the wake of the crime, tens of thousands of people, including Čaputová, took to the streets to protest the governing party, forcing the resignation of Prime Minister Robert Fico and several other government officials.

Inspired to become involved on a deeper level, Čaputová joined the fledgling Progressive Slovakia party, and in January 2018, she was elected as a deputy chair at its first congress. In 2019, she became the party's presidential candidate. In stark contrast to the populist, antidiversity rhetoric espoused by most of her opponents, she campaigned on a platform of public civility and transparent government, adopting as a slogan the phrase "Stand up to evil." She explained to Shaun Walker for the *Guardian* (1 Apr. 2019), "There needs to be a change in the way politics is done, and the tone with which people approach debates."

Čaputová handily won the first round of the election on March 16, with more than 40 percent of the vote, and in the runoff, held on March 30, she trounced Šefčovič, 58 percent to 42 percent. (Observers have pointed out, however, that Čaputová's election is hardly ironclad proof of Slovakia's tolerance and progressiveness: a sizeable number of people still voted for conservative and far-right candidates during the first round, including more than 10 percent who opted for neo-fascist Marian Kotleba, who at times appears in public dressed as a member of Slovakia's Hlinka guard, which appropriated Jewish property and rounded up Jews for deportation during World War II.)

Although Prime Minister Peter Pellegrini is largely responsible for leading the government, Čaputová's role is not merely ceremonial. Inaugurated on June 15, Čaputová, as president of Slovakia, is commander in chief of Slovakia's armed forces, has the authority to appoint top judges, and holds strong legislative blocking powers. She has announced her intention to introduce reforms to Slovakia's police and judicial systems to make them more equitable, supports LGBT rights, and continues to advocate for strong environmental protections.

Naysayers have wondered whether she will be able to maintain her relatively liberal stances in the face of fearmongering, xenophobic leaders in neighboring countries, including President Miloš Zeman of the Czech Republic and Hungarian Prime Minister Viktor Orbán. "We'll try to have a constructive relationship with neighboring countries but at the same time have clear stances and positions based on values," she asserted to Walker.

PERSONAL LIFE

Čaputová has two teenage daughters, Ema and Leo, and is divorced from her husband, Ivan Čaputa. Her partner, Peter Konečný, is a musician and photographer. She continues to reside in Pezinok, which is now much cleaner and more livable thanks to her environmental activism. She considers herself a "religious believer and a spiritual person" and has stressed to interviewers that Christian values are compatible with liberalism.

In addition to the Goldman Environmental Prize, her laurels include the European Prize for Political Culture, which she received in August 2019 for her efforts in the service of European democracy.

SUGGESTED READING

Čaputová, Zuzana. "Q&A with Zuzana Čaputová." Interview. *The Goldman Environmental Prize*, Goldman Environmental Foundation, 9 Nov. 2016, www.goldmanprize.org/blog/qa-zuzana-caputova/. Accessed 11 Oct. 2019.

Jancarikova, Tatiana. "Anti-Graft Campaigner Wins First Round of Slovak Presidential Vote." *Reuters*, 15 Mar. 2019, www.reuters.com/article/us-slovakia-election-president/anti-graft-campaigner-wins-first-round-of-slovak-presidential-vote-idUSKCN1QW2Z3. Accessed 11 Oct. 2019.

Roache, Madeline. "What to Know about Zuzana Caputova, Slovakia's First Female President." *Time*, 2 Apr. 2019, time.com/5561925/zuzana-caputova-slovakias-first-female-president/. Accessed 11 Oct. 2019.

Santora, Marc. "Slovakia's First Female President, Zuzana Caputova, Takes Office in a Divided Country." *The New York Times*, 15 June 2019, www.nytimes.com/2019/06/15/world/europe/zuzana-caputova-slovakia-president.html. Accessed 11 Oct. 2019.

Santora, Marc, and Miroslava Germanova. "Zuzana Caputova Is Elected Slovakia's First Female President." *The New York Times*, 30 Mar. 2019, www.nytimes.com/2019/03/30/world/europe/slovakia-election-president.html. Accessed 11 Oct. 2019.

Tait, Robert. "Slovakia's New President Buoys Czech Liberals on First Foreign Visit." *The Guardian*, 20 June 2019, www.theguardian.com/world/2019/jun/20/slovakias-liberal-president-zuzana-caputova-makes-first-visit-to-czech-republic. Accessed 11 Oct. 2019.

Walker, Shaun. "Zuzana Čaputová, the Spiritual Liberal Who Beat Slovakia's Populists." *The Guardian*, 13 Apr. 2019, www.theguardian.com/world/2019/apr/13/zuzana-caputova-slovakia-president-spiritual-liberal-progressive-values. Accessed 11 Oct. 2019.

—*Mari Rich*

Sean M. Carroll

Date of birth: October 5, 1966
Occupation: Theoretical physicist

"Science isn't a separate kind of human endeavor, utterly different from other things that we do," Sean M. Carroll stated in a press release from the American Institute of Physics (AIP) (24 July 2014). "It's part of what makes us human, a natural outcome of our intrinsic curiosity and urge to better understand the world." Indeed, that curiosity and urge to understand have driven the theoretical physicist since childhood and have fueled his research into phenomena such as dark energy and the complex field of quantum mechanics. At times, his diverse research interests have proven troublesome. "I've been told, 'When you apply for grants, don't mention you work on the foundations of quantum mechanics.' It's not seen as serious physics. It's not something government agencies want to give you money to do," he revealed to Sophia Chen for *Wired* (18 Sept. 2019). Nevertheless, Carroll has succeeded in establishing himself not only as a noted researcher in his field—he holds a research professorship at the California Institute of Technology (Caltech) and received a 2015 Guggenheim Fellowship—but also as a skilled science communicator. He has published popular-science best sellers that convey such complex topics as cosmology, the Higgs boson particle, quantum mechanics, and the possibility of a multiverse.

EARLY LIFE AND EDUCATION
Sean Michael Carroll was born on October 5, 1966. He grew up in Yardley, Pennsylvania, near Philadelphia on the eastern edge of the state. Drawn to science from a young age, Carroll developed an interest in physics by age ten and was fascinated by topics related to the underpinnings of reality. "I was always attracted to the biggest possible questions. I was never interested in how a telephone works," he recalled to Chen.

Carroll graduated from Pennsbury High School in Fairless Hills, Pennsylvania, in 1984. Following high school, he attended Villanova University on a full-tuition scholarship. An astronomy and astrophysics major, he minored in

Photo by Sgerbic via Wikimedia Commons

philosophy, a subject in which he began to develop an intense interest. "While science was my first love and remains my primary passion, the philosophical desire to dig deep and ask fundamental questions continues to resonate strongly with me, and I'm convinced that familiarity with modern philosophy of science can be invaluable to physicists trying to tackle questions at the foundations of the discipline," he later wrote in a personal narrative posted to his blog on April 9, 2015. Carroll earned both a bachelor's degree in astronomy and astrophysics and an honors program bachelor of arts degree from Villanova in 1988.

Carroll pursued doctoral studies in astronomy at Harvard University under adviser George Field. His studies were funded largely through fellowships from the National Science Foundation (NSF) and the National Aeronautics and Space Administration (NASA). In addition to performing research, Carroll taught a course in astronomy and found that he enjoyed teaching. He earned his doctorate with the dissertation "Cosmological Consequences of Topological and Geometric Phenomena in Field Theories" in 1993.

WORK IN ACADEMIA
Carroll began his career in academia at the Massachusetts Institute of Technology (MIT) as a postdoctoral researcher within the Center for Theoretical Physics and a lecturer in physics beginning in 1993. In 1996 he moved to the Institute for Theoretical Physics at the University of California, Santa Barbara, where he took on another postdoctoral research position. In 1999, Carroll became an assistant professor at the University of Chicago. There he conducted research and taught a number of physics courses for undergraduate and graduate students.

Carroll remained active in research and received accolades for his teaching work at the University of Chicago. He was thus surprised to learn in the spring of 2005 that he had been denied tenure, the expected next step in his career trajectory as an academic. Unable to determine the specific reasons for the rejection, he would later attribute it to his engagement in activities outside of scientific research, including writing. "Probably the worst thing I personally did was to write [the 2003 textbook] *Spacetime and Geometry*," he wrote in an article for *Discover* magazine (30 Mar. 2011). "You might think that a long volume filled with equations that provides a real service to the community would help your case. It won't; it will hurt it. Why? Because while you were writing that book, you weren't doing research." He left the university in 2006.

Despite that setback, Carroll soon found a new position at Caltech. He joined that institution as a senior research associate in 2006. He later worked as a research professor in its physics department. Beginning in 2019 Carroll also held the position of external professor at the Santa Fe Institute, an independent research facility in New Mexico. In addition, he has delivered lectures at many colleges and universities, was an National Science Foundation (NSF) Distinguished Lecturer in 2007 and created several lecture courses sold as part of the Great Courses series.

RESEARCH INTERESTS

A theoretical physicist, Carroll has explored multiple areas of interest during his career, including the concepts of dark energy and modified gravity. His research interests were more varied than those of some other researchers, and after being denied tenure in Chicago, he contemplated giving up his writing work and focusing on a single area of research to improve his success in academia. Ultimately, however, he decided against that approach. "After a great deal of contemplation, I decided that such a strategy was exactly what I didn't want to do," he wrote in his personal narrative. "I would remain true to my own intellectual passions, and let the chips fall where they may." Following his move to Caltech, Carroll continued to work in multiple areas of theoretical physics, most of which deal with what he describes as "trying to figure out how nature works at a deep level."

Carroll is perhaps best known for his work within quantum mechanics, an area of research that features heavily in his writing for general audiences. "We see tables and chairs and people and planets moving through spacetime. Quantum mechanics says that there are no such things as tables and chairs—there's just something we call a wave function," he told Chen about the concept. "The job of physicists and philosophers is to show how, if we live in a world that is just a wave function, then why does it look like there are people and planets and tables and chairs?"

In recognition of his work, Carroll has received numerous honors, including induction as a fellow of the American Physical Society (APS). He won the 2014 Andrew Gemant Award from the American Institute of Physics (AIP) and the following year received the prestigious Guggenheim Fellowship, a grant designed to support individuals who have demonstrated excellence in a creative field or in research.

PUBLICATIONS

In addition to numerous papers published in venues such as the *Astrophysical Journal*, *Physical Review Letters*, and the *International Journal of Modern Physics*, Carroll is the author of many articles for general audiences and the blog *Preposterous Universe*, which he created in 2004. His first book, the textbook *Spacetime*

and Geometry: An Introduction to General Relativity, was published in 2003. In addition to his short-form and academic writing, Carroll authored several popular-science books that seek to explain complex topics within theoretical physics to general audiences. *From Eternity to Here: The Quest for the Ultimate Theory of Time* (2010) concerns cosmology and deals with topics such as time and entropy, while *The Particle at the End of the Universe: How the Hunt for the Higgs Boson Leads Us to the Edge of a New World* (2012) chronicles the search for the titular particle and the research taking place at the Large Hadron Collider at the European Organization for Nuclear Research (CERN).

Although research remained Carroll's "primary focus," as he told Gourav Khular for *Astrobites* (14 July 2016), writing was nevertheless an important part of his life and an experience that he appreciated. "Once every few years I can write a book, and I really enjoy writing books!" he told Khular. "The ability to stretch yourself for a hundred thousand words or more, and get things right, and explain things the way they should be explained—I think that's something I adapt very naturally to."

Carroll has received particular attention for two New York Times Best Sellers: *The Big Picture: On the Origins of Life, Meaning, and the Universe Itself* (2016), which deals with topics such as the nature of reality; and *Something Deeply Hidden: Quantum Worlds and the Emergence of Spacetime* (2019). Again delving into quantum mechanics, *Something Deeply Hidden* explores the Many Worlds interpretation of quantum mechanics, which suggests that the universe is constantly splitting and implies the existence of a multiverse. Along with his physics-related work, Carroll has published a variety of articles on philosophy and science, and the transcript of a 2014 debate between Carroll and philosopher William Lane Craig formed the basis of their 2016 publication *God and Cosmology: William Lane Craig and Sean Carroll in Dialogue*, edited by Robert B. Stewart.

SCIENTIFIC OUTREACH

Alongside his other work, Carroll hosts the podcast *Mindscape*, a multidisciplinary interview program that, according to its website, brings together "science, society, philosophy, culture, arts, and ideas." Launched in mid-2018, the podcast originated in Carroll's interviews for *The Big Picture*. "I talked to major philosophers, thinkers, and experts on a lot of different things, and I found that a lot of fun," he told Melinda Baldwin for *Physics Today* (21 Mar. 2019). "I realized that maybe there was room for a podcast that was more along those lines." Alongside increasing public engagement with science through projects such as *Mindscape*, Carroll hopes to foster discussions between scientists from different fields. "We talk about disciplines interacting with each other, but it's very rarely scientific disciplines interacting. I want to lower that barrier between physics and the rest of science," he told Baldwin.

In addition to performing scientific outreach through his books and podcast, Carroll has bridged the scientific community and popular culture through his work as a science consultant for a variety of major films, including *TRON: Legacy* (2009), *Terminator: Genysis* (2015), and *Avengers: Endgame* (2019). He has also appeared in television documentary programs such as the NOVA series *The Fabric of the Cosmos* and the Discovery series *How the Universe Works*.

PERSONAL LIFE
Carroll and his wife, science writer Jennifer Ouellette, encountered each other's blogs online and first met in person at a physics conference. The couple married in 2007. They live in Los Angeles.

SUGGESTED READING
Carroll, Sean. "Author Q&A: Cosmologist Sean Carroll on Podcasting." Interview by Melinda Baldwin. *Physics Today*, 21 Mar. 2019, doi:10.1063/pt.6.4.20190321a. Accessed 13 July 2020.

———. "5 Questions with Sean Carroll, Physicist at CalTech and the Santa Fe Institute." *Cool NYC Events*, 10 Sept. 2019, www.coolnycevents.com/2019/09/10/5-questions-with-sean-carroll-physicist-at-caltech-and-the-santa-fe-institute. Accessed 13 July 2020.

———. "How to Get Tenure at a Major Research University." *Discover*, 30 Mar. 2011, www.discovermagazine.com/the-sciences/how-to-get-tenure-at-a-major-research-university. Accessed 13 July 2020.

———. "Our Cosmology and The Big Picture: An Interview with Sean Carroll." Interview by Gourav Khular. *Astrobites*, 14 July 2016, astrobites.org/2016/07/14/our-cosmology-and-the-big-picture-an-interview-with-sean-carroll. Accessed 13 July 2020.

———. "A Personal Narrative." *Sean Carroll*, 9 Apr. 2015, www.preposterousuniverse.com/blog/2015/04/09/a-personal-narrative. Accessed 13 July 2020.

———. "Sean Carroll Thinks We All Exist on Multiple Worlds." Interview by Sophia Chen. *Wired*, 18 Sept. 2019, www.wired.com/story/sean-carroll-thinks-we-all-exist-on-multiple-worlds. Accessed 13 July 2020.

"'Outspoken' Caltech Scientist Wins 2014 Gemant Award." *American Institute of Physics*, 24 July 2014, www.aip.org/news/2014/outspoken-caltech-scientist-wins-2014-gemant-award. Accessed 13 July 2020.

SELECTED WORKS
Spacetime and Geometry: An Introduction to General Relativity, 2003; *From Eternity to Here: The Quest for the Ultimate Theory of Time*, 2010; *The Particle at the End of the Universe: How the Hunt for the Higgs Boson Leads Us to the Edge of a New World*, 2012; *The Big Picture: On the Origins of Life, Meaning, and the Universe Itself*, 2016; *Something Deeply Hidden: Quantum Worlds and the Emergence of Spacetime*, 2019

—Joy Crelin

Ruth E. Carter
Date of birth: April 10, 1960
Occupation: Costume designer

Ruth E. Carter built a reputation as one of the most accomplished and respected costume designers in Hollywood, with a résumé that "reads like a tour through the past three decades of black cinema," as Kyle Buchanan wrote for *T: The New York Times Style Magazine* (10 Dec. 2019). She launched her career in the late 1980s, notably working with legendary director Spike Lee on such classic films as *Do the Right Thing* (1989) and *Malcolm X* (1992). After earning an Academy Award nomination for her work on the latter, Carter was propelled into the Hollywood mainstream. She would go on to be involved in a wide variety of film and television projects, joining forces with other high-profile directors such as Steven Spielberg, Robert Townsend, Lee Daniels, and Ava DuVernay.

Photo by Gage Skidmore via Wikimedia Commons

Known for her exhaustive research and strict attention to historical accuracy, Carter received a second Oscar nomination for her work on Spielberg's nineteenth-century slave trade drama *Amistad* (1997). Then, in 2019, she earned her first Oscar victory for her work on the blockbuster Marvel superhero film *Black Panther* (2018). That project exemplified the stylings of Afrofuturism—an aesthetic that explores the melding of African diaspora culture with technology—and made Carter the first African American to win the Academy Award for best costume design.

EARLY LIFE AND EDUCATION

The youngest of eight children, Ruth E. Carter was born on April 10, 1960, in Springfield, Massachusetts. Along with her five brothers and two sisters, she was raised by her mother, who worked as a counselor. In an interview with Kandia Johnson for *Black Enterprise* (17 Oct. 2017), Carter recalled that her mother would often stop and talk to people on the street to hear out their problems, helping to instill in her an openness to the complexities of the human condition—a value that would later inform her work as a costume designer. "Ultimately," she noted to Johnson, "I was groomed to be a storyteller at a young age."

Carter first developed an interest in the arts through her older brothers, who regularly painted and sketched at the family's dining room table. She also dabbled in sewing as a girl; using a Singer sewing machine, she would make articles of clothing for herself and refashion her mother's old dresses. Still, Carter was largely "anti-fashion" growing up, as she admitted to Buchanan. "I just wanted to be a free spirit."

At Springfield's Technical High School, Carter became heavily involved in theater and wanted to become an actor. After graduating she enrolled at the Hampton Institute (later Hampton University), a historically black college in Hampton, Virginia, with strong family ties. Coming from a family of teachers and encouraged by her mother, Carter initially studied special education. She planned to learn sign language and work in theater for the deaf. However, after two years she switched her major to theater arts, inspired by her active role in Hampton's drama department.

It was after auditioning unsuccessfully for a play that Carter found her true calling. The drama instructor asked her instead to make costumes for the production, and she agreed, as she saw an opportunity to rekindle her childhood passion for drawing. As she already knew how to sew, she made many of the costumes from scratch with materials purchased from a local fabrics store. "Once I did that, it caught on like wildfire," she told Tre'vell Anderson for the *Los Angeles Times* (29 Nov. 2018). "By my senior year, I was the costume designer on campus."

CAREER BEGINNINGS

Carter earned her degree in theater arts from Hampton in 1982, though she had no formal training in costume design due to the school's limited curriculum. She instead learned by working on productions and through independent study. Following her college graduation, Carter spent a season interning at a local theater company in Springfield. She then won an internship with the Santa Fe Opera in New Mexico, where she worked as a stitcher, "living the life of hand sewing and immersing into all of the craft work," as she put it to Anderson. Though invaluable from an educational standpoint, the monotonous work, combined with opera's rigid hierarchy, prompted her to refocus her energies on design.

To pursue costume design, Carter moved to Los Angeles. She landed a job with the Los Angeles Theatre Center (LATC), where she quickly worked her way up to head of the costume shop. Through the LATC she met the well-known choreographer Otis Sallid, who accepted her offer to work as an unpaid freelance costume designer for his traveling dance company's popular show "A Night for Dancing" in 1986.

Following a performance of that show, a friend introduced Carter to the then unknown filmmaker Spike Lee, who was about to release his breakthrough first feature *She's Gotta Have It* (1986). Eager to facilitate Carter's entrée into Hollywood, Lee advised her to sign up in the film department of one of Los Angeles' big local universities, so she could volunteer on a student project using professional equipment. Heeding this advice, Carter began to see the potential of working in cinema. However, she continued to work in theater as her friendship with Lee developed.

Carter received her big break in 1988, when Lee asked her to do the costumes for his second feature, *School Daze*, a musical-comedy film that chronicles fraternity life at a historically black college. She quit her job at the LATC and dived headlong into designing clothes for the highly stylized film. It proved the beginning of a decades-long collaborative partnership with Lee, who would soon be recognized as a prominent auteur. "Spike Lee was my greatest support and biggest mentor," she told Johnson. "I am indebted to him for the life and career I have now."

ACADEMY AWARD NOMINEE

After serving as costume designer for Keenan Ivory Wayans's blaxploitation parody *I'm Gonna Git You Sucka* (1988), Carter collaborated with Lee again on his simmering 1989 masterpiece *Do the Right Thing* (1989). For the landmark dramatic comedy, which unflinchingly tackles contemporary race relations in the Bedford-Stuyvesant neighborhood of Brooklyn, she crafted bold and vibrant outfits that celebrated street style trends of the era—high-top sneakers, graphic tees, jerseys, knee-length shorts, and various Afrocentric accoutrements. One of the most acclaimed films of the 1980s, *Do the Right Thing* helped popularize urban streetwear and offered the first glimpses of Carter's Afrofuturist style.

Carter would go on to design the costumes for Lee's next five feature films. Perhaps most notable of these was *Malcolm X* (1992), which established her reputation for period detail and painstaking historical research. During preproduction for the epic biopic, which traces the tumultuous life of the eponymous black nationalist leader, Carter pored over mountains of Malcolm X's letters and police records to gain a better understanding of the man. The film, which stars Denzel Washington in the title role, is highlighted by Carter's brash and colorful zoot suits. It resulted in Carter's first Academy Award costume design nomination, which also made her the first black person to earn a nomination in that category.

Soon Carter was on the radar of other noted directors, and she worked on a wide variety of projects. In addition to Lee, she frequently collaborated with filmmakers Robert Townsend and John Singleton. For example, Carter worked with Townsend on the period musical drama *The Five Heartbeats* (1991), the superhero comedy *The Meteor Man* (1993), and the screwball comedy *B.A.P.S.* (1997). "Ruth can do whatever is in front of her because she's got amazing taste," Townsend told Anderson. "She's a true artist and can take on any assignment."

Steven Spielberg hired Carter to create costumes for his nineteenth-century historical drama *Amistad* (1997), named after the Spanish slave-trading vessel on which a real-life rebellion took place in 1839. For the film, which centers around the contentious legal battle that ensued in the wake of the rebellion, Carter traveled all over the world to find period-specific clothes. Her resultant work was rewarded with a second career Oscar nomination for costume design.

IN-DEMAND DESIGNER

Carter's versatility and openness to taking on assignments across a wide range of genres helped make her one of the most in-demand costume designers in Hollywood. Known for her collaborative nature, she formed long associations with a number of prominent actors. For example, she worked with Eddie Murphy on five feature films in the first decade of the 2000s alone. In the twenty-first century she also increasingly ventured into television projects (her first had been the 1989 pilot for the groundbreaking sitcom *Seinfeld*).

Still, Carter repeatedly found herself drawn back to historically minded period pieces, particularly ones concerning the African American experience. As she told Rob Haskell for the *Wall Street Journal* (1 Nov. 2018), "My wheelhouse is the African-American journey in this country. . . . Stories rooted in the politics of the time." For Salim Akil's *Sparkle* (2012), a musical loosely based on the all-female group The Supremes, Carter designed 1960s-era dresses inspired by avant-garde fashion designers. For *Lee Daniels' The Butler* (2013), a historical drama about longtime White House butler Eugene Allen, she perused vintage Los Angeles clothing shops to outfit such stars as Oprah Winfrey and Jane Fonda. On Ava DuVernay's *Selma* (2014), a chronicle of Martin Luther King Jr.'s landmark 1965 voting rights marches, she helped carefully reproduce the fashions worn by the iconic civil rights leader and those around him.

Carter's meticulous approach on such films involved studying photographs and old film clips to identify period details or the exact appearance of real-life figures being portrayed. Her design process would begin with mood boards reflecting the key visual elements of a film's characters, with the intention of helping the costumes enhance the performances. "A lot of times we get clothes onto a person and we think our job is done," she told Haskell. "But I like to see the sweat on the clothes. I like to see how people wear them and embody them."

Carter continued this meticulous attention to detail for the 2016 remake of the miniseries *Roots*. For this epic historical drama she immersed herself in slave narratives and sifted through an archive of early-nineteenth-century clothing. The work brought her first career Emmy Award nomination.

BLACK PANTHER AND BEYOND

Carter's career reached new heights in 2018 with the Marvel superhero film *Black Panther*. With its highly distinctive, African-inspired aesthetic, the film in many ways represented a culmination of all her previous work, with her designs highlighted on a blockbuster scale. Directed by Ryan Coogler, *Black Panther* follows the eponymous heroic character, also known as T'Challa (portrayed by Chadwick Boseman), as he leads his fictional African kingdom of Wakanda through an array of challenges. To realize her and Coogler's vision for the traditional but technologically advanced nation, Carter traveled to Africa and studied the garments of various tribes across the continent, such as the Maasai people of Kenya and Tanzania and the Ndebele ethnic group of South Africa.

Over the course of a six-month preproduction process, Carter crafted and sourced roughly 1,500 costumes, overseeing an international team of researchers, shoppers, embroiderers, tailors, and engineers. She followed a strict Afrocentric color palette and incorporated traditional materials but also made extensive use of advanced technology such as 3D printing. This effort at "melding sci-fi with global fashion history" earned Carter widespread critical praise "as one of the essential visual storytellers of Afrofuturism," as Doreen St. Félix wrote for the *New Yorker* (10 Sept. 2018).

Black Panther received rave reviews from critics and became a cultural phenomenon, taking in over $1.3 billion at the worldwide box office. Carter's standout costumes were frequently noted as a highlight. St. Félix called it "a rare thing: a big-budget superhero movie that is unabashedly serious about great clothes." The film received seven Academy Award nominations, including for best costume design. When Carter was announced as the Oscar winner in early 2019, she made headlines as the first African American to earn the award in that category.

Following the wave of publicity around her first Oscar win, Carter continued to work steadily. In 2019 she reunited with Eddie Murphy again on the 1970s blaxploitation parody *Dolemite Is My Name*. She was also attached to Murphy's sequel to his 1988 comedy *Coming to America*.

PERSONAL LIFE
Carter lives in Los Angeles. In 2020 she partnered with the Swedish clothing retailer H&M to launch her first fashion collection, which drew inspiration from 1980s and '90s clothing styles.

SUGGESTED READING
Anderson, Tre'vell. "'Black Panther' Costume Designer Ruth E. Carter Is Hollywood Royalty—with or without the Awards." *Los Angeles Times*, 29 Nov. 2018, www.latimes.com/entertainment/movies/la-ca-mn-ruth-e-carter-black-panther-20181129-story.html. Accessed 16 Jan. 2020.

Carter, Ruth. "Meet Ruth E. Carter: The Costume Designer behind Marvel's Black Panther (Part 1 of a 2-Part Interview." Interview by Kandia Johnson. *Black Enterprise*, 17 Oct. 2017, www.blackenterprise.com/meet-the-hollywood-costume-designer-behind-marvels-black-panther/. Accessed 16 Jan. 2020.

Carter, Ruth, and Cynthia Erivo. "Ruth Carter and Cynthia Erivo on Clothes, Culture and Self-Expression." Interview by Kyle Buchanan. *T: The New York Times Style Magazine*, 10 Dec. 2019, www.nytimes.com/2019/12/10/t-magazine/ruth-carter-cynthia-erivo.html. Accessed 16 Jan. 2020.

Haskell, Rob. "In 'Black Panther,' Costume Designer Ruth E. Carter Found a Career-Defining Challenge." *The Wall Street Journal*, 1 Nov. 2018, www.wsj.com/articles/in-black-panther-costume-designer-ruth-e-carter-found-a-career-defining-challenge-1541083028. Accessed 16 Jan. 2010.

Ryzik, Melena. "The Afrofuturistic Designs of 'Black Panther.'" *The New York Times*, 23 Feb. 2018, www.nytimes.com/2018/02/23/movies/black-panther-afrofuturism-costumes-ruth-carter.html. Accessed 16 Jan. 2020.

Schmidt, Ingrid. "10 Surprising Facts about Oscar Winner Ruth E. Carter and Her Designs." *The Hollywood Reporter*, 1 Mar. 2019, www.hollywoodreporter.com/lists/10-surprising-facts-oscar-winner-ruth-e-carter-her-designs-1191544/item/ruth-e-carter-siblings-1191561. Accessed 16 Jan. 2020.

St. Félix, Doreen. "Ruth E. Carter's Threads of History." *The New Yorker*, 10 Sept. 2018, www.newyorker.com/magazine/2018/09/10/ruth-e-carters-threads-of-history. Accessed 16 Jan. 2020.

SELECTED WORKS
School Daze, 1988; *Do the Right Thing*, 1989; *Malcolm X*, 1992; *Amistad*, 1997; *Lee Daniels' The Butler*, 2013; *Selma*, 2014; *Roots*, 2016; *Black Panther*, 2018; *Dolemite Is My Name*, 2019

—*Chris Cullen*

Sukhinder Singh Cassidy

Born: 1970
Occupation: Entrepreneur

Sukhinder Singh Cassidy perennially appears on lists of the most interesting and powerful businesspeople in the world. She has been named one of "tech's next-gen leaders" by *Fortune*, one of the "Silicon Valley 100" by *Business Insider*, a "power woman" by *Forbes*, and one of the "most creative people in business" by *Fast Company*, to name just a few of her accolades.

The list of companies Cassidy has either founded or helmed is equally impressive. Although she began her career by working in finance and media, she was lured in the 1990s to the Silicon Valley–based world of tech. She later launched such enterprises as Yodlee, a pioneering data aggregation platform; Polyvore, a user-generated online fashion magazine of sorts; and Joyus, an e-commerce site that displays its wares via video. Along the way she also worked as president of tech giant Google's Asian Pacific and Latin America operations and head of event-ticketing giant StubHub. She explained to Aarti Virani and Parizaad Khan Sethi for *Vogue India* (Mar. 2015) that not having a tech background was no impediment to her success: "We've moved from an era of engineers as rock stars to product visionaries as rock stars," she asserted.

Cassidy is perhaps most celebrated, however, for her activism and efforts to increase gender diversity in the business and tech worlds. She founded theBoardlist, a curated networking site aimed at matching talented female leaders to open board positions. "Instead of putting the onus on women to try to fix a problem they didn't create or have the power to change, I created a platform for decision-makers and those in power—who are still overwhelmingly male and non-diverse—to promote qualified women," she wrote in a piece for *Time* (16 Nov. 2017). "We didn't want to shame companies for their track records on women. We simply wanted to put more brilliant and talented women in contention for an empty board seat."

EARLY YEARS AND EDUCATION
Sukhinder Singh Cassidy was born in Dar es Salaam, a major city on the coast of Tanzania. Her parents were both physicians. When she was two years old, she moved with them and her two sisters to St. Catharines, a city in Ontario, Canada. The family spent its early years there trying to assimilate into Canadian culture while still stressing Sikh values. Until her uncle joined them, her father was the only Sikh sardar in the immediate area.

Cassidy has described herself as a particularly intense, academically driven child. By the time she was in middle school, she was helping her father keep the records at his medical practice and prepare his income taxes; when she was a teen, she computerized his office system. She

Photo by TechCrunch via Wikimedia Commons

also enjoyed watching him as he perused the financial pages of the newspaper each morning and called his broker to make trades.

Her father encouraged her to prepare for a business career, but Cassidy instead treated college as something of a lark. "Interestingly, college was my revolt period after growing up in a highly conservative household," Cassidy recalled to Adam Bryant for the *New York Times* (8 July 2016). "So when I went away to college, I was going to have a good time. My grades were good, but I was mostly enjoying the freedom to make my own choices." Cassidy attended the Ivey School of Business Administration at the University of Western Ontario, graduating in 1992.

EARLY CAREER
Despite getting decent grades, studying abroad in Belgium for a semester, and successfully completing her degree, Cassidy had little direction after college. "For somebody who was so intense, I actually didn't know what I wanted to do. I went through a recruiting cycle after graduating but didn't get a job. So I went from feeling great about myself as a high school student to wondering what's wrong with me. I felt pretty demoralized," she admitted to Bryant. Eventually, through a classmate, she was invited to interview at the investment banking and wealth management firm Merrill Lynch, in New York City. Although she had no idea how serious the recruiters were, she bought a train ticket to New York at her father's urging and was surprised to be hired almost immediately.

Cassidy remained at Merrill Lynch as a financial analyst—handling mergers and acquisitions, initial public offerings, and other such tasks—from 1993 to 1995, dividing her time between the company's New York and London offices. During a stint in London she accepted an analyst's post at British Sky Broadcasting. She stayed for just over a year, before undertaking an extended period of travel. During that year, she visited Egypt and Israel, spent several months skiing in British Columbia, and drove the coast of California in an old Mazda.

MOVING TO TECH
In late 1997, intrigued by the tales emerging from the section of the San Francisco Bay area known as Silicon Valley—a hotspot for entrepreneurs and tech innovators—Cassidy moved permanently to California. However, she wrote for *Time* that her career as a tech executive almost ended before it had hardly begun. "Before chasing the startup dream in the late 90s, I had built a successful track record in the very male-dominated traditional media and investment banking industries. I had a thick skin and a lot of hustle—and I knew how to make things happen" she recalled. "But when I got to Silicon Valley,

what had worked for me in New York and London in my early career suddenly became a liability. On my second day of work, my first tech boss told me that I 'scared the secretaries.'"

She was infuriated to see that supervisors started giving her increasingly menial tasks, while male colleagues with similar work styles were praised and promoted. Determined to succeed despite Silicon Valley's difficult-to-bear office culture, in January 1998 she joined forces with the founders of Junglee, an Indian e-commerce startup that was soon purchased by the growing e-commerce company Amazon for $250 million. She worked as a business development manager there until mid-1999, when she was recruited to help launch Yodlee, a new entry in the still novel realm of financial technology. Serving as special vice president of business development, Cassidy helped sell Yodlee's data aggregation services to global banks, brokerages, and other institutions.

She remained with Yodlee until 2003, when she joined Google as the head of Asian Pacific and Latin America operations. During her six years in that position, those regions became the fastest growing in the company, with nine new research and development centers established and well over a dozen sales centers. Although she was considered a rising star at the tech giant, she eventually felt the urge to do something more entrepreneurial. From 2009 to 2010 she served as CEO-in-residence at Accel Partners, a top venture capital firm that she considered a valuable training ground.

Cassidy's next interim stop was a short stint at Polyvore, a site that allowed users to assemble fashion spreads by dropping in images of clothes and accessories from across the web, from March to September 2010. She called the company's model "social commerce." Watching the growing popularity of the video streaming platform YouTube, along with the continued success of shopping channels like QVC, sparked her next idea. In 2011, with the help of a $7.9 million investment from Accel, she founded Joyus, an online retailer coupled with a video platform that allowed customers to watch engaging content and then purchase the products featured. Joyus was acquired by StackCommerce in 2017.

ON THE BOARD

In addition to her individual work in tech, Cassidy promoted the inclusion of other women in the industry. She won widespread praise for an op-ed in which she exhorted women in tech fields to "choose possibility." Posting on the site *Recode* (13 May 2015), she called Silicon Valley "the place that fanned the flames of my ambition and my irrational faith in what I could achieve" and asserted, "Every part of the startup ecosystem has the opportunity to increase the rate of progress for women in tech entrepreneurship."

Over the course of her career Cassidy sat on several boards, including those of Ericsson, TripAdvisor, and Urban Outfitters. Her experiences as a board member led her to work to change the lack of gender diversity in corporate America by getting more women on more boards. In 2015 she founded theBoardlist, hoping to connect interested CEOs with qualified women board members. Within its first two years more than four hundred companies had used the service, and well over one hundred women had been offered board seats.

Having left Joyus in 2017, Cassidy next became the president of StubHub in May 2018. The popular ticket exchange and resale company had been founded in 2000 and acquired by eBay seven years later. By the time Cassidy joined as CEO, it had grown into the largest company of its kind in the world. She oversaw its acquisition by Viagogo for $4 billion in early 2020, right before the global COVID-19 pandemic virtually shut down the live entertainment and sports industries. In May 2020, she announced that she was stepping down from her post in the wake of a massive restructuring.

"I've learned that my risk tolerance is high," Cassidy replied when asked by Bryant how she felt about switching jobs frequently. "I always say to people, once you realize you're employable, everything else is O.K." She continued, "The other part of it is that I'm very impatient. Whenever I think I'm stagnating and not going to get where I'm meant to go, I have this anxiety. So the anxiety of not getting there overwhelms the fear of uncertainty. I guess I just trade one fear for another. People see that as risk tolerance, but it's more this sense that I'm supposed to contribute something more or learn something more."

PERSONAL LIFE

In addition to English, Sukhinder Singh Cassidy learned to understand Punjabi but does not fluently speak it. She married Simon Cassidy, a former hedge-fund manager who later ran an investment firm, in 2003. They have three children. In her rare spare time, she enjoys playing tennis.

SUGGESTED READING

Brooks, Dave. "Sukhinder Cassidy Exits StubHub Amid Restructuring, Job Cuts." *Billboard*, 28 May 2020, www.billboard.com/articles/business/9391903/sukhinder-singh-cassidy-exits-stubhub-restructure-job-cuts. Accessed 28 July 2020.

Cassidy, Sukhinder Singh. "The Boss: Sukhinder Singh Cassidy Is on a Mission to Get More Women on Company Boards." *Time*, 16 Nov. 2017, time.com/5022322/

sukhinder-singh-cassidy-sexism-tech.   Accessed 28 July 2020.

————. "Sukhinder Singh Cassidy: Either You Manage Me or I Manage You." Interview by Adam Bryant. *The New York Times*, 8 July 2016, www.nytimes.com/2016/07/10/business/sukhinder-singh-cassidy-either-you-manage-me-or-i-manage-you.html. Accessed 28 July 2020.

————. "Tech Women Choose Possibility." *Recode*, 13 May 2015, www.vox.com/2015/5/13/11562596/tech-women-choose-possibility. Accessed 28 July 2020.

————. "15 Questions with Sukhinder Singh Cassidy." Interview by Aimee Rawlins. *CNN Tech*, 2015,money.cnn.com/interactive/technology/15-questions-with-sukhinder-singh-cassidy/index.html. Accessed 28 July 2020.

Rao, Pallavi. "Ascent of a Woman." *Economic Times*, 27 Feb. 2006, economictimes.indiatimes.com/ascent-of-a-woman/articleshow/1417956.cms. Accessed 28 July 2020.

Segall, Eli. "Sukhinder Singh Cassidy: CEO of Polyvore's 'Appetite for Change' Creates Silicon Valley Success." *Silicon Valley Business Journal*, 21 Mar. 2010, www.bizjournals.com/sanjose/stories/2010/03/22/focus4.html. Accessed 28 July 2020.

Virani, Aarti, and Parizaad Khan Sethi. "Valley Girls." *Vogue India*, Mar. 2015, static1.squarespace.com/static/561a86b0e4b0b66177b71a25/561a9157e4b0e20307ed3345/561a9159e4b0e20307ed34f4/1444581721461/Valley-Girls-Vogue-India-March-2015.pdf. Accessed 28 July 2020.

—*Mari Rich*

Noah Centineo

Born: May 9, 1996
Occupation: Actor and model

Rising actor Noah Centineo became best known for his role in the 2018 teen romantic comedy *To All the Boys I've Loved Before*, an adaptation of the 2014 first entry in a best-selling young-adult book series by Jenny Han. The instant popularity of the Netflix film, in which Centineo played charming jock Peter Kavinsky, earned him viral fame as the "Internet Boyfriend of 2018," Brooke Marine wrote for *W* magazine (21 Aug. 2018). "Everyone fell in love with Noah Centineo seemingly overnight." The film was declared one of the streaming service's original works with the most views up to that point, earning fans among adults as well as teens and earning multiple watches from many Netflix subscribers.

To All the Boys I've Loved Before might have been his big break, but Centineo's career began years earlier. The Florida-born actor started out in community theater, and around the age of eight he secured agency representation that saw him land modeling jobs. He eventually moved to Los Angeles, where guest spots in shows like Disney Channel's *Austin & Ally* (2011–12) led to a meatier role on the Freeform family drama *The Fosters* in 2015 that lasted until 2018. Appearing in a slew of romantic comedies in 2018 and 2019 solidified his status within the genre and continued to foster a dedicated fan base. Centineo, who was able to reprise his role as Peter in the 2020 sequel *To All the Boys: P.S. I Still Love You*, attributed his success as a romantic lead to his own love of romance. "I think everybody's into love. I think when you're young, being in love for the first time is like this fantasy," he told Hanh Nguyen for *IndieWire* (21 Aug. 2018). "It's this concept that no one quite understands, but everyone thinks about it all the time. And these films really give the younger adults and the younger kids a chance and a peek into that world, maybe prematurely, before they've been able to see it."

EARLY LIFE AND EDUCATION

Noah Centineo was born in Miami, Florida, on May 9, 1996. He grew up in Boynton Beach, in Palm Beach County, as well as other locations in the state. His father, Greg, was a pastor before becoming an entrepreneur while his mother, Kellee, was a fitness instructor. He has an older sister named Taylor. He cited his performance as Mowgli in a fifth-grade production of *The Jungle Book* as one that contributed most directly to his

Photo by Cris e Panda via YouTube and Wikimedia Commons

developing love of acting. "I think, just honestly, maybe it was the adoration, you know, the applause at the end and then the rush of just like being in front of people and making them laugh. Maybe it was the attention, I don't know, but I started just knowing that I felt euphoric when I was doing it, and I wanted to keep doing it," he recalled to Lulu Garcia-Navarro for National Public Radio (NPR) (23 Feb. 2020).

When Centineo was eight years old, though he was more interested at the time with things such as the drums and soccer, he was asked by his parents to accompany his sister on an open-call audition at the John Robert Powers agency in West Palm Beach. Drawing attention to himself, he ended up signing with the company. The representation won him some work locally as a model and in commercials. While a student at BAK Middle School of the Arts in West Palm Beach, he landed his first larger film role, starring in the 2009 independent family adventure-comedy *The Gold Retrievers*, with Billy Zane and Steve Guttenberg, when he was twelve years old. In it, Centineo's character and his dog embark on a treasure hunt to prevent the foreclosure of his family's home.

Centineo attended Boca Raton Community High School for approximately two years, where he played on the soccer team. However, his agent told him that if he was serious about acting, he needed to move to Los Angeles. "That's when I looked at my parents and was like, 'Yo, I'm about it. If you move me there I'll be successful. This is what I want to dedicate my life to,'" he recalled to Max Berlinger for the *New York Times* (21 Sept. 2018). His parents, who ultimately divorced around that time, gave him their blessing, and Centineo, then fifteen, moved with his mother to Los Angeles to pursue his dreams.

DISNEY CHANNEL AND *THE FOSTERS*

In 2011 Centineo starred in the family film *Turkles*, about a group of kids who set out to find some missing sea turtle eggs. He then landed a role on Disney Channel's *Austin & Ally* (ironically, it was set in Miami). The show follows two teens: Austin (Ross Lynch), an outgoing musician, and Ally (Laura Marano), a quiet singer-songwriter. Centineo appeared in three episodes in season one between 2011 and 2012 as a character named Dallas, Ally's crush. The role led to others with Disney, including guest spots on the show *Shake It Up*, starring Bella Thorne and Zendaya, in 2013, and *Jessie*, starring Debby Ryan, in 2014. That same year, 2014, he was part of the cast in the Disney Channel original movie *How to Build a Better Boy*, which drew in millions of viewers upon its premiere. Reviewing the made-for-television film for the *Huffington Post* (13 Aug. 2014), Denette Wilford described it as a "tamer version of *Weird Science*," the 1985

teen comedy in which two boys design their ideal woman on a computer and bring her to life. In *How to Build a Better Boy*, China Anne McClain and Kelli Berglund play two intelligent teenage students who design an advanced robotic boyfriend. Centineo played Jaden Stark, not the product of the girls' experiment, but one of their tutees. Branching out beyond Disney, he also appeared on an episode of the Nick at Nite comedy series *See Dad Run* in 2014. Meanwhile, he briefly continued his studies at Beverly Hills High School, though he ultimately completed his education in independent study.

Centineo's biggest breakthrough in television up to that point came in 2015, when he was cast as a regular in the ABC Family (changed to Freeform in 2016) drama *The Fosters*, about a lesbian couple raising five children, one biological and, eventually, four adopted, in San Diego. The show premiered in 2013, and Centineo joined the cast after one of its stars, Jake T. Austin, departed at the end of the second season. Taking over Austin's role, he played Jesus Adams Foster, the teenage adopted son of matriarchs Stef (Teri Polo) and Lena Adams Foster (Sherri Saum). Cierra Ramirez played his twin sister, Mariana. The show won praise for tackling heavy subject matter without sentimentality. Writing for the *New Yorker* (3 Feb. 2014), Emily Nussbaum described it as "wise, funny and insightful." After a successful run, *The Fosters* was brought to an end in 2018. The following year, Freeform premiered a spin-off series titled *Good Trouble*, starring *The Fosters'* Maia Mitchell and Ramirez, and Centineo reprised his role as a guest star in two episodes of its first two seasons.

TO ALL THE BOYS I'VE LOVED BEFORE

Meanwhile, in between shooting scenes for *The Fosters*, Centineo participated in other projects. These included appearing in the music video for the Camila Cabello song "Havana" as well as in the teen romantic comedy *SPF-18*. (The film received middling reviews but enjoyed a brief resurgence after the release of *To All the Boys I've Loved Before*, while Cabello's video went on to win Video of the Year at the 2018 MTV Video Music Awards.)

To All the Boys I've Loved Before, another teen romantic comedy and surprise smash hit, premiered on Netflix in 2018. Based on young-adult author Jenny Han's book of the same name, *To All the Boys I've Loved Before* follows Lara Jean (Lana Condor), a shy teenager who writes private love letters to her crushes, past and present. Lara Jean intends to keep the letters a secret, but when her little sister mails them out, she is forced to publicly reckon with her private feelings. Centineo plays Peter Kavinsky, a charming jock who Lara Jean once kissed during a childhood game of spin-the-bottle. The two agree to enter a fake relationship—Peter to make his ex-girlfriend jealous, and Lara Jean to provide cover for her real crush on her sister's ex-boyfriend. Ultimately, the two kindle their own romance.

To All the Boys I've Loved Before became one of Netflix's most-viewed original films ever. Centineo's portrayal of the sensitive and charming Peter won him the admiration of millions of fans, both young adults and adults alike. As Allison P. Davis put it for The Cut (14 Sept. 2018), "What Centineo does well . . . is play a simple, suburban-mall kind of crush with Stanislavski dedication. That's it. He's just fully nice and hot at a time that feels like 'nice and hot' is a rare resource." Emily Yoshida, writing for Vulture (15 Aug. 2018), echoed this observation in the first line of her positive review: "I didn't appreciate what a unicorn-like rarity a good, solid boy is in a teen comedy until To All the Boys I've Loved Before."

FURTHER ROMANTIC COMEDIES AND A SEQUEL

Further cementing his place as an increasingly beloved star of the romantic comedy genre, Centineo appeared in another Netflix romantic comedy, Sierra Burgess Is a Loser, a modern retelling of Edmond Rostand's 1897 play Cyrano de Bergerac, in 2018. In it, a less popular teenage girl named Sierra (Shannon Purser) catfishes a handsome jock at another school (Centineo) who thinks he is texting with a cheerleader named Veronica (Kristine Froseth). The film earned moderately positive reviews but did not seem to capture the zeitgeist in the way that To All the Boys I've Loved Before had. Increasingly in demand, Centineo additionally costarred in Swiped in 2018, playing, in a departure from his previous roles, the womanizing college roommate of a gifted coder (Kendall Ryan Sanders) whom he persuades to create an app to coordinate discreet hookups. The 2019 film The Perfect Date, based on Steve Bloom's 2016 novel The Stand-In, follows a high schooler (Centineo) who, via an app of his own creation, rents himself out as an ideal date. While Centineo embraced his niche, relating to Davis that as there are "so many degrees to love" he felt that he had "a lot more to offer the space," he also maintained an open mind as an actor. This included taking on a small role in the 2019 Charlie's Angels reboot and confirming that he would appear as the iconic character He-Man in a new live-action film.

In 2020 Centineo starred in the sequel to To All the Boys I've Loved Before, titled To All the Boys: P.S. I Still Love You and based on the second book (2015) in Han's series. Peter and Lara Jean's nascent relationship is put to the test by another of Lara Jean's old crushes. Though critics expressed disappointment with the film,

suggesting that it lacked the novelty and verve of the original, Centineo's fans remained loyal.

PERSONAL LIFE

Noah Centineo struggled with excessive drinking and drug use as he was breaking into the industry, he told Amy Kaufman for the Los Angeles Times (3 Aug. 2018). "Everything's available in Los Angeles to those who do go out or want it—and you're not borrowing Mom or Dad's money," he said. "If you have your own money, you feel entitled to spending your own money how you'd like to, and that's a slippery slope." After a year of sobriety, he embraced a life of moderation. He lives in Los Angeles and enjoys working out and practicing yoga.

SUGGESTED READING

Berlinger, Max. "Noah Centineo Is Hot. If Only He Could Cool Off." The New York Times, 21 Sept. 2018, www.nytimes.com/2018/09/21/style/noah-centineo-to-all-the-boys-ive-loved-before.html. Accessed 12 Sept. 2020.

Centineo, Noah. "Noah Centineo from To All the Boys I've Loved Before Responds to Becoming the Internet's Newest Boyfriend." Interview by Brooke Marine. W, 21 Aug. 2018, www.wmagazine.com/story/noah-centineo-to-all-the-boys-ive-loved-before-peter-kavinsky-instagram/. Accessed 13 Sept. 2020.

Davis, Allison P. "Noah Centineo, Shameless Heartthrob." The Cut, Vox Media, 14 Sept. 2018, www.thecut.com/2018/09/my-date-with-noah-centineo.html. Accessed 13 Sept. 2020.

Garcia-Navarro, Lulu. "'To All the Boys' Star Noah Centineo Has an 'Inner Mr. Potato Head.'" NPR, 23 Feb. 2020, www.npr.org/2020/02/23/808079501/to-all-the-boys-star-noah-centineo-has-an-inner-mr-potato-head. Accessed 13 Sept. 2020.

Kaufman, Amy. "Move Over, Zac Efron: Noah Centineo Is This Summer's New Teen Heartthrob." Los Angeles Times, 3 Aug. 2018, www.latimes.com/entertainment/movies/la-ca-mn-noah-centineo-netflix-20180803-story.html. Accessed 13 Sept. 2020.

Nguyen, Hanh. "'To All the Boys I've Loved Before': Noah Centineo Was Almost Cast as Boy Next Door Josh, Not Peter." IndieWire, 21 Aug. 2018, www.indiewire.com/2018/08/to-all-the-boys-ive-loved-before-noah-centineo-peter-josh-netflix-1201996135/. Accessed 13 Sept. 2020.

Wilford, Denette. "'How to Build a Better Boy' Review: A Tamer Version of 'Weird Science.'" Review of How to Build a Better Boy, directed by Paul Hoen. HuffPost, 13 Aug. 2014, www.huffingtonpost.ca/denette-wilford/how-to-build-a-better-boy-review-family_b_5676158.html. Accessed 12 Sept. 2020.

SELECTED WORKS
The Fosters, 2015–18; *To All the Boys I've Loved Before*, 2018; *Sierra Burgess Is a Loser*, 2018; *To All the Boys: P.S. I Still Love You*, 2020

—Molly Hagan

Gemma Chan

Date of birth: November 29, 1982
Occupation: Actor

Although British actor Gemma Chan had appeared in numerous film and television projects prior to 2018, a turning point in her career came that year, when she was introduced to audiences worldwide as a part of the ensemble cast in the romantic comedy *Crazy Rich Asians*. With her role as Astrid in the film, which proved popular among audiences and received largely positive reviews from critics, she both benefited from that commercial and critical success and joined a pop-cultural moment that she had never expected would come to pass. "I look back on it now and I couldn't have imagined that film being made, even five years ago," she told Rebecca Nicholson for the *Observer* (28 July 2019).

A professional actor since the first decade of the twenty-first century, Chan began her career with small roles in films as well as memorable guest appearances in UK television series such as *Doctor Who* (2009) and *Sherlock* (2010). A starring role in the science-fiction series *Humans* gained her further recognition between 2015 and 2018, and she would go on to join one of the most popular film franchises of all time in 2019, when she played a supporting role in the Marvel superhero film *Captain Marvel*. She remained thankful for the films and television series that had led her to that point, particularly those that enabled her to explore a diverse array of characters and experiences. "I feel very lucky and very proud to have been part of all of [those] projects," she told Yolanda Machado for *Harper's Bazaar* (2 Apr. 2019).

EARLY LIFE AND EDUCATION
Gemma Chan was born on November 29, 1982, in London, England. The oldest of two children born to a pharmacist mother and an engineer father, she has a younger sister. She grew up in Kent, in an environment that she would later describe as suburban. As a child, she aspired to become a marine biologist or an astrophysicist, among other professions, but did not consider that she might go on to become an actor. Nevertheless, she would eventually draw connections between her childhood dreams and her later profession. "I suppose, actually in many ways, I

Photo by Collider Video via Wikimedia Commons

liked the idea of playing all these different roles or living these different lives, which I kinda get to do to a little extent in my acting career, which is nice," she explained to Michelle Lee for *Allure* (11 Nov. 2019). As a child and teenager, Chan participated in a variety of extracurricular activities, including ballet, competitive swimming, and violin performance. Although she did not opt to pursue a career as a professional musician, she would later play violin for a portion of the soundtrack to the science-fiction television series *Humans*, in which she costarred.

After completing her secondary education, Chan enrolled in Worcester College, part of the University of Oxford, to study law. Although she initially hoped to work in that field, she discovered during her first year that the practice of law did not actually appeal to her. After completing her degree program in 2001, she secured a training position with the prestigious London law firm Slaughter and May but decided to pursue acting instead. "I realized that what had initially attracted me to law was watching films that were courtroom dramas and barristers giving these amazing speeches," she told Nicholson about that decision. After successfully auditioning for acceptance and taking up modelling work for a time as a source of funding, she attended the Drama Centre London at Central Saint Martins, part of the University of the Arts London.

EARLY CAREER
Upon completing her studies at the Drama Centre London in 2008, Chan was forced to decide whether to seek out acting opportunities abroad, particularly in the United States, or to remain in the United Kingdom. Although some of those

around her warned her that opportunities for actors of Asian descent were limited in the United Kingdom, she ultimately chose to remain in the country and began her career with small roles in films such as *Exam* (2009), *Pimp* (2010), and *Shanghai* (2010).

Throughout the first years of her career as a professional actor, Chan became best known for her work on television, which included an appearance in a 2009 episode of the long-running science-fiction series *Doctor Who*, "The Waters of Mars," as well as two episodes of the comedy series *The IT Crowd* (2010). In 2010, she costarred in "The Blind Banker," the second episode of the popular and critically acclaimed television series *Sherlock*, a twenty-first-century take on the established literary character Sherlock Holmes. "We had no idea it would be so popular, but [stars Benedict Cumberbatch and Martin Freeman] were so brilliant and had such a good dynamic that I had a feeling about it," she told William Martin for the website CultBox (1 Feb. 2011) about the series, which would become an influential addition to British popular culture over the next several years. "I think Sherlock Holmes will always be a fascinating character and the modern update of the show felt fresh and exciting, which people seemed to like."

TELEVISION SUCCESS

As Chan's career developed further, she continued to find work on television, taking on significant roles in existing series. In 2011, she had a recurring role in the fourth and final season of the television series *Secret Diary of a Call Girl*, playing a rival to the show's protagonist. "I was already a fan of the show before I was cast," she told Martin about the opportunity. "I think it's great fun, well written and although it's a little bit of fantasy, it's got an emotional core that people can relate to." She also appeared in several episodes of the comedic series *Fresh Meat* in 2011 and in 2012 took on a supporting role in the second season of the supernatural drama series *Bedlam*. In addition to television and film, Chan was active in theater during her early career, costarring in the David Henry Hwang play *Yellow Face* at the National Theatre in 2014 and in a production of the Harold Pinter play *The Homecoming* at Trafalgar Studios between late 2015 and early 2016.

The year 2015 saw the premiere of Chan's next major project, the science-fiction series *Humans*. In the world of the series, human beings exist alongside synths, humanoid robots that fill a variety of roles, including the role of domestic helper. Chan played a synth known as Anita, who is brought into a family's household but is soon revealed to be more than she appears. To prepare for their roles, Chan and her fellow actors who played synths went through training that they referred to as "synth school," learning to move in ways that would distinguish them from the actors playing humans. "We tried to come up with a universal physical language that all synths share," she explained to Kathryn Shattuck for the *New York Times* (26 June 2015). "What this boils down to is that ultimately machines run on battery power, and every move has to be specific and economic and with a grace, eliminating all the little extras. Perfect steps, very precise, nothing very robotic, but something other than human." *Humans* premiered in the United Kingdom and the United States in June 2015 and was subsequently renewed for a second and third season, which aired beginning in 2016 (2017 in the United States) and 2018, respectively. In 2016, the series was nominated for the British Academy of Film and Television Arts (BAFTA) TV Award for Best Drama Series.

INTERNATIONAL BREAKTHROUGH

Alongside her work in television, Chan continued to take on roles in a variety of major films, including *Jack Ryan: Shadow Recruit* (2014), *Fantastic Beasts and Where to Find Them* (2016), *Transformers: The Last Knight* (2017), and *Mary Queen of Scots* (2018). In 2018, she was introduced to a wider audience thanks to the major romantic comedy film *Crazy Rich Asians*. Adapted from the 2013 Kevin Kwan novel of the same name, the first book in a series, *Crazy Rich Asians* features a large ensemble cast and costars Chan as Astrid, a cousin of one of the protagonists and a character with a significant personal story arc in the film.

In addition to providing Chan with a breakthrough role, *Crazy Rich Asians* was particularly significant due to its focus on characters of Asian descent and its incorporation of elements of East Asian culture. "I took my mum and dad with me to the premiere in London, and they were just in tears," she told Nicholson about the film's significance. "My mum said to me, she never expected to see people [on screen] who looked like her family, the food that we ate, music that was in the soundtrack that she hadn't heard since her childhood. It was really personal and really special." Chan went on to be nominated for the Screen Actors Guild Award (SAG) for Outstanding Performance by a Cast in a Motion Picture alongside the rest of the film's ensemble cast, and the success of *Crazy Rich Asians* sparked rumors that she might reprise her role in future films based on later books in Kwan's series, in which the character of Astrid plays a larger role.

Another key moment in Chan's career came in 2019, when she appeared in a supporting role in the film *Captain Marvel*, the twenty-first installment in the Marvel Cinematic Universe (MCU) series of superhero films. She played Minn-Erva, a member of the alien military body

Starforce who serves alongside the amnesiac human Carol Danvers (Brie Larson), later known as Captain Marvel. The first MCU film to feature a solo female lead, *Captain Marvel* was particularly meaningful to Chan, who appreciated the film's inspiring message. "This one in particular is really important for little girls and young women to watch and to feel empowered and to feel that anything is possible for them—that they can dream big," she told Machado. "Some of them may fall, but then they can get back up, and that's okay."

WIDE-RANGING PROJECTS

In addition to *Captain Marvel*, the year 2019 saw the premiere of *I Am*, an anthology miniseries in which each episode follows a different woman. The episode starring Chan, "I Am Hannah," follows the titular Hannah as she navigates life in her thirties and confronts the pressures society places on women of that age, including the pressure to have children. "I feel like we have more freedom these days, but we don't necessarily feel as free as we should to make different choices for ourselves," she explained to Yasmin Omar for *Harper's Bazaar* (1 Aug. 2019) about the tensions underlying the episode. "If we saw a wider spectrum of honest portrayals of women who have made different kinds of choices, maybe the more accepting we'll become and the less judgmental we'll be." Alongside her work on screen, she has sought to expand her reach behind the scenes of the film industry and in June 2019 announced that she had started her own production company. With that company, she hoped to make films focusing on unappreciated but pioneering women. In August 2019, it was announced that Chan would be returning to the MCU as one of the stars of the film *The Eternals*.

PERSONAL LIFE

When not filming elsewhere, Chan, an avid fan of the Arsenal soccer club, lives primarily in London.

SUGGESTED READING

Chan, Gemma. "The *Allure* Podcast: Gemma Chan on Aging, Self-Acceptance, and Being a Kid of the '90s." Interview by Michelle Lee. *Allure*, 11 Nov. 2019, www.allure.com/story/allure-podcast-gemma-chan-interview-recording-transcript. Accessed 8 Mar. 2020.

——. "Gemma Chan Explains the Art of Being a Robot on 'Humans.'" Interview by Kathryn Shattuck. *The New York Times*, 26 June 2015, www.nytimes.com/2015/06/28/arts/television/gemma-chan-explains-the-art-of-being-a-robot-on-humans.html. Accessed 8 Mar. 2020.

——. "Gemma Chan Interview: 'Actors of East Asian Descent Don't Get the Opportunities White Actors Do.'" Interview by Andrzej Lukowski. *Time Out*, 10 Apr. 2014, www.timeout.com/london/theatre/gemma-chan-interview-actors-of-east-asian-descent-dont-get-the-opportunities-white-actors-do. Accessed 8 Mar. 2020.

——. "Gemma Chan ('Secret Diary of a Call Girl') Interview." Interview by William Martin. *CultBox*, 1 Feb. 2011, cultbox.co.uk/interviews/exclusives/gemma-chan-secret-diary-of-a-call-girl-interview. Accessed 8 Mar. 2020.

Machado, Yolanda. "Gemma Chan Knows Hollywood Has a Long Way to Go with Inclusion." *Harper's Bazaar*, 2 Apr. 2019, www.harpersbazaar.com/culture/film-tv/a26897937/gemma-chan-captain-marvel-interview/. Accessed 8 Mar. 2020.

Nicholson, Rebecca. "Gemma Chan: 'Nothing Will Top the Night I Pole-Danced with Celine Dion on a Bus.'" *The Observer*, Guardian News and Media, 28 July 2019, www.theguardian.com/global/2019/jul/28/gemma-chan-film-interview-nothing-will-top-the-night-i-pole-danced-with-celine-dion. Accessed 8 Mar. 2020.

Omar, Yasmin. "Gemma Chan: We Need to Be Less Quick to Judge." *Harper's Bazaar*, 1 Aug. 2019, www.harpersbazaar.com/uk/culture/entertainment/a28350652/gemma-chan-interview/. Accessed 8 Mar. 2020.

SELECTED WORKS

Secret Diary of a Call Girl, 2011; *Bedlam*, 2012; *Humans*, 2015–18; *Crazy Rich Asians*, 2018; *Captain Marvel*, 2019; *I Am*, 2019

—Joy Crelin

David Chariandy

Date of birth: 1969
Occupation: Writer

By early 2020, David Chariandy had published only three books—two novels and one work of nonfiction. This small body of work had, however, firmly established him as a major voice in Canadian literature, particularly regarding the experience of Caribbean immigrants in the country. In 2019 he gained international recognition when he won the US–based Windham-Campbell Prize in the fiction category for his body of work. As quoted by Sue Carter in *Quill & Quire* (13 Mar. 2019), the award selection committee called Chariandy's work "entirely humane and immensely tender" and praised its depiction of "the intimacies found within fraught and fraying social spaces."

Photo by Simon Fraser University via Wikimedia Commons

EARLY LIFE AND EDUCATION

David Chariandy was born in Toronto, Ontario, Canada, in 1969 to parents who had emigrated from the Caribbean nation of Trinidad; his mother, who was black, was a domestic worker and his father, who was of South Asian descent, worked briefly in a poorly paid position at a publishing house and then gave that job up to work at a furniture factory. Chariandy and his brother grew up in the suburban Scarborough neighborhood of Toronto.

As a teenager, Chariandy read mostly science-fiction and fantasy novels until he came upon the works of Canadian novelist Robertson Davies, which led him to develop an interest in literature. He was, however, frustrated to realize that his own experiences as a person of color and the child of immigrants were rarely represented in the Canadian literary canon. "There was a very powerful sense that it was not worthy of representation—none of my life," he told Mark Medley for the *Globe and Mail* (22 Sept. 2017). "My parents were not worthy of representation. My experiences were not worthy of representation." This experience of seeking reflections of his life in literature and failing to find them motivated him to become a writer and create the kinds of books he had wanted to read as a teenager.

Chariandy earned bachelor's and master's degrees from Carleton University in Ottawa. There, he encountered for the first time books by Canadian authors of color such as Joy Kogawa and Maria Campbell, whose writing dealt with experiences that were more familiar to him. "These writings shook and inspired me in profound ways," he told Manahil Bandukwala for

Carleton's website (25 Jan. 2019). In particular, he discovered the work of black Canadian author Austin Clarke, who became a mentor to Chariandy as he attempted to forge a career as a writer. Though he did not actually take a creative writing course until his third year at Carleton, Chariandy published his first short story in the school's student newspaper. He went on to receive a PhD from York University, writing a thesis on black Canadian literature.

SOUCOUYANT: A NOVEL OF FORGETTING

Chariandy's first novel, *Soucouyant: A Novel of Forgetting*, was published in 2007. The novel is narrated by an unnamed teenaged boy growing up in Scarborough, following him as he copes with his father's death in an industrial accident and his mother's early-onset dementia. His mother, a Trinidadian immigrant, is obsessed with the soucouyant, a wicked spirit in Caribbean folklore who sheds her skin at night to travel in the form of a fireball and suck the blood of her victims. The narrator's mother claims to have had an encounter with a soucouyant as a child, and the narrator seeks to understand what actually happened and learn more about his family's history before his mother loses her memory completely. The book was nominated for several literary awards, including the 2007 Governor General's Literary Award for fiction in English and the 2007 Scotiabank Giller Prize as well as the 2009 IMPAC Dublin Literary Award. It won the 2007 Foreword INDIES Book of the Year Award for Literary Fiction.

In an interview with Charles Demers for the *Tyee* (17 Oct. 2007), Chariandy noted that he had begun with the intention to explore dementia as a medical condition, but that as he worked on the book, the condition became "a way to explore the fragility of cultural memory, and how difficult it can be for us to know the past." He further explained, "I was interested not only in establishing a connection with the past, but in foregrounding the oftentimes very difficult *process* of establishing that connection, particularly for historically disenfranchised peoples." The mother's loss of memory thus stands, according to Chariandy, as a metaphor for the way that the history of people of color is often systematically erased or simply not recorded, leaving younger generations struggling to understand where they come from.

BROTHER AND I'VE BEEN MEANING TO TELL YOU

Ten years after the publication of *Soucouyant*, Chariandy published his sophomore novel, *Brother*, which he described as arising from things he wished he could have explored more in *Soucouyant* and was dedicated to his mentor Clarke, who had died the previous year.

Explaining to Ryan B. Patrick for the CBC (27 Sept. 2017) why he had taken so long between books, Chariandy said, "I wanted to do justice to these stories. How do you adequately tell the story of the resilience of mothers, of everyday youth and of these particular communities? I had to be careful about what I was emphasizing."

The story of two boys growing up in Scarborough in the 1980s and 1990s, *Brother* draws more on Chariandy's own life than his previous novel did. "I'm a fiction writer and this is clearly the work of the imagination," Chariandy told Patrick. "But I still wanted to capture what Scarborough was really like for a child in the early 1990s, particularly a child with a black mother and a South Asian father growing up at that particular time." The book deals primarily with the aftermath of an incident of police violence in that community, a topic that had received increased attention in both Canada and the United States for several years preceding the book's publication. "It may have been almost a decade in the making, but it could not be more timely," Chariandy's editor, Martha Kanya-Forstner, told Medley. "I think we had that sense . . . that the book had become the book it needed to be at just the moment that it needed to come." Chariandy told Medley, however, that recent events had not influenced the book's subject matter. "The thing I've always tried to remind people is that the issue has always been front and center for specific communities," he said. *Brother* won the 2017 Rogers Writers' Trust Fiction Prize, the 2018 Toronto Book Award, and the 2018 Ethel Wilson Fiction Prize, and many periodicals named it one of the best books of the year.

While working on *Brother*, Chariandy was also writing *I've Been Meaning to Tell You: A Letter to My Daughter*, published in 2018. His first nonfiction book, *I've Been Meaning to Tell You* was inspired by interactions with his teenaged daughter. In interviews, Chariandy explained that the 2016 US presidential election was the first time his daughter, then twelve years old, had paid attention to politics and that she was distressed by the anti-immigrant sentiment that had come to the fore during that time. "She had started asking questions about the politics of race and belonging. She always knew that certain things were a reality, but it was surprising for her to hear those things from figures of authority," he told Brian Bethune for *Maclean's* (29 May 2018). "So I wanted to give her a deeper story of ancestry and struggle and love and the politics of the very land that we both belong to."

Chariandy thus decided to write an account of the family's recent history in the form of a letter addressed to his daughter, illustrating the Chariandys' connection to Canada while also recounting many of the instances of racism and xenophobia they had endured over the decades.

Chariandy showed each chapter to his daughter as he finished writing it and asked for her feedback. She was surprised to learn of many of the incidents in the book, even the ones that had occurred during her lifetime. "Parents only show so much to their kids because they have to stay strong and be parents," she told Kate Kellaway for the *Observer* (14 Apr. 2019). "Although I knew he goes through struggles on a daily basis, the book was a revelation."

The following year, Chariandy's work garnered particularly high-profile recognition when he was chosen as one of eight international authors to be awarded a 2019 Windham-Campbell Prize. The awards, administered annually by Yale University, were established with the aim of highlighting literary achievement and allowing writers some financial independence to devote time to their work. As the only recipient that year representing Canada, he claimed the prize for fiction.

OTHER WORK

Chariandy has been a strong advocate for Canadians of color in the publishing industry. Around 2006, he cofounded Commodore Books, the first black publishing company in western Canada, along with Wayde Compton and Karina Vernon. The company's inaugural publication was *Adventures in Debt Collection* (2007), by Fred Booker, a collection of linked short stories. Chariandy has also served as a mentor for young writers of color attempting to break into the publishing business through less traditional routes.

Alongside his career as an author, Chariandy has maintained a career in academia, through which he has explored many of the same themes that are dealt with in his creative work. In the early 2000s, he began a lengthy teaching tenure at Simon Fraser University. He has continued to write scholarly articles on black Canadian literature and Caribbean literature; these have been published in numerous journals as well as in books such as *The Routledge Companion to Anglophone Caribbean Literature* (2011) and *The Oxford Handbook of Canadian Literature* (2016). He has also edited several special issues of journals.

Chariandy is married to Sophie McCall, an academic. They have a daughter and a son and live in Vancouver.

SUGGESTED READING

Bethune, Brian. "David Chariandy Writes to His Daughter, in Wary Hope." *Maclean's*, 29 May 2018, www.macleans.ca/culture/books/david-chariandy-writes-to-his-daughter-in-wary-hope/. Accessed 5 Mar. 2020.

Carter, Sue. "David Chariandy Wins Windham-Campbell Prize." *Quill & Quire*, 13 Mar. 2019, quillandquire.com/omni/

david-chariandy-wins-windham-campbell-prize/. Accessed 5 Mar. 2020.

Chariandy, David. "Forgotten Son: David Chariandy on 'Soucouyant.'" Interview by Charles Demers. *The Tyee*, 17 Oct. 2007, thetyee.ca/Books/2007/10/17/Soucoyant/. Accessed 5 Mar. 2020.

——. "How David Chariandy Brought His Novel Brother to Life." Interview by Ryan B. Patrick. *CBC Books*, 27 Sept. 2017, www.cbc.ca/books/canadareads/how-david-chariandy-brought-his-novel-brother-to-life-1.4310129. Accessed 5 Mar. 2020.

——. "The Open Magic of Literature: A Discussion with David Chariandy." Interview by Manahil Bandukwala. *Faculty of Arts and Social Sciences*, Carleton University, 25 Jan. 2019, carleton.ca/fass/a-discussion-with-david-chariandy/. Accessed 5 Mar. 2020.

Kellaway, Kate. "David Chariandy: 'To Make Sense of Prejudice, Tell the Story of the Past.'" *The Observer*, Guardian News and Media, 14 Apr. 2019, www.theguardian.com/books/2019/apr/14/david-chariandy-ive-been-meaning-to-tell-you-father-advice-to-daughter. Accessed 5 Mar. 2020.

Medley, Mark. "In Brother, David Chariandy Shines a Light on Scarborough." *The Globe and Mail*, 22 Sept. 2017, www.theglobeandmail.com/arts/books-and-media/in-brother-david-chariandy-shines-a-light-on-scarborough/article36363666/. Accessed 5 Mar. 2020.

SELECTED WORKS

Soucouyant: A Novel of Forgetting, 2007; *Brother*, 2017; *I've Been Meaning to Tell You: A Letter to My Daughter*, 2018

—*Emma Joyce*

Wendy Clark

Born: ca. 1970–71
Occupation: Advertising executive

In April 2020, the announcement was made that Wendy Clark, then the president and CEO of agency holding company DDB Worldwide, would take the reins of Dentsu Aegis Network—which consists of more than twenty advertising, marketing, media, and data companies—as its global CEO in September. Although Clark might not be a household name among the general public, chances are good that most consumers in the United States have used at least one product with which she has been involved. Considered a major player in the advertising world, she has worked with such powerhouse brands as Coca-Cola, McDonald's, and AT&T, and her laurels include mention as one of *Fast Company*'s Top-10 Business Disruptors in 2011, the 2014 New York Women in Communications Matrix Award, *Ad Age*'s 2017 Executive of the Year title, and induction into the American Advertising Federation's Advertising Hall of Achievement in 2019.

"She is rewriting the rules of the advertising industry," Charles Cooley, host of the *Fearless Leaders Podcast* (8 Sept. 2017), asserted, alluding to the fact that throughout her career, Clark has been known for her empathy, work ethic, moral compass, and determination. "I'm pretty sure at the end of my life no one is going to wax lyrical about some advertising campaign I launched in 1999," she wrote in an undated essay for the *Lean In* website. "But, if I do my best to lead with values, purpose and principles, they just might say that I was a decent person. And to me, that's a far greater achievement."

EARLY LIFE AND EDUCATION

Wendy Clark was born Wendy Ludla in the United Kingdom to an American mother and a British father. Her parents separated when she was just three years old, and until she attended a sleepover party with a friend in first grade, she was unaware that mothers and fathers often remained together in one house. Although she has three half-sisters from her father's second marriage, she told Cooley that she was "an only child from an only mom."

Clark's mother was determined that her daughter would grow up to be ambitious and self-sufficient. "She just put all her energy into my broadest development and outlook, and I knew from an early age that I would work," Clark recalled to Cooley. "I knew I was going to have a career. I couldn't have really even told you what it was but I knew I was very clear I was going to college. I was going to have an education."

When Clark was eleven years old, she moved with her mother to Florida to be closer to extended family. "America was Mickey Mouse and hamburgers," she told Cooley. "I thought it was fantastic." Her early years in Florida were somewhat peripatetic, and between the ages of eleven and fifteen, she attended five different schools. She credits that experience with teaching her that she could walk into any room, meet people, and make friends.

Needing to help her cash-strapped mother, Clark began working at McDonald's as a teen, and she has considered it a foundational life experience. "At 16 years old I was running an entire shift of a restaurant and you learn leadership the hard way that way," she said to Cooley. "I had to deal with customer satisfaction, cash management, insubordination. It's unbelievable what I was dealing with at 16 years old and it just shaped me." By then she had shed her British accent and mannerisms and felt truly American.

Because of her financial constraints, she considered only in-state colleges, and she eventually decided on Florida State University (FSU), where she studied English and creative writing starting in 1988. She served for a time as leader of her sorority and has described herself as an average student. She graduated from FSU with a bachelor's degree in 1991.

LAUNCHING A CAREER

After she graduated, Clark moved to Atlanta, where her mother had recently settled. In a time before online job applications, she sent out countless printed résumés by mail, hoping to land a job in advertising—the only industry she knew of in which a degree in creative writing might be put to practical use. She finally heard back from a small, woman-owned agency called the Denmark Group that had an opening—not for a copywriter but for a receptionist. Although Clark had few secretarial skills, she jumped at the chance to get a foot in the door. She was excited to be earning $14,000 a year, a sum that allowed her to avoid being a burden on her mother but did not always guarantee that she could purchase enough groceries to feed herself.

One day, she was asked by her boss to write a press release, but she became discouraged after her piece went through the editorial process. "The only word left that I had written was 'the,'" she recalled to Cooley. She subsequently abandoned her ambition to write copy and moved into account services as an account coordinator, ensuring that client needs were met, and project schedules were on track. After two years at the Denmark Group, Clark took on a variety of other jobs, including creating employee newsletters at Information America, a data company.

In the mid-1990s Clark was contacted by Linda Smith, a former client of the Denmark Group who was then working as a marketer at Bell South, a telecom company. Smith invited Clark, who had been considering returning to school to earn an MBA, to join her in Florida. Realizing that a challenging, hands-on job could be more valuable than another degree, Clark agreed. Making the move turned out to be a wise choice; Clark was able to learn about pricing, research and development, and other areas that were new to her, and in 2001, she parlayed that experience into a job at GSD&M, a full-service ad agency. There she led an account services team of 120, dealing with such major clients as Southwest Airlines, Walmart, and Land Rover.

In 2004 Clark made the move to an in-house position at AT&T, which had been a GSD&M client. Although she had not been contemplating a move at that time, once she was approached, she reasoned that being on the client side of the business might be less stressful than agency work. Somewhat ironically, soon after she started, AT&T became the largest telecommunications company in the world through a series of acquisitions, and Clark was forced to oversee a major rebranding effort. "I've never worked as hard," she recalled to Cooley. "The agency business looked like a walk in the park next to rebranding hard hats and trucks and rebranding launch campaigns."

Clark's next major move came in 2008 when she was recruited by chief marketing officer Joe Tripodi to join Coca-Cola North America (Coke) as senior vice president of integrated marketing communications and capabilities. Initially, she was met with some distrust on the part of longtime employees, who questioned why she was being brought in from the outside with no background in packaged goods. Others gossiped that she had been hired only because she was a woman, and that Tripodi was under pressure to diversify his team. Rather than being bothered by naysayers, Clark, who later became the president of the company's sparkling brands and strategic marketing division, set out to prove them wrong. "I don't have my MBA, so . . . that was my master's, working with the world's best marketers, unquestionably," she told an interviewer for *Sports Business Journal* (2 Oct. 2017). "There's a wheat-and-chaff thing that happens at Coke, and if you can't keep up, you need to consider doing something else."

At Coke, Clark—who was responsible for the popular "Share a Coke" campaigns of 2014 and 2015—also became an influential leader of Coke's women's leadership council, and during her time there the percentage of women in senior leadership positions jumped from about 19 percent to 32 percent.

DDB AND BEYOND

In late 2015 Clark left Coke for DDB North America, just as McDonald's announced it was seeking to consolidate its advertising with a single agency holding company. The plan set off a fierce competition between Omnicom (DDB's parent company) and rivals Publicis Groupe and WPP; Clark was largely credited with winning Omnicom the business and orchestrating the launch of the fast food giant's dedicated ad agency, We Are Unlimited. Thanks in large part to that feat, she was promoted to CEO of DDB Worldwide in 2018. The high-profile promotion put her in charge of a team of more than two thousand people in DDB offices around the world, so industry observers were surprised when it was announced in early April 2020 that Clark would be leaving DDB to become global CEO of Dentsu Aegis Network (DAN) that September. DAN, a conglomerate started in 1901, counts among its clients American Express,

Disney, General Motors, Microsoft, and Procter & Gamble, and executives there expressed hope that Clark's hiring would greatly expand its creative capabilities.

Clark, whose role at DAN positioned her as head of forty-two thousand employees around the world, told Gideon Spanier for *PR Week* (6 Apr. 2020), "I've had the privilege of working for brands and companies with powerful heritages and that's informed my enduring belief that great brands and companies benefit from having a foot in their past and a foot in their future."

PERSONAL LIFE
Clark and her husband have three children. She explained to Rezwana Manjur for *Marketing* (28 June 2018) that she does not try to achieve the clichéd ideal of work-life balance. "I think balance is the wrong paradigm," she said. "What I like to push for is work-life integration in a way it works for you."

Although Clark had signed a nondisclosure agreement, during the 2016 WikiLeaks incident, it was revealed that she had consulted with the Hillary Clinton campaign on their logo and marketing strategy.

SUGGESTED READING
Clark, Wendy. "The Poet: Wendy Clark." Interview by Charles Cooley. *Fearless Leaders Podcast*, 8 Sept. 2017, www.thelookinglass.com/fearless-episodes/fearless-ep-21-the-poet-wendy-clark. Accessed 18 Aug. 2020.

———. "The Sit-Down: Wendy Clark, CEO DDB North America." *Sports Business Journal*, 2 Oct. 2017, www.sportsbusinessdaily.com/Journal/Issues/2017/10/02/People-and-Pop-Culture/The-sit-down.aspx. Accessed 18 Aug. 2020.

———. "Wendy Clark." *Lean In*, 2020, leanin.org/stories/wendy-clark. Accessed 18 Aug. 2020.

Manjur, Rezwana. "From Receptionist to CEO: Meet DDB's First Female Global CEO Wendy Clark." *Marketing*, 28 June 2018, www.marketing-interactive.com/from-receptionist-to-ceo-meet-ddb%E2%80%99s-first-female-global-ceo-wendy-clark. Accessed 18 Aug. 2020.

Sellers, Patricia. "How Ad Giant DDB Stole Coke Star Marketer Wendy Clark." *Fortune*, 11 Sept. 2015, fortune.com/2015/11/11/wendy-clark-coke-ddb/. Accessed 18 Aug. 2020.

Spanier, Gideon. "DDB's Wendy Clark Quits to Become Dentsu Aegis Network Global CEO." *PR Week*, 6 Apr. 2020, www.prweek.com/article/1679485/ddbs-wendy-clark-quits-become-dentsu-aegis-network-global-ceo. Accessed 18 Aug. 2020.

Weissbrot, Alison. "Wendy Clark Named Global CEO Of Dentsu Aegis Network." *Ad Exchanger*, 6 Apr. 2020, www.adexchanger.com/agencies/wendy-clark-named-global-ceo-of-dentsu-aegis-network/. Accessed 18 Aug. 2020.

—*Mari Rich*

Marie-Louise Coleiro Preca
Date of birth: December 7, 1958
Occupation: President of Malta

As the ninth president of Malta, Marie-Louise Coleiro Preca is the youngest person to hold the office, as well as the only nominee to receive unanimous approval from the Malta House of Representatives.

EARLY LIFE AND EDUCATION
Marie-Louise Coleiro Preca was born on December 7, 1958, in Qormi, Malta. She attended St. George's Primary School, Maria Regina Girls' Grammar School, and the Polytechnic before studying at the University of Malta. There she earned a bachelor's degree in legal and humanistic studies (international studies), as well as a notary public diploma.

Coleiro Preca developed a strong interest in politics as a youth. When she was sixteen, she volunteered for the Partit Laburista (PL; Labour Party in English). Later, she became a member of the National Youth Socialists Bureau, the National Bureau of Socialist Youths (now the Labour Youth Forum), and the PL's national council. She was a founding member of the Ġużè Ellul Mercer Foundation, an editor of the PL's newspaper *Il-Ħelsien*, and the president of the Socialist Women's Group.

POLITICAL CAREER
Coleiro Preca's involvement in national politics deepened when she became a national executive for the PL. She advanced to the post of assistant general secretary and then general secretary. She served in the latter position for nine years, from 1982 until 1991. From 1996 to 2001, she was the president of the PL women's section.

In 1998, she became a member of Parliament (MP) in the House of Representatives of Malta. While part of the opposition, she served as the shadow minister for social policy, tourism, and health, and as a member of the Standing Committee for Social Affairs. As an MP, she dealt with social issues, such as housing, education, welfare, and poverty. She also focused on international communication and issues and served as a delegate to the Council of Europe.

In March 2013, Coleiro Preca became the minister of family and social solidarity. She strove to improve the delivery of social services to better serve vulnerable members of society while also creating mechanisms to prevent abuse and fraud. She implemented single means testing and simplified the benefit system for social welfare programs, such as for retirees, widows, and persons eligible for marriage grants or children's allowances. She established family resource centers and regional centers to provide more effective and integrated delivery of social services. She also initiated pension and child-supplement reforms.

Coleiro Preca was serving as the minister of family and social solidarity in March 2014 when she was nominated for the post of president. Prime Minister Joseph Muscat assured the reluctant Coleiro Preca that he planned to expand the role of the presidency from a primarily ceremonial position to one that would incorporate the same type of work she had performed as a minister. In accepting the nomination, Coleiro Preca emphasized her intent to continue to serve the public and to work on social issues, particularly to combat poverty.

On April 1, 2014, every member of the House of Representatives approved Coleiro Preca's nomination for president. She was sworn in as president three days later, becoming the youngest president in Maltese history. In her inaugural speech, Coleiro Preca emphasized unity, inclusion, tolerance, and diversity and pledged to make them the hallmarks of her tenure.

As president, Coleiro Preca has earned the support of the opposition party and helped to promote unity within Malta's political system. Other accomplishments include establishing several organizations that allow her to continue the work she started as a minister. She founded the President's Foundation for the Wellbeing of Society, the National Forum of Trade Unions, and the National Cancer Platform. The purpose of these groups is to promote dialogue and collaboration among individuals and organizations with common goals and challenges. She also founded the Malta Community Chest Fund, which supports cancer patients, people with disabilities, and other people in need either financially or materially, and the Children's Hub, which promotes self-expression and empowerment of children as well as intergenerational communication. She continues to work on issues related to poverty, housing, and education, believing that they are essential to creating and supporting a just society and healthy economy.

IMPACT

Coleiro Preca has increased Malta's participation in the global community and worked with other countries to address issues related to migration, terrorism, sustainable development, social justice, and poverty. She has welcomed heads of states to Malta, visited other countries, and participated in several meetings with presidents of other European Union (EU) nations.

In September 2015, she attended the Arraiolos Group summit in Wartburg and Erfurt, Germany, the first time that Malta had been invited to a meeting. There she spoke about strategies to implement social justice and stressed that the well-being of countries was dependent on the well-being of its population and that to foster a country's well-being, it was necessary to eradicate poverty and provide quality education. She also explained that education was the best way to protect youth from susceptibility to extremist groups.

PERSONAL LIFE

Coleiro Preca is married to Edgar Preca. She has one daughter, Angie.

SUGGESTED READING

"Biography of the President of Malta, H.E. Marie-Louise Coleiro Preca." Presidents of Malta (2014-2019). www.gov.mt/en/Government/Government%20of%20Malta/Presidents%20of%20Malta/Pages/Marie-Louise-Coleiro-Preca.aspx. Accessed 31 Jan. 2020.

Coleiro Preca, Marie Louise. "Address by Her Excellency Mrs. Marie-Louise Coleiro Preca. President of Malta, the Palace, Valletta—Friday, 4th April 2014." Government of Malta, Department of Information. Dept. of Information, 4 Apr. 2014. foreignaffairs.gov.mt/en/Government/Press%20Releases/Pages/Address-by-Her-Excellency-Marie-Louise-Coleiro-Preca,-President-of-Malta,-on-the-Occassion-of-the-Exchange-of-the-New-Year'.aspx. Accessed 31 Jan. 2020.

"It's Official: Marie Louise Coleiro Preca Will Be Malta's Ninth President; PN Reaction." Malta Independent, 4 Mar. 2014. www.independent.com.mt/articles/2014-03-04/news/pm-opposition-leader-in-meeting-on-presidency-4146462720/. Accessed 31 Jan. 2020.

"Marie Louise Coleiro Preca Sworn in as Malta's Ninth President." Maltese Community Council of Victoria, Inc. MCCV, 5 Apr. 2014. mccv.org.au/news/marie-louise-coleiro-preca-sworn-in-as-maltas-ninth-president/. Accessed 31 Jan. 2020.

"Tearful Marie-Louise Coleiro Preca Bids Farewell to Parliament, Promises to Be Catalyst of Unity." Times of Malta, 1 Apr. 2014. timesofmalta.com/articles/view/tearful-marie-louise-coleiro-preca-bids-farewell-to-parliament-promises-to-be-catalyst-of-unity.513160. Accessed 31 Jan. 2020.

"Updated: Education Keeps Young Migrants from Becoming Victims of Extremism—President." Malta Independent, 22 Sept. 2015. Web. 10 Oct. 2015. www.

pressreader.com/malta/malta-independent/20150923/281539404756901. Accessed 31 Jan. 2020.

—*Barb Lightner*

Jodie Comer

Date of birth: March 11, 1993
Occupation: Actor

In September 2019, British actor Jodie Comer was stunned when she was announced as the recipient of that year's Emmy Award for Outstanding Lead Actress in a Drama Series for her performance as the assassin Villanelle in the BBC America series *Killing Eve*. For fans of the series, however, that recognition was both perhaps expected and highly deserved. Comer began starring in the role of Villanelle, the nemesis of British intelligence agent Eve Polastri (portrayed by Sandra Oh), upon the series' premiere in 2018, bringing depth and a highly engaging level of unpredictability to the complex and challenging character. "What I love about playing her is I am always encouraged to take risks," Comer told Yvonne Villarreal for the *Los Angeles Times* (6 Apr. 2019) about the character. "You don't want people to underestimate her or not believe her danger, but ultimately, people should have fun with her, they should live through her mischief and naughtiness and her, this may sound weird, but her kind of honesty."

Raised in England, Comer began studying acting at local workshops around the age of eleven and started appearing on television as a young teenager, though she would later take a self-deprecating approach when discussing her early work. "If I saw any of my performances from then, I'd want to punch myself in the face," she told Zoe Williams for the *Guardian* (20 Dec. 2018). Roles in projects such as the series *My Mad Fat Diary* (2013–15) and *Doctor Foster* (2015–17) and the miniseries *Thirteen* (2016), the latter of which earned Comer her first British Academy of Film and Television Arts (BAFTA) TV Award nomination, further established her as an actor to watch. It was the debut of *Killing Eve* in 2018, however, that truly represented her international breakthrough, leading not only to critical recognition but also further opportunities within and outside of the United Kingdom.

EARLY LIFE AND EDUCATION

Jodie Comer was born on March 11, 1993, in Liverpool, England. One of two children, she has a brother named Charlie. Her mother, Donna, worked in public transportation, while her father, Jimmy, was a sports massage therapist

Photo by Steve Granitz/WireImage

who worked for the Everton FC soccer team. She grew up in Childwall, a suburb of Liverpool and attended St. Julie's Catholic High School. As a student, she participated in school-sponsored theater productions.

Although Comer did not initially plan to pursue a career in acting, she displayed a penchant for performing from a young age. "I was always doing impressions—of [singer and television personality] Cilla Black, of the singer Anastacia," she recalled to Danielle Stein Chizzik for *Town & Country* (8 Apr. 2019). "I was very extroverted, very in touch with my emotions. I loved to talk, and I was probably a bit of a nuisance in the classroom because I never shut up." Comer began studying drama and dance locally when she was about eleven years old, attending local drama workshops. She first received substantial notice for her work when she participated in and won a monologue competition at a drama festival in Liverpool, impressing both judges and audience with an intensely emotional performance of a monologue about a real-life British tragedy.

EARLY ACTING CAREER

Around the age of twelve or thirteen, Comer obtained her first paying acting gig, performing in a radio play produced for the BBC. She eventually signed with an agent and began to appear in small roles on television, including in episodes of series such as *The Royal Today* (2008), *Holby City* (2010), and *Waterloo Road* (2010). In addition to acting on stage while in school, she at times performed in theater productions elsewhere, such as a 2010 production of the play *The Price of Everything* at England's Stephen

Joseph Theatre. Comer appeared in the television miniseries *Justice* in 2011 and continued to take on small roles on television over the next several years, including an appearance in the procedural series *Law & Order: UK* (2013).

Between 2013 and 2015, Comer costarred in the television series *My Mad Fat Diary*, playing the best friend of the series' protagonist. Although a supporting role, her part in the series represented a new level of success for Comer, who had previously appeared largely in single episodes of shows. "I look back on that, and it's so iconic," she told Rebecca Nicholson for the *Observer* (2 June 2019). "I remember getting off the phone, going, oh my God, I'm doing a whole six episodes! *This is so cool.* Filming in London. Whooaaa." *My Mad Fat Diary* received critical acclaim during its three seasons and drew widespread attention to the talents of its young cast members, including Comer.

Beginning in 2015, Comer appeared in a dramatically different sort of role in the television series *Doctor Foster*, playing the woman with whom the titular doctor's husband is having an affair. During the run of that series, in which she appeared between 2015 and 2017, Comer also starred in the 2016 miniseries *Thirteen*, about a young woman who has escaped from captivity after being abducted thirteen years before. In recognition of her performance, she was nominated for the BAFTA TV Award for Leading Actress. She likewise starred in the 2017 miniseries *The White Princess*, a work of historical fiction based on a novel by author Philippa Gregory. Although she appeared to be starring in back-to-back projects, Comer later noted in interviews that her work was far less in demand during that period than some observers might assume. "People get the impression that you're working all year round because things come out one after another on the television," she explained to Williams. "They don't realize that was filmed a year-and-a-half ago and you've been unemployed ever since."

KILLING EVE

A turning point in Comer's career came in 2018, when she began to star in the internationally acclaimed thriller series *Killing Eve*. Inspired by a series of novellas by writer Luke Jennings, the show was created for television by critically acclaimed showrunner Phoebe Waller-Bridge, who had previously won extensive praise for the series *Fleabag* and whom Comer had first met at a BAFTAs afterparty. Upon auditioning for the series, Comer impressed Waller-Bridge and her colleagues with both her own performance and her chemistry with actor Sandra Oh, who had been cast in the role of protagonist Eve Polastri. In the series, Polastri is an intelligence agent working in the United Kingdom who becomes aware of the threat posed by a mysterious assassin known as Villanelle, played by Comer. Over the course of the show's first season, the two characters become caught in a tangled relationship in which each is tracking the other.

For Comer, the role of Villanelle presented an opportunity to explore the craft of acting in a new way. "I had this impression that, to do good acting, everything is minimal, really whispered, less is more," she told Williams. "What I learned playing Villanelle is that there is acting that can be so full of life and bold that it is ridiculous at times." Following *Killing Eve*'s debut on BBC America in April 2018 and subsequent UK debut on BBC One in September of that year, both critics and viewers widely praised Comer's performance, citing both her characterization of Villanelle and the character's interactions with Polastri as some of the program's highlights. Although the critical and popular reception of the show's first season created dauntingly high expectations for its follow-up, Comer preferred to devote her attention to the task at hand, no matter how demanding. Oh has praised her costar's acting ability and work ethic, telling Stein Chizzik, "I'd be very hard-pressed to do some of the things Jodie does. She was born with an uncanny ear, and she just has tremendous innate talent." The second season of *Killing Eve* premiered in the United States and the United Kingdom in 2019, and the series was renewed for a third season in mid-2019. *Killing Eve* was then renewed for a fourth season in January 2020, prior to the premiere of season three.

CRITICAL ACCLAIM

Though widely praised for her performance as Villanelle, Comer was floored when she was awarded the Emmy Award for Outstanding Lead Actress in a Drama Series in 2019. "I was in a complete state of shock," she told Michael Schneider for *Variety* (Sept. 2019) about her unexpected win. "During the day I was strangely calm because I didn't think it would be me. But it also happened so fast. . . . You want to soak it up, not rush it, and take it all in." In addition to Comer's award, *Killing Eve* was nominated for several other trophies, including the award for Outstanding Drama Series, at the Emmys and likewise won several BAFTA TV Awards. This time, Comer took home the award for Leading Actress.

In addition to her continuing work on *Killing Eve*, Comer worked on a variety of other projects following her international breakthrough and in 2019 played a small role in the blockbuster film *Star Wars: The Rise of Skywalker*. That same year, she shot scenes, alongside costar Ryan Reynolds, for her largest major film role up to that point in the action feature *Free Guy*. "What I am really appreciating is that people now want to meet me and have conversations with me and see what I want to do and what films interest me," she told Villarreal. "I've never been in that position."

PERSONAL LIFE

When not filming elsewhere, Comer lives with her parents in Childwall. She has described herself as a private person and, unlike many other actors, rarely uses social media for purposes unrelated to work. "I want to work. I don't want to be *seen*," she explained to Nicholson. "If I'm going out, I want it to be with my closest mates in a flat, with my hair tied up, doing something really embarrassing. I want that to be in a private world."

SUGGESTED READING

Chizzik, Danielle Stein. "Jodie Comer Is Hollywood's Next Great Chameleon." *Town & Country*, 8 Apr. 2019, www.townandcountrymag.com/style/fashion-trends/a26932487/jodie-comer-killing-eve-interview-may-2019/. Accessed 17 Jan. 2020.

Desta, Yohana. "*Killing Eve*'s Jodie Comer Is Ready to Creep You Out Now." *Vanity Fair*, 13 Apr. 2018, www.vanityfair.com/hollywood/2018/04/killing-eve-jodie-comer-interview. Accessed 17 Jan. 2020.

McIntosh, Steven. "*Killing Eve*: Why Jodie Comer 'Confuses' People." *BBC News*, 4 June 2019, www.bbc.com/news/entertainment-arts-48341381. Accessed 17 Jan. 2020.

Nicholson, Rebecca. "Jodie Comer: 'Mum and Dad Took My Bafta on a Pub Crawl.'" *The Observer*, Guardian News & Media, 2 June 2019, www.theguardian.com/tv-and-radio/2019/jun/02/jodie-comer-everyones-favourite-psychopath-is-back-in-killing-eve-season-two. Accessed 17 Jan. 2020.

Schneider, Michael. "No One Was More Surprised by Jodie Comer's Emmy Win Than Jodie Comer." *Variety*, Sept. 2019, variety.com/2019/tv/features/jodie-comer-emmys-killing-eve-sandra-oh-1203347900/. Accessed 17 Jan. 2020.

Villarreal, Yvonne. "'Killing Eve's' Jodie Comer on Her Bewitching Killer Villanelle—and Bruce Springsteen." *Los Angeles Times*, 6 Apr. 2019, www.latimes.com/entertainment/tv/la-et-st-killing-eve-jodie-comer-20190406-story.html. Accessed 17 Jan. 2020.

Williams, Zoe. "The Chic Assassin: Jodie Comer on Playing *Killing Eve*'s Villanelle." *The Guardian*, 20 Dec. 2018, www.theguardian.com/tv-and-radio/2018/dec/20/the-chic-assassin-jodie-comer-on-playing-killing-eves-villanelle. Accessed 17 Jan. 2020.

SELECTED WORKS

My Mad Fat Diary, 2013–15; *Doctor Foster*, 2015–17; *Thirteen*, 2016; *The White Princess*, 2017; *Killing Eve*, 2018–

—Joy Crelin

Christopher Comstock

Date of birth: May 19, 1992
Occupation: Musician

The names and faces of most chart-topping musicians may be intrinsically linked to their popular work, but musician Christopher Comstock is undoubtedly an exception. Though an active member of the electronic dance music (EDM) community since as early as 2011, Comstock is best known not as himself but as the internationally popular EDM artist Marshmello, a mysterious figure known for hiding his face under his signature marshmallow-shaped mask. That anonymity not only drew attention to the artist, sparking speculation about his true identity since his emergence in EDM circles around 2015, but also granted Comstock the freedom to experiment with his music in ways never before possible while largely avoiding interviews and scrutiny of his personal life. "I don't take my helmet off because I don't want or need fame," he explained on the social network Twitter, as quoted by Natalie Robehmed for *Forbes* (14 Nov. 2017). "I'm genuinely trying to create something positive for people to connect with." With the albums *Joytime* (2016), *Joytime II* (2018), and *Joytime III* (2019) and standalone singles featuring artists such as Selena Gomez, Logic, and Bastille, Comstock-as-Marshmello has succeeded in doing just that, developing a devoted fan base and a reputation for putting on energetic and positive live shows.

Photo by Stefan Brending via Wikimedia Commons

EARLY LIFE AND CAREER

Comstock was born on May 19, 1992, and grew up around Philadelphia, Pennsylvania. He began attending St. Joseph's University in Pennsylvania in 2010. A longtime fan of EDM, he was already experimenting with making music in that genre during his college years. "As soon as EDM started getting bigger, before it blew up, I realized I wanted to try to make the music and started DJing parties. At the time it wasn't the 'cool' thing to do yet," he recalled to *EDM Sauce* (2 Oct. 2013). "EDM took off and I started my mashups and I ended up being really good at it. Ever since then I fell in love with it."

Under the name Dotcom, Comstock released a variety of tracks online, including numerous mashups—songs consisting of two or more existing songs that have been edited together and transformed into a new work. He also released dubstep remixes as well as original tracks, some of which went on to be featured in EDM-focused radio programs on stations such as BBC Radio 1. He continued to release music under the Dotcom name on a regular basis through 2015 and would sporadically return to that alias over the subsequent years, offering up new Dotcom songs in 2016 and 2019.

BECOMING MARSHMELLO

While still releasing music as Dotcom, Comstock met Moe Shalizi, an up-and-coming manager of EDM musicians who soon became Comstock's manager as well. Although Comstock had found some success in the EDM world as Dotcom, the pair worked together to develop a new identity for the musician, one that would give him a fresh start and enable him to reach a far wider audience. "For us it was, how do you create a brand that is accessible to everybody, that everyone can be and relate to?" Shalizi told Zack O'Malley Greenburg for *Forbes* (7 Nov. 2018). "The concept we had in mind . . . was, How do you create a universal character?" Working in collaboration with Shalizi, Comstock developed the identity of Marshmello, an EDM artist whose true identity would be kept secret from the public and whose face would be hidden by a distinctive and highly brandable marshmallow-shaped mask.

Over the next several years, Marshmello's popularity and financial success, as well as the allure of his mysterious identity, prompted widespread discussion among EDM fans and publications regarding the human being behind the mask. Although some observers suggested that Marshmello might be one or more EDM artists who had already achieved worldwide fame, those intrigued by the mystery soon came to focus on Comstock, based on a variety of clues, including similar tattoos visible in photographs of both Comstock and Marshmello, the absence of Dotcom while Marshmello was performing, and

an interview with the established EDM artist Skrillex in which Skrillex referred to Marshmello as "Chris." A conclusive reveal of Marshmello's identity came in 2017, when *Forbes* entertainment journalist Robehmed reported that a major music-licensing database returned the same song results for the names Marshmello and Christopher Comstock. *Forbes* later confirmed Marshmello's age and identity prior to his inclusion in the publication's 30 Under 30 list for music in 2018.

INDEPENDENT ARTIST

Just as he had as Dotcom, Comstock made significant use of the internet to promote his early work as Marshmello, releasing tracks for free through streaming services such as SoundCloud. In addition to remixes of songs by popular EDM artists, he released a variety of original works, including the 2015 song "WaVeZ." As Marshmello gained popularity online, the artist began touring as well, establishing a reputation for energetic and entertaining live shows. He gained further attention in 2016 for a publicity initiative in which he rented a billboard that was strategically placed outside the music festival Coachella, at which he was not a performer. Featuring a photograph of Marshmello as well as text reading, "I'm working hard now so my future daughter doesn't have to sell detox tea on her social media," as quoted by Tim Ingham for *Music Business Worldwide* (19 Mar. 2019), the billboard went viral among Coachella attendees and their social-media followers, further increasing recognition of Marshmello among young people.

Although Marshmello's early success as an artist won him attention from mainstream record labels as well as EDM listeners, he opted not to sign with any of those companies, believing that none would be a good fit for him. "They wanted to sign us just to sign us," he explained to Greenburg. Rather than sign a record deal, Marshmello remained an independent artist who retained his artistic freedom as well as ownership of his songs and master recordings. He likewise continued to work closely with his manager, Shalizi, who in 2018 left his previous employer, Red Light Management, to found an independent management company, the Shalizi Group.

MAINSTREAM SUCCESS

A multi-instrumentalist, Comstock plays piano, guitar, and drums in addition to creating electronic music. He has contributed his own vocals to Marshmello songs such as "Alone" and "You & Me," often using vocal-manipulation technology both to protect his identity and to meet the sonic needs of particular songs. Having first made a name for himself with standalone tracks released online, Marshmello released his first full-length album, *Joytime*, in 2016. The album reached the number-five position on the Billboard US Dance chart, and several individual songs from the album appeared on the dance songs chart, including the single "Keep It Mello," which featured artist Omar LinX, and the songs "Summer" and "Find Me." His second album, 2018's *Joytime II*, proved an even greater success, peaking at number one on Billboard US Dance.

Although Marshmello received significant attention for his albums and solo songs, he reached a broader audience through a series of collaborations with popular artists, including the 2017 single "Danger," which featured the hip-hop group Migos and was included on the soundtrack to the film *Bright*. The 2017 song "Silence," featuring Khalid, not only topped the dance singles chart but also hit number thirty on the Billboard Hot 100 following its release as a standalone single. Marshmello followed that track with "Wolves," a collaboration with singer Selena Gomez that reached number twenty on the Hot 100 chart. For Marshmello, the opportunity to work with Gomez—a popular solo artist and a previous collaborator with EDM musicians such as Kygo and Zedd—was a particularly exciting one. "I met her at a party . . . and she was like, 'I'm a huge fan, I'm excited for our song,'" he told Matt Medved for *Billboard* (22 Mar. 2018). "And I'm freaking out, like, 'Whoa, did Selena Gomez just say that?'" In addition to being released as a single, "Wolves" was later included as a bonus track on Gomez's 2020 album, *Rare*.

Having demonstrated his crossover appeal through his collaborations with pop and hip-hop artists—which also included the singles "Friends," featuring British singer Anne-Marie; "Happier," featuring British band Bastille; "Everyday," featuring the rapper Logic; and "Here with Me," featuring the Scottish band Chvrches—Marshmello further displayed his success among both EDM fans and general pop-music audiences in 2019 with the release of *Joytime III*, his third studio album. In addition to reaching the number-one position on the Billboard US Dance chart, *Joytime III* reached as high as number fifty on the Billboard 200 chart, his highest position on that chart to date. Marshmello's work to cultivate a broad audience also paid off financially: in late 2018, Forbes reported that the artist had earned an estimated $44 million over the previous two years.

ONLINE PRESENCE

Having long made use of the Internet as a means of distribution and promotion, Comstock continued to promote his work as Marshmello online through often-unconventional means in the years following his debut under that name. Such efforts included a cooking series titled *Cooking with Marshmello*, posted to the video-sharing service YouTube, which he developed in collaboration with Shalizi. "The typical musician can only upload so much content to YouTube, right? You can do a music video, a cover, and that's kind of it. So what else do you put up on your channel?" Shalizi told Ingham about their strategy. "Marshmello is a costume; it's a character. So we have the luxury of being able to do more than other artists. We started this cooking show, and the whole idea behind it was to create a deeper cultural connection with our global audience." The series specifically worked to promote that cultural connection by featuring dishes from around the world, including Nigerian jollof rice, Argentinian churrasco, and Indian pani puri.

Marshmello has likewise expanded the reach of his music and brand through outreach to the video-gaming community, including through his *Gaming with Marshmello* series of YouTube videos. In February of 2019, the artist performed a live virtual concert within the popular video game *Fortnite*, becoming the first artist ever to do so. "We made history today!" he wrote on Twitter following the event, as quoted by Riley Little for *ScreenRant* (2 Feb. 2019). "The first ever live virtual concert inside of @fortnite with millions of people in attendance. So insane, thank you [*Fortnite* creator Epic Games] and everyone who made this possible!"

PERSONAL LIFE

When not performing elsewhere, Comstock lives in Los Angeles.

SUGGESTED READING

Comstock, Christopher. "Interview with Dotcom [EDM Sauce Exclusive]." *EDM Sauce*, 2 Oct. 2013, www.edmsauce.com/2013/10/02/interview-with-dotcom/. Accessed 9 Feb. 2020.

Greenburg, Zack O'Malley. "Forbes 30 Under 30 Cover Story: How Marshmello Became a $44 Million DJ." *Forbes*, 7 Nov. 2018, www.forbes.com/sites/zackomalleygreenburg/2018/11/07/forbes-30-under-30-cover-story-how-marshmello-became-a-44-million-dj/#252ed96d618b. Accessed 9 Feb. 2020.

Ingham, Tim. "Masterminding Marshmello: 'How Do We Turn This into the Next Disney?'" *Music Business Worldwide*, 19 Mar. 2019, www.musicbusinessworldwide.com/masterminding-marshmello-how-do-we-turn-this-into-the-next-disney/. Accessed 9 Feb. 2020.

Little, Riley. "Fortnite Players Are Losing Their Minds over In-Game Marshmello Concert." *ScreenRant*, 2 Feb. 2019, screenrant.com/fortnite-marshmello-concert-epic-games/. Accessed 9 Feb. 2020.

Medved, Matt. "How Marshmello and Manager Moe Shalizi Built Dance Music's Most

Irresistible Brand." *Billboard*, 22 Mar. 2018, www.billboard.com/articles/news/magazine-feature/8255794/marshmello-interview-billboard-dance-music-cover-story-2018. Accessed 9 Feb. 2020.

Robehmed, Natalie. "Unmasking Marshmello: The Real Identity of the $21 Million DJ." *Forbes*, 14 Nov. 2017, www.forbes.com/sites/natalierobehmed/2017/11/14/unmasking-marshmello-the-real-identity-of-the-21-million-dj/#6e8b883d4ffe. Accessed 9 Feb. 2020.

Shotwell, James. "Marshmello: One Crazy Night with Music's Silent Sensation." *Substream Magazine*, 24 Apr. 2018, substreammagazine.com/2018/04/marshmello-one-crazy-night-with-musics-silent-sensation/. Accessed 9 Feb. 2020.

SELECTED WORKS

Joytime, 2016; *Joytime II*, 2018; *Joytime III*, 2019

—*Joy Crelin*

Giuseppe Conte

Date of birth: August 8, 1964
Occupation: Politician and jurist

Giuseppe Conte was sworn in as Italy's prime minister in June 2018. Conte, a civil law professor at the University of Florence, was not affiliated with any political party, but perhaps more surprisingly, had no previous government experience. Conte's appointment was the result of an uneasy alliance between two political parties in Italy. The populist Five Star Movement and the nationalist League offered Conte's name to Italian president Sergio Mattarella for approval because Conte was the only person on whom both parties could agree. As prime minister, Conte, a verbose technocrat, was tasked with leading this divisive coalition, implementing harsh anti-immigration measures and advocating for improved public services. His first year in office was fraught with political infighting, and in August 2019, Matteo Salvini, the leader of the anti-immigrant League party and Conte's deputy prime minister, sought a no-confidence vote in Conte, aiming to usurp the coalition's political power and install himself as prime minister. Up until that point, Conte, a political novice who was often eclipsed by the more charismatic Salvini, had been seen as a puppet of the two parties that had elevated him. But in a remarkable moment of political gamesmanship, Conte tendered his resignation, upbraiding Salvini in a forceful parliamentary address. In September, Conte, who ultimately kept his job, brokered a new coalition, uniting the Five Star Movement and Italy's Democratic Party, to suppress Salvini's power grab.

EARLY LIFE AND EDUCATION

Conte was born on August 8, 1964, in a small village called Volturara Appula in the southern region of Puglia. His father, Nicola, was a local government administrator; his mother, Lilliana Roberti, worked as an elementary school teacher. A childhood friend told Angela Giuffrida for the *Guardian* (23 May 2018) that Conte "studied hard at school and was very reserved," adding, "He has always been very elegant, even at school he was impeccably dressed." Conte's dapper taste remained one of his most distinctive characteristics. Conte earned a degree from Rome's Sapienza University in 1988. He opened a law practice in Rome and later began teaching civil law at the University of Florence.

After his appointment as prime minister, Conte was accused of inflating his résumé, overstating his relationship to schools like New York University (NYU). When contacted about Conte's claim that he had "perfected and updated his studies" at NYU every summer between 2008 and 2012, NYU spokespeople told multiple outlets that while there is no official record of Conte's having attended the school, he was granted permission to conduct research at the NYU law library. Similarly, Conte claimed to have taught at the University of Malta in the summer of 1997; the university has no record of Conte's time there, though they concede he may have been a lecturer through the now defunct Foundation for International Studies (FIS), a separate

Photo by Massimo Di Vita/Archivio Massimo Di Vita/Mondadori Portfolio via Getty Images

entity. There is also no evidence to prove that Conte, as he claimed, conducted research at the Sorbonne in Paris in 2000, or Yale University in 1992. Conte also claimed to have conducted research in affiliation with Villa Nazareth, a Roman cultural institution, at Duquesne University in Pittsburgh the same year; Duquesne said Conte did research there but was not enrolled as a student.

STAMINA FOUNDATION CASE

In 2013, Conte represented the family of a four-year-old girl named Sofia de Barros, who was suffering from metachromatic leukodystrophy, an incurable neurodegenerative disease. De Barros, who died in 2017, was part of a group of terminally ill patients who had undergone an experimental stem cell treatment through the Stamina Foundation, founded by Davide Vannoni, an entrepreneur with no medical training. After an investigation, the treatment was discontinued and the Stamina Foundation was banned. De Barros's family sued to continue their daughter's treatment, even though there was no scientific evidence for its effectiveness. The ensuing legal battle was emotionally fraught and highly publicized. Conte won the case. De Barros was allowed to continue her treatment, and the Health Ministry issued an official decree allowing any patient who had been undergoing the treatment to continue it. A group of European scientists wrote a letter denouncing the decree. They argued that Stamina's therapies were potentially dangerous and a scam. They accused Italy's health minister, Renato Balduzzi, as quoted by Catherine Hornby for *Reuters* (28 Mar. 2013), of setting a "dangerous precedent" regarding patient safety and medical licensing criteria. The Stamina Foundation was eventually shuttered, and Vannoni, who died in 2019, was convicted of conspiracy and fraud.

Conte's support for the de Barros family and the Stamina treatments was mirrored by a rising populist political party called the Five Star Movement, with which Conte would soon become involved.

THE FIVE STAR MOVEMENT

The Five Star Movement was founded by comedian Beppe Grillo in 2009 as a response to the 2008 financial crisis and the corruption of the former prime minister Silvio Berlusconi's government. The populist party identifies as anti-corruption and antiestablishment, rather than left-wing or right-wing. For instance, the "five stars" represent five left-leaning policy goals: access to public water, public transportation, sustainable development, internet access, and environmentalism. But the Five Star Movement also supports some traditionally right-wing policies too, expressing skepticism about the European Union (EU) and supporting action against illegal immigration. Growing support for the party was solidified in the Italian general election in March 2018. The Five Star Movement and the right-wing League parties emerged with the most support, though neither won a clear majority.

APPOINTMENT AS PRIME MINISTER OF ITALY

After the election, the leader of the Five Star Movement, Luigi Di Maio, and the leader of the League, Matteo Salvini, agreed to form a coalition government, widely expected to be populist and antiestablishment. The League (Lega, formerly known as the Northern League or Lega Nord) under Salvini was considerably farther to the right than the Five Star Movement, with a strong anti-immigrant platform. After two months of fraught negotiations, Di Maio and Salvini offered Conte's name as an inoffensive compromise nominee for prime minister for President Sergio Mattarella's approval. Di Maio, who had offered Conte as a potential public administration minister on the campaign trail, praised Conte, whom he met in 2013 and who was little known to the Italian public. Di Maio described him, as quoted by Jason Horowitz in the *New York Times* (21 May 2018), as a "professional of the highest level," "a self-made man," and a "tough guy." Conte used different terminology to describe himself to the press: "I will be the defense attorney for all Italians," he said, as quoted by *CNN* (1 June 2018). He took office on June 1, 2018.

GOVERNMENT COLLAPSE

Though Mattarella ultimately approved Conte's appointment, he had reportedly expressed serious reservations about Conte's ability to manage the volatile coalition, which came to power on promises to overturn politics as usual. Reports about Conte's inflated résumé did little to instill confidence, nor did reports early in his tenure that Conte was planning to take an English proficiency exam in preparation for a teaching position at a Rome university. Conte was tasked with mediating between the two main coalition partners, each led by a man who had expressed desire to serve in the role of prime minister himself, and each of whom served as deputy prime ministers under Conte. In June, Salvini, who also served in the cabinet as minister of the interior, announced plans to close all Italian ports to ships carrying migrants, and duly turned away a rescue ship carrying more than six hundred migrants. Conte supported the decision.

In July, Conte visited the White House, where President Trump, as quoted by David M. Herszenhorn in *Politico* (30 July 2018), congratulated Conte on his "tremendous victory"—although Conte was appointed, not elected—and praised Conte's hardline anti-immigrant stance.

Conte did his best to implement the rest of the coalition's agenda. In defiance of the rest of the EU, he demanded a review of Italy's sanctions against Russia, while the Five Star–led Health Ministry sought to loosen laws making vaccines mandatory for children.

Over the course of Conte's first year as prime minister, animosity between the Five Star Movement and the League intensified and Salvini's popularity grew. According to Horowitz, writing for the *New York Times* (29 Aug. 2019), Conte was often "overshadowed" by his fiercely conservative deputy. In the May 2019 election for the European Parliament, the League won twice as many seats as the Five Star Movement for the Italian delegation, a huge gain for Salvini's party. In June, Conte called a press conference in which he threatened to resign if the warring factions of his coalition did not find a way to work together. Horowitz and Elisabetta Povoledo, writing for the *New York Times* (3 June 2019), described the news conference as "remarkable," particularly for Conte, who was "widely considered a puppet of his deputy prime ministers," Di Maio and Salvini. "I'm not here just to scrape by or drift," Conte said of his role, as quoted by Horowitz and Povoledo. "I can and want to do more."

CONTE II

In August, Salvini sought to bring a no-confidence vote against Conte, in hopes of collapsing the coalition government and bringing snap elections that would install him as prime minister. On August 20, Conte frustrated this plan by offering his resignation. In a scorching address to Parliament, Conte—speaking with Salvini and Di Maio seated on either side of him—accused Salvini of "political opportunism." By placing his own interests above those of the country, Conte said, as quoted by Horowitz in the *New York Times* (20 Aug. 2019), Salvini had thrust the country into a "vortex of political uncertainty and financial instability." In another article for the *New York Times* (29 Aug. 2019), Horowitz described the speech as "filled with previously unseen flashes of gravitas and steel." If it was, as Horowitz suggested, a "last-ditch audition" for the leadership role that Conte had been shirking, he won it.

Mattarella asked Conte to form a new government, which he did by freezing out Salvini and the League, turning instead to the center-left Democratic Party. The unlikely coalition, united in their opposition to Salvini and dubbed Conte II by the Italian media, received a vote of confidence from Parliament in September. The government's aims were very different from those espoused by the previous coalition. Conte promised to seek less punitive anti-immigration measures and strengthen Italy's role in the EU,

while focusing on education and sustainability initiatives. "We must recover sobriety and rigor so that our citizens can see renewed confidence in our institutions," he said upon resuming power, as quoted by the *New York Times* (11 Sept. 2019).

PERSONAL LIFE

Conte is separated from his wife. They have a young son.

SUGGESTED READING

Borghese, Livia, Gianluca Mezzofiore, and Barbie Latza Nadeau. "Giuseppe Conte: The Political Unknown Who Will Lead Italy." *CNN*, 1 June 2018, www.cnn.com/2018/05/23/europe/italy-giuseppe-conte-resume-ntl/index.html. Accessed 17 Dec. 2019.

Giuffrida, Angela. "'They Throw Mud': New PM Facing Up to Messy World of Italian Politics." *The Guardian*, 23 May 2018, www.theguardian.com/world/2018/may/23/parents-of-lawyer-nominated-as-italys-pm-worry-about-political-mudslinging. Accessed 17 Dec. 2019.

Horowitz, Jason. "How Giuseppe Conte of Italy Went from Irrelevant to Irreplaceable." *The New York Times*, 29 Aug. 2019, www.nytimes.com/2019/08/29/world/europe/italy-conte-government-salvini.html. Accessed 17 Dec. 2019.

———. "Italy's Government Collapses, Turning Chaos into Crisis." *The New York Times*, 20 Aug. 2019, www.nytimes.com/2019/08/20/world/europe/italy-pm-giuseppe-conte-resign.html. Accessed 17 Dec. 2019.

———. "Italy's Populists Offer Giuseppe Conte for Prime Minister; N.Y.U. Claim in Question." *The New York Times*, 21 May 2018, www.nytimes.com/2018/05/21/world/europe/italy-government-giuseppe-conte-di-maio.html. Accessed 17 Dec. 2019.

Horowitz, Jason, and Elisabetta Povoledo. "Italy's Prime Minister Delivers Ultimatum to Warring Coalition Partners." *The New York Times*, 3 June 2019, www.nytimes.com/2019/06/03/world/europe/giuseppe-conte-matteo-salvini-italy.html. Accessed 17 Dec. 2019.

"In Italy, a Sharp Turn Back to the Center." *The New York Times*, 11 Sept. 2019, www.nytimes.com/2019/09/11/opinion/giuseppe-conte-italy.html. Accessed 17 Dec. 2019.

—*Molly Hagan*

Kizzmekia Corbett

Date of birth: January 26, 1986
Occupation: Immunologist

As a scientist working in vaccine development for infectious respiratory diseases, National Institutes of Health (NIH) researcher Kizzmekia Corbett was long aware that were a pandemic to begin, her already important work would take on a new degree of urgency. That moment came in early 2020, when the newly identified SARS-CoV-2 virus and COVID-19, the respiratory disease it causes, began to spread throughout the world. "We predicted pandemics, but the extent to which this one is happening is mind-blowing," Corbett told Kate Murphy for the *News & Observer* (26 June 2020). "It's surreal to be in the middle of it and watching it all play out." As head of a team of researchers within the NIH's Vaccine Research Center, Corbett led the group's efforts to develop a safe and effective vaccine to guard against the virus—efforts that began in January 2020, long before the true extent of the coronavirus pandemic became known.

A full-time researcher at the NIH since 2014, Corbett spent much of her time in college and in her early career effectively preparing to combat a novel coronavirus pandemic like the one in 2020. A graduate of the University of Maryland, Baltimore County, and the University of North Carolina at Chapel Hill, she honed her laboratory skills through summer programs at the NIH, during which she studied viruses such as the respiratory syncytial virus, and immersed herself further in the field of vaccine development through her graduate research into the dengue virus. Combined with her research into coronaviruses after arriving at the NIH, her graduate experience made Corbett one of the most qualified researchers to the task of developing a vaccine amid a global health emergency. Even if the coronavirus pandemic were immediately resolved, however, Corbett's work in vaccine development would undoubtedly continue. "There will always be more questions," she once told the website *UNC Healthtalk* (14 Feb. 2014). "That's what science is; question after question. There will always be another one to answer."

EARLY LIFE AND EDUCATION

Kizzmekia Shanta Corbett was born on January 26, 1986, in Hurdle Mills, North Carolina. She spent her early years in Hurdle Mills before moving with her family (her mother, stepfather and six siblings) to the nearby town of Hillsborough. As a child, Corbett displayed a high level of curiosity and scientific inquisitiveness and was known for seeking out answers to the questions she had. In addition to taking advanced classes

Photo by Nehrams2020 via Wikimedia Commons

at school, Corbett had the opportunity to work in a science laboratory at the University of North Carolina (UNC) as a teenager through the summer program Project SEED (Summer Experiences for the Economically Disadvantaged), run by the American Chemical Society (ACS). "Our parents were adamant that if we had jobs in the summer, that they much be educational, and so, for whatever reason, I chose to get a job in a laboratory," she recalled to Sandra Jordan for the *St. Louis American* (18 May 2020) about that key early experience. Corbett attended Orange High School in Hillsborough, from which she graduated in 2004.

After high school, Corbett enrolled in the University of Maryland, Baltimore County (UMBC), where she was part of the university's Meyerhoff Scholars Program and pursued a double major in biological sciences and sociology. In addition to furthering her education in the classroom, she gained valuable skills and experiences through a variety of practical programs, including a summer internship in a lab at the Stony Brook School of Health Technology and Management at Stony Brook University and a period spent working as a laboratory technician at the University of Maryland School of Nursing. Perhaps the most influential of those experiences, however, was her work as biological sciences trainee at the NIH through the government research agency's Undergraduate Scholarship Program. Through that program, administered by the NIH Office of Intramural Training and Education, Corbett was able to spend her summers working at the NIH, where she helped conduct research related to vaccines. Much of her research during that period concerned the respiratory syncytial virus, a virus that, though largely harmless for much of the population, can severely harm infants or elderly people who contract it. Corbett was intrigued by vaccines' lack of effectiveness in addressing respiratory syncytial virus, and her experience researching the virus gave her "a passion for vaccine development, specifically for viruses that evade vaccine responses," she later told *MEDdebate* (21 Mar. 2020). Corbett earned her bachelor's degree from UMBC in 2008.

GRADUATE RESEARCH

Intent upon pursuing further studies leading toward a career in vaccine development, Corbett applied to multiple graduate schools but was drawn to the UNC at Chapel Hill, an institution she found to be particularly supportive of its graduate students. "It was really organized," she told *UNC Healthtalk*. "UNC clearly cares about students; they were more interested in what they could do for students to further our careers than they were about what we could bring to their research factories." After enrolling in UNC, Corbett began her graduate research under the supervision of professor and laboratory researcher Aravinda de Silva. De Silva specialized in the dengue virus, the virus responsible for the tropical disease dengue fever. Corbett was also active in student government and the school's Science Policy Advocacy Group during her time at UNC.

Working alongside de Silva and various colleagues, Corbett devoted much of her time at UNC to the study of dengue. She was particularly focused on the efforts to prevent human beings from contracting it. Transmitted by mosquitos, the dengue virus has a number of characteristics that make developing vaccines for it a particularly tricky prospect. For example, antibody responses to the virus can vary widely from person to person. "Not understanding these issues is one reason why vaccine trials have failed in the past," Corbett explained to *UNC Healthtalk*. "We need to know what happens naturally in people when a virus infects someone." For her dissertation, titled "Dissecting Human Antibody Responses to Dengue Virus Infection," Corbett traveled to Sri Lanka on a research fellowship and studied samples taken from a group of children who had been infected with dengue, analyzing their immune systems' antibody response to the virus. In addition to writing her dissertation, she coauthored several papers during her time at UNC and following her graduation published the paper "Preexisting Neutralizing Antibody Responses Distinguish Clinically Inapparent and Apparent Dengue Virus Infections in a Sri Lankan Pediatric Cohort" (2015), for which she received first author credit, in the *Journal of Infectious Diseases*. Corbett earned her doctorate

in microbiology and immunology from the UNC School of Medicine in 2014.

NATIONAL INSTITUTES OF HEALTH

In October 2014, Corbett returned to the NIH, this time joining the Vaccine Research Center (VRC) within the National Institute of Allergies and Infectious Diseases (NAID) as a research fellow. Working under deputy director Barney Graham, she joined a team that specialized in researching and developing vaccines for respiratory viruses. Corbett specifically studied coronaviruses, viruses that cause a number of respiratory diseases in humans, ranging from the common cold to the far more deadly Severe Acute Respiratory Syndrome (SARS), first identified in 2003, and Middle East Respiratory Syndrome (MERS), first identified in 2013. Over the next several years, Corbet coauthored a variety of papers on coronaviruses and contributed substantially to the VRC's efforts to respond to such viruses.

For Corbett, the NIH was the ideal workplace. "I fell in love with the NIH because of just the vast amount of different things that are happening on campus, not just science," she said in an interview for the NIH podcast *Speaking of Science* (21 May 2020), going on to reference the art and music programs held there. "The NIH was from my perspective at that time, the place to be when it came to science," she explained. Working within the NIH likewise enabled Corbett to work on cutting-edge public-health research.

SARS-COV-2 AND COVID-19

In late 2019, Corbett's team at the VRC was completing its typical tasks, working on continuing research within the field of vaccine development. "We were doing assays, really looking at specific details about the immune response that we would hypothetically like to elicit from a vaccine perspective," she recalled in her interview for *Speaking of Science*. Quickly, however, the team's priorities changed. In December 2019, a novel coronavirus was detected in Wuhan, China. The virus was soon designated severe acute respiratory syndrome coronavirus 2 (SARS-CoV-2), while the respiratory disease it caused became known as COVID-19. In a matter of months, SARS-CoV-2 spread around the world, and in March 2020, the World Health Organization (WHO) declared that the outbreak had officially become a pandemic.

For Corbett and her colleagues, who had previously studied respiratory diseases such as SARS and MERS, the timing of the outbreak and subsequent pandemic was a surprise, but the existence of an outbreak and pandemic was less of one. "SARS and MERS, two coronaviruses, had already caused massive outbreaks,"

Corbett told Janell Ross for *NBC* (12 Apr. 2020). "And these big, challenging questions remained, along with the fact that it was clear that it could happen again. It was looming out there and just a matter of time." In light of the major public-health threat that the novel coronavirus presented, Corbett and her colleagues shifted their focus to developing a vaccine, building upon their previous work and expertise related to earlier coronaviruses.

DEVELOPING A VACCINE

As scientific lead for the VRC's coronavirus vaccine program, Corbett was responsible for overseeing the center's response to the crisis. Although the virus was not identified in the United States until late January 2020, and did not begin spreading through community transmission until the following month, she emphasized the importance of developing a vaccine for the virus as early as possible. "In pandemic preparedness, our job as vaccinologists, enviro-immunologists, immunologists, epidemiologists, is to plan ahead of time, so that we had a vaccine ready to go, in case there was a pandemic like there is now," she later told Jordan. NIH researchers began their efforts to develop a vaccine in January 2020, working in conjunction with the company Moderna. In March of that year they began a phase-one clinical trial for a vaccine, becoming the first research group in the world to do so.

Although efforts to prevent the spread of the novel coronavirus through social distancing, the wearing of masks, and the washing and sanitizing of hands and surfaces proved somewhat successful throughout the first half of 2020, the development of a vaccine remained a priority throughout the world, as a vaccine would prevent the virus from taking hold within the human body. "Viruses have surface proteins that solely function to help the virus to bind to a human cell. So that initial step, the attachment of the viral protein to a human cell is what is the first step at facilitating infection," Corbett explained in her interview for *Speaking of Science*. "From a vaccine development standpoint, if you can stop that initial step in some form, then you can essentially stop infection and then that means you can stop transmission." The initial trial of the NIH vaccine proved promising, and further clinical trials to assess the safety and efficacy of the proposed vaccine continued throughout mid-2020.

PERSONAL LIFE

Corbett lives in Maryland.

SUGGESTED READING

"Corbett Continues Quest for Dengue Fever Vaccine." *UNC Healthtalk*, 14 Feb. 2014, healthtalk.unchealthcare.org/ kizzy-goes-to-sri-lanka. Accessed 13 July 2020.

Corbett, Kizzmekia. "Dr. Kizzmekia Corbett— The Novel Coronavirus Vaccine." *Speaking of Science*, 21 May 2020, irp.nih.gov/podcast/2020/05/dr-kizzmekia-corbett-the-novel-coronavirus-vaccine. Accessed 13 July 2020.

———. "*MEDdebate* Interviews Dr. Kizzmekia Corbett, the Viral Immunologist Leading the Race to Develop a Covid-19 Vaccine." *MEDdebate*, 21 Mar. 2020, www.meddebate.com/2841. Accessed 13 July 2020.

Fears, Darryl. "Kizzmekia Corbett Spent Her Life Preparing for This Moment. Can She Create the Vaccine to End a Pandemic?" *The Washington Post*, 6 May 2020, www.washingtonpost.com/climate-environment/2020/05/06/kizzmekia-corbett-vaccine-coronavirus. Accessed 13 July 2020.

Jordan, Sandra. "COVID-19 Vaccine Researcher Kizzmekia Corbett Tells STEM Students to Stay Focused, Seek Mentors, Let Their Work Address the Haters." *The St. Louis American*, 18 May 2020, www.stlamerican.com/news/local_news/covid-19-vaccine-researcher-kizzmekia-corbett-tells-stem-students-to-stay-focused-seek-mentors-let/article_d152046e-994d-11ea-81bf-070ad512581c.html. Accessed 13 July 2020.

Murphy, Kate. "This Young, Black, Female Scientist from NC Leads Efforts to Find a COVID-19 Vaccine." *News & Observer*, 26 June 2020, www.newsobserver.com/news/local/article243758962.html. Accessed 13 July 2020.

Ross, Janell. "Working on Coronavirus Vaccine Trials, Kizzmekia Corbett Is 'Not Your Average' Scientist." *NBC News*, 12 Apr. 2020, www.nbcnews.com/news/nbcblk/scientist-kizzmekia-corbett-leads-way-covid-19-vaccine-trials-dedication-n1181626. Accessed 13 July 2020.

—*Joy Crelin*

William Cordova

Date of birth: 1971
Occupation: Artist

William Cordova has become highly renowned for employing a wide variety media—photography, film, painting, sculpture, illustration, to name a few—to examine the ways in which objects maintain meaning for culturally diverse communities and within his own Peruvian community. His work began receiving notice in the art world beginning in the early 2000s and has subsequently been displayed in numerous group exhibitions at international museums

Photo by Jmrykim via Wikimedia Commons

and galleries as well as over two dozen solo exhibitions.

Dividing his time between Peru, South Florida, and New York, the Peruvian American has come to be considered among the best artists to demonstrate the power of cultural flux and change both in an individual and in society. On its website, the contemporary art gallery Sikkema Jenkins & Co. noted: "Utilizing a variety of materials, including found and discarded objects, feathers, collage, and other reclaimed detritus, Cordova's multimedia practice weaves coded statements on contemporary social systems and economies within the personal history of objects."

EARLY LIFE AND EDUCATION

William Cordova was born in Lima, Peru, in 1971. His family immigrated to the United States around 1977, settling in Miami, Florida. However, the move was not permanent, and young William found himself moving often. This lack of permanency led him to find preciousness in objects, usually found items, but also photographs. "Photographs were the only things that I could grasp as a child. They were the only things that we brought to the US," he explained in an interview with Stacy Lynn Waddell for *Daylight* (1 Oct. 2012). "They were the only things that we could afford." He noted that the family could not afford toys, so he photographed them as well as clothes and other photos.

Cordova has recalled how the unsettled nature of his childhood prevented him from making friends or excelling in school. In Miami, where he attended public schools, he explained

to Elisa Turner for a profile in the *Hamptons Art Hub* (26 Oct. 2017), "I was very slow in learning anything. . . . The only things I ever excelled at were visual arts and writing. My spelling and grammar were terrible, though."

In spite of his academic struggles, Cordova graduated from Miami Central High School in 1988 and began studying medicine and psychology at Miami Dade Community College. This period of his life showed his growing interest in art. He drew political cartoons in high school, then began putting up unsigned posters on city buses of a picture of a soda can, painted white but dripping with bloody bullet holes. A professor at his community college discovered Cordova was the artist behind the posters and nominated him for a scholarship. Cordova left Miami Dade Community College in 1994 to study fine arts degree at the School of the Art Institute of Chicago in Illinois. He completed his BFA in 1996. Two years later he returned to Miami, where he continued making art.

In 2002, Cordova continued his studies at the Yale School of Art in New Haven, Connecticut. The following year he attended the Skowhegan School of Painting and Sculpture, a summer intensive residency in Maine, and received the 2003 Yale Graduate Residency scholarship. Cordova completed his MFA, with a concentration in painting/printmaking, at Yale in 2004.

ARTIST IN RESIDENCE

After Cordova finished at Yale, he participated in artist-in-residence programs at the Art Omi International Arts Center in Ghent, New York, and at the Studio Museum in Harlem, New York, both in 2004, and the LMCC/Workspace program at the Lower Manhattan Cultural Council in 2005. In 2006, he became an artist-in-residence at the Headlands Center for the Arts in Sausalito, California, and at the Core Program at the Glassell School of Art in Houston, Texas. Between 2007 and 2019, Cordova was invited to participate in some fifteen additional artist-in-residence programs across the country, including in Chicago, New Orleans, Miami, and Texas, as well as in Berlin, Germany. Most notably, he was chosen for the highly selective MacDowell Colony Fellowship in 2008.

Cordova believes such experiences have aided his work tremendously. "Being in a residency program gives you time and space and allows you to take a lot of risk with your work," he explained to Turner. "Your work evolves to a certain point where it isn't about commerce."

CAREER HIGHLIGHTS

Even before graduate school, Cordova's work was featured in several international group exhibitions. Among them were the traveling exhibition *Mass Appeal: The Art Object and Hip Hop*

Culture, which debuted in Ottawa, Ontario, in August 2002; *Americas Remixed* in Milan, Italy, in October 2002; and the highly prestigious Venice Biennale in the summer of 2003. He also had his first solo exhibitions at that time, *You Shook Me All Night Long* at the Institute of Contemporary Art in Winnipeg, Manitoba, in 2002 and *No More Lonely Nights* at the Museum of Contemporary Art in Miami, Florida, in 2003–04.

After Cordova left Yale, museums and universities began to seek him out to do projects, some of which began attracting the notice of art reviewers and ultimately led to higher-profile exhibition opportunities. As Cordova explained to Turner, "That [press coverage] eventually caught the interest of curators in New York and also galleries."

Project representatives were intrigued by many aspects of Cordova's work, most notably his idea of alchemy—changing one object into another. This is particularly notable when one understands how often the artist uses found materials, such as lumber, cardboard, feathers, or paper bags, to create his art. Thematically, his conceptual works (and their titles) tend to foreground the experiences and histories of people of color in the Americas. For instance, his brown-bag-and-feather assemblage *untitled (geronimo)* references both the Apache leader and a Black Panther. He also evokes universal ideas of truth-telling, impermanence, absence, fragmentation, and memory. The Guggenheim Museum website describes his practice thus: "Cordova treats found objects as carriers of their own particular memories; by juxtaposing these symbols, his work offers new cross-cultural narratives that resist the traditionally linear understanding of history."

By the end of the 2010s, Cordova had displayed his artwork in more than twenty-five solo exhibitions and dozens of group exhibitions. Some of his more notable solo shows were at the prestigious Sikkema Jenkins & Co. gallery in New York City: *laberintos* (October to December 2009), *yawar mallku: temporal landscapes* (March to April 2013), and *Smoke Signals: Sculpting in Time* (April to May 2017). He also exhibited in such US cities as Chicago, Miami, New York, San Antonio, Austin, Los Angeles, San Francisco, Atlanta, Boston, and Seattle—as well as Lima; Havana, Cuba; Murcia, Spain; Zurich, Switzerland; and Berlin, Germany. He was also invited to show his work at the 2008 Whitney Biennial, the 2008 Prague Triennial, and the 2015 and 2019 Havana Biennials. Some of his artworks appear in the public collections of museums like the Whitney Museum of American Art and the Guggenheim.

RECOGNITION

Wherever his work has been put on display, it has been met with considerable praise from art critics. Several have noted its capacity to influence social change. Paul Boshears, writing for *New American Paintings* (28 Sept. 2011), declared that Cordova's acts of reclamation are about "apprehending the lessons of the relationships that interacted and produced these objects. This apprehension leads to appreciation, an increase in the value of what is at hand. It is in this process of making familiar and sitting-with that social change is possible and Cordova's attempts at sparking those conversations is to be lauded." Similarly, Bryan Granger wrote for the *Daily Serving* magazine (11 June 2014): "In trying to navigate a complex, interconnected web of meaning, these open-ended works connect these particular histories to the personal histories of each viewer. . . . Cordova's exhibition provides a platform for social change, one that is more capable than other, more traditional curatorial models." Granger further noted that the apparent simplicity and unconventional arrangement of his installations requires viewers' active engagement in making meaning of the pieces.

Throughout his career, Cordova has also earned numerous awards for his artistry, including the 2001 South Florida Cultural Consortium Fellowship, the 2013 Guna S. Mudheim Fellowship in Visual Arts, and a 2017 Florida Prize in Contemporary Art from the Orlando Museum of Art. He has also received a great deal of financial support for his artistic endeavors, primarily through grants, among them a 2005 Rema Hort Mann Foundation Emerging Artist Grant, a 2009 Art Matters Foundation grant, and a 2011 Joan Mitchell Foundation Painters and Sculptors Grant.

ADDITIONAL PURSUITS

From 2001 onward, Cordova has curated other artists' work, either as a co-organizer or exhibition curator, primarily in Florida, Georgia, Texas, and Illinois. He was inspired in this work by Howardena Pindell, who was both a painter and a curator for a dozen years at the Museum of Modern Art (MOMA) in New York City. "It was necessary for Howardena to do that at the time because there was a lack of African American artists or just artists of color in general," he told Turner. "She felt obligated to take on the task and create these exhibits."

Cordova is dedicated to communicating about art as well. He is a published art essayist whose writings have been published in journals and magazines such as *Ante Journal*, *Art Lies*, *Wax Poetics*, and *Art in America*, among other publications. When not living elsewhere for a residency, he also gives lectures at universities and teaches and mentors youth at the nonprofit Arts for Learning Miami.

SUGGESTED READING

Cordova, William. "To Retrieve and Protect: Stacy Lynn Waddell Interviews William Cordova." Interview by Stacy Lynn Waddell. *Daylight,* 1 Oct. 2012, daylightbooks.org/blogs/news/17201901-to-retrieve-and-protect-stacy-lynn-waddell-interviews-william-cordova. Accessed 27 Dec. 2019.

Granger, Bryan. "William Cordova: Ceiba: Reconsidering Ephemeral Spaces at MDC Museum of Art + Design." Review of *Ceiba: Reconsidering Ephemeral Spaces,* by William Cordova. *Daily Serving,* 11 June 2014, www.dailyserving.com/2014/06/william-cordova-ceiba-reconsidering-ephemeral-spaces-at-mdc-museum-of-art-design. Accessed 16 Jan. 2020.

Turner, Elisa. "William Cordova: Now's the Time for His 'New Type of Perspective.'" *Hamptons Art Hub,* 26 Oct. 2017, hamptonsarthub.com/2017/10/26/artists-william-cordova-nows-the-time-for-his-new-type-of-perspective. Accessed 27 Dec. 2019.

Uszerowicz, Monica. "The Wondrous Alchemy of William Cordova's Sculptures." *Hyperallergic,* 13 Sept. 2018, hyperallergic.com/454339/william-cordova-nows-the-time-narratives-of-southern-alchemy-pamm. Accessed 27 Dec. 2019.

"William Cordova." *Guggenheim,* Solomon R. Guggenheim Foundation, www.guggenheim.org/artwork/artist/william-cordova. Accessed 27 Dec. 2019.

"William Cordova." *Sikkema Jenkins & Co.,* www.sikkemajenkinsco.com/william-cordova. Accessed 27 Dec. 2019.

SELECTED WORKS

You Shook Me All Night Long, 2002; *No More Lonely Nights,* 2003–04; *laberintos,* 2009; *yawar mallku: temporal landscapes,* 2013; *Smoke Signals: Sculpting in Time;* 2017

—Christopher Mari

Jai Courtney

Born: March 15, 1986
Occupation: Actor

Australian actor Jai Courtney rose to prominence in Hollywood as a leading man in the late 2010s, a decade after making a name for himself in the television series *Spartacus.* While he began his career battling alongside A-list actors like Tom Cruise, Bruce Willis, Arnold Schwarzenegger,

and Emilia Clarke in action films, he later took a more central role in both popular movies, like *Suicide Squad* (2016), in which he played the villain-turned-antihero Captain Boomerang, as well as in real-life dramas like *Stateless* (2020), a television series produced by Cate Blanchett about the plight of undocumented immigrants in Australia. For his part, Courtney feels blessed to have had such a diverse acting experience thus far in his career. In speaking with Marc Malkin for *Variety* (25 June 2020), Courtney declared, "I am lucky that sometimes I'm making these small-budget gritty dramas like 'Stateless,' and sometimes I'm out shooting big ridiculous action comedies like 'Suicide Squad.' To have feet on both of those trains is a lot of fun—and it also means that I never get tired of it."

EARLY LIFE AND EDUCATION

Jai Stephen Courtney was born in Sydney, New South Wales, Australia, on March 15, 1986. He came to love acting early in life, when he and his sister were dropped off at an after-school improvisational class. Courtney was then just six but remembers clearly playing all the games and activities with relish. He recalled to Christopher McQuarrie for *Interview* magazine (1 June 2015), "I was a show-off as a kid and loved to dress up. I was constantly in costume, drawing mustaches on with eyeliner and letting my sister plait my hair and all that. I was always trying to perform, but never with some dream to be on the stage. The stage was wherever I was standing at the time." He remained with the program throughout high school.

Photo by Eva Rinaldi via Wikimedia Commons

Courtney attended Cherrybrook Technology High School, where in addition to theater, he enjoyed playing rugby and hanging out with friends. He graduated from the school around 2004. As his friends went off to college, he decided that he was done with school—he especially disliked writing papers—and instead, took a job working in a warehouse. He quit after six months.

It was not until after watching an Australian television show with his mother that listed a casting agent in the credits that Courtney considered a career in acting. His mother suggested calling the agent; Courtney did and the agent politely explained that an aspiring actor needed a theatrical representative to be considered for a part. The person he spoke to on the phone provided a list of agents. He called many, but all of them said their client lists were full.

Courtney began to consider going to college, but to study acting and theater instead of a more traditional major. After applying to a number of drama schools across his native Australia, he was accepted to the Western Australian Academy of Performing Arts in Perth. Courtney told McQuarrie about his experience at the school: "I could be honest with myself and not try to fit the mold for something else, and that I actually had something to offer. And once I got comfortable with the fact that I was training to be an actor, I loved it. I've always been clear about the fact that I was going to make it happen." Courtney graduated from the school in 2008.

EARLY FILM CAREER

Courtney got his first roles in Australian television shows like *All Saints* (2008) and *Packed to the Rafters* (2008–09), as well as in the comedy film *Stoned Bros* (2009). His breakout role came in 2010, when he was cast in the television series *Spartacus: Blood and Sand*, which starred the late actor Andy Whitfield in the titular role. During the series, Whitfield was diagnosed with stage IV non-Hodgkin lymphoma, a serious cancer diagnosis, especially for someone who was then in his late thirties. The second season of the series was delayed until he recovered. For a time, it appeared that he was in remission, but Whitfield eventually succumbed to the illness, dying on September 11, 2011. Courtney contributed his recollections of his friend to the documentary *Be Here Now: The Andy Whitfield Story*, which was released in 2015. In an interview with Christina Radish for *Collider* (19 Apr. 2016), Courtney remembered, "Andy was a lovely, generous, funny, handsome, humble, committed actor. He didn't come from a world where that was always what he wanted to do. He grew into that through exploring some insecurities within himself." Courtney continued, describing the effect Whitfield had on set, "He felt lucky to be there,

and he was going to make the most of it. I think that attitude is infectious."

After concluding his run on *Spartacus*, Courtney earned several roles in action films starring major Hollywood actors, including *Jack Reacher* (2012), starring Tom Cruise as the titular character taken from the book series written by novelist Lee Child. Courtney followed *Jack Reacher* with a role starring alongside Bruce Willis in *A Good Day to Die Hard* (2013), the fifth entry in the Die Hard series, which began in 1988. In the film, Courtney portrayed Jack, the estranged son of Willis's character, New York Police Department detective John McClane. Although brimming with possibility, the sequel did not stand up to critical scrutiny. The same year, he also appeared in the crime drama *Felony*, which earned him more positives reviews than his previous film, as well as nominations for best supporting actor from the Australian Film Critics Association Awards and the Film Critics Circle of Australia Awards.

BREAKING OUT ON THE BIG SCREEN

After appearances with such big-name action stars, Courtney's career in Hollywood began to take off. A number of projects came his way, including a role in *Divergent* (2014) and *Insurgent* (2015), the first two films of the science-fiction trilogy series based on the best-selling novels by Veronica Roth. He mixed such big-budget action films with more dramatic roles, including his part of Cup in the biographical drama *Unbroken* (2014) and Lt. Colonel Hughes in the war drama *The Water Diviner* (2014). The former film, directed by Angelina Jolie, is based on the real-life experiences of Louis Zamperini, an Olympian who survived being adrift in a raft for forty-five days and time in Japanese prison camps during World War II.

In 2015, Courtney starred in *Terminator Genisys*, a reboot of *The Terminator* (1984). In the film, he portrayed Kyle Reese, a soldier sent back in time from a post-apocalyptic 2029 to 1984 to prevent the death of Sarah Connor, played by Emilia Clarke, who is the mother of their world's savior. When Kyle arrives in the past, however, he learns that the timeline has been altered from the original film. Now, Sarah has been brought up by a reprogrammed Terminator robot, portrayed by Arnold Schwarzenegger, as he had been in the original series. *Terminator Genisys* was intended to reboot the long-running science fiction series with a new timeline, but the film was critically and commercially unsuccessful.

After costarring with Shia LaBeouf in the thriller *Man Down* (2015), Courtney joined the ensemble cast of the supervillain film *Suicide Squad* (2016). In the latter, Courtney portrayed Captain Boomerang, a supervillain who agrees to go along on a black-ops mission to save the world in exchange for a reduced sentence. The film, directed by David Ayers, is based on the DC Comics series of the same name and features an ensemble cast with such noted actors as Will Smith, Margot Robbie, and Jared Leto. Although DC had high hopes that the film would help establish a shared universe with other DC comic characters, *Suicide Squad* was critically panned. Despite bland reviews, Courtney was praised by critics for his performance. When asked about filming the movie, Courtney told Radish, "What was most surprising was the comradery on set. It's easy to imagine, on a film of that scale with a cast of that scale, you wouldn't find the family that we did in each other. . . . It really was a familial experience for all of us, which was really cool." The same year, he costarred in the romantic drama *The Exception* alongside Lily James and Christopher Plummer.

Courtney returned to television in 2017, appearing in several episodes of the Netflix comedy *Wet Hot American Summer: Ten Years Later*. In 2019, he costarred in a number of films, including the family drama *Storm Boy*, the comedy *Buffaloed*, and the military drama *Semper Fi*. The following year, he lent his voice to a character in the animated film *100% Wolf* (2020), before starring in the six-part miniseries *Stateless* (2020), about Australia's real-life mandatory detention system for immigrants who arrive without visas. The program places undocumented immigrants in centers where they must live until their asylum cases are processed. In the series, which was produced by actor Blanchett, Courtney portrayed a local man who takes a job as a guard because it pays well. Reviewing the series for the *New York Times* (7 July 2020), Mike Hale wrote, "There's a tinge of . . . high-minded obviousness throughout 'Stateless,' in the way it strategically deploys the Australian legal designation 'unlawful noncitizens' and satirically frames statements about 'duty of care' and handling prisoners in culturally appropriate ways. And its finale, unsurprisingly, offers bittersweet catharses for the Australian authority figures and sentimental irresolution for the detainees."

UPCOMING PROJECTS

Although the coronavirus (COVID-19) pandemic of 2020 put most industries, including the film industry, on pause, Courtney had several projects already completed or in postproduction. By that time, Courtney had concluded filming the action-crime drama "Honest Thief" and the action film "Jolt," as well as "The Suicide Squad," the highly anticipated sequel to the similarly named film in which he portrayed Captain Boomerang. Unlike the first movie, Courtney remarked that the sequel promised to have more humor, due in large part to new

director James Gunn. Courtney told Malkin, "James Gunn has an approach to things that is uniquely his; he pulls a lot of that into the 'Suicide Squad' world. And I think that it fits really well, and audiences are going to have a lot of fun with it."

SUGGESTED READING

Courtney, Jai. Interview: Jai Courtney Interview by Christopher McQuarrie. *Interview*, 1 June 2015, www.interviewmagazine.com/film/jai-courtney-1. Accessed 23 July 2020.

———. "Jai Courtney on Remembering Andy Whitfield with 'Be Here Now' and Pushing Boundaries with 'Suicide Squad.'" Interview by Christina Radish. *Collider*, 19 Apr. 2016, collider.com/jai-courtney-suicide-squad-be-here-now-interview. Accessed 23 July 2020.

———. "Listen: Jai Courtney on Netflix's 'Stateless' and Filming the 'Suicide Squad' Sequel." Interview by Marc Malkin. *Variety*, 25 June 2020, variety.com/2020/streaming/podcasts/jai-courtney-suicide-squad-sequel-netflix-series-1234648559. Accessed 23 July 2020.

Hale, Mike. "Review: In 'Stateless' on Netflix, Cate Blanchett (and Immigration)." Review of *Stateless*. *The New York Times*, 7 July 2020, www.nytimes.com/2020/07/07/arts/television/review-stateless-netflix-cate-blanchett.html. Accessed 27 July 2020.

SELECTED WORKS

Spartacus, 2010; *Jack Reacher*, 2012; *A Good Day to Die Hard*, 2013; *Unbroken*, 2014; *Divergent*, 2014; *The Water Diviner*, 2014; *Insurgent*, 2015; *Terminator Genisys*, 2015; *Suicide Squad*, 2016; *Stateless*, 2020

—*Christopher Mari*

Brian Cox

Born: March 3, 1968
Occupation: Physicist

Throughout physicist Brian Cox's career, after he transitioned from a focus on music to scientific study and work, what he has wanted more than anything in the world has been to make science both more accessible and central to the lives of people in his native United Kingdom and around the world. In an interview with Bryony Gordon for the *Telegraph* (22 Jan. 2013), Cox lamented the popular perception of science: "It is sometimes seen as the preserve of very clever old men and that's clearly untrue and clearly problematic." As a particle physicist affiliated with the University of Manchester beginning with his earning of a PhD in the late 1990s and

Photo by The Royal Society via Wikimedia Commons

followed by a lengthy tenure as a professor in the institution's physics and astronomy department, Cox has had significant impact in the world of academia and research in changing that public perception about science. He has faced similar hurdles as a longtime member of the team of the ATLAS detector experiment at the Large Hadron Collider (LHC) at the European Council for Nuclear Research (CERN) near Geneva, Switzerland. As an acclaimed and well-recognized television presenter on a slew of science-based television programs starting in the mid-2000s, he has also proven to have enormous influence in increasing more mainstream genuine interest in the sciences across the United Kingdom.

Although Cox is well regarded among his colleagues as a dedicated physicist, he is also admired by television audiences for his affable personality and the fact that in a previous career he had been a pop star with bands like Dare and D:Ream. By the end of the second decade of the twenty-first century his television work had offered him a compelling platform to advocate for funding of the sciences, believing that the future of his country's (and the world's) economy lay in developing the next generation of scientists, engineers, and thinkers.

EARLY LIFE AND EDUCATION
Brian Cox was born on March 3, 1968, in Oldham, Lancashire, England. His parents both worked in banking. In interviews he has described his childhood as being a happy one, in which he became impassioned about astronomy and space exploration while also nurturing a love for music. By the age of sixteen, he had taught

himself to play the keyboard and had begun going to music clubs, finding an outlet for his creativity. Meanwhile, his musical focus contributed to a decline in performance and drive in some areas of school, particularly math.

Around 1986, Cox joined the rock band Dare, which had been formed by Darren Wharton of Thin Lizzy, and, upon earning a record deal, left any thoughts of higher education behind him. "When you're 18, 19, 20 years old, you're not thinking: pop music is a waste of my intellect. You're thinking: this is brilliant," he said to Tom Lamont for the *Guardian* (5 Oct. 2014). He recorded two albums with Dare, *Out of the Silence* (1988) and *Blood from Stone* (1991), before leaving the band in the early 1990s, in part due to what has been cited as a disagreement between members that had turned physical. While out on tour, he had reignited his interest in science, particularly physics, as he spent time reading books on subjects like quantum mechanics.

Returning home, he decided to study physics and earn his bachelor's degree at age twenty-three. Drawn to its history and level of research despite his initial instinct to move away from home, he called the University of Manchester and said, "I want to come to university now and do physics," he recalled to David Smith for the London *Observer* (13 Sept. 2008). While earning his undergraduate degree, he joined a second band, D:Ream, which had some commercial success, including a dance hit, "Things Can Only Get Better." That song went to the top position on the official United Kingdom chart in 1994 and served as a campaign song for the Labour Party in the lead-up to the 1997 parliamentary election. Although the band was relatively successful, as Cox has explained it, D:Ream was only ever a part-time job, as he was working at the same time to complete his doctorate at the University of Manchester.

CAREER IN ACADEMIA AND RESEARCH
While working on his thesis to receive a PhD in high-energy particle physics, which he completed by 1998, Cox worked at the Hadron Elektron Ring Anlange (HERA) particle accelerator in Hamburg, Germany. "He was a breath of fresh air—he'd done something else with his life," Jeff Forshaw, a particle physics professor who taught him and became one of Cox's future collaborators and colleagues, recalled of Cox's graduate work to Smith. "The first impression was of someone enthusiastic and very capable. We worked together during his PhD, have written a lot of papers together since then." Cox soon began what would prove to be a lengthy professional affiliation with the University of Manchester, which included his appointment as a professor within the department of physics and

astronomy; his lectures covered such topics as relativity and quantum mechanics.

In 2005, Cox received a research fellowship from the Royal Society University. By that time, he had already been conducting research at the Large Hadron Collider (LHC) at the European Council for Nuclear Research (CERN) facility near Geneva, Switzerland. Over several years, his work at CERN largely concerned the ATLAS particle detector project, which was designed, along with other detectors, to help scientists learn more about the early universe's conditions by capturing and recording the proton collisions occurring within the LHC and picking up on any products of these collisions, such as the long-theorized Higgs particle (evidence of which was considered discovered in 2012). With his team, he contributed to the design, construction, and installation of parts of the detector as well as other efforts. His research in particle physics additionally enabled him to author or coauthor a large number of scientific papers.

BECOMING A FACE OF TV SCIENCE

It was Cox's research and work at CERN that led to his presence on television, a path that had initially been unexpected for the scientist and academic but would eventually earn him further recognition for his ability to use the medium effectively to garner greater interest in and understanding of science, including in younger generations. After contributing impressive interviews to documentaries for the BBC's long-running and acclaimed science series *Horizon*, which included the 2005 installation "Einstein's Unfinished Symphony," his first prominent brush with televised fame came when he was given the opportunity to host *The Big Bang Machine*, a 2008 BBC Four program that describes the work being done at the LHC. The largest machine of its kind in the world at more than 16 miles (approximately 27 kilometers) in circumference, it was built between 1998 and 2008 beneath the France–Switzerland border near Geneva. It is designed to smash energy particles together at speeds nearly equal to that of light to better understand how the universe was formed.

Following that program, Cox, who had increasingly acquired a reputation for being able to explain complicated scientific concepts and convey information accessibly and enthusiastically in an engaging, storytelling manner, worked as a presenter on a handful of *Horizon* episodes through 2009 as well as many other science-based programs. Some of the more notable included *Wonders of the Solar System* (2010), a popular miniseries in which he explores different areas of the planet to discuss how phenomena and features on Earth can provide insights into the workings of the solar system. His next series, *Wonders of the Universe* (2011), considered the

entire universe through the lens of the fundamental natural principles that apply on Earth: energy, time, gravity, light, and matter. Another notable presenting opportunity came in the form of *A Night with the Stars* (2011), which helps to explain quantum theory—essentially the physical properties of nature on an atomic scale—to a lay audience.

As the title suggests, the third part of the Wonders franchise, *Wonders of Life* (2013), combined physics and biology as it delves into the origins and miraculous variety of life on Earth and the connections between them. Gordon declared, "In many ways, *Wonders of Life* is a departure from the previous programmes, which spawned complaints that the music was too loud, the presenting style too effusive, the locations across the globe too numerous given that the cost was picked up by the licenced-payer. *Wonders of Life* is still beautifully shot but it is less bombastic, a little calmer."

MAINTAINING A SCIENTIFIC INFLUENCE ON TELEVISION AND IN BOOKS

Another notable program Cox hosted was *The Science of* Doctor Who (2013), which aired in time for the fiftieth anniversary of the long-running BBC science-fiction show following the adventures of a Time Lord known only as the Doctor. Filmed from a lecture theater and incorporating celebrity guests, the largely praised program features Cox providing *Doctor Who* fans with authoritative knowledge of the science behind relevant concepts such as time travel as well as extraterrestrials.

In 2014, Cox served as presenter for *Human Universe* (2014), which examines significant questions about the existence of human beings, whether they are alone in the universe, and what their future might consist of. "The series, as a whole, is physics- and cosmology-based," Cox said of *Human Universe* to Lamont. "But it really addresses the human response to ideas as much as the ideas themselves. Was the universe around forever? Is the universe eternal? What does that mean? The questions cosmology raises are essentially inward-looking."

Continuing to remain popular with audiences and be trusted to front varied television projects, his hosting roles into the end of the 2010s included those for *The Entire Universe* (2016), a humorous musical about the universe; *The 21st Century Race for Space* (2017), which looks at how private companies are finding innovative ways to launch human beings into and beyond Earth's orbit; and the largely well-received *The Planets* (2019), which takes a deep dive into the stories of the solar system's eight major planets. By 2019, he had also conducted live science tours, breaking records with single-show ticket sales; that year, he traveled around the world for his *Universal: Adventures in Space and Time* show, which featured high-resolution photographs as part of the experience. "When you look at images of thousands of galaxies in one photograph, then your reaction is to feel absolutely insignificant, so the aim is to discuss why that might not be the case, and to celebrate that," he explained to Alice Lascelles for the *Financial Times* (23 Feb. 2018).

Although he has become best known for serving as a presenter for popular science programs, despite his continued impact on the world of academia as a professor and researcher, he has admitted to being uncomfortable with being recognized and that he has typically preferred the relative anonymity of teaching first-year physics students. "Suddenly you're famous," he told Lamont. "I didn't like it very much. You're no longer anonymous. . . . It's odd, at first, and then you get used to it."

In addition to his science advocacy on television, Cox has coauthored a number of books on scientific subjects. With Forshaw he wrote *Why Does E=mc²? (And Why Should We Care?)* (2009), *The Quantum-Universe (And Why Anything That Can Happen, Does)* (2011), and *Universal: A Guide to the Cosmos* (2016). With Andrew Cohen he has written *Wonders of the Solar System* (2010), *Wonders of the Universe* (2011), *Human Universe* (2014), and *Forces of Nature* (2016).

PERSONAL LIFE AND ACCOLADES

Cox married Gia Milinovich, a television producer, in 2003. They have a son, George. Cox also has a stepson, Moki, from Milinovich's previous relationship.

Throughout his career, Cox has been the recipient of a number of honors for his commitment to scientific research and popular science. These awards have included the 2006 Lord Kelvin Award from the British Association; the 2010 Institute of Physics' Kelvin Prize, the 2012 Institute of Physics' President's Medal, and the 2012 Royal Society's Michael Faraday Prize. Meanwhile, in 2010 he was named an officer of the Order of the British Empire (OBE). In 2016, he was elected a fellow in the Royal Society.

SUGGESTED READING

Cox, Brian. "Prof Brian Cox: 'Being Anti-Expert—That's the Way Back to the Cave.'" Interview by Decca Aitkenhead. *The Guardian*, 2 July 2016, www.theguardian.com/tv-and-radio/2016/jul/02/professor-brian-cox-interview-forces-of-nature. Accessed 17 July 2020.

———. "Brian Cox Interview: Stars in His Eyes." Interview by Bryony Gordon. *The Telegraph*, 22 Jan. 2013, www.telegraph.co.uk/culture/tvandradio/9803162/Brian-Cox-interview-stars-in-his-eyes.html. Accessed 17 July 2020.

Lamont, Tom. "Physicist Brian Cox: 'The Side of Me That People Don't Tend to See Is the Side That Argues.'" *The Guardian*, 5 Oct. 2014, www.theguardian.com/theobserver/2014/oct/05/physicist-brian-cox-interview-human-universe. Accessed 17 July 2020.

Lascelles, Alice. "Physicist Brian Cox: 'I Think within the Next 10 or 20 Years, We'll Be on Mars.'" *Financial Times*, 23 Feb. 2018, www.ft.com/content/3544fee8-169e-11e8-9376-4a6390addb44. Accessed 10 Aug. 2020.

Smith, David. "Putting the Fizz into Physics." *The Observer*, Guardian News and Media, 13 Sept. 2008, www.theguardian.com/science/2008/sep/14/cern.particlephysics. Accessed 20 July 2020.

SELECTED WORKS

The Big Bang Machine, 2008; *Wonders of the Solar System*, 2010; *Wonders of the Universe*, 2011; *Wonders of Life*, 2013; *Human Universe*, 2014; *The 21st Century Race for Space*, 2017; *The Planets*, 2019

—Christopher Mari

Fletcher Cox

Born: December 13, 1990
Occupation: Football player

On February 4, 2018, defensive tackle Fletcher Cox and his team, the Philadelphia Eagles, achieved the ultimate distinction in American football: winning the Super Bowl. The Eagles defeated the highly favored, defending champion New England Patriots in Super Bowl LII to claim the first such title in franchise history. The win was likewise a first for Cox, who had played for the Eagles since entering the National Football League (NFL) as a first-round draft pick in 2012. "I tell you what, there's no greater feeling, you know, to be world champions," Cox said following the game, in an interview with *NFL GameDay Prime* (4 Feb. 2018).

A football player from the age of thirteen, Cox established himself as a defensive star while a student at Yazoo City High School in Mississippi and went on to hone his skills further at Mississippi State University, where he played three seasons with the Bulldogs. After beginning his professional career in 2012, he distinguished himself as a premier defensive force both for the Eagles and in the NFL, earning Pro Bowl and All-Pro honors, among others. For Cox, however, such accomplishments were only the beginning. "I just want to keep setting the bar because

Photo by Jeffrey Beall via Wikimedia Commons

records are made to be broken," he told Graham Foley for the *Eagles'* website (20 Dec. 2018). In 2020, the NFL and the Pro Football Hall of Fame selected Cox for their 2010s All-Decade Team, further solidifying his status as one of the era's most significant players.

EARLY LIFE AND EDUCATION

Cox was born on December 13, 1990, in Yazoo City, Mississippi. He grew up there, living with his mother, Malissa, and three siblings. An athletic child, Cox played sports such as basketball and track but particularly aspired to play football, a sport his mother considered to be too dangerous. "My Mom would never, ever sign the papers for me to play football," he recalled to Sheil Kapadia for *Philadelphia* magazine (30 June 2015). "She wouldn't sign it no matter what. The thing about it was, 'I don't want my baby to get hurt.' That's what my Mom would always say. 'I don't want my baby to get hurt.'" Despite his mother's objections, Cox remained persistent. "I kept bugging her about it, kept bugging her about it," he told Kapadia. "And she finally said, 'Alright, I'm doing it.'"

Having at last gained permission to play football, Cox began playing the sport at the age of thirteen and continued to do so throughout his time at Yazoo City High School, playing on both offense and defense. He completed more than one hundred tackles per season during both his junior and senior seasons, which, among other impressive statistics, earned him media recognition as one of the best high school players in Mississippi. In recognition of Cox's achievements over the course of his career, the school

would later rename its football stadium in his honor. "It's just a great accomplishment," he told Foley about that recognition. "It's something I can always go back to when I'm done playing and say I had a stadium named after me." Cox graduated from Yazoo City High School in 2009.

MISSISSIPPI STATE

Recruited by many college and university football programs during his high school years, Cox decided to remain in his home state and attend Mississippi State University. Upon joining the Mississippi State Bulldogs football team, he played on a regular basis throughout his freshman season in 2009 and served as a member of the starting lineup for four games. "I learned a lot," he later recalled about that first season, as quoted by Will Sammon for the *Mississippi Clarion Ledger* (4 Feb. 2018). "No. 1, just being a man. Coach (David) Turner in my first year, his whole thing was, 'I'm gonna help you mature as a man before I help you mature as a football player.'"

Cox's strong performance during his freshman season earned him Freshman All-Southeastern Conference (SEC) honors. He then saw an increase in playing time in his sophomore season, during which he started eleven of the twelve games. Further honing his skills throughout that period, Cox filled multiple defensive positions during his tenure with the Bulldogs, including the positions of defensive tackle and defensive end. In his junior season Cox achieved totals of fifty-six tackles and five sacks and earned first-team All-SEC honors. He did not return to Mississippi State for his senior season, opting instead to leave school after three years to pursue a career in professional football.

PHILADELPHIA EAGLES

In January 2012, Cox declared for that year's NFL Draft, putting himself forward for selection by any of the participating teams. By that time he was widely considered one of the top defensive tackle prospects in the country, and even among the best available players overall. For Cox, the draft and the potential NFL career it represented were in many ways the culmination of years of effort. "This shows that hard work pays off," he told Pete Thamel for the *New York Times* (3 Jan. 2012). "Coach [Dan] Mullen always told me that I'd play in the NFL. I said, 'Yes, sir, that's something that I want to do.' To be able to play in the NFL, that's something that a lot of people don't get to do."

Prior to the draft many NFL experts expected Cox would be selected in the second round or possibly near the end of the first round. However, the Philadelphia Eagles upended that thinking by trading up to select Cox with the twelfth overall pick in the first round. The team later signed him to a four-year contract. He made his regular season debut with the Eagles in their first game of the 2012 season, against the Cleveland Browns, and contributed two tackles in Philadelphia's victory. Cox showed considerable promise as a rookie, playing in all but one of the team's games and starting nine of them. Though the Eagles finished with only four wins and twelve losses, Cox was named to the 2012 All-Rookie Team compiled by the Pro Football Writers Association.

In addition to being the culmination of a longtime dream, Cox's entry into the NFL represented a valuable opportunity to work alongside and learn from older and more established defensive players. "You have to respect those guys," he told Foley about his teammates. "Just to be around that experience, just to be around guys like that who add so much. They're guys I respect, and I try to pick their brains about some things, what do they do, what do they do to play in the league for this long." Cox's learning experiences continued throughout the 2013 season, during which he became a full-time starter. With a new coaching staff and new defensive strategy in place, the Eagles finished the season with a 10–6 record, placing first in National Football Conference (NFC) East Division. They entered the playoffs as the third seed in the NFC but lost to the New Orleans Saints in the Wild Card Round.

SUPER BOWL CHAMPION

Cox remained a key member of the Eagles over the next several seasons, earning numerous honors in recognition of his contributions to the team's defensive play. He earned the title of the NFC Defensive Player of the Week for the first time in 2015, and in September 2016 was named NFC Defensive Player of the Month. He was also selected for his first Pro Bowl in 2015. Although rumors that Cox might be traded to another team spread through the sports media in 2015, no deal materialized, and he signed a six-year, $103 million contract extension with the Eagles in June 2016.

Although Cox had established himself as one of the best defensive players in the league, the Eagles continued to struggle overall, missing the postseason three years in a row. That changed in 2017, when Philadelphia went 13–3 in the regular season and finished first in the NFC East despite losing star quarterback Carson Wentz to injury. Earning the number one seed in the NFC playoffs, the Eagles beat the Atlanta Falcons in the divisional round and the Minnesota Vikings in the NFC Championship to reach Super Bowl LII. There they faced the defending champions, the New England Patriots, who were favored to repeat by most analysts. Despite being underdogs, Cox and his teammates pulled off an upset

victory, winning 44–33 behind backup quarterback Nick Foles. "I'm proud of this team," Cox told *NFL GameDay Prime* after the championship. "Everybody doubted us . . . and we just went out and showed the world, man, that we could go against anybody and win when it comes down to it." In addition to marking Cox's first Super Bowl outing and victory, the championship was a significant milestone for the Eagles as the franchise's first Super Bowl win.

RECOGNITION AND SERVICE

Cox was named one of the Eagles' defensive captains in September 2018. He continued to play a prominent role on the team over the course of the 2018 season, earning first-team All-Pro honors from the Associated Press. The 9–7 Eagles returned to the postseason as a wild card team and defeated the Chicago Bears in the first round before losing to the Saints in the divisional playoffs. The team finished with an identical record the following year, this time winning the NFC East, but lost in the playoffs to the Seattle Seahawks.

In April 2020, the NFL and the Pro Football Hall of Fame announced that Cox was one of fifty-two players named to the All-Decade Team representing the 2010s, a list highlighting many of the best NFL players of the era. "To me it means a lot. I sure can appreciate that," Cox said of his inclusion, as quoted by Dave Zangaro for *NBC Sports Philadelphia* (17 May 2020). "Gotta thank the coaching staff, my teammates and everybody who helped me get to this point to be able to be on there. It's such an honor. And I'm truly blessed to be on there."

In addition to playing football, Cox worked to promote the sport in his home state of Mississippi and in 2015 established an annual free football camp for local youth. "Kids, coaches don't have to pay a dime and that's one of my way of giving back, making it special for the kids, making it special for the state of Mississippi," he explained to Samaria Terry for *WJTV* (22 June 2019). He especially sought to serve as a role mode specifically for the young people of Yazoo City, frequently mentioning his hometown as a way to show that lofty goals—such as playing in the NFL—can be achievable for small-town residents.

PERSONAL LIFE

In addition to football, Cox developed a passion for cars and the sport of drag racing, thanks in large part to the influence of his older brother, who died in 2015. "My brother, Shaddrick, introduced me to cars and he introduced me to working on cars and really what hard work was. And that's helped me in all areas I work. I just fell in love with it," he told Foley. Alongside working on cars in his spare time, Cox owns the drag racing team Cox Racing, which competes in Mississippi and beyond.

SUGGESTED READING

Cox, Fletcher. "Kevin Hart Crashes Fletcher Cox's Post Super Bowl LII Interview . . . and It's Hilarious!" *YouTube*, uploaded by NFL Media Originals, 4 Feb. 2018, www.youtube.com/watch?v=3HhK7HbX3Qs. Accessed 9 Aug. 2020.

———. "A Q&A with Pro Bowl DT Fletcher Cox." Interview by Graham Foley. *Philadelphia Eagles*, 20 Dec. 2018, www.philadelphiaeagles.com/news/fletcher-cox-questions-one-on-one. Accessed 9 Aug. 2020.

Kapadia, Sheil. "Showing Up: Inside Fletcher Cox's Journey." *Philadelphia*, 30 June 2015, www.phillymag.com/birds247/2015/06/30/showing-up-inside-fletcher-coxs-journey/. Accessed 9 Aug. 2020.

Sammon, Will. "Super Bowl Star Fletcher Cox Has Never Forgotten Yazoo City." *Mississippi Clarion Ledger*, 4 Feb. 2018, www.clarionledger.com/story/magnolia/2018/02/01/super-bowl-eagles-star-fletcher-cox-never-forgotten-yazoo-city/1077986001/. Accessed 9 Aug. 2020.

Terry, Samaria. "Fletcher Cox Holds 4th Annual Free Football Camp." *WJTV*, 22 June 2019, www.wjtv.com/news/fletcher-cox-holds-4th-annual-free-football-camp-2/. Accessed 9 Aug. 2020.

Thamel, Pete. "Mississippi State Defensive Tackle Declares for N.F.L. Draft." *The New York Times*, 3 Jan. 2012, www.nytimes.com/2012/01/04/sports/ncaafootball/mississippi-states-fletcher-cox-declares-for-nfl-draft.html. Accessed 9 Aug. 2020.

Zangaro, Dave. "Fletcher Cox Honored by All-Decade Nod That Will Help His HOF Chances." *NBC Sports Philadelphia*, 17 May 2020, www.nbcsports.com/philadelphia/eagles/fletcher-cox-nfl-all-decade-hall-of-fame. Accessed 9 Aug 2020.

—*Joy Crelin*

Kendall Coyne Schofield

Date of birth: May 25, 1992
Occupation: Hockey player

Hockey player Kendall Coyne Schofield is an Olympic gold medalist and six-time world champion. She is considered one of the fastest players in the sport. In 2019, she became the first woman to appear in the National Hockey League (NHL) All-Star Skills Competition, competing for fastest skater. Her inclusion was not planned.

Four hours before the competition began, Coyne Schofield, who was supposed to demonstrate the drill, was asked to fill in for a male player. "The most pressure I felt was the self-inflicted pressure of knowing that I had the weight of our sport on my shoulders," she told Kristina Rutherford for Canada's *Sportsnet* website in 2019. "The skate had to be perfect, otherwise the narrative turns to: 'I told you so. They don't belong.'"

While Coyne Schofield credits her incredible speed to training, her haphazard trajectory also illustrates the lack of opportunities for women in hockey, from the minor to the professional leagues. As a teenager she realized the height of her ambition was the Olympics—an incredible, coveted feat, to be sure, but the games happen only once every four years. As she has observed in multiple interviews: girls win gold medals; boys win Stanley Cups. Despite a handful of professional women's leagues emerging in the 2010s, with pay as low as two thousand dollars per season, their continued existence is unsustainable. Coyne Schofield began playing part-time for the National Women's Hockey League (NWHL) Minnesota Whitecaps in 2016. Although she and other players have successfully pressured the league to increase compensation, unequal pay for female players remains an issue in the sport, and she and other players opted to sit out the 2019–20 season in North America as part of their struggle to establish a viable women's professional league.

EARLY LIFE

Coyne Schofield was born to John and Ahlise Coyne in Oak Lawn, Illinois, on May 25, 1992.

Photo by Dave Sandford/NHLI via Getty Images

She has two older brothers, Jake and Kevin, and a younger sister, Bailey. Her brother Kevin played hockey growing up and later played for Becker College in Massachusetts. Inspired by him, Coyne Schofield put on her first pair of figure skates when she was three years old. "She looked up at me as a little tiny girl and said, 'This is boring,'" her mother told Madeline Sattler for Northeastern University's *Huntington News* (1 Mar. 2012). "So we took those figure skates off her, put the hockey skates on her and she never looked back." Love for the sport was also passed on to Coyne Schofield's sister, who plays for Northeastern. Hockey was more than a hobby for Coyne Schofield. "I realized hockey was my thing when other kids were being forced to the rink by their parents, and I went every day purely for the love of the game," Coyne Schofield said during an interview for Berkshire School in 2013. "Every day with hockey felt like Christmas."

Growing up in Palos Heights, a suburb of Chicago, Coyne Schofield played on local boys' teams. She wanted to play travel hockey, which was more competitive than other local youth hockey outlets, but was cut multiple times from the Orland Park Vikings AA travel team. When she was eleven, she made the Chicago Trail AAA boys' team and began playing with boys a year older. "Now that I'm older, I can understand what might've happened, why I might've been cut [in Orland Park]," she told Rutherford. "My parents are pretty positive it was because I had a ponytail coming out of my helmet."

Coyne Schofield's early experiences are similar to those of other female hockey players, in that they are defined by a lack of opportunity for girls and a reluctance on the part of competitive boys' teams to include them. The same year Coyne Schofield won a spot on the Chicago Trail AAA travel team, she was recruited by Manon Rhéaume—a former Team Canada goalie and the first and only woman to play in an NHL game—to join the first all-girls team at the Quebec Pewee Tournament, a long-running international competition for players aged twelve and under. Again, Coyne Schofield would be younger than her teammates, but for the first time in her life, those teammates would be girls. The team lost in the semifinals; they were not invited to play again the next year.

HIGH SCHOOL CAREER

In 2007, at age fifteen, Coyne Schofield was recruited to become the youngest member of the Under-18 National Team. It was an impressive feat considering her diminutive size; Coyne Schofield was five feet tall and weighed just over 100 pounds. She has always been small, but this has proven to be an asset, and she learned to compensate for her lack of bulk with speed. In

2009, she scored the game-winning goal, leading the Under-18 team its second consecutive world championship title. Coyne Schofield also played for the Under-22 National Team, all while still attending school at Carl Sandburg High School in Orland Park, Illinois.

Coyne Schofield graduated from Carl Sandburg in 2010 and had committed to play for Boston University (BU), but when she approached the school's coach, he told her that the school was no longer offering her a scholarship. Coyne Schofield then decided to extend her high school career by playing for the Berkshire School, a preparatory school in Sheffield, Massachusetts, for the 2010–11 season, while also studying in hopes of gaining admission to Harvard University the next year. She enjoyed her time at Berkshire; it was the first time she had ever played for a school team. "I never played hockey for my high school. No one at school really knew why I was always traveling or whom it was with," she explained in an interview with Berkshire. "They just knew I played hockey." Coyne Schofield won the team's most valuable player award and was named New England Prep School Player of the Year.

NCAA CAREER AND 2014 OLYMPICS

In 2011, Coyne Schofield enrolled at Northeastern University and began playing for the Huskies. At the end of the season, she was unanimously named Hockey East Rookie of the Year. The same year she joined the women's national team and helped lead them to a world championship title. She garnered national attention after scoring the team's first goal in the tournament against Slovakia. At eighteen, she was the team's youngest member. She was praised for her incredible speed, but Coyne Schofield was humble. "For me, my speed is genetics—both my parents are fast, my father especially fast," Coyne Schofield told Laura Gottesdiener for the *Huffington Post* (19 Apr. 2011). "The other half is training."

In 2013, Coyne Schofield was again invited to try out for the US Olympic team. She was one of forty-one players invited to try out for the 2010 Olympic team but did not make the cut that year. With more experience under her belt, she made the team nearly four years later. "It was a very emotional day. It was so surreal," she told Berkshire of the day she found out. "All that kept going through my head were the times of adversity and all the hard work, and sacrifices that have been made for this single moment, have finally paid off."

Coyne Schofield took the year off from school to train with a national team in suburban Massachusetts and, in January 2014, traveled to compete in the Winter Olympic Games in Sochi, Russia. She was the co-lead scorer for Team

USA, but her efforts were not enough to beat back rival Canada in the final game on February 20. Before the games, Coyne Schofield recalled how, at seven years old, she had met former Team USA captain Cammi Granato at a hockey camp in 1999. Granato had let a young Coyne Schofield hold her 1998 gold medal; the moment inspired Coyne Schofield to work for one of her own. The loss at Sochi was heartbreaking. She accepted the silver medal with tears in her eyes.

Coyne Schofield returned to Northeastern in the fall of 2014. In 2015, she won her third world championship and was also selected by the Boston Pride as the third overall pick for the inaugural NWHL draft. As a senior in 2016, she won the coveted Patty Kazmaier Memorial Award, given to the top player in women's college hockey. She graduated with a bachelor's degree in communications and signed with the Minnesota Whitecaps, an independent women's pro team, the same year.

2018 OLYMPICS AND AN UNCERTAIN PROFESSIONAL FUTURE

In 2017, Coyne Schofield and other Team USA players announced that they would boycott the world championships if they did not receive fair pay. The team's governing body, USA Hockey, had only paid female players one thousand dollars a month for six months during Olympic years; they agreed to pay annual stipends of fourteen to twenty-one thousand. Coyne Schofield and the team went on to win another world championship that year, and she began training for the 2018 Olympic Games in PyeongChang, South Korea.

As in 2014, Team USA faced Canada in the final Olympic round. The game ended in a dramatic shootout, with the US winning, 3–2. It was the first gold medal for the team since the one Coyne Schofield had held almost twenty years earlier. "I got a text from Cammi [Granato] offering her congratulations," Coyne Schofield told Lucas Aykroyd for the *New York Times* (27 Nov. 2018). "I can get teary-eyed talking about it." The team's victory—which won Best Game at the 2018 ESPY Awards—drew Coyne Schofield into the national spotlight. She appeared in an episode of the competition reality show *American Ninja Warrior*. She was inducted into the Chicagoland Sports Hall of Fame and became the first woman to receive the Stan Mikita Lifetime Achievement Award.

In July 2018, Coyne Schofield also became the first woman to play in the newly created Chicago Professional Hockey League (CPHL), a competitive league for NHL players and veterans to compete in the offseason. Her inclusion won a lot of attention, but it also highlighted the dearth of professional opportunities for female hockey players.

In 2019, Coyne Schofield scored the game-winning goal in overtime to win her sixth world championship title. Still at the height of her career, she has had to chase opportunities to play. She plays for enthusiastic crowds on weekends, commuting from her homes in California, where she trains with the under-18 Anaheim Junior Ducks boys' team, and Chicago, where she works in fan development for the Chicago Blackhawks. "I get, 'Well, how come you didn't move to Minnesota?'" Coyne Schofield told Aykroyd. "I said: 'You're paying me $7,000. I'm not moving to Minnesota.' If this league was more sustainable, I would consider it. But I'm not moving away from my family for that amount of money."

In March 2019, the Canadian Women's Hockey League (CWHL) announced that it was shutting down on May 1, 2019, leaving the NWHL as the only women's league in North America. That same month, a group of two hundred top female hockey players led by Coyne Schofield, American player Hilary Knight, and Canadian player Shannon Szabados announced on social media that they would not play any professional hockey in North America for the 2019–20 season in an effort to establish a single, economically sustainable professional league.

PERSONAL LIFE

Coyne Schofield married Michael Schofield III, an offensive guard for the Los Angeles Chargers, in 2018. The two attended the same high school but did not know one another at the time. They met at the gym in 2014, while Schofield awaited news of the NFL Draft and Coyne Schofield was nursing an old wrist injury. The couple split their time between Los Angeles and Chicago.

SUGGESTED READING

Aykroyd, Lucas. "A Whirlwind Year for the Fastest Woman in Hockey." *The New York Times*, 27 Nov. 2018, www.nytimes.com/2018/11/27/sports/kendall-coyne-schofield.html. Accessed 21 Jan. 2020.

Coyne, Kendall. "Interview with Kendall Coyne, '11." *Berkshire School*, 2013, www.berkshire-school.org/uploaded/photos/Alumni/Interview_with_Kendall_Coyne.pdf. Accessed 21 Jan. 2020.

Gottesdiener, Laura. "Kendall Coyne Scores First Goal for U.S. in Women's Hockey World Championships." *HuffPost*, 19 Apr. 2011, www.huffpost.com/entry/kendall-coyne-hockey-championship_n_850970. Accessed 21 Jan. 2020.

Rutherford, Kristina. "'What's Right for the Game.'" *Sportsnet*, 2019, www.sportsnet.ca/hockey/nhl/inside-cwhl-nwhl-mess-big-read. Accessed 21 Jan. 2020.

Sattler, Madeline. "Coyne Shines in First Year with Northeastern." *Huntington News*, Northeastern University, 1 Mar. 2012, huntnewsnu.com/21153/sports/coyne-shines-in-first-year-with-northeastern. Accessed 21 Jan. 2020.

—*Molly Hagan*

Samantha Cristoforetti

Date of birth: April 26, 1977
Occupation: Astronaut

In November 2014, Samantha Cristoforetti took a journey to a destination that fewer than six hundred human beings before her had reached: space. An officer in the Italian air force with a lifelong dream of spaceflight, Cristoforetti had been selected by the European Space Agency (ESA) as an astronaut candidate in 2009 and spent several years training for the role, waiting for her opportunity to join an expedition crew. That moment came in late 2014, when she and the other crew members for Expedition 42/43 made the voyage from their launch site in Kazakhstan to the International Space Station (ISS), where they would live and conduct scientific experiments for the next several months. Along with the two fellow crew members with whom she arrived, Cristoforetti remained in space for just under two hundred full days, setting a record for the longest uninterrupted spaceflight on a single mission by an ESA astronaut.

Such a record, however, was far less important to Cristoforetti than her scientific work and the sense of perspective that traveling into space gives to the few fortunate enough to do so. "When you look at the Earth from space, it looks like a big space ship that is flying through space, and oh, by the way, carrying all of humanity on it," she told Jonathan D. Woods and Jeffrey Kluger for *Time* (10 Aug. 2015). "You start to get this feeling that, just as on the space station, we can only function if we all work together as a crew and we're all crew members. None of us is a passenger. . . . You have to take care of each other." Following her return to Earth in June 2015, Cristoforetti remained active in the European space program and in 2018 published a memoir about her experiences in space.

EARLY LIFE AND EDUCATION

Samantha Cristoforetti was born in Milan, Italy, on April 26, 1977. She grew up in a resort village in the Italian Alps, where her parents, Sergio and Antonella, operated a hotel. As a child, Cristoforetti was given a great deal of independence and had the opportunity to roam extensively outdoors. She would later comment in interviews

Photo by Andreas Schepers via Wikimedia Commons

that those experiences played a significant role in shaping her later life. In addition, there was little light pollution in her childhood village, so the young Cristoforetti was able to take in a largely unimpeded view of the night sky, which sparked her curiosity about space. "I don't remember a precise moment in my childhood when I decided that, as an adult, I would be an astronaut," she wrote in her 2018 memoir, as quoted in translation by Silvia Donati for *Italy Magazine* (8 Mar. 2019). "Rather, I think it was a piling up of many stimuli that, at some point, reached critical mass. Then yes, I started telling everyone."

Over the course of her childhood, Cristoforetti attended a primary school in her village and later enrolled at a *liceo scientifico*, a variety of Italian secondary school that offers a five-year program emphasizing sciences as well as languages and philosophy. As a teenager she spent a year studying abroad in the United States, having enrolled in a high school in Saint Paul, Minnesota. "I was very fascinated by the idea of not much traveling, but really discovering other places, other cultures, really learning other languages," she explained to Alessandra Potenza for *The Verge* (14 May 2017). She returned to Italy following her school year abroad and subsequently completed her final year of secondary school, graduating in 1996. Still craving further cultural exposure, she went on to travel to Germany to attend the Technical University of Munich, where she studied mechanical engineering and focused particularly on aerospace-related topics; she also spent periods working on research projects at institutions in France and

Russia. In 2001, she earned her master's degree from the Technical University of Munich.

BECOMING AN ASTRONAUT

In late 1999, the Italian military announced that it would begin accepting the voluntary enlistment of women into the armed forces the following year. Hoping to become a pilot and still focused on her longtime dream of serving as an astronaut, Cristoforetti became one of the earliest women to join the Italian Air Force, enrolling in the country's air force academy in 2001 after completing her studies in Munich. "In a way I was throwing away my engineering studies fully because I had to start again from scratch with colleagues that basically were out of school and, and so do undergraduate studies again, but in the end it was worth it," she recalled in a 2014 interview, the transcript of which was posted on the website of the United States' *National Aeronautics and Space Administration* (NASA). During her years in air force training she pursued studies in aeronautical sciences at the University of Naples Federico II, completing a degree in 2005. Having successfully become an officer in the air force, she went on to pursue pilot training at a facility in the United States and particularly worked to master Italy's AMX combat aircraft.

Approximately seven years after Cristoforetti's entrance into the Italian air force academy, her trajectory shifted yet again with the announcement that the European Space Agency (ESA) was preparing to select a new group of potential astronauts. "There is no unsolicited application. You have to wait for a selection to come up and there had not been one for 15 years or so," she explained about the selection process in her 2014 interview for NASA. "I was in a very demanding training program in the air force, fully engaged in that, and I was very happy in doing what I was doing. But then this news came out and the selection was open . . . so I really had to grab that chance." In 2009, Cristoforetti learned that she was one of six individuals chosen out of thousands to join the ESA's astronaut program.

Cristoforetti completed her initial astronaut training, which involved testing survival skills and learning the basics of orbital mechanics, in 2010. She then went on to train in essential areas such as robotics, ISS systems, and flight engineering while waiting to be assigned to an expedition. In 2012, it was announced that she would take part in Expedition 42/43, a joint initiative of the ESA, the Italian Space Agency (ASI), NASA, and the Russian space agency (Roscosmos) that would see her travel to and live for a time aboard the ISS.

EXPEDITION 42/43

Cristoforetti's first space expedition launched on November 23, 2014. In her role as a flight engineer, she was part of a three-person crew at launch that included Russian cosmonaut Anton Nikolaevich Shkaplerov and American astronaut Terry W. Virts. Upon docking with the ISS, the trio joined the personnel already on board, which included American astronaut and mission commander Barry Wilmore as well as Russian cosmonauts Aleksandr Mikhailovich Samokutyayev and Yelena Olegovna Serova. Following the departure of Wilmore, Samokutyayev, and Serova in March 2015, Virts took on the role of commander, and Cristoforetti and her remaining colleagues were subsequently joined by Russian cosmonauts Gennady Ivanovich Padalka and Mikhail Borisovich Kornienko and American astronaut Scott Joseph Kelly.

Although Cristoforetti had trained extensively to go into space, her time on the ISS was nevertheless marked by new experiences. "I was very open, like a blank page," she told Woods and Kluger. "I discovered many things, like how it feels to float—just that sensation of being so light to the point of having no weight whatsoever, of being able to move in three dimensions. Everything is just effortless." During their time on the space station Cristoforetti and her colleagues were responsible for conducting or supervising hundreds of scientific experiments, many of them heavily reliant on the microgravity and corresponding weightlessness experienced by all beings and objects aboard the station. "Microgravity is an exceptional opportunity to highlight a number of mechanisms that help us understand how our body works and that we would not see on the Earth because they are hidden or inhibited by the presence of gravity," she explained for the website *ResearchItaly* (20 Nov. 2014). Among other efforts, the astronauts sought to observe and document how plants grow, bones lose density, and fruit fly immune systems develop in microgravity, collecting data for further analysis back on Earth.

In addition to conducting scientific research and performing her duties related to the operation and upkeep of the ISS, Cristoforetti engaged in substantial public-outreach efforts during her months in space. She became particularly known for blog posts and photographs posted to the Internet from the station. She also starred in a memorable series of videos about life on the ISS in which she demonstrated how astronauts eat, exercise, and use the restroom while in space.

RETURN TO EARTH

Although they were originally set to return to Earth on May 13, 2015, Cristoforetti, Virts, and Shkaplerov remained on board the ISS nearly a month longer than planned after a problem with a cargo vehicle delayed their return flight. The astronauts ultimately returned to Earth on

June 11, 2015, after 199 days and sixteen hours in space. That lengthy span, often rounded up to an even 200 days in media reports, meant that Cristoforetti set a record for the longest spaceflight without interruption by an ESA astronaut as well as the longest spaceflight by a woman. Though she had already been the center of much media attention thanks to her videos and other outreach efforts, her return to Earth as a record holder drew further media interest. Still, Cristoforetti considered the records to be of little significance. "I think records are more something for media to write about because it's potentially a piece of news. But of course for me, it really doesn't make a huge difference having been in space 200 days as opposed to 190, which would not have been the record," she explained to Woods and Kluger. In addition to receiving widespread media attention following her return, she was also honored with the prestigious Knight Grand Cross of the Order of Merit by the Italian government.

Following her return from the ISS, Cristoforetti continued to work for the ESA, primarily leading teams at the European Astronaut Centre (EAC) in Cologne, Germany. Among other projects, she worked on research simulations for potential moon habitat technology, contributed to a project aiming to establish a lunar orbital space station, and participated in collaborations with the China National Space Administration. Her memoir *Diario di un'apprendista astronauta* was published in Italy in 2018. Two years later, she announced on social media that an English translation of the work, *Diary of an Apprentice Astronaut*, had also been prepared.

PERSONAL LIFE

Outside of work, Cristoforetti participates in activities such as hiking and scuba diving. Having long enjoyed drinking espresso, she made headlines in 2015 for drinking the first cup of espresso to be brewed in space, made using the ISS's newly installed "ISSpresso" coffee machine. Cristoforetti and her partner, Lionel Ferra, an astronaut instructor, had a daughter, Kelsey, in late 2016.

SUGGESTED READING

Cristoforetti, Samantha. "Astronaut Samantha Cristoforetti on Tweeting from Space and Brewing the First Zero-G Espresso." Interview by Alessandra Potenza. *The Verge*, 14 May 2017, www.theverge.com/2017/5/14/15626640/esa-astronaut-samantha-cristoforetti-interview-italy-space-espresso. Accessed 7 June 2020.

———. "Expedition 42/43 Crew Interview: Samantha Cristoforetti—Flight Engineer 5." *NASA*, 2014, www.nasa.gov/sites/default/files/cristoforetti_transcript.pdf. Accessed 7 June 2020.

———. "Interview with Samantha Cristoforetti, Heading to Space." *ResearchItaly*, 20 Nov. 2014, www.researchitaly.it/en/interviews/interview-with-samantha-cristoforetti-heading-to-space/#null. Accessed 7 June 2020.

———. "A Life in the Day: The Italian Astronaut Samantha Cristoforetti." Interview by Jeremy Taylor. *The Times*, 3 May 2015, www.thetimes.co.uk/article/a-life-in-the-day-the-italian-astronaut-samantha-cristoforetti-q3b2t8p6rjk. Accessed 7 June 2020.

———. "Meet the Woman Who Has Spent 200 Days in Space." Interview by Jonathan D. Woods and Jeffrey Kluger. *Time*, 10 Aug. 2015, time.com/3990462/samantha-cristoforetti-space/. Accessed 7 June 2020.

Donati, Silvia. "To the Stars and Back: Why We Love Samantha Cristoforetti." *Italy Magazine*, 8 Mar. 2019, www.italymagazine.com/featured-story/stars-and-back-why-we-love-samantha-cristoforetti. Accessed 7 June 2020.

O'Brien, Joe, and Amy Sherden. "Astronaut Samantha Cristoforetti Returns from Record-Breaking Space Mission, Becomes Internet Sensation." *ABC News*, 23 Feb. 2016, www.abc.net.au/news/2015-07-08/astronaut-samantha-cristoforetti-internet-sensation/6604868. Accessed 7 June 2020.

—Joy Crelin

Carmen Yulín Cruz

Date of birth: February 25, 1963
Occupation: Politician

Polls regularly show that up to half of all Americans do not realize that Puerto Rico's 3.4 million residents are citizens of the United States. Given that general lack of knowledge about the unincorporated territory, located in the Caribbean Sea some one thousand miles southeast of Florida, it is unsurprising that before 2017 few had heard of Carmen Yulín Cruz, the mayor of the Puerto Rican capital of San Juan. That changed, however, in September 2017, when Hurricane Maria hit the island. Maria destroyed most of Puerto Rico's infrastructure; killed 2,975 people, according to 2018 estimates by the Puerto Rican government; and left countless others without food, water, electricity, or shelter.

Thanks to her no-holds-barred rhetoric and empathetic style, Cruz became a media spokesperson for those suffering in the wake of the storm. She waded through the flooded streets of San Juan with a bullhorn, helping to rescue and comfort her constituents. She also described to

Photo by Melvin Alfredo via Wikimedia Commons

journalists the horrors she witnessed and called upon the federal government to send desperately needed aid. Media coverage of Maria's aftermath frequently included video of Cruz criticizing the Federal Emergency Management Agency (FEMA) for its inadequate response and pleading for more to be done. In one widely aired news conference, she bluntly said, "People are dying in this country. I am begging, begging anyone that can hear us, to save us from dying. If anybody out there is listening to us, we are dying, and you are killing us with the inefficiency and the bureaucracy."

Cruz's criticism attracted the ire of US President Donald Trump, who attacked the mayor's leadership. Yet despite Trump's disdain, Cruz earned widespread respect, and in 2018 the editors of *Time* named her as one of the hundred most influential people of the year. She did not see her actions as especially heroic or noteworthy, however. "That is my job," she told Richard Fausset and Frances Robles for the *New York Times* (30 Sept. 2017). "My job is to make life better for people, and you cannot make life better if you are [viewing from afar] in a helicopter. You can't make life better for them if you can't touch them." She cares little, she says, for the political ramifications of being so outspoken. "Sometimes you have to shake the tree in order to make things happen," she asserted to Fausset and Robles. "And if that has a political cost, I will take it, as long as it saves lives."

EARLY LIFE AND EDUCATION

Carmen Yulín Cruz Soto was born in San Juan on February 25, 1963, to Pedro Cruz Vega, a maintenance worker, and his wife, Carmen Irene Soto Molina. She has one brother, Pedro José Cruz. In speeches, she has mentioned her family's poverty and her great-grandfather's toil in the sugar cane fields. As a child she sometimes accompanied her father to watch the cane cutters working at dawn, gaining an appreciation for her family history. By all accounts a strong-willed and opinionated youngster, she would later credit one of her grandmothers with imbuing her with spirit. "She told me: never start a fight, but always finish one," Cruz recalled to John Paul Rathbone for the *Financial Times* (7 Sept. 2018).

While Cruz has made reference in interviews and public speaking events to her dyslexia, she was an honor student at San Juan's Julio Sellés Solá Elementary School. At her secondary school, which was affiliated with the University of Puerto Rico, she served as both the head of the student council and a presidential youth summit representative.

Like many Puerto Rican students, Cruz left the island for the mainland to attend college. In 1984 she graduated, cum laude, from Boston University, with a bachelor's degree in political science and a concentration in human resources management. She was then offered a scholarship to study at Carnegie Mellon University's Heinz College of Information Systems and Public Policy. She received a master's degree in public policy and management in 1986 and became the inaugural winner of the Spirit Award (later known as the Barbara Jenkins Award), given to students who have made important contributions to college life.

Cruz remained on the mainland to start her career, choosing to focus on human resources. She worked at a series of organizations that included Colgate-Palmolive, Scotiabank, and the US Treasury Department. Fausset and Robles referred to her during this period as a "star in the blue-chip world of corporate America." In 1992 she returned to Puerto Rico to enter politics.

POLITICAL CAREER

With her political science and public policy background, Cruz eventually found work as an adviser to Sila María Calderón, a San Juan mayor who later became Puerto Rico's governor. Cruz also advised the head of the Puerto Rico House of Representatives. In 2000, as a member of the centrist Partido Popular Democrático (Popular Democratic Party or PPD), she ran unsuccessfully for a House seat in District One.

In 2005 the governor of Puerto Rico appointed Cruz to the San Juan Reorganization Commission. In 2008 Cruz ran once again for the Puerto Rico House of Representatives. That year she fared better, winning an at-large seat representing the entire island.

As San Juan's 2012 mayoral election neared, Cruz toyed with the idea of throwing her hat into the ring against three-time incumbent Jorge Santini, considered by political observers to be a formidable opponent. When she finally decided to enter the race, a confident Santini found her to be little threat, referring to her repeatedly as "esa señora," or "that woman." She, by contrast, took to invoking the image of the "pitirre," a tiny but tenacious bird known for valiantly attacking larger ones.

As Santini attempted to tar the admittedly left-leaning Cruz as a socialist, she began building a strong grassroots coalition comprised of taxi drivers, immigrants from the Dominican Republic, students, and the LGBTQ community. Thanks to that support, on November 6, 2012, she was elected as mayor of San Juan.

Cruz, a member of the PPD's small left wing, coasted easily to reelection in 2016. Among her popular actions as two-term mayor were allowing San Juan government health workers to unionize and supporting student-led strikes. She also met with approval from her constituents for appearing before Congress to demand that Puerto Rico, while remaining a US territory, be given more independence and control over its own affairs. Her popularity—and international profile—skyrocketed even more, however, when tragedy hit the island.

HURRICANE MARIA
A fierce Category 5 hurricane, Maria struck Puerto Rico on September 20, 2017, after making landfall on Dominica two days before. The storm destroyed communications and power infrastructure, flooded roads, flattened entire neighborhoods, and cut the island off almost entirely from the mainland. With little way to contact the outside world, residents relied on their towns' mayors for instruction and guidance.

Cruz was forced to live with her family and staffers at the Roberto Clemente Coliseum, a concrete venue she later took to ironically calling "the Trump Tower Presidential Suites" or "my Mar-a-Lago," after President Trump's well-known properties. When not strategizing there, she was out in the streets of San Juan, wearing what would soon be considered her trademark work boots. She handed out solar-powered lanterns, tried to organize emergency food supplies, and attempted to otherwise aid the people she encountered. Chief among her missions was to spread the word to the wider world about Puerto Rico's plight, and as journalists managed to make their way to San Juan, she exhorted them to help.

Cruz quickly became known among the international press for her sometimes-sharp tongue and impatience with the Trump administration. When acting Homeland Security Secretary Elaine Duke defended the federal government's response to the storm, saying, "It is really a good-news story, in terms of our ability to reach people," Cruz shot back that it was not good news for those who were still hungry, thirsty, and homeless. When Trump intimated that Cruz was in the pocket of Democrats (despite the fact that Puerto Rico has different political parties than the mainland) and called her a "nasty woman" she began wearing a t-shirt emblazoned with the word "nasty."

In contrast to Trump and his followers, many commentators celebrated Cruz and helped elevate her public profile even further. Many saw her as an important voice drawing attention to the often-overlooked complications of Puerto Rico's territorial status. In an essay celebrating Cruz's inclusion on the prestigious *Time* 100 2018 list, actor Benicio Del Toro noted how Puerto Rico's 3.4 million American citizens have no representation in Congress and are unable to vote for president—making the attention Cruz was able to capture even more remarkable and important. Calling her "passionate, courageous and articulate," Del Toro concluded, "Cruz's legacy will be marked by her uncompromising refusal to let anyone ignore the lives of those affected by the hurricane."

LOOKING TO THE FUTURE
In March 2019, Cruz announced that she would be running in Puerto Rico's November 2020 gubernatorial race. "I've been thinking for a long time, what's the best way I can serve Puerto Rico," she said, as quoted by Nicole Acevedo for *NBC News* (22 Mar. 2019). "I'm going to do so by becoming the next governor."

Cruz also served as one of four national cochairs on Senator Bernie Sanders's 2020 presidential campaign. She told Scott Barsotti for the Heinz College website (Aug. 2018), that she values honesty and building consensus in the political arena. "Leaders need to respect people enough not to play with the truth," she said. Later in the same interview she explained, "It isn't about your position, but your conviction. You have world leaders who do not inspire trust or empathy because they are incapable of putting that out there or seeing past their own biases. . . . Coming up with what the problem is from an unbiased perspective, that gives people a common ground to build a solution."

PERSONAL LIFE
In 2010 Cruz married her third husband, psychologist and university professor Alfredo Carrasquillo, just three months after meeting him. They divorced within a year but remarried in 2013, only to divorce again in 2017. She has one daughter, Marina Yulín Paul Cruz, from an earlier marriage.

A dog owner, Cruz's hobbies included teaching herself to play the ukulele and reading biographies. She prefers to do all her own cooking, laundry, and shopping. "It's important," she told Rathbone. "Otherwise, as a politician, you can feel different from others. That's dangerous. It's a disservice."

SUGGESTED READING

Acevedo, Nicole. "San Juan Mayor Carmen Yulín Cruz to Run for Puerto Rico Governor in 2020." *NBC News*, 22 Mar. 2019, www.nbcnews.com/news/latino/san-juan-mayor-carmen-yul-n-cruz-run-puerto-rico-n986331. Accessed 19 Feb. 2020.

Barsotti, Scott. "Carmen Yulín Cruz: The Most Resilient Mayor in the United States." *Heinz College*, Carnegie Mellon University, Aug. 2018, www.heinz.cmu.edu/media/2018/August/carmen-yulin-cruz-most-resilient-mayor. Accessed 19 Feb. 2020.

Del Toro, Benicio. "Time 100 2018: Carmen Yulín Cruz," *Time*, time.com/collection/most-influential-people-2018/5217603/carmen-yulin-cruz/. Accessed 19 Feb. 2020.

Fausset, Richard, and Frances Robles. "Who Is Carmen Yulín Cruz, the Puerto Rican Mayor Criticized by Trump?" *The New York Times*, 30 Sept. 2017, www.nytimes.com/2017/09/30/us/san-juan-mayor-cruz.html. Accessed 19 Feb. 2020.

Hernández, Arelis R., et al. "Trump Called San Juan's Mayor a Weak Leader. Here's What Her Leadership Looks Like." *The Washington Post*, 30 Sept. 2017, www.washingtonpost.com/news/post-nation/wp/2017/09/30/trump-called-san-juans-mayor-a-weak-leader-heres-what-her-leadership-looks-like/. Accessed 19 Feb. 2020.

Menendez, Alicia. "Carmen Yulin Cruz on Puerto Rico's Future & What She Learned from Tangling with Trump." *Bustle*, 12 Apr. 2019, www.bustle.com/p/carmen-yulin-cruz-on-puerto-ricos-future-what-she-learned-from-tangling-with-trump-17034244. Accessed 19 Feb. 2020.

Rathbone, John Paul. "The Puerto Rico Mayor Who Took On Trump." *Financial Times*, 7 Sept. 2018, www.ft.com/content/241991d2-b02d-11e8-8d14-6f049d06439c. Accessed 19 Feb. 2020.

—*Mari Rich*

Alex Cuba

Date of birth: 1974
Occupation: Singer-songwriter

Alex Cuba is an award-winning Cuban Canadian singer-songwriter. He has won four Latin Grammy Awards, including the award for best new artist in 2010, and was nominated for five more Latin Grammys and three Grammy Awards. He has also won multiple Juno Awards, which recognize musical artists in Canada. Cuba grew up playing traditional Cuban dance music, called Cuban son (*son cubano*), a style made internationally popular by the Buena Vista Social Club. Cuba's career trajectory illustrates his love for traditional Cuban music, as well as his desire to set himself apart from it. Cuba began his career as a bassist, but after settling in Canada in 1999, he discovered his voice as a singer and guitarist, playing Cuban music influenced by American pop, jazz, and soul. "Cuba laid the foundation," Cuba told Roger Levesque for the *Edmonton Journal* (3 Nov. 2017), "but in many ways Canada shaped me."

EARLY LIFE

Alex Cuba was born Alexis Puentes in the small town of Artemisa, Cuba, in 1974. He and his fraternal twin brother, Adonis Puentes, grew up in a musical family. Their father, Valentín Puentes, was a guitarist and music teacher at a neighborhood cultural center across the street from their childhood home. In an interview in 2000, Adonis, who is also a singer-songwriter,

Photo by Tibrina Hobson/Getty Images

recalled meeting and jamming with renowned Cuban artists like the late singers Ibrahim Ferrer and Celina González, the latter considered the queen of campesina, or Cuban country music. "We'd be there every day," Adonis told Tim Perlich for *Now Toronto* (27 July 2000) of the school where their father taught, "surrounded by musicians and bands rehearsing." When Cuba was four years old, he performed with his father's students on television. He played a Cuban percussion instrument. "I remember playing it. I remember people looking at me. I remember feeling nervous because I was in front of a camera. I remember people saying 'Oh, look how cute he is,'" Cuba told a reporter for British Columbia's *Columbia Valley Pioneer* (2 Aug. 2018). "I was having fun. I liked what I was doing."

Cuba began taking guitar lessons at age six. At fourteen, he took up the electric bass. The instrument led him to American music, including funk, jazz, blues, and pop. Cuba is also influenced by Cuban trova music, a style that features a singer-songwriter accompanied by a guitar. Early on, Cuba's father discouraged him from singing, arguing that his voice did not have the booming quality integral to Cuban music. As a young man, Cuba played bass for the jazz-fusion group the Tempermentos and joined his father's band, Los Puentes. In 1995, the band toured across Canada.

THE PUENTES BROTHERS

Cuba immigrated to Victoria, British Columbia, in 1999. In 2000, he and Adonis released an album called *Morumba Cubana* as the Puentes Brothers. The brothers, both living in Canada, longed to create the traditional music of their youth in their own image. "What I've always wanted to play was traditional music updated with our modern ideas about harmony and lyrics," Cuba told Perlich. "With this band we formed, I finally have that opportunity." *Morumba Cubana* was nominated for a 2001 Juno Award for World Album of the Year.

EARLY SOLO CAREER

Cuba moved to his wife's hometown of Smithers, British Columbia, in 2003. Smithers is small, with a population of just over five thousand people, and surrounded by mountains. Cuba found the solitude inspiring; he traded his bass for a guitar and eschewed the big band sound of traditional Cuban music in favor of a solo acoustic sound. He adopted the stage name Alex Cuba, and released his first solo album, *Humo de tabaco* [Tobacco Smoke], in 2005. All the songs were in Spanish, though the mid-tempo ballad "Lo mismo que yo" ["Same as Me"] featured English verses by the Canadian singer-songwriter Ron Sexsmith. Upon the launch of the album, Cuba met Andres Mendoza, who would later become

his manager. "I was blown away by his talent, his stage presence, his charisma and his lyrical quality," Mendoza told Nicholas Jennings for *Words & Music* (21 Mar. 2011). "I was like, 'This guy is a star.'" *Humo de tabaco* won a Juno Award for World Music Album of the Year in 2006.

US label Blue Note Records hoped to sign Cuba for his second solo album. They were in negotiations with him for eight months over the album's production and release but could not agree on the artistic direction and parted ways amicably. Cuba later launched his own label, Caracol Records, and became an independent artist. Caracol released his second solo album, *Agua del pozo* [Well Water], in 2007, for distribution in the United States and Canada through EMI. It included the hit "Si pero no" ["Yes but No"], as well as the popular song "Vampiro." The album also won a Juno Award for World Music Album of the Year in 2008.

In 2008, Canadian singer-songwriter Nelly Furtado, best known for her 2000 top-ten hit "I'm Like a Bird," contacted Cuba about writing for her first Spanish-language album, *Mi plan* (2009). It proved to be a fruitful collaboration. Cuba cowrote more than half of the songs on the album, including the title track, a duet between him and Furtado. Another song, the pop tune "Manos al aire" ["Hands in the Air"], hit number one on the Billboard Latin Songs chart. The album went on to win a Latin Grammy Award for Best Female Pop Vocal Album in 2010.

ALEX CUBA

Cuba released his third solo album, the self-titled *Alex Cuba*, in 2009. "This record finds Cuba sounding less moody than usual, and appropriately surrounded by funky and lighthearted music," Jasmine Garsd wrote for National Public Radio (NPR) (30 May 2010). In multiple interviews, Cuba has said that he is more inspired by happiness than sadness; his music reflects that. The pop-influenced "Caballo"—in which Cuba asks a woman to ride a horse with him—features a joyful horn section. The reggae-inspired "Directo" is similarly playful, with the lyric, "I send you this song that says nothing, but it goes directly to your heart." *Alex Cuba* also features "If You Give Me Love," the first song he wrote entirely in English. "It's contagiously funky," Garsd wrote, "though his English lyrics pale in comparison to his Spanish-language creations." *Alex Cuba* was nominated for a Latin Grammy Award for Best Male Pop Vocal Album in 2010. Although he did not win that award, Cuba took home a Latin Grammy Award for Best New Artist.

RUIDO EN EL SISTEMA

In 2012, Cuba released *Ruido en el sistema* [Static in the System]. In a statement before the album's release, he wrote, as quoted by Alex Hudson for Toronto's *Exclaim* magazine (15 Aug. 2012), that it referred to "the amount of static/noise that we have now in our lives covering up the truth from us in so many ways." In the title track, Cuba sings about the numbing distractions of life, while the upbeat "Nadie como tu" ["No-one Like You"] features vocals by Furtado. The album, which incorporates elements of jazz and rock, earned him a Socan Hagood Hardy Award for outstanding achievement in jazz and world music. The same year, Cuba won a Latin Grammy Award for Best Tropical Song for writing Dominican singer Milly Quezada's exuberant hit, "Toma mi vida" ["Take My Life"]. In 2013, a song from *Ruido en el sistema* [System Noise] called "Eres tu" [It's You] won a Latin Grammy for Best Music Video.

HEALER

Cuba's fifth album, *Healer* (2015), features a handful of English-language songs and a host of collaborators. The half-English, half-Spanish pop song "Half a Chance" features Sexsmith, while the percussive "Beautiful Mistakes" features Canadian jazz singer Alejandra Ribera. Michael J. Warren, who reviewed the album for *Exclaim* (27 Mar. 2015), wrote that *Healer* "largely continues down the same sonic lane as Cuba's previous work . . . and remains a pleasant merging of traditional Cuba and contemporary soul music," he concluded. *Healer* won a Latin Grammy Award for Best Singer-Songwriter Album and was nominated for a Grammy for Best Latin Pop Album in 2016.

LO ÚNICO CONSTANTE

Cuba's sixth album, *Lo único constante* [The Only Constant] (2017), was influenced by a style of Cuban music called *filin* (from the English word "feeling") based on traditional trova music, which became popular in Havana in the 1940s. The style combines acoustic guitar and romantic American jazz. "*Lo único constante* is superbly minimalistic yet profoundly full," Marisa Arbona-Ruiz wrote for NPR (22 Apr. 2017). "Get ready for a sensory upload of sublime playing, creative arrangements and melodic delight." She offered particular praise for the album's catchy first single, "Todas las cabezas están locas" ("All Heads Are Crazy"), for its "upbeat polyrhythms and syncopated hand claps." *Lo único constante* was nominated for a Latin Grammy Award for Best Singer-Songwriter Album, as well as a Grammy Award for Best Latin Pop Album.

SUBLIME

Cuba wrote his seventh album, *Sublime* (2019), in Canada and Mexico, where he has found tremendous popularity. Cuba wanted the album "to be more intimate, naked, and more vulnerable," he told Kerry Doole for *Words & Music* (8 Oct. 2019). To that end, Cuba self-produced the album and plays every instrument—including the congas for the first time in his life. Cuba collaborated with guest singers, including the eighty-nine-year-old Cuban legend Omara Portuondo, on the song "Y si mañana" ("And If Tomorrow"). Of the album, Cuba told Doole: "It took a lot of courage to get to this point. I'm coming out with a somewhat quiet and very melodic album. That may not fit this climate of music, but it's exactly what I wanted to do," he said, noting the popularity of the reggaeton dance hit "Despacito" ["Slowly"].

PERSONAL LIFE

Cuba met his wife, Sarah Goodacre-Puentes, then a student at Simon Fraser University, in Vancouver in 1995. "It was a very powerful moment that would shape my entire life," Cuba told François Marchand for the *Vancouver Sun* (3 Feb. 2016). "We met in March and that same year in December we got married." The couple co-own Caracol Records, which Goodacre-Puentes manages, and have three children. The family lives in Smithers, British Columbia.

SUGGESTED READING

"Alex Cuba on Love, Latin Music and Little Hands." *The Columbia Valley Pioneer*, 2 Aug. 2018, www.columbiavalleypioneer.com/entertainment/alex-cuba-on-love-latin-music-and-little-hands/. Accessed 19 Jan. 2020.

Arbona-Ruiz, Marisa. "Songs We Love: Alex Cuba, 'Todas Las Cabezas Están Locas.'" *NPR*, 22 Apr. 2017, www.npr.org/sections/altlatino/2017/04/22/524282306/songs-we-love-alex-cuba-todas-las-cabezas-est-n-locas. Accessed 20 Jan. 2020.

Garsd, Jasmine. "First Listen: Alex Cuba, 'Alex Cuba.'" *NPR*, 30 May 2010, www.npr.org/templates/story/story.php?storyId=127215122. Accessed 20 Jan. 2020.

Levesque, Roger. "Cuban Roots Inspire Essential Songs for Acclaimed Canadian Singer." *Edmonton Journal*, 3 Nov. 2017, edmontonjournal.com/entertainment/local-arts/cuban-roots-inspire-essential-songs-for-acclaimed-canadian-singer. Accessed 19 Jan. 2020.

Marchand, François. "B.C. Singer-Songwriter Alex Cuba Sets Sights on Grammys." *Vancouver Sun*, 3 Feb. 2016, vancouversun.com/entertainment/music/b-c-singer-songwriter-alex-cuba-sets-sights-on-grammys. Accessed 19 Jan. 2020.

Perlich, Tim. "Puentes Discover Cuban Roots in Canada." *Now Toronto*, 27 Jul. 2000, nowtoronto.com/music/puentes-discover-cuban-roots-in-canada/. Accessed 19 Jan. 2020.

Warren, Michael J. "Alex Cuba—Healer." *Exclaim*, 27 Mar. 2015, exclaim.ca/music/

article/alex_cuba-healer. Accessed 20 Jan. 2020.

SELECTED WORKS
Alex Cuba, 2009; *Healer*, 2015; *Lo único constante*, 2017; *Sublime*, 2019

—*Molly Hagan*

Sharice Davids

Born: May 22, 1980
Occupation: Lawyer and politician

"Sharice Davids' story may not sound like the average biography of a lawmaker," Eugene Daniels wrote for *Politico* (9 Apr. 2019), and, indeed, most profiles of Davids have tended to focus on the elements of her background that made her a political trailblazer. She became one of the first two American Indian women elected to the US Congress (along with New Mexico's Debra Haaland), winning a House of Representatives seat from Kansas in 2018 as a Democrat. She also became the first openly LGBTQ person to represent Kansas. Furthermore, Davids earned attention for her working-class background—she was the first member of her family to attend college—and, perhaps more unusually, for her previous experience as a mixed martial arts (MMA) fighter, facts that she touted in her campaign to convey her determination and spirit. When Daniels asked how her identity might impact her work on Capitol Hill, Davids replied "It helps me see that there are lots of different lenses and experiences that shape the way people experience this world. Your experience . . . might be slightly different than mine, or vastly different than mine, depending on what we're talking about, but it's still just as real and valid and should be heard and be part of how we come up with our policy."

A member of the Ho-Chunk Nation, Davids earned a law degree and worked in community development. After serving as a 2016–17 White House Fellow she initially sought to support others as political candidates, particularly women, before determining to run for office herself. In winning Kansas's Third Congressional District she flipped a seat long held by Republicans and became part of a historically diverse congressional class. Once in office Davids turned her attention to the details of policy rather than her identity; she recognized the groundbreaking nature of her success and its potential influence. "My day-to-day feels very much like the focus is on the specific topics and issues and legislation," she told Vincent Schilling of *Indian Country Today* (22 Apr. 2019). "But then when I have that

Photo by Kristie Boyd, U.S. House Office of Photography via Wikimedia Commons

chance to take a step back and realize that folks like Deb Haaland and I are bringing a completely different lived experience and perspective to all of this. . . . It will be a part of making sure that other people after us see that not only is it a possibility, but it is likely."

EARLY LIFE AND EDUCATION
Sharice Davids was born on May 22, 1980, in Frankfurt, West Germany, where her mother, Crystal Herriage, was then stationed as a member of the US Army. Because of Herriage's military career, Davids and her brother moved frequently throughout their childhoods. Eventually the family settled in Leavenworth, Kansas, where Herriage took a job with the US Postal Service. It was sometimes a struggle to make ends meet, and although Davids became deeply interested in martial arts—as a child she was obsessed with film star and martial artist Bruce Lee—she could not afford formal lessons.

After graduating from Leavenworth High School in 1998, Davids entered Haskell Indian Nations University in Kansas, becoming the first in her family to attend college. "I didn't know what I wanted to do with my life at that point, but I was drawn to Haskell because it was inexpensive and I was able to take classes that interested me," she recalled to Suzette Brewer for the *Tribal College Journal of American Indian Higher Education* (8 Nov. 2018). "It had the kind of environment that allowed us as Native students to challenge baseline assumptions and have all these different conversations with people from other tribes about things we were passionate about."

Paying her way through college with a variety of jobs, Davids later attended Johnson County Community College and the University of Kansas before enrolling at the University of Missouri-Kansas City, where in 2007 she earned a degree in business administration. It was during her college years that she realized that she could now arrange for her own martial-arts lessons. She began with Brazilian capoeira before taking up tae kwon do and karate, and at the suggestion of a coach she debuted as an amateur MMA competitor in 2006. She won her first MMA fight in less than two minutes.

Despite demonstrating her skills in the ring, Davids decided to continue her education rather than immediately pursue a career in MMA—a sport that at the time provided few opportunities for women. While she continued to fight on an amateur level, she embarked on studies at Cornell Law School, where she earned a JD in 2010. The considerable student debt she incurred along the way would later inform her political platform.

BEFORE POLITICS
After earning her degree from Cornell, Davids joined SNR Denton, a large law firm, in 2010. After less than two years she left that job to serve as director of economic development at the Red Cloud Indian School on South Dakota's Pine Ridge Indian Reservation, home to the Oglala Lakota people, where she worked to develop an entrepreneurial program. She then became the deputy director of the Thunder Valley Community Development Corporation, a nonprofit that undertook various social initiatives on the Pine Ridge reservation.

On the reservation Davids founded Hoka! Coffee, a small entrepreneurial venture. However, it failed to take off. She also advised tribal clients on legal matters. Meanwhile, witnessing the growth in women's MMA, Davids decided to attempt a professional fighting career in 2013. She won her first professional fight and in 2014 tried out for an edition of the reality show *The Ultimate Fighter*, which offered contestants a chance to win a lucrative Ultimate Fighting Championship (UFC) contract. She did not make the cut, however, and eventually realized she wanted to take a different path. "You train for 12 years of your life and you get three minutes to demonstrate that to a panel of people who will be deciding if you get to be in the UFC or not," she told Karim Zidan for the *Guardian* (6 Aug. 2018). "I felt that—while I would always be a martial artist—I was done trying to take MMA fights."

Davids refocused on reservation community projects, and from 2015 to 2016 she served on the board of directors for Twelve Clans Inc., an economic development organization owned by the Ho-Chunk Nation. Then in 2016 she was chosen for the highly selective White House Fellows program and assigned to the US Department of Transportation. Her time in that position coincided with the transition between the administrations of President Barack Obama and President Donald Trump, which furthered her desire to work for social change. She returned to Kansas after the fellowship with a new level of political determination.

Davids set about joining the search to find a female Democratic Party candidate capable of unseating incumbent Republican representative Kevin Yoder, who had entered Congress in 2003 but was viewed as vulnerable. She ran into constant roadblocks. "No one was interested," she explained to Brewer. "We had talked to probably six different people and were getting nowhere. So I thought, if I'm this worked up about it then I'm just gonna do it. That's when I made the decision to run."

US HOUSE OF REPRESENTATIVES
Davids announced her candidacy in February 2018, joining a fairly crowded primary field. Her most notable primary opponent was Brent Welder, who ran a more left-wing campaign and had support from several national progressive figures. Yet Davids narrowly defeated Welder as well as several others to take the Democratic nomination. She made gun control a centerpiece of her platform, along with accessible health care and improved education.

With the financial support of national Democratic leaders and organizations, Davids went on to beat Yoder in the midterm with about 54 percent of the vote. The win made her the first Democrat to represent the Third District in a decade and helped the Democrats take control of the House. Media coverage of the victory, however, focused largely on her status as one of the first two American Indian women elected to Congress and Kansas's first openly gay representative. To her supporters, her personal background was just part of her appeal. "Sharice won the hearts of voters by putting forward a positive and solutions-oriented agenda while explaining how her experiences as a Native American LGBTQ woman influenced her policy positions and beliefs," Annise Parker, head of the LGBTQ Victory Fund, told Brooke Sopelsa and Tim Fitzsimons for *NBC News* (7 Nov. 2018). "Sharice's victory tonight will become a model for other LGBTQ leaders considering a run for office in red states or districts."

Davids was sworn in on January 3, 2019. She was assigned to the Committee on Small Business and the Committee on Transportation and Infrastructure and became a cochair of the Congressional LGBT Equality Caucus and vice-chair of the Congressional Native American

Caucus. Many in the media considered her part of a group of newly elected young, female progressives. Yet Davids earned a reputation for keeping a lower profile than some of her more left-wing peers. Although she won much praise among centrists for her relationship-building skills and quiet advocacy for her district, she also drew criticism from some progressives disappointed in her moderate positions on issues such as universal health care. However, in a show of Democratic Party unity, she was the only representative from Kansas to vote to impeach President Trump in December 2019.

As the 2020 election approached, Davids was increasingly seen as a rising Democratic star, distinguished by her studious approach to legislation. "Sharice Davids may be the only person that reads every sentence of every bill, of every amendment," Missouri representative Emanuel Cleaver admiringly told Bryan Lowry for the *Kansas City Star* (13 Apr. 2019). For her part, Davids took her title of "representative" seriously, aiming to listen to constituents from across the political spectrum. As she told Lowry, "When I talk to folks I've asked them . . . when you had the chance to talk to my predecessor what were the things that were helpful and what were the things that you would like to see different and asking those questions I think gets to core of why somebody should be sent to DC."

PERSONAL LIFE
Davids noted that at times she faced discrimination as an LGBTQ person. For example, when working on the Pine Ridge Indian Reservation she and her then partner were ineligible for an employee housing benefit.

In 2017 Davids and her brother debuted the video podcast *Starty Pants*, featuring entrepreneurs in the Greater Kansas City area with a focus on women, people of color, and members of the LGBTQ community.

SUGGESTED READING
Brewer, Suzette. "Sharice Davids and the Rise of the Native Electorate." *Tribal College Journal of American Indian Higher Education*, 8 Nov. 2018, tribalcollegejournal.org/sharice-davids-and-the-rise-of-the-native-electorate/. Accessed 14 July 2020.

Davids, Sharice. "Rep. Sharice Davids Reflects on Her First 100 Days in Congress." Interview by Vincent Schilling. *Indian Country Today*, 22 Apr. 2019, indiancountrytoday.com/news/rep-sharice-davids-reflects-on-her-first-100-days-in-congress-B8agleznl0GSs-BTEw7TF7g. Accessed 14 July 2020.

Hignett, Katherine. "Who Is Sharice Davids? Kansas Democrat Becomes First Openly LGBT Native American Woman Elected to House." *Newsweek*, 7 Nov. 2018, www. newsweek.com/who-sharice-davids-kansas-democrat-becomes-first-openly-lgbt-native-american-1205319. Accessed 14 July 2020.

Lowry, Brian. "'Not a Showoff.' Sharice Davids' Quiet Approach Endears Her to Democratic Leaders." *The Kansas City Star*, 13 Apr. 2019, www.kansascity.com/news/politics-government/article229177954.html. Accessed 14 July 2020.

___, and Katy Bergen. "Sharice Davids Makes History: Kansas' 1st Gay Rep, 1st Native American Woman in Congress." *The Kansas City Star*, 7 Nov. 2018, www.kansascity.com/news/politics-government/election/article221156115.html. Accessed 14 July 2020.

Sopelsa, Brooke, and Tim Fitzsimons. "Sharice Davids, a Lesbian Native American, Makes Political History in Kansas." *NBC News*, 7 Nov. 2018, www.nbcnews.com/feature/nbc-out/sharice-davids-lesbian-native-american-makes-political-history-kansas-n933211. Accessed 6 Aug. 2020.

Zidan, Karim. "How Sharice Davids Traded in MMA for a Shot at Political History." *The Guardian*, 6 Aug. 2018, www.theguardian.com/sport/2018/aug/06/sharice-evans-us-congress-mixed-martial-arts. Accessed 14 July 2020.

—*Mari Rich*

Shane Dawson

Date of birth: July 19, 1988
Occupation: YouTuber

Shane Dawson is "a legit YouTube star," as Tom Ward wrote for *Forbes* (27 July 2017) when Dawson was named sixth on the Forbes Top Influencers List of 2017. "That term is thrown around loosely these days, but he's the real deal." Dawson joined the video-sharing platform relatively early in its development and became one of the first people to rise to fame under its auspices. His various YouTube channels—which feature comedy sketches, personal confessionals, biographical profiles, and conspiracy theories—amassed well over twenty-two million subscribers by 2019. Thanks to banner ads and product tie-ins, he was estimated to be worth some $12 million.

"It's easy to dismiss YouTube and its stars as anything but the juggernaut it's become," Jeff Slate wrote for *Quartz* (10 July 2015). "Most of us use it to watch news clips, conveniently hear our favorite music (sorry Tidal), or just to pass the time at work, the way we used to spend evenings channel-surfing. But to at least a generation, YouTube is its own ecosystem, with stars as

Photo by heartrayna via Wikimedia Commons

then I'd open my mouth and they'd be like, 'He's funny. We don't know what to do with this.' So I said, 'I'm just gonna do my own thing.'"

THE START OF A YOUTUBE CAREER

YouTube launched in 2005, and Dawson originally considered it as little more than a place to simply store content he created in high school. In 2008, after being rejected from multiple acting jobs, he began uploading those videos, which included short comedic sketches, to the still relatively new platform. "I just wanted to make movies," Dawson told Slate. "I'd wanted to be a director since I was five, and had been making videos since I was a kid." It came as something of a shock to him when a raunchy video he had made of himself pole dancing at the Jenny Craig location garnered enough attention to get him, his mother, and his brother fired. He later found work as a security guard at an aquarium in Long Beach. The post was undemanding enough that he had ample time to make new videos each week. His early efforts involved Dawson playing such offensively stereotypical characters as Barb the Lesbian, Guadalupe/Fruit Lupe, and Shanaynay the ghetto girl, but despite the problematic nature of the material, the videos began amassing a large, loyal viewership. Among his most popular sketches was "Fred Is Dead," (2008) which depicted Shanaynay murdering a well-liked rival YouTuber at Dawson's behest.

In addition to his comedic content, Dawson also won fans with his seemingly heartfelt video diaries, in which he explored sensitive subjects like his own body dysmorphia and angst. "I kind of made the decision early on to be extremely open about everything and just pretend like all of these people watching were my close friends that I could tell stuff to and be honest with," he explained to Considine.

When his videos began regularly attracting fifty thousand views each, YouTube approached Dawson to join its new partnership program, which allowed the platform to run advertising along with a creator's content and split the revenues. Because of the often offensive nature of his work, Dawson did not earn a large sum of money at first, but it was enough to pay for a new apartment in a somewhat better neighborhood. Eventually his mother was able to quit her job and devote herself to helping him with the videos, and he began to get offers for small brand deals, earning money to promote products or services directly within his videos. By September 2011, Dawson had the fifth most-subscribed-to YouTube channel.

In addition to YouTube, Dawson soon began reaching fans through other outlets. He released several songs and music videos on both his YouTube Channel and on iTunes, including "Maybe This Christmas" (2012) and "Wanna Make Love

big as any in movies or on television." Dawson undeniably set the tone for numerous other YouTubers who followed in his wake. "He wasn't the first person to realize that his brand of one-man variety show—equal parts teen confessional, pop satire and really great hair—might appeal to legions of angsty, wry-minded teens," Austin Considine opined for the *New York Times* (2 Apr. 2010). "But he got in early and well, with little more than a camera, a laptop and a burning need to communicate."

EARLY LIFE AND EDUCATION

Dawson was born Shane Lee Yaw on July 19, 1988, to Kyle Yaw Jr., an abusive alcoholic who ultimately left the family, and Teresa Yaw. He has two older brothers, Jacob Thomas Yaw and Jerid Yaw. Dawson grew up in Long Beach, California. He began making short videos when he was seven or eight years old. At Lakewood High School, which he attended as a teen, he was bullied mercilessly for both his low socioeconomic status and his weight, but he found some escape in writing and videography. At eighteen, Dawson lost almost 150 pounds on Jenny Craig, a diet program in which clients purchase pre-prepared frozen meals and check in regularly with a counselor. He soon accepted a job at a local Jenny Craig storefront operation where his mother and brothers also found work.

At the same time, Dawson, determined to be involved in the film industry in some capacity, auditioned for any acting job he learned of. "I was auditioning for stuff, commercials, and wasn't getting any work because my 'type' was suicidal gay teenager," he quipped to Ward. "But to You" (2013). In 2013, he began hosting the podcast *Shane and Friends*, which continued until 2017. He also wrote two best-selling collections of autobiographical essays: *I Hate My-selfie* (2015) and *It Gets Worse* (2016). In 2014, Dawson participated in the Starz reality series *The Chair*, during which two aspiring directors are given the same script and must each make a film. Dawson's directorial entry, which he titled *Not Cool*, was pilloried by professional critics as tasteless and unfunny but was nonetheless chosen by viewers to win the $250,000 prize. The full film, in which Dawson also starred, was released later that year.

CONTROVERSIES

Dawson's journey to YouTube stardom was marked by regular drama and controversy. He is often called upon to apologize for racist tropes and other objectionable content. "Comic sketches that include a vampire drinking menstrual blood can't be everyone's idea of entertainment," Considine wrote. "But considering that that video alone has earned nearly six million views, perhaps there's a more appropriate question: Does it matter?" Attempting to explain Dawson's immense popularity to the older and more culturally conventional readers of the *New York Times*, Considine approached Robert J. Thompson, the founding director of the Bleier Center for Television and Popular Culture at Syracuse University. Thompson explained, "This isn't something that you'd watch as your only form of entertainment. But when you're sitting around, looking at videos and sending them to other people, I guess he is developing this new, comic style that is unique to the Internet." Answering those who assert that his work is unsuitable for young people, he somewhat tautologically told Slate, "I've never made videos for teenagers. They should not be watching my videos. They're not for them. But that's the medium, that's who's watching."

In 2014, Dawson found himself accused of copyright infringement when he released a parody of singer Taylor Swift's hit song "Blank Space," only to have her labels, Big Machine Records and Sony, insist upon the video's removal. (It was later restored to the platform.) He also faced allegations of purposely tagging his videos with misleading labels to attract unwitting viewers—a charge that he strenuously denied.

NEW DIRECTIONS

In 2018, Dawson launched a series of documentaries aimed at exploring the lives of other viral internet stars. The first series covered YouTuber Jake Paul, a prankster whose stunts include tossing furniture into an empty pool and setting it on fire and hiding in a restroom at the White House undetected for several hours. The first installment of the eight-part series, *The Mind of Jake Paul* (2018), was watched seven million times within the first few hours it was posted. Dawson also released a series about Tana Mongeau, a YouTuber whose attempts to organize the 2018 fan convention TanaCon ended in chaos. Dawson's popularity skyrocketed thanks to the documentaries. Julia Alexander wrote for the youth-oriented entertainment site *Polygon* (3 Aug. 2018), "Dawson has spearheaded an entirely new genre of video on YouTube that somehow makes it feel fresh all over again. It feels like new era of entertainment, echoing the past, and kicking off a trend that everyone will soon be replicating."

His third documentary series focused on Jeffree Star, a would-be singer, longtime internet sensation, and successful cosmetics entrepreneur who is well known for starting feuds with other online celebrities. The five-part *Secret World of Jeffree Star* attracted tens of millions of viewers with its video tour of Star's jam-packed closet and its insider look at the cutthroat world of the cosmetics industry. A second season featuring Star, titled the *Beautiful World of Jeffree Star*, followed the creation and 2019 release of Dawson and Star's collaborative makeup line.

Deemed less praiseworthy were Dawson's conspiracy theory videos of early 2019, in which he put forth offbeat ideas involving Chuck E. Cheese (which he claimed served patrons' uneaten pizza to other diners), children's television shows (which he asserted spread nefarious subliminal messages), iPhones (which supposedly secretly recorded their owners' every word), and the California wildfires (which had, according to him, been started by high-powered military lasers). The videos attracted tens of millions of views and helped precipitate a change in YouTube's recommendation algorithms, which were tweaked to reduce the spread of misleading or harmful content.

PERSONAL LIFE

In 2015, Dawson announced that he was bisexual. Shortly thereafter he became romantically involved with internet personality Ryland Adams. The couple got engaged in March 2019. They live together in Calabasas, California, with a menagerie of pets.

SUGGESTED READING

Alexander, Julia. "Shane Dawson's New Documentaries Crack YouTube Culture's Kardashian Problem." *Polygon*, 3 Aug. 2018, www.polygon.com/2018/8/3/17642862/shane-dawson-jeffree-star-documentary-keeping-up-kardashians. Accessed 13 Nov. 2019.

Considine, Austin. "Shane Dawson, YouTube's Comic for the Under-30 Set." *The New York Times*, 2 Apr. 2010, www.nytimes.

com/2010/04/04/fashion/04youtube.html. Accessed 13 Nov. 2019.

Dawson, Shane. "All Aboard the Shane Train." Interview by Tom Ward. *Forbes*, 27 July 2017, www.forbes.com/sites/tomward/2017/07/27/all-aboard-the-shane-train-an-interview-with-shane-dawson. Accessed 13 Nov. 2019.

Leskin, Paige. "The Rise of Shane Dawson, the Veteran YouTuber Who's Been Embroiled in Multiple Controversies and Is Worth an Estimated $12 Million." *Business Insider*, 12 Nov. 2019, www.businessinsider.com/shane-dawson-net-worth-youtube-career-chuck-e-cheese-controversies-2019-9. Accessed 13 Nov. 2019.

Roose, Kevin. "YouTube Unleashed a Conspiracy Theory Boom. Can It Be Contained?" *The New York Times*, 19 Feb. 2019, www.nytimes.com/2019/02/19/technology/youtube-conspiracy-stars.html. Accessed 13 Nov. 2019.

Slate, Jeff. "Shane Dawson: The Most Popular, Successful Comedian You've Never Heard Of." *Quartz*, 10 July 2015, qz.com/436482/shane-dawson-the-most-popular-successful-comedian-youve-never-heard-of/. Accessed 13 Nov. 2019.

Wei, William. "Meet the YouTube Stars Making $100,000 Plus Per Year." *Business Insider*, 19 Aug. 2010, www.businessinsider.com/meet-the-richest-independent-youtube-stars-2010-8. Accessed 13 Nov. 2019.

—*Mari Rich*

Ajay Devgn

Born: April 2, 1969
Occupation: Actor, director, and producer

Ajay Devgn is recognized in Bollywood—as the Hindi-language movie industry based in Mumbai, India, is known—for his extreme versatility. Appearing in more than one hundred films, he played everything from action heroes to comedic roles, romantic leads to real-life historical figures. Although considered prolific by Western standards, Devgn's number of credits was not particularly unusual for Bollywood, where many top actors appear in hundreds of films. He also remains levelheaded about his success. Discussing his hundredth picture, *Tanhaji: The Unsung Warrior*, which was released in early 2020, Devgn was matter-of-fact: "I did not even realize that it is my 100th film and, honestly, it does not matter to me," he told Udita Jhunjhunwala for the Indian news site *Scroll.in* (5 Jan. 2020). "Whether it is your first film, your 99th film or your 100th film, you have to work just as hard,

put in as much effort and you want it to do well, or maybe even better than the previous one."

After bursting onto the scene in the early 1990s, Devgn watched India's film industry evolve along with his career. "The working style has changed; technology has changed," he explained to Jhunjhunwala. "Things are more professional now. The audience has also evolved. They are quality-conscious. As for the younger directors, they are confident and clear. We [have] worked and learned. They have come prepared. That's the difference." As his career progressed, Devgn also welcomed the chance to play characters of greater depth. "Earlier, a Hindi film hero was invariably shown as a college-going guy. Now, it is no longer the case. In fact, the meatier roles are written for people who are of a certain age," he told Meena Iyer for *DNA India* (6 May 2019). "[Before], when an actor reached 35, he didn't know what to do with himself. He was too old to run around trees and too young to play father or elder brother. Now, these stereotypes are fast disappearing."

EARLY LIFE AND EDUCATION

Ajay Devgn was born Vishal Devgan on April 2, 1969. His father, Veeru Devgan, was a well-known stunt choreographer and director who oversaw fight and action scenes for more than eighty films, and his mother, Veena, was a producer. He grew up with three siblings: sisters Neelam and Kavita and brother Anil.

Devgn graduated from Silver Beach High School, in the upscale Mumbai neighborhood of Juhu. He later attended Mithibai College of Arts, part of the University of Mumbai. "Luckily,

Photo by Bollywood Hungama via Wikimedia Commons

I never had to go through struggle in my life," Devgn admitted to Sugandha Rawal for the Indian entertainment and news site *Sify.com* (15 Sept. 2019). "Everything just fell in place."

LAUNCHING A CAREER

Devgn made his major debut in *Phool Aur Kaante* (*Flowers and Thorns*) (1991), playing the estranged son of an underworld crime boss. When his own son is kidnapped, he must reunite with his father to get the child back. Devgn immediately established himself as an action hero to watch; in one scene, now considered iconic, he rides down the road astride two motorcycles, with one foot on each seat and hair ruffling slightly in the wind. When the bikes are forced to veer apart because of a road obstacle, he does a perfect split, sunglasses still perched firmly on his face and leather jacket still pristine. *Phool Aur Kaante* attracted legions of fans and won Devgn a 1992 Filmfare Award for Best Male Debut. (The Filmfare Awards, given annually since 1954, are sometimes referred to as the Bollywood equivalent to the Academy Awards.)

He followed that auspicious start with a string of other successful pictures. These included *Vijaypath* (*Path of Victory*) (1994), which costarred the popular actor Tabu, and *Major Saab* (1998), whose cast included iconic actor Amitabh Bachchan. Those films were viewed as proof that Devgn could hold his own against even scene-stealing colleagues.

In 1998, Devgn made what many characterized as a breakthrough film, *Zakhm* (Wound). Set amidst the political unrest that plagued Mumbai in the early 1990s, *Zakhm* stars Devgn as a son trying to fulfill his late mother's wishes to be buried according to Muslim tradition. While Devgn had been known for his action roles, the film established him as a serious actor with wide range and garnered him a prestigious National Film Award.

A PLACE IN THE PANTHEON

Industry observers sometimes mark *Zakhm* as a dividing line in Devgn's career, and, while some of his later films were more critically or commercially successful than others, he began earning his place in the pantheon of Bollywood A-listers as an actor as well as a producer and director. In 2000, Devgn founded Ajay Devgn Ffilms, an eponymous production company. In 2008, he made his directorial debut with *U Me Aur Hum* (*You, Me, and Us*), a romantic drama in which he appeared alongside his wife, Kajol.

In 2003, Devgn won his second National Film Award for his starring role in *The Legend of Bhagat Singh*. The 2002 biopic tells the story of the titular revolutionary who fought against the British for Indian independence and was executed in 1931 at the age of twenty-three. Singh's

exploits made him a revered folk hero in India, and the film played there and in Indian communities around the globe to appreciative audiences. In addition to the National Film Award, Devgn won a 2003 Filmfare Award for best actor. He captured a second Filmfare Award at that same ceremony, in the category of best villain for his work in *Deewangee* (*Obsession*) (2002), a psychological thriller in which he plays an accused murderer.

In 2006, Devgn starred in *Omkara*, a crime thriller adapted from Shakespeare's *Othello*. In a move that strengthened his reputation for versatility, that year he was also part of an ensemble cast in the first of a series of screwball comedies that, while not critically acclaimed, became enormous box-office draws. *Golmaal: Fun Unlimited* (2006), *Golmaal Returns* (2008), *Golmaal 3* (2010), and *Golmaal Again* (2017) follow a band of appealing young troublemakers as they fall in love, marry, start businesses, and cause general mayhem. The films constitute one of the highest-grossing series in Bollywood history, and *Golmaal 3* played a large part in Devgn being named most profitable actor at the 2011 ETC Bollywood Business Awards. It had not been his only successful film of 2010, however; adding to his collective box-office take were *Once Upon a Time in Mumbaai*, *Raajneeti* (*Politics*), *Atithi Tum Kab Jaoge?*(*Guest, When Will You Leave?*), *Aakrosh* (*Anger*), and *Toonpur Ka Superrhero*.

Despite their popularity with audiences, some of Devgn's efforts earned him criticism from reviewers. Writing for the *New York Times* (18 Oct. 2009), Rachel Salz noted Devgn's willingness to forgo drama and dive into relatively low-brow comedy. Reviewing the 2009 action comedy *All the Best: Fun Begins*, which Devgn produced and starred in, she wrote: "Where has all the drama gone? Hindi cinema has a serious case of the giggles these days. So perhaps it's not surprising that an actor like Ajay Devgn, who played a powerful, brooding Othello in *Omkara*, should want in on the comedy fun." Calling the film a "more-is-more farce set in Goa that features spectacular car crashes, a mute villain who communicates by tapping a spoon on a glass, torture by ice, and rock 'n' roll mayhem on the beach," she lamented that it was not a successful combination. "While the movie has plenty of energy, it rarely hits the comic peaks it's working so hard to achieve." She also criticized the film's use of "gratuitous blackface."

THE ROHIT SHETTY COP UNIVERSE AND BEYOND

Salz was more complimentary of Devgn's next film, *Singham* (2011), in which he stars as a morally upright police officer who is much beloved in his small village near the Goa-Maharashtra border. Calling it "a fists-of-steel throwback of a Bollywood film," Salz wrote for the *New York Times* (21 July 2011), that the film was "old-fashioned" for its lengthy 140-minute running time and its "full complement of songs and dances—a treat, now that so many movies forgo musical numbers or include them only as spoofs." She also noted that unlike Bollywood's tendency to make films with urban themes for urban audiences, the film had an "uncomplicated, even cartoonish insistence on the benefits of village soil over city dirt for cultivating bedrock Indian values."

Directed by Rohit Shetty, who also helmed the *Golmaal* series, *Singham* grossed more than 100 crore, equivalent to a billion rupees and considered a benchmark of success in Bollywood. It went on to inspire other works that also take place in what Devgn called the "Rohit Shetty cop universe": a 2014 sequel, *Singham Returns*; *Little Singham*, a 2018 animated children's series; and a 2018 spin-off, *Simmba*, in which Devgn makes a cameo appearance.

Throughout the 2010s Devgn maintained a grueling filming schedule and lengthened his list of honors. In 2012, for example, he was named Cinematic Icon of the Year at the GQ Awards, India, and in 2016 he was recognized by the government of India with the Padma Shri, one of the highest civilian honors given by the country. His films of the period include *Mahabharat* (2013), an animated picture for which he provided a voice; *Fitoor* (*Madness*) (2016), a loose adaptation of Charles Dickens's *Great Expectations*; *Shivaay* (2016), an action-adventure in which he races to save his mute daughter from human traffickers; and *De De Pyaar De* (Give Me My Love) (2019), a romantic comedy in which he plays a middle-aged man who falls in love with a woman half his age. Devgn's hundredth film, *Tanhaji: The Unsung Warrior*, tells the story of a famed warrior in the army of the seventeenth-century Maratha ruler Shivaji.

PERSONAL LIFE

Devgn and Kajol married in a traditional Hindu ceremony on February 24, 1999. They have two children together: a daughter, Nysa, born in 2003, and a son, Yug, born in 2010.

SUGGESTED READING

Devgn, Ajay. "Ajay Devgn on Staying Ahead of the Curve: The Day You Think You Know Everything, You Should Quit.'" Interview by Udita Jhunjhunwala. *Scroll.in*, 5 Jan. 2020, scroll.in/reel/948801/ajay-devgn-on-staying-ahead-of-the-curve-the-day-you-think-you-know-everything-you-should-quit. Accessed 18 May 2020.

———. "'50 Is the New 40': Ajay Devgn." Interview by Meena Iyer. *DNA India*, 6 May 2019, www.dnaindia.com/bollywood/interview-dna-exclusive-50-is-the-new-40-ajay-devgn-2746294. Accessed 18 May 2020.

———. "'I Don't Think about My Stardom': Ajay Devgn." Interview by Sugandha Rawal. *Sify.com*, 15 Sept. 2019, www.sify.com/movies/i-don-t-think-about-my-stardom--ajay-devgn-ians-interview--news-bollywood-tjpjuKgjbgajf.html. Accessed 18 May 2020.

———. "Interview: 'People Come Less with Romantic Scripts to Me.' Ajay Devgn." Interview by Subhojit Ghosh. *CineSpeaks*, 12 May 2019, cinespeaks.com/interview-people-come-less-with-romantic-scripts-to-me-ajay-devgn/. Accessed 18 May 2020.

Salz, Rachel. "Where Comedy and Complexity Meet." Review of *All the Best*, directed by Rohit Shetty. *The New York Times*, 18 Oct. 2009, www.nytimes.com/2009/10/19/movies/19all.html. Accessed 18 May 2020.

———. "A Cop Meets Bollywood." Review of *Singham*, directed by Rohit Shetty. *The New York Times*, 21 July 2011, www.nytimes.com/2011/07/22/movies/singham-a-bollywood-cop-film-review.html. Accessed 18 May 2020.

SELECTED WORKS

Phool Aur Kaante (*Flowers and Thorns*), 1991; *Vijaypath* (*Path of Victory*), 1994; *Major Saab*, 1998; *Zakhm* (*Wound*), 1998; *The Legend of Bhagat Singh*, 2002; *Deewangee* (*Obsession*), 2002; *Omkara*, 2006; *Golmaal: Fun Unlimited*, 2006; *Singham*, 2011; *Mahabharat*, 2013; *Fitoor* (*Madness*), 2016; *De Pyaar De* (Give Me My Love) , 2019; *Tanhaji: The Unsung Warrior*, 2020

—*Mari Rich*

Marina Diamandis

Date of birth: October 10, 1985
Occupation: Singer

"I don't care about being a star or 'idol,'" singer Marina Diamandis told Brittany Spanos for *Rolling Stone* (2 May 2019). "I love connecting with humans through music." Diamandis, who self-released her earliest music in 2007 as Marina and the Diamonds, indeed forged strong connections with an international body of fans who appreciate her songs' strong emotional resonance, catchy melodies, and compelling vocal performances. Following her successful debut album, *The Family Jewels* (2010), she further established herself as an alt-pop performer with global appeal on the 2012 concept album *Electra Heart*, which also introduced her alter ego of the same name. Her 2015 album *Froot* continued

Photo by Kevin Winter/Getty Images for Coachella

her penchant for bending genres and reached the top ten on the charts in both the United States and the United Kingdom.

Amid that success, however, Diamandis found herself feeling drained and disconnected from her creative abilities, feelings that she later linked to the persona of Marina and the Diamonds. "It took me well over a year to figure out that a lot of my identity was tied up in who I was as an artist, and there wasn't much left of who I was," she explained to Douglas Greenwood for *Dazed* (31 Jan. 2019). Yet rather than quit music altogether in the face of such an identity crisis, Diamandis took a different approach, renaming herself simply Marina in 2018. Under that name she made her return to music with the album *Love + Fear* (2019).

EARLY LIFE AND EDUCATION

Marina Lambrini Diamandis was born in Wales in 1985. She was the second of two daughters born to Esther and Dimos Diamandis, who separated when Diamandis was a young child and later divorced. Following that separation and her father's return to his native country of Greece, she remained largely in Wales with her mother, growing up in the small town of Pandy. Diamandis attended the Haberdashers' Monmouth School for Girls, located in Monmouth, Wales.

Although not yet sure of her future career path, the young Diamandis was intrigued by the entertainment industry from a young age. As she told Alyssa Bailey for *Express* (6 Sept. 2010), she "knew from around ten years old that I would become a performer. My heart just hadn't told me what kind." She discovered that she enjoyed

singing, but preferred to sing mostly in private throughout her teen years. Although she did not undergo formal vocal or instrumental training, she eventually learned to play piano—and later additional instruments such as the glockenspiel—after realizing that doing so would grant her a greater ability to write her own music.

While in her mid-teens, Diamandis moved to Greece to live with her father. She completed her secondary education through an International Baccalaureate program there before returning to the United Kingdom, where she struggled to find a satisfying educational path for herself. She enrolled in a series of universities to study topics such as music composition and dance but ultimately quit each program, preferring instead to strike out on her own as a singer.

MARINA AND THE DIAMONDS

Although intent upon pursuing a career in music, Diamandis did not initially consider the possibility of writing and recording her own songs. Seeking a way to break into the business, she steadily attended auditions for musicals and manufactured pop groups, to little success. Over time, however, the idea of writing her own songs and making music on her own terms appealed to her, especially after being introduced to the homemade recordings of cult favorite singer-songwriter Daniel Johnston. She bought basic recording equipment and began to develop what would become some of the first songs released under the performing name Marina and the Diamonds. While that name led many to assume the project was a band rather than a solo artist, Diamandis later stated repeatedly in interviews and on social media that "the Diamonds," in fact, referred to her fans.

And indeed, despite being unsigned, Diamandis began to develop a dedicated fan base early on in her career. She first captured the attention of listeners in the United Kingdom and elsewhere by sharing her work through avenues such as the popular social-networking website *MySpace*. Diamandis's extensive use of *MySpace* also gave her a way of connecting directly with her growing number of fans. This personal engagement would contribute significantly to her popularity, and even after the decline of *MySpace* she would continue similar activity on platforms such as the social media service *Twitter* and various blogs. Music she released independently through *MySpace* included the 2007 EP *Mermaid vs. Sailor*, which included early versions of two songs that would later appear on versions of Marina and the Diamonds' debut album.

In late 2008, Diamandis signed a deal with the Warner Music Group label 679 Recordings. Promotional efforts for her debut full-length album began the following year and included the release of a three-track EP titled *The Crown*

Jewels as well as the singles "Obsessions" and "Mowgli's Road" in 2009. The buzz around these releases led to her second-place ranking on the BBC's Sound of 2010 list. The full album, titled *The Family Jewels*, was released in February 2010. Building upon Diamandis's prior work, it features a unique take on pop music built around her songwriting and distinctive vocals. "I suppose it can be loosely defined as alternative or left-field pop," she explained to Bailey about her work. "The two defining elements are theatre and humor. I like laughing at how tragic and dramatic my brain can get."

Prior to the US release of *The Family Jewels*, Diamandis also released the promotional EP *The American Jewels*, which featured a selection of songs from the album as well as a remix. Although the album experienced limited success in the US market, it proved popular in the United Kingdom, peaking at number five on the Official UK Albums chart. Many critics compared Diamandis to 1980s art-pop icon Kate Bush, whereas others categorized her among a new wave of artists combining contemporary pop with quirkier influences.

ELECTRA HEART AND FROOT

Following the release of *The Family Jewels*, Diamandis began work on her second album, which would undergo significant changes throughout the development process. The album was originally conceived as a side project in which Diamandis would explore a variety of female archetypes found in American pop culture. Although the resulting work, *Electra Heart* (2012), instead became the second full-length Marina and the Diamonds album, some of that original concept remained. Diamandis also developed a satirical alter ego—Electra Heart—for the album, which was much more dance-pop oriented than her earlier music. She would later reflect on the change in sound, which proved controversial with some fans, as part of her developmental process. "I feel like I kind of used that mode of expression to explore my identity, because it was so shaky in my early twenties," she explained to Greenwood.

Despite a somewhat mixed critical reception, *Electra Heart* reached number one on the UK Albums chart and thirty-one on the US Billboard 200 chart. Yet even as the album proved popular among listeners in a number of countries, Diamandis was struck by the way in which her use of the Electra Heart alter ego and a concept album structure had affected the public perception of Marina and the Diamonds and her work. "I realised, OK, this is why I don't like being a pop star because people assume you don't know anything and you don't make your own music. I saw that change as soon as I dyed my hair blond and created music that had a different

production style," she explained to Michael Cragg for the *Guardian* (30 Jan. 2015). "It was fascinating but it made me think: 'I'm not going to do this again.'" Diamandis later commented in interviews that she had killed the Electra Heart character, whom she had only intended to exist for only a limited time.

For the next Marina and the Diamonds album, *Froot*, released in March 2015, Diamandis moved away from *Electra Heart*'s high-concept nature and slick production values. "I didn't really have a conscious plan for what I was going to write or what the album was going to be like," she told Brodie Lancaster for *Rookie* (24 Feb. 2015). "I think I was just really relieved to do things in an uncomplicated way." The first of Diamandis's albums to chart higher in the United States than in the United Kingdom, *Froot* peaked at number eight on the Billboard 200 and number ten on the UK Albums Chart. Yet despite the album's success, Diamandis found that the process of touring and promoting her music had become draining. "I just felt like I couldn't cope anymore, but I had a commitment to be on tour," she recalled to Greenwood. "I was on stage every night realising I didn't want to be looked at, but I couldn't speak about that publicly because I didn't want to spoil the illusion for people coming to see you, who've paid for a ticket and waited outside." Following the end of the tour—known as the Neon Nature Tour—in 2016, Diamandis took a break from music, hoping to reconnect with the emotions that fueled her songwriting.

LOVE + FEAR

While on hiatus Diamandis considered stepping away from music altogether. "I felt like Marina and the Diamonds had just become this shell and I was trying to break free of it," she told Spanos about that decision. "I just felt completely blocked. It was easier for me to just stop being an artist, which wasn't the right solution." She briefly studied acting and went on to enroll in psychology courses at Birkbeck, University of London. The experience ultimately reinvigorated her, and she soon resumed writing songs. Diamandis took another important step in 2018, when she announced on social media that she would be changing her performing name from Marina and the Diamonds to simply Marina, sometimes written as MARINA.

The new name freed her to explore new directions in her writing, and she also worked with a fresh set of collaborators. Diamandis released her first album under the name MARINA, *Love + Fear*, in April 2019. In addition to the album itself, she released an EP featuring acoustic versions of *Love + Fear* tracks. Proving popular among longtime fans and new listeners, *Love + Fear* reached the number-five spot on the UK

Albums chart and hit number twenty-eight on the Billboard 200. Not long after the album's release, Diamandis revealed that she was already working on her next project. In late 2019 she appeared as a featured vocalist on the song "If I Left the World" by electronic artist Gryffin.

PERSONAL LIFE

Diamandis began dating fellow musician Jack Patterson, of the electronic group Clean Bandit, around 2015. The two collaborated on several songs. These included the 2017 single "Disconnect" and the song "Baby," the latter of which was included on both *Love + Fear* and the 2018 Clean Bandit album *What Is Love?*

SUGGESTED READING

Diamandis, Marina. "America's Sweetheart: Marina and the Diamonds, 'The Family Jewels,' at 9:30 Club." Interview by Alyssa Bailey. *Express, The Washington Post*, 6 Sept. 2010, www.washingtonpost.com/express/wp/2010/09/06/marina-diamandis-marina-and-the-diamonds-family-jewels-930-club/. Accessed 15 Nov. 2019.

———. "Marina and the Diamonds: 'I Killed Electra Heart with Sleeping Pills.'" Interview by Michael Cragg. *The Guardian*, 30 Jan. 2015, theguardian.com/music/2015/jan/30/marina-and-the-diamonds-interview-new-album-froot. Accessed 15 Nov. 2019.

———. "Marina Diamandis Mines the Future." Interview by Alex Chapman. *Interview*, 26 Apr. 2012, www.interviewmagazine.com/music/marina-and-the-diamonds-electra-heart. Accessed 15 Nov. 2019.

———. "Trust Your Gut: An Interview with Marina and the Diamonds." Interview by Brodie Lancaster. *Rookie*, 24 Feb. 2015, www.rookiemag.com/2015/02/marina-and-the-diamonds/. Accessed 15 Nov. 2019.

Greenwood, Douglas. "My Name Is Marina." *Dazed*, 31 Jan. 2019, www.dazeddigital.com/music/article/43131/1/marina-and-the-diamonds-name-change-new-music-interview. Accessed 15 Nov. 2019.

Mele, Sofia. "Marina and the Diamonds on the Struggle to Record New Album: 'I Thought I Wasn't Going to Do This Anymore.'" *Billboard*, 11 July 2019, www.billboard.com/articles/columns/pop/8465030/marina-and-the-diamonds-abbey-road-interview. Accessed 15 Nov. 2019.

Spanos, Brittany. "The Reeducation of Marina Diamandis." *Rolling Stone*, 2 May 2019, www.rollingstone.com/music/music-features/marina-love-and-fear-album-interview-821048. Accessed 15 Nov. 2019.

SELECTED WORKS

The Family Jewels, 2010; *Electra Heart*, 2012; *Froot*, 2015; *Love + Fear*, 2019

—*Joy Crelin*

Steven Dillingham

Date of birth: May 12, 1952
Occupation: Government official

On January 7, 2019, Steven Dillingham was sworn in as the twenty-fifth director of the US Census Bureau, a US Department of Commerce organization charged with conducting a population and housing count of all fifty states, the District of Columbia, Puerto Rico, and the Island Areas every ten years, as required by the US Constitution. "The census is at once prosaic and giant, requiring a level of meticulous planning and execution comparable to a major military operation or a space-probe launch," Emily Bazelon wrote for the *New York Times Magazine* (28 Nov. 2018). "The data provide the most detailed national self-portrait we have, showing us where we are collectively and how we are changing."

Dillingham was nominated for Census Bureau director by Republican President Donald Trump and became director of the bureau at a contentious time. Critics of Trump and his administration feared they were politicizing the census, seeking to manipulate the findings in such a way that immigrants, and black,

Photo by US Department of Commerce via Wikimedia Commons

indigenous and people of color (BIPOC) would be undercounted, and thus denied accurate redistricting and representation in Congress, as well as federal funding for needed services. There were also fears that rural communities would be granted disproportionate representation in the US House of Representatives. These fears were fueled in large part by Secretary of Commerce Wilbur Ross's decision to include a citizenship question on the census forms—a course of action ultimately halted by the Supreme Court. Because the 2020 census is the first to be conducted largely online and by mail, security and privacy concerns also arose.

Dillingham has maintained, however, that he is nonpartisan and devoted to conducting the most precise count possible. "Accurate data is an essential underpinning for representative and responsive government, as well as a thriving economy," he said during an address to the Senate Homeland Security and Governmental Affairs Committee (3 Oct. 2018). "While the Census Bureau faces challenges, I know that it has the talent and commitment for meeting them."

EARLY LIFE AND EDUCATION

Steven Dean Dillingham was born on May 12, 1952, in Orangeburg, South Carolina. His father was a career military man who entered the service during World War II, at the age of seventeen, and remained for two decades. Dillingham has two brothers, and all three boys were named for military leaders who served with their father.

Dillingham, an Eagle Scout, attended Rock Hill High School, in Rock Hill, South Carolina. He graduated in 1970 as a member of the first racially integrated cohort in the school's history. He then entered the US Air Force Academy, in Colorado, thanks to a recommendation by South Carolina Congressman Tom Gettys, and after being honorably discharged from the academy in 1972, he transferred to Winthrop College, in Rock Hill. Dillingham graduated from Winthrop with a bachelor's degree in political science in 1973.

Dillingham next entered the University of South Carolina (USC) in Columbia, earning a Juris Doctor degree (JD) in 1976 and a Master's Degree in Public Administration (MPA) in 1978. He remained at the school to earn a PhD in political science, and while pursuing his doctoral studies he coauthored a journal article on the civil liability of police officers. "A lot of people were writing about how to sue the police, but there was very little talk of how police could avoid lawsuits," coauthor and retired professor of criminology Harry Barrineau recalled to Jeffrey Mervis for *Science* (20 July 2018). "So, we wanted to give them some advice." Dillingham has also published several scholarly papers on such

topics as prison violence, probation and parole, and federal drug policy.

Dillingham earned his doctoral degree in 1987, and he also holds a Master of Business Administration degree (MBA) from George Washington University and a Master of Laws (LLM) from Georgetown University. He held a variety of jobs during his school years. During law school, for example, he worked as a grocery store manager and at an electric company, and during graduate school he worked as a residential supervisor for the South Carolina Commission for the Blind, a research analyst for the state's department of corrections, and a USC teaching assistant. He served as a visiting assistant professor (1980–81) and then as an assistant professor (1981–86) in the University of South Carolina (USC)'s College of Criminal Justice.

CAREER IN THE PUBLIC AND PRIVATE SECTORS

Dillingham first arrived in Washington, DC, in 1985, serving that year as counsel to Senator Strom Thurmond, Sr., a staunch segregationist, on the Senate Judiciary Committee. From 1985 to 1986 Dillingham worked as an attorney in the Office of Personnel Management (OPM), which operates as the federal government's chief human resources and personnel policy agency. Dillingham then worked as an attorney for the US Department of Energy (DoE), and in 1988 he made a move to the Department of Justice (DOJ), serving as its deputy director for policy and special programs until 1990, when President George H. W. Bush appointed him director of the Bureau of Justice Statistics (BJS), whose mission was to collect, analyze, and publish information on crime, criminal offenders, victims of crime, and the operation of governmental justice systems.

When Dillingham was being confirmed for that post, according to an anecdote he related to the Senate Homeland Security and Governmental Affairs Committee during his 2018 confirmation as director of the Census Bureau, his infant daughter, Abigail, began to cry, just as Senator Joe Biden, who was chairing the confirmation hearing, lifted his gavel to end the proceedings. "Senator Biden smiled and remarked, 'Let the record show that Abigail has the last word,'" Dillingham recalled. Among his accomplishments at Bureau of Justice Statistics (BJS) was updating major surveys on crime victims and law enforcement practices, making them much more relevant and useful to researchers working on the front lines of those fields.

When President Bill Clinton, a Democrat, took office in 1993, Dillingham left government service to practice law, but he returned when President George W. Bush tapped him in 2007 as director of the Bureau of Transportation Statistics (BTS), a post he held until 2011.

Dillingham—who has served as the deputy director for the National District Attorneys Association (NDAA), administrator of the American Prosecutors Research Institute (APRI), and academic adviser to the law and justice task force of the American Legal Exchange Council (ALEC), also spent three years during the mid-2010s as the associate registrar at George Mason University in Fairfax, Virginia, where he concurrently taught a course on the economics of the sports industry. In 2017 he returned to the OPM as an associate general counsel for the Trump administration, and he subsequently became the director of the Peace Corps Office of Strategic Information, Research, and Planning.

THE CENSUS

After John Thompson, the head of the US Census Bureau, abruptly resigned in the spring of 2017, the agency went without permanent leadership for more than a year, as the Trump administration scrambled to deal with other crises and vacancies. Trump formally nominated Dillingham for the post in July 2018. According to Mervis, not only did Dillingham have sufficient government experience and appropriate academic qualifications for the job, but he was also capable of nonpartisanship. "Democrats and civil rights groups worry [Dillingham] will do the bidding of his political bosses and undermine the integrity of the decennial head count. But those who know him, including liberal academics, say he's a straight shooter with good management skills and someone who doesn't let his conservative political views interfere with day-to-day operations."

Dillingham, who was confirmed unanimously on January 2, 2019, and sworn in five days later, repeatedly declared his intention to remain impartial and data-driven. Even as debate heated up about Ross's proposed addition of a citizenship question to the 2020 census, he refused to comment. When Trump issued a tweet on April 1 criticizing Democrats who wanted to leave out the citizenship question, Dillingham assured Hansi Lo Wang for *NPR* (1 Apr. 2019), "I don't follow tweets. . . . We think the courts will decide the issue. Our job at Census will be to conduct a census whether the question's in there or if it isn't, whatever the court decides." Ultimately, after dozens of lawsuits were filed by states, cities, and human-rights groups, the issue made its way to the Supreme Court, which upheld a lower-court ruling that the question could not be included. Opponents of the question were relieved, pointing out that misusing census data can have dire repercussions.

While nearly all US Census respondents in 2020 are being invited to respond online, by phone, or by mail, Dillingham, as had been a bureau tradition since 2000, chose one remote Alaskan village to be the site of the first in-person counting. In late January, he traveled to Toksook Bay (population 590 according to the 2010 census) to meet Lizzie Chimiugak Nenguryarr, an elder of the Nunakauyarmiut Tribe and the first person to be officially counted. By mid-March, amid concerns about cost overruns, lack of staffing, outreach to communities without internet access, cybersecurity risks, privacy violations, and other such pitfalls, the 2020 Census, estimated to cost more than $15 billion, was fully underway. Dillingham's term is scheduled to expire at the end of 2021.

PERSONAL LIFE

Dillingham lives in Alexandria, Virginia. He is married to Kimberly Kent Dillingham, a part-time social worker and public-school teacher who is the daughter of the late Glenn A. Kent, an Air Force lieutenant general and defense analyst who developed strategic arms control agreements during the Cold War era. The couple's daughter, Abigail, also works as a teacher, and during her summer breaks, she often travels to volunteer in village schools in Southeast Asia, Central America, and Africa. Dillingham's own volunteer efforts have included helping the Justice Ministry of Iraq establish a system of data collection. During his stint there, he saw Iraqi officials "risk life and limb traveling in unsafe and hazardous conditions across deserts stretching hundreds of miles to deliver this data," as he told the Homeland Security and Governmental Affairs Committee, an experience that informed his "personal perspective on the importance of data collection."

SUGGESTED READING

Administration of George Bush. *Public Papers of the Presidents of the United States: George Bush*, Book 1, 1990, www.govinfo.gov/app/details/PPP-1990-book1. Accessed 23 May 2020.

Bazelon, Emily. "In Donald Trump's Census, Who Counts?" *The New York Times Magazine*, 28 Nov. 2018, www.nytimes.com/2018/11/28/magazine/donald-trump-census.html. Accessed 23 May 2020.

Dillingham, Steven. "Opening Statement of Steven Dillingham." *US Senate Committee on Homeland Security and Governmental Affairs*, 3 Oct. 2018, www.hsgac.senate.gov/imo/media/doc/Prepared%20Statement-Dillingham-2018-10-03.pdf. Accessed 23 May 2020.

Maxwell, Lauren. "Head of US Census Arrives in Alaska for Start of 2020 Count." *KTVA*, 17 Jan. 2020, www.ktva.com/story/41580558/head-of-us-census-arrives-in-alaska-for-start-of-2020-count. Accessed 23 May 2020.

Mervis, Jeffrey. "Census Bureau Nominee Becomes Lightning Rod for Debate over 2020
Census." *Science*, 20 July 2018, www.sci-
encemag.org/news/2018/07/census-bureau-
nominee-becomes-lightning-rod-debate-
over-2020-census. Accessed 23 May 2020.

Wang, Hansi Lo. "Census Bureau Must Be
'Totally Objective' on Citizenship Question,
Director Says." *NPR*, 1 Apr. 2019, www.npr.
org/2019/04/01/707628958/census-bureau-
must-be-totally-objective-on-citizenship-
question-director-says. Accessed 23 May
2020.

—*Mari Rich*

Hannah Dreier

Date of birth: ca. 1986–87
Occupation: Journalist

Hannah Dreier won the 2019 Pulitzer Prize
for Feature Writing, based on a series of three
articles she wrote for the investigative news organization ProPublica in 2018 about the consequences of flawed investigations into the gang
MS-13. According to the Pulitzer website, the
prize is awarded "for distinguished feature writing giving prime consideration to quality of writing, originality and concision, using any available
journalistic tool." The award included a $15,000
stipend. Among her many honors, in 2017 Dreier also was unanimously chosen to receive the
2016 James Foley Medill Medal for Courage in
Journalism for her reporting for the Associated
Press on the political chaos of Venezuela and
its consequences. As one of the judges, *Chicago Tribune* investigative reporter David Jackson, stated for the Medill Medal press release
(1 Sept. 2017), "I think people will be reading
her dispatches in order to understand this huge
event for years. This is really enduring work, extremely enterprising. In that very dangerous environment, she is sticking her nose everywhere
and confronting authorities and going into places where reporters haven't been."

EARLY LIFE AND EDUCATION
Hannah Dreier was born in the 1980s and raised
by her mother in San Francisco. While Dreier
was growing up, she and her mother sometimes
had little money and experienced eviction from
their home. Dreier went to the Urban School of
San Francisco for high school, starting in 2000.
A research paper she wrote as a junior became
required reading for a class in the history of
Southeast Asia. Dreier's curiosity even as a high
school student was a component of her later career as a journalist.

After graduating from high school in 2004,
Dreier went on to attend Wesleyan University
in Middletown, Connecticut. During her senior
year, she roomed with the editor-in-chief of the
Wesleyan Argus, the university newspaper. Although she had written a few articles for the *Argus*, she had not expected to enter journalism as
a profession, as she told Brooke Kushwaha and
William Halliday for the paper (23 Apr. 2019):
"When I was at Wesleyan, I was really politically active, and I thought I was going to be an
activist and do some sort of social justice job in
DC. But it turned out I really didn't like that
kind of work. I think I'm naturally too skeptical
and have some natural problems with authority." She graduated from Wesleyan in 2008 with
a Bachelor of Arts with honors in English, history, and philosophy.

EARLY CAREER
In 2009, Dreier began working as a metro reporter for the Bay Area News Group. She wrote
about local political issues and more for three
small area newspapers: the *Contra Costa Times*,
Oakland Tribune, and the *San Jose Mercury News*.
As Dreier told Kushwaha and Halliday, "I got an
internship at a newspaper in the Bay Area, and
they were just willing to teach me everything. I
came in with very few reporting skills and really
learned on the job, covering these small towns. I
made a lot of mistakes early on, and the people
there were really generous."

ASSOCIATED PRESS
In 2012, Dreier began reporting on California
state government and politics for the Associated Press (AP). With a focus on government
accountability, her reporting prompted state
audits and inspired new legislation. The following year the AP offered her a full-time job
covering Las Vegas and the gambling industry.
Dreier had never been to Las Vegas, but she accepted the job. The AP was the only national
news agency in the city. She wrote reviews that
were featured in newspapers across the country
and learned how to write to appeal to a mass
audience.

In 2014, Dreier, who is fluent in Spanish,
took an assignment in Venezuela, a country on
the brink of collapse, where she was the AP's
only English language reporter. As she told
Julissa Treviño for *Columbia Journalism Review*
(20 June 2017), "I wanted to live abroad and
translate one culture to another. That's always
what I've liked the most about reporting, is going somewhere totally unfamiliar and seeing how
things unfold." Dreier tried to focus on reporting
on areas of the country other than Caracas, the
capital, where most of the journalists were concentrated. Once she had filed her stories on hap-
penings considered newsworthy, Dreier pursued

her own interests. In her articles, she wanted to include hope wherever possible as well as highlight the beauty of the country.

Dreier and the other journalists faced not only difficulties but danger. The country was ranked as the most dangerous in the world outside of a war zone. Dreier was mugged by motorcyclists during the day and had a gun pointed at her during her first month in Venezuela. She learned to carry money whenever she went out so that muggers would be satisfied and not harm her. When state security forces kidnapped her and held her in custody, Dreier was relieved, knowing that there were limits to what they could do to her as an American journalist. Her editors put a tracker on her phone so they could know where she was at all times. She also had to deal with inflation that reached 800 percent in 2017 and chronic food shortages, with bare shelves and long lines to buy any food. To survive, she had to rely on the black market, which she learned about from her colleagues.

Dreier's reporting was published in 2016 and 2017 as part of the AP series entitled "Venezuela Undone," which includes stories, photos, videos, and interactive features. In one of Dreier's articles for the series, "A Child's Scraped Knee a Life or Death Matter in Venezuela," published 4 Oct. 2016, she details the medical shortages and consequent danger that Venezuelans were facing on a regular basis, using a three-year-old girl's experience. Dreier also wrote about how she and her editors wrestled with whether and when to interfere. Ultimately, they decided to become involved to purchase medicine only if the child's life was in danger. Dreier told Kushwaha and Halliday, "In Venezuela especially, I got obsessed with how I was going to get U.S. readers to engage with this story that's just so depressing. . . . I'm just interested in finding ways to get readers to read to the end of the story, even if it's hard to take."

For her work on the article, Dreier earned the Ancil Payne Award for Ethics in Journalism, given by the University of Oregon's School of Journalism and Communication. As Andra Brichacek wrote for the school's news site, "During the course of planning and reporting the story, she and her editors continually balanced the well-being of her subjects against her journalistic imperative to stay uninvolved. When considering such difficult questions as whether to supply life-saving medicine, or whether to put sources at risk in an environment that does not allow media, the AP team made careful decisions to uphold the integrity of her story while protecting sources and responding to subjects' needs."

PROPUBLICA AND A PULITZER

Dreier left Venezuela in 2017 to return to the United States, where she accepted a position as a reporter with ProPublica, based in New York City. Upon her return to the United States, she was shocked by the change in the climate around newspaper and reporting that had followed the election of Donald Trump. The targeting of journalists and credible news outlets, as well as the repeated instances of "fake news" and the falsehoods being communicated, reminded her of Venezuela.

In 2018, Dreier began investigating a federal and local crackdown on MS-13, a gang originally founded in the 1980s by Salvadoran immigrants who had fled civil war in El Salvador for Los Angeles. The gang had previously killed five Hispanic students at Brentwood High School on Long Island. Her investigation focused on the ways that police bias and anti-immigrant rhetoric hindered efforts to stop MS-13 and adversely affected young Hispanic immigrants. As *Wesleyan University Magazine* (7 Sept. 2018) reported, Dreier told an audience at a forum of journalists, "The truth is immigration policy hasn't changed that dramatically under Trump. The rhetoric has changed, but what he's really done is put immigration in the center of the national conversation."

Dreier's resulting series of three articles, "Trapped in Gangland: How the MS-13 Crackdown Shattered Immigrant Lives," was published over several months in 2018. In the first article, "A Betrayal," copublished in April by ProPublica and *New York* magazine, Dreier tells the story of Henry, a young Salvadoran immigrant and MS-13 member who was detained by the Immigration and Customs Enforcement (ICE) agency and slated for deportation despite his having turned informant against the gang. "The Disappeared," which was released in September, follows a mother who searched MS-13's Long Island killing grounds for answers regarding the fates of missing immigrant teens after police had written them off as runaways. The final story in the series, "He Drew His School Mascot—and ICE Labeled Him a Gang Member," was published in December as a collaboration between ProPublica and *The New York Times Magazine*.

Dreier's series led to some policy changes at both the Department of Homeland Security and Long Island's police departments and school systems. In addition, she changed some readers' minds; as she told Kushwaha and Halliday, "Someone wrote to me and told me that, for the first time, they feel compassion for an illegal immigrant. . . . I think that's the highest thing these stories can do, to open people's minds to a more empathetic view of the world." Because of the danger that the stories would make their way to MS-13 leaders in Central America, they were not translated into Spanish or promoted in the communities they covered. The series earned Dreier a Pulitzer Prize in Feature Writing, which was announced in April 2019, as well as a 2019 Robert F. Kennedy Human Rights Journalism Award for New Media.

THE WASHINGTON POST
In September 2019, Dreier joined the *Washington Post* as a staff writer. In a February 2020 article, "Trust and Consequences," she reported that therapists' notes from counseling sessions with detained migrant children were being shared with immigration officers. The therapists told the children that their sessions were confidential, but the information they shared in confidence eventually went to ICE and was used against them in court without the therapist or the child being aware that this would happen or granting their consent. In the case of a young man named Kevin Euceda from Honduras, not only did he remain in detention as a result of his confidential information being shared, but his therapist resigned.

In response to Dreier's article, such information sharing was denounced by mental health organizations, therapists, and politicians as a breach of trust between therapist and client that violated professional standards of confidentiality. In March 2020, members of Congress introduced legislation to prevent the Trump administration and ICE from continuing the practice. Twenty-three senators formally requested that the inspector general investigate how the practice had started in the first place.

SUGGESTED READING
Dreier, Hannah. "Bill Would End Practice of Using Confidential Therapy Notes against Detained Immigrant Children." *The Washington Post*, 4 Mar. 2020, washingtonpost.com/national/bill-would-end-practice-of-using-confidential-therapy-notes-against-detained-migrant-children/2020/03/04/0ab73d52-5e46-11ea-9055-5fa12981bbbf_story.html. Accessed 9 Mar. 2020.

——. "Q and A: Hannah Dreier on Covering a Country Headed for Economic Collapse." Interview by Julissa Treviño. *Columbia Journalism Review*, 20 June 2017, www.cjr.org/q_and_a/hannah-dreier-venezuela.php. Accessed 9 Mar. 2020.

——. "'Washington Post': Therapy Notes Are Being Used against Migrant Children." Interview by Noel King. *Morning Edition*, NPR, 18 Feb. 2020, www.npr.org/2020/02/18/806886958/washington-post-therapy-notes-are-being-used-against-migrant-children. Accessed 9 Mar. 2020.

Holder, William. "Alumni Panel: What's Really Going on in Journalism Today." *Wesleyan University Magazine*, 7 Sept. 2018, magazine.blogs.wesleyan.edu/2018/09/07/alumni-panel-whats-really-going-on-in-journalism-today/. Accessed 9 Mar. 2020.

King, Noel. "ProPublica Reporter Delves into Covering MS-13 Street Gang." *Morning Edition*, NPR, 26 June 2018, www.npr.org/2018/06/26/623451416/propublica-reporter-delves-into-covering-ms-13-street-gang. Accessed 9 Mar. 2020.

Kushwaha, Brooke, and William Halliday. "Hannah Dreier '08 Talks Pulitzer Win for MS-13 Coverage." *The Wesleyan Argus*, 4 Apr. 2019, wesleyanargus.com/2019/04/23/hannah-dreier-08-talks-pulitzer-win-for-ms-13-coverage-1/. Accessed 9 Mar. 2020.

—*Judy Johnson*

Alexander Dreymon

Date of birth: February 7, 1983
Occupation: Actor

Actor Alexander Dreymon is best known for playing Uhtred of Bebbanburg on the hit historical drama series *The Last Kingdom*, which began airing in 2015 and was renewed for a fifth season in 2020. Adapted from a series of novels by Bernard Cornwell and set in the ninth and tenth centuries, *The Last Kingdom* centers on the story of Alfred the Great, seen as the founder of England, but it is told through the perspective of Uhtred, a fictional Saxon who is kidnapped as a child and raised by the brutal invaders, the Danes. When the series begins, Uhtred seeks to conquer the lands of his birth as Alfred the Great hopes to bring the disparate kingdoms together as one. In a show about war and the identity of nations, Dreymon plays Uhtred with a hint of swagger. "Even though he is super cheeky . . . he's very truthful, very loyal, very trustworthy," he told Cher Martinetti for *SyFy Wire* (26 Nov. 2018). "Even though he's being tested from both sides again and again and being distrusted, the truth is that he does do what he says, and is a man of his word."

The affable, German-born Dreymon, who has credited his acting career to hard work and politeness, does not share his famous character's cruder attributes, or his penchant for brutality. When discussing how he chooses which parts to pursue, he told Julie Sagoskin for *Resident* magazine (Apr. 2019), "I am drawn to a challenge. So, if there's a character that feels very different from me, I love the idea of trying to figure out how to bridge that gap."

EARLY LIFE AND EDUCATION
Born Alexander Doetsch in Germany on February 7, 1983, Dreymon grew up across Europe

© Foto: Ra Boe via Wikipedia

and in the United States, eventually achieving fluency in German, French, and English. "It sort of happened," he explained to Luaine Lee for central Oregon's *The Bulletin* (14 Oct. 2015) of his unusually itinerant upbringing. "There were family circumstances that made us move to France because my aunt had had a very grave horse riding accident, and my mom wanted to take care of her." He has attributed other moves to a far-flung, though close-knit, extended family. His mother was a teacher, and though he maintained a good relationship with his father, a doctor, he was often not around. After his mother re-married, they moved to Switzerland. In later interviews, he would cite his displaced youth as a reason behind his ability to connect with the character of *The Last Kingdom*'s Uhtred. Between the ages of twelve and sixteen, he stayed on and off with close friends on the Pine Ridge Indian Reservation in South Dakota, where he picked up skills such as riding horses and driving a car.

Growing up, Dreymon was drawn to psychology and architecture in addition to entertaining notions of becoming an astronaut, but acting was a persistent love. He later recalled his friendship with a cousin with whom he was close growing up and how he once asked at what age someone could get married after seeing Princess Leia for the first time in *Star Wars: Episode VI—Return of the Jedi* (1983). "We used to take themes from movies and then just reenact them and film them," he recalled to Martinetti. "And I think, I just knew that that's what I wanted to do later on, if I could."

Following high school, Dreymon participated in acting classes in Paris. Looking back on his beginnings as an actor, he would ultimately describe his level of inherent ability as negligible. "My first steps on stage felt embarrassing and humiliating, and I had no idea what I was doing," he wrote for *Backstage* (26 Nov. 2018). Still, his acting teacher, Lesley Chatterley, saw, in Dreymon's words, an "inkling of talent," and helped him cultivate it. After three years of theater training, he went on to study drama at the Drama Centre of Central Saint Martins, a college that is part of the University of the Arts London (UAL). He relished the challenge. "I loved my three years there," he wrote for *Backstage*. "They taught me discipline, resilience, humility, and how to take pride in hard work."

EARLY CAREER AND *AMERICAN HORROR STORY: COVEN*

Though Dreymon completed his studies at the Drama Centre, he did not immediately find real success in the industry and endured through several years of office work and unsuccessful auditions. Remaining committed, in 2010 he landed his debut professional role in the made-for-television French film *Ni reprise, ni échangée* (*Neither Taken Back nor Exchanged*). The following year, he appeared in the dramatic BBC Two film *Christopher and His Kind*, starring English actor Matt Smith as the writer Christopher Isherwood. Dreymon played a gay sex worker in 1930s Germany. Also in 2011, he had a part in an Italian film titled *Sotto il vestito niente* (*Nothing under the Dress*) and a British World War II drama titled *Resistance*. The latter would be his last film under the name Alexander Doetsch.

In 2013, Dreymon made a bigger impression when he was cast in the third season of Ryan Murphy's anthology series *American Horror Story: Coven*. The story, set in contemporary New Orleans, follows a coven of witches. Dreymon played a recurring character named Luke Ramsey, who lives with his religious mother (played by Broadway legend Patti LuPone) but is drawn to the women at the heart of the show. The independent vampire film *Blood Ransom* (2014) saw Dreymon take on his first starring role as a man who unwittingly helps a vampire-in-the-making escape her undead captors. However, the film ultimately received poor reviews.

THE LAST KINGDOM

After a months-long audition process in 2014 that involved several rounds of self-taping and screen tests, Dreymon was cast in the BBC Two and BBC America television series *The Last Kingdom*. The show was developed and adapted from Bernard Cornwell's novel series that had been launched with the first installment in 2004 and was initially known as the Warrior Chronicles/Saxon Stories before later being referred to as the Last Kingdom series. Cornwell's novels revolve around the story of Alfred the Great, the ruler of the Saxon kingdom of Wessex, and his descendants. The small screen iteration *The Last Kingdom* was able to capitalize in part on the popularity of the HBO series *Game of Thrones*, which had debuted in 2011; however, it is historical fiction rather than historical fantasy. Combining fiction with historical events, figures, and context, *The Last Kingdom* takes place in the ninth and tenth centuries, when England was a land of disparate kingdoms vulnerable to Viking attacks. Alfred the Great, recognized as the creator of England, envisioned one unified kingdom, and while this series tells this story, it is done from the point of view of a fictional character named Uhtred of Bebbanburg, the son of a Saxon lord who is captured as a child and raised by Danes.

To prepare for his role as Uhtred, Dreymon first immersed himself in Cornwell's books. "Once the theoretical part is done, I like to spend as much time as possible in character and try him out on people I don't know," he explained to the men's fashion magazine *Da Man* (5 Oct. 2015). "Not an easy feat when you're working on a 9th-century warlord." When the show begins, Uhtred, hoping to reclaim his birthright, returns to his Saxon roots, encountering Alfred (David Dawson) in Wessex, the "last kingdom" standing against the relentless and brutal Danes. There, Alfred and Uhtred will make their stand to begin to bring the kingdoms together as one. Uhtred's unusual backstory sets him apart from his compatriots, except for Brida (Emily Cox), who was also captured by the Danes as a child and was raised alongside Uhtred.

The Last Kingdom, shot in Hungary, premiered in 2015. Critics, who gave the show's first season positive reviews overall, often noted that Uhtred's clashing identities effectively mirrored the discordance of the emerging state of England. Additionally, they praised the show's realism. "Alexander Dreymon is a canny choice for Uhtred," Dennis Perkins wrote for the *A.V. Club* (9 Oct. 2015). He compared it to the popular History channel show *Vikings*, which began in 2013 and explores a similar historical period. "Depicted as brave and skilled in battle but no visionary, the boyishly bearded Uhtred may lack the eerie magnetism of his *Vikings* counterpart Ragnar, but . . . Uhtred's exploits appear less like those of a man ahead of his time, and more like a man without options improvising ways to stay alive."

Netflix joined *The Last Kingdom* as a coproducer during the show's second season, bringing it to several other countries and greatly enhancing its appeal. After the streaming service became the only distributor and producer for the third season, it continued in this capacity and further renewed the series that continued to attract loyal fans, with a fifth season ordered in 2020.

OTHER WORK

In between filming for *The Last Kingdom*, Dreymon occasionally appeared in projects outside of the series. In 2016, he starred in an independent fantastical drama titled *Guys Reading Poems*, directed by Hunter Lee Hughes. The film was a stark departure from the swashbuckling *Last Kingdom*; in it, a boy escapes his trauma by imagining men reading famous poems. Dreymon played the boy's father. In 2018, he starred in another independent film titled *Heartlock*, a crime drama and romance set in an American prison. Dreymon played an incarcerated man who works at the prison infirmary. He manipulates a female prison guard, Tera (Lesley-Ann Brandt), to help him escape. Inevitably, Dreymon's character develops feelings for Tera, complicating his plans. *Heartlock* received lackluster reviews, though Frank Scheck, writing for the *Hollywood Reporter* (23 Jan. 2019), wrote, "Dreymon and Brandt, both exuding charisma and sensuality to spare, are magnetic as the illicit lovers. Their excellent work almost, but not quite, compensates for the pic's familiar-feeling aspects." After securing a place in the cast, Dreymon began shooting scenes for a new film, *Horizon Line*, a survival thriller, in 2019.

PERSONAL LIFE

In addition to his acting career, Dreymon is passionate about wildlife conservation. He began developing a charitable foundation called Tiger Burning Bright with a childhood friend to help protect the dwindling tiger population in Thailand. Also interested in work behind the camera, he served as an associate producer or coproducer for a number of episodes of *The Last Kingdom* through its fourth season.

Dreymon lives in Los Angeles. He enjoys writing, reading, and connecting with his family when he is not filming or traveling.

SUGGESTED READING

Dreymon, Alexander. "Alexander Dreymon: Diving into the Depths of Fame, Fashion and Future Projects." Interview by Julie Sagoskin. *Resident*, Apr. 2019, residentpublications. com/alexander-dreymon/. Accessed 20 July 2020.

———. "Interview with Alexander Dreymon: Alexander Dreymon Talks 'The Last Kingdom' and His Music Career." Video Interview by Pedro Correa. *Da Man*, 21 Dec. 2015, da-man.co.id/alexander-dreymon-talks-the-last-kingdom-and-his-music-career/. Accessed 16 July 2020.

——. "Netflix Star Alexander Dreymon on the Power of Politeness and Never Giving Up." *Backstage*, 26 Nov. 2018, www.backstage.com/uk/magazine/article/1-netflix-star-on-the-power-of-politeness-never-giving-up-66126/. Accessed 16 July 2020.

Lee, Luaine. "Alexander Dreymon Is a Man of the World." *The Bulletin* [Bend, Oregon], 14 Oct. 2015, www.bendbulletin.com/lifestyle/alexander-dreymon-is-a-man-of-the-world/article_3af4025e-7426-52da-a841-a67204079d01.html. Accessed 20 July 2020.

Martinetti, Cher. "The Last Kingdom's Alexander Dreymon, The True King of the North." *SyFy Wire*, 26 Nov. 2018, www.syfy.com/syfywire/the-last-kingdoms-alexander-dreymon-the-true-king-of-the-north. Accessed 16 July 2020.

Perkins, Dennis. "The Epic but Human *The Last Kingdom* Proves There's Always Room for More Vikings." Review of *The Last Kingdom*, Created by Gareth Neame and Nigel Marchant. *A.V. Club*, Onion, Inc., 9 Oct. 2015, tv.avclub.com/the-epic-but-human-the-last-kingdom-proves-there-s-alwa-1798185158. Accessed 16 July 2020.

Scheck, Frank. "'Heartlock': Film Review." Review of *Heartlock*, directed by Jon Kauffman. *The Hollywood Reporter*, 23 Jan. 2019, www.hollywoodreporter.com/review/heartlock-1178514. Accessed 16 July 2020.

SELECTED WORKS

Resistance, 2011; *American Horror Story: Coven*, 2013; *Blood Ransom*, 2014; *The Last Kingdom*, 2015– ; *Heartlock*, 2018

—*Molly Hagan*

Christian Drosten

Born: 1972
Occupation: Virologist

One of the most influential figures inside Germany is Christian Drosten, an unassuming academic and virologist who developed the testing protocols necessary to determine whether someone is infected with COVID-19, the novel coronavirus that began in China in late 2019 and has reached pandemic proportions across the world. Even before that pandemic made him a household name in Europe, Drosten was renowned in his field for having helped identify and test for the severe acute respiratory syndrome (SARS), a related predecessor to COVID-19, in 2003.

In addition to Drosten's research and input on the German government's response to the pandemic, he has also been featured in a frequent podcast, where he explains plainly the challenges facing the world in developing effective treatments and vaccines. That podcast has proved immensely popular, with over a million listeners streaming it each time Drosten records an episode.

The German response to the COVID-19 pandemic has impressed virologists. Far fewer Germans have been dying of the disease than many of their European counterparts. By early May, the case fatality rate (CFR)—the ratio between known deaths from the disease and total confirmed cases—in Italy reached 14 percent and was about 15 percent in France. In Germany, however, the CFR was just 4.4 percent. Part of this was due to Germany's intense work in the early months of 2020 to track, test, and contain those who were contagious in order to prevent them from infecting others. But the lockdown of society weighed on many, who believe the German government did too much and is restricting movements unnecessarily. Discussing the public pressure for a return to normal, Drosten noted in an interview with Laura Spinney for the UK *Guardian* (26 Apr. 2020): "The federal plan is to lift lockdown slightly, but because the German states, or Länder, set their own rules, I fear we're going to see a lot of creativity in the interpretation of that plan. I worry that the reproduction number [of new cases] will start to climb again, and we will have a second wave."

EARLY LIFE AND EDUCATION

Born in 1972 in Lingen, West Germany (now part of the Federal Republic of Germany), Christian Heinrich Maria Drosten was raised on a pig farm in the Emsland region. The eldest son, he completed his secondary schooling at the Gymnasium Marianum in Meppen, a large private Catholic school, in 1991 and became the first member of his family to attend college. For two years, he studied chemistry and biology in Dortmund and Münster before pursuing medicine.

In 2000 Drosten earned his medical degree from the University of Frankfurt, where his thesis was on blood donor screening in transfusion virology. From there he completed a doctorate with the German Red Cross (DRK) Institute for Transfusion Medicine and Immunohaematology in 2003.

START AMID SARS

Drosten's virology career began in earnest in March 2003, when Dr. Leong Hoe Nam of Singapore was rushed from a plane to a university hospital in Frankfurt. There, it became clear that the doctor was experiencing respiratory symptoms consistent with a viral disease that had emerged in Asia the preceding November, the newly named "severe acute respiratory syndrome" (SARS). The authorities at the Frankfurt hospital sent a sample of Leong's blood to the Bernhard Nocht Institute for Tropical Medicine (BNITM) in Hamburg for Drosten to analyze. The various molecular diagnostic tests he ran turned up empty, however.

Days later, the same hospital virologists gave Drosten a sample of the actual virus that they had grown in a petri dish. Having the virus itself enabled him to use a method he had developed, in which he sequenced the genetic material of a previously unknown virus and compared it against known viral sequences. He soon found that the new virus was similar to a coronavirus in cattle that did not harm humans; only two coronaviruses were then known to infect humans and those produced low numbers of the common cold. Drosten and his colleague Dr. Stephan Günther then concluded that SARS was a previously unrecorded virus. "At the time, medical students learned hardly anything about coronaviruses," Drosten recalled to Kai Kupferschmidt in Science (28 Apr. 2020).

From there, Drosten and Günther devised the first rapid diagnostic test and made it available just two days after the virus was identified. By that July, SARS was contained, but not before it killed about 9.6 percent of the nearly 8,100 people it infected worldwide. For his part in helping to curb the pandemic, Drosten received numerous accolades, including the Federal Cross of Merit, Germany's highest civilian award.

During his tenure at BNITM, Drosten also worked on diagnostic procedures for identifying Lassa fever, created the first blood test to detect rabies effectively, and oversaw the development of a new, inexpensive blood test for hepatitis C. By April 2007 he had risen to head of the clinical virology working group.

Drosten went on to direct the Institute for Virology at the University Hospital of Bonn in 2007. There he and his group investigated viral evolution to better understand how viruses make the leap to humans from other animals, such as bats and rodents, in order to identify potential future threats. Explaining his focus on animal-to-human transmission, Drosten said in an undated interview for the *Charité* website, "A virus appears out of the blue, taking the world by complete surprise because it belongs to a family of viruses so far only known to veterinary medicine. The moment it appears, the world is already facing a pandemic."

CAMEL-BORNE CORONAVIRUS

In 2012 a slower moving, but deadlier coronavirus emerged: Middle East respiratory syndrome (MERS). It first came to Drosten's attention when an older patient from the United Arab Emirates died in Germany while being treated for a respiratory condition. The patient had been caring for an ill-racing camel, which Drosten suspected might have been the source of the infection. Explaining coronaviruses' tendency to change animal hosts, he said to Spinney, "We [humans] create such opportunities through our non-natural use of animals—livestock. Livestock animals are exposed to wildlife, they are kept in large groups that can amplify the virus, and humans have intense contact with them . . . so they certainly represent a possible trajectory of emergence for coronaviruses. Camels count as livestock in the Middle East."

With his colleagues, Drosten detected the virus's RNA and showed that camels in the area might have been responsible for intermittent MERS transmission to humans for decades. He later collaborated closely with the Saudi Arabian health ministry for disease monitoring. Explaining the possibility that MERS had become more contagious in 2015, Drosten told Michaeleen Doucleff for WBUR (4 June 2015), "It's always possible that a virus can change. That's a general rule. But such a virus usually needs not just one but several of these changes, and the probability for these to happen together is really very low."

By January 2020, nearly eight years after its emergence, MERS had infected more than 2,500 people total and killed 866—a global CFR of 34.3 percent.

COMBATTING THE COVID-19 PANDEMIC

Drosten became the head of Charité University Hospital's Institute of Virology in 2017, precipitating a move to Berlin. A year later he was named the research director of Charité Global Health. There he studied emerging diseases such as the Zika virus, as well as more established diseases, such as dengue and hepatitis B.

While serving in these capacities, Drosten learned of a new coronavirus, SARS-CoV-2, emerging in Wuhan, China, in late 2019. The associated disease, COVID-19, can cause severe pneumonia in those who are infected and is especially deadly to older people and those with preexisting health conditions. In the first few months of 2020, COVID-19 quickly spread out from Wuhan, China, sparking a worldwide pandemic not seen since the influenza of 1918–19, which killed roughly 50 million people. Governments around the world were initially reluctant to take measures to control the spread of the new virus. By mid-May 2020, COVID-19 had infected more than 4 million people in 215 countries, with some 300,000 deaths.

In early January 2020, Drosten's group developed a laboratory test able to detect SARS-CoV-2 based on its genetic sequence. The group released their work publicly online, and the World Health Organization (WHO) publicized it on January 13, allowing other countries to detect and test for the disease. Researchers also used it to determine that human-to-human transmission was possible. "Now that this diagnostic test is widely available, I expect that it won't be long before we are able to reliably diagnose suspected cases. This will also help scientists understand whether the virus is capable of spreading from human to human," Drosten explained for *Global Biodefense* (17 Jan. 2020). "This is an important step in our fight against this new virus."

Germany had its first confirmed case of COVID-19 by January 27. In March, the federal government banned large public gatherings like sporting events and, like other governments around the world, began initiating large-scale restrictions. Even Drosten was not initially sure if all the closures were necessary but later came to see the error in his original thinking. "I was thinking too short-term," Drosten said of his initial reluctance to close schools, as quoted by Sven Siebert for the news site *Deutschland. de* (24 Mar. 2020). He and his colleagues later showed that children with COVID-19 had similar viral loads as infected adults, despite showing fewer symptoms, and, therefore, could spread infection if schools were opened.

PREVENTION PARADOX

Unlike other developed countries hard hit by COVID-19, including the United States, France, Italy, and Spain, Germany's CFR has remained comparatively low, hovering at around 4.4 percent by early May. Drosten credits that to widespread, decentralized testing, which began in earnest in Germany in late February by medical labs around the country. Germans were being tested at a rate of about 120,000 a week throughout March. "I believe that we are just testing much more than in other countries, and we are detecting our outbreak early," Drosten explained to Rob Schmitz for *NPR* (25 Mar. 2020).

Although the CFR in Germany has proved to be quite low, Drosten believes that the country is now facing what he terms a "prevention paradox," in which some people, eager to get back to work and normal lives and seeing few cases locally, believe government overreacted in implementing widespread lockdowns. Some countries, including Germany, began easing their restrictions on people's movements in April and May 2020, but Drosten and other virologists expressed concern that the virus would resurge as people begin to interact with one another once more.

CORONAVIRUS PODCAST

Drosten, although private by nature and preferring the confines of his laboratory to advising on public policy, has become the face of the German response to COVID-19 as an adviser to Chancellor Angela Merkel. Multiple times a week, he also sits for a thirty-minute, interview-format podcast, *Das Coronavirus-Update (The Coronavirus Update)*, in which he attempts to explain simply the challenges facing the world with regard to the COVID-19 pandemic. More than a million people in Germany listen to his podcast. Volker Stollorz, head of the German Science Media Center, told Kupferschmidt: "It's a stroke of luck that we have someone here in Germany who is recognized worldwide as an expert on coronaviruses and who is willing and able to communicate so well."

As Germany's go-to expert on COVID-19, Drosten is seen as a reasonable, factual voice of clarity amid the anxiety and fear surrounding the pandemic. He has stressed in his podcasts that much remains unknown about the virus; for example, half of the infections appear to be occurring among people who have yet to display symptoms of infection. Although many in Germany are eager for a reopening of society, many others, including those in the Merkel government, carefully consider what he has to say about issues such as schools reopening. "At this point, if Drosten says it is too early, that carries as much weight as Merkel saying it," noted Marcel Fratzscher, president of the German Institute for Economic Research (DIW Berlin), told Kupferschmidt.

For his work as a public health communicator, Drosten received a special prize from the German Research Foundation. Although the

COVID-19 crisis has made him a popular figure among many, it has also made him a target of mockery and even death threats from Germans who have become disaffected with the political response to the pandemic.

PERSONAL LIFE

Drosten lives with his wife and son in Berlin, where he cycles to work. He has told interviewers that he prefers the energy of city life to the countryside.

SUGGESTED READING

Drosten, Christian. "Staying a Step Ahead of the Virus." *Charité*, 2017, www.charite.de/en/research/themes_research/test/. Accessed 12 May 2020.

Drosten, Christian, and Vincent Munster. "Viral Superspreader? How One Man Triggered a Deadly MERS Outbreak." Interview by Michaeleen Doucleff, *WBUR*, 4 June 2015, www.wbur.org/npr/412046893/viral-super-spreader-how-one-man-triggered-a-deadly-mers-outbreak. Accessed 12 May 2020.

"German Researchers Develop 1st Test for New Coronavirus." *Global Biodefense*, 17 Jan. 2020, globalbiodefense.com/newswire/german-researchers-develop-1st-test-for-new-coronavirus. Accessed 7 May 2020.

Kupferschmidt, Kai. "How the Pandemic Made This Virologist an Unlikely Cult Figure." *Science*, 28 Apr. 2020, www.sciencemag.org/news/2020/04/how-pandemic-made-virologist-unlikely-cult-figure. Accessed 7 May 2020.

Schmitz, Rob. "Why Germany's Coronavirus Death Rate Is Far Lower Than in Other Countries." *NPR*, 25 Mar. 2020, www.npr.org/2020/03/25/820595489/why-germanys-coronavirus-death-rate-is-far-lower-than-in-other-countries. Accessed 7 May 2020.

Siebert, Sven. "The Virologist Who Explains the Virus to Us." *Deutschland.de*, 23 Mar. 2020, www.deutschland.de/en/topic/knowledge/christian-drosten-corona-researcher-and-government-advisor. Accessed 7 May 2020.

Spinney, Laura. "German's Covid-19 Expert: 'For Many, I'm the Evil Guy Crippling the Economy." *The Guardian*, 26 Apr. 2020, www.theguardian.com/world/2020/apr/26/virologist-christian-drosten-germany-coronavirus-expert-interview. Accessed 7 May 2020.

—*Christopher Mari*

Ree Drummond

Born: January 6, 1969
Occupation: Blogger and television personality

Blogger and television personality Ree Drummond told Eliza Borné for *BookPage* in 2011, "I think everyone has a story—I've just found a fun way to tell my story and convey my day-to-day life." By the time of that interview, however, Drummond's story and day-to-day life had already spent several years reaching a far wider audience than most. In 2006 she launched *The Pioneer Woman*, a food and lifestyle blog documenting her life on a large Oklahoma cattle ranch, and it quickly amassed an avid fan base with its wholesome, down-to-earth tone. The blog's runaway success earned her a book deal, and she released a series of popular cookbooks as well as a memoir about her marriage and several children's books. Drummond also made television appearances; and in 2011 she debuted her own program, also called *The Pioneer Woman*, a Food Network cooking show that became a key part of the channel's programming.

Drummond would go on to expand her Pioneer Woman brand further through the opening of a retail and restaurant facility, the Mercantile, as well as through the publication of a print of *The Pioneer Woman* magazine, which debuted in 2017. In retrospect, Drummond's rise to culinary prominence could perhaps have seemed inevitable, but Drummond continually expressed disbelief that her career rose out of such unlikely beginnings. "I just started with a personal blog, free software online and no plan at all except that I would post photos and my mom would read it," she told Tracy Nicholson for *Design & Living Magazine* (5 May 2017).

EARLY LIFE AND EDUCATION

Drummond was born Ann-Marie Smith on January 6, 1969, in Bartlesville, Oklahoma. One of four children, she had two older brothers and a younger sister. Her father, William, was a surgeon, while her mother, Gerre, was a homemaker. Drummond's parents divorced when she was in her twenties.

As a teenager Drummond attended Bartlesville High School. After graduating in 1987, she left Oklahoma for Los Angeles, a city that had long captured her interest, and enrolled in the University of Southern California. "There was just something about Los Angeles. It was the biggest city I could think of to go," she recalled to Rene Lynch for the *Los Angeles Times* (23 Sept. 2009). "I couldn't wait to get there." While living in California Drummond became increasingly drawn to city life and particularly enjoyed exploring the many restaurants and varying cuisines available to her, an experience that would shape her love of food and cooking. Although she initially planned to major in broadcast journalism and pursue a career in that field, she later switched her major to gerontology. She earned her bachelor's degree from the University of Southern California in 1991.

Drummond remained in California for a time following college, having found a job in marketing, but after about two years decided to leave her job and attend law school. While preparing to apply to a law school in Chicago, she returned to Oklahoma for what was planned to be a brief visit. That visit proved to be a fateful one, as she unexpectedly met and began a relationship with Ladd Drummond, a member of an established cattle-ranching family and the owner of a large rural property near Pawhuska, Oklahoma. The couple later married, and Drummond began a new lifestyle on the rural ranch that was vastly different from her days as a city dweller. Though the transition was not always easy for her, Drummond later considered it a positive change. "I am thoroughly convinced that I am where I was meant to wind up," she explained to Borné. "In the country we really lead an isolated life . . . we're just together, we're out here, we're on the land and in the quiet. It's not that everyone needs that to maintain some level of peace and contentment, but I needed it. It centered me."

BECOMING THE PIONEER WOMAN

Drummond first entered the public eye beginning in May 2006, when she began blogging to share stories about her home life and photographs of her children and surroundings with far-flung members of her family. Despite the casual nature of her blog, she was a committed writer who posted updates, ranging from poetry to humorous anecdotes, on a regular basis. "It enabled me to express a creative side that I didn't know I had," Drummond later told Nicholson about her blog. "I lived in the country for ten years at that point, so maybe it stored up and needed to come out somehow."

Over time, the blog—which came to be known by the title *The Pioneer Woman*—attracted visitors outside of Drummond's family, and her readership continued to grow as she expanded the focus of her content and established a distinctive authorial voice. Above all, she became best known for her posts about food and cooking. Beginning in 2007, when she posted step-by-step instructions for cooking a steak, *The Pioneer Woman* drew many readers as a source of detailed recipes that Drummond illustrated heavily with photographs of each step of the process. In recognition of her work, Drummond received several Weblog Awards (known as "Bloggies") from 2007 to 2010.

Building upon the success of her blog, Drummond published her first cookbook, *The Pioneer Woman Cooks: Recipes from an Accidental Country Girl*, in 2009. "Obviously, I had no idea what I was doing," she recalled to Nicholson about the book. "I look back at the photos and I cover my face with my hands because the photos were not good, but I love it because it was me. I wasn't trying to make it something it wasn't, so I just did photos of my kids and my dogs interspersed with the food."

Drummond also covered other topics on her blog, perhaps most notably chronicling the story of her relationship with her husband from their first meeting through the early years of their marriage. This content, which was romantic yet realistic also provided insight into working ranch life and resonated with her fan base, much like her recipes. A memoir based on those posts, *The Pioneer Woman: Black Heels to Tractor Wheels*, was published in 2011. Drummond's memoir was also optioned for film, although the adaptation eventually stalled in the developmental stages. The success of her early books allowed Drummond to branch out into writing for children, beginning with *Charlie the Ranch Dog* (2011). Inspired by the Drummond family's real-life basset hound, the picture book became the first in a series for beginning readers.

TELEVISION PERSONALITY

As Drummond's popularity as a blogger increased, she began to extend her reach into the medium of television as well, making guest appearances on Food Network programs such as *Throwdown with Bobby Flay* and *Paula's Best Dishes*. She would go on to appear as a judge in food competition shows such as *Iron Chef America*, *Christmas Cookie Challenge*, and *Beat Bobby Flay*, and was also a recurring guest on talk shows such as *Good Morning America*, *Today*, and the Food Network program *The Kitchen*. Perhaps the most significant moment in Drummond's television career, however, came with the premier of her own cooking series, *The Pioneer Woman*, on the Food Network. Airing in August 2011, the debut episode of the series introduced television viewers to Drummond's hearty style of cooking and featured recipes for chicken-fried steak, mashed potatoes, and what Drummond described as cowboy breakfast sandwiches. "I'm not a trained chef, and so I have a level of accessibility," she later told *CBS News* (10 Mar. 2019) about her approach to the program. "I'm not going to show [viewers] anything that is beyond their skill. And also, I use a lot of ingredients that are pretty easy to get."

Though the success of her blog had long demonstrated the appeal of her culinary approach, the move to television was a challenging one for Drummond, who was initially unsure of how to navigate that new medium. "Everything I'd done up to this point was on the other side of the camera," she explained in an interview for the magazine *Imbibe*. "When I started my show I wasn't really sure if I'd translate to TV, since I'm most comfortable in my blogging realm where I can pause, and TV moves so fast. On the other hand, the thing I really love about TV is that it shows more dimension." Despite Drummond's concerns, *The Pioneer Woman* proved highly popular among Food Network viewers. The show went on to air twenty-two seasons and more than 280 episodes between August 2011 and June 2019. Drummond signed a new three-year deal with the Food Network in September 2019.

EXPANDING THE PIONEER WOMAN BRAND

With her blog and her television show established as ongoing hits, Drummond continued to expand her reach in other areas. She published additional best-selling cookbooks under the Pioneer Woman Cooks banner, including *Food from My Frontier* (2012), *A Year of Holidays* (2013), *Dinnertime* (2015), *Come and Get It!* (2017), and *The New Frontier* (2019). She also released further installations of the Charlie the Ranch Dog series and launched a new children's series with the publication of the picture book *Little Ree* in 2017. Another work of nonfiction focusing on Drummond's life and family, *Frontier Follies: Adventures in Marriage and Motherhood in the Middle of Nowhere*, appeared in 2020.

Alongside such work, Drummond played an active role in transforming her area of Oklahoma into a popular destination for fans of *The Pioneer Woman*. In 2012 she and her husband purchased a long-unused building in Pawhuska, which they subsequently renovated. Featuring a restaurant, store, and bakery, the facility opened to the public under the name the Mercantile in 2016. "It's very exciting, and honestly a little surreal," Drummond told Shay Spence for *People* (16 Nov. 2016). "I've never actually opened the doors of a business, so it's totally new territory for me." In addition to hosting tourists at the Mercantile, Drummond and her family at times allowed visitors to tour their ranch's guest house, the filming location for the *Pioneer Woman* television show.

Drummond grew the Pioneer Woman brand again in 2017 with the launch of *Pioneer Woman Magazine*, a print periodical published by Hearst Magazines. Drummond also continued to develop her blog over the years, partnering with online-media companies as the business expanded, including Hearst Digital Media. In 2020, her team revamped the website significantly to incorporate a variety of new content.

PERSONAL LIFE

Ree Drummond met Ladd Drummond, better known to readers of her blog and first memoir as Marlboro Man, while visiting Oklahoma in the early 1990s. They married in 1996 and went on to have four children. Drummond's blog and other writings frequently feature her immediate family, as well as some extended relatives and friends.

Even as television and writing work as well as other aspects of managing her businesses ventures took up much of her time, Drummond remained devoted to the culinary interests that shaped her career. "As much as possible, I do hang on to the home cooking and at least make sure there's a casserole or two in the freezer and soup ready to go," she told Spence. "I feel like if I stop that, what's the point? That's who I am."

SUGGESTED READING

Borné, Eliza. "Ree Drummond: A City Girl Finds Her Home on the Range." *BookPage*, Feb. 2011, bookpage.com/interviews/8663-ree-drummond-biography-memoir#.X1Osw-eSlPZ. Accessed 7 Sept. 2020.

Drummond, Ree. "Exclusive Interview with the Pioneer Woman, Ree Drummond." Interview by Tracy Nicholson. *Design & Living Magazine*, 5 May 2017, www.designandliving-magazine.com/the-pioneer-woman-ree-drummond/. Accessed 7 Sept. 2020.

———. "Q & A with Ree Drummond." *Imbibe*, imbibemagazine.com/q-a-with-ree-drummond/. Accessed 7 Sept. 2020.

Fortini, Amanda. "O Pioneer Woman!" *The New Yorker*, 2 May 2011, www.newyorker.com/magazine/2011/05/09/o-pioneer-woman. Accessed 7 Sept. 2020.

Lynch, Rene. "O Pioneer!" *Los Angeles Times*, 23 Sept. 2009, www.latimes.com/archives/la-xpm-2009-sep-23-fo-pioneer23-story.html. Accessed 7 Sept. 2020.

"The Pioneer Woman: Ree Drummond on Food, Fame and Family." *CBS News*, 10 Mar. 2019, www.cbsnews.com/news/the-pioneer-woman-ree-drummond-on-food-fame-and-family/. Accessed 7 Sept. 2020.

Spence, Shay. "Look Inside Pioneer Woman Ree Drummond's Gorgeous New Restaurant." *People*, 16 Nov. 2016, people.com/food/pioneer-woman-ree-drummond-restaurant-mercantile/. Accessed 7 Sept. 2020.

SELECTED WORKS

The Pioneer Woman Cooks: Recipes from an Accidental Country Girl, 2009; *The Pioneer Woman: Black Heels to Tractor Wheels*, 2011; Charlie the Ranch Dog series, 2011– ; *The Pioneer Woman Cooks: Food from My Frontier*, 2012; *The Pioneer Woman Cooks: A Year of Holidays*, 2013; *The Pioneer Woman Cooks: Dinnertime*, 2015; *The Pioneer Woman Cooks: Come and Get It!*, 2017; Little Ree series, 2017– ; *The Pioneer Woman Cooks: The New Frontier*, 2019; *Frontier Follies:*

Adventures in Marriage and Motherhood in the Middle of Nowhere, 2020

—*Joy Crelin*

Jackie Sibblies Drury

Date of birth: ca. 1982
Occupation: Playwright

Jackie Sibblies Drury first came to the attention of theatergoers thanks to a play with an unwieldy title: *We Are Proud to Present a Presentation about the Herero of Namibia, Formerly Known as Southwest Africa, from the German Sudwestafrika, between the Years 1884–1915.* The plot involves six actors trying—with great difficulty—to mount a production about the genocide of the African Herero tribe by German colonists in the late 1800s. Developed as Drury's graduate playwriting thesis, it went on to win the 2010 Ignition Festival of New Plays and was subsequently staged at Chicago's Victory Gardens Theatre and New York City's Soho Repertory Theatre (Soho Rep).

In 2019 Drury received the Pulitzer Prize for Drama, among other honors, for *Fairview,* another thought-provoking play that explored pressing societal issues. The Pulitzer committee described it as "a hard-hitting drama that examines race in a highly conceptual, layered structure, ultimately bringing audiences into the actors' community to face deep-seated prejudices."

Despite the seriousness of those themes, Drury's work contains strong elements of humor. "Occasionally when you're watching a Drury play, you may find yourself laughing, then wondering if you're supposed to, or allowed to," Diep Tran wrote for *American Theatre* (29 May 2019). Drury, who has said she counts the legendary comedian Richard Pryor as an inspiration, told Tran, "It's my favorite kind of laughter. The kind that feels like, Ugh, you're not supposed to be doing it, or I can't believe I'm laughing at this, or I hope that no one hears me laughing at this. I like to go to plays to feel stuff, and that is a way to deeply feel something."

EARLY LIFE AND EDUCATION

Jackie Sibblies Drury grew up in Plainfield, New Jersey, raised as an only child in a middle-class family by her mother and grandmother, both Jamaican immigrants. She attended a small, multicultural private school. Although the school was diverse, students often still divided themselves along racial and socioeconomic lines—a lesson, Drury has told interviewers, in how persistent such segregation can be, even in otherwise inclusive settings.

Photo by Linda Fletcher via Wikimedia Commons

Drury's mother, a successful businesswoman, regularly took her to Manhattan to see Broadway shows; the two were particularly fond of *Phantom of the Opera,* and on long car trips they sang along to the soundtrack together.

Drury embarked on her undergraduate studies at Yale University, where she studied theater. Her mother, as she recalled to Lawrence Goodman for the *Brown Alumni Magazine* (July/Aug. 2013), "was terrified at first. She was like, 'You're going to this big fancy school and studying theater? What a waste.'" One of her classes was taught by the artist and playwright Deb Margolin, who required her students to write their own pieces about their lives and then perform them; that exercise sparked in her a desire to try her hand at playwriting, and after graduating from Yale in 2003, she began investigating master of fine arts (MFA) programs.

GRADUATE SCHOOL AND THE HERERO GENOCIDE

"When I wasn't applying to different graduate school programs I would also work on various play ideas, and one of them was an idea about this actor who is in a lot of [Rainer Werner] Fassbinder movies," Drury told Christopher Heaney for the *Appendix* (12 June 2013). "He was this black dude who is the son of an American GI and a German woman, who was born in Germany and speaks German, but in these Fassbinder movies he always plays an American GI and speaks English with a German accent. It's weird." Fascinated by the idea of a black German actor who was never cast as a German character due to his race, Drury Googled "Black People in

Germany." During her research, she came across information about the Herero genocide, which took place in the late nineteenth century in Namibia, when it was a German colony. The Herero and Nama peoples had rebelled when the Germans began confiscating their land to build a railroad. In response, the Germans issued an "extermination order" that resulted in the killing of tens of thousands of Herero people.

Drury kept that knowledge in the back of her mind while pursuing an MFA degree from Brown University, and when the time came to prepare her playwriting thesis, she decided to use the little-known historical event as the basis. She also brought her own personal experience to bear on the project. In graduate school, Drury noticed that "whenever they touched on cultural studies, or race, or other things that make us uncomfortable . . . students' presentations would either become really ironic and removed and silly, or would latch on to a dry, super-earnest and politically correct script of how we've been taught to talk about it," she explained to Heaney. "So I realized that in talking about the Herero it became necessary to talk about race in general, because from the vantage point of an American audience it is really hard to talk about Africa and not imprint American racial dynamics onto it."

Drury earned her master's degree from Brown in 2010, the year *We Are Proud to Present* triumphed at the Chicago-based Ignition Festival. In early 2012, Drury's play was produced at Victory Gardens Theater in Chicago, and later that year it made its Off-Broadway debut at the Soho Rep.

WE ARE PROUD TO PRESENT

We Are Proud to Present takes place as a group of actors (listed simply as Black Woman, Black Man, White Man, Another Black Man, and so forth) find themselves stymied in their attempts to make a play about the Herero because the only written records of the time were created by the Germans. "A thorny set-to arises over whether black Americans in the 21st century can truthfully represent the experience of Africans living more than a century before, when no firsthand testimony has been left behind to guide them," Charles Isherwood wrote for the *New York Times* (16 Nov. 2012), ultimately concluding that the play "impressively navigates the tricky boundaries that separate art and life, the haunted present and the haunting historical past."

"Though *We Are Proud to Present* was written in 2010," *American Theater* reviewer Diep Tran wrote in 2019, "what it talks about is still so heated and unresolved that it could have been written today. And if it seems lately there's been a surfeit of Black playwrights tackling race onstage in formally inventive ways, it can be partly traced to Drury's work at the beginning of the decade."

SOCIAL CREATURES AND REALLY

Drury next gained attention for *Social Creatures* (2013), which follows a group of survivors as they hide inside a theater during a zombie apocalypse. When a fellow survivor, who happens to be black, seeks refuge, they deem him infected and imprison him. "It's about how we become scared of anything outside your own group, however you define it," Drury told Goodman. "We're divided and suspicious of each other. People are terrified of everyone that they don't know."

In between productions, Drury took on a variety of temp jobs—although she admits that monetary awards like the $150,000 Windham Campbell Prize and the $40,000 Jerome Fellowship made things easier for her than for many playwrights. She also accepted teaching jobs, first at Fordham University and then at the Yale School of Drama, where she is a faculty member.

In 2016, Drury's *Really* premiered at New York City's Abrons Arts Center, directed by experimental auteur Richard Maxwell and performed by his troupe, the New York City Players. A sparse, three-person drama, it explores the relationships between the mother of a recently deceased young photographer and his girlfriend. Although the production attracted little attention outside the city's downtown theater scene, Drury's next play, *Fairview*, brought her the most media attention of her career.

FAIRVIEW AND MARYS SEACOLE

Fairview was co-commissioned by Berkeley Repertory Theatre and Soho Rep, and it debuted to sold-out audiences on both coasts in 2018. The play starts as a good-natured family comedy centered on preparations for a grandmother's birthday party before morphing into something darker. "Let me give you fair warning on *Fairview*, Jackie Sibblies Drury's dazzling and ruthless new play: If you see it—and you must—you will not be comfortable," Ben Brantley warned in a review for the *New York Times* (17 June 2018). "And some time after the show has ended, when you're thinking straight again, you'll realize just how artfully you have been toyed with before the final kill, as the mouse to one canny cat of a play."

From February to April 2019 New York City audiences flocked to Lincoln Center Theater's LCT3 (a venue for new works) to see Drury's *Marys Seacole*, which moves back and forth in time between Mary Seacole, a nineteenth-century British Jamaican nurse, and Mary, a nurse working in modern America. An exploration of what it means to be a caretaker, the play garnered solid reviews and an Obie.

WRITING PROCESS AND REACH

Drury told Tran that her writing process could be considered relatively haphazard. "It's lots and lots of pages of notes, and short exchanges of text and some stage directions and some impressionistic gathering of things," she said. When she finally has enough material to rehearse, she gathers a group of actors to run through the manuscript. "Somehow you find a simple and direct but nuanced way of explaining something that you've been trying to figure out how to articulate," she continues. "When you find those moments, then you're like, 'Yes! I found my "to be or not to be"!'"

Drury's plays have been performed at theaters across the country, as well as internationally. In addition to New York's Soho Rep, Victory Gardens, Abrons Art Center, and Lincoln Center, her work has been staged at theaters in Providence, Louisville, Philadelphia, Boston, London, and Washington, DC. She has developed projects and received artistic support at the Rockefeller Foundation Bellagio Center, Sundance Institute, Ground Floor at Berkeley Rep, Manhattan Theatre Club, American Conservatory Theatre, Ars Nova, Soho Rep Writer/ Director Lab, New York Theatre Workshop, PRELUDE, the Bushwick Starr, and the MacDowell Colony.

PERSONAL LIFE

Drury is married to Mark Drury, an anthropologist who teaches at Princeton University. The couple live in Brooklyn.

SUGGESTED READING

Brantley, Ben. "Review: Theater as Sabotage in the Dazzling 'Fairview.'" Review of *Fairview*, by Jackie Sibblies Drury. *The New York Times*, 17 June 2018, www.nytimes.com/2018/06/17/theater/review-theater-as-sabotage-in-the-dazzling-fairview.html. Accessed 5 Nov. 2019.

Drury, Jackie Sibblies. "Interview with Jackie Sibblies Drury: The Reenactors." Interview by Christopher Heaney. *Appendix*, 12 June 2013, theappendix.net/issues/2013/4/interview-with-jackie-sibblies-drury-the-reenactors. Accessed 5 Nov. 2019.

Goodman, Lawrence. "The Monstrous Unknown." *Brown Alumni Magazine*, 2 July 2013, www.brownalumnimagazine.com/index.php/articles/2013-07-02/the-monstrous-unknown. Accessed 5 Nov. 2019.

Isherwood, Charles. "Acting Out a Blood Bath Brings Dangers of Its Own." Review of *We Are Proud to Present a Presentation about the Herero of Namibia, Formerly Known as Southwest Africa, from the German Sudwestafrika, between the Years 1884–1915*, by Jackie Sibblies Drury. *The New York Times*, 16 Nov. 2012, www.nytimes.com/2012/11/17/theater/reviews/we-are-proud-to-present-a-presentation-at-soho-rep.html. Accessed 5 Nov. 2019.

Maxwell, Richard. "Jackie Sibblies Drury Explores the Role of Art in 'Really.'" Review of *Really*, by Jackie Sibblies Drury. *American Theatre*, 23 Sept. 2016, www.americantheatre.org/2016/09/23/jackie-sibblies-drury-explores-the-role-of-the-arts-in-really/. Accessed 5 Nov. 2019.

Tran, Diep. "Jackie Sibblies Drury: Thinking and Feeling." Review of *Fairview*, by Jackie Sibblies Drury. *American Theatre*, 29 May 2019, www.americantheatre.org/2019/05/29/jackie-sibblies-drury-thinking-and-feeling/. Accessed 5 Nov. 2019.

Weinert-Kendt, Rob. "Writes Well with Others." *The New York Times*, 16 Apr. 2013, archive.nytimes.com/query.nytimes.com/gst/fullpage-9D02EFDB113EF93B-A25757C0A9659D8B63.html. Accessed 5 Nov. 2019.

SELECTED WORKS

We Are Proud to Present a Presentation about the Herero of Namibia, Formerly Known as Southwest Africa, from the German Sudwestafrika, between the Years 1884–1915, 2012; *Social Creatures*, 2013; *Really*, 2016; *Fairview*, 2018; *Marys Seacole*, 2019

—Mari Rich

Alain Ducasse

Date of birth: September 13, 1956
Occupation: Chef and restaurateur

"A restaurant must tell a story to clients—even more than storytelling, it's a matter of story-feeling," Alain Ducasse told Jennifer Parker for *Skift Table* (6 May 2019). A successful chef since the 1980s and the owner of more than thirty individual restaurants by 2020, the French-born Ducasse is perhaps uniquely suited to tell such stories. As head of restaurants such as Le Louis XV in Monaco, Alain Ducasse at the Plaza Athénée in France, and Alain Ducasse at the Dorchester in the United Kingdom, he has established a reputation for providing diners with high-quality French cuisine that often highlights local and seasonal ingredients, to extensive critical acclaim. In recognition of his work and that of the chefs working in his kitchens, Ducasse has held more than twenty Michelin stars at points in his career and at one time owned three restaurants that had each achieved the top rating of three stars. Although the breadth of his culinary empire—which, in addition to his restaurants, includes a cooking school and a chocolate

Photo by Wikialainducasse via Wikimedia Commons

factory, among other businesses—prevents him from spending as much time in his restaurants' kitchens as he did early in his career, Ducasse has emphasized that his role as executive is not separate from the cooking process but an essential part of it. "Cooking is much more than peeling and mincing turnips," he explained to Rooksana Hossenally for *Forbes* (3 Feb. 2016). "It's about creating recipes, it is about sourcing the produce, it is about working with interior designers, choosing tableware, defining the style of service"—all elements for which the restaurants under the DUCASSE Paris umbrella are well known.

EARLY LIFE AND EDUCATION

Alain Ducasse was born in southwestern France on September 13, 1956. He grew up on a farm in the small town of Castel-Sarrazin, where his family planted and tended produce and raised poultry as well as other livestock. As a child, Ducasse was greatly influenced by his family's relationship with food, particularly his grandmother's cooking and use of fresh produce and meats. "My room smelled of foie gras, and mushrooms, and blanquette of veal," he recalled to Craig R. Whitney for the *New York Times* (11 Mar. 1998). "I liked to eat, and we had a garden, and animals, and I'd go picking mushrooms with my grandfather—it was a sort of extra-cultural richness." His family's emphasis on fresh, seasonal, and locally produced ingredients would continue to guide Ducasse throughout his career, shaping his approach to developing dishes and menus.

By the time he was twelve years old, Ducasse had determined that he wanted to pursue a career as a professional cook, to the dismay of his parents. "My parents were cool, very cool . . . but at the beginning, when I said I wanted to cook,

they were against the idea because they thought I'd take over the business," he recalled to David Ellis for *ES* (20 Mar. 2018). Nevertheless, he began his culinary education as a teenager, taking his first restaurant apprenticeship at the age of sixteen. In addition to his hands-on training, he went on to pursue a formal education at a hotel school in the southeastern French city of Bordeaux.

EARLY CAREER

Over the course of the 1970s, Ducasse worked alongside several of the era's notable chefs, honing his culinary skills in the kitchens of their restaurants. For a time, he worked at Michel Guérard's Les Prés d'Eugénie, which had the distinction of first being awarded three Michelin stars in 1977. Publicized through the tire manufacturer Michelin's series of city guidebooks, Michelin star ratings are among the most prestigious honors in the restaurant world. Even a single star indicates that a restaurant has reached a significant level of culinary excellence; the three-star rating is reserved only for restaurants deemed by the guide's creators to be the best of the best. In addition to gaining insight into culinary creativity at Guérard's highly awarded restaurant, Ducasse was educated in pastry arts by Gaston Lenôtre and went on to work for the chef Roger Vergé at Le Moulin de Mougins. Working for the acclaimed chef Alain Chapel in Mionnay, France, he learned more about focusing on ingredients' natural flavor before serving as chef at Vergé's L'Amandier de Mougins.

In 1981, Ducasse took on his most significant role to that point, becoming head chef of the restaurant La Terrasse. A hotel restaurant, like many of his later establishments, La Terrasse was situated in the Hôtel Juana in Juan-les-Pins, on France's Mediterranean coast. After several years under Ducasse's leadership, La Terrasse was awarded two Michelin stars in 1984. Although that year was in some ways a triumphant one for Ducasse, it was also a devastating one. In August 1984, he and a group of colleagues set out from southern France in a small plane, heading to a hotel restaurant in the Alps. The plane crashed in the mountains, and Ducasse, who was thrown from the aircraft, was the sole survivor. His injuries required numerous surgeries as well as an extended recovery period, during which he remained active in the operations of La Terrasse. "I had to keep working, even if I might never walk again," he recalled in an interview with the *Harvard Business Review* (May 2014). "I managed my restaurant from my hospital bed, by writing the menus, for example. It really improved my ability to delegate, and I understood that I was able to lead without being physically present." Though undeniably challenging, the experience proved valuable to him and set the stage for his later work as a restaurateur, which entailed operating numerous restaurants from a distance.

THREE-STAR CHEF

During the late 1980s, Ducasse learned of a new opportunity to make a mark on the culinary world, this time not in France but in the neighboring principality of Monaco. "It was the Prince of Monaco's ambition to create a fine dining restaurant, with the goal of obtaining three Michelin stars," he explained to Johannes Pong for the *South China Morning Post* (9 Mar. 2017). After presenting his ideas for the restaurant to Prince Rainier III, Ducasse was hired to take on that mission. "He was shocked that my vision was completely different to what was being served at a grand hotel at that time," he told Pong about the prince's response. "I wanted to deliver a totally different narrative from the culinary codes of the time." Located at the Hôtel de Paris in the Monte Carlo district of Monaco, Ducasse's restaurant, Le Louis XV, opened in 1987. The restaurant's cuisine, much of it inspired by the culinary traditions of southern France, earned him and the establishment widespread acclaim, and in 1990, the Michelin guide awarded Le Louis XV three stars.

In addition to operating Le Louis XV, Ducasse opened a variety of new establishments throughout the 1990s. In 1995, he opened his first inn in the Provence region of France, La Bastide de Moustiers. He opened a second inn in 1999 and remained involved in the hotel business over the next decades through the hospitality arm of his company, initially known as Alain Ducasse Entreprise and later known as DUCASSE Paris. A particularly key moment for Ducasse came in 1996, after veteran chef Joël Robuchon sought to retire from running his restaurant at the Hotel du Parc in Paris. "Everybody knew Joel Robuchon was going to retire, but nobody called him," he recalled to Whitney. "So I said, 'All right, to keep myself busy on weekends, I'll do it.'" Upon taking over the space, he set up the restaurant Alain Ducasse, where, over the next years, the establishment would secure a reputation for high-quality, fine dining. The restaurant was awarded three Michelin stars not long afterward, and though he had to wait for one more year until Le Louis XV's temporarily demoted star status had once again been raised to three, that honor made Ducasse the first chef in over six decades to have two three-star restaurants at the same time in 1998. After operating at Hotel du Parc for some time, he moved Alain Ducasse to the Plaza Athénée in 2000, where it was again awarded three stars.

GLOBAL EXPANSION

The first decades of the twenty-first century represented a period of rapid global expansion for Ducasse, who opened numerous restaurants both within and outside of France. He opened his first US restaurant, Alain Ducasse at the Essex House in New York, in 2000. The restaurant received three Michelin stars in 2005, an achievement that meant that Ducasse was the first chef, up to that point, to be the owner of three restaurants claiming three stars simultaneously. The restaurant closed in 2007, however. Meanwhile, he had opened his first restaurant in Asia, Japan's Beige, in 2004, marking the beginning of an extensive effort to expand into East Asia and the Middle East. The year 2007 saw the opening of Alain Ducasse at the Dorchester in London, which went on to receive two Michelin stars in 2009 and three beginning in 2010. During that time, he also furthered his involvement in culinary-education initiatives, which included creating a cooking school designed for nonprofessionals in 2009.

As well as realizing another longtime goal by establishing a chocolate boutique and combined manufacturing workshop in Paris in 2013, Ducasse was the focus of the 2017 documentary *The Quest of Alain Ducasse*, and he started a new coffee shop and roasting venture in Paris in 2019. By June 2020, the parent company DUCASSE Paris operated thirty-four restaurants around the world. Though perhaps most associated with fine-dining fixtures such as costly fixed-price menus, some of those restaurants took a more casual approach, offering more accessible bistro cuisine or similar options. In addition to restaurants in Monaco, France, Japan, and the United Kingdom, Ducasse-led establishments operating by 2020 included Rivea and Benoit in the United States, BBR in Singapore, Blue in Thailand, and miX Dubai in the United Arab Emirates.

As a restaurateur, Ducasse was particularly interested in the creative opportunities such expansion offered him as well as the role his company could play in meeting the needs of hotel groups and other stakeholders. "I am yearning to explore various forms of dining, and I organized my teams to realize these challenges. We want and we can!" he explained to Parker. "We also owe this expansion to our clients. [Investors] organize calls for [concepts] and choose us because our offers get the best evaluation." To ensure the success of his establishments, Ducasse focused on building a team of skilled and dependable chefs capable of achieving the desired level of quality. In addition to overseeing his restaurant group, he has published numerous cookbooks.

CULINARY APPROACH

Although his many restaurants have varied in terms of menu offerings, Ducasse has long been committed to showcasing local and seasonal fresh ingredients in conjunction with both his culinary point of view and his desire to work toward a more sustainable culinary industry. "When talking about sustainability and the future of food, it's important to take into account the good health of my clients, as well as the health of the planet. Only take from the earth what you consume," he told Pong. He has also emphasized the importance of culinary diversity, particularly within the ever-changing culinary landscape of the early twenty-first century. "New countries emerge, discovering and reshaping their food culture, young talents blossom everywhere, the dialogue between chefs is becoming more intense," he explained to Hossenally. He added that such factors have resulted in "a much more diversified offer and a buoyant culinary scene." Though Ducasse's best-known restaurants heavily feature French cuisine, he and his chefs have sought to explore a wider range of foods through restaurants such as Ômer in Monaco, which specializes in broader Mediterranean cuisine, and Cucina Byblos, an Italian restaurant in Saint-Tropez, France.

PERSONAL LIFE

Ducasse and his first wife, Michèle, had a daughter together. He married Gwénaëlle Gueguen in 2007. They have three children. Although he spends a great deal of time in France, Ducasse is a citizen of Monaco, having gained citizenship in the principality in 2008. He has been featured in numerous cooking programs and documentaries.

SUGGESTED READING

Ducasse, Alain. "Interview: Alain Ducasse on Running a Successful Restaurant Empire." Interview by Jennifer Parker. *Skift Table*, 6 May 2019, table.skift.com/2019/05/06/interview-alain-ducasse-on-running-a-successful-restaurant-empire/. Accessed 7 June 2020.

———. "Life's Work: An Interview with Alain Ducasse." *Harvard Business Review*, May 2014, hbr.org/2014/05/alain-ducasse. Accessed 7 June 2020.

———. "The Story behind the Michelin Stars: An Interview with Alain Ducasse, France's Most Famous Chef." Interview by Rooksana Hossenally. *Forbes*, 3 Feb. 2016, www.forbes.com/sites/rooksanahossenally/2016/02/03/the-story-behind-the-michelin-stars-an-interview-with-alain-ducasse. Accessed 7 June 2020.

———. "Alain Ducasse Interview: I Am Not ahead of the Competition at All." Interview by David Ellis. *ES*, 20 Mar. 2018, www.standard.co.uk/go/london/restaurants/alain-ducasse-on-jason-atherton-diversity-in-food-retirement-a3793711.html. Accessed 7 June 2020.

Pong, Johannes. "Alain Ducasse on His New Hong Kong Restaurant Rech, Places in the City He Loves to Eat at, and the Sunny Side of Life." *South China Morning Post*, 9 Mar. 2017, www.scmp.com/lifestyle/food-drink/article/2077019/alain-ducasse-his-new-hong-kong-restaurant-rech-its-seaside. Accessed 7 June 2020.

Whitney, Craig R. "The Brightest, Seventh Star: Ducasse Himself." *The New York Times*, 11 Mar. 1998, www.nytimes.com/1998/03/11/dining/the-brightest-seventh-star-ducasse-himself.html. Accessed 7 June 2020.

—*Joy Crelin*

Channing Dungey

Born: March 14, 1969
Occupation: Television executive and producer

Entertainment executive Channing Dungey has served since 2018 as the vice president of original content for Netflix, following a two-year turn as president of ABC Entertainment Group, a role that made her the first African American head of a major broadcast network. Dungey has been dubbed the "Shonda Rhimes whisperer" for her many successful collaborations with the powerhouse writer and producer. As a development executive for ABC, Dungey adopted a blunt, yet compassionate approach while working closely with Rhimes on her pilot script for the medical drama *Grey's Anatomy*. "I think of myself as a creative partner," Dungey told Nicole Laporte for *Fast Company* (16 Oct. 2018). "It's my job to [point out] aspects of a story that aren't landing for the audience. . . . I try not to intercede too often. When I do, I want to make it count." Dungey's technique proved to be quite effective: In its sixteenth season (2019–20), *Grey's Anatomy* has surpassed *ER* as the longest-running prime-time medical drama in history.

During her tenure at ABC, Dungey also partnered with Rhimes in developing and launching some of the network's other successful dramas, including *Scandal* and *How to Get Away with Murder*. Dungey's hard work was rewarded in February 2016 when Ben Sherwood, Disney/ABC Television president, handpicked Dungey to head up ABC Entertainment. Earlier in her career, Dungey was a film production executive, meaning when she left ABC and moved to Netflix in 2018, she had reached the upper echelons of three different entertainment platforms: film, television, and streaming.

EARLY LIFE AND EDUCATION

Channing Nicole Dungey was born on March 14, 1969, to Judith and Don Dungey in Sacramento, California, where she attended Rio

Americano High School, alongside her younger sister, Merrin. Growing up, the siblings also shared a childhood fascination with television, religiously buying fall preview issues of *TV Guide* and making audio recordings of their favorite television series, including *Charlie's Angels*, *Remington Steele*, and *Hart to Hart*. It was a trait that they developed, under the watchful eye of their mother, a retired schoolteacher, and their father, a manager with Sacramento Municipal Utility District's general services department.

Upon completing high school in 1986, Dungey briefly flirted with studying political science at the University of California at Los Angeles (UCLA), intending to practice international law before switching to film studies and deciding to pursue a career in entertainment—a passion she rediscovered after taking several film and television electives, especially her beloved screenwriting class. Although Dungey realized that screenwriting was not her forte, she soon found her ideal niche. "I loved working with the other students and reading their material and offering feedback," she told Jenny Hontz for *Emmys.com* (5 June 2018). With the help of her screenwriting professor, Dungey quickly figured out her future career: script development.

EARLY CAREER

Dungey's foray into the entertainment industry occurred following her 1991 graduation from UCLA's School of Theater, Film, and Television, where she earned a bachelor's in fine arts with honors. Dungey started out as a development assistant to producer John Davis, helping to pitch movie concepts at Davis Entertainment, a 20th Century Fox production partner. Next came a two-and-a-half-year stint at actor Steven Seagal's LA–based Steamroller Productions. As story editor, Dungey was involved in developing and producing such Seagal blockbusters as *Under Siege* (1992) and *On Deadly Ground* (1994).

In 1994, Dungey accepted a production executive post at Warner Brothers studios. Over the next four years Dungey, alongside mentor Lucy Fisher, oversaw the development of a vast roster of critically and commercially successful movies that included *Bridges of Madison County* (1995), *Twister* (1996), *Space Jam* (1996), and *Practical Magic* (1998). By February 1998 Dungey had joined Jorge Saralegui's production company, Material Film, in the role of senior vice president of production. Not only was she in charge of procuring the rights to new projects in the development stages, but she was also tasked with supervising several projects that she already had under development at Warner Brothers, which had just inked a first-look agreement with Material. Dungey rose to serve as coproducer of the Eddie Murphy–Robert De Niro buddy comedy *Showtime* (2002), as well as the big-screen

adaptations of Anne Rice's *Queen of the Damned* (2002) and Elmore Leonard's *The Big Bounce* (2004).

TOUCHSTONE TELEVISION

At the time, major Hollywood movie studios were increasingly gravitating toward big-budget, special effects–laden action flicks that had the possibility for sequels. Dungey responded to this growing trend by cofounding Dexterity Pictures (with Pamela Post) in January 2003, committed to producing more meaningful independent and studio features and creating new television shows. A year and a half later, Dungey had scheduled a pitch meeting with friend Suzanne Patmore Gibbs, then the outgoing senior vice president of drama series at Touchstone Television, later known as ABC Studios. "I think a lot of the really interesting storytelling was starting to migrate from film to television, so I started casting my sights toward television, and that's what led me to Touchstone and ABC Studios," she told R. Thomas Umstead for *Next TV* (28 Oct. 2019). At Patmore Gibbs's suggestion, Dungey met with Patmore Gibbs's successor, Morgan Wandell, who offered her a job.

As vice president of drama development at Touchstone, Dungey was responsible for developing and acquiring Touchstone's drama programming. One project in particular that caught Dungey's eye during her first year was *Grey's Anatomy*, a pilot that focused on the professional and personal lives of Seattle surgical residents. "I had no idea who Shonda [Rhimes] was, but I really responded to her narrative voice," she recalled to Hontz. Dungey was tapped to oversee *Grey's*, along with two other pilots: *Desperate Housewives*, about four women whose seemingly idyllic suburban lives are rocked by their neighbor's suicide; and *Lost*, about plane crash survivors trapped on a mysterious island.

In May 2004 all three series were picked up for ABC's fall schedule, with *Grey's* debuting midseason. They each became breakout hits for ABC in 2004–05, earning renewals and catapulting the network to third place among adults aged eighteen to forty-nine. The three shows would remain in the ABC lineup over the next four seasons (2005–09), and Touchstone Television would be renamed ABC Television Studios. During that period, Dungey oversaw the development of *Grey's* spinoff *Private Practice*, whose May 2007 pilot featured Dungey's sister, though she did not ultimately appear in the series. Dungey's second collaboration with Rhimes, *Private Practice* premiered in September 2007 and became an instant hit and ran until 2013. Dungey's next success came in 2009, with the police procedural *Castle*, about a best-selling crime writer turned amateur detective; it ran until 2016.

CLIMBING THE RANKS AT ABC

In June 2009 Dungey was promoted to senior vice president of drama development for the ABC Entertainment Group, where she reported to Patmore Gibbs. Dungey was reunited with another familiar face in 2010, when Rhimes's production *Off the Map* was added to ABC's 2010–11 lineup. However, *Off the Map*, which was set in a remote Amazon clinic, was cancelled after one season. The procedural *Body of Proof*, about a neurosurgeon-turned-medical examiner, fared better, scoring a second-season pickup.

Dungey's next collaboration with Rhimes proved more successful. *Scandal*, a political drama centering around a powerful black female crisis manager embroiled in DC politics, debuted in April 2012 as a seven-episode midseason replacement and was renewed a month later. Dungey also collaborated closely with *Lost* producers Edward Kitsis and Adam Horowitz on *Once upon a Time*, which chronicles fairy tale characters trapped in a mythical town by an evil witch's curse. The fantasy series became one of the season's top-rated new dramas and was awarded a second season. Dungey had a surprise hit with *Revenge*; the soapy drama about a mysterious woman's return to Hamptons' high society on a quest for vengeance consistently performed well among the popular eighteen-to-forty-nine demographic, earning a second season renewal.

Buoyed by country music's increasing mainstream appeal, Dungey greenlit *Nashville* for 2012–13—the first season ABC employed a split-season plan for its dramas and incorporated the limited series in midseason. Despite ratings struggles, the show's critical acclaim and chart-topping two-volume soundtrack led to a sophomore season. Following the blockbuster success of the 2012 film *The Avengers*, based on the Marvel Comics series, Dungey oversaw the development of the ABC spinoff *Agents of S.H.I.E.L.D.* The series became the focus of ABC's 2013–14 lineup, giving the network the biggest drama debut in four years. It was renewed in May 2014—nearly a year after Dungey's promotion to executive vice president of drama development, movies and miniseries, for ABC Entertainment.

For the 2014–15 season, ABC embraced diversity, as reflected in the network's prime-time lineup featuring multiracial casts. This included *How to Get Away with Murder*, the latest Rhimes offering, starring Viola Davis as a criminal defense attorney and professor/mentor to a group of ambitious law students; and *Quantico*, in which Bollywood actress Priyanka Chopra played a fugitive FBI rookie accused of terrorism. Dungey continued the trend with *American Crime*, a limited anthology series exploring race relations. The first season dealt with a young white military couple who are victims of a violent home invasion and the four African American and Hispanic men suspected of murder. All three dramas returned for the 2015–16 season.

PRESIDENT OF ABC ENTERTAINMENT

Dungey made headlines of her own in February 2016, when Ben Sherwood, Disney/ABC Television president, tapped her to replace Paul Lee as head of ABC Entertainment. With this promotion, she became the first African American to head a major television network. One of Dungey's first moves involved the cancellation of fan favorites *Nashville* and *Castle* in May 2016, to make way for new productions. Her first major appearance came that August at the Television Critics Association (TCA) press tour, where she addressed the network's creative direction, teasing a possible *Star Wars* series while also continuing to tout diversity and inclusion.

Dungey's strategy was reflected in the network's 2016–17 lineup, which boasted a sitcom about a special-needs child (*Speechless*); a miniseries chronicling the modern gay rights movement (*When We Stand*); and a *Bachelorette* installment featuring the first lead of color in the franchise's history. Dungey applied a similar approach to several 2017–18 shows, including one about an autistic surgeon (*The Good Doctor*) and another about a rapper turned politician (*The Mayor*), as well as a second *Grey's* spinoff (*Station 19*). She also brought back successful revivals of *American Idol* and *Roseanne*.

TACKLING CONTROVERSY AND HEADING TO NETFLIX

However, Dungey's tenure was not without controversy. While attending the 2017 Television Critic's Association (TCA) summer press tour in early August, she defended *Last Man Standing*'s surprise cancellation, citing cost-cutting and new programming strategy and denying star Tim Allen's claim that his conservative politics played any role in her decision. A week later, Dungey lost longtime collaborator Rhimes, who defected to streaming service Netflix. Dungey found herself in the midst of another firestorm in February 2018, when a *Black-ish* episode spotlighting the hot-button kneeling protests of professional football players was shelved over creative differences, much to the outrage of series creator Kenya Barris. She was then thrust into the spotlight again, courtesy of the *Roseanne* reboot's April 3 episode, during which Barr's character mocked *Fresh Off the Boat* and *Black-ish*, ABC sitcoms about families of color. Barr was at the center of another controversy surrounding her racially incendiary May 29 tweet comparing Valerie Jarrett, former senior advisor to President Barack Obama, to an ape. That same day, Dungey, who had defended the show in April, issued a statement announcing *Roseanne*'s cancellation.

At the 2018 TCA summer press tour, Dungey unveiled a 2018–19 lineup featuring several family comedies (*Roseanne* offshoot *The Conners*, *Single Parents*) and ensemble dramas (*A Million Little Things*, *The Rookie*). That would be Dungey's last major appearance as ABC president; prior to Disney's merger with 21st Century Fox, she resigned her post in mid-November, despite efforts to keep her.

A month later Dungey signed with Netflix, also home to former collaborator Barris. Since February 2019, she has served as the company's vice president of original content. In this newly created role, Dungey will oversee projects from the likes of Rhimes, Barris, as well as Barack and Michelle Obama, whose production house has a deal with Netflix.

PERSONAL LIFE

Since 2003, Dungey has been married to Scott Power, with whom she has two children.

SUGGESTED READING

Hontz, Jenny. "Season of Change," *Emmys.com*, Television Academy, 5 June 2018, www.emmys.com/news/features/season-change-0. Accessed 10 May 2020.

Laporte, Nicole. "ABC Entertainment's Channing Dungey Discusses 'The Conners,'" *Fast Company*, 16 Oct. 2018, www.fastcompany.com/90245269/the-network-effect. Accessed 10 May 2020.

Nelson, Valerie. "Sister, Sister." *Emmys.com*, Television Academy, 4 June 2014, www.emmys.com/news/mix/sister-sister. Accessed 10 May 2020.

Umstead, R. Thomas. "Channing Dungey." *Next TV*, 28 Oct. 2019, www.broadcastingcable.com/news/channing-dungey. Accessed 10 May 2020.

—*Bertha Muteba*

Billie Eilish

Date of birth: December 18, 2001
Occupation: Singer-songwriter

Billie Eilish became a SoundCloud sensation with the upload of the song "Ocean Eyes" in 2015, generating an enormous fandom through her angsty, self-reflective, confessional alternative pop that included millions of followers on Instagram and leading to *When We All Fall Asleep, Where Do We Go?*, her 2019 debut full-length record. Topping the Billboard 200 chart as well as the UK albums chart, the album spawned several popular singles, including the Billboard Hot 100 number-one hit "Bad Guy."

Just seventeen at the time of the record's release, her work on it earned her six Grammy Award nominations, two American Music Awards, and three MTV Video Music Awards. Of those six Grammy nods, she became the youngest musician in Grammy history to earn spots in the four categories of Record of the Year, Album of the Year, Song of the Year, and Best New Artist at the same time. She ultimately took home the trophies in each of these four categories as well as for Best Pop Vocal Album at the awards ceremony in January 2020.

In discussions about the appeal of Eilish's music surrounding her rather intense rise to stardom, commentators often focused on her unique style and authenticity. "There are countless aspiring teenage musicians producing remixes on SoundCloud or uploading YouTube videos in their bedrooms, but Eilish's disregard for conventions in music and fashion is exactly what has captured the attention of Generation Z," Charlie Harding wrote of her for *Vox* (19 Aug. 2019). For Eilish, she expressed in interviews that she did not care for labels and that remaining true to herself and the type of music she wanted to create remained crucial.

EARLY LIFE

Billie Eilish Pirate Baird O'Connell was born on December 18, 2001, and raised in Los Angeles. Her parents, Maggie Baird and Patrick O'Connell, were actors who met in Alaska while working on a theatrical production. For many years, they found small parts on television and in films, and Baird performed with the Groundlings, an improvisational comedy troupe. After settling in Los Angeles, when they were not

Photo by Gary Miller/Getty Images

getting many acting jobs, they also looked for work outside of that career.

After Eilish and her older brother, Finneas, were born, their parents decided that they would homeschool them, giving them freedom to be creative and explore their interests. "Our whole stance was, general knowledge is all," O'Connell said to Josh Eells for *Rolling Stone* (31 July 2019). "You need to know why the sky is blue, but you don't need to memorize a bunch of esoterica you'll never use." Drawn to performing from as early as she can remember and always singing, Eilish participated in talent shows and became part of the Los Angeles Children's Chorus when she was eight. Also interested in the visual world of photography and film, she would set up scenes outside her house featuring her toys and use a camera to tell a story in pictures, and at other times she would make music videos. The other art that was integral to her life outside of her studies was dance, as she was a member of a local dance company.

Music also had a significant presence in the household, fueling a passion within Eilish and her brother. Eilish learned to play the ukulele and had access to three pianos. Baird taught her children the fundamentals of how to write songs, a method of expression that Eilish really took to. "We kind of had a rule in the house that no one would ever make you go to sleep if you were playing music," Baird told Eells. "Music trumped everything."

SOUNDCLOUD BREAKTHROUGH AND FIRST EP

After a time, Eilish and Finneas, who had already been writing and creating together, began recording songs. These sessions, which took place at home, marked the beginning of a strong collaboration in which they would continue to return to her brother's small bedroom to write and produce. Their musical influences included Avril Lavigne, the Beatles, and Green Day. "We're listening to everything—all genres, new music, old music, and it all just gets sort of synthesized and boiled down into a broth that we make," Finneas explained, as quoted by Harding.

In late 2015 the pair uploaded the song "Ocean Eyes," which Finneas had composed, to the SoundCloud music platform so that Eilish's dance teacher could access it for use in a recital. Unexpectedly, many people began listening to and sharing the song, playing it one thousand times within the first day of its posting, and its mention on sites like *Hillydilly*, which is dedicated to discovering new music, brought Eilish to the attention of the music industry. Though shocked by the amount of attention that the song had attracted so quickly, she knew that if she were to make a career out of her talent, she wanted to have as much control over it as possible. After signing with Darkroom and Interscope

Records in 2016 and rereleasing "Ocean Eyes," in an effort to generate even more interest in her music and style, she began releasing additional singles, including "Bellyache" and "Bored." The latter of which was included on the soundtrack to the Netflix series *13 Reasons Why*.

In August 2017 Eilish released her first EP, *dont smile at me*. Containing previously released singles as well as songs such as "Copycat" and "Watch," the album eventually hit number fourteen on the Billboard 200 chart. Finneas cowrote most of the tracks for the EP and produced it at home. In interviews, Eilish described the benefits of working with her brother in such a creative capacity, particularly being able to be honest with one another. "We take criticism really well, so he'll do something and I'll be like, 'No. That's terrible,' and he'll be like, 'Okay. You're right,'" she told Haley Weiss for *Interview* (27 Feb. 2017). "We're a team."

Her work successfully communicated her unique artistry to fans and critics. Prior to the release of her first full-length record, *When We All Fall Asleep, Where Do We Go?*, reviewer Jon Pareles noted for the *New York Times* (29 Mar. 2019), "She doesn't play innocent, or ingratiating, or flirtatious, or perky, or cute. Instead, she's sullen, depressive, death-haunted, sly, analytical, and confrontational, all without raising her voice."

WHEN WE ALL FALL ASLEEP, WHERE DO WE GO?

Following the release of her EP, Eilish, along with her family, embarked on a tour with impressive ticket sales. In addition to traveling and performing, throughout 2018, she put out a series of songs, including a cover of Drake's "Hotline Bling," "Lovely" (a collaboration with Khalid), "You Should See Me in a Crown," "When the Party's Over," and "Come Out and Play." *Forbes* magazine also named her to its 30 Under 30 list in November 2018.

Before releasing *When We All Fall Asleep, Where Do We Go?* in March 2019, Eilish put out another pair of singles: "When I Was Older" and "Bury a Friend." Once again written and produced with her brother, her long-expected full-length debut features an intro in which she removes her Invisalign. When her long-expected full-length debut was finally released, it hit the top of the charts in both the United States and the United Kingdom. Within short order, every song on the album (once again stylized in all lowercase letters), apart from "Goodbye," had made the Billboard Hot 100 chart; "Bad Guy" even reached the number-one position. This success allowed Eilish to further accomplish a goal for her music that she had expressed to Weiss: "I want to touch people in the way that it touches me, and have somebody feel a certain way that they didn't know they felt."

Eilish's fans were not the only ones who loved the record; music critics did as well. Pareles noted, "Eilish began her career establishing what kind of pop star she doesn't intend to be. With her debut album, she's even tougher: tough enough to show some heart." As he broke down a number of the tracks on *When We All Fall Asleep, Where Do We Go?*, he commended the work's cohesiveness with respect to the discernible progression in tone. In a review for *Rolling Stone* (29 Mar. 2019), Suzy Exposito said of Eilish's debut LP, "It's an album full of dressed-down avant-pop with D.I.Y. immediacy and intimacy that can still hold its own amid Top 40 maximalists like Ariana Grande and Halsey. Eilish's sound is hyper-modern, but still feels classic; evoking another Billie in history, she sets the jazz-aware swing in her vocals over skittering trap beats and doo-wop piano asides."

Eilish went on to promote the album's release with another family-aided tour and perform in front of a roaring crowd at Coachella for the first time in April of that year. As further evidence of her rise to mainstream fame, in September she was honored with the opportunity to open the forty-fifth season of *Saturday Night Live* as the sketch comedy series' musical guest. Following the announcement that she had been nominated for six Grammy Awards based on her work for *When We All Fall Asleep, Where Do We Go?*, it was revealed that *Billboard* had chosen her as its 2019 Woman of the Year. Making further Grammy history, she won five of the six Grammys for which she was nominated, walking away from the ceremony in January 2020 with the awards for Record of the Year and Song of the Year for "Bad Guy" as well as Album of the Year, Best New Artist, and Best Pop Vocal Album.

PERSONAL LIFE

In interviews, Eilish has been open about her struggles with mental illness, particularly depression and body dysmorphia from around the age of thirteen, after a serious dance injury kept her from dancing. She has also mentioned how she was diagnosed both with Tourette syndrome (a neurological disorder that involves involuntary movements and vocalizations) and with synesthesia (a condition in which sensory perceptions are mingled). For Eilish, the latter means that she perceives people, places, and things by colors, numbers, and shapes.

Known for her interest in fashion, when not touring or recording, she has said that she enjoys spending time with friends and learning the basics of music production.

SUGGESTED READING

Eells, Josh. "Billie Eilish and the Triumph of the Weird." *Rolling Stone*, 31 July 2019, www.rollingstone.com/music/music-features/billie-eilish-cover-story-triumph-weird-863603. Accessed 2 Jan. 2020.

Eilish, Billie. "Discovery: Billie Eilish." Interview by Haley Weiss. *Interview*, 27 Feb. 2017, www.interviewmagazine.com/music/discovery-billie-eilish. Accessed 2 Jan. 2020.

Exposito, Suzy. "Review: Billie Eilish's 'When We All Fall Asleep, Where Do We Go?' Is Noir Pop with Bite." Review of *When We All Fall Asleep, Where Do We Go?* by Billie Eilish. *Rolling Stone*, 29 Mar. 2019, www.rollingstone.com/music/music-album-reviews/review-billie-eilish-when-we-all-fall-asleep-where-do-we-go-814754. Accessed 2 Jan. 2020.

Harding, Charlie. "Billie Eilish, the Neo-Goth, Chart-Topping 17-Year-Old Pop Star, Explained." *Vox*, 19 Aug. 2019, www.vox.com/culture/2019/4/18/18412282/who-is-billie-eilish-explained-coachella-2019. Accessed 2 Jan. 2020.

Pareles, Jon. "Billie Eilish Redefines Teen-Pop Stardom on a Haunted, Heartfelt Debut Album." Review of *When We All Fall Asleep, Where Do We Go?* by Billie Eilish. *The New York Times*, 29 Mar. 2019, www.nytimes.com/2019/03/29/arts/music/billie-eilish-when-we-all-fall-asleep-where-do-we-go-review.html. Accessed 2 Jan. 2020.

Yeung, Neil Z. "Billie Eilish." *AllMusic*, www.allmusic.com/artist/billie-eilish-mn0003475903/biography. Accessed 2 Dec. 2020.

—*Christopher Mari*

Jeremy Farrar

Born: September 1, 1961
Occupation: Medical researcher and physician

Since its establishment in 1936, the charitable organization the Wellcome Trust has funded medical research in a wide range of areas, contributing portions of its multibillion-dollar endowment to researchers and institutions investigating many of the diseases that most threaten humankind. For the trust's director, UK medical researcher Sir Jeremy Farrar, the fund's unique position within the medical community enables the Wellcome Trust to make substantial contributions that might otherwise be impossible. He explained to Helen Branswell for *STAT* (6 May 2016), "We are in the privileged position of being an independent, philanthropic organization.

Photo by Wellcome Images

If we can't act boldly and with flexibility, then who can?"

Prior to joining the Wellcome Trust in 2013, Farrar—an expert in infectious diseases and tropical medicine—spent nearly two decades at the Oxford University Clinical Research Unit in Vietnam, where he served as director. In addition to more commonplace disease outbreaks, his years in Vietnam encompassed two of the most concerning outbreaks of the early twenty-first century: avian influenza and severe acute respiratory syndrome (SARS). Farrar's experiences during that period convinced him of the importance of swift, well-funded, internationally consistent responses to disease outbreaks and fueled his efforts to prepare the global medical community for future crises. "There is now a window of opportunity to build global scientific capacity before another crisis—such as a new pandemic—hits," he wrote in a 2012 article for *Nature*. "This means collaborating with the people who share a vested interest in using the money efficiently and effectively to prevent outbreaks and address daily public-health and clinical issues in their own countries." As director of the Wellcome Trust, Farrar has worked to achieve that goal—a mission that proved more vital after COVID-19 reached pandemic proportions in early 2020.

EARLY LIFE AND EDUCATION

Jeremy James Farrar was born in Singapore on September 1, 1961. He was the youngest of six children. His father was an English teacher and an artist and writer. The Farrar family lived in a variety of countries both prior to and following Farrar's birth because of his father's teaching

job. In addition to Singapore, Farrar spent his childhood living in New Zealand, Cyprus, and Libya. "Inevitably it has a big influence, I think, on the way you see things and your approach to the world," he told Branswell about his childhood experiences. "It has some downsides. You don't have a very strong sense of belonging somewhere." After leaving Libya, Farrar moved to the United Kingdom to attend university. He initially planned to study humanities subjects such as language, history, philosophy, politics, and economics, but finding languages too difficult for him, he soon switched his focus to medicine. "It is amazing how these things change," he told James Ashton for the *Independent* (18 Jan. 2015) about that revelation. "You think you plan your life and career but in reality you don't."

While a medical student at University College London in the early 1980s, Farrar developed a love of research that would shape the trajectory of his career. Then planning to work in neurology, he pursued a residency in that discipline at the University of Edinburgh and went on to complete doctoral studies in neuroimmunology at the University of Oxford. Farrar earned his PhD with the dissertation "Analysis of Combinatorial Immunoglobulin Libraries from a Myasthenia Gravis Patient" in 1997.

Despite his initial plans, Farrar determined during that period that he was not interested in pursuing a career in neurology and was far more interested in infectious diseases. Nevertheless, Farrar later found that his background in neurology was highly relevant to his work in infectious diseases, as many cause neurological symptoms in affected individuals.

CLINICAL RESEARCH UNIT

While at Oxford, Farrar learned that the university's disease research unit located in Vietnam was hiring and applied. He was ultimately selected to head the group, which then had fewer than a dozen members but would encompass five hundred by the end of Farrar's tenure. He officially took the position of director of the Oxford University Clinical Research Unit in Vietnam in 1995 and continued to fill that role until 2013, when he was succeeded by researcher Guy Thwaites.

Over nearly two decades at the research unit in Vietnam, Farrar gained expertise in numerous infectious diseases through hands-on experience. He worked to prevent devastating outbreaks and combat phenomena such as drug resistance, which causes traditional means of combatting a virus or bacteria to become less effective. "I was terrified," he recalled to Ashton. "I did two ward rounds a day for 18 years and those patients had horrible, multi-drug resistance to TB [tuberculosis], bird flu, SARS." Farrar was active in the response to the SARS outbreak that began in 2002 as well as the 2003 outbreak of H5N1, the virus commonly known as "avian influenza" or "bird flu." For his contributions to the study of infectious disease, he received substantial recognition from the Vietnamese government, including the Ho Chi Minh City Medal.

In 2011, while still in Vietnam, Farrar also established the UK–registered Farrar Foundation, a family charity that offers grants to organizations conducting educational, medical, or other beneficial programs in Southeast Asia.

COMBATTING INFECTIOUS DISEASE

Farrar, a widely acknowledged expert in tropical medicine and emerging infectious diseases, has published his work extensively in scientific journals, contributing to some six hundred papers. He has also served as an adviser for the World Health Organization (WHO) and co-chair of the World Economic Forum.

As a highly qualified commentator on policies and procedures for identifying, limiting the spread of, and treating infectious diseases, he has often urged medical policymakers to consider the full context of an affected region or culture when addressing a disease outbreak, noting that policymakers at times institute methods of containing or treating an outbreak that are inappropriate for a given area or cause additional harm to a region's residents. "We risk making interventions in one sphere without considering the consequences for the other sphere," he told Branswell. "And as a result, you'll get it wrong." In interviews, he has cited as an example the response to avian influenza, during which infected chickens were set to be killed but the owners of the birds were insufficiently compensated for the loss, which thus caused financial hardship and created an incentive to move or hide the infected birds.

Having worked in Asia during serious avian flu and SARS outbreaks, Farrar also often cites the importance of strong communication and long-term partnerships between international medical organizations and the medical workers and researchers on the ground in the affected areas. "Too often, [infectious disease] surveillance is crisis-driven, ad hoc and reactive; it is incorporated into overextended and under-resourced systems. It frequently relies on outside experts, who arrive with little understanding or appreciation of the country, local infrastructure or culture," he wrote in *Nature*. "Inevitably, a lot of time and resources get wasted."

Farrar continued to speak out about the need for effective outbreak responses during and after an outbreak of Ebola in West Africa that began in December 2013 and remained a cause of concern within the medical community for several years. Among other objections to the international Ebola response, he decried vaccine studies not having begun until seven months after the outbreak was first detected and was incredulous over the slow progress in making experimental drugs and vaccines available for testing. "It's ridiculous that we haven't got these (experimental) products out of labs and animal trials and into human testing, and at least offered to people," he opined, as quoted by Kate Kelland for *Reuters* (2 July 2014). He added, "This is not the first time this has happened, and it will happen again—we know that." Farrar argued that the failures in the international approach to addressing the Ebola outbreak demonstrated the weaknesses in existing methods of handling disease outbreaks in general and further called attention to the dangers of drug-resistant bacteria and viruses, against which vaccines could be the greatest protection.

WELLCOME TRUST

On April 24, 2013, the charitable organization the Wellcome Trust announced that Farrar would be joining the trust as its next director, succeeding Sir Mark Walport. The Wellcome Trust was established in 1936 in accordance with the will of Sir Henry Wellcome, a deceased businessman whose pharmaceutical company eventually became part of the pharmaceutical firm GlaxoSmithKline. The trust is dedicated to funding medical research, including work conducted at Oxford's Clinical Research Unit in Vietnam.

Officially joining the Wellcome Trust as director in October 2013, Farrar set out to continue the organization's mission of funding research in key areas of health and ensuring that the medical community would be poised to address the health concerns of the future. "I have inherited the strategic plan, which takes [the Wellcome Trust] from 2010 to 2020," he told Daniel Cressey for *Nature Medicine* (6 Feb. 2014). "Within that, there are five high-level areas [genetics and genomics; understanding the brain; infectious diseases; aging and chronic disease; and environment, nutrition and health]. But I've always said that the most important emerging infection of the twenty-first century is going to be drug resistance. I think it's going to be one of many areas that I focus on."

With an endowment of £26.76 billion (nearly $33 billion) in fiscal year 2019, the Wellcome Trust is well equipped to fund research in those areas, including research in countries such as India that Farrar identified as underfunded. He has likewise called attention to the importance of funding not only veteran researchers but also those still early in their careers, telling Ashton, "The really bright ideas don't come from people my age, they come from people in their twenties."

The board of directors, pleased with his leadership, renewed Farrar's term as director for another five years in March 2018.

CORONAVIRUS 2019 (COVID-19)

A novel coronavirus began causing a serious respiratory illness, later termed COVID-19, in China in late 2019. After COVID-19 became a worldwide pandemic in early 2020, Farrar and his colleagues at the Wellcome Trust joined the international response to the pandemic and called for further research and cooperation on the global level. The organization dedicated billions to financing diagnostic testing, antiviral drug and vaccine development, and production, as well as aiding low-income countries in stockpiling needed supplies, such as masks and medications, in preparation for future outbreaks.

"Support from enlightened Governments, with commitment to the global research effort is vital if we are to end this pandemic and prevent future tragedies. The pace and impact of the spread of this virus is unprecedented, our global response must be too," Farrar said in a Wellcome Trust press release (26 Mar. 2020). He continued, "Science is the only exit strategy from this pandemic—it needs greater financial support with all advances available to those that need them, regardless of where they live." Farrar further urged financial bodies such as the International Monetary Fund (IMF) to intervene and for world leaders to coordinate their efforts to end the pandemic.

In addition to issuing guidance and funding research, the Wellcome Trust sought to provide tangible support for frontline workers. On April 6, 2020, it announced that the trust's headquarters in London would be transformed into a space for National Health Service (NHS) workers to sleep, eat, or access mental-health support during the COVID-19 crisis.

PERSONAL LIFE

Farrar and Christiane Dolecek, a medical researcher specializing in typhoid fever, wed in June 1998. They have three children and live in North Oxford, England. In his leisure time, Farrar enjoys cricket, poetry, tennis, and skiing.

Farrar has received numerous scientific and civic honors for his efforts. A commander of the Order of the British Empire since 2005, Farrar was later named a knight bachelor by Queen Elizabeth II in 2019. He was also elected a fellow of the Royal Society in 2015.

SUGGESTED READING

Ashton, James. "Jeremy Farrar Interview: Wellcome Trust Director Says 'I'm Not a Great Believer in the Power of Prayer.'" *The Independent*, 18 Jan. 2015, www.independent.co.uk/news/science/jeremy-farrar-interview-wellcome-trust-director-says-im-not-a-great-believer-in-the-power-of-prayer-9986626.html. Accessed 12 Apr. 2020.

Branswell, Helen. "With Billions in the Bank, a 'Visionary' Doctor Tries to Change the World." *STAT*, 6 May 2016, www.statnews.com/2016/05/06/jeremy-farrar-wellcome-trust. Accessed 12 Apr. 2020.

Farrar, Jeremy. "'The Most Dangerous Emerging Disease Is Drug Resistance.'" Interview by Katrin Elger and Veronika Hackenbroch. *Der Spiegel International*, 8 Dec. 2014, www.spiegel.de/international/world/infectious-disease-expert-jeremy-farrar-on-ebola-epidemic-a-1006019.html. Accessed 12 Apr. 2020.

———. "Shift Expertise to Where It Matters." *Nature*, vol. 483, 28 Mar. 2012, pp. 534–35, doi: 10.1038/483534a. Accessed 12 Apr. 2020.

———. "Straight Talk with . . . Jeremy Farrar." Interview by Daniel Cressey. *Nature Medicine*, vol. 20, no. 112, 6 Feb. 2014, doi:10.1038/nm0214-112. Accessed 12 Apr. 2020.

Kelland, Kate. "Experimental Ebola Drugs Should Be Tried in Africa, Disease Expert Says." *Reuters*, 2 July 2014, www.reuters.com/article/us-health-ebola-medicines/experimental-ebola-drugs-should-be-tried-in-africa-disease-expert-says-idUSKBN-0F714C20140702. Accessed 14 Apr. 2020.

"Wellcome Statements on Novel Coronavirus (COVID-19)." *Wellcome*, 26 Mar. 2020, wellcome.ac.uk/press-release/wellcome-statements-novel-coronavirus-covid-19. Accessed 12 Apr. 2020.

—*Joy Crelin*

Allyson Felix

Born: November 18, 1985
Occupation: Track-and-field sprinter

American runner Allyson Felix is widely regarded as one of the greatest sprinters of all time. She first competed in the Olympic Games in 2004 at the age of eighteen, earning a silver medal. Across the 2008, 2012, and 2016 Games, running both individual and relay events, she would win two more silver medals and six gold. The haul made her the most decorated female track-and-field star in Olympic history, tying the record with nine total medals and setting the record for gold. Felix also achieved record-setting success beyond the Olympics, and in 2018 was ranked sixteenth on ESPN's list of the twenty most dominant athletes of the past two decades. In 2019 she became the most decorated athlete

Photo by Fernando Frazão / Agência Brasil

of all time in World Championships in Athletics competition (overseen by World Athletics, formerly the International Association of Athletics Federations, or IAAF). That year she surpassed legendary sprinter Usain Bolt's record with her twelfth and thirteenth World Championships titles, bringing her to eighteen championship medals overall.

However, it was not only on the track that Felix proved an influential figure. After she gave birth to her daughter in late 2018, she made headlines for a dispute with her sportswear sponsor, Nike, over maternity support. She subsequently became a dedicated activist and champion of women's rights and maternal health. "We are talking about the next generation," she told Tom Reynolds for *BBC Sport* (7 Oct. 2019). "When I think about the word legacy those are the things I want to change and those are the things I want to be remembered for."

EARLY LIFE AND EDUCATION

Allyson Felix was born on November 18, 1985, in Los Angeles, California. Her father, Paul, was an ordained minister who at various times taught at several different institutions. Her mother, Marlean, was an elementary school teacher who was also very active in their church. Felix grew up with one brother, Wes, who would also become an accomplished runner and eventually work as her manager.

Felix's favorite sport as a child was basketball, but as a freshman at Los Angeles Baptist High School she discovered she had a notable talent for running. Just weeks after joining the private school's track team she finished seventh in the 200-meter race at a statewide meet, and

over the course of her high school career she would record five first-place finishes at the state meet. She quickly earned the nickname "Chicken Legs" among her teammates for her disproportionately spindly limbs, but was also well known for her physical strength. Felix was only fifteen years old when she won her first international title, taking gold in the 100-meters at the 2001 World Youth Championships in Hungary. Under the tutelage of sprint coach Jonathan Patton, in 2003 Felix was named female high school athlete of the year by *Track and Field News*. That year she completed a 200-meter race in 22.11 seconds, the fastest ever recorded for a high school girl to that date.

Upon graduating from high school in 2003 Felix entered the University of Southern California (USC). Although she had been offered an athletic scholarship and a spot on the school's track team (the Trojans), she decided to forgo college eligibility by signing a professional contract with apparel company Adidas, which paid her tuition plus a salary. "It was kind of crazy going to school and doing track at the same time," Felix recalled to David Leon Moore for *USA Today* (30 July 2012). "With all the traveling and not being a student in an athletic program and not having tutors or extra help that the student-athletes get, it was hard. . . . Somehow, I made it work." Felix eventually graduated from USC in 2008 with a bachelor's degree in elementary education. Meanwhile, she began racking up record-breaking performances on the world stage while still a student.

OLYMPIC DEBUT AND WORLD CHAMPIONSHIPS SUCCESS

Touted as an up-and-coming track star, Felix made her first Olympic appearance during the 2004 Games in Athens, Greece. She garnered a silver medal in the 200-meters, her signature event, finishing just behind Veronica Campbell-Brown of Jamaica. The following year, at the 2005 World Championships in Helsinki, Finland, the nineteen-year-old Felix became the youngest ever sprinter to win gold in that competition's 200-meters. She successfully defended the title in 2007 in Osaka, Japan, finishing the race in 21.81 seconds. That year she also helped her team to victory in the 4×100-meter and 4×400-meter relays, thus becoming only the second woman ever to earn three golds at a World Championships.

While Felix was thrilled to have broken the 22-second mark for the individual 200-meters, she told interviewers that she had no intention of resting on her laurels and was keeping the 2008 Olympics foremost in mind. At the 2008 Games in Beijing, China, however, she was once again narrowly bested by Campbell-Brown in the 200-meters and finished with her second

Olympic silver. Felix did end up taking home her first Olympic gold medal as a member of the US women's 4×400-meter relay team.

In 2009 Felix once again successfully defended the World Championships title, claiming her third 200-meters gold medal by clocking 22.02 seconds. However, she continued to note to the press that her goal was to win Olympic gold in an individual event. "I hate to lose," she told Moore of her unwillingness to settle for silver. "For me, it's about winning." She characterized this mindset not as resentment, but as a motivational strategy to help her do her best.

In 2010 Felix became the first person ever to win two IAAF Diamond League trophies in the same year, acing both the 200-meters and 400-meters. In contrast, the 2011 World Championships were disappointing by her standards, as her streak of titles in the 200-meters ended with a third-place finish and she earned silver in the 400-meters. However, she did claim two more gold championship medals as part of Team USA's efforts in the 4×100-meter and 4×400-meter relays.

2012 AND 2016 OLYMPICS

Though she had already proven herself one of the best sprinters in the world, Felix elevated her profile considerably with her performance at the 2012 Olympic Games in London, England. There, her quest for an individual Olympic gold finally came to fruition when she completed the 200-meters in 21.88 seconds. Two days later she won a second gold, this time helping the US women's relay team set a new world record of 40.82 seconds in the 4×100-meters. The team also took the gold in the 4×400-meters, with Felix running the second leg. Her three gold medals made her the winningest female athlete at the London Games, and she also finished fourth in the 100-meters.

A hamstring injury waylaid Felix at the 2013 World Championships, but she returned in 2015 to earn gold in the 400-meters and silver in both the 4×100-meters and 4×400-meters. This made her the first female runner to win titles in both the 200-meter and 400-meter individual events, as well as the most decorated US athlete in World Championships history. Felix then focused on qualifying for the 2016 Olympics in Rio de Janeiro, Brazil. Battling another injury, she qualified for the 400-meters but then narrowly missed the cut to compete for the 200-meters as well.

Despite not competing in her trademark event, Felix still managed to make history at the 2016 Games. She lost the 400-meters by a heartbreaking seven-hundredths of a second to Bahamian sprinter Shaunae Miller, who used the controversial tactic of diving across the finish line. Yet Felix won two more gold medals in the relay events, bringing her career Olympic total to nine medals. This tied her with Jamaican sprinter Merlene Ottey for the most all-time among female track-and-field athletes, and her six golds placed her alone at the top. In addition, only three male runners—Paavo Nurmi, Carl Lewis, and Usain Bolt—could boast more Olympic medals.

Once again Felix was not content to rest on her past achievements. In the 2017 World Championships she continued to prove her dominance, taking gold medals in both the 4×100-meter and 4×400-meter relays as well as bronze in the 400-meters. However, she did begin to reflect on her success and formulate new goals. "It's really about the journey," she told Meghan Roos for *Women's Running* (24 July 2018). "Throughout my various experiences, I've learned that it's not so much about one specific destination or goal but the process and the journey to get there. That's where I feel like character and integrity are built and tested."

DISPUTE WITH NIKE AND ACTIVISM

Some observers were surprised to see Felix appear to slow down in 2018, reducing her schedule and posting slower than normal times at races. "People started to wonder why," she told Ramona Shelburne for *ESPN* (13 Dec. 2018). "It was time to tell them what was really going on. I was pregnant."

In interviews Felix often openly and proudly discussed her pregnancy experience, including overcoming life-threatening pre-eclampsia. However, it also earned considerable media attention for another reason. Felix's contract with Nike—a hugely influential sponsor in the sports world—had run out in late 2017, and renewal negotiations proved tense. In an op-ed for the *New York Times* (22 May 2019), Felix noted that she had originally signed with Nike in part because of its ostensible commitment to empowering women and girls, but was disappointed by the company's treatment of her and other female athletes in maternity. "Despite all my victories, Nike wanted to pay me 70 percent less than before," she wrote in the op-ed. "If that's what they think I'm worth now, I accept that. What I'm not willing to accept is the enduring status quo around maternity. I asked Nike to contractually guarantee that I wouldn't be punished if I didn't perform at my best in the months surrounding childbirth. I wanted to set a new standard. If I, one of Nike's most widely marketed athletes, couldn't secure these protections, who could?"

Felix's op-ed helped bring public and political attention to the challenges facing sponsored female athletes. In response, several sports apparel companies—eventually including Nike—agreed to adopt maternity protections. For Felix (who ultimately left Nike to sign on as the face of the Gap's new sportswear brand Athleta), the episode marked her entry into social activism. In May 2019 she testified before a US House of Representatives committee on the issue of maternal mortality, particularly among black women. "To me it is so much bigger than track and field," she told Reynolds. "I love the sport but I love that it has given me a platform to talk about issues that change lives. That is where I find the most meaning."

RETURN TO RUNNING

Felix returned to athletic competition in 2019. That July she ran in the USA Track and Field (USATF) Outdoor Championships, qualifying for the 4×400-meter relay pool for the 2019 World Championships in Doha, Qatar. In Doha in early autumn she secured two gold medals, in the mixed relay and women's relay, the twelfth and thirteenth of her career. This gave her the most golds in World Championships history, surpassing Bolt's eleven.

PERSONAL LIFE

Felix married fellow sprinter Kenneth Ferguson. Their daughter Camryn was born in November 2018. In addition to her athletic career, Felix actively supported various causes, including the children's advocacy group Right to Play and the voluntary athlete drug-testing program Project Believe. She also served on the Council for Fitness, Sports and Nutrition under US President Barack Obama and as a US State Department sports diplomacy ambassador.

SUGGESTED READING

"Allyson Felix." *Team USA*, 2020, www.teamusa. org/usa-track-and-field/athletes/Allyson-Felix. Accessed 2 Apr. 2020.

Felix, Allyson. "Allyson Felix: My Own Nike Pregnancy Story." *The New York Times*, 22 May 2019, www.nytimes.com/2019/05/22/opinion/allyson-felix-pregnancy-nike.html. Accessed 2 Apr. 2020.

———. "Allyson Felix on Pregnancy and Motherhood: 'Only So Much of This You Can Predict, Much Less Control.'" As told to Ramona Shelburne, *ESPN*, 13 Dec. 2018, www.espn. com/espnw/voices/story/_/id/25526785/allyson-felix-pregnancy-motherhood-only-much-can-predict-much-less-control? Accessed 2 Apr. 2020.

———. "Meet the Elite: Our Q&A with Allyson Felix." Interview by Meghan Roos. *Women's Running*, 24 July 2018, www.womensrunning.com/culture/meet-the-elite-allyson-felix/. Accessed 2 Apr. 2020.

Moore, David Leon. "Allyson Felix Determined to Get 200 Olympic Gold." *USA Today*, 30 July 2012, usatoday30.usatoday.com/sports/olympics/london/track/story/2012-07-19/Allyson-Felix-200-meters-London-Olympics-gold/56418576/1. Accessed 2 Apr. 2020.

Reynolds, Tom. "Allyson Felix: World Athletics Championships Record-Breaker on Life-Changing Year." *BBC Sport*, 7 Oct. 2019, www.bbc.com/sport/athletics/49952710. Accessed 2 Apr. 2020.

Zaccardi, Nick. "Allyson Felix: Everything Is on the Table in 2020." *NBC Sports*, 7 Jan. 2020, olympics.nbcsports.com/2020/01/07/allyson-felix-track-and-field-400-200/. Accessed 28 Feb. 2020.

—*Mari Rich*

Teresita Fernández

Date of birth: May 12, 1968
Occupation: Visual artist

"The first thing I do when I start a new work is ask the very simple question, 'Where am I?'" visual artist Teresita Fernández explained to Nick Ducassi for *FIU Magazine* (19 Jan. 2016). She added, "I start excavating and researching where I am historically, economically, socially, geographically, visually, emotionally, physically—where exactly is this site located? Not just physically, but in people's imaginations and in history and in the entire context of place." As Fernández's extensive body of work demonstrates, place and landscape can inform not only the shape or visual characteristics of a piece but also its placement within an indoor or outdoor exhibition space, its function, and its relationship with the people viewing it.

Primarily a sculptor who works with materials such as metal, graphite, ceramics, and polycarbonate tubing, Fernández has received extensive recognition for works such as *Fata Morgana*, an eye-catching reflective canopy of sorts that spanned a walking path in New York's Madison Square Park from June 2015 into January 2016. Fernández, a 2005 MacArthur Fellow and a former member of the US Commission of Fine Arts, has participated in scores of group exhibitions for over more than thirty years and exhibited dozens of solo shows across the United States, Western Europe, and Japan. The first retrospective of her work, titled *Elemental*, debuted at the Pérez Art Museum Miami in 2019, calling further attention to the beauty and depth of the sculptor's art.

Despite the widespread recognition Fernández has received, she remains deeply aware that the questions fueling her art require ongoing investigation. "I cull from a lot of established ideas of landscape, but I'm also questioning them and trying to provide a very different series of lenses

Photo by KRG Img via Wikimedia Commons

to amplify what the word 'landscape' means," she told Lindsey Davis for *Art21 Magazine* (21 Sept. 2016).

EARLY LIFE AND EDUCATION

Fernández was born in Miami on May 12, 1968 to Cuban immigrants who had fled the communist revolution as teenagers. Her father worked in a yacht factory and later in life opened his own business in the same industry. Many of the women in Fernández's family worked in the clothing industry, and the young Fernández and her three siblings at times amused themselves by creating their own arts-and-crafts projects out of fabric scraps left over from their relatives' work. Fernández also enjoyed drawing and was an avid reader, thanks in part to the encouragement of her parents, who ensured that their home was filled with books. "They would always tell us the only thing they can never take away from you is your education," she explained to Carol Kino for *WSJ Magazine* (31 Mar. 2015) about her childhood. "And you were taught to carry yourself with dignity."

After graduating from Southwest Miami High School, Fernández enrolled in the arts program at Florida International University (FIU). Although she did not initially plan to focus on sculpture, she took her first sculpting course as a sophomore and was immediately drawn both to the artform and to metal as a medium. Because of the architectural nature of some of her work, Fernández has often been asked whether she studied architecture in college, but she has made it clear in interviews that she did not. "I was very much a sculptor, a conceptual artist,

whose practice was rooted in sculpture. But I always said that my connection to architecture had to do with human scale," she explained to Helen Stoilas for the *Art Newspaper* (4 Dec. 2019). "It had to do with that immersive component, of you as a viewer being immersed in a spatial context and negotiating that." After completing a Bachelor of Fine Arts degree at FIU in 1990, Fernández went on to earn a Master of Fine Arts degree at Virginia Commonwealth University in 1992.

EARLY CAREER

After completing graduate school, Fernández returned to Miami but soon set off to various locations throughout the United States and the world in search of work opportunities, residencies and fellowships, and artistic inspiration. "I was traveling a lot, living out of a suitcase for five years," she recalled to Sara Roffino for *Brooklyn Rail* (July–Aug. 2014). Although deeply influenced by all her experiences abroad, Fernández identified her time in Japan in 1997 for the ARCUS Project as a particular inspiration that greatly shaped her understanding of place and color, among other elements of her work. That year she moved to New York to complete a residency with the Marie Walsh Sharpe Foundation and began to establish a home for herself in that city, which would remain her home base for more than two decades. A couple years later, in 1999, she spent time in Rome as a fellow at the American Academy. Fernández later completed arts residencies in Philadelphia in 2005, Singapore in 2010, Bali in 2011, and Rome in 2018.

Fernández had numerous opportunities to display her sculptural work over the first years of her career, contributing both large installations and smaller works to a variety of exhibitions and venues. She contributed an installation to the Museum of Contemporary Art in North Miami in 1996 and in 1998 installed the work *Borrowed Landscape*, inspired greatly by her travels in Japan and by European formal gardens, at the San Antonio venue Artpace. Another early work was *Waterfall* (2000), a large aluminum-and-plastic installation that evokes the titular natural feature, displayed at the New Mexico art museum SITE Santa Fe.

For the strength of her work and her contributions to her chosen artform, Fernández began to receive significant recognition through awards such as a 1999 Louis Comfort Tiffany Biennial Artist Award and prestigious opportunities such as a 2003 Guggenheim Fellowship. A milestone in her career came in 2005, when Fernández was selected as one of the twenty-five members of that year's class of MacArthur Fellows. Granted by the John D. and Catherine T. MacArthur Foundation, the MacArthur Fellowship—sometimes referred to as the "genius grant"—awards a five-year stipend to talented individuals who show exceptional promise in their respective fields.

A SENSE OF LANDSCAPE

As an artist, Fernández has been particularly intrigued by the idea of landscapes and worked to communicate senses of place and landscape through many of her pieces. At times, that focus on place and landscape extends to her use of materials; for example, one of her many installations to feature chunks of graphite, *Drawn Waters (Borrowdale)* (2009), is named in part after a valley in England where a large deposit of graphite was discovered during the late sixteenth century. Fernández also often incorporates materials such as glass, ceramic, and polycarbonate tubing in her work and is known for her work with metals, such as aluminum, gold, and brass. Conscious of the places from which such materials originated, she uses that knowledge to add depth to her work. The raw material "becomes simultaneously the landscape it came from . . . but also the secondary image that's created, which may be entirely different and unrelated," she explained to Davis. "So I'm playing with this notion that we're always in many places at once and that each place that we think of is really a sort of layering, a stacking, of many places, whether they're physical, or imagined, or remembered."

Fernández's devotion to landscape likewise extends to the shape and format of the works she creates, many of which are site-specific installations designed to conform to the needs of an indoor or outdoor location or are otherwise immersive pieces that require specific positioning. The positioning of works was particularly important in the 2014 solo exhibition *As Above So Below*, for example, in which the sculpture *Black Sun* was suspended overhead while works such as *Lunar (Theatre)* and *Nocturnal (30 Days)* were placed next to each other to call attention to the moon's natural cycles. Other artistic efforts, such as the mosaic-like ceramic installations of the Viñales series, directly reflect the idea of landscape, having been inspired by the landscapes Fernández encountered in the Viñales valley and cave system during her first visit to Cuba in 2015.

In much of Fernández's early works, she eschewed issues of identity or origin in favor of exploring such universal themes as gaze and the creation of place. Her works have become increasingly political, however, addressing such issues as migration, colonial history, and climate disruption.

PUBLIC RECOGNITION

Fernández, having established herself as a major contributor to the artistic community of the United States, was appointed to the US Commission of Fine Arts by President Barack Obama in 2011. She remained in that advisory role into 2014.

Fernández gained further public recognition in 2015, when her sculpture *Fata Morgana* was installed in New York City's Madison Square Park. Consisting of metal pillars holding up panels of polished metal twelve feet above a path through the park, the work reflects both tens of thousands of people who walk underneath each day as well as light and glimpses of the surrounding landscape. "Regardless of whether they [those walking the path] were choosing to or not, they became projected onto the piece and they also became projected onto a shared space with other commuters and passersby," Fernández explained to Davis. Unlike many of Fernández's previous works, *Fata Morgana* was located not in a gallery or institution but in a public space where anyone could view and participate, which she noted to Davis created a "democratizing effect."

Dedicated to promoting the work of visual artists of Latin American descent, Fernández organized the US Latinx Arts Futures Symposium, held in September 2016 with the backing of the Ford Foundation and Andy Warhol Foundation for the Visual Arts. The event focused on inclusivity within the artistic community. She was named a National Academician by the National Academy of Design in 2017.

In October 2019, the Pérez Art Museum Miami launched a retrospective of Fernández's work to date. Although Fernández had not lived there for decades, she was pleased that the retrospective, titled *Elemental*, would be held in the city of her birth. "It's really important that my first mid-career retrospective is in my hometown because so much of my work is about place and about unravelling one's relationship to place," she explained to Stoilas. "So it was loaded in lots of ways, personally as well, to be able to contextualise it within that framework." After closing in Miami in February 2020, *Elemental* moved to Arizona's Phoenix Art Museum in March of that year.

PERSONAL LIFE

Fernández lives and works in Brooklyn, New York. After moving to New York, she met and married Tom Downs, a video artist, with whom she had two children, Caspian (b. 2001) and Cypress (b. 2004). The couple eventually divorced.

SUGGESTED READING

Ducassi, Nick. "On the Cusp of Greatness: Alumna Teresita Fernandez Takes New York City Art World by Storm." *FIU Magazine*, 19 Jan. 2016, news.fiu.edu/2016/on-the-cusp-of-greatness-alumna-teresita-fernandez. Accessed 9 Feb. 2020.

Fernández, Teresita. "Finding Yourself in the Landscape: Teresita Fernández in Conversation." Interview by Monica Uszerowicz. *Cultured*, 15 Oct. 2019, www.culturedmag.com/teresita-fernandez-in-conversation. Accessed 9 Feb. 2020.

——. "Teresita Fernández, an Artist of Place, Brings Her Art Home to Miami." Interview by Helen Stoilas. *The Art Newspaper*, 4 Dec. 2019, www.theartnewspaper.com/interview/teresita-fernandez-the-world-was-always-burning. Accessed 9 Feb. 2020.

——. "Teresita Fernández with Sara Roffino." Interview by Sara Roffino. *Brooklyn Rail*, July–Aug. 2014, brooklynrail.org/2014/07/art/teresita-fernndez-with-sara-roffino. Accessed 9 Feb. 2020.

——. "Unearthing Place: An Interview with Teresita Fernández." Interview by Lindsey Davis. *Art21*, 21 Sept. 2016, magazine.art21.org/2016/09/21/unearthing-place-an-interview-with-teresita-fernandez/#.Xjx9hndFxPY. Accessed 9 Feb. 2020.

Kino, Carol. "Artist Teresita Fernández Transforms New York's Madison Square Park." *WSJ Magazine*, 31 Mar. 2015, www.wsj.com/articles/artist-teresita-fernandez-transforms-new-yorks-madison-square-park-1427814775. Accessed 9 Feb. 2020.

Sheets, Hilarie M. "For Teresita Fernández, Personal Is Political." *The New York Times*, 24 Oct. 2019, www.nytimes.com/2019/10/23/arts/design/teresita-fernandez-latinx-artists.html. Accessed 9 Feb. 2020.

SELECTED WORKS

Borrowed Landscape, 1998; *Waterfall*, 2000; *Drawn Waters (Borrowdale)*, 2009; *Fata Morgana*, 2015; Viñales series, 2015–19

—Joy Crelin

Sutton Foster

Born: March 18, 1975
Occupation: Actor and performer

Although actor and performer Sutton Foster had begun to build a successful career for herself by the year 2000, appearing in touring productions of the musicals *Grease* and *Les Misérables* as well as on Broadway, perhaps the most significant development of her career came in the form of unexpected news. She had been hired to serve as an understudy for the new musical *Thoroughly Modern Millie* during its 2000 run at California's La Jolla Playhouse, and prior to the production's premiere, the lead actor left the production and she was asked to take over the title role of Millie.

"My career changed in one phone call," she recalled to Debra Birnbaum for *Variety* (13 Feb. 2015). "It was like a dream." Foster remained with the production following its move to Broadway in 2002, ultimately winning the Tony Award for Best Actress in a Musical in recognition of her work.

In addition to her later roles in musicals such as *The Drowsy Chaperone* (2006–07), *Shrek the Musical* (2008–10), and *Anything Goes* (2011–12), Foster gained attention for her work on television, including in the short-lived ABC Family series *Bunheads* (2012–13) and the popular TV Land original series *Younger*, which aired its sixth season in 2019, and she has attributed much of her success to her willingness to take chances. "I've had some amazing breaks, but then you have to be ready to seize the moment when the timing and the luck line up," she told the television writer Amy Sherman-Palladino in an interview for *Interview* magazine (23 Aug. 2017). "You can't be afraid. You have to be open. I feel like I've always been a leaper, and I've always leapt into things without thinking."

EARLY LIFE

Sutton Lenore Foster was born on March 18, 1975, in Statesboro, Georgia. The second of two children born to Robert and Helen Foster, she spent her early years in Georgia, where she grew up alongside older brother Hunter, who would also go on to become a Tony Award–nominated actor. Foster was interested in the performing arts from a young age, and her parents encouraged her in her pursuits, signing her up for dance lessons by the time she was four years old. Also

Photo by The Huntington Theatre Company via Flickr

drawn to singing, Foster particularly enjoyed experimenting with operatic vocal styles during her early years, despite her lack of formal training. "I think it was the style of singing—I wanted a grand, really loud sound," she told Anthony Tommasini for the *New York Times* (11 May 2011). She began her career in musical theater at the age of ten, when she starred in a local production of *Annie*. Foster would go on to appear in a number of other local productions as a child and continued to do so following her family's move to the Detroit suburb of Troy, Michigan, in the late 1980s.

EARLY CAREER AND EDUCATION

Foster began to pursue performing opportunities more seriously as a teenager, and in 1990 she appeared on the televised talent show *Star Search*. "I lost to this guy named Richard Blake who's actually now a Broadway performer," she recalled in an interview with Ophira Eisenberg for the NPR program *Ask Me Another* (9 Sept. 2015). "And so every time I see him, I give him squinty eyes 'cause he beat me by a quarter star." She later left Troy High School to perform in the ensemble for a national tour of the musical *The Will Rogers Follies*; though she did not attend class in person, she was able to take advantage of correspondence courses to finish her credits and graduate. Following her time with that tour, she enrolled at Carnegie Mellon University in the early 1990s but ultimately chose to leave the university after a year and focus instead on pursuing a career in theater.

After leaving Carnegie Mellon, Foster lived with her parents in Tennessee for a brief period and entertained the idea of becoming a teacher before spending time in New York, where she lived with her brother while auditioning for shows. Although she felt somewhat directionless during that period, she hit a turning point in her career after auditioning for and securing a role in the musical *Grease*, which was set to begin a national tour. Having gained experience with the musical over the course of the tour, she would appear in the Broadway production of *Grease* in 1996. Additional roles followed, including parts in the Broadway productions of *Annie* and *The Scarlet Pimpernel* in 1997. After serving as a member of the ensemble and as an understudy for the role of Éponine in the popular musical *Les Misérables* on Broadway in 1998, she returned to the world of touring, joining a touring production of the show as Éponine into 1999.

THOROUGHLY MODERN MILLIE

A key period in Foster's career began around 2000, when she auditioned for the lead role in the new musical *Thoroughly Modern Millie*, a work set to be staged at California's La Jolla Playhouse that year. Although she did not succeed

in winning the title role, she was hired on as an understudy, an actor who would typically appear in the show's ensemble but was prepared to take over the lead role if the regular actor was unavailable. Although Foster had been offered the opportunity to return to the Broadway production of *Les Misérables* to play Éponine full time, she decided to turn down that role in order to pursue her new project. "Everyone thought I was crazy," she told Birnbaum about that decision. "I just really wanted to do something new and move forward. I didn't have ulterior motives."

Foster's "crazy" decision proved to be a fortunate one: prior to the La Jolla premiere of *Thoroughly Modern Millie*, the actor originally cast as Millie left the production, and Foster was suddenly promoted into that role. After proving herself through her work during the musical's California run, she remained with the show upon its move to Broadway in 2002. Set in the 1920s, the show is a romantic comedy about a young woman who moves to New York City to seek out a wealthy husband and becomes embroiled in a human-trafficking conspiracy. Impressing critics and audiences with her performance during her time on stage, Foster won the 2002 Tony Award for Best Actress in a Musical, and the show itself received the Tony Award for Best Musical. Ultimately, she remained with the production until February 2004.

BROADWAY SUCCESS

Having achieved success on Broadway, Foster sought to develop her talents further and began to take lessons with longtime voice teacher Joan Lader. "I had always been a big belter," she told Tommasini. "Joan taught me how to develop my mixed voice. I never knew I had that. It opened up a whole new world. I learned that there was power in subtlety, stillness and tenderness." Her vocal skills and dramatic abilities went on to win her further high-profile parts, including the roles of Jo in *Little Women* in 2005 and Janet Van De Graaff in *The Drowsy Chaperone* between 2006 and 2007, both of which earned her Tony Award nominations. She also costarred in two musicals based on popular films, *Young Frankenstein*, in which she played the role of Inga from late 2007 to mid-2008, and *Shrek the Musical*, for which she earned another Tony nomination for her performance (she stayed with the production from its opening in late 2008 to its closing in early 2010) as Princess Fiona.

In 2011, Foster again returned to Broadway in a revival of the 1930s musical *Anything Goes*, playing the character of Reno Sweeney. She won the Tony Award for Best Actress in a Musical for her work in the production, with which she remained into 2012. Although Foster had received widespread recognition for her work as Reno and similarly loud, energetic characters, she began to seek out other types of roles following her time in *Anything Goes*, hoping to explore a more diverse array of characters. "I realized I couldn't keep going in that same direction because I didn't know where else to go, beyond that," she explained to Adrienne Gaffney for *Vanity Fair* (30 May 2014). "I think if someone [told me to] look at my career as a whole, I think variety, and I think challenging myself as an actor, and even doing the unexpected—is so much more exciting." Over the next several years, she starred in the Broadway debut of the musical *Violet* (2014), for which she turned in a performance that saw her receive her sixth Tony Award nomination, and went on to appear in off-Broadway productions of shows such as *The Wild Party* (2015) and *Sweet Charity* (2016–17). In addition to appearing in cast-recording albums for many of her shows, she also recorded several solo albums, including *Wish* (2009), *An Evening with Sutton Foster* (2011), and *Take Me to the World* (2018).

TELEVISION CAREER

Over the course of her career in theater, Foster had also made intermittent appearances on television, beginning in the first decade of the twenty-first century in episodes of series such as *Flight of the Conchords* (2007) and *Law & Order: Special Victims Unit* (2010). In 2012, she began to turn more of her attention to television as the star in the ABC Family show *Bunheads*, a dramedy focused on the world of ballet. Her character in *Bunheads* was her first starring role, and the show gave her the opportunity to gain a deeper understanding of acting for the screen. "It felt like I had gone to college to learn how to work on camera, because before then I really had very limited camera experience," she told Gaffney. "I primarily had done stage work and I feel so at home on stage and when I first started working on *Bunheads* it felt so foreign." Although *Bunheads* was canceled after a single season, the show gained a cult following among some viewers, particularly fans of showrunner Sherman-Palladino's body of work.

Foster returned to television in 2015 with the starring role in *Younger*, a series based on a 2005 novel by Pamela Redmond Satran and broadcast on the television channel TV Land. The series centers on a woman named Liza—played by Foster—who, facing ageism within the workplace, decides to begin her career in publishing while pretending to be in her mid-twenties when she is really in her early forties. Over the course of its first season and beyond, *Younger* follows Liza as she navigates work, friendships, and romance while working to keep her secret. Proving popular among viewers, *Younger* aired six seasons between 2015 and 2019, offering Foster the opportunity to explore her character at length. "It's been really cool for me to play a character that's evolved," she told Julie Musbach for the website *BroadwayWorld* (26 Aug. 2019). "When you do theatre you tell the same story every night and there is opportunity in that, you can kind of go back, you can develop a character, but this has been wonderful to be able to truly grow with the character." *Younger* was renewed for a seventh season in July 2019.

RETURN TO THE STAGE

Although Foster had appeared in a variety of stage productions during breaks from filming *Younger*, she began working toward a particularly high-profile return to Broadway in 2019, when it was announced that she would star in a revival of the 1957 musical *The Music Man*. She was set to play librarian Marian Paroo opposite screen and stage actor Hugh Jackman, who had been cast as traveling con man Harold Hill. "I'm really excited to come back to Broadway with *The Music Man*," she told Musbach. "I haven't done a big Broadway musical since *Anything Goes*. . . . It's going to be a big show; I'm really looking forward to diving into it."

PERSONAL LIFE

Foster was married to actor Christian Borle from 2006 to 2010. She married screenwriter Ted Griffin in 2014. Their adopted daughter, Emily, was born in 2017. In addition to singing and acting, Foster enjoys crocheting and making art.

SUGGESTED READING

Foster, Sutton. "BWW interview: Checking In with *Younger*, *The Music Man* Star Sutton Foster on National Dog Day!" Interview by Julie Musbach. *BroadwayWorld*, 26 Aug. 2019, www.broadwayworld.com/article/BWW-Interview-Checking-In-with-Younger-the-Music-Man-Star-Sutton-Foster-on-National-Dog-Day-20190826. Accessed 12 Apr. 2020.

———. "Sutton Foster: Really, Anything Goes." Interview by Ophira Eisenberg. *Ask Me Another*, NPR, 9 Sept. 2015, www.npr.org/2015/09/10/438902767/sutton-foster-really-anything-goes. Transcript. Accessed 12 Apr. 2020.

———. "Sutton Foster on Going Without Stage Makeup in *Violet*, the Cancellation of *Bunheads*, and Overly Enthusiastic Fans." Interview by Adrienne Gaffney. *Vanity Fair*, 30 May 2014, www.vanityfair.com/culture/2014/05/sutton-foster-violet-no-makeup. Accessed 12 Apr. 2020.

———. "'Younger' Star Sutton Foster on Her 'Thoroughly' Classic First Big Role." Interview by Debra Birnbaum. *Variety*, 13 Feb. 2015, variety.com/2015/legit/features/younger-star-sutton-foster-on-her-thoroughly-classic-first-big-role-1201432711. Accessed 12 Apr. 2020.

———. "*Younger*'s Sutton Foster Isn't Afraid to Win All the Awards." Interview by Amy Sherman-Palladino. *Interview*, 23 Aug. 2017, www.interviewmagazine.com/culture/youngers-sutton-foster-isnt-afraid-to-win-all-the-awards. Accessed 12 Apr. 2020.

Tommasini, Anthony. "A Big Belter Who Found a True Voice." *The New York Times*, 11 May 2011, www.nytimes.com./2011/05/15/theater/theaterspecial/sutton-foster-stars-in-anything-goes.html. Accessed 12 Apr. 2020.

SELECTED WORKS
Thoroughly Modern Millie, 2000 and 2002–4; *The Drowsy Chaperone*, 2006–07; *Anything Goes*, 2011–12; *Bunheads*, 2012–13; *Younger*, 2015–

—Joy Crelin

Mette Frederiksen

Date of birth: November 19, 1977
Occupation: Politician

Photo by The White House via Wikimedia Commons

Politician Mette Frederiksen was elected prime minister of Denmark in June 2019. At forty-one, she was the youngest person to ever serve the role. Frederiksen has been a familiar figure among the center-left Social Democrats since she was a teenager in the party's youth wing. Early in her career, she gained a reputation for speaking her mind, even when it meant challenging fellow party members on their conservative views. But since Frederiksen became the leader of the Social Democrats in 2015, she has aligned with the right-wing nationalist Danish People's Party (DPP) to push anti-immigration, anti-Muslim policies that have alarmed human rights advocates and the United Nations (UN) refugee agency. Supporters describe her as an idealist-turned-realist; others deride her as a cynic willing to sacrifice long-held leftist beliefs for power. Regardless, her ideological about-face on immigration is stark. As a parliamentarian in 2002, she criticized her party, saying that they had contributed to "the national lie that the number of immigrants was the big problem instead of focusing on integration," as quoted by Nikolaj Rytgaard for the Copenhagen daily, *Berlingske* (10 Oct. 2014). Over a decade later, Frederiksen took the exact opposite view, going as far as to propose quotas on how many "non-Western" immigrants Denmark would accept.

Across Europe, left-wing political parties are moving rightward on immigration, but even in this context, Frederiksen and Denmark's Social Democrats are outliers. "While other social-democratic parties have adopted tougher immigration laws in times of 'crisis' and used anti-immigration and Islamophobic language, no party has so openly ran on a nativist and welfare-chauvinist agenda as the Danish Social Democrats," Cas Mudde, a political scientist at the University of Georgia, told Karina Piser for the *Nation* (7 June 2019).

The party's rhetoric under Frederiksen, while reflective of the larger will of the Danish people, has deeply disturbed some Danes. "When I came to Denmark in the 1990s, it was more welcoming and open. I decided to build my life here, and I gave my children to Denmark, to Danish society, with the expectation that they would be fully accepted," Sabah Qarasnane, a Moroccan Danish community organizer from Copenhagen, told Emma Graham-Harrison for the UK *Guardian* (12 Aug. 2018). "And now it is not clear if that is happening."

UPBRINGING AND EARLY CAREER
Mette Frederiksen was born on November 19, 1977, in Aalborg, a city in the Jutland region of northern Denmark. Her father, Flemming, is a former typographer. Her mother, Anette, a teacher, died of cancer in 2013. Frederiksen is a fourth-generation Social Democrat, and both of her parents engaged in political activism. According to her father, she expressed an interest in politics as a child of six or seven. "I've never doubted that Mette could go all the way, if she wanted," he said later, as quoted by a journalist for *BBC News* (27 June 2019). At twelve, she joined campaigns to protect the rainforest and save whales. She also joined the ANC Youth

League, a part of the South African antiapartheid movement. At fifteen, she joined the youth wing of the Social Democratic Party and became the county chair in North Jutland.

Frederiksen attended the Aalborghus Gymnasium, where she was a student council member. She earned a degree in administration and social science at Aalborg University in 2007 and a master's degree in African Studies from the University of Copenhagen in 2009.

In 2000, Frederiksen served as the youth consultant for the Danish Federation of Trade Unions. The following year she was elected to Denmark's Folketing, or parliament, at twenty-four. She quickly earned a reputation as an idealist and impassioned speaker who occasionally butted heads with party leadership. "In her youth she created edge, or put less popularly, she created division," Noa Redington, an adviser to former prime minister Helle Thorning-Schmidt, told Martin Selsoe Sorensen and Richard Pérez-Peña for the *New York Times* (22 Aug. 2019). Frederiksen had a heated exchange about immigration with Social Democratic interior minister Karen Jespersen during this time. Jespersen had suggested in 2000 that asylum seekers who had committed crimes should be interned on a desert island. Jespersen also supported measures that would effectively separate immigrant families. Frederiksen dismissed these ideas, asserting that preserving families seeking asylum was a matter beyond debate.

Frederiksen was named deputy party leader of the Social Democratic Party in 2005. In 2010, she was criticized for enrolling her young daughter in a private school after having spoken out against parents who eschewed Denmark's public-school system to send their children to private schools. She later said that the experience taught her the importance of tempering her views.

Frederiksen was named minister of employment in 2011 and minister of justice in 2014.

A SHIFT TO THE RIGHT

A brief overview of Denmark's political history over the past two decades puts Frederiksen's political shift and election to the premiership in 2019 into context. In 2002, Anders Fogh Rasmussen's center-right government, spurred by the nationalist DPP, passed a series of laws restricting immigration, mostly aimed at Muslim migrants coming from war-torn Iraq and Afghanistan. At the time, Frederiksen spoke out vehemently against the laws. Politicians like Jespersen, who cowrote a 2005 book in which she compared Islam to Nazism and communism, stoked fears that migrants were inherently dangerous and posed a threat to Danish values.

In 2014 and 2015 global upheaval, including civil war in Syria, contributed to mass migration

on a scale unseen since World War II. Refugees fled their countries of origin by any means available to them, often crossing the Mediterranean Sea in dangerous rubber dinghies. The European Union (EU) was wholly unprepared to receive them. Some countries, like Sweden and Germany, scrambled to absorb and accommodate refugees pushed out of their homes by war and poverty. Other countries moved to block them. Denmark was among the latter.

In 2015, some twenty-one thousand people sought asylum in Denmark. Many Danes feared that the influx would strain the country's robust welfare system. In response, Danish officials introduced a host of policies, large and small, aimed at discouraging refugees from settling in Denmark. The country cut social benefits to refugees by 45 percent—Denmark advertised this and other disincentives in newspapers in Lebanon, a country with a large refugee population—while in 2016 a Danish city council decreed that schools and daycares serve pork once a week because observant Muslims do not eat it. In 2016, the Folketing passed the so-called jewelry law, which empowers authorities to seize refugees' assets exceeding $1,450, exempting wedding rings or similar items of sentimental value.

Helle Thorning-Schmidt, a Social Democrat and Denmark's first female prime minister, was elected in 2011 but lost power amid this ideological shift in 2015. Lars Løkke Rasmussen of Venstre, the liberal party, became prime minister. Thorning-Schmidt resigned as the leader of the Social Democrats, and Frederiksen took her place.

ANTI-IMMIGRANT RHETORIC

By 2015 Frederiksen, like the rest of her party, including Thorning-Schmidt, supported more punitive, discriminatory policies against immigrants and Muslims living in Denmark. Under Frederiksen, Richard Orange for the *Guardian* (10 June 2018) wrote, the Social Democrats adopted "rhetoric on Islam" that "rival[ed] that of the populist right." "They are almost fighting about who has the most extreme ideas," one local Danish politician told Orange. Frederiksen said, as quoted by Orange, that some Muslims "do not respect the Danish judicial system" and called for all Muslim schools in the country to be closed. In June 2018, the left-wing Social Liberals and the Social Democrats, led by Frederiksen, broke ties over their respective immigration proposals. This ended a twenty-five-year electoral partnership.

In the run-up to the election in June 2019, Frederiksen doubled down on her anti-immigration, anti-Muslim rhetoric, setting herself and the Social Democrats apart from Venstre. In a policy proposal called "Realistic and Fair Immigration," published by the journal *International*

Politics and Society (14 May 2019), Frederiksen observed that eight percent of Denmark's population was of "non-Western origin." (In Denmark, the term "non-Western" is widely understood as a euphemism for individuals who are Muslim and/or have dark skin.) She said that while those who had integrated into Danish society by learning the language, working, and sharing so-called Danish values had become Danish, other immigrants "had come to Denmark without becoming part of Denmark." She proposed a cap on how many "non-Western" immigrants would be allowed in Denmark each year. She also proposed abolishing ghettos by ensuring that "no residential areas, schools or educational institutions have more than 30 percent non-Western immigrants and descendants."

More controversially still, Frederiksen campaigned on support for what is known as the 2018 "ghetto package" or "ghetto plan," a series of policies aimed at integrating Denmark's heavily Muslim immigrant population. These policies looked to regulate ghettos—more than twenty-five residential areas defined, among other criteria, as places where more than half of residents are "non-Western." The venom of the word *ghetto*, and its evocation of the Jewish ghettos of the Nazi era, is not lost on Danes who oppose the policies. Ghetto residents are subject to different laws than other Danish citizens, and those laws often carry harsher sentences. Other restrictions impose disturbing levels of social control widely criticized by the international community. For instance, children living in the ghettos must complete twenty-five hours a week of state-sanctioned Danish language and cultural schooling from the age of one; if parents refuse to comply, their families are stripped of social benefits.

PRIME MINISTER OF DENMARK

In the June 2019 election, Frederiksen's Social Democrats won 91 of 179 parliamentary seats. The outcome was touted as a victory for the Left, particularly as the DPP saw its votes cut by more than half. But as Piser wrote, the result "says less about the far right's demise than about its steady creep into the mainstream." The Social Democrats allied with several other left and center-left parties to form a minority government. Frederiksen was formally appointed as prime minister on June 27.

Early in her tenure, in August 2019, Frederiksen made a quip about President Donald Trump's expressed desire to buy Greenland, an autonomous territory, from Denmark. "Thankfully, the time when you buy and sell other countries and populations is over," she said, as quoted by Sorensen and Pérez-Peña. Trump was so displeased with her comments that he

called her "nasty" and canceled a planned visit to Denmark.

Frederiksen had planned to make climate change and childcare political priorities in 2020, but the coronavirus 2019 (COVID-19) pandemic forced her to shift gears politically. On March 12, 2020, Frederiksen appeared on television to announce that she was shutting Denmark down in response to COVID-19. The shutdown included schools, public offices, and restaurants, as well as international borders. Parliament passed an amendment to the nation's Epidemic Act that same day to transfer power from regional epidemic commissions to the federal health ministry and thus centralize Denmark's disease response. Frederiksen and the government's swift response were credited with limiting the impact of the novel coronavirus within Denmark and allowing it to be the first EU nation to reopen its primary schools, in April 2020.

PERSONAL LIFE

Frederiksen married cinematographer Bo Tengberg in July 2020. She was previously married to Erik Harr, with whom she has a daughter, Ida Feline, and a son, Magne. The couple divorced in 2014 after eleven years of marriage.

SUGGESTED READING

"Danish PM Frederiksen Takes Power and Joins Nordic Swing to the Left." *BBC News*, 27 June 2019, www.bbc.com/news/world-europe-48784508. Accessed 8 July 2020.

Frederiksen, Mette. "Realistic and Fair Immigration." *International Politics and Society*, 14 May 2019, www.ips-journal.eu/regions/europe/article/show/realistic-and-fair-immigration-3460/. Accessed 10 July 2020.

Graham-Harrison, Emma. "Stigmatized, Marginalized: Life Inside Denmark's Official Ghettos." *The Guardian*, 12 Aug. 2018, www.theguardian.com/world/2018/aug/12/denmark-official-ghettos-cultural-assimilation-country-once-tolerant. Accessed 11 July 2020.

Orange, Richard. "Denmark Swings Right on Immigration—And Muslims Feel Besieged." *The Guardian*, 10 June 2018, www.theguardian.com/world/2018/jun/10/denmark-swings-right-immigration-muslims-besieged-holbaek. Accessed 10 July 2020.

Piser, Karina. "The European Left's Dangerous Anti-Immigrant Turn." *The Nation*, 7 June 2019, www.thenation.com/article/archive/denmark-social-democrats-welfare-chauvinism/. Accessed 11 July 2020.

Sorensen, Martin Selsoe, and Richard Pérez-Peña. "Denmark's Leader Didn't Want a Fight with Trump. She Got One Anyway." *The New York Times*, 22 Aug. 2019, www.nytimes.com/2019/08/22/world/

europe/-trump-greenland-denmark-mette-frederiksen.html. Accessed 10 July 2020.

—*Molly Hagan*

Limor Fried

Date of birth: ca. 1979
Occupation: Electrical engineer

Limor Fried founded Adafruit Enterprises, a company specializing in do-it-yourself (DIY) electronics, in 2005 while still a student at the Massachusetts Institute of Technology (MIT). The venture quickly proved successful, and she soon became a notable figure in various overlapping areas within the worlds of business and technology. She was even the first female engineer ever to be pictured on the cover of *Wired* magazine, in 2011. "Fried has become a poster child for a number of causes—women in engineering, female entrepreneurship, manufacturing in Manhattan, open-source and hacker culture, the maker movement," Nicola Twilley wrote in a profile for the *New Yorker* (3 Mar. 2016). "But her greater goal is to help the rest of us see electrical engineering the way that she does, as an artistic endeavor."

Indeed, thinking creatively has informed Fried's entire approach to her business and her social advocacy. Her products and initiatives have often emphasized the joy of creation, especially as a way to promote education. *Adafruit* has attracted particular attention for its user-friendly kits aimed at people of any ages or level of experience. And the company distinguished itself as much more than a mere online retailer of parts: the Adafruit website has become a knowledge portal for the DIY engineering community, featuring numerous video tutorials, blog posts, and user forums to guide visitors through the process of making their own devices. Many videos have featured Fried herself. "We want to show that you don't need years of higher education in electrical engineering to make something fun and cool," she told Jean Kumagai for *IEEE Spectrum*, a magazine published by the Institute of Electrical and Electronics Engineers (22 Apr. 2013). "Everyone has an engineer or maker inside them."

EARLY LIFE AND EDUCATION

Fried grew up with three siblings in Brookline, Massachusetts, a suburb of Boston. Her father was a professor at Boston University, and her mother was a highly regarded piano teacher. As a child, Fried loved watching *Mr. Wizard's World*, a television show that aired on the Nickelodeon network and featured a kindly host who

Photo by Max Morse / TechCrunch via Wikimedia Commons

performed a simple scientific experiment each episode while explaining it to his young viewers. She soon exhibited an interest in and aptitude for science and technology. "I just loved being creative, and I loved science," she noted in an undated video profile for *Makers* magazine. "I loved building things, like taking things apart, understanding how they worked."

Once, when she was about seven, Fried spied a bunch of balloons stuck to the ceiling at a local mall. She went home and, with her father's help, constructed a mechanical arm to retrieve the balloons, which she gave away to other children. By the time she was in third grade, she was reverse-engineering household electronics, including the family VCR, disassembling them to see how they worked. One of her favorite projects involved a Radio Shack tone-dialer—a device used to access touch-tone voice menus when calling from a rotary-dial phone—that she modified to allow her to make free phone calls. She would later fondly recall that in her youth it was permissible to even experiment with explosives, as long as the fire department was notified.

Although she was bright and intellectually curious, Fried did not enjoy high school. Often, instead of attending classes, she and her friends hung out on the nearby MIT campus, sneaking into the computer center to tinker or attending meetings of the anime club. She ultimately dropped out of high school before graduating, but because of her father's connection to Boston University, she was allowed to take classes there. She became a computer science major, and eventually transferred to MIT. There she was a regular visitor to MITERS, a student-run lab filled with electrical engineering equipment.

BEGINNING ADAFRUIT

At MIT Fried immersed herself in hacker and DIY culture, regularly posting photographs and detailed instructions of her latest hardware-hacking experiments online. She became known in the community by the handle "Ladyada," a homage to nineteenth-century mathematician Ada Lovelace, who is considered by many to be the world's first computer programmer. Among the projects receiving the most positive feedback from her growing audience were the MiniPOV, an LED display that made words appear to float in air, and several devices designed to fit inside an Altoids mint tin, including the Minty MP3 player and the MintyBoost phone charger. As she told Rob Matheson for *MIT News* (31 May 2013), "I would spend a few hours doing class-work, then at night work on projects."

Eventually Fried began receiving messages from frustrated do-it-yourselfers: the projects she was showcasing looked fun, but it could be difficult to find and purchase the many needed parts, particularly for those who did not have access to well-equipped electrical engineering labs. She decided to offer parts herself, neatly packaged into kits for anyone interested in following her designs. She borrowed some of her tuition money to buy components, began assembling kits in her dorm room, and added a PayPal button to the tutorials she was posting. (Although it was sometimes a race to make back the money before her tuition bill became due, Fried would later tout the fact that she got her company off the ground without asking for loans or venture capital.)

Meanwhile, Fried was active in MIT's Media Lab, a research facility whose members come from the worlds of technology, media, science, art, and design. However, she was not always an ideal student in the eyes of university administrators. For example, she once attached a black box with protruding wires to a parking garage girder, along with a note explaining that the device was an art project for an electrical engineering course. She quickly received a sternly worded letter from MIT's administration chastising her for potentially causing a bomb scare and noting that "art is not usually associated with electrical engineering," as she quoted on her personal website. Nevertheless, Fried earned a bachelor's degree and then a master's in electrical and electronics engineering, graduating in 2005. Her master's thesis project was titled "Social Defense Mechanisms: Tools for Reclaiming Our Personal Space" and detailed her development of glasses that darkened when a television was turned on and a radio-frequency jammer that prevented cell phones from operating in a user's personal space. (She got the idea for the latter while trying to study in a café, only to be disrupted by the loud phone conversations of her fellow patrons.)

By Fried's final year at MIT her DIY-kit business had grown into a company she called Adafruit (also inspired by Lovelace). She next applied for and was accepted into a one-year residency program at Eyebeam, a New York City–based organization dedicated to allowing artists and innovators of all types to engage and experiment with technology. She moved into a converted warehouse with eight other people and worked in Eyebeam's Open Lab on various new-media and electronic projects.

GROWING HER COMPANY

When her Eyebeam residency ended, Fried elected to remain in New York to grow the enterprise she had started back in her dorm room. She reasoned that there she would have ready access to talented workers, plenty of design inspiration, and the benefits of a fast-paced, energized environment. She initially ran Adafruit out of her small New York City apartment. "My goal was to create the best place online for learning electronics and making the best designed products for makers of all ages and skill levels," she told Katherine Hague for the *Blueprint* (23 Feb. 2015).

Undaunted when that first apartment was condemned, Fried found another nearby, and by 2010 the company had eight employees and was shipping more than $3 million worth of kits annually. By the mid-2010s Adafruit had some one hundred employees and operated from a 50,000-square-foot industrial space in downtown Manhattan. Its annual revenue, according to most business sources, reached more than $40 million.

Fried and Adafruit thrived financially despite promoting the concept of open-source hardware, in which all mechanical drawings, schematics, circuit board layout data, and other specifications for a product are freely shared at no charge. Therefore, someone could technically, and legally, build a device Fried had developed by purchasing parts elsewhere and paying her nothing. Although this unconventional model and her support for hacking led some observers to wonder if she subscribed to an anticorporate agenda, Fried often asserted that she was a staunch capitalist, and indeed found it particularly exciting whenever she heard that she had inspired another entrepreneur. At the same time, however, she acknowledged that having a strong social mission was also very important to her. "I think of Adafruit as a cause, not just a company," she declared to David Zax for *Fast Company* (10 Jan. 2011). "There's a company that sustains me, but that's not enough to drive what I do. What we're trying to do is make electrical engineering exciting, cool, and fun."

ELECTRONICS ICON

Under Fried's leadership, Adafruit both drew on and contributed to the growth of the Maker Movement—which emphasizes curiosity, innovation, and a do-it-yourself ethos—in the first decades of the twenty-first century. The company's website became a socially oriented resource providing not just parts and kits for sale but also resources for sharing projects and collaborating. It hosted several regular video features, including "Ask an Engineer," in which Fried fields user questions; and a live show-and-tell during which anyone with a webcam could demonstrate what they are building. "People who used to do this stuff alone now have even more community," she told Chris Anderson for *Wired* (29 Mar. 2011). "It used to be just freaks in garages; now it's freaks in garages working together."

Fried also spearheaded educational efforts, including a video series aimed at inspiring the very youngest budding electrical engineers. Called *Circuit Playground*, it stars Adabot, a Muppets-style robot who explains terms and concepts in ten-minute episodes such as "A Is for Ampere" and "D Is for Diode." With increasing public attention to the value of STEM education, Fried became something of an icon for her success in inspiring young people. Her status as a trailblazer for women in the traditionally male-dominated world of engineering also earned attention and accolades. She related a story to Anderson that reflected her efforts to showcase women engineers: a viewer of one of her videos wrote in to report that his daughter had also seen the program and asked, "Dad, are there boy engineers too?"

As her reputation grew Fried earned a number of awards and honors in both the business and technology fields. In 2009, she garnered a Pioneer Award from the Electronic Frontier Foundation for her work with open-source hardware. She was named one of the most influential women in technology by *Fast Company* magazine in 2011 and *Entrepreneur* magazine's entrepreneur of the year in 2012. In 2016, she was honored by the White House as a Champion of Change for her efforts to promote diversity in the technology world, including education and entrepreneurship. In 2018, Forbes named Fried one of America's Top 50 Women in Tech, and the Manufacturing Institute presented her with a 2019 STEP (Science, Technology, Engineering and Production) Ahead Award.

PERSONAL LIFE

Fried is married to fellow engineer Phillip Torrone. She has told interviewers that she dislikes domestic duties like laundry and preparing meals because she much prefers creating new projects.

Among her personal quirks is her longtime refusal to own a cell phone. Fried also often earned attention for her facial piercings and bright pink hair. "The traditional image of engineer is being changed," she said in her *Makers* video profile. "And that's good. That means that we're getting more brains, more experience, more people that have new exciting problems to solve."

SUGGESTED READING

Fried, Limor. "Q&A: Open Source Electronics Pioneer Limor Fried on the DIY Revolution." Interview by Chris Anderson. *Wired*, 29 Mar. 2011, www.wired.com/2011/03/ff_adafruit/. Accessed 7 Nov. 2019.

———. "ShopLocket Talks with Limor Fried: Founder of Adafruit." Interview by Katherine Hague. *The Blueprint*, archive.is/20150223015216/https://theblueprint.com/stories/limor-fried/#selection-393.1-405.20. Accessed 7 Nov. 2019.

Kumagai, Jean. "Profile: Limor Fried." *IEEE Spectrum*, 22 Apr. 2013, spectrum.ieee.org/geek-life/profiles/profile-limor-fried. Accessed 7 Nov. 2019.

"Limor Fried: Founder & CEO, Adafruit Industries." *Makers*, www.makers.com/profiles/5aa3d982b36ef856656f6172. Accessed 7 Nov. 2019.

Matheson, Rob. "Meet the Maker." *MIT News*, Massachusetts Institute of Technology, 31 May 2013, news.mit.edu/2013/limor-fried-adafruit-0531. Accessed 7 Nov. 2019.

Twilley, Nicola. "Limor Fried's Artful Electronics." *The New Yorker*, 3 Mar. 2016, www.newyorker.com/tech/annals-of-technology/limor-frieds-artful-electronics. Accessed 7 Nov. 2019.

Zax, David. "2011 Most Influential Women in Technology: Limor Fried." *Fast Company*, 1 Oct. 2011, www.fastcompany.com/3016954/the-most-influential-women-in-technology-2011-limor-fried. Accessed 7 Nov. 2019.

—*Mari Rich*

Adena Friedman

Date of birth: July 15, 1969
Occupation: Businessperson

Adena Friedman became the head of the National Association of Securities Dealers Automated Quotations (Nasdaq), the second largest stock exchange in the world, in January 2017. At the time of her promotion, Friedman had spent over twenty years working her way through the company after starting as an intern in 1993. As she told Samantha Sharf for *Forbes* (May 2016),

Photo by Financial Times via Wikimedia Commons

"If you really think about the fabric of the United States, or the finance of any economy, finance is a true underpinning of what makes the economy great, if it can be done successfully, responsibly and with a client orientation." Her successes have led Friedman to become a formidable leader in the finance industry. In 2016, *Forbes* ranked her among Wall Street's top ten winners. She was also ranked thirtieth in *Forbes*'s 2019 ranking of the most powerful women in the world.

EARLY LIFE AND EDUCATION

Born in 1969, Adena Robinson Testa Friedman grew up in Baltimore, Maryland. Friedman knew from a young age that she was interested in finance. On Saturdays, she and her brother frequently accompanied their father, David Testa, to his office at T. Rowe Price, where he was chief investment officer. Her mother, Adena, attended law school when her daughter was nine, becoming the first woman partner in the law firm she later joined. Friedman sometimes went with her to classes and has stated that she regards her mother as a hero for pursuing a career after initially dropping out of college. Both Friedman and her brother ultimately pursued careers in finance.

Friedman attended all-girls schools from age eight until she went to college. That ten-year experience shaped her, as she told David Gelles for the *New York Times* (23 Mar. 2018), "It was a really important part of me growing up, being in an environment where being smart was celebrated. They constantly talked about going as far as you can go in your life." At her schools, Friedman

was surrounded by peers who shared her love of math and science, and teachers who worked with students to create realistic paths to achieve their goals. After watching Sally Ride, the first woman in space, Friedman grew interested in becoming an astronaut; she later considered a political career. During high school she participated in Model UN.

When she was wait-listed for admission to Williams College, her first choice for college, Friedman wrote a letter to the admissions office, explaining why she was the right fit for the school. She was then accepted and began attending Williams after graduating high school in 1987. She earned her Bachelor of Arts in political science from Williams College in 1991.

EARLY CAREER

The summer before her senior year of college, Friedman worked on Capitol Hill for then Senator Al Gore. That experience changed her direction away from politics, as she told Ryan Underwood for *Vanderbilt Magazine* (29 May 2017), "The pay was $15,000 a year. You couldn't earn a living. That was a little bit shocking. The second thing was that I realized government wasn't quite as idealistic as I thought it was." Unsure of what to do after college, Friedman went on to Vanderbilt University. She earned her master's degree in business administration in 1993 from Vanderbilt's Owen Graduate School of Management. Within the business field, she was most interested in product management. She thought the work of financial products was more interesting than that of consumer goods, so entered the world of finance.

Friedman joined Nasdaq, the trading company that manages about one-fifth of all stock transactions in the United States, as an unpaid intern researcher in 1993. The fee-based plan she created during her internship to monetize one of the company's functions remained in place more than twenty years later. She was eventually hired by the company, serving as its head of data products for nine years, before becoming the head of corporate strategy. During that time, Friedman was key in Nasdaq's 2008 acquisition of the nation's oldest stock exchange, the Philadelphia Stock Exchange (PHLX), as well as of the Boston Stock Exchange (BSE), the Offset Market Exchange (OMX)—a Nordic and Baltic financial services company—and the Institute for New Economic Thinking (INET). In 2009, Friedman was named chief financial officer (CFO) of Nasdaq.

In 2011, Friedman left Nasdaq to work as CFO and managing director for the Carlyle Group, a private equity firm. Her decision shocked her colleagues at Nasdaq, where she was being groomed for the top position. One of the motivations for changing companies was the opportunity to remain in Washington, DC, rather than commuting to New York. She was key in taking the Carlyle Group public in 2012. When the Carlyle Group promoted Curt Buser, a thirty-year industry veteran, to a position that threatened Friedman's path to chief executive officer (CEO), she decided to leave the company.

CEO OF NASDAQ

Friedman returned to Nasdaq in 2014, where she began serving as president of global corporate and information technology solutions. The following year, she added chief operating officer (COO) to her title. She was the obvious choice to replace Nasdaq's CEO, Bob Greifeld, after his retirement. She accepted the position in January 2017, becoming, as many news sources noted, the first woman to head a global stock exchange. In response to questions about her position as CEO, Friedman told Alexandra Gibbs and Elizabeth Schulze for *CNBC* (6 Dec. 2017), "I don't feel any extra pressure, honestly, as a female CEO. . . . I'm hoping that I can achieve the sense of being a really great leader and the fact that I happen to be a woman is just part of that equation, but it isn't the defining part of it." She also stated that she prefers the risk-taking aspect of CEO to the advisory role of CFO.

Nasdaq is the second-largest stock exchange in the world; the company owns several European stock exchanges, including those in Helsinki, Stockholm, and Copenhagen, Denmark. In addition to being a capital market, Nasdaq also provides technology to nearly one hundred other markets and clearinghouses around the globe. Friedman told Thomas Heath for the *Washington Post* (12 Oct. 2018), "Nasdaq is really an engine for capitalism. It is the core engine. It sits in the center, and it allows for all those entrepreneurs to come to a place and find money. That's a great thing for society." Following in Greifeld's footsteps, Friedman remained committed to diversifying the company by expanding its influence into financial technology, as well as enhancing the potential for artificial intelligence in systems that can spot fraud or theft at banks and strategize the best stock trading options. As she told Alexander Osipovich for *Wall Street Journal* (3 Feb. 2017) about the potential of artificial intelligence, "We think in the next decade it could really transform the business." Nasdaq's approach appealed to a growing number of technology companies. It has continued to forge new ideas in stocks, including using blockchains to manage income, as well as using artificial intelligence to make investment decisions.

SUCCESS AS CEO

Nasdaq competes with the New York Stock Exchange (NYSE) in terms of number of initial public offerings (IPOs) and total worth. Both exchanges now have a focus on the technology sector. As Joseph N. DiStefano of *The Philadelphia Inquirer* (6 Oct. 2018) reported, Friedman considers Nasdaq "a technology company that happens to work in the financial services industry." Under her leadership, Nasdaq signed the Parity Pledge, an agreement to interview at least one qualified woman for any senior executive position, in the late 2010s. Friedman is also committed to equity, diversity, and inclusion in the company's recruiting and hiring practices, as she told DiStefano, "Diversity results in better outcomes for companies and consumers." Nasdaq has placed less emphasis on revenue from stock trades and more on new sources of income, such as data research. In 2019, 78 percent of all companies that went public did so through Nasdaq.

During the coronavirus (COVID-19) pandemic of 2020, Friedman decided to split Nasdaq's employees into two teams that would alternate working one week in the office and one week at home. Over the weekend, the offices would be thoroughly cleaned. If one of the company's teams became infected with the virus, the other one could keep the business going.

Friedman was elected as a Class B director to the New York Federal Reserve Bank in 2018. Federal Reserve Banks have three classes of directors—A, B, and C—with three people in each of those classes. Class B directors are charged with representing the public. She is the only CEO of a stock exchange to have been elected to the bank. In 2020, Friedman was also elected to a five-year term at Vanderbilt University's Board of Trust.

PERSONAL LIFE

Friedman lives with her husband, Michael, a college classmate and former lawyer who became a potter, and their two sons in Chevy Chase, Maryland. She also has an apartment in New York City, where Nasdaq is headquartered. After taking her sons to classes in taekwondo, she began studying the martial art also, earning a second-degree black belt. In addition, she played second base for Nasdaq's softball team and enjoys keeping statistics at baseball games.

SUGGESTED READING

DiStefano, Joseph N. "Nasdaq Chief Calls Philly a Fertile Place for Tech to Grow." *The Philadelphia Inquirer*, 6 Oct. 2018, www.inquirer.com/philly/blogs/inq-phillydeals/nasdaq-chief-philly-fintech-fmc-stock-20181005.html. Accessed 28 May 2020.

Friedman, Adena. "How Nasdaq C.E.O. Adena Friedman Beat the Odds on Wall Street." Interview by David Gelles. *The New York Times*, 23 Mar. 2018, www.nytimes.com/2018/03/23/business/adena-friedman-nasdaq-corner-office.html. Accessed 20 May 2020.

Gibbs, Alexandra, and Elizabeth Schulze. "How Attending and All-Girls School Helped Prepare the CEO of Nasdaq for a Career on Wall Street." *CNBC*, 6 Dec. 2017, www.cnbc.com/2017/12/06/nasdaq-ceo-adena-friedman-on-her-upbringing-education-and-working-on-wall-street.html. Accessed 20 May 2020.

Heath, Thomas. "Nasdaq CEO Is on a Mission—For the Little Guy." *The Washington Post*, 12 Oct. 2018, www.washingtonpost.com/business/economy/nasdaq-ceo-is-on-a-mission--for-the-little-guy/2018/10/12/5b655fdc-c0df-11e8-90c9-23f963eea204_story.html. Accessed 20 May 2020.

Sharf, Samantha. "Nasdaq's Adena Friedman on Why Young People Should Want to Work in Finance." *Forbes*, 12 May 2016, www.forbes.com/sites/samantha-sharf/2016/05/12/nasdaqs-adena-friedman-on-why-young-people-should-want-to-work-in-finance/#53c9eca37792. Accessed 20 May 2020.

Underwood, Ryan. "Markets Master: Nasdaq CEO Adena Friedman, MBA'93 Charts the Future of Finance." *Vanderbilt News*, Vanderbilt University, 29 May 2017, news.vanderbilt.edu/2017/05/29/markets-master-adena-friedman-begins-her-tenure-as-ceo-of-nasdaq-looking-to-emerging-technologies-to-help-reshape-world-financial-markets/. Accessed 20 May 2020.

—*Judy Johnson*

component, just like traits such as height. "As nutrition has improved over the past 200 years, Americans have gotten much taller on average, but it is still the genes that determine who is tall or short today," Friedman explained in an article for *Newsweek* (9 Sept. 2009). "The same is true for weight." In his research, Friedman set out to identify a defective gene that was causing a particular strain of mice to become obese. The discovery of this gene—the "ob" gene—led to the discovery of a hormone called leptin. Leptin sends signals to the brain, regulating food intake. The discovery is widely considered a landmark in modern physiology.

Friedman has won many awards for his work, including the Bristol-Myers Squibb Award for Distinguished Achievement in Metabolic Research in 2001, and the Banting Lecture Award in 2002. In 2005, he received both the Gairdner Foundation International Award and the Passano Foundation Award and received the Jessie Stevenson Kovalenko Medal and the Danone International Prize in 2007. In 2009, he received the prestigious Shaw Prize, worth $1 million, as well as the Keio Medical Science Prize. He went on to receive the Albert Lasker Basic Medical Research Award (2010), the Robert J. and Claire Pasarow Foundation Medical Research Award (2011), the BBVA Foundation Frontiers of Knowledge Award in Biomedicine (2012), the Foundation IPSEN Endocrine Regulation Prize (2012), the King Faisal International Prize (2013), the Harrington Prize for Innovation in Medicine (2016), the Wolf Prize in Medicine

Jeffrey M. Friedman

Date of birth: July 20, 1954
Occupation: Molecular geneticist

Jeffrey M. Friedman is an award-winning molecular geneticist, known for his 1994 discovery of the hormone leptin, whose role in regulating body weight has provided key insights into the genetic causes of obesity. Molecular geneticists investigate the function and structure of genes, with the aim of understanding how genes control behavior. As Friedman explained to Debra M. Katz of the *New York Times* (5 Feb. 1995), his focus on genes linked to obesity stems from his interest "in the molecular mechanisms that regulate behaviors." He added: "One of the crucial behaviors that every organism has to regulate is food intake. And so the idea was that by trying to identify genes that related to obesity we could maybe get a peek into the ways in which a particular behavior is regulated." Friedman's research revealed that obesity, rather than being merely a result of individual choices, has a strong genetic

Photo by Duncan Hull and The Royal Society via Wikimedia Commons

(2019), and a Breakthrough Prize in Life Sciences in 2020.

EARLY LIFE AND EDUCATION

Jeffrey M. Friedman was born on July 20, 1954, in Orlando, Florida, and he grew up in North Woodmere on Long Island, New York. His father was a radiologist, and his mother was a teacher. His younger brother, Scott, also a doctor, is the Dean for Therapeutic Discovery at the Icahn School of Medicine at Mount Sinai, where he specializes in liver disease. As a child, Friedman dreamed of becoming an athlete or a veterinarian. It never occurred to him to pursue an academic career as a scientist. "In my family, the highest level of achievement was to become a doctor," he recalled in a short autobiography on the Shaw Prize website in 2009. Friedman graduated from Hewlett High School in 1971 and enrolled as a student at Rensselaer Polytechnic Institute (RPI) in Troy, New York. He earned a bachelor's degree in biology in 1973 and earned his medical degree from Albany Medical College of Union University, New York, in 1977, at the age of twenty-two.

Friedman trained in internal medicine and gastroenterology. He participated in some research studies as a medical student and during his two residencies at Albany Medical Center Hospital. Friedman's first piece of work, under the tutelage of Patrick Wong, related to the effects of dietary salt on the regulation of blood pressure. "After completing this project, I excitedly submitted a paper for publication. I remember one of the reviews verbatim: 'This paper should not be published in the *Journal of Clinical Investigation* or anywhere else,'" Friedman recalled for the Shaw Prize website. "Fortunately, one of my mentors in medical school still thought I might have some aptitude for research." That mentor recommended that Friedman work in the basic science research laboratory at Rockefeller University in Manhattan. Friedman heeded the advice, and in 1980, joined the laboratory of Dr. Mary-Jeanne Kreek to study the effects of endorphins in the development of narcotic addiction.

EARLY RESEARCH WORK

From 1980 to 1981, Friedman also served as a postgraduate fellow at Cornell University Medical College. Back at Rockefeller, he met another scientist named Bruce Schneider. Schneider was studying cholecystokinin (CCK), a peptid hormone that aids in digestion. In the 1970s, it was discovered that subjects injected with CCK reduced their food intake. Friedman was interested in CCK, he wrote, as an example of how "a single molecule can change behavior." His interest was such that he set out to establish the possible role of CCK in the development of obesity in mice. "The starting point for this work was the prior observation that a particular strain of mouse, the ob mouse, is obese because of a defect in a single gene, and no one had ever been able to identify this defective gene before," Friedman explained to Katz. He wondered if CCK could be the ob gene.

To complete this research, Friedman wrote for the Shaw Prize, "I was going to need additional training in basic research, so I abandoned my plans to continue medical training in gastroenterology," and he entered the PhD program at Rockefeller University. He began his studies in the lab of Professor James E. Darnell Jr., studying gene expression in the liver, while also learning the basics of molecular biology. He continued to pursue the interests he had cultivated with Schneider, though, and by the end of his studies he had successfully isolated the CCK gene from mice. This was an achievement in itself, though it suggested that CCK was not, in fact, the ob gene. (Friedman knew that the ob gene mapped to chromosome 6; CCK was later found to map to chromosome 9.)

Friedman finished his PhD degree in 1986. He continued his research as an assistant professor at Rockefeller University. He also became an assistant investigator at the Howard Hughes Medical Institute (HHMI) in Maryland. In 1991, he was promoted to associate professor and named head of Rockefeller's molecular genetics laboratory. In 1995, he became a full professor, and in 1999, he was named the school's Marilyn M. Simpson Professor.

POSITIONAL CLONING OF OB GENE

As the head of his own lab at Rockefeller University, Friedman redoubled his efforts to identify the ob gene. (Recall that the ob gene itself, which regulates body weight and food intake, does not cause obesity; obesity is caused—though not exclusively—by a defect in that gene.) Building on work done by Doug Coleman at the Jackson Laboratory in the 1960s and 1970s, Friedman and his team used a then-new technology called positional cloning, a technique that has been used to identify the cystic fibrosis gene and the colon cancer gene, among others. Though Friedman knew approximately where the ob gene was located, he still needed to search for a marker close enough to the gene so he could clone it. The marker, Friedman told Sarah Allan for *Disease Models & Mechanisms* (2012) "would need to map to a segment approximately equal to 1/3000 of the genome. We took several approaches to enrich for markers in this very small region, but it was difficult and it took a long time." In fact, the search took years, but once a marker was found the project accelerated.

Later, in a 2016 article for the *Journal of Clinical Investigation*—the same publication that had so harshly rejected him years before—Friedman would recall: "This was a painstaking, anxiety-provoking, repetitive, and in many ways stultifying process that, after a ten-year odyssey ended with a moment of discovery and a sense of exhilaration that is one of the defining moments of my life."

DISCOVERY OF LEPTIN
In 1994, Friedman published a landmark paper detailing the findings of his near-decade-long study. Friedman and his team identified the ob gene in mice and humans, further discovering that the gene encodes a hormone, which they chose to call leptin. (As Friedman explained to Katz, he and his team were able to isolate the human counterpart of the ob gene in mice and found them profoundly similar.) The word leptin comes from the Greek word *leptos*, for thin, meaning that the presence of leptin keeps a mouse—or a human—from becoming obese. Leptin, Friedman explained in his article for *Newsweek*, "sends a signal informing the brain that there are adequate stores of energy. When leptin drops, appetite increases." He used the example of a young boy in England who, because of a genetic error, could not produce leptin. He was hungry all the time because his body did not understand that he had eaten and stored enough energy. After receiving leptin injections, the boy was able to eat normally, and his body weight came under control. "This example illustrates that feeding behavior is a basic drive, similar to thirst and other life-sustaining drives," Friedman wrote. "The key role of leptin and other molecules to control feeding behavior undercuts the common misconception that food intake is largely under voluntary control."

In the years since the discovery, Friedman's lab has continued to research leptin and how it functions. They have shown that leptin has powerful effects on reproduction, metabolism, other endocrine systems (a collection of glands that produce hormones that regulate behavior) and immune function. "Jeff's research has transformed the way we think about obesity," Rockefeller University President Richard P. Lifton said, as quoted by the Rockefeller University website (5 Sept. 2019), when Friedman was named the recipient of a 2020 Breakthrough Prize in Life Sciences, worth $3 million. "He discovered an endocrine system that informs the brain about the state of energy storage in the body. When fat stores are low, leptin is low, driving food seeking and consumption. People who can't make leptin have seemingly insatiable appetite. This spectacular work establishes a biological basis for obesity and provides clear evidence that overeating is not always a simple failure of willpower."

SUGGESTED READING
Allan, Sarah. "Leading the Charge in Leptin Research: An Interview with Jeffrey Friedman." *Disease Models and Mechanisms*, vol. 5, no. 5, 2012, pp. 576–79, www.ncbi.nlm.nih.gov/pmc/articles/PMC3424452/. Accessed 8 Mar. 2020.
Friedman, Jeffrey M. "Autobiography of Jeffrey M. Friedman." *The Shaw Prize*, 7 Oct. 2009, www.shawprize.org/en/shaw.php?tmp=3&twoid=12&threeid=40&fourid=16&fiveid=7. Accessed 7 Mar. 2020.
——. "Finding the Gene That Makes Mice, and Maybe Others, Fat." Interview by Debra M. Katz. *The New York Times*, 5 Feb. 1995, www.nytimes.com/1995/02/05/nyregion/long-island-qa-jeffrey-m-friedman-finding-the-gene-that-makes-mice.html. Accessed 8 Mar. 2020.
——. "The Long Road to Leptin." *The Journal of Clinical Investigation*, vol. 126, no. 12, 2016, pp. 4727–34, www.ncbi.nlm.nih.gov/pmc/articles/PMC5127673/. Accessed 8 Mar. 2020.
——. "Obesity Is Genetic." *Newsweek*, 9 Sept. 2009, www.newsweek.com/obesity-genetic-79383. Accessed 8 Mar. 2020.
"Jeffrey M. Friedman to Receive 2020 Breakthrough Prize in Life Sciences." *The Rockefeller University*, 5 Sept. 2019, www.rockefeller.edu/news/26554-jeffrey-m-friedman-to-receive-2020-breakthrough-prize-in-life-sciences/. Accessed 9 Mar. 2020.

—*Molly Hagan*

Marcelo Gleiser
Date of birth: March 19, 1959
Occupation: Physicist; astronomer; author

Marcelo Gleiser is an award-winning theoretical physicist, astronomer, and author known for focusing his decades-long career on providing a better understanding of scientific inquiry to a lay audience, while at the same time being mindful of the limits of that same inquiry. In addition to serving as a professor of physics at Dartmouth College, he has authored several popular science books and wrote extensively for both popular media and scientific journals. The many subjects he has covered include the origin of life, the nature of the early universe, and the interface between cosmology and particle physics.

In 2019 Gleiser received the Templeton Prize, an award that acknowledges individuals who have sought to make connections between science, the humanities, and spirituality. "To me, science is one way of connecting with the mystery of existence," he noted to Lee Billings

Photo by Gleiser via Wikimedia Commons

for *Scientific American* (20 Mar. 2019). "And if you think of it that way, the mystery of existence is something that we have wondered about ever since people began asking questions about who we are and where we come from. So while those questions are now part of scientific research, they are much, much older than science."

EARLY LIFE AND EDUCATION

Marcelo Gleiser was born in Rio de Janeiro, Brazil, on March 19, 1959, the youngest of Haluza (née Schneider) and Izaac Gleiser's three sons. His father was a dentist, amateur musician, and gardener, while his mother had graduated from the University of Brazil with a bachelor's degree in pedagogy. His grandfathers were prominent leaders of Rio's Jewish community.

Gleiser would later recall how the beauty of the natural world that surrounded him in his youth inspired his scientific curiosity. In particular, he grew up living very close to the ocean and was also able to regularly visit other impressive landscapes. "It's impossible not to be amazed by the enormity of nature when you have that huge, beautiful Atlantic Ocean in front of you. And I was lucky that my grandparents had a house in the mountains about two hours from Rio," he noted in an interview with Krista Tippett for the National Public Radio (NPR) program *On Being* (8 Jan. 2012). "So I think from a very early age I was just mystified by the beauty of this, and I wanted to understand how was that all possible."

When Gleiser was six years old, his mother died. This devastating experience

greatly influenced his search for understanding the meaning of existence. Born into a Jewish family, he initially sought understanding in the religious scriptures of his faith; later, science would be the means by which he would continue his quest. Gleiser told Billings: "I think it was a very early sense of loss that made me curious about existence. And if you are curious about existence, physics becomes a wonderful portal, because it brings you close to the nature of the fundamental questions: space, time, origins. And I've been happy ever since."

For his bar mitzvah, Gleiser received an autographed picture of the famed theoretical physicist Albert Einstein, who had been hosted by Gleiser's grandfather during Einstein's visit to Brazil in 1925. The picture of Einstein with his grandfather inspired him to study astronomy and physics. Gleiser earned his bachelor of science degree from the Catholic University of Rio de Janeiro in 1981. A year later he received his master of science degree from the Federal University of Rio de Janeiro. In 1986, he completed his doctorate in theoretical physics at King's College London. His thesis was titled "Kaluza-Klein Cosmology"; his adviser was J. G. Taylor.

ACADEMIC CAREER

Gleiser's academic career began in the fall of 1986, when he served as a postdoctoral research associate at the Fermilab Theoretical Astrophysics Group. He remained there until August 1988, when he moved to California for a postdoctoral fellowship at University of California, Santa Barbara's Institute for Theoretical Physics. That position lasted until the fall of 1991, when he became an assistant professor of physics and astronomy at Dartmouth College. After becoming an associate professor at Dartmouth in 1995, he became a full professor in 1998 and the Appleton Professor of Natural Philosophy in 1998. In 2016, he founded and became the director of the college's Institute for Cross-Disciplinary Engagement (ICE), which, according to the institute's website, "is dedicated to transforming the dialogue between the sciences and humanities . . . in order to explore fundamental questions where a cross-disciplinary exchange is essential."

At Dartmouth, Gleiser had three main research topics: the origin of life on Earth and possibly on other planets (known as astrobiology); the physics of the early universe just after the Big Bang; and the ways in which particle physics and cosmology connect—essentially the study of the very small and the very large. With regards to life on Earth and in the universe, his primary research focused on understanding how nonliving chemicals became living creatures and how that process might be replicated in other places in the universe. He considered himself a believer in the "Rare Earth" hypothesis, which argues that the various elements needed to produce life—the right temperate climate, the presence of liquid water, planets being the right distance from their parent stars, etc.—may have occurred elsewhere but not often.

Gleiser also asserted his belief that the best way to understand the history of the early universe is to study both cosmology and particle physics, the latter of which looks at the subatomic particles that make up the universe. Without an understanding of both, he suggested, human beings cannot come to the most comprehensive understanding of the natural world. In 1994, his research in this area led him to co-discover "oscillons," particle field configurations that exist for a very long time, both in small particles and in cosmology at large.

POPULAR SCIENCE WRITER

Over the course of his career Gleiser wrote more than one hundred papers for peer-reviewed journals. At the same time he became known as a highly regarded popular science writer. He authored hundreds of science essays, including a weekly essay for *13.8*, his blog with fellow physicist Adam Frank for the online magazine *Orbiter*. The *Orbiter* blog grew as a continuation of the *NPR* blog *13.7: Cosmos and Culture*, which the pair cofounded in 2009 and which featured their own essays as well as pieces by writers such as Alva Noë, Barbara J. King, and Tania Lombrozo. Both blogs featured commentary on science, culture, and meaning.

Gleiser also wrote several popular science books that earned praise for the way in which they tackle complex subjects and present them to a lay audience. His first book, *The Dancing Universe: From Creation Myths to the Big Bang*, was published in 1997. In it, Gleiser surveys about 2,500 years of intellectual inquiry into the question of how the universe began. He compares various scientific, religious and philosophical viewpoints to demonstrate how humanity's questioning and understanding has evolved over that expansive period of history.

Gleiser's next book, *The Prophet and the Astronomer: A Scientific Journey to the End of the World* (2001), looked at the opposite subject: how the universe might end. Again taking on a macro perspective, he discusses how many religious denominations have apocalyptic traditions, and highlights how these came into the world of scientific inquiry during the Renaissance. The book also covers how contemporary scientists look at the ways in which our existence might end, such as meteor impacts, environmental degradation, and war, to the collapse of our sun or the end of the universe as a whole. A reviewer for *Kirkus* (15 Mar. 2002) found that Gleiser "wears his knowledge of astronomy, physics, and philosophy lightly as he

surveys centuries of thought for the nonspecialist reader."

Gleiser's third book was *A Tear at the Edge of Creation: A Radical New Vision for Life in an Imperfect Universe* (2010). Within its pages, he argues that humanity's search for an overarching unifying theory of everything that would tie together all avenues of scientific theory is misguided because nature is imperfect and, therefore, not completely knowable. Instead, he proposes a new way of viewing the universe, a "humanocentrism" that both acknowledges the exceeding rareness of intelligent life and asks us to undertake the responsibility that that entails—by caring for ourselves, our planet, and all of the other life forms with which we come into contact.

In *The Island of Knowledge: The Limits of Science and the Search for Meaning* (2014), Gleiser uses a metaphor to explain the evolution of human understanding. He describes our knowledge as an expanding island, always growing larger, but ever surrounded by an ocean of ignorance. New knowledge leads to new questions that had been unasked or unexpected earlier, leading to a never-ending unknown that humanity will be unable to comprehend. Among the subjects he covers in the book are multiverses, superstring theory, curved spaces, and particle physics. He explained the premise of *The Island of Knowledge* to Charlene Brusso for *Publishers Weekly* (11 Apr., 2014): "This book is intended to be a grounding exercise. If you cannot get any data to test a theory, I believe it cannot be considered a physical theory. I think it's wonderful to have these great, ambitious ideas, but we have to listen to nature. We have to be extremely careful about how to incorporate new ideas in the scientific enterprise."

Gleiser's released *The Simple Beauty of the Unexpected: A Natural Philosopher's Quest for Trout and the Meaning of Everything* in 2016. The book explores his lifelong love of fishing and how the pastime has informed his view of the world.

WINNING THE TEMPLETON PRIZE AND OTHER AWARDS

In 2019, Gleiser won the Templeton Prize, an award that is given to individuals who explore spirituality in life. Presented by the John Templeton Foundation each year, it carries a stipend of nearly $1.5 million. Among its previous recipients are the Dalai Lama, Desmond Tutu, and Mother Teresa. Gleiser, the first Latin American to receive the honor, felt it was his willingness to maintain an open mind with regards to scientific inquiry and religion that earned him the prize. Although he described himself as a religious agnostic, he criticized both religious people who deny scientific evidence and scientists who are strongly atheistic. "I honestly think atheism is inconsistent with the scientific method," he told

Billings. "It's a statement, a categorical statement that expresses belief in nonbelief. 'I don't believe even though I have no evidence for or against, simply I don't believe.' Period. It's a declaration. But in science we don't really do declarations. We say, 'Okay, you can have a hypothesis, you have to have some evidence against or for that.'"

In addition to winning the Templeton Prize, Gleiser received numerous awards and honors for his research and writing. He earned the Presidential Faculty Fellows Award from the White House and the National Science Foundation (NSF) (1994–1999). He won the Jabuti Award, Brazil's highest literary award, for *The Dancing Universe*, *The Prophet and the Astronomer*, and *The Simple Beauty of the Unexpected*. He also claimed the National Research Council of Brazil's 2001 José Reis Prize for the Public Understanding of Science; the 2011 Distinguished Alumnus Award from the Pontifical Catholic University of Rio de Janeiro; and the 2015 Brazilian Diaspora Prize, presented by the Brazilian government. Gleiser was named a fellow of the American Physical Society (APS) and was elected to the General Council of the American Physical Society, serving from 2013 to 2016. In 2017, he was elected a professor extraordinarius at the University of South Africa.

PERSONAL LIFE

Gleiser became a naturalized US citizen. He married Wendy Lynn Martin in 1987 and had three children with her: Andrew Philip (b. 1988), Eric Izaac (b. 1993), and Tali Sarah (b. 1996). The couple divorced in 1996. He married his second wife, psychologist Kari Amber Mc-Cadam, in 1998. They have two sons together, Lucian Jacob (b. 2006) and Gabriel Lennon (b. 2011).

SUGGESTED READING

"About." *Marcelo Gleiser*, 2019, marcelogleiser.com/about. Accessed 18 Dec. 2019.

Gleiser, Marcelo. "Atheism Is Inconsistent with the Scientific Method, Prizewinning Physicist Says." Interview by Lee Billings. *Scientific American*, 20 Mar. 2019, www.scientificamerican.com/article/atheism-is-inconsistent-with-the-scientific-method-prizewinning-physicist-says/. Accessed 18 Dec. 2019.

———. "Cosmic Conundrums: PW Talks with Marcelo Gleiser." Interview by Charlene Brusso. *Publishers Weekly*, 11 Apr. 2014, www.publishersweekly.com/pw/by-topic/authors/interviews/article/61822-cosmic-conundrums-pw-talks-with-marcelo-gleiser.html. Accessed 18 Dec. 2019.

"Marcelo Gleiser." *Dartmouth Department of Physics and Astronomy*, 18 Dec. 2019, physics.dartmouth.edu/people/marcelo-gleiser. Accessed 18 Dec. 2019.

"Marcelo Gleiser CV." *Dartmouth College*, 2019, faculty-directory.dartmouth.edu/sites/dartmouth.edu.faculty-directory/files/cvnew_1.pdf. Accessed 18 Dec. 2019.

Robison, Marilynne, and Marcelo Gleiser. "Marilynne Robison and Marcelo Gleiser: The Mystery We Are." Interview by Krista Tippett. *On Being*, 8 Jan. 2012, onbeing.org/programs/marilynne-robinson-marcelo-gleiser-the-mystery-we-are/#transcript. Accessed 18 Dec. 2019.

SELECTED WORKS

The Dancing Universe, 1997; *The Prophet and the Astronomer*, 2001; *A Tear at the Edge of Creation*, 2010; *The Island of Knowledge*, 2014; *The Simple Beauty of the Unexpected*, 2016

—*Christopher Mari*

Gennady Golovkin

Date of birth: April 8, 1982
Occupation: Boxer

Although some athletes undoubtedly remain the same person both on and off the field of play, Kazakh boxer Gennady Golovkin thinks of his in-ring and out-of-ring selves as two distinctly different beings. "When I'm talking to you outside the ring I'm Gennady Golovkin," he said, as quoted by Brian Harty for the *Ring* (10 Sept. 2017). "When I step through the ropes I'm Triple-G." Indeed, over the course of his lengthy career in amateur and professional boxing, Golovkin—whose first name is sometimes written as Gennadiy and whose nickname, based on his initials, is often rendered as GGG—has established himself as an intimidating force within the ring, winning the majority of his matches and at times holding as many as four separate middleweight boxing titles.

Although a 2018 loss to fellow boxer Canelo Álvarez put an end to his undefeated record, Golovkin continued to push for greatness in 2019, signing a $100 million deal with sports streaming service DAZN and beginning a new string of victories fueled not only by a desire to win titles and prizes but also by the feeling that competition awakens within him. "My body knows the feeling. When you want something so badly. You crave the feeling until it's there in front of you," Golovkin wrote in an essay for the *Players' Tribune* (14 Sept. 2017). "Sometimes, I just want to just fight. Your body just wants it. Sometimes, you just want to destroy this guy, to show you know more, to show that you're better. You want to beat him just to show that you can."

Photo by Box Azteca via Wikimedia Commons

EARLY LIFE AND EDUCATION

Gennady Gennadyevich Golovkin was born on April 8, 1982, in Karaganda, Kazakhstan, which was then part of the Soviet Union. His parents were Kazakhs from different ethnic backgrounds: his father, a Russian also named Gennady, was a coal miner, while his mother, Elizabeth, of Korean heritage, worked in a chemical laboratory. One of four children, he has a twin brother named Maxim, and two older brothers, Sergey and Vadim. An athletic child, Golovkin was particularly drawn to the sport of soccer, which he hoped to pursue professionally one day. His aspirations changed, however, by the late 1980s, during which his older brothers introduced him to the sport of boxing and took him to a local boxing club to try the sport himself. "When we went, I didn't like it," he recalled in his essay for the *Players' Tribune*. "Who wants to get hit in the face? It's a dangerous sport and I liked playing on my soccer teams. But, it came easy to me. I got it. I understood it. And I was very, very good. Right away."

With Golovkin having immediately demonstrated his potential as a boxer, his older brothers encouraged him to develop his skills further through bouts with other aspiring athletes, including competitors far older than him. "I just followed what my brothers told me to do," he told Dave Golokhov for *AskMen India* (21 Feb. 2015). "It [was] a test to see who was the best in the neighborhood." The Golovkin brothers also spent time watching televised boxing matches, including amateur bouts and highly publicized matches featuring major boxers who competed

in the United States. Although Golovkin's older brothers were both killed while serving in the military during the early 1990s, he continued to progress in the sport to which they had introduced him and would later note in interviews that he had in part continued boxing as a way of honoring their memories. Both Golovkin and his twin brother competed extensively on the junior amateur level throughout their teen years, proving themselves to be talented boxers. Golovkin competed in a variety of events overseen by the International Boxing Association (l'Association Internationale de Boxe Amateur, or AIBA) and in 2000 won the gold medal for his weight class at AIBA Junior World Boxing Championships in Hungary.

AMATEUR CAREER

Golovkin distinguished himself as a strong competitor on the international level throughout his career as an amateur boxer, winning a variety of competitions throughout Europe and Asia. He won the gold medal in the light middleweight class at the 2002 Asian Games in South Korea and the following year claimed the gold at the World Amateur Boxing Championships in Thailand, his first major victory in the middleweight class. During the summer of 2004, Golovkin traveled to Athens, Greece, to participate in the middleweight boxing competition at that year's Olympic Games. After progressing through the early rounds of competition, he defeated US boxer Andre Dirrell in the semifinals but lost to Russian competitor Gaydarbek Gaydarbekov in the finals, claiming a silver medal.

Although Golovkin continued to compete as an amateur in 2005, participating in competitions such as the World Amateur Boxing Championships and the Boxing World Cup, he found himself growing dissatisfied with his career prospects during that period. "After the Olympics, I went as far as I could with boxing in Kazakhstan," he explained in his essay for the *Players' Tribune*. "There was only amateur fighting for me there, and I wanted to go pro. But I couldn't get a professional contract in my country." Although he initially planned to retire from boxing altogether, Golovkin eventually decided to pursue a professional career outside of his home country and signed a deal with Universum, a boxing promotions company based in Germany.

PROFESSIONAL DEBUT

After signing with Universum, Golovkin made his professional debut in Germany on May 6, 2006, in a match against boxer Gabor Balogh. He won the match by knockout, beginning a string of successes that would build Golovkin's reputation as a skilled, relentless, and intimidating fighter. Competing largely in Germany throughout the next several years, he won eighteen bouts between 2006 and 2010, when he ended his association with Universum following a contract dispute. After cutting ties with the company, Golovkin traveled to the United States in search of new opportunities. He soon began training with accomplished boxing trainer Abel Sanchez at Summit Gym in Big Bear, California, beginning a professional relationship that would continue for nearly a decade.

Throughout his years with Sanchez, Golovkin committed to a challenging training regimen that saw him dedicate as many as five hours per day to his sport. "I usually train for two hours in the morning for cardio work and stretching," he told Golokhov. "Then three hours in the afternoon for my boxing work, sparring, and bag work." His intensive training proved particularly valuable as Golovkin began to compete against higher-level opponents in matches that earned him both increasing acclaim and world titles. In August of 2010, he beat Colombian boxer Milton Nunez in a bout in Panama City to claim the interim World Boxing Association world middleweight title. He became the full titleholder later that year. The following year, Golovkin claimed another title, the middleweight title from the International Boxing Association (IBA), after beating Lajuan Simon by knockout in a fight in Germany.

A key moment for Golovkin came in August 2012, when he made his US debut in a fight against Polish boxer Grzegorz Proksa. Held at the Turning Stone Casino Resort in Verona, New York, the fight was his first to be televised by the premium channel HBO, one of the leading broadcasters of professional boxing during that period. For Golovkin, the fight represented an opportunity to exhibit his skills in a new level of competition. "This is my dream, my first fight in America," he told the Associated Press in an article published by *ESPN* (31 Aug. 2012). "Maybe the next fight is in New York, in Vegas, but now, I'm very happy." Golovkin won the match decisively, defeating Proksa in just five rounds. He competed in his second US fight early the following year, defeating American boxer Gabriel Rosado by technical knockout at New York City's prestigious Madison Square Garden.

WORLD TITLEHOLDER

Over the years following his US debut, Golovkin continued to compete in fights held in the United States and abroad. In 2014, he claimed the interim World Boxing Council world middleweight title after beating Mexican boxer Marco Antonio Rubio by knockout in two rounds at a match in California. He went on to claim the International Boxing Federation (IBF) world middleweight title by defeating Canadian boxer David Lemieux by technical knockout at Madison Square Garden the following year.

Although Golovkin had succeeded in fighting a number of professional boxers and accumulating an array of titles, his intensity in the ring had made him a feared competitor, and he and his team noted in interviews that his reputation appeared to prompt some major boxers to avoid competing against him. However, a turning point came in September 2017, when Golovkin had the opportunity to face the popular and successful Mexican boxer Saúl "Canelo" Álvarez at the T-Mobile Arena in Las Vegas, Nevada. A highly anticipated match among fans of professional boxing, the fight was likewise a key one for Golovkin himself, who relished the opportunity to face Álvarez. "It was frustrating when the other big names or champions wouldn't fight me, but now I have the opportunity to show that I'm the best," he told Gareth A. Davies for the *Telegraph* (9 Sept. 2017) prior to the fight. "This is a huge fight and first-class boxing, and the winner between myself and Canelo will have the respect of the fans as being the best." To the surprise of both the competitors and their fans, the fight ended not in a conclusive victory for either boxer but in a draw, a controversial decision that prompted calls for a rematch. Golovkin and Álvarez returned to Las Vegas for a second fight in September of the following year, and Golovkin lost the match—and his titles—to his opponent in a razor-thin majority decision.

DAZN DEAL

In early 2019, it was announced Golovkin had signed a deal with the streaming service DAZN, a subscription-based broadcaster of sports content, including televised boxing matches. Under the terms of the three-year deal, Golovkin would receive an estimated $100 million for six fights, becoming one of a number of major boxers—including Álvarez—to sign with the service. That year also saw Golovkin end his relationship with Sanchez and begin working with trainer and former professional boxer Johnathon Banks. Golovkin's first DAZN fight came in June of 2019, when he faced off against Canadian boxer Steve Rolls at Madison Square Garden, winning by knockout in four rounds. He went on to fight Ukrainian boxer Sergiy Derevyanchenko at Madison Square Garden in October of that year. Winning by unanimous decision, Golovkin claimed the interim world middleweight titles from the International Boxing Federation and the International Boxing Organization.

Following a successful 2019, Golovkin was scheduled to compete in his next fight for DAZN in the first half of 2020, during which he was set to face Polish boxer Kamil Szeremeta. Perhaps more significant to both Golovkin's fans and Golovkin himself, however, were rumors that he would soon face off against Álvarez for a third match, possibly even before the end of 2020. "I think we're going to have that fight," Golovkin said of those rumors in 2019, as reported by Scott Christ for *Bad Left Hook* (24 Apr. 2019). "It will be different and it will be a more definitive result—and it will be honest."

PERSONAL LIFE

Golovkin and his wife, Alina, had their first child, a son named Vadim, in 2009. They had a daughter in 2017, shortly before Golovkin's first fight with Álvarez. Golovkin lives and trains in Southern California. He remains close to his twin brother, who accompanies him to many of his fights.

SUGGESTED READING

Boyd, Flinder. "GGG: Inside the Come-Up." *Bleacher Report*, 15 Sept. 2017, bleacher-report.com/articles/2733225-ggg-life-story-gennady-golovkin-what-next-fight. Accessed 8 Mar. 2020.

Christ, Scott. "Gennady Golovkin Wants a Definitive Conclusion to Rivalry with Canelo Alvarez." *Bad Left Hook*, 24 Apr. 2019, www.badlefthook.com/2019/4/24/18513817/gennady-golovkin-interview-canelo-alvarez-third-fight-2019-dazn-steve-rolls. Accessed 8 Mar. 2020.

Davies, Gareth A. "Gennady Golovkin Exclusive Interview: My Brothers Would Pick Fights for Me with Grown Men 'From When I Was in Kindergarten.'" *The Telegraph*, 9 Sept. 2017, www.telegraph.co.uk/boxing/2017/09/09/gennady-golovkin-exclusive-interview-brothers-would-pick-fights. Accessed 8 Mar. 2020.

Golovkin, Gennady. "The Things I Can't Forget." *The Players' Tribune*, 14 Sept. 2017, www.theplayerstribune.com/en-us/articles/gennady-golovkin-boxing-canelo-alvarez. Accessed 8 Mar. 2020.

——. "Will Gennady Golovkin Score a KO Tonight? Here's How He Does It." Interview by Dave Golokhov. *AskMen India*, 21 Feb. 2015, in.askmen.com/celeb-interviews/1102423/interview/gennady-golovkin-interview. Accessed 8 Mar. 2020.

"Golovkin Heads to US with Middleweight Title Hopes." *ESPN*, 31 Aug. 2012, www.espn.com/espn/wire?section=boxing&id=8321185. Accessed 8 Mar. 2020.

Harty, Brian. "Gennady Golovkin: The Quiet Man." *The Ring*, 10 Sept. 2017, www.ringtv.com/516530-gennady-golovkin-quiet-man/. Accessed 8 Mar. 2020.

—Joy Crelin

Hala Gorani

Born: March 1, 1970
Occupation: Television journalist

Emmy Award–winning television broadcast journalist Hala Gorani, who began her professional tenure with CNN in 1998, became the host of *Hala Gorani Tonight* for CNN International in 2017. Born to Syrian parents in Seattle and brought up in Paris, Gorani has spent more than two decades covering events that have transformed the Middle East. In 2011, she was part of a team that earned CNN a News and Documentary Emmy Award, covering the Egyptian revolution live from Tahrir Square in Cairo. She went on to cover the larger Arab Spring, of which the revolution was a part, and, beginning in 2014, the displacement of millions of Syrians during the country's civil war—another event triggered, in large part, by the spate of uprisings known as the Arab Spring. Her early work with CNN, including her special program *Inside the Middle East*, which aired in the 2000s, provided social and cultural context for these events, highlighting the stories of everyday people across the region. She was the anchor involved with the news feature story "Syria: Gasping for Life in Khan Sheikhoun," about a 2017 chemical attack in Syria, which won a News and Documentary Emmy Award in 2018. Regardless of such recognition, she remained dedicated to her responsibility to educate the public as a member of the media. "I think the desire to get the truth out there, and make sure people see all sides of an

Photo by the Association for International Broadcasting via Wikimedia Commons

important story, is what gets me out of bed in the morning," she explained to Roula Allam in an undated interview for *About Her*.

EARLY LIFE AND EDUCATION

Hala Gorani was born in Seattle, Washington, on March 1, 1970, though both of her parents were from Aleppo, Syria. She spent her earliest years in various locations such as St. Louis, Missouri, and Algeria, where her father worked for an American company. After her parents separated, she and her older brother moved to Paris with their mother. Gorani attended a French boarding school and was most directly inspired to become a journalist after watching the 1984 film *The Killing Fields*, based on Sydney Schanberg, a Pulitzer Prize–winning *New York Times* journalist, and his experiences covering the Khmer Rouge's rise to power in Cambodia. "I watched that film and thought what a noble career a journalist has and knew it was what I wanted to do," Gorani recalled to Kelly Crane for the *Gulf News* (5 May 2008). "I made the decision there and then and started a student magazine." Also drawn to photography and storytelling, she recognized that she did not possess the right talent to pursue a career as a photojournalist. Returning to the United States to attend George Mason University in Virginia, she studied economics but cut her teeth writing for the student newspaper, *Broadside*, cementing her desire to work as a journalist. She graduated in 1992.

EARLY CAREER

Gorani settled back in Paris and launched her journalism career as a writer for *La Voix du Nord* (*The Voice of the North*), one of France's daily newspapers, and the Agence France-Presse (AFP) news agency. She later described her foray into television journalism as an intern around 1994, while she was a student at the Institut d'Études Politiques de Paris, or Sciences Po, as "quite accidental." "I had gathered enough experience so that I convinced them to let me write the TV scripts," she told Rana Nawas for the podcast *When Women Win* (25 June 2018). "That wasn't necessarily my primary ambition to be on television." During that time, she was employed by the French network France 3 and worked on stories for the French cable network Paris Premiere.

After graduating from Sciences Po in 1995, Gorani, upon seeing a newspaper advertisement, applied with a résumé and demo tape for a job as an anchor with Bloomberg Television's new French-language station in London. The company eventually offered her the position once she had been flown in to conduct an interview. She told Nawas that she still adheres to the advice she was given by a BBC trainer and consultant during the interview process. He told her, she

recalled to Nawas, "When you're reading the news, you're not, you're talking to people. Always remember that you're talking to people. So the things that you naturally do when you're talking to someone in real life, do those things. . . . Nobody really ever talks to you in real life by staring you down for half an hour without once looking away or once taking a breath."

ANCHOR FOR CNN

In 1998, Gorani was hired as an anchor and reporter for CNN International. Among other locations, she reported from Paris, covering France's adoption of the euro in 2002, and anchoring coverage of the French presidential election the same year. After the beginning of the Iraq War in 2003, she was at the helm of a monthly show for CNN International called *Inside the Middle East*. Tending to focus more on issues related to Middle Eastern society and culture rather than conflicts, she covered various human-interest stories across the region, including stories about artists, poverty, security, and the LGBTQ community. Her coverage of the latter group earned her a GLAAD (Gay and Lesbian Alliance Against Deformation) Award nomination. When describing why she considered her time contributing to *Inside the Middle East*, which she viewed as having a more unique journalistic take on the region, as an especially significant period of her personal and professional life, she told Nawas, "It was always going somewhere where we're the only camera crew and we just decided to follow up on some interesting story and I think I learned more about the Middle East in those five years than in my entire career."

In 2006, Gorani covered the Hajj, the annual pilgrimage to Mecca, from within the holy city in Saudi Arabia. Her reporting on the 2006 war between Israel and Hezbollah (based in Lebanon) helped CNN win an Edward R. Murrow Award for coverage of the Middle East conflict in 2007. She again covered the French presidential election in 2007, and in 2008, she oversaw a panel that included former British prime minister Tony Blair and Nobel Peace Prize–winning author Elie Wiesel, among others, at the World Economic Forum in Davos, Switzerland. In 2009, she hosted an hour-long special called *The Middle East Challenge*, synthesizing her work of the previous years to present a snapshot of political, economic, and religious issues in the entire region.

INTERNATIONAL DESK AND THE ARAB SPRING

Gorani was an anchor, alongside Jim Clancy, of CNN's *Your World Today* between 2006 and 2009, when she became the host of a new show called *International Desk*. Still, she continued to work as a correspondent, and her reporting of the 2010 earthquake in Haiti, a catastrophic event that killed thousands of people, played a significant part in CNN winning the prestigious Golden Nymph Award at the Monte Carlo Television Festival that year. When answering a later interview question regarding the worst scenes that she had encountered in the field, she responded that the devastation of the earthquake in Haiti had been one of the most difficult to witness: "Seeing tens of thousands of people dead, and the sheer scale of that disaster was hard to fathom, and I still think about it pretty regularly, even to this day," she told Allam.

In 2011, she covered the Egyptian revolution that led to the removal from power of Hosni Mubarak, who had served as Egypt's autocratic president for approximately thirty years. Inspired by similar events in Tunisia, the revolution was a part of a larger series of uprisings across the Middle East known as the Arab Spring. Gorani covered the eighteen-day revolution on the ground in Cairo's Tahrir Square. Her fluency in Arabic—she is also fluent in English and French—allowed her to navigate the various and conflicting factions protesting in the street. Along with other journalists at the network, she received a News and Documentary Emmy Award for her reporting.

In 2012, Gorani covered the Egyptian election, in which Mohamed Morsi of the Muslim Brotherhood was named Egypt's first democratically elected president. (Morsi, who died in 2019, was removed from office in a coup a year later.) After leaving *International Desk* in 2014, she began hosting a show called *The World Right Now*. She also began covering the Syrian refugee crisis. When a wave of protests had erupted in Syria in 2011, President Bashar al-Assad's government cracked down on dissenters, engendering a brutal, multisided civil war. Gorani, who covered aspects of the Syrian refugee crisis starting around 2014, saw the events in Syria as indicative of the change taking place across the entire region.

The violence forced millions of Syrians from their homes. (Gorani's own family members left in 2012, when fighting reached Aleppo.) Refugees fled to nearby Turkey, Lebanon, Iraq, and Jordan, but as these countries grew concerned about the increasing influx of immigrants, Syrians traveled further, to North America, Europe, and Asia. Although European countries did not face the strain of countries like Turkey and Lebanon, some moved to limit refugee programs, exacerbating an already dire crisis. Gorani reported the unfolding story from Lebanon.

HALA GORANI TONIGHT

In 2015, Gorani was part of a team that covered the events following a terrorist attack at the Paris offices of *Charlie Hebdo*, a satirical French magazine. That same year, Gorani was criticized for interviewing the older sister of Samy Amimour, who had been identified as one of the terrorists who executed the attacks at the Bataclan concert hall in Paris on November 13, 2015. She defended the interview at the 2016 Women World Changers Summit in Melbourne, Australia, saying, as quoted by Nassim Khadem for the *Sydney Morning Herald* (21 Oct. 2016), "We do these stories precisely because they give us understanding of the very things that make us uncomfortable, that disgust us and that scare us as well."

It was announced in late 2017 that *The World Right Now* was being replaced with *Hala Gorani Tonight*. A CNN press release (3 Nov. 2017) quoted the senior vice president of CNN International's programming, Mike McCarthy, as saying, "The world has changed almost beyond recognition in the past three years, and the need to put such change into context has never been greater. There are few people who can do that like Hala, and this new show will allow her to use her formidable skill and intellect to give viewers the full picture." In 2018, Gorani and her team won a News and Documentary Emmy Award for Outstanding Hard News Feature Story in a Newscast for a special called "Syria: Gasping for Life in Khan Sheikhoun." The special provided an in-depth report on a chemical attack that occurred in Khan Sheikhoun, Syria, on April 4, 2017. The attack killed dozens of people, including many children, and footage as well as photographs from Khan Sheikhoun provoked international outrage. That same year, Gorani was also one of the anchors nominated for an Emmy Award for CNN for Outstanding Breaking News Coverage based on reporting on the suicide bombing outside of an Ariana Grande concert in Manchester, England, on May 22, 2017. Continuing to speak with high-profile figures, in early 2020 she aired an interview with model Naomi Campbell on *Hala Gorani Tonight* that included discussion of diversity in the fashion industry.

PERSONAL LIFE

In 2015, Gorani married photojournalist Christian Streib in Morocco. That same year, she was awarded an honorary doctorate from George Mason University and gave the school's commencement address. Based in London, Gorani has a dog named Louis.

SUGGESTED READING

Crane, Kelly. "The Other Side of CNN Anchor Hala Gorani." *Gulf News*, 5 May 2008, gulfnews.com/lifestyle/the-other-side-of-cnn-anchor-hala-gorani-1.103575. Accessed 28 July 2020.

Gorani, Hala. "Hala Gorani Reveals What It Takes to Be an Experienced International

Journalist." Interview by Roula Allam. *About Her*, www.abouther.com/node/2101/people/features/hala-gorani-reveals-what-it-takes-be-experienced-international-journalist. Accessed 13 Aug. 2020.

———. "Season Finale with CNN's Hala Gorani—Her Story, Parity in Media, and Patterns in Politics." Interview by Rana Nawas. *When Women Win*, 25 June 2018, whenwomenwinpodcast.com/season-finale-with-cnns-hala-gorani-her-story-parity-in-media-and-patterns-in-politics/. Transcript. Accessed 28 July 2020.

"Hala Gorani Tonight Debuts on CNN International." *CNN Press Room*, 3 Nov. 2017, cnnpressroom.blogs.cnn.com/2017/11/03/hala-gorani-tonight-debuts-on-cnn-international/. Accessed 13 Aug. 2020.

Khadem, Nassim. "Why the US Media Turned on Donald Trump, According to CNN Anchor Hala Gorani." *The Sydney Morning Herald*, 21 Oct. 2016, www.smh.com.au/business/companies/why-the-us-media-turned-on-donald-trump-according-to-cnn-anchor-hala-gorani-20161021-gs7f9i.html. Accessed 10 Aug. 2020.

—*Molly Hagan*

Photo by Aspect Ventures via Wikimedia Commons

Theresia Gouw

Date of birth: 1968
Occupation: Venture capitalist

Theresia Gouw, a venture capitalist, began her career as a partner at the well-known venture capital (VC) firm Accel in the early 2000s, where she became an early investor in the social networking site Facebook. In 2014 she partnered with a former colleague, Jennifer Fonstad, to found Aspect, a VC firm that was notable for focusing on early investment in women-led companies; Gouw and Fonstad parted ways in 2018. Gouw cofounded Acrew, the rare multigenerational VC firm, in 2019.

Gouw was named alongside people like Bill Gates, Jeff Bezos, and Larry Page on *Time* magazine's annual list of the forty most influential people in tech in 2013. She has also appeared on *Forbes's* annual Midas List of the best venture capital investors nine times, including in 2020. Gouw is also featured in Julian Guthrie's 2019 book, *Alpha Girls: The Women Upstarts Who Took on Silicon Valley's Male Culture and Made the Deals of a Lifetime*, about female venture capitalists.

EARLY LIFE AND EDUCATION

Theresia Gouw, who is also known as Theresia Gouw Ranzetta, was born to parents of Chinese descent in Jakarta, Indonesia. In the early 1970s, when she was about three years old, she and her family fled the persecution of the Suharto regime, which was targeting the country's ethnic Chinese minority. In Indonesia, her father, Steve, was an orthodontist and her mother, Bertha, was a nurse. Upon arrival in the United States, however, they were initially forced to pursue different careers. The family, including Gouw's younger sister, Andrea, settled in Middleport, near Buffalo, New York. There her mother waited tables at a Chinese restaurant. "My dad got a job as a dishwasher and went back to school at SUNY Buffalo in order to get his dental certification to work in America," Gouw told Angel Au-Yeung for *Forbes* (11 July 2018).

Gouw attended a local high school, where her parents, particularly her father, pushed her to achieve perfect grades. She also played sports and was elected homecoming queen and prom queen. Gouw studied engineering—one of two acceptable majors set forth by her parents—at Brown University and graduated magna cum laude in 1990. Her engineering graduating class, she told Rebecca Jarvis for the podcast *No Limits* (1 Nov. 2018), "was 90 percent male, 10 percent female. Interestingly in venture capital today depending on which numbers you look at it's either 91 or 93 percent male and either 9 or 7 percent female on the investing partner side. So I guess without knowing it, it prepared me well; it was fairly similar."

Gouw took a summer internship as an engineer at a General Motors (GM) plant outside of Buffalo, where she was one of just five women. There she discovered that she was more interested in the work of the company's product managers. "I was working in a building with a thousand engineers, and I realized what I liked most was product management," she told Au-Yeung. "But the people who moved out of frontline engineering and into [product management] roles all had MBAs." Gouw began studying for the Graduate Management Admission Test (GMAT) and got a job as a management consultant at Bain and Company in Boston before enrolling as a graduate student at Stanford University. Later, she recalled downloading Mosaic, an early web browser, in the Stanford computer lab in 1994. The moment solidified Gouw's interest in the burgeoning tech sector. She earned her MBA degree in 1996.

ACCEL

The same year Gouw graduated from Stanford, she and several classmates raised $1 million in venture funding to cofound Release Software. By 1999, she was looking for other opportunities. A Release investor suggested venture capital. "He thought my experience coupled with my engineering degree and MBA, plus my inherent interest in the early stages of startups, would be a good fit for this field," she told Diana Kapp for *Marie Claire* (10 Apr. 2013).

Gouw joined Accel, a VC firm in Palo Alto, as an investment associate at the height of the tech bubble. Her first several years at Accel were shaped by the ensuing economic downturn. She described sitting with a founder and looking at the company's balance sheet after the 2000 crash as one of her toughest days on the job.

Within a few years, however, business turned around. In her interview with Jarvis, Gouw described VC as "an apprenticeship business" and credited partners Breyer and Arthur Patterson as mentors. In 2005 Gouw following Breyer's lead, investing in a fifteen-month-old social media company called Facebook. "We had looked at a lot of other social media platforms before and some of them actually had a larger number of users," Gouw told Au-Yeung. "But we'd never seen anything like Facebook's daily active usage at the time. Two thirds of users were using it every day, and half of them were using it two hours a day. That's a really meaningful service and platform, and that was the thing that really stood out at the time."

Gouw eventually became a partner at Accel. During her tenure, she oversaw investments in Interlace Systems, which was purchased by Oracle in 2007; the open-source email platform Zimbra, purchased by Yahoo in 2007; and an email organization tool called Xoopit, which was also purchased by Yahoo in 2009. Gouw oversaw investment in the real estate listing platform Trulia and in Glam Media, a digital lifestyle media company that, at its height, was worth over $1 billion; it shut down in 2016. She also oversaw investment in Birchbox, a subscription beauty service, that experienced a similar boom-and-bust trajectory.

ASPECT VENTURES

In 2014 Gouw left Accel to launch her own VC firm, Aspect Ventures, with Jennifer Fonstad, a former partner and managing director at Draper Fisher Jurvetson. The two had met twenty years earlier when they both worked at Bain and Company and then had worked together at Release. Gouw later described their relationship as a mentorship-turned-collaboration, with Fonstad as the mentor.

Aspect's mission focused on early-stage mobile start-ups. "I co-founded Aspect with the idea to create venture the way it was in the late 1990s, by creating a fund that was just laser-focused on the early stage," Gouw explained to Au-Yeung. Fonstad and Gouw also emphasized the value of investing in diverse companies. "We think as women we bring a different perspective to the boardroom and these companies in how they approach problem-solving and strategic thinking," Fonstad told Claire Cain Miller for the *New York Times* (5 Feb. 2014). "It's clearly not an industry that puts a lot of women in it, and we're trying in our own way to illustrate how diversity makes a difference." For instance, between 2011 and 2013, according to a Babson College study cited by Davey Alba for *Wired* (14 May 2015), just three percent of companies that received VC funding had female CEOs. By contrast, 40 percent of the companies Aspect invested in its first year had female founders or cofounders.

In their first year Fonstad and Gouw invested in ten companies with their own capital. Among those companies were Forescout, a cybersecurity company that Gouw had discovered at Accel, and *The Muse*, a career advice website aimed at millennials. Gouw sits on the board of both companies. Aspect introduced its first official fund, worth an impressive $150 million, in 2015, and oversaw investments in companies including Chime, a banking app, and Vida Health, a self-described virtual care company. "We have a motto that if we invest in a company, we reserve and plan to invest in that company all the way through until a liquidity event," Gouw explained to Murray Newlands for *Forbes* (2 Sept. 2016). Forescout was the first Aspect investment to go public in 2017.

Aspect raised its second fund, worth $181 million, in 2018. Backers for the second fund included Melinda Gates, of the Gates Foundation, and Cisco CEO Chuck Robbins. Aspect reupped funding for networking and security company Cato Networks and the security intelligence company Exabeam, among others.

Gouw and Fonstad parted ways in 2019, citing, Fonstad told the *Wall Street Journal* (16 Sept. 2019), "different leadership styles and different ways of operating at the portfolio level."

ACREW CAPITAL

Gouw, along with several former Aspect employees, founded their own firm called Acrew Capital. Though she has declined to speak about why she left Aspect, she has emphasized the governing philosophy of Acrew. "I have four co-founders in Acrew Capital, so there's five of us, and we operate as a team, and we all have equal say in investment decisions, and that's my management style," she said, as quoted by Connie Loizos for *Tech Crunch* (18 Dec. 2019). She has also noted that Acrew is "multigenerational," a rarity among VC firms. Within a few months of its founding, Acrew raised a $250 million debut fund. Early investments included Chime, as well as Klar, a similar banking app, in Mexico City.

PERSONAL LIFE

Gouw married Tim Ranzetta, whom she met at Bain. They have two children.

SUGGESTED READING

Alba, Davey. "Women-Led VC Firms Are on the Rise—and Raising Lots of Cash." *Wired*, 14 May 2015, www.wired.com/2015/05/aspect-ventures-150m-fund. Accessed 13 July 2020.

Au-Yeung, Angel. "How Theresia Gouw Became America's Richest Female Venture Capitalist." *Forbes*, 11 July 2018, www.forbes.com/sites/angelauyeung/2018/07/11/theresia-gouw-newcomer-self-made-women-2018/#46484b6554ca. Accessed 12 July 2020.

Jarvis, Rebecca. "'The Biggest Mistake That Entrepreneurs Often Make Is Underestimating the Competition'—Theresia Gouw." *No Limits*, 1 Nov. 2018, www.linkedin.com/pulse/biggest-mistake-entrepreneurs-often-make-competition-rebecca-jarvis. Accessed 12 July 2020.

Kapp, Diana. "Theresia Gouw: Silicon Valley Big Shot." *Marie Claire*, 10 Apr. 2013, www.marieclaire.com/career-advice/news/a7557/theresia-gouw-silicon-valley/. Accessed 12 July 2020.

Loizos, Connie. "Theresia Gouw's 'Multigenerational' New Firm, Acrew, Just Closed a $250 Million Debut Fund." *Tech Crunch*, 18 Dec. 2019, techcrunch.com/2019/12/18/theresia-gouws-multigenerational-new-firm-acrew-just-closed-a-250-million-debut-fund. Accessed 13 July 2020.

Miller, Claire Cain. "Two of Venture Capital's Senior Women Start a New Firm." *The New York Times*, 5 Feb. 2014, bits.blogs.nytimes.com/2014/02/05/two-of-venture-capitals-senior-women-start-a-new-firm/. Accessed 12 July 2020.

Newlands, Murray. "Bridging the Funding Gap: An Interview with the Women behind Aspect Ventures." *Forbes*, 2 Sept. 2016, www.forbes.com/sites/mnewlands/2016/09/02/bridging-the-funding-gap-an-interview-with-the-women-behind-aspect-ventures. Accessed 13 July 2020.

—Molly Hagan

Alan Gratz

Born: January 27, 1972
Occupation: Author

On *Alan Gratz*'s official website in 2020, one of his banner mottos was "Putting Fictional Kids in Danger Since 2006"—a more than apt description of the type of novels he loves to produce. His work for middle schoolers involves dropping young adults into serious peril and having them embark on daring exploits, often in historical contexts. In an interview with Sarah Grochowski for *Publishers Weekly* (18 Oct. 2018), Gratz explained why he felt it was important to write for middle school: "Middle schoolers particularly are at this amazing time when they're beginning to look beyond the world of their school, their street, their home. They're starting to look at the larger world and ask bigger questions. . . . Those are the kids I am writing for."

The novels Gratz published in the late 2010s are works of historical fiction about young adults from past eras. These include *Refugee* (2017), about three young refugees from different times escaping dangers in their homelands; *Grenade* (2018), about a Japanese schoolboy who is charged with defending Okinawa from invading US forces during World War II; and *Allies* (2019), about a multinational group of young people facing the challenges of the D-Day invasion of France together.

Although his books often detail harrowing historical subjects, Gratz believes that the object of his work is to entertain as well as inspire young readers to have hope. In an interview with Jon Little for *BookPage* (3 Aug. 2017), he remarked, "I'm a naturally hopeful person. I like to think the best of people, and I always expect the world will (over time—if not in the short term!) get better and better. . . . I don't require a Hollywood ending for every story; I'm not that naive.

But I cannot write a book in which there is no hope."

EARLY LIFE AND EDUCATION

Alan Michael Gratz was born in Knoxville, Tennessee, on January 27, 1972. A love of storytelling came to him early, when he used to make up bedtime stories for his younger brother, some of which involved acting them out with action figures. Despite this interest in storytelling, he was not an impassioned reader at this time. On his official website, Gratz recalled, "I didn't read a lot of books when I was a kid. I was more likely to be out building a fort in the woods or inventing a fake country or playing video games."

Decades before he became a young-adult writer, Gratz's aunt dug into their family's history and discovered that their ancestor, Louis Alexander Gratz, had a secret. "He was a penniless Prussian orphan who came to the United States in the 1860s, joined the Union Army and fought his way south with [General William Tecumseh] Sherman's troops," Gratz recalled in an interview with Tina Jordan for the *New York Times* (3 Aug. 2018). "He was Jewish, but had abandoned his religion and heritage when he made his new start in America. Family lore has it that learning our ancestors were Jewish is what gave my anti-Semitic grandfather a fatal heart attack."

For middle school and high school, Gratz attended Knoxville's Webb School, where his father, Ron Gratz, taught for thirty years. As an undergraduate he studied creative writing at the University of Tennessee, Knoxville, and earned a College Scholars degree. Later he completed a master's degree in English education at the same institution.

TEACHER AND PLAYWRIGHT

Prior to becoming a young-adult author, Gratz worked as an eighth grade teacher for some years. He thoroughly enjoyed the experience and believes his students helped to inspire his novels, recalling of teaching to Grochowski, "My favorite part was the eighth graders. I could do without administration, grading, and parents, but being in the classroom with the students was awesome." He added that he enjoys visiting schools as a young-adult novelist, because it allows him to be in the classroom without doing all the work of a teacher. In addition to his teaching, he also wrote plays, magazine articles, and more than six thousand radio commercials.

After becoming a published novelist, he continued to teach on occasion. In 2010, he taught historical fiction writing to middle school students at Tokyo's American School as their first artist in residence. The following year, he was the children's writer in residence at Columbus, Ohio's Thurber House, a nonprofit literary center and museum that was once the home of New *Yorker* humorist and writer James Thurber. In 2017, Gratz was the writer in residence at the Jakarta Intercultural School in Jakarta, Indonesia.

BEGINNING A CAREER WRITING FOR YOUNG ADULTS

Gratz began steadily publishing for young adults in 2006, when he published his first novel, *Samurai Shortstop*. He was inspired to write the novel after finding a picture of a man in a kimono throwing out the first pitch at a baseball game in Japan in 1915, but it explores the relationship of a boy and his father after his uncle commits ritual suicide. The following year, the novel was selected as one of the American Library Association's (ALA) Top Ten Best Books for Young Adults.

Gratz then penned the first book in his Horatio Wilkes Mystery series, *Something Rotten* (2007), which was quickly followed by a sequel, *Something Wicked* (2008). The idea for a teen detective character had been percolating in Gratz's brain since he had taken a mystery and detective fiction class as a teenager in college. Each book was inspired by a Shakespearian play: the first was inspired by *Hamlet*; the second by *Macbeth*. *Something Rotten* was honored as a 2008 ALA Quick Pick for Young Adult Readers, and Gratz had planned additional novels in the series, but unfortunately it did not sell well enough for his publisher to continue.

For his next pair of books, *The Brooklyn Nine* (2010) and *Fantasy Baseball* (2011), Gratz used his favorite sport, baseball, as inspiration. In *The Brooklyn Nine*, he imagines nine generations of a family playing the sport against the backdrop of American life in each of those periods. In the latter, he concocts a fantasy baseball tournament in which characters from classic children's novels, like *Peter Pan* and *The Wonderful Wizard of Oz*, compete against one another. *The Brooklyn Nine* was one of the ALA's Top Ten Sports Books for Youth and Top Ten Historical Books for Youth.

After completing a Star Trek novel, *Starfleet Academy: The Assassination Game* (2012), Gratz took a deep dive into a new series, which he told his wife that he wanted to be "full of awesome," according to his official website. To that end, he threw in airships and brains in jars, secret societies and ray guns, clockwork machine men and mad scientists, and more. The first book in the series, *The League of Seven*, proved so popular when it was published in 2014 that Gratz was able to complete the League of Seven trilogy with *The Dragon Lantern* (2015) and *The Monster War* (2016). On his website, he wrote that he would have loved *The League of Seven* as a middle school student. In his interview with Grochowski, Gratz explained his goal in writing page turners: "My number one goal is to write a book that a kid can't put down. I'm trying to write a book that will grab you by the lapels and won't let you go."

CONTINUING TO WRITE AND EXPLORE HISTORY

With that in mind, Gratz explored more historical contexts for his fiction in the next phase of his career. His novel *Prisoner B-3087* (2013) was based on the experiences of a real-life Holocaust survivor as he attempted to live through the horrific experience of being interred at a Nazi concentration camp. In 2014, the novel was named one of the Young Adult Library Services Association's (YALSA) Best Fiction for Young Readers.

Gratz next published *Code of Honor* (2015), a 2016 YALSA Quick Pick for Reluctant Readers. The novel tells the story of an Iranian American teenager named Kamran Smith who joins the US military because he wants to follow in his big brother Darius's footsteps. But when Darius is falsely accused of being a terrorist, Kamran races to clear his brother's name.

For *Projekt 1065* (2016), Gratz explored the Hitler Youth and their role in Nazi Germany during World War II. While researching his novel, he discovered that Ireland had remained neutral during the war but had employed spies among its diplomatic ranks. The main character in *Projekt 1065* is Michael O'Shaunessey, the son of the Irish ambassador to Nazi Germany who infiltrates the Hitler Youth.

After penning *Ban This Book*, a 2017 novel about modern students challenging adults who wish to ban certain books from libraries, Gratz again returned to a (partially) World War II theme in his *New York Times* Best Seller *Refugee* (2017), which tells the interconnected stories of three young refugees from different places and eras: Josef, a Jewish refugee from the Nazis; Isabel, a refugee from Cuba's Communist dictatorship; and Mahmoud, a refugee from the civil war in Syria. *Refugee* went on to earn several awards and honors, including the Sydney Taylor Book Award, the National Jewish Book Award, the Cybils Middle Grade Fiction Award, a Charlotte Huck Award Honor, and a Malka Penn Award for Human Rights Honor. It was also named a 2018 Global Read Aloud Book.

In *Grenade* (2018), Gratz delved into the Japanese perspective of World War II, as seen in the story of Hideki, a middle school student who is pulled from school to serve in the Blood and Iron Student Corps. He and the other young soldiers are given a grenade and told not to come back until they have killed an American soldier. The novel also follows a young US Marine named Ray, who has landed on Okinawa to fight his first battle.

His 2019 book *Allies* (2019) is about a multinational group of young adults seeking to save Europe following the D-Day invasion of June 1944. Like many of its predecessors, Gratz's book received excellent reviews. A reviewer for *Kirkus* (14 July 2019) noted about *Allies*, "The horrors of war and the decisions and emotions it entails are presented with unflinching honesty through characters readers can feel for. In the end, all the threads come together to drive home the point that allies are 'stronger together.' Both an excellent, inclusive narration of important historical events and a fast-paced, entertaining read."

PERSONAL LIFE

Gratz resides in Asheville, North Carolina, with his wife, Wendi, and their daughter, Jo. In addition to working as a full-time author, Gratz counts among his hobbies reading widely; playing board games, video games, and role-playing games; and building things like chicken coops, woodsheds, and catapults. A baseball fanatic, he supports the Ashville Tourists, a minor league club, the Los Angeles Dodgers, and the Hiroshima Carp, a pro team in Japan.

SUGGESTED READING

"Frequently Asked Questions." *Alan Gratz*, 2020, www.alangratz.com/frequently-asked-questions/. Accessed 9 July 2020.

Gratz, Alan. "Exclusive Interview with Alan Gratz, Author of *Refugee*." Interview by Stephanie Renae Johnson. *The Passed Note*, 26 July 2017, thepassednotereview.com/exclusive-interview-with-alan-gratz-author-of-refugee/. Accessed 9 July 2020.

———. "*Refugee*." Review of *Refugee*. *Kirkus*, 10 May 2017, www.kirkusreviews.com/book-reviews/alan-gratz/refugee/. Accessed 9 July 2020.

———. "Interviews: Alan Gratz, Following Young Refugees across History." Interview by Jon Little. *BookPage*, 3 Aug. 2017, bookpage.com/interviews/21676-alan-gratz-childrens. Accessed 9 July 2020.

———. "Q & A with Alan Gratz." Interview by Sarah Grochowski. *Publishers Weekly*, PWxyz, LLC, 18 Oct. 2018, www.publishersweekly.com/pw/by-topic/childrens/childrens-authors/article/78345-q-a-with-alan-gratz.html. Accessed 9 July 2020.

———. "*Allies*." Review of *Allies*. *Kirkus*, 14 July 2019, www.kirkusreviews.com/book-reviews/alan-gratz/allies/. Accessed 9 July 2020.

Jordan, Tina. "That Huge Surprise in His Own Family Genealogy? It's Playing Out in His Novels." *The New York Times*, 3 Aug. 2018, www.nytimes.com/2018/08/03/books/review/refugee-alan-gratz-best-seller.html. Accessed 7 July 2020.

—*Christopher Mari*

Guo Pei

Date of birth: March 12, 1967
Occupation: Fashion designer

"The measurement of a person's success is how far you can go, not which road you take," fashion designer Guo Pei explained to Jane Gayduk for *Interview* magazine (29 Sept. 2017). "It is also necessary to be loyal to your initial choices. If you choose and change unceasingly, there will be no time for you to achieve success. Time is [a] human's most precious asset. We have to use the time we have to do the things we love." Indeed, Guo has dedicated much of her career to doing just that, designing ornate garments—often intricately embroidered gowns—that reflect Chinese textile-arts techniques and design motifs as well as the influence of both real and fairytale history. A particularly popular designer among Chinese celebrities, she rose to fame in the United States in 2015, when the pop star Rihanna wore one of her eye-catching designs to that year's Met Gala. After gaining entrance into the prestigious, highly selective French haute couture community the following year, Guo expanded her reach further, all the while designing garments that reflected her own unique artistic vision.

EARLY LIFE AND EDUCATION
Guo Pei was born in China on March 12, 1967. Her father served as an officer in the Chinese army, and her mother was a teacher. She spent her early years in Beijing, where she lived with her parents and maternal grandmother. Guo developed an interest in designing and making clothing at a young age and first began to learn to sew as a toddler. Her mother made much of the family's clothing, and as Guo grew older, she played an increasingly important role in assisting her mother, whose poor eyesight made the work difficult. Although utilitarian, unembellished clothing was in favor during Guo's childhood, the era of Cultural Revolution, Guo was nevertheless deeply influenced by the Chinese fashion of earlier periods. This was thanks largely to her grandmother, who told her numerous stories about the designs and fashion landscape of the pre-Communist era.

Photo by Richard Bord/Getty Images

In 1982, at the age of fifteen, Guo enrolled in the newly founded fashion design program at what became the Beijing Institute of Fashion Technology (BIFT). Vocational in focus, the program was designed to teach its participants the skills necessary to work in ready-to-wear clothing manufacturing. Although Guo already had strong sewing skills and a creative approach to fashion, she was inexperienced in other key areas, including sketching designs. In her interview with Gayduk, she admitted that she created her first ever fashion sketch during a vocational exam. "At that time, out of the 500 candidates, only 26 passed. I was very lucky to be selected as one of these 26 people and I entered the fashion profession," she told Gayduk. "I'm still very shocked when I think of that moment." After completing the four-year fashion design program, Guo graduated in 1986.

EARLY CAREER
After completing her training in fashion design, Guo began her career with a state-owned manufacturer of children's clothing. Less than two years later she moved to a private company specializing in women's apparel, which would remain her primary focus over the next decades. In that role, Guo was responsible for designing ready-to-wear fashion, with a wide audience in mind as opposed to an individual client. Her focus began to shift, however, when a prospective customer approached her to design a custom ensemble. Despite an initial skepticism of designing for a single customer rather than for many potential customers, which Guo later

noted in interviews felt like a waste, her perspective changed after she saw how the customer responded to her work. "I was so pleased and realized I was doing a very meaningful thing—improving my customer's image," she explained to Chen Xi for the *Global Times* (31 July 2019). "This was a different kind of joy than what I got designing mass-produced garments."

During the period that followed, Guo took on an increasing number of private commissions and even delved into costume design, creating pieces for a televised historical drama. Yet despite her increasing devotion to custom work, she did not yet consider herself to be a couturier (a designer specializing in creating one-of-a-kind custom pieces) or to be working within the realm of high fashion. "At the time, I didn't think about it as haute couture, I was just following my heart and enjoying making my customers look beautiful and gorgeous," she told Chen Xi. "After designing a number of outfits and gaining a lot of experience, I realized that I was in the field of haute couture." In 1997 Guo decided to dedicate her career entirely to high fashion, founding the couture label Rose Studio.

HAUTE COUTURE

Guo has become known for her ornate, highly embellished garments that often feature adornments such as beadwork, natural materials such as feathers and fur, and gold and silver thread, and for her substantial use of embroidery—particularly Chinese embroidery techniques that had all but disappeared from public use during the mid-to-late twentieth century. The imagery in her pieces often alludes to Chinese history and symbolism, such as imperial dragons and popular porcelains, but also incorporates inspirations from Western architecture, royalty, and art movements. To produce garments featuring such detailed and time-intensive elements, she employed a sizable group of skilled artisans, eventually working with as many as five hundred workers. "The artisans are my most precious assets," Guo told Vivian Chen for the *South China Morning Post* magazine *Style* (7 Nov. 2017). "I nurtured them from day one. When we first started, we didn't have many references or role models that we could follow. We started from scratch and I'm very proud of the work they do today."

As Guo built her reputation as a designer, her work gained popularity among China's celebrities and wealthy residents and was featured in high-profile events such as the CCTV New Year's Gala, an annual television special that reaches an audience numbering in the hundreds of millions. She held her first fashion show, titled *Samsara*, during the 2006 China International Fashion Week. The pieces presented during the show drew inspiration from a variety of natural and historical influences, including the passage of time and French military attire of the Napoleonic era.

The garments created by Guo and her employees ranged from expensive but wearable evening gowns and wedding dresses to ornate gowns and other garments intended more as display pieces than as wearable clothing. Although she worked exclusively as a couturier during the first decades of Rose Studio's existence and did not produce ready-to-wear items, Guo eventually turned to ready-to-wear Chinese bridal apparel as a means to fund the creation of additional high-fashion garments that would be costly to produce but unlikely to sell. She also later collaborated with MAC to produce a cosmetics line.

Given the substantial amount of time and labor needed to create many of her pieces, Guo held relatively few fashion shows compared to other couture designers. She preferred to devote her time to designing and constructing original work rather than to planning and traveling for shows. Yet despite their relative rarity, Guo's fashion shows came to attract significant attention in China. Her work also gained further international exposure through her contribution of garments to the 2008 Beijing Olympic Games opening ceremony.

GLOBAL REACH

A new audience took note of Guo's designs in mid-2015, when New York City's Metropolitan Museum of Art (commonly known as the Met) featured examples of her work in the exhibit *China: Through the Looking Glass*. At that year's Met Gala, the annual fundraiser for the museum's Costume Institute, the singer Rihanna wore a Guo-designed garment known as "The Great Queen." A striking yellow cape gown, "The Great Queen" featured extensive embroidery, a flowing train, and more than fifty pounds of silk fabric and other materials. Although the Guo pieces featured in the museum's exhibit likewise drew attention, the piece worn by Rihanna became the center of widespread media and social media discussion that substantially raised Guo's profile within the United States. The following year saw the premiere of the making-of documentary *The First Monday in May*, which chronicled the development of the *China: Through the Looking Glass* exhibit and featured appearances by Guo, among other designers. In light of her work, Guo was included in the Time 100 Most Influential People list for 2016.

The year 2016 was key for Guo as an influential member of the global high-fashion community. That year the Chambre Syndicale de la Haute Couture (now the Fédération de la Haute Couture et de la Mode), the French body that regulates haute couture, admitted Guo as a guest member. This rendered her eligible to show her couture during Paris Haute Couture Week and recognized her membership in that prestigious and highly regulated community. The first Chinese designer to be admitted to that body, Guo was pleased to have the opportunity to show her work in Paris. "I respect the values of the couture federation as they respect their members' passion, craftsmanship and how they can contribute to the living art—haute couture—in the future," she told Vivian Chen. "Being on the official couture calendar has really taken me and my team to new heights. I feel that we are growing with every collection." In addition to debuting her first collection in Paris, Guo opened a studio there in keeping with the couture federation's requirements.

FASHION AS ART

Throughout her career, Guo was deeply invested in promoting the understanding of clothing as art. For Guo, haute couture "shows many years of culture and art, and it's very historical and emotional. It transcends memory and challenges those who experience it to continue to be creative in their roles within society," as she put it to Ali Webb for the magazine *L'Officiel* (6 Sept. 2019). "It also challenges our view of the past." She also saw it as a means of transcultural exchange, telling Chen Xi, "As a kind of artwork, [clothing design] does not have a border. Everyone can enjoy its beauty because my designs are also a language, touching people's souls."

In addition to the 2015 Met exhibit, Guo displayed her designs at museums in a variety of countries, including the Musée des Arts Décoratifs in Paris and the Asian Civilisations Museum in Singapore. A solo exhibition featuring dozens of Guo-designed garments, footwear, and accessories opened at the Savannah College of Art and Design's SCAD FASH Museum of Fashion and Film in September 2017.

In 2019, Guo signed a contract with the high-end auction house Sotheby's to both auction off some of her work and display other pieces alongside complementary works of visual art. "It's rare to see haute couture collaborate with art and transcend the two spheres at the same time. It's rare and it's great," she told Webb following the announcement of her partnership with Sotheby's. "Because it's not something you see on a daily basis, this is a great opportunity to show haute couture to the world." Guo went on to curate the Sotheby's auction GOLD: The Midas Touch, held in October 2019 and featuring more than sixty golden items and works of art, including an ornate bridal gown designed by Guo herself.

PERSONAL LIFE

Guo is married to Cao Bao Jie, an international textile dealer. They have two daughters together. In addition to her work in fashion, Guo was known to collect teddy bears. She lives with her family outside Beijing.

SUGGESTED READING

Chen, Vivian. "Chinese Fashion Designer Guo Pei Goes Global with Army of Artisans." *Style*, 7 Nov. 2017, www.scmp.com/magazines/style/fashion-beauty/article/2118731/chinese-fashion-designer-guo-pei-goes-global-army. Accessed 13 Dec. 2019.

Chen Xi. "An Interview with China's Queen of Haute Couture: Guo Pei." *Global Times*, 31 July 2019, www.globaltimes.cn/content/1159855.shtml. Accessed 13 Dec. 2019.

Gayduk, Jane. "Life Lessons from Couture Queen Guo Pei." *Interview*, 29 Sept. 2017, www.interviewmagazine.com/fashion/life-lessons-couture-queen-guo-pei. Accessed 13 Dec. 2019.

"Guo Pei." *Business of Fashion*, 2018, www.businessoffashion.com/amp/community/people/guo-pei. Accessed 13 Dec. 2019.

Guo Pei: Couture Beyond; Curriculum Guide. SCAD, 2017, www.scadfash.org/sites/all/themes/scadfash/images/Guo-Pei-lesson-plan.pdf.

Thurman, Judith. "China's Homegrown High-Fashion Designer." *The New Yorker*, 2019, www.newyorker.com/magazine/2016/03/21/guo-pei-chinas-homegrown-high-fashion-designer. Accessed 16 Dec. 2019.

Webb, Ali. "For Guo Pei, Fashion Is an Eclectic Art." *L'Officiel*, 6 Sept. 2019, www.lofficielusa.com/fashion/guo-pei-sothebys-interview-2019. Accessed 13 Dec. 2019.

—Joy Crelin

Hildur Guðnadóttir

Born: September 4, 1982
Occupation: Musician and composer

For cellist and composer Hildur Guðnadóttir, obtaining fame and recognition was never a goal. "I'm not really a person who seeks out attention much," she told Jon Blistein for *Rolling Stone* (13 Jan. 2020). "I've always felt more comfortable in the shadows." Yet while Guðnadóttir may not have actively pursued the spotlight, her critically acclaimed work as a composer drew her considerable attention nonetheless. In particular, her contributions to the television miniseries *Chernobyl* (2019) and the supervillain film *Joker* (2019) earned the Icelandic musician widespread recognition as one of film and television composing world's major forces.

A cellist from the age of five, Guðnadóttir was born into a musical family and studied at prominent music schools in Iceland and Germany. She began performing with bands as a teenager, later launched a career as a solo artist, and by 2011 had begun to establish herself as a composer of scores for films and television shows. That career shift was not a calculated one for Guðnadóttir, who told Valentin Maniglia for *Score It* (21 Aug. 2019), "I didn't have any ambition to become a film composer, I just loved doing music." Over the next years her love of making music led her to contribute partial or total scores to numerous films as well as to the Icelandic television series *Ófærð* (*Trapped*), for which she earned an Edda Award (the Icelandic equivalent of a Grammy Award). It was *Chernobyl* and *Joker*, however, that fueled her true international breakthrough, winning Guðnadóttir an Emmy Award, a Grammy Award, and an Academy Award, among other honors.

EARLY LIFE AND EDUCATION

Hildur Ingveldardóttir Guðnadóttir was born in Iceland on September 4,1982. She grew up in Hafnarfjörður, a coastal city in the southwestern region of the country. Born into a musical family, Guðnadóttir was surrounded by music from a young age: her mother, Ingveldur Guðrún Ólafsdóttir, was a singer, while her father, Guðni Franzson, played clarinet and worked as a conductor. Her brother would similarly pursue a career in music, and other members of her extended family were also musicians. The musical environment in which she spent her childhood proved to be a memorable one. "Because I spent so much time hanging out at rehearsals, as a child, the instruments were coloured by the people that played them," she recalled in an interview for the website *Fifteen Questions*. "For example, the oboe not only has its sound, but it also has the personality of my aunt Eydís. Most instruments have a personality attached to them in my mind."

With the encouragement of her mother, who selected the instrument for her, Guðnadóttir began playing the cello at the age of five. She also sang in choirs as a young child. As the young musician's skills progressed, she studied at multiple music schools in Iceland, including the Reykjavík Music Academy and the Iceland Academy of the Arts (IAA). She later traveled to Germany to study at the Berlin University of the Arts and would remain in Berlin for many years, living and working in that city.

EARLY CAREER

In addition to studying classical cello technique, Guðnadóttir began to expand her repertoire in more experimental directions as a teenager. By the age of fifteen she had begun playing in bands. For the young musician, that period was essential to her development as an artist. "There are just so many dos and don'ts in classical upbringing," she explained to Alex Godfrey for the *Guardian* (13 Dec. 2019). "But when I started to play with bands, none of those rules applied, and I just felt such a sense of freedom. It really changed the way I saw music." After first performing with Icelandic bands such as Múm beginning in the late 1990s, Guðnadóttir went on to perform with numerous additional musical acts over the next decades, most of them broadly classifiable as either experimental or indie, including Schneider TM, Nico Muhly, the Knife, and Sunn O))).

In addition to working on her numerous collaborations, which included both traditional cello performances and more avant-garde work, Guðnadóttir began to establish herself as a solo artist during the first decade of the twenty-first century. Many of her compositions allowed her to explore her own psyche. "My solo music started as a way to really look inwards, and to spend time completely by myself with an instrument, without any outside dialogue," she recalled to Tim Greiving for *NPR* (3 Oct. 2019). "A lot of my music is kind of contemplative, and somehow that always tends to tilt on the darker side. My inner conversation is apparently quite dark."

Guðnadóttir released her first solo album, *Mount A*, under the name Lost in Hildurness in 2006. She followed that release with several additional albums released under her own name, including *Without Sinking* (2009), *Leyfðu Ljósinu* (Let the Light) (2012), and *Saman* (2014). Though considered solo albums rather than works with bands or other ensembles, Guðnadóttir's recordings remained highly collaborative works, featuring contributions from close friends, family members, and frequent creative partners.

COMPOSING FOR FILM AND TELEVISION

Although during her early career Guðnadóttir was best known for her solo recordings and work with bands, she also began to make a name for herself as a composer for film. Among her early works in that realm were scores for projects such as the American horror film *The Bleeding House* (2011), the Turkish-German production *Jîn* (2013), and the Icelandic thriller *The Oath* (2016). In addition to composing entire scores, she contributed individual songs to major films such as the award-winning 2015 historical drama *The Revenant* and played cello for the scores of films such as *Sicario* (2015) and *Arrival* (2016). The latter two films were both scored by the Icelandic composer Jóhann Jóhannsson, a frequent creative collaborator of Guðnadóttir.

She subsequently took over composing the score for the 2018 film *Mary Magdalene* from Jóhannsson following his death in 2018. That year also saw the release of the *Sicario* (Hitman) sequel *Sicario: Day of the Soldado*, which featured a score by Guðnadóttir.

As a composer, Guðnadóttir worked to develop scores that both fit the mood and tone of the project at hand but also actively enhanced the project's ability to convey its narrative. "When I tell a story—I say that because music is a big part of the storytelling—I try to dive as deep as I can into it, much like an actor who becomes the character he plays," she explained to Maniglia about her process. Though most often composing for feature films, Guðnadóttir also had the opportunity to explore the similar, yet distinct medium of television through her work for the Icelandic television series *Ófærð* (released in Anglophone countries under the title *Trapped*), which began airing in 2015. The following year, Guðnadóttir received Iceland's Edda Award for best music for her work on *Ófærð*, just one of many honors she would go on to receive for her compositions.

CHERNOBYL

The year 2019 represented a high point in Guðnadóttir's career, with the release of two major projects that would draw international attention to her work and earn her substantial critical acclaim. The first of those was the HBO miniseries *Chernobyl*, a historical television work about the 1986 accident at the titular Soviet nuclear power plant and its aftermath. Serving as composer for the five-part miniseries, Guðnadóttir appreciated the script's straightforward approach to depicting historical events and sought to avoid creating music that was overly dramatic, instead seeking to create a score that would be reminiscent of the sounds of machinery and radiation and would evoke appropriate levels of fear and claustrophobia.

To that end, Guðnadóttir traveled to Chernobyl to record audio from the site itself, which she, in turn, edited and reworked to create the miniseries' powerful score. "I wanted to understand the feeling of what must have gone through people's heads as they were trying to navigate through that disaster," she explained to Godfrey. "I didn't know what it was going to sound like. It was like treasure hunting. You go in there with completely open ears and you just listen." Guðnadóttir's efforts were ultimately well-received by audiences and critics alike. She went on to receive the 2019 Emmy Award for Outstanding Music Composition for a Limited Series as well as the 2019 Grammy Award for Best Score Soundtrack for Visual Media in recognition of her work.

JOKER

Guðnadóttir became the center of further attention later in 2019, following the premiere of the feature film *Joker* at the Venice Film Festival in August of that year. Based on the DC Comics villain of the same name, *Joker* sought to present a serious and dramatic take on the well-established character and was aided significantly by Guðnadóttir's work on its score. She received the film's script prior to the start of filming, and began composing based on that outline. After sending early versions of the resulting music to the filmmakers, they in turn at times adjusted the film itself to fit around her music.

In one memorable scene in the film, the character of the Joker, played by actor Joaquin Phoenix, performs an improvised dance set to one of Guðnadóttir's pieces. "He was basically responding in real time and just performing," the composer told Blistein. "It was so beautiful to see Joaquin completely embody what I had felt when I wrote the music. That was exactly the way I experienced the character and it was so magical to see his connection without having to explain it." Though not originally planned, Phoenix's dance combined with Guðnadóttir's music became a key moment in the film, underscoring the protagonist's development as a character. The music in that scene and others received substantial praise following *Joker's* release, earning Guðnadóttir the 2020 Academy Award for Best Original Score, among other awards.

Although the cello remained Guðnadóttir's primary instrument throughout her career, she also played a variety of other instruments, including other stringed instruments such as the zither, and occasionally contributed vocals to her work. She became particularly recognized for her work with experimental instruments such as the halldorophone, a cello-like electro-acoustic instrument that she helped develop and used extensively when creating the score for *Joker*. "It's a feedback instrument," she explained to Greiving. "A lot of the electronic sounds that you hear in the score, it's all performed live, and it's all coming from that instrument and the connection with the amplifiers."

Guðnadóttir also embraced digital recording technology, which she noted in her interview for *Fifteen Questions* enabled her to record and mix much of her music on her own. "That is only possible because of technology advancing so much in recent years," she explained. Such technology further facilitated the sorts of creative exchange that took place during her time composing for *Joker*, enabling Guðnadóttir to send demo versions of her score to the filmmakers with ease, despite the geographic distance between them.

PERSONAL LIFE

Guðnadóttir settled in Berlin, Germany, where she shared studio space in a converted factory building with a group of other artists. She married British-born musician and producer Sam Slater, with whom she had a son named Cody. Guðnadóttir and Slater worked together on a variety of projects, including the scores for *Chernobyl* and *Joker*, for which he served as a producer.

SUGGESTED READING

Blistein, Jon. "Oscars: 'Joker' Composer Hildur Guðnadóttir Is Making History." *Rolling Stone*, 13 Jan. 2020, www.rollingstone.com/movies/movie-news/oscars-joker-hildur-gudnadottir-936322/. Accessed 10 May 2020.

Godfrey, Alex. "*Joker* and *Chernobyl* Composer Hildur Guðnadóttir: 'I'm Treasure Hunting.'" *The Guardian*, 13 Dec. 2019, www.theguardian.com/music/2019/dec/13/joker-and-chernobyl-composer-hildur-gunadottir-im-treasure-hunting. Accessed 10 May 2020.

Greiving, Tim. "Composer Hildur Guðnadóttir Finds the Humanity in 'Joker.'" *NPR*, 3 Oct. 2019, www.npr.org/2019/10/03/766172923/composer-hildur-gu-nad-ttir-finds-the-humanity-in-joker. Accessed 10 May 2020.

Guðnadóttir, Hildur. "'Anyone Can Write Music'—An Interview with Hildur Guðnadóttir." Interview by Valentin Maniglia. *Score It*, 21 Aug. 2019, magazine.scoreit.org/anyone-can-write-music-an-interview-with-hildur-gudnadottir/. Accessed 10 May 2020.

———. "Fifteen Questions Interview with Hildur Guðnadóttir." *Fifteen Questions*, 15questions.net/interview/fifteen-questions-interview-hildur-gudnadottir/page-1/. Accessed 10 May 2020.

———. "No Emails on the Cello: An Interview with Hildur Guðnadóttir." Interview by Lucia Udvardyova. *SHAPE*, 11 Mar. 2015, shapeplatform.eu/2015/no-emails-on-the-cello-an-interview-with-hildur-gudnadottir/. Accessed 10 May 2020.

Hajdu, David. "Expect the Unexpected: On the Music of Hildur Guðnadóttir." *The Nation*, 5 Feb. 2020, www.thenation.com/article/culture/hildurg-gudnadottir-music-profile/. Accessed 10 May 2020.

SELECTED WORKS

The Bleeding House, 2011; *Jîn*, 2013; *Ófærð*, 2015–19; *The Oath*, 2016; *Sicario: Day of the Soldado*, 2018; *Chernobyl*, 2019; *Joker*, 2019

—*Joy Crelin*

Rachel Haurwitz

Born: May 20, 1985
Occupation: Biochemist

Rachel Haurwitz could not have possibly predicted what lay ahead for her when, as a graduate student in 2008, she took a position in researcher Jennifer Doudna's laboratory at the University of California, Berkeley. Joining Doudna's research group, she became a key contributor to the laboratory's groundbreaking work on the CRISPR-Cas9 gene-editing technology, which built upon the natural ability of a specific enzyme within bacteria to create "basically a way to go inside of cells and precisely change DNA-sequences," she explained to Nicolas Kristen for *Metropole* (7 June 2017). (CRISPR stands for Clustered Regularly Interspaced Short Palindromic Repeats and Cas9 stands for the enzyme CRISPR-associated protein 9.) Haurwitz, Doudna, and their colleagues were aware of the potential applications for that technology, and by mid-2012, Haurwitz was serving as president and CEO of Caribou Biosciences, a start-up dedicated to licensing CRISPR-Cas9 technology to pharmaceutical companies, agricultural corporations, and government research organizations, among other partners.

An aspiring biologist as early as middle school, Haurwitz developed an even greater passion for science as a teenager and went on to pursue a bachelor's degree in biological sciences at Harvard. She later completed a doctorate from the University of California, Berkeley,

Photo by TechCrunch Disrupt 2019 via Wikimedia Commons

submitting a CRISPR-related thesis in 2012. It was her time in Doudna's laboratory and later work with Caribou, however, that made Haurwitz a high-profile figure within the biotechnology community, earning her a place on lists such as the 2018 *Forbes* ranking of the top fifty US women in technology. "It makes me feel incredibly lucky," she told Andrew Joseph for *STAT* (22 June 2016) about the sequence of events that led to her success. "I am here because I was in the right place at the right time, with the right people and the right science around me." Though being in the right place at the right time undoubtedly played a role in her success, Haurwitz's passion for biology and dedication to her company, which had entered licensing agreements with more than ten individual companies or research organizations by 2020, were also significant factors.

EARLY LIFE AND EDUCATION

Rachel Elizabeth Haurwitz was born on May 20, 1985, in Pittsburgh, Pennsylvania . She spent her early years in the Pittsburgh suburb of Mount Lebanon, where she lived with her parents, Ralph and Linda, and her brother, Aaron. Haurwitz's mother was a teacher, while her father worked as an environmental reporter for one of Pittsburgh's daily newspapers. After that paper ceased operations, her father found a position at a newspaper in Austin, Texas, and the family moved there when Haurwitz was eight years old.

As a child, Haurwitz was exposed to a variety of environmental and scientific topics thanks to her father, who studied those topics to remain informed about the areas he covered as a journalist. One summer when she was in middle school, her father took a course at the Marine Biological Laboratory in Woods Hole, Massachusetts, and the rest of the family traveled to Woods Hole with him. "While he was in classes all day, my mom would put my brother and me in the car and drive us around and take us to a variety of the labs, where professors would really kindly show us their research," Haurwitz recalled to Brady Huggett for the *Nature Biotechnology*'s *First Rounder* podcast (26 Apr. 2017). "I just thought it was the coolest thing in the world." Having decided that she wanted to become a biologist thanks to her experiences that summer, she committed further to that goal after taking a biology class in her freshman year of high school, during which she was able to explore college-level biological concepts and design her own research project.

After graduating from Anderson High School in Austin in 2003, Haurwitz enrolled at Harvard College, Harvard University's undergraduate college. Although drawn to biology, she was initially unsure of her specific academic path. "I didn't

really know where in the grand world of biology I thought I might fit," she explained to Huggett. However, her undergraduate program was a flexible one, offering the aspiring scientist opportunities to explore a variety of areas of interest. Haurwitz chose to major in biological sciences and completed her bachelor's degree in that field in 2007. After Harvard, she went on to attend the University of California, Berkeley, where she pursued doctoral studies in molecular and cell biology and completed a thesis titled "The CRISPR Endoribonuclease Csy4 Utilizes Unusual Sequence- and Structure-Specific Mechanisms to Recognize and Process CrRNAs." Haurwitz earned her PhD from Berkeley in 2012. She also completed a certificate in management of technology at the university's Haas School of Business.

INTRODUCTION TO CRISPR-CAS9

Haurwitz began her graduate research career at Berkeley in a laboratory studying topics related to ribonucleic acid (RNA) but in 2008 moved to the laboratory of Jennifer Doudna, a researcher and professor within the university's chemistry and molecular and cell biology departments. After joining the Doudna Lab, she was tasked with working on a specific niche project within the laboratory's purview. "[Doudna] pitched to me the project that she wanted me to join," Haurwitz recalled to Joseph. "There was one scientist in the lab working on it, and it was something she called CRISPR." The research was related to CRISPR deoxyribonucleic acid (DNA) sequences and the enzyme Cas9, which occur naturally in the immune system of some bacteria. In nature, Cas9 can cleave, or cut, portions of DNA. Over the course of the work carried out at Berkeley and simultaneously at other institutions, including the University of Vienna and the Massachusetts Institute of Technology (MIT), researchers determined that those processes could be harnessed as a means of deliberately cutting and editing genomes for genetic-engineering purposes. Doudna was one of the foundational researchers in the field, and Haurwitz, as a graduate student in her laboratory, was at the forefront of that research. Indeed, at the start of Haurwitz's work on the project, Doudna and her team knew relatively little about the phenomenon or its potential uses; by the end of Haurwitz's time in the lab, however, the researchers had devised a practical means of programming Cas9 to edit DNA in specific ways.

In addition to representing a major breakthrough in biological research, the development of CRISPR-Cas9 technology was key because of its relative ease of use, which, as Haurwitz noted to Jonasz Tołopiło for *Papaya.Rocks* (29 Apr. 2019), "democratizes the techniques of gene editing." Although gene-editing processes were already in existence, they were "much more technically challenging," she told Tołopiło. "With previous methods, in order to edit the genome, one would actually need to engineer the entire new protein capable of reaching it. Practically, this meant that someone needed to have a PhD in the field of genome editing." CRISPR, on the other hand, made gene editing accessible to scientists outside of that field and opened it to numerous applications within the broader discipline of biotechnology.

CARIBOU BIOSCIENCES

In 2011, Haurwitz, Doudna, and fellow researchers Martin Jinek and James Berger founded a new biotechnology company, Caribou Biosciences, to oversee the licensing of intellectual property developed at the Doudna Lab. Though Haurwitz's primary work experience was in research prior to that point, she quickly took charge of the operations of the small start-up. "I was incredibly excited because the idea was real, and I was terrified," she told Megha Satyanarayana for *C&EN* (8 Mar. 2020). "I was incredibly naive as to exactly how challenging all this was. I jumped in, feet first." By mid-2012, Haurwitz held the positions of president and chief executive officer (CEO) of Caribou Biosciences, roles she would continue to hold into 2020.

Over the next several years, Caribou Biosciences expanded significantly, not only in size but also in scope and reach within its industry. "One day was pipetting clear liquids from one tube to the other and the next was trying to figure out how to build and grow a company," Haurwitz told Molly Fosco for *OZY* (16 Mar. 2018). Though challenging, overseeing Caribou's evolution was a rewarding process for Haurwitz, who led the company as it expanded from a tiny start-up within a basement incubator in 2012 to an established company with its own office, laboratory, and staff of nearly fifty by early 2018. In addition to managing the company's growth, she was responsible for overseeing the acquisition of funding from investors. Haurwitz and her colleagues raised $11 million in Series A funding, which concluded in 2015, and an additional $30 million in Series B funding in 2016.

LICENSING AND APPLICATIONS

Through their work with Caribou Biosciences, Haurwitz and her colleagues hoped to facilitate the use of CRISPR–based gene-editing technology for a variety of research applications, including the development of innovative treatments for conditions such as cancer. To that end, the company has established licensing partnerships with a variety of research groups and in 2014 cofounded the medical-research company Intellia Therapeutics, which licenses CRISPR-Cas9 technology for health-related purposes.

Haurwitz served as a member of the board of directors for Intellia Therapeutics between 2014 and 2016. Other companies that signed licensing agreements with Caribou Biosciences have included the Jackson Laboratory, which uses CRISPR-Cas9 technology to genetically engineer mice; the health-care company Novartis, which was also an investor in the start-up; Danisco US, which sought to use CRISPR-related technology to address the COVID-19 pandemic; and the United Kingdom's Medical Research Council.

Caribou's licensees represent a diverse array of scientific fields, demonstrating the broad appeal of relatively accessible gene-editing technology. "Any market with bio-based products will be changed by gene editing," Haurwitz explained to Fosco. In addition to working with research groups in a variety of fields, Caribou Biosciences seeks to enable continuing research into specific mechanisms of CRISPR-Cas9 technology that will facilitate further applications of the technology in the future. "Today we're pretty proficient in deleting one gene in certain cells. We're not particularly good at deleting more than one gene at a time. And we're also still figuring out how best to actually insert new sequences rather than just deleting genes," Haurwitz told Tołopiło about the limitations of the existing technology—limitations that she and her colleagues were seeking to overcome.

PERSONAL LIFE

Haurwitz lives in California. In recognition of her work with Caribou Biosciences, she has been named to many lists of influential science and technology professionals, including the 2014 Forbes 30 Under 30 list for science and health care and the 2018 Forbes America's Top 50 Women in Tech list.

SUGGESTED READING

Fosco, Molly. "This Scientist Turned CEO Wants to Gene-Edit a Way to Cure Cancer." *OZY*, 16 Mar. 2018, www.ozy.com/the-new-and-the-next/this-scientist-turned-ceo-wants-to-gene-edit-a-way-to-cure-cancer/85243/. Accessed 10 Aug. 2020.

Haurwitz, Rachel. "First Rounder: Rachel Haurwitz." Interview by Brady Huggett. *First Rounders*, 26 Apr. 2017, www.stitcher.com/podcast/nature-biotechnologys-first-rounders-2/nature-biotechnologys-first-rounders/e/first-rounder-rachel-haurwitz-49963904. Accessed 10 Aug. 2020.

———. "Rachel Haurwitz: A Pair of Genetic Scissors—Will CRISPR Change Our Life?" Interview by Jonasz Tołopiło. *Papaya.Rocks*, 29 Apr. 2019, papaya.rocks/en/trendbook/rachel-haurwitz-genetyczne-nozyczki-czy-crispr-zmieni-nasze. Accessed 10 Aug. 2020.

Joseph, Andrew. "At 31, She Runs One of the Hottest Biotech Companies in the Country." *STAT*, 22 June 2016, www.statnews.com/2016/06/22/rachel-haurwitz-crispr-caribou/. Accessed 10 Aug. 2020.

Kristen, Nicolas. "15 Minutes with Rachel Haurwitz at Pioneers Festival 2017." *Metropole*, 7 June 2017, metropole.at/pioneers-17-interview/. Accessed 10 Aug. 2020.

Regalado, Antonio. "Rachel Haurwitz." *MIT Technology Review*, www.technologyreview.com/innovator/rachel-haurwitz/. Accessed 10 Aug. 2020.

Satyanarayana, Megha. "CRISPR Technology: Where Female Entrepreneurs Thrive." *C&EN*, 8 Mar. 2020, cen.acs.org/biological-chemistry/gene-editing/CRISPR-technology-Where-female-entrepreneurs-thrive/98/i9. Accessed 10 Aug. 2020.

—*Joy Crelin*

Josh Hawley

Date of birth: December 31, 1979
Occupation: Politician and lawyer

Joshua David Hawley became the youngest serving member of the United States Senate at thirty-nine when he was inaugurated in 2019. A Republican representing Missouri, Hawley is both conservative and a populist. During his tenure as Missouri's attorney general, he led the state's largest anti–human trafficking bust in its history. Hawley opposes the pervasiveness of social media companies. He asked John McCormack for *National Review* (20 June 2019), "Are these platforms—the social-media platforms in particular—are those really good for the economy, for society, for the country? Are they really adding anything at all?"

EARLY LIFE AND EDUCATION
Joshua David Hawley was born in Springdale, Arkansas, Hawley grew up in rural Lexington, Missouri. His mother was a schoolteacher; his father was a banker who hosted George W. Bush when Bush was campaigning for his father, George H. W. Bush, during his run for president in 1988. Hawley was in third grade.

Hawley's parents wanted their son to have a solid education. Although not Catholics, they sent him to a Catholic school, Rockhurst High School in Kansas City, driving an hour each way. He graduated from Stanford University in 2002 with a major in history. He credits his time there with his interest in constitutional law, and he cites Stanford history professor David M. Kennedy as a mentor. As he told John J. Miller for

National Review (26 Apr. 2018), "We don't share political views, not by a long shot, but he taught me how to read and understand documents the way they were written and not how we wish they were written." One summer, Hawley interned at the conservative think tank Heritage Foundation.

Hawley taught American history at St. Paul's School in London before attending Yale Law School, from which he graduated in 2006. While at Yale, he led the student branch of the Federalist Society, a conservative group, and started a Bible study group.

EARLY CAREER
Hawley clerked for Michael W. McConnell of the US Court of Appeals for the Tenth Circuit. He also had a clerkship with Chief Justice John Roberts. Hawley greatly admired President Theodore Roosevelt, the early twentieth century icon of the Progressive Era. While working for Roberts, he expanded his Stanford honors thesis into a full biography, Theodore Roosevelt: Preacher of Righteousness, published in 2008.

That same year Hawley began as an appellate litigator at Hogan & Hartson in Washington, DC. From 2011 to 2015, he worked for the public-interest law firm Becket Fund for Religious Liberty. He argued on the 2011 *Hosanna-Tabor Evangelical Lutheran Church and School* v. *EEOC* (Equal Employment Opportunity Commission) case, which resulted in a unanimous victory for church rights, due to the "ministerial exception" rule that protects churches from government interference. A teacher had sued

Photo by Chip Somodevilla/Getty Images

because she was asked to resign due to illness and then fired. Because she was also ordained and taught religious classes, she was exempt from employment protection, as part of the church's First Amendment rights.

Hawley was also on the team that in 2014 successfully argued *Burwell v. Hobby Lobby* before the Supreme Court. The Green family, which owns more than 500 Hobby Lobby stores, sued for the right not to provide coverage for contraceptives to their employees, believing that contraceptive use was contrary to God's plan. In a 5–4 decision, the business won the right not to comply with the provisions of the Patient Protection and Affordable Care Act (PPACA). The verdict allowed family businesses to be run as they chose according to their religious beliefs. Peter Dobelbower, Hobby Lobby's senior vice president and general counsel, told Miller, "Josh was instrumental in providing expertise, based on his knowledge of the Constitution."

Hawley returned to Missouri to become an associate professor of constitutional law at the University of Missouri while continuing to work for Becket.

ATTORNEY GENERAL

Hawley campaigned successfully in 2016 to become Missouri's attorney general; he became the first Republican to hold that office in more than two decades. One of his first acts was to close the office's environmental and agricultural division. Created in 1993, it was designed to prosecute illegal pollution.

A new Federalism Unit was created to dispute federal regulations and laws. Mary Compton, spokeswoman for the Office of the Attorney General (AG), issued a statement quoted by Jack Suntrup for the *St. Louis Dispatch* (22 Oct. 2018), saying, "The Federalism Unit works to limit how the federal government and overregulation interferes in the lives of Missourians. The Unit fights to protect the interests of Missouri's farmers, small business owners and workers." Former employees of the AG's office viewed this as a drain on resources for dealing with state-related issues such as consumer protection and cases brought against the state.

Hawley faced criticism for his handling of the attorney general's office; judges complained about the slow rate of discovery. He also failed to thoroughly investigate one of his top supervisors, who was forced to leave due to complaints about his behavior by a staff member.

Hawley claimed he was streamlining the office, but the departure rate under his administration was unusually high. In 2017, the first year he held the position, ninety-eight employees left the office; another eighty-one had left by October 2018.

As experienced litigators left the staff, settlement costs increased, leading to increased costs for taxpayers. Twenty-five to thirty lawyers comprised the usual size of the civil litigation staff; it decreased to eight when those Hawley appointed left.

SENATE CAMPAIGN

Ten months after taking office, Hawley announced his candidacy for the United States Senate, hoping to unseat Democratic incumbent Claire McCaskill. Having campaigned for the job of attorney general using advertisements that targeted politicians who were just climbing the ladder, Hawley faced a barrage of criticism suggesting that he was a hypocrite, using the attorney general position as a stepping stone to the US Senate. He denied the charge, insisting that political strategist Karl Rove and Senate Majority Leader Mitch McConnell had urged him to run against McCaskill, and assuring people that he was in touch with the AG's office even while campaigning for Senate. Hawley told Miller, "I had not planned to do this. But ultimately I came to believe that this is an urgent moment. We're at an inflection point. The choices we make today will set the trajectory for the next fifty years."

He campaigned with President Donald Trump's approval and endorsement. He also garnered an endorsement from the National Rifle Association (NRA). He and McCaskill spent millions of campaign dollars on airtime advertisements, making it one of the most expensive Senate races in history. McCaskill lost the November 2018 election as conservative rural voters flocked to Hawley, despite ads run by Emily's List highlighting his desire to repeal insurance coverage provisions for pre-existing conditions, including diabetes and cancer.

Though Republicans lost control of the US House of Representatives in the midterm elections, Hawley's victory helped strengthen the Republican hold on the Senate—increasing their majority from fifty-one to fifty-three—and turned Missouri from a purple state to a solidly red state. As Nicholas Fandos reported for *New York Times* (6 Nov. 2018), in his election night victory speech, Hawley said, "Tonight the people of Missouri have said that our way of life and our values are going to renew this country and that is what we are about, and that is what we are for." Hawley was sworn in as a US senator in January 3, 2019.

CONFRONTING BIG TECH

Hawley's Senate committee assignments include those on the Judiciary; Armed Services; Homeland Security and Governmental Affairs; Small Business and Entrepreneurship; and the Special Committee on Aging.

Early in his term in the Senate, Hawley pursued a cause he had also favored as a state attorney general (and that his erstwhile hero, the trust-buster Theodore Roosevelt, would have supported): challenging the power of big tech companies. He introduced several bills to regulate tech giants such as Facebook and Google. Some were aimed at protecting children, such as removing "loot boxes," which are marketed to minors and permit players in video games to pay to win. As Hawley told McCormack, "This is gambling. These are casinos essentially getting inserted into kids' games, and this speaks to a larger issue we ought to be talking about, which is the addiction economy." Another measure to protect children would give parents the ability to remove profiles of their children that companies created.

Hawley proposed another bill, the Social Media Addiction Reduction Technology (SMART) Act, that would curtail the use in apps like *Facebook* and *Twitter* of features such as infinite scrolling and autoplay videos, which Hawley said encourages internet addiction. he said, "Too much of the 'innovation' in this space is designed not to create better products, but to capture more attention by using psychological tricks that make it difficult to look away," said Hawley, as Katie Mettler reported for the *Washington Post* (30 July 2019). "This legislation will put an end to that and encourage true innovation by tech companies."

Hawley also proposed decreasing tech's ability to monitor children's use of the Internet, with an update of the Children's Online Privacy Protection Act (COPPA), which is more than two decades old. He coauthored that bill with a Democrat, Edward Markey of Massachusetts. That and his approval of Elizabeth Warren's critique of social media made him seem like a senator likely to work across the aisle with Democrats.

OTHER ISSUES

Hawley supported President Trump in many areas, including the need for a border wall with Mexico. He opposed a general path to citizenship for the many undocumented immigrants already in the United States.

Like President Trump, Hawley supports a nationalistic, rather than a global, outlook. At the July 2019 National Conservatism Conference held in Washington, DC, as Ben Sales reported for *Jewish Telegraphic Agency* (19 July 2019), Hawley condemned "a powerful upper class and their cosmopolitan priorities. This class lives in the United States, but they identify as 'citizens of the world.' They run businesses or oversee universities here, but their primary loyalty is to the global community." Hawley's rhetoric condemning "cosmopolitan elites" disturbed some in the Jewish community, as the phrase has at times been used in anti-Semitic contexts. In the wake of his remarks, the Anti-Defamation League asked Hawley to be more careful with his rhetoric.

In April 2019 Hawley joined Republican senators Tom Cotton of Arkansas and David Perdue of Georgia in re-introducing the Reforming American Immigration for a Strong Economy (RAISE) Act; it had first been put forward in 2017. As reported on Cotton's website, Hawley said, "We need an immigration system that puts American workers first. Our broken immigration policies hurt hardworking Americans and the talented individuals who are stuck in line, waiting to contribute to our country. With the RAISE Act, the United States can finally end chain migration and move to a merit-based system. All Americans deserve rising wages, a growing economy, and an equal shot at the American Dream."

PERSONAL LIFE

Hawley met his wife, Erin, when both were law clerks for Chief Justice Roberts. As he told Miller, "We shared an office and started dating but didn't tell the chief and went to great lengths to conceal our relationship. The office manager figured it out, but she kept it to herself." The couple has two sons, Elijah and Blaise.

SUGGESTED READING

Appiah, Kwame Anthony. "Why Do Politicians Blame 'Cosmopolitans' for Local Problems?" *The New York Times Magazine*, 21 Aug. 2019, www.nytimes.com/2019/08/21/magazine/why-do-politicians-blame-cosmopolitans-for-local-problems.html. Accessed 30 Oct. 2019.

McCormack, John. "Josh Hawley's Virtue Politics." *National Review*, 20 June 2019, www.nationalreview.com/magazine/2019/07/08/josh-hawleys-virtue-politics/. Accessed 23 Oct. 2019.

Mettler, Katie. "A Lawmaker Wants to End 'Social Media Addiction' by Killing Features That Enable Mindless Scrolling." *The Washington Post*, 30 July 2019, www.washingtonpost.com/technology/2019/07/30/lawmaker-wants-end-social-media-addiction-by-killing-features-that-enable-mindless-scrolling/. Accessed 30 Oct. 2019.

Miller, John J. "Josh Hawley's Worthy Climb." *National Review*, 26 Apr. 2018, www.nationalreview.com/magazine/2018/05/14/josh-hawley-senate-race-worthy-candidate-missouri/. Accessed 23 Oct. 2019.

Stack, Liam. "Republicans Had a Plan for Josh Hawley in Missouri. He's Working on It." *The New York Times*, 13 July 2018, www.nytimes.com/2018/07/13/us/politics/josh-hawley-missouri-senate.html. Accessed 29 Oct. 2019.

—*Judy Johnson*

Phil Heath

Date of birth: December 18, 1979
Occupation: Bodybuilder

Phil Heath learned a number of valuable lessons throughout his career as an amateur and professional bodybuilder. "The most important one is to remain a student of my own physical, mental and emotional attributes," he told *Edgar* magazine (11 Nov. 2019). "Implementing a constant willingness to learn new things has also yielded some great successes." Given the nature of Heath's successes, "great" is perhaps an understatement. A college basketball player turned competitive strength athlete, he earned his bodybuilding pro card in 2005 and won the prestigious title of Mr. Olympia for the first time in 2011. He went on to defend his title for the next six consecutive years, becoming one of the most successful Mr. Olympia titleholders of all time.

Mr. Olympia winners receive substantial monetary prizes as well as widespread attention from bodybuilding fans and potential sponsors. Yet Heath tended to focus simply on stunning the public with his muscular physique, built through an intensive exercise program and carefully planned diet. "Everyone knows I'm going to come in shape, but they don't know exactly how big I'm going to be or where I'm going to improve," he told an interviewer for *Flex* magazine (24 Sept. 2018). "So my job is just to make sure that nothing changes to the negative—that my proportions stay the same, but I just get better. And just try to shock the world again."

EARLY LIFE AND EDUCATION

Phillip Jerrod Heath was born on December 18, 1979. He grew up in Seattle, Washington, where he attended Rainier Beach High School. An athlete from early in life, he specialized in basketball during his teen years and was a key contributor to his high school's team, which would later retire his jersey number. His skills on the court earned him a full scholarship to the University of Denver, a National Collegiate Athletic Association (NCAA) Division I school, after graduating from high school in 1998. During his time at the University of Denver, Heath studied business administration and information technology.

Despite enjoying basketball, Heath was dissatisfied with the amount of playing time he was given. He later admitted that his college-aged self had felt that he was owed more opportunities on the court. A particularly difficult moment came during his senior postseason, when the University of Denver men's basketball team was eliminated early during the Sun Belt Conference Tournament. As the last game of his senior

Photo by Dave Kotinsky/Getty Images

season, that final game was also Heath's last as a basketball player. "Something was just not easy with that. I didn't like it," he recalled to Greg Glasgow for the *University of Denver Magazine* (28 Aug. 2013). "Hearing the buzzer sound and your career is done. I was going to class, and I was still living in the basketball house, so I'm still seeing the guys compete, and it hurt. I despised basketball for a long time. I didn't go to a game for three years."

Following the end of Heath's collegiate basketball career, he found a new direction after a classmate introduced him to the sport of bodybuilding. Having struggled with depression and thoughts of suicide in college, he found that bodybuilding training helped him attain a better mental and emotional state. "It really kind of helped me focus on myself," he told a seminar audience in a *Generation Iron Fitness Network* video (13 Nov. 2014). "If I was angry, I went to the gym. If I was happy, I went to the gym." Planning to focus more seriously on bodybuilding, Heath left the university in 2002, without completing his degree. He later returned and earned his bachelor's degree in information technology in 2012.

BODYBUILDING CAREER

After leaving college, Heath worked as a bouncer to support himself while training to compete as a bodybuilder. He made his debut in a bodybuilding competition in 2003, competing as a novice in the light-heavyweight category of that year's National Physique Committee (NPC) Northern Colorado event. Heath won an overall title in that competition, and his success served as further motivation to move forward in the sport. Two years later he claimed first place in the men's heavyweight category and in the overall competition at the NPC USA Championships, earning his pro card and the right to compete in professional-level events held by the International Federation of Bodybuilding and Fitness (IFBB). Heath made his professional debut at the 2006 IFBB Colorado Pro Show, winning first place. He went on to compete in other IFBB events over the next several years, including the 2008 IFBB Ironman Pro and the 2007, 2008, and 2010 IFBB Arnold Classics. During this period he earned the nickname the Gift.

As a professional bodybuilder who at times competed for substantial monetary prizes in addition to titles, Heath devoted a significant amount of time to his physical training. This included an array of free-weight and machine-based exercises aimed at promoting muscle hypertrophy, or excessive growth. Unlike some of his peers, Heath believed that bodybuilders should work with heavy weights not only during their main training periods but also during the periods leading up to their contests. "I'm making sure that the weights being lifted are heavy all the time. Saying, 'Oh, I'm just going to focus on higher reps and shred up'—that's a fallacy," he explained to *Flex* magazine. He added, "I realize that a strong muscle is always a bigger one and that you should be able to lift heavy throughout your contest prep until maybe the last ten days." Although the size of one's muscles plays an important role in one's performance in competitive bodybuilding, the discipline also focuses heavily on aesthetic factors, such as muscle symmetry and the overall shape of the competitor's physique.

From early on in Heath's professional career, he focused particularly on attaining the prestigious title of Mr. Olympia, given to the winner of the bodybuilding competition at the annual Joe Weider's Olympia Fitness and Performance Weekend. Previous winners of that title included actor-turned-politician Arnold Schwarzenegger as well as other prominent bodybuilders such as Frank Zane, Lee Haney, and Ronnie Coleman. For Heath and others, the title of Mr. Olympia represented the pinnacle of bodybuilding achievement. "You win the Mr. Olympia, you are the best in the world," he explained to Glasgow. Heath competed in his first Mr. Olympia contest in 2008, ultimately placing third behind Dexter Jackson and Jay Cutler. He returned to the competition in 2009, placing fifth, and vied for the title again in the 2010 contest, during which he placed second behind Cutler.

MR. OLYMPIA

A key point in Heath's career came in September of 2011, when the bodybuilder again traveled to Las Vegas, Nevada, to compete for the title of Mr. Olympia. Despite strong competition, Heath succeeded in claiming first place, beating previous champion Cutler as well as a major rival such as Kai Greene. "Words cannot describe how I feel right now," he said in an interview following the competition, as quoted by Matt Faulconer for *Bleacher Report* (21 Sept. 2011). "I'm so happy I was able to do it and able to have fun while doing it." After securing the title of Mr. Olympia, Heath next traveled to Mumbai, India, to compete in the first annual Sheru Classic Asian Grand Prix. He took first place in that competition as well, claiming his second title in as many weeks. He would go on to repeat that feat in 2012, defending his Mr. Olympia title and again placing first at the Sheru Classic.

Over the next several years, Heath became a fixture of the Mr. Olympia contest, competing in and winning the high-profile event every year between 2013 and 2017. In achieving his seventh win in 2017, he tied Schwarzenegger for the second-most Mr. Olympia titles, remaining behind only Haney and Coleman, who had each won eight. Although Heath was pleased to have won the title numerous times, he frequently stated in interviews that he hoped eventually to win a total of ten times. "Barring injury, I'll smash it," he told John Branch for the *New York Times* (28 Oct. 2016). "I'll get to ten. The question is: Can I continue to be a better version of myself?"

In 2018, Heath sought to win his eighth Mr. Olympia title but ended up placing second behind first-time winner Shawn Rhoden. He opted not to compete in the following year's competition, which was ultimately won by first-time winner Brandon Curry. "As many people have known me throughout my career to compete at our sport's biggest event, I am sitting this one out as I continue to work on other projects inside and outside of bodybuilding," Heath said of his absence, as quoted by Rose McNulty for *Muscle & Fitness* (Sept. 2019). Despite his absence from the 2019 Mr. Olympia contest, he remained a prominent member of the bodybuilding community and in September of that year was named *Muscular Development* magazine's bodybuilder of the year.

OTHER WORK

Heath also became a prolific public speaker in addition to his bodybuilding work. He conducted many seminars and public appearances, often in conjunction with fitness expositions and similar events. As a longtime competitor in professional bodybuilding, he also appeared in more than a half-dozen bodybuilding documentaries, perhaps most notably 2013's *Generation Iron*, which follows a group of bodybuilders as they prepare for the Mr. Olympia contest. Heath like-wise marketed his own brand of athletic apparel and accessories, Gifted Athletics, as well as the Phil Heath Labs line of supplements.

Heath frequently suggested in interviews that the true focus of his speaking engagements, his business initiatives, and even his appearances in competitions has been to inspire those watching him, much as he was once inspired to begin bodybuilding. "It can be ten people or thousands of people, I want them to see something special," he told Branch. "I want them to say, 'I saw the best in the world at something,' and maybe that will inspire them to go do something in their life with the same vigor."

PERSONAL LIFE

Heath was married to Jennie Laxson, but the couple later divorced. He later married Shurie Cremona. Heath lives near Denver and trains at local gyms such as Armbrust Pro Gym in the suburb of Wheat Ridge. "I keep to myself, but I watch people," he told Branch about his gym-going habits. "You don't know what that person on the treadmill is going through."

SUGGESTED READING

Branch, John. "No One Is Looking at This Headline." *The New York Times*, 28 Oct. 2016, www.nytimes.com/2016/10/29/sports/phil-heath-mr-olympia-bodybuilder.html. Accessed 15 Nov. 2019.

Faulconer, Matt. "Mr. Olympia 2011: Phil Heath Goes from Basketball Star to Bodybuilding Legend." *Bleacher Report*, 21 Sept. 2011, syndication.bleacherreport.com/amp/860026-mr-olympia-2011-phil-heath-goes-from-basketball-star-to-bodybuilding-legend.amp.html. Accessed 15 Nov. 2019.

Glasgow, Greg. "Body of Work: Alumnus Phil Heath Talks about His Journey to Mr. Olympia." *University of Denver Magazine*, 28 Aug. 2013, magazine-archive.du.edu/alumni/body-of-work-alumnus-phil-heath-talks-about-his-journey-to-mr-olympia. Accessed 15 Nov. 2019.

Heath, Phil. "Show Stopper." *Edgar*, 11 Nov. 2019, edgardaily.com/interviews/phil-heath-exclusive-interview. Accessed 15 Nov. 2019.

———. "Training with the Gift." *Flex*, 24 Sept. 2018. *Bodybuilding.com*, www.bodybuilding.com/fun/training-with-the-gift.html. Accessed 15 Nov. 2019.

McNulty, Rose. "Phil Heath Is Officially Out of the 2019 Olympia." *Muscle & Fitness*, Sept. 2019, www.muscleandfitness.com/athletes-celebrities/news/phil-heath-officially-out-2019-olympia. Accessed 15 Nov. 2019.

"Phil Heath Reveals Dark Past." *Generation Iron Fitness Network*, 13 Nov. 2014, generation-iron.com/phil-heath-reveals-dark-past. Accessed 15 Nov. 2019.

—*Joy Crelin*

Ada Hegerberg

Date of birth: July 10, 1995
Occupation: Soccer player

By the age of twenty-three, the Norwegian striker Ada Hegerberg was already considered an icon in the sport of soccer (known internationally as football), outperforming even contemporary legends like Lionel Messi and Cristiano Ronaldo. In just her first five seasons with the famed French soccer club Olympique Lyonnais Féminin (Lyon) she amassed 120 goals, and by late 2019 she had over 300 career goals to her name. She scored a record-breaking fifteen goals in the 2018 Union of European Football Association (UEFA) Women's Champions League alone, and in 2019, she became the highest-scoring player in Champions League history. Hegerberg led Lyon to four consecutive Champions League titles, leading Rory Smith to write for *New York Times* (17 May 2019) that "There may not be a team on earth that can match its [Lyon's] talent advantage, or its dominance of its sport."

Photo by Harold Cunningham - UEFA/UEFA via Getty Images

Hegerberg's dominance brought her many honors and awards, including recognition as the 2015–16 UEFA Women's Player of the Year. Her contract renewal with Lyon in 2018 reportedly made her the world's highest-paid female soccer player, and also set a record for women's soccer with its three-year term. She went on to win the inaugural Ballon d'Or Feminin, an award that recognizes the best female soccer player in the world, in 2018. Hegerberg also became a strong advocate of equality in sports, shocking fans when she quit the Norwegian national team in 2017 because she did not believe that the country was doing enough to invest in female players. She put herself at the forefront of a campaign for better treatment and better pay for female players.

EARLY LIFE
Ada Martine Stolsmo Hegerberg was born to Stein Erik Hegerberg and Gerd Stolsmo in Molde, Norway, on July 10, 1995, and spent her early years in Sunndalsøra in northern Norway. In a piece for the *Players' Tribune* (16 Dec. 2018), Hegerberg fondly described her family as "a real football family." Her older brother, Silas, played the sport as a child, and her older sister, Andrine, later played midfield for professional clubs, including Paris Saint-Germain and AS Roma. When Hegerberg was young the family moved to Kolbotn, south of Oslo, so she and her sister could play for the youth team there. In Kolbotn, young boys and girls played together. Hegerberg's mother was the team's coach; her sister was the captain.

The Hegerbergs instilled in their children the importance of hard work and never drove them to soccer practice. "They had to go to training by running or by bike," her father recalled to Andrew Keh for the *New York Times* (11 Dec. 2018). "If it's not important for you, then you won't go." The Hegerbergs also encouraged humility. "You can always criticize upward," her father told Keh, "but never kick downward." That advice would prove valuable in Hegerberg's fight for gender equality in soccer.

ENTRY INTO SOCCER
Hegerberg had little interest in soccer as a young child on the sidelines, preferring to read books instead. While watching one of her sister's games, a man asked Hegerberg what she wanted to be when she grew up and whether she wanted to play soccer like her sister. "Apparently, I just looked at him with disgust and said, 'No, I'm going to have a *real* job,'" Hegerberg recalled for the *Players' Tribune*. However, she took up the game around age seven and soon was utterly captivated by it. From then on soccer was "almost like life or death" for her, as she put it. That competitive spirit would be another important

aspect of her social advocacy as well. "The one thing I would say to any girl who is reading this right now is this: You can't lose your fire," she wrote. "You can't let anybody take your fire away from you. If you have big dreams, the fire is the only thing that will get you there."

As a teen in Kolbotn, Hegerberg gained a reputation as an enormously talented, if intense, player. Tales of Hegerberg "screaming, scolding teammates twice her age, demanding and disdaining," persist, Tom Kershaw wrote in the *Independent* (12 Jan. 2019). Yet Hegerberg later took a different view of her young self. "I just wanted something so badly that I could tell people around me that were ten years older that they had to play and perform," she told Kershaw. "I would still say that I had respect."

EARLY PROFESSIONAL CAREER
In 2009 Hegerberg and her sister joined Kolbotn IL, a professional club in the women's league Toppserien. At sixteen she became the youngest player to score a hat trick (three goals in one game) in the league's history, and she finished the season as the league's top scorer. She appeared in the 2011 Norway Women's Cup with Kolbotn. She and her sister then moved to the club Stabaek Fotball, based outside of Oslo, for which Hegerberg scored twenty-five goals in eighteen games. The sisters made their debut in the Champions League, an annual competition hosted by the UEFA, in 2012 and led Stabaek to win the Norwegian Women's Cup.

During this period Hegerberg also competed internationally with the Norwegian national team. She appeared at the 2010 UEFA European Women's Under-17 Championship, where Norway lost in the second qualifying round. She later helped lead the team to greater successes: progressing to the finals in the 2011–13 UEFA Women's EURO championship and the quarterfinals at the 2012 Under-20 Women's World Cup, sponsored by the Fédération Internationale de Football Association (FIFA).

Hegerberg had long dreamed of playing abroad, but it was her growing frustration with women's soccer in Norway that pushed the seventeen-year-old to join FFC Turbine Potsdam, a German professional club, in 2012. "Football is the biggest sport in Norway for girls and has been for years but at the same time girls don't have the same opportunities as the boys," she opined to Suzanne Wrack in an interview for the *Guardian* (3 July 2018). Potsdam offered Hegerberg her first taste of truly rigorous training. "We would train three times per day," she wrote. "We would train in the freezing rain, in the snow. It didn't matter."

OLYMPIQUE LYONNAIS

In 2014 Hegerberg received a call from Lyon, France. "The best club called me and wanted to know if I wanted to go there and play and I was like: 'Yeah, I'm totally doing this,'" she recalled to Wrack. "The best players were there, I thought it was a dream. I knew it would be tough to get a spot in the team but I knew I had to trust in my own qualities and go for it." She signed with Olympique Lyonnais that July. For Hegerberg, the difference between training with Lyon and training in Norway was night and day. She described the club as a model, with male and female players treated exactly alike. Hegerberg finished her first season at Lyon as the league's top scorer, with thirty-four goals in thirty-two matches.

The following season Hegerberg pulled off an incredible goal—Kershaw argued that it could be counted as "one of the best in history"—to win the 2015 UEFA Champions League. For her performance, she was named UEFA Best Women's Player in Europe and UEFA Women's Player of the Year for the 2015–16 season.

NORWEGIAN NATIONAL TEAM

Also in 2015 Hegerberg made her Women's World Cup debut for Norway. She scored a goal in the team's early win over Thailand, but as Kim McCauley observed for *SB Nation* (7 June 2015), "her performance was so much more than that." McCauley predicted that Hegerberg could be a star of the Norwegian team. However, Hegerberg's place on the team would ultimately be short-lived, despite helping the team to the round of sixteen and scoring three goals in four World Cup matches.

In 2017, Hegerberg played for the Norwegian national team in the UEFA Women's EURO championship. The team lost several games running, and Hegerberg stormed off the field. It was the last time she played for the team. She expressed frustration with the stifling atmosphere and management of the team—rooted, she suggested, in a lack of respect for female players. Norwegian Football Federation, for its part, portrayed her as difficult, outspoken, demanding, and entitled.

Around the same time, the federation and the national players' association struck a deal for equal pay for male and female players and introduced further investments in women's soccer. The reforms put Norway ahead of other countries in terms of equality, but Hegerberg insisted they were not enough.

BALLON D'OR AND THE BATTLE FOR RESPECT

Hegerberg led Lyon to another Champions League victory in the 2018 tournament, scoring a record-breaking fifteen goals. She was shortlisted for the 2017–18 UEFA Women's Player of the Year, coming in second behind Pernille Harder.

In December 2018 Hegerberg became the first woman to win a Ballon d'Or, which originated in the 1950s to honor male soccer players. Although she would later call the night she received the award as the best of her life, it was marked by an awkward moment that drew considerable controversy. After she received her trophy, the show's cohost, the DJ Martin Solveig, greeted her by asking if she knew how to twerk (perform a sexually provocative dance). She dismissed it. Fans and fellow athletes were outraged, however, that Solveig had undercut Hegerberg's moment with a sexist joke; many took to social media to express their support and condemn Solveig's remark. Hegerberg insisted in subsequent interviews that for her, the incident barely registered because she was so focused on the award and on being in the company of other star athletes, her peers.

In 2019 Hegerberg scored a hat trick for Lyon against Barcelona to win the Champions League final, their fourth consecutive title and sixth ever. The feat made Hegerberg the highest scorer in the competition's history, with fifty-three goals scored in Champions League matches. She was nominated for UEFA Women's Player of the Year as well as Best FIFA Women's Player 2019.

Meanwhile, fighting for equality within soccer remained a top priority for Hegerberg. In May 2019, ahead of the Women's World Cup, she became a face of Time for Action, the first five-year UEFA campaign to equalize the sport. The campaign aimed not only to double the number of female players in Europe by 2024, but also to change standards for and cultural attitudes about girls' and women's soccer. "I could speak for hours about equality, and what needs to change in football, and in society as a whole," Hegerberg wrote for the *Players' Tribune*. "But in the end, everything comes back to respect."

PERSONAL LIFE

Soccer remains a family affair for Hegerberg outside of her playing career. She and her sister cohosted Hegerberg Fotball, an annual soccer-training academy for Norwegian girls. Their mother also wrote a memoir about raising the two soccer stars, *Fotball-Mamma: Historien om Andrine og Ada Hegerberg* (Soccer mom: The story of Andrine and Ada Hegerberg), published in September 2019.

In May 2019 Hegerberg married fellow Norwegian soccer player Thomas Rogne, a defender who played for the Glasgow Celtics FC and the Polish club Lech Poznań.

SUGGESTED READING

Hegerberg, Ada. "Not Here to Dance." *The Players' Tribune*, 16 Dec. 2018, www.theplayerstribune.com/en-us/articles/ada-hegerberg-not-here-to-dance. Accessed 13 Nov. 2019.

Keh, Andrew. "Ada Hegerberg Would Prefer to Talk about Soccer." *The New York Times*, 11 Dec. 2018, www.nytimes.com/2018/12/11/sports/ada-hegerberg-lyon-ballon-dor-twerk.html. Accessed 13 Nov. 2019.

Kershaw, Tom. "Ada Hegerberg: Unflinching, Uncompromising, the Making of the World's Greatest Female Footballer." *Independent*, 12 Jan. 2019, www.independent.co.uk/sport/football/womens_football/ada-hegerberg-exclusive-interview-ballon-dor-norway-lyon-womens-world-cup-a8720156.html. Accessed 13 Nov. 2019.

Olmstead, Molly. "Why the World's Best Soccer Player Isn't Playing in the Women's World Cup." *Slate*, 8 June 2019, slate.com/culture/2019/06/ada-hegerberg-world-cup-norway-protest-why.html. Accessed 20 Nov. 2019.

Smith, Rory. "The World's Most Dominant Team Isn't Who You Think." *The New York Times*, 17 May 2019, www.nytimes.com/2019/05/17/sports/olympique-lyon-womens-champions-league.html. Accessed 13 Nov. 2019.

Wrack, Suzanne. "Lyon's Ada Hegerberg: 'Girls in Norway Don't Have the Same Opportunities as Boys.'" *The Guardian*, 3 July 2018, www.theguardian.com/football/2018/jul/03/lyon-ada-hegerberg-ronaldo-champions-league-goals. Accessed 13 Nov. 2019.

—*Molly Hagan*

Wim Hof

Born: April 20, 1959
Occupation: Extreme sports athlete

Dutch extreme sports athlete and wellness influencer Wim Hof has long been dissatisfied with the state of the world. "We can shoot people to the moon, but we don't have solutions for mental disorders?" he asked in an interview with Vivienne Tang for *Destination Deluxe* (2019). "We can master mathematics, languages, history, and how to make money, but not how to balance ourselves and become happy. That's ridiculous!" For Hof, the solution to such pervasive twenty-first-century wellness problems lies within a group of physical and mental practices that he has dubbed the Wim Hof Method, which encompasses exposure to the cold, breathing exercises, and meditation and can, according to Hof, help practitioners gain an unprecedented level of control over their own bodies. Because of this belief, he was continuing efforts to teach the method by 2020.

Although aspects of the Wim Hof Method and its purported results might sound farfetched to some, Hof's own accomplishments while adhering to the method have been undeniable. A proponent of cold-water swimming since early adulthood, he made a name for himself by breaking multiple cold-related Guinness World Records, including the records for longest period in an ice bath and fastest barefoot half marathon run on snow or ice, in addition to performing risky climbs of some of the world's tallest mountains. For Hof, his ability to withstand lengthy ice baths and other physical challenges is attributable to his practice of the Wim Hof Method and specifically to his long-standing engagement with cold temperatures. "The impact of severe cold makes you aware of your deeper physiology," he explained to Sam Parker in an undated interview for *Conrad Magazine*. "This is something we have lost in modern life. But we can rediscover it with practice."

EARLY LIFE AND CAREER

Hof was born on April 20, 1959 in Sittard, the Netherlands. He was one of nine children born to his parents and has a twin brother named Andre. Hof's birth was a traumatic one, and as an adult, he would come to believe that there was a connection between the circumstances of his birth and his affinity for the cold. Intrigued by a variety of religions, languages, and philosophies as a child, he began reading about belief

Photo by Stefan Brending via Wikimedia Commons

systems such as Buddhism and Hinduism by the age of twelve and immersed himself deeply in such topics during his teen years. "I was learning about meditation, yoga, and any philosophy I could get my hands on," he recalled to Vikas Shah for *Thought Economics* (22 Nov. 2018). In addition to such pursuits and finding enjoyment in snow and playing in the woods, the young Hof was active in sports such as running and martial arts.

A key moment in Hof's early life came when he was around seventeen years old. While walking near a canal in Amsterdam one day, he was suddenly struck by the need to jump into the canal, where he swam in the intensely cold water. The incident kindled a passion for cold-water swimming in Hof, who felt that swimming in very cold water helped him to clear his mind and reinvigorate his body. He continued to practice cold-water swimming in his free time over the next years but did not pursue a career in that area at the time, instead supporting himself by working as a mail carrier, among other jobs.

Over the decades following his first encounter with the cold water of the Amsterdam canal, Hof came to believe that immersing himself in cold temperatures was an essential means of connecting with his body's inner workings. "Swimming in cold water was just able to bring me right back into the depth of my physiology, more than any of those disciplines were able to do. So I got hooked on the cold, and to use it to get into this deep connection with my mind and my body," he explained to Tang. Though initially an obscure figure within the Netherlands, he gained more widespread attention after being featured on a local television program in the late 1990s. Due to his partiality for ice-filled water and cold exposure, Hof gained the nickname "the Iceman," a moniker the media would continue to reference over the course of his career.

WORLD RECORDS

Considered by some to be a professional daredevil or extreme sports athlete, Hof first became well known on the international stage for performing a host of risky feats—many involving the cold—and setting numerous world records. Though he had experienced a dangerous situation during a rehearsal of the swim when his sight became compromised by the frigid water temperature, he set his first Guinness World Record in 2000, swimming an impressive distance under a sheet of ice in Finland. In addition to such ventures, Hof braved the cold in a different environment in 2007, when he performed a partial climb of Mount Everest, reaching an altitude of more than seven thousand meters (over twenty-four thousand feet). Unlike most mountaineers, who wear warm clothing designed to withstand the harsh mountain weather, Hof made his climb while wearing only a pair of shorts and a pair of shoes. His potential ascent to the top of the mountain was stopped by a foot injury.

The year 2007 also saw Hof discard his shoes as well to run a barefoot half marathon in Finland, which he completed in two hours, sixteen minutes, and thirty-four seconds. His half marathon time earned him the Guinness World Record for fastest half marathon run barefoot on ice or snow, a record he continued to hold by mid-2020. Returning to mountains, in 2009, after a two-day journey, he summited Mount Kilimanjaro, Africa's tallest peak; once again his only article of clothing was his shorts. Many of his other records during this time involved submersion in ice baths for increasingly lengthy periods of time: by 2013, after having broken the record a number of times before, he held the record after having been immersed in ice for one hour, fifty-three minutes, and two seconds. In addition to breaking numerous cold-related world records, he tackled a variety of other physical challenges, including completing a desert marathon in Africa's Namib in 2011 without any water. Yet despite his many accomplishments, he preferred to focus not on the records themselves but on the response of the public, and of medical and scientific experts, to the challenges he had overcome. "They brought a lot of attention but what was most important was that I got the attention of the scientific community, who were telling me what I was doing was physiologically not possible," he explained to Stuart Kenny for *Mpora* (27 Jan. 2017). "But I was doing it."

THE WIM HOF METHOD

Hof has credited his ability to endure extreme temperatures and complete strenuous physical challenges to his evolved implementation of what he refers to as the Wim Hof Method, a set of practices that emphasize exposure to the cold, breathing exercises, and the study of meditation and mindfulness; he had devoted more and more of his time to developing and advocating this method by the end of the second decade of the twenty-first century. Exposure to the cold is an especially key component to the method, as Hof believes that experiencing cold temperatures can help make people more in touch with their own bodies and even grant them control over the body's responses to temperature and other stimuli. "The cold brings back our cardiovascular system to its original condition, where the mind-body connection is being reset. Our will has a direct influence on our vascular system," he told Tang. "Once we have an inborn connection with our cardiovascular system, we're able to 'travel' within and influence that system." In addition to promoting swimming in cold water and exposing one's bare skin to snow, he believes that practitioners of the Wim Hof Method should regularly take cold showers.

Likewise, Hof asserts that the breathing exercises he champions can not only improve one's ability to hold one's breath for lengthy periods—a helpful skill when swimming under ice, as Hof has notably done—but can also change one's body chemistry in beneficial ways, and he further believes that meditation and mindfulness can grant practitioners of the Wim Hof Method even greater control over their bodies' stress levels and unconscious responses to the outside world. Though Hof has identified his practice of the method as essential to the attainment of his world records and completion of other physical feats, he believes that the method can have far greater applications and has claimed at times that practicing the method can reduce stress, decrease inflammation, and even help treat chronic illnesses. To promote the Wim Hof Method, Hof has taught classes around the world, offered online courses for sale on his website, and implemented training programs for those interested in becoming teachers of the method themselves. "I want to bring something to the world that makes people stronger, happier, and healthier—that's it," he told Shah about his motivations. Although Hof and other practitioners of the Wim Hof Method are enthusiastic about his recommendations, the method has received some criticism from within the medical community over the years, particularly in response to Hof's claims that the method can alleviate or treat certain mental and physical conditions.

TESTING AND RECOGNITION

Having demonstrated an uncommon tolerance of cold temperatures and taxing physical conditions over the course of his decades as the Iceman, Hof became the focus of several scientific studies designed to understand his capabilities and the factors underlying his body's responses. In 2011, researchers affiliated with the Netherlands' Radboud University Medical Center conducted a study in response to Hof's assertion that he could control his immune system's response to threats. The researchers injected Hof with a toxin that typically engenders an extreme response from the immune system; however, Hof appeared to suppress his immune response through meditation. "I showed within a quarter of an hour to have complete control over the symptoms and also the cytokines, which are the inflammatory beings in the blood created by the immune response," he told Tim Ferriss for the Tim Ferriss Show (7 Sept. 2015). The researchers went on to repeat the experiment, the findings of which were published in 2014, with a group of volunteers that Hof had trained in the Wim Hof Method, with similar results. Hof later participated in a 2017 study carried out by researchers from the Wayne State University School of Medicine in the United States, who found, using scanning equipment as he underwent cold exposure experiments, that Hof appeared to have a degree of mental control over his body's responses to cold temperatures.

The author of several books published in both Dutch and English, Hof was also one of the subjects of the 2017 book *What Doesn't Kill Us*, written by journalist Scott Carney. He has been featured in numerous television programs, including *Ripley's Believe It or Not!* (2000–01), the Discovery Channel documentary *The Real Superhumans and the Quest for the Future Fantastic* (2007), and the Netflix series *The Goop Lab* (2020). In June 2020, the production studio Genesius Pictures announced plans to produce a film about Hof's life, set to star actor Joseph Fiennes as Hof.

PERSONAL LIFE

Hof had four children with his first wife prior to her suicide in 1995. He later revealed in interviews that the difficult period following his wife's death, during which he attempted to navigate his grief while raising his children on his own, deepened his commitment to the physical and mental practices for which he would become known. "Unhappiness brings on necessity," he explained to Kenny. "You need to find a way to bring joy and happiness back again, to raise kids and show them love. I found it through practice in nature, in the cold and in breathing." Hof later had two more children with other partners. In addition to teaching his method and pursuing world records in countries around the world, Hof has held retreats at his property in Przesieka, Poland.

SUGGESTED READING

Hedegaard, Erik. "Wim Hof Says He Holds the Key to a Healthy Life—But Will Anyone Listen?" *Rolling Stone*, 3 Nov. 2017, www.rollingstone.com/culture/culture-features/wim-hof-says-he-holds-the-key-to-a-healthy-life-but-will-anyone-listen-196647/. Accessed 10 Aug. 2020.

Hof, Wim. "A Conversation with Wim Hof, 'The Iceman.'" Interview by Vikas Shah. *Thought Economics*, 22 Nov. 2018, thoughteconomics.com/wim-hof-iceman/. Accessed 10 Aug. 2020.

———. "*The Tim Ferriss Show* Transcripts: Episode 102; Wim Hof." Interview by Tim Ferriss. *The Tim Ferriss Show*, 7 Sept. 2015, tim.blog/wp-content/uploads/2018/08/102-wim-hof.pdf. Accessed 10 Aug. 2020.

———. "Wim Hof: The Iceman on Breathwork, Ice Baths, and How to Reset and Control Your Immune System." Interview by Vivienne Tang. *Destination Deluxe*, 2019, destinationdeluxe.

com/wim-hof-method-iceman-breathwork/. Accessed 12 Aug. 2020.

———. "The Wim Hof Interview | The 26-Time World Record Holder Who Believes He Can Cure Depression Forever." Interview by Stuart Kenny. *Mpora*, 27 Jan. 2017, mpora.com/wellbeing/wim-hof-interview-happiness/. Accessed 10 Aug. 2020.

Parker, Sam. "Breaking the Ice with Wim Hof." *Conrad Magazine*, conradmagazine.com/interview-daredevil-adventurer-iceman-wim-hof/. Accessed 10 Aug. 2020.

Shea, Matt, and Daisy-May Hudson. "The Man Who Uses Meditation to Conquer Extreme Cold." *Vice*, 16 July 2015, www.vice.com/en_us/article/exqzqk/iceman. Accessed 10 Aug. 2020.

—*Joy Crelin*

Alex Honnold

Born: August 17, 1985
Occupation: Rock climber

In 2017, Alex Honnold became the first person to complete a free-solo climb of El Capitan, a rock face measuring approximately three thousand feet in Yosemite National Park. Free-solo climbing is the most difficult—and most dangerous—form of rock climbing, as climbers ascend without the use of ropes, harnesses, or any of the other protective equipment that is usually used in the sport. El Capitan, meanwhile, is notorious among rock climbers as a particularly difficult climb, on which even seasoned veterans sometimes take falls.

At the time of his historic climb, Honnold had been undertaking free-solo climbs of famously difficult rock walls for around ten years, and he had gained some recognition for his combination of athletic prowess and fearlessness. His El Capitan ascent, however, which he completed in just under four hours, catapulted him to a new level of fame—with the help of the documentary *Free Solo* (2018), which documented the climb and his extensive preparation for it. The film was critically well received and won the 2019 Academy Award for Best Documentary (Feature).

Despite this recognition, Honnold remained modest about his athletic talent, maintaining that what set him apart was not so much skill as a willingness to do something most climbers are not interested in doing. Often asked about his approach to and process behind climbing, especially for such particularly dangerous ascents, he told Joe McGovern for *Rolling Stone* (26 Sept. 2018), "It's about imagining it and thinking it

through and feeling my body float through the moves. Climbing moves are all about feeling it, and that is something I've spent my whole life doing."

EARLY LIFE
Alex Honnold was born on August 17, 1985, in Sacramento, California, to Dierdre Wolownick, a French teacher, and Charles Honnold, an English as a second language (ESL) teacher. He discovered his love of climbing at an early age. "When I was a kid, I was always climbing trees and buildings and anything else I could find," he told Chris Noble for the book *Why We Climb: The World's Most Inspiring Climbers* (2017). When he was about eleven years old, a climbing gym opened in his area; he began going to the gym regularly, honing his skills. He was determined to master the sport despite what he felt was a lack of natural aptitude. "I was never like gifted in the way that a lot of people are gifted rock climbers. . . . I was never super strong. But I just like loved climbing all the time," he explained to Tim Ferriss for the podcast *The Tim Ferriss Show* (17 May 2016).

Honnold graduated from Mira Loma High School in 2003 and enrolled at the University of California, Berkeley, studying civil engineering. However, during his freshman year he had trouble focusing on his studies. In part, this was due to personal struggles—his grandfather had recently died, and his parents had divorced—but he also found that he was more interested in climbing at nearby Indian Rock Park than spending time at school. Though his hard work

Photo by Et3115009 via Wikimedia Commons

up to that point paid off when he made the US Youth National Team in the summer of 2004 and placed second, he suffered further tragedy when his father died unexpectedly of a heart attack that same month. After that, he dropped out of university to focus on climbing, eventually venturing out to different locations in his mother's van despite having relatively little experience climbing outside.

In December 2004, Honnold had a serious accident while snowshoeing in the mountains and suffered a concussion and some broken bones. After a slow recovery from his injuries, he began experimenting with solo climbs, initially because of his innate shyness, and he sought out routes at places like Joshua Tree National Park. These short climbs piqued his interest in free soloing on the larger rock formations that climbers refer to as "big walls."

EARLY CLIMBS
Honnold grabbed the attention of the climbing world in 2007, when he pulled off a series of challenging climbs in Yosemite National Park. In May of that year, he completed a free ascent of the climbing route known as Freerider in one day, and then in September he free soloed two other routes in the park, Astroman and the Regular North Face of the Rostrum, in a single day. According to the Yosemite Decimal System, a system of grading the difficulty of climbs that ranges from 5.0 at the easiest to 5.15 at the hardest, the difficulty of the Regular North Face is 5.10, Astroman is 5.11, and Freerider is 5.12. Only two other climbers had ever free soloed Astroman, and only one had done both Astroman and the Rostrum in the same day. These ascents took him rapidly from complete obscurity to fame among rock-climbing enthusiasts. "In the mind of the climbing world, Honnold emerged from the goo fully formed," Alex Lowther wrote in a profile for *Alpinist* (Summer 2011).

In 2008, Honnold followed up this achievement with still more impressive feats. On April 1, he set a speed record of eighty-three minutes for free soloing Moonlight Buttress (5.12) in Zion National Park. Given the date and the unlikely nature of the accomplishment, when news of the climb was reported, many climbers initially assumed it was a joke. In September, he became the first person to free solo the Regular Northwest Face (5.12) of Half Dome, also in Yosemite.

GROWING FAME
In 2009, Honnold signed his first major sponsorship contract, becoming a professional athlete. Around that same time, he recreated his solo climbs of Moonlight and Half Dome for a short documentary titled *Alone on the Wall* (2009); though the routes he took were easier than the ones he had previously climbed, they were still challenging by the standards of the average climber. Filmmaker Peter Mortimer, as quoted by Lowther, described the experience of watching Honnold begin his ascent of the notoriously difficult Moonlight, only to pause and ask the film crew, "So do you guys, like, want me to make this look like it's hard for me?" Meanwhile, Honnold himself told Lowther, "I've never soloed anything hard on camera." He then added, "When I go and pose, it's just a workday for me, you know? It's just for fun." The film screened at festivals, including Mountainfilm in Telluride, where it earned the 2010 Charlie Fowler Award, and secured Honnold an appearance on *60 Minutes* in October 2011. This media attention garnered Honnold a new level of mainstream recognition.

Honnold's noteworthy achievements were not limited to free-solo climbing. In 2012, he set a speed record for completing what is known as the Yosemite Triple Crown—climbing El Capitan, Mt. Watkins, and Half Dome—in eighteen hours and fifty minutes. He reportedly completed about 90 percent of the climb as a free-solo climb, using ropes for only short stretches. Less than two weeks later, he and fellow climber Hans Florine set a speed record for climbing the El Capitan route known as the Nose, reaching the summit in two hours and twenty-three minutes.

In 2015, Honnold published *Alone on the Wall*, a memoir cowritten with fellow climber David Roberts.

PREPARING FOR EL CAPITAN
As far back as 2011, Honnold was considering the possibility of free soloing El Capitan. "That's the elephant in the room, you know? 'Are you going to do that?'" he said to Lowther. "If I did El Cap, I could ride that the rest of my life." However, he worried that sponsorship and media attention would overcomplicate the endeavor and was initially unsure whether he wanted to deal with the resulting logistics. Furthermore, he was worried about the pressure that it would put on him to be watched the whole time by the media or other spectators.

Nevertheless, he found the challenge impossible to resist. By 2015, after having climbed El Capitan seven times in seven days with David Allfrey in June of the previous year, he was training in earnest for his planned free solo, making ascents with rope of El Capitan over and over to ensure that he knew the rock as well as possible in addition to training in other spots in Yosemite as well as outside of the United States. These practice climbs were important to Honnold, not only for the purpose of mastering the physical movements needed to make the climb, but for minimizing his nervousness when the time came to make his solo ascent. "The important part of being able to climb El Cap was for it to feel slightly normal, for it to feel slightly business as usual," he told Ben Church for *CNN* (25 Feb. 2019). "For me to look up at the wall and to think I'm just going to climb this like I usually climb this, even though I don't have a rope on."

At about that time, Jimmy Chin—a friend and fellow climber who had dabbled in filming climbing documentaries in the past and had filmed some of Honnold's solos—and Elizabeth Chai Vasarhelyi talked with Honnold about making a documentary of his training process and, eventually, the actual climb. They followed Honnold for several months, filming his training climbs as well as his daily life in the van he then lived in.

EL CAPITAN AND BEYOND

On June 3, 2017, Honnold finally made his ascent of El Capitan without a rope. People with cameras were stationed on ledges along his route to film his progress, and despite Honnold's fears when he first considered the climb, he was not bothered by the attention. "When I passed the cameramen on the wall, it was just really nice to be able to see my friends up there and celebrate with them," he told Church. He completed the climb in just under four hours, achieving something he described to Mike McPhate for the *New York Times* (6 June 2017) as an "all-consuming dream."

Shortly after his historic free solo, Honnold climbed El Capitan again, using ropes, with his mother, who became the oldest woman to climb El Capitan. For his efforts, he was awarded the American Alpine Club's 2018 Robert and Miriam Underhill Award, given annually to the individual who demonstrates "the highest level of skill in the mountaineering arts." The 2018 Piolets d'Or, one of the most prestigious awards for climbers, gave him a special mention for his "outstanding contribution to climbing." The documentary, *Free Solo*, was released in 2018 and went on to win the 2019 Academy Award for Best Documentary (Feature).

Although after his El Capitan free solo, Honnold had difficulty finding another driving goal of similar magnitude, he did continue to seek out new challenges. In 2019, for example, he completed a roped climb of a route called Arrested Development on Mt. Charleston in Nevada. At a difficulty of 5.14, it was the most difficult climb he had ever completed. In March 2020 he, with Colin Haley, completed what was likely the first ascent of Cerro Eléctrico Oeste, a mountain peak in Patagonia.

PERSONAL LIFE

For much of his adult life, Honnold lived in a van, traveling constantly from one climbing site to the next. In 2017 he bought a house in Las Vegas; he later purchased a second home in Lake Tahoe, a cabin that had been his family's vacation home when he was a child. In 2019, he became engaged to his longtime girlfriend, Sanni McCandless, a life coach.

Honnold is a proponent of renewable energy and in 2012 founded the Honnold Foundation, a nonprofit dedicated to funding solar energy projects. He has often worked as a volunteer to install solar panels.

SUGGESTED READING

Church, Ben. "'If He Slips, He Falls. If He Falls, He Dies'—Climbing 3,000 Feet without Ropes." *CNN*, 25 Feb. 2019, www.cnn. com/2019/02/21/sport/free-solo-alex-honnold-rock-climbing-el-capitan-spt-intl/index. html. Accessed 15 Apr. 2020.

Honnold, Alex. "Assessing Risk and Living without a Rope—Lessons from Alex Honnold." Interview by Tim Ferriss. *The Tim Ferriss Show*, episode 160, 17 May 2016, tim. blog/2016/05/17/alex-honnold/. Transcript. Accessed 16 Apr. 2020.

———. "California Today: An 'Incomprehensible' Climb in Yosemite." Interview by Mike McPhate. *The New York Times*, 6 June 2017, www.nytimes.com/2017/06/06/us/california-today-alex-honnold-el-capitan-climb.html. Accessed 15 Apr. 2020.

———. "Climber Alex Honnold on Filming 'Free Solo,' Facing Death and Rejecting Religion." Interview by Joe McGovern. *Rolling Stone*, 26 Sept. 2018, www.rollingstone.com/ movies/movie-features/climber-alex-honnold-free-solo-interview-728944/. Accessed 16 Apr. 2020.

Lowther, Alex. "Less and Less Alone: Alex Honnold." *Alpinist*, Summer 2011, www.alpinist. com/doc/web17s/wfeature-alp35-alex-honnold-profile-less-and-less-alone. Accessed 15 Apr. 2020.

Noble, Chris. *Why We Climb: The World's Most Inspiring Climbers*. Falcon, 2017.

Serrels, Mark. "Alex Honnold's Next Big Climb Isn't Free Solo, It's Free Solar." *CNET*, 26 Sept. 2019, www.cnet.com/features/alex-honnold-next-big-challenge-isnt-free-solo-its-free-solar. Accessed 15 Apr. 2020.

—*Emma Joyce*

Mamoru Hosoda

Born: September 19, 1967
Occupation: Filmmaker and animator

Mamoru Hosoda is a leading anime filmmaker whose films have received acclaim from fans and critics alike. He has often been compared with the legendary Hayao Miyazaki, whose work has been celebrated in Japan for decades. Unlike many anime directors who work mainly in the digital realm, Hosoda creates his animated films primarily by hand, in the hopes of continuing a long-running, beloved art form. In return for his dedication to his craft, his films, which he writes or cowrites, have been rewarded with considerable popularity and accolades. For example, *The Boy and the Beast*, his feature-length film from 2015, was the highest-grossing Japanese film of the year, while *Mirai*, his 2018 film, was nominated for an Academy Award for Best Animated Feature Film—cementing his international reputation as a premier anime director.

Hosoda's body of work has several major recurring themes, but two of the more notable are an interest in family relationship dynamics, as well as the way in which people change over time. He invariably explores his themes through a world filled with fantastical elements, including interactions with mythical creatures, shape-shifting, and time travel. Some of his fans have suggested he develop a film without fantasy, but he has been reluctant to do so. In an interview with Brian Camp for *Otaku Magazine* (21 May 2013), Hosoda said of the fantasy element in his work, "I believe that fantasy stories, including western folk tales and children's books, have some reality in them. There's always something that reflects real life in the fantasy stories. People can learn and see and reflect their own life in the fantasy tales."

EARLY LIFE AND EDUCATION

Mamoru Hosoda was born on September 19, 1967, in Kamiichi, Toyama Prefecture, Japan. His hometown, surrounded by mountains, would later inspire many of the worlds his anime characters inhabit. He recalled of his hometown to Camp, "There's a famous mountain in my hometown, in the area where I grew up, called Tsurugi-dake (Mount Tsurugi). It's known to be the harshest mountain in Japan. . . . It's still the same. And that inspired the nature and background that I drew."

His father worked as a railroad engineer, and his mother worked as a tailor. In interviews, he described his relationship with them as being quite close, with both parents living into his adulthood. As a child, Hosoda was inspired to become an animator after seeing *The Castle of Cagliostro* (1979), a Japanese action, adventure,

Photo by Et3115009 via Wikimedia Commons

and comedy. The film was cowritten and directed by Hayao Miyazaki, whose body of work led to him becoming one of Hosoda's anime heroes. Hosoda began creating his own animations in middle school.

In 1986, Hosoda began studying oil painting at the Kanazawa College of Art in Ishikawa. The school was also the alma mater of notable creators like Shigeru Miyamoto, the developer of the Nintendo video game system, and filmmaker Hiromasa Yonebayashi, who worked at Studio Ghibli, which was cofounded by Miyazaki.

TOEI ANIMATION

In 1991, shortly after graduating from college, Hosoda began work as a key animator at Toei Animation, a studio perhaps best known in the United States for producing the cartoon series *The Transformers* (1984–87). His first projects included animating television films for such series as *Dragon Ball Z* and *Sailor Moon Super S.* "Everybody does everything in animation. It's very collaborative," he recalled of his experience to Tara Brady for the *Irish Times* (30 Oct. 2018). He served solely as an animator until 1998, at which point he became interested in also working as a director. Hosoda explained to Brady, "I think the relationship between a director and the animators is really, really important. It's not always easy to find good animators, who are not just good animators, but people who you get on with. It helps when you have experience of both sides."

Hosoda began his career as a director by working on television episodes and films related to the Digimon series, about a virtual-reality work that grew out of the Earth's various communication networks. He directed seven episodes of *Digimon: Digital Monsters* between 1999 and 2001. He also directed the related short films *Digimon Adventure* (1999) and *Digimon Adventure: Our War Game!* (2000) as well as the television film *Digimon: The Movie* (2000). Hosoda credited Toei for giving him the opportunity and confidence to become an anime director.

DIFFICULTIES WITH STUDIO GHIBLI

Hosoda's work on *Digimon: The Movie* earned him attention from Miyazaki's Studio Ghibli. In late 2001, Studio Ghibli announced that Hosoda was chosen to direct *Howl's Moving Castle*, a fantasy about a young woman who was transformed into an old woman and must rely on a young magician who inhabits a walking castle to break the spell. The film was scheduled to be released in 2003; however, creative differences between Hosoda and the studio's executives created delays. "I was told to make [the movie] to similar to how Miyazaki would have made it, but I wanted to make my own film the way I wanted to make it," he said to Allegra Frank for *Polygon* (20 Oct. 2018). "The difference between the film I wanted to do and how they wanted to do it was too great, so I had to get off the project."

With Hosoda forced off the film, Miyazaki took over the directing duties for *Howl's Moving Castle*, which earned critical acclaim upon its release in 2004. The experience for Hosoda, however, proved disappointing; Miyazaki had been one of his role models, and he feared that his career as a director might be limited—or at an end—after leaving. Fortunately for Hosoda, he was welcomed back to Toei Animation. He served as a director for a number of their projects, including the short film *Superflat Monogram* (2003), an episode of the series *One Piece* (2004), and the feature film *One Piece: Baron Omatsuri and the Secret Island* (2005). He also directed twenty-six episodes of the series *Samurai Champloo* (2004–05).

MADHOUSE STUDIO

Although he was working steadily, Hosoda hoped to direct more ambitious projects. In 2005, he began working at a new animation studio, Madhouse. His directorial debut with that studio was *The Girl Who Leapt Through Time* (2006). The film was based on the novel by Yasutaka Tsutsui and adapted for the screen by Satoko Okudera. In it, Makoto, a high school student, discovers she has the ability to travel back in time. As she does, she attempts to fix things that she believes are wrong in her life, without realizing that she is changing other people's lives as well.

Hosoda followed this film with the action adventure *Summer Wars* (2009), about an eleventh grader who must fix a problem he caused in OZ, a digital world, while at the same time dealing with the complexities of spending time with the family of the girl he has a crush on. Hosoda crafted the original story, while Okudera wrote the screenplay. Like its predecessors, the film was a hand-drawn effort. When asked why he preferred hand-drawn anime, he explained to Gavin J. Blair for the *Hollywood Reporter* (1 Nov. 2016), "It's like the difference between a photograph and a painting. Both of them have their own value, but the appeal of paintings is very broad. Painting has thousands of years of history, and the newest way to express that culture is through anime films drawn by hand, that's the way I see it." Hosoda continued, stating, "If you go to an art museum you can see that context of painting history, and I see the continuation of that line as the production of anime, expressing through pictures and adding something contemporary to those thousands of years of history."

FOUNDING STUDIO CHIZU

In 2011, Hosoda left Madhouse Studio to cofound his own studio, Studio Chizu, with Yuichiro Saito, who had served as a producer for his two films with Madhouse. Having his own studio to write and direct his own films allowed Hosoda to make the kinds of films that were not beholden to any anime genres. Hosoda noted to S. Takemori for *Tokyo Otaku Mode News* (9 Nov. 2016), "I want my films to be avant-garde in what they express. . . . Animated films are based on pictures, which make the possibilities of expression much broader than other types of films. I want my films to show that we all have more ideas and methods of expression than we might think." With Studio Chizu, Hosoda used fantasy landscapes and stories to explore his prevailing theme: how people grow and change, primarily through their relationships with their families.

The first film he wrote and directed for his new studio was *Wolf Children* (2012), which chronicles the relationship of a mother with her two shape-shifting children after their werewolf father dies. To allow her children the opportunity to decide who they will become—more human or more wolf—she moves them to the countryside, where the local farmers do not know what to make of them. He stated in interviews that the film was heavily inspired by his mother and the landscape of his childhood home.

Hosoda's next film, the action adventure *The Boy and the Beast* (2015), also explores family relationships. After a nine-year-old boy's mother dies, he discovers a mythical world of intelligent beasts while living on the streets of Japan. Of the film, Hosoda said to Takemori, "I am a father, but I was unsure of how I should behave as one. That same sense of confusion can be found in *The Boy and the Beast*, where one of the characters does his best to serve as a father figure. It's quite possible that my own experiences and emotions—hesitation, confusion, heartbreak—as well as the ways in which I handle them may match the way I create my films." Hosoda wrote, directed, and designed the character animation for the film, which became the highest-grossing Japanese film that year.

In 2018, Hosoda wrote and directed *Mirai*, which centers on a four-year-old boy who encounters his younger sister from the future. Through a magical garden, they visit relatives from different time periods. The film was celebrated internationally, with nominations for Best Animated Feature Film at the Golden Globe Awards, Best Animated Feature at the Critics' Choice Awards, and Best Animated Feature at the Academy Awards.

PERSONAL LIFE

Mamoru Hosoda is married. He and his wife have a son and a daughter. His marriage, the birth of his children, and the death of his parents all influenced different films he created through Studio Chizu.

SUGGESTED READING

Brady, Tara. "Mamoru Hosoda's Poignant and Strange Inversion of It's a Wonderful Life." *The Irish Times*, 30 Oct. 2018, www.irishtimes.com/culture/film/mamoru-hosodas-poignant-and-strange-inversion-of-it-s-a-wonderful-life-1.3676853. Accessed 10 Aug. 2020.

Hosoda, Mamoru. "Getting Fired from a Miyazaki Movie Was 'a Good Thing' for This Anime Director." Interview by Allegra Frank. *Polygon*, 20 Oct. 2018, www.polygon.com/2018/10/20/18001588/mamoru-hosoda-fired-howls-moving-castle-interview. Accessed 10 Aug. 2020.

———. "Anime Director Mamoru Hosoda on Drawing by Hand and the Industry Post-Hayao Miyazaki (Q&A)." Interview by Gavin J. Blair. *The Hollywood Reporter*, 1 Nov. 2016, www.hollywoodreporter.com/news/anime-director-mamoru-hosoda-drawing-by-hand-industry-post-hayao-miyazaki-q-a-942844. Accessed 10 Aug. 2020.

———. "Mamoru Hosoda Exclusive Interview." Interview by Brian Camp. *Otaku Magazine*, 21 May 2013, otakuusamagazine.com/mamoru-hosoda-exclusive-interview. Accessed 10 Aug. 2020.

———. "Tokyo International Film Festival—Interview with Director Hosoda Mamoru [Event Report]." Interview by S. Takemori. *Tokyo Otaku Mode News*, 9 Nov. 2016, otakumode.com/news/581c5141da3a593270590c2e/Tokyo-International-Film-Festival-Interview-with-Director-Hosoda-Mamoru-Event-Report. Accessed 10 Aug. 2020.

SELECTED WORKS

Digimon: The Movie (with Shigeyasu Yamauchi), 2000; *The Girl Who Leapt through Time*, 2006; *Summer Wars*, 2009; *Wolf Children*, 2012; *The Boy and the Beast*, 2015; *Mirai*, 2018

—*Christopher Mari*

Hou Yifan

Date of birth: February 27, 1994
Occupation: Chess grandmaster

Chinese chess player Hou Yifan became a grandmaster at fourteen and, as one of the game's top players, earned the moniker "the Queen of Chess." In late 2019 she was ranked as the top women's player in the world and eighty-seventh among all active players regardless of gender. She was just the third woman, after Judit Polgar and Maia Chiburdanidze, to break into the overall top one hundred since 1971. Hou won her first Women's World Chess Championship (WWCC) in 2010, becoming the youngest person to win that title. She secured WWCC victories again in 2011, 2013, and 2016, solidifying her status as a major prodigy.

Despite her historic success, Hou set her sights on the greater goal of becoming the first female player to win the World Chess

Photo by Valery Sharifulin\TASS via Getty Images

Championship (WCC). That prestigious competition, overseen by the Fédération Internationale des Échecs (FIDE, also known as the International Chess Federation or the World Chess Federation) and held every two years dating back to 1886 (the WWCC was not established until 1927), is considered open—meaning that both men and women can compete. Many observers suggested that Hou indeed had the potential to become the overall champion. By late 2019 she had stopped competing in women's tournaments, preferring instead to compete in open contests. Hou herself noted her belief that victory against any competitor would be possible if she modeled herself after her favorite chess piece: the pawn. "When the pawn gets to the other side, it can become anything except the king," Hou remarked to Charlie Campbell for *Time* (May 17, 2018). "To me it shows that regardless of your background, if you stick to your goals and strive, eventually you will become a better version of yourself."

EARLY LIFE

Hou Yifan was born on February 27, 1994, in Xinghua, Jiangsu, China. She was acknowledged as a chess prodigy at just three years of age, when she began regularly beating both her father and grandmother at the game. Two years later, she was training with a local professional coach. Before long, the coach was urging her family to find a better coach, in a bigger city, because she had already advanced well beyond his expertise.

In an interview with David Cox for *Chess. com* (28 Sept. 2019), Hou recalled, "When I was seven, I got the opportunity to move to another province to study chess with a grandmaster. And then after I won the World under-10 girls' title in 2003, I got invited to the national training center, which earned me opportunities to play tournaments all over the world, and then more tournament organizers noticed me and invited me to strong international tournaments."

Becoming the youngest member of the Chinese national chess team provided extraordinary opportunities for the young Hou. Now she could train and compete against the top players in the country. But the experience of being away from home, beginning at age seven, proved to be difficult. "I left my parents behind," Hou noted in her *Chess.com* interview. "I was living at the home of a local chess player, but I was also too young and curious about this new world to be suffering too much. But it wasn't a boarding school; it was just a chess club and so there wasn't anyone taking care of my daily life." Soon after, her mother decided to quit her own job to focus on Hou's growing talent, taking her from tournament to tournament. Hou would later note that having a parent looking out for her greatly benefited her personal development.

THE CHESS QUEEN

With her mother at her side, Hou began competing internationally. She won her first tournament in the girls' under-10 division at the FIDE World Chess Championship in Greece. At age ten she moved to Beijing, where she studied at the National Chess Center.

When she turned twelve Hou went to Russia to compete in the 2006 WWCC. After besting Nadezhda Kosintseva and Natalia Zhukova, she lost in the third round. In 2007, however, Hou won the Chinese National Chess Championship, becoming the youngest women's champion in her nation's history. That same year FIDE named her a women's grandmaster. Once again, she was the youngest person ever to earn that honor.

Hou lost the 2008 WWCC final to Russia's Alexandra Kosteniuk. Still, that November she became the youngest female player to be awarded overall grandmaster status by FIDE, meaning she had met the league's qualifications for types of tournaments played, opponents played, and personal performance ratings. In 2010, when she was sixteen, she became the youngest-ever women's world champion at the WWCC in Antioch, Turkey. She initially tied Ruan Lufei in the final round, then bested her in a series of "speed" tie-breaking games.

Hou would win the FIDE women's title three more times before the age of twenty-five. At the 2011 WWCC in Tirana, Albania, she held her title in a ten-game match against Humpy Koneru. Although she lost her championship to Anna Ushenina in 2012, she regained it from Ushenina in 2013 in China, then won it again in Lviv, Ukraine, in 2016, after defeating defending champion Mariya Muzychuk six to three.

Part of what is remarkable about Hou's success is that it was due far more to her natural ability than to any intense training regimen. Unlike many players, Hou did not make chess the central focus of her life. "She told me she never really worked extremely hard," Vladimir Kramnik—then the world's third-ranked player—told Alex W. Palmer for *ESPN* (7 Sept. 2017). "And, of course, that's a big compliment to her—never working like the professional male top players are doing and yet achieving so much."

For her own part, Hou believed that the difference in her approach to chess was part cultural, part personal preference. In China, it is customary for male players to train relentlessly, while female players are allowed to make time for going to college, having families, and maintaining a healthy work-life balance. That said, Hou's coaches were frustrated with her decision in 2012 to attend Peking University, one of China's leading universities, to study international relations instead of continuing to train and compete. Her coach believed she could be one of the top overall players in the world if she continued her training. Yet Hou believed she had made the right decision. "I want my life to be rich and colorful, not narrow," she said to Palmer. "I knew it would impact my chess, but that's how I wanted to live my life."

MOVING BEYOND THE WOMEN'S CHAMPIONSHIP

In 2016 Hou applied for the University of Chicago's graduate program in social work, but then deferred acceptance. Her undergraduate work later enabled her to earn a postgraduate Rhodes Scholarship to study public policy at the University of Oxford in the United Kingdom.

Meanwhile, with her reputation as the Queen of Chess well established, Hou sought to expand her goals. "To be the best female player has no attraction to me," Hou told Palmer. "I've been there for years." To that end, she stopped competing in women's championships, hoping to establish herself as a towering force in open competition. But she did face considerable challenges. Notably, FIDE's championship systems are significantly different. The women's champion must defend her title each year, with no preferences given to winners by strength or experience. By comparison, the open title champion must defend their title every other year against a single competitor who has advanced through the ranks to become the official challenger.

Hou often noted that she found those divisions frustrating and hoped that she might be instrumental in effecting a change. Along those lines, she took an unusual action in February 2017, setting a record for the quickest loss by a grandmaster when she forfeited her final match at the Tradewise Gibraltar Chess Festival after five moves. Hou threw the match to protest the fact that she had been matched against female competitors seven times over ten rounds, even though there was a four-to-one ratio of male to female players in the tournament. The tournament's organizers countered her protest by noting that a computer was picking the pairings, but Hou felt she had no other recourse. "It makes me really, really upset," Hou told Peter Holley for the *Washington Post* (2 Feb. 2017). "Not just for me but for the other women players."

In her interview with *Chess.com*, Hou explained that while studying at Oxford she competed very little professionally, taking part in just one chess tournament and some other smaller events. In January 2018 she competed in the Tata Steel tournament and was the only female player among the fourteen competitors. In May 2018, she competed in the Grenke Chess Classic. She recognized that to reach her goal of winning the overall chess championship, she would need to put in considerably more training and effort. At the same time, she admitted that chess was not a career for her, but a passion, one that she loved but that she would continue to keep from dominating her life. Away from the chess board, she discussed her fascination with international relations and her desire to pursue a career that might help underprivileged people. While continuing her graduate studies at Oxford, in May 2019 Hou led her chess team from the university to their third consecutive win over their rivals at the University of Cambridge.

GENDER-GAP CONTROVERSY

In September 2019, Hou sparked controversy with comments she made about the gender gap in competitive chess. "Theoretically there should be a possibility that a woman can compete for the title in the future, but practically I think that the chances of this happening in the next few decades are very small," she told Cox. "If you look at any sport, it's hard to imagine girls competing at the same level as men." Although she conceded that statistically there were more men than women playing competitive chess and, therefore, men had better chances of becoming a top player, she suggested that the physical stamina needed for long matches put women at a natural disadvantage. She also pointed to social and cultural factors, including the longstanding tendency for men to train harder and from an earlier age.

Hou further elaborated on her points, telling Cox "I suspect that the male perspective on chess favors men, perhaps when it comes to the emotional aspect of the game and making practical and objective decisions. To put it simplistically, I think male players tend to have a kind of overview or strategy for the whole game, rather than focusing too much attention on one part of the game." However, she also mentioned that questions about the gender gap in chess deserved further research. Nevertheless, her comments sparked considerable debate in the chess community. For example, English grandmaster Nigel Short, who had previously been criticized for his comment that men and women are "hardwired very differently," told the *Telegraph*'s Leon Watson (12 Oct. 2019) that he "would have been ripped to shreds as a misogynist dinosaur" if he had said what Hou did about gender differences.

SUGGESTED READING

Campbell, Charlie. "Blazing a Trail." *Time*, 17 May 2018, time.com/collection-post/5277965/hou-yifan-next-generation-leaders/. Accessed 18 Nov. 2019.

"FIDE Chess Profile: Hou, Yifan." *International Chess Federation*, 2019, ratings.fide.com/card.phtml?event=8602980. Accessed 19 Nov. 2019.

Holley, Peter. "This Chess Grandmaster Was Tired of Being Paired against Women—So

She Just Threw a Game." *The Washington Post*, 2 Feb. 2017, www.washingtonpost.com/news/worldviews/wp/2017/02/02/this-chess-grandmaster-was-tired-of-being-paired-against-women-so-she-just-threw-a-game/. Accessed 18 Nov. 2019.

Hou Yifan. "Hou Yifan Interview: 'Competing with Top Males Is Talent and Opportunity.'" Interview by David Cox. *Chess.com*, 28 Sept. 2019, www.chess.com/article/view/hou-yifan-interview-chess. Accessed 18 Nov. 2019.

Palmer, Alex W. "The Exceptional Genius of Hou Yifan." *ESPN*, 7 Sept. 2017, www.espn.com/espn/story/_/id/20619175/inspiring-greatness-exceptional-genius-hou-yifan-one-china-greatest-chess-players. Accessed 18 Nov. 2019.

Watson, Leon. "'Queen of Chess' Says It's Hard to Imagine Women Competing at the Same Level as Men." *The Telegraph*, 12 Oct. 2019, www.telegraph.co.uk/news/2019/10/12/queen-chess-says-hard-imagine-women-competing-level-men/. Accessed 18 Nov. 2019.

—*Christopher Mari*

Eva Illouz

Date of birth: 1961
Occupation: Professor

Long affiliated with the department of sociology and anthropology at Hebrew University in Jerusalem, Eva Illouz is widely recognized for exploring a wide variety of topics and their relevancy to the way we live, work, and build relationships. "She's analyzed everything from love's leap into leisure, to Freud's popularity in the American workplace, to psychobabble as a new lingua franca," Jesse Tangen-Mills wrote for *Guernica* (1 June 2010). "Historian? Philosopher? For lack of a better term, Illouz is a cultural theorist. Unlike other theorists, however, her ideas are more than just complex complaining; they are surprising and poignant, perhaps because all of her investigations come from the heart."

Illouz—named by the German newspaper *Die Zeit* in 2009 as one of a dozen thinkers with the potential to impact the future—is the author of numerous books. These include: *Consuming the Romantic Utopia: Love and the Cultural Contradictions of Capitalism* (1997), *Cold Intimacies: The Making of Emotional Capitalism* (2007), and *Why Love Hurts: A Sociological Explanation* (2012). Many of her works revolve around a common theme: "the connection between the development of the capitalist world and the development of people's emotional world," as Koby Ben-Simhon wrote for the Israeli daily

newspaper *Haaretz* (25 June 2009). Illouz first began to explore the issue early in her career and was intrigued to find that when most subjects were asked to define romance, they did so largely as a consumer experience: candlelit restaurants, tropical vacations, gifts of flowers and jewelry. She told interviewers that her goal in many of her books is to show readers that their emotional lives are heavily influenced by politics, economics, and the outside forces surrounding them—effectively holding a mirror up to their behavior.

EARLY LIFE AND EDUCATION

One of five siblings, Eva Illouz was born into a Jewish family in Fes, Morocco, in 1961. "I mostly remember the old quarter, the mellah, where the streets were dark and narrow, and full of life," she told Ben-Simhon of her earliest years. "But it's hard for me to know if these are genuine memories or if they come from postcards and movies." Her father was a jeweler and her mother a housewife. As it was inexpensive at that time in Morocco to hire household help, the family maintained a large staff and lived in great comfort.

Morocco had been a French protectorate between 1912 and 1956, and France's cultural influence was still very much apparent in Fes during Illouz's childhood. She attended a small French private school and socialized with Muslim and French neighbors. "On the one hand, the Jews were similar to the Muslims in manners, in rituals and in placing such a high value on hospitality, but at the same time, they also identified with France," she recalled to Ben-Simhon.

Photo by Tzachi Lerner via Wikimedia Commons

"The French were able to present themselves like the rest of the West, as the universal nation that espoused liberty. As a young girl, I felt that in France, Jews could be assimilated as equal citizens. I was very attracted to, and am still very attracted to, the dream of universality."

Like many Moroccan Jews, Illouz's mother had been expelled from school during World War II, and as a result she held a fierce belief in the importance of education for her children. Despite being staunch Zionists, Illouz's parents reasoned that the young state of Israel would not present the best educational opportunities for their children. When she was ten, Illouz and her family moved to France, settling in a suburb of Paris that was home to many Jews.

Her new school introduced her to a wide array of cultures; there were students in her class from Africa, Spain, and Portugal—a pleasant surprise to Illouz, who had feared that France would be more homogenous. She would later fondly recall her high school teachers, who introduced her to ancient Greek philosophy and transmitted a love of knowledge for its own sake.

Illouz spent her summer breaks from school visiting an aunt in Herzliya, Israel, where she immersed herself in the older woman's romance novels and reveled in the sense of informality that pervaded the country. "There was a strong feeling of belonging and of liberation, on the most basic level," she asserted to Ben-Simhon. "As someone who grew up in a very formal milieu, being in Israel, where you could go out to the street in your pajamas or a robe seemed both bizarre and charming to me. . . . I was enchanted by this kind of laxity and disorder."

Upon graduating from high school in 1978, Illouz entered Paris Nanterre University, often referred to as Paris X. There she remained until 1982, earning an undergraduate degree in literature with minors in sociology and communications. In 1986, she earned a master's degree in communications from Hebrew University. She won a Fulbright Scholarship that year and next traveled to the United States to attend University of Pennsylvania's Annenberg School for Communication in Philadelphia, where she received her PhD in communication and cultural studies in 1991.

ACADEMIC CAREER

Upon earning her doctoral degree, Illouz embarked upon a teaching career. She returned to Israel, where she served as a lecturer in the department of sociology at Tel Aviv University until 1999. She later described that period—during which she also spent two years as a visiting professor at Northwestern University, in Illinois—as very intellectually fruitful. She was, however, denied tenure, a decision she attributed to the fact that sociology, unlike math or chemistry,

elicits high levels of debate and questions about the legitimacy of one's research. Although she was disappointed, she told interviewers that the rejection spurred her to work even harder. She noted that she eventually gained a large measure of satisfaction in knowing that her scholarship is accepted and disseminated throughout the world.

In 2000, Illouz joined the faculty of Hebrew University as a senior lecturer of sociology. There she steadily climbed the ranks of academia, making full professor in 2006. She was named the Rose Isaac Chair in Sociology (a post earlier held by the legendary sociologist Shmuel N. Eisenstadt) in 2010. In 2006, she became a member of Hebrew University's multidisciplinary Center for the Study of Rationality.

Illouz also became affiliated in various capacities with the Institute for Advanced Studies at Princeton University; the School for Advanced Studies in the Social Sciences (École des hautes études en sciences sociales) in Paris; the Institute for Advanced Study of Berlin (Wissenschaftskolleg zu Berlin); and the University of Zurich. In 2012 she became president of Bezalel National Academy of Art and Design in Jerusalem, holding that post until 2015. Illouz's scholarly work garnered her Hebrew University's Outstanding Researcher Award in 2008, the Annaliese Maier Research Award 2013 from the Alexander von Humboldt Foundation, and a 2018 EMET Prize for Science, Art and Culture in Social Sciences, among other honors. She also became an occasional contributor of opinion pieces for *Haaretz*.

BOOKS

Illouz published her first book, *Consuming the Romantic Utopia: Love and the Cultural Contradictions of Capitalism*, in 1997. The seed for the book was planted while she was pursuing her doctoral studies in Pennsylvania, with little in the way of disposable income, and set out to have a romantic dinner for her boyfriend's birthday. "I thought, Well, I can't really invite him to a restaurant because I just didn't have money at all, so I'm going to cook for him," she recalled to Tangen-Mills. "But then, when I thought I was going to cook for him, it was obvious to me that I needed to cook some kind of fancy food. I needed to buy candles and I didn't even have a tablecloth because I was living, you know, like a student. And so then I realized actually in order to produce the effect of a romantic dinner for this boyfriend I needed to put out money, which at the time I didn't have."

In a review of the book for the *American Sociological Journal* (July 1998), Scott Coltrane praised Illouz's "forceful and compelling case that romance has become commodified and commodities have become romanticized." He went on to assert that, "Although more questions are raised than answered in this book, the questions are important and the emergent understandings are delectable."

Illouz's next volume, *Oprah Winfrey and the Glamour of Misery* (2003), took top honors in the culture category at the American Sociological Association book awards. It examines the cultural significance of the popular talk show host Oprah Winfrey. In preparing the book, Illouz watched Winfrey's show for more than a year and read hundreds of transcripts. Illouz also read numerous mass-market biographies of Winfrey; regular issues of *O*, the magazine Winfrey spearheaded; the self-help books Winfrey fervently promoted; and fan messages posted on Winfrey's website. The revolving narratives of self-improvement and suffering that Winfrey promulgated apparently resonated deeply with her audience, and Illouz believed the phenomenon warranted serious study.

Illouz's next two books, *Cold Intimacies: The Making of Emotional Capitalism* (2007) and *Saving the Modern Soul: Therapy, Emotions, and the Culture of Self-Help* (2008), received similarly solid reviews in academic journals. The volume that followed, *Why Love Hurts: A Sociological Explanation* (2012), which featured a tattooed wrist against a stark red background on its cover, attracted even wider attention. "In more than one way, I started writing this book in my head many years ago, while still an adolescent," she wrote in an introductory section. "It is the product of hundreds, perhaps thousands, of conversations with close friends and strangers that left me perplexed and puzzled by the chaos that pervades contemporary romantic and sexual relationships."

Equally provocative and timely was Illouz's 2014 volume *Hard Core Romance: Fifty Shades of Grey, Best Sellers, and Society*. The book delves into the reasons why certain books—such as the Fifty Shades of Grey series by E. L. James, with its lurid descriptions of sadomasochism—become so popular with female readers despite being formulaic and not especially well-written. Illouz's later works include *Manufacturing Happy Citizens: How the Science and Industry of Happiness Control Our Lives* and *The End of Love: A Sociology of Negative Relations*, both released in 2019.

PERSONAL LIFE

Illouz was dubbed a Chevalier de la Légion d'Honneur in 2018. She and her husband, Elhanan Ben-Porat, a professor of economics at Hebrew University, have three sons together.

SUGGESTED READING

Ben-Simhon, Koby. "The Tyranny of Happiness." *Haaretz*, 25 June 2009, www.haaretz.com/1.5069841. Accessed 3 Nov. 2019.

Coltrane, Scott. Review of *Consuming the Romantic Utopia: Love and the Cultural Contradictions of Capitalism*, by Eva Illouz. *American Sociological Journal*, vol. 104, no. 1, July 1998, pp. 242–44, doi.org/10.1086/210014.

Illouz, Eva. "Love in the Time of Capital." Interview by Jesse Tangen-Mills. *Guernica*, 1 June 2010, www.guernicamag.com/illouz_6_1_10/. Accessed 3 Nov. 2019.

———. *Why Love Hurts: A Sociological Explanation*. Polity, 2012.

Park, David W. Review of *Oprah Winfrey and the Glamour of Misery*, by Eva Illouz. *Journal of Communication*, vol. 55, no. 4, 2005, pp. 874–75, doi.org/10.1111/j.1460-2466.2005.tb03029.x.

SELECTED WORKS

Consuming the Romantic Utopia, 1997; *Oprah Winfrey and the Glamour of Misery*, 2003; *Cold Intimacies*, 2007; *Saving the Modern Soul*, 2008; *Why Love Hurts*, 2012; *Hard Core Romance*, 2014; *Manufacturing Happy Citizens* (with Edgar Cabanas), 2019; *The End of Love*, 2019

—Mari Rich

Christone Ingram

Born: January 19, 1999
Occupation: Blues musician

Grammy-nominated artist Christone "Kingfish" Ingram hails from the Mississippi Delta, a region in northwestern Mississippi widely recognized as the birthplace of the musical genre known as the Delta blues. Typically featuring wailing slide guitars and lyrics that embody pain and hardship, Delta blues originated in the 1920s and had a deep influence on American popular music. Breaking onto the scene in his teens, Ingram was immediately praised by many critics as a virtuoso of the form and an important figure in keeping the music alive. Reviewers often referred to him with such superlatives as "blues savior," "torchbearer," "prodigy," "young blues aristocrat," and "the future of the blues." "I do think I have an old soul, that I've been here before," Ingram was quoted as saying in a press release issued when he signed with *Alligator Records* (19 Feb. 2019), explaining why he was so intent upon mastering a genre whose most celebrated practitioners died decades before he was born. "I'm moving forward with one foot in the past."

Photo by Rory Doyle via Wikimedia Commons

Ingram took the responsibility of being a steward of a long and treasured musical heritage seriously, but he also expressed his interest in putting his own mark on the traditional blues. "The tradition is always going to be there. That's the root for everything," he asserted in an interview with Alison Richter for *Guitar* magazine (2 July 2019). "But I feel if you want to attract young people to the blues, how about mixing in some of the modern elements that we have, such as rap and a few other styles? Once we get them in, then we can show them the real deal and show them the history. That's what I'm trying to do. I love all genres of music, and I want to keep this thing going but still attract a younger audience."

EARLY LIFE AND EDUCATION

Christone "Kingfish" Ingram was born on January 19, 1999, and grew up in the small Mississippi Delta town of Clarksdale. The town is associated with many of the seminal figures of Delta blues music. Famed singer-songwriter Muddy Waters (1913–83) lived in the vicinity, and among the most storied locales in the area is the crossroads of Highways 61 and 49, where the legendary Robert Johnson (1911–38) was said to have sold his soul to the devil in exchange for his blistering musical talent. "If you're a young musician aspiring to join the blues conversation, Clarksdale is a good cred-conferring hometown to have," Tom Moon wrote for National Public Radio (*NPR*) (9 May 2019). In the *Alligator Records* press release, however, Ingram pointed out that his own skill did not come from any variant of the Johnson myth: "I just practice all the time. That's the only deal I made, and it's with myself."

Ingram's father, Christopher, and his mother, the former Princess Latrell (Pride), both hailed from musical families—Princess was a first cousin of country singer Charley Pride—and they instilled a love of music, particularly gospel, in their son early on. When Ingram was eight years old, he watched a PBS documentary on Muddy Waters with his father, and it sparked a fervent interest in the blues. "It was a sound that I had never heard before—just a powerful, captivating sound that caught my ear," he recalled to John Wirt for *Offbeat Magazine* (27 Feb. 2020). "I just knew, whatever it was, I liked it."

Ingram began exhibiting an uncanny ability to independently learn any song he heard, and his parents decided to enroll him in the Arts and Education Program at Clarksdale's Delta Blues Museum, where he studied with Bill "Howl- N-Madd" Perry and Richard "Daddy Rich" Crisman. It was Perry who gave Ingram the nickname "Kingfish," saying his young student reminded him of a character from *Amos 'n' Andy*, a popular radio show that aired in the late 1920s and early '30s and was adapted as an equally popular television program in the 1950s. (The Kingfish character was known for his get-rich-quick schemes and tendency to ensnare his friends in trouble.) Although Ingram began by studying the drums and bass, he ultimately settled on the guitar. At age eleven he played back-up for Perry at the Ground Zero Club, a well-attended venue not far from the Delta Blues Museum.

THE BUZZ BEGINS

Ingram was soon performing with other local musicians, despite not yet being out of middle school. "Juke joints, dive bars, the whole nine yards—but where I come from, that's a normal thing," he explained to Wirt. "The guys who are old and gray now, that's what they were doing back when they were kids. It wasn't an out of the box thing. Here in Mississippi, way before my generation, the people who came before me always did that."

Higher-profile gigs followed. In 2014, Ingram was part of a delegation of young artists from the Delta Blues Museum invited to the White House to perform for First Lady Michelle Obama, who presented them with the National Arts and Humanities Youth Program Award. The following year, Ingram garnered the 2015 Rising Star Award from the Rhythm & Blues Foundation. He also appeared in the 2016 film *Sidemen: Long Road to Glory*, which documents the lives of piano player "Pinetop" Perkins, drummer Willie "Big Eyes" Smith, and guitarist Hubert Sumlin, who backed Muddy Waters and other venerable bluesmen of their era.

Ingram began touring widely, both through the United States and internationally, playing on stage with such acts as Buddy Guy and the Tedeschi Trucks Band and appearing at such gatherings as the Chicago Blues Festival and the Beale Street Music Festival. One high-profile fan, the funk star Bootsy Collins, began telling his social media followers about Ingram and sharing his YouTube videos, some of which attracted millions of views as a result.

Viewers of daytime television were introduced to Ingram through performances on the *Rachael Ray Show* and *The Steve Harvey Show*. In 2018, he was hired as a featured onscreen performer during the second season of the Netflix show *Luke Cage*, which follows the adventures of an ex-con who is endowed with superhuman strength thanks to a botched experiment. The soundtrack album for the series features Ingram performing two classic cover songs: "I Put a Spell on You" and "The Thrill Is Gone."

DEBUT ALBUM

In late 2017 Ingram, not satisfied with singing only covers, began cowriting songs for an album. The result, *Kingfish*, was released in early 2019, thanks in part to Buddy Guy, who reportedly funded some of the production costs and who can be heard on one track, "Fresh Out." Produced by Tom Hambridge, a long-time collaborator of Guy, *Kingfish* was released on Alligator Records, an independent label whose founder, Bruce Iglauer, had first met Ingram when the latter was just fourteen and playing a gig on Beale Street in Memphis.

Reviewers were lavish in their praise. "It's almost like he's singing through the guitar," Tom Moon wrote for the *NPR* piece. "Every utterance, every little ghost phrase, is rendered with exactitude. He might be landing on the lowdown dirty notes, but he's hitting them cleanly. . . . This emphasis on crisp execution makes literally every Ingram solo on the album a dramatic event. On the up-tempo stuff, he tears through blistering lines with the easygoing assurance of a road-dog veteran. Then when it's slow-blues time, he makes the guitar moan."

The occasional dissenting quibble tended to be from listeners questioning how someone as young as Ingram could sing the blues with any degree of authenticity. "I didn't have to pick cotton, [I wasn't] enslaved, my woman didn't leave me or anything, but I've had some things in my life that I've been through where I had the blues," Ingram explained to Rudi Greenberg for the *Washington Post* (13 Nov. 2019). "Did I have to go through all that? No. But I think I earned my right to play and sing the blues. It's in me."

In a huge statement of industry affirmation for the young artist, *Kingfish* garnered a nod in the category of Best Traditional Blues Album at the Sixty-Second Annual Grammy Awards. Ingram attracted further attention for the non-traditional music video he made with animator Lyndon Barrois for the track "Outside of This Town." The surreal stop-motion video features sculptures made from gum wrappers and was created solely on iPhones.

Ingram expressed a desire to push the envelope in other ways as well. While he told Greenberg, "You have to live up to what the guys before you brought. You gotta respect that ground before you even talk about moving anything forward," he also worked to expand beyond the boundaries of traditional blues. Ingram collaborated with (and opened for) the indie rock band Vampire Weekend, and often noted his intention to explore hip-hop more fully, citing rappers Snoop Dogg and Kendrick Lamar as figures he would like to work with.

PERSONAL LIFE

Ingram was diagnosed with Asperger syndrome, a form of autism spectrum disorder. He became active in multiple arts-education programs, including United by Music, aimed at encouraging aspiring performers with developmental challenges such as autism. He also works with Blues in the Schools, an initiative of the Blues Foundation, which introduces children across the country to traditional music and includes lessons about the importance of cultural and racial diversity.

Ingram's mother, Princess, died in December of 2019, just a day before her fiftieth birthday. At her funeral, held in Sardis, Mississippi, Ingram performed a rendition of "Amazing Grace."

As with many noted guitarists, Ingram's choice of musical equipment earned attention from fans and the press. In part due to his large stature, he noted his preference for a guitar with some heft and a wide neck, such as those custom made by luthier Mike Chertoff. He also owned models by both best-known electric guitar brands, Fenders and Gibson, and played various acoustic guitars. He recalled to journalists that his first amplifier, purchased by his father from a pawnshop, was from the Mississippi-based company Peavey, and he remained loyal to that brand.

SUGGESTED READING

"Alligator Records Signs Christone 'Kingfish' Ingram." *Alligator Records*, 19 Feb. 2019, www.alligator.com/news/index.cfm/nID/797/t/Alligator-Records-Signs-Christone-"Kingfish"-Ingram/. Accessed 11 Apr. 2020.

"Bio." *Christone "Kingfish" Ingram*, www.christonekingfishingram.com/bio. Accessed 11 Apr. 2020.

Greenberg, Rudi. "A Music Prodigy Finds His Calling: Singing the Blues." *The*

Washington Post, 13 Nov. 2019, www.wash-ingtonpost.com/goingoutguide/music/a-music-prodigy-finds-his-calling-singing-the-blues/2019/11/12/47a6ed56-00e6-11ea-8501-2a7123a38c58_story.html. Accessed 11 Apr. 2020.

Hiatt, Brian. "Is Christone 'Kingfish' Ingram the Future of the Blues?" *Rolling Stone*, 31 Oct. 2018, www.rollingstone.com/music/music-features/christone-kingfish-ingram-future-blues-747484/. Accessed 11 Apr. 2020.

Moon, Tom. "Christone 'Kingfish' Ingram Breathes Life into the Blues." *NPR*, 9 May 2019, www.npr.org/2019/05/09/721047827/first-listen-christone-kingfish-ingram-king-fish. Accessed 11 Apr. 2020.

Richter, Alison. "All Hail Young Blues Aristo-crat Christone 'Kingfish' Ingram." *Guitar*, 2 July 2019, guitar.com/features/interviews/interview-christone-kingfish-ingram-blues/. Accessed 11 Apr. 2020.

Thomason, Cody. "The Blues Isn't Dead, It's Just 19 Years Old." *The Vicksburg Post*, 26 Apr. 2018, www.vicksburgpost.com/2018/04/26/at-19-kingfish-keeping-the-blues-alive/. Accessed 11 Apr. 2020.

Wirt, John. "Christone 'Kingfish' Ingram Talks Back." *Offbeat Magazine*, 27 Feb. 2020, www.offbeat.com/articles/christone-kingfish-in-gram/. Accessed 11 Apr. 2020.

—*Mari Rich*

Junji Ito

Date of birth: July 31, 1963
Occupation: Horror mangaka

Japanese artist Junji Ito is the creator of doz-ens of horror comics featuring disturbing bodily transformations, unknowable supernatural forc-es, and uncanny creatures. Although not well known to the general public, Ito has had a cult following among horror fans for several decades. In 2019 he won an Eisner Award—one of the most prestigious awards in comics—for his ad-aptation of Mary Shelley's 1818 novel *Franken-stein*, causing a surge of renewed interest in his works. Two of Ito's most famous works, *Tomie* and *Uzumaki*, have been adapted for film. In Japan, *Junji Itô: Korekushon (The Junji Ito Col-lection)* miniseries started airing in 2018, while a Cartoon Network Adult Swim miniseries based on *Uzumaki* is slated to begin airing on the chan-nel's anime programming block, Toonami, in 2020, potentially bringing Ito and his work to the attention of a wider audience.

In an October 25, 2019, interview for Toon-ami, Ito attributed his interest in horror to a

Photo by Niccolò Caranti via Wikimedia Commons

fascination with the unknown. "You could say I'm exploring mysteries," he told Toonami. "It's like when you see something scary, or you're wondering what is beyond the darkness. I want to know those kinds of things."

EARLY LIFE AND EDUCATION

Junji Ito was born on July 31, 1963, in Japan's Gifu Prefecture. His childhood home had a basement with a dirt floor that made it easy for bugs such as centipedes and cockroaches to get in; this instilled in him a lifelong fear of insects that eventually became an influence on his art.

He showed an early interest in both reading and creating manga, or comics, telling Japanese news outlet *Rocket News 24* in 2012 that he drew his first manga when he was in preschool and bound the pages together himself with string to mimic a real book. He frequently borrowed hor-ror manga by Kazuo Umezu—most famously the creator of *Hyōryū kyōshitsu (The Drifting Class-room)*, which ran from 1972 to 1974—from his older sisters. "When I was very small, maybe 4 or 5 years old, my two older sisters would read Kazuo Umezu and Shinichi Koga in magazines and I read them too," Ito told Ben K. for the Japanese culture website Grape (10 June 2019). "I was hooked." The first manga he purchased was Umezu's *Orochi*, but he stated in the 2012 *Rocket News 24* interview that he was too young at the time to understand the story.

In middle school he became interested in science fiction and wanted to become a science fiction novelist, writing several short stories in the genre.

TOMIE

After high school, he studied to become a dental technician. He entered that field in 1984 but found the work grueling, especially as the hours were often long. He began drawing manga shortly afterward, publishing his first work, the manga *Tomie*, in 1987. He told Grape that while studying anatomy in vocational school had some influence on his later artistic career, the most significant influence of his dental experience on his art was related to the tools he used to draw. "I learned techniques I could use to customize those tools, such as cutting and whittling down pens to make them shorter, cutting grooves into the base so they would be easier to hold, sanding them down to make them smooth and clean," he said. "That all came from the techniques I learned to shape and finish dentures." In 1990 he quit his day job to draw manga full-time. "For a while I had a few regrets about not pursuing that career," he told Mira Bai Winsby for *78 Magazine* (Feb.–Mar. 2006). "However, creating comics is so much more exciting than dentistry, and I don't regret anything now."

Ito's decision to devote himself to art full-time was motivated in part by receiving an honorable mention for a Kazuo Umezu Prize (for which Umezu himself was a judge) for *Tomie*. The eponymous Tomie is a beautiful, arrogant girl whose preternatural perfection literally drives her classmates insane, leading them to kill her. However, she appears in school the next day as if nothing had happened.

Despite initially intending *Tomie* to be a standalone, he received some criticism from a friend who felt that the reasons for Tomie's murder did not make sense and was motivated by this to turn it into a series so that he could further explore the themes suggested by the original comic. In the series, which ran in the teenage girl–aimed magazine *Gekkan Halloween* (*Monthly Halloween*) from 1987 through 2000, Tomie is a sort of twisted femme fatale. She seduces men and drives them to madness; however, this leads not to their deaths, but to hers. She regenerates each time she dies, and the bloody sequence of events inevitably repeats itself. "Her beauty is her weapon, a tool she wields to get people to do her bidding, and yet it's also ultimately her downfall," Meagan Navarro wrote for the horror-fiction web magazine *Bloody Disgusting* (29 Nov. 2019). "Power always comes at a price." Ito noted in his interview for Grape, however, that many of the girls reading *Tomie* in *Monthly Halloween* wrote fan letters indicating that they saw the title character as an aspirational figure rather than a cautionary tale. "Tomie lives her life completely as she wishes," he said. "They envy Tomie's freedom, that's what I think."

A sequel, *Atarashii Tomie* or *Tomie Again*, was published in 2001. A film series based on the property produced nine films between 1999 and 2011. Ito was lukewarm on these adaptations, telling Winsby, "Comics utilize images, angles, and feelings that are hard to create in the real world. I think it's hard to reproduce the overall atmosphere of a comic into a movie." *Tomie* was first translated into English in 2016, published as a single hardcover volume.

FRANKENSTEIN MANGA

In 1994 Ito was commissioned to create a manga adaptation of the novel *Frankenstein* as a tie-in to the film adaptation by Kenneth Branagh that was released that year. The manga was received largely without fanfare at the time, but its English translation, released in 2018 as part of a collection of some of Ito's shorter works, won an Eisner Award and was widely praised by critics. Ito told Tom Speelman for the entertainment magazine *Polygon* (26 Oct. 2018) that he tried in his adaptation to bring out some aspects of the original that had been neglected in many previous versions. "Unlike the *Frankenstein* movies that had been released up until that point, the original novel is a piece of literature that poses deep philosophical questions," he said. "I wanted my adaptation to reflect that aspect."

UZUMAKI

Ito found even greater fame with *Uzumaki*, which was serialized from 1998 to 1999. The series depicts a town whose residents become obsessed with spirals; the shapes begin to distort their surroundings and, eventually, their bodies. "In Ito's hands, a silly concept on paper becomes downright unsettling," Navarro wrote, echoing a sentiment that many critics and fans have expressed regarding various of Ito's works. "Something that starts so innocuous slowly builds to an oppressive force, a perversion of the ordinary rendered bone-chilling in Ito's hands." The inexplicable and uncontrollable nature of the supernatural force in *Uzumaki* drew comparisons to seminal American horror author H. P. Lovecraft, whom Ito has cited as an influence. *Uzumaki* was published in English from 2001 to 2002; this translation was nominated for an Eisner Award for Best US Edition of Foreign Material in 2003 and was many English-speaking readers' first introduction to Ito's work. A hardcover English-language omnibus edition, combining all three volumes, was released in 2013. *Uzumaki* was also adapted into a live-action film in 2000.

GYO

Ito's third series, *Gyo: Ugomeku Bukimi* (Fish: Ghastly wriggling), was first serialized from 2001 through 2002 and released in English, under the abbreviated title of *Gyo*, in two volumes published in 2003 and 2004. In the series, fish, sharks, and whales begin scuttling onto land on insectile mechanical legs, the product of failed experiments by the Japanese military during World War II. Amid the visceral horror of the sea creatures dying and rotting on land and the mechanical legs seeking humans as new sources of energy, there is a suggestion of concern regarding the ways that a country's past transgressions can return to haunt its citizens in the present. Ito acknowledged the antiwar themes of *Gyo* and told Grape that his beliefs on the matter were influenced by the "tragic and frightening war stories" his parents, who had survived World War II, told him when he was a child. Director and writer Takayuki Hirao adapted *Gyo* into an animated film in 2012; its English release was titled *Gyo: Tokyo Fish Attack!*

The second volume of *Gyo* also included several bonus short stories, one of which, "Amigara Dansō no kai" ("The Enigma of Amigara Fault"), became one of Ito's best-known and best-regarded stories. The story concerns person-shaped holes appearing in the side of a cliff; each hole appears to be made in the shape of a specific individual, and people are inexorably drawn to find and enter "their" holes.

SHORT WORKS, COLLECTIONS, AND ADAPTATIONS

Ito has published many other short works; these have been collected in volumes such as *Yōkai kyōshitsu* (2015; *Dissolving Classroom*, 2017); *Ma no kakera* (2014; *Fragments of Horror*, 2015); and *Ito Junji jisen kessaku-shu* (2015; *Shiver: Junji Ito Selected Stories*, 2017), the original title of which translates to "Junji Ito's self-selected best works collection." Ito told *Grape* that his short comics were the works he was proudest of, adding, "I don't think I'm very good at long stories, so I don't have any which I'm personally satisfied with."

An anthology anime adapting some of Ito's more famous short works, *Junji Itô: Korekushon* (*Junji Ito Collection*), aired in 2018. It was not well received by fans, who felt that Ito's trademark aesthetics translated poorly to the screen, but Ito, despite his reputation for not caring for adaptations of his work, praised the series. He told Speelman, "Several episodes are actually better [than] the original manga versions. I really appreciate how faithful they were to my original stories."

OTHER WORK

Outside of the horror genre, Ito created the series *Ito Junji no Neko Nikki: Yon & Mu* (*Junji Ito's Cat Diary: Yon & Mu*), a comedy in which he portrays the everyday antics of his cats, Yon and Mu, in the same style as his horror works. It was serialized from 2008 to 2009 and published in English in 2015. He described the series to

Speelman as a "great change of pace" from his usual works.

In 2017 he published a graphic novel adaptation of the Japanese literary classic *Ningen shikkaku* (1948; *No Longer Human*, 1957), by Osamu Dazai. While the setting and events of the semiautobiographical novel are entirely mundane, Ito employs his typical horror imagery in places as a metaphorical representation of the narrator's depression and suicidal tendencies.

Although Ito has rarely ventured into other media, he did official artwork for the Pokémon video game franchise in 2014. He was also slated to collaborate with video-game auteur Hideo Kojima and award-winning film director Guillermo del Toro on the horror game *Silent Hills*. Although a playable demo was released in 2014, the game was ultimately canceled. Kojima later gave Ito and del Toro cameos in his 2019 video game *Death Stranding*.

PERSONAL LIFE

In 2006 Ito married artist Ishiguro Ayako, a painter whose work often focuses on supernatural, fantastical, and monstrous creatures. Ishiguro is also the creator of several children's picture books about cats. They have two children. In 2013 the family had two cats, Tenmaru and Tonichi, which they had fostered and then adopted.

SUGGESTED READING

Bestor, Nicholas. "Itō, Junji." *The Encyclopedia of Japanese Horror Films*, edited by Salvador Jimenez Murguia. Rowman & Littlefield, 2016, pp. 146–48. *eBook Collection (EBSCOhost)*, search.ebscohost.com/login.aspx?direct=true&db=nlebk&AN=1285761&site=ehost-live&scope=site. Accessed 19 Feb. 2020.

Ito, Junji. "An Interview with Master of Horror Manga Junji Ito (Full Length Version)." Interview by Ben K. *Grape*, 10 June 2019, grapee.jp/en/116016. Accessed 12 Feb. 2020.

——. "Into the Spiral: A Conversation with Japanese Horror Maestro Junji Ito." Interview by Mira Bai Winsby, interpretation by Miyako Takano. 78 *Magazine*, Feb.–Mar. 2006, www.78magazine.com/issues/03-01/arts/junji.shtml. Accessed 12 Feb. 2020.

Ito, Junji, et al. "Uzumaki: Creation." *YouTube*, uploaded by Adult Swim, 25 Oct. 2019, www.youtube.com/watch?v=iQwVaPMRya0. Accessed 12 Feb. 2020.

Navarro, Meagan. "Exploring the Visceral Horrors of the Legendary Junji Ito." *Bloody Disgusting*, 29 Nov. 2019, bloody-disgusting.com/comics/3595513/exploring-visceral-horrors-junji-ito. Accessed 12 Feb. 2020.

Speelman, Tom. "Manga Legend Junji Ito Reflects on the Power of Frankenstein."

Polygon, 26 Oct. 2018, www.polygon.com/comics/2018/10/26/18027234/junji-ito-frankenstein-mary-shelley-translation. Accessed 12 Feb. 2020.

SELECTED WORKS

Tomie, 1987–2000; *Frankenstein*, 1994; *Uzumaki*, 1998–99; *Gyo*, 2001; *Ito Junji no Neko Nikki: Yon & Mu (Junji Ito's Cat Diary: Yon & Mu)*, 2008–09; *Ito Junji jisen kessaku-shu (Shiver: Junji Ito Selected Stories)*, 2015; *Ningen shikkaku (No Longer Human)*, 2017

—*Emma Joyce*

Jarrod Jablonski

Date of birth: April 24, 1969
Occupation: Cave diver

One of the world's most accomplished and respected exploration divers, Jarrod Jablonski has dedicated his life to uncovering and preserving underwater environments. A lifelong native of Florida, Jablonski started scuba diving in his teens before graduating to cave and technical diving. Beginning in the 1990s he earned international attention for his diving achievements with the Woodville Karst Plain Project (WKPP), an ongoing effort to map the vast limestone cave systems underlying the eponymous plain, which runs from the southern edges of Tallahassee, Florida, to the Gulf Coast. Through various projects with the WKPP he set several cave diving world records, including one for the longest cave traverse in 2007. Across his career he accumulated more than ten thousand dives.

Jablonski is credited with pioneering the "Doing It Right" (DIR) system of diving, which he helped advance through his nonprofit training and research organization Global Underwater Explorers (GUE). Established in 1998, the organization provides "a quest for divers to get the most they can out of their diving and their lives," as Jablonski wrote in a self-penned article for the diving blog *InDepth* (5 Dec. 2018). GUE has conducted far-reaching exploration projects that have placed Jablonski in some of the most remote and inhospitable places on Earth. He also founded the dive equipment company Halcyon Manufacturing, serving as its president and chief executive officer (CEO). In addition, he has written extensively about diving for various publications.

EARLY LIFE AND EDUCATION

Jarrod Jablonski was born on April 24, 1969, in West Palm Beach, Florida. He developed an interest in water at a young age. A self-described "water baby," Jablonski "could swim before I learned to walk and swam regularly for years," as he noted to David Strike in an interview for the diving blog *Nektonix* (8 Feb. 2016). Growing up near South Florida's famous beaches, Jablonski became a competitive swimmer, and after entering Forest Hill Community High School, in West Palm Beach, his interests expanded to scuba diving. He was first certified as a recreational diver, along with his father, in 1984.

Upon graduating from Forest Hill in 1987, Jablonski enrolled at the University of Florida in Gainesville. It was there that he discovered cave diving for the first time. He was instantly fascinated by the discipline, a more difficult and dangerous form of scuba diving. "I loved the quiet, serene beauty of the environment and the unique challenges particular to cave diving," he recalled to Strike, though noting that he still enjoyed diving of any kind. "In truth I just love to be under the water and exploring some of the world's most unique scenery."

Jablonski was certified as a cave diver in 1989. The following year he started teaching cave diving at Ginnie Springs, a privately owned park near the town of High Springs, Florida, as a way to channel his passion and simultaneously pay for college. He continued to teach at Ginnie Springs until 1996. Early on he was inspired by famed diver and oceanographer Jacques Cousteau in the effort to combine exploration and education.

Jablonski graduated from the University of Florida with a degree in English in 1992, and earned a second bachelor's degree, in geology, in 1994. Afterward, he evaluated whether to turn diving into a full-time pursuit or take up a more traditional career. As he told Strike, "I decided to give diving my all for two years, at the end of which time I'd evaluate where I was. I have never looked back."

HALCYON MANUFACTURING AND GLOBAL UNDERWATER EXPLORERS

Upon launching his diving career, Jablonski aspired to follow in the footsteps of Cousteau, whose extensive undersea explorations helped raise awareness of the world's oceans and its inhabitants. He noted to Strike that "the opportunity to educate people, conduct valuable research and protect a fragile environment" was just as motivating as the thrill of exploring and witnessing incredible scenery. This aim prompted Jablonski to become intimately involved in the Woodville Karst Plain Project (WKPP). He eventually became training director for the project, through which he turned his attention to technical diving, a realm that takes practitioners far beyond recreational diving limits.

Joining forces with a small group of like-minded explorers and researchers, Jablonski began diving "with near maniacal obsession," as he recalled in his *InDepth* (5 Dec. 2018) article. While participating in exploratory diving projects, he recognized the need for greater safety practices in the rapidly evolving industry. At the time, he and his fellow divers relied more on a relatively haphazard approach when conducting deep technical dives, one which left people extremely vulnerable in inhospitable environments. As Jablonski revealed in the *InDepth* article, "I helped recover the bodies of numerous people that died in caves around the world and mourned the loss of leading explorers and dear friends along the way."

During this period Jablonski constantly had to modify his breathing equipment to safely cover the dives he and his friends were undertaking in Florida's underwater caves. This ultimately led him to cofound, with fellow diver Robert Carmichael, the company Halcyon Manufacturing in 1996. Based in High Springs, Halcyon, for which Jablonski would serve as president and CEO, specialized in cutting-edge diving equipment and hardware, offering such products as breathing regulators, masks, light systems, and handheld dive vehicles. Though initially only geared toward highly technical divers, the company later broadened its product line to the recreational realm; its products would eventually be sold in hundreds of dive shops around the world. Jablonski also opened his own dive shop, Extreme Exposures, in High Springs in 1998, carrying Halcyon products and other brands.

Meanwhile, Jablonski's desire to improve diver training and practices led him to establish the nonprofit organization Global Underwater Explorers (GUE). Also started in 1998, it aimed to provide forward-thinking training and educational opportunities for recreational, technical, and cave divers. Commenting on GUE's mission, Jablonski explained in the *InDepth* article, "We hoped to develop training that encouraged greater safety, allowed more fun and empowered divers with enough capacity to join a variety of projects, including our many conservation and exploration projects."

"DOING IT RIGHT" PHILOSOPHY AND EXPEDITIONS

Through GUE and his projects with the WKPP, Jablonski developed and popularized the groundbreaking "Doing It Right" (DIR) system of diving, which "was born from the knowledge that even seemingly simple diving can get pretty complicated," as he told Strike. The DIR system introduced a number of diving procedures and protocols, among which have included requiring instructor requalification and renewals, devising pre-dive checklists, prohibiting smoking, and using helium-enriched breathing gases. Focusing on quality over quantity, the system promotes

uniformity and safety among dive teams. This simple ethos helped spawn DIR groups all over the world. However, over the years it also met with resistance from some members of the standardization-averse scuba diving community.

Using the DIR model, Jablonski successfully led thousands of dives around the world, reaching record-breaking depths and distances on several occasions. In particular, he earned attention from the international diving community for his achievements with the WKPP. In 1999 he and a diving partner, Andrew Georgitsis, completed a 19,000-foot journey through the underwater caves of Wakulla Springs, near Tallahassee, while reaching depths of 300 feet. Using Halcyon equipment that Jablonski specifically invented for such dives, the two established a dual record for the world's longest and deepest cave diving penetrations.

In 2007 Jablonski eclipsed the world record again when he and another regular diving partner, Casey McKinlay, conducted a seven-mile underwater traverse between Turner Sink and Wakulla Springs. Besides setting the record for longest cave diving traverse, the dive established the Wakulla-Leon Sinks cave system, which is located within the Woodville Karst Plain, as the longest of its kind in the United States. This and other explorations helped raise awareness of the area's importance as a natural resource, leading the Florida House of Representatives to adopt a resolution recognizing the WKPP's work in 2011. Jablonski was directly cited in the resolution.

Concurrently with his work for the WKPP, Jablonski carried out numerous exploration and conservation projects around the world with GUE. In 2007 the organization helped to discover the oldest near-complete human skeleton found in the Americas, in an underwater chamber called Hoyo Negro in Quintana Roo, Mexico. In 2014 GUE took part in the mission to locate and document the German submarine *U-576* from the Battle of the Atlantic during World War II, in collaboration with the National Oceanographic and Atmospheric Administration (NOAA). The organization was also active in an ongoing Italian government archaeological project off the western coast of Sicily investigating artifacts from the first Punic War (264–241 BCE).

OTHER ENDEAVORS AND PROJECTS

Throughout his career Jablonski authored dozens of articles about GUE-specific protocols, procedures, and philosophies, as well as several diving books. In 2008 he became a fellow of the Explorers Club, a US–based international multidisciplinary professional society that promotes the advancement of field research and scientific exploration. In 2014 he assumed a diver training and safety role at the Nad Al Sheba Sports Complex in Dubai, United Arab Emirates.

Meanwhile, Jablonski continued to run and grow his companies, keeping him closely tied to the diving industry. By the mid-2010s Halcyon had more than two dozen employees and was considered a worldwide leader in diving equipment. "Thousands of people around the world are using our equipment in a wide range of environments," he said to Anthony Clark for *Gainesville.com* (15 Mar. 2015). "I feel really fortunate and proud of what everyone's helped us accomplish."

In 2018 Jablonski received the Divers Alert Network (DAN) Rolex Diver of the Year Award for his significant contributions to diver training and safety. The award, given annually, is regarded as one of the most prestigious awards in scuba diving. Yet even as one of the highest-profile figures in his field, Jablonski maintained a down-to-earth approach. Speaking of his general philosophy toward life and diving, he told Strike, "I like to keep things as simple as possible because I find that things get very complicated on their own with very little help from me. . . . I like to keep simple and squeeze every bit of fun out of each endeavor that I pursue."

SUGGESTED READING

Clark, Anthony. "World-Renowned Local Scuba Outfitter Halcyon Now Has Room to Grow." *Gainesville.com*, 15 Mar. 2015, www.gainesville.com/article/LK/20150315/News/604153587/GS. Accessed 11 Jan. 2020.

Gillman, Greg. "Staying Alive While Looking Good: Local Stores Lead the Way in Setting Scuba Trends." *High Springs Herald*, 29 July 2004, web.archive.org/web/20040803001246/http://highspringsherald.com/articles/2004/07/29/sports/sports01.txt. Accessed 11 Jan. 2020.

"Jablonski, Jarrod." *Diving Almanac*, 12 May 2018, divingalmanac.com/jablonski-jarrod/. Accessed 17 Feb. 2020.

Jablonski, Jarrod. "GUE History: Towards a New and Unique Future (2004)." *InDepth*, 23 Apr. 2019, gue.com/blog/gue-history-towards-a-new-and-unique-future-2004/. Accessed 11 Jan. 2020.

——. "In Retrospect: Twenty Years of Global Underwater Explorers." *InDepth*, 5 Dec. 2018, gue.com/blog/in-retrospect-twenty-years-of-global-underwater-explorers/. Accessed 11 Jan. 2020.

——. "An Interview with Jarrod Jablonski." Interview by David Strike. *Nektonix*, 8 Feb. 2016, nektonix.com/2016/02/08/an-interview-with-jarrod-jablonski/. Accessed 11 Jan. 2020.

"Jarrod Jablonski Selected as 2018 DAN Rolex Diver of the Year." *DiveNewsWire*, 15 May 2018, www.divenewswire.com/jarrod-jablonski-selected-as-2018-dan-rolex-diver-of-the-year/. Accessed 11 Jan. 2020.

—*Chris Cullen*

Bert and John Jacobs

BERT JACOBS
Born: ca. 1965

JOHN JACOBS
Born: ca. 1968
Occupation: Founders of Life is Good Company

Bert and John Jacobs are the founders of the Life is Good apparel company, best known for their brand logo, which features the three-word phrase and a crudely drawn, grinning mascot named Jake. John Jacobs, the younger of the two brothers, drew Jake in an attempt to create a figure that evoked boundless positivity in a negative world. Jake sports sunglasses and a beret. He is, as one friend told the brothers early on, a guy who's "got life figured out." Jake's goofy smile proved to be a huge hit, laying the groundwork for a multimillion-dollar company selling various goods—including t-shirts, dog beds, hats, socks, and coffee mugs—emblazoned with Jake's image and the words, "Life is good." The Jacobs brothers decided to launch a t-shirt business when they were on a road-trip in their early twenties. Working out of a van and selling their designs to college students along the East Coast, they were nearly broke when they hit upon Jake in 1994. By 1995, they had made over $82,000 in sales. "The reason people bought those shirts was because they understood it instantly," Bert Jacobs told Glenn Rifkin for the *New York Times* (22 Nov. 2007). "It made them smile, and it was tangible. They could reach out and get a little sunshine." In addition to their retail company, the brothers also fund the nonprofit charity Life is Good Playmakers, and wrote the self-help book *Life is Good: How to Live with Purpose and Enjoy the Ride* (2015).

EARLY LIFE AND EDUCATION

Bert and John Jacobs, the two youngest of six siblings, were born in Needham, a suburb of Boston, Massachusetts. Growing up, their family of eight shared a small house. Money was always tight. In an interview with the Boston public radio station WBUR (2 Oct. 2015), Bert described their mother, Joan, as "the first powerful optimist in our lives." Their father, Al, was a World War II and Korean War veteran, and worked in a machine shop. When Bert and John were in elementary school, their parents were in an auto accident. Joan suffered some broken bones, but Al lost the use of his right hand. Depression and frustration with his physical therapy made him quick to anger. Joan did her best to keep the family's spirits high. "The huge thing that we look back at that had such great impact was every night at the dinner table she'd look around at each of us and say, 'Tell me something good that happened today.' And as simple as that sounds, it changed the energy in the room," John told WBUR. "Instead of us moaning about a tough assignment or a teacher or something like that, we were riffing on something absurd or funny or positive and that kind of thing creates momentum in a house." After high school, Bert attended Villanova University, from which he graduated with a bachelor's degree in communication in 1987. John studied English literature and art at the University of Massachusetts, Amherst, and graduated in 1990.

JACOB'S GALLERY

In 1988, Bert and John embarked on a seven-week, cross-country road trip from California, where John was spending a semester for school, to Boston. "We began with a thin stack of cash, a map of the United States, some mixtapes custom-made by our big brother Allan, and a strict plan of no plan," the brothers write in their book, *Life is Good*. During the trip, they began to discuss the possibility of starting a business together. They landed on t-shirts. "T-shirts were an accessible way to blend art and business," John told WBUR.

Upon arriving in Boston, the brothers moved back in with their parents and launched a ragtag T-shirt company called Jacob's Gallery. They hawked their wares at street fairs and in college dorms. Business was poor, but they were undeterred. They bought a used Plymouth Voyager minivan—a "soccer mom van," as Bert described it to Janean Chun for the *Huffington Post* (21 Mar. 2012)—and began planning month-long and six-week road trips along the East Coast. They jokingly called the van, which served as their home and office, the Enterprise. Bert and John knocked on dorm room doors selling their shirts. "We pulled the seats out of the back of the van and would sleep there on top of the T-shirts," John told Chun. When they returned to Boston after each sojourn, the brothers tested different designs by throwing a party for their friends and asking for feedback. Nearly five years passed. The brothers worked briefly as substitute teachers, but their focus remained on their fledgling business. "Back in Boston, we'd bump into people we knew, and they would politely ask, 'What are you doing? You guys have a college education,'" Bert recalled to Chun.

After a particularly demoralizing run—they had just $78 in their bank account—Bert and John philosophized about how to stay positive in a negative world. The discussion led John to doodle the character they would eventually name Jake.

LIFE IS GOOD

As per their tradition, Bert and John threw a party in Boston and showed their friends their new design. The response was surprisingly positive. One friend's comment—"This guy's got life figured out"—inspired a tagline: life is good. Days later, Bert and John printed forty-eight T-shirts with their new design and took them to a street fair in Cambridge. The shirts, including the two they were wearing, sold out in forty-five minutes. "We were searching for so many years for, 'What do we stand for?'" John said, as quoted by Natalie Walters for *Business Insider* (3 Feb. 2016). "Then when we put out this design, the response was so immediate. It was exactly what we had hoped for."

High off their early success, the brothers shopped the shirts around Boston, but retail stores were not interested. They found one taker in Cape Cod; the owner of a beach shop, bought twenty-four shirts. When the owner asked Bert and John for the character's name, they told her his name was Jake—short for their last name, Jacobs. It was a fortuitous answer; they later discovered that *jake* is an old slang term meaning "everything is alright." The shirts in the store sold out in two weeks. From there, business exploded. By the end of the year, Bert and John had made over $80,000.

Retailers began asking to see Jake doing different activities, like fishing or riding a bike, and the business expanded. The brothers admit that they made a lot of mistakes at the beginning. Their company, officially called Life is Good, was taking off, but they could not manage it themselves. Bert and John hired their first employee, their twenty-three-year-old neighbor, Kerrie Gross, for $17,000 a year. "We had a financial guy tell us we'd need to make $250,000 in sales in order to afford to hire an employee," John told Rebecca Knight for the London *Financial Times* (19 May 2009). "He might as well have told us we'd need to make $50 billion." By the end of their second year, the brothers had more than doubled their profits, making about $262,000 in top line sales; Gross's meager salary was paid in full. In 1996, they staked out a new office space, a forty-foot shipping container on a dirt lot, but they did not stay there long. In 1997, Life is Good broke $1 million in sales, and they moved to a more traditional space in Needham.

The company continued to expand, producing different products in addition to T-shirts. Bert and John moved beyond their iconic mascot, creating new products lines in 2008, among them, Good Karma, Good Kids, Good Dog, and Good Vibes. Around the same time, Life is Good broke over $100 million in annual sales. By 2015, the Life is Good brand was sold in 4,500 stores across the United States, as well as in thirty other countries. The same year, the brothers published the self-help book *Life Is Good: How to Live with Purpose and Enjoy the Ride*, which focuses on their message of embracing optimism.

PLAYMAKERS AND OTHER CHARITABLE WORK

In 2000, Bert and John planned to begin buying radio advertisements, but a slew of fan letters from customers telling them how much the brand inspired them in dark times made the brothers change their mind. They instead used the advertising money to sponsor a pumpkin festival in Keene, Maine, in 2003. The first festival raised $52,000 for camps for children with life-threatening conditions, and they soon spread to other communities around New England. The 2006 Life is Good Pumpkin Fest in Boston broke the Guinness world record for most carved, lit jack-o-lanterns in one place at one time and raised over $500,000. Buoyed by the festivals' success, in 2005, Bert and John founded Life is Good Kids Foundation, a charity that helped fund programs for children facing poverty, illness, and violence. In 2010, the charity merged with the nonprofit Project Joy, founded by their friend Steve Gross, and was rebranded Life is Good Playmakers. Additionally, 10 percent of all Life is Good sales go to supporting the company's charitable agenda; Life is Good Playmakers is fully funded by Life is Good profits. These "positive vibes," as Bert and John call their mission, are also good for business. "The profitability of the for-profit side should always feed the nonprofit side. . . . You don't have to choose between for profit and nonprofit. You can integrate these things," Bert told Sarah Whitten for CNBC (19 May 2015). "It is important to our customer base. They react positively to it."

After the terrorist attacks of September 11, 2001, Life is Good created a T-shirt with an American flag and donated all the proceeds to the families of victims. They did a similar fundraiser after the Boston marathon bombings, which took place blocks from their offices, in 2013. It was one of their best-selling T-shirts ever. In 2020, when the coronavirus pandemic hit, Bert and John found themselves in a similar position. The company outfitted their distribution center in accordance with safety guidelines and introduced a line of shirts with slogans such as "Class of 2020: 'Virtually' the greatest class of all time" and "Stay calm, stay cool, stay home." Business continues to thrive, though Bert and John are cautious. "We're fortunate to have built up a community of what we call 'rational optimists,'" Bert told Derek Catron for *USA Today* (10 July 2020). "Our customers, like ourselves, recognize that there are obstacles. . . . We like to say, 'Life isn't easy, and life isn't perfect. But life is good.'"

SUGGESTED READING

Catron, Derek. "Life Is (Still) Good: T-Shirt Company Finds Not Even Coronavirus Can Kill Optimism." *USA Today*, 10 July 2020, www.usatoday.com/story/news/2020/07/10/life-is-good-t-shirt-covid/5363131002. Accessed 15 July 2020.

Jacobs, John, and Bert Jacobs. "Bert and John Jacobs, Life is Good: From Living in Van to Running a $100 Million Company." Interview by Janean Chun. *HuffPost*, 21 Mar. 2012, www.huffpost.com/entry/bert-john-jacobs-life-is-good_n_1345033. Accessed 14 July 2020.

———. "The Needham-Born Brothers behind 'Life is Good' and Its Positive Mantra." Interview. *WBUR*, 2 Oct. 2015, www.wbur.org/radioboston/2015/10/02/life-is-good. Accessed 14 July 2020.

Knight, Rebecca. "A Fortune Coined from Cheerfulness." *Financial Times*, 19 May 2009, www.ft.com/content/80274aa0-448a-11de-82d6-00144feabdc0. Accessed 15 July 2020. [Paywall]

Rifkin, Glenn. "Millions of Sales from 3 Simple Words." *The New York Times*, 22 Nov. 2007, www.nytimes.com/2007/11/22/business/smallbusiness/22sbiz.html. Accessed 14 July 2020.

Walters, Natalie. "The Fascinating Story of How Two Brothers Went from Running a Failing Business Out of their Van to Building a $100 Million Company." *Business Insider*, 3 Feb. 2016, www.businessinsider.com/the-success-story-of-life-is-good-2016-2. Accessed 14 July 2020.

Whitten, Sarah. "Life is Good's $100 Million Ad-Free Global Success Story." *CNBC*, 19 May 2005, www.cnbc.com/2015/05/19/life-is-good-for-bert-and-john-jacobs.html. Accessed 15 July 2020.

—Molly Hagan

John Asher Johnson

Date of birth: January 4, 1977
Occupation: Astrophysicist

John Asher Johnson is best known for his work in detecting planets outside our solar system, known as extrasolar planets or exoplanets. In 2012, he and his team made a groundbreaking

Photo by Johnjohn3141 via Wikimedia Commons

discovery of three rocky planets orbiting a distant star known as Kepler-42. These were the first confirmed exoplanets known to be smaller than Earth. (According to the National Aeronautics and Space Administration (NASA), more than 4,000 exoplanets had been found as of January 2020; small, rocky examples often drew media attention due to their potential for Earth-like environments.) The success of his work earned Johnson a distinguished reputation as a notable astrophysicist. In 2013, he joined Harvard University, where he became the school's first tenured African American professor in a physical science field. Known for his work in support of people of color in the sciences, he went on to help found the Banneker Institute at Harvard to promote diversity in astronomy and astrophysics.

Johnson's professional success was driven by his curiosity, tenacity, and willingness to work in a relatively new field—the first exoplanets were not confirmed until the 1990s. He was part of a wave of researchers who overcame early challenges to expand the field greatly in the 2010s. As he noted in an interview for NASA's website (16 Feb. 2012), "To be a good scientist, you spend a great amount of time being stuck. Because that means you are doing something interesting. That means you are at the cutting edge."

EARLY LIFE AND EDUCATION

John Asher Johnson (also known professionally as John A. Johnson or just John Johnson) was raised in St. Louis, Missouri. In interviews he noted that he faced few academic challenges in high school and continued to be successful in

college. He earned his BS degree in physics from the University of Missouri at Rolla, later known as the Missouri University of Science and Technology. It was as an undergraduate that Johnson first became interested in astronomy, after a friend convinced him to view a meteor shower. Soon he found himself noticing other features of the night sky, sparking a curiosity that would shape his life.

Upon graduation in 1999, Johnson decided to pursue astronomy further. He first completed a summer undergraduate research project at the LIGO Project at the California Institute of Technology (Caltech). LIGO, formally known as the Laser Interferometer Gravitational Wave Observatory, was created to detect cosmic gravitational waves and then use those observations as an astronomical tool. Johnson then began graduate studies in astronomy at the University of California, Berkeley, despite having no previous formal schooling in the field. There he struggled academically for the first time. He considered himself much less experienced than his classmates, and had to adapt to the nature of truly cutting-edge research. "When I got to graduate school, it was the first time that I encountered questions no one on Earth knew the answer to," he said in his NASA interview. "There was no answer in the back of the book. There was not a right way to answer that question. I was looking at a difficult problem and trying to devise the method for reaching the answer."

Johnson took on these challenges and eventually thrived thanks to dedication and a strong network of support. Especially influential was a course taught by Doug Finkbeiner, then a postdoctoral researcher and later Johnson's colleague at Harvard. Johnson initially intended to focus on cosmology (the branch of astronomy concerned with the studies of the origin and evolution of the universe), particularly on developing vehicle-borne instruments. However, this plan soon changed when he learned of a newly emerging subfield: exoplanets. Such planets were long believed to exist, but no exoplanet had ever been confirmed prior to 1992. More began to be discovered throughout the last decade of the twentieth century. Johnson explained his shift in focus to Melinda Baldwin for *Physics Today* (21 Nov. 2016): "Fortunately, I was pursuing my PhD at one of the few institutions that had researchers specifically focusing on exoplanets. I found the opportunity to find planets orbiting other stars irresistible. Once I learned that this was a viable career path, I immediately hopped on board."

Johnson earned his master's degree in astrophysics in December 2002. While pursuing his doctorate, also at UC Berkeley, he served as a lecturer at the university in 2005. He then completed his PhD in astrophysics in May 2007.

EXOPLANET HUNTER

Upon completing his doctoral degree, Johnson was a National Science Foundation (NSF) Astronomy and Astrophysics Postdoctoral Fellow at the University of Hawaii Institute for Astronomy from 2007 to 2009. In 2009, he became an assistant professor of astronomy and astrophysics at Caltech, where he also worked as a scientist at NASA's Exoplanet Science Institute at Caltech. While exoplanet science had already come a long way from the 1990s, Johnson was still part of a rapidly developing field with new findings around every corner. "In the early days of planet detection, we didn't have any hard data, other than our solar system," he remarked to Pat Brennan for NASA's *Exoplanet Exploration* website (27 Feb. 2017). "Every class of planets could be considered a surprise if you're expecting something to look like our solar system. Nothing does. In that sense, we're still in a state of constantly being surprised."

In 2012, Johnson's own significant exoplanet discovery further helped to dismantle the notion that planetary systems would mirror our own. Using data from NASA's Kepler program, he and his research team identified a system of three small, rocky planets orbiting a red dwarf star known as Kepler-42. At the time they were the smallest exoplanets known. The finding drew attention because the system was much more like that of Earth, Mars, and Venus than previously discovered exoplanets. However, Johnson noted that the new planets were too close to their star to be in the so-called habitable zone suitable for liquid water, and, therefore, potential life as we know it.

For Johnson, discovering a new planetary system was "absolutely thrilling," as he said in his NASA interview. "I couldn't believe it. It was an exciting time to be a researcher."

HARVARD AND MINERVA

Johnson left Caltech in 2013 to become a professor of astronomy at Harvard University, where he continued to conduct research into the study of exoplanets. Some of his research interests included using Doppler measurements and transit photometry to detect exoplanets; the spin-orbit angles of exoplanets; the ways in which stars allow exoplanets to develop; and studying dwarf stars using broadband photometry and high-resolution spectroscopy. He was also involved with building the next generation of instruments aimed at improving the ability to detect exoplanets.

During this time Johnson became the principal investigator of the Miniature Exoplanet Radical Velocity Array (MINERVA) project, which began operations in 2015. An Earth-bound telescope array, MINERVA used radial velocity and planetary transits to detect very

distant planets. With this and other tools, Johnson and his colleagues found multiple compact planetary systems, as well as other discoveries such as an asteroid-like body orbiting a white-dwarf star and in the process of disintegrating. Johnson also led the team that has established the "Kepler dichotomy" of planetary development, which notes that planetary systems either come in neat orbits, like our own solar system, in which planets all orbit on the same plane, or they come in highly eccentric orbits, misaligned from both their parent stars and other planets in their systems. The disorder of such planetary systems is either the result of the way they were formed or due to some galactic collision at some point in their history.

In 2015, Johnson published *How Do You Find an Exoplanet?*, a book that serves as a primer for undergraduate students who are interested in the common methods by which scientists look for and confirm the existence of exoplanets. "For a long time I've wanted an introductory book in exoplanets that I could hand to an aspiring undergraduate researcher that would quickly get her or him up to speed in the field," he told Baldwin, noting that there were already similar texts for graduate-level students and plenty of popular science works on the subject. "I hope that this book fills an important niche and enables young researchers an accessible entry point to the field."

BANNEKER INSTITUTE

In addition to his own astrophysics research and his regular duties as a professor, Johnson looked for opportunities to provide extra help to learners from marginalized backgrounds. Along these lines he founded the Banneker Institute, a summer program hosted at the Harvard-Smithsonian Center for Astrophysics that debuted in 2015. Named for Benjamin Banneker (1731–1806)—an African American almanac author, surveyor, naturalist, and farmer who was the first professional astronomer in the United States—the institute aimed to support undergraduate students of color studying astronomy. "There are a number of obstacles that a student of color will encounter when they are in a historically white institution like Harvard," Johnson told Mia C. Karr for the *Harvard Crimson* (2 Mar. 2017). "One of the biggest problems is that everyone that they interact with is in a society that constantly sends a message that the intelligence and that the industriousness of black people is less than that of white people.

In the Banneker Institute course, Johnson sought to balance the curriculum by providing students with an understanding of both astrophysics and social justice. The program reflects the structure of other, more traditional summer research programs for undergraduates, but also makes investigation of issues of race and racism a significant part of the experience. The institute and Johnson's other work in mentoring students have drawn much praise from colleagues, activists, and students themselves.

ACCOLADES AND PERSONAL LIFE

Johnson has received numerous awards for his work throughout his career. These have included the 2002 UC Berkeley Teaching Effectiveness Award; the 2002 UC Berkeley Outstanding Graduate Student Instructor Award; the 2007 UC Berkeley Uhl Prize for Outstanding Scholarly Achievement; the 2012 American Astronomical Society (AAS) Newton Lacy Pierce Prize; the 2012 Associated Students of the California Institute of Technology (ASCIT) Teaching Award; the 2012 Richard P. Feynman Prize for Excellence in Teaching; and Harvard's Fannie Cox Prize for Excellence in Science Teaching (2015). He has also held numerous fellowships, including from the David and Lucile Packard Foundation, the Alfred P. Sloan Foundation, and the Kavli Foundation. Upon winning the Newton Lacy Pierce Prize, Johnson told Brian Bell for the *Caltech* website (24 Jan. 2013), "Thanks to powerful new instruments and an emerging generation of highly motivated explorers, planetary astronomy is an exciting field to be in right now. I am happy to be part of it."

Johnson and his wife, Erin, have two sons, Owen and Marcus. His hobbies include bicycling, playing basketball, and building Legos with his kids.

SUGGESTED READING

Bell, Brian. "John Johnson Wins Astronomy Prize." *Caltech*, 24 Jan. 2013, www.caltech.edu/about/news/john-johnson-wins-astronomy-prize-38267. Accessed 17 Dec. 2019.

"John Asher Johnson." *Harvard Magazine*, Jan./Feb. 2014, harvardmagazine.com/2014/01/john-asher-johnson. Accessed 17 Dec. 2019.

"John Asher Johnson." *Harvard University*, scholar.harvard.edu/jjohnson/cv. Accessed 17 Dec. 2019.

Johnson, John Asher. "Black History Month—Profile of a Scientist." Interview. *NASA*, 16 Feb. 2012, https://www.nasa.gov/mission_pages/kepler/news/johnson20120216.html. Accessed 20 Dec. 2019.

——. "Exoplanet Astronomer Searches for a Brighter Future." Interview by Pat Brennan. *NASA Exoplanet Exploration*, 27 Feb. 2017, exoplanets.nasa.gov/news/1420/exoplanet-astronomer-searches-for-a-brighter-future/. Accessed 17 Dec. 2019.

——. "Questions and Answers with John Asher Johnson." Interview by Melinda Baldwin. *Physics Today*, 21 Nov. 2016, physicstoday.scitation.org/do/10.1063/PT.5.3041/full/ Accessed 17 Dec. 2019.

Karr, Mia C. "Harvard Astronomer, Institute Offer Support for Students of Color in Sciences." *The Harvard Crimson*, 2 Mar. 2017, www.thecrimson.com/article/2017/3/2/john-johnson-banneker/. Accessed 20 Dec. 2019.

—*Christopher Mari*

Tyshawn Jones

Date of birth: December 24, 1998
Occupation: Skateboarder

In 2014, the skateboarding and apparel brand Supreme released a full-length skateboarding video titled *Cherry*. While any video released by Supreme would receive widespread attention thanks to the brand's overall popularity, *Cherry* proved especially significant due to one of the skateboarders it featured: a talented teenage New Yorker remarkably adept at street skateboarding named Tyshawn Jones. Though he was already known as a young skateboarder to watch among the skaters of New York City, *Cherry* proved to be a key breakthrough for Jones, who gained widespread recognition for his skating in that video and others despite his characteristically casual approach to promoting himself. "When I was filming for *Cherry*, I feel like I didn't take it as serious. It wasn't every day I was thinking about getting clips for this video. We were just skating," he told Lui Elliott and William Strobeck for *Thrasher* magazine (26 Dec. 2018). "I didn't think it was serious until the end."

Over the next several years, Jones continued to hone his skills, and in 2018 *Thrasher* magazine awarded him the title of Skater of the Year in recognition of his work. Jones, however, continued to look forward to future challenges. "Skateboarding, that's impossible to master," he explained to Cam Wolf for *GQ* (9 Sept. 2019). "So that's why I like it. I feel like I can always push myself and learn something new."

EARLY LIFE AND THE ORIGIN OF A SKATEBOARDER

Tyshawn Jones was born in New York City on December 24, 1998. He spent much of his early life living with his family in Hackensack, New Jersey, but had returned to New York by the time he was around twelve, settling in the Soundview neighborhood of the Bronx borough of New York City. During that period, he lived with his mother, Termisha Henry, who would later oversee the operations of the restaurant he would open in the borough in 2018.

Introduced to the sport of skateboarding at a young age, Jones was first exposed to the movements and culture of skateboarding through *Skate*, a video game he enjoyed playing with his older brother and other relatives. When, following their mother's wish that they would go outside more, his brother acquired a skateboard and began to practice skating in real life; Jones also got a skateboard from Target and began to learn to skate as well in order to keep up with his brother. "I was following him around all the time," he told Felix Petty for *i-D* (8 Sept. 2019). "I wanted to be him. . . . I wanted to do whatever he did and he wanted to skate so I was gonna skate too." While he initially struggled to learn the basics of skateboarding, he soon demonstrated a talent for the sport that he honed by practicing daily. Although he initially attended local schools, he ultimately preferred to focus on skateboarding rather than academics. "In Middle School they asked me what I was going to do with my life, and I was like, I don't care about school, I'm gonna be a pro-skateboarder, I don't need a diploma," he recalled to Petty.

In addition to his preferred sport of skateboarding, Jones played basketball at times as a child and teenager but found it to be less challenging—and thus less interesting—than his primary passion. "Basketball ain't even that hard," he explained to Alexis Castro for *Jenkem* (31 Jan. 2018). "I'm not saying it's easy to be a pro basketball player, but the way I see it, if you give a random person a basketball and say throw this in that hoop and give them 100 tries, they're gonna do it. If you tell someone to do a kickflip and give them 1,000 tries, they're probably not gonna do it."

BREAKTHROUGH VIDEO

Following his family's move to the Bronx, Jones began to study specific parts of skating videos and started skating at local venues such as the River Avenue skate park. Growing more committed to learning and experiencing skateboarding well enough to make something of himself, he later began to travel, taking buses and trains, into Manhattan to visit the skate parks there, as well as the impromptu skate parks that the city landscape represented. "I always knew that if I wanted to keep getting better, I'd have to move on from the Bronx," he explained to Castro. Over the next several years, he mastered the streets and structures of Manhattan—from stairs and railings to trash cans and subway entrances—which provided many opportunities for a young skater to train and exhibit his skills.

Jones had begun to receive attention for his skateboarding talents when he was as young as twelve, and that attention only increased in his teen years. A key factor in his escalating profile was his relationship with the company Supreme, a major brand within the skateboarding world. Having started as a New York skate shop in the mid-1990s, Supreme had evolved into a cultural force by the second decade of the twenty-first century, retaining its ties to the skateboarding community while developing a devoted fan base among streetwear aficionados. After an employee of the shop saw a video of Jones skating and recognized his abilities, he offered the young skateboarder, who eventually accepted, free merchandise from the company. Jones regularly frequented the shop and went on to appear in a short skateboarding video, "Buddy," produced by Supreme in 2012.

While "Buddy" and other video clips drew further attention to Jones, his true breakthrough came in 2014, when he appeared in the Supreme skateboarding video *Cherry*. In addition to featuring more extensive footage than "Buddy," the much lengthier *Cherry* documented increasingly complex and daring maneuvers performed by Jones, including impressive skateboarding carried out on the exterior of the New York County Supreme Court building in Manhattan. *Cherry* made Jones a progressively more recognized figure within the skateboarding communities both inside and outside of New York, bringing him fame in addition to a host of new opportunities. That same year, he signed a major sponsorship deal with Adidas, and he would go on to have a solo part in the first full-length skate film, which had been several months in the making and was titled *Away Days*, released by the brand in 2016. However, Jones preferred to focus on continuous improvement rather than his newfound status as a celebrity, an attitude he retained throughout the next several years. "I feel like, if I believed I was great, I could just put my hands up in the air and say, 'I'm already there. I did it already,'" he told Wolf. "Instead, I say, 'That was cool—it happened.' Gives me a chance to do it again, to do it better."

SKATE STAR

In the years following Jones's breakthrough with *Cherry*, he continued to skate extensively throughout New York and elsewhere. During some outings, the young skateboarder and his colleagues filmed new skate footage and posted it online, earning him even greater admiration, a dedicated audience, and fans who would at times approach him in public. In addition to Supreme, which provided increasing financial and material support to Jones over the years and featured him in promotional content, and Adidas, Jones forged partnerships with a number of sponsors as his career progressed, including FA. Meanwhile, he also branched into business. Around 2015, he cofounded and further developed the skateboard hardware and apparel company Hardies Hardware, which sold an array of branded clothing items and skate products. Four years after the debut of *Cherry*, he costarred in the 2018 Supreme video *Blessed*, further solidifying his status as one of the skateboarding world's major figures. "Nothing's changed in my eyes really: just more people watching but that's a good thing," he told Ben Powell for *Slam City Skates'* blog (9 Aug. 2019). "It's fine though; I'm chill with people coming up to me and all that—it's no pressure or anything. It's all love."

In recognition of Jones's accomplishments, the skateboarding publication *Thrasher* magazine, a significant cultural force within the skateboarding world, named him the Skater of the Year for 2018. He was notably the first New York–based skateboarder to win that title, as the sport had long been dominated by athletes based on the West Coast. Though pleased to have been awarded the title, he minimized that achievement somewhat, focusing as usual on the sport itself. "I'm very proud to have achieved it," he told Josh Davis for *HYPEBEAST* magazine (28 May 2019). "But at the end of the day, you should just have fun and skate."

OPENING A RESTAURANT AND DESIGNING FOR ADIDAS

Continuing to pursue business ventures of his own, Jones established the restaurant Taste So Good in 2018. Located in the Bronx, Taste So Good served a variety of Caribbean dishes—including jerk chicken and oxtail—as well as sandwiches, wings, and other items. Though the restaurant proved successful during its first years of operation, Jones once again preferred to focus on the future. "It opened up and I just thought, Tight and kept it moving," he told Elliott and Strobeck. "That's with everything. Even when I get a new shoe or anything. I'm grateful, I enjoy it to myself and I'll post about it but I don't dwell on it. I did that. What can I do next?" In addition to his existing business ventures, he expressed interest in investing in real estate.

While promoting Adidas, Jones also had the chance to design a pair of signature skate shoes for the company. "I was very involved and I always knew what I wanted to do if I was presented with the opportunity to create my own pro shoe," he told Powell about the design process. "There's a lot of basketball inspiration in the design and I took some inspiration from the Adidas 'Top Ten' shoe too. I always loved the look of that one." Named after Jones, the first release of his shoes was made available for purchase in mid-2019.

OTHER PROJECTS

In addition to Jones appearing in Supreme videos and other video clips, a short documentary about his life was released online by the magazine *i-D* in 2019. In June 2020, the video game company Activision Blizzard announced that he would be one of eight new skaters to appear in the forthcoming video game *Tony Hawk's Pro Skater 1+2*, a remastered version of the classic skateboarding games from two decades earlier. As well as winning him a spot in a high-profile video game, his level of skill in skateboarding also prompted speculations that he would one day compete in the sport in the Summer Olympic Games following skateboarding's debut in the event—which had been postponed in 2020 due to the coronavirus pandemic—though Jones remained somewhat skeptical of the concept. "If they told me, 'Come to the Olympics,' I'd be like, 'All right,'" he told Wolf. "But I'm not about to go try to qualify. I don't like contests, anyway."

PERSONAL LIFE

Jones lives and skateboards in New York.

SUGGESTED READING

Davis, Josh. "Tyshawn Jones Is Here for the Long Run." *HYPEBEAST*, 28 May 2019, hypebeast.com/2019/5/tyshawn-jones-interview-hypebeast-mania-issue-25. Accessed 13 July 2020.

Greenwood, Douglas. "Watch the World's First Tyshawn Jones Documentary." *i-D*, 9 Oct. 2019, i-d.vice.com/en_us/article/evjm9m/watch-the-worlds-first-tyshawn-jones-documentary. Accessed 13 July 2020.

Jones, Tyshawn. "The Hustle to the Top with Tyshawn Jones." Interview by Alexis Castro. *Jenkem*, 31 Jan. 2018, www.jenkemmag.com/home/2018/01/31/hustle-top-tyshawn-jones/. Accessed 13 July 2020.

———. "Tyshawn Jones Interview." Interview by Ben Powell. *Slam City Skates*, 9 Aug. 2019, blog.slamcity.com/tyshawn-jones-interview/. Accessed 13 July 2020.

———. "Tyshawn Jones Interview." Interview by Lui Elliott and William Strobeck. *Thrasher*, 26 Dec. 2018, www.thrashermagazine.com/articles/tyshawn-jones-interview/. Accessed 13 July 2020.

Petty, Felix. "Tyshawn Jones Is Skateboarding's New Superstar." *i-D*, 8 Sept. 2019, i-d.vice.com/en_us/article/9kebxe/tyshawn-jones-skateboarder-interview-cover. Accessed 13 July 2020.

Wolf, Cam. "Tyshawn Jones, Supreme Being." *GQ*, 9 Sept. 2019, www.gq.com/story/tyshawn-jones-skateboarder-interview. Accessed 13 July 2020.

—Joy Crelin

Phoebe Judge

Born: September 2, 1983
Occupation: Journalist and podcaster

As a journalist, Phoebe Judge earned multiple Edward R. Murrow and Associated Press Awards. Her wide-ranging interests led to interviews with people as varied as photographer Annie Leibovitz; CIA agents who helped track Osama bin Laden; writers Alexandra Fuller and Robert MacFarlane; a resident at the National Leprosarium in Carville, Louisiana; real-life superheroes; a skinhead; and distance swimmer Lynne Cox, who befriended a baby whale named Grayson. However, she became best known as a creator and host of podcasts, earning a dedicated following of listeners. In 2014, she and colleague Lauren Spohrer launched the Webby Award–winning program *Criminal*, helping to popularize the true-crime genre in the podcast world. The duo then had another success in a rather different genre with *This Is Love*, which was first released in 2018 and focused on love stories.

Judge often noted that the podcast format gave her more control over content than most traditional media channels. As she told Tanysha Bolger for *Ezra Magazine* (6 Mar. 2019), "That freedom to pursue stories that you're curious about is so wonderful. And I think that's what makes the work so enjoyable, is that we're telling stories that interest us, that our bar for a good story, is a story that we're curious about."

EARLY LIFE AND EDUCATION

Phoebe Valentine Judge was born on September 2, 1983, and raised in Chicago, IL. Her parents, Valentine and Tony Judge, named her for her aunt, Phoebe Legere, a musician and painter. Judge's parents raised her and her three siblings strictly; for example, the children could not leave the table until they had finished drinking a glass of milk, which Judge hated. Soda pop was not permitted, nor more than an hour of television per week.

As a child, Judge secretly took money from her father's pants pockets to buy candy, particularly red Swedish fish. She credits her listening skills to childhood attempts to be sure her parents would not catch her. When she was seven or eight, she decided to steal a pack of gum from a store; her sister, Chloe, threatened to tell their parents and blackmailed Judge for months.

Judge left Chicago for Vermont to attend Bennington College, where she earned a Bachelor of Arts degree, with emphases in politics, literature, and liberal arts. After graduating in 2005, she studied at the Salt Institute for Documentary Studies, a program of the Maine College of Arts in Portland, Maine. Judge focused

Photo by Lauren Spohrer via Wikimedia Commons

on radio documentary, producing *Hunting for the Hungry* (2007), which told the story of Sportsmen Against Hunger, a group that donated wild game to food shelters.

EARLY CAREER

Judge began as a reporter in 2007 when she covered a murder trial on the island of Nantucket in Massachusetts for WCAI, a National Public Radio (NPR) station for the Cape Cod area. Another of her early jobs was with Mississippi Public Broadcasting, where she worked as the Gulf Coast reporter from 2008 to 2010. In that role she covered the April 20, 2010, BP *Deepwater Horizon* oil spill in the Gulf of Mexico. She filed several stories on NPR's *All Things Considered* and other programs about the spill's ramifications.

After leaving Mississippi Public Radio, Judge went to India to research and produce a documentary on the health of the Ganges River, which is considered sacred in the Hindu tradition but is terribly polluted.

In 2012, Judge moved to Durham, North Carolina, to become a producer, reporter, and guest host of *The Story with Dick Gordon*, a radio program produced for North Carolina Public Radio affiliate WUNC in Chapel Hill and broadcasted nationally. There she met producer, editor, and director Lauren Spohrer. After an eight-year run, the show ended in October 2013, when Gordon retired, and the show's producers decided not to continue the show with a new host.

CRIMINAL

Judge and Spohrer had worked well together on *The Story* and teamed up to brainstorm ideas to replace it after it ended. Spohrer, a fan of Cornell Woolrich and Raymond Chandler's mystery and detective novels, noted the appetite for the multiple *Law and Order* police procedural series on television. The two colleagues realized that there was no radio equivalent and that such a show would never run out of material. They decided to focus not only on perpetrators of crime but also witnesses, enforcers, and victims. They also determined that not every episode would be dark in tone. In 2013 Judge and Spohrer, along with Eric Mennel, worked independently to create *Criminal*, a true-crime podcast they launched in January 2014.

Judge and Spohrer recorded and edited the *Criminal* podcasts in the evening. To save money they began recording in Spohrer's bedroom closet. Both continued to work full-time jobs in radio; Judge worked at WUNC as a reporter and host for *Here & Now*, a popular interview show.

The podcast network Radiotopia, which hosts artist-owned, listener-supported podcasts, picked up *Criminal* in 2015. The network managed business aspects such as advertising and marketing, as well as finding sponsors, thus freeing Judge and Spohrer to work on the creative side. Spohrer was the first to work on the show full-time, but by 2016 Judge had also made *Criminal* her sole job. The show remained an independent production, which for the creators meant continuing to search for an audience and creative ways to make the show better.

The show, broadcast every other Friday, varies in length but is generally no more than half an hour long. It delves into sociological aspects of crime, as well as historical cases. For example, one episode, "In Plain Sight," covered the case of William and Ellen Craft, who assumed disguises to escape slavery. Even Judge was surprised by *Criminal's* success. As she told Bolger, "When Lauren Spohrer and I created the show, we really wanted it to be successful and we told ourselves, 'Even if no one listens, we're going to take this really seriously.' And the fact that somehow that worked, is still shocking to me and I appreciate it all the time."

PUTTING A SHOW TOGETHER

Both Judge and Spohrer committed themselves to doing background research for each story. The show reinforced Judge's idea that a successful interviewer requires the person asking questions to do more listening than talking. In her view, success also relied on an interviewer who is both curious and willing to accept the answer an interviewee gives, even if it seems to be a lie. In addition, some shows required fact-checking information for accuracy. Depending on how many people needed to be interviewed and how much fact-checking must occur, a show could take between twenty-five and more than forty hours to complete.

Concerning the requisite personal connection *Criminal* required, Judge told Leonard Sipes for *DC Public Safety Radio* (18 Mar. 2016), "We won't do it unless we have a very strong personal story at the center of it. . . . I think for us hearing that firsthand account, hearing the emotion and the way someone has seen one of these events through their own eyes, having someone who can give us that type of perspective is critical for us." Judge and Spohrer were also adamant about not forcing moral conclusions, sensationalizing stories, or resolving endings.

In addition to the broadcasts, the team sometimes took the show on the road for a live audience in nightclubs or small theaters. These sessions also included a question-and-answer opportunity with the audience, along with other interactive segments, such as stop-motion animated graphics done by the show's artist, Julienne Alexander.

BRANCHING OUT

Following the success of *Criminal*, Judge and Spohrer decided to expand the reach of their show and move in new directions, though in areas equally as complicated as crime. They began by adding two story-oriented podcasts, *This Is Love* and *Phoebe Reads a Mystery*.

The former began on February 14, 2018, after Judge and Spohrer brainstormed ideas to expand their storytelling. They thought "Why not try a topic like love?" as Judge told Evie Hemphill for *St. Louis Public Radio* (23 Apr. 2020). "People have these preconceived notions of what love is and what it should be and what a love story is. Let's do the same thing. Let's confuse people, let's open up this word." Judge found similarities between the passions of crime stories and those of love stories. Described as warmer than *Criminal*, the show features some of the same elements of that podcast, including music and interviews.

Soon Judge and Spohrer had another hit on their hands. In 2019, *Time* recommended *This Is Love*, which published an episode each week, as one of the best podcasts in the area of society. As Eliana Dockterman wrote for *Time* (20 Dec. 2019), "The podcast tries to decode the mystery of how our romances, obsessions and relationships drive us. Listening to it can feel like a contact high."

Phoebe Reads a Mystery began for Judge out of her own comfort reading of mysteries in 2020, when a planned road show for her podcast was canceled amid the COVID-19 pandemic. As Sarah Hotchkiss reported for KQED (2 Apr. 2020), in the first episode, Judge told listeners,

"One thing that's been making me feel a little more at ease has been reading fiction. I started reading Agatha Christie's first published novel, *The Mysterious Affair at Styles* and I thought, maybe I could read it to you. A chapter a day until we get to the end." Listeners appreciated Judge's efforts; after five shows, the show was ranked number twenty-two on Apple podcasts. She moved on to other classic novels with a flair of mystery and suspense, including Wilkie Collins's *The Moonstone* and *Jane Eyre* by Charlotte Brontë.

PERSONAL LIFE
Phoebe Judge lives in Durham, North Carolina, with her partner, Sara. She enjoys cooking and has dabbled in making beer; she also tends a vegetable garden in the front yard. Judge runs, enjoys long walks, and keeps to a regular schedule of meals and sleep. She was also known to take an annual two-week vacation in northern Maine in a location without Internet access. As she told *Durham Magazine* (27 Oct. 2015), "As much as I love North Carolina, I'll never get used to warm ocean water. North Carolina beaches will never be cold enough for me."

SUGGESTED READING
Capewell, Jillian. "Before 'Serial,' Two Women Set Out to Bring True Crime to Podcasts." *HuffPost*, 3 Feb. 2016, www.huffpost.com/entry/criminal-podcast-true-crime-phoebe-judge_n_56afd185e4b0b8d7c230436f. Accessed 5 Sept. 2020.

Hemphill, Evie. "'Criminal' Co-Creators Phoebe Judge and Laura Spohrer Talk Crime, Love, and St. Louis." *St. Louis Public Radio*, 23 Apr. 2020, news.stlpublicradio.org/show/st-louis-on-the-air/2020-04-23/criminal-co-creators-phoebe-judge-and-lauren-spohrer-talk-crime-love-and-st-louis. Accessed 25 Aug. 2020.

Judge, Phoebe. "'Criminal' Podcast Host Phoebe Judge Interview." Interview by Tanysha Bolger. *Ezra Magazine*, 6 Mar. 2019, ezramagazine.com/criminal-podcast-host-phoebe-judge-interview/. 22 Aug. 2020.

———. "5 Burning Questions with WUNC's Phoebe Judge." Interview. *Durham Magazine*, 27 Oct. 2015, durhammag.com/5-burning-questions-with-wuncs-phoebe-judge/. Accessed 17 Sept. 2020.

___, and Lauren Spohrer. "This Is Criminal—An Interview with Phoebe Judge and Lauren Spohrer." Interview by Leonard Sipes and CSOSA. *DC Public Safety*, 18 Mar. 2016, media.csosa.gov/podcast/transcripts/this-is-criminal-an-interview-with-phoebe-judge-and-lauren-spohrer/. Accessed 17 Sept. 2020.

Mallenbaum, Carly. "Why the 'Criminal' Podcasters Are Moving from Murder to Love Stories in New Show 'This Is Love.'" *USA Today*, 13 Feb. 2018, www.usatoday.com/story/life/entertainthis/2018/02/13/love-criminal-podcast/322565002/. Accessed 17 Sept. 2020.

SELECTED WORKS
Criminal, 2014– ; *This Is Love*, 2018– ; *Phoebe Reads a Mystery*, 2020–

—Judy Johnson

Kersti Kaljulaid
Date of birth: December 30, 1969
Occupation: Politician

In 2016, the parliament of Estonia, a Baltic nation of some 1.3 million people that borders Russia and Latvia, elected Kersti Kaljulaid president. Kaljulaid is Estonia's fifth president since 1938, and the fourth since the end of the country's Soviet occupation in 1991. She is also the youngest person and first woman to ever hold the office.

The experience of growing up under an oppressive regime shaped Kaljulaid's core views, including her fierce advocacy of democratic institutions, human rights, and freedom of speech. At the Brussels Forum in 2017, she derided the tendency to equate democracy with consumerism. "Too many people in the world associate democracy with their ability to go and buy more and more every year," she said, as quoted by Jonathan Capehart for the *Washington Post* (28 Mar. 2017). "I come from a country where it's much more popular to remind people that democracy is available at every income level and this is something which you need to protect. . . . The freedom of speech. The freedom of thinking. The freedom of coming and going." Her advocacy is particularly important given threats at home—the rise of the far-right Conservative People's Party, or EKRE—and abroad, specifically, the resurgence of Russia, and its threat to Estonia's nascent democracy. A former auditor for the European Union (EU), which Estonia joined in 2004, Kaljulaid is also a fierce defender of Estonia's participation in that body. "The hysterical rise of 'Europe is bad' and 'Europe is regulating too much' limits our space for rational debate," she told Benjamin Bathke for *Foreign Policy* magazine (18 July 2019). "I'm trying to overcome it by pointing out the basics so that our populations finally understand that the European Union is good for them."

EARLY LIFE AND CAREER
Kersti Kaljulaid was born in Tartu, Estonia's second-largest city, on December 30, 1969. She attended high school in Tallin, Estonia's capital.

Photo by Annika Haas via Wikimedia Commons

She had a specific interest in ornithology and was a member of the student scientific association.

Kaljulaid was attending the University of Tartu's Faculty of Natural Sciences when Estonia gained its independence from the Soviet Union in 1991. She recalled that turbulent time in an interview with Capehart for his podcast *Cape Up with Jonathan Capehart* (28 Mar. 2017), saying: "We were indeed very poor, but we were proud that we were free." Kaljulaid graduated from the university with a degree in genetics.

After the Soviet occupation ended, Estonia, under Prime Minister Mart Laar and President Lennart Meri, invested heavily in computer and internet literacy, and became a haven for start-up companies, boasting some of the lowest business tax rates in the EU and liberal laws regulating tech research. Kaljulaid entered the workforce during this period as a sales manager for Eesti Telefon, Estonia's state-owned telecom company. After that, she was a project manager at the now defunct bank Hoiupank. She then took a job in investment banking at Hansapank, which was then the most successful bank in Estonia; it was later sold to the Swedish bank Swedbank.

GOVERNMENT OFFICIAL

In 1999, Kaljulaid was appointed economic advisor to Laar during his second term as prime minister. In this capacity, she advised Laar during budget negotiations with other ministers, collaborated with the ministers of social affairs and finance on pension reform, and organized cooperation between the prime minister's office,

other ministries, and Estonia's central bank. She also managed relations between the prime minister's office and international financial institutions such as the International Monetary Fund (IMF), World Bank, and the European Bank for Reconstruction and Development. While serving as Laar's economic advisor, she earned a master's degree in business and economics from the University of Tartu's Faculty of Economics and Business Administration, graduating in 2001. In 2002, Kaljulaid left the prime minister's office to accept a role as the chief financial officer and chief executive officer of Iru Power Plant, a subsidiary of Eesti Energia, a state-owned energy company.

When Estonia joined the EU in 2004, Kaljulaid was chosen as the country's representative to the European Court of Auditors (ECA) in Luxembourg, which is comprised of one auditor from each EU member state. The body monitors and implements the budget of the EU. As an ECA auditor, Kaljulaid organized a financial audit of the EU's research and development funds (2004–06), audited the EU's Galileo project (2004–07), audited the EU's structural policies (2007–10), and worked on the agriculture audit (2016). Between 2010 and 2016, she coordinated the ECA's Annual Report and State of Assurance. Additionally, she served as the chair of several of the ECA committees for the Europol audit and administrative affairs.

PARLIAMENT'S CONSENSUS CANDIDATE

Prior to Kaljulaid's election in 2016, Estonian politics were in turmoil. Toomas Hendrik Ilves, Estonia's president from 2006 to 2016, described the turmoil, and Russia's role in promoting it, in an interview with Nick Douglas for *Lifehacker* (16 Oct. 2019). "The worst situation I faced was in 2007, when we had a massive cyberattack from Russia. And riots. I had to go and calm people down," he said. In 2014, Russia invaded Crimea, detained an Estonian security officer, and began a military buildup in the Baltic region. Estonia in turn stepped up its defense measures—even training citizens to fight as insurgents—in the event of conflict with Russia. In 2015, Europe was rattled by waves of migrants and refugees fleeing Africa and the Middle East, including Syria. Anti-immigration sentiment gripped Europe, buoying racist, far-right parties to power across the EU. These events had a profound impact on Estonia's political milieu at the time of Kaljulaid's election in 2016.

In 2016, Ilves was finishing his second and final five-year term, but the Riigikogu, the Estonian parliament, with its ruling three-party coalition, could not agree on a successor. Members of parliament (MPs) were unable to choose among four candidates in August, nor among five candidates in September, as no candidate met the sixty-eight-vote threshold. Kaljulaid was not among the first two sets of candidates. Instead, her candidacy arose from an agreement among six parties in parliament to nominate a political outsider. Not only was Kaljulaid outside of local politics—her position as Estonia's representative on the European Court of Auditors required her to work abroad in Luxembourg—but she was not affiliated with a particular political party, though she had described herself in 2013 as a liberal conservative who is liberal on social issues like LGBTQ rights, but economically conservative. When the *Post*'s Capehart asked Kaljulaid how she became parliament's consensus candidate, she politely steered the conversation toward her pride in accepting the job. In October 2016, Kaljulaid won the election unanimously, with 81 votes out of 101 MPs. The remaining twenty MPs were absent or abstained, but no one voted against her.

In November 2016, about a month after Kaljulaid's election, prime minister Taavi Rõivas's coalition government—including his own center-right Reform party, the left-leaning Social Democrats and the conservative IRL party—collapsed. Rõivas resigned, and was replaced by Jüri Ratas of the populist Center party, which has historic ties to Vladimir Putin's Russia.

PRESIDENT OF ESTONIA

With Russia as a looming threat, Kaljulaid has made impassioned speeches in support of democracy and democratic processes. In 2017, she pointedly reiterated Estonia's support of the EU and NATO (North Atlantic Treaty Organization), both of which Estonia joined in 2004, to stand against Russian aggression in the region, and calling on the West to recognize it as a threat to democracy everywhere. "I trust NATO," she told Capehart, when he asked her how worried she was about Russia invading Estonia, as it had Ukraine. "I also trust the international value-based community to make sure that Russia recognizes that our democratic architecture is not going to fail."

In April 2019, Kaljulaid traveled to Moscow for the opening of the new Estonian embassy, making her the first Estonian leader to visit Russia in eight years. Kaljulaid also met with Putin, who expressed displeasure with Estonia and the rest of the EU for imposing sanctions on Russia. Kaljulaid and Putin spoke just after NATO sent a thousand troops to the Estonian border. Many Estonians criticized Kaljulaid for agreeing to the meeting at all, but she was firm in her decision. "Neighbors should talk," Kaljulaid said, as quoted by a reporter for *Radio Free Europe* (19 Apr. 2019), "even if we have certain disagreements."

Kaljulaid has had to contend with domestic threats as well, namely the rise of the right-wing populist EKRE party. In 2013, EKRE member Martin Helme proclaimed his immigration stance, as quoted by Estonia's *ERR News* (29 May 2013), as: "If you're black, go back," adding, "I want Estonia to be a white country." Kaljulaid has emerged as an outspoken critic of EKRE, telling Bathke just before the parliamentary elections in March 2019: "I hate them for their behavior, and I apologize for the image this might give." Kaljulaid attributes the rise of the EKRE to Estonia's rapid democratization and industrialization after 1991. She suggested that some Estonians felt left behind by change and were looking for someone—namely the EU and asylum seekers—to blame. "In the last thirty years, we caught up on decades of industrialization under Soviet rule. It's been an extremely quick change. Depopulation of rural areas, concentration in the cities, and therefore the need to constantly react to social inequalities, happened to us at double the speed," she explained to Bathke. "This has created a feeling among people in rural areas that life and developments pass them by."

The EKRE party tripled its seats in the 2019 elections, winning five key ministries in the ruling coalition. During the government swearing-in ceremony, Kaljulaid wore a sweatshirt that read, in Estonian, "Speech is free." When Marti Kuusik, a man accused of domestic violence, was sworn in as the new minister of technology and foreign trade, Kaljulaid walked out of the ceremony, forcing Kuusik to salute an empty chair. Afterward, another EKRE minister, Mart Helme criticized her behavior, calling her an "emotionally heated woman," as quoted by the Associated Press (2 May 2019). Kuusik resigned the next day.

PERSONAL LIFE

Kaljulaid married Georgi-Rene Maksimovski in 2011. The couple have two sons. Kaljulaid also has two children—a son and a daughter—from a previous marriage and is a grandmother.

SUGGESTED READING

Bathke, Benjamin. "Estonia Battles Its Elected Racists." *Foreign Policy*, 18 July 2019, foreignpolicy.com/2019/07/18/estonia-battles-its-elected-racists/. Accessed 9 Mar. 2020.

Capehart, Jonathan. "Does Estonia Understand Democracy Better Than Any of Us?" *Cape Up with Jonathan Capehart*, Washington Post Opinions, 28 Mar. 2017, www.washingtonpost.com/podcasts/cape-up/does-estonia-understand-democracy-better-than-any-of-us/. Accessed 10 Mar. 2020.

——. "'I'm Not Afraid': The President of Tiny Estonia Gives a Giant Lesson in Leadership." *The Washington Post*, 28 Mar. 2017, www.washingtonpost.com/blogs/post-partisan/wp/2017/03/28/

im-not-afraid-the-president-of-tiny-estonia-gives-a-giant-lesson-in-leadership/. Accessed 9 Mar. 2020.

"Conservative Politician: 'If You're Black, Go Back.'" (Estonia) *ERR News*, 29 May 2013, news.err.ee/107416/conservative-politician-if-you-re-black-go-back. Accessed 11 Mar. 2020.

Douglas, Nick. "I'm Former Estonian President Toomas Hendrik Ilves, and This Is How I Work." *Lifehacker*, 16 Oct. 2019, lifehacker.com/im-former-estonian-president-toomas-hendrik-ilves-and-1838158082. Accessed 10 Mar. 2020.

"Estonia Minister Calls First Female President 'Emotionally Heated Woman.'" *The Guardian*, 2 May 2019, www.theguardian.com/world/2019/may/03/estonia-minister-calls-first-female-president-emotionally-heated-woman. Accessed 11 Mar. 2020.

"Estonian President Meets with Putin on Rare Visit to Russia." *Radio Free Europe*, 19 Apr. 2019, www.rferl.org/a/estonian-president-meets-with-putin-on-rare-visit-to-russia/29891517.html. Accessed 11 Mar. 2020.

—*Molly Hagan*

Caroline Kepnes

Born: November 10, 1976
Occupation: Author

Caroline Kepnes has written for numerous pop culture venues, including Walt Disney and *Entertainment Weekly*. She has written magazine columns, scripts, and television episodes, but her greatest success has come from her *New York Times* best-selling novels. Her first novel, *You*, published in 2014, has been translated into nearly twenty languages and was short-listed for a 2015 Crime Writers Association Dagger Award in the United Kingdom. *You* drew praise from prolific and popular writer Stephen King and has been compared to *American Psycho* (1991), by Bret Easton Ellis, and *Gone Girl* (2012), by Gillian Flynn, among other works. Of the male protagonist in *You*, Joe Goldberg, Kepnes told Laura Barcella for *Slate* (29 Sept. 2014), "There is something timeless about his loneliness to me, but I think it's particularly interesting to tell a story about someone disconnected when we, as an increasingly virtual society, are grappling with connectivity." As of mid-2020, two novels in the You series had been made into a television series on Netflix, featuring Penn Badgley.

EARLY LIFE AND EDUCATION

Kepnes was born on November 10, 1976. She grew up in Centerville, a village of the town of Barnstable on Cape Cod. In 1990 she started attending Barnstable High School, where she was the editor of the school newspaper and her English and journalism teachers sharpened her love for reading and writing. As she told Laurie Higgins for *Cape Cod Times* (28 Dec. 2018), "I cannot say enough about my teachers at Barnstable High School. They were like Robin Williams's character in 'Dead Poets Society.' They were absolutely amazing."

In 1991, Kepnes got her first taste of journalism beyond the school paper when her older brother Alex was an extra in the movie *School Ties*, which was filming in Concord, Massachusetts. Encouraged by her journalism teacher, Kepnes talked the movie producers into letting her interview one of the stars; she chose Chris O'Donnell, and *Cape Cod Times* published the article. As she told Gwenn Friss for *Cape Cod Times* (24 June 2018), "It was my first story in the real world."

Kepnes sharpened her observational skills when she babysat for families vacationing on Cape Cod and worked the ticket office at Hy-Line Cruises, a ferry company. Reading books in the Nancy Drew series helped her realize she wanted to write stories with a bit of danger in them. While still in high school she won a Smith Corona typewriter when one of her stories received honorable mention in *Sassy* magazine's Fabulous Fiction Contest.

Kepnes graduated from Barnstable High in 1994. She went on to attend Brown University in Providence, Rhode Island, where she designed her own major, notions of normalcy in American culture, under the broad category of American civilization. The major allowed her to combine psychology and writing, and as part of it, she completed an independent study on the show *South Park* and the culture of repetition. She also studied fiction and playwriting.

EARLY CAREER

After graduating from Brown in 1999, Kepnes declined a job at a law firm and moved to New York City. She took temporary jobs, including one in the mammalogy department at the Museum of Natural History, and wrote in her spare time. She also worked at a bookstore and had an internship at *Conan O'Brien* but determined that the pace of television did not suit her.

When Kepnes saw an ad in the *New York Times* that asked, "Do you like boy bands?" she responded and began writing for *Tiger Beat*. About that job, which she held from 1999 to 2000, she told Meredith Goldstein for the *Boston Globe* (30 Aug. 2018), "My favorite thing in the world was the reader mail, because this was before the Internet had taken over, so we had a section in the magazine called 'Tiger Talk.' It's unthinkable now. . . . In a more innocent time, this is how the kids would find each other and be pen pals."

Kepnes became an editorial assistant at *Entertainment Weekly* from 2000 to 2002. In addition, she wrote *Stephen Crane*, a children's biography of the writer Stephen Crane, which was published in 2004. During this time, she also wrote and submitted a spec script for an episode of *7th Heaven*, a feel-good television series that aired in the 1990s and 2000s. Her script was accepted and produced and aired in 2006.

WRITING ON TWO COASTS

Kepnes moved to Los Angeles. She next worked at E! Online in 2007. During her tenure at E!, she worked on Ted Casablanca's gossip column, The Awful Truth, covering celebrities on the red carpet and at movie premieres. Working on The Awful Truth led to her landing her own column, Reel Girl, covering movies and television shows, which she worked on through 2008. She subsequently worked as a staff writer for the Walt Disney Company's *Secret Life of the American* from 2008 to 2009. She also wrote, produced, and directed the 2012 short film *Miles Away*, which was distributed by Thirty-Seven Fifty Productions. The film, nominated for the Audience Award for Best Short Comedy at the 2014 Woods Hole Film Festival, was about aliens and alienation.

Kepnes moved back to Cape Cod to help her family during a difficult time. Her father died in 2013 after a two-year battle with cancer. She carried additional burdens; she was a victim of identity theft and also needed emergency throat surgery within a few months of her dad's death. In addition, she developed vocal cord nodules, leading to a period when she could not use her voice. She told Goldstein, "When they talk about the spheres of your life, every sphere of my life was a disaster, and that's why I started writing my first novel." Kepnes moved back to Los Angeles, where she started writing her novel, and supported herself by writing for Yahoo TV, from 2013 to 2014.

YOU, THE NOVEL

Written from both first and second person points of view, *You* is a romance in the style of Nora Ephron, particularly her film *You've Got Mail* (1998). In addition, it is also a psychological thriller, told primarily from the point of view of a sociopathic stalker, Joe Goldberg, an antihero who manipulates and harms the women he loves. In the novel, his latest obsession is Guinevere Beck—her friends call her Beck—a New York University graduate student, aspiring writer, and customer at the bookstore where Joe works as a manager.

Kepnes considers her novel to be a love letter to some of her own favorite novels. As she told Higgins, "Ever since I was a little kid I've loved stories and simply loved making things up. I've gotten to do some really exciting things, but along the way I always wrote short stories. I love prose so much and I always wanted to write my own novel."

In writing *You*, she followed the principle familiar to many writers to "write what you know." The story borrows from her experiences working in a used bookstore, as well as her time living in New York and Los Angeles. The fact that Kepnes did not have secure passwords for her phone or computer while writing also fueled some of the invasive aspects of the plot, which relies on modern technology devices and platforms. As she explained to Shaazia Ebrahim for *Daily Vox* (2 Apr. 2019), "We have so much connection right now, access to so many stories at all times, the sense of knowing people. . . . There's a breakdown of boundaries that turns us all into mild voyeurs." Joe not only tweets from his own Twitter account, but also breaks into other people's accounts and poses as those people. Atria/Emily Bestler Books acquired *You* in a two-book deal and released it in 2014.

HIDDEN BODIES

Kepnes's second novel featuring Joe Goldberg, *Hidden Bodies*, was published in 2016 and includes social satire, as well as dark humor and suspense. Explaining the genre-bending of both novels, Kepnes told Mara White in an interview for *Huffpost* (6 Dec. 2017), "Joe's relationships are the driving force. The only rule is that I have to believe in it. If I read it over and don't feel like I'm in him then I'm not done."

In *Hidden Bodies*, Kepnes pays homage to many facets of contemporary culture, including music and books, particularly to Woody Allen's 1986 film *Hannah and Her Sisters*. Joe has moved from New York to Los Angeles; he is out of the bookstore and in love, but still carrying grudges. He meets twins named for scores in tennis, Love and her brother Forty. The novel ends in a suspenseful manner, all but guaranteeing more work to come.

YOU, THE TELEVISION SERIES

You reached another audience when it premiered in 2018 as a *Lifetime* series, with Greg Berlanti and Sera Gamble's assistance in adapting the novel for television. The following year it was picked up by Netflix as a streaming series and season two, based on *Hidden Bodies*, was released.

In an interview with Emma Gray for *Huffpost* (13 Sept. 2018), commenting on Joe's character, actor Penn Badgley said, "If we can't turn away from Joe's humanity, then we have to accept how we've somehow also been supportive and complicit in allowing Joe to reach the conclusions he's reached [about love]. We can't just point the finger and call people evil."

The television series departs from Kepnes's novel in allowing access to Beck's thoughts and feelings, as well as Joe's. Its timeliness was heightened by the accusations of sexual harassment against Hollywood producer Harvey Weinstein. Even before the charges against Weinstein were made public, however, Gamble had added a professor who had the power to destroy Beck's academic career, as Weinstein had threatened to destroy the careers of young actors who refused his sexual advances. As Gamble told Judy Berman for the *New York Times* (7 Sept. 2018), "The Me Too movement did not invent the problem; it's just the current iteration of a conversation trying to address a problem that's been going on since long before we were born."

PROVIDENCE
Kepnes's stand-alone third novel, *Providence* (2018), was the first full-length novel that Lena Dunham and Jenni Konner published at Random House under their imprint Lenny, which they launched in 2017. Like the You series, *Providence* is a romantic thriller. In contrast to the series, *Providence* is also a detective story and weaves the stories of three main characters, rather than remaining in one character's mind. The novel is set in the title city, which Kepnes recalls from her college years. As she told Kim Kalunian for *WPRI.com* (15 Feb. 2019), "There is something so mystical and dreamy about that city. . . . Every time that Providence evolves, it still feels like Providence, and that, to me, speaks to the strength of Rhode Island and that really unique personality."

MORE OF YOU
In 2019, Kepnes announced she was working on two more books in the You series, with the third book taking place in a small town in the Pacific Northwest. In January 2020 Netflix announced that the series' third season, based on book three, was scheduled to debut in 2021, with Badgley continuing the role of Joe Goldberg. In August 2020, Kepnes announced on Twitter that she had finished the third book, *You Love Me*, which was due to be released on April 6, 2021.

PERSONAL LIFE
Kepnes divides her time between Cape Cod—which she enjoys visiting in winter when the tourists are gone—and Los Angeles. She told Goldstein, "To me, it is a miracle that my main job, my primary job every day, is writing books. That blows my mind." She enjoys writing in coffee shops as well as at home; she also plays blackjack.

SUGGESTED READING
Berman, Judy. "The Women Behind 'You' on Creating This Season's Darkest, and Most Timely, Romance." *The New York Times*, 7 Sept. 2018, www.nytimes.com/2018/09/07/arts/you-lifetime-sera-gamble-caroline-kepnes.html. Accessed 13 July 2020.

Goldstein, Meredith. "Shiny Happy People Give Carolyn Kepnes the Creeps." *The Boston Globe*, 30 Aug. 2018, www.bostonglobe.com/arts/2018/08/30/shiny-happy-people-give-author-caroline-kepnes-creeps/EYabuQjJfgT-2k6bdyJqXXP/story.html. Accessed 14 July 2020.

Greene, Doyle. "Who's on First? (Or, Anyone for Seconds?)." *Film Criticism*, vol. 42, no. 4, 2018, pp. 1–4, doi:10.3998/fc.13761232.0042.407. Accessed 4 Aug. 2020.

Higgins, Laurie. "Centerville Native's Debut Hits the Mark with Twisted Tale of Passion." *Cape Cod Times*, 28 Dec. 2018, www.capecodtimes.com/article/20141228/ENTERTAINMENTLIFE/141229508. Accessed 14 July 2020.

Kepnes, Caroline. "Caroline Kepnes on Suffering, Categories as Comfort, and the Dissonance between the Said and the Unsaid." Interview by Mara White. *Huffpost*, 29 Jan. 2016, updated 6 Dec. 2017, www.huffpost.com/entry/caroline-kepnes-on-suffer_b_9094480. Accessed 17 Aug. 2020.

———. "The Dark Side of Twitter: A Digital-Age Tale of Brooklyn Hipsters Gone Mad." Interview by Laura Barcella. *Salon*, 29 Sept. 2014, www.salon.com/test2/2014/09/29/the_dark_side_of_twitter_a_digital_age_tale_of_brooklyn_hipsters_gone_mad/. Accessed 17 Aug. 2020.

———. "'You' Author Caroline Kepnes Talks Stalking, Book Snobs and Writing." Interview by Shaazia Ebrahim. *The Daily Vox*, 2 Apr. 2019, www.thedailyvox.co.za/you-author-caroline-kepnes-talks-stalking-book-snobs-and-writing/. Accessed 17 Aug. 2020.

SELECTED WORKS
You, 2014; *Hidden Bodies*, 2016; *Providence*, 2018

—*Judy Johnson*

Asma Khan

Date of birth: July 1969
Occupation: Chef

For chef Asma Khan, operating a successful London restaurant was about far more than business from the beginning. "It isn't about the money, the accolades, it is a platform for me to talk about politics and race," she explained to Anna Sulan Masing for *Eater London* (22 Feb. 2019). As owner and chef of Darjeeling Express, Khan sought to promote the profession of cooking among South Asian women, whom she noted are underrepresented in restaurants and are often discouraged from pursuing cooking work outside of the home. To address that issue, when it came time to hire staff, she employed an all-female kitchen staff made up of women who were home cooks rather than formally trained culinary school graduates.

Indeed, the backgrounds of the restaurant's other cooks echoed that of Khan herself. Raised in a food-loving family, Khan nevertheless had few cooking skills upon her move from India to the United Kingdom in the early 1990s and initially struggled to recapture the flavors she had enjoyed earlier in life. After making a concerted effort to learn to cook, however, she soon displayed a passion and a talent for the culinary arts. She set out to share this talent through a series of supper club dinners in her home—and, eventually, a pop-up restaurant. That successful pop-up, launched in 2015, led directly to the opening of Darjeeling Express to substantial critical acclaim in mid-2017. Although pleased to have the opportunity to serve her food to hungry patrons from London and beyond, Khan particularly focused on the deeper significance of her work. "I have always seen myself as a vehicle to acknowledge the silent, nameless and faceless women in my family who cooked wonderful food but were never recognised or appreciated for their skills," she told Hope Howard for the *Independent* (3 May 2018).

EARLY LIFE

Asma Khan was born in India in July 1969. She was the second child—and second girl—born to parents with royal Rajput and Bengali ancestry. Due to her status as a second daughter, Khan grew up confronting the societal perception that second daughters are a burden, which she would later attribute in interviews to the traditional practice of providing costly dowries when a young woman marries. "It left me with a huge desire to do good, to make a difference, to lift other women," she told Katie Quinn for *Food52* (8 Mar. 2019) about that experience. In addition to fulfilling those goals, Khan would later seek to help improve the lives of her fellow second

Photo by Erik Voake/Getty Images for Netflix

daughters by dedicating a portion of her restaurant's proceeds to a charity created to support second daughters.

As a child Khan lived for a time in the southern Indian city of Hyderabad, where she was introduced to foods that would greatly influence her culinary point of view. She spent most of her early life in Kolkata (formerly Calcutta), where her mother owned a catering business. An athletic child, Khan enjoyed playing cricket with the other children in her neighborhood. The primary form of entertainment for her family, however, was food. "At lunchtime we would talk about what we were going to have for dinner. At dinner, we would talk about how we would use the leftovers for breakfast," she recalled to Ellie Costigan in an interview for the website of *Borough Market* (31 Dec. 2018). Yet despite the family's love of food, her mother's culinary business, and the presence of talented household cooks, Khan's own cooking skills were severely limited. By the time she was in her early twenties, she was reportedly unable even to boil an egg.

A CULINARY AND LEGAL EDUCATION

In 1991, Khan moved to the United Kingdom to be with her husband, who had obtained a university position in Cambridge, England. Not long after her arrival, she began to experience a degree of homesickness and especially missed the smells and tastes of the foods she had eaten throughout her early life. As she was unable to obtain those foods otherwise, she decided to learn to cook them herself. "When you can't change anything around you as an immigrant, having no family and friends, the only thing you can do is infuse your kitchen with aromas of home," she explained to Quinn. After learning basic recipes and cooking techniques from an aunt, Khan returned to India for a time to learn additional family recipes, particularly those based on the royal cuisine of the Mughal culture. "The most difficult thing to master with Mughlai cuisine is to get the spice layering right," she told Howard. "Spicing is an art form. . . . The flavours and spicing of well-made Mughlai food should not be overwhelming—there is a lightness and delicacy in this cuisine." Over the subsequent years, Khan honed her newfound cooking skills in her home kitchen, developing a passion for cooking that would shape her career going forward.

By midway through the 1990s, Khan decided to pursue studies in law and was accepted as a student by Hughes Hall, a college of the University of Cambridge. After her husband's work led them to move to London, however, Khan transferred to King's College, where she completed her law degree. She went on to pursue graduate studies at the university, earning her doctorate in British constitutional law in 2012. Khan particularly enjoyed developing her skills in historical research during her time as a student and later noted in interviews that that experience proved useful when she was researching historical recipes.

DARJEELING EXPRESS

In 2012, while living in the South Kensington district of London, Khan began to hold supper club dinners at her home. For those events, Khan invited diners into her home, where she—and eventually a small team of fellow home-trained cooks—prepared and served relaxed, informal dinners. Although she began by holding these supper club meals on a limited basis, they eventually became a regular event for Khan, who enjoyed the process. "It is a good way of doing it: you know how many people are coming, they've already paid, there is minimal waste," she told Costigan. "They come, they eat, they leave, and you wash up." Despite the popularity of the dinners, Khan eventually stopped holding them after her children objected, instead moving on to pursue other ventures.

A new opportunity arose in 2015, when Khan opened a pop-up restaurant in the private dining room of the Sun and 13 Cantons, a pub in London's Soho neighborhood. Although the new environment required that she and her team of cooks adjust to cooking in a restaurant setting, the experience was an overwhelmingly positive one for Khan's burgeoning career as a chef, and the pop-up received positive reviews from diners. Perhaps more significant was that one of the guests who had tried and enjoyed Khan's cooking was the landlord of a restaurant property in London's Kingly Court complex, and he approached Khan to offer her the space. She faced some setbacks during the planning process, including the loss of a potential investor, but was ultimately able to secure funding for the restaurant. She named the business Darjeeling Express. Prior to opening the permanent restaurant, she opened a Darjeeling Express pop-up at Druid Street Market in mid-2016.

Darjeeling Express's Kingly Court location opened in June 2017. In keeping with Khan's previous pop-ups and supper club, the restaurant was staffed largely by women, with the women working in the kitchen being home cooks rather than formally trained cooking professionals. "Home cooks are brilliant because we can multitask, we're used to cooking in very cramped spaces, we have very limited resources and we don't shout at each other! Because you don't need to shout—we just look at each other," Khan explained to Quinn. "There's no hierarchy in my kitchen, no one has any ranks." She was particularly interested in promoting cooking as a career among South Asian women, a demographic underrepresented in most restaurants.

SUCCESS OF DARJEELING EXPRESS AND CHEF'S TABLE

Following its opening, Darjeeling Express won widespread acclaim from London food critics and became a popular destination among diners. As part of the London culinary community, Khan took pride in cooking locally produced vegetables and other fresh ingredients rather than those shipped in from elsewhere. "Okra packed in India would arrive jet-lagged in my kitchen. I don't want to cook a jet-lagged okra," she told Costigan. "I'd rather cook something fresh and vibrant." Khan also took an environmentalist approach to restaurant ownership, seeking to limit Darjeeling Express's food waste and minimize use of disposable plastics. In addition to operating Darjeeling Express itself, Khan opened the pop-up restaurant Calcutta Canteen in 2018. She published her first cookbook, *Asma's Indian Kitchen*, in October of that year.

In 2018, Khan was selected to be featured in an episode of *Chef's Table*, an Emmy Award–nominated documentary series produced by the streaming service Netflix. Launched in 2015, the series features a different chef in each episode and delves into their culinary background and ongoing work. The first British chef to be featured in the program, she was chosen as the focus of the third episode of the show's sixth season. Khan enjoyed filming the episode, which documented her work at Darjeeling Express as well as her travels in India, and particularly appreciated working with director Zia Mandviwalla.

"She did not ask me pointless questions about my husband and marriage, I did not need to explain what my mother meant to me, she got it," she told Masing. "She noticed things like I took my shoes off after a filming session, so before a shot she would call out 'Asma put your shoes on,' just like my sister would—little things, but they made me feel she understood what made me tick." Khan's episode of *Chef's Table* was released on Netflix in February 2019.

PERSONAL LIFE

Khan married Mushtaq Khan, a professor in the Department of Economics at SOAS University of London. They have two sons together. Khan lives and works in London.

SUGGESTED READING

Khan, Asma. "Asma Khan on Her All-Female Kitchen, Mughal Cuisine and Chinese Takeaway." Interview by Hope Howard. *Independent*, 3 May 2018, www.independent.co.uk/life-style/food-and-drink/asma-khan-darjeeling-express-indian-food-mughal-cuisine-sexism-chef-a8301666.html. Accessed 15 Nov. 2019.

———. "How 'Chef's Table' Star Asma Khan Is Breaking Down Barriers with Her All-Women Kitchen." Interview by Katie Quinn. *Food52*, 8 Mar. 2019, food52.com/blog/23896-chefs-table-asma-khan-darjeeling-express-second-daughters. Accessed 15 Nov. 2019.

———. "'I Am Grateful to This Soil, to This Land and City. If I Don't Use Its Produce, What's the Point?'" Interview by Ellie Costigan. *Borough Market*, 31 Dec. 2018, boroughmarket.org.uk/articles/i-am-grateful-to-this-soil-to-this-land-and-city-if-i-don-t-use-its-produce-what-s-the-point. Accessed 15 Nov. 2019.

Masing, Anna Sulan. "Britain's First 'Chef's Table' Star Explores Identity on Her Own Terms." *Eater London*, 22 Feb. 2019, london.eater.com/2018/10/3/17904894/chefs-table-asma-khan-netflix-darjeeling-express-london-chef. Accessed 15 Nov. 2019.

O'Neill, Holly. "Darjeeling Express: The Amateur Cooks Turned Professional Chefs." *The Guardian*, 17 Sept. 2017, www.theguardian.com/lifeandstyle/2017/sep/17/darjeeling-express-the-amateur-cooks-turned-professional-chefs. Accessed 15 Nov. 2019.

—*Joy Crelin*

Angélique Kidjo

Born: July 14, 1960
Occupation: Singer-songwriter

For nearly four decades, singer-songwriter Angélique Kidjo has forged a prolific career by merging traditional rhythms from her West African homeland of Benin with a vast array of musical genres, ranging from R&B, jazz, funk, and rock to Afro-Cuban and Latin diaspora influences. The willingness to push boundaries has proven successful for the world-renowned, multilingual Kidjo, who had more than a dozen albums under her belt and four Grammy Awards to her credit by mid-2020. In addition to her music career, she has made a name for herself as a humanitarian dedicated to the empowerment of African women and girls.

PURSUIT OF MUSIC

Angélique Kpasseloko Hinto Hounsinou Kandjo Manta Zogbin Kidjo was born to Yvonne and Franck Kidjo on July 14, 1960, in the port city of Ouidah, Dahomey, on the brink of its independence from France. She was the seventh of ten children. Growing up in Cotonou, Kidjo enjoyed listening to her father's diverse record collection, which featured American artists ranging from rock icons Jimi Hendrix and Carlos Santana to R&B legends James Brown, Aretha Franklin, and Otis Redding. At age nine she was introduced to the music of South African singer Miriam Makeba, after hearing her cover of "Malaïka," a Swahili love ballad.

Photo by Schorle via Wikimedia Commons

Kidjo learned the value of education from her liberal parents. "The deal I had with my father was: You want to sing, you go to school," she shared with Conor Gaffey for *Newsweek* (8 May 2016). She explained, "My mum and dad believed that the best tool and weapon and wealth they could give all of us [children] was school." Kidjo's father also defied societal norms by ensuring that all three of his daughters would be educated.

Kidjo first graced the stage at six years old, when she performed the traditional Beninese tune "Atcha Houn" for her mother's theatrical troupe. At nine years old, Kidjo started singing with her brothers' R&B cover band, often being chaperoned to weekend gigs by her father. In her teens, she joined the high school band Les Sphinx and penned her first tune.

Before age twenty, Kidjo had decided to pursue music. She enlisted her brother Oscar and Cameroonian singer-producer Ekambi Brilliant to record her first album. After *Pretty*, Kidjo's full-length debut, was released in September 1981, she embarked on a tour of West Africa, including Ivory Coast and Togo.

EXILE IN PARIS

Kidjo's burgeoning fame elicited unwelcome demands by the government to record political anthems and praise the communist regime. In 1983 Kidjo, who was desperate to escape those constraints, fled to Paris, France, where two of her brothers were attending school. After a brief stint studying law, she enrolled at the renowned jazz school Le CIM. There she met Jean Hébrail, a French musician and producer who became a longtime collaborator.

While working various jobs, such as a hotel cleaner, Kidjo honed her vocal chops singing with the Afro-funk group Alafia. A chance encounter with Dutch pianist Jasper van't Hof during a 1985 gig led to an invitation to front the Afro-European funk-jazz group Pili Pili. Kidjo toured Europe and released four albums—*Jakko* (1987), *Be in Two Minds* (1988), *Pili Pili* (1989), and *Hotel Babo* (1990)—with the band before launching a solo career.

Kidjo collaborated with Hébrail on *Parakou* (1989), which included an appearance by van't Hof on the Bella Bellow cover "Blewu." The self-produced album drew the attention of Island Records founder Chris Blackwell, who signed Kidjo to the label's Mango imprint in 1991—the same year she released *Logozo*, her major-label debut. The disc, a blend of African beats, reggae, Latin influences, and dance/electronic music, topped the *Billboard* World Albums chart in June 1992. Kidjo reached second place in that *Billboard* category with her follow-up, 1994's *Ayé*, which fuses elements of pop and dance music with traditional African sounds. The music video for the

ecofriendly hit "Agolo" earned Kidjo a Grammy Award nod.

That same year Kidjo returned to Benin for the first time in over a decade, following its peaceful transition to a democratic republic. Accompanied by Hébrail and a team of audio engineers, she toured villages throughout the country, capturing field recordings of traditional instruments, including cowbells, flutes, berimbaus, and drums. Those indigenous sounds became the basis of her next album, which also incorporates modern African pop, gospel, and hip-hop. *Fifa* (1996) boasts an appearance by Carlos Santana and Kidjo's first English-language tracks, including "Wombo Lombo," a Top-20 hit on the *Billboard* Dance Club Songs chart.

MOVE TO AMERICA AND COLUMBIA RECORDS

Kidjo subsequently settled in New York City, with the intention of examining the origins of African music and their impact on contemporary North and South American music and cultures. "I came to America, where black people have been brought through slavery," Kidjo told Phylicia Oppelt for the *Washington Post* (23 Sept. 1998). "As an artist from Africa, I want to meet people from the diaspora . . . to find the sound of the moment."

Released in 1998 through Island Records, *Oremi*, the first of a three-part project, features collaborations with celebrated jazz vocalist Cassandra Wilson and R&B singer Kelly Price. To promote the disc, whose first single was a reinterpretation of Hendrix's "Voodoo Child," Kidjo hit the road as part of 1998's female-centric Lilith Fair Tour. She earned her second Grammy Award nod in 1998, when *Oremi* was recognized in the best world music album category. She also appeared on the soundtrack for Disney's *Lion King 2: Simba's Pride*.

Following Blackwell's departure from Island Records, Kidjo joined the Columbia Records roster. For the second installment of her project, she explored the connection between African rhythms and the music of Salvador de Bahia, Brazil, a former slave-trading port and home to a vibrant Afro-Brazilian culture. Kidjo's collaborators on *Black Ivory Soul* (2002) included South African–born musician Dave Matthews and Ahmir "Questlove" Thompson, drummer for the hip-hop band the Roots. In addition to placing second on the World Albums chart, *Black Ivory Soul* earned Kidjo her third Grammy nod and yielded another hit with "Tumba," which reached the top thirty of the Dance Club Songs chart.

Latin and Caribbean music were the centerpiece of *Oyaya!* (2004), which capped off the trilogy. It cracked the *Billboard* World Albums top five and landed a fourth Grammy nomination, in the best contemporary world music album category.

HER FIRST GRAMMY

After signing with New York City–based Razor & Tie, an independent label, Kidjo started work on her next album, recruiting percussionists from Benin's Gangbé Brass Band as well as an all-star lineup that included Joss Stone, Peter Gabriel, Alicia Keys, and Josh Groban. *Djin Djin* (2007), Kidjo's ode to her West African origins, features her unique take on several covers, including Sade's haunting ballad "Pearls," the Rolling Stones' rock classic "Gimme Shelter," and Maurice Ravel's best-known opera, *Boléro.* "I like music that gives me the ability to try anything I want to try," she told Roberta MacInnis for *Chron.com* (19 Apr. 2007).

The effort paid off in early 2008, when Kidjo won her first-ever Grammy and National Association for the Advancement of Colored People (NAACP) Image Awards. That summer she sang at jazz artist Quincy Jones's seventy-fifth birthday celebration. In December, Kidjo debuted at London's Royal Albert Hall and was featured in the charity music-video project *The Price of Silence.*

After appearing at US President Barack Obama's inaugural Peace Ball in January 2009, Kidjo performed at tributes for Makeba, Nina Simone, and Nelson Mandela, as well as high-profile events including the 2009 United Nations (UN) Day Concert.

Kidjo kicked off 2010 with the release of *Õÿö,* an homage to her late father. It celebrates the music of her childhood, ranging from traditional African songs to classic 1960s and 1970s funk and Bollywood tunes. Along with renditions of "Atcha Houn" and the South African song "Lakutshona Llanga," the Grammy-nominated *Õÿö* includes covers of James Brown's "Cold Sweat" and Curtis Mayfield's "Move on Up."

Kidjo went on to perform at the 2010 Fédération Internationale de Football Association (FIFA) World Cup hosted by South Africa. The following spring she was named an officer of the Ordre des Arts et des Lettres (Order of Arts and Letters) by the French government.

CELEBRATION OF MOTHER AFRICA

Kidjo's March 2011 greatest-hits performance at WGBH Studios in Brighton, Massachusetts, became the subject of *Spirit Rising,* a PBS special that aired in June 2011, and a live concert recording released in February 2012. Two years later she released a similarly titled memoir and unveiled the classical orchestra piece "Ifé, Three Yoruba Songs," which incorporates her poems set to the music of world-renowned composer Philip Glass.

For Kidjo's next album, her first under 429 Records, she incorporated recordings of female choirs from villages in Kenya and Benin, singing in indigenous languages. *Eve* (2014), a celebration of African women, boasts Dr. John, the Orchestre Philharmonique du Luxembourg, and the Kronos Quartet as collaborators. The album not only topped the *Billboard* World Album charts, it also earned Kidjo her second Grammy Award for Best World Music Album.

She subsequently reteamed with Luxembourg's philharmonic for 2015's *Sings,* which features nine reinterpreted songs and two new tunes. The collaboration helped Kidjo snag her second consecutive Grammy Award for Best World Music Album.

TRIBUTES TO THE TALKING HEADS AND CELIA CRUZ

Kidjo also revisited the past with her next effort: a reinterpretation of the Talking Heads' 1980 classic *Remain in Light*—an album she first discovered after fleeing to Paris. "I'm a very rhythmic person. Music is part of my heartbeat and every part of my body," Kidjo shared with Kory Grow for *Rolling Stone* (22 Mar. 2018). "This had an African touch to it." Kidjo released the album in June 2018.

Kidjo's 2019 project *Celia* is a tribute to Afro-Cuban salsa queen Celia Cruz. "As an African girl, when I first heard Celia Cruz sing 'Quimbara,' it just struck a chord. . . . From the first time I heard it, I heard Africa in it. I just felt it in my gut," she explained to Judy Cantor-Navas for *Billboard* magazine (20 May 2019). The album, which reimagines Cruz's well-known hits with an Afrobeat sound, was well received, winning her a fourth Grammy.

Additional projects included performances of composer Ibrahim Maalouf's *Queen of Sheba* (2018) and Glass's Symphony No. 12 (2019). To raise awareness of hygiene measures amid the coronavirus 2019 (COVID-19) pandemic, she recorded a reimagined version of Makeba's "Pata Pata" that was released in April 2020.

PERSONAL LIFE

Kidjo and her husband, Jean Hébrail, live in New York. Their daughter, Naïma, is a Yale-educated actor and playwright.

Along with her recording career, Kidjo, who speaks and sings in eight languages, established the Batonga Foundation for girls' education in Africa. She has served as a UNICEF (United Nations Children's Fund, originally called the United Nations International Children's Emergency Fund) goodwill ambassador and received the Amnesty International Ambassador of Conscience Award in 2016.

SUGGESTED READING

Cantor-Navas, Judy. "Angélique Kidjo on Recording the Songs of Celia Cruz: 'The World Cannot Forget Her.'" *Billboard*, 20 May 2019, www.billboard.com/articles/columns/latin/8512133/angelique-kidjo-celia-cruz-album-interview. Accessed 10 Aug. 2020.

Gaffey, Conor. "Angélique Kidjo. Singing to Educate Africa's Girls." *Newsweek*, 8 May 2016, www.newsweek.com/angelique-kidjo-africa-must-be-more-organized-girls-education-456639. Accessed 10 Aug. 2020.

Grow, Kory. "Angelique Kidjo Talks Reinventing Talking Heads' 'Remain in Light' on New LP." *Rolling Stone*, 22 Mar. 2018, www.rollingstone.com/music/music-features/angelique-kidjo-talks-reinventing-talking-heads-remain-in-light-on-new-lp-203888/. Accessed 10 Aug. 2020.

MacInnis, Roberta. "Angélique Kidjo Is Truly an International Performer." *Chron.com*, Houston Chronicle, 19 Apr. 2007, www.chron.com/entertainment/music/article/Angelique-Kidjo-is-truly-an-international-1801165.php. Accessed 10 Aug. 2020.

Oppelt, Phylicia. "Angelique Kidjo's Song of Herself." *The Washington Post*, 23 Sept. 1998, www.washingtonpost.com/archive/lifestyle/1998/09/23/angelique-kidjos-song-of-herself/5f06b735-3a38-46a1-b396-73850ebee672/. Accessed 10 Aug. 2020.

Russonello, Giovanni. "It's Angélique Kidjo's Birthday, and Her Country's Too." *The New York Times*, 12 Mar. 2020, www.nytimes.com/2020/03/12/arts/music/angelique-kidjo-carnegie-hall.html. Accessed 13 Aug. 2020.

SELECTED WORKS

Logozo, 1991; *Oremi*, 1998; *Black Ivory Soul*, 2002; *Oyaya!*, 2004; *Djin*, 2007; *Õÿö*, 2010; *Eve*, 2014; *Sings*, 2015; *Remain in Light*, 2018; *Celia*, 2019

—*Bertha Muteba*

Christine Sun Kim

Date of birth: 1980
Occupation: Sound artist

Christine Sun Kim is generally referred to as a "sound artist," a term that has been used with increasing frequency since the 1970s. Kim and others active in the burgeoning world of sound art (sometimes also called sonic art or audio art) create interdisciplinary works that connect sound to painting, performance, and other formats. Her involvement with the artform might seem counterintuitive to some observers, since

Kim has been Deaf since birth, however, she believes that being deaf has given her a unique relationship with sound. "As I acquired American Sign Language and English, I became aware of my relationship with sound and its social currency," she explained in an artist statement posted on the website of the London-based gallery *Carroll / Fletcher*. "I identified the parameters of each language and how they interrelate with social behavior. In part, my art practice is an attempt to shift my relationship to sound away from society's strictures; that is, rather than seeking approval for making what are generally perceived to be correct sounds, I produce and translate sounds based on my own perception."

Kim has exhibited and performed her work in such prestigious venues as the Museum of Modern Art (MoMA) and the Whitney Biennial in New York City. Her most widely viewed performance, however, came on February 2, 2020, when she was tapped to perform both the National Anthem and "America the Beautiful" in American Sign Language (ASL) at that year's National Football League (NFL) Super Bowl. Although Kim's performance on the forty-yard line was broadcast in real time on the jumbo screens in the stadium, she was visible to television audiences for just a few seconds, with cameras breaking away to show several players during the middle of both songs. "Why have a sign language performance that is not accessible to anyone who would like to see it?" she wrote the next day in an op-ed for the *New York Times* (3 Feb. 2020). "To be honest, it was a

Photo by Joi Ito via Wikimedia Commons

huge disappointment—a missed opportunity in the struggle for media inclusiveness on a large scale."

Kim has never shied away from expressing the frustration of living in a world geared toward the hearing, nor has she avoided discussing the political ramifications of deafness. "There's a long history of oppression, not enough support to American Sign Language," she told Lucy Martirosyan not long after the Super Bowl, in an interview for the Public Radio International show *The World* (13 Feb. 2020). "Being Deaf [has] always been a political thing. I don't know if it will ever stop being political. It would be nice to be Deaf and not have to deal with all of this, having to fight for everything and have this tension."

She hopes that exposure to her art might help advance the struggle. "Often hearing people are the ones who are looking and creating history and we are just pushed to the side," she asserted to Martirosyan. "But as my art becomes bigger and I have a larger platform, I think it's a nice way for me to look at myself almost as an archivist. I've made work. I've put it in history, and as that continues to grow, hopefully so does the awareness."

EARLY LIFE AND EDUCATION
Christine Sun Kim was born in Orange County, California, in 1980. She has one sister, who is also Deaf. In the 1980s ASL was beginning to gain widespread acceptance; before then, Deaf people were expected to rely on lip-reading or on the limited help hearing aids provided to some. Kim's parents, immigrants from Korea, decided to learn English and ASL concurrently. "It [was] really one of the biggest examples of respect . . . for me and my sister," Kim recalled to Martirosyan. "We felt seen, we felt valued, we felt important. Like, I am here, I exist. And growing up, that was an important feeling to have. And I think it helped me to develop a strong self-identity."

From 1994 to 1998, Kim attended University High School, in Irvine, participating in the Ocean County Department of Education's Deaf and Hard of Hearing Program. While she loved art from an early age, the program emphasized science, math, and literature, with little time devoted to other subjects. She competed on swimming and gymnastics teams; she has recalled that in the 1990s, local California papers often covered Deaf high school athletes—a trend she dismissively called "pre-social media inspiration porn," to Zachary Small for *ArtNet News*. Although she did not make a cheerleading team, Kim sustained a fascination with the sport, pointing out the similarities in the large, dramatic movements performed by both cheerleaders and ASL interpreters.

After high school, Kim attended Rochester Institute of Technology's National Technical Institute for the Deaf. While there, she asked to take an evening art class, but the school could not find a suitable interpreter, and she was denied. She graduated with a bachelor's degree in applied arts and sciences in 2002.

ARTS EDUCATION
Kim subsequently decided to attend the School of Visual Arts (SVA) in New York City. It was there she was first exposed to art in a formal setting. She made her first sale—a painting she had done of her dog, which she sold to a boyfriend's father for $500—during her time at the school. In 2006, she earned an MFA.

Kim first supported herself with various jobs, including education specialist at a museum and digital archivist at a publishing company. In 2008, she earned an artist residency in Berlin, Germany, where sound art was wildly popular. Although she had been devoting herself mainly to painting, Kim realized that she possessed an unusual and rare understanding of sound, honed during her formative years by closely observing how people behaved and responded to different noises.

Returning to school for a master's degree in sound and music at Bard College, however, Kim discovered that some people were skeptical. About her time in graduate school, Kim recalled to Tim Auld for the *Guardian* (25 Nov. 2015) that some of her classmates doubted her abilities. "I think the perception was they'd been working on music and sound for years and years and here I am, you know, I just kind of show up, and so people were kind of looking at me like, 'What are you bringing to this?' and I have to deserve and earn their respect." Despite the negative response, Kim earned her MFA from Bard in 2013.

ART CAREER
Shortly after graduating, Kim was chosen to participate in the MoMA show *Soundings*, the institution's first-ever exhibition dedicated to sound art. Among her pieces at the show was *All. Day.*, a multimedia work in which she traces the path an ASL speaker's hand would take to communicate the concept "all day," a sign that mimics the arc of the sun and explores the concept of rest bars (musical symbols indicating a silent interval).

Kim continued to explore ways to represent sound visually: employing vibrating objects, creating visual scores, and conducting a choir that used evocative facial expressions. In 2015, she gave a widely viewed TED Talk in which she discussed the similarities between music and sign language and described her artistic journey. "I decided to reclaim ownership of sound and to put it into my art practice," she said. "And when I presented this to the art community, I was blown away with the amount of support and attention I received. I realized: sound is like money, power, control—social currency. In the back of my mind, I've always felt that sound was *your* thing, a hearing person's thing. And sound is so powerful that it could either disempower me and my artwork, or it could empower me. I chose to be empowered."

Kim received a flurry of attention in the art world during the 2019 Whitney Biennial, when she was one of eight artists who threatened to withdraw her pieces in protest if the museum did not remove Warren B. Kanders—whose company sells military supplies, including tear gas—from its board of directors. Kanders resigned from the board and Kim allowed her work to be shown. *Degrees of Deaf Rage*, a collection of charcoal drawings, was based on infuriating experiences she and other Deaf people regularly undergo, including "being given a Braille menu at a restaurant" and "offered a wheelchair at an airport."

Kim later exhibited a series called *Off the Charts* at the Massachusetts Institute of Technology's List Visual Arts Center in Cambridge, Massachusetts, in early 2020. *Off the Charts* is a series of drawings broken down in chart form of the various factors involved in her life as a Deaf person ("Why I Do Not Read Lips" and "Why I Work with Sign Language Interpreters," for example). Visitors to the Arts Center could also listen to the audio installation *one week of lullabies for roux* for which Kim had commissioned several friends to create alternative lullabies for her daughter, specifying that they omit lyrics and speech and focus on low frequencies.

THE SUPER BOWL

In 2020, Kim was invited by the National Association for the Deaf (NAD) and the NFL to perform at that year's Super Bowl. Although she initially wondered if she should refuse in solidarity with quarterback Colin Kaepernick—who had been banned from the NFL for taking a knee in peaceful protest against the oppression of Black people and other people of color—and in memory of the many Deaf people who had been mistreated or killed by police in the last decade, Kim ultimately agreed. In her *New York Times* op-ed, she explained: "I wanted to express my patriotism and honor the country that I am proud to be from—a country that, at its core, believes in equal rights for all citizens, including those with disabilities."

Before the Super Bowl, Fox Sports, the network broadcasting the game, announced that they would provide a dedicated feed of Kim's performance on their website. During the live performance, however, the camera's cut away

from her within seconds to show several of the players. The event received criticism from the Deaf community, and two days later, the NAD released a full video of Kim's song interpretations. Although she was disappointed, she wrote in her op-ed, "Still, my pride in being chosen for this performance was genuine. . . . I had hoped to provide a public service for deaf viewers, and believed that my appearance might raise awareness of the systemic barriers and the stigmas attached to our deafness—and move some people to action. I hope that despite the failure of Fox to make the performance accessible to all, it did do that."

PERSONAL LIFE

Kim moved to Berlin, Germany, around 2013. She and her husband, the conceptual artist Thomas Mader, have a daughter. They are raising her to use ASL, German Sign Language or *Deutsche Gebärdensprache* (DGS), and German. Mader and their child are both hearing.

SUGGESTED READING

Auld, Tim. "Christine Sun Kim: 'I'm Not Trying to Be a Freakshow.'" *The Guardian*, 25 Nov. 2015, www.theguardian.com/artand-design/2015/nov/25/christine-sun-kim-sound-artist-deaf-london-exhibition. Accessed 22 June 2020.

Kim, Christine Sun. "An Artist Who Channels Her Anger into Pie Charts." Interview by Anna Furman. *The New York Times Style Magazine*, 21 May 2019, www.nytimes.com/2019/05/21/t-magazine/christine-sun-kim-artist.html. Accessed 22 June 2020.

———. "The Aural Artist." Interview by Emily McDermott. *Interview*, 14 Dec. 2015, www.interviewmagazine.com/art/christine-sun-kim-16-faces-of-2016. Accessed 22 June 2020.

———. "Christine Sun Kim, the Transgressive Deaf Artist, Will Sign the National Anthem Alongside Demi Lovato During the Super Bowl." Interview by Zachary Small. *ArtNet*, 28 Jan. 2020, news.artnet.com/art-world/christine-sun-kim-national-anthem-super-bowl-1763775. Accessed 22 June 2020.

———. "The Enchanting Music of Sign Language." TED Fellows Retreat, Aug. 2015, www.ted.com/talks/christine_sun_kim_the_enchanting_music_of_sign_language/transcript?language=en. Accessed 22 June 2020.

———. "I Performed at the Super Bowl. You Might Have Missed Me." *The New York Times*, 3 Feb. 2020, www.nytimes.com/2020/02/03/opinion/national-anthem-sign-language.html. Accessed 22 June 2020.

Martirosyan, Lucy. "Artist Christine Sun Kim on 'Deaf Rage,' the Super Bowl and the

Power of Sound." *The World*, Public Radio International, 13 Feb. 2020, www.pri.org/ stories/2020-02-13/artist-christine-sun-kim-deaf-rage-super-bowl-and-power-sound. Accessed 22 June 2020.

SELECTED WORKS

All. Day., 2013; *Degrees of Deaf Rage*, 2019; *Off the Charts*, 2020

—*Mari Rich*

Mikyoung Kim

Date of birth: ca.1968
Occupation: Landscape architect and designer

Award-winning landscape architect and designer Mikyoung Kim is known for work that challenges the traditional notions of her field with unique deployment of both natural and processed materials. Since the early 1990s her visionary work has drawn praise from the architectural and design community, as well as from ordinary visitors, who see her creations as places to reset, disengage and unwind. One of Kim's most notable pieces was done in Seoul, South Korea, in which she took the ChonGae Canal—once one of the city's most polluted waterways—and turned it into a pedestrian's paradise that draws some 90,000 visitors daily. Additionally, she and her firm, Mikyoung Kim Design, are highly regarded for their work in the development of healing gardens, including the Crown Sky Garden at the Anne & Robert H. Lurie Children's Hospital of Chicago and the Miami Healing Garden at the Jackson South Community Hospital. According to Kim, healing gardens have the potential to not only help patients and their caregivers relax, but also help recover them mentally, physically, and spiritually.

Kim suggested that her success comes largely from a close collaboration with her clients, because she seeks to understand what they need. In an interview with Jared Green at the American Society of Landscape Architects (ASLA) 2017 Annual Meeting in Los Angeles and published on the group's website, Kim noted, "Our clients often have very high expectations—they are patients in a hospital, developers who are building very high-end developments, etc. Through our process, they enter a shared design space with us; one that is a collective experience that hopefully yields a unique landscape in the end."

EARLY LIFE AND EDUCATION

Mikyoung Kim was born around 1968 and raised in Hartford, Connecticut, the daughter of parents who had immigrated from South Korea. She recalled her experience as a child of immigrants in an interview with Carley Thornell for *Boston Magazine* (23 July 2014): "Even though I was born here and I'm an American citizen, I grew up at a time when there weren't many Asians where I was living. People tell me I have an uncanny ability to go to a new place and really listen or hear and understand what that place is about."

From about the age of six, Kim was a serious piano player and planned to become a concert pianist. Her love of music was aided by her having a mild form of synesthesia, in which she could "see" colors that went along with the music she heard or played. She earned a bachelor's degree in sculpture and art history, with a minor in music, at Oberlin College. However, she gave up piano when she learned she had tendinitis, a chronic inflammation of the tendons that would prevent her from achieving her musical goals. Although the diagnosis was extremely difficult for her to take, she decided to seek another creative outlet. She told Julie Lasky for the *New York Times* (6 Feb. 2013): "I had to find another form of expression, which was public and performative, used the body and had a kind of creativity to it." To that end, Kim studied landscape architecture at Harvard University's Graduate School of Design, from which she graduated with a master's degree in landscape architecture in 1992.

CHEONGGYECHEON URBAN RENEWAL PROJECT

In 1994 Kim established her own company, Mikyoung Kim Design (MYKD), in Boston, Massachusetts. Kim and MYKD went on to work on numerous projects that have been widely celebrated. Chief among them was Seoul's Cheonggyecheon Urban Renewal project and the Chon-Gae Canal Source Point Park (2005), with its Sunken Stone Garden, a restoration project that was especially dear to her because of her family connection to South Korea.

The canal had once been the seven-mile long Cheonggyecheon, a stream that collected water from mountains surrounding Seoul, but over the decades it became a festering mix of wastewater and raw sewage. It was eventually covered by a highway, which divided Seoul in two. After the government tore down the highway, Kim and her team started working in the early 2000s to improve the water quality, while ensuring that the canal would be able to withstand difficult storms like monsoons. At the same time, she converted the area near the source into a park that would serve as an attraction. For the stone garden at the start of the canal, Kim and her team sourced local stone from North Korea and South Korea to highlight hopes for Korean reunification. The stone garden included large, canal-bank steps that allowed visitors to sit by the water and cool off.

Through Kim's work the canal was beautified to the extent that it became a major attraction for the city. The rehabilitation project was completed in 2005, and was credited with restoring more than 213 birds, fish, and other species; making the water safe for public use; and drawing tens of millions of visitors. It also brought in private investment to the tune of roughly $600 million. In 2010, Kim's work on the ChonGae Canal earned her the Veronica Rudge Green Prize in Urban Design from Harvard University, First Place in the International Design Competition Seoul, and an Urban Waterfront Commission Honor Award.

WORLD-RENOWNED LANDSCAPE DESIGNER

The Cheonggyecheon Urban Renewal project helped make Kim a star in the landscape design community, and she took on further high-profile contracts. In particular, she became known for her work on parks and healing gardens. In 2011 Kim and MYKD constructed Ripple Garden at Miami Jackson, also known as Project Ripple, at the entrance of Jackson South Medical Center (formerly Miami Jackson South Community Hospital) in Miami, Florida. The healing garden featured private areas separated by plant materials and running water that masked conversations. She also employed a mist that could cool people at the center of the garden during hot days. She described her feelings about healing gardens to Lasky in the following way: "When we look for a place to call home and we nurture a garden we call our own, we are looking for a place that's restorative, that's regenerative and that has a kind of humanity." In 2012, Kim and MYKD's work was recognized by the Americans for the Arts Public Art Network (PAN) Year in Review as one of the most outstanding public art projects of 2011.

In 2013, Kim and her firm completed work on 140 West Plaza: Exhale, in Chapel Hill, North Carolina. The leaders of the town wanted to create a new downtown park but also wanted to solve the problem of the considerable amount of surface storm water runoff that was then in the area. Her solution was a sculpture, *Exhale*, which was constructed to take the cleansed runoff through a misting system that could cool people who visited the park on hot days. "If there is no extraneous water from the site, there is no mist," she explained in an interview with Green for *The Dirt* (3 June 2015). "It's like the sculpture is breathing." For their design, MYKD won the 2013 Architizer A+ Award and the CODAworx CODA Award.

Kim's artistry and innovation were again on display in the creation of another healing garden project in 2013, the Crown Sky Garden at the Ann & Robert H. Lurie Children's Hospital of Chicago. The project, which comprised a healing garden on the eleventh floor and a tree house on the twelfth floor of a twenty-three-story hospital, posed considerable limitations. No organic materials like soil or plants could be employed that might harm patients with weakened immune systems, and water features were also ruled out to protect patients from infectious diseases. To get around these problems, Kim used bamboo as a natural material, with soil that was 98 percent inorganic. She also created water systems that bubble up through marble but are not open to the public. The garden also used interactive furniture, so that when a human hand touches an embedded brass one, the brass emits sounds.

In 2017, Kim and MYKD won an ASLA National Honor Award for work on the Chicago Botanic Garden, which included the five-acre Regenstein Learning Campus, with its grassy mounds, waterway, tree tunnels, and discovery gardens. In a 2017 interview with Green for ASLA, she said that she designed the Botanic Garden as a multisensory engagement experience that encouraged visitors of all ages to touch objects, listen to the sounds of nature, discover natural processes, and ask questions. She also commented on her concerns about children's use of mobile phones and other technology, and how landscape architects can play a key part in mitigating technology's adverse effects. "There's clearly a connection between childhood obesity and technology. As landscape architects, we can help municipalities and cities plan their neighborhoods better because it's the daily rituals that really matter," she told Green. "Instead of focusing on large centralized parks, it's important for us to also advocate for a more atomized green neighborhood plan where kids can walk through a pocket park, a neighborhood park, every day, or even twice a day."

ACADEMIC CAREER

From 1994 to 2012 Kim was a professor at the Rhode Island School of Design (RISD), teaching a wide variety of sculpture and design courses. For five of those years she served as a department head, and she was named professor emeritus at the school. She also taught classes in design and sculpture in other academic settings, including at the Harvard Graduate School of Design from 2017 to 2018. In 2018 she was the Glimcher Distinguished Visiting Professor at Ohio State University's Knowlton School of Architecture.

As Kim told Thornell: "Teaching really taught me to love engagement and learn that other people have these ideas that can open a door in your mind. I think that my studio is very much like a studio in school in that we try to practice the open engagement of ideas. It's really a healthy reminder for designers to have young people around that keep your ideas fresh, so the mind is limber. I think it's very easy for designers to become predictable or stale and that's probably my biggest fear."

AWARDS

Kim's long and distinguished career earned her and her company more than fifty awards, according to her firm's official website. She was named an AD Innovator by *Architectural Digest*, and in 2018 she received the Design Medal from the American Society of Landscape Architects (ASLA) while her firm won the National Design Award from Cooper Hewitt, Smithsonian Design Museum. "It is a tremendous honor to be recognized and supported by my peers and clients. This recognition is an amazing moment for me because it not only honors the work of my office, but also highlights the importance of resiliency, restoration, and creative thinking," Kim said in a press release upon receiving the Design Medal, as quoted by the *Harvard University Graduate School of Design* website. In 2019 the editors of *Fast Company* named MYKD on its most innovative companies list. That same year, Boston mayor Marty Walsh appointed Kim to serve as commissioner of the Boston Civil Design Commission.

PERSONAL LIFE

Kim and her husband—a doctor, who often advised her on her healing garden projects—live in Boston. They have a son, named Max.

SUGGESTED READING

Green, Jared. "Mikyoung Kim's Fractal Landscapes." *The Dirt*, 3 June 2015, dirt.asla.org/2015/06/03/mikyoung-kims-fractal-landscapes/. Accessed 3 June 2020.

Kim, Mikyoung. "Interview with Mikyoung Kim, FASLA." Interview by Jared Green. *American Society of Landscape Architects*, 2017, www.asla.org/ContentDetail.aspx?id=52172. Accessed 2 June 2020.

———. "10 Questions with Landscape Architect Mikyoung Kim." Interview by Carley Thornell. *Boston Magazine*, 23 July 2014, www.bostonmagazine.com/property/2014/07/23/10-questions-landscape-architect-mikyoung-kim/. Accessed 4 June 2020.

Lasky, Julie. "Summoning Nature for Healing." *The New York Times*, 6 Feb. 2013, www.nytimes.com/2013/02/07/garden/mikyoung-kims-healing-gardens.html. Accessed 3 Feb. 2013.

"Mikyoung Kim." *Landscape Architects' + Designers' Profile*, ladprofile.weebly.com/mikyoung-kim.html. Accessed 4 June 2020.

"Mikyoung Kim MLA '92 Receives 2018 ASLA Design Medal." *Harvard University Graduate School of Design*, 2018, campaign.gsd.harvard.edu/alumni_updates/mikyoung-kim-mla-92-receives-2018-asla-design-medal/. Accessed 3 June 2020.

"Most Innovative Companies: Mikyoung Kim Design." *Fast Company*, 2020, www.fastcompany.com/company/mikyoung-kim-design. Accessed 3 June 2020.

SELECTED WORKS

Cheonggyecheon Urban Renewal and ChonGae Canal Source Point, 2005; Ripple Garden at Miami Jackson, 2011; 140 West Plaza: Exhale, 2013; Crown Sky Garden, 2013; Chicago Botanic Garden, 2017

—Christopher Mari

Tom King

Born: July 15, 1978
Occupation: Comic book author

Tom King became one of the most sought-after comic book authors in the early 2010s, following the publication of his first novel, *A Once Crowded Sky*, in 2012. He is best known for his limited series, *Mister Miracle* and *The Sheriff of Babylon* for DC, and *The Vision*, for Marvel; both *The Vision* and *Mister Miracle* won King Eisner Awards. The three stories follow known superheroes but explore contemporary events and ideas. *The Sheriff of Babylon* is set during the Iraq War, and *Mister Miracle*, which many comics fans have dubbed a masterpiece, explores the anxiety of living in a frightening and uncertain time. Like the superhero characters he writes about, King has an unusual origin story. He grew up a self-proclaimed comic book–loving nerd in Southern California, who, after graduating from Columbia University, took a job with the Justice Department in the summer of 2001. After watching terrorists attack the Pentagon on September 11, he joined the Central Intelligence Agency (CIA). King spent nearly a decade working in counterterrorism in Iraq and Afghanistan, until the desire to be a more present father—his own dad had walked out on his mother when he was a child—drew him back to Washington, DC.

In 2019, the multiple Eisner Award–winning writer finished a stint as the writer for DC Comics' iconic *Batman* series. The same year, King began writing the screenplay for director Ava DuVernay's *New Gods* adaptation. He will undoubtedly bring his own spin to the world, created by Jack Kirby in the 1970s. "In comic books, so many of the stories are just the same types of stories, but with variations that make them interesting," King told Vaneta Rogers for the comics website *Newsarama* (1 Sept. 2017).

"It's like watching a great symphony being played by different people."

EARLY LIFE AND EDUCATION
Thomas K. King was born on July 15, 1978, and grew up in Southern California. He was raised by his mother, a studio executive who played an important role in the invention of the DVD, and his grandmother. King's mother wanted him to become a doctor or a lawyer, but visits to the Warner Brothers' lot where *Die Hard* (1988) was shot, as well as his early interest in comic books, seeded a different dream. He remembers the first comic that captured his imagination: *Avengers* #300 by Walt Simonson and John Buscema. King pored over the glossary at the back of the issue. "They had a list of every Avenger and they had a little John Buscema picture of them and what issues they had been in," King told Brian Michael Bendis and Susana Polo for the gaming website *Polygon* (25 Sept. 2018). "It was like there was this sort of hidden mythical history that I had just found to dip into, I couldn't believe it was all connected and all through one story." When he was twelve, King called Archie Comics in Los Angeles and asked if he could work there, sweeping floors. They politely declined.

After high school, King enrolled as a student at Columbia University, a school he chose in part because Matthew Michael "Matt" Murdock, the alter ego of the fictional superhero Daredevil, went there. King studied philosophy and history, and interned at Vertigo, an imprint of DC Comics. He mostly worked the copy machine but recalled being in the room as writer

Photo by Luigi Novi via Wikimedia Commons

Garth Ennis and editor Axel Alonso were devising the end of the series *Preacher*. The next year, King interned for Marvel Comics, where he was an assistant to *X-Men* writer Chris Claremont, who was then in charge of reviewing and revising scripts. It proved to be an invaluable writing education. "My job was to sit there and sort of listen to him as he examined each script and broke it down and said what works and what doesn't work," King recalled to Rogers. King graduated from Columbia in 2000.

TIME IN THE CIA
Shortly after graduating, King sold a script for Marvel's *Black Knight* series, and seemed poised to embark on a fruitful career as a comics writer when Marvel declared bankruptcy. When King's former bosses were laid off, he decided to pursue the path his mother had encouraged him to follow. He moved to Washington, DC, in hopes of becoming a lawyer.

King took a job at the Justice Department, working for the Radiation Exposure Compensation Act (RECA) program, where he distributed funds to people who had developed cancer after being exposed to radiation from atomic weapons testing or uranium mining. After the terrorist attacks on September 11, 2001, however, King felt compelled to join the CIA. He had heart, but little else. He had not traveled overseas, and he spoke no foreign language. But King was persistent. He applied for a job through the CIA website, completed grueling rounds of tests and interviews, and eventually, he was hired.

King worked as an operations officer and a counterterrorism operations officer, recruiting people to penetrate terrorist networks and designing operations. He spent time in Iraq, Pakistan, and Afghanistan, though he stated that being in the CIA was less glamorous than it might sound. "I remember I worked in the ops room, you know, like Tom Clancy's ops room. It was during the Iraq War. 'This is going to be amazing, I'm working in an ops room,'" he told Jason Concepcion for the *Ringer* (3 Aug. 2016), describing his initial expectations. "And it's mostly just dudes watching CNN trying to get through the night. The work gets done, but it's not what you think it is."

A ONCE CROWDED SKY
King left his job with the CIA in 2009 because it required too much time away from home and from his young family. "I couldn't really be the father I wanted to be and the operations officer I wanted to be at the same time," he told Concepcion. King became a stay-at-home dad and began writing at night. In 2012, he published a novel called *A Once Crowded Sky*. It takes place in a world in which superheroes and villains have lost all of their powers. Interspersed with

illustrated panels, James Floyd Kelly of *WIRED* (26 July 2012) favorably described it as a comic book in novel form. "Everything we love about comics—origin tales, a worthy villain, team-ups . . . conspiracies, super technology, disgraced heroes, redeemed villains—it's all here," he wrote. "And it's a fun read."

Buoyed by positive reviews—if not enthusiastic sales—King began pitching editors at DC and Marvel. In 2013, he published a story, illustrated by Tom Fowler, called "It's Full of Demons" for the Vertigo anthology *Time Warp*. The story imagined a time traveler going back in time and killing Adolf Hitler; it was told from the perspective of Hitler's sister.

THE SHERIFF OF BABYLON AND THE VISION

From 2014 to 2016, King gained some renown as a cowriter for the DC series *Grayson*, about a superhero-turned-spy. In 2015 and 2016, he wrote *The Omega Men*, also for DC. At the same time, he wrote *The Sheriff of Babylon*, for DC/ Vertigo, the first comic series to define his career. *The Sheriff of Babylon* was a project that King initially resisted writing. He had pitched it in his early, freelance days, when he was still clawing for a foothold in the industry. Illustrated by Mitch Gerads, *The Sheriff of Babylon* is classic noir. It follows the story of a cop-turned-military-consultant named Chris Henry as he attempts to solve the murder of an Iraqi police recruit. Scott Beauchamp for *Vulture* (4 Aug. 2016) wrote that it was "both politically and psychologically more complex than any conventional gumshoe narrative." The series explores King's own conflicted feelings about the invasion and war that characterized his experience overseas.

His next career defining publication, *The Vision*, for Marvel, followed in 2016. Vision, the android superhero of the Avengers, has a complicated origin story. He was originally created by the villain Ultron to kill the Avengers, but ended up joining the team instead. Through years of story, the Vision was forced to square his synthetic body with his desire to be human. This tension inherent in the Vision's identity is at the heart of King's telling in which the character and his family move to a house in the suburbs of Washington, DC. *The Vision* received effusive reviews and won a prestigious Eisner Award in 2017. David Cantwell for the *New Yorker* (22 Mar. 2018) wrote: "Even in an era when our pop-cultural skies are more jammed with Zeitgeist-powered superheroes than ever before, 'The Vision' goes down as one of the great comic-book stories—an examination of the limits built into each of us, a superhero tale not about saving the world but about simply fighting to make sure that you, and your family, fit into it."

BATMAN AND MISTER MIRACLE

In 2016, King was hired as the writer for *Batman*, a series that debuted in 1939. Writing such an iconic character was its own kind of challenge, King told Concepcion. "I write these very thinky comics where there's no hero," he said. *Batman*, however, is a simple "story about a hero triumphant." He wrote over one hundred comics for the series until 2019.

In 2017, King and Gerads published the limited series *Mister Miracle*, based on a character of the *New Gods* mythology. In King's telling, Mister Miracle contends with post-traumatic stress disorder as he attempts to put his dark past behind him. The series opens after the hero's failed attempt at suicide. The story sprang from what King describes as a near-death experience in 2016, a panic attack that King thought was a heart attack. The episode was compounded by King's unease with the state of the politically divided world at the time. He decided to explore these feelings through the story of Mister Miracle, a master escape artist. "I didn't want to write about the politics of it, because a lot of people were doing better work than me, but to write about the anxiety of it and the emotion of it and to write about what it felt like to be alive in sort of this latter-half of this decade when it just feels like we're living in something that's not real," he told David Betancourt of the *Washington Post* (14 Nov. 2018). "And we feel like we're trapped. And we don't know how to get out." The series earned King two 2019 Eisner Awards, for Best Limited Series and for Best Writer.

In 2019, King shifted mediums when he began working as a cowriter on the screenplay for the film *New Gods*. Directed by Ava DuVernay, the film is an adaptation of the comic series of the same name based on characters created by Jack Kirby in 1971.

PERSONAL LIFE

King met his wife Colleen, a lawyer, while working for the Justice Department. They have three children and live in Washington, DC.

SUGGESTED READING

Beauchamp, Scott. "The Best Retelling of the Iraq War Story Is a Comic Book." *Vulture*, 4 Aug. 2016, www.vulture.com/2016/07/sheriff-of-babylon-comic-book-iraq-war.html. Accessed 15 May 2020.

Betancourt, David. "'Mister Miracle' Turned Real-World Anxiety into a Hit Superhero Series." *The Washington Post*, 14 Nov. 2018, www.washingtonpost.com/arts-entertainment/2018/11/14/mister-miracle-turned-real-world-anxiety-into-hit-superhero-series. Accessed 16 May 2020.

Cantwell, David. "The Wisdom of 'The Vision,' a Superhero Story about Family and Fitting In."

The New Yorker, 22 Mar. 2018, www.newyorker.com/books/page-turner/the-wisdom-of-the-vision-a-superhero-story-about-family-and-fitting-in. Accessed 15 May 2020.

Concepcion, Jason. "The Spy Who Came into the Comic Book Store." *The Ringer*, 3 Aug. 2016, www.theringer.com/2016/8/3/16045554/tom-king-cia-batman-vision-comics-20d24c021406. Accessed 15 May 2020.

Kelly, James Floyd. "Heroes and Villains Are Gone from *A Once Crowded Sky*." Review of *A Once Crowded Sky*, by Tom King. *WIRED*, 26 July 2012, www.wired.com/2012/07/a-once-crowded-sky. Accessed 15 May 2020.

King, Tom. "From CIA to Comic Books: The Secret Origin of Batman's Tom King." Interview by Vaneta Rogers. *Newsarama*, 1 Sept. 2017, www.newsarama.com/36229-from-cia-to-comic-books-the-secret-origin-of-batman-s-tom-king.html. Accessed 15 May 2020.

King, Tom, et al. "The World's Finest: Batman's Tom King and Superman's Brian Bendis in Conversation." *Polygon*, 25 Sept. 2018, www.polygon.com/comics/2018/9/25/17895756/batman-tom-king-superman-brian-bendis-interview. Accessed 15 May 2020.

SELECTED WORKS

A Once Crowded Sky, 2012; *Grayson*, 2014–16; *Omega Men*, 2015–16; *The Sheriff of Babylon*, 2015–16; *The Vision*, 2016; *Batman*, 2016–19; *Mister Miracle*, 2017–18

—*Molly Hagan*

Eliud Kipchoge

Date of birth: November 5, 1984
Occupation: Long distance runner

In October 2019, Eliud Kipchoge—a long distance runner with numerous marathon wins under his belt—became the first person to run a marathon in under two hours. It was a barrier once thought to be unbreakable, akin to running a mile in under four minutes, which was first broken in 1954 by Roger Bannister. At the 1908 Olympics, Johnny Hayes ran that same 26.2-mile distance in just under three hours. Since that time, other competitors have beaten Hayes's time, yet none but Kipchoge performed so consistently in race after race. Between 2013 and 2019, Kipchoge competed in twelve marathons and won eleven of them. The one he did not win, he came in second.

Kipchoge set the official marathon world record with a time of 2:01:39 at the 2018 Berlin Marathon. He bested that record at the 2019 INEOS 1:59 Challenge in Vienna, Austria, when he ran the marathon in 1:59:40. Because that latter event was not an open competition, it was not officially regarded; nevertheless, Kipchoge himself sees it as a human accomplishment equivalent to landing men on the moon back in 1969—something once deemed impossible until it was done. After his historic achievement, Kipchoge declared, as quoted by Joshua Law for *Forbes* (13 Oct. 2019): "I am the happiest man in the world to be the first human to run under two hours, and I can tell people that no human is limited."

EARLY LIFE

The youngest of four children, Eliud Kipchoge was born on November 5, 1984, in Kapsisiywa, Kenya. His mother was a schoolteacher; his father died when he was very young. Running was a part of his daily life from a very early age. In order to get to school each day, he had to jog there. As a teenager, he had to stop his education to help support his family. His job was to collect milk from neighbors and bring it to market, where it would be sold.

In 2001, when he was sixteen, Kipchoge met Patrick Sang, an Olympic silver medalist in the steeplechase and a local legend. Kipchoge was not running seriously but asked Sang for pointers. Sang readily gave him advice on how to improve. When he finally learned Kipchoge's name, they were mutually stunned to learn that Kipchoge's mother had been Sang's kindergarten teacher. After Sang discovered that the teenager

Photo by Denis Barthel via Wikimedia Commons

had won a regional race in 2002, he officially became Kipchoge's coach and mentor, even giving him his own Timex watch. "When you're young, you always hope that one day you'll be somebody," Sang said to Scott Cacciola for the *New York Times* (14 Sept. 2018). "And in that journey, you need someone to hold you by the hand. It does not matter who that person is, so long as they believe that your dreams are valid. So for me, when you find a young person with a passion, don't disappoint them. Give them a helping hand and see them grow."

EARLY SUCCESSES AND OLYMPIC GLORY

Kipchoge has stated that he believes his life would have been extremely different had he not met Sang. They began their partnership by training for local 3,000-meter and 5,000-meter races. He began competing seriously in junior competitions in 2002, winning just one international 3,000-meter race in Cagliari, Italy. His breakout moment came in 2003, when he won the 5,000-meter race at the World Athletics formerly known as the International Amateur Athletic Federation and International Association of Athletic Federation World Championships in Paris, France, beating racing legend Hicham El Guerrouj. Kipchoge was then just eighteen.

The following year, Kipchoge won three 3,000-meter races, in Qatar, Belgium, and Monaco, and one 5,000-meter race in Italy, before placing first in the 5,000 meters at the Olympic Trials in Nairobi, Kenya. He then earned the bronze medal in the 5,000 meters at the 2004 Olympic Games held in Athens, Greece. In that final event, he finished just behind El Guerrouj and Kenenisa Bekele. Over the next four seasons, Kipchoge continued to rack up successes at major international events, including winning the San Silvestre Vallecana—a ten-kilometer road race—in 2006, and earning the silver medal in the 5,000 meters at the 2007 IAAF World Championships held in Osaka, Japan.

Kipchoge returned to the Olympics in Beijing, China, in 2008. There he won the silver medal in the 5,000 meters, again finishing just behind Bekele. Following the 2008 Olympics, Kipchoge continued to compete internationally in 5,000-meter events, but his finishes were not always consistent. He finished third in the 2010 Nairobi Commonwealth Games, and when he ran in the 2012 Olympic Trials in Kenya, he finished seventh and did not qualify for the team.

REINVENTING HIMSELF AS A MARATHON MAN

At this point Kipchoge began to reevaluate his career. He still loved to run, but he had begun to believe that the event he was competing in was no longer suited to him. He instead began to train to run the marathon—a grueling 26.2-mile race. To train effectively, Kipchoge committed to understanding both himself and his training as thoroughly as possible. He began training judiciously at a camp near his home in Eldoret, Kenya. He then recorded each workout in a notebook. He has stated that during his training he never pushes himself to 100 percent, preferring to give his all on race days.

His self-discipline and his almost monastic approach to running earned him not only worldwide admirers but also a series of stunning victories. Kipchoge's first victory came during his debut in the 2013 Hamburg Marathon, where he not only came in first but set a course record of 2:05:03. His next competition, the 2013 Berlin Marathon, found him coming up just short, finishing second behind Wilson Kipsang, a fellow Kenyan. He credits his success to simple, old-fashioned hard work. "I always tell people that this is a really simple deal: Work hard," he said, as quoted by Cacciola. "If you work hard, follow what's required and set your priorities right, then you can really perform without taking shortcuts. If you're taking shortcuts, you can't be free."

Between 2014 and 2016, Kipchoge remained undefeated, winning the 2014 Chicago Marathon, the 2015 London Marathon, the 2015 Berlin Marathon, and the 2016 London Marathon, where he set a course record of 2:03:05. He was the odds-on favorite to win the marathon at the 2016 Olympic Games in Rio de Janeiro and did so, with a time of 2:08:44. Although it was his slowest marathon time to date, it was enough to secure a gold medal. He was just the second male Kenyan marathoner to win Olympic gold. The first was Samuel Wanjiru, who won it in Beijing in 2008.

SETTING MARATHON RECORDS

Following the Olympics, Kipchoge earned a first place finish in the 2017 Berlin Marathon, finishing with a time of 2:03:32. Also in 2017, he partnered with Nike in a sponsored attempt to run the marathon in under two hours, a feat that had never before been accomplished. Nike organized the event, called Nike Breaking2, to have peak running conditions. It was held on a looped Formula 1 course in Monza, Italy, however, Kipchoge came up just short of breaking the record, finishing the marathon with a time of 2:00:25. Despite the time being his new personal best and fastest marathon in history, the time was not recorded as a record because it was not attained in a regular marathon race.

Kipchoge started 2018 by winning the London Marathon, finishing with a time of 2:04:17. On September 16, 2018, he entered the Berlin Marathon looking like the man to beat, owing to the enormous amount of victories under his belt. Leading up to the race, Kipchoge explained to Cacciola, "I am just going to try to run my personal best. If it comes as a world record, I would appreciate it. But I would treat it as a personal best." He completed the event that day, which had mild temperatures and little wind, with the staggering final time of 2:01:39, beating the marathon world record, held by Dennis Kimetto since 2014, by a full minute and 18 seconds. Kipochoge noted after the Berlin Marathon, as quoted by Cindy Boren for the *Washington Post* (16 Sept. 2018): "I have trained so well for this race and have full trust in the programs of my coach. I am just so incredibly happy to have finally run the world record as I have never stopped believing in myself."

Kipchoge's next major event came on April 28, 2019, when he entered the London Marathon. He had already won that event three previous times, but this one proved particularly special, when he set a course record of 2:02:37, the second-fastest marathon time ever run on a record-eligible course. The win was also his tenth consecutive marathon win.

Not content with these phenomenal achievements, Kipchoge again set his goal on running a marathon in under two hours. At an event organized by the petrochemical company INEOS, called the INEOS 1:59 Challenge, he set out to do just that, running 26.2 miles in world record time on October 12, 2019. When he hit the course in a park in Vienna especially chosen for speed, he managed to break the mythical two-hour barrier, completing it in 1:59:40, a full ten seconds better than his team had hoped. The effort, however, was symbolic in many ways. The course was designed for speed; it was not an open competition; and a rotation of professional pacesetters ran around him in an open-V formation. These differences likely aided Kipchoge's time, which is why it was not officially recorded; nevertheless, he still managed to do what seemed impossible. "This shows no-one is limited," Kipchoge said, as quoted by *BBC News* (12 Oct. 2019). "Now I've done it, I am expecting more people to do it after me."

At the finish line, he embraced his wife, Grace, and their three children, without whom he believes he could not ever have committed to his record-shattering career. It was the first time his family had ever watched him race in person.

SUGGESTED READING

Boren, Cindy. "Eliud Kipchoge Smashes Marathon World Record by 78 Seconds in Berlin." *The Washington Post*, 16 Sept. 2018, www.washingtonpost.com/news/early-lead/wp/2018/09/16/eliud-kipchoge-smashes-marathon-world-record-by-78-seconds-in-berlin. Accessed 28 Jan. 2020.

Cacciola, Scott. "Eliud Kipchoge Is the Greatest Marathoner, Ever." *The New York Times*, 14 Sept. 2018, www.nytimes.com/2018/09/14/sports/eliud-kipchoge-marathon.html. Accessed 28 Feb. 2020.

Chavez, Chris. "Eliud Kipchoge: Running under Two Hours for the Marathon Is Like the Moon Landing." *Sports Illustrated*, 14 Aug. 2019, www.si.com/olympics/2019/08/14/eliud-kipchoge-sub-two-hour-marathon-ineos-159-challenge-moon-landing. Accessed 28 Jan. 2020.

"Eliud Kipchoge and Six Landmark Record Breakers." *BBC News*, 13 Oct. 2019, www.bbc.co.uk/newsround/50026229. Accessed 3 Mar. 2020.

"Eliud Kipchoge: The Stats behind His World Record at the Berlin Marathon." *BBC Sport*, 17 Sept. 2018, www.bbc.com/sport/athletics/45547435. Accessed 3 Mar. 2020.

Keh, Andrew. "Eliud Kipchoge Breaks Two-Hour Marathon Barrier." *The New York Times*, 14 Oct. 2019, www.nytimes.com/2019/10/12/sports/eliud-kipchoge-marathon-record.html. Accessed 28 Feb. 2020.

Law, Joshua. "Eliud Kipchoge Thrusts Himself into Sports Pantheon, But His Sub-Two-Hour Marathon Is Tainted by Association." *Forbes*, 13 Oct. 2019, www.forbes.com/sites/joshualaw/2019/10/13/eliud-kipchoge-has-thrust-himself-into-the-pantheon-of-all-time-greatsbut-his-sub-two-hour-marathon-is-tainted-by-association/#74f0eed11cdc. Accessed 28 Feb. 2020.

—*Christopher Mari*

Jürgen Klopp

Born: June 16, 1967
Occupation: Professional football manager

Jürgen Klopp is a German football (soccer) manager who led Liverpool to its first Premier League title in thirty years in 2020. Klopp, originally from the Black Forest region of Germany, arrived at the storied football club in 2015, coming off of a successful seven-year tenure with Borussia Dortmund, in which he led the team to back-to-back Bundesliga titles in 2011 and 2012. Before that, Klopp coached Mainz, another German club, where he had also spent over a decade as a player, scoring fifty-six league goals over the course of his career.

Klopp, an enthusiastic presence on the sidelines, is best known for popularizing a tactical philosophy known as *gegenpressing*, German for "counter pressing." Michael Baumann, writing for the sports website the *Ringer* (13 Dec. 2019), described gegenpressing as a style of play "in which a relentless and ferocious defensive press . . . feeds a fast-paced counterattack."

Photo by Дмитрий Голубович via Wikimedia Commons

Gegenpressing is proactive and requires incredible stamina; Klopp has famously referred to it as "heavy metal football." As he explained to Ryan Kelly for *Goal* (8 May 2020), "Gegenpressing lets you win back the ball nearer to the goal. It's only one pass away from a really good opportunity. No playmaker in the world can be as good as a good gegenpressing situation, and that's why it's so important."

EARLY LIFE

Klopp was born in Stuttgart, Germany, on June 16, 1967. He grew up in his mother's hometown of Glatten, a spa village in the Black Forest region of Germany, with his two older sisters. As a child, Klopp wanted to be a doctor, but his love of soccer—and a fortuitous opportunity—would set him on a different path. His father, a traveling salesman, encouraged him to play soccer. "Norbert had a big influence on him, he shaped him," Klopp's first coach, Ulrich Rath, told Sam Sheringham for the BBC (23 Mar. 2020). Rath recalled Klopp as a "bad loser," but also a "natural leader." "He was always right at the forefront and he spoke up when something was not right," Rath said. Klopp was a midfielder and captain for SV Glatten's youth teams. When he was a teenager, he began playing for TuS Ergenzingen, a larger team in a nearby town. Around the same time, he tried unsuccessfully to make the professional team in Stuttgart.

PROFESSIONAL PLAYING CAREER WITH MAINZ

Klopp left Glatten to study sports business at Goethe University Frankfurt while working part-time jobs and playing as an amateur with various teams including Pforzheim, Eintracht Frankfurt II, Viktoria Sindlingen, and Rot-Weiss Frankfurt. In 1990, Klopp signed a semiprofessional contract with the second division team Mainz 05; he was twenty-three. "When he came to us he was a forward," club captain Michael Schumacher recalled to Sheringham. "He was fast and good with his head but he struggled with the technical side of the game." Klopp, famously self-deprecating, was blunt about his weaknesses as a player. "I had fourth-division talent and a first-division head," he told Uli Hesse for the soccer magazine *FourFourTwo* (22 Mar. 2018). "That resulted in the second division."

One of Klopp's career highlights during his time with Mainz 05 was a 5–0 game at Erfurt in 1991, in which he scored four goals—a club record that he held for more than twenty years. The game prompted hopes that Klopp would move up to the Bundesliga, Germany's top league, but that dream never came to pass. Klopp spent the rest of his eleven-year career with Mainz, where he was moved to midfield, and then defense, under coach Wolfgang Frank, who joined the team in 1995.

COACHING CAREER WITH MAINZ

Klopp, considered a leader among his teammates, took an interest in becoming a coach upon his eventual retirement. Twice a week, he traveled to Cologne, nearly 120 miles away, to study for his football coaching license at the German Sports Academy. Klopp was widely considered a candidate to coach Mainz at some point in the future, but an opportunity for him to do so came much sooner than he anticipated. After Coach Frank left the team, Mainz went through three managers in less than a year. Coach Eckhard Krautzun was abruptly fired in February 2001, just two days before an important game. In an emergency summit among senior players and staff, Klopp was chosen to take his place. Christian Heidel, the club's sporting director at the time, later attributed the decision to gut instinct, a choice "made with the stomach and not the head," he told Aimee Lewis for *CNN* (2 July 2020). Klopp accepted the job without hesitation, and the team rallied around him. "In the first game, against MSV Duisburg, who were the clear favourites, we had the most motivated Mainz team ever," Heidel told Andy Hunter for the *Guardian* (31 May 2019). "Although we won only 1–0, Duisburg had no chance that day."

When Klopp became manager, stakes were high for the team, as they faced the possibility of demotion to the third tier. Yet, despite being a first-time manager, he led Mainz to win six of their first seven games, staving off demotion with one game to spare. In his early years with Mainz, Klopp began to develop his take on gegenpressing, the distinctive style of play for which he would become known. Klopp did not invent the concept of "pressing"—one of his mentors, Frank, was an enthusiastic proponent of this approach—but Klopp came up with his own distinct way of using it. The team embraced his methods. In his first two full seasons as manager, Mainz came close to qualifying for the Bundesliga, missing the promotion by a few points and a goal. Mainz finally won the coveted promotion, for the first time in club history, in 2004.

Mainz spent three seasons in the Bundesliga, and in 2006, the team qualified for the Union of European Football Associations (UEFA) Cup but dropped out of the first round after losing to Sevilla FC. Mainz was demoted in 2006–07. Klopp resigned his position in 2008, with a record of 109 wins, 78 draws, and 83 losses.

BORUSSIA DORTMUND

In 2008, Klopp was appointed the new manager of Borussia Dortmund, also known as die Borussen or Dortmund. The club had finished thirteenth in the Bundesliga the previous season and were looking to reclaim the glory they had enjoyed in the 1990s. Klopp began to deliver early; in his first season as coach, Dortmund remained unbeaten at home, and won the 2008 DFL-Supercup. They finished a respectable sixth in the Bundesliga. Klopp's strategy involved both implementing gegenpressing and finding the players to support it. Will Sharp of *These Football Times* (7 May 2019) wrote that, early on, Klopp "set upon orchestrating a multifaceted revolution" at Dortmund. "In close collaboration with the club's renowned scouting and player recruitment setups, Klopp stacked his squad with a very particular caliber of player, notably recruiting from lesser leagues and drawing astutely from his club's youth academy," Sharp wrote.

In 2009–10, Dortmund finished fifth in the league. Then, despite high hopes, they lost their opening game in 2010, a seemingly inauspicious beginning to what turned out to be a historic season. The loss lit a fire that fueled Dortmund on an incredible winning streak through the first half of the season. The unforgiving pace of gegenpressing dogged them in the second half, but by then they had amassed enough points to win the Bundesliga title, Klopp's first, in 2011. In the 2011–12 season, Dortmund lost three of their first six league games, but then went unbeaten for the next twenty-eight, winning twenty-three games, tying five, and scoring an incredible seventy-three goals. They had successfully defended their title by the season's end.

Dortmund finished second in the Bundesliga in 2013–14 and narrowly missed the Champions League title. The club won the DFL-Supercup in 2013–14 and 2014–15 but finished the season a disappointing seventh in the league.

LIVERPOOL

In 2015, Klopp ended his tenure with Dortmund and accepted a position as the manager of the Liverpool club in England. Like Dortmund in 2008, Liverpool's best days seemed to be behind them. A storied club with a dramatic, and occasionally tragic, history, Liverpool had not been a significant force since the early 1990s. As Ryan O'Hanlon put it for the *Ringer* (24 May 2018), before Klopp, Liverpool fandom was sustained by nostalgia. "Every game felt like a historic act, an attempt to reclaim past glories," he wrote. The club's co-owner, Boston Red Sox owner John W. Henry, sought to rejuvenate the team. He selected Klopp through a statistics-mathematical model devised by Cambridge physicist Ian Graham, who was hired as the club's head of analysis.

Klopp joined Liverpool in October, after the season had already begun. Without time to implement his strategy in full, Klopp simply instructed his players to run—the foundational skill of the gegenpressing system. In his first full season with the club, Liverpool qualified for the Champions League. In 2017–18, Klopp guided the team to their first Champions League final since 2007, though they ultimately fell to Real Madrid.

In 2018–19, Liverpool outscored opponents by sixty-seven goals, and finished the season with ninety-seven points, the third-highest total in Premier League history. (They were a point shy of the Premier League title.) Liverpool also staged a return to the Champions League final in 2019, beating Tottenham Hotspur 2–0 for the coveted title. Rory Smith wrote for the *New York Times* (1 June 2019) that the historic victory capped the club's "extraordinary rise," adding of Klopp, "Liverpool's players know precisely who to thank for that."

Arguably, the crowning achievement of Klopp's tenure up to that point at Liverpool came at the end of the 2019–20 season, when he led the club to its first Premier League title in thirty years. The event was not without its own drama, however. By March, Liverpool seemed all but certain to claim the coveted prize, but the onslaught of the coronavirus 2019 (COVID-19) pandemic threatened to halt the season entirely. When the Premier League resumed play in June, Liverpool finally clinched the long-awaited title, but in a stadium devoid of fans. Usually known for his enthusiastic celebratory displays, Klopp greeted the moment with subdued emotion. "It's for you out there. It's for you," he told fans in an internet video, as quoted by Nicholas Mendola for *NBC Sports* (26 June 2020). "I hope you stay at home. Go in front of your house maybe. But it's in here," he said, pointing to his heart and head.

PERSONAL LIFE

Klopp and his first wife, Sabine, separated in 2001. They have a son named Marc. Klopp married Ulla Sandrock in 2005. She is the author of a 2008 children's book titled *Tom and the Magic Football*.

SUGGESTED READING

Baumann, Michael. "Jürgen Klopp Has Shaped Liverpool in His Image—and They're Winning Because of It." *The Ringer*, 13 Dec. 2019, www.theringer.com/year-in-review/2019/12/13/21013189/jurgen-klopp-liverpool-premier-league-leaders. Accessed 12 Aug. 2020.

Hesse, Uli. "How Klopp's Playing Career Shaped His Coaching Style." *FourFourTwo*, 22 Mar. 2018, www.fourfourtwo.com/performance/training/how-klopps-playing-career-shaped-his-coaching-style#vmWBXyU328DRQaRG.99. Accessed 11 Aug. 2020.

Hunter, Andy. "How a Gut Decision Began Jürgen Klopp's Managerial Rollercoaster." *The Guardian*, 31 May 2019, www.theguardian.com/football/2019/may/31/jurgen-klopp-champions-league-final-liverpool-mainz. Accessed 12 Aug. 2020.

Kelly, Ryan. "Gegenpressing: How Does the Tactical Style Made Famous by Klopp Work?" *Goal*, 8 May 2020, www.goal.com/en/news/gegenpressing-how-does-the-football-tactical-style-made/1wc20wx6qtkkq1t36xj0px9mel. Accessed 12 Aug. 2020.

Lewis, Aimee. "Changing Doubters to Believers. How Jurgen Klopp Turned Liverpool into Title Winners." *CNN*, 2 July 2020, www.cnn.com/2020/06/25/football/jurgen-klopp-liverpool-premier-league-title-spt-int/index.html. Accessed 12 Aug. 2020.

Sharp, Will. "How Jürgen Klopp Built an Empire out of Ruin at Borussia Dortmund." *These Football Times*, 7 May 2019, thesefootballtimes.co/2019/07/05/how-jurgen-klopp-built-an-empire-out-of-ruin-at-borussia-dortmund/. Accessed 13 Aug. 2020.

Sheringham, Sam. "Jurgen Klopp: Liverpool Manager's Journey from Black Forest to Heroic Status at Anfield." *BBC*, 23 Mar. 2020, www.bbc.com/sport/football/51989229. Accessed 11 Aug. 2020.

—Molly Hagan

Karlie Kloss

Date of birth: August 3, 1992
Occupation: Model and entrepreneur

Beginning her high-profile career at age fifteen, supermodel Karlie Kloss has told interviewers that she counts walking the runway for such designers as John Galliano and Jean Paul Gaultier as career highlights. Kloss has since appeared in such high-profile televised projects as the annual Victoria's Secret fashion show, served as the face of brands including Nike and Estée Lauder, and used her platform to inspire other young girls. Kloss told Elaine Welteroth for British *Vogue* (1 July 2019), "I am deeply ambitious and driven, and there are a lot of big things I want to do—big things. But I also want to enjoy the people I love and who love me." In addition to her modeling career, Kloss began hosting the fashion competition show *Project Runway* in 2019.

Kloss has been forthright about considering the profession to be a steppingstone for loftier pursuits. "I started high school, and that same week, I flew to New York City to begin what would become my career. In that way, my profession took me by surprise, but the beauty of being fifteen was that I was driven by pure curiosity and the promise of adventure," she recalled in a blog entry posted on *LinkedIn* (4 May 2018). "Nothing was holding me back. I had big dreams to travel the world and help others and make a meaningful impact with my life and my profession." After gaining a following of young girls as a model, Kloss used her platform—and her

Photo by Stephane Cardinale - Corbis/Corbis via Getty Images

interest in computer coding—to launch the non-profit Kode with Klossy, a coding camp for teenage girls, in 2015.

EARLY LIFE AND EDUCATION

Karlie Elizabeth Kloss was born in Chicago, Illinois, on August 3, 1992. Her father, Kurt, was a doctor, and her mother, Tracy, was an art director. Kloss has three sisters: Kristine, now a fashion marketing executive, and twins Kariann and Kimberly, who work as a program coordinator at Kode with Klossy and as a VIP relations assistant at Christian Louboutin, respectively.

When Kloss was three years old, the family moved to St. Louis, Missouri. There, she developed an avid interest in science and math; her sisters have joked to interviewers that Karlie was the nerdy one among them. She also studied classical ballet at Caston's Ballet Academy, a local studio. She has credited that extracurricular activity with helping her greatly in her career, asserting to journalists that the key to modeling is movement, rhythm, and muscle control.

In 2006, when Kloss was thirteen years old, she appeared in a charity fashion show, where she was spotted by Jeff and Mary Clarke of Mother Model Management, who are perhaps best known for discovering a young Ashton Kutcher. Among her first professional jobs were a campaign for Abercrombie Kids shot by well-known photographer Bruce Weber and, at age fourteen, a cover shoot for the June issue of Chicago's *Scene Magazine*.

HER BIG BREAK

In 2008—the same year she started her freshman year at Webster Groves High School—Kloss was signed by Elite Model Management. At age fifteen, she won her first truly high-profile job, jetting to New York City to make her catwalk debut for Calvin Klein during Fashion Week. "When I walked that runway, I didn't know a single person in the audience and I was thinking, 'OK, I gotta do my chemistry homework,'" she recalled to Andrew Bevan for *Porter* (4 Apr. 2018). "Every moment of that first trip to New York was a Cinderella experience, and had it not happened, there is a high likelihood I would have taken a very different route and not pursued this in a serious way." That season she also walked for such design houses as Alexander McQueen, Valentino, and Gucci.

Kloss worked throughout her high school years, flying around the world for jobs when she wasn't in class. "I had such normal high school experiences, like the awkward first kiss," she explained to Bevan. "None of my friends at school understood the magnitude of this other life that I had."

Despite her average high school life, Kloss had an illustrious early career, landing her first *Teen Vogue* cover in 2008. She was deemed to be one of fashion's favorite faces by the editors of the American edition of *Vogue* in 2009, and in 2010, she was chosen for a feature toasting the supermodels of the decade in British *Vogue*'s December issue. In 2011, Kloss attended her senior prom wearing a striking Dior gown.

RISE TO SUPERMODEL ELITE

By 2011, the year she graduated from high school, Kloss had become the face of the Marc Jacobs fragrance Lola and appeared in campaigns for such prestigious brands as Dolce & Gabbana, Oscar de la Renta, and Hermes. The same year, she made her debut as a Victoria's Secret angel, becoming a popular fixture of the lingerie giant's annual televised fashion shows for the next several years. In 2012, Kloss partnered with the popular high-end bakery Milk Bar to create a special recipe called Karlie's Kookies, whose sales benefit children's charities, and hosted that year's season of the MTV series *House of Style*. She also became a face of the athletic wear brand Nike in 2014 and a brand ambassador for Swarovski in 2016.

In 2015, Kloss enrolled in New York University's Gallatin School to explore feminist theory. At the same time, she gave up her lucrative Victoria's Secret contract, explaining to Welteroth, "I didn't feel it was an image that was truly reflective of who I am and the kind of message I want to send to young women around the world about what it means to be beautiful." Kloss continued, stating, "I think that was a pivotal moment in me stepping into my power as a feminist, being able to make my own choices and my own narrative, whether through the companies I choose to work with, or through the image I put out to the world."

Although she again made an appearance at the 2017 Victoria's Secret fashion show, Kloss focused on a variety of other magazine and television appearances. In addition to several international editions of *Vogue*, she appears regularly in such publications as *W*, *Elle*, *Allure*, and *Vanity Fair*, and she has served as global spokesmodel and brand ambassador for such companies as L'Oréal and Estée Lauder.

Kloss's modeling career has not been without some measure of controversy, however. In March 2017 she was featured in a *Vogue* spread dressed as a geisha and was subsequently forced to apologize for what critics decried as a blatant case of cultural appropriation. In a similar incident that occurred later that same year, she was cut from a Victoria's Secret broadcast when producers realized that the Native American headdress she was wearing could be construed as offensive.

KODE WITH KLOSSY

Kloss is known as a particularly savvy user of social media. She was an early adopter of Instagram and has several million followers who avidly peruse pictures of her professional projects and exotic vacation snaps. Her similarly popular *YouTube* channel features weekly vlogs and Q&A sessions with fans. "Before the dawning of social media, I think the role of the model was more to be seen," she told Chioma Nnadi for *Vogue* (11 Sept. 2018). "I've always wanted to use my voice for positive impact. Now I can speak in real time." She has also used her platform to advocate for women in science, technology, engineering, art, and mathematics (STEAM) careers and encouraged young girls to pursue STEAM education.

In 2014, Kloss took a two-week computer coding boot camp at the Flatiron School in New York City. Following her experience and new-found interest in coding, Kloss became passionately dedicated to helping other young women interested in technology. In 2015, she underwrote twenty-one scholarships—in partnership with the Flatiron School—for girls aged thirteen to eighteen to attend the school's program. The following year, she launched her own Kode with Klossy coding camps, providing free two-week programs for the same demographic. "I had an audience of young women paying attention to me on social media and in my career, and I wanted to connect them to opportunities that could really open their minds and open doors in their lives," she explained to Stephanie Schomer for *Entrepreneur* magazine (8 Oct. 2019). "It's not only a responsibility but a real privilege to be able to point someone in a direction that could be valuable to them." Starting with three camps in Los Angeles, New York, and St. Louis, the program grew to eleven camps in nine cities by 2017. In 2018, Kode with Klossy began awarding one thousand scholarships across fifty camps in twenty-five cities.

In addition to her other successes, Kloss spearheaded Freeform's 2018 *Movie Night with Karlie Kloss*, during which she screened such varied films as *The Goonies*, *Dirty Dancing*, and *Finding Nemo*, and served as a correspondent on the Netflix show *Bill Nye Saves the World* (2017). In 2019, she took over from fellow supermodel Heidi Klum to host the popular reality competition *Project Runway*, which provides a forum for aspiring fashion designers. She also serves as an executive producer on the show.

PERSONAL LIFE

On October 18, 2018, Kloss married venture capitalist Josh Kushner, whom she had been dating since 2012. Kloss converted to Judaism before the marriage, a move that some observers have criticized as subservient or weak. She has vociferously defended her decision, however, asserting that she did not undertake the conversion process simply for the sake of Kushner, who is an Orthodox Jew, but only after many years of studying and soul searching.

The couple is often featured in the tabloid media, with much of the coverage stemming from their family ties to President Donald Trump: Trump's daughter Ivanka is married to Kushner's brother Jared. Despite that, they are fervent Democrats and are regularly photographed at marches for liberal causes.

SUGGESTED READING

Adams, Susan. "Model Karlie Kloss Sees Big Growth for Her Coding Camp for Teen Girls." *Forbes*, 16 Mar. 2018, www.forbes.com/sites/susanadams/2018/03/16/model-karlie-kloss-sees-big-growth-for-her-coding-camp-for-teen-girls/#17138c0d78d3. Accessed 16 Oct. 2019.

Bevan, Andrew. "Karlie Kloss: The Surprising Supermodel." *Net-a-Porter*, 4 Apr. 2018, www.net-a-porter.com/us/en/porter/article-32d50515ce34bbdf/reporter/news/karlie-kloss. Accessed 16 Oct. 2019.

De Klerk, Amy. "Karlie Kloss." *Vogue: Britain*, 2 Aug. 2012, www.vogue.co.uk/article/karlie-kloss. Accessed 16 Oct. 2019.

De Valle, Jane Keltner. "At Home with Supermodel Karlie Kloss and Her Sisters." *Teen Vogue*, 31 Oct. 2012, www.teenvogue.com/gallery/karlie-kloss-and-family. Accessed 16 Oct. 2019.

Nnadi, Chioma. "Karlie Kloss Gets Candid about Politics, Her Relationship, and Women in Tech." *Vogue*, 11 Sept. 2018, www.vogue.com/article/karlie-kloss-interview-vogue-october-2018-issue. Accessed 16 Oct. 2019.

Schomer, Stephanie. "Supermodel Karlie Kloss's Lesson to Young Women: Never Be Afraid to Ask Questions!" *Entrepreneur*, 8 Oct. 2019, www.entrepreneur.com/article/339381. Accessed 16 Oct. 2019.

Welteroth, Elaine. "Karlie Kloss: 'Only Now Do I Have the Confidence to Stand Tall & Know the Power of My Voice.'" *Vogue: Britain*, 1 July 2019, www.vogue.co.uk/article/karlie-kloss-on-modelling-faith-philanthropy-business. Accessed 16 Oct. 2019.

—*Mari Rich*

Christina Koch

Born: January 29, 1979
Occupation: Astronaut and electrical engineer

By the beginning of the third decade of the twenty-first century, a total of around 560 people from countries all over the world had ventured into space. Despite many achievements, only a few of those individuals, however, became household names. As of early 2020, Christina Koch, an American electrical engineer and National Aeronautics and Space Administration (NASA) astronaut, proved to be an exception to the norm. A member of NASA's 2013 astronaut class, Koch completed her astronaut candidate training in 2015 and spent several years preparing for her first journey into space. That journey began in March 2019, when she embarked on a long-duration NASA mission aboard the International Space Station (ISS), one which would earn her a place in history. During her mission, on which she was involved in performing over two hundred important scientific investigations designed, in part, to learn more about human health in microgravity and the human body's ability to adjust to factors such as stress and weightlessness, she spent 328 consecutive days in space, which set a record for the longest single spaceflight in history by a woman. She also conducted six spacewalks, including executing the first-ever all-female spacewalk with Jessica Meir in October 2019.

Prior to becoming a NASA astronaut, Koch, a graduate of North Carolina State University (NC State), worked as an engineer in a variety of remote locales, serving time at research stations in Antarctica, Greenland, and Alaska. She also helped develop space science instruments for NASA and Johns Hopkins University. Such multifaceted experiences ultimately put Koch on a path toward contributing to human spaceflight. During a press conference held before her first mission to space, Koch said, as quoted by the Jacksonville, North Carolina, *Daily News* (27 Feb. 2019), "I believe that one of the greatest honors of flying into space is . . . our responsibility to carry the dreams of everyone into space with us."

EARLY LIFE AND EDUCATION

Born Christina Hammock on January 29, 1979, in Grand Rapids, Michigan, Koch grew up in Jacksonville, in eastern North Carolina, where she developed her penchant for exploration and adventure. From a young age, she became particularly drawn to science through her parents, Ronald and Barbara, whose interests included biology, chemistry, astrophysics, and astronomy. She has recalled that her parents always had *National Geographic*, *Astronomy*, and *Popular*

Photo by NASA

Science magazines lying around the house when she was a youngster.

Koch was as young as five years old when she began expressing the desire to become an astronaut, a career choice that her parents and others encouraged. Enamored with outer space, she adorned her bedroom walls with pictures of celestial bodies as well as a space shuttle and often observed the stars using a telescope in her family's backyard. During her youth, she also spent significant amounts of time at space camp, including one in Huntsville, Alabama, where she was shown a checklist of requirements for prospective astronauts. The idea of following a vocational checklist, however, prompted Koch's resolve to live according to her own passions and interests. "Down the road, if I looked at the experiences that I had gathered, and I thought that I really could contribute to the human spaceflight program as an astronaut, I would apply," she explained, as quoted by Jimmy Ryals for *NC State News* (27 Sept. 2016).

Koch went to the North Carolina School of Science and Mathematics (NCSSM), a prestigious high school located in Durham that is a constituent institution within the University of North Carolina system. While the school's rigorous curriculum centered around math, science, and technology, she was also able to broaden her interests to other subjects, such as photography, which became a lifelong passion. During time away from school, she took regular sailing trips with her father around coastal areas near Jacksonville, further sparking her thirst for exploration.

Upon graduating from NCSSM in 1997, Koch enrolled at North Carolina State University (NC State) in Raleigh, North Carolina, where she continued to immerse herself in a wide range of activities. While double-majoring in electrical engineering and physics, she served as a staff photographer for the school's student-run newspaper, volunteered with social justice organizations, and became fervently involved in rock climbing. Besides becoming a favorite avocational pursuit, the latter activity would later aid Koch in her astronaut training, both physically and mentally. Between 2001 and 2002, she earned bachelor's degrees in electrical engineering and physics and a master's in electrical engineering, all from NC State.

BEYOND THE CHECKLIST
Koch began her association with NASA in 2001, when, while still a student at NC State, she received the university's sole astronaut research scholarship. The scholarship funded a prestigious summer internship with the NASA Academy program at the Goddard Space Flight Center in Greenbelt, Maryland. Following her graduation from college, this experience paved the way for her to secure a position working for NASA full time: from 2002 to 2004, she was employed as an electrical engineer at the Goddard Space Flight Center's Laboratory for High Energy Astrophysics. In that role, she helped develop scientific instruments, including some that were for planetary probes, for a number of NASA missions.

In 2004, Koch, seizing an opportunity for adventure and to fulfill another dream, quit her job at NASA to work in Antarctica. She spent three years as a research associate in the US Antarctic Program, during which she worked out of several remote research stations; she worked on scientific instruments and served on the fire-fighting and ocean and glacier search and rescue teams. Braving minus-100-degree temperatures and twenty-four-hour-periods of darkness during the winter that, along with the harsh and remote landscape, would later lead her to compare her time there to space, Koch noted to Kristen Bobst for *Teen Vogue* (27 Sept. 2017) that Antarctica's extreme conditions pushed her to succeed even further in her job responsibilities. "When pure performance is the criteria," she said to Bobst, "I've noticed women naturally excel."

Koch went back to designing space science instruments in 2007, when she accepted a position as an electrical engineer at the Johns Hopkins University Applied Physics Laboratory in Laurel, Maryland. Following a two-year stint there, during which she was a member of a team that developed an instrument for a NASA probe orbiting Jupiter, she returned to scientific pursuits in more remote locations, spending time

again in Antarctica and stationing during some winters in Greenland. By around 2011, she had joined the National Oceanic and Atmospheric Administration (NOAA), working to better understand Earth's climate with the agency's Global Monitoring Division Atmospheric Baseline Observatory in Barrow, Alaska, before being appointed station chief of its observatory in American Samoa. Commenting on Koch's more non-traditional career path, Cecilia Townsend, her advisor at NC State, explained to Kate Murphy in an interview for the Raleigh, North Carolina, *News & Observer* (23 Aug. 2019), "She didn't just check the boxes to become [an astronaut]. She's very adventurous, and I think that's what it takes to be an astronaut. She's not afraid of anything."

RECORD-BREAKING NASA ASTRONAUT
A significant accumulation of career skills led Koch to apply from her remote location in Alaska to become an astronaut in 2011. In June 2013, following an extensive interview process that required her to travel from American Samoa to Houston, Texas, she realized her childhood dream when she was one of eight astronauts selected for NASA's twenty-first astronaut class, which included four women and four men; she was chosen from a pool of more than 6,100 applicants. During the notoriously rigorous candidate training process, Koch highlighted the role that many of her avocational pursuits played in shaping her intrepid mindset. She finished her astronaut candidate training in 2015. In addition to learning such skills as flying, systems maintenance, and spacewalking, she also received instruction in the Russian language.

Koch spent nearly six years training for her first journey to space, which officially began on March 14, 2019, when she embarked on a long-duration mission aboard the International Space Station (ISS). Launching to the ISS from the Baikonur Cosmodrome in southern Kazakhstan in a Soyuz MS-12 spacecraft, she was part of a crew that included Russian cosmonaut Alexey Ovchinin and fellow NASA astronaut Nick Hague. The three were charged with maintaining, as well as conducting, various scientific experiments on board the ISS, which orbits the Earth from about 250 miles above its surface and has been continuously occupied by international crews since 2000.

Koch served as a flight engineer for NASA expeditions 59, 60, and 61 to the ISS. In total, she spent 328 continuous days in space, which set a record for a female astronaut on a single spaceflight, surpassing Peggy Whitson's 2016–17 record of 288 days. (As of early 2020, retired NASA astronaut Scott Kelly held the overall American record at 340 days.) Besides setting a new mark for longevity, Koch, who orbited the Earth over 5,200 times, was also recognized for her part in conducting the first all-female space-walk, doing so with NASA astronaut classmate Jessica Meir in October 2019. The spacewalk was one of six that Koch performed during her stay aboard the ISS, which included two more all-female spacewalks with Meir in January 2020.

In addition to her spacewalks, which helped maintain and bolster the capabilities of the ISS, Koch contributed to more than two hundred scientific experiments, including those that focused on protein crystallization and the investigation of kidney cells. Many of these experiments were aimed at investigating the effects of microgravity and radiation on long-term space fliers, ultimately yielding greater insights into deep-space travel for NASA, which planned on sending more astronauts to the moon in preparation for future human missions to Mars. Commenting on such plans, Koch, who returned safely from space on February 6, 2020, explained to Kate Murphy in another article for the *News & Observer* (1 July 2019), "As astronauts one of the things that we sign up for is to be ready for any eventuality." She then added, "We would all be ready and it would be an honor for all of us to be able to do that."

PERSONAL LIFE

Koch resides with her husband, Robert, in Galveston, Texas. Among her honors include winning the US Congress Antarctic Service Medal with Winter-Over distinction in 2005 and NASA Group Achievement Awards in 2005 and 2012. Besides photography and rock climbing, she enjoys traveling, running, surfing, and practicing yoga. "I also love community service, tutoring or anything that spreads the love of science or reading," she noted to Bobst.

SUGGESTED READING

"Christina Hammock Koch NASA Astronaut." *NASA*, 18 Feb. 2020, www.nasa.gov/astronauts/biographies/christina-hammock-koch/biography. Accessed 6 Apr. 2020.

"Jacksonville Astronaut Will 'Carry the Dreams of Everyone' to Space." *The Daily News* [Jacksonville, NC], 27 Feb. 2019, www.jdnews.com/news/20190227/jacksonville-astronaut-will-carry-dreams-of-everyone-to-space. Accessed 6 Apr. 2020.

Koch, Christina. "Interview with Astronaut Christina Koch." Interview by Kristen Bobst. *Teen Vogue*, 27 Sept. 2017, www.teenvogue.com/story/interview-with-astronaut-christina-koch. Accessed 6 Apr. 2020.

Kowal, Mary Robinette. "Christina Koch Lands on Earth, and Crosses a Threshold for Women in Space." *The New York Times*, 10 Feb. 2020, www.nytimes.com/2020/02/06/science/christina-koch-nasa-astronaut.html. Accessed 6 Apr. 2020.

Murphy, Kate. "As Moon Landing Anniversary Arrives, Astronaut Christina Koch Makes History of Her Own." *The News & Observer* [Raleigh, NC], 1 July 2019, www.newsobserver.com/news/nation-world/article232163512.html. Accessed 6 Apr. 2020.

Murphy, Kate. "Christina Koch, Tar Heel of the Month, Explores from the International Space Station." *The News & Observer* [Raleigh, NC], 23 Aug. 2019, www.newsobserver.com/news/local/article234229227.html. Accessed 6 Apr. 2020.

Ryals, Jimmy. "To the Stars." *NC State News*, NC State, 27 Sept. 2016, news.ncsu.edu/2016/09/christina-koch-astronaut/. Accessed 6 Apr. 2020.

—*Chris Cullen*

Fyodor Konyukhov

Date of birth: December 12, 1951
Occupation: Survivalist and adventurer

Whether it be scaling Mount Everest, sailing around the world, or jumping from the Earth's stratosphere, extreme adventurers have repeatedly pushed the boundaries of human endeavor. Few, if any, however, have realized feats that match the breadth and ambition of Russian survivalist and adventurer Fyodor Konyukhov, whose "resume ranges wider than James Bond himself," as Ross Collicutt wrote for the men's

Photo by the Press Office of the President of the Russian Federation via Wikimedia Commons

lifestyle website *The Manual* (9 Mar. 2020). Widely regarded as the most prolific and versatile explorer in the world, Konyukhov has successfully completed more than fifty expeditions—across the disciplines of sailing, trekking, mountaineering, skiing, rowing, and hot-air ballooning, to name a few—since the late 1970s, many of which have established new world records. He is the first and only person in history to have achieved the following five feats: trekking to the North and South Poles as well as the Arctic pole of inaccessibility (the point in the Arctic farthest from any landmass), climbing Mount Everest, and sailing around Cape Horn, at the south end of South America. He is also the first Russian and the third person to have completed the Explorers Grand Slam, a series of feats that includes reaching the North and South Poles and climbing all Seven Summits (the highest peaks on each of the seven continents). Other notable accomplishments include completing the first solo circumnavigation of Antarctica in a sailboat in 2008 and setting the speed record for a solo nonstop hot-air balloon flight around the world in 2016.

A true modern-day Renaissance man, Konyukhov, who has sailed around the world five times, is also an artist, author, and Russian Orthodox priest. As active as ever in his sixties, with a number of projects on the horizon, Konyukhov has attributed his restlessness to an irrepressible sense of wonder and discovery. "There are seven billion people on this planet but we lack curiosity, we don't seek adventures," he asserted to Claire Bigg for *RFERL.org* (26 Sept. 2016). "Humans should be more curious—they should strive to discover new worlds."

EARLY LIFE AND EDUCATION

Fyodor (also spelled Fedor) Konyukhov was born into a peasant family on December 12, 1951, in Chkalovo, a village in the Zaporizhzhya region of southeastern Ukraine, then part of the Soviet Union. His father, Filipp, was a generational fisherman who plied his trade on the Sea of Azov. Konyukhov's father often took him on fishing runs as a boy, sparking what would become a lifelong enchantment with the sea. Konyukhov additionally became enamored of adventure through stories told by his grandfather, an imperial army officer who served in the same garrison as the Arctic explorer Georgy Sedov.

When Konyukhov was nine years old, the Russian cosmonaut Yuri Gagarin became the first human to travel into space. The milestone helped further cultivate Konyukhov's imagination and adventurous spirit. "At the time, I was convinced that by the twenty-first century we would already have scientific stations on Mars and settlements on the Moon," Konyukhov told Bigg. With such ambitious expectations in tow,

Konyukhov began embarking on expeditions of his own: at age fifteen he rowed solo across the Sea of Azov, which is roughly 210 miles long and 85 miles wide.

Konyukhov went on to study navigation at the Odessa Maritime College in Ukraine. After graduating from there, he attended the Leningrad Arctic School, where he majored in ship mechanics. He then served a tour with the Soviet armed forces, after which he resumed his studies, enrolling at the Bobruisk College of Arts in Belarus (also then part of the Soviet Union), to study woodcarving. This ultimately enabled him to pursue a secondary career as a professional artist.

Konyukhov was admitted to the Soviet Artists Union in 1983 and became a member of the Moscow Artists Union in 1992. A gold medal laureate and honorary academician of the Russian Arts Academy, he has created over 3,000 pieces of art—paintings, lithographs, sculptures—and taken part in more than 100 Russian and international art exhibitions.

MULTIFACETED ADVENTURER

Concurrently with his art projects, Konyukhov began leading scientific and sporting expeditions across a wide array of disciplines. In the late 1970s, he organized yachting voyages that followed routes of the eighteenth-century Danish explorer Vitus Bering, who, as a member of the Russian Navy, famously discovered what would later be called the Bering Strait. Then, in 1981, Konyukhov undertook a dog sled trip through the Chukotka Peninsula, Russia's easternmost region. That trip paved the way for skiing expeditions to the Arctic pole of inaccessibility, the point on the Arctic ice pack that is furthest away from land, in 1986, and to the North Pole, the northernmost point on Earth, in 1988. (Konyukhov returned to the North Pole again in 1989 and 1990.)

During the 1990s Konyukhov turned his attention to sailing and mountaineering. In 1991, he became the first Russian to complete a solo nonstop round-the-world sailing journey, doing so on a thirty-six-foot yacht. The following year, he summited Russia's Mount Elbrus, the highest peak in Europe, and Mount Everest, the highest peak in Asia and indeed the world. Those successes marked Konyukhov's first efforts to scale the seven highest mountains of the world's seven continents, collectively known as the Seven Summits. By 1997, Konyukhov had reached the summits of the other five mountains—Antarctica's Vinson Massif, South America's Aconcagua, Africa's Kilimanjaro, Australia's Kosciuszko, and North America's Denali. Reaching the South Pole for the first time during his ascent of the Vinson Massif, he became the first Russian and the third person in history to complete the Explorers Grand Slam.

Konyukhov broadened his list of adventurous endeavors in 2000, when he participated in the historic Iditarod, an annual thousand-mile sled dog race that runs between Anchorage and Nome, Alaska. In 2002, he helped organize the first camel caravan expedition in modern Russian history, completing a 650-mile route through southern Russia along parts of the ancient Silk Road. That same year he became the first Russian to cross the Atlantic Ocean on a rowboat, accomplishing the feat in forty-six days and four hours to set a world record. Commenting on the satisfying aspects of his work, Konyukhov told Anna Malpas in an article for *Smith Journal*, as republished on *Adventure.com* (7 Feb. 2019): "You gain most when you set yourself a goal—any goal—and carry it out."

HOT AIR BALLOON RECORD

Konyukhov continued to conduct record-breaking exploits in his fifties and sixties. In 2004, he set a solo transatlantic record for crossing the Atlantic Ocean on a maxi, or racing, yacht, doing so in just fourteen days and seven hours. Then, in 2008, he became the first person to make a solo circumnavigation of Antarctica in a sailboat, taking 102 days to complete the journey. Konyukhov's sailing expeditions gradually became more daring in nature, and in 2014, he completed the first nonstop east-to-west crossing of the Pacific Ocean on a rowboat. Traveling from coastal Chile to eastern Australia, he covered more than ten thousand miles in 159 days, setting new world records for both distance and duration.

Konyukhov spent roughly the next two years learning how to pilot a hot air balloon in preparation for an attempt to fly around the world in one. He earned considerable international attention when, in July 2016, he successfully fulfilled that endeavor. Taking just eleven days and six hours to complete the 22,000-mile journey, Konyukhov set a new speed record for hot-air ballooning around the world and became the first person to circumnavigate the globe in a balloon on the first attempt.

The adventure proved to be the most dangerous of Konyukhov's career, however, as he was forced to brave sleep and food deprivation, equipment failures, subzero temperatures, and lightning storms before landing in a field in Perth, Australia, near the site he disembarked from. "I thought I was going to die," Konyukhov wrote in a piece for the *Guardian* (16 Sept. 2016). "It was both physically and emotionally draining."

FUTURE EXPEDITIONS

The breathtaking but harrowing adventure failed to slow Konyukhov down, and in 2019, he made the first successful solo crossing of the Southern Ocean on a rowboat, covering 6,400 nautical miles from New Zealand to Chile in 154 days. This marked the longest number of days ever spent in the Southern Ocean, which is widely regarded as the most dangerous ocean on the planet. He also set the record for being, at sixty-seven, the oldest lone rower in history.

In January 2020, at age sixty-eight, Konyukhov summitted Mount Kilimanjaro for a second time. He next plans to fulfill a childhood dream by ballooning into the Earth's stratosphere. The stratosphere expedition, set for 2020, aims to break a world high-altitude record for a hot-air balloon. Konyukhov plans to reach at least 83,000 feet in a 230-foot-tall balloon—the biggest that has ever been constructed.

Konyukhov's other plans include completing the first solar powered nonstop round-the-world flight in a plane called the *Albatross* and descending to the bottom of the Pacific Ocean's Challenger Deep, the deepest seabed in the world. "I am getting older and wiser," he acknowledged to Malpas, but added, "When you've done fifty expeditions, people believe in you more."

PERSONAL LIFE

When Konyukhov is not adventuring, he resides in Moscow, Russia. He is married and has three children: sons Oscar and Nikolay and daughter Tatiana. In addition to his many other exploits, he has authored more than twenty books and is a member of the Union of Writers of the Russian Federation. In 2010, he became an ordained priest with the Ukrainian Orthodox Church. Upon summitting Mount Everest for the second time in 2012, he became the first priest in the church's history to accomplish the feat.

SUGGESTED READING

Bigg, Claire. "Record-Breaking Russian Adventurer Says the World Needs More Explorers." *RFERL.org*, 26 Sept. 2016, www.rferl.org/a/russia-adventurer-konyukhov-balloon-exploration/28014872.html. Accessed 19 Mar. 2020.

Bisharat, Andrew. "Russian Adventurer Completes Round-the-World Ballooning Record." *National Geographic*, 22 July 2016, www.nationalgeographic.com/adventure/features/athletes/hot-air-balloon-circumnaviation-record-fedor-konyukhov/. Accessed 19 Mar. 2020.

Collicutt, Ross. "Fedor Konyukhov, the 69-Year-Old Adventurer, Plans to Balloon into Space." *The Manual*, 9 Mar. 2020, www.themanual.com/outdoors/fedor-konyukhov-ultimate-adventurer/. Accessed 19 Mar. 2020.

Delbert, Caroline. "69-Year-Old Russian Daredevil Will Balloon into the Stratosphere." *Popular Mechanics*, 10 Mar. 2020, www.popularmechanics.com/space/a31356117/russian-daredevil-balloon-stratosphere/. Accessed 19 Mar. 2020.

Konyukhov, Fedor. "Experience: I Flew Solo around the World in a Hot-Air Balloon." *The Guardian*, 16 Sept. 2016, www.theguardian.com/travel/2016/sep/16/experience-flew-solo-round-world-hot-air-balloon. Accessed 19 Mar. 2020.

Malpas, Anna. "Meet 21st-Century Russia's Most Tireless Adventurer." *Adventure.com*, 7 Feb. 2019, adventure.com/russias-adventurer-fedor-konyukhov/. Accessed 19 Mar. 2020.

Winsor, Peter. "Fyodor Konyukhov: The World's Busiest Adventurer Begins His Latest Expedition." *Explorersweb.com*, 19 Nov. 2018, explorersweb.com/2018/11/19/fedor-konyukhov-the-worlds-busiest-adventurer-begins-his-latest-expedition/. Accessed 19 Mar. 2020.

—*Chris Cullen*

Rodrigo Koxa

Date of birth: September 22, 1979
Occupation: Surfer and waterman

In November 2017, Brazilian surfer Rodrigo Koxa entered the water off the coast of Nazaré, Portugal, with the simple yet daunting goal of surfing one of the world's largest—and most dangerous—waves. Indeed, Koxa was well aware of the danger the area's waves posed to surfers; three years before, he had suffered a traumatic wipeout at Nazaré that nearly drove him away from surfing entirely. By the time of his return, however, he was determined to overcome his fear and fulfill a longtime dream. "I think I put all the fear somewhere else," he recalled to Amy Crawford for *Smithsonian Magazine* (July 2018). "I don't know where. But I felt so confident!" Koxa's confidence proved well founded: after entering the water, he successfully surfed an immense wave that was later determined to have been a record-breaking eighty feet tall.

A surfer since childhood, Koxa has specialized in the sport of big wave surfing since he was a teenager and has spent decades traveling the world in search of large waves, which he refers to as "bombs." Although his earlier efforts earned him a degree of acclaim within the world of surfing, including nominations for the XXL Biggest Wave Award and the Big Wave Award for wipeout of the year, none garnered him as much recognition as his wave at Nazaré, which both the World Surf League (WSL) and the Guinness World Records organization certified as the largest wave ever surfed. "Only God blesses out in the ocean and I feel so fortunate to have surfed the biggest wave of all time," Koxa told Dylan Heyden for *The Inertia* (28 June 2018) about the experience. In addition to international recognition and the title of record holder, Koxa's accomplishment at Nazaré earned him the Quiksilver XXL Biggest Wave Award in 2018.

EARLY LIFE AND EDUCATION

Koxa was born Rodrigo Augusto do Espírito Santo on September 22, 1979, in Jundiaí, Brazil. Though typically used as his surname within the surfing community, "Koxa" is a nickname derived from the Brazilian food coxinha, a type of fried dumpling or croquette. Koxa's mother, Sandra, was a psychotherapist, while his father, Hélio, was a businessman. Growing up in Guarujá in eastern Brazil, Koxa was introduced to the sport of surfing at an early age and began surfing himself by the age of eight. He soon began to participate in surfing competitions, and he won his first event at the age of twelve.

A turning point in Koxa's early life came in the mid-1990s, when he was fifteen years old. While visiting Puerto Escondido, Mexico, the young surfer had the opportunity to surf waves larger than those to which he was accustomed, a key feature of Puerto Escondido that draws numerous surfers and surf competitions to its beaches. Koxa decided that he wanted to become a big wave surfer, a surfer who specializes in surfing large waves and often dedicates their career to seeking out the largest and most challenging waves in the world, despite the numerous dangers such waves represent. He began to seek out such waves and by 2000 had relocated to the surfing hotspot of Hawaii. There, Koxa lived for a time with Garrett McNamara, an established big wave surfer who would go on to become one of the most widely recognized athletes in the sport. "He was different, crazy and always looking to do things differently from others . . . a leader!" he told Heyden about McNamara, whom Koxa often identified in interviews as a significant career influence.

SEARCH FOR BIG WAVES

Over the decades following his teenage commitment to big wave surfing, Koxa traveled around the world in search of large waves, spending time not only in Brazil, Mexico, and the United States but also locations such as Tahiti, Chile, and Portugal. Although he began his surfing career doing traditional paddle-in surfing, in which a surfer paddles out into the water while lying on a surfboard in order to catch a wave, he began to experiment with the newer, alternative method of tow-in surfing while visiting Teahupo'o, a coastal locale in Tahiti known for unique waves shaped by a nearby reef. In tow-in surfing, a driver, often driving a Jet Ski or similar vehicle, tows the surfer and surfboard out into the water so that the surfer can attain the optimal position and ride larger waves than would otherwise be possible.

Koxa continued to practice tow-in surfing over the next few years, building a team of colleagues whose assistance made his efforts—and his safe recovery from less successful attempts—possible. "My goal is always to make sure I have my team in place so that we all have a safe session and we go home to our families uninjured and alive," he explained to Eric Akiskalian for *Towsurfer.com* (16 Nov. 2017). "When you have the crew that you trust and can rely on to do their part, you are inspired to be your best and ride the biggest waves you can find out there." Koxa eventually formed a particularly strong working partnership with driver Sérgio Cosme, who would tow Koxa to some of his most impressive waves. "He has so much sense of speed and timing," Koxa told Akiskalian about Cosme.

Though he had not yet been invited to participate in major big wave surfing competitions such as the Big Wave Tour, held by the WSL (known as the Association of Surfing Professionals from 1983 to 2015), Koxa experienced significant success as an independent surfer throughout the first decades of the twenty-first century, at times receiving international recognition for his accomplishments. In August 2010, he set a record for largest wave surfed in South America while surfing at Punta Docas in Chile. He went on to be nominated for the 2011 Billabong XXL Biggest Wave Award, an award given by the WSL as part of the Big Wave Awards, for his work in Chile. Although he did not win that year, he continued to seek out large waves and earned recognition for both his successes and his failures. In 2012, Koxa was nominated for the Verizon Wipeout of the Year Big Wave Award for a wipeout he experienced at Teahupo'o in August 2011.

NAZARÉ

While Koxa has surfed extensively in North America, South America, and the Pacific, his worst moments and greatest triumphs have come on the coast of Nazaré, a town in Portugal that in the early twenty-first century became one of the best-known centers of the big wave surfing world. Not far off the coast of Nazaré is a deep underwater canyon, which enables characteristically large waves to form. While the area is potentially deadly to surfers due to both the sheer size and force of the waves and the presence of dangerous rocks, Nazaré's waves represented a compelling challenge to big wave surfers such as McNamara, who set a world record

for largest wave surfed there in 2011. Koxa first visited Nazaré in 2013, two years after McNamara's feat, with the goals of both challenging himself on its waves and one day breaking the record set by his longtime friend. Attempts to do so, however, soon proved almost fatal: in 2014, Koxa suffered a severe wipeout at Nazaré and, unable to escape the water with the aid of his driver, was nearly pushed into the rocks. Although he survived, the experience was psychologically damaging, and Koxa was later diagnosed with post-traumatic stress disorder (PTSD). "Four months later, I had bad dreams, I didn't travel, I got scared," he later recalled, as quoted by *SurferToday* (29 Apr. 2018). Koxa avoided surfing large waves for a year following the incident, a decision that cost him his sponsorships but was necessary for his recovery. Following that period, he worked to reacclimate himself to big wave surfing, easing back into his sport.

A new opportunity to master the waves of Nazaré came in late 2017, when Koxa returned to the area in conjunction with particularly advantageous water conditions. Prior to his attempt, he had a dream that he took as prophetic. "My dream said, 'go straight down, go straight down, go straight down,'" he explained at the Big Wave Awards, as quoted by Anna Dimond for the *World Surf League* (30 Apr. 2018). "It was something talking to me. I didn't know what it meant." On November 8, 2017, however, Koxa took his dream's advice to heart. After he and Cosme noticed a wave forming, Cosme towed him out to it. "I remember the shadow of it," Koxa told Crawford of the wave. "It was super-powered, super-fast." As he later explained in interviews, the wave had a different angle and shape than the typical wave at Nazaré, which enabled Koxa to ride the wave straight down for a longer time than usual before having to surf out of the crashing wave's path. After he did so and returned to shore, Koxa reviewed the video footage taken of the wave and was stunned to realize that the giant wave not only seemed to be the largest wave he had ever surfed but also appeared to be the largest to be tackled successfully by any surfer at Nazaré or elsewhere.

WORLD RECORD

Following Koxa's success at Nazaré, the WSL set out to certify the height of the wave, measuring it based on the photographs and video footage taken at the scene. The WSL announced that the wave had been eighty feet (about twenty-four meters) tall, two feet taller than the record-setting wave surfed by McNamara in 2011. In recognition of Koxa's accomplishments, the WSL awarded him the 2018 Quiksilver XXL Biggest Wave Award at the Big Wave Awards ceremony, held in California in April 2018. Alongside a trophy and extensive professional recognition, the award carried a prize of $25,000 for Koxa as well as a $5,000 prize for the photographers who documented the wave.

For Koxa, receiving the award was both the culmination of nearly a decade of efforts to reach the highest levels of his challenging sport and a signal that he should continue to challenge himself further. "When I was nominated to the XXL finals for the first time back in 2011, I realized that I could win someday so I worked very hard to conquer this dream," he told Heyden. "Now, I'll work even harder to be invited to compete on the Big Wave Tour. I intend to expand my structure to be able to live the big surf magic more intensely." In addition to receiving recognition from the WSL, Koxa became the center of international media attention and was also recognized as holding the official world record for largest wave surfed, as recorded by the Guinness World Records organization.

PERSONAL LIFE

When not surfing elsewhere, Koxa lives in Guarujá, Brazil. He is married to Aline Cacozzi, a psychologist and university instructor.

SUGGESTED READING

Akiskalian, Eric. "'The Biggest Wave of My Life': Rodrigo Koxa on 'Nazare Big Wednesday.'" *Towsurfer.com*, 16 Nov. 2017, towsurfer.com/2017/11/the-biggest-wave-of-my-life-rodrigo-koxa-on-nazare-big-wednesday/. Accessed 7 June 2020.

Crawford, Amy. "What It Took to Set the World Record for Surfing." *Smithsonian Magazine*, July 2018, www.smithsonianmag.com/science-nature/what-took-set-world-record-surfing-180969334/. Accessed 7 June 2020.

Dimond, Anna. "Koxa on His Winning Nazaré Wave: It Was a Present from God." *World Surf League*, 30 Apr. 2018, www.worldsurfleague.com/posts/322236/rodrigo-koxa-on-his-winning-nazare-wave-it-was-a-present-from-god. Accessed 7 June 2020.

"'A Dream Come True': Brazil's Rodrigo Koxa Surfs the Biggest Wave on Record." *NZ Herald*, 30 Apr. 2018, www.nzherald.co.nz/sport/news/article.cfm?c_id=4&objectid=12042377. Accessed 7 June 2020.

Heyden, Dylan. "Who the Hell Is Rodrigo Koxa, Guinness World Record Holder for Biggest Wave Ever Ridden?" *The Inertia*, 28 June 2018, www.theinertia.com/surf/who-the-hell-is-rodrigo-koxa-guinness-world-record-holder-for-biggest-wave-ever-ridden/. Accessed 7 June 2020.

Hodgetts, Rob. "Brazilian Sets Record for Biggest Wave Ever Surfed." *CNN*, 30 Apr. 2018, www.cnn.com/2018/04/30/sport/surfing-big-wave-awards-wsl-nazare-portugal-spt/index.html. Accessed 7 June 2020.

"Rodrigo Koxa Breaks the World Record for the Biggest Wave Ever Surfed." *SurferToday*, 29 Apr. 2018, www.surfertoday.com/surfing/rodrigo-koxa-breaks-the-world-record-for-the-biggest-wave-ever-surfed. Accessed 7 June 2020.

—*Joy Crelin*

Zoë Kravitz

Born: December 1, 1988
Occupation: Actor and model

Zoë Kravitz is no stranger to fame. Having grown up accustomed to the concept of the spotlight as the daughter of music legend Lenny Kravitz and *The Cosby Show* actor Lisa Bonet, it seemed to be only a matter of time before she would become a star in her own right. From a young age she began to passionately pursue her interests in both music and acting, reminiscent of her parents' vocations. However, her road to stardom was ultimately not an easy one. As she told James Mottram for *Independent* (6 Mar. 2015), "I definitely got opportunities that other people wouldn't have gotten. I got an agent very quickly. But people want to shoot you down. They want to say, 'you're only getting this and that because of who your parents are.'"

Photo by Gage Skidmore via Wikimedia Commons

Kravitz began to establish her own identity within the entertainment industry, playing supporting roles in films, including *It's Kind of a Funny Story* (2010), while maintaining a parallel career as a model, representing famed brands and fashion designers such as Vera Wang. At the same time, she also expressed her creative talents through her passion for her music as the lead singer of bands such as Elevator Fight and Lolawolf. After making her mark in the X-Men franchise with 2011's *X-Men: First Class* and the Divergent film series (2014–16), she gave the performance of a lifetime in the Emmy Award–winning HBO series *Big Little Lies* (2017–19), wholeheartedly throwing herself into the role of Bonnie, a young woman with a difficult past. Her role in the short-lived but critically acclaimed Hulu series *High Fidelity* (2020) further showed her prowess as a leading actor and producer.

EARLY LIFE
Zoë Kravitz was born Zoë Isabella Kravitz on December 1, 1988, in Los Angeles, California, into a family of musicians and entertainers. At the time of her birth, both her parents were involved in the entertainment business. Her father, Lenny Kravitz, was a singer-songwriter trying to break into the music industry going by the alter ego Romeo Blue. Her mother, Lisa Bonet, was a twenty-one-year-old actor known for her role as Denise Huxtable in the long-running NBC series *The Cosby Show* between 1984 and 1991 as well as the spin-off *A Different World* (1987–89). Kravitz's connection to show business did not end with her parents, however. Her paternal grandparents, Sy Kravitz and Roxie Roker, were a television news producer and an actor, respectively.

After Bonet left *The Cosby Show* in 1991—over what was reported as creative disagreements with producers—and separated from Kravitz (their divorce was finalized in 1993), she and her daughter relocated to a more secluded spot: a house on a five-acre property nestled in the mountains of the Los Angeles community Topanga Canyon. There, Kravitz grew up surrounded by nature, attending school, watching old VHS tapes such as the original 1976 *Freaky Friday* film (though only during her limited TV time), and nurturing her imagination and inner artist away from the world of celebrity.

When Kravitz was eleven, she exchanged the scenic mountains of Topanga Canyon for the vibrant, fast-paced city of Miami, Florida. She moved in with her father, who by then had gotten rid of the Romeo Blue name and released several successful albums, becoming an iconic musician. The move was a significant change for Kravitz, who told Alex Pappademas for the *New York Times* (13 Feb. 2020), "I just wanted to feel normal," before continuing to say, "and

the way my mother was raising me felt very abnormal, even though looking back, it was the coolest." Although attending the Miami Country Day School she felt like an outcast, experiencing firsthand the work of her father opened her eyes to a world of possibilities within the entertainment industry—a world to which she saw herself belonging.

CAREER BEGINNINGS
During high school Kravitz moved with her father to New York City, where she attended the Rudolf Steiner School in Manhattan. She found that compared to her classmates in Miami, students at Rudolf Steiner School were more community oriented—an environment that permitted her to develop her acting skills. This period proved to be a pivotal one for the future star, as she became involved with the drama club and acted in as many ways, including in plays, as possible. "I used to make my grandparents pay a dollar to watch me sing *Grease* songs and 'Somewhere Over the Rainbow' in their living room. I was always an entertainer and I would always do all that stuff, but it slowly evolved into a career, which is great, but it wasn't a plan," Kravitz explained to Mottram. This time also coincided with her first appearances on the big screen, including in the 2007 romantic comedy *No Reservations* costarring actors Catherine Zeta-Jones and Aaron Eckhart, and in the 2007 crime-drama *The Brave One* starring Jodie Foster. Both premiered the same year she graduated from high school.

Kravitz continued to focus on acting, enrolling at the acting conservatory at Purchase College (State University of New York) for a year. However, the pressures of her blossoming career combined with continued teenage insecurities became a bit overwhelming, contributing to an ongoing battle with bulimia that had begun not long after she entered her teen years. While she ultimately sought treatment and began her recovery journey, during this challenging time she was also able to find solace in music. As she told Fiona Golfar for *Elle* (8 Jan. 2020), "I, too, found being a teenager and young adult hard to navigate, and music was a refuge for me, somewhere to hide." Aside from enjoying making music and singing with her band, Elevator Fight, her acting and modeling careers soon began to take off. After having a role in 2008's dramatic comedy *Birds of America*, in 2009 she became the face of fashion designer Vera Wang's Princess perfume collection, and, the following year, she appeared in a supporting role in the comedy-drama film *It's Kind of a Funny Story* and modeled in Alexander Wang's fall clothing campaign.

Kravitz's career as an actor only kept growing in 2011, when she portrayed a character named Pearl for eight episodes on the hit television series *Californication*, which starred actor David Duchovny as Hank Moody, a narcissistic novelist with a bad case of writer's block. Perhaps, however, the highest-profile role she landed to that point was as Angel Salvadore, one of the mutants with superhuman powers in the action film *X-Men: First Class* (2011). The film, which starred the likes of James McAvoy, Michael Fassbender, and Jennifer Lawrence, was a box-office success, amassing $352.6 million worldwide.

DYSTOPIAN, INDEPENDENT, AND ACTION MOVIES

While continuing to feed her love of music by writing and performing music, which included beginning to sing and record with her newly formed band Lolawolf around 2013, Kravitz remained committed to acting. The year 2014 saw her become part of the Divergent film series, a dystopian trilogy based on the book series (2011–13) of the same name by author Veronica Roth. The first film installment, *Divergent*, introduces Kravitz's character: an intelligent, bold young woman named Christina. Early in the first film, Christina befriends central character Tris (Shailene Woodley), beginning a long-lasting relationship that plays a central role as the story progresses, though not without its fair share of problems.

That same year, Kravitz was part of a different type of film, this one titled *The Road Within*. Unlike the action-filled *Divergent*, *The Road Within* is an independent comedy-drama that follows Vincent (Robert Sheehan), a young man with Tourette syndrome who is enrolled at a behavioral facility. There, he meets Alex (Dev Patel), an English man with obsessive-compulsive disorder, and Kravitz's Marie, a young woman struggling with anorexia. Soon the three embark on a road trip of a lifetime, taking the ashes of Vincent's mother to be released in the ocean.

After reprising her role as Christina in *The Divergent Series: Insurgent* in March 2015, Kravitz was next seen in the role of Toast the Knowing in *Mad Max: Fury Road*, which premiered in May. Directed by George Miller and featuring the performances of an ensemble cast that included Tom Hardy, Charlize Theron, and Nicholas Hoult, this action-packed, postapocalyptic film tells the story of a rebellious lieutenant (Theron) who decides to escape the tyranny of ruler Immortan Joe (Hugh Keays-Byrne) with five female captives, including Toast the Knowing.

In 2016 came the release of *The Divergent Series: Allegiant*, the conclusion of the trilogy. This installment marked Kravitz's third collaboration—though it would not be the last—with Woodley; they became close friends in the process. When Woodley talked with Pappademas, she only spoke highly of her friend: "Zoë's

constantly looking at the world around her, thinking, 'How can I leave this place better than it was when I got here? How can I continue to use my talents and gifts as a singer, as a writer, as an actor in a way that's meaningful and impactful for future generations and have fun doing it?'"

BIG LITTLE LIES AND HIGH FIDELITY

Returning to the television medium, from 2017 to 2019 Kravitz was part of the cast of the Emmy-winning HBO series *Big Little Lies*. An adaptation of the popular 2014 novel by Liane Moriarty, the show stars Woodley, Reese Witherspoon, Nicole Kidman, and other big-name actors. Set in Monterey, California, it follows the story of five women who find themselves involved in a murder investigation. Due in large part to its success in drawing in viewers, it would go on to air a second season. Although Kravitz's Bonnie is more of a background character in the first season, this changes in season two when her role becomes more prominent. The actor's characterization of Bonnie, who has a painful backstory involving child abuse, allowed her to display raw emotion and vulnerability in a largely acclaimed performance.

Between seasons one and two of *Big Little Lies*, in addition to proving herself a capable voice actor, Kravitz appeared in *Fantastic Beasts: The Crimes of Grindelwald* in 2018, a film within the Harry Potter universe. She portrays Leta Lestrange, an outcast who, during her time at Hogwarts, befriends Newt Scamander—the main protagonist, who loves magical creatures—eventually becoming his love interest. Discussing her representation of the biggest role portrayed by a person of color in the Harry Potter franchise (her character had briefly been introduced in the 2016 predecessor *Fantastic Beasts and Where to Find Them*) with Amy Kaufman for the *Los Angeles Times* (8 Nov. 2018), Kravitz praised writer J. K. Rowling and the casting directors for including more diverse characters in the story. "I think they were mostly only auditioning women of color for this role. I know it was an important thing for Jo. She was very aware of what she was doing," Kravitz told Kaufman.

In 2020 Kravitz was seen playing the lead role in the Hulu series *High Fidelity*, an adaptation of the 1995 novel of the same name by Nick Hornby. She also served as an executive producer of the show. Playing the part of Robyn "Rob" Brooks, the owner of a record store in the gentrified Brooklyn neighborhood of Crown Heights, Kravitz's interpretation of a young woman with a string of failed relationships was particularly lauded, though it did not save the show from being canceled at the end of season one. Nonetheless, more high-profile projects had continued coming her way, including the 2019 announcement that she would portray the iconic role of

Catwoman in the newest installment in the Batman superhero franchise.

PERSONAL LIFE

Zoë Kravitz and fellow actor Karl Glusman married in July 2019 in Paris, France. They recited their vows in front of a small number of family members and friends gathered at her father's house. Kravitz has two half siblings, sister Lola and brother Nakoa-Wolf, who are the children of Bonet and her husband Jason Momoa, an actor and model.

SUGGESTED READING

Golfar, Fiona. "Zoë Kravitz Has Finally Found Her Zen." *Elle*, 8 Jan. 2020, www.elle.com/culture/movies-tv/a30419740/zoe-kravitz-interview-high-fidelity-the-batman. Accessed 5 Sept. 2020.

Kravitz, Zoë. "Zoë Kravitz Loves Her *Fantastic Beasts* Role but Is Fed Up with Hollywood Tokenism." Interview by Amy Kaufman. *Los Angeles Times*, 8 Nov. 2018, www.latimes.com/entertainment/movies/la-et-mn-zoe-kravitz-conversation-20181108-story.html. Accessed 5 Sept. 2020.

———. "Zoë Kravitz Interview: On *Mad Max: Fury Road*, *Insurgent* and Becoming More Successful Than Her Showbiz Parents." Interview by James Mottram. *Independent*, 6 Mar. 2015, www.independent.co.uk/arts-entertainment/films/features/zoe-kravitz-interview-on-mad-max-fury-road-insurgent-and-becoming-more-successful-than-her-showbiz-10088795.html. Accessed 5 Sept. 2020.

Pappademas, Alex. "Sooner or Later, Zoë Kravitz Was Going to Be a Star." *The New York Times*, 13 Feb. 2020, www.nytimes.com/2020/02/13/arts/television/zoe-kravitz-high-fidelity.html. Accessed 5 Sept. 2020.

SELECTED WORKS

X Men: First Class, 2011; The Divergent Series, 2014–16; *The Road Within*, 2014; *Mad Max: Fury Road*, 2015; *Big Little Lies*, 2017–19; *Fantastic Beasts: The Crimes of Grindelwald*, 2018; *High Fidelity*, 2020

—*Maria del Pilar Guzman*

Sebastian Kurz

Born: August 27, 1986
Occupation: Politician

Sebastian Kurz was first elected chancellor of Austria in 2017. At thirty-one, he was both the youngest person to ever serve that role and as the youngest democratic head of government anywhere in the world. A self-styled modern leader in the mold of France's Emmanuel Macron or Canada's Justin Trudeau, Kurz, who entered politics at sixteen, cultivated a progressive-presenting brand that belied his conservative views. A member of Austria's center-right People's Party (Österreichische Volkspartei; ÖVP), many political observers considered his rhetoric more in line with the country's far-right populist Freedom Party (Freiheitliche Partei Österreichs; FPÖ), with whom he formed a coalition government in 2017. Long associated with fascism, racism, and anti-Semitism, the FPÖ surged in popularity in the 2010s and sought to distance itself from its past, but remained controversial.

To some, Kurz's embrace of the FPÖ was a pragmatic way of harnessing its growing support and moderating its radical elements. "If mainstream politics wants to survive, you have to do a Kurz," Alexander Stubb, the former center-right prime minister of Finland, told Ben Hall and Ralph Atkins for the *Financial Times* (6 Jan. 2019). Others argued that, as an establishment politician, Kurz inappropriately enabled and legitimized the once vehemently derided group. "You don't fight fire with kerosene," former center-left chancellor Christian Kern told Hall and Atkins. "They are shifting the red lines of what is morally and politically acceptable permanently to the right."

As chancellor, Kurz drew international attention with nationalist policies, such as efforts to block refugees and migrants from entering the country and curtailing the freedoms of Austria's

Photo by the Austrian Council Presidency

Muslim population. He remained popular, but in 2019 a scandal involving his FPÖ vice chancellor resulted in the collapse of his government and his removal from office. Incredibly, Kurz managed to reclaim the chancellorship months later, and formed a surprising alliance with Austria's environmentalist Green Party.

EARLY LIFE AND EDUCATION

Sebastian Kurz was born in Vienna on August 27, 1986, and grew up an only child in the city's Meidling district, known for its culturally diverse working-class population. His mother was a high school teacher, and his father an engineer. At sixteen, Kurz called the offices of Austria's conservative ÖVP, asking to join. "It didn't go too well," Kurz recalled in a campaign video, as quoted by Melissa Eddy for the *New York Times* (16 Oct. 2017). "They gave me the sense that I should get back to them in a couple of years. That experience left me with the idea that politics should actually be something where everyone can participate. Where anyone who wants to can get involved."

Kurz joined the party at seventeen, and in 2009, while he was a law student at the University of Vienna, became the national leader of its youth wing. In that position, Kurz came up with several controversial advertising campaigns hoping to draw other young people to the party. One slogan for the 2010 Viennese state elections, "Schwarz macht geil," referencing the ÖVP's official color, was a pun that translates to both "Black makes you cool," and "Black makes you horny." By all accounts, Kurz was successful at his job, and he created a powerful network of political operatives and allies.

EARLY POLITICAL CAREER

Kurz was a member of the Vienna City Council from 2010 until 2011, when he was appointed state secretary of the Interior Ministry for social integration. He quit his law studies to devote himself to his new job, which required him to facilitate immigrants' participation in Austrian society. Kurz proposed a fast-track for citizenship for immigrants who exhibited strong German language skills, or participated in some form of volunteer work. He won praise from liberal commentators, and even came out against a FPÖ proposal seeking to limit immigrant access to welfare—a proposal he would later actively pursue. Kurz became known for his excellent communication and managerial skills. "He has a great feeling for how the public opinion changes," Stefan Lehne, a scholar and former official with the Austrian Ministry of Foreign Affairs, told Anna Goldenberg for the *Atlantic* (3 July 2018). "He's a great communicator, but you don't really know what he is thinking."

In 2013 Kurz was elected foreign minister at the age of twenty-seven, becoming the youngest person to serve a similar post in the world. Early in his tenure he began espousing more hardline right-wing views on immigration and multiculturalism. He singled out Muslim Austrians, who made up about 6 percent of the country's population in 2014, for special scrutiny, claiming to fear the spread of extremism. For instance, he sought to authorize a German-language version of the Qur'an "to discourage interpretations that incite radical Islamists," as Christopher Cermak wrote for Germany's *Handelsblatt* newspaper (19 Dec. 2014). The proposal sparked a furious debate in Austria, as did a proposed ban on foreign funding for mosques and a call for imams to deliver their sermons in German.

In 2015 Kurz's staunch nationalism found growing support among Austrians as record numbers of refugees, fleeing Syria, Afghanistan, Iraq, and other countries in the Middle East and Africa, surged into Europe seeking asylum. Germany, led by Prime Minister Angela Merkel, mobilized to welcome them. Kurz, in his position as foreign minister, did all he could to bar their entrance, creating tensions between the two neighboring countries. Early on, when asked why he refused to greet refugees arriving at train stations, as other politicians had done, Kurz told his biographer, as quoted by Goldenberg: "It's the wrong signal to criminal smugglers that people who gave them that much money and made it across the Mediterranean are greeted with smiles."

In 2016, Kurz met with leaders of the Balkan states in Vienna, forging an agreement to close the European Union's (EU) eastern borders to refugees and migrants. The United Nations (UN) and the EU, particularly Merkel, were outraged. Merkel was working on a different deal with Turkey, which was ultimately successful, to stem the flow of migrants into Europe. Simon Shuster, writing for *Time* magazine (29 Nov. 2018), described Kurz's actions as a "disaster for EU solidarity" and a humanitarian crisis. Closing the border between Greece and Macedonia left tens of thousands of people stranded in a "squalid" camp near the Greek village of Idomeni, Shuster reported. Greek prime minister Alexis Tsipras begged fellow EU leaders to intercede. "When kids are born and old people die in the mud of Idomeni," Tsipras said, as quoted by Shuster, "that's the political work of Sebastian Kurz."

CHANCELLOR OF AUSTRIA

Kurz's push to close the eastern border was popular among Austrians. "The closing of the Balkan route made Kurz a political star in Austria," Kurz's biographer, Paul Ronzheimer, wrote, as quoted by Shuster. "He enjoyed that role."

In May 2017, Kurz was named chair of the People's Party. He renamed it the New People's Party, and changed its official color from black to turquoise. The cosmetic changes were aimed at rebranding the party as a larger conservative movement. Kurz himself became the face of that movement; his use of social media, youth, and fashion won him comparisons to more liberal leaders like Macron, Trudeau, and former US President Barak Obama.

Kurz launched his campaign for the chancellery with a pledge to limit immigrant access to Austria's social-welfare system. His rhetoric came directly from the FPÖ—so much so that members of that party complained. As Eddy put it for the *Times* (13 Oct. 2017), Kurz co-opted "the far-right's push to limit immigration and to reinforce a national identity, but in a more moderate and polite tone." In October 2017 the People's Party finished first in legislative elections, making Kurz the youngest chancellor in Austria's history.

As many predicted, the newly elected Kurz formed a coalition government with the Freedom Party. (Though the center-left Social Democrats earned the second most votes in the election, they and the People's Party had earlier refused to work together; the Freedom Party, winning just over a quarter of the vote, came in third.) The alliance made some officials uneasy, based on the rocky history of similar alliances. In 2000, Israel and some members of the EU had introduced sanctions against Austria after the ÖVP formed a coalition government with the FPÖ, arguing that the coalition legitimized extremism.

Austrian President Alexander Van der Bellen took the extraordinary step of eliciting several promises from Kurz's government before he agreed to administer the oath of office in December 2017. Given that the Freedom Party had long lobbied for Austria to leave the EU, Van der Bellen required the incoming administration support Austria's membership in the EU, and further put in place checks and balances to prevent them from seeking a referendum on the issue. Citing the country's Nazi past, the president also insisted that the new government abandon plans to set up a home security ministry, and pointedly reminded the new leaders that they represented all Austrians, including immigrants.

Kurz awarded FPÖ leaders key government posts, including the defense and interior ministries. He also adopted a number of the Freedom Party's proposed restrictions on Muslim citizens. By June 2018 his government had banned full-face coverings, closed seven mosques (including six run by a group called the Arab Cultural and Religious Community, which was dissolved), and asked for a number of Turkish imams to be expelled from the country. The actions were part of a broader crackdown under a 2015 law that allowed regulation of the Islamic community. Kurz expressed commitment to fighting what he described as illegal migration to the EU, calling for Austria, Germany and Italy to form an "axis of the willing" to do so. His choice of phrase was criticized for recalling the former Axis powers of World War II, an alliance that included Nazi Germany (of which Austria was a part).

In July 2018 Kurz assumed the six-month rotating presidency of the EU's council. In that role, he was able to set the term's agenda. He called it "A Europe That Protects," and listed his first priority as: "Security and the fight against illegal migration." His rhetoric was not totally out of step with EU leaders, who weeks earlier, had reached a deal to create a series of camps, or secure migrant processing centers, to identify and deport economic migrants while allowing asylum seekers to be resettled in the EU.

THE "IBIZA AFFAIR" AND POLITICAL COMEBACK

In May 2019 a video emerged in which Heinz-Christian Strache, chair of the Freedom Party and Kurz's vice-chancellor, appeared to engage in corrupt financial dealing with a woman posing as the daughter of a Russian oligarch. Shot in Ibiza, Spain, in 2017, the video resulted in Strache's resignation and the collapse of Kurz's coalition government. In a matter of hours, Kurz went from one of the most successful right-wing politicians in Europe to being the first Austrian chancellor since World War II to be ousted by his peers, after the Austrian Parliament declared no confidence in his leadership and voted for his removal.

In the wake of the "Ibiza affair," as it became known, Kurz managed to distance himself from the FPÖ. After courts ruled that raids conducted by the Freedom Party–led interior ministry against Austria's own domestic intelligence service were largely illegal, Kurz characterized his relationship with the party as strained. He lamented, as quoted by Rick Noack for the *Washington Post* (2 Jan. 2020), "There were many situations that were hard for me to put up with."

In the September 2019 elections, Kurz managed to reclaim the chancellorship. He came to the role with a new outlook, forging a coalition government with the Green Party. Their January 2020 coalition contract reflected a blend of conservative and progressive policies, with its inclusion of a ban on headscarves for Muslim girls and women and a proposal to set up deportation centers for unsuccessful asylum seekers alongside a carbon tax on airline tickets and a goal of making Austria carbon neutral by 2040.

PERSONAL LIFE

Kurz has maintained a long-term relationship with Susanne Thier. He lives in Meidling, Vienna.

SUGGESTED READING

Cermak, Christopher. "Reforming Islam, Austrian-Style." (Düsseldorf, Germany) *Handelsblatt*, 19 Dec. 2014, www.handelsblatt.com/today/politics/sebastian-kurz-reforming-islam-austrian-style/23616128.html. Accessed 11 Apr. 2020.

Eddy, Melissa. "Austria Is Poised to Shift Sharply Right in Election." *The New York Times*, 13 Oct. 2017, www.nytimes.com/2017/10/13/world/europe/austria-election-freedom-party.html. Accessed 13 Apr. 2020.

———. "For Sebastian Kurz, Austria's 31-Year-Old Leader, a Swift Rise." *The New York Times*, 16 Oct. 2017, www.nytimes.com/2017/10/16/world/europe/sebastian-kurz-austria.html. Accessed 11 Apr. 2020.

Goldenberg, Anna. "Europe's Agenda Is in the Hands of a 31-Year-Old." *The Atlantic*, 3 July 2018, www.theatlantic.com/international/archive/2018/07/sebastian-kurz-eu-presidency-immigration/564350/. Accessed 11 Apr. 2020.

Hall, Ben and Ralph Atkins. "Sebastian Kurz: Saviour of Europe's Mainstream or Friend of the Far-Right?" *Financial Times*, 6 Jan. 2019, www.ft.com/content/9396664c-044d-11e9-9d01-cd4d49afbbe3. Accessed 13 Apr. 2020.

Noack, Rick. "Sebastian Kurz Is Poised to Become the World's Youngest Government Leader—For the Second Time." *The Washington Post*, 2 Jan. 2020, www.washingtonpost.com/world/2020/01/02/world-is-likely-get-new-youngest-government-leader-hes-familiar-face/. Accessed 13 Apr. 2020.

Shuster, Simon. "Austria's Young Chancellor Sebastian Kurz Is Bringing the Far-Right into the Mainstream." *Time*, 29 Nov. 2018, time.com/5466497/sebastian-kurz/. Accessed 12 Apr. 2020.

—*Molly Hagan*

Ravyn Lenae

Date of birth: January 22, 1999
Occupation: R&B singer-songwriter

Many listeners initially heard Ravyn Lenae, who has claimed such influences as Erykah Badu and India.Arie, when she was featured on a track of rapper Noname's long-awaited 2016 mixtape *Telefone*. On that song, "Forever," Noname sings, "They ain't tryna' see me shine, shine," but in fact many critics did feel that the album did shine,

Photo by Bruce from Sydney via Wikimedia Commons

praising its richness and emotional intelligence. In the wake of that success, Lenae toured with Noname and opened for the R&B artist known as SZA in 2017. Although those gigs brought her more widespread attention, Lenae had been singing for years and had even already put out an EP, *Moon Shoes* (2015). As Tara Mahadevan wrote for the music magazine *The Fader* (1 Feb. 2018), "For those who've had their ears to Chicago's innovative R&B scene, Ravyn's rise was only a matter of time."

Making her accomplishments even more noteworthy for commentators and critics, Lenae was not yet out of high school when she began her breakout. Before she toured with Noname, her teachers had worked with her to create a plan for her to complete virtual learning while on the road. *Rolling Stone* magazine cited such early talent and dedication as a reason for including her in its March 2017 list of "10 New Artists You Need to Know." Indeed, Lenae continued to attract industry and fan buzz with her eclectic blend of styles as she released two more EPs, *Midnight Moonlight* and *Crush*, in 2017 and 2018, respectively. Interviewers consistently commented on the rarity of someone so young being so musically gifted. When Mahadevan asked if Lenae felt unduly pressured by such comments, she replied, "In a way, there's a lot of pressure, in a way there is not, because I'm really hard on myself when it comes to my music and my achievements. And I have to remember . . . that I have so much time to do everything that I want to do."

EARLY LIFE AND EDUCATION

Born Ravyn Lenae Washington on January 22, 1999, in Chicago, Illinois, Lenae was raised on the city's South Side. In interviews, she remembered her earliest years fondly. She was close to her grandfather, Richard Williams, a native of Panama who had been a doo-wop singer in a group based there. A soprano in his youth, he abandoned his musical aspirations when his voice began to change, and after coming to the United States he eventually became the pastor of the Pullman Christian Reformed Church. The church, which was central to Lenae's childhood, had been founded around the 1970s, at a time of heightened racial tensions on Chicago's South Side. Williams, who remained pastor for several decades after taking on the role in 1981, encouraged reconciliation, and Pullman Christian thus attracted a relatively diverse group of worshippers. Lenae sang in the choir and later credited her early interest in music to her time there.

When Lenae was around ten years old, her grandmother bought her a guitar. "[It] was very random," she recalled to Tosten Burks for *Spin* (14 Feb. 2018). "My grandma just knew that I liked music and was like, oh, a guitar. It was a typical Walmart guitar. I started taking private lessons. I don't know if I really played it. I think I was just honestly curious." She later took up piano as well but found that she most enjoyed singing rather than playing an instrument and focused instead on honing her vocal talents.

Lenae had always loved listening to music, and after aging out of her Disney *High School Musical* phase, she played a constant stream of R&B, rap, pop, and neo-soul. Beyoncé was a particular favorite, as were OutKast, Timbaland, India.Arie, and Badu. Inspired to perfect an assignment to write and sing a song, she began composing her own tunes while in middle school and recognized her passion and talent. "I grew up having an ear for what was hot and was not," she told Mahadevan, "What sounds good in music and what doesn't."

Lenae auditioned for and was accepted into the Chicago High School for the Arts (more casually referred to as ChiArts), which had been established in 2009. There she attended academic classes from early in the morning until two o'clock in the afternoon before studying classical music until the early evening. As a high schooler she also had the opportunity to attend a program at Chicago's House of Blues. Although she had considered becoming a music therapist or teacher, the program, which put her in touch with music industry professionals and gave her experience performing original work, solidified for her the idea of forging a singing career.

FIRST EP AND LAUNCHING A MUSIC CAREER

Lenae uploaded her first single, "Greetings," early in 2015. That year, as a high school sophomore, she joined forces with Monte Booker, an aspiring music producer who had also grown up on the South Side. Along with rapper Smino, they became members of a collective called Zero Fatigue, which met at Classick Studios, in Chicago's Humboldt Park neighborhood. Managed by recording engineer Chris "Classick" Inumerable, the studio was known as a warm and welcoming place where local young artists could bond and collaborate.

Fitting in work on the project after her long school days and dedicating money she had earned working after classes to pay for studio time, with Booker's help Lenae created a debut EP (extended play), *Moon Shoes*. They made the work available online as a free download in August 2015. The album, as Mahadevan wrote, "pair[s] her candied voice with Booker's trademark idiosyncratic beats," and it caught the attention of major label Atlantic Records, which signed her to a deal and rereleased the EP in 2016. Additionally, she had been invited to collaborate with rapper Noname on a track included on her debut project, *Telefone* (2016). *Moon Shoes* eventually racked up a large number of plays on the audio streaming service SoundCloud, helped in some part by fans who discovered her through her work with Noname. Lenae soon began to get increasingly admiring media attention: she was, for example, named Verizon's Big Break Artist on WGCI in Chicago, as well as one of BBC Radio's "New Names of 2016."

TOURING AND *MIDNIGHT MOONLIGHT*

Further building a reputation, in the early months of 2017 Lenae spent time on the road as part of Noname's tour promoting *Telefone*. Meanwhile, she and Booker had teamed up again for the EP *Midnight Moonlight*, which Atlantic released in March 2017, not long before she graduated from ChiArts in May. Around the time of the album's release and her impending graduation, she reflected on having already made serious forays into the music business. Explaining how pivotal ChiArts was to her development, she told Sydney Gore for *Nylon* (15 Feb. 2017), "I'm a singer now, I've been trained classically, taken acting lessons, music technology; I'm a well-rounded artist, I feel, and I owe it to [school]." She continued, "I feel like I want to take everything [the school] gave me and apply it to who I am as an artist today and go out in the world and basically spill my puzzle pieces."

Reviewing *Midnight Moonlight* for the respected music magazine *Pitchfork* (25 Apr. 2017), Marcus J. Moore wrote, "Lenae doesn't *sing*, per se; instead, her blend of atmospheric hums speaks directly to you." Describing the album's vibe, Moore continued, "*Midnight* brims with quiet intensity, bringing singers like Syd and Aaliyah to mind. Yet while their art focuses strictly on hip-hop and R&B, Lenae's sound feels a bit more atmospheric, blending modern bounce, dream pop, and electronica." Later in 2017, Lenae got the opportunity to open on select dates for SZA, one of the year's more popular artists, during her North American tour.

A CHANGE OF DIRECTION

For her next effort, *Crush*, Lenae collaborated with up-and-coming producer and guitarist Steve Lacy, with whom she had become acquainted online through social media following the increased hype created by *Midnight Moonlight*. In interviews, she explained that the pairing led to a different writing and recording process than she had previously been used to with Booker, a change that she ultimately found beneficial. Released in February 2018 and preceded by the well-received single "Sticky," the five-song EP was widely seen as the next step in her evolution as an artist. Burks explained that while Lenae had first established herself with "intimate, romantic confessions that floated gently over local hip-hop producer Monte Booker's jittery brand of neo-soul," *Crush* "is driven by surf rock licks and group harmonies that reframe Lenae's lonely relationship studies as sunny pop jams."

To support *Crush* and this next phase in her growing career, Lenae embarked on tour, performing her new music at venues and events around the world between 2018 and 2019. In April 2020, a new song by Lenae, "Rewind," was featured on an episode of the popular HBO series *Insecure*. Discussing her plans for the future, she told Sydney Scott for *Essence* (27 Mar. 2017), "I try not to create a bucket list or timeline for my life, mainly because I'd rather it flow naturally and organically without the stress of my expectations. However, I would really like to travel the world a few times. Music has taken me to heights I couldn't imagine and would love to see how far it is able to stretch."

PERSONAL LIFE

Lenae, who remains based in Chicago, often spoke of her love of colors and the influence certain hues have on her music—she said, for example, that *Midnight Moonlight* was inspired by blues and purples, while *Crush* was intended to invoke pinks and reds. This led some music journalists to speculate that she had synesthesia, a condition in which one sense is simultaneously perceived by another, such that a person can for example "hear" color or "taste" sounds. However, she dispelled that conjecture, emphasizing that she simply loves colors and patterns of all sorts. For this reason, she became known for often wearing brightly colored outfits and dyes her hair. A great fan of Chicago's vintage and thrift shops, she also got a series of tattoos, including a raven perched on a cherry blossom, the Aquarius symbol, and a French proverb that translates as, "Dream your life, live your dreams."

SUGGESTED READING

Lenae, Ravyn. "New & Next: Ravyn Lenae Is a New Voice out of Chicago That You Have to Hear." Interview by Sydney Scott. *Essence*, 27 Mar. 2017, www.essence.com/entertainment/new-next-ravyn-lenae. Accessed 11 May 2020.

———. "Ravyn Lenae's Brand of Soul Is Already in the Future." Interview by Kristin Corry. *Noisey*, Vice, 24 Apr. 2018, www.vice.com/en_us/article/xw79zq/ravyn-lenae-4-leaf-clover-interview-video. Accessed 11 May 2020.

———. "Ravyn Lenae Doesn't Want to Be a Star." Interview by Sydney Gore. *Nylon*, 15 Feb. 2017, www.nylon.com/articles/ravyn-leane-interview. Accessed 11 May 2020.

———. "Ravyn Lenae Is Feeling Lovey Dovey." Interview by Tosten Burks. *Spin*, 14 Feb. 2018, www.spin.com/2018/02/interview-ravyn-lenae-crush-ep-steve-lacy/. Accessed 11 May 2020.

———. "Ravyn Lenae Makes Vital Songs to Fall in and out of Love To." Interview by Tara Mahadevan. *The Fader*, 1 Feb. 2018, www.thefader.com/2018/02/01/ravyn-lenae-crush-interview-steve-lacy. Accessed 11 May 2020.

Moore, Marcus J. "Review of *Midnight Moonlight*, by Ravyn Lenae." *Pitchfork*, 25 Apr. 2017, pitchfork.com/reviews/albums/23183-midnight-moonlight-ep/. Accessed 11 May 2020.

SELECTED WORKS

Moon Shoes, 2015; *Midnight Moonlight*, 2017; *Crush*, 2018

—Mari Rich

Jane Levy

Date of birth: December 29, 1989
Occupation: Actor

At age eighteen, Jane Levy made the fateful decision to leave college to seriously follow her dream of an acting career. "I remember feeling that [being onstage] was the most at home I've ever felt while doing something," she shared with Noah Lehava for *Coveteur* (29 May 2019). Her choice would prove serendipitous. Shortly after completing a drama program in 2010, she nabbed her first-ever television part: the recurring character of Mandy Milkovich on the

Photo by Gage Skidmore via Wikimedia Commons

Showtime series *Shameless*; the five episodes in which she was featured began airing in early 2011. Her other big break also came in 2011, when she nailed her first audition for pilot season and was cast as Tessa, a snarky Manhattan teen whose father makes her move to the suburbs, on the critically acclaimed but ratings-challenged ABC sitcom *Suburgatory*—her first regular series role.

Thanks to appearances in films such as the remake of *Evil Dead* (2013) and the suspenseful home invasion thriller *Don't Breathe* (2016) as well as on television in the Stephen King—influenced Hulu series *Castle Rock*, Levy also distinguished herself as a recognizable figure in the entertainment industry's horror genre. Throughout her career, she has dedicated herself to being a versatile performer by tackling a wide range of dramatic and comedic roles. Nowhere is this more evident than in her involvement as the star of *Zoey's Extraordinary Playlist*, which began airing in early 2020 and marked her return to network television. For the NBC musical dramedy, she took on the role of a woman who can hear people's thoughts, which are interpreted as musical numbers.

EARLY LIFE AND EDUCATION
Jane Colburn Levy was born to Mary Tilbury and Lester Levy on December 29, 1989, in California. She grew up with her older brother, Simon, in the San Francisco suburb of San Anselmo. She hails from a highly creative family, and though she entertained notions of acting, her first real love was sports. When she was

around five years old, she started playing soccer, after her mother enrolled her in a camp. Her first brush with performing would come two years later, with appearances in a local stage adaptation of the musical *Oklahoma!* and subsequent productions of *Annie* and *The Wizard of Oz*.

Soccer remained a passion of Levy's while she was attending Sir Francis Drake High School in San Anselmo. At the end of her freshman year, she decided to concentrate on playing for the varsity girls soccer team, partly due to frustration with her drama teacher. However, she continued to hone her performing skills as part of the school's hip-hop dancing troupe. By her senior year, she had been promoted to captain of the varsity soccer squad.

Having also received some worldly experience while living in England for several months, after graduating from high school, Levy accepted an offer to attend Goucher College, a private liberal arts institution in Baltimore, Maryland. However, two weeks prior to the start of sophomore year, realizing she did not feel fulfilled by her coursework, she left Goucher to pursue her true calling. With her parents slightly concerned but having given their blessing, she moved to New York City around 2008 to study at the Stella Adler Studio of Acting. About her training there, she explained to Jenelle Riley for *Backstage* (2 May 2012), "Acting school was about exercising that acting muscle and doing it every single day—and having people tell you that you're bad every single day! Which pushes you to work even harder." Before completing the conservatory program, which she participated in for about a year and a half, she submitted her headshot and résumé to, among others, New York City–based talent manager James Suskin, who agreed to represent her.

BREAKING INTO TELEVISION
Levy's acting career quickly took off. Two weeks after returning to her native California in 2010, she successfully auditioned to play promiscuous teen Mandy Milkovich on *Shameless*, a new Showtime dramedy starring William H. Macy as the alcoholic, down-on-his-luck father of six children. Levy, who had darkened her naturally blonde hair color in preparation for the recurring role, made her television debut on the series' January 23, 2011, episode before appearing in a total of five episodes during the inaugural season of the show, which would eventually become the network's best-performing freshman series.

Shortly after she had finished filming for *Shameless*, Levy prepared to try out for pilot season, a period between January and April when studios cast many of their potential series for the upcoming fall television season. Despite her limited acting experience, the newcomer, now sporting red hair, made a favorable impression at her very first pilot audition for a sitcom about a sarcastic teenage girl whose father uproots her from the big city to live in suburbia. "Because she doesn't come from a TV comedy background, she has a different rhythm," series creator Emily Kapnek told AJ Marechal for *Variety* (20 Oct. 2011). "When people are seasoned in the comedy world, that timing and cadence creeps into their performance. There was none of that with Jane."

In February 2011, Levy was tapped to play the lead, opposite Jeremy Sisto, as Tessa in the ABC comedy pilot *Suburgatory*, which was officially unveiled as part of the network's 2011–12 fall schedule. When *Suburgatory* debuted in late September, she went from being relatively unknown to gaining greater critical and viewer attention. Tim Goodman was complimentary in his review for the *Hollywood Reporter* (27 Sept. 2011), calling Levy "pitch-perfect" and also adding, "She's not only got the snark but the facial expressions that illuminate her disdain for the Disneyland she finds herself in." Television audiences were equally charmed; *Suburgatory* earned a full-season pickup in October 2011.

MAKING A NAME FOR HERSELF

After being named to the *Forbes* 30 Under 30 list in 2011, Levy appeared in a feature film for the first time as part of the cast of the indie drama *Nobody Walks*, which, in part, earned its producers a Special Jury Prize upon its premiere at the 2012 Sundance Film Festival in January. She received more positive news that May, when *Suburgatory* was renewed for a second season. Following her part in the Halloween comedy *Fun Size* (2012), for her next project, *Evil Dead* (2013), Fede Álvarez's remake of the 1981 horror flick, she tackled much darker material, starring as a heroin addict who attempts to get clean at a seemingly secluded cabin and falls prey to demonic forces. "I really wanted to work on *Evil Dead* because of how different it is from *Suburgatory*. I guess that's my main goal in this industry . . . to play a wide range of characters," she confided to Vicki Larson for *Marin Independent Journal* (17 Apr. 2012). "That process of creating a new person is so fun for me."

When *Evil Dead* made its US premiere in April 2013, the film grossed around $26 million in its opening weekend, eventually taking in $97.5 million worldwide. By May, ABC had renewed *Suburgatory* for a third season, despite the show's ratings struggles. However, instead of a fall premiere, the series returned in mid-January 2014, as part of the network's midseason schedule. Though production cuts designed to focus attention on the core characters were made, the series was ultimately canceled in May 2014—less than one month after her next film,

the ensemble millennial drama *About Alex*, had premiered at the Tribeca Film Festival.

Levy's singing voice was on display in *Bang Baby* (2014), which features her playing an aspiring teenage singer whose idol ends up in her small town after his car breaks down, just as a chemical leak results in many townspeople experiencing mutations. The 1960s-set sci-fi musical, which was shot over four weeks, won the City of Toronto Award for Best Canadian First Feature Film at the Toronto International Film Festival, where it had its world premiere in September 2014. Following appearances in three 2015 films—the short films *Nicholas & Hillary* and *Here Now* as well as the indie comedy *Frank and Cindy*—Levy reteamed with Álvarez on the psychological horror-thriller *Don't Breathe*. In it, she played yet another troubled character: a desperate young woman who hopes to get away from abuse she suffers at home by breaking into a blind veteran's house and stealing cash but winds up becoming the hunted. After its August 2016 release, *Don't Breathe* became a surprise late summer smash, grossing over $157 million worldwide.

RETURNING TO FAMILIAR TERRITORY

On the heels of that sleeper hit, Levy embraced much lighter fare. In 2016, she costarred in the live-action, computer-animated film *Monster Trucks* (2016), which filmmakers reportedly hoped could be considered on the same level as the blockbuster Transformers franchise but which did not fare well at the box office. The following year saw her appear in the dark satire *I Don't Feel at Home in This World Anymore* (2017), which claimed the US Dramatic Grand Jury Prize at Sundance and aired on Netflix.

Shifting her focus to the small screen, she had a guest appearance in Showtime's 2017 revival of *Twin Peaks* and a starring role as a talent coordinator in the drama *There's . . . Johnny!*, a fictional behind-the-scenes look at Johnny Carson's iconic late-night talk show that streamed on Hulu in November 2017. Also around that time, she appeared opposite Glenn Close in *Sea Oak*, a half-hour dramedy pilot about a vengeful zombie that was passed over by Amazon; zombies were also at the center of her big-screen comedy *Office Uprising* (2018).

Levy revisited the horror genre with Hulu's *Castle Rock* (2018), a Stephen King–inspired anthology series about an attorney who goes back to his sleepy Maine hometown to represent a death-row inmate while confronting his grim past. For the show's first season, she portrayed Diane "Jackie" Torrance, a sarcastic taxi driver and aspiring writer who harbors a morbid curiosity. When asked about her continued involvement in horror projects, she told Tom Philip for *GQ* (17 Aug. 2018), "I like things that push buttons and push boundaries, and horror and comedy are genres that do that." Next came another anthology drama: Netflix's *What/ If*, the first season of which was released on the platform in 2019. She starred as a financially strapped start-up founder who receives a life-changing offer from a ruthless venture capitalist (played by Renée Zellweger).

ZOEY'S EXTRAORDINARY PLAYLIST

In February 2019, Levy had secured the lead role in *Zoey's Extraordinary Playlist*, a new NBC musical drama about an ambitious young coder who, after suffering an MRI mishap, is able to hear people's private thoughts, expressed through song-and-dance numbers. She was offered the role outright, despite not having a musical theater background. "This part was going to require a wide range of comedy and drama and singing and dancing. I also needed somebody who felt a little quirky . . . someone who was really smart as well," show creator Austin Winsberg told Sydney Bucksbaum for *Entertainment Weekly* (6 Jan. 2020). "To have that razor-sharp comedic timing to be as expressive as she is for all the musical numbers, Jane was the first person we thought of that checked all those boxes."

To prepare for the title role, Levy underwent vocal training. After the series kicked off with a preview episode in January 2020, her first opportunity to showcase her voice came in mid-February during the show's second episode, when Zoey performs Kiki Dee's "I've Got the Music in Me." In episode eight, which aired in late March 2020, Levy experienced another milestone: the first time that her character performs every single song; it took three days to rehearse. Following the May 3, 2020, season finale, it was announced in June that a second season of the series had been ordered by NBC.

PERSONAL LIFE

Levy married Jaime Freitas, an actor, in March 2011. The couple separated, and she filed for divorce in 2013. She counts fellow actors Jenny Slate and Mae Whitman among her closest friends.

SUGGESTED READING

Bucksbaum, Sydney. "*Zoey's Extraordinary Playlist* Helped Jane Levy Discover Her Inner 'Secret Musical Theater Nerd.'" *Entertainment Weekly*, 6 Jan. 2020, ew.com/tv/2020/01/06/jane-levy-zoeys-extraordinary-playlist-series-preview/. Accessed 5 June 2020.
Goodman, Tim. "Review of *Suburgatory*, created by Emily Kapnek." *The Hollywood Reporter*, 27 Sept. 2011, www.hollywoodreporter.com/review/suburgatory-tv-review-240705. Accessed 5 June 2020.
Levy, Jane. "Jane Levy Is Horror's Secret Weapon." Interview by Tom Philip. *GQ*, 17 Aug. 2018, www.gq.com/story/castle-rock-jane-levy-interview. Accessed 12 June 2020.
———. "Jane Levy on Being Horror's Secret Sauce and Her Newest Musical TV Drama." Interview by Noah Lehava. *Coveteur*, 29 May 2019, coveteur.com/2019/05/29/jane-levy-talks-working-with-renee-zellweger-what-if/. Accessed 5 June 2020.
———. "Jane Levy's *Suburgatory* Background Was San Anselmo." Interview by Vicki Larson. *Marin Independent Journal*, 17 Apr. 2012, www.marinij.com/2012/04/17/jane-levys-suburgatory-background-was-san-anselmo/. Accessed 5 June 2020.
Marechal, AJ. "Jane Levy: 21-Year-Old Moves to *Suburgatory*." *Variety*, 20 Oct. 2011, variety.com/2011/tv/news/jane-levy-21-year-old-moves-to-suburgatory-1118044532/. Accessed 5 June 2020.
Riley, Jenelle. "*Suburgatory* Star Jane Levy on Her First Season." *Backstage*, 2 May 2012, www.backstage.com/magazine/article/suburgatory-star-jane-levy-first-season-52126/. Accessed 12 June 2020.

SELECTED WORKS

Shameless, 2011; *Suburgatory*, 2011–14; *Evil Dead*, 2013; *Bang Baby*, 2014; *Don't Breathe*, 2016; *Castle Rock*, 2018; *Zoey's Extraordinary Playlist*, 2020–

—*Bertha Muteba*

Lil Nas X

Date of birth: April 9, 1999
Occupation: Singer-songwriter

In late 2018 Lil Nas X made a thirty-dollar purchase that would change his life: an instrumental track created by producer YoungKio that mixes hip-hop beats with country-style guitar samples, which immediately made Lil Nas X think of a cowboy whose emotions and desires echoed his own. After recording the resulting song, "Old Town Road," in a local studio, Lil Nas X released the track online, just as he had for previous musical projects such as the 2018 mixtape *NASARATI*.

Unlike many of his earlier songs, however, "Old Town Road" became a surprise hit, spreading rapidly throughout social networks and apps such as *Twitter* and *TikTok*—thanks in large part to Lil Nas X's mastery of memes and internet humor—before finding its way out into the wider world. Though thrilled with the song's popularity, Lil Nas X found the rise of "Old Town Road" to

Photo by Jason Kempin/Getty Images

be a stressful period. "I'm always thinking: What if I'm not promoting the song hard enough? What if this never goes for me?" he told Joe Levy for *Billboard* (19 Sept. 2019). He added, "I was stressing so much more during that period because it was my first song to move at this height, this speed. One wrong step and it can all slip up." Despite such worries, nothing prevented "Old Town Road" from claiming the top spot on the Billboard Hot 100 chart, and remixes featuring artists such as country singer Billy Ray Cyrus further cemented the song's status as a pop-cultural phenomenon. "Everything lined up for this moment to take me to this place," he told Andrew R. Chow for *Time* (15 Aug. 2019).

EARLY LIFE AND EDUCATION

Lil Nas X was born Montero Lamar Hill on April 9, 1999. The youngest of six children, he grew up near Atlanta, Georgia, living for periods in the city itself as well as the nearby city of Austell. His parents separated when he was six years old, and he lived with each of them at various points. His father was a gospel singer, and music was an important part of his life from an early age. As a teenager, Hill attended Lithia Springs High School, from which he graduated in 2017.

After graduating from high school, Hill enrolled in the University of West Georgia to study computer science. Long immersed in social media and mobile technology, he was interested in learning skills such as app design but soon found that undergraduate studies did not appeal to him. "I was doing good in school, but I didn't want to do school anymore," he explained

to Lakin Starling for *Teen Vogue* (3 June 2019). After his first year, Hill left school and moved in with one of his sisters who was providing for two of his other siblings as well. He took jobs in hospitality and entertainment to make ends meet.

During that period, he remained heavily connected to the Internet and further developed the meme-heavy internet persona, first explored during his high school years, that would make him popular on social media websites such as *Twitter* but also serve as the launching point for his music career. "It'd never have made it out there without the meme culture that embraced it," he later told Al Horner for *GQ Hype* (5 Aug. 2019).

EARLY WORK

Although Hill came from a musical background, he did not initially consider pursuing a career in music, instead beginning to record songs simply as a hobby. "At first, I was just bored, like, 'Hey, Twitter, I made a song,'" he told Starling. "But I'm like, 'Wait, this is really hard.'" Over time, however, he became increasingly invested in his work, which he made available to stream freely online. "I made another one, and it didn't make any noise. I was overtrying. A lot of it was me trying to be something that people would like instead of making music that I would like," he explained to Starling. "Around my fifth song, the melodies and flows were coming to my head with no effort. I was like, 'This is something I want to do.'" Releasing his music under the name Lil Nas X, Hill began to develop an audience for his work, which at the time fell primarily within the rap genre.

In July 2018 Lil Nas X released his first mixtape, *NASARATI*. A compilation of independently recorded songs, *NASARATI* features many of the characteristics for which Lil Nas X's work would become known, including references to contemporary political figures, such as US president Donald Trump and North Korean leader Kim Jong Un, as well as to pop-culture characters, including the video-game character Sonic the Hedgehog and the Marvel Comics villain Thanos. Made available through popular music sites such as *SoundCloud*, *NASARATI* received some attention among hip-hop listeners but did not produce a major hit.

"OLD TOWN ROAD"

In late 2018, while searching for new beats to use as instrumental tracks for his songs, Lil Nas X discovered a beat created by a Dutch producer known as YoungKio; it also, unbeknown to him, contained an unlicensed Nine Inch Nails sample. "When I first heard the beat and its guitar sample, I was like, 'This is a sad cowboy going through some s——,'" he recalled to Starling. After purchasing the beat for thirty dollars, he spent a month working on what would become the song "Old Town Road," a song blending the country and hip-hop genres and expressing the artist's own feelings, including about his desire to leave home, through a Western-inspired narrative. Intent upon making the song sound as good as possible, Lil Nas X moved away from his former at-home recording processes and instead sought out an affordable recording venue in the Atlanta area. "It was my first studio made song, because I was like this can't be no butt-quality song," he told Rodney Carmichael for *NPR Music* (10 Apr. 2019).

After completing "Old Town Road" and releasing it online in late 2018, Lil Nas X began to work on promoting the new track, creating memes and videos related to it in the hope of drawing widespread attention to his work. "Old Town Road" attracted attention particularly from users of the app *TikTok*, which allows its userbase to create short mobile videos featuring clips from songs. In the case of "Old Town Road," *TikTok* users began to create so-called Yeehaw Challenge videos, in which the stars of the videos transform into cowboys or cowgirls while the song plays in the background. The popularity of the Yeehaw Challenge meme—and the YeeHaw Agenda movement to popularize black cowboy depictions—directed further public and media attention to Lil Nas X's work, just as his own efforts to promote the song had intended. "People were like, 'Where are these memes coming from?'" he told Chow. "If you see something going around the Internet, people want to join in."

CONTROVERSY AND RECOGNITION

As "Old Town Road" gained popularity online, the song entered the Billboard Hot 100 chart and moved steadily upward. Due to the song's unique genre, which Lil Nas X described as "country trap," "Old Town Road" also entered Billboard's Hot Country chart and remained there for a time. However, in March 2019, *Billboard* removed the song from the Hot Country chart with the stated reasoning that "Old Town Road" did not adhere to enough of the characteristics of contemporary country music. The decision proved to be a controversial one. Many commentators accused *Billboard* of gatekeeping the country genre and removing "Old Town Road" because Lil Nas X is African American, particularly considering that other crossover songs by white artists had recently been allowed.

For the artist himself, the genre debate surrounding "Old Town Road" was less about race than about fear of change. "Initially I was like, 'I think I'm being discriminated against,'" Lil Nas X told Carmichael. "But then as I went on to think about it, I felt like it was more of a purist situation, like, 'We want this to stay this way.' . . . One of those scared [responses], like, 'We don't want this to evolve this far,' basically."

Though controversial, *Billboard*'s decision ultimately directed further public attention toward "Old Town Road," and in early April Lil Nas X emphasized the song's country elements further by releasing a remix featuring additional vocals by country singer Billy Ray Cyrus. That remix was the first in a string of "Old Town Road" remixes featuring various artists, including child yodeler Mason Ramsey, producer Diplo, and rapper RM, the latter a member of the Korean pop band BTS. Proving popular among listeners, the "Old Town Road" remix featuring Cyrus spent a record-setting nineteen weeks atop the Hot 100 and won the award for musical event of the year from the 2019 Country Music Association Awards and song of the year at the 2019 MTV Video Music Awards.

EP 7

In March 2019, amid the publicity surrounding "Old Town Road," Lil Nas X signed a record deal with Columbia Records. Columbia helped him avoid legal woes with Nine Inch Nails and released his debut extended-play (EP) record, 7, in June of that year. Unlike *NASARATI*, 7 features songs that incorporate a variety of genres, including rap, country, rhythm and blues, alternative rock, pop, and electronic music. "I'm still in the first stage of figuring out who I am. . . . I want to do everything and I'm still learning how I work," Lil Nas X told Horner of his eclectic approach. "But the one thing I'll always know is that people don't know what they want until they get it. They didn't know they wanted a song about taking a horse to the old town road in 2019. But they did."

The EP 7 features both the original version of "Old Town Road" and the remix featuring Cyrus in addition to six new songs, including Lil Nas X's second single, "Panini." The other songs on the EP include contributions from several other artists, such as drummer Travis Barker and rapper Cardi B. Among the most personally significant songs on the EP was "C7osure (You Like)," in which Lil Nas X discusses his need to be true to himself rather than doing what others want or expect of him. The album opened at number two on the Billboard 200 chart, boding well for his future beyond "Old Town Road." Following the release of 7, Lil Nas X continued to work on his first full-length album, hoping to continue his musical success on his own terms. "Seeing digital numbers, it's a good feeling. It goes so quickly, though," he told Chow. "You have to keep going." In November 2019 the internet-bred sensation was nominated for a half dozen Grammy Awards, including in the coveted categories of record of the year, album of the year, and best new artist.

PERSONAL LIFE

Lil Nas X pointed particularly to "C7osure (You Like)" when he came out as gay on social media in June 2019, encouraging fans to listen closely to its lyrics. "It's something I was considering never doing, ever. Taking to the grave," he told *BBC Breakfast* about coming out, as quoted by Jazz Monroe for *Pitchfork* (5 July 2019). "But I don't wanna live my entire life—especially how I got to where I'm at—not doing what I wanna do." He has since spoken of both longstanding homophobia in the hip-hop and country music communities and the support of fans.

Lil Nas X owns an apartment in Los Angeles, California, that he shares with his two dogs.

SUGGESTED READING

Carmichael, Rodney. "Wrangler on His Booty: Lil Nas X on the Making and the Magic of 'Old Town Road.'" *NPR*, 10 Apr. 2019, www.npr.org/2019/04/10/711167412/wrangler-on-his-booty-lil-nas-x-on-the-making-and-the-magic-of-old-town-road. Accessed 15 Nov. 2019.

Chow, Andrew R. "'It Feels Like I'm Chosen to Do This.' Inside the Record-Breaking Rise of Lil Nas X." *Time*, 15 Aug. 2019, time.com/5652803/lil-nas-x. Accessed 15 Nov. 2019.

Horner, Al. "Lil Nas X: 'I'm Still in the First Stage of Figuring Out Who I Am.'" *GQ Hype*, 5 Aug. 2019. www.gq-magazine.co.uk/culture/article/lil-nas-x-interview. Accessed 15 Nov. 2019.

Levy, Joe. "How Lil Nas X Sees His Future after 'Old Town Road.'" *Billboard*, 19 Sept. 2019, www.billboard.com/articles/news/8530101/lil-nas-x-billboard-cover-story-interview. Accessed 15 Nov. 2019.

Monroe, Jazz. "Lil Nas X Discusses Coming Out as Gay in New Interview: Watch." *Pitchfork*, 5 July 2019, pitchfork.com/news/lil-nas-x-discusses-coming-out-as-gay-in-new-interview-watch. Accessed 15 Nov. 2019.

Starling, Lakin. "Lil Nas X Talks Fame, Going Viral, and More in His First Cover Story." *Teen Vogue*, 3 June 2019, www.teenvogue.com/story/lil-nas-x-june-2019-cover. Accessed 15 Nov. 2019.

Yahr, Emily. "Billboard Said Lil Nas X's 'Old Town Road' Wasn't Country Enough. Then Billy Ray Cyrus Stepped In." *The Washington Post*, 5 Apr. 2019, www.washingtonpost.com/arts-entertainment/2019/03/29/billboard-pulled-lil-nas-xs-viral-old-town-road-country-chart-it-ignited-controversy. Accessed 15 Nov. 2019.

—*Joy Crelin*

Ken Liu

Date of birth: 1976
Occupation: Author

"Science fiction can't tell us a lot about the future. It's more interesting for what it says about the society that produces it," writer and translator Ken Liu told Boyd Tonkin for *Newsweek* (30 Oct. 2016). From the publication of his first work of short fiction in 2002 onward, Liu has worked to express a great deal about society through his writing, much of which has been categorized as science fiction or fantasy. Along the way, he has developed both a dedicated readership and an impressive body of work, which encompasses more than 150 works of short fiction, including the widely lauded short story "The Paper Menagerie," as well as the critically acclaimed Dandelion Dynasty novels.

Just as significant, however, has been Liu's role in bringing Chinese science fiction to the United States through his work as a translator. Though not initially drawn to translation, he has built a productive career in that area thanks, in part, to his dedication to capturing the intent and meaning of the writing in question. "It's not a sentence-by-sentence or word-by-word recreation," he told Alexandra Alter for the *New York Times Magazine* (3 Dec. 2019), about his approach to translation. "It's about, how do I recreate the overall effect?" Much like his own writing, Liu's translations of novels—including Liu Cixin's award-winning *Three-Body Problem* (2014), and short stories, including those

Photo by Larry D. Moore via Wikimedia Commons

collected in his anthologies *Invisible Planets* (2016) and *Broken Stars* (2019)—have earned widespread recognition and have introduced a host of intriguing, powerful new narratives to readers throughout the United States.

EARLY LIFE AND EDUCATION

Ken Liu was born Liu Yukun in Lanzhou, China, in 1976. When he was a young child, his parents—students of chemistry and statistics, respectively—left the country to pursue studies abroad, and Liu remained in China with his paternal grandparents. Growing up in a household that valued books and reading, he became an avid reader in multiple genres, including science fiction. "The first science fiction work I read was the Chinese translation for *Do Androids Dream of Electric Sheep?* by Philip K. Dick, which turned into [the 1982 film] *Blade Runner*," he recalled to David Barr Kirtley for the *Geek's Guide to the Galaxy* podcast, a transcript of which was published in *Lightspeed Magazine* (Sept. 2015). "I thought that was a fascinating story." After about seven years with his grandparents, Liu rejoined with his parents, who by that time were residing in the United States. The family briefly lived in Palo Alto, California, before moving to Connecticut, where they lived in the towns of Stonington and Waterford.

Still a dedicated reader, Liu began writing his own fiction while in high school, though he did not begin to submit his work for potential publication until college. He was also active in cross-country running. After graduating from Waterford High School in 1994, Liu enrolled in Harvard University, where he studied English and computer programming. He earned his bachelor's degree from the institution in 1998.

ENGINEER AND LAWYER

Following college, Liu initially found work as a software engineer with the technology company Microsoft and later worked for a start-up, Idiom Technologies. After several years, however, he decided to pursue a different path and returned to Harvard for law school, earning his juris doctorate in 2004.

Although Liu considered software engineering and law to be similar fields due to the importance of defined rules in both, his career transition was at times a challenging one. "When you're a software engineer, you learn that it's really terrible to copy and paste, because that increases the chances of error. In law, however, you take the same thing and put it in multiple places verbatim, because there's an inherent culture of conservatism," he told Mary Wang for *Guernica* (28 May 2020). Liu would later have to unlearn habits from both fields in his career as a writer but at times noted in interviews that his prior experiences served as fruitful sources of creative inspiration. He was particularly inspired by his years of work as a litigation consultant specializing in patent law, which improved his understanding of the development of technology.

SHORT FICTION

While still in college, Liu began submitting stories to magazines but met with rejection. He continued to seek publication over the next years in an effort that he described to Jing Tsu for *Logic* magazine (1 May 2019) as "just a lot of try, try, try again." Liu's participation in online writing groups proved key during that period, enabling him to improve his work in response to critiques.

A turning point came in 2002, which saw the publication of Liu's first published story, "Carthaginian Rose," in the anthology *Empire of Dreams and Miracles*. He went on to publish sporadically over the next several years, placing stories in publications such as *Strange Horizons* and the 2009 anthology *Thoughtcrime Experiments*. Liu's work began to be published more extensively in 2011, appearing in major magazines such as *Crossed Genres*, *Clarkesworld*, *Nature*, and *Lightspeed*. Among the stories published that year was "The Paper Menagerie," which originally appeared in the *Magazine of Fantasy & Science Fiction* and went on to win the 2011 Nebula Award, 2012 Hugo Award, and 2012 World Fantasy Award, three significant awards within the genres of science fiction and fantasy.

Having published more than 150 pieces of short fiction by mid-2020, Liu is a prolific writer whose work is often characterized as science fiction but who does not necessarily set out to write in that genre. "Genre-wise, I don't really pay attention to labels," he explained to Tsu. "I simply like writing stories that literalize metaphors. I enjoy writing stories in which some metaphorical concept is made literally true, tangible, so that you can manipulate it, touch it, and play with it, as an actual thing." Liu's approach to writing, as well as his incorporation of scientific and historical elements into his work, continued to earn him acclaim after 2012: He won a second Hugo Award in 2013 for the short story "Mono no aware," originally published in the 2012 anthology *The Future Is Japanese*, and also earned award nominations for works such as "The Regular" (2014) and "Thoughts and Prayers" (2019).

ADAPTATIONS AND COLLECTIONS

Several of Liu's works have inspired screen adaptations. The story "Good Hunting" (2012), for instance, formed the basis of a 2019 episode of the animated Netflix series *Love, Death + Robots*. In March of 2020, the television channel AMC announced that it had greenlit two seasons of a new animated series *Pantheon*, based on a series of Liu's short stories.

In addition to their appearances in magazines and anthologies, some of Liu's short stories have appeared in collections dedicated to his own writing. The first such collection, *The Paper Menagerie and Other Stories* (2016), encompasses a carefully curated selection of the author's work. "My editor, Joe Monti, and I wanted to pick sample stories that represented what I was interested in writing, and what I liked and thought I was good at writing about; a variety sampler pack for people who are not familiar with my short fiction," Liu told Kirtley of his approach. Following its publication, *The Paper Menagerie and Other Stories* was nominated for the 2017 World Fantasy Award for Best Collection and won the 2017 Locus Award in that category. Liu went on to publish *The Legends of Luke Skywalker* (2017), a collection of linked short stories set within the Star Wars universe, and a second collection in wholly original worlds, *The Hidden Girl and Other Stories* (2020).

DANDELION DYNASTY

In addition to his short fiction, Liu began to make a name for himself as a novelist in 2015 with the publication of *The Grace of Kings*, the first installment in his Dandelion Dynasty series. A work of epic fantasy set in the fictional island nation of Dara, the novel blends a host of influences, including Chinese history and Western literary forms. "I said, 'I'm going to take this period of history—when a lot of heroes were rising up all around China; it was a time of war, of great change and social contention—and try to reimagine the story as a Western epic fantasy, and create a whole new world with new cultures and people in it,'" Liu told Kirtley about the novel's origins.

Grace and the subsequent work in the Dandelion Dynasty series, *The Wall of Storms* (2016), are in some ways celebrations of engineering, a subject to which Liu has long been drawn. "I've always wanted to read a fantasy book in which the heroes are not wizards, but engineers," he told Wang. For Liu, engineers "are a lot like poets," he explained to Wang. "You acquire the tropes and techniques of your literary or engineering tradition, and then you innovate and combine them into new poems or machines. This is the view of engineering I wanted to get across." The novels feature the development of technology that relies on what is known as "silkmotic force," or electromagnetism, which has prompted Liu to refer to the series' subgenre as "silkpunk," analogous to steampunk. Notably, Liu built a number of models and experimented with electrostatic force while working on the novels, seeking to ensure that the technological principles described in the books were sound.

Following its debut, the Dandelion Dynasty series received both critical acclaim and widespread attention from readers. *Grace* won the 2016 Locus Award for Best First Novel, and *Wall* was short-listed for another Locus Award. A third installment, *The Veiled Throne*, is scheduled for publication in 2021.

TRANSLATIONS

Though an established author in his own right, Liu is particularly known for his work translating Chinese science fiction into English for publication in the United States. Liu did not intend to pursue a career in translation but instead fell into it largely by chance through his friendship with Chinese writer Chen Qiufan. "I just loved their [Chinese speculative-fiction writers'] work—the narrative techniques were new; the ideas fresh; the voices sharp, poignant, and funny," he recalled to Tsu. "I wished more American readers beside myself got to read them." Liu began by translating works of short fiction, some of which went on to be published in English-language magazines as early as 2011. Over the course of the decade, stories translated by Liu appeared in major science-fiction magazines such as *Clarkesworld*, the *Magazine of Fantasy and Science Fiction*, and *Lightspeed*. They were also included in reprint anthologies such as *Year's Best Science Fiction and Fantasy* and *The Best Science Fiction of the Year* as well as themed collections such as *Upgraded* (2014) and *Current Futures: A Sci-Fi Ocean Anthology* (2019).

Liu is perhaps best known for his translation of the Liu Cixin novel *The Three-Body Problem*, published in the United States in 2014. Originally published in China in 2006, *The Three-Body Problem* earned widespread critical acclaim in the United States, winning the 2015 Hugo Award for Best Novel and earning nominations for several other prestigious science-fiction awards. Liu went on to translate Liu Cixin's 2010 novel *Death's End* in 2016, as well as the 2011 spin-off *The Redemption of Time* by Baoshu in 2019. His translations of *Waste Tide* (2013), by Chen Qiufan, and *Vagabonds* (2016), by Hao Jingfang, debuted in the United States in 2019 and 2020, respectively.

In addition to translating novels, Liu has edited the anthologies *Invisible Planets* (2016) and *Broken Stars* (2019), which collect his translations of works by authors such as Liu Cixin, Chen Quifan, Xia Jia, Cheng Jingbo, Tang Fei, and others. Both anthologies also include a selection of essays on Chinese science fiction and its cultural significance.

PERSONAL LIFE

Liu met his wife, software engineer turned professional photographer Lisa Tang Liu, at Idiom. The couple cocreated a mobile game for infants and toddlers. They have two daughters and live in the Greater Boston area.

SUGGESTED READING

Alter, Alexandra. "How Chinese Sci-Fi Conquered America." *The New York Times Magazine*, 3 Dec. 2019, www.nytimes.com/2019/12/03/magazine/ken-liu-three-body-problem-chinese-science-fiction.html. Accessed 13 July 2020.

Liu, Ken. "How Ken Liu Translates, and Why He Writes." Interview by Nick Admussen. *Public Books*, 13 Sept. 2019, www.publicbooks.org/how-ken-liu-translates-and-why-he-writes. Accessed 13 July 2020.

————. "Interview: Ken Liu." Interview by David Barr Kirtley. *Lightspeed Magazine*, no. 64, Sept. 2015, www.lightspeedmagazine.com/nonfiction/interview-ken-liu. Accessed 13 July 2020.

————. "Ken Liu on Writing, Translating, and the Future of the Dandelion Dynasty." *Tor.com*, 1 Apr. 2020, www.tor.com/2020/04/01/highlights-from-ken-lius-r-books-ama. Accessed 13 July 2020.

————. "Paper Animals: Ken Liu on Writing and Translating Science Fiction." Interview by Jing Tsu. *Logic*, no. 7, 1 May 2019, logicmag.io/china/ken-liu-on-writing-and-translating-science-fiction. Accessed 13 July 2020.

Tonkin, Boyd. "Meet the Man Bringing Chinese Science Fiction to the West." *Newsweek*, 30 Oct. 2016, www.newsweek.com/man-bringing-chinese-science-fiction-west-514893. Accessed 13 July 2020.

Wang, Mary. "Ken Liu: 'We Get to Define the Stories We Want to Be Told about Us.'" *Guernica*, 28 May 2020, www.guernicamag.com/miscellaneous-files-ken-liu. Accessed 13 July 2020.

SELECTED WORKS

Dandelion Dynasty series, 2015–; *The Paper Menagerie and Other Stories*, 2016; *The Legends of Luke Skywalker*, 2017; *The Hidden Girl and Other Stories*, 2020

—*Joy Crelin*

Marjorie Liu

Born: ca. 1979
Occupation: Author and comic book writer

Although Marjorie Liu began her writing career as a prolific author of fantasy novels, she has become a highly celebrated comic book writer. She has written extensively for Marvel Comics, specializing in titles related to the X-Men and other superhero mutants. She has also branched out into writing her own fantasy/steampunk series, *Monstress*, for Image Comics. The fantastical

Photo by Luigi Novi

series, which began in 2015, garnered tremendous support from fans, who are thrilled by its portrayal of complex female characters, and has earned Liu a host of awards, including the 2018 Eisner Award for Best Writer. She became the first female comic book writer to win an Eisner since the awards began in 1988.

She discussed the evolution of her writing career with Lenika Cruz for the *Atlantic* (14 Sept. 2017), saying: "There is something deeply invigorating about the comic-book medium. It's not just the kinds of stories we're able to tell, but it's also the relationships that are built and the collaborative force that generates between you and your whole team when things are going right."

EARLY LIFE

Marjorie M. Liu was born in 1979 in Philadelphia, Pennsylvania, to a Chinese father and a white mother. Her parents raised her in Washington State, where her father worked as a chemical engineer for a paper mill. They also frequently visited her father's family in Vancouver, British Columbia.

Although she considered herself Chinese, her experience as a biracial child often left her feeling out of place. She has recounted the racism against her family, and her father in particular, that she witnessed. She herself was prevented from participating in Chinese American clubs at school because of her appearance. "I felt very Chinese," she recalled to Mallory Yu for NPR's *All Things Considered* (22 July 2016). "But then I was trying to reconcile that with not feeling welcome." Those experiences, along with weight-related bullying, would later inform the types of stories she chose to write.

As a child she read widely. She recalled to Claire E. White in an interview for the *Internet Writing Journal* (May 2005): "When I was little, Laura Ingalls' *Little House on the Prairie* books were an endless source of enjoyment, and from that time on I've soaked in everything from Robert Louis Stevenson to Joseph Campbell to Charles DeLint to [Jorge Luis] Borges." She also began writing her own stories from a young age.

Liu attended public schools through fourth grade. She was then enrolled in the Lakeside School, a private coed school, in Seattle for middle and high school. She graduated in 1996.

EDUCATION

In 2000, Liu completed an undergraduate degree at Lawrence University in Appleton, Wisconsin. There she studied biomedical ethics and East Asian languages and cultures. While at Lawrence, she honed her web design skills by creating *WolverineandJubilee.com*, a fan site devoted to two popular X-Men characters Wolverine and Jubilee. Liu had never read any comics or watched superhero cartoons, but the websites she admired most were those devoted to comics, so when she sought to create her own website, she emulated those. She later began reading comics and writing fan fiction, which she posted online. The experience of writing fan fiction—fiction devoted to established characters but written by fans and usually posted anonymously—was liberating for her. It allowed her to be creative and develop her storytelling powers. That said, neither fan fiction nor her undergraduate degree seemed likely to secure her a well-paying job, so the one-time premedical student began looking at becoming a lawyer.

Liu was accepted into the University of Wisconsin Law School in Madison, Wisconsin, and graduated with her juris doctorate in 2003. She largely enjoyed her legal studies, but by the time she was admitted to the bar, she felt she was on the wrong path. Recalling her "defining moment" in a negotiation role play for her corporate law class, she told White: "Almost everyone in that class went through a radical personality shift—myself, included. I became a mean person. . . . I've never touted myself as some sweet doe-eyed pussycat—but I shocked myself." She added, "Given enough time and enough opportunity, that was who I could become. Ten or twenty years down the line, I would be the person I used to hate."

TAKING THE PLUNGE INTO NOVEL WRITING

During this time, Liu was still writing fan fiction, original short fiction, poetry, and nonfiction pieces. After a point, she decided to take the plunge and write a novel. She told Yu, "I felt completely free to write whatever the hell I wanted, and to go in and be bananas."

Writing in a month-long creative fury, she completed her first novel-length manuscript. She then sent it to agents, each of whom passed on it. She then began sending her manuscript directly to publishers who accepted non-agented submissions. Chris Keeslar at Dorchester Publishing ultimately accepted the book in 2004, while she was attending the Clarion Workshop, a six-week-long speculative fiction bootcamp then held in East Lansing, Michigan. That first novel was published as a mass-market paperback under the title *Tiger Eye* (2005) and formed the basis of the Dirk & Steele series. She initially landed a four-book contract, but the series evolved into twelve paranormal fantasy romances, in which people with extraordinary powers risk their lives to help others. Liu began writing full time and wrote much of that series from her family farm in Indiana, where she relocated after leaving Clarion.

Although Liu was writing and publishing these novels at a brisk pace—often more than one a year—she also found time to write urban fantasy fiction. The Hunter Kiss series is about the last living demon hunter on the planet. She uses the tattoos covering her body as her personal army to battle the forces of evil. The series came to encompass five books and two novellas, beginning with *The Iron Hunt* (2008) and concluding with *Labyrinth of Stars* (2014).

Despite living her dream, Liu found that for her, writing alone for hours and days on end was not conducive to her mental health. She wrote a tie-in novel for Pocket Star Books for Marvel Comics, *Dark Mirror* (2006), and then offered her writing services to Marvel editors for their comic series, which would allow her to collaborate with a team of creators, including an artist. Liu recalled to Lenika Cruz for the *Atlantic*: "Writing is very isolating, and I didn't have a lot of balance in my life. There was always a reason for me not to be out in the world, because I could just say, 'I have a deadline.' For someone who is already sort of shy and occasionally socially phobic, that was a very deadly trap to fall into." She soon decided to give up writing novels but to continue writing comics in order to earn money and also because she found it satisfying.

AWARD-WINNING COMIC BOOK WRITER

Unlike writing novels, writing comic books tends to be a collaborative effort between author and illustrator. The illustrator needs to understand exactly what the author wants illustrated not only on each page, but in each panel on each page. For Liu, it required her to rethink how to tell a story, given that she would need to provide descriptions to her artist collaborators for how she wanted every action to look as well as dialogue for each character. "I didn't know how to write comics, I had to teach myself," she told Milena Veselinovic for *CNN* (18 Dec. 2014). "I had never been a comic book person before really because I had no access to them. Once I had access I thought that these are just another avenue for telling stories and delving into the imagination."

For her first assignment for Marvel Comics, she worked on the X-Men spinoff series, *NYX: No Way Home* (2008–9), about a group of homeless teenage mutants in New York City. Mutants, in Marvel Comics, are people born with superhuman powers who are often ostracized by the world at large. Multiple series of X-Men comics have been published since the early 1960s; the X-Men and other mutants have often been stand-ins for oppressed groups. Liu went on to write many X-Men and mutant titles for Marvel, including *Dark Wolverine* (2009–10) and *Daken: Dark Wolverine* (2010–11), with Daniel Way; *X-23* (2010–12); *Wolverine: Road to Hell* (2010); and *X-Men: X-Termination* (2013). Liu received considerable attention for penning the wedding of the X-Man Northstar to his partner Kyle during her time on *Astonishing X-Men*, in 2012 and 2013. This work earned her a nomination for the 2013 GLAAD Media Award for Outstanding Comic Book. In addition to writing mutant titles, she has also written stories for Marvel's most popular female superheroes, including Black Widow.

Her last Marvel work was *Star Wars: Han Solo* in 2016. The limited series takes place between the films *Star Wars Episode IV: A New Hope* (1977) and *Star Wars Episode V: The Empire Strikes Back* (1980), which describes Solo's evolution from lovable rogue to a hero of the Rebellion against the Galactic Empire. That series launched among the top ten on the *New York Times* Best Seller list and earned her a nomination for an Eisner Award, the comic industry's most prestigious award.

MAKING A *MONSTRESS*

Although Liu loved working for Marvel, because of its rich characters and their interconnected history, she often cautioned herself to be mindful not to get attached to any one title, knowing it could be taken from her or cancelled at any time. She wanted greater artistic freedom as well. So, with the help of artist Sana Takeda, her collaborator for *X-23*, Liu produced a creator-owned series for Image Comics, *Monstress*, which takes place in an alternate, matriarchal Asia following a period of warfare between humans and magical creatures called Arcanics. The main character is Maika Halfwolf, a teenaged Arcanic who passes as human. Throughout the series, Liu and Takeda explore issues of racism,

feminism, and power against a richly wrought world influenced by World War II and the Cold War. Primarily, however, Liu wanted to create a fantasy series with women at the forefront of the action. She explained to Yu: "That was my goal through this book to show women in all their great and wonderful diversity. Women who are good, women who are evil, women who are in uniform, women in all straits of life and power—and that they are fully realized."

In addition to being a commercial and critical hit, *Monstress* earned numerous awards after it began in November 2015. The best-selling first collection, *Monstress, Vol. 1: Awakening* (2016), received the 2017 British Fantasy Award for Best Comic/Graphic Novel. *Monstress, Vol. 2: The Blood* (2017) won the 2018 British Fantasy Award for Best Comic/Graphic Novel and the 2018 Eisner Awards for Best Writer, Best Continuing Series, and Best Publication for Teens. *Monstress, Vol. 3: Haven* (2018) was named the 2018 Harvey Award Book of the Year. *Monstress* also received the Hugo Award for Best Graphic Story three consecutive times (2017–19). The fourth collection, *Monstress, Vol. 4: The Chosen*, was published in 2019. Volumes 2 through 4 were each nominated for a Bram Stoker Award, given by the Horror Writers Association.

In addition to writing comics and graphic novels, Liu has taught graphic novel writing at the Clarion Workshop and the Massachusetts Institute of Technology (MIT), as well as popular fiction at the Voices of Our Nation workshop. She lectures widely as well.

PERSONAL LIFE

Liu lives in Boston, Massachusetts. She has been romantically involved with Junot Díaz, a fellow writer who won the Pulitzer Prize for his novel *The Brief Wondrous Life of Oscar Wao*. At her encouragement, Díaz published his first children's book, *Islandborn*, in 2017.

SUGGESTED READING

"About." *MarjoriemLiu.com*, marjoriemLiu.com/about. Accessed 5 Mar. 2020.

Liu, Marjorie. "A Conversation with Marjorie M. Liu." Interview by Claire E. White. *The Internet Writing Journal*, May 2005, www.writerswrite.com/journal/marjorie-m-Liu-5052. Accessed 5 Mar. 2020.

Liu, Marjorie. "Comic Book Writer Marjorie Liu on How Rejection Shaped Her Writing." Interview by Mallory Yu. *All Things Considered*, NPR, 22 July 2016, www.npr.org/2016/07/22/487078939/graphic-novelist-marjorie-Liu-on-how-rejection-shaped-her-writing. Accessed 5 Mar. 2020.

Liu, Marjorie. "Marjorie Liu: Making a Monstress." Interview by Lauren K. Alleyne.

Guernica, 15 Feb. 2016, www.guernicamag.com/making-a-monstress. Accessed 13 Apr. 2020.

Liu, Marjorie. "Marjorie Liu on the Road to Making Monstress." Interview by Lenika Cruz. *The Atlantic*, 14 Sept. 2017, www.theatlantic.com/entertainment/archive/2017/09/marjorie-Liu-monstress-interview/539394. Accessed 5 Mar. 2020.

Quaintance, Zack. "NYCC '19: MONSTRESS Creators Marjorie Liu, Sana Takeda Discuss Hit Comic." *Comics Beat*, 3 Oct. 2019, www.comicsbeat.com/nycc-19-monstress. Accessed 12 Mar. 2020.

Veselinovic, Milena. "How a Lawyer Left the Courtroom to Discover She Had X-Men Powers." *CNN*, 18 Dec. 2014, edition.cnn.com/2014/12/16/world/asia/marjorie-Liu-bestselling-author-lawyer/index.html. Accessed 5 Mar. 2020.

SELECTED WORKS

Dirk & Steele novel series, 2005–12; *Dark Mirror*, 2006; Hunter Kiss novel series, 2008–14; *NYX: No Way Home*, 2008–09; *Dark Wolverine* (with Daniel Way), 2009–10; *X-23*, 2010–12; *Black Widow: The Name of the Rose*, 2011; *Astonishing X-Men*, 2012–13; *Monstress*, 2015–; *Star Wars: Han Solo*, 2016

—*Christopher Mari*

Lizzo

Date of birth: April 27, 1988
Occupation: Singer

Lizzo is a Grammy Award–winning pop star, who rose to fame after the unusual breakout success of her catchy single, "Truth Hurts," in 2019. In 2020, she was nominated for eight Grammy Awards, more than any other artist that year. She won three awards, including Best Urban Contemporary Album for her major label debut, *Cuz I Love You* and Best Pop Solo Performance for "Truth Hurts." Hits like "Truth Hurts," "Juice" and "Good as Hell" are demonstrative of the Lizzo brand: they exude optimism, self-empowerment, and body positivity. As Brittany Spanos put it for *Rolling Stone* (22 Jan. 2020): Lizzo has sought to make "the type of songs she wanted to hear at the end of a rough day, songs that want you to feel beautiful, successful, booked and busy, because Lizzo feels all those things."

A classically trained flautist who studied to become a professional musician, Lizzo's dreams of becoming a rapper and a rock star led her to pursue other paths. After the astonishing success of her 2019 year, Lizzo might seem like an overnight success, but she has been performing for over a decade. A mainstay of the Minneapolis music scene in the early 2010s, the pop superstar Prince once offered to be her manager. Her presence in pop culture has become ubiquitous; videos of her twerking, playing flute—or, incredibly, twerking while playing the flute—and joyfully cackling one of her catchphrases have made her one of the most beloved stars of the moment. In 2019, *Time* named her Entertainer of the Year.

EARLY LIFE AND EDUCATION

Melissa Viviane Jefferson was born in Detroit, Michigan, on April 27, 1988. Her father, Michael Jefferson, and her mother, Shari Johnson-Jefferson, owned a real estate business. She has two older siblings: a sister, Vanessa, and a brother, Mikey. Lizzo grew up singing gospel music with her family in the Pentecostal church. When she was nine, the family moved to Houston. At school, Lizzo was a self-described nerd, raising her hand to answer every question. She was assigned to learn to play the flute for band class and knew she had hit on a talent that would serve her throughout her life. "I was just so good at flute," she told Spanos. "[I thought], 'This is it for me. I'm going to college for this sh——t.' I knew back then." Lizzo became a virtuoso, memorizing Giulio Briccialdi's "Carnival of Venice" at thirteen. Manny Gonzales, her band director at Elsik High School, later recalled to Houston's *KTRK News* (4 Feb. 2020), "I thought she would play for a major symphony or be a flute player or recording artist. As a matter of fact, my assistant

Photo by Raph_PH via Wikimedia Commons

band director at the time said one day, 'Hey, let me have your autograph. I want to be the first one to get your autograph.' And I remember she autographed a piece of paper for him."

As a teen, Lizzo also joined a girls singing group in the mold of Destiny's Child. She wrote a ballad for them called "Broken Households," but insisting that she could not sing, she directed the other girls on how to perform it. Later, she formed her own group called Cornrow Clique, with members Nino, Lexo, and Zeo. Lizzo called herself Lisso, short for Melissa, which latter changed to Lizzo.

EARLY CAREER

Lizzo won a music scholarship to the University of Houston but struggled as a student. A combination of academic and financial pressure, as well as her father becoming ill, forced her to drop out at the age of twenty. "I was sad and disappointed in myself, because I'd always been so advanced in school, the golden child," she recalled to Julia Smith for *Texas Music* (25 Oct. 2019). "So when I wasn't successful, I was like, 'Who am I?' I thought my life was going to be something else, and it wasn't happening." It was a dark period. Her family moved to Denver, and Lizzo spent time living on the couches of various friends. At one point, she lived out of her car for six months. In 2008, she answered a Craigslist ad for a lead vocalist for a prog-rock band called Ellypseas. It was the first time she seriously considered singing. She auditioned and got the job, though performing made her anxious. She quit the band after her father died in 2010.

After spending some time in Denver with her family, where she formed a short-lived rock band called Lizzo & the Larva Ink, she moved to Minneapolis in 2011. There, she continued to perform as a rapper, guesting on a host of indie mixtapes. She formed a group, with Sophia Eris and Claire de Lune, called the Chalice the same year. The Chalice became a major part of the local scene after the release of their hit song, "Push It." "I think for a long time, Minneapolis hip-hop was pretty serious," Claire de Lune recalled to Steven Marsh in an oral history of Lizzo's rise for *Mpls St. Paul* magazine (7 Oct. 2019). "We were just fun. We sang songs about going out and getting your nails done and partying. We did choreography; we had matching outfits." The Chalice took off quickly; three months after their very first show they were performing at Austin's South by Southwest (SXSW) music festival.

LIZZOBANGERS

After appearing on a local news program, the Chalice got a call from Minneapolis music legend Prince. The late superstar asked them to perform at Paisley Park in 2013, as well as on his 2014 song "Boytrouble." True to Prince's eccentricities, Lizzo and the Chalice communicated with him through surrogates and over the phone—even when they were recording at his house. At one point, Prince even considered becoming Lizzo's manager even though the two had never met in person. At the same time, Lizzo also joined the female rap collective GRRRL PRTY. Their 2013 hit song, "Wegula," further raised Lizzo's profile.

The Chalice and Lizzo's popularity were on the rise, but Lizzo longed to make her own music. She released her solo debut, *Lizzobangers*, in 2013. One of her collaborators, producer Ryan Olsen, told Marsh that Lizzo was confident about what she wanted the record to be. "She had a really strong sense of what she wanted to pull off. What she was musically leaning towards," he said. The Chalice broke up shortly after *Lizzobangers* was released, and Lizzo went on tour to promote it. In 2014, she performed the song "Bus Passes and Happy Meals" from *Lizzobangers* on the *Late Show with David Letterman*, and her song "Paris" was featured on an episode of the television show, *Girls*.

Lizzo released her second studio album, *Big GRRRL Small World*, in 2015. Katherine St. Asaph for the music website *Pitchfork* (10 Dec. 2015) wrote that Lizzo is "a true triple threat, equally searing as a rapper, soul singer, and personality. . . . *Big GRRRL Small World* comes off as the work of an already minted star—her introduction to the small world, which she's already stepped over, laughing." Included on that album was a ballad called "My Skin," about learning to love oneself. The empowerment ethos of that song would inform Lizzo's later work.

THE VIRAL SUCCESS OF "TRUTH HURTS"

Lizzo was signed to Atlantic Records in 2015, and in 2016, she released an EP called *Coconut Oil*. The EP included "Good as Hell," a song that would become a hit two years later. The titular song, Lizzo told Spanos, was written as an ode to black women. "As a black woman, I make music for people, from an experience that is from a black woman," she said. "I'm making music that hopefully makes other people feel good and helps me discover self-love. That message I want to go directly to black women, big black women, black trans women. Period." The album did not enjoy the success that Lizzo had hoped it would. In 2017, she released a single called "Truth Hurts." She knew it was a hit, but like her EP, it too seemed to fall flat. She briefly considered quitting music altogether.

On tour in 2018, Lizzo posted a video of herself playing flute while covering Kendrick's Lamar's "Big Shot." During the interlude, Lizzo and her back-up dancers hit the shoot—a popular dance move—before Lizzo returns to the flute. The video, and Lizzo's impressive performance, became a viral hit, inspiring the #FluteAnd-ShootChallenge. Riding on her viral success, Lizzo created videos of herself riding escalators and golf carts, villainously laughing, which were viewed thousands of times.

She released her major label debut, *Cuz I Love You*, in 2019. The same day, Netflix released a film called *Someone Great*, starring Gina Rodriguez and Lakeith Stanfield. It included a scene in which Rodriguez's character dances along to Lizzo's "Truth Hurts"—a song that had disappeared so quickly that it did not even appear on her new album. The synergy of Lizzo's social media fame and the film catapulted "Truth Hurts" to the top of the charts, two years after it was initially released. Lizzo performed a medley of "Truth Hurts" and "Good as Hell" at the MTV Music Awards. Both songs became number-one hits.

CUZ I LOVE YOU

Cuz I Love You yielded songs like "Tempo" featuring Missy Elliott, and the Grammy Award–winning ballad, "Jerome," in which Lizzo turns down a guy who does not deserve her. Though the song is slower than her usual fare, "Jerome" is classic Lizzo, punctuated by runs and interjections, half-rapped and half-sung in belting, soul style. In a review for *Pitchfork* (22 Apr. 2019), Rawiya Kameir offered praise but also criticism: "Despite her obvious skill and charisma, some of the album's eleven songs are burdened with overwrought production, awkward turns of phrase, and ham-handed rapping." Elsewhere, Kameir described Lizzo's self-empowerment message as coming across more as schtick than sincere. Lizzo read the review and took to Twitter to voice her displeasure, writing, as quoted by Spanos, that critics who "don't make music themselves should be unemployed." It was not Lizzo's first Twitter dust-up; in 2018, she praised the use of one of her songs in a Weight Watchers commercial, which some fans felt was at odds with her body-positive ethos.

Regardless of either criticism or social media scandal, *Cuz I Love You*, was a hit record, going platinum by the end of the year. Lizzo's success was rewarded with eight Grammy Award nominations—the most nominations for a single artist that year—including for the top four prizes: album of the year for *Cuz I Love You*, song of the year and record of the year for "Truth Hurts," and best new artist. Although she did not take home those awards, she did win three other Grammy Awards: best pop solo performance for "Truth Hurts," best traditional R&B performance for "Jerome," and best urban contemporary album for *Cuz I Love You*. She was also named 2019 Entertainer of the Year by *Time*.

Her success in the music industry also opened avenues in the film industry. In 2019, Lizzo lent her voice to the animated musical film *Ugly Dogs* and appeared in the crime comedy *Hustlers*, costarring Jennifer Lopez and Constance Wu.

PERSONAL LIFE

In interviews, Lizzo has suggested that she is queer and open to dating more than one gender. She moved to Los Angeles in 2016.

SUGGESTED READING

"Here's How Lizzo's Former Elsik HS Band Director Knew She Would Make It." *KTRK News*, 4 Feb. 2020, abc13.com/5709484. Accessed 13 Mar. 2020.

Kameir, Rawiya. "Lizzo, *Cuz I Love You*." Review of *Cuz I Love You*, by Lizzo. *Pitchfork*, 22 Apr. 2019, pitchfork.com/reviews/albums/lizzo-cuz-i-love-you/. Accessed 13 Mar. 2020.

Marsh, Steve. "An Oral History of Lizzo's Rise to Fame." *Mpls St. Paul Magazine*, 7 Oct. 2019, mspmag.com/arts-and-culture/oral-history-lizzo-minneapolis. Accessed 13 Mar. 2020.

Smith, Julia. "Lizzo's Moment." *Texas Music*, 25 Oct. 2019, txmusic.com/features/lizzos-moment. Accessed 13 Mar. 2020.

Spanos, Brittany. "The Joy of Lizzo." *Rolling Stone*, 22 Jan. 2020, www.rollingstone.com/music/music-features/lizzo-cover-story-interview-truth-hurts-grammys-937009. Accessed 13 Mar. 2020.

St. Asaph, Katherine. "Lizzo, *Big GRRRL Small World*." Review of *Big GRRRL Small World*, by Lizzo. *Pitchfork*, 10 Dec. 2015, pitchfork.com/reviews/albums/21312-big-grrrl-small-world. Accessed 13 Mar. 2020.

SELECTED WORKS

Lizzobangers, 2013; *Big GRRRL Small World*, 2015; *Coconut Oil*, 2016; *Cuz I Love You*, 2019

—Molly Hagan

Tove Lo

Date of birth: October 29, 1987
Occupation: Singer-songwriter

Electropop sensation Tove Lo first made her mark penning tunes for Icona Pop and Girls Aloud, among other artists, before beginning to provide the vocals for her work herself and stepping into the international spotlight with 2013's sleeper hit "Habits." Lo's deeply personal breakup anthem sparked some controversy for its unabashedly candid lyrics about embracing hedonism to combat heartache and its equally

Photo by Daniel Åhs Karlsson via Wikimedia Commons

provocative video depicting her drinking heavily. After following up her debut EP *Truth Serum* (2014) with full-length albums that included 2014's *Queen of the Clouds*, 2016's *Lady Wood*, 2017's *Blue Lips*, and 2019's *Sunshine Kitty*, Lo has developed a solid fan base and has made a career out of pushing boundaries, unapologetically and honestly celebrating female empowerment and sexuality through her music and videos. "I like challenging people," she said to Nolan Feeney for *Entertainment Weekly* (17 Nov. 2017), "[and] forcing them to think about or feel things they usually try to stay away from."

EARLY LIFE AND EDUCATION
Tove Lo was born Ebba Tove Elsa Nilsson on October 29, 1987, in Stockholm, Sweden, and raised in the affluent suburb of Djursholm with her brother. The daughter of a therapist mother and an entrepreneur father, Lo was just three years old when, after becoming fascinated by the lynx exhibit at her local zoo, she earned the moniker that would later be famous. "I was standing with my face pressed against the glass," she related to Mark Savage for *BBC News* (11 Apr. 2014). "So my parents started calling me Tove Lo and it stuck." Despite her comfortable childhood, she battled anxiety and depression. Around the age of nine, she began journaling as a creative outlet, and she found herself writing poems and short stories that she considered rather dark. By the time she was twelve, she had penned her first tune, "Crazy," and discovered the grunge music of Kurt Cobain after listening

to Nirvana's 1994 *MTV Unplugged in New York* record.

Lo first showed interest in pursuing music at age thirteen, when she accompanied a friend to the recording studio. "I went in and tried the microphone," she told Kathleen Johnston for *British GQ* (26 July 2019). "That's the moment I remember realising, 'This is amazing. I want to spend the rest of my life in this room.'" Upon completing junior high, she successfully auditioned for the singing program at the renowned secondary music academy Rytmus Musikergymnasiet, where she was exposed to several different musical genres, including rock, jazz, and blues. While there, she received vocal training (private and group); as part of the school's ensemble classes, she cut her performing teeth rehearsing and playing live alongside classmates such as Caroline Hjelt, who later became half of the Swedish duo Icona Pop.

EMBARKING ON A SONGWRITING CAREER
Following her graduation around 2006, Lo shared a Stockholm apartment with Hjelt. Joining forces with other local musicians, she helped create the experimental rock group Tremblebee, whose complicated music relied on assorted time signatures and unusual tunings. Lo served as the lead singer for the band, which performed on the local bar circuit and independently released some songs before disbanding in 2009, after which she decided to pursue a solo career. "I started playing around with producing on my own and making tracks," she told Mathias Rosenzweig for *Vogue* (13 Sept. 2016). "I realized that I'm way simpler in my tastes than this band was. I wanted to go in a more pop direction."

While writing and recording demos in a converted shed studio outside her cousin's home, Lo supported herself financially with cover gigs and stints as a backing vocalist and session singer. Her professional songwriting career took off when she turned an encounter with an A&R representative at a party into a networking opportunity. After sending him her demos, she was eventually signed to Warner Chappell Music, Warner Music Group's publishing arm, in 2011. Not long after, she attended a birthday celebration for producer and songwriter Alexander Kronlund, who was captivated by her impromptu onstage performance with the live band. After a few recording studio sessions with Kronlund, she accompanied him to Los Angeles, where she first met and performed for legendary pop songwriter and producer Max Martin.

Lo earned some of her first songwriting credits for two dance tracks: Icona Pop's "We Got the World" and "Something New," the comeback tune from the quintet Girls Aloud. While initially thinking of it as a cathartic side job, she also worked on her own solo material, collaborating with the production team the Struts on the debut song "Love Ballad," self-released under the name Tove Lo in October 2012. They reteamed for "Habits," Lo's somber post-breakup ode, which she partially penned while in New York in 2012 during Hurricane Sandy and which she released independently in Sweden in early 2013. The song garnered the attention of Universal Music executives, who subsequently offered her a recording contract under Island Records.

TRUTH SERUM AND QUEEN OF THE CLOUDS
American audiences quickly became familiar with Lo's music in 2014, following the release of her debut EP, *Truth Serum*, in March and her full-length debut, *Queen of the Clouds*, in September. Both albums boasted the breakout hit "Habits (Stay High)," which topped the Billboard Mainstream Top 40 and Hot Rock & Alternative Songs charts; it also cracked the Hot 100's top three. In the emotionally raw accompanying music video, a drunken, disheveled Lo copes with a bad breakup by acting out, partying, and drinking. "I can't lie," she told Savage when discussing the very real nature of "Habits." "What I'm singing about is my life. It's the truth." She also worked with Alesso and Lucas Nord on two other charting songs: "Heroes (We Could Be)" and "Run on Love," respectively. Both collaborations reached number one on the Billboard Dance Club Songs chart.

Lo spent the year promoting her music, including a performance on *Late Night with Seth Meyers*, a South by Southwest (SXSW) festival appearance, a North American tour (presented by VH1's *You Oughta Know* series), and a gig opening for Katy Perry during the Australian leg of her Prismatic World Tour. As she continued to write tracks for other artists, including Zara Larsson and Cher Lloyd, her promising singing career was almost cut short when she was diagnosed with vocal cord cysts. However, those fears were laid to rest after she underwent successful surgery in January 2015.

During the recovery period after the surgery, Lo began work on her next album and released her follow-up single, "Talking Body," along with a music video, in which she and her lover visit a sex club while also evading the police on a motorcycle. The song eventually topped the Billboard Dance Club Songs chart while Ellie Goulding's "Love Me Like You Do," for which she contributed lyrics, received award nods from the Grammy Awards and more. Lo returned to the stage at 2015's SXSW festival before continuing to perform, including at events such as the Rock in Rio, Bonnaroo, and Lollapalooza festivals, followed by her first headlining tour.

MAINTAINING MOMENTUM
Not long after her single "Scars" was released in February 2016 as the lead single from the soundtrack for *The Divergent Series: Allegiant*, Lo was featured on the sultry duet "Close" with Nick Jonas, who had sought her out while working on his third solo record. "There's this honesty and vulnerability to her work," Jonas confided to Jessica Pressler for *The Cut* (Oct. 2016), "and not a lot of people will go to that place." Lo costarred opposite Jonas in the accompanying video. Between mid-April to late May, the duo reunited on several occasions to perform the song, and by July, "Close" had reached the top ten of the Billboard Mainstream Top 40 and Dance Club Songs.

For her sophomore full-length effort, *Lady Wood* (2016), Lo continued to embrace female empowerment and sexuality while also reflecting upon her personal and professional rollercoaster journey. "*Lady Wood* is about the pattern of chasing rushes for me," she admitted to Brennan Carley for *GQ* (27 Oct. 2016). "That goes in love, in music, in doing drugs—everything that I do to feel the most alive at all times." The album reached number eleven on the Billboard 200 album chart and spawned two singles: "Cool Girl," a tech-house feminist anthem that turns the tables on the power dynamics in romantic relationships, and "True Disaster," a synth-pop tune about staying in an inevitably doomed relationship. In October 2016, Lo, inspired by the album's first half, costarred opposite Lina Esco in *Fairy Dust*, a short film spotlighting the rush and excitement associated with newfound romance while also addressing drug use, mental health, sexuality, and obsession.

Lo embarked on a tour across North America and Europe to support *Lady Wood* in February 2017. Meanwhile, she also starred in the sequel to *Fairy Dust*, the dark, contemplative short *Fire Fade*, which highlights *Lady Wood*'s remaining tracks and depicts Lo's emotional breakdown.

BLUE LIPS AND SUNSHINE KITTY
By November 2017, Lo had released *Blue Lips*, representing the continuation and culmination of her emotional journey. Like its predecessor, *Blue Lips* is a concept album made up of two chapters focusing on the climax ("Light Beams") and the comedown ("Pitch Black") of a love affair. Its lead single alludes to Lo's new relationship status and its accompanying video addresses losing oneself in a newfound relationship. After guesting on "Out of My Head," the main single from Charli XCX's *Pop 2* mixtape, Lo recruited the singer, along with Icona Pop, Alma, and Elliphant, to join her on the second single from *Blue Lips*, a remix that was released in June. That same month, she served as a co-headliner at the LA Pride Festival 2018.

Inspired by *Blue Lips*, Lo unveiled a short film chronicling two girlfriends who escape heartbreak by embarking on a road trip. Her visual ode to female friendship debuted in October 2018, along with "Blow That Smoke," her first collaboration with Major Lazer. She ended the year with a fan appreciation video for her track "Hey You Got Drugs?" that provided fans with an intimate peek into her life on tour. Her follow-up record, 2019's *Sunshine Kitty*, marked a clear departure from the melancholy of her previous material, reflecting her self-confidence and budding relationship. "All my music is very vulnerable, but there was an anger about being vulnerable," she confided to Salvatore Maicki for *Fader* (24 Sept. 2019). "Now, there's an acceptance in being vulnerable."

In May 2019, Lo released the lead track "Glad He's Gone," whose companion video earned her another Grammy nod—her second up to that point and her first for a song she had both written and performed. Subsequent singles included the Kylie Minogue collaboration "Really Don't Like U" (2019) and 2020's "Bikini Porn," cowritten by Grammy-winning producer Finneas. After completing shows in North America and Europe into March 2020, further dates for Lo's Sunshine Kitty 2020 tour were postponed due to the coronavirus pandemic.

PERSONAL LIFE

Lo, who identifies as bisexual, purchased a home in Los Angeles around 2019. Along with a few others, she began quarantining there in March 2020 during the coronavirus pandemic, casually working on music production and hosting themed dinners. In July 2020, she announced her marriage to her partner, creative director and producer Charlie Twaddle.

SUGGESTED READING

Carley, Brennan. "Tove Lo, Music's Realest Real-Talker." *GQ*, 27 Oct. 2016, www.gq.com/story/tove-lo-lady-wood. Accessed 21 July 2020.

Lo, Tove. "Tove Lo: 'My First Diva Moment? When I Played Coachella with Alesso.'" Interview by Kathleen Johnston. *British GQ*, 26 July 2019, www.gq-magazine.co.uk/culture/article/tove-lo-interview. Accessed 15 July 2020.

———. "Tove Lo Isn't Afraid to Get Messy." Interview by Salvatore Maicki. *Fader*, 24 Sept. 2019, www.thefader.com/2019/09/24/tove-lo-sunshine-kitty-interview-glad-hes-gone-kylie-minogue. Accessed 15 July 2020.

___ "Tove Lo on Her New Album and Pushing the Limits of Censorship; 'When Are They Going to Stop Me?'" Interview by Nolan Feeney. *Entertainment Weekly*, 17 Nov. 2017, ew.com/music/2017/11/17/tove-lo-blue-lips-interview/. Accessed 15 July 2020.

———. "Tove Lo on Her New Album and Redefining the 'Cool Girl.'" Interview by Mathias Rosenzweig. *Vogue*, 13 Sept. 2016, www.vogue.com/article/tove-lo-lady-wood-album-interview. Accessed 15 July 2020.

Pressler, Jessica. "Lo, and Behold." *The Cut*, New York Media, Oct. 2016, www.thecut.com/2016/10/tove-lo-lady-wood-c-v-r.html. Accessed 15 July 2020.

Savage, Mark. "Tove Lo: A Swedish Pop Star in Waiting." *BBC News*, 11 Apr. 2014, www.bbc.com/news/entertainment-arts-26954021. Accessed 15 July 2020.

SELECTED WORKS

Truth Serum, 2014; *Queen of the Clouds*, 2014; *Lady Wood*, 2016; *Blue Lips*, 2017; *Sunshine Kitty*, 2019

—Bertha Muteba

Joey Logano

Date of birth: May 24, 1990
Occupation: Race car driver

Joey Logano had been racing cars for more than a dozen years by the time he made his official NASCAR Cup Series debut in 2009, but the experienced young driver was nevertheless struck by the intensity of the competition he faced upon entering the highest level of stock-car racing. "It's all so different. You're racing against forty-three of the best drivers in the world," he told Viv Bernstein for the *New York Times* (25 July 2009). "The guys that struggle to make the show, they're no slackers. They're good. So every one of those guys are good. It makes it tough, no doubt."

Despite the challenge that awaited him, Logano soon established himself as a Cup Series competitor to watch, winning his first series race in June 2009 and going on to win more than twenty additional races over the next decade. His 2015 Daytona 500 victory further bolstered his status as one of NASCAR's rising stars, a reputation that only grew after his highly successful performance in the 2018 series earned Logano the title of Cup Series champion. He has also at times faced disappointments over the course of his NASCAR career, including an unsuccessful attempt to defend his Cup Series championship in 2019; nonetheless, Logano has long preferred to look ahead to the next race. "I think you just realize you'll get through it, and [must] move onto the next challenge ahead of you," he told

Photo by Sean Gardner/Getty Images

Andy Frye for *Forbes* (14 Dec. 2018). "Some things you can't control, some things you can."

EARLY LIFE AND EDUCATION

Joseph "Joey" Thomas Logano was born on May 24, 1990, in Middletown, Connecticut, to Tom and Deborah "Debbie" Logano. His father owned a hazardous waste–disposal company when Logano was young, and his parents later opened and operated a skating rink in North Carolina. Both Logano and his older sister, Danielle, were active ice skaters during their childhoods: Logano played ice hockey for five years, while Danielle went on to become a professional figure skater and skating instructor.

Despite his interest in hockey, Logano was particularly drawn to racing after his first encounter with the sport when he was five years old. "I fell in love right away and from that point on, all I wanted to do was race," he recalled to Asher Fair in an interview for the racing website *Beyond the Flag* (17 Jan. 2019). Logano participated in quarter-midget racing, a motorsport in which children race scaled-down race cars over short distances and raced at the Silver City Quarter Midget Club in Meriden and Little T Speedway in Thompson, Connecticut.

As Logano gained experience as a racer, he demonstrated a substantial talent for and dedication to the sport, earning victories while still in elementary school. He won the junior stock-car quarter midget division at the Eastern Grand National Championship in 1997 and at the next two consecutive national championships. In 1999, when Logano was nine, his family moved

to Alpharetta, Georgia, and later to Huntersville, North Carolina, to pursue further sports opportunities for the Logano children, who also began homeschooling. Logano progressed to the higher-level Bandolero racing in 1999 and then the Pro Legends Series in 2002. Over the subsequent years, Logano competed in various racing series, including the ASA Late Model Series and Pro Cup Series. He signed with the racing team Joe Gibbs Racing in 2005, at the age of fifteen.

NASCAR

Logano made his National Association for Stock Car Auto Racing (NASCAR) debut in 2007, competing in developmental regional series such as the Busch East Series. His performance during that series earned him the title of K&N Pro Series Rookie of the Year and demonstrated his readiness to progress to more challenging levels of competition. The 2008 season saw Logano compete in the NASCAR Nationwide Series, another developmental series, and achieve more than a dozen top-ten finishes. He also first appeared in a race on the highest-level NASCAR circuit in September of that year, ultimately finishing thirty-second at the 2008 Sylvania 300 at the New Hampshire Motor Speedway.

For stock-car drivers competing in the United States, the NASCAR Cup Series represents the highest level of competition. It is the tournament through which up-and-comers test their skills against those of seasoned competitors. Consisting of twenty-six races per regular season, the main tournament is followed by an additional ten races known as the playoffs (or, formerly, the Chase), in which all of the season's racers compete but only qualifying competitors vie for the championship.

Logano, having demonstrated his readiness for that level of racing during his previous seasons, entered the Cup Series as a serious contender for the 2009 season and achieved his first series victory in June of that year, at the abbreviated Lenox Industrial Tools 301, in New Hampshire. Although the prospect of racing against experienced drivers many years his senior represented a daunting challenge, Logano focused on the fundamentals of his sport. "He's [veteran] Dale Earnhardt Jr., yeah, but I mean, you don't race him different because he's Dale Earnhardt Jr.," he explained to Bernstein. "You race everyone the same. You race everyone with respect." For his performance over the 2009 series, which included seven top-ten finishes, Logano was named the 2009 NASCAR Cup Series Rookie of the Year.

TEAM PENSKE

Over the next several seasons, Logano continued to demonstrate his talents in the Cup Series, completing more than twenty top-ten finishes between 2010 and 2011. He claimed his second Cup Series victory, at the Pocono 400, in 2012 and also won seven races on the Nationwide Series; he continued to compete in that tournament (renamed the NASCAR Xfinity Series in 2015) through 2019, making fewer appearances there as he excelled at the higher level, however.

Logano was dropped from Joe Gibbs Racing after the 2012 series but joined Team Penske for the 2013 season. The year was a successful one for Logano, who won the Pure Michigan 400, finished in the top ten in twelve Cup Series races, and qualified for his first playoffs. He experienced even greater success in 2014, winning five Cup Series races, including the Toyota Owners 400 in Richmond, Virginia, and the Hollywood Casino 400 in Kansas.

Perhaps the most significant achievement of Logano's career to that point, however, came at the start of the 2015 Cup Series, when Logano won the Daytona 500. His achievement at the prestigious series opener called attention to Logano's continuing development as a racer and potential for further success on the track. After the race, he acknowledged, "I've been through a lot in my career already and still have a long ways to go," as reported by Brant James for *USA Today* (23 Feb. 2015). He went on to note, "I'm so happy and thankful that I went through the times of trying to figure this out, the tougher times worrying about if you're going to have a job or not. . . . When you get to the point of worrying about winning races, that's where you want to be in your career." Although Logano did not replicate his success in Daytona immediately, he accrued six Cup Series victories over 2015 and put forth strong performances in 2016 and 2017, winning four more races and achieving forty-three top-ten finishes.

CUP SERIES CHAMPION

Another milestone for Logano came during the 2018 Cup Series, a strong tournament for the racer. In addition to winning the Geico 500 at the Talladega Superspeedway, the First Data 500 at Martinsville Speedway, and the Ford EcoBoost 400 at the Homestead-Miami Speedway, he managed to finish in the top ten in twenty-three additional races. "We were maximizing our finishes and knew if we could keep that execution, we'd get some wins and come playoff time really have a shot at this thing," he told Frye about his team's performance in the events of the series. He added, "Our speed came in, we were leading more laps, winning stages, and grabbed some important wins. But you never know you've got the win until you cross the last finish line since so many things can happen." Logano's strong performance during the main series and the playoffs paid off, and he was named the 2018 NASCAR Cup Series champion that November.

Returning to the series in 2019, Logano won two races and managed an additional nineteen top-ten finishes, ultimately ranking fifth among the competitors by the end of the series. Despite being unable to claim a second consecutive championship in 2019, he managed a new achievement that November, when the Guinness World Records organization confirmed that Logano had constructed the longest Hot Wheels toy car track in the world to date. Looping throughout Logano's garage in Charlotte, North Carolina, the track measured 1,941 feet (about 597 meters) and was 103 feet longer than that of the previous record holder. In a statement quoted by Chris Chin for the *Drive* (28 Nov. 2019), Logano described the record as "a dream come true" and characterized the effort as one fueled by both nostalgia and continuing devotion to the sport of racing. "I have so many memories playing with my Hot Wheels cars as a kid," he explained. "Hot Wheels basically founded my passion for racing—the first car I ever had was a Hot Wheels car." Logano returned to the world of full-sized race cars in early 2020.

PHILANTHROPY

In addition to his racing pursuits, Logano is an active philanthropist and the founder of the Joey Logano Foundation, which provides funds to children's and youth organizations throughout the United States. "We have an amazing platform as NASCAR Drivers and professional athletes and it would be a shame to waste that," he told Fair about his charity work. "Using the power of NASCAR and the reach we can generate from our fan base we can turn that to a positive for the Joey Logano Foundation because NASCAR fans are extremely generous with their resources, whether it's money, time or special skills." In recognition of his work, Logano was named Comcast Community Champion of the Year 2018.

PERSONAL LIFE

Logano married Brittany Baca, whom he had met at his family's ice rink, in 2014. Their son, Hudson, was born in January 2018. The family lives in North Carolina. When he is not racing, Logano enjoys spending time with family and friends, four-wheeling, and restoring classic cars.

SUGGESTED READING

Bernstein, Viv. "After Slow Start, Logano Shows He Belongs in Sprint Cup." *The New York Times*, 25 July 2009, www.nytimes.com/2009/07/26/sports/autoracing/26nascar.html. Accessed 17 Jan. 2020.

Chin, Chris. "NASCAR Champ Joey Logano Builds World's Largest Hot Wheels Track in His Garage." *The Drive*, 28 Nov. 2019, www.thedrive.com/news/31245/

nascar-champ-joey-logano-builds-worlds-lon-gest-hot-wheels-track-in-his-garage. Accessed 17 Jan. 2020.

Courchesne, Shawn. "Logano Back Home in Connecticut after Daytona Win." *Hartford Courant*, 23 Feb. 2015, www.courant.com/sports/auto-racing/hc-joey-logano-daytona-500-0224-20150223-story.html. Accessed 17 Jan. 2020.

Fair, Asher. "NASCAR: Joey Logano Talks Joey Logano Foundation and More in Exclusive Interview." *Beyond the Flag*, 17 Jan. 2019, beyondtheflag.com/2019/01/17/nascar-joey-logano-talks-joey-logano-foundation-more-exclusive-interview. Accessed 17 Jan. 2020.

James, Brant. "Joey Logano's Daytona 500 Win Validates All the Hype." *USA Today*, 23 Feb. 2015, www.usatoday.com/story/sports/nascar/2015/02/22/joey-logano-daytona-500-win-team-penske-chase/23860865. Accessed 17 Jan. 2020.

Logano, Joey. "Joey Logano Interview: I'm the Guy Who Worries about Everything." Interview by Jeff Gluck. *SBNation*, 7 Mar. 2012, www.sbnation.com/nascar/2012/3/7/2851634/joey-logano-nascar-joe-gibbs-racing-2012. Accessed 17 Jan. 2020.

——. "Racing 2018: Interview with NASCAR Champion Joey Logano." Interview by Andy Frye. *Forbes*, 14 Dec. 2018, www.forbes.com/sites/andyfrye/2018/12/14/racing-2018-interview-with-nascar-champion-joey-logano/#388979972896. Accessed 17 Jan. 2020.

—*Joy Crelin*

Oliver Luck

Date of birth: April 5, 1960
Occupation: Sports executive

In 2018 Oliver Luck, a former National Football League (NFL) quarterback turned sports executive, accepted the position as the commissioner of the newly rebooted XFL. The XFL, a professional football league founded by billionaire World Wrestling Entertainment (WWE) CEO Vince McMahon, launched in 2001. That first iteration of the league earned a negative reputation as it incorporated the kind of spectacle, violence, and attitude associated with professional wrestling. Players wore jerseys with silly nicknames and famously participated in an opening "scramble" for the ball in lieu of a coin toss. The XFL enjoyed novelty success for its first few games but shuttered after a single season. After McMahon announced in early 2018 that he was bringing the league back, Luck was initially skeptical about taking the job as commissioner.

"But I was assured that we would build this the right way with 100% focus on football," he told Michel Martin for the National Public Radio program *All Things Considered* (8 Feb. 2020). "And all the other stuff that the XFL was known for—some of the gimmicks, if you will—those are all consigned to the dustbin."

Building a league from the ground up was undeniably a formidable task, but Luck—who ran for Congress, served as the general manager of a Houston-based soccer team, and worked as an executive for the National Collegiate Athletic Association (NCAA)—had unique experience in that arena, having helped shape NFL Europe (defunct as of 2007) in the 1990s. As the general manager of the Frankfurt Galaxy, and later president of the league, Luck found ways to draw a European crowd, most of them unfamiliar with American football. When the XFL officially relaunched with its first four games on the second weekend in February 2020, he was in attendance at the debut matchup in Washington, DC, to witness the initial result of his work.

EARLY LIFE AND EDUCATION

Luck was born on April 5, 1960, and was raised in University Heights, a suburb of Cleveland, Ohio. His family was not particularly inclined toward sports, but he took an interest in and displayed a talent for sports at a young age. At the all-boys prep school Saint Ignatius High School, he was a top student, a basketball player, and a football star. Luck led the Saint Ignatius Wildcats to the city championships in 1976 and 1977.

After graduating in 1978, he attended West Virginia University (WVU) in Morgantown, where he studied history. Playing quarterback for the Mountaineers, he started three seasons. In addition to setting a school record with forty-three touchdown passes over his career there, as a senior, he led the team to victory at the Peach Bowl. He ended his college career having passed for 5,765 yards.

Later, when Hua Hsu interviewed Luck for the now-defunct ESPN website Grantland (3 Sept. 2013), he observed, "Even though Luck is famous for being the ex-quarterback turned businessman, you get the sense that he still sees himself as the honors student who happened to play football, not the football player with some smarts." Indeed, Luck excelled in academics, and he recalled his favorite German professor and the joy of learning to read the works of writers Bertolt Brecht and Franz Kafka in their original language. (Luck's mother was born in Germany.) A Rhodes Scholar finalist in 1981, Luck graduated from WVU the following year.

PROFESSIONAL FOOTBALL, LAW, AND A

CONGRESSIONAL CAMPAIGN

In 1982 Luck entered the NFL as a second-round draft pick for the Houston Oilers. (The Oilers became the Tennessee Titans in the 1990s.) He played only eleven games in his first three seasons, though he started six. In 1985 he saw more play after starting quarterback Warren Moon was injured. "Luck has been getting a chance to show what he can do," Frank Litsky wrote for the *New York Times* (4 Dec. 1985). "He is an intense, courageous player who does not always look like a picture-book quarterback and does not try to strong arm the opposition." However, Luck never eclipsed Moon, who went on to become a Hall of Famer. Luck stayed in the league long enough to be eligible for an NFL pension, taking the field in only four games in 1986, and retired in 1987.

Knowing that he would not play football forever, Luck began studying for a law degree while still with the Oilers. He attended classes in the offseason throughout his NFL career and graduated from the University of Texas at Austin's law school in 1987, the same year he retired. After living in Germany for a year to complete a legal fellowship, he spent time in Washington, DC, working as part of a commercial transactions group for a law firm. In 1990 he briefly switched gears toward politics and ran as a Republican for a seat in the US House of Representatives representing West Virginia's Second Congressional District. Though he ultimately lost the election to incumbent Democrat Harley Staggers Jr., a new opportunity to break into the business side of the sports world soon presented itself.

WORLD LEAGUE OF AMERICAN FOOTBALL AND NFL EUROPE

Shortly after the election, in late 1990, Luck was offered a job as the general manager of the Frankfurt Galaxy, a football team with the fledgling World League of American Football (WLAF). Though Luck only had his experience as a player and his German-language skills as a foundation for the position, he accepted. The job proved particularly challenging, as he was required to build the franchise team from the ground up. "I can't emphasize how little had been done to prepare to launch a pro sports franchise," he later told Jon Gold for ESPN (23 June 2017). "There was no stadium deal, not one employee. No local staff, marketing, PR. Nor was there any football staff. It was a true truncated startup."

Luck began by hiring a staff and furnishing his office with desks and chairs from the Frankfurt army base. Troops were leaving the city after the fall of the Berlin Wall the year prior. He hired coach Jack Elway and dealt with a host of farcical logistical problems, such as forgetting to book flights for the team to compete in games back in the United States. Still, Luck and his team managed to draw twenty-three thousand people to the Galaxy's first game.

Although the WLAF enjoyed some success in its first year, interest flagged in its second, and it was put on hold in 1992. Luck was still in Germany when the league restarted in 1995, and he served as general manager of the new Rhein Fire in Dusseldorf that same year. By 1996 he had been named president of the league. Bringing to that role expertise culled from his experiences with the Galaxy and the Fire, he emphasized the spectacle of the game, combining entertainment and play. As most Europeans knew American football through the NFL's Super Bowl, Luck explained to Hsu, the Galaxy had had to bring their games to that level every time they played at home. The WLAF (rebranded as NFL Europe for the 1998 season) officially folded in 2007. Meanwhile, Luck had resigned his position around 2000 and returned to the United States.

HOUSTON DYNAMO AND WVU ATHLETIC DIRECTOR

In 2001 Luck was named CEO of the Harris County-Houston Sports Authority. In that role, he helped oversee deals to build sports stadiums including the Toyota Center, Reliant Stadium, and Minute Maid Park. In late 2005 he was named general manager of Houston's professional soccer team, the Houston Dynamo, which had been formed from a team relocated out of San Jose, California. Again, he was charged with building a team. Luck knew little about soccer, but the team won two Major League Soccer (MLS) Cup championships during his tenure (2006 and 2007). He also helped lobby for the construction of the soccer-specific BBVA Compass Stadium, which began hosting games in 2012.

Luck left in 2010 to take a job as the athletic director at WVU. He oversaw a host of changes in the program, most notably the school's move from the Big East Conference to the Big 12 in 2012. As part of the shift, he was able to argue for a greater focus on and investments in improving the university's baseball program to compete, which included plans that led to the building of a new stadium that opened in 2015. In discussing his commitment to bolster the baseball program, he explained to John Antonik for WVUSports.com (29 May 2019), "I always thought that Mountaineer fans needed more than just football in the fall and basketball in the winter." Luck also brought men's golf as a varsity sport back to the school after more than thirty years and instituted beer sales during football games.

At the same time, Luck became famous for reasons beyond his résumé. His son, Andrew, was the number-one overall pick of the NFL Draft in 2012. At WVU, Luck often joked that his position title, AD, also stood for "Andrew's Dad."

NCAA AND XFL

By early 2015 Luck had left WVU and begun serving as the executive vice president of regulatory affairs with the NCAA at the institution's Indianapolis headquarters. His hiring was seen by many commentators as a move to appease athletic directors who felt the organization was disconnected and did not have their interests in mind. During his tenure, Luck sought to build relationships with schools and athletes.

After more than three years, he resigned to accept the position as the commissioner of Vince McMahon's newly rebooted XFL professional football league in 2018. At the time, negative perceptions of the XFL lingered from its first failed iteration in 2001, controversies swirled around the sport of football in general, including safety and rules, and recently created leagues such as the Alliance of American Football had collapsed. Luck nevertheless took on the seemingly uphill task and remained confident that the XFL would be different in many ways. As chief architect, he spent many months conducting strategy meetings and working with teams to build the XFL, negotiating players, coaches, formats, and rules as well as making efforts to generate interest.

The XFL held its first game on February 8, 2020, a week after the NFL's Super Bowl. Sports writers largely noted that the game was significantly more professional than those of the XFL of yore. While the old XFL boasted the brute violence of the game, the new XFL appeared to find other ways to innovate. Luck even argued that the league's rules of play, many of them different from the NFL, could make the game safer. Summing up what he saw as the promise of the XFL, he told Martin, "We know it's a challenge, and we're going into this eyes wide open. But we think we've got a pretty good shot at establishing a league that people want to watch."

PERSONAL LIFE

Luck married Kathy Wilson, whom he met in law school. They have four children: Mary Ellen, Emily, Addison, and Andrew, who retired from the NFL after a series of injuries in 2019.

SUGGESTED READING

Antonik, John. "WVU 'All in' on College Baseball." *WVUSports.com*, 29 May 2019, wvusports.com/news/2019/5/29/wvu-now-all-in-on-college-baseball.aspx. Accessed 14 Feb. 2020.

Greene, Dan. "The XFL: A Second-Chance League and Its Not-My-First-Rodeo Commish." *Sports Illustrated*, 1 May 2019, www.si.com/nfl/2019/05/01/new-xfl-oliver-luck-spring-football-league-2020. Accessed 14 Feb. 2020.

Hsu, Hua. "The Residue of Design." *Grantland*, 3 Sept. 2013, grantland.com/features/the-life-career-oliver-luck-athletic-director-west-virginia-andrew-luck-father. Accessed 10 Feb. 2020.

Litsky, Frank. "Oliver Luck Gets Role with Oilers." *The New York Times*, 4 Dec. 1985, www.nytimes.com/1985/12/04/sports/oliver-luck-gets-role-with-oilers.html. Accessed 11 Feb. 2020.

Luck, Oliver. "The Relaunch of XFL." Interview by Michel Martin. *All Things Considered*, NPR, 8 Feb. 2020, www.npr.org/2020/02/08/804163433/the-relaunch-of-xfl. Accessed 11 Feb. 2020.

Luck, Oliver, et al. "10 Years after NFL Europe's Demise, Alumni Remember League Fondly." Interview by Jon Gold. *ESPN*, 23 June 2017, www.espn.com/nfl/story/_/id/19638357/oral-history-10-years-nfl-europe-demise-alumni-such-kurt-warner-remember-developmental-league-fondly. Accessed 11 Feb. 2020.

—*Molly Hagan*

Robert Macfarlane

Born: August 15, 1976
Occupation: Writer

Photo by David Levenson/Getty Images

"For nearly two decades," British writer Robert Macfarlane wrote for the *Guardian* on April 20, 2019, "I have been writing about the relationships of landscape and the human heart." Though perhaps most simply described as nature writing, Macfarlane's popular and critically acclaimed work does, in fact, focus heavily on those relationships, exploring the multitude of ways in which human beings interact with, shape, and speak or write about their natural surroundings. He is known for his works dealing with nature and language, including the 2015 book *Landmarks* and the best-selling 2017 project *The Lost Words*, the latter of which calls attention to nature terminology that was removed from a children's dictionary. Macfarlane is likewise well known for several books dealing with wilderness spaces in Britain and the ancient paths and roadways that continue to divide the landscape in the early twenty-first century.

A writer and university lecturer, Macfarlane first established himself as a strong voice in nature writing with the publication of the 2003 book *Mountains of the Mind*. Over the later decades, he continued to reinforce that reputation, earning awards such as the E. M. Forster Prize for Literature in recognition of his work.

Though aware that writing about the natural world and humankind's relationship with it can often take on a nostalgic tone, Macfarlane champions an alternate approach, preferring to write about the natural world in its contemporary state. "I suppose that I'm keen, if possible, to free the idea of writing about place from the sense that it always has to be retrospective," he explained to Boyd Tonkin for the *Independent* (8 Mar. 2015) about his approach. "There are forms of experience and encounter that are absolutely of the moment." His critically acclaimed 2019 book, *Underland: A Deep Time Journey*, aptly demonstrates that perspective, exploring the underground realm of the present and dealing, in part, with the reemergence of once-buried beings and structures due to the effects of climate change on the modern landscape.

EARLY LIFE

Robert Grant Macfarlane was born in England on August 15,1976. He grew up in Hallam, Nottinghamshire, a coal mining region where he lived with his younger brother and parents. Macfarlane's father, John, was a respiratory specialist and professor who worked for the Nottingham City Hospital and Nottingham University prior to his retirement, while his mother, Rosamund, worked in medical research. Both parents later became dedicated nature and wildlife photographers and received widespread recognition for their work.

As a child, Macfarlane often visited his grandparents in the mountainous Scottish Highlands. There, encouraged by his grandparents' love of such activities, he became an avid hiker and mountain climber. Those visits proved formative for Macfarlane, instilling in him a deep appreciation of the outdoors and planting the roots for what would become his first book. "I have some pristinated memories from those places, where everything else from those years, those early years, is a mist," he recalled to Krista Tippet in an interview for the podcast *On Being* (14 Nov. 2019). "I can't remember anything from my Nottinghamshire childhood, but I can remember picking up a roe deer's antler that was as exotic as coral, to me, on the side of a highland river. So I think the power of that place, those arctic mountains of Britain, they grooved deep into me."

By the time he reached his late teens, however, Macfarlane felt the need to take an extended break from his outdoor pursuits. His experience at sixteen of summitting all four 3,000-foot mountains of England's Lake District within twenty-hours left him "absolutely broken," as he told Rachel Cooke for the *Observer* (26 May 2012).

EDUCATION AND ACADEMIC CAREER

An aspiring poet during his teen years, Macfarlane completed his secondary education at Nottingham High School, an independent day school in Nottingham proper. After the conclusion of his time there, he enrolled in Pembroke College at the University of Cambridge, from which he earned his bachelor of arts degree in 1997. Macfarlane studied at Magdalen College, Oxford, for two years and later returned to Cambridge to earn a doctorate. His doctoral research concerned plagiarism and originality in nineteenth-century British literature, and he published a book on that topic, *Original Copy*, in 2007.

Between his time at Magdalen College and his doctoral studies at Cambridge, Macfarlane spent a year in Beijing, China, where he taught at a university while also beginning the manuscript for his first book. While still a doctoral student, he established himself as a fellow in English at Emmanuel College, Cambridge, in 2002. Macfarlane later held the positions of university reader in literature and the environmental humanities and, later, reader in English and the geohumanities." In those roles, he has taught courses on writing and literature as well as on topics related to nature, environmentalism, and the landscape. He has also served as director of studies in English.

Macfarlane's teaching career and writing career often overlap, with the findings of each at times contributing to the other. "My books take five, six or seven years to write and tend to become pretty consuming," he explained to Tobias

Grey in a profile for the *New York Times* (28 May 2019), describing himself as "an absolutely obsessive reviser and editor." He added that his books "become the ways I organize my time and also part of the conversation I have with my students when I teach."

NATURE WRITING

Macfarlane's debut book, *Mountains of the Mind: A History of a Fascination* (2003), focuses on humankind's longstanding fascination with mountains and apparent drive to climb and summit them. The work emerged initially out of Macfarlane's own interest in mountain climbing, a passion of his early life that he later largely gave up for safety reasons: "I was very bad at it, but I was quite bold, and that's a bad combination," he told Grey. Reprinted the following year in the United States with the subtitle "Adventures in Reaching the Summit," the book also formed the basis of a documentary film titled *Mountain: A Breathtaking Voyage into the Extreme*. A critically acclaimed work of nonfiction, *Mountains of the Mind* won the Best First Book Award from the *Guardian* newspaper in 2003 and became a first in a string of genre-defying publications dealing with nature and humankind's multifaceted engagement with it.

Macfarlane's next nature-focused work, *The Wild Places* (2007), is part wilderness travelogue, part natural history, and concerns the limited remaining wilderness areas in the British Isles. His books *The Old Ways: A Journey on Foot* (2012) and *Holloway* (2013)—the latter a collaboration with Stanley Donwood and Dan Richards—deal with means of traversing the landscape and the lingering signs, including ancient trails and sunken paths, left behind from recurring use.

In addition to humankind's physical interactions with nature, Macfarlane is fascinated by the intersections between nature and language. In *Landmarks* (2015), he discusses noteworthy writers who were heavily influenced by natural landscapes and highlights regional nature terminology with roots in the diverse languages and dialects of the United Kingdom, both to preserve such terminology and to promote the exploration of both the linguistic and the natural world. He told Tonkin, "It's not that I think we should all be spouting dialect to one another. It's more a sense of wanting to send people out into the fields and back into the dictionary."

Macfarlane engaged further with the connections between language and nature with *The Lost Words: A Spell Book*, a 2017 collaboration with illustrator Jackie Morris. "The simplest form of the book is just twenty words that fell out of a widely used children's dictionary because they weren't being used enough, and they were words for nature: acorn, bluebell, kingfisher, conker,

wren, willow," he told Tippet. "And so, we just wanted to make a spell book that might conjure them back." To that end, *The Lost Words* presents Morris's paintings of the plants and animals at hand alongside Macfarlane's "spells," acrostic poems designed to be read aloud. A popular schoolbook within the United Kingdom, *The Lost Words* earned critical praise and inspired a number of artistic and multimedia projects, including a musical album, *Spell Songs* (2019), and extensive murals in UK children's hospitals. A companion volume of theirs, titled *The Lost Spells*, was published in the United Kingdom in January 2020. The international edition was scheduled for publication in late 2020.

UNDERLAND

Alongside those works and contributions to books concerning the interactions between humans and the natural world at ground level, Macfarlane also delved into the subterranean world, a vast realm that serves as the focus of his 2019 book, *Underland: A Deep Time Journey*. He began work on the book around 2012 and spent many years researching and writing the work, during which he descended into cave systems and visited underground facilities designed to contain scientific research and nuclear waste. Speaking of the natural, yet human-shaped realm his work explores, he said to Grey, "Much of the underland is massively regulated space. It's where states and individuals and corporations have gone to put things that are most precious and dangerous to them."

As Macfarlane reveals, some of the things long buried are increasingly being revealed: the increase in average global temperature and melting of ice and permafrost associated with climate change, for instance, has revealed human and animal corpses both ancient and contemporary, at times with potentially dire consequences. "They are not curios—they are horror shows," he wrote for the *Guardian* about the once-buried things now revealed. "Nor are they portents of what is to come—they are the uncanny signs of a crisis that is already here, accelerating around us and experienced most severely by the most vulnerable." A powerful and enlightening work, *Underland* received extensive critical praise upon its publication, calling further attention to Macfarlane's talents as a nature writer and characteristically complex approach to the topics he explores.

In recognition of his contributions as a writer, Macfarlane was elected a fellow of the Royal Society of Literature in 2012 and received honorary doctorates from the Universities of Gloucestershire and Aberdeen in 2013 and 2014, respectively. He is also the recipient of numerous literary awards, including the 2004 Somerset Maugham Award, the 2017 E. M. Forster

Prize for Literature from the American Academy of Arts and Letters, and the 2019 Wainwright Prize for nature writing.

PERSONAL LIFE

Macfarlane is married to Julia Lovell, a scholar on China, translator, and author of a handful of books on Chinese history. They have two sons and a daughter, and live in Cambridge, England.

In keeping with his research interests, Macfarlane enjoys spending significant periods of time outdoors, which he has noted in interviews has given him a broad but at times incomplete knowledge of the natural world. "I really am very poor with plants," he admitted to Cooke. "I know my birds, though I'm not a birder. I know my trees . . . *reasonably*. It's a vernacular acquaintance born of spending a long time outside."

SUGGESTED READING

Cooke, Rachel. "Robert Macfarlane: 'Paths Are Human; They Are the Traces of Our Relationships.'" *The Observer*, 26 May 2012, www.theguardian.com/books/2012/may/27/robert-macfarlane-old-ways-interview. Accessed 10 May 2020.

Grey, Tobias. "Robert Macfarlane and the Dark Side of Nature Writing." *The New York Times*, 28 May 2019, www.nytimes.com/2019/05/28/books/robert-macfarlane-underland.html. Accessed 10 May 2020.

Macfarlane, Robert. "Robert MacFarlane The Hidden Human Depths of the Underland." Interview by Krista Tippet. *On Being*, 14 Nov. 2019, onbeing.org/programs/robert-macfarlane-the-hidden-human-depths-of-the-underland. Accessed 10 May 2020.

———. "Speaking the Anthropocene: An Interview with Robert MacFarlane." Interview by Emmanuel Vaughan-Lee. *Emergence Magazine*, 2019, emergencemagazine.org/story/speaking-the-anthropocene. Accessed 10 May 2020.

———. "What Lies Beneath: Robert Macfarlane Travels 'Underland.'" *The Guardian*, 20 Apr. 2019, www.theguardian.com/books/2019/apr/20/what-lies-beneath-robert-macfarlane. Accessed 10 May 2020.

"Robert MacFarlane Wins Book Award." *BBC Local Nottingham*, BBC, Dec. 2003, www.bbc.co.uk/nottingham/culture/2003/12/robert_macfarlane_first_book_award.shtml. Accessed 10 May 2020.

Tonkin, Boyd. "Robert Macfarlane Interview: A Linguistic Wander through Britain's Wild Landscapes." *Independent*, 8 Mar. 2015, www.independent.co.uk/arts-entertainment/books/features/robert-macfarlane-interview-a-linguistic-wander-through-britains-wild-landscapes-10087939.html. Accessed 10 May 2020.

SELECTED WORKS

Mountains of the Mind, 2003; *The Wild Places*, 2007; *The Old Ways: A Journey on Foot*, 2012; *Holloway* (with Stanley Donwood and Dan Richards), 2013; *Landmarks*, 2015; *The Lost Words: A Spell Book* (with Jackie Morris), 2017; *Underland: A Deep Time Journey*, 2019

—Joy Crelin

Rebecca Makkai

Date of birth: April 20, 1978
Occupation: Writer

Rebecca Makkai is the award-winning author of the 2018 novel *The Great Believers*. The novel is mostly set during the early days of the AIDS epidemic in Chicago, Illinois, in the 1980s. Makkai, the daughter of academics, grew up in Chicago around the same time. Pulitzer Prize–winning author Michael Cunningham gave *The Great Believers* a rave review for the *New York Times* (25 June 2018), describing it as "an absorbing and emotionally riveting story about what it's like to live during times of crisis." *The Great Believers* is Makkai's third novel—she also has a collection of short stories called *Music for Wartime* (2015)—but it is widely considered to be her literary breakout. The novel solidified Makkai's literary standing when it was named a finalist for the National Book Award and the Pulitzer Prize. Makkai teaches in the MFA writing program at Northwestern University and is the artistic

Photo by Manny Carabel/Getty Images

director of StoryStudio, a small school that offers storytelling workshops.

EARLY LIFE

Rebecca Makkai was born in Chicago on April 20, 1978. She grew up in Lake Bluff, a community on Lake Michigan's North Shore, though her roots, on her father's side, extend to Budapest. Her grandmother was the famous leftist Hungarian novelist Rózsa Ignácz, who died shortly after Makkai was born. Her grandfather, János Makkai, was a member of Hungarian parliament who advocated for a law removing Jews from the country in 1939. Makkai writes about her relationship to her grandfather and discovering his anti-Semitic past in her short story collection *Music for Wartime* (2015). Makkai's father, Adam Makkai, who is also a poet, arrived in the United States in 1957, a refugee of the failed Hungarian Revolution. While Hungary was under Soviet rule, Makkai's grandmother and father smuggled writing in and out of the country. Makkai's mother, an American from Iowa, once smuggled two of Ignácz's novels to the United States in her girdle.

Both of Makkai's parents were linguistic professors at the University of Illinois, Chicago. They also ran a linguistics press and an organization, the Linguistics Association of Canada and the United States, out of the family home. Each summer, the family traveled to a different college campus for the association's annual conference. "Linguists love to talk to children; they want to know how children process language. So I would have these amazing conversations with adults," Makkai recalled to Matt Jennings for *Middlebury Magazine* (26 July 2019), a publication of Middlebury College. Makkai grew up surrounded by academics, artists, and ex-pats. "My parents would host a lot of visiting artists and musicians (from Hungary) and have concerts in the house," she recalled to Christopher Borrelli for the *Chicago Tribune* (20 June 2018). "We were the first stop for a lot of expats who got out." Encouraged by her family's relationship to the arts, Makkai knew early on that she wanted to be a writer. She wrote her first short story when she was three years old. By the time she was in high school, she was scouring literary magazines and researching writing programs, seriously considering her path.

As an adult, Makkai wrote an essay for the *New Yorker* in which she revealed that she had been sexually molested by a family friend, who occasionally lived at her family's house, from the ages of seven to thirteen. She recalls writing a victim impact statement and delivering it to her abuser in court when she was a teenager. The defense lawyer accused her of plagiarizing her account, arguing that other teenagers he knew could not write that well.

EDUCATION AND EARLY CAREER

Makkai studied English at Washington & Lee University in Lexington, Virginia. The university houses a major literary magazine called *Shenandoah*; Makkai spent three years as a student assistant on the magazine. The job gave Makkai an insider's view of the process of selecting and rejecting stories. "I was so grateful for all that time spent sending out hundreds of rejections at a time; I knew better than to take things personally, and I knew the patience I'd need," she recalled to Tracy Richardson for *Shenandoah* (2011) years later. As a student, Makkai published a handful of stories in the student literary magazine, then called *Ariel*. Her writing was different then, she recalled in her interview with Richardson. Her stories were more lyrical and "much more concerned with voice than with plot." Her narrators were often people with a limited point of view—a child or an outsider. "A few years after college, someone gave me the very liberating advice that it was okay to have a narrator as smart as—or smarter than—I am," she recalled. The advice changed the way she approached the story. Makkai graduated with a degree in English in 1999.

Makkai went on to study for her master's degree in English at Middlebury College's Bread Loaf School of English in Vermont. The program took place over the course of five summers; during that time, Makkai worked as an elementary school teacher at a Montessori school. As a graduate student, she studied with the Pulitzer Prize–winning poet Paul Muldoon and the short story writer David Huddle. She also studied the work of authors like James Joyce, Marcel Proust, and Thomas Mann. Makkai graduated in 2004.

EARLY SHORT STORIES AND NOVELS

Makkai spent twelve years working as an elementary school teacher, developing her writing on nights and weekends. She found some early success as a short story writer. From 2008 to 2011, her stories appeared in four consecutive editions of the annual anthology *Best American Short Stories*. One of those stories, "The Briefcase" (2009), is about a political prisoner being held in an unnamed country at an unspecified time. It draws on elements of Makkai's family history and illustrates the cyclical cruelty of repressive regimes. "I've always been fascinated by the revolutions—both political and personal—that will make someone abandon everything and start over," Makkai said to Richardson regarding the story.

The popularity of her short stories helped Makkai land influential agent Nicole Aragi. Makkai had sent Aragi a query letter that included a synopsis of her first novel, *The Borrower*. Aragi read the manuscript and signed her soon after. Makkai published *The Borrower* in 2011. Set in Hannibal, Missouri, the hometown of iconic American writer Mark Twain, the book follows a local librarian named Lucy who befriends a ten-year-old boy. After coming out to his fundamentalist Christian family, the boy's parents have decided to send him to gay-conversion therapy. In an effort to protect her young friend, Lucy kidnaps him, and the two embark on a road trip adventure. In a short review for the *New York Times* (15 June 2011), Susannah Meadows wrote: "Although the inadvertent kidnapping isn't entirely believable, this failure doesn't sink Ms. Makkai's first novel. It's an appealing, nonromantic love story about an unexpected pairing—and a surprisingly moving one."

Makkai published her second novel, *The Hundred-Year House*, in 2014. The book, which follows one hundred years in the life of a house on Chicago's North Shore, began as a short story. In it, a group of artists and intellectuals uncover the house's secret past. In 2015, Makkai published a collection of short stories, including "The Briefcase" and other early stories, called *Music for Wartime*. Dwight Garner of the *New York Times* (7 July 2015) gave the collection a critical review. He described Makkai's writing as "self-conscious," though he noted that "the very good writer in her pops up often enough . . . to keep you alert."

THE GREAT BELIEVERS

Makkai third novel, *The Great Believers*, was published in 2018. Makkai originally envisioned the novel as a story about an artist's muse in Paris between the world wars, with a subplot about the early days of the AIDS crisis in Chicago. Ultimately, that equation was reversed, with numerous subplots and characters emerging from the connection between the two time periods. "The more research I did, the more convinced I became that this world"—Chicago in the 1980s—"should be at the heart of the plot and not a subplot," she told Jennings. The novel's protagonist became Yale Tishman, a young man working to establish a permanent art collection at Northwestern University.

While Makkai was working on the novel, she worried that Yale's story was not hers, as a straight woman, to tell. "If I was going to do it well, I needed to be convinced that I could talk to the right people, that I could avoid cliché, that I could be accurate down to the most granular level, that I could get the psychology right," she recalled to Jennings. She read hundreds of issues of the *Windy City Times*, a gay Chicago weekly, and conducted interviews, reaching out to friends and friends of friends on *Facebook* and moving outward from there. "I wanted someone who had lived through this in Chicago in the 80s to read it to not to be taken out of it by some little thing that made it apparent to them that it

was fiction," she told Rachel León for the *Chicago Review of Books* (19 June 2018).

The Great Believers won the Andrew Carnegie Medal for Excellence in Fiction, the Stonewall Book Award, the Chicago Review of Books Award, and the *Los Angeles Times* Books Prize for Fiction; and was a finalist for the National Book Award and the Pulitzer Prize. It was also named one of the ten best books of the year by the *New York Times*.

PERSONAL LIFE

Makkai is married to Jon Freeman, whom she met at Bread Loaf. Freeman is a teacher and assistant dean of students at Lake Forest Academy, a boarding school in suburban Chicago. They have two daughters and live on the Lake Forest campus.

SUGGESTED READING

Borrelli, Christopher. "Rebecca Makkai, Author of Chicago-Set 'The Great Believers,' Knows the Value of Diligence." *Chicago Tribune*, 20 June 2018, www.chicagotribune.com/entertainment/ct-ent-rebecca-makkai-0624-story.html. Accessed 9 Nov. 2019.

Cunningham, Michael. "Surviving AIDS, but at What Cost?" Review of *The Great Believers*, by Rebecca Makkai. *The New York Times*, 25 June 2018, www.nytimes.com/2018/06/25/books/review/rebecca-makkai-great-believers.html. Accessed 9 Nov. 2019.

Garner, Dwight. "Review: Rebecca Makkai's 'Music for Wartime,' Stories with Echoes of Loss." Review of *Music for Wartime*, by Rebecca Makkai. *The New York Times*, 7 July 2015, www.nytimes.com/2015/07/08/books/review-rebecca-makkais-music-for-wartime-stories-with-echoes-of-loss.html. Accessed 10 Nov. 2019.

Makkai, Rebecca. "A Conversation with Rebecca Makkai." Interview by Matt Jennings. *Middlebury Magazine*, 26 July 2019, middleburymagazine.com/features/a-conversation-with-rebecca-makkai/. Accessed 10 Nov. 2019.

———. "How Rebecca Makkai Wrote 'The Great Believers.'" Interview by Rachel León. *Chicago Review of Books*, 19 June 2018, chireviewofbooks.com/2018/06/19/great-believers-rebecca-makkai-interview/. Accessed 10 Nov. 2019.

———. "Interview with Rebecca Makkai." By Tracy Richardson. *Shenandoah*, 2011, shenandoahliterary.org/61/interview-with-rebecca-makkai-2/. Accessed 10 Nov. 2019.

Meadows, Susannah. "Newly Released Books." Review of *To Be Sung Underwater*, by Tom McNeal; *The Borrower*, by Rebecca Makkai; *Maine*, by J. Courtney Sullivan; *Sister*, by Rosamund Lupton; *Bloodmoney*, by David

Ignatius; and *Witches of East End*, by Melissa de la Cruz. *The New York Times*, 15 June 2011, www.nytimes.com/2011/06/16/books/new-novels-by-david-ignatius-melissa-de-la-cruz-and-others.html. Accessed 10 July 2019.

SELECTED WORKS

The Borrower, 2011; *The Hundred-Year House*, 2014; *Music for Wartime*, 2015; *The Great Believers*, 2018

—Molly Hagan

Sanna Marin

Date of birth: November 16, 1985
Occupation: Politician

When Sanna Marin was sworn in as prime minister of Finland on December 10, 2019, she became the Nordic country's youngest prime minister and the youngest sitting head of government in the world. A former minister for transport and communication and city councilor for Tampere, Finland's third-largest city, Marin led a coalition government with four other women in top spots—three of whom were, like her, under the age of thirty-five. "I have never thought about my age or gender," she told reporters after being tapped to head Finland's Social Democratic Party, as quoted by Robert Greenall for *BBC News* (10 Dec. 2019). "I think of the reasons I got into politics and those things for which we have won the trust of the electorate."

When Marin became the youngest prime minister in the nation's history, she also was its third female prime minister: she was preceded by Anneli Jäätteenmäki, who served in that capacity in 2003, and Mari Kiviniemi, who served from 2010 to 2011. Finland, a Northern European nation bordering the Baltic Sea, has a long history of supporting women leaders. All the way back in 1907 Finnish voters elected nineteen women as members of Parliament (MPs), and in April 2019, women won a record ninety-four seats (47 percent) in the two-hundred-seat unicameral parliament. Given that context, "Marin's background and gender are far less interesting than her character and accomplishments," Fredrik Erixon asserted in an opinion piece for the *Spectator* (14 Dec. 2019). "She is an inspiring person who has packed an extraordinary career into just a few years."

EARLY LIFE AND EDUCATION

Sanna Mirella Marin was born on November 16, 1985, in Helsinki, Finland's capital. Her background was far from privileged. Her mother had grown up in an orphanage, and her father struggled with alcohol. The couple divorced when Marin was young, and her mother later entered a same-sex relationship. Although Finland is now known as relatively liberal, and same-sex marriage was legalized in 2017, Marin told interviewers that during her formative years, her "rainbow family," as she has called it, was not fully accepted by society, and she sometimes felt marginalized. Despite that state of affairs—and despite some lack of material comforts—she described her childhood as one full of love.

When Marin was seven, her family moved to Pirkkala, just outside Tampere, a major industrial center located about 180 kilometers north of Helsinki. Much of the social life in Pirkkala revolved around the church, which provided a place for young people to gather for coffee and games of billiards. At age fifteen Marin got her first job, at a bakery in Tampere, and she later sold magazines door to door to earn money. During her adolescence she spent her spare time walking her dog, playing basketball, and dancing.

By her own account, Marin was an indifferent student, earning mediocre grades (including the poorest marks of all the students in her German-language elective) and putting little effort into homework. Still, she would later remember most of her teachers fondly. She graduated from Pirkkala Upper Secondary School in 2004, despite her lackluster performance.

Marin worked for a time as a cashier before deciding to attend college, the first person in her family to do so. She enrolled in the University of Tampere (later Tampere University), working as a salesperson at times to avoid student loan debt. Marin completed a bachelor's degree in administrative studies there in 2012. Eventually, in 2017, after she had already embarked on a career in government, she also earned a master's degree in administration, with a thesis entitled "Finland, a Country of Mayors."

While in college Marin belonged to the student union and Tampere Region Student Housing Foundation and chaired the political club. She later served as a trainee at the Treasury in 2010 and at the nonprofit Amnesty International Finland in 2012.

EARLY POLITICAL CAREER

Marin did not arrive at the idea of forging a political career easily. She told interviewers that while she always voted as a matter of civic pride and responsibility, she simply assumed that politicians came from more privileged backgrounds than hers. Still, her mother had always stressed the importance of having a strong value system, and the family had often benefited from Finland's social-welfare policies. "I got to live a safe childhood, have an education and pursue my dreams," she wrote in a letter to colleagues, as reported by Johanna Lemola and Megan Specia for the *New York Times* (10 Dec. 2019).

"Enabling it for everyone has driven me into politics."

Although Marin initially considered Finland's Green Party, the Social Democrats ultimately seemed more aligned with her beliefs. In 2006, she joined the Social Democratic Youth. She became the organization's first vice president in 2010 and remained in that post for two years.

Marin clerked for the city of Tampere from 2006 to 2007. She first ran for municipal office in 2007 but did not win. She had better luck in 2009, when she was elected a deputy city councilor for Tampere, a position she held until 2012. During that time she also represented the city for the Secondary Education Board. From 2013 to 2017 she was not only a full member but also chaired the council. She gained a national reputation and grew in popularity thanks to social media videos of her calm demeanor in sometimes heated meetings.

While chairing the city council, Marin also served as a member of the Pirkanmaa regional council. In Finland, regional councils are joint municipal administrations that function primarily as economic development and planning authorities.

PARTY ROLES

In 2014, concurrent with her other duties, Marin was elected as the second deputy chairperson of the Social Democratic Party. The following April she was elected as an MP representing the electoral district of Pirkanmaa. During her tenure in parliament she served briefly on various committees, including finance, administration, legal affairs, and environment. In 2017, she was reelected to the city council and became the first deputy chairperson for the Social Democrats.

Marin's star continued to rise, and in early 2019 she served as interim leader while Prime Minister Antti Rinne took two months medical leave of absence. On June 6, 2019, she became Finland's minister of transport and communications. While serving in that role, she launched negotiations toward rail-service improvements and participated in European Union (EU) discussions on transportation-related carbon emissions. During that period she also floated a vision of the future in which Finns might work just four six-hour workdays, an idea that was later incorrectly dubbed a new government policy.

BECOMING PRIME MINISTER

The year 2019 proved a turbulent one in the Finnish parliament. During the national elections in April the Social Democrats barely defeated the right-wing, populist Finns Party, and no one party garnered more than 18 percent of the vote. With little popular support, on December 3, Rinne was forced to step down due to coalition criticism over the way he was handling an ongoing strike by the state-run postal service. A few days later, on December 8, the Social Democrats narrowly nominated Marin—who had ably served as Rinne's deputy on the campaign trail—over parliamentary group leader Antti Lindtman, 32–29, to succeed Rinne. She was sworn in on December 10. Despite that major change, Rinne retained his post as the chair of the party; Marin was considered the favorite to win party leadership at the next convention, scheduled for June 2020, however.

In addition to the Social Democratic Party, the partners in Marin's ruling coalition government were the Center Party (led by Katri Kulmuni, aged thirty-two), the Greens (led by Maria Ohisalo, aged thirty-four), the Left Alliance (led by Li Andersson, aged thirty-two), and the Swedish People's Party of Finland (led by Anna-Maja Henriksson, aged fifty-five). In all, twelve of the nineteen ministers in the five-party coalition were women. These demographic facts drew considerable international media attention to the Finnish government, and to Marin in particular.

Some of Finland's pundits agreed that the women's ascendancy "exceptional" and "pretty amazing," as gender-studies scholar Elina Penttinen put it to Jan M. Olsen and Vanessa Gera for the Associated Press (10 Dec. 2019). Other, however, expressed frustration at the tone of international coverage. "We have actually a very broad base of women in politics, and we have had a pretty equal situation in the political sphere for more than 35 years . . . one can kind of expect this sooner or later," Anne Holli, a professor of political science at the University of Helsinki, asserted to Lemola and Specia. Holli and fellow political scientist Tuomas Ylä-Anttila called greater attention to the ages of the prime minister and cabinet members, noting a significant generational shift was underway in Finnish politics.

POLICIES

In his *Spectator* piece, Erixon argued that considering the Social Democrats' slim victory over more populist parties and the evolving priorities of a country long known for its strong social welfare system, the success of Marin's tenure was far from assured. "She represents a green and tech-friendly social liberalism, backed up by more taxes and spending," he wrote. He further noted that that change in political landscape is "an experiment—and one that could easily backfire in a country whose rapidly ageing population is jaded about politics. But the Finns have a proverb for the experiment. . . . 'Ladies first, even on to thin ice.'"

Indeed, Marin was considered far to the left of the political spectrum, even by the standards of her very liberal party. Under the coalition government, she was expected to pursue ambitious clean-energy goals, such as making the country carbon neutral by 2035, and intended to create tens of thousands of jobs while shoring up Finland's social safety net, which faced financial challenges as the population aged. Marin opposed both a cap on refugees and the idea of NATO membership. Among the challenges facing her government were the population's growing support for more right-leaning parties, disputes over labor union compensation, relatively high unemployment, and a downturn in the economy.

Nevertheless, Marin adopted an optimistic tone. "Finland will not be finished in four years, but it can get better," she wrote on Twitter, as reported by Specia for the *New York Times* (10 Dec. 2019). "That's what we're working on. I want to build a society where every child can become anything and every person can live and grow in dignity."

PERSONAL LIFE

Marin married entrepreneur Markus Räikkönen. In January 2018 she gave birth to their daughter, Emma. The family lives in Tampere.

Marin speaks Finnish, English, Swedish, and some German. She became known for often posting both private and work-related entries on social media, a practice she stated she would continue while in office.

SUGGESTED READING

Erixon, Fredrik. "Finland's New PM Has Wowed the World. But What about Finland?" *The Spectator*, 12 Dec. 2019, www.spectator.co.uk/2019/12/finland-is-rebooting-its-politics-and-its-new-centrism-is-defined-by-youth. Accessed 12 Dec. 2019.

Greenall, Robert. "Sanna Marin: The Rising Star Who Leads Finland's 5.5 Million." *BBC News*, 10 Dec. 2019, www.bbc.com/news/world-europe-50712230. Accessed 11 Dec. 2019.

Lemola, Johanna, and Megan Specia. "Sanna Marin of Finland to Become World's Youngest Prime Minister." *The New York Times*, 10 Dec. 2019, www.nytimes.com/2019/12/09/world/europe/finland-prime-minister-sanna-marin.html. Accessed 11 Dec. 2019.

Olsen, Jan M., and Vanessa Gera. "At 34, Sanna Marin Is the World's Youngest Sitting Head of Government." *Time*, 10 Dec. 2019, time.com/5747062/worlds-youngest-government-leader. Accessed 11 Dec. 2019.

Pohjanpalo, Kati, and Leo Laikola. "'I've Proven My Abilities': Finland's Sanna Marin Becomes the World's Youngest Prime Minister." *National Post*, 9 Dec. 2019, nationalpost.com/news/world/ive-proven-my-abilities-finlands-sanna-marin-becomes-the-worlds-youngest-prime-minister#comments-area. Accessed 11 Dec. 2019.

Specia, Megan. "Who Is Sanna Marin, Finland's 34-Year-Old Prime Minister?" *The New York Times*, 10 Dec. 2019, www.nytimes.com/2019/12/10/world/europe/finland-sanna-marin.html. Accessed 11 Dec. 2019.

—*Mari Rich*

Lieke Martens

Date of birth: December 16, 1992
Occupation: Soccer player

When soccer player Lieke Martens was a child, she had no idea that the Netherlands had a women's national soccer team. By the end of 2017, however, there was little chance that anyone in the Netherlands—or in any country that follows women's soccer closely—could remain unaware of the team's existence. Having previously put forth a strong performance in the 2015 FIFA (Fédération Internationale de Football Association) Women's World Cup, the first World Cup in the Netherlands women's team's history, the team went on to win the 2017 UEFA (Union of European Football Association) Women's Championship, held that year in the Netherlands. Martens herself scored three goals during the championship tournament, helping to secure not only her team's victory but also widespread recognition of her own talents and those of her teammates. "Now, every little girl knows that Holland has a women's national team," she wrote in an essay for the *Players' Tribune* (8 Mar. 2018). "We all feel we are heroes for them. That they look up to us. That we can inspire them." Martens and her teammates gained even more fame in 2019, when the team achieved a second-place finish in the FIFA Women's World Cup in France. Yet for Martens, who plays for the women's Barcelona soccer club when not representing the Netherlands on the international level, there is even more to come. "I don't think I'm at my peak yet," she told Ramiro Aldunate for *MARCA* (17 Nov. 2017). "I have moved to a new country, I have to adapt to everything. It's a new language, new people. I'm giving myself time to adjust. I'm patient."

EARLY LIFE

Lieke Elisabeth Petronella Martens was born on December 16, 1992, Nieuw-Bergen, Netherlands. One of four children born to Bert and Thea Martens, she grew up in Bergen. Martens developed an interest in soccer at a young age,

Photo by Ailura via Wikimedia Commons

and some of her earliest memories are of watching her two older brothers play the sport. She soon began playing as well, practicing her skills with her brothers and devoting time to kicking soccer balls against any available wall.

Martens dreamed of one day playing soccer professionally, but because opportunities for women to play soccer were limited in the Netherlands at the time, she believed that she would need to join a men's team to do so. "I didn't have any female heroes. I couldn't look up to someone who was doing what I wanted to do. I didn't even know that a Dutch women's national team existed," she explained in her essay for the *Players' Tribune*. In addition to the Dutch professional men's soccer team Ajax, which she aspired to join herself, Martens was a fan of the Barcelona soccer club and was particularly inspired by the Brazilian player Ronaldinho, who played for Barcelona during the 2000s. Martens played on boys' teams throughout her childhood and into her teens, at times playing on teams coached by her father.

EARLY CAREER

When Martens was fifteen years old, she was selected to join the Netherlands' national women's under-nineteen (U19) team and left home for the city of Amsterdam to join her new teammates. Although excited by the opportunity to represent her country in international competition, she found that living away from home for the first time was a challenging experience. "I was living with girls who were eighteen or nineteen years old," she wrote in her essay for the

Players' Tribune. "We were team-mates, but we mostly did things on our own, so I'd have to figure stuff out by myself. Things like cooking and washing my clothes. Of course, I didn't have a clue." Competing with the U19 national team during 2010 and 2011, Martens was a member of the squad that competed in the 2010 UEFA Women's U19 Championship, during which the Netherlands made it to the semifinals before losing to England.

In addition to the U19 national team, Martens competed with a variety of soccer clubs within the women's division of the Eredivisie—the Netherlands' professional soccer league—during her early years as a professional player, including SC Heerenveen Vrouwen and VVV-Venlo. In 2011, she moved to Belgium to play for the team Standard Liège. She then played two seasons with MSV Duisburg, part of the German Frauen-Bundesliga league, and in 2014 began playing in the Swedish Damallsvenskan league with Göteborg FC. "Everywhere I've been has been good for me, and I think I've made the right decisions so far," Martens told Nick Aitken for *Women's Soccer United* (24 Sept. 2015) about her club career to that point. "Even so, it'd be good to stay in one place for a little longer now, to help my development more." Martens switched teams yet again in November 2015, signing with the Swedish team FC Rosengård. She played for FC Rosengård in 2016 and 2017 and assisted the team in claiming the Swedish Cup in August 2016.

NATIONAL TEAM SUCCESS

In addition to playing professional soccer in the Netherlands, Belgium, Germany, and Sweden, Martens represented her native country in international competition frequently throughout the years after her debut with the senior national team in 2011. In 2013, she joined the roster for the UEFA Women's Championship, during which the team was unable to make it out of the tournament's group stage. The Netherlands experienced far greater success during the 2015 FIFA Women's World Cup, the first World Cup for which the women's national team had ever qualified. While competing in the host country of Canada, Martens achieved a major career milestone, scoring a goal in a game against New Zealand. "It was a great feeling when that shot went in," she recalled to Aitken. "It was a wonderful feeling to score that goal, the Netherlands' first at a Women's World Cup, particularly as it turned out to be the winner." Although the Netherlands did not progress past the round of sixteen, the 2015 Women's World Cup was a key turning point for the team, demonstrating the Netherlands' ability to compete on the international tournament level.

In 2017, the Netherlands served as the host country for the UEFA Women's Championship, Martens's second since joining the senior national team. During the tournament, the Netherlands proceeded through the group stage and secured a spot in the knockout stage. "We felt good after the group stage—we had nine points, we won all the games," Martens told Suzanne Wrack for the *Guardian* (24 Apr. 2018). "I really felt then that something was possible. When we beat England 3–0 in the semi-final I thought: 'Right, now we have to win this final.'" The Netherlands went on to do so, defeating Denmark with a score of four points to two. Having scored a total of three goals and two assists over the course of the tournament, including a goal in the final game, Martens was named the UEFA women's EURO player of the tournament and won the Best FIFA Women's Player award for 2017.

BARCELONA
In addition to experiencing success on the international level, Martens found further success in her club career beginning in July 2017, when she signed a deal with the Barcelona women's team, FC Barcelona Femení. A longtime fan of Barcelona, she was excited to relocate to Spain and join the women's team. "It's a big club and here everything is impressive," Martens told Aldunate. "I love the club, they gave me a great welcome, plus the team is strong and the people are really nice. There's a good level here." The 2017–18 season proved to be a successful one for Barcelona, which ended the season ranked second in the Primera División. At the end of the season, Barcelona competed in the Copa de la Reina de Fútbol, the national championship for Spanish women's soccer. Martens contributed a goal to the team's victory in the semifinals, and the team went on to defeat the Atlético Madrid women's team to claim the championship. Martens remained with Barcelona during the subsequent two seasons, and in 2019, she aided the team in achieving a second-place finish in that year's UEFA Women's Championship League.

2019 WORLD CUP
In June 2019, the Netherlands competed in the FIFA Women's World Cup, held that year in France. After progressing through the group stage of the tournament, the team faced Japan in the round of sixteen. Martens scored both of the Netherlands' two goals during the game, which won them the match and the ability to progress to the quarterfinals for the first time in the team's history. Named player of the match, Martens was pleased with the victory but immediately hampered by a toe injury incurred during the postgame celebration, which threatened her ability to compete in the remaining rounds. "As a

player you always want to play in one of the biggest games of your career and this is one of the biggest ones," she said prior to the World Cup final, as reported by Simon Evans for *Reuters* (3 July 2019). "I am hopefully going to play. I am going to do the recovery and I really believe in the medical staff and that something can happen, so let's see every single day, how it goes." After beating Italy and Sweden in the quarterfinals and semifinals, respectively, Martens and her teammates faced the defending champions, the United States, in the final round. The Netherlands ultimately lost the match, becoming runners up in the World Cup.

Internationally known through her affiliation with Barcelona and success in the Women's World Cup, Martens has sought to use her increased international profile both to promote the sport of soccer among girls and young women and to advocate for equal pay for female soccer players, who are frequently paid less than their male counterparts. "I think it's important that federations and teams talk about money because we aren't talking about buying extra cars, but of being able to go to the supermarket and buy good food. We want to be valued more and have the right to ask them to discuss wage equality," she explained to Aldunate. "Women's football is growing, and it's normal to pay more." In speaking out about the issue of wage equality, Martens added her voice to those of players from numerous countries, including the United States, who have sought to raise awareness of the financial disparities female athletes face within professional soccer and other sports.

SUGGESTED READING
Aitken, Nick. "Lieke Martens: 'Scoring at Canada 2015 Was Wonderful.'" *Women's Soccer United*, 24 Sept. 2015, www.womenssoccerunited.com/lieke-martens-interview. Accessed 8 Mar. 2020.

Evans, Simon. "Dutch Star Martens Hopes to Make Final Despite Injury." *Reuters*, 3 July 2019, www.reuters.com/article/us-soccerworldcup-nld-swe-martens/dutch-star-martens-hopes-to-make-final-despite-injury-idUSKCN1TY30C. Accessed 8 Mar. 2020.

"Lieke Martens Named Player of the Tournament." *UEFA.com*, 6 Aug. 2017, www.uefa.com/womenseuro/news/023c-0e169fc95c3a-961bb8bc2e14-1000--lieke-martens-named-player-of-the-tournament/. Accessed 8 Mar. 2020.

Martens, Lieke. "Be Like Ronaldino." *The Players' Tribune*, 8 Mar. 2018, www.theplayerstribune.com/en-us/articles/lieke-martens-be-like-ronaldinho. Accessed 8 Mar. 2020.

——. "Martens: Women Have the Right to Demand the Same as Men." Interview by Ramiro Aldunate. Adapted by Sam Leveridge.

MARCA, 17 Nov. 2017, www.marca.com/en/football/barcelona/2017/11/17/5a0e176d468aeb6e098b472f.html. Accessed 8 Mar. 2020.

McIntyre, Doug. "Meet Lieke Martens, the Breakout Star of the 2019 Women's World Cup." *Yahoo! Sports*, 4 July 2019, sports.yahoo.com/meet-lieke-martens-the-netherlands-striker-and-breakout-star-of-the-2019-womens-world-cup-120755501.html. Accessed 8 Mar. 2020.

Wrack, Suzanne. "Lieke Martens: 'Ronaldinho Was My Idol. Long Hair, Great Dribbles . . . I Loved Him.'" *The Guardian*, 24 Apr. 2018, www.theguardian.com/football/blog/2018/apr/24/lieke-martens-barcelona-ronaldinho. Accessed 8 Mar. 2020.

—*Joy Crelin*

Arthur B. McDonald

Date of birth: August 29, 1943
Occupation: Physicist

Arthur B. McDonald is a Nobel Prize–winning Canadian astrophysicist and particle physicist credited with the joint discovery that neutrinos possess mass and can change identity.

EARLY LIFE AND EDUCATION
Arthur B. McDonald was born on Cape Breton in Sydney, Nova Scotia, on August 29, 1943. As a child, he loved fishing and science. His mother, Valerie McDonald, told the CBC in 2016 that McDonald was always a curious child who, even as a toddler, tried to understand how their family clock worked.

In 1964, McDonald graduated with a bachelor's degree from Dalhousie University in Halifax, Nova Scotia, and went on to earn a master's degree in physics at the university in 1965. He then attended the California Institute of Technology (Caltech) in Pasadena, California, where he earned a PhD in nuclear physics in 1969.

Having completed his university studies, McDonald worked for the Chalk River Nuclear Laboratories of Atomic Energy of Canada from 1969 until 1982. He became a professor in Princeton University's physics department in 1982, where he had access to the Palmer Cyclotron, a noteworthy tool for studying particle physics, which was built in the 1930s and decommissioned in 1998.

As a particle physicist and astrophysicist, McDonald has studied neutrinos for most of his career. Neutrinos are a type of lepton, one of the basic particles that make up all matter. In the 1980s, he helped to develop a neutrino observatory center 6,800 feet (2,070 meters) underground in Sudbury, Ontario. In 1989, he became the Sudbury Neutrino Observatory's first director and began teaching as a professor at Queens University in Kingston, Ontario.

The Sudbury Neutrino Observatory (SNO) was built underground to allow neutrinos to pass through layers of rock and reach a large water tank that made up the observatory's detector. The underground position of the detector also allowed the scientists to observe neutrinos in isolation from cosmic rays. It was at SNO that McDonald began to develop his research into the question of whether solar neutrinos possess mass.

NOBEL PRIZE WINNER
Despite being the second-most abundant particle in the universe after photons, little was understood about neutrinos and their properties as matter prior to research McDonald directed at SNO. Theoretical physicist Wolfgang Pauli theorized the existence of neutrinos in 1930, but he believed that they were undetectable and did not collide with matter.

McDonald's SNO team studied a group of electron neutrinos originating at the sun. The tests had shown two-thirds of these neutrinos disappearing when they reached the earth, raising the question of whether the particles were dissipating.

McDonald's findings proved that the neutrinos were changing identity from electron neutrinos to other neutrino types, tau and muon neutrinos. This ensured that the neutrinos were not disappearing on their way to the earth from the sun, and consequently proved that neutrinos have mass. In fact, McDonald's team's findings suggest that neutrinos, which are created by cosmic rays, may collectively have as much mass as the collective weight of stars.

Having successfully proven that neutrinos do have mass and can change identities, McDonald won the 2015 Nobel Prize in Physics. He shared the award with Takaaki Kajita, whose research team at Japan's Super-Kamiokande neutrino detector developed the same findings about neutrinos. In 2016, McDonald's SNO team was one of five teams to split the Breakthrough Prize in Fundamental Physics, worth $3 million. Japan had three winning teams, one of which was Kajita's Super-Kamiokande team.

IMPACT
McDonald has authored more than 120 scientific papers and is a decorated scientist, having won many awards. In 2006, he earned one of Canada's highest national honors when he was made an Officer of the Order of Canada. In addition to the Nobel Prize and the Fundamental Physics Prize, his other honors include a Herzberg Medal (2003) and a Benjamin Franklin

Medal in Physics (2007). McDonald was elected as a Fellow of the Royal Society of London in 2009 and was promoted to Companion of the Order of Canada in 2015.

The neutrino mass question had been investigated for more than fifty years prior to McDonald's breakthrough findings. The *Wall Street Journal* noted that the outcome of McDonald's research "opened the door to a new world of physics." The finding that neutrinos have mass has forced particle physicists to revise their understanding of how the universe works.

PERSONAL LIFE

McDonald lives in Canada with his wife. He serves as professor emeritus at Queens University, where he has taught since 1989.

SUGGESTED READING

"Arthur McDonald, Nobel Winner, Snags 2nd Major Science Honour." *CBCnews*. CBC/Radio Canada, 9 Nov. 2015, www.cbc.ca/news/canada/nova-scotia/arthur-mcdonald-breakthrough-prize-1.3310308. Accessed 27 July 2020.

"Arthur McDonald's Mother Proud of Nobel Prize–winning Son." *CBCnews*. CBC/Radio Canada, 7 Oct. 2015, www.cbc.ca/news/canada/nova-scotia/mom-of-nobel-prize-winner-arthur-mcdonald-proud-1.3261329. Accessed 27 July 2020.

Gregersen, Erik. "Arthur B. McDonald." *Encyclopedia Britannica Online*. Encyclopedia Britannica, 12 Feb. 2016, www.britannica.com/editor/Erik-Gregersen/6723. Accessed 27 July 2020.

Grodin, Claire. "Nobel Prize in Physics Awarded for Discovering Neutrinos Have Mass." *Fortune*. Fortune Media, 6 Oct. 2015, fortune.com/2015/10/06/nobel-prize-physics-neutrino/. Accessed 27 July 2020.

Naik, Gautam, and Anna Molin. "Nobel Prize in Physics Won by Takaaki Kajita and Arthur B. McDonald for Work on Neutrinos." *The Wall Street Journal*. Dow Jones, 6 Oct. 2015, www.wsj.com/articles/nobel-prize-in-physics-won-by-takaaki-kajita-and-arthur-b-mcdonald-for-work-on-neutrinos-1444126197. Accessed 27 June 2020.

Overbye, Dennis. "Takaaki Kajita and Arthur McDonald Share Nobel in Physics for Work on Neutrinos." *The New York Times*, 7 Oct. 2015, www.nytimes.com/2015/10/07/science/nobel-prize-physics-takaaki-kajita-arthur-b-mcdonald.html._Accessed 27 July 2020.

"Past Winner 2003 NSERC Award of Excellence: Arthur McDonald." *Natural Sciences and Engineering Research Council of Canada*. NSERC, 13 Aug. 2010, www.nserc-crsng.gc.ca/Prizes-Prix/Herzberg-Herzberg/Profiles-Profils_eng.asp?ID=1005. Accessed 27 July 2020.

—*Richard Means*

Judith McKenna

Born: 1966
Occupation: Businesswoman

By 2020 the retail giant Walmart had around 6,000 stores operating in twenty-six countries outside the United States, with a workforce of more than 700,000 associates serving the needs of more than 200 million customers every week. Analysts pointed out that the company's global arm generated more revenue than the gross domestic product of many countries. It is therefore little surprise that as Walmart International's president and CEO, overseeing more than $120 billion in revenue, Judith McKenna became widely acknowledged as one of the most influential businesspeople in the world and a fixture on such annual lists as *Fortune*'s 50 Most Powerful Women.

Formerly the chief operating officer of the retailer's US operations, McKenna rose to be considered the second highest-ranked member

Photo by Walmart

of Walmart's administrative hierarchy, behind only CEO Doug McMillon. Both McMillon and his predecessor, Mike Duke, once held her role as head of the company's international division, seen as an important testing ground for those hoping to lead the entire company. "It's McKenna's job to transform the retailer from an American company that happens to have an international business into a truly global enterprise," as Beth Kowitt wrote for *Fortune* (25 Sept. 2018). She pursued that goal by acknowledging that different countries have different business needs, and by making decisions on a market-by-market basis. Although all of the company's stores around the world operate under the Walmart umbrella, they retain individual names depending on locality (for example, Seiyu in Japan and Changomas in Argentina), and McKenna expressed a commitment to ensuring that every store functions as a strong, local business, responsive to the needs of its customers and providing value to its community. "I'm a retailer at heart," she asserted in a *YouTube* video accompanying *Fortune*'s 2019 Most Powerful Women feature (23 Sept. 2019).

EARLY LIFE AND EDUCATION

Judith McKenna was born in 1966 and raised in Middlesbrough, a postindustrial town in North Yorkshire, England. Her parents were both teachers, a fact that some journalists have used to explain her establishment and promotion of dozens of "Walmart Academies," employee training programs intended to facilitate career advancement. She grew up with an older sister, who became a social worker.

McKenna has told interviewers that her upbringing was normal and uneventful. She attended the local comprehensive school, a type of secondary school in England and Wales that does not have selective admissions. She got her first job at age sixteen, working at a local dress shop. She would later credit the experience with teaching her invaluable customer service skills and an awareness of the challenges of running a small business. The owner, she recalled, often left her alone to manage the store on her own—a practice, she admitted, that would probably not be allowed today.

Upon graduating from her comprehensive school, McKenna entered England's Hull University, where she studied law. (The university later awarded her an honorary doctorate in law.) Somewhat reluctant to map out a firm career plan and wanting to see what opportunities presented themselves, she next moved to London. There she joined KPMG, considered one of the "Big Four" global accounting firms, and earned certification from the Institute of Chartered Accountants in England and Wales.

EARLY CORPORATE CAREER

In 1992 McKenna became an account executive at the Leeds-based Tetley Pub Company. Of working for a pub management company, she told Emma De Vita for *Management Today* (1 Apr. 2012), "It's a very big world with some very big characters. And, boy, do you have to be able to stand up for yourself when you walk into a working men's club and negotiate a loan." McKenna became known for her ability to connect with both the pub owners, who learned she had a sense of empathy and fair play, and her subordinates, who became so loyal that some continued sending her holiday cards for years after working with her.

In 1993, Tetley was acquired jointly by Danish brewer Carlsberg and British restaurant and spirits company Allied Domecq, and McKenna became a corporate accountant with Allied Domecq. She remained there until 1996, when she was recruited by Asda, a British supermarket chain headquartered in Leeds, England. She served in various capacities, including comptroller, and when Walmart acquired the company in 1999 for £6.7 billion, she was closely involved in the negotiations. "Actually, it didn't feel like a takeover," McKenna recalled to De Vita. "It felt much more like a merger, which sounds extraordinary when the world's biggest retailer has just bought you."

WALMART BEGINNINGS

With Walmart now Asda's parent company, McKenna was officially an employee of the retail giant, which in 2001 promoted her to chief financial officer of Asda. She remained in that capacity for a decade, taking on increasing responsibilities in the realms of real estate, construction, and store development. In a turn of events that was particularly exciting for her, in 2010 she oversaw the £778 million acquisition of rival chain Netto and the subsequent conversion of its stores to the Asda brand.

In 2011, following the departure of Asda's chief operating officer (COO), Simon King—whose ouster after just six months was the cause of some gossip in the retail world—McKenna was named to fill the position. Some inside observers were surprised that she agreed to leave her CFO post, which she greatly enjoyed and had thrived in. She admitted to Kowitt, "I didn't really want to do anything else [initially]. I thought I had the best job in the universe, and I had broken every ceiling going, and I was quite happy with it, thank you."

Once she was ensconced as COO, McKenna led all of Asda's retail operations, including its brick-and-mortar stores, online presence, and distribution network. She was widely credited with helping Asda fend off fierce competition from popular chains like Tesco, Sainsbury, and

Aldi. Buzz began circulating that she was being groomed for a senior executive role within the parent company.

That buzz was quickly proven right when she was named executive vice president of strategy and international development for Walmart International in 2014. Her career trajectory steepened even further in early 2015, when she was made chief development officer of Walmart US's business unit. Credited for an initiative to integrate digital commerce into the physical stores, she was promoted within months to executive vice president and COO for Walmart US and given responsibility for more than 4,500 retail locations and 1.5 million employees.

During her tenure in that post McKenna introduced some of the systems she had developed at Asda to Walmart's domestic stores. These included a labor-saving method of storing excess inventory above shelves, rather than in out-of-the-way stock rooms. She also won praise for her launch of the Walmart Academy program, which trained 250,000 employees in its first year alone, and for the relatively smooth rollout of Online Grocery Pickup, a program in which customers order online and then pull their cars into specially designated store parking spots, where workers load their orders.

HEAD OF WALMART INTERNATIONAL

In early 2018, after Walmart International CEO David Cheesewright announced his retirement, McKenna was named to replace him, taking over that February. Now at the top of an increasingly vital part of the Walmart empire, she faced several challenges. Soon after accepting the post she found herself at the center of a whirlwind of deals, including the proposed merger of Asda with competitor Sainsbury and the sale of the majority of the shares in Walmart's Brazilian operation to an equity firm—signs of a pullback in major markets. But these were just preliminary deals ahead of what many called one of the company's riskiest moves ever: the $16 billion purchase of a majority stake in Flipkart, India's biggest online retailer. That investment was the most expensive in Walmart history and set a record in the global e-commerce sector.

Quoting financial experts who called the Flipkart deal "jaw-dropping," Kowitt wrote: "In a span of just a few weeks, it seemed to throw the scripture handed down by founder Sam Walton out the window, by essentially trading a reasonably stable, profitable business in the United Kingdom for a money-losing venture in India that may take a decade to even begin to show signs of paying off." In other words, Walmart was departing from its historic reliance on big-box stores to make a long-term investment in e-commerce. Kowitt asserted, "McKenna and her team bear a Walmart-size responsibility with

Walmart-size consequences. In reprioritizing the company's global footprint, they are effectively placing bets on the future of retail." Still, there was considerable belief among observers that McKenna was up to the task. In an article for *Kantar US Insights* (25 Jan. 2018), Tim Campbell listed attributes that McKenna was seen as bringing to Walmart International as CEO, including international experience in maximizing operational efficiency and rigor, a deep knowledge of e-commerce, and the ability to connect with and support employees at all levels.

However, all did not go flawlessly during the first year or so of McKenna's tenure as head of Walmart International. When the Flipkart deal was first announced, Walmart stock immediately tumbled 3 percent, and experts predicted that it would drag down earnings per share by 60 cents over the next fiscal year. (Though others pointed out that while expensive in the short term, the deal might pay off down the line, giving Walmart a strong toehold in e-commerce in one of the fastest-growing markets in the world.) Then, in early 2019, UK regulators blocked Sainsbury's proposed $9.5 billion merger with Asda, charging that the cost would come out of consumers' pockets and squelch competition. At that year's World Retail Congress in Amsterdam, McKenna defended the failed merger and said it would have resulted in lower, not higher prices. She told Paul Skeldon for *Internet Retailing* (15 May 2019), "I've worked in the UK market for a very long time and anybody who thinks that [the deal would have raised] prices . . . perhaps doesn't know the environment and the market dynamics very well and certainly doesn't know what our business stands for."

In 2020 Walmart, like all global businesses, suddenly faced the challenges of the global coronavirus pandemic. In China, where the pandemic started, the company had grown to do $10 billion in business at its more than four hundred stores. (One of these, a Sam's Club in Shenzhen, had the highest sales of any Walmart location in the world.) Under McKenna's direction, in January and February 2020 the company cut store hours at its locations in China and strengthened its partnership with Chinese delivery and logistics firm Dada-JD Daojia. McKenna also noted that her focus was on ensuring that her employees stayed healthy and that customer needs were met as efficiently as possible.

PERSONAL LIFE

McKenna married to Phil Dutton, a retail executive she met while both were working at Asda. She told Zoe Wood for the *Guardian* (15 Nov. 2008) that she and her husband avoided shop talk at home and were "more likely to talk about what's for tea." The couple had two children together, a girl (born early in McKenna's career at Asda) and a boy (born seven years later).

Often asked about being a woman in a male-dominated business, McKenna took the issue in stride. "You have to be yourself. There's no point in pretending you're a male, it just wouldn't work," she asserted to Skeldon. She did, however, note that she would like to see more women in senior roles. "I think there is an obligation on everybody in the industry to be very thoughtful about finding people and bringing them through, making sure you have diverse candidate lists," she said in the same interview. "I've got a 24-year-old daughter and I'd like to think that the world is her oyster and there is no barrier to her to do whatever she wants to do, and I think we've all got to think that way."

SUGGESTED READING

Campbell, Tim. "Here's What Judith McKenna Brings to Walmart International." *Kantar US Insights*, 25 Jan. 2018, us.kantar.com/business/retail/2018/what-judith-mckenna-brings-to-walmart-international/. Accessed 17 Feb. 2020.

De Vita, Emma. "Judith McKenna: The MT Interview." *Management Today*, 1 Apr. 2012, www.managementtoday.co.uk/judith-mckenna-mt-interview/article/1124087. Accessed 17 Feb. 2020.

Iyengar, Rishi. "Walmart Spent $16 Billion to Go Big in India. She Has to Make It Work." *CNN Business*, 11 Mar. 2019, www.cnn.com/2019/03/10/business/walmart-international-ceo-judith-mckenna-profile/index.html. Accessed 17 Feb. 2020.

Kowitt, Beth. "Meet the Woman Running Walmart's Biggest Deal Ever." *Fortune*. 25 Sept. 2018, fortune.com/longform/walmart-international-flipkart-judith-mckenna/. Accessed 17 Feb. 2020.

McKenna, Judith. "Most Powerful Women: Judith McKenna," *YouTube*, uploaded by *Fortune Magazine*, 23 Sept. 2019, www.youtube.com/watch?v=QbsaTe4RiCA. Accessed 17 Feb. 2020.

Skeldon, Paul. "Walmart International CEO Judith McKenna Defends Asda Sainsbury's Merger as 'Bold' Bid to Drive Down Prices." *Internet Retailing*, 15 May 2019, internetretailing.net/industry/industry/walmart-international-ceo-judith-mckenna-defends-asda-sainsburys-merger-as-bold-bid-to-drive-down-prices--19612. Accessed 17 Feb. 2020.

Wood, Zoe. "How Asda Takes Sting out of the Crunch." *The Guardian*, 15 Nov. 2008, www.theguardian.com/business/2008/nov/16/asda-interview-judith-mckenna. Accessed 17 Feb. 2020.

Photo by NASA

—*Mari Rich*

Jessica Meir

Born: July 1, 1977
Occupation: Astronaut and scientist

Jessica Meir joined the National Aeronautics and Space Administration (NASA) at age thirty-five after a career as a scientist to follow her long-held passion to go to space. As Meir explained to students at her alma mater, the Scripps Institution of Oceanography at University of California San Diego (30 Jan. 2020), "I've been saying I wanted to be an astronaut since I was five years old, and because I had identified that as my passion, and also identified other aspects of science and exploration that led me down that road and pursued it—with a lot of hard work and dedication and perseverance—and then a lot of luck, all wrapped together to actually get me where I am today."

EARLY LIFE AND EDUCATION

Jessica Ulrika Meir was born in 1977 and grew up in Caribou, Maine, the youngest of five children. Her parents, Josef and Ulla-Britt Meir, supported her interest in science. Her mother, a former nurse, is Swedish; her father, a surgeon, is an Iraqi-Israeli Jew. Her first-grade teacher asked her when she was five years old to draw a picture of what she wanted to be when she grew up. Meir drew an astronaut in space.

The summer before she began high school, she attended a space camp at Purdue University. As she told Julia Bayley for *Bangor Daily News* (18 June 2013), "I have been very interested in science from a young age. I was mostly interested in biology and physiology and always interested in space flight, so I involved myself in as many space-related activities as I could." She graduated from Caribou High School in 1995 as valedictorian.

She then attended Brown University in Rhode Island. Between her sophomore and junior years, she was part of a six-week summer program, the Space and Life Sciences Training Program at Kennedy Space Center in Florida. For her study abroad semester, Meir chose to go to Stockholm, Sweden, to connect with her maternal heritage. While in college she also became a certified scuba diver. During a summer program at Brown to study the effects of space biology, she and other students designed a program the National Aeronautics and Space Administration (NASA) later used as part of the Reduced Gravity Student Flight Opportunities Program. Meir graduated from Brown in 1999 with a degree in biology. Meir earned a master's degree in space studies in 2000 from the International Space University, located near Strasbourg, France.

EARLY CAREER

Meir spent three years, from 2000 until 2003, doing physiology research for Lockheed Martin's Human Research Facility at NASA's Johnson Space Center in Houston, Texas. She worked as a liaison between astronauts on the space station and Earth-bound scientists, studying the effects of being in space on the human body. While living in Houston she also earned her pilot's license.

In addition, she studied to become an aquanaut (a person who remains in an underwater shelter for an extended period), traveling to Florida's Aquarius underwater habitat and research station, located near Key Largo about fifty feet below the surface, for NASA Extreme Environment Mission Operations (NEEMO), an astronaut training program. As she explained to Tom Ireland for *Biologist* (Feb. 2016), "NASA got interested in using [Aquarius] as an analogue for space, as it has the small space, small crew, life support systems and all the other psychological aspects and crew dynamics of a space module. We were collecting data for coral research, but also building structures as if we were on a spacewalk."

Meir went on to earn a doctorate in marine biology from the Scripps Institution of Oceanography in San Diego in 2009. She studied the physiology of deep-diving animals that live in extreme environments, such as elephant seals in northern California and emperor penguins in Antarctica. She learned that elephant seals can dive for two hours before needing to come up for air, while emperor penguins need to come up every thirty minutes.

After completing her doctorate, Meir did postdoctoral research at Vancouver's University of British Columbia (UBC). In 2010, Meir raised a dozen bar-headed geese, which can fly three miles high over the Himalayas, from the time they hatched so that they would imprint on her, regarding her as their mother. As she told Ben Guarino for the *Washington Post* (4 Sept. 2019), "It was one of the most amazing things I've ever experienced in my life. I say this jokingly, but there's a little bit of truth to it, too: I was a woman in my mid-30s when I was imprinting these geese . . . so there's a lot going on, with the imprinting of my 12 baby goslings." UBC had a thirty-yard long wind tunnel in which Meir could study the birds' flight. Using improvised masks fitted to the geese's bills so the team could regulate the amount of oxygen they were getting, Meir was able to recreate the low-oxygen conditions of their thousand-mile migrations over the world's tallest mountain range. She and her fellow researchers discovered that the birds lowered their body temperature and slowed their metabolism to survive such flights.

When selected for the NASA mission, Meir was an assistant professor of anesthesia at Harvard Medical School and Harvard-affiliated Massachusetts General Hospital in Boston. That position, which she accepted in 2012, was in part a result of her research with the geese.

ASTRONAUT

Meir was part of the 2009 cohort of astronauts training for a chance to spend time aboard the International Space Station (ISS), which orbits about 250 miles above Earth at about 17,000 miles per hour. Although she was a finalist, she was not chosen as one of the nine people ultimately selected for the ISS.

When the next astronaut class, the twenty-first, formed in 2013, Meir went through the rigorous process again, and, as she told Bayly, "The second time's the charm." Out of 6,300 applicants to the program, four men and four women, including Meir, were selected for NASA's twenty-first astronaut class. It was the first class that had equal gender representation. The ensuing training program included learning to fly a jet and to speak and understand enough Russian to communicate with her Russian counterparts on the ISS. As she told Sarah Kaplan for the *Washington Post* (28 April 2015), "While you're conducting this science and learning along the way, you're also testing your body and your strength."

On September 25, 2019, after six years of training, Meir left Earth in a Russian Soyuz spacecraft that took off from Kazakhstan, bound for the International Space Station. Also in the spacecraft were Russian cosmonaut Oleg Skripochka and the first astronaut in space from the United Arab Emirates, Hazzaa Ali Almansoori. When she arrived for her six-month stint at the ISS, she became the second female crew member, joining Christina Koch and four male crew members.

Speaking to a group of students at Brown University on February 13, 2020, from her perch in space, Meir challenged the group, saying, "It was a decision I had to make to do that—to take the risk and not be afraid to fail again. And because I did that, that's really the only reason why I ended up here today. If you don't try, then of course it's not going to happen."

MAKING HISTORY

Along with Koch, Meir made history by being part of the first all-female spacewalk on October 18, 2019. The announced spacewalk, originally planned for Koch and another woman and scheduled for March 2019, was delayed, because NASA did not have two medium-sized spacesuits. Meir and Koch were the fourteenth and fifteenth women to participate in a spacewalk. All but one of the women who have been on a spacewalk have been from the United States. During the seven-hour and seventeen-minute spacewalk, the women replaced a faulty charger for the lithium ion batteries that distribute solar power to the station. In recognition of that feat, the twenty-five women in the United States Senate introduced a resolution honoring the first all-female spacewalk, which passed unanimously.

In January 2020 the two went on another spacewalk, to complete upgrades to the ISS's power grid. They replaced nickel-hydrogen batteries that had been in place for decades with lithium-ion batteries, which last longer and are more powerful.

The spacewalk, Meir told Christian Davenport and Lateshia Beachum for the *Washington Post* (19 Oct. 2019), "shows all the work that went in for the decades prior—all of the women who worked to get us to where we are today. The nice thing for us is we don't even really think about it on a daily basis. It's just normal. We're part of the team. . . . It's really nice to see how far we have come."

PERSONAL LIFE

Meir holds both United States and Swedish citizenship and speaks Swedish, as well as the Russian she learned as an astronaut. She is the first Swedish woman and the fourth Jewish woman to participate in a space mission. Meir is musical, playing saxophone, flute, and piccolo. Of her dream come true, Meir told Alvin Powell for the *Harvard Gazette* (6 Sept. 2013), "The vision I've always had, the thing I've always wanted, was that feeling of looking back at the Earth, with the entirety of everything you ever knew below you. I can't imagine how that would feel." Meir's six months on the ISS included Thanksgiving, of which she has fond family memories. She told Graham Gillian for the *Portland Press Herald* (26 Nov. 2019), "As I got older and lived in various places, Thanksgiving turned into an even broader extended family. I have adopted families all over the country. So I'll be thinking this year about everyone down on the ground celebrating together."

SUGGESTED READING

Bayly, Julia. "Caribou High School Graduate among Newest NASA Astronauts." *Bangor Daily News*, 18 June 2013, bangordailynews.com/2013/06/17/news/aroostook/caribou-high-school-graduate-among-newest-nasa-astronauts/. Accessed 28 Mar. 2020.

Davenport, Christian, and Lateshia Beachum. "All-Female Spacewalk Makes History for NASA." *The Washington Post*, 19 Oct. 2019, www.washingtonpost.com/technology/2019/10/18/nasa-live-spacewalk-christina-koch-jessica-meir/. Accessed 28 Mar. 2020.

Guarino, Ben. "NASA Astronaut as Mother Goose." *The Washington Post*, 4 Sept. 2019, www.washingtonpost.com/science/2019/09/04/this-astronaut-raised-geese-study-their-hearts-birds-stole-hers/. Accessed 28 Mar. 2020.

Kaplan, Sarah. "Journey to Mars: Meet NASA Astronaut Candidate Jessica Meir." *The Washington Post*, 28 Apr. 2015, www.washingtonpost.com/lifestyle/kidspost/journey-to-mars-jessica-meir/2015/04/28/29d206a0-b11b-11e4-886b-c22184f27c35_story.html. Accessed 28 Mar. 2020.

Meir, Jessica. "One Small Step for a Physiologist." Interview by Tom Ireland. *The Biologist*, Feb. 2016, thebiologist.rsb.org.uk/biologist/162-biologist/biologist-interviews/1451-one-small-step-for-a-physiologist. Accessed 28 Mar. 2020.

———. "An Out of This World Conversation with Astronaut Jessica Meir." Interview. *Scripps Institution of Oceanography*, UC San Diego, 30 Jan. 2020, scripps.ucsd.edu/news/out-world-conversation-astronaut-jessica-meir. Accessed 28 Mar. 2020.

Zraick, Karen. "NASA Astronauts Complete the First All-Female Spacewalk." *The New York Times*, 19 Oct. 2019, www.nytimes.com/2019/10/18/science/space/nasa-female-spacewalk.html. Accessed 28 Mar. 2020.

—Judy Johnson

Photo by Anthony Quintano

Ari Melber

Born: March 31, 1980
Occupation: Attorney and television journalist

Ari Melber, a lawyer by training, became widely known for his various television roles. He served as an NBC News legal analyst, reporting and commenting on stories related to law and justice across all the network's platforms, and was named MSNBC's chief legal correspondent in 2015. He raised his profile further in 2017, when he began hosting *The Beat with Ari Melber*, a weeknight television program on MSNBC featuring reporting, commentary, and in-depth interviews. Additionally, he was frequently called upon to step in as a guest host for shows such as *The Last Word with Lawrence O'Donnell* and *The Rachel Maddow Show*. Indeed, he appeared so frequently in NBC's programming that some observers joked that the "M" in "MSNBC" could stand for "Melber."

Few could joke about Melber's ratings, however. *The Beat* drew 1.8 million viewers in January 2019, the most MSNBC had ever attracted in the six-p.m. timeslot. Online viewership also proved impressive; some thirteen million YouTube watchers clicked on his channel each month in 2019. Praising his "precision wonkiness" and disdain for political "white noise," Alyson Krueger wrote for the *Columbia Journalism Review* (Nov./Dec. 2014): "Melber has disrupted cable news' regular rhythm of political speculation, rants, and breathless coverage with conversations about public policy and his own view of

right and wrong. He approaches journalism as though he were working the courtroom, probing witnesses, circumventing circumventers, and pushing for resolution." As Melber explained to Krueger, "It doesn't seem to me that my ideal role is trying to mimic something that is already out there. I spent so much time practicing law, it would seem that I would try to bring something in . . . to be part of the solution."

EARLY LIFE AND EDUCATION

Melber was born in Seattle, Washington, on March 31, 1980. His mother, Barbara Melber, was a University of Chicago–educated sociologist who taught at the University of Washington and Boston University and worked in the nonprofit sector. His father, Daniel Melber, was an Israeli-born neurologist whose parents had fled Germany for Jerusalem to escape the Nazis. Melber grew up with one older brother, Jonathan.

For a while Melber attended a Jewish Day School, splitting his time between religious and secular studies. When he was in third grade, he wrote, directed, and starred in a play about a major oil company on trial for an oil spill. The production was memorable for props such as an oil-soaked fish that was brandished dramatically in a plastic bag and a Super Soaker water gun wielded by the student playing the bailiff.

At Garfield High School, a public high school in Seattle that counts music icons Jimi Hendrix and Quincy Jones among its alumni, Melber was elected class president and developed a love for rap music and jazz. He specifically recalled purchasing the Fugees' 1996 album *The Score* his freshman year and feeling that a whole new world was opening to him.

Upon graduating Garfield, Melber entered the University of Michigan at Ann Arbor. In 2002 he earned a bachelor's degree in political science.

TRYING TO FORGE A CAREER IN POLITICS

Melber subsequently moved to Washington, DC, finding work as an aide to Senator Maria Cantwell, a Democrat representing Washington State. He quickly became disillusioned by the empty rhetoric and political theater that seemed to characterize Congress, however. Unwilling to fully abandon politics, Melber next joined Senator John Kerry's campaign for the 2004 presidential election. "I felt that at least campaigning with a finite goal and trying to change who would be in the White House could make a big difference," he recalled to Krueger. He was devastated when Kerry lost, admitting later that he cried so hard on the way home from election headquarters that he had to pull his car to the side of the road.

LEGAL CAREER

Following Kerry's defeat, Melber enrolled in Cornell Law School, seeking to address the injustices of the world that way, rather than through politics. He did, however, travel with Barack Obama's 2008 presidential campaign as a *Washington Independent* correspondent while in law school. In January 2010 he published a well-regarded special report for *techPresident. com* titled "Year One of Organizing for America: The Permanent Field Campaign in the Digital Age." The report presented an analysis of the Obama for America Campaign's transition into Organizing for America, an arm of the Democratic National Committee, during Obama's first year as president.

As a law student, Melber was an editor of the *Cornell Journal of Law and Public Policy*. He also interned with the New York County public defenders' office. There he became deeply immersed in the criminal justice system and gained first-hand knowledge of its flaws. He was deeply invested in the cases of his mostly indigent clients, who were typically pressured by administrators to plead guilty to save time, and he found himself getting depressed each day. "I didn't have the emotional grit and toughness and I found it really sad," Melber told Grove. "I felt helpless because of the way the system was set up. I thought I'm not cut out for this."

Upon graduating in 2009, Melber joined the international law firm Cahill Gordon & Reindel, where he worked under renowned First Amendment lawyer Floyd Abrams. Concurrently, he began writing op-eds and commentary for such publications as the *Atlantic*, *Politico*, the *Nation*, and *Reuters*. Executives at MSNBC took notice of his well-reasoned, evenhanded pieces and began asking him to appear on the air.

JOINING MSNBC

In 2013 Melber left the law firm and became a regular on MSNBC's *The Cycle*, an afternoon panel show that also featured conservative journalist Abby Huntsman, music critic Touré, and Democratic strategist Krystal Ball. He also began appearing as a substitute host for vacationing primetime personalities, increasing his visibility considerably. He found the move from arguing cases to working on camera was an interesting one. "In journalism, you have the opportunity to reach so many people with substantive arguments instantly," Melber told Krueger. "Whether they respond or agree or anything happens is an open question, but that immediate access and impact is, to me, extraordinary."

Melber quickly became a staple on MSNBC and other programming under the NBC News umbrella. Named the network's chief legal correspondent in 2015, he won a 2016 Emmy Award for his reporting on the Supreme Court. That honor came even as he admitted to finding it a challenge to discuss breaking decisions quickly and accurately, as the court's cases are always complex and nuanced. (He pointed out that in law school a student may spend days trying to grasp a single case, whereas on television, an analyst has just minutes.) Another of the biggest challenges of his job, Melber noted, was being called upon to cover the FBI and criminal proceedings, because that agency's internal processes are largely kept concealed, with leaks punishable by law. He attempted to face such challenges with optimism. "Anchoring breaking news from the studio can be thrilling," he admitted to Mark Miller for the *Jewish Journal* (23 May 2018), "but is probably the part of the job that requires the most coffee."

THE BEAT WITH ARI MELBER

The launch of Melber's own MSNBC show, *The Beat*, in 2017 helped push his already rising profile to even greater heights. It found great ratings success both on the air and online, setting records for the network. Crucially, many of those tuning in belonged to the 25-to-54 demographic coveted by advertisers. (By contrast, the median ages of CNN, MSNBC, and Fox News viewers were measured at 60, 65, and 65, respectively, in 2018.) Reviewers have credited Melber's success to his training as a lawyer, his political background, his fairness and integrity, and his ability to connect intellectually and emotionally with viewers. His widely respected status was reflected in his interviews with such politically disparate subjects as former attorney general Eric Holder; Supreme Court Justice Stephen Breyer; senators Kamala Harris, Ted Cruz and Rand Paul; and Joe Arpaio, the controversial former sheriff of Maricopa County, Arizona.

Indeed, Melber soon became known for attracting a wide variety of high-profile guests, including many supporters of Donald Trump, the real-estate tycoon and reality television personality who unexpectedly became the Republican presidential nominee and then won the presidency in 2016. This was significant as many conservatives tended to shun MSNBC (and other news outlets they considered overtly liberal) for the politically right-leaning Fox News. Melber sought to correct this imbalance through an even-handed approach. "We want everyone who's credible and can bring something to the table to be on," he explained to Grove. "They're not there just because they want to talk to me—they could do that off-air. They're there because they think this forum is fair enough that they can get their views out." At the same time, Melber acknowledged that President Trump's frequent hiring and firing of high-level staffers, his continual tweeting, and his chaotic style of governing did pose challenges for anyone covering him.

Melber also stood out for his frequent evocation of pop culture references, perhaps most notably from rap and hip-hop music. "Law and politics are often overly complicated because there are people that don't want the rest of us to know what's going on," he asserted to Miller. "It always rankled me—in law school and the legal profession—when lawyers would speak to each other in their own exclusive language. My job is to be accurate and clear. I'll reach for just about any reference or analogy that might help. That includes rap lyrics, which have great wisdom, especially about the criminal justice process."

PERSONAL LIFE

Melber lives in the New York City borough of Brooklyn. He was married to culture reporter Drew Grant for three years, from 2014 to 2017.

SUGGESTED READING

Berg, Madeline. "Mixing Rap and Politics, MSNBC's Ari Melber Produces a Hit." *Forbes.* 16 Jan. 2018, www.forbes.com/sites/maddieberg/2018/01/16/mixing-rap-and-politics-msnbcs-ari-melber-produces-a-hit/#333655ec6b7f. Accessed 23 Feb. 2020.

Grove, Lloyd. "Even Trump's Personal Attorney Jay Sekulow Likes MSNBC's Ari Melber." *The Daily Beast,* 26 Apr. 2019, www.thedailybeast.com/ari-melbers-message-to-trump-fans-be-like-jay-sekulow-and-come-on-my-msnbc-show. Accessed 23 Feb. 2020.

Hill, Jarrett. "Charlamagne tha God, Ari Melber Dish on Hip-Hop and Politics." *The Hollywood Reporter,* 28 July 2017, www.hollywoodreporter.com/news/charlamagne-tha-god-ari-melber-dish-hip-hop-politics-1025173. Accessed 23 Feb. 2020.

Krueger, Alyson. "Is Ari Melber the Future of Cable-News Anchors?" *Columbia Journalism Review,* Nov./Dec. 2014, archives.cjr.org/feature/mission-driven.php. Accessed 23 Feb. 2020.

Miller, Mark. "Marking the Beat with Ari Melber." *Jewish Journal,* 23 May 2018, jewishjournal.com/culture/just-asking/234433/marking-beat-ari-melber/. Accessed 23 Feb. 2020.

Thorp, Charles. "Why MSNBC's Ari Melber Embraces Carbs—and Cinnamon Rolls." *Men's Journal,* 2020, www.mensjournal.com/entertainment/why-msnbcs-ari-melber-embraces-carbs-and-cinnamon-rolls/. Accessed 23 Feb. 2020.

—*Mari Rich*

Stipe Miocic

Date of birth: August 19, 1982
Occupation: MMA fighter

Photo by Arturo Pardavila via Wikimedia Commons

In the world of mixed martial arts (MMA), few competitors stand out as being as formidable as Stipe Miocic. In 2016, he became the heavyweight champion of the Ultimate Fighting Championship (UFC), which is the premier MMA organization in the United States. After his MMA debut in 2010, Miocic continuously impressed fans of the sport. By 2019, he had amassed a record of nineteen wins and three losses by combining his incredible wrestling skills with his lightning-quick striking capabilities, which were honed during his time as a Golden Gloves amateur boxing competitor. His speed and power enabled him to beat his UFC opponents in the first round nine times. In 2018, Miocic beat the league record for the most consecutive successful heavyweight title defenses, having defended his title three times. As Justin Barrasso pointed out in *Sports Illustrated* (17 Aug. 2019): "Miocic is now the most accomplished heavyweight in UFC history." He subsequently lost the title to Daniel Cormier in July 2018, before winning it back in August 2019. The third fight between Miocic and Cormier is scheduled for August 15, 2020.

EARLY LIFE AND EDUCATION

Stipe Miocic was born in Independence, Ohio, on August 19, 1982, to Kathy and Bojan Miocic. His parents, immigrants from Croatia, separated before his first birthday. During much of his early childhood, he lived with his mother and his grandparents in Euclid, Ohio. His mother worked for two decades at Penske Logistics, then worked as a paralegal at the Elk and Elk

Company law firm. In about 1993, his mother had another son, Jonathan, with her partner, Steve Bancsi. Although there is an eleven-year age difference between the brothers, they are exceedingly close, so much so that Stipe was initially inspired to become a kindergarten teacher because of the time he spent with Jonathan.

Throughout his childhood, Stipe developed a love of sports, which was encouraged by his mother. She also encouraged him to have a strong work ethic. "My mom says, 'You work hard, you get your opportunity,'" Miocic said to Jason Brill for *Cleveland Magazine* (7 Sept. 2016). "She ingrained it in my head." While attending North High School, Miocic excelled at baseball, wrestling, and football. He later competed in baseball and wrestling at Cleveland State University, where he majored in marketing and communications. As an undergraduate, he decided to quit wrestling to focus on baseball, in which he played third base. His baseball success led him to transfer to Trevecca Nazarene University in the fall of 2004, in the hopes of attracting major league scouts. As he helped his college team win the TranSouth Athletic Conference (TSAC), scouts came from the San Diego Padres, the Cincinnati Reds, and the Pittsburgh Pirates, but he received no offers.

Without an athletic outlet, Miocic began to realize that his communications degree was not the direction he wanted to go in. "I didn't want to sit behind a desk," Miocic explained to Brill. "A bunch of my buddies are firemen and I like to help people, so I did that." According to different sources, he worked as a bartender and at a gym called Elite Fitness while he was taking classes to become a firefighter paramedic at Cuyahoga Community College.

MIXED MARTIAL ARTS CAREER

While working at Elite Fitness, one of the gym's owners asked Miocic to train with Dan Bobish, a UFC fighter. "I was helping a guy train for a fight and never left the gym," Miocic recalled for his official UFC fighter profile on UFC. It was during one of those training sessions that Strong Style owner Marcus Marinelli, who would become Miocic's coach and friend, saw his raw potential as an MMA fighter. He began training in earnest as a fighter in 2005, with Marinelli suggesting that he take up amateur boxing to improve his striking ability, a skill that needed to be added to his already formidable wrestling skills. Miocic did so, and ultimately moved up the ranks to compete in a national Golden Gloves tournament in 2009. "Stipe had been boxing for six or seven months and he was beating guys with like 150 or 200 amateur fights," Marinelli told Brill.

Miocic began his MMA career with North American Allied Fight Series, which serves as a kind of MMA minor league for the UFC. After besting his first opponent with a knockout punch seventeen seconds into the first round, Miocic went on to win his next five bouts. In mid-2011, he signed with the UFC and made his debut against Joey Beltran on October 8, 2011. He won that fight by unanimous decision in the third round.

He returned to the octagon—the eight-sided cage where UFC athletes battle—on February 15, 2012, in a fight with Phil De Fries. There he secured his first knockout, in the first round, earning him a Knockout of the Night award. His next fight, against Shane Del Rosario, was held on May 26, 2012, and again ended with Miocic knocking out his opponent, this time in the second round. The first loss of his professional career came at the end of that year, on September 29, at the hands of Stefan Struve, but the match earned both men a Fight of the Night award.

As 2013 began, Miocic came back from his defeat determined to beat his opponents. He bested Roy Nelson in a third-round unanimous decision on June 15, and earned another unanimous decision on January 25, 2014, against Gabriel Gonzaga. His next bout, on May 31, 2014, against Fabio Maldonado earned him a Performance of the Night award when he scored a win via technical knockout (TKO).

Miocic's next loss came on December 13, 2014, at the hands of Junior Dos Santos, who won a unanimous decision in the fifth round. He restarted a winning streak on May 9, 2015, however, by knocking out Mark Hunt in the fifth round. During this battle Miocic set a record for the most strikes landed in a single UFC bout and for the widest strike margin against an opponent with 361–48. He then fought Andrei Arlovski on January 2, 2016, beating him in the first round by knockout and earning the Performance of the Night award.

Miocic's phenomenal success up until that point allowed him to face Fabricio Werdum for the UFC Heavyweight Championship on May 14, 2016. He won the championship by devastating Werdum with a short right hook in the first round, knocking him out and earning a Performance of the Night award. Of winning the title, Miocic said, as quoted by Brill, "All I care about is my city. I brought it home to them. That was my goal. I did what I said I was going to do." On September 10, 2016, he put his brand-new championship up against Alastair Overeem, scoring a first round knockout and earning the Fight of the Night award. His second title defense was a rematch against Dos Santos, on May 13, 2017. Unlike their previous bout, Miocic came out on top, besting Dos Santos in the first round and earning a Performance of the Night. He then faced Francis Ngannou on January 20,

2018, during which Miocic kept his title via unanimous decision in the fifth round. The win made Miocic the first person to successfully defend a heavyweight title three consecutive times.

RIVALRY WITH DANIEL CORMIER

Miocic's greatest challenge has come in the form of Daniel Cormier, a former Olympic wrestler who became the first simultaneous heavyweight and light heavyweight world champion in UFC history. During their first bout, held on July 7, 2018, Cormier made quick work of the champion, scoring a knockout in the very first round. With the second bout, held on August 17, 2019, Miocic wore down the new champion over the course of four rounds, not only winning back the belt by knockout but also securing a Performance of the Night award. Miocic's regaining of the title impressed devoted fans of the sport. "Eras differ but there's no denying Miocic's reign as a two-time champion," Mark Podolski noted for the *News-Herald* (11 June 2020). "He's the only heavyweight in the history of the sport to defend the belt three straight times."

Following that fight, Cormier was eager for a rematch, but Miocic was unable to give him one because he had to recover from surgery to repair a torn retina. In addition, his job as a firefighter paramedic required him to be on the front lines during the coronavirus (COVID-19) pandemic, which began in China in December 2019 and spread around the world throughout 2020. Miocic also wanted to resume full-time training before the fight, something that he was unable to do under the pandemic restrictions that shuttered many businesses and forced people to maintain social distancing. The third match in the Miocic-Cormier trilogy is scheduled to take place on August 15, 2020.

On the third bout between Miocic and Cormier, Brett Okamoto, a commentator on *ESPN* (10 June 2020), declared, "Miocic is the only man to ever defend the title three consecutive times. Daniel Cormier has lost to two men in his entire career. Just two—Miocic and the greatest fighter of all time, Jon Jones." Okamoto concluded, "A belt is on the line in this one, but more important, the winner will be able to call himself the best heavyweight of his era."

PERSONAL LIFE

Miocic works as a part-time firefighter paramedic in Oakwood and Valley View, Ohio, and plans to work full-time when he retires from MMA competition. Miocic married Ryan Marie Carney in 2016; the couple welcomed a daughter in 2018.

SUGGESTED READING

Barrasso, Justin. "Daniel Cormier Champing at the Bit to Fight Stipe Miocic for a Third Time." *Sports Illustrated*, 7 May 2020, www.si.com/mma/2020/05/07/ufc-daniel-cormier-stipe-miocic-fight-contract. Accessed 15 June 2020.

———. "UFC 241: Stipe Miocic Knocks Out Daniel Cormier to Regain Heavyweight Title." *Sports Illustrated*, 17 Aug. 2019, www.si.com/mma/2019/08/18/ufc-241-cormier-miocic-updates-analysis. Accessed 16 June 2020.

Brill, Jason. "King of the Cage." *Cleveland Magazine*, 7 Sept. 2016, clevelandmagazine.com/in-the-cle/the-read/articles/the-king-of-the-cage. Accessed 15 June 2020.

Helwani, Ariel, et al. "Stipe Miocic vs. Daniel Cormier 3—Retirement, Jon Jones or Francis Ngannou for Winner?" *ESPN*, 10 June 2020, www.espn.com/mma/ufc/story/_/id/29288012/stipe-miocic-vs-daniel-cormier-3-retirement-jon-jones-francis-ngannou-winner. Accessed 16 June 2020.

Podolski, Mark. "Everything on the Line for Stipe Miocic in Trilogy Fight vs. Daniel Cormier." *News-Herald*, 11 June 2020, www.news-herald.com/sports/stipe-miocic/everything-on-the-line-for-stipe-miocic-in-trilogy-fight-vs-daniel-cormier/article_58b183f0-ab5d-11ea-a36e-7360e6e1b8e6.html. Accessed 15 June 2020.

"Stipe Miocic." *ESPN*, www.espn.com/mma/fighter/_/id/2504951/stipe-miocic. Accessed 16 June 2020.

"Stipe Miocic—Official UFC Fighter Profile." *UFC*, media.ufc.com/fighter/stipe-miocic. Accessed 15 June 2020.

—*Christopher Mari*

Mikhail Mishustin

Born: March 3, 1966
Occupation: Politician

On January 15, 2020, Russian president Vladimir Putin proposed changes to the country's constitution that could allow him to retain power long past 2024, when his current, and ostensibly final, term was set to expire. Many Kremlin watchers predicted that Putin would join the newly empowered State Council (comprised of legislative and federal district leaders and chaired by the president) in 2024, allowing him to wield considerable influence over his successor. In response, Prime Minister Dmitri Medvedev and his entire cabinet resigned within hours of the president's speech, and Putin appointed a new prime minister, Mikhail Mishustin. "When Russians woke up on Wednesday morning, most had likely never heard of Mikhail Mishustin, the head of the country's tax service. But by the time

Photo by the Government of Russia (premier.gov.ru) via Wikimedia Commons

they went to bed that night, Mishustin had been named as Russia's new prime minister," Reid Standish and Amy MacKinnon wrote for *Foreign Policy* (16 Jan. 2020).

A career bureaucrat, Mishustin had kept an exceptionally low profile; he did not profess an allegiance to a specific political party and exhibited no outward ambitions to gain political power. Observers thus hypothesized that Putin, who had held sway over Russia for two decades, installed the low-key taxman in a calculated attempt to ensure that he would have no strong rival in 2024. "The president is laying the groundwork as he prepares for a transition in 2024 that analysts say will likely see him abandon the presidency but remain Russia's dominant politician in a beefed-up role as Russia's prime minister or in the government's State Council instead," Andrew Roth explained for the *Guardian* (15 Jan. 2020). "The 67-year-old has, in effect, ruled Russia since 2000, making him the longest-serving leader since Stalin, and what he plans to do in 2024 remains the most important political question in the country."

EARLY LIFE AND EDUCATION
According to his official biography on the Russian government website, Mikhail Mishustin was born on March 3, 1966, in Moscow. The biography did not give further information about his early years or his parents.

Mishustin attended the Stankin Moscow Machine-Instrument Institute, a leading engineering school later known as Stankin Moscow State Technological University, graduating in 1989 with a degree in computer-aided design.

After several years in the working world, Mishustin entered the Plekhanov Russian University of Economics, a large and highly regarded institution in Moscow, where in 2003 he earned a PhD in economics with a thesis on the topic of state fiscal administration in Russia. In 2010, he earned a second doctoral degree in economics from the Academy of National Economy under the Government of the Russian Federation. (The school was later renamed the Russian Presidential Academy of National Economy and Public Administration.)

TECH CAREER
In 1992, shortly after the dissolution of the Soviet Union (USSR), Mishustin began working at the International Computer Club, a nonprofit group that had been founded by a group of scientists and engineers during perestroika—the period of economic and political reform that took place in the former USSR under Mikhail Gorbachev in the 1980s. Among the organization's activities was publishing a journal and staging exhibitions of new high-tech products, and its goal was to introduce Western tech firms to the Russian market. Mishustin initially worked as head of the International Computer Club's testing facility, where he reviewed software projects and published reports in the group's journal, and in the mid-1990s he was elevated to the post of deputy director.

GOVERNMENT SERVICE
In 1998, Mishustin accepted a post as the deputy head of the state tax service under Boris Fyodorov. In that capacity, he took charge of the agency's IT systems and helped modernize its accounting and revenue-monitoring processes. The following year, the office was reorganized as the ministry of taxes and revenues, and Mishustin was named a deputy minister. He continued to modernize, and it was thanks to his efforts that digital signatures and other such innovations were implemented.

In 2004, Mishustin was placed in charge of the federal agency for real estate cadastre, housed within the ministry of economic development. A cadastre, compiled for tax purposes, is a record of a property's boundaries, value, and ownership. In his new role, Mishustin launched large-scale tech systems and developed a unified system for real-estate accounting by the government. He took on his next public role in 2006, when he was named head of the newly created federal agency for the management of special economic zones. (The zones were devoted to such sectors as heavy industry, tourism, and electronics and were meant to encourage development and investment.)

Mishustin left government service from 2008 to 2010 to become president of the UFG Group, whose cofounder was former finance minister Boris Fyodorov, under whom Mishustin had worked at the Federal Tax Service. In the spring of 2010 Mishustin accepted a post as head of the Federal Tax Service. He is widely credited for transforming the service into one of the most technologically advanced agencies of the Russian government. His aim, as he has explained during rare interviews, was to bring service entirely online, so that citizens could simply log into their accounts, see what they owe, and pay their bills seamlessly. He also saw online technology as a way to fight corruption, as individual taxpayers would no longer have direct contact with potentially bribable officials.

Although he was not in the limelight, Mishustin was media savvy. In addition to creating new ads and slogans for the tax service, under his direction, the tax service launched a 2012 television special, hosted by journalist Larisa Katysheva, that aimed to make Russia's tax code more accessible to the public. The following year he arranged for cosmonaut Pavel Vinogradov to make a streaming video of himself paying taxes online while in orbit, which set a Guinness World Record for highest altitude financial transaction.

In 2018, Mishustin claimed that the digital technologies he spearheaded had resulted in greatly increased revenue for the state: thanks to new systems for collecting value-added taxes (VAT), taxes on the unemployed, and other previously hard-to-enforce taxes, revenue grew almost 70 percent within his first five years as head of the tax service—and that was during a period when Russia's gross domestic product (GDP) rose very little.

BECOMING PRIME MINISTER

To understand why Putin chose Mishustin to be prime minister, it is helpful to understand Putin's role over the past two decades as Russia's foremost political figure and how Mishustin might help Putin hold onto power. In December 1999, President Boris Yeltsin resigned and named Putin, then acting prime minister, to serve as acting president. Putin won his first election to the presidency in 2000, when he was popular, and the Russian economy was doing well. After that point, he essentially circumvented limits on his power even as the economy and his popularity waned. He served two four-year terms as president, as allowed by Russia's constitution at the time. He then served four years as prime minister, before winning reelection as president with 60 percent of the vote in 2012, when the constitution was amended to extend presidential terms to six years. In the 2018 presidential election, he won reelection by a landslide, yet again.

When Mishustin was put forth as Prime Minister Medvedev's replacement, observers guessed that Putin saw the successful tax expert as someone with great bureaucratic ability but little desire to erode Putin's hold on the country. "Mishustin remains an inoffensive choice whom Putin is relying on to deliver economic progress and focus on the day-to-day work of turning the president's proclamations into reality," Standish and MacKinnon wrote. "Through his low profile and experience with the country's vast and cumbersome bureaucracy, Mishustin is now positioned to enact unfulfilled government policies and help quell socioeconomic discontent as Putin's slow-motion power transfer winds toward 2024."

Mishustin was confirmed by the State Duma, the lower house of Russia's Federal Assembly, with 383 out of 424 votes in favor, no votes against, and 41 abstentions. He assumed his new post on January 16, 2020. After entering office, he won some praise in the media for bringing back a number of former ministers, including Foreign Minister Sergei Lavrov and Defense Minister Sergei Shoigu, along with some new faces, resulting in a balance of experience and fresh perspective.

FINANCIAL QUESTIONS AND HEALTH CRISES

As soon as Mishustin entered the glare of public scrutiny, questions arose about his personal finances. While investigating how it was possible for Mishustin's wife, Vladlena Mishustina, to have earned 789 million rubles ($12.5 million) over the preceding nine-year period, reporters discovered that he had transferred his personal wealth to her before entering public service again in 2010. Several independent investigations were also launched into the Mishustins' real estate holdings, which included a sprawling mansion and a luxury Moscow apartment. Most eventually accepted that the family had made several lucrative, but legal, investments.

On April 30, 2020, Russia reported a record 7,099 cases of COVID-19. Mishustin was diagnosed with COVID-19 that same day and sent to the hospital to isolate. Although First Deputy Prime Minister Andrey Belousov stepped in, Mishustin participated in occasional governmental meetings via videoconferencing. He recuperated and returned to work by the middle of May.

PERSONAL LIFE AND HONORS

Mishustin and his wife have three sons. He holds Russia's Order of Honour (2012) and Order for Service to the Fatherland (2015), and he is known among his colleagues for his attention to detail and painstaking preparation for any public appearance. He is an avid hockey fan who plays in Putin's own Night Hockey League and sits on the board of Russia's Ice Hockey Federation. His other passion is music, particularly the piano, and he has composed a song for well-known Russian singer Grigory Leps.

SUGGESTED READING

Esfandiari, Sahar. "Everything We Know about Russia's New PM Mikhail Mishustin, the Hockey-Playing Former Tax Official Who Is a Key Part of Putin's Plan to Tighten His Grip on Power." *Business Insider*, 17 Jan. 2020, www.businessinsider.com/russia-prime-minister-mikhail-mishustin-everything-we-know-2020-1. Accessed 18 July 2020.

Ilyushina, Mary, and Rob Picheta. "Russian Prime Minister Tests Positive for Covid-19." *CNN*, 30 Apr. 2020, www.cnn.com/2020/04/30/europe/mikhail-mishustin-russia-pm-coronavirus-positive-intl/index.html. Accessed 18 July 2020.

Klomegah, Kester Kenn. "Meet Mikhail Mishustin, Russia's New Prime Minister." *Eurasia Review*, 17 Jan. 2020, www.eurasiareview.com/17012020-meet-mikhail-mishustin-russias-new-prime-minister-oped/. Accessed 18 July 2020.

"New Russian PM Transferred His Wealth to Wife—Kommersant." *The Moscow Times*, 20 Jan. 2020, www.themoscowtimes.com/2020/01/20/new-russian-pm-transferred-earnings-to-wife-kommersant-a68969. Accessed 18 July 2020.

Roth, Andrew. "Russian Government Quits as Putin Plans to Stay in Power Past 2024." *The Guardian*, 15 Jan. 2020, www.theguardian.com/world/2020/jan/15/putin-calls-for-constitution-changes-that-would-weaken-successor. Accessed 18 July 2020.

Rustamova, Farida. "Russia's PR Minister Mikhail Mishustin Is Obsessed with His Image Online and in the Media. Here's How This Fixation Shapes His Cabinet." *Meduza*, 3 June 2020, meduza.io/en/feature/2020/06/03/russia-s-pr-minister. Accessed 18 July 2020.

Standish, Reid, and Amy MacKinnon. "Who Is Russia's New Prime Minister?" *Foreign Policy*, 16 Jan. 2020, foreignpolicy.com/2020/01/16/who-is-russias-new-prime-minister-mikhail-mishustin/. Accessed 18 July 2020.

—*Mari Rich*

Richard Mofe-Damijo

Born: July 6, 1961
Occupation: Actor

Though little known in the West, Richard Mofe-Damijo rose to become one of the biggest stars of Nigeria's film industry, popularly known as Nollywood. Despite only getting its start in the 1990s, by 2009 Nollywood was the second-largest film industry in the world in terms of output, after India's Bollywood. Its films are exported to many other countries. Yet while many Nollywood stars have appeared in well over one hundred films, Mofe-Damijo—often called RMD by his fans—focused on quality over quantity. "During the prolific period, let me not say crazy period of Nollywood, I didn't jump on any movie that came my way," he told Odion Okonofua for the Nigerian online news platform *Pulse* (27 Aug. 2020). "I have always tried to be selective of the kind of movies I did." In an interview with Ferdinand Ekechukwu for *This Day* (27 Oct. 2018), he elaborated, "I have probably turned down 20 times more roles than I have accepted. I'm not afraid to say that."

This strategy worked well for Mofe-Damijo. In recognition of his great contributions to the arts, the governor of his native Delta state appointed him as a special adviser of culture and tourism in 2008. He then became the commissioner of culture and tourism for the state in 2009, remaining in that role until 2015. Widely respected as a Nollywood veteran, Mofe-Damijo was honored by the Africa Movie Academy Awards with a lifetime achievement award in 2016. Not content to rest on his laurels, he continued to star in a variety of films and television shows in the following years.

EARLY LIFE AND EDUCATION

Richard Mofe-Damijo was born on July 6, 1961, in Warri, Nigeria. His mother was a trader and his father worked for the Nigerian Ports Authority. His father had multiple wives, and Mofe-Damijo grew up with sixteen half-sisters.

Mofe-Damijo had an early interest in acting, discovering his love for the art while playing

Photo by the Government of Russia (premier.gov.ru) via Wikimedia Commons

make-believe as a child. He joined his school drama club in secondary school and went on to study theater arts at the University of Benin, where he was surprised to be offered the lead role in the first production he auditioned for. While still an undergraduate he was cast in the lead role in the made-for-television film *Echoes of Wrath*, which won the Nigerian Television Authority National Annual Drama Competition. Mofe-Damijo graduated with a Bachelor of Arts degree in 1983.

Before fully entering the entertainment industry Mofe-Damijo worked as a journalist for several years, writing for a number of publications and producing Nigeria's first all-gloss men's magazine, *Mister*. As his acting career began to take off, in 1997 Mofe-Damijo enrolled in the University of Lagos to study law, graduating in 2004. He was called to the bar the following year. Explaining to Kemi Ajumobi for *Business Day* (4 Mar. 2016) why he decided to get a second degree in a very different area from his first, he said, "When you become a lawyer, a new world opens up to you; I began to see the world from different angles."

RISE TO FAME

Mofe-Damijo's first professional role after graduating from university was on the soap opera *Ripples* in the late 1980s. His career then received a significant boost when he was cast in the popular soap opera *Checkmate* (1991–94) as the villain Segun Kadiri. He had his first film role, in the drama *Violated*, in 1995. He appeared in its sequel the following year. Not content to merely appear in front of the camera, Mofe-Damijo soon tried his hand at screenwriting, writing and producing the 1997 film *Out of Bounds*. Other significant early films included *Hostages* (1997), *Diamond Ring* (1998), and *Freedom* (1999).

As Nollywood entered the "prolific period" that Mofe-Damijo spoke of in his interview with Okonofua, the actor's career picked up steam; he was soon starring in multiple films each year. In his busiest year, 2004, he appeared in over thirty films, with lead roles in thirteen of them. One of the films he starred in that year, *The Mayors*, went on to win five awards at the first African Movie Academy Awards in 2005, including Best Actor in a Leading Role for Mofe-Damijo. Other works released in 2004 included *I Want Your Wife*, *Deadly Desire*, and *Critical Assignment*, with many spawning sequels. The following year saw him appear in many more roles, including *Darkest Night* and *Behind Closed Doors*.

POLITICAL CAREER

By 2008 Mofe-Damijo was firmly established as one of Nollywood's biggest stars. It was, therefore, a surprising move when he put his acting career on hiatus to serve as a special adviser to the governor of Nigeria's Delta state. He was adamant, however, that despite this new position, he was still an actor first and foremost. "I'm going to be doing a lot of local work [in Delta state] to build the industry here, so there's really no leaving the art," he told Funmi Johnson for the *Nigerian Voice* (24 Feb. 2008). "I am going to teach, I am going to coach and I'm going to inspire, so I'm still involved in acting one way or the other." To maintain some involvement with acting during this time, he gave lectures at the Film and Broadcast Academy in Ozoro.

During his tenure as special adviser and subsequently commissioner of culture and tourism, Mofe-Damijo oversaw the opening of Delta Leisure Resorts, consisting of a theme park and water park in Warri and an animal reserve and wildlife park in Asaba. Speaking to Sam Umukoro for *Africa Interviews*, he called this project his "biggest contribution to the tourism industry." The region also saw increased use as a movie and television filming location while Mofe-Damijo was commissioner.

Despite these accomplishments, Mofe-Damijo found that there were frustrating limitations on what he was able to do. "No matter how good the development programme is, when a new government comes in, there is the possibility of a change or complete overhaul sometimes to the detriment of the people they are supposed to be serving," he told Ajumobi. "The challenge I found is that democracy is slow."

RETURN TO ACTING

Mofe-Damijo returned to television in 2011, appearing on the primetime soap *Tinsel*. In 2012, he received a special recognition at the Best of Nollywood Awards. He began appearing in films again in 2014, performing in the crime drama *To Rise Again* and the comedy *30 Days in Atlanta* that year. *30 Days in Atlanta* was the top-grossing Nigerian film of 2014.

When his tenure as a state commissioner ended in 2015, Mofe-Damijo returned to acting full time. That year he appeared in the film *Oloibiri*, which explores the impact of the oil industry's arrival in Nigeria on the titular small village in Bayelsa state. Mofe-Damijo played Gunpowder, a disillusioned local who eventually takes up arms against the oil companies to defend his people. The role was a personal one for Mofe-Damijo, whose home region of Warri was itself negatively affected by the oil industry. "I am a very angry young man in terms of some of the things that I think are wrong with our system and that sort of fuels the angst in the character," he told *cityVoice* (4 May 2015). Though the film does not portray the character in an unambiguously positive light, Mofe-Damijo told *TV Continental* (25 Oct. 2016), "I didn't consider my part in the movie evil, I considered him the modern day Robinhood." *Oloibiri* was screened at the 2015 Cannes Film Festival. It won the Best

Movie West Africa award at the Africa Magic Viewers Choice Awards in 2017 and had a limited theatrical release in the United States that year.

In 2016, Mofe-Damijo starred in the hit television series *Hush*, a drama described as a "Nigerian telenovela" taking inspiration from Latin American soap operas. Mofe-Damijo's character, Bem, is a phenomenally successful fashion designer who marries a powerful politician, Arinola (Thelma Okoduwa). Both have secrets and powerful enemies, and their marriage sets off a chain of intrigue. The show ran for two seasons and received significant social media buzz during its run.

Following his turn in *Oloibiri* Mofe-Damijo appeared, albeit in secondary roles, in a string of highly successful films. He played the father of the groom in the romantic comedy *The Wedding Party* (2016), which went on to become Nigeria's top-grossing film of all time. It was followed a year later by a sequel, *The Wedding Party 2*, which joined its predecessor in the top ten, becoming the second highest-grossing Nigerian film. In 2018, Mofe-Damijo appeared in *Chief Daddy*, a family dramedy that became the third highest-grossing Nigerian film.

Mofe-Damijo produced his first television series, *The Mr. X Family Show*, in 2018. He also starred in it as a single father trying to balance running a successful business with caring for his three children. This role reunited him with Ego Boyo, with whom he had costarred in *Checkmate* and *Violated*. That year, he also won his second Africa Movie Academy Award for Best Actor in a Leading Role for his performance in the film *Crossroads* (2018). Discussing with Ajumobi his sustained success after decades in the business, Mofe-Damijo said, "For some people, after the first hit, they tend to take their audience for granted. I never take my audience for granted."

PERSONAL LIFE

Richard Mofe-Damijo was married to the journalist May Ellen-Ezekiel, who died in 1996. They had one son. In 2000 he married television personality Jumobi Adegbesan, with whom he had two sons and two daughters. In his spare time, he enjoys traveling and writing poetry.

Mofe-Damijo owned the PR company White Water Limited and the production company RMD Productions Limited. In 2018, he became a brand ambassador for the real estate company Landlagos, which works to provide affordable housing in Lagos, Nigeria's largest city.

SUGGESTED READING

Ajumobi, Kemi. "Richard Mofe-Damijo . . . Still the King of the Screen." *Business Day*, 4 Mar. 2016, businessday.ng/personality/article/richard-mofe-damijo-still-the-king-of-the-screen. Accessed 8 Sept. 2020.

Ekechukwu, Ferdinand. "For RMD, It's Good News from Kigali." *This Day*, 27 Oct. 2018, www.thisdaylive.com/index.php/2018/10/27/for-rmd-its-good-news-from-kigali/. Accessed 8 Sept. 2020.

"The Film 'Oloibiri' Would Shed Light on Our Problems in Niger Delta—RMD." *TV Continental*, 25 Oct. 2016, tvcontinental.tv/2016/10/25/film-oloibiri-shed-light-problems-niger-delta-rmd. Accessed 8 Sept. 2020.

Mofe-Damijo, Richard. Interview by Sam Umukoro. *Africa Interviews*, www.africainterviews.com/richard-mofe-damijo. Accessed 8 Sept. 2020.

———. "Special Adviser or Not, I'm Still an Actor—RMD." Interview by Funmi Johnson. *The Nigerian Voice*, 24 Feb. 2008, www.thenigerianvoice.com/amp/movie/3968/special-adviser-or-not-im-still-an-actor-rmd.html. Accessed 8 Sept. 2020.

Okonofua, Odion. "Know Your Celebrities: 7 Things You Didn't Know about Veteran Actor Richard Mofe Damijo." *Pulse*, 27 Aug. 2020, www.pulse.ng/entertainment/celebrities/7-interesting-facts-you-didnt-know-about-richard-mofe-damijo/vnqxdqk. Accessed 8 Sept. 2020.

"Playing Gunpowder in Oloibiri Was a Piece of Cake—RMD." *cityVoice*, 4 May 2015, cityvoiceng.com/playing-gunpowder-in-oloibiri-was-a-piece-of-cake-rmd. Accessed 8 Sept. 2020.

SELECTED WORKS

Violated, 1995; *Out of Bounds*, 1997; *The Mayors*, 2004; *Darkest Night*, 2005; *30 Days in Atlanta*, 2014; *Oloibiri*, 2015; *The Wedding Party*, 2016; *The Wedding Party 2*, 2017; *Chief Daddy*, 2018; *Crossroads*, 2018

—*Emma Joyce*

Kento Momota

Date of birth: September 1, 1994
Occupation: Badminton player

In April 2016, Kento Momota's promising badminton career came to an abrupt halt. A skilled athlete who had won a number of Badminton World Federation (BWF) titles by then, Momota was favored to represent Japan in the upcoming Summer Olympics in Rio de Janeiro, Brazil, but charges of illegal gambling derailed those plans. To avert a possible prison sentence, he agreed to a one-year ban from competing in badminton that cost him the chance to represent his country abroad and sank his player ranking. "That one-year in the wilderness was the darkest period of my life, and I really

Photo by Shi Tang/Getty Images

missed the competition," he recalled to Shirish Nadkarni for *Firstpost* (9 July 2018). "But I resolved to keep practising and working out to stay fit; vowed that I would come back even stronger than before."

Indeed, Momota's performance following his return to competition in mid-2017 aptly demonstrated the success of that strategy. After rebuilding his ranking over the course of 2017, he re-entered the highest level of BWF play in 2018, winning several tournaments and claiming his first BWF World Championships title. His success throughout 2019, which included a second consecutive World Championships victory, established him as a likely 2020 Olympic contender and cemented his place within a wave of young athletes bringing their energy and skills to the sport of badminton. "A new generation of players is taking over and I am pleased to be part of it," he told the Agence France-Presse (AFP) for an article published in *Yahoo! Sports* (28 Apr. 2019).

EARLY LIFE AND JUNIOR CAREER

Kento Momota was born on September 1, 1994. Growing up in Mitoyo, Kagawa Prefecture, he first learned the sport of badminton while in first grade. "My [older] sister played it and before realizing I was doing the same," Momota recalled to Matthew Hernon for *Tokyo Weekender* (Oct. 2019). "In the sixth grade, I participated in the All Japan Elementary School Championships. If I hadn't won that I would have switched to baseball, but I did win so decided to carry on. At junior high school, I began to think that I could have a talent for badminton."

As Momota's performance in badminton competitions soon demonstrated, he did, in fact, have a talent for the sport. He continued to hone his abilities as a teenager through training and appearances in various junior-level Badminton World Federation (BWF) events. His early international appearances included competitions such as the Korea International Challenge 2009 and the Osaka International Challenge 2010. In April 2010 Momota competed in his first BWF World Junior Championships, where he progressed past the group stage but was subsequently defeated. He returned to that event the following year and claimed a bronze medal in the men's singles division. He also tied for third at the Badminton Asia Youth Under 19 Championships in 2011, beginning a long string of successes on the regional level.

INTERNATIONAL CONTENDER

The year 2012 was in many ways a breakthrough year for Momota, who claimed gold medals at both the under-19 and world junior championships. His participation in BWF's lower-level Grand Prix and World Superseries tournaments gave him valuable experience that would benefit him in the years to come. After his junior eligibility ended, Momota committed to playing in a wide variety of international BWF events, seeking to qualify for the highest level of competition. He began the year 2013 on a strong note, winning the men's singles competition at the Yonex Estonian International. Momota went on to claim additional titles at the Swedish International Stockholm and the Austrian International Challenge, both held as part of the BWF's lower-level International Challenge series. He also put forth strong performances in other events. He even progressed to the quarterfinals of the Li Ning Singapore Open and the Adidas China Masters and to the semifinals of the Yonex OCBC US Open and the Victor China Open.

Over the next years Momota continued to establish himself as an up-and-coming player to watch, appearing frequently in BWF competitions and demonstrating the speed and technique that became his hallmark. The year 2015 was particularly successful for him, as he won the OUE Singapore Open in April and the BCA Indonesia Open two months later. That August, he tied for the bronze medal at the Total BWF World Championships, becoming the first Japanese player to medal in the men's singles division of that competition.

SUSPENSION

By early 2016 Momota appeared to be poised for a year of competition that would include not only the typical slate of BWF tournaments but perhaps also the highest-profile international sporting event of all: the Summer Olympic Games, held that year in Rio de Janeiro, Brazil.

His journey to the Olympics ended however, in April 2016. On the heels of his win at the Yonex Sunrise India Open, allegations surfaced that Momota and another Japanese badminton player had repeatedly gambled in an illegal casino in Japan. While certain forms of gambling are permitted in Japan, casino-based gambling is not, and the Nippon Badminton Association, the nation's badminton leadership, deemed that Momota's actions violated the principles of their sport. Momota did not deny the allegations and later described his behavior to Nadkarni as "immature and foolish." Individuals charged with illegal gambling could face several years' prison time in Japan, but Momota agreed to a deal in which the association would not file charges and would instead bar him from international competition for a year.

For Momota, who had been devoted to badminton since early childhood, his sudden departure from competition amid a promising year was difficult, both emotionally and professionally. "I couldn't play, I couldn't see any goals and my future career looked extremely dicey," he told Hernon. "I didn't watch any of the 2016 Olympics because I felt too regretful. It was a tough time, but thanks to people who supported me I was able to get through it. I really appreciate everyone who was there for me." Despite his disappointment, he later admitted that he was not yet truly ready to compete at the Olympic level, telling Hernon that it would likely have been "impossible to take home the gold."

RETURN TO BADMINTON
Momota's yearlong suspension also took a toll on his world men's singles ranking, which fell from 4th in April 2016 to a low of 282nd in July 2017 due to his period of inactivity. Upon his return, his ranking disqualified him from high-level BWF tournaments, and he instead sought to re-establish himself through lower-level BWF International Challenge and Grand Prix events. He made his official return in July 2017, claiming second place in the Yonex Canada Open. He earned his first title of 2017 in August, winning the Yonex/K&D Graphics International Series, and went on to further victories at the Yonex Belgian International, Li Ning Czech Open, the Yonex Dutch Open, and the Macau Open. His strong performance enabled him to rebuild his reputation quickly and lifted his ranking to 48th by the start of 2018.

In 2018, Momota focused on the newly established BWF World Tour (formerly part of the BWF Superseries). The year saw a dramatic return to form for Momota, who claimed the men's singles title at several events, including the Blibli Indonesia Open, the Daihatsu Yonex Japan Open, and the Danisa Denmark Open. He also remained somewhat active in lower levels of competition, winning the Yonex Sunrise Vietnam International Challenge. In April, he won the 2018 Badminton Asia Championships, defeating Chinese player Chen Long to claim the gold medal. He also competed again in the BWF World Championships, held that year in China. After defeating Liew Daren of Malaysia in the semifinals, Momota achieved a decisive victory over Chinese player Shi Yu Qi to win his first BWF World Championships title. In so doing, he also claimed the first Japanese men's victory at that event.

OLYMPIC HOPEFUL
In early 2019, Momota experienced a disappointing setback at the Indonesian Masters. There he lost in the finals to Danish player Anders Antonsen, despite his belief that he had been "in form," as he told the AFP for an article published in the *Straits Times* (10 Nov. 2019). Nevertheless, Momota learned from his defeat and allowed it to fuel him as the year progressed. "I used that as motivation to work harder," he explained to the AFP. "I didn't want to lose another final so I've put in a lot of effort." His effort proved successful: in March 2019 he progressed through the rounds at the Yonex All England Open and defeated Danish player Viktor Axelsen to claim the singles title. It was not only his first victory at an event where he first competed five years before, but also assured him that he was well prepared for the challenges to come. "The 2020 Olympic (qualifying) race begins in May and it gives me a lot of confidence that I was able to win the pre-Olympic event that everyone wanted to win," he explained after the victory, as quoted by the *Japan Times* (11 Mar. 2019).

Over the course of 2019 Momota defended his Badminton Asia Championships title against challenger Shi Yu Qi; won the Yonex German Open, the Daihatsu Yonex Japan Open, the Danisa Denmark Open, and the Fuzhou China Open; and retained the World Championships title. By November 2019 he ranked first in the overall and World Tour rankings.

Momota, however, focused primarily on the challenge awaiting him in 2020, when he would seek to win a medal for Japan in the Tokyo Summer Olympics. He also sought to overcome his biggest rival: himself. "I can only become stronger by overcoming my own weaknesses," he told Hernon. "I need to work harder so I can give back to those people who've supported me."

SUGGESTED READING
"Badminton: Japan Star Kento Momota Defends Fuzhou Crown for 10th Title This Year." *The Straits Times*, 10 Nov. 2019, www.straitstimes.com/sport/badminton-japan-star-kento-momota-defends-fuzhou-crown-for-10th-title-this-year. Accessed 15 Nov. 2019.
"Badminton World Championships: Kento Momota Becomes First Japanese Man to Claim

Crown as Carolina Marin Also Salutes." *South China Morning Post*, 5 Aug. 2018, www.scmp.com/sport/other-sport/article/2158354/badminton-world-championships-kento-momota-becomes-first-japanese. Accessed 15 Nov. 2019.

Hernon, Matthew. "Meet the 2020 Athletes: Badminton Champ Kento Momota." *Tokyo Weekender*, Oct. 2019, www.tokyoweekender.com/2019/10/meet-the-2020-athletes-badminton-champ-kento-momota/. Accessed 15 Nov. 2019.

Jiwani, Rory. "Kento Momota: Why I Am My Own Biggest Rival." *Olympic Channel*, 10 Nov. 2019, www.olympicchannel.com/en/stories/features/detail/kento-momota-badminton-japan-tokyo-2020. Accessed 15 Nov 2019.

"Kento Momota Wins Historic First All England Open Title." *The Japan Times*, 11 Mar. 2019, www.japantimes.co.jp/sports/2019/03/11/more-sports/kento-momota-wins-historic-first-england-open-title. Accessed 15 Nov. 2019.

"Momota Hails 'New Badminton Generation' after Japan Double." *Yahoo! Sports*, 28 Apr. 2019, sports.yahoo.com/japan-double-golden-delight-badminton-asia-championships-112631665--spt.html. Accessed 15 Nov. 2019.

Nadkarni, Shirish. "Japan's Kento Momota Battles Depression with New-Found Maturity to Prove His Worth, Eyes Gold at 2020 Tokyo Olympics." *Firstpost*, 9 July 2018, www.firstpost.com/sports/japans-kento-momota-battles-depression-with-new-found-maturity-to-prove-his-worth-eyes-gold-at-2020-tokyo-olympics-4699221.html. Accessed 15 Nov. 2019.

—*Joy Crelin*

Kent Monkman

Date of birth: November 13, 1965
Occupation: Artist

Kent Monkman is among the most successful and versatile visual artists in Canada. His work has been exhibited in such high-profile venues as the National Gallery of Canada, the Smithsonian National Museum of the American Indian, and the Metropolitan Museum of Art (the Met), and private collectors have paid up to $150,000 for individual paintings at auction.

Monkman, an illustrator, painter, performance artist, videographer, photographer, and sculptor, is best known for subverting large-scale, classically rendered paintings by incorporating Indigenous figures and alternative narratives. Notably, many of his works feature a gender-bending figure in stiletto boots and a feathered headdress, the artist's alter ego and muse often known as Miss Chief Eagle Testickle (a wordplay on "mischief egotistical").

In exploring the complexities of historical and modern Indigenous experiences, Monkman's provocative works have at times attracted both respect and opprobrium, often from the same quarters. "Provocation is Monkman's M.O.," Nick Martin, an enrolled Sappony tribal member and staff writer for the *New Republic* (21 May 2020), explained. "He wants to press audiences to venture outside the heteronormative comfort levels defined by colonialism's religion of choice." While applauding Monkman's "stunning" hyperrealism, specificity, grand scale, and "eye-popping color palettes," he also questioned, "But is that enough? Just because Monkman alludes to terrible history does not mean he has anything really profound to say about it."

EARLY LIFE

Kent Monkman was born on November 13, 1965 in St. Mary's, Ontario, Canada. He was the youngest of three sons, and the family later adopted a daughter. His mother, Rilla Unger, was of Anglo-Irish descent, and his father, Everet Monkman, was a member of the Fisher River Cree Nation. Devout Christians, they served for a time as missionaries on the Shamattawa Reserve, in a remote area of northern Manitoba. Because his mother spoke no Cree and their cabin was cramped and cold, the family relocated around 1967 to Winnipeg, where his father worked for a church, driving taxis, doing social work, and flying. (He died in a plane crash when Monkman was in his twenties.)

The relative who had perhaps the most influence on Monkman's future work was his paternal great-grandmother, Caroline Everett, who lived with the family until Monkman was ten years old. She was born in 1875, the year several First Nations chiefs signed a treaty with Queen Victoria that resulted in multiple forced relocations throughout her life. Monkman's grandmother, Elizabeth Monkman, one of thirteen children and one of the few to survive to adulthood, was forcibly sent to a residential boarding school run by a religious order. Such institutions were used by the Canadian government for decades as a means to encourage assimilation, and physical and sexual abuse were common; among Monkman's best-known works is *The Scream* (2016), which depicts priests, nuns, and Mounties wresting children from their distraught families.

The elder members of the family spoke rarely of this troubled history, and Monkman has told interviewers he sometimes felt alienated from his Cree heritage as a result, particularly since his formative years were relatively comfortable. He lived in a largely white, gentrified neighborhood, excelled in school, and was well-liked by his classmates at Kelvin High School in Winnipeg.

EDUCATION

At the age of seventeen, dreaming of becoming an artist, Monkman enrolled at Sheridan College in Ontario. Although he had little interest in studying conceptual art, he reveled in his painting, drawing, and color-theory classes, seeking to develop practical skills. Monkman earned his diploma in illustration in 1989 and found work rendering storyboards for television commercials. Using felt markers, he ultimately created thousands of storyboards that were unceremoniously discarded by directors once they were no longer needed. The job, he has asserted, taught him to draw speedily and intuitively.

He later worked as a set and costume designer for the Native Earth Performing Arts theater before turning exclusively to making art. He also continued to take classes, completing programs at the Banff Centre in Alberta in 1992, the Sundance Institute in Los Angeles, California, in 1998, and the Canadian Screen Training Institute in 2001.

ART CAREER BREAKTHROUGH

Throughout the 1990s Monkman focused on abstract art, seeking to distance himself from illustration. He enjoyed a half-dozen solo shows that decade but found little success otherwise. Among his work during this period was a series of abstract paintings incorporating Cree syllabics (the written form of the language), which he arranged to suggest grappling male bodies—an early attempt to address intertwined themes of colonialism and sexuality. He was fascinated, however, by the Old Masters, admiring their rich color palettes and skillful techniques, and he was attracted, as well, to nineteenth-century landscape paintings by Edward Church and Thomas Cole, among others.

Some art critics note 2004 as a transformational year for Monkman—one that launched him on a path to relative wealth and fame. That year the National Gallery of Canada bought *Portrait of the Artist as Hunter* (2002), a representational depiction of a buffalo hunt with Miss Chief and a seminude cowboy as participants. The National Gallery gradually acquired other works, including seven-by-eleven-foot *The Triumph of Mischief* (2007), which Gerald Hannon described for *Toronto Life* (6 Sept. 2011) as "crammed with libidinous revelry that somehow manages to be a complete history of both Western art and the troubled interactions between First Nations and European colonizers, all playing out before the world-weary eyes of Miss Chief (who is carrying a chic little birchbark clutch and studiously ignoring Picasso)." Although those high-profile acquisitions did

not bring overnight fame and fortune, they "assure[d] collectors of his credibility and, perhaps more importantly, his bankability," as Hannon explained.

Monkman was inspired to create Miss Chief by George Catlin, a nineteenth-century American artist and showman who collected Indigenous artifacts and sometimes painted himself into his depictions of First Nations life, and Paul Kane, a similar Canadian artist. Monkman has told interviewers that he intended Miss Chief to challenge the self-declared authority of the European gaze. He sometimes appears in video pieces and at public events dressed as Miss Chief, doing so for the first time in 2004 at the McMichael Canadian Collection, a notoriously tradition-bound venue.

By 2017 Monkman was running his studio much like Renaissance masters did: he designs the overall concept and oversees a cadre of seven or eight apprentices, whom he instructs and who do the bulk of the painting before he steps in for finishing touches. Unlike those artists, he often conducts photo shoots with costumed models to use as a guide in creating his larger and more detailed paintings. "When you have the structure of your source material really nailed in your photograph, it really liberates and give you freedom to express with paint," he explained to Dakshana Bascaramurty for the *Globe and Mail* (1 Dec. 2017).

NOTABLE EXHIBITS

The Triumph of Mischief was part of an exhibition of the same name that traveled nationally from 2007 to 2010. In addition to displaying a selection of paintings, Monkman showed works on video, many created with his longtime collaborator Gisèle Gordon, and transformed the gallery spaces he visited into interactive tipi camps. (The tipis were said to belong to Miss Chief and contained elaborate chandeliers, velvet drapery, and other fixtures.)

In 2017 *Shame and Prejudice: A Story of Resilience*, organized by the Art Museum at the University of Toronto, began touring cities throughout Canada and was set to conclude in late 2020. The exhibit was mounted in response to Canada 150, the 150th anniversary celebrations of the Confederation of the Canadian provinces. "Most Indigenous people are thinking, what does this mean to us personally? What does it mean for our families and communities to be inside a country that has perpetrated a genocide against us?" Monkman told Robert Enright for *Border Crossings* (Sept. 2017). He continued, "I wanted it [this exhibition] to resonate on that personal level because sometimes people think of these things in an abstract way and don't connect it to real lives." Among the most talked-about pieces in the exhibit was *The Daddies*, a near-reproduction of the government-commissioned *Fathers of*

Confederation, an iconic depiction of the 1864 Charlottetown Conference. While Monkman's version included the same twenty-three men in nineteenth-century garb, it had one unmistakable addition: Miss Chief in stilettos grandly gesturing before the group.

Monkman was later commissioned by New York City's Metropolitan Museum of Art to create two works to hang in the building's famed, vaulted Great Hall beginning in 2019. Titled *mistikôsiwak (Wooden Boat People)*, the exhibition's two complex figural artworks upend conventional heroic representations of European colonizers. One depicts weak, shipwrecked Europeans and an enslaved African being rescued and welcomed by robust, vibrantly colored Indigenous figures. In the other, modern-day Indigenous people and others of color in a wooden boat rescue a few whites from stormy waters as a white supremacist, a soldier, and couple of law enforcers brandish weapons on a nearby island. The latter references George Washington crossing the Delaware River, while the former echoes several Renaissance paintings. Monkman, Tim Barringer asserted in *The Art Newspaper* (6 Feb. 2020), "offer[s] a coruscating Indigenous critique of the project of European colonialism and the forms of art integral to it. He does so with a witty, in places camp, inversion of the machinery of history painting—the genre held in academic theory to represent the zenith of Western art. The result is both delicious for the contemporary viewer and deadly to the Eurocentric and heteronormative certainties of the Met's founders."

CONTROVERSIES

Despite such positive sentiments, some critics like Nick Martin question whether Monkman and other Indigenous artists should agree to exhibit at major North American institutions such as the Met and the Smithsonian, given their histories and ongoing displays of Indigenous sacred and cultural artifacts. Martin acknowledged that reputational and financial success often depends on such relationships and expressed concern, echoed by others, that this can compromise the artistic output of Indigenous artists. Who, critics ask, is the work for?

Others have noted that Monkman's use of European artistic conventions puts his work into a context of shared history versus alternative history. To some, like Daniel Baird, this hints that Monkman believes in the possibility of reconciliation. To others, like art historian Regan de Loggans (Choctaw), his artwork "pander[s] to the erasure of Indigenous sovereignty through the narrative of a shared history between settlers and colonizers as though their experiences are commensurate," as quoted by Martin.

Monkman also came under fire in early 2020, after unveiling the painting *Hanky Panky*, which depicts Prime Minister Justin Trudeau pants down, surrounded by a crowd of laughing Indigenous women and Miss Chief holding aloft a sex toy shaped much like a symbol used in the Missing and Murdered Indigenous Women movement. Some Indigenous observers objected to the implication of sexual violence—an interpretation Monkman later refuted, citing subtle clues indicative of consent in the work, but for which he apologized. Others, including Senator Murray Sinclair (Ojibway), applauded the role reversal as a critique not only of present-day politics but also the long history of sexual violence against Indigenous people.

PERSONAL LIFE

Monkman identifies as two spirit, a gender-fluid identity recognized, and historically respected, among many Indigenous cultures in North America. During his adult life, he has had a number of romantic partners, including his artistic collaborator Gisèle Gordon, musician-composer Dustin Peters, and civic leader Ben Bergen. He divides his time between Toronto and Prince Edward County and travels often.

Among Monkman's many honors are a 2014 Indspire Award, given to Indigenous Canadians who demonstrate outstanding achievement; a 2017 Bonham Centre for Sexual Diversity Studies Award; an honorary doctorate from the Ontario College of Art and Design (OCAD) University; and a 2017 Premier's Award for Excellence in the Arts from the Province of Ontario.

SUGGESTED READING

Baird, Daniel. "The Alternative Realism of Kent Monkman." *The Walrus*, July–Aug. 2020, thewalrus.ca/the-alternative-realism-of-kent-monkman. Accessed 25 June 2020.

Barringer, Tim. "The Big Review: Kent Monkman at the Met.'" *The Art Newspaper*, 6 Feb. 2020, www.theartnewspaper.com/review/the-big-review-kent-monkman-at-the-metropolitan-museum-of-art. Accessed 25 June 2020.

Bascaramurty, Dakshana. "The Modern Touch of an Old Master." *The Globe and Mail*, 1 Dec. 2017, www.theglobeandmail.com/arts/inside-the-process-behind-kent-monkmans-art/article37126241/. Accessed 25 June 2020.

Martin, Melissa. "Former Winnipegger Stoking Passion in a New Generation of Indigenous Artists." *Winnipeg Free Press*, 6 Oct. 2017, www.winnipegfreepress.com/local/once-inspired-now-inspiring-449794323.html. Accessed 14 July 2020.

Martin, Nick. "The Provocations of Kent Monkman." *The New Republic*, 21 May 2020, newrepublic.com/article/157742/provocations-kent-monkman. Accessed 25 June 2020.

Monkman, Kent. "The Incredible Rightness of Mischief." Interview by Robert Enright. *Border Crossings*, no. 43, Sept. 2017, bordercrossingsmag.com/article/

the-incredible-rightnes-of-mischief. Accessed 25 June 2020.

Porter, Catherine. "'Genius' or 'Amoral'? Artist's Latest Angers Indigenous Canadians." *The New York Times*, 28 May 2020, www.nytimes.com/2020/05/28/world/canada/painting-canada-monkman-trudeau-indigenous.html. Accessed 25 June 2020.

SELECTED WORKS

Portrait of the Artist as Hunter, 2002; *The Triumph of Mischief*, 2007; *The Daddies*, 2016; *mistikôsiwak (Wooden Boat People)*, 2019; *Hanky Panky*, 2020

—*Mari Rich*

Arte Moreno

Born: August 14, 1946
Occupation: Major League Baseball team owner and businessman

Arte Moreno made his fortune in billboard advertising; in September 2020, *Forbes* estimated his net worth to be $3.4 billion. Yet, he became perhaps best known for his investment in baseball. In 2003 he and his wife, Carole Moreno, spent $184 million to acquire the Anaheim (later Los Angeles) Angels, a Major League Baseball (MLB) team. The acquisition made Moreno the first Mexican American to own a major league sports team. Under the Morenos' ownership, the Angels' franchise value grew to an estimated $1.9 billion by 2020.

Throughout Moreno's tenure as the Angels' co-owner, he sought to grow the team's market share by pulling fans from the team's nearby competitors, the Los Angeles Dodgers, an older and more established franchise, as well as by acquiring marquee players like power-hitting first baseman Albert Pujols. Under Moreno's ownership the Angels won the American League (AL) Western Division in 2004, 2005, 2007, 2008, 2009, and 2014, though they were unable to secure a World Series championship. By 2020 the team had drawn a total of 52 million fans—more than 3 million each season—to the team's home stadium. Moreno also drew attention in 2020 when he released plans for a new Angels ballpark.

EARLY LIFE AND EDUCATION

Arturo "Arte" Ricardo Moreno was born on August 14, 1946 in Tucson, Arizona. He was one of Arturo Elias Moreno and Mary Moreno's eleven children. His parents met when Moreno's father was in his mid-thirties and his mother was a twenty-five-year-old widow with a young daughter. After the couple married they had ten

more children, including Arte, and raised them in a two-bedroom house in Tucson. Arte and his four brothers slept in a pair of bunk beds in an enclosed porch while their six sisters shared a bedroom.

A penchant for running businesses ran in Moreno's family. His father owned a small printing business and often printed friends' wedding invitations or the local church bulletin free of charge. His grandfather was the proprietor of Tucson's first Spanish-language newspaper. Although proud of their Mexican heritage, the family required all their children to speak English at home. Moreno's father also made sure they attended church services every Sunday.

Moreno and his father did not always get along, particularly during the turbulent 1960s, during which different family generations were often divided over cultural issues. They did, however, share a love of baseball. His father "walked around with the box scores in his hand," Moreno recalled to Sam Farmer for the *Los Angeles Times* (18 June 2006). "He always knew who was doing what, who pitched, who made the errors, who was doing a crummy job."

Shortly after graduating from high school, Moreno was drafted into the United States Army in 1966 and served in the Vietnam War. After his tour of duty ended in 1968, he went to the University of Arizona on the GI Bill and earned his bachelor's degree in marketing.

ENTERPRISING BUSINESS CAREER

Moreno worked in the advertising industry for a number of years before eventually being hired by Outdoor Systems, a billboard company in which he eventually took a controlling interest. His real fortune, however, was made in the late 1990s, when Outdoor Systems proved so profitable that he was able to sell it to Infinity Broadcasting for more than $8 billion in 1999.

During the 1980s, while working in advertising, Moreno became interested in applying his business acumen to his favorite pastime: baseball. In 1985, with seventeen other investors, he purchased the Salt Lake Trappers, a Single-A minor league team in the Pioneer League. The Trappers would win three championships during the Moreno-led ownership before Moreno sold his shares in 1992.

In 1998 Moreno became one of the original investors in the Arizona Diamondbacks, an expansion team then new to MLB. He was a part owner of the team when the Diamondbacks won the World Series in 2001. According to reports, Moreno attempted to buy a majority ownership in the team around this time, but his offer was not accepted.

LEADING THE ANGELS

On May 22, 2003, Arte and Carole Moreno completed their purchase of the Anaheim Angels from the Walt Disney Company, becoming the third owners in the team's history. The team was established in 1961 as one of MLB's first expansion teams; its original owner was the actor Gene Autry. In order to boost the franchise's profile, which was somewhat lower in the southern California area than the more established Los Angeles Dodgers, Moreno immediately made efforts to draw fans by lowering ticket and concession prices at Angel Stadium. He also began to spend money to attract top players to the Angels, including Vladimir Guerrero, an outfielder who was then the best free agent available and was signed to a contract worth $70 million. In 2004, the team's performance on the field drew 3.4 million fans over the course of the season, and the Angels made the playoffs. Moreno hoped the team's efforts would culminate in a World Series championship. "A lot of people talk about getting to the World Series," Moreno said to Sean Gregory for *Time* (22 Aug. 2005). "All I want is to win one." The Angels had previously won their first World Series title in 2002.

In 2005, Moreno further expanded his efforts at escalating the rivalry with the Dodgers by officially changing the team's name from the Anaheim Angels to the Los Angeles Angels of Anaheim—a mouthful, but one that would both allow the team to expand its fan base from Orange County to Los Angeles, while at the same time satisfying the team's lease with the city of Anaheim. City officials ultimately went to court about the name change, but the team officially retained the new name, though they are commonly referred to as the Los Angeles Angels.

Moreno hoped to pull fans from the Dodgers, though he did acknowledge that the Dodgers' fan base is old and deep. "We are starting to get a nice little market rivalry," Moreno remarked, as quoted by David Leon Moore for *USA Today* (23 Feb. 2005). "I think it's a real exciting time for baseball in Southern California."

Another of Moreno's attempts to promote the Angels' franchise was in his outreach to children. In an interview with Nathaniel Penn for *GQ* (21 Mar. 2012), he noted, "When I came in, I started talking about marketing to 8-year-olds, and everybody thought I was nuts. Now those kids are 20 years old, right? . . . So if you're saying, 'Are you marketing for young people in the area?' Yes, I am."

Part of Moreno's marketing push was to recruit All-Star players with lucrative contracts. He oversaw signings such as pitcher Bartolo Colón in 2004 (Colón would go on to win the 2005 American League (AL) Cy Young Award in 2005 with the Angels); Gold Glove–winning outfielder Torii Hunter before the 2008 season; and reigning World Series Most Valuable Player (MVP) Hideki Matsui for the 2010 season. Perhaps the most notable free agent signing, however, was three-time National League (NL) MVP

Albert Pujols, who joined the Angels on a ten-year, $254 million contract in 2012. Yet not all the Angels' stars came from other teams; Moreno and his front office also drafted and developed talented players, as exemplified by Mike Trout, who was selected by the team in the 2009 MLB draft and would come to be widely acknowledged as one of the greatest players of all time. In March 2019, Moreno signed Trout—who already had two AL MVP awards and would add another that season—to a record-setting twelve-year, $426.5 million contract meant to keep him with the Angels for his entire playing career.

Recruiting and maintaining a solid stable of exceptional players enabled the Angels to regularly make the postseason throughout Moreno's ownership. The team won the AL Western Division championship in 2004, 2005, 2007, 2008, 2009, and 2014. However, they struggled to find postseason success, failing to reach the World Series in any of those playoff runs. Critics noted that despite the skills of position players such as Trout, the franchise had less success with pitchers, and massive contracts such as Pujols's were less beneficial than hoped and restricted the team's financial flexibility. Nonetheless, Moreno continued his efforts to build a World Series contender. In 2017 he approved the signing of Japanese phenom Shohei Ohtani, who went on to be named AL Rookie of the Year in 2018. Before the 2020 season he signed another All-Star, Anthony Rendon, who was fresh off a World Series victory with his former club, the Washington Nationals.

In June 2020 it was reported that Moreno and the investment group of which he was a partner, SRB Management, had agreed to purchase 153 acres of land around the site of Angel Stadium with the idea of redeveloping it. Bought from the city for approximately $325 million (the final price was subject to change once the development was completed), the site was composed primarily of low structures and parking lots. Moreno and SRB Management were interested in turning it into a vibrant walkable neighborhood composed of transportation hubs, parks, shops, restaurants, theaters, offices, and the like, with the potential for creating more than 45,000 jobs and infusing the local economy with some $7 billion, according to SRB's estimates. What to do with Angel Stadium remained a question, however. One plan was to renovate the existing stadium to bring it back to its original design while also adding restaurants and bars. Another option was building a new state-of-the-art stadium in the newly renovated neighborhood and tearing down the old one, similar to what the New York Yankees did with their stadium in the Bronx. Either way, the real estate deal meant the Angels would stay in Anaheim through at least 2050.

PERSONAL LIFE AND PHILANTHROPIC EFFORTS

Together Arte and Carole Moreno had a son and daughter, Rico and Nikki. Moreno also had a son, Bryan, from a prior marriage. Dedicated to philanthropy, the Morenos donated millions of dollars to underprivileged youth and educational nonprofits and other charitable organizations. In 2004, shortly after buying the Angels, they established the Angels Baseball Foundation, which invests in "education, health care, arts and sciences, and community-related youth programs to experience the positive attributes of baseball," according to the couple's official *MLB.com* web page.

SUGGESTED READING

"Arte and Carole Moreno: Ownership." *MLB. com*, www.mlb.com/ana/team/moreno_arte. jsp. Accessed 5 Aug. 2020.

"Arte Moreno." *Forbes*, 6 Aug. 2020, www.forbes. com/profile/arturo-moreno/#17e726df1ecc. Accessed 6 Aug. 2020.

Farmer, Sam. "Generosity and Work Ethic Were the Gifts That Helped Turn His Son into a Billionaire Owner." *Los Angeles Times*, 18 June 2006, www.latimes.com/archives/la-xpm-2006-jun-18-sp-moreno18-story.html. Accessed 4 Aug. 2020.

Gregory, Sean. "Arturo Moreno." *Time*, 22 Aug. 2005, content.time. com/time/specials/packages/rinto ut/0,29239,2008201_2008200_2008188,00. html. Accessed 4 Aug. 2020.

Moore, David Leon. "City of Angels . . . and Dodgers." *USA Today*, 24 Feb. 2005, usatoday30.usatoday.com/sports/baseball/2005-02-23-dodger-angels-cover_x.htm. Accessed 4 Aug. 2020.

Penn, Nathaniel. "Arte Moreno Is a New (Nice) Steinbrenner." *GQ*, 21 Mar. 2012, www. gq.com/story/arte-moreno-mlb-baseball-owner-los-angeles-angels-anaheim. Accessed 4 Aug. 2020.

Reichard, Kevin. "Angels Unveil Ambitious Development Plan—But No Ballpark Decision." *Ballpark Digest*, 24 June 2020, ballparkdigest. com/2020/06/24/angels-unveil-ambitious-development-plan-but-no-ballpark-decision/. Accessed 4 Aug. 2020.

—*Christopher Mari*

Adam Mosseri

Date of birth: January 23, 1983
Occupation: Tech executive

"You might not know Adam Mosseri's name, but I think you should," Laurie Segall asserted on the December 16, 2019, episode of her podcast *First Contact*. "He is one of the most influential people in tech today. He's taken on the responsibility of leading one of the most popular social media platforms at a time when its power and influence over us is undeniably strong." The platform to which she was referring is Instagram, which has more than a billion monthly active users.

"Instagram has revolutionized shopping, dealt a near-death blow to women's magazines, taken celebrities from TV and movie screens to our fingertips and made Shih Tzus and personal trainers household names," Amy Chozick wrote for the *New York Times* (17 Jan. 2020), describing the platform's enormous reach. Segall, by contrast, took a more sober view of its effects. "Instagram and its parent company Facebook sit at the center of many complicated human issues these days," she said. "Between Russian interference in political elections, the debate on free speech and expression, and the larger implications of social media's impact on our mental health—there's a lot to navigate and none of it is black and white."

Mosseri, who joined Instagram in 2018 after a stint overseeing Facebook's News Feed function, has been at the center of many of those issues—both serious (it was on his watch that many Facebook users were exposed to misleading political posts by Russian trolls) and seemingly frivolous (Instagram's decision to hide "like" counts, which reportedly angered some high-profile users).

"In the early days, we were so excited and optimistic about the value that comes from

Photo by TechCrunch via Wikimedia Commons

connecting people and, just quite frankly, under-focused and somewhat naive about the negative consequences of connecting people at scale," Mosseri admitted to Audie Cornish during an episode of the National Public Radio (NPR) show *All Things Considered* (24 Sept. 2019). "[But] you have to shift [tech developers'] mind-sets. When they have an idea that they're excited about, you need to get them to a place where they naturally not only think about all the good that can come from it but how that idea might be abused."

EARLY LIFE AND EDUCATION

Adam Mosseri was born on January 23, 1983, and raised in Chappaqua, a wealthy hamlet some thirty miles north of New York City. His Israeli-born father, Rami, is a highly regarded psychotherapist, and his mother, Shauna, is an architect. Mosseri and his brother, Emile, now a musician and composer, attended Chappaqua's Horace Greeley High School, consistently ranked among the top public secondary schools in the nation.

After graduating from Horace Greeley, Mosseri won admission to the Gallatin School of Individualized Study. A constituent school of New York University (NYU), Gallatin encourages students to develop their own academic programs and majors, and Mosseri chose to focus on media and information design. As a first-year student, he lived with five roommates, sharing a single bathroom and sleeping in a small, windowless bedroom. He earned extra money designing websites, and he eventually joined forces with a partner, Sidney Blank, to launch Blank Mosseri, a design consultancy. (Some sources have referred to it as an architectural firm.) Despite the youth of its founders, the firm attracted some relatively prestigious clients, including Brown University and the Architectural League of New York.

Mosseri helped open an outpost of the firm on the West Coast in 2005 and began working as an adjunct professor at San Francisco's Academy of Art University during that period. He remained as creative director and partner of Blank Mosseri until 2007, when he left to become a product designer at TokBox, a live-video startup that has since become part of the larger company Vonage.

Inspired by the tech entrepreneurship scene in the San Francisco Bay area, he next tried launching a music-sharing app but was served a cease-and-desist order from the Recording Industry Association of America.

JOINING FACEBOOK

Mosseri had long harbored ambitions of joining Facebook but had never had any luck scoring an interview. That changed once he had an entry on his résumé related to music sharing. In 2008 he signed on as a Facebook product designer. Thanks to his solid work ethic—he often slept on a sofa in the office rather than heading home at night—within a year he had been promoted to design manager. In 2012, by then a member of Facebook founder Mark Zuckerberg's inner circle, he was named director of product management, and another promotion, this time to vice president of product management, followed four years later.

As part of his project management duties, Mosseri helped design and oversee Facebook Home, a smartphone interface he launched in 2013 that let users easily access apps, receive Facebook notifications, and send messages. However, Facebook Home never gained popularity, and the company discontinued it. Mosseri next worked on Facebook's News Feed, the constantly updated list of stories in the middle of a user's home page. The News Feed generates billions of dollars in ad revenue for the company; however, when it emerged that foreign actors, including the Russian government, were manipulating the feature to sway the 2016 presidential election in Donald Trump's favor, Mosseri became deeply involved in one of Facebook's biggest imbroglios to date.

In the wake of the tumult, Facebook announced that the News Feed was being revamped. Algorithms were tweaked so that users saw more content from family and friends (and less from unknown publishers and brands) to foster meaningful social connections. Use of membership groups, where users who shared hobbies or interests could interact in a lively but respectful way, was encouraged, while video, essentially a passive experience, was de-emphasized—despite being a reliable source of revenue.

Discussing the issue with Cornish, Mosseri stressed that he felt a deep responsibility to consider, right from the start, how tech platforms and features could be used, both for good *and* ill, and to immediately address any abuses that occur despite the best efforts of developers and administrators. "The most important lesson to me is that when you build a new feature or idea . . . That's awesome. That's exciting. We should be enthusiastic about that, but we need to also think about how [it] might be misused." He continued, "It makes everything you do much more complicated because, honestly, trying to build a feature that people use is difficult enough." He pointed out, however, that social media companies like Facebook had to be careful not to overstep and veer into censorship. "There are certain things that we cannot and should not do, given our scale," he explained. "We're not going to weigh on one ideological point of view or one religious point of view, for instance."

INSTAGRAM

The photo-sharing platform Instagram had been founded in 2010 by Kevin Systrom and Mike Krieger; even as the company grew explosively, the two remained respected and beloved by their employees. By 2012, when Instagram was acquired by Facebook for a reported $1 billion in cash and stock, it had some 30 million registered users.

Systrom and Krieger remained at the helm until the end of September 2018. Although rumors swirled about the reasons for their departure, with many insiders blaming tensions with Zuckerberg, the pair publicly stated that they simply wanted to be free to explore creatively. It was announced that Mosseri, who had quietly been appointed head of product development at Instagram just a few months before, would be stepping in to lead the whole company.

Some industry experts saw Mosseri's ascension as a win-win situation and predicted that the move would allow Instagram to integrate more seamlessly into Facebook, thus creating a stronger revenue model that would benefit both companies' advertisers and users. In their widely publicized formal statement, Systrom and Krieger wrote: "We are thrilled to hand over the reins to a product leader with a strong design background and a focus on craft and simplicity—as well as a deep understanding of the importance of community. These are the values and principles that have been essential to us at Instagram since the day we started, and we're excited for Adam to carry them forward."

Since assuming his new post in October 2018, Mosseri has overseen several changes to the platform, which allows users to upload photos and videos, edit them with various filters, and organize them with tags. Among these was the removal in October 2019 of the "Following" tab, which allowed users to see what their friends had been looking at and commenting on—intended as a way to introduce users to new content, but in practice often a source of social competition or emotional upset, since, for example, someone could see that their partner was liking the posts of an ex, or that their friends were interacting heavily with a social rival. Additionally, when a fourteen-year-old British girl committed suicide in early 2019 after seeing graphic images of self-harm on the platform, Mosseri moved quickly to ban such images and develop tools to prevent bullying behavior.

Most buzzed about, however, was Mosseri's move toward removing publicly displayed "like" counts, on the theory that they lead to unfair comparisons among users and contribute to low esteem, especially in Instagram's legions of adolescent users. This is an enormously controversial initiative, as "likes" are the main way Instagram users gauge one another's popularity, but Mosseri has been adamant about trying to ameliorate what is now widely acknowledged as the psychologically harmful aspects of social media, especially for young people. "We will make decisions that hurt the business if they help people's well-being and health," Mosseri said at the WIRED25 conference in San Francisco in November 2019. According to the plan, which has been tested for Instagram users in Australia, Brazil, Canada, Ireland, Italy, Japan, and New Zealand, as well as for a limited number of US users, people will be able to see their own "like" counts, but not those of other users, with the intention of making Instagram a "less pressured environment," according to the company. The change is expected to be rolled out nationwide in the United States later in 2020.

Mosseri undeniably faces multiple challenges at the helm of Instagram. He must meet Zuckerberg's expectations of growth and revenue, all while appeasing employees who want to maintain independence from Facebook and contending with complaints from longtime users vociferously uncomfortable with change of any sort. There has been pressure, as well, from politicos, with Massachusetts senator and former 2020 Democratic presidential candidate Elizabeth Warren calling for Facebook's acquisition of Instagram to be reversed because of the company's formidable size and power. Perhaps most concerning as election season approaches, independent studies have ascertained that Instagram, like its parent company, is being used by Russian trolls who are again seeking to foment national discord ahead of the 2020 election—a state of affairs that Mosseri and his developers are actively battling.

As Chozick wrote, however, citing the examples of a couple who fell off a cliff to their deaths while trying to snap an Instagram "selfie" and the ill-fated 2017 Fyre music festival that was hyped by Instagram advertising and then canceled: "The most obvious dark forces—pornography, self-harm, disinformation—seem almost simple compared to the largely unknown long-term impact of a platform that has turned every vacation, every dinner party, every parental milestone into an online performance."

PERSONAL LIFE

Mosseri, an avid amateur cook, has been married to his wife, Monica, an interior designer, since 2013. They have two sons, Nico and Blaise. The family lives in San Francisco.

SUGGESTED READING

"Adam Mosseri Unfiltered: How Instagram's CEO Navigates Chaos, Anxiety and Making Bold Moves." *First Contact with Laurie Segall*, Apple Podcasts, 16 Dec. 2019, podcasts.apple.com/us/podcast/adam-mosseri-unfiltered-how-instagrams-ceo-navigates/

id1487530250?i=1000459738831. Accessed 20 Jan. 2020.

Chan, Rosalie. "Instagram Head Adam Mosseri Says the App Will Test Hiding 'Likes' for Some Users in the US Starting Next Week." *Business Insider*, 8 Nov. 2019, www.businessinsider.com/instagram-to-test-hiding-like-counts-in-us-wired25-2019-11. Accessed 20 Jan. 2020.

Chozick, Amy. "This Is the Guy Who's Taking Away the Likes." *The New York Times*, 17 Jan. 2020, www.nytimes.com/2020/01/17/business/instagram-likes.html. Accessed 20 Jan. 2020.

Constine, Josh. "Meet Adam Mosseri, the New Head of Instagram." *TechCrunch*, 1 Oct. 2018, techcrunch.com/2018/10/01/adam-mosseri-head-of-instagram/. Accessed 20 Jan. 2020.

Cornish, Audie. "Instagram Head Adam Mosseri on the Lessons He's Learned about Social Media Abuse." *All Things Considered*, NPR, 24 Sept. 2019, www.npr.org/2019/09/24/763958806/instagram-head-adam-mosseri-on-the-lessons-hes-learned-about-social-media-abuse. Accessed 20 Jan. 2020.

Rodriguez, Salvadore. "Facebook's Adam Mosseri Fought Hard against Fake News—Now He's Leading Instagram." *CNBC*, 31 May 2019, www.cnbc.com/2019/05/31/instagram-adam-mosseri-must-please-facebook-investors-and-zuckerberg.html. Accessed 20 Jan. 2020.

Wagner, Kurt. "Meet Adam Mosseri, Instagram's New Boss." *Vox*, 1 Oct. 2018, www.vox.com/2018/10/1/17924592/instagram-new-ceo-adam-mosseri-kevin-strom-replacement. Accessed 20 Jan. 2020.

—*Mari Rich*

Katie Moussouris

Date of birth: November 25, 1974
Occupation: Computer security expert

In 2016, Katie Moussouris founded Luta Security, a cybersecurity firm specializing in managing vulnerability disclosure for governments and other large, complex organizations. Just two years later she was named one of the world's top fifty women in technology by *Forbes* magazine. Before launching her company, she led vulnerability research efforts for the technology giant Microsoft and was also instrumental in building Hack the Pentagon, the federal administration's first bug bounty initiative, completed under the auspices of the US Department of Defense. (Bug bounties are cash rewards offered

to "white-hat" hackers—those who use their skills for legitimate activities, versus malicious or "black-hat" hackers—in exchange for finding computer vulnerabilities so that they can be corrected.) "Hackers are humans above all else, and like most humans, we want to help," she noted in an op-ed piece for the *New York Times* (30 Mar. 2016). "Building things more securely is the first step. For everything else, hackers will show the way, if you let us."

Moussouris first became immersed in hacker culture as a teen and would earn a reputation as one of its staunchest defenders. For example, she supported bug bounties despite controversy around such programs, both from other hackers wary of being mistaken for the criminals they are actually attempting to stop and from some observers arguing that the practice of paying hackers, no matter what their intentions, only encourages bad behavior. Moussouris recognized that laypeople hold many misconceptions about hacking, but suggested the practice has been invaluable to society. "We and our culture are largely misunderstood as being at best, mischief-makers, and at worse, criminals," she told Ashley Perks for *The Hill* (25 Oct. 2017). "The fact of the matter is, we wouldn't have the internet today without hackers. We wouldn't have all of this amazing technology without people who are willing to see the technology of today and envision something different."

EARLY LIFE AND EDUCATION

Katherine Moussouris was born in 1974 and grew up in the Boston suburb of Arlington,

Photo by Omar Marques/SOPA Images/LightRocket via Getty Images

Massachusetts. She mentioned to interviewers that her father was a jeweler of Greek descent but referred to her mother as a single parent.

Moussouris's mother hailed from the Northern Mariana Islands, a US Commonwealth in the Pacific Ocean near Guam. As a young woman, she settled in the Boston area to study biochemistry thanks to an academic scholarship, and she later became an embryologist, helping thousands of infertile couples become parents and contributing to the advancement of stem cell research over the course of her career. She died of breast cancer in 2011; in a Twitter tribute on October 9, 2017, Moussouris wrote of her mother: "I like to believe that a stem cell line she preserved will be instrumental in better cures for her fatal cancer and so many others."

Moussouris's mother greatly valued education, an ethos she instilled in her daughter. Moussouris shunned Barbie dolls in favor of the rudimentary Commodore 64 computer she received as a gift when she was about eight. Armed with the manual that came in the box, she taught herself the early computer programming language BASIC and, bored by the simple version of Pac-Man that came preloaded in the Commodore 64, she began to create her own games.

She recalled to Perks that she came of age in the pre-internet era of dial-up bulletin board systems, which allowed anyone with a modem and a home computer to call in and interact with others. "I happened to dial into the same bulletin board system as a bunch of hackers known as The L0pht," she said, noting that several of those individuals would go on to prominence in the cybersecurity world, including working for DARPA (Defense Advanced Research Projects Agency). "These were the folks I grew up with as a teenager. So as a hobbyist, I kind of learned online with my friends."

Moussouris was the only female member of her high school's computer club. When the team traveled for competitions, she had to stay in a hotel room either by herself or with the rare female competitor from another school. She and her teammates were, as she would later quip to interviewers, the "nerdiest of the nerds."

Despite her deep interest in computers, Moussouris opted not to study computer science when she entered Simmons College (later Simmons University), an all-women school in Boston. Wanting to forge a career that would be more action-oriented than programming, she opted to study molecular biology and mathematics, figuring that she would eventually do cancer or AIDS research.

A CAREER START

While still in school, Moussouris found a job working on the Human Genome Project at the MIT Whitehead Institute. From 1995 to 1997 she served as part of the world's first bioinformatics team, managing the data analysis for all the institute's genotyping projects. When she discovered that data science was not for her, she moved into the role of systems administrator. She later managed IT for the school's Department of Aeronautics and Astronautics, which was often the target of hackers. "I learned the pain of having to defend your own network from attackers and polished my penetration-testing skills," she recalled to Gary McGraw for *IEEE Security & Privacy* magazine (July–Aug. 2015).

In 1999, Moussouris moved to San Francisco to become a Linux developer at a company called Turbolinux. (Linux is a group of open-source systems originated by the now-legendary software engineer Linus Torvalds.) There she evaluated threats and vulnerabilities and spearheaded a robust security response program. Within a few years, as she told Perks, "I finally realized I can write code, but I'm way better at breaking it. So, I decided to become a professional penetration tester, which is a person who is hired by, let's say, a bank to find the holes in the bank and show you how to fix it."

Moussouris subsequently worked for such security companies as Intrusion and @stake. The latter was ultimately purchased by Symantec, where Moussouris developed the Symantec Vulnerability Research Program. When she launched the initiative, she printed shirts for her team that read: "Don't Hate the Finder. Hate the Vuln." (In hacking and gaming circles, "vuln" is a commonly used abbreviation for "vulnerability.") In a column for the blog *Dark Reading* (12 May 2015), she explained the importance of her work at Symantec—and the resistance many outside executives felt to it: "When vendors lack a process and ability to receive, investigate, remediate, and communicate about security vulnerabilities, often the first reaction is to call in the lawyers. However, software bugs are not usually fixed by lawyers, threats, or intimidation. They simply distract all parties from the only route that ensures our collective security," she asserted. "All software contains bugs. . . . Those who are unable to gracefully deal with external parties who are trying to warn them of security holes are putting their users, and possibly the Internet as a whole, at risk."

MICROSOFT

In 2007, Moussouris joined Microsoft as a security strategist. In that capacity, she created and led several new initiatives, including a program called Defend the Flag that trained IT professionals to recognize and stop attacks on the company's Windows operating system. Among her signature accomplishments was launching the technology giant's first bug bounty program. It would pay out more than $250,000 in rewards to hackers who helped the company detect and fix vulnerabilities in its platform.

Moussouris became a leading public spokesperson for the company's cybersecurity efforts, appearing often in such media outlets as the *BBC*, *Reuters*, *Engadget*, and *ZDNet*. During her time at Microsoft she also served as a lead subject matter expert for the International Organization for Standardization (ISO). She edited a new ISO vulnerability handling process for the group, which promotes global proprietary, industrial, and commercial standards in a wide variety of industries.

Moussouris's time at Microsoft was marred, however, by what she saw as systematic gender discrimination. In September 2015, after she had left its employ, she became one of three plaintiffs in a lawsuit that charged that more than 8,600 women collectively lost $238 million in pay and 500 promotions because of bias in the company's performance review process.

HACK THE PENTAGON AND LUTA

In 2014, Moussouris left Microsoft to become the chief policy officer at HackerOne, an enterprise that had launched a few years earlier to negotiate agreements between helpful, white-hat hackers and organizations with security vulnerabilities. Several major companies, including Yahoo and Twitter, signed on, as did the Department of Defense, which launched the Hack the Pentagon bug bounty program in 2016. Moussouris hailed such programs as vehicles to build trust between traditional adversaries: hackers and the government. "It is not only a green light for hackers to come forward, it's a tangible incentive for them to do so, and a much-needed recruiting exercise for Uncle Sam," Moussouris wrote for the *New York Times*. "I know because I am a hacker. I hack policies instead of computers these days, but the principles are the same: Learn the secrets about the system you are trying to hack and turn it to do your will." Her confidence was not misplaced. Over 1,400 hackers registered in advance to participate, and within six hours of the platform becoming operational, 200 reports of bugs had been sent.

In 2016, Moussouris struck out on her own, founding the security startup Luta. (She named the enterprise after the island in the Northern Marianas where her mother was born.) The company aimed to go beyond simply identifying vulnerabilities, building solid back-end processes to prioritize and handle them. Thanks to Moussouris's work with the ISO, her clients soon included several foreign governments and national Computer Emergency Response Teams (CERTs), as well as major private-sector organizations.

PERSONAL LIFE

According to remarks she made on social media, Moussouris went through a divorce, but she disclosed little else publicly about her personal life.

Aside from her main professional endeavors, she served as an adviser for the Washington-based nonprofit Center for Democracy and Technology. She was also a cybersecurity fellow at the nonpartisan New America think tank and a former affiliate member of Harvard's Belfer Center for Science and International Affairs.

SUGGESTED READING

Lee, Timothy B. "Judge Deals Blow to Women Suing Microsoft over Gender Discrimination." *Ars Technica*, 26 June 2018, arstechnica.com/tech-policy/2018/06/judge-denies-class-action-status-to-women-in-microsoft-discrimination-case/. Accessed 17 Nov. 2019.

Moussouris, Katie. "Hackers Can Be Helpers." *The New York Times*, 30 Mar. 2016, www.nytimes.com/roomfordebate/2016/03/30/should-hackers-help-the-fbi/hackers-can-be-helpers. Accessed 17 Nov. 2019.

——. "How I Got Here: Katie Moussouris." Interview by Dennis Fisher. *Threatpost*, 4 Nov. 2013, threatpost.com/how-i-got-here-katie-moussouris/102784/. Accessed 17 Nov. 2019.

——. "Q&A with Katie Moussouris, Cybersecurity Professional." Interview by Ashley Perks. *The Hill*, 25 Oct. 2017, thehill.com/policy/cybersecurity/356983-qa-with-katie-moussouris-cybersecurity-professional. Accessed 17 Nov. 2019.

——. "Silver Bullet Talks with Katie Moussouris." Interview by Gary McGraw, *IEEE Security & Privacy*, vol. 13, no. 4, pp. 7–9, 2015, doi:10.1109/MSP.2015.89. Accessed 17 Nov. 2019.

——. "Vulnerability Disclosure Deja Vu: Prosecute Crime Not Research." *Dark Reading*, 12 May 2015, www.darkreading.com/vulnerabilities---threats/vulnerability-disclosure-deja-vu-prosecute-crime-not-research/a/d-id/1320384. Accessed 17 Nov. 2019.

—*Mari Rich*

John Mulaney

Date of birth: August 26, 1982
Occupation: Comedian

Comedian John Mulaney scored his first big break at twenty-six years old, when he joined the writing team for *Saturday Night Live* (*SNL*). Soon he made his mark behind the scenes. Within months he had helped create one of the franchise's most recognizable characters: Stefon, the nightlife correspondent and Weekend Update fixture. "There is a learning curve with any new writer at 'SNL,'" head writer/cast member Seth Meyers told Christopher Borrelli for the *Chicago Tribune* (4 Oct. 2014). "And [with]

Photo by Mingle Media TV via Wikimedia Commons

John, it wasn't just the quality right away, but how quickly . . . that quality came." Over the next four-plus years, he excelled in the role, even winning a 2011 Emmy Award for cowriting Justin Timberlake's monologue.

Mulaney's wry, self-deprecating sense of humor has not only evoked comparisons to Jerry Seinfeld but also made him a hot commodity on the comedy circuit. In addition to the four stand-up specials under his belt, one of which earned him his second Emmy, Mulaney has also distinguished himself in front of the *SNL* cameras, with several impressive hosting stints, including a 2019 Emmy-nominated turn. But fame and recognition are not what are most important to Mulaney. "I'm an entertainer, not an artist," he told Jonah Weiner for *Esquire* (12 Sept. 2019). "I do it for audiences. I do it for people to consume."

ASPIRING COMEDIAN

Chicago, Illinois, native John Mulaney was born on August 26, 1982. He is the third of Ellen Stanton Mulaney and Charles "Chip" Mulaney Jr.'s four surviving children: older siblings Carolyn and Chip as well as younger sister, Claire. Both parents worked in law. At age four Mulaney experienced the tragic death of his newborn brother, Peter.

After joining the Rugrats, a children's improv/sketch comedy group, seven-year-old Mulaney was invited to audition for the comedy caper *Home Alone*—an offer his strict parents rebuffed and a part that ultimately launched Macauley Culkin to stardom. He continued to hone his performance chops while attending

Saint Clement School in Lincoln Park, eschewing written assignments in favor of performing original skits alongside classmate John O'Brien. Mulaney often visited the Museum of Broadcast Communications to binge on archived episodes of classic television shows, such as the sitcom *I Love Lucy*, and listened to comedy albums from Bob and Ray before bed.

Upon completing Saint Clement's in 1996, Mulaney attended Saint Ignatius College Prep, a strict Jesuit high school in downtown Chicago. Mulaney, who had his first drink at age thirteen, increasingly turned to alcohol and cocaine. "I drank for attention," he confided to Weiner. "I was really outgoing, and then at twelve, I wasn't. I didn't know how to act. And then I was drinking, and I was hilarious again." Mulaney's hard partying and excessive drinking escalated, resulting in blackouts and destructive behavior, including swigging perfume by mistake. Nevertheless, Mulaney graduated in 2000.

COLLABORATION WITH KROLL

Mulaney went on to study English and theology at Georgetown University, his parents' alma mater. There he gravitated toward comedy. As a first-year student, Mulaney was cast in the Georgetown Players Improv Troupe by director Nick Kroll. Mulaney performed with the group and thrived in the setting. "One way long-form improv is done is one person . . . steps forward and does a monologue and then you go off that," he told Andy Downing for *Madison.com* (27 Feb. 2013). "I started to realize I really liked doing the monologues, and I also started realizing I would hog the scenes a lot."

After graduating from Georgetown in 2004, Mulaney joined Kroll in New York City, where he worked at Comedy Central and enjoyed his first collaboration with Kroll: *Cavalcade of Personalities* (2004), a spoof of 1930s high-society newsreels featured on *Jump Cuts*, Comedy Central's short-film series. The two also collaborated on the parody series *I Love the 30s*, which aired on Motherload, Comedy Central's online network.

In 2005, Mulaney went sober and poured his energy into performing. He had a regular gig at Rififi, taking part in the alternative-comedy venue's weekly showcases, including "Invite Them Up" and Kroll's *Welcome to Our Week*.

Mulaney experienced another pivotal moment in 2005. While browsing the historic Strand Bookstore with Kroll, they observed a pair of crotchety, turtleneck-and-blazer-wearing friends buying hardcover copies of Alan Alda's 2006 memoir, *Never Have Your Dog Stuffed*. The older men inspired Gil Faizon and George St. Geegland, two grumpy, disheveled Upper West Side septuagenarians who engage in politically incorrect dialogue. As cohost of *Welcome to Our Week*, Mulaney fleshed out the persona of Geegland, alongside Kroll's Faizon. Along with uttering "Oh, hello" in unison, the duo would drink "tuna martinis" and interview performers after each set.

Mulaney gained national attention after opening for fellow Georgetown alum Mike Birbiglia's 2006 Medium Man on Campus Tour and a *Late Night with Conan O'Brien* appearance in 2007. In early 2008, Mulaney and Kroll reprised their Geegland and Faizon characters for a pair of shorts, *Video Club* and *Gil and George Visit Mona*, featured on the comedy site Funny or Die. Subsequently Mulaney appeared on VH1's pop-culture series *Best Week Ever* and graced the stage at June's Bonnaroo Music and Arts Festival.

Mulaney went on to join the writing staff of sketch-comedy series *Important Things with Demetri Martin* while maintaining a presence at New York's Upright Citizens Brigade (UCB). There he caught the attention of *Saturday Night Live* (SNL) cast members Amy Poehler and Seth Meyers, who recommended him for the late-night variety show.

SNL AND FIRST EMMY

At his *SNL* cast tryout, Mulaney focused on familiar material. "I'd done impressions on there [*Best Week Ever*], like Kevin Federline and George Takei, but I decided to adapt my standup into more of a character form," he told Dave Itzkoff for the *New York Times* blog the 6th Floor (20 Jan. 2012). "I had a joke about how Donald Trump is not just a rich man, but what a hobo imagines a rich man to be." The *Law and Order* superfan included a spoof regarding the type of characters regularly featured on the procedural.

Although Bobby Moynihan was cast, Mulaney landed a coveted job among *SNL's* writing staff and later helped develop the character of Stefon, a flashy partier played by Bill Hader, the character's other cocreator. Mulaney drew inspiration from another Culkin film: the 2003 club culture–influenced *Party Monster*. Stefon's debut came during a November 1, 2008, sketch, in which he played the brother of guest host Ben Affleck. Another first-season highlight included Mulaney's on-camera debut, playing a stagehand during an Activia sketch.

Mulaney experienced other career milestones. In addition to the release of his debut album, *The Top Part*, in late March 2009, Mulaney's first half-hour television special premiered on Comedy Central less than a week later. As a member of *SNL's* writing staff, Mulaney received an Emmy Award nomination for Outstanding Writing for a Variety, Music or Comedy Series shortly after his first season. That September, Mulaney served as consultant for the 2009 MTV Video Music Awards before returning to *SNL* for his second season. He performed double duty on the April 24, 2010, episode, penning Stefon's "Weekend Update" debut and also appearing on a "Weekend Update" segment, critiquing Girl Scout cookies.

By season's end, Mulaney and the *SNL* writers had received a 2010 Writers Guild of America (WGA) Award for Best Comedy/Variety Series and their second consecutive Emmy nod. The comedian won his first-ever Emmy a year later, when he shared the prize for outstanding original music and lyrics for guest host Justin Timberlake's opening monologue on the season finale.

GOODBYE *SNL* AND *OH, HELLO*

Mulaney would spend another season at *SNL* before leaving in 2012, with three Emmy nods for writing, an WGA Award, and a nomination from the Producers Guild of America (PGA) under his belt. Mulaney, who had already starred in a Comedy Central special—*New in Town*—and released a chart-topping accompanying disc, was hard at work on his next project: developing the script for a loosely biographical television pilot. "I was writing for other people and really wanted to strike out on my own," he told Kevin Fallon for the *Daily Beast* (14 Apr. 2017). After NBC rejected the script in May 2013, Mulaney pitched a revamped version to the Fox network, which committed to sixteen episodes. His eponymous sitcom premiered in October 2014, but only twelve episodes of the show were aired before it was canceled in February 2015.

Mulaney briefly joined the writing staff of the spoof series *Documentary Now!* before returning to the comedy stage in November, with the premiere of his next stand-up special. *The Comeback Kid* (2015) earned Mulaney his first individual Emmy nod in the outstanding writing for a variety special category. He was also nominated that year for his work on *SNL's* fortieth anniversary special.

Mulaney spent part of 2015 revisiting the character of George St. Geegland during the third—and final—season of sketch program *Kroll Show*. He next collaborated with Kroll on a play, *Oh, Hello*, centered on George and Gil that also incorporates a high degree of ad-libbing. "These characters in particular are so insane sometimes that it's probably the most liberating thing to do on stage because we can kind of do whatever the hell we want," Mulaney told Graham Piro for the *Georgetown Voice* (8 Feb. 2016). "It feels like we deeply know the characters and we're willing to go off in various directions every single night." Following workshops in Los Angeles, California, and Nashville, Tennessee, the critically acclaimed *Oh, Hello* enjoyed a three-week engagement at New York's Cherry Lane Theatre in December 2015 before embarking on a national tour.

BROADWAY AND *SNL* HOSTING DEBUT

In September 2016, after a successful Off-Broadway stint, *Oh, Hello on Broadway* kicked off an equally triumphant four-month run at the Lyceum Theatre. (The streaming service Netflix later aired a performance of the show in 2017.) Mulaney reunited with Kroll to host the 2017 Independent Spirit Awards before collaborating on Kroll's animated sitcom *Big Mouth*, which premiered on Netflix in 2017. Mulaney voiced several characters and served as consulting producer.

By then Mulaney had already concluded the first leg of his Kid Gorgeous comedy tour; in September 2017 he embarked on his second leg, which ended in February 2018. A Netflix companion special, *John Mulaney: Kid Gorgeous at Radio City*, aired in May 2018, and an accompanying CD was released in late September. At the 2018 Emmys Mulaney won the prize for outstanding writing for a variety special.

Following his second hosting gig at the 2018 Independent Spirit Awards, Mulaney returned to the *SNL* fold, becoming one of the program's few writers to return as host (following in the footsteps of Conan O'Brien and Larry David). Highlights of the April 14, 2008, episode included a skit first written by Mulaney in 2010, in which he played an indifferent lobster diner waiter opposite cast member and close friend Pete Davidson, and another where he played a sassy server in drag.

In another year-end highlight, Mulaney voiced the character of Spider-Ham in Marvel Comics' critically acclaimed December 2018 release *Spider-Man: Into the Spider-Verse*. The full-length animation went on to win best animated feature at the Oscars and Golden Globes.

Mulaney started the year 2019 by launching Sundays with Pete and John, a seven-week comedy tour with Davidson. The duo also shared the stage in early March 2019, when Mulaney hosted *SNL* again; they appeared in a bodega bathroom skit—a sequel to their previous lobster diner sketch.

Mulaney's performance earned him a 2019 Emmy nod and a third *SNL* hosting gig in late February 2020—two months after the unveiling of his Netflix children's musical comedy/variety special, *John Mulaney and the Sack Lunch Bunch* (2019), inspired by educational children's programs such as *3-2-1 Contact* and *Sesame Street*. The critically hailed seventy-minute program featured Mulaney and a cast of child actors performing songs and sketches, alongside scripted chats and unscripted interviews.

PERSONAL LIFE

Mulaney lives in New York with his wife, make-up artist and stylist Annamarie Tendler, and their French bulldog, Petunia. His wife did work for *Oh, Hello on Broadway* and has been mentioned often in his shows.

SUGGESTED READING

Borrelli, Christopher. "Comedian John Mulaney Is the Throwback Kid." *Chicago Tribune*, 4 Oct. 2014, www.chicagotribune.com/entertainment/ct-ae-1005-john-mulaney-20141004-column.html. Accessed 10 June 2020.

Downing, Andy. "A Stand-Up Guy: 'SNL' Vet John Mulaney Takes the Barrymore Stage." *Madison.com*, 27 Feb. 2013, madison.com/entertainment/arts_and_theatre/a-stand-up-guy-snl-vet-john-mulaney-takes-the/article_551ca6fe-802a-11e2-9ed6-0019bb2963f4.html. Accessed 10 June 2020.

Fallon, Kevin. "Is John Mulaney the Next Seinfeld?" *The Daily Beast*, 14 Apr. 2017, www.thedailybeast.com/is-john-mulaney-the-next-seinfeld. Accessed 10 June 2020.

Itzkoff, Dave. "The Big Profile: John Mulaney." *The 6th Floor, The New York Times*, 20 Jan. 2012, 6thfloor.blogs.nytimes.com/2012/01/20/the-big-profile-john-mulaney. Accessed 10 June 2020.

Piro, Graham. "'Oh, Hello' Again: Georgetown Welcomes Back Comedic Duo." *The Georgetown Voice*, 8 Feb. 2016, georgetownvoice.com/2016/02/08/oh-hello-again-georgetown-welcomes-back-comedic-duo. Accessed 10 June 2020.

Weiner, Jonah. "Mulaney Is More Than a Funny Guy in a Suit and Tie," *Esquire*, 12 Sept. 2019, www.esquire.com/entertainment/tv/a28900498/john-mulaney-interview-2019. Accessed 10 June 2020.

SELECTED WORKS

Saturday Night Live, 2008–12; *John Mulaney: New in Town*, 2012; *Mulaney*, 2014–15; *John Mulaney: The Comeback Kid*, 2015; *John Mulaney: Kid Gorgeous at Radio City*, 2018; *John Mulaney and the Sack Lunch Bunch*, 2019

—Bertha Muteba

Alyssa Nakken

Date of birth: June 13, 1990
Occupation: Baseball coach

Alyssa Nakken made headlines in the sports media and beyond in January 2020, when it was announced she had been hired as an assistant coach with the San Francisco Giants baseball team, making her the first female full-time coach in the history of Major League Baseball (MLB). The Giants, in the midst of a major rebuild among both players and staff, did not make mention of the groundbreaking nature of Nakken's appointment in their initial press release, preferring to focus on her credentials. "She's simply an assistant coach, another piece to help the organization return to prominence," Alex Pavlovic explained for *NBC Sports* (5 Feb. 2020). "But there's no downplaying how important this all will be for a sport that was far behind the times." Nakken acknowledged the significance of her MLB position, particularly as an inspiration to others. "When I was growing up and trying to figure out what it was I wanted to do, I never saw this as an opportunity, being in baseball as an adult," she told Alyson Footer for a *Baseball Digest* article republished on *MLB.com* (14 May 2020). "You didn't see women in uniform, on the field, working with male athletes. You just didn't see it. I never thought it was a possibility."

Nakken's rise to fame was relatively quick. A softball star at Sacramento State College, she impressed those around her as a natural and effective leader. She first joined the Giants as an intern in 2014 and steadily worked her way up. Soon she caught the attention of others in the organization, and after Gabe Kapler was hired as the team's new head coach in late 2019 he saw her as a good fit for his staff, which sought to include a wide range of perspectives rather than focus on typical baseball experience. "Sure, it's not the traditional lineup of coaches," Nakken told Pavlovic. "But the fact that I've been with this organization, I know how it runs, this whole staff is brand new and it needs to come together and come together quickly and we have a lot of work to do. I'm the right person for that job."

EARLY LIFE AND EDUCATION

Alyssa Nakken was born on June 13, 1990, in Woodland, California, near the state capital of Sacramento. (In a fitting coincidence, exactly one year later softball was first included in the Olympics, leading June 13 to be celebrated as World Softball Day.) She grew up with two older brothers, Ryan and Jason. Their father, Bob, was a partner in a local law firm, and their mother, Gaye, coordinated the food pantry at the Woodland Christian Church.

Nakken attended her first San Francisco Giants game when she was just three weeks old, as her parents and brothers were fans of the team. Growing up in an athletics-oriented family, Nakken played many sports as a child, including soccer, basketball, and volleyball. However, she showed a passion for softball, often waking up before her parents and heading out by herself to a local park to pitch into the backstop. When she was nine years old, she began playing in travel league softball. Soon she was demonstrating not just talent as a player, but also leadership qualities. Her father recalled how he was once

forced to step in to coach his daughter's team after the regular coach was ejected, but as he knew little about coaching, it was Nakken who ultimately rallied her fellow players. "Alyssa then took them together and said, 'Look, let's just get this done'—words to that effect," he told Mark W. Sanchez for the website of the sports-focused radio station *KNBR* (5 Feb. 2020).

Nakken enjoyed a comfortable upbringing, and she found herself to be a natural people person. By the time she was a teenager she was known for having many friends. She also continued to develop her sports prowess and became considered one of the best softball players ever to attend Woodland High School. When she graduated in 2008, she was heavily recruited by colleges. Deciding to stay relatively close to home, she chose California State University, Sacramento, more commonly known as Sacramento State.

COLLEGE SOFTBALL STAR

At Sacramento, Nakken, a psychology major, proved to be a star both in the classroom and on the field. For all four years of her college career she was named National Fastpitch Coaches Association (NFCA) Scholar-Athlete, as well as Pacific Coast Softball Conference (PCSC) Commissioner's Honor Roll recipient. In her senior season, 2012, she was also named the PCSC Scholar-Athlete of the Year. Nakken was a full-time starter across 184 games played for the Sacramento State Hornets, most often at first base.

Just as in high school, in college Nakken's statistics earned her consideration as one of the best softball players in team history. In 562 career at-bats she racked up 171 hits, 34 doubles, 19 home runs, 83 runs batted in (RBIs), 115 runs scored, 18 stolen bases, and a .304 batting average. By the time of her graduation she had set a school record for putouts (1,265) and was ranked in the top six of all-time in several other statistical categories, including runs scored and home runs. She was selected to the all-conference team three times.

Nakken once again stood out as a leader, serving as team captain during both her junior and senior seasons. Known for her grit and determination, she was fondly nicknamed "Pig Pen" because her uniform was seemingly always dirty from her physical efforts. But her dedication and team spirit extended beyond her own play. In one telling episode, she was sidelined for a time after suffering a serious car accident while racing home to see her ill grandmother, but she nonetheless showed up at every practice to cheer on her teammates. She also built a reputation for serving as a bridge between players and coaches and effectively dealing with any contention, earning respect from both sides.

Nakken earned her bachelor's degree in psychology in 2012. She briefly considered attending law school before deciding to remain in the sports world. She later entered the University of San Francisco, where she earned a master's degree in sport management in 2015. While in graduate school she undertook a major research project examining the internal and external factors that motivate individuals to perform at their physical peak—knowledge that was becoming increasingly important in pro sports, as teams tried to find next-generation, science-based methods to get the most from their roster. Nakken's outgoing nature proved an advantage in her studies: "She's the kind of person that can walk in a room, has a great smile, gets along with people, that she can quickly make friends," a professor told Sanchez. "She just has that very engaging kind of personality."

JOINING THE GIANTS

After college Nakken held several jobs, including as chief information officer for the University of San Francisco baseball team. Then, in 2014, she was selected for a highly competitive internship in the Giants' operations department. There her duties included inputting scouting reports—a task that strengthened her interest in player development—and preparing for trading deadlines. As the Giants progressed in the play-offs that year, she became involved in running analytics for the team. San Francisco ended up winning the 2014 World Series, and Nakken participated in the celebration parade and was given a championship ring (which are sometimes presented to team staff in addition to players and coaches). In the wake of the victory, she helped plan postseason travel and World Series parties, and she gradually began working her way up in the organization.

Hired as a full-time Giants employee, Nakken assumed responsibility for producing and directing several of the team's health and wellness events. These included the popular Giant Race series, which invited runners to take part in a succession of runs in various California cities, with each one ending on the field of the local baseball stadium. She also chaired an employee group dedicated to increasing diversity and equity in the organization. In 2019, Nakken earned the Sprinkles of Love Award, a team honor recognizing front office employees for ethics, professionalism, and humanitarianism.

Although she enjoyed her work, Nakken began to seek new professional challenges, especially as the Giants went from World Series contention to franchise rebuilding. She set out to interview various team executives about what they hoped for the future of the organization. "I felt after each conversation, there could be an opportunity for me to come in and make an impact for this team and this staff," Nakken told Kerry Crowley for the *Mercury News* (6 Feb. 2020). "What role? I don't know, but I want to be there. Title? I don't care, but let me help."

Nakken's initiative caught the attention of Giants manager Gabe Kapler soon after he was hired in November 2019. Kapler was invested in assembling a youthful, diverse coaching staff, and initiated a series of discussions with Nakken. "What Alyssa was able to demonstrate was a strong ability to listen and break down information into very digestible bits," Kapler told Sanchez. "And that essentially makes her a) a good teacher, b) a good communicator and c) a good coach." He soon offered Nakken an assistant coaching position. "I honestly didn't even know the interview was happening," she told Pavlovic. "It was just me having conversations with Gabe and some of the staff about my thoughts on the clubhouse and the team and how do we put the best team on the field every single night."

MAKING HISTORY

Nakken's hiring was announced in a Giants press release on January 16, 2020. Although the organization was aware of the historic nature of the appointment, there was little fanfare. Instead, Kapler and others focused on her sports background and her years of involvement with the team. "It was never about being a female," Nakken told Crowley. "It was never about being the first. It was about, 'Hey, we have a brand-new staff, there's a lot going on. We need somebody to come in here and make an impact.'"

Nevertheless, the media quickly took hold of the fact that Nakken was the first woman in MLB history to hold a full-time coaching job. Nakken found herself in headlines across the sports press and national news outlets. "Your phone starts to blow up, and then you turn on the TV and there are news reporters in the childhood bedroom you grew up in your parents' house," she told Crowley of the tumult surrounding the announcement. "It was like, 'God, that escalated quickly.' But it's an incredible feeling." Most coverage was positive, with many characterizing her hiring as a victory for gender equality. Congratulations came pouring in from friends as well as from high-profile public figures. However, there were some negative reactions, including from former Giants player Aubrey Huff, who posted on social media that he could not imagine being coached by a woman.

Nakken's role as an assistant coach did not involve on-field appearances during games, as the maximum number of coaches allowed in the dugout during an MLB game is seven. However, she would don a uniform for games like more senior coaches and participate in field warmups during pregame activities. Her duties included throwing batting practice, hitting practice ground balls to fielders, and assisting the first base coach with base-running and outfield drills. She was also involved in behind-the-scenes work such as planning meetings and various team-building tasks.

Other specific aspects of Nakken's position were expected to be clarified as she grew into the role. She expressed her excitement to be part of an operation that was much younger and more experimental than the typical model for MLB coaches. "Gabe is taking a huge leap. Not just with me, but this entire coaching staff," she asserted to Pavlovic. "This is so exciting and it's so rad because it's literally the most brilliant people I've ever talked to."

In April 2020, as spring training began, it was announced that Nakken and Rachel Balkovec, a minor league coach in the New York Yankees farm system, would appear on the cover of the May/June issue of *Baseball Digest*. During spring training Nakken reported adjusting smoothly to her new responsibilities. However, her regular season coaching debut was delayed after the 2020 MLB season was postponed indefinitely due to the coronavirus pandemic.

PERSONAL LIFE

Nakken has largely kept her personal life private, though she remains in touch with many of her close friends from childhood and beyond. She enjoys athletic activities such as yoga, running, and surfing.

SUGGESTED READING

"Alyssa Nakken to Coach MLB, Makes History." *World Softball Confederation*, 23 Jan. 2020, www.wbsc.org/news/alyssa-nakken-to-coach-mlb-makes-history. Accessed 1 June 2020.

Corrales, Raul. "Woodland's Alyssa Nakken Working to Stay 'True to Herself.'" *Daily Democrat*, 8 Feb. 2020, www.dailydemocrat.com/2020/02/08/woodlands-alyssa-nakken-working-to-stay-true-to-herself/. Accessed 1 June 2020.

Crowley, Kerry. "Poker, Churros and Making History: Inside Alyssa Nakken's First Days as a Giants Coach." *The Mercury News*, 6 Feb. 2020, www.mercurynews.com/2020/02/06/poker-churros-and-making-history-inside-alyssa-nakkens-first-days-as-a-giants-coach/. Accessed 1 June 2020.

Footer, Alyson. "These Women Are Taking Their Turn at Bat." *MLB.com*, 14 May 2020, www.mlb.com/news/alyssa-nakken-rachel-balkovec-spearheading-women-s-role-in-baseball. Accessed 1 June 2020.

"Giants Complete Gabe Kapler's Major League Coaching Staff with Additions of Mark Hallberg and Alyssa Nakken as Assistant Coaches." *MLB.com*, 16 Jan. 2020, www.mlb.com/press-release/press-release-giants-hire-mark-hallberg-and-alyssa-nakken-as-assistant-coaches. Accessed 1 June 2020.

Pavlovic, Alex. "Alyssa Nakken Wanted New Challenge, Will Make MLB History with Giants." *NBC Sports*, 5 Feb. 2020, www.nbcsports.com/bayarea/giants/alyssa-nakken-wanted-new-challenge-will-make-mlb-history-giants. Accessed 1 June 2020.

Sanchez, Mark W. "Behind the Rise of Alyssa Nakken, from Memorable Softball Captain to Giants' Trailblazing Coach." *KNBR*, 5 Feb. 2020, www.knbr.com/2020/02/05/behind-the-rise-of-alyssa-nakken-from-memorable-softball-captain-to-giants-trailblazing-coach/. Accessed 1 June 2020.

—*Mari Rich*

Natti Natasha

Born: December 10, 1986
Occupation: Singer

The most-viewed female artist on YouTube at the start of 2019, singer Natti Natasha solidified her hold on that platform's userbase further with the release of her debut album, *ilumiNATTI*, later that year. Encompassing seventeen tracks and mixing genres such as reggaetón, urban pop, and bachata, *ilumiNATTI* was, in many ways, the culmination of Natasha's lengthy journey from unknown featured artist to full-fledged star. Born and raised in the Dominican Republic, Natasha began her career as a young teenager, performing music with a group of friends. She later moved to the United States to pursue her goal, working low-paying factory jobs to support herself.

Photo by Cmoro005 via Wikimedia Commons

Though an early appearance on the 2012 Don Omar single "Dutty Love" and the later release of the EP *All About Me* seemed poised to earn her a new level of recognition, the aspiring singer struggled to make a name for herself over the next several years. She repeatedly encountered the belief that female artists could not succeed in reggaetón or related genres. Ultimately, such setbacks made her later success both more satisfying and more meaningful. "I'm in love with music, with my career," Natasha said in an interview for *Hola! USA* (27 Mar. 2020). "It's been so much work to get to where I am. I still have a long way to go. I love what I'm doing, and I feel that everything has a moment." In 2019, she was named the Best Female Artist of the Year at the Billboard Latin Music Awards.

EARLY LIFE AND EDUCATION

Natasha was born Natalia Alexandra Gutiérrez Batista on December 10, 1986, in Santiago de los Caballeros, Dominican Republic. Her father was a teacher. Natasha demonstrated a particular talent for singing while still young and later enrolled in a school of fine arts in Santiago, where she honed her skills further with the goal of one day becoming a successful performer. "When you're a little girl," she told Suzy Exposito for *Rolling Stone* (15 Mar. 2019), "you never think anyone's gonna tell you 'no.' If you believe in something, and you start playing the part enough, [you think] it's just magically gonna happen! Because why not?"

By the time Natasha was in her early teens she had begun pursuing a career in music more seriously, forming a music group called D'Style with her friends. "I had some friends where one of them rapped and one sang and I was the female voice so that's how we started," she recalled to Roytel Montero for *Forbes* (18 Feb. 2020). "Then we started having a couple of songs and then we were on the radio, and then we went to clubs here and there when reggaetón started to be a little more popular and a little more accepted." Despite the efforts of its members, D'Style did not progress further, stalling Natasha's career for a time. After finishing high school, she enrolled in Pontificia Universidad Católica Madre y Maestra in Santiago de los Caballeros, where she studied industrial engineering.

EARLY CAREER

Still focused on pursuing a career in music, Natasha left both university and the Dominican Republic and moved to the United States in the late 2000s. She settled in the New York City borough of the Bronx. The period following her arrival in New York was a difficult one for the aspiring singer, who struggled to support herself and worked a number of low-paying and at times exploitative jobs. "I cleaned the house where I stayed; that was how I paid my way, by cleaning," she recalled in her interview with *Hola! USA*. "[I also worked] in a factory, and I remember that they had me do different things. One day, I was on the cosmetics production line; another day, I was wrapping packages." She has told interviewers that she spent a short period of time as an undocumented immigrant.

Beginning around 2010 Natasha found opportunities to sing, making small appearances in a number of songs. She soon came to the attention of established reggaetón singer and music executive Don Omar, who signed her to his record label Orfanato Music Group. A key moment in her early career came in 2012, with the release of the single "Dutty Love," performed by Don Omar and featuring Natasha. The single proved popular among reggaetón listeners and earned three Billboard Latin Music Awards.

Natasha then released a solo extended-play (EP) recording, called *All About Me* (2012), later that year. To her disappointment, however, *All About Me* received relatively little attention. Opportunities to take her career further were limited. "It was scary. I was lost and lonely. I didn't think anyone was going to help me," she told Raquel Reichard for the *Fader* (5 Dec. 2018). "After you get a high like that, and they don't give you the opportunity to keep doing more, but you have so much more to give, it's frustrating. But that frustration, if you're positive, turns into a good hunger." In interviews, Natasha would later attribute the setbacks of her early career to a belief among industry personnel that women would not be successful or profitable artists in genres such as reggaetón, which had long been dominated by men.

RISE TO FAME

Despite the disappointing results of her early attempts to break into the recording industry, Natasha remained focused on her music. In 2017, she signed with the Puerto Rican record label Pina Records. Over the next several years she became known for recording collaborations with a number of major artists in genres such as reggaetón and pop, including Daddy Yankee, Bad Bunny, and Thalía. One of her most popular singles from that era was the 2017 song "Criminal," a collaboration with singer Ozuna, which peaked at number five on the Billboard Hot Latin Songs chart. Natasha experienced even greater success with the single "Sin Pijama," released the following year. A collaboration with singer Becky G, the song peaked at number four on that Billboard Hot Latin Songs weekly chart and at number seventy on the Billboard Hot 100 chart.

For Natasha, the success of the singles released from 2017 only confirmed that she had made the correct decision in continuing to pursue a singing career despite the obstacles she faced. "I was a girl who believed in the color of my voice, and what I had to say," she told

Exposito. "I was not going to listen to any man [who would say], 'Girls don't sell.' I mean, so many women are making it around the world! You're gonna put that down?" In recognition of her newfound popularity, Natasha was nominated for a 2018 Billboard Latin Music Award in the category of Hot Latin Songs Artist of the Year, Female. She won the award the following year, at which time she was also nominated for the 2019 Billboard Latin Music Award for new artist of the year.

ILUMINATTI
After several years of releasing singles but no albums, Natasha released her debut album, *ilumiNATTI*, in February 2019. The album was preceded by several singles, including "Quién Sabe (Who Knows);" later singles from the album included the ballad "La Mejor Versión de Mí (The Best Version of Me)." Encompassing seventeen tracks, *ilumiNATTI* features songs in a multitude of genres, including genres featured in Natasha's existing body of work and others she had not previously explored. "I made it a point to not only include urban, because music is universal," she explained to Jessica Roiz for *Billboard* (13 Feb. 2019) about her approach to the album. "I could do reggaetón, I could do trap, I could do bachata, I could do dancehall, all of that, and then a ballad. I think that's what sums up the whole album and it's very special." In keeping with Natasha's history of collaborations, the album featured guest appearances from two fellow artists, the Brazilian singer Anitta and the Puerto Rican singer Kany García.

Popular among listeners, *ilumiNATTI* peaked at 149 on the US Billboard 200 chart and reached the number-three position on the US Top Latin Albums chart. Alongside her earlier work, the music videos produced to accompany singles from the album gained substantial audiences on the video-sharing site YouTube, making Natasha the most-viewed female music artist on the site in March 2019. The album also earned her Billboard Latin Music Award nominations for top Latin album and hot Latin Songs artist. However, she remained more focused on the public reception of her music than on the awards themselves. "Even if I don't win, I won because just being there to me is big already," she explained to Montero. "It's a celebration, you're a part of it, you get to share your music with the world and that's the goal." In addition to performing and recording music, Natasha walked in New York Fashion Week for the clothing label Custo Barcelona and in 2019 began to serve as a mentor for the Univision singing competition show *Reina de la Canción* (*Singing Queen*).

PERSONAL LIFE
Natti Natasha was married in the Dominican Republic earlier in her life; however, she confirmed following her rise to fame that she had been divorced for some time. Although relatively private regarding some aspects of her personal life, she noted in interviews that she believed in the importance of forging personal and emotional connections with listeners through her music.

SUGGESTED READING
Natti Natasha. "Latin Pop Superstar Natti Natasha Taps into the Power of Sisterhood." Interview by Suzy Exposito. *Rolling Stone*, 15 Mar. 2019, www.rollingstone.com/music/music-latin/natti-natasha-iluminatti-interview-807179/. Accessed 8 Sept. 2020.
———. "Music Interview: Natti Natasha." Interview by Anthony Guivas. *The Young Folks*, 15 Feb. 2019, www.theyoungfolks.com/music/129680/music-interview-natti-natasha. Accessed 8 Sept. 2020.
———. "Meet Natti Natasha: The Latin Artist Taking Música Urbana by Storm." Interview by Roytel Montero. *Forbes*, 18 Feb. 2020, www.forbes.com/sites/roytelmontero/2020/02/18/meet-natti-natasha-the-latin-artist-taking-msica-urbana-by-storm/#136f2a6d5954. Accessed 8 Sept. 2020.
———. "Natti Natasha Holds Down the Throne as the Reggaeton Pop Queen" Interview. *SoundExchange*, 8 Oct. 2019, www.soundexchange.com/2019/10/08/natti-natasha-holds-down-the-throne-as-the-reggaeton-pop-queen. Accessed 8 Sept. 2020.
———. "Natti Natasha on Pouring Her Heart Out in Debut Album "ilumiNATTI': 'It's All About Empowerment.'" Interview by Jessica Roiz. *Billboard*, 13 Feb. 2019, www.billboard.com/articles/columns/latin/8498202/natti-natasha-interview-iluminatti. Accessed 8 Sept. 2020.
———. "Natti Natasha Shares How She Went from Being Undocumented to Living Her 'American Dream.'" Interview. *Hola! USA*, Dec./Jan. 2019/2020, us.hola.com/celebrities/20191126fighemggmm/natti-natasha-hola-usa-interview. Accessed 8 Sept. 2020.
———. "Natti Natasha Is Ushering in a Brighter Future for Reggaeton." Interview by Raquel Reichard. *The Fader*, 5 Dec. 2018, www.thefader.com/2018/12/05/natti-natasha-la-baby-criminal-interview. Accessed 8 Sept. 2020.

—*Joy Crelin*

Lisa Nishimura
Occupation: Business executive

Photo by Steve Granitz/WireImage

"I never lack awe at people," Lisa Nishimura told Joy Press for *Vanity Fair* (15 June 2018). "Why people react the way they do, what are they hoping to achieve, what holds us back." In her role with the streaming-media company Netflix, Nishimura has proved herself uniquely able to facilitate the exploration of such topics through both long- and short-form programming. A former employee of multiple independent record labels and the film distributor Palm Pictures, she joined Netflix in 2007 as vice president of independent content acquisition, a role in which she was tasked with expanding the genre, topical, and geographical boundaries of the company's library of content. As Netflix moved into producing and distributing its own original content, Nishimura took charge of its original comedy programs—most notably standup specials—and documentaries. She was then promoted to vice president of independent film and documentary features in early 2019.

In addition to the strength of the original content itself, Nishimura focused significantly on the ways in which Netflix's approach to acquiring and distributing work benefited both filmmakers and the viewers of their work. "I believe documentary filmmakers want three things: They want to be fairly compensated, they want to be supported in their creative vision, and they want an audience," she explained to Natalie Jarvey for the *Hollywood Reporter* (17 Nov. 2016). As the popular and critical success of documentary series such as *Making a Murderer* (2015–18) and *Wild Wild Country* (2018) and feature-length documentaries such as *13th* (2016) demonstrated, Netflix and Nishimura

have distinguished themselves as major players within that space, earning numerous accolades while bringing new and thought-provoking stories to viewers around the world.

EARLY LIFE AND EDUCATION

Nishimura was born in California. The daughter of a chemist father and a violinist mother, she grew up in the Silicon Valley region of northern California. Nishimura's parents had both been born in Japan, and they raised their daughter to speak both English and Japanese. "I was lucky in that I grew up in a bilingual household. In addition to having American television, we had [the Japanese broadcast network] NHK in our house," she recalled to Audrey Ryu for *Character Media*. To Nishimura, her childhood experiences significantly shaped her later approach to acquiring content that represents a diverse array of perspectives. "I think it was the idea that each story is completely different—the craft and form and the resonance—and therefore the importance was ensuring that the right people to tell this story were given that opportunity," she told Ryu. A dedicated viewer of documentary content from a young age, Nishimura grew up watching programs such as the PBS documentary series *NOVA*. She was also drawn to music and studied piano as a child.

After graduating from high school, Nishimura enrolled in the University of California (UC) San Diego. A psychology student, she initially planned to attend medical school after completing her degree, with the goal of entering a medical profession. During her time in college, she remained interested in the music industry and managed various bands during her spare time. She earned her bachelor's degree in psychology from UC San Diego in 1993.

EARLY CAREER

Though she still planned to attend medical school following her graduation from UC San Diego, the timing of Nishimura's graduation gave her the opportunity to seek out an internship to fill her time before enrolling. She obtained a position with Windham Hill Records, a small record label specializing in instrumental music that was based in northern California during that period. "When I got it, they said, "It pays $4.70 an hour, and there's absolutely no full-time job on the other end," Nishimura told *Fast Company* (29 Oct. 2018) about the internship. Soon, however, Nishimura's job prospects—and career trajectory as a whole—changed significantly. "To my surprise, after three months, they offered me a full-time gig . . . so I took it," she told *Fast Company*. Having traded her medical aspirations for a career in the media industry, Nishimura went on to work as director of international film and music distribution for Valley Media in 1995 and 1996.

Midway through 1996, Nishimura moved further into the music industry, joining Six Degrees Records as head of sales. Founded by former employees of Windham Hill Records, Six Degrees Records was affiliated with Island Records, a label cofounded by record executive Chris Blackwell. Blackwell would go on to found the independent film and home-video distributor Palm Pictures, and Nishimura joined that company as general manager in January 2002. She remained with Palm Pictures until September 2007. During her time with the company, Nishimura gained experience in producing independent content and met top executives from the DVD-rental service Netflix, further shaping her career to come.

NETFLIX

Having become familiar with Nishimura through her work with Palm Pictures, Netflix executives recruited her to join the company in 2007. Moving to Netflix in October of that year, Nishimura became the company's vice president of independent content acquisition. Although Netflix had introduced its streaming video platform—soon to become its primary service—that year, the company was still primarily focused on renting DVDs and did not produce any original content. To stock Netflix's library film and television library, Nishimura was tasked with acquiring content from a broad range of genres and from all over the world. "What was exciting was [that] it was the first global job," she recalled to Press. "So I was buying anime from Japanese studios, I was buying Scandinavian horror shows, I was buying French drama, American independents."

Nishimura's efforts proved successful, and Netflix leadership encouraged her to continue to seek out new and exciting content. "I remember early on being told, 'Hey! Your metrics look really good,' and I thought it was just going to be a little compliment at the end of the sentence," Nishimura told Ryu. "But the comment was, 'I wonder if you're taking enough risks!' That was my first year at the company, and I thought, 'OK, this is a different place.'"

As Netflix shifted its focus toward streaming video, Nishimura continued to acquire a broad range of content for the service's users to enjoy through that platform. In 2012 the company began a new push toward releasing original content, initially focusing on scripted television series. In keeping with the interests and viewing habits of Netflix customers, Nishimura suggested that the company also specifically look into producing original documentaries and comedy content, both of which were popular among the service's user base. "Thinking about our global membership is really the driver," she told Ryu about her approach. "That's the north star: What's going to bring the member joy? What stories are going to be really resonant?" By the end of 2012,

she had been named vice president of original documentary and comedy programming and was tasked with seeking out opportunities to provide viewers with high-quality original content in those genres. Among Netflix's earliest successes in that mission were a series of original comedy specials for which Nishimura served as executive producer, including standup specials by comedians such as Chelsea Peretti, John Mulaney, Hannibal Buress, Patton Oswalt, and Ali Wong.

DOCUMENTARY CONTENT

While Netflix's entry into the realm of original comedy specials proved successful among viewers and influential within the comedy community, its development as a prominent producer of documentary content under Nishimura's leadership was perhaps of even greater significance. The company's first original feature-length documentary, The Square (Al midan), debuted in 2013. Nishimura served as executive producer for the film, which focused on political unrest in Egypt during the period known as the Arab Spring. The Square was nominated for the Academy Award for best documentary and won three Emmy Awards for nonfiction programming, signaling the critical establishment's willingness to recognize Netflix's achievements within the documentary space.

The success of The Square and Netflix's later feature-length documentaries likewise signaled a significant shift in the life cycle of such films, which often struggled to reach interested viewers. "A documentary might come out at a festival, be beautifully reviewed, and people would be excited to see it," Nishimura explained to Ryu. "But if it didn't get distribution—except for the handful of people who were lucky enough to see it at the festival—nobody got to see it." Distribution via Netflix, however, enabled documentaries to attain wider viewership, which Nishimura cited as one of the key benefits for filmmakers working with the company.

In addition to feature-length documentaries, Netflix became well known for the documentary series format. This was popularized by the series Making a Murderer, introduced to Netflix subscribers in 2015 and focusing on accused killer Steven Avery and the legal proceedings surrounding his case. Although the subject matter and format of the series might have dissuaded other media executives, Nishimura was intrigued by its promise. "I was completely engrossed in the story," she told Press. "On paper, the fact that these are first-time filmmakers might raise your blood pressure a little bit, but [not] if you looked them in the eye and saw the materials and the rigor." In addition to winning four Emmy Awards for its debut season, Making a Murderer proved particularly popular among Netflix viewers. It helped the trend of watching multiple episodes in a single sitting—known popularly as binge watching—become the subject of external media attention.

Netflix replicated the viral success of *Making a Murderer* with the 2018 documentary series *Wild Wild Country*, which Nishimura acquired for the service based on a 2015 pitch from filmmakers Chapman Way and Maclain Way. Focusing on clashes between residents of a small Oregon town and the followers of a spiritual leader who moved to the area during the 1980s, the documentary drew particular attention thanks to its unusual subject matter, unique setting, and thought-provoking lesson that "life is messy and all sides of a story have 100 percent conviction that they are on the right side of reason," as Nishimura told Press.

In addition to her work acquiring such series, Nishimura served as a producer for several major Netflix documentary programs. These included *13th* (2016), created by acclaimed filmmaker Ava DuVernay, as well as for food-related documentary content such as the series *Chef's Table* (2015) and *Ugly Delicious* (2018). She also executive produced the 2016 documentary short *The White Helmets*, which won the Academy Award for best documentary short subject. In March 2019, Nishimura was named Netflix's vice president of independent film and documentary features.

PERSONAL LIFE

Nishimura, who also sometimes uses the name Lisa Nishimura-Seese, is married to former Palm Pictures coworker Greg Nishimura-Seese. Together they have a son, named Royal Kai. In addition to developing content for Netflix, she enjoys cooking, gardening, hiking, and working with ceramics.

SUGGESTED READING

Jarvey, Natalie. "Top Netflix Exec on 'Making a Murderer' Season 2 and Chris Rock's $40M Payday." *Hollywood Reporter*, 17 Nov. 2016, www.hollywoodreporter.com/news/top-netflix-exec-making-a-murderer-season-2-chris-rocks-40m-payday-947227. Accessed 13 Dec. 2019.

Low, Elaine. "Netflix's Lisa Nishimura Named Indie Film, Documentary Features Head." *Variety*, 20 Mar. 2019, variety.com/2019/tv/news/netflix-lisa-nishimura-brandon-riegg-1203168827/amp/. Accessed 13 Dec. 2019.

Nishimura, Lisa. "Lisa Nishimura on How She Picks Documentaries for Netflix." Interview with Matt Holzman. *KCRW*, 10 Dec. 2018, www.kcrw.com/culture/shows/the-business/kristoffer-polaha-on-hallmark-movies-netflixs-lisa-nishimura/lisa-nishimura-on-how-she-picks-documentaries-for-netflix. Accessed 13 Dec. 2019.

———. "Netflix's Lisa Nishimura Is One of the Most Powerful Asian Americans in Hollywood." Interview with Audrey Ryu. *Character Media*, 28 Nov. 2018, charactermedia.com/netflixs-lisa-nishimura-is-one-of-the-most-powerful-asian-americans-japanese-in-hollywood/. Accessed 13 Dec. 2019.

———. "Netflix's Lisa Nishimura on Patagonia, Nike, and Jane Austen." *Fast Company*, 29 Oct. 2018, www.fastcompany.com/90248445/netflixs-lisa-nishimura-on-patagonia-nike-and-jane-austen. Accessed 13 Dec. 2019.

———. "Our Diverse 100: Meet Lisa Nishimura, the Executive Finding Audiences (and Oscars) for Netflix Comedies and Documentaries." Interview with Rebecca Keegan. *Los Angeles Times*, 2 June 2016, www.latimes.com/entertainment/movies/la-et-mn-academy-diversity-candidates-lisa-nishimura-20160525-snap-htmlstory.html. Accessed 13 Dec. 2019.

Press, Joy. "This Is the Netflix Exec to Thank for Your *Wild Wild Country* Binge." *Vanity Fair*, 15 June 2018, www.vanityfair.com/hollywood/2018/06/lisa-nishamura-netflix-documentary-wild-wild-country/amp. Accessed 13 Dec. 2019.

—*Joy Crelin*

Samin Nosrat

Born: November 7, 1979
Occupation: Chef and food writer

In the oversaturated world of food television, the Iranian American chef, writer, and teacher Samin Nosrat stands out. A native of California, she led a virtually anonymous culinary career for almost two decades before earning widespread attention in 2017 with the publication of her James Beard Award–winning first cookbook *Salt, Fat, Acid, Heat: Mastering the Elements of Good Cooking*, which highlights a groundbreaking cooking philosophy based around those four eponymous elements. The highly acclaimed book spawned a four-episode companion series of the same name starring Nosrat that was released in 2018 on the streaming service Netflix. The popularity of her book and series helped Nosrat, a protégé of the noted American chef Alice Waters, become a "darling of the food world" and reach "full-blown food celebrity" status, as Amanda Shapiro declared for *Bon Appétit* (21 Mar. 2019).

Known for her infectiously charming demeanor, Nosrat has been credited with breaking down cultural barriers through her relaxed, empowering, and accessible approach to home cooking. As she explained to Helen Rosner in an interview for the *New Yorker* (23 Feb. 2020), "What I tried to do with my show is convey this idea that good food around the world is more similar than it is different, and that we, as humans, are more similar than we are different."

EARLY LIFE

Samin Nosrat was born on November 7, 1979, in San Diego, California. Along with her twin brothers, who are four years younger, she was raised in the city's middle-class University City neighborhood. (Nosrat had an older sister who died of a brain tumor at the age of three.) Nosrat's parents emigrated from Iran to the United States in 1976, unsure about whether they would be able to return there. As a result, her mother "made it a priority to immerse us in the culture of our homeland," as Nosrat wrote in an article for the *Guardian* (20 Aug. 2017).

Nosrat grew up almost exclusively eating Iranian cuisine. She would later recall spending a good portion of her childhood accompanying her mother on trips all over San Diego and its surrounding counties in search of the proper ingredients. Though intensely fond of eating, Nosrat did not demonstrate an interest in cooking until adulthood; her early experiences in the kitchen were mostly limited to menial tasks like peeling eggplants. Still, "food was always this incredible thing bringing our family together," she told Kelly Hensel for *Food Technology Magazine* (1 May 2017), adding that it helped keep them connected to their culture.

While her palate was unwaveringly Iranian, Nosrat, like many other children of immigrants, struggled with identity issues throughout her youth and adolescence. "I grew up a brown kid in a super-white world," she told Rosner. "I was called a 'terrorist' in second grade. I was always aware that I was different, and I didn't fit in." Nonetheless, she made concerted attempts to "fit in" with her white peers by becoming a high-achieving people pleaser. To challenge herself both academically and socially, Nosrat attended La Jolla High School, a prestigious institution located in one of San Diego's most affluent areas, where she first discovered her passion and talent for writing. Upon graduating from high school in 1997, she enrolled at the University of California, Berkeley.

CHEZ PANISSE

At Berkeley, Nosrat majored in English and intended to follow a path that would help her become a professional writer. However, she admittedly did not know how to implement that plan. The idea of pursuing a culinary career did not occur to Nosrat until May 1999, when she had dinner at Alice Waters's world-renowned Berkeley restaurant Chez Panisse, which has been credited with pioneering California cuisine and with launching the modern farm-to-table movement. Nosrat's meal that day included frisée aux lardons salad, halibut in broth, guinea hen, and a chocolate soufflé filled with raspberry sauce. She later recalled to Hensel that, "Eating there was an illuminating experience, both as a diner, but certainly as just a person experiencing what it is to be in a restaurant and be really cared for."

After spending her junior year abroad in London, Nosrat, still inspired by her life-changing meal at Chez Panisse, personally wrote Waters a letter asking for a job bussing tables there. Waters obliged, and Nosrat worked at the restaurant part time as a busser throughout her senior year at Berkeley. It was during this time that Nosrat began to immerse herself in the intricacies of food and cooking. Surrounded by like-minded overachievers and perfectionists at Chez Panisse, Nosrat recounted in the *Guardian* article, "Everyone had something to teach me, from how to vacuum quickly and efficiently to how to hold three plates without dropping them and how to properly slice crusty bread."

Nosrat's burgeoning passion for food culture was such that she even skipped her college graduation ceremony in the spring of 2001 to work a nighttime bussing shift. By then, she had already made unsuccessful attempts to join Chez Panisse's kitchen staff. She was eventually given that opportunity, serving as an unpaid apprentice before rising to become the restaurant's *garde manger*, a paid position in which she was charged with such tasks as making staff meals and accepting deliveries. In these roles Nosrat intently observed the cooking styles of her chef colleagues, nearly all of whom worked off pure instinct, without following recipes and directions. She would later note that Chez Panisse, more than anything else, taught her how to use all five of her senses both in and out of the kitchen.

TRANSITION TO FOOD WRITING AND TEACHING

Wanting to expand her culinary education, Nosrat left Chez Panisse and moved to Italy, where she spent two years apprenticing under the noted Florentine chef Benedetta Vitali. Upon returning to the United States in 2004, Nosrat landed a job as a line cook at Eccolo, an Italian bistro in Berkeley founded by her former Chez Panisse colleague Christopher Lee. There, she ascended to the position of sous chef, which put her in charge of the restaurant's kitchen staff. She held that role until Eccolo closed in 2009.

While at Eccolo, Nosrat met and befriended the acclaimed food journalist, author, and teacher Michael Pollan. Pollan allowed her to audit one of his classes at UC Berkeley's School of Journalism in the spring of 2007. Encouraged by her performance in the class, Nosrat started writing about food for local publications such as *Edible San Francisco* and the *San Francisco Chronicle*. Around this time, she also segued into teaching private cooking classes, which ultimately led Pollan to hire her as his personal cooking instructor in 2010. Her tutelage helped inform Pollan's 2013 book *Cooked: A Natural History of Transformation*.

The same year of that book's publication, Nosrat sold the manuscript for her first cookbook, which was acquired by Simon & Shuster in a bidding war. Her manuscript focused on the science behind the four elements in which Nosrat's cooking philosophy is grounded: salt, fat, acid, and heat. Nosrat—who had previously abandoned two other book projects—considered the work "a distillation of my cooking experiences into a way to simplify and think about cooking," as she explained to Hensel. "I wanted to try to create a roadmap for people to be able to understand what sensory cues to look for as they cook. And how to develop their palate so they know what it is they're tasting for."

SUCCESS AND ACCLAIM FOR *SALT, FAT, ACID, HEAT*

Nosrat took three years to finish her manuscript, during which time she also appeared in an episode of Pollan's Netflix series *Cooked* in 2016. When *Salt, Fat, Acid, Heat* was published in April 2017, the 480-page, photo-less book received rapturous praise from critics. Reviewers heralded its unpretentious and unvarnished approach to home cooking. In addition to espousing her cooking philosophy, the book, which features illustrations by Wendy MacNaughton, highlights Nosrat's many culinary mishaps in her journey toward becoming a capable chef both in professional kitchens and at home. In her *New Yorker* article, Rosner called the book "a clear-eyed, conversational, often strikingly funny explication of the fundamental principles of good cooking."

Salt, Fat, Acid, Heat became a *New York Times* Best Seller only weeks after its release and went on to receive a number of culinary honors. Perhaps most notable was the 2018 James Beard Award for best cookbook—"the food equivalent of Best Picture," as Shapiro put it. It would remain a best seller for years, and came to be widely regarded as one of the best and most influential cookbooks of the twenty-first century. The book's enormous popularity led to the creation of a four-episode Netflix food and travel documentary series of the same name, which helped transform Nosrat into a global food celebrity.

Debuting on the streaming service in October 2018, *Salt Fat Acid Heat*, like its source material, won wide acclaim. In each of the series' four episodes, Nosrat explores a component from its title: salt in Japan, fat in Italy, acid in Mexico, and heat in California. Netflix's first instructional cooking show, the women-centric series earned much praise for uprooting the social conventions of food television. In a representative review for the *Washington Post* (15 Oct. 2018), Maura Judkis commented on the groundbreaking nature of a woman of color hosting such a series: "Most travel food shows are about white male discovery. And most home cooking shows are about white female domesticity. Nosrat gently rejects all of that."

Rather than give an air of perfection in a glossy show kitchen like many other cooking shows, Nosrat endeared herself to viewers with imperfections, ones that are celebrated through her magnetic and at times goofy personality and a perpetually exuberant enthusiasm about food. As Nosrat explained to Mayukh Sen for the *Guardian* (4 Jan. 2019), "Silliness and wackiness and clumsiness can disarm people, and are a beautiful way of balancing the more serious things I have to offer."

In addition to her book and series, Nosrat also wrote for various outlets, including as a regular columnist for *New York Times Magazine*'s *Eat* blog beginning in 2017. In March 2019 she announced she was working on her second cookbook, *What to Cook*, again with illustrations by MacNaughton.

PERSONAL LIFE

Though known for her charisma and joyfulness as seen on screen, Nosrat noted that at times she found fame challenging. "I'm grateful about people who are moved enough by the work to want to say something. But I mourn the loss of anonymity," she told Sen. Nosrat also often discussed other personal challenges with interviewers, from her struggles to pursue a more vegan diet to facing bouts of depression.

SUGGESTED READING

Judkis, Maura. "Netflix's New 'Salt Fat Acid Heat' Is Unlike Any Other Food Show on TV." *The Washington Post*, 15 Oct. 2018, www.washingtonpost.com/news/voraciously/wp/2018/10/15/netflixs-new-salt-fat-acid-heat-is-unlike-any-other-food-show-on-tv/. Accessed 22 Apr. 2020.

Nosrat, Samin. "How to Cook Like a Pro. Step One: Listen to the Sound Your Food Makes." *The Guardian*, 20 Aug. 2017, www.theguardian.com/lifeandstyle/2017/aug/20/how-to-cook-like-a-pro-listen-to-your-food-samin-nosrat-chez-panisse-chef-alice-waters. Accessed 22 Apr. 2020.

———. "'I Fail Almost Every Day': An Interview with Samin Nosrat." Interview by Helen Rosner. *The New Yorker*, 23 Feb. 2020, www.newyorker.com/culture/the-new-yorker-interview/i-fail-almost-every-day-an-interview-with-samin-nosrat. Accessed 22 Apr. 2020.

———. "Mastering the Elements of Good Cooking." Interview by Kelly Hensel. *Food Technology Magazine*, 1 May 2017, www.ift. org/news-and-publications/food-technology-magazine/issues/2017/may/columns/culinary-point-of-view-samin-nosrat. Accessed 22 Apr. 2020.

Sen, Mayukh. "Success Comes with Its Own Heart Attack: Netflix Chef Samin Nosrat on the Reality of Fame." *The Guardian*, 4 Jan. 2019, www.theguardian.com/food/2019/jan/04/samin-nosrat-salt-fat-acid-heat-netflix. Accessed 2 Apr. 2020.

Shapiro, Amanda. "Everybody Loves Samin." *Bon Appétit*, 21 Mar. 2019, www.bonappetit.com/story/samin-nosrat. Accessed 22 Apr. 2020.

Zhang, Jenny G. "'Salt, Fat, Acid, Heat' Changes the Rules for Who Gets to Eat on TV." *Eater*, 24 Oct. 2018, www.eater.com/2018/10/24/18014782/salt-fat-acid-heat-samin-nosrat-eating-cooking-food-tv-netflix. Accessed 22 Apr. 2020.

—*Chris Cullen*

Kia Nurse

Born: February 22, 1996
Occupation: Basketball player

Women's National Basketball Association (WNBA) player Kia Nurse got her start with the Canadian junior national team at the age of sixteen. Inspired by her older sister, who also played basketball for the Canadian junior team, Nurse took up the sport at the age of four and "just fell in love with basketball really quickly," she told Kennedi Landry for *SBNation* (21 Aug. 2019). Nurse's dedication to the game and skills on the court won her early international recognition. Following four successful seasons and two championship victories with the University of Connecticut (UConn) Huskies, Nurse began her professional basketball career with the New York Liberty in mid-2018, becoming one of the most talked-about young players in the WNBA. Yet, despite those accomplishments, Nurse prefers to focus not on the past, but on the challenges and victories yet to come. "I try not to sit back and think about what I've already accomplished and feel like, 'OK. Well, it was good enough, my career's gonna have a legacy,'" she told Ben Forrest for *Sports Illustrated* (5 May 2020). "I feel like I want it to be a lot more than what it is."

EARLY LIFE AND EDUCATION

Nurse was born on February 22, 1996, in Hamilton, Ontario, Canada. The youngest of three children born to Richard and Cathy Nurse, she grew up within a family of athletes: her father had played in the Canadian Football League (CFL) during the early 1990s, and her mother had played basketball while in college. Nurse's older brother, Darnell, played hockey throughout his childhood and went on to play in the National Hockey League (NHL), while her older sister, Tamika, played basketball in college as well as in junior-level international tournaments.

Although Nurse was active in multiple sports over the course of her childhood, including soccer, she was particularly drawn to basketball thanks to the influence of her older sister, whom she greatly admired. "I wanted to be everything she was," she told Landry. Nurse began playing basketball at the age of four and continued to play throughout her schooling, including during her years at St. Thomas More Catholic Secondary School. As a member of the school's girls' basketball team, Nurse helped lead the team to three consecutive championships, in 2011, 2012, and 2013. She also represented Ontario during that period, competing for her province in multiple championships. Nurse graduated from high school in 2014.

TEAM CANADA

Alongside competing at the high school and provincial levels, Nurse began to represent Canada in junior-level international competitions in 2011, when she joined the country's under-sixteen (U-16) girls' team at the U-16 International Basketball Federation (FIBA) Americas Championship. The next year, she served as captain of the under-seventeen (U-17) Canadian girls' team

Photo by FIBA via Wikimedia Commons

at the U-17 FIBA World Championship, where Canada claimed the bronze medal. Beginning in 2013, Nurse moved up to the senior-level team, where she trained and played alongside much older, more established players. "School was still going on, and I was like, 'These are grown women. They talk about taxes, marriage. I don't even know what's happening over here,'" she recalled to Kristina Rutherford for *Sportsnet*. As a member of the senior team, Nurse contributed to the Canadian women's second-place finish in the 2013 FIBA Americas Championship.

Having established herself as a key member of Team Canada, Nurse continued to play with the senior national team over the next several years, appearing in competitions such as the 2014 FIBA World Championship. A key moment came in 2015, when the team claimed the gold medal at that year's Pan American Games and drew widespread attention to the skills and dedication of Nurse and her teammates. "No one ever talked about Canadian players coming up on the women's side," she later told Rutherford about the period prior to the 2015 win. "Once Pan-Ams happened, everybody started noticing, 'Hey, there's some really good women coming up and this team has been performing really well on the world stage.' People finally actually looked at us like we were serious, and that we were actually good at what we were doing." Fueled by their success at the Pan American Games, Nurse and her teammates went on to compete in the 2016 Olympic Games in Brazil, where the Canadian women's team progressed through the group stage but ultimately lost to France in the quarterfinals.

UNIVERSITY OF CONNECTICUT

As Nurse's high-school career approached its end, she drew the attention of recruiters from numerous college basketball programs and began to develop a list of potential choices. She eventually decided to travel to the United States to enroll at the University of Connecticut (UConn), an institution that competed within Division I of the National Collegiate Athletic Association (NCAA) and was particularly known for the strength of its women's basketball team. Indeed, the team had such a strong reputation that Nurse believed she would struggle to attain a spot as a player. "I thought it was a risk to go to UConn, because I figured I'm going to sit on the bench for two years behind some really good players, and try to learn as much as I can from them and see what happens," she explained to Rutherford.

After enrolling at UConn in late 2014, however, Nurse found that her concerns were largely unwarranted: Joining the Huskies women's basketball team as a freshman, she went on to score 399 points over the course of her debut season and was named to the American Athletic

Conference's All-Freshmen Team in recognition of her performance on the court. The 2014–15 college basketball season also saw Nurse compete in her first NCAA Division I Women's Basketball Championship, during which her team claimed the championship title. She remained a key member of the team over the next three seasons, consistently accompanying the Huskies to the NCAA Championship and winning an additional title in 2016. In recognition of her contributions, she received a variety of honors and was named to several different American Athletic Conference and All-America teams. A sports management major, Nurse graduated from UConn in May 2018.

NEW YORK LIBERTY

In April 2018, the New York Liberty of the WNBA selected Nurse in the first round of that year's WNBA Draft. The tenth overall draft pick, Nurse signed a four-year deal with the team, becoming the sixteenth athlete from Canada to join the league. After appearing in a selection of exhibition games, Nurse made her regular-season debut with the Liberty on May 20, 2018, in a game against the Chicago Sky. She scored 17 points during her debut game, the second most of any Liberty player; she beat the franchise record for most points by a rookie in her fourth game with 34 points. Nurse went on to play in a total of thirty-four games over the course of the season, starting seven of them. She scored a total of 310 points during the season and achieved an average of 8.7 points per game, second on her team and seventh in the league for rookies.

Although the 2018 season was a disappointing one for the Liberty, which ended the season with a record of only seven wins and twenty-seven losses, Nurse received significant attention among fans and the sports media due to her substantial contributions to the team. Though preferring to focus on self-improvement rather than accolades, she was pleased to be able to promote the sport of basketball in Canada, where hockey had long been dominant. "There's a huge, huge, huge love for the sport right now," she told Landry. "If a young kid wants to pick up a stick and a puck and some skates, go for it, but I'm all for a kid picking up a ball and going outside and playing." Nurse remained with the Liberty for the 2019 season, during which she started all thirty-four games and scored a total of 465 points. She achieved a total of 116 free throws, the fifth most in the league, as well as the sixth-most three-point field goals (65) in the WNBA. In recognition of her strong performance, Nurse was selected as a starting player for the 2019 WNBA All-Star Game.

CANBERRA CAPITALS

Many of the WNBA's players choose to spend their off seasons playing abroad to develop their skills further and earn additional income to offset the relatively low salaries available to WNBA athletes. Nurse chose that path in mid-2018, signing a contract with the University of Canberra Capitals of Australia's Women's National Basketball League (WNBL). She spent the 2018–19 and 2019–20 WNBL seasons with Canberra, during which the team won two consecutive WNBL championships. Nurse earned a number of honors during her time with Canberra, including player of the week honors and most valuable player for the 2019–20 season.

In addition to proving financially beneficial, Nurse's seasons in Australia proved productive on a more personal level as well. "I was allowed to be in a system in Australia where I was a lot more free than any system I've played in since my high school days," she explained to Forrest. "That allowed me to kind of get confidence back into my offensive game . . . and that was pretty exciting." In early 2020, however, Nurse announced that she did not plan to return to Canberra for the 2020–21 season, as she planned to pursue other ventures in North America and hoped to give herself more time to rest and recuperate between WNBA seasons.

PREPARING FOR THE FUTURE
Though the 2020 WNBA season was initially scheduled to begin in May, the emergence of the coronavirus (COVID-19) pandemic in early 2020 forced league leadership to delay the start of the season until July and devise a new, condensed schedule of games. While the period was one of uncertainty, Nurse preferred not to dwell on the delay, focusing instead on spending time with her family and continuing her workouts at home. "I'm not gonna forget how to shoot just because I haven't shot in a couple weeks and that's how I've kinda seen it," she told Sarah Valenzuela for the *New York Daily News* (29 Apr. 2020). "I've been doing this for many years now. It's ingrained in what I do." The New York Liberty's 2020 season began on July 25, 2020, with a game against the Seattle Storm. Despite spraining an ankle during that opening game, Nurse remained a key member of the team and contributed seventeen points toward the Liberty's first win of the season, which took place in an August game against the Washington Mystics.

The COVID-19 pandemic likewise prompted the delay of the 2020 Olympic Games, in which Nurse had planned to represent Canada in the women's basketball tournament. In March 2020, the International Olympic Committee postponed the event—initially set to take place in Tokyo, Japan, during the summer of that year—to July 2021. Though some might consider the postponement of the Olympics to be a setback, Nurse maintained a positive attitude and continued to look forward to Team Canada's return to competition. "We've had a lot of time together in the last three years to prepare for this," she told Forrest. "So hopefully another year won't be anything of an issue for us."

PERSONAL LIFE
Nurse lives in the New York Liberty's home state of New York during the WNBA season and spends a portion of her time in Hamilton with her family. In addition to playing basketball in the WNBA, the WNBL, and international competitions, she has worked as a basketball analyst for the sports television channel TSN. Nurse has signed endorsement deals with companies such as Nike and its basketball-themed offshoot Jordan Brand.

SUGGESTED READING
Forrest, Ben. "Kia Nurse Is Riding a Remarkable High . . . and She's Not Done Yet." *Sports Illustrated*, 5 May 2020, www.si.com/nba/raptors/canada-basketball/canadas-kia-nurse-quickly-becoming-womens-basketball-star. Accessed 9 Aug. 2020.

Landry, Kennedi. "Kia Nurse Is Becoming the Face of Canadian Women's Basketball." *SB-Nation*, 21 Aug. 2019, www.sbnation.com/wnba/2019/8/21/20806139/kia-nurse-wnba-canada-new-york-liberty. Accessed 9 Aug. 2020.

Magliocchetti, Geoff. "New York Liberty: Kia Nurse Comments on Injury, New Efforts in 2020." *Empire Sports Media*, 27 July 2020, empiresportsmedia.com/liberty/new-york-liberty-kia-nurse-comments-on-injury-new-efforts-in-2020/. Accessed 9 Aug. 2020.

Nurse, Kia. "Watch: Interview with New York Liberty Rookie Kia Nurse." Interview by Ian Bethune. *UConn Blog*, 20 May 2018, www.theuconnblog.com/2018/5/20/17373550/interview-with-new-york-liberty-rookie-kia-nurse-uconn-huskies-womens-basketball-canada. Accessed 9 Aug. 2020.

Rutherford, Kristina. "Just Getting Started." *Sportsnet*, www.sportsnet.ca/basketball/nba/kia-nurse-canada-new-york-liberty-wnba-profile. Accessed 9 Aug. 2020.

Valenzuela, Sarah. "Liberty G Kia Nurse Makes the Most of Her Indefinite Offseason." *New York Daily News*, Tribune Publishing, 29 Apr. 2020, www.nydailynews.com/sports/basketball/ny-liberty-kia-nurse-offseason-coronavirus-20200429-ocjckmk5gjhgvdaezn3p4v7kje-story.html. Accessed 9 Aug. 2020.

—*Joy Crelin*

Adriana Ocampo

Date of birth: January 5, 1955
Occupation: Planetary geologist

Photo by BugWarp via Wikimedia Commons

Longtime NASA researcher Adriana Ocampo fell in love with space exploration at a young age and never looked back. During her childhood she daydreamed of exploring space herself as an astronaut. As a teenage immigrant to the United States she began volunteering at NASA's Jet Propulsion Laboratory (JPL) in the early 1970s, working her way to become a full-time employee. She would go on to earn considerable acclaim for her groundbreaking work, and in 2005 she was named the lead executive for NASA's New Frontiers program. In that capacity she oversaw the New Horizons mission to the dwarf planet Pluto, the Juno mission to the planet Jupiter, the OSIRIS-REx asteroid sample mission, and other major projects.

As a planetary geologist, Ocampo also studied Earth along with other celestial bodies. In fact, arguably her best-known achievement was helping to prove the existence of the Chicxulub impact crater in Mexico. This crater is all that remains of a large object—either an asteroid or comet—that struck the Earth about 65 million years ago, wiping out more than half of all species, including the dinosaurs. Its discovery made Ocampo a leading figure in her field, known for her expertise in remote sensing. She subsequently used her recognition to bring attention to causes such as international cooperation, education, and advocacy for women and minorities in science. On her official NASA webpage, Ocampo advised anyone who might want to follow in her footsteps: "Dream and never give up. When thinking about the great adventure that you have ahead, dream and never give-up, be

persistent and always be true to your heart. Live life with gusto."

EARLY LIFE AND EDUCATION

Adriana C. Ocampo was born in Barranquilla, Colombia, on January 5, 1955, though her family soon moved to Buenos Aires, Argentina. She grew up there with two sisters. Her mother was a teacher at a Montessori school, while her father was an electrician who often also held additional jobs. Above all else, her parents were encouraging of their daughters' dreams. "When I was a little girl I would go on the roof of my house and look at the stars and wonder how far they were away from me," Ocampo recalled on her NASA profile. "I would also make 'spacecraft' with the pots and pans from my mother's kitchen. I would dress my doll up as an astronaut, and my dog Taurus was my co-pilot."

Although the school system provided few opportunities for girls to pursue science, Ocampo maintained her interest as she got older. In particular she became obsessed with the US National Aeronautics and Space Administration (NASA), which at the time was continually pushing the boundaries of space travel and research. "I ended up writing a letter addressed only to 'NASA'; it made its way there and they wrote back!" she noted on the website *Share Your Road* (2019). "That crystalized my interest in space exploration."

Ocampo and her family moved again when she was fourteen, this time to Pasadena, California. She was somewhat nervous about moving to the United States because she had studied French in school and not English, but her struggles with the language were short-lived. Meanwhile, she was excited to find out all she could about NASA, including the nearby Jet Propulsion Laboratory (JPL). Thanks to a program through her high school, Ocampo was able to volunteer at the JPL and then get a summer job there after her junior year. She kept working at the JPL after graduating from high school and entering college. She first enrolled at Pasadena City College, where she earned an associate degree in physical sciences in 1977, and then studied geology at California State University, Los Angeles, graduating with a bachelor's degree in 1983. (Ocampo would later receive a master's degree in planetary geology from California State University, Northridge in 1999 and a PhD in planetary geology from the Vrije Universiteit Amsterdam in 2013.)

NASA RESEARCHER

Ocampo's career at NASA built steadily from her high school years onward. From 1973 to 1983 she served as a student researcher at the JPL, essentially working part time as an assistant to help pay her way through college. She then accepted a full-time position as a research scientist at the JPL. She would later reflect on the incredible opportunity that NASA presented, despite the challenges she had to overcome. "Obviously there were not many girls, and on top of being a girl I spoke English with a 'funny' accent, so I was kind of a double minority," she told Claire van den Broek for the academic research–focused *Mendeley Blog* (5 Aug. 2014). "But they were really open and gave me a chance."

Over her decades at NASA, Ocampo was involved with numerous space missions. In the 1970s she worked on the Viking missions to Mars, processing the images the landers sent back to Earth. Her work would eventually result in an important photo atlas of Mars's moon Phobos, published in 1984. Another early career highlight was Ocampo's time as a member of the navigation and mission planning teams for the Voyager missions to the outer planets of Jupiter, Saturn, Uranus, and Neptune. The Voyager probes were launched in 1977 and continued to send back telemetry even after they went far beyond their planetary targets and reached interstellar space. Ocampo helped formulate data on the movement of Saturn and its moons and rings that the craft used to navigate. She was also involved in the Hermes program researching the inner planet Mercury.

Ocampo's role increased with the *Galileo* spacecraft, which was launched in 1989 and arrived at Jupiter in late 1995. She led the mission's Near Infrared Mapping Spectrometer (NIMS) operation using one of *Galileo*'s instruments. The NIMS team collected valuable data about composition of the asteroid Gaspra as it passed the probe, as well as much information about Jupiter and its moons. Ocampo focused on the moon Europa and the makeup of its surface. Through missions like these she developed an expertise in the field of remote sensing, and specifically tools that allow planetary geologists and geographers to better understand how planetary surfaces have been reshaped over millions of years, including by impacts from asteroids or comets. This knowledge would prove critical to one of the crowning episodes of her career—one that focused on Earth rather than outer space.

CONFIRMING THE CHICXULUB CRATER

By the early 1980s several researchers had proposed that a large asteroid or other celestial body impacted the Earth roughly 65 million years ago, causing a mass extinction that included the dinosaurs (known as the Cretaceous-Paleogene (K-Pg) or Cretaceous-Tertiary (K-T) extinction event). However, at the time there was very little hard evidence to support that theory. Meanwhile, oil exploration led to the discovery of a massive buried crater on the coast of Mexico's Yucatán peninsula. During 1989 and 1990 Ocampo and fellow researchers Kevin O. Pope and Charles Duller were involved in a mapping project in

that area and discovered a cluster of cenotes, or sinkholes, aligned in a semicircle. They realized that the formation was linked to the crater, potentially indicating it as a major impact site that would fit the timeframe of the K-Pg extinction. In May 1991, the trio published their findings in the prestigious scientific journal *Nature*.

The work by Ocampo and her colleagues on what became known as the Chicxulub crater was the first real scientific proof of a catastrophic impact that may have wiped out as much as half of the life that was then abundant on Earth. In addition to the devastation of the impact itself, the event likely sent up a dust cloud and ignited fires that blocked out the sun, killing off plant life and further stressing surviving populations. The planet likely saw a drop in temperature that led to near-freezing conditions worldwide. As Ocampo noted in her NASA profile, "this amazing event . . . changed the evolution of life on our planet."

The Chicxulub crater became a central focus of Ocampo's career, providing the foundation for both her master's and PhD thesis work. She was involved with numerous expeditions to the site over the years, adding further data to support the K-Pg impact theory. With teams of fellow scientists, she collected hundreds of pounds of samples, including drill cores and fossils. Among the important discoveries were sites of ejecta, or material that was expelled from the impact site. Some of these rare features include tektites, small spheres of glass that strongly indicate extreme heat from an impact event. They are also significant for what they can tell researchers about similar features on other planets. "The discovery of these new ejecta sites is very exciting," Ocampo said, as quoted on the *JPL* website (12 Mar. 1998). "It is like seeing a bit of Mars on Earth."

NEW FRONTIERS

Ocampo would go on to apply her experience with the Chicxulub crater to other impact sites around the world. In 1996 she studied ejecta in Gubbio, Italy. That same year she announced that radar imaging conducted by the space shuttle program had led to the discovery of a chain of impact craters in Chad, Africa. Her team hypothesized that those impacts, though much smaller than at Chicxulub, may have been related to another extinction event approximately 360 million years ago. "Could these impacts be part of a larger event? Were they, perhaps, part of comet showers that could have added to the extinction?" she speculated to Douglas Isbell and Mary Hardin for the *JPL* website (20 Mar. 1996). "Little by little, we are putting the puzzle together to understand how Earth has evolved."

In 1998 Ocampo took a new position with NASA as a program executive in Washington, DC. There her work focused on promoting international cooperation on space science, something she had advocated for throughout her career. As part of her duties she contributed to joint missions with other space agencies around the world, including the European Space Agency (ESA). From 2002 to 2004 she also served as a senior scientist with the ESA.

In 2005 Ocampo was named lead program executive for NASA's series of missions known as New Frontiers. That program focused on studying the outer solar system with several next-generation space probes. The first of these spacecraft was *New Horizons*, which was launched in 2006 and traveled to Pluto, becoming in 2015 the first space probe to photograph the former ninth planet of the solar system in any detail. The second was *Juno*, which was launched in 2011 and entered orbit around Jupiter in 2016. It was the first solar-powered probe to study an outer planet, and collected a variety of data about the gas giant. The third New Frontiers probe was *OSIRIS-REx*, which was launched in September 2016 with a mission to conduct detailed studies of the asteroid Bennu and return a sample to Earth.

Ocampo described her great responsibility on these missions for *Share Your Road*: "A big part of my job involves ensuring proper communication between people and teams, and making sure we're on budget. Almost everything NASA does is something no one's ever done before, so we have to be very creative every single day."

ACCOLADES AND MEMBERSHIPS

Throughout her distinguished career, Ocampo earned numerous awards for her work. In 1992 she received the Woman of the Year Award in Science from the Comisión Femenil in Los Angeles. Four years later she won the JPL's Advisory Council for Women Award. In 1997 she won the Science and Technology Award from the Chicano Federation. In 2002 the editors of *Discover* named her one of the magazine's 50 Most Important Women in Science. In 2016 she was named National Hispanic Scientist of the Year.

Ocampo also held memberships in a number of distinguished professional organizations. These included the American Institute of Aeronautics and Astronautics (AIAA), the Association of Women in Geoscience (AWG), the Society of Hispanic Professional Engineers (SHPE), the Society of Women Engineers (SWE), and the Planetary Society. She also helped found the Pan American Space Conference.

PERSONAL LIFE

Ocampo was married to fellow researcher Kevin O. Pope for a time. She noted some of her personal interests in her NASA profile: "I love nature and anything that has to do with flying. Also, I love exploring and living life like it is a grand adventure."

SUGGESTED READING

"Adriana Ocampo," *Physics Today*, 5 Jan. 2017, physicstoday.scitation.org/do/10.1063/pt.5.031391/full/. Accessed 18 Nov. 2019.

"Adriana Ocampo." *Share Your Road*, 2019, roadtripnation.shareyourroad.com/profile/bfb61a38. Accessed 18 Nov. 2019.

Hopping, Lorraine Jean. *Space Rocks: The Story of Planetary Geologist Adriana Ocampo*. Joseph Henry, 2006.

Isbell, Douglas, and Mary Hardin. "Chain of Impact Craters Suggested by Spaceborne Radar Images." *NASA Jet Propulsion Laboratory*, 20 Mar. 1996, www2.jpl.nasa.gov/sl9/news80.html. Accessed 18 Nov. 2019.

"More Evidence Points to Impact as Dinosaur Killer." *NASA Jet Propulsion Laboratory*, California Institute of Technology, 12 Mar. 1998, www.jpl.nasa.gov/news/news.php?feature=5186 Accessed 18 Nov. 2019.

Ocampo, Adriana. Interview. *Solar System Exploration*, NASA, solarsystem.nasa.gov/people/1780/adriana-ocampo/. Accessed 18 Nov. 2019.

Van den Broek, Claire. "'You Need Perseverance to Realise Your Dreams' Meet Adriana Ocampo, Lead Program Executive at NASA's New Frontier Program." *Mendeley Blog*, 5 Aug. 2014, blog.mendeley.com/2014/08/05/you-need-perseverance-to-make-your-dreams-come-true-meet-adriana-ocampo-the-woman-who-is-the-lead-program-executive-at-nasas-new-frontiers-program/. Accessed 18 Oct. 2019.

—*Christopher Mari*

Ilhan Omar

Date of birth: October 4, 1982
Occupation: Politician

Democrat Ilhan Omar was elected in 2018 to represent Minnesota's Fifth District in the US House of Representatives. Omar, a former state representative, was the first Somali American ever elected to Congress. She was also, along with Rashida Tlaib, a congresswoman representing Michigan's Thirteenth District, one of the first two Muslim women to serve in Congress. Omar was born in Somalia and immigrated to the United States when she was twelve years old, ultimately settling in Minneapolis. She first ran for office, for a seat in Minnesota's state legislature, in 2016, the same year that real estate magnate and reality television personality Donald Trump won the presidency. Omar, a black woman, Muslim, and refugee, became one of the president's favorite targets. At a rally in Omar's district in October 2019, he called her a "fraud" and a "disgrace to our country." Months earlier, in July 2019, he criticized Omar at a rally in Greenville, North Carolina, as the crowd chanted, "Send her back," a racist dig at Omar for not being born in the United States. That same month, Trump also insulted Omar as part of "the Squad," a group of four progressive Democratic freshmen that also included Representatives Tlaib, Ayanna Pressley of Massachusetts's Seventh District, and Alexandria Ocasio-Cortez of New York's Fourteenth District.

Omar has been called out by some on the left for her own controversial remarks in her criticism of the American Israel Public Affairs Committee (AIPAC) and Israel's policies regarding Palestinians. Omar was elected with the support of young progressives in Minneapolis and endorsed progressive Democratic candidate Senator Bernie Sanders for president in the 2020 campaign.

EARLY LIFE AND EDUCATION

Omar was born the youngest of seven children in Mogadishu, Somalia's capital city, on October 4, 1982. Her mother, a woman of Yemeni descent, died just two years later. In 1991, when Omar was eight years old, civil war between rival clan-based militias broke out in Somalia, causing her family to flee. "One night militia tried to break into our home, and the exterior was riddled with bullets," Omar recalled to Jeff Nelson for *Time* magazine (8 Nov. 2019). "My family left our neighborhood, passing through dead bodies and debris." For four years, they lived in a refugee camp near Mombasa, Kenya, where Omar has recalled her astonishment at the lack of privacy, and watching movies in a makeshift movie theater in a hut. Omar and her family immigrated to the United States as asylum-seekers in 1995. They first settled in Arlington, Virginia, where Omar, who spoke little English, began middle school and experienced her first brush with American racism. Bullies at her school stuck chewing gum on her headscarf and pushed her down stairs. Omar recalled to Sheryl Gay Stolberg for the *New York Times* (30 Dec. 2018) that her father sat her down and said, "'Listen, these people who are doing all of these things to you, they're not doing something to you because they dislike you. They are doing something to you because they feel threatened in some way by your existence.'"

Two and a half years later, the family moved to the Cedar-Riverside neighborhood of Minneapolis. Cedar-Riverside has often been called Little Mogadishu for its large population of Somali and other East African immigrants. When Omar and her family arrived, there were only a handful of Somali families. Her father, who had been a teacher in Somalia, found work as a cab driver and later got a job working for the post office. Omar enrolled as a student at Edison High

School. "There were a lot of racial conflicts and cultural divides that were happening there," she told Drew Wood for *Mpls.St.Paul Magazine* (21 Oct. 2016). Recalling her difficulties in middle school, Omar launched a unity and diversity program, bringing together students of various backgrounds for lunches and retreats.

Omar was granted US citizenship in 2000, at the age of seventeen. She began wearing a hijab in 2001, after the terrorist attacks on September 11, in solidarity with other Muslims who were being vilified and marginalized for their identity.

EARLY POLITICAL CAREER

Omar has said that her interest in politics began at fourteen, when she was called upon to translate for her grandfather at a local caucus for Minnesota's Democratic-Farmer-Labor (DFL) Party. She went on to study political science at North Dakota State University. Omar told Stolberg that her political impulse is motivated by injustice. "I think back to the orientations I went through a little over 20 years ago in the process of coming to this country, and in those orientations they did not have people who were homeless. There was an America that extended liberty and justice to everyone. There was an America where prosperity was guaranteed regardless of where you were born and what you looked like and who you prayed to," she said. "I wasn't comfortable with that hypocrisy."

After graduating in 2011, Omar was a nutrition outreach coordinator for the Minnesota Department of Education. Two years later, she managed engineer Andrew Johnson's campaign when he ran for a Minneapolis City Council seat. He won the race and hired Omar as a policy aide. In this role, she pushed initiatives involving juvenile justice reform and hunger. In 2014, at an event for Mohamud Noor, a local Somali American candidate running for state congress, Omar was held down and beaten by multiple assailants. She suffered a concussion; her attackers were never identified. Given the violence and hostility she faced, Omar was reluctant to run for office herself. But with the encouragement of a group called Women Organizing Women, led by Somali American organizer Habon Abdulle, Omar decided to run in District 60B for the Minnesota House of Representatives in 2016.

MINNESOTA STATE REPRESENTATIVE

The same year Omar ran to represent District 60B, then presidential candidate Donald Trump denigrated the Somali community in Minnesota, lamenting at a rally the large number of Somali immigrants who lived in the state. Minnesotans, he said, had "suffered enough" for opening their doors to "large numbers of Somali refugees." His comment demonstrated the vast differences in ideology that found traction that election year. Meanwhile, Omar was running to unseat Phyllis

Kahn, a forty-four-year incumbent affiliated with the DFL party. Her campaign was chronicled in the 2018 documentary *Time for Ilhan*. Buoyed by the support of newly energized, young, progressive voters, Omar won the primary handily. Despite allegations of bigamy—her personal life is complicated, though not bigamous—and the claim by a conservative blogger, Scott Johnson, that she committed immigration fraud by marrying her own brother (she did not), she went on to beat her Republican challenger, Abdimalik Askar, in the general election. It was an easy victory; though Askar's name still appeared on the ballot, he had suspended his campaign in August. Nonetheless, it was a historic election; Omar was not merely the first Somali American representative in Minnesota, but the first Somali American lawmaker in the United States.

2018 US CONGRESSIONAL ELECTION

In June 2018, Democratic congressman Keith Ellison stepped down from office to run for Minnesota attorney general. (Ellison, elected to the US House in 2006, was the first Muslim to serve in Congress.) Omar, and other progressive Democrats, threw their hats in the ring to replace him. Minnesota's Fifth District has been reliably Democratic for half a century, and the election of Donald Trump pushed constituents further left. Omar's opponents in the Democratic primary included the state's first Latina lawmaker, Senator Patricia Torres Ray, a Colombian immigrant who was arrested for protesting President Trump's family separation immigration policy. Omar also faced Margaret Anderson Kelliher, a former state House speaker, known for having gone to bat against Minnesota's Republican governor Tim Pawlenty. Fighting Trump administration policies was at the heart of the race, and Omar was able to convince voters that her fight was personal, noting that she and her family would have been subjected to Trump's proposed Muslim ban. "For so long, so many of us felt you needed permission to get involved politically and that you needed an invitation," Omar told Youssef Rddad for the *Associated Press* (5 Aug. 2018). "I think we are at a moment that we've been building up that's part of a movement that says if you want things done, you have to do them yourself."

In August 2018, one of Omar's campaign events, featuring Tlaib, was interrupted by Laura Loomer, a far-right activist known for her racist, anti-Muslim views. (In November 2018, Loomer was banned from *Twitter* for her racist posts about Omar.) The disruption, and other racist attacks, did not deter Minnesotans from voting for Omar, who ran on a policy platform that included universal Medicare, a fifteen-dollar minimum wage, and tuition-free college. In November, she defeated Republican Jennifer Zielinski in a landslide victory with 78 percent of the vote.

FIRST TERM AS A US CONGRESSWOMAN

Omar was sworn in as a member of the US House of Representatives on January 3, 2019. The next day, she successfully pushed Congress to overturn a 181-year-old ban on headwear in the chamber so that she would be allowed to wear her hijab. Omar began serving on the foreign affairs committee, the budget committee, and the education and labor committee. She joined the Congressional Black Caucus and became the whip for the Congressional Progressive Caucus. Alana Abramson, who profiled Omar for *Time* magazine (18 July 2019), wrote that Omar is known among the progressive faction as "a workhorse who deals with less sexy pieces of legislation like rules packages and budget caps," though in June 2019, along with Senator Bernie Sanders and Representative Pramila Jayapal of Washington, she sponsored the Student Debt Cancellation Act of 2019. That October, she and Sanders also introduced the Universal School Meals Program Act, which would ensure that every student in the United States would have access to school meals. In November 2019, she introduced the Homes for All Act, which would provide $1 trillion in funds for building twelve million new public and affordable housing units.

Still, in terms of attention, Omar's freshman term became defined by controversy. Some of her tweets and comments about AIPAC and Israel invoked anti-Semitic tropes. Although she apologized for her remarks and reached out to local Jewish groups to mend her relationship with them, her remarks prompted critical responses across the political spectrum. In March 2019, the House passed a resolution condemning anti-Semitism, anti-Muslim discrimination, and other forms of bigotry against minorities by a vote of 407 to 23. That August, the Alabama Republican Party approved its own resolution asking for Omar to be expelled from Congress for rhetoric that "runs counter to American values and patriotism," specifically citing her controversial comments about terrorism and Israel. The Democratic-controlled House did not pass the resolution, however, and Omar remained staunch in her criticism of Israel, particularly the country's treatment of Palestinians.

In large part thanks to President Trump, Omar became a right-wing target. Upstart Republican lawmakers repeatedly sought to tie Omar to terrorist groups like ISIS, based solely on their biases against her ethnicity and religion. In October 2019, a Republican state senator in North Dakota posted a photo of a female Somali soldier from the 1970s, claiming that the girl was Omar at an al-Qaeda training camp. In November 2019, a New York man pleaded guilty and was convicted after threatening to kill Omar. She has said that she refuses to humble herself to those who see her as a threat. "I don't have a way of making myself less threatening as a black person, as a black woman, as a Muslim person," she told Benjamin Wallace-Wells for the *New Yorker* (27 Mar. 2019). "And so it is just living with the reality that there are people who will see you as a threat. And figuring out how do you not allow that to deter the work that you have to get done."

PERSONAL LIFE

Omar began a romantic partnership with Ahmed Hirsi in 2002. Omar has said that they were married according to Islamic custom but had not completed their application for a civil marriage. The couple had three children together and separated in 2008. In 2009, Omar married Ahmed Nur Said Elmi, a British citizen; they separated in 2011 and Omar filed for divorce in 2017. In 2018, she wed Hirsi in a civil marriage, but they divorced in November 2019. Omar's daughter, Isra Hirsi, is a cofounder of the US Youth Climate Strike; she also became known for documenting Omar's 2018 campaign on social media.

SUGGESTED READING

Abramson, Alana. "'I Believe in My Work.' How Rep. Ilhan Omar Rose from Refugee to Trump's Top Target." *Time*, 18 July 2019, time.com/5628844/ilhan-omar-profile/. Accessed 12 Dec. 2019.

Nelson, Jeff. "Making US History." *Time*, 8 Nov. 2019, time.com/collection-post/4641521/ilhan-omar-american-voices/. Accessed 11 Dec. 2019.

Omar, Ilhan. "Meet Ilhan Omar." Interview by Drew Wood. *Mpls.St.Paul Magazine*, 21 Oct. 2016, mspmag.com/arts-and-culture/coffee-and-conversation-with-ilhan-omar/. Accessed 11 Dec. 2019.

Rddad, Youssef. "As Ellison Departs Congress, Omar Chases Another First." *Associated Press*, 5 Aug. 2018, apnews.com/ecd-d8c06f7c546429d8f6df1daa44525. Accessed 12 Dec. 2019.

Stolberg, Sheryl Gay. "Glorified and Vilified, Representative-Elect Ilhan Omar Tells Critics, 'Just Deal.'" *The New York Times*, 30 Dec. 2018, www.nytimes.com/2018/12/30/us/politics/ilhan-omar-minnesota-congress.html. Accessed 11 Dec. 2019.

Wallace-Wells, Benjamin. "Ilhan Omar's Embattled First Months in Office." *The New Yorker*, 27 Mar. 2019, www.newyorker.com/news/the-political-scene/ilhan-omars-embattled-first-months-in-office?verso=true. Accessed 12 Dec. 2019.

—*Molly Hagan*

Satoshi Ōmura

Date of birth: July 12, 1935
Occupation: Biochemist

Satoshi Ōmura shared the 2015 Nobel Prize in Physiology and Medicine for his work identifying compounds produced by soil microbes that were used to develop the antiparasitic drug Ivermectin, which treats diseases such as river blindness and filariasis.

EARLY LIFE AND EDUCATION

Satoshi Ōmura was born on July 12, 1935, in Japan's Yamanashi Prefecture. His father was a farmer, his mother was a teacher, and he and his five siblings all helped tend the family farm. Ōmura's grandmother helped to raise the children, and she instilled a strong sense of public service in Ōmura.

Ōmura was not interested in studying or in academic pursuits as a child, but his father's encouragement led him to focus on his studies and pursue a university education. He received an undergraduate degree from the University of Yamanashi in 1958.

After graduation, Ōmura hoped to teach, but no jobs were available locally, so he accepted a position teaching science night school classes in Tokyo. Seeing the effort his students exerted in his classes inspired him to return to school to pursue an advanced degree. He studied organic chemistry at the Tokyo University of Science, which awarded him a Master of Science degree in 1963.

After graduation, Ōmura accepted a research associate position at the University of Yamanashi where he became interested in microorganisms while working under Professor Motoo Kagami researching alcohol production. Microbes and their potential to produce useful compounds would from then on form the focal point of Ōmura's professional career.

DEVELOPING MEDICINE FROM MICROBES

Ōmura remained at the University of Yamanashi until 1965, when he joined the Kitasato Institute as a researcher and took up leadership of the drug discovery group. Simultaneously, he began studying organic chemistry at the Tokyo University of Science. In 1968, he received a PhD in pharmaceutical sciences from the University of Tokyo and became an associate professor at Kitasato University. He earned a PhD in chemistry from the Tokyo University of Science in 1970.

Shortly after completing his second PhD, Ōmura received an offer from the general manager of the Japan Antibiotics Research Association, Yukimasa Yagisawa, to study in the United States. At the time, Ōmura was considering positions in several labs, including an offer from Max Tishler, retired head of research at the pharmaceutical company Merck and then-professor in Wesleyan University's chemistry department. Tishler's offer was lower in pay than any other offer, but Ōmura explained that he felt there must be a hidden value behind the offer, so he accepted it.

In 1971, Ōmura took the position as a visiting professor in Wesleyan's newly established chemistry department that was headed by Tishler. Shortly afterward, Tishler became president of the American Chemical Society (ACS), which, coupled with his reputation as the man who had steered Merck into position as a world-leading pharmaceutical company, meant that a stream of internationally renowned people from science and industry visited the department on a regular basis. This became a source of professional and scientific resources that Ōmura was able to draw from. Ōmura was called back to the Kitasato Institute in 1971, but the year he spent in the United States established his strong ties to both academic and industrial leaders.

Upon returning to Japan, he established a lab dedicated to discovering useful compounds made by microorganisms in soil that could be turned into veterinary drugs. In 1974, he discovered *Streptomyces avermectinus*, a bacteria that produces an extremely effective antiparasitic compound. This was quickly developed into the antiparasitic drug Ivermectin, which entered the market in 1981. At first it was used exclusively to treat helminth worm infections in livestock, but the human benefits were quickly discovered: It was highly effective against several debilitating diseases caused by parasitic worms, in particular onchocerciasis, or river blindness. In 1988, the World Health Organization (WHO) approved the drug and began distributing it free of charge in affected areas.

In 1990, Ōmura's long tenure and groundbreaking work earned him the presidency of the Kitasato Institute. In 2008, he oversaw the merger of the Kitasato Institute with Kitasato Gakuen (academy) where he served as president emeritus from 2008 to 2012. In 2005, he was appointed the first Max Tishler Professor of Chemistry at Wesleyan.

IMPACT

In 2015, Ōmura was one of three people awarded the Nobel Prize in Physiology or Medicine for his work developing antiparasitic drugs. He shared half of the $960,000 award with William C. Campbell, who was then affiliated with Drew University, for their collaborative but independent work on the development of the drugs Avermectin and its refined form, Ivermectin. In the years since its development, Ivermectin has all but eliminated river blindness and has greatly reduced the incidence of filariasis, another parasitic disease that can lead to elephantiasis.

Over the course of his long career, Ōmura has revolutionized the methods scientists use to find and isolate new microbes as well as the potentially useful organic compounds they produce. He has personally discovered more than a dozen new genera of microbes and has described more than forty new species.

PERSONAL LIFE

Ōmura married his wife, Fumiko, in 1963. They had one child, a daughter named Ikuyo. Fumiko died in 2000, and Ōmura has said he believes that he was able to win the Noble Prize thanks to his wife's support over the years.

In addition to his academic and scientific accomplishments, Ōmura has published several collections of personal essays. His hobbies include calligraphy, golf, and cross-country skiing. He is also a patron of Japanese art and opened a museum in his hometown.

SUGGESTED READING

Altman, Lawrence K. "Nobel Prize in Medicine Awarded to Three Scientists for Parasite-Fighting Therapies." *The New York Times*, 5 Oct. 2015, www.nytimes.com › 1987/10/13 › science › mit-scientist-wins-nobel-pri… . Accessed 31 Jan. 2020.

Callaway, Ewen, and David Cyranoski. "Anti-Parasite Drugs Sweep Nobel Prize in Medicine 2015." *Nature*. Macmillan, 5 Oct. 2015, www.nature.com/news/anti-parasite-drugs-sweep-nobel-prize-in-medicine-2015-1.18507. Accessed 30 Jan. 2020.

Klass, Perri. "War of the Worms." *The New Yorker*. Condé Nast, 14 Dec. 2015. , www.newyorker.com/tech/annals-of-technology/war-of-the-worms. Accessed 31 Jan. 2020.

Ōmura, Satoshi, and Andy Crump. "The Life and Times of Ivermectin—A Success Story." *Nature*. Macmillan, 1 Dec. 2004, www.nature.com/articles/nrmicro1048. Accessed 31 Jan. 2020.

"People: Professor Satoshi Ōmura." *Kitasato*. Kitasato Inst., 2013, www.satoshi-omura.info/. Accessed 1 Feb. 2020.

"Professor Satoshi Ōmura." *Satoshi-Omura*. Satoshi Ōmura, 2015, satoshi-omura.info/biography/index.html. Accessed 1 Feb. 2020.

Tatsuta, Kuniaki. "Celebrating the 2015 Nobel Prize in Physiology or Medicine of Dr. Satoshi Ōmura." *Nature*. Macmillan, 21 Oct. 2015, www.nature.com/articles/ja2015113. Accessed 31 Jan. 2020.

—*Kenrick Vezina*

Heather O'Neill

Date of birth: October 4, 1973
Occupation: Author

Heather O'Neill is an award-winning Canadian author, known for her lyrical visions of the gritty, bohemian underbelly of Montreal. Her writing has been shaped by her upbringing, growing up poor in Montreal's Red-Light district, and becoming a single mother at the age of twenty. In 2006, she published her first novel, *Lullabies for Little Criminals*, about an observant young teenager and her relationship with her father, a heroin addict. *Lullabies* won the Hugh MacLennan Prize for Fiction in 2007 and was a finalist for the Governor General's Literary Award. It also won Canada Reads 2007, an annual contest in which one book is selected for all Canadians to read. In 2008, it was short-listed for the Orange Prize for Fiction, which became known as the Bailey's Women's Prize for Fiction from 2014 through 2017 and was thereafter known as the Women's Prize for Fiction. O'Neill's second novel, *The Girl Who Was Saturday Night* (2014), is set in Montreal in 1995, against the backdrop of the Quebec independence referendum. Her 2017 novel *The Lonely Hearts Hotel*, a period novel set in the early twentieth century, was long-listed for the Bailey's Women's Prize for Fiction.

EARLY LIFE AND EDUCATION
Heather O'Neill was born in Montreal on October 4, 1973. When she was five years old, her parents divorced. She moved with her mother to Virginia, but two years later, her mother sent her and her two sisters back to Montreal to live with their father. O'Neill was later inspired by her father and his tales of being a petty criminal as a child during the Great Depression. "He worked sneaking into windows for older hardened criminals," she told the *CBC* (31 Jan. 2018). "He was in prison when he was 11 years old." When O'Neill was a child, her father worked as a janitor but wryly described himself as a professor of philosophy. He encouraged O'Neill's early love of reading, though he had only finished the third grade. "It was almost magical to him that I was able to read everything and keep up. Once he . . . bought me a pile of Charles Dickens novels at a garage sale," she recalled. "He was incapable of reading them himself, but [he told me], 'I'll give you two bucks for each one you read.'"

O'Neill grew up in Notre-Dame-de-Grâce, or NDG, on Montreal's West End. At the time, people derisively joked that the neighborhood's initials stood for "No Damn Good." O'Neill was acutely aware of her family's poverty. Her father saw her early knack for reading as an opportunity for social and financial advancement. In the fifth grade, a teacher praised O'Neill's story about a cockroach who tries to pass himself off as a cricket—perhaps inspired by her family's run-down apartment, which "was ugly, tiny and filled with cockroaches," she wrote for the *New York Times* (7 May 2006). The teacher encouraged her to become a writer. In high school, O'Neill began writing poetry and sold her poems outside of metro stations.

O'Neill described her high school experience to the magazine *Quill & Quire* (2006) as "post-apocalyptic." Still, she enjoys writing about teenage characters, living during the era in which she was a teenager. "It's one of those fun transitional ages when you don't know who you are, but you feel all the excitement of becoming someone new," she told Juliet Waters for *McGill News* (2014).

EARLY LIFE AND EDUCATION
O'Neill won a modest scholarship to McGill University in Montreal. She enjoyed the freedom of her college years, living in a huge, run-down apartment with six other students, getting high, and having philosophical conversations deep into the night. She graduated from McGill in 1994.

After college, she studied poetry and creative writing at Concordia University in Montreal. Later, she would speak against Concordia's creative writing department and its culture of sexual harassment. During her time as a student, O'Neill was groped and harassed by a certain professor, who offered to help edit her book of poetry if she agreed to sleep with him. She refused. In 1998, O'Neill published the book, a collection of poetry called *Two Eyes Are You Sleeping*, as part of the DC New Writers Series edited by Robert Allen. She collaborated with director John L'Ecuyer to adapt one of her short stories for the Canadian feature film *Saint Jude*, which was released in 2000. O'Neill also published essays for magazines and was a regular contributor to the popular Chicago-based NPR program *This American Life*.

LULLABIES FOR LITTLE CRIMINALS
In 2003, *Toronto Life* published an excerpt from O'Neill's unpublished novel in the magazine's summer fiction issue. The story won her an agent, and her novel, *Lullabies for Little Criminals*, was published in 2006. *Lullabies* follows the story of a twelve-year-old girl named Baby. Baby lives with her eccentric father, Jules, who is addicted to heroin but eager to share the wonder and adventure of life with his daughter. When Jules enters rehab, Baby is placed in foster care and bounced from one home to another. She eventually reunites with her newly sober father, but slides into addiction and prostitution. On its face, *Lullabies* sounds like a sad story, but the book won rave reviews for the spark and verve

of its narrator. "Baby is the real triumph here; Jules's charm is utterly believable, but Baby's yearning for him, even for his cruelties, aches to the bone," a reviewer wrote for *Kirkus* (1 Aug. 2006). "Baby believes she is guided by reason and conviction, but O'Neill shows us that Baby is all emotion and instinct."

THE GIRL WHO WAS SATURDAY NIGHT

Canada Reads helped *Lullabies* become a best seller, and O'Neill's life was forever changed. "We felt like we were rolling in the money. We had always been so broke, broke, broke. Like we couldn't even buy a T-shirt," O'Neill told Waters. "Suddenly we were taking cabs from the corner dépanneur [convenience store]." But the popularity of her debut made writing a follow-up a daunting task. In 2014, she published her second novel, *The Girl Who Was Saturday Night*. The book is set in 1995, just before the Quebec independence referendum, a period of political uncertainty during which the province contemplated national sovereignty. O'Neill remembered preparing to cast her first electoral vote during this time, having just turned of age to do so. "Everything seemed strange and magical and absurd, and you had no idea what was going to happen. . . . There was this heightened sense of being," she recalled to Mark Medley for Canada's *National Post* (13 Mar. 2014).

O'Neill's book follows the story of twins Nicolas and Nouschka Tremblay. Children of a famous folk singer, the Tremblay twins were beloved members of their father's act. As teenagers, their deep and specific bond begins to unravel. Quebec's independence referendum serves as a metaphor, though the story's connection to the province is more than superficial. "It's impossible to talk about *The Girl Who Was Saturday Night* without talking about Quebec," poet Emma Healey wrote in her enthusiastic review for the *National Post* (2 May 2014). "This novel isn't technically about the province or its culture, but Quebec is all about this novel—as in, around everything, like air." Writing francophone characters as an anglophone writer, O'Neill was careful to capture the essence of Quebec, particularly Montreal. She later said she read a hundred books about the province's history. Taken alongside *Lullabies*, Healey wrote, "The two books form an incredibly specific historical record of a very particular Montreal—one overflowing with cats and trash and petty crime, whose spine is Boulevard Saint-Laurent and whose primary chroniclers are sharp-eyed, large-hearted young women."

DAYDREAMS OF ANGELS AND THE LONELY HEARTS HOTEL

In 2015, O'Neill published a collection of short stories called *Daydreams of Angels*. It was praised for its strangeness—a reviewer for *Kirkus* (14 July 2015) described it as "endearingly weird"— and magical realism. "The plots are grounded with kindness and pain," Carmen Maria Machado wrote for *NPR* (8 Oct. 2015). "[O'Neill's] prose is restrained but lovely, and her images crackle."

O'Neill's 2017 novel *The Lonely Hearts Hotel*, like her previous novels, is also set in Montreal, though it takes place in the early twentieth century. Although it is told in the third person, *Lonely Hearts* is "ferociously direct," André Forget wrote for the Canadian magazine *The Walrus* (13 Dec. 2016). He described it as O'Neill's "most gripping book to date." In it, Rose and Pierrot meet as children in a Montreal orphanage in the 1910s. Separated as teenagers, they spend the rest of their lives searching for one another, all while falling in and out of luck and grace. Though Molly McCloskey offered some criticism in a review for the *Guardian* (30 Mar. 2017), she praised the book for its "big-heartedness," and "its defiant affirmation of the whole seedy, sad, beautiful burlesque that is the life of these characters."

PERSONAL LIFE

O'Neill gave birth to a daughter named Arizona in 1994. She moved in with Arizona's father, a man named Chris, but as his drug addiction spiraled out of control, O'Neill realized that she needed to break out on her own. "The gravity of being 20 and about to become a single mother sank in," she wrote in an essay for the *Guardian* (18 Feb. 2017). With some regret, she moved back into the apartment building where she had grown up, where her father was able to care for Arizona while O'Neill worked a series of minimum wage jobs. O'Neill has said that the experience of being a young, single mother shaped her writing. Her adventures with her young daughter "deeply affected my style, making it more lyrical," she wrote for *Chatelaine* magazine (20 Mar. 2014).

O'Neill lives in Montreal.

SUGGESTED READING

"Bringing Up Baby." *Quill & Quire*, Nov. 2006, quillandquire.com/authors/bringing-up-baby/. Accessed 12 June 2020.

Forget, André. "Heather O'Neill at the Height of Her Literary Powers." *The Walrus*, 13 Dec. 2016, thewalrus.ca/heather-oneill-at-the-height-of-her-literary-powers/. Accessed 12 June 2020.

Healey, Emma. "*The Girl Who Was Saturday Night*, Heather O'Neill: Review." Review of *The Girl Who Was Saturday Night*, by Heather O'Neill. *National Post*, 2 May 2014, nationalpost.com/entertainment/books/book-reviews/

the-girl-who-was-saturday-night-by-heather-oneill-review. Accessed 12 June 2020.

McCloskey, Molly. *"The Lonely Hearts Hotel* by Heather O'Neill Review—Descent into a Fairytale Underworld." Review of *The Lonely Hearts Hotel*, by Heather O'Neill. *The Guardian*, 30 Mar. 2017, www.theguardian.com/books/2017/mar/30/lonely-hearts-hotel-review-by-heather-oneill-review. Accessed 12 June 2020.

Medley, Mark. "Heather O'Neill: Divide and Conquer." *National Post*, 13 Mar. 2014, nationalpost.com/afterword/heather-oneill-divide-and-conquer. Accessed 12 June 2020.

Waters, Juliet. "The Main Is Her Muse." *McGill News*, 2014, mcgillnews.mcgill.ca/s/1762/news/interior.aspx?sid=1762&gid=2&pgid=730. Accessed 12 June 2020.

"Writer Heather O'Neill Finds Wisdom in an Eccentric Father's Advice." *CBC*, 31 Jan. 2018, www.cbc.ca/radio/deas/writer-heather-o-neill-finds-wisdom-in-an-eccentric-fathers-advice-1.4512242. Accessed 12 June 2020.

SELECTED WORKS

Two Eyes Are You Sleeping, 1998; *Lullabies for Little Criminals*, 2006; *The Girl Who Was Saturday Night*, 2014; *Daydreams of Angels*, 2015; *The Lonely Hearts Hotel*, 2017

—*Molly Hagan*

Ryan O'Reilly

Date of birth: February 7, 1991
Occupation: Hockey player

Professional hockey player Ryan O'Reilly joined the opening-day roster of his first National Hockey League (NHL) team in 2009 at the age of eighteen. "In games, there are always ups and downs. But it's about living those downs and riding the ups as long as you can," O'Reilly told Tracey Myers for the *NHL* website (23 Oct. 2018). Like any athlete, O'Reilly has extensive personal experience with both the ups of his sport—which for the Canadian-born center have included competing in two postseason tournaments during the first five years of his NHL career—and the lows—which included three lackluster seasons with the Buffalo Sabres. O'Reilly's move to the St. Louis Blues for the 2018–19 season proved to be another career high, reinvigorating O'Reilly's love of his sport and leading to a meaningful milestone in the form of a Stanley Cup Finals victory for the Blues. "The Cup is the ultimate goal," O'Reilly explained following the tournament, as quoted by Stephen Whyno for CBC (13 June 2019). Although named the Most Valuable Player (MVP) of the 2019 NHL postseason and widely recognized for his contributions during both the regular season and the playoffs, O'Reilly downplays his own role in the Blues' success. "[I was] just trying to go out there and be the spark and try to make a difference," he said, as quoted by Whyno.

EARLY LIFE

Ryan O'Reilly was born on February 7, 1991, in Clinton, Ontario, Canada. One of four children born to Bonnie and Brian O'Reilly, he grew up in Bluewater, Ontario, where his family owned a home that had once been a schoolhouse. Both of his parents had educational and professional backgrounds in social work. Bonnie worked for a children's aid organization, and Brian was a sports psychologist. They also served as foster parents and took in more than forty individual children over the years, sometimes welcoming as many as four at a time. Due to the number of children in the household, hockey took on particular significance for O'Reilly, who began playing the sport as a preschooler. "It was a big thing that I could do [alone]," he told Adam Kimelman for the *NHL* website (10 June 2009). "It was a lot better for me to have that." While O'Reilly enjoyed practicing his hockey skills on his own, he also played the game with his siblings, including older brother and future NHL and American Hockey League (AHL) player Cal O'Reilly. "We'd have 4-on-4 hockey games at home every night. I was lucky to have other kids to play with

Photo by Bruce Bennett/Getty Images

like that, because it really did make me a better player," he recalled to Adrian Dater for the *Denver Post* (14 Jan. 2010). "In a way, I have some of those kids to thank for where I am today."

Having first learned the basics of hockey at home, O'Reilly went on to hone his skills on several different youth teams, including the Seaforth Stars, the Huron-Perth Lakers, and the Toronto Jr. Canadiens. In 2007, he became the first player to be selected in that year's Ontario Hockey League (OHL) draft. Made up of players in their late teens and early twenties, the OHL is a junior-level league that is considered professional rather than amateur. Drafted by the Erie Otters, O'Reilly had a strong debut season with the team, scoring a total of 52 points over the course of sixty-one games. He remained with the team for the 2008–09 season as well, scoring 16 goals and 50 assists in sixty-eight games and serving as assistant captain. In addition to playing for the Erie Otters, O'Reilly represented Canada in junior-level international competitions held by the International Ice Hockey Federation (IIHF) and served as captain of the country's under-17 and under-18 teams.

COLORADO AVALANCHE

Having attracted a great deal of attention from professional hockey organizations over the course of his junior career, the eighteen-year-old O'Reilly entered the 2009 NHL draft as a strong contender for selection by a team. He was ultimately chosen by the Colorado Avalanche, which selected O'Reilly in the second round of the draft, making him the thirty-third overall pick. Due to his age and placement in the draft, O'Reilly did not expect to be immediately added to the team's roster, instead believing that he would be sent to train elsewhere. To his surprise, Avalanche leadership placed him on the roster for the team's opening-day game against the San Jose Sharks. O'Reilly scored an assist during the game, contributing to the Avalanche's victory over the Sharks and demonstrating his value to his new team. "This is where I want to be," he later explained to Rick Sadowski for the *NHL* website (7 Oct. 2009). "To make it reality is a great feeling. I hope to be here the whole year. I know it's a day-by-day thing, and I have to do whatever I can do to impress them." O'Reilly put forth a strong performance over the course of his first season in the NHL, playing in eighty-one games and scoring 8 goals and 18 assists. Following the regular season, the Avalanche competed in the conference quarterfinals of the 2010 Stanley Cup Playoffs but were eliminated by the Sharks.

O'Reilly continued to play with the Colorado Avalanche over the next several years, adapting to life in the NHL and working toward his further development as a player. In late 2012,

a labor dispute within the league led to a lockout, delaying the start of the 2012–13 season. O'Reilly traveled to Russia during that period, joining Metallurg Magnitogorsk of the Kontinental Hockey League for part of late 2012 and early 2013 before rejoining the Avalanche. The following season was another success, with O'Reilly scoring 28 goals and 36 assists. He was awarded the 2014 Lady Byng Memorial Trophy in recognition of his sportsmanship, conduct, and hockey skills. At the end of the season, the Avalanche became champions of the Western Conference's Central Division and proceeded to compete in the playoffs, where the team lost to the Minnesota Wild in the first round. During the 2014–15 season, his last with the Avalanche, O'Reilly put forth another strong effort, scoring 17 goals and 38 assists over the course of eighty-two games.

BUFFALO SABRES

Prior to the 2015–16 season, the Avalanche traded O'Reilly to the Buffalo Sabres. Although the team itself performed relatively poorly during the season, finishing seventh in the NHL's Atlantic Division, O'Reilly scored a total of 60 points over seventy-one games and was selected to play in the 2016 NHL All-Star Game, the first of his career. The 2016–17 season likewise went relatively poorly for the Sabres, which finished eighth in the Atlantic Division. The team's bad luck continued into the following season, during which the Sabres amassed only twenty-five wins out of the season's eighty-two games and ultimately placed last in the NHL. O'Reilly, however, simultaneously represented Canada in senior-level IIHF events, including the Ice Hockey World Championships, and assisted Canada in claiming consecutive first-place championship finishes in 2015 and 2016.

For O'Reilly, who played in eighty-one games and scored a total of 61 points over the course of the 2017–18 season, the Sabres' frequent losses became draining. "We're stuck in this mindset of just being OK with losing," he said in an interview at the end of the season, as quoted by John Vogl for the *Buffalo News* (9 Apr. 2018). "I feel it, too. I think it's really crept into myself. Over the course of the year, I've lost myself a lot, where it's just kind of get through, just being OK with just not making a mistake. That's not winning hockey at all, and it's crept into all of our games." O'Reilly's candid comments, as well as his admission that he had "lost the love of the game multiple times," proved controversial among Buffalo Sabres fans and leadership, and hockey journalists later linked those comments to the team's decision to trade O'Reilly to the St. Louis Blues during the summer of 2018.

ST. LOUIS BLUES

O'Reilly began his first season with the St. Louis Blues with one substantial goal in mind: to win the Stanley Cup. The ultimate sign of an NHL team's success, the Cup had evaded O'Reilly during his time with the Avalanche and had been utterly out of reach during his three seasons with the Sabres. With the Blues, however, O'Reilly was bolstered not only by his teammates, but also by the team's dedicated fans. "I didn't know a whole lot about the city but quickly found out how great it was," he told Myers of the move to St. Louis, Missouri. "It's a hockey town, they love their Blues and it's nice to be a part of it." A strong performer during his first season with the team, O'Reilly played in eighty-two games, scored 28 goals, and managed a career high of 49 assists. He was also selected to compete in his second NHL All-Star Game.

Having earned a spot in the playoffs thanks to their regular-season performance, the Blues beat the Winnipeg Jets and the Dallas Stars during the first and second rounds of the tournament before defeating the San Jose Sharks in the conference finals. Although O'Reilly dealt with multiple injuries during the early stages of the competition, he remained intent on achieving his goal. "There was a couple tough games, but once you kind of get going and the adrenaline takes over, I didn't notice it," he said, as quoted by Whyno. The Blues faced the Boston Bruins during the 2019 Stanley Cup Finals, ultimately defeating the Bruins four games to three. O'Reilly personally scored 23 points over the course of the playoffs, the most of any player on the Blues, and was delighted by his new team's victory. "You dream of this for so long," he said afterward, as quoted by Whyno. "As a kid, that feeling comes back to you of just what it means to win this thing. I still can't believe this. I can't believe I'm here right now and a Stanley Cup champion with this group of guys." In recognition of his contributions during the postseason, O'Reilly was named MVP and awarded the prestigious Conn Smythe Trophy. He remains with the Blues for the 2019–20 season.

PERSONAL LIFE

O'Reilly married Dayna Douros, a yoga instructor, in June 2018. The wedding took place the day before O'Reilly learned that he had been traded to the Blues. The couple's son, Jameson, was born in 2017.

SUGGESTED READING

Dater, Adrian. "Avs Rookie O'Reilly Credits Maturity to His Upbringing." *Denver Post,* 14 Jan. 2010, www.denverpost.com/2010/01/14/avs-rookie-oreilly-credits-maturity-to-his-upbringing/. Accessed 15 Nov. 2019.

Fox, Luke. "Ryan O'Reilly's Passion Bleeds through for Blues in Stanley Cup Win." *Sportsnet,* 13 June 2019, www.sportsnet.ca/hockey/nhl/ryan-oreillys-passion-bleeds-blues-cup-win/. Accessed 15 Nov. 2019.

Kimelman, Adam. "O'Reilly Fostering Attention in This Year's Draft." *NHL,* 10 June 2009, www.nhl.com/news/oreilly-fostering-attention-in-this-years-draft/c-424826. Accessed 15 Nov. 2019.

O'Reilly, Ryan. "Five Questions with Ryan O'Reilly." Interview by Tracey Myers. *NHL,* 23 Oct. 2018, www.nhl.com/news/five-questions-with-st-louis-blues-center-ryan-oreilly/c-301161270. Accessed 15 Nov. 2019.

Sadowski, Rick. "Rookies Duchene, O'Reilly Rely on Friendship." *NHL,* 7 Oct. 2009, www.nhl.com/news/rookies-duchene-oreilly-rely-on-friendship/c-501337. Accessed 15 Nov. 2019.

Vogl, John. "Sabres' Ryan O'Reilly Says He Lost Love of Game, Lacked Mental Toughness." *Buffalo News,* 9 Apr. 2018, buffalonews.com/2018/04/09/sabres-oreilly-says-he-lost-love-of-game-lacked-mental-toughness/. Accessed 15 Nov. 2019.

Whyno, Stephen. "'Fired Up' Ryan O'Reilly Awarded Conn Smythe Trophy after Goals in 4 Straight." *CBC,* 13 June 2019, www.cbc.ca/sports/hockey/nhl/stanley-cup-final-blues-bruins-game-7-conn-smythe-1.5173331. Accessed 15 Nov. 2019.

—Joy Crelin

George Osborne

Born: May 23, 1971
Occupation: Politician

George Osborne is a British Conservative politician who has served as the Chancellor of the Exchequer since 2010 and the First Secretary of State since 2015.

EARLY LIFE AND EDUCATION

George Osborne was born Gideon Oliver Osborne on May 23, 1971, in London, England. The eldest of four children, his father was Sir Peter Osborne, the seventeenth baronet of Ballintaylor, who founded the wallpapering firm Osborne & Little. Osborne grew up in the Notting Hill section of London and attended St. Paul's School. When he was thirteen, he changed his given name to George. His full name became George Gideon Oliver Osborne.

Osborne attended Magdalen College, Oxford, where he studied history and was an editor of the university magazine, *Isis.* After graduating college, he initially pursued a journalism career. When that did not work out, he turned to politics.

POLITICAL CAREER

Osborne began his political career working as a researcher in the Conservative Party's headquarters in 1994. He quickly rose through the ranks of the Conservative Party, and that same year he was appointed the special adviser in the Ministry of Agriculture, Fisheries, and Food. He held various positions in the Conservative Party over the next few years. In 1997, he worked on then–Prime Minister John Major's campaign. After the Conservatives lost the election, Major resigned as party leader and William Hague replaced him as leader of the Conservative Party. That same year, Osborne became Hague's political secretary.

In 2001, Osborne entered Parliament as the representative for Tatton, becoming the youngest Conservative member in the House of Commons. Also entering Parliament in 2001 was David Cameron, a fellow member of the Conservative Party. Osborne and Cameron became friends and allies, and they both rose rapidly through the party. During his first term as a Member of Parliament (MP), Osborne was a member of the Public Accounts Committee and the Transport Committee. He briefly served as the opposition whip in 2003. In September 2004, Osborne was appointed to the shadow cabinet as the shadow chief secretary to the treasury, a post he held until May 2005.

During Osborne's early years in parliament, the Conservative Party went through a tumultuous period in which subsequent leaders attempted to restore the public's confidence and regain the government. Following the party's defeat in the 2005 general election, party leader Michael Howard resigned. Osborne, who had been favored by Howard as his successor, briefly considered running for party leader. Instead, he gave his support to Cameron and ran his successful campaign for leader. Cameron and Osborne then partnered and attempted to modernize the Conservative Party and make it more responsive to voters' concerns. Moving away from the right, they espoused more moderate stances on issues related to tax cuts and public spending in an effort to recast the image of the Conservative Party and appeal to a broader segment of the population.

Osborne was reelected to Parliament in 2005. He again was appointed to the shadow cabinet, serving as the shadow Chancellor to the Exchequer from May 2005 to May 2010. He shadowed Gordon Brown until June 2007 and Alistair Darling until 2010.

In the 2010 election, Osborne was elected to a third term. For the first time since 1992, the Conservatives won a majority in England, but they failed to gain a majority in Scotland and Wales. Osborne served on the Conservative's negotiating team that helped to form a coalition government with the Liberal Democrats, and Cameron became the prime minister. Cameron appointed Osborne the Chancellor of the Exchequer. As chancellor, Osborne's primary responsibilities are setting monetary and fiscal policies, including creating the budget, raising revenue, and controlling public spending.

Osborne implemented many austerity measures in an attempt to help the United Kingdom recover from the 2008 recession. In his first budget speech, in June 2010, he announced plans to reduce public spending, freeze public sector wages, raise the capital gains tax, implement a bank levy, and decrease the corporation tax. In October 2010, he announced a five-year economic plan that included: additional cuts in public spending and public sector jobs, increased taxes, establishment of a permanent bank levy, and increased the pension age earlier than expected. These measures affected a wide range of public services, including government agencies such as policing, community groups, foreign ministry, and defense. Despite these measures, by the end of 2010 the economy had shrunk by 0.5 percent and inflation had increased. Critics, particularly members of the Labour Party, faulted Osborne's strategies and as the economy failed to rebound as expected over the next years, called for Osborne to change course.

Osborne continued to make cuts and introduced austerity measures, saying long-term economic measures were necessary rather than those that would produce immediate results. By 2013, the economy had begun to recover. In 2015, Osborne was reelected to Parliament, and the Conservatives won the general elections. He was again appointed Chancellor of the Exchequer and named the First Secretary of State.

IMPACT

Although George Osborne's harsh austerity measures made him unpopular among some Britons, by early 2015 it appeared his measures had produced positive results and were leading to economic stability. Britain's borrowing was reduced, and unemployment had declined, and the economy showed signs of growth. These successes helped the Conservative Party win the 2015 election and improved Osborne's stature, leading some political analysts to speculate he had ambitions for higher office. Following the 2015 election, Osborne announced his plan to continue to cut public spending through 2020, saying that recovery was dependent on long-term economic measures. His 2016 budget introduced a tax on sugary drinks, several tax cuts, and a 30 percent budget decrease for the National Health Service.

PERSONAL LIFE

George Osborne is married to the writer Frances Osborne. They have two children, Luke and Liberty.

SUGGESTED READING

Beckett, Andy. "The Real George Osborne." *The Guardian.* Guardian News and Media, 28 Nov. 2011, www.theguardian.com/politics/2011/nov/28/real-george-osborne. Accessed 2 Oct. 2020.

Chan, Szu Ping. "Budget 2016: Can Osborne Keep His Economic Plan on Course?" *Telegraph.* Telegraph Media Group, 13 Mar. 2016, www.telegraph.co.uk/business/2016/03/11/budget-2016-can-osborne-keep-his-economic-plan-on-course/. Accessed 2 Oct. 2020.

"Chancellor of the Exchequer and First Secretary of State: The Rt. Hon George Osborne MP." *Gov.UK.* Govt. of the United Kingdom, www.gov.uk/government/ministers/chancellor-of-the-exchequer. Accessed 2 Oct. 2020.

Osborne, George. "A Conversation with George Osborne." Interview by Stephen J. Friedman. *Council on Foreign Relations.* , 7 Dec. 2015, www.cfr.org/event/conversation-george-osborne. Accessed 2 Oct. 2020.

Parker, George. "The Reinvention of George Osborne." *Financial Times.* 6 Mar. 2015, www.ft.com/content/d1d65690-c2ae-11e4-a59c-00144feab7de. Accessed 2 Oct. 2020.

"Rt. Hon George Osborne MP." *UK Parliament.* UK Parliament, n.d., members.parliament.uk/member/1458/career. Accessed 2 Oct. 2020.

"Profile: Chancellor George Osborne." *BBC News.* Nov. 2012, www.bbc.com/news/10343316. Accessed 2 Oct. 2020.

—*Barb Lightner*

Zaza Pachulia

Date of birth: February 10, 1984
Occupation: Basketball executive; former basketball player

For former basketball player Zaza Pachulia, life in the National Basketball Association (NBA) was characterized by a mastery of skills on the court but near-ignorance of the work taking place behind the scenes. "We were so spoiled as players, because they would provide us something already decided—thought about it, discussed, and decided," he told Bill DiFilippo for *Dime* (5 Nov. 2019). "We never knew what was taking place behind the scenes, who were the people making decisions, or coming up with ideas?" After joining the Golden State Warriors organization as an executive, however, Pachulia's understanding of team operations evolved dramatically. "Sitting in the room with smart people, people who work very hard, it's pretty cool, it's pretty interesting," he told DiFilippo.

Born in the country of Georgia, Pachulia played basketball professionally in Turkey before being drafted by the Orlando Magic in the 2003 NBA Draft. Over the next sixteen seasons he played for six different teams, among them the Warriors during that team's championship-winning 2017 and 2018 postseason campaigns. Following a single-season stint with the Detroit Pistons, Pachulia announced his retirement in August of 2019 and soon afterward rejoined the Warriors as a consultant. His deep affinity for all things basketball drove his decision to remain connected to the sport in a professional capacity, and he even joked about being ready to get back on the court at a moment's notice. "I love this game so much," he told Connor Letourneau for the *San Francisco Chronicle* (6 Oct. 2019). "That's the reason why I keep working out every day. For me to play basketball, you don't need to say it twice. I'm ready."

EARLY LIFE AND EDUCATION

Pachulia was born Zaur Pachulia in the Georgian capital of Tbilisi, on February 10, 1984. He later changed his legal first name to Zaza. Pachulia's parents, Davit (David) and Marina, were both athletes: his father competed in judo, while his mother was an accomplished basketball player who had played for the Soviet Union. Although his father hoped that Pachulia would train in wrestling, his mother greatly encouraged

Photo by Jane Tyska/Digital First Media/The Mercury News via Getty Images

Pachulia's early love of her own sport, taking him to games as a spectator from a young age. "My mom helped me a lot, taking me to every single game, putting us in the good seats," he recalled to Spencer Davies for *CloseUp360* (24 Oct. 2018). "Sometimes I had to sit on the stairs since the arena was always packed and always full. But I didn't care about it where I was sitting. As long as I could watch the game as a kid, it was amazing to me." He began playing basketball himself while still a child and had established himself as a talented player by the time he reached his teens.

In 1997, the Turkish national basketball team recruited Pachulia, who was over six feet tall by the time he was thirteen, encouraging him to move to Turkey and play in a junior league. For the young player, this represented an opportunity to play his sport at a higher level and have a better shot at eventually reaching the NBA. With the support of his parents, he decided to take that opportunity, moving to Istanbul, Turkey, and eventually received Turkish citizenship. "It wasn't easy to leave the country. To make the decision to leave everything? I was born and raised with all my friends and family members," he recalled to Mark Medina for *AJC* (25 Dec. 2017). "It was a huge step in my career. Now you're committed to basketball."

Pachulia enrolled in a local school following his arrival in Turkey and remained based in that country while completing his education. He would later take classes from several university businesses schools, including Harvard Business School and the Kellogg School of Management at Northwestern University.

EUROPEAN BASKETBALL TO THE NBA

Following his move to Turkey, Pachulia first played for the developmental affiliate of the basketball team Ülker GSK. In 2000, at the age of sixteen, he joined the club's adult-level roster, which competed in the EuroLeague, the top professional basketball league in Europe. With Ülker, Pachulia made a name for himself as a star center in major tournaments such as the Turkish Basketball Presidential Cup, which the team won for three consecutive years beginning in 2001.

Although a successful player in Turkey, Pachulia nevertheless continued to dream of playing in the NBA. In 2003, he declared his eligibility for that year's NBA Draft, at the age of nineteen. Having demonstrated his potential during his years in Turkey, Pachulia captured the attention of the Orlando Magic organization, which ultimately selected him in the second round as the forty-second overall pick. He subsequently signed with the team.

Pachulia made his debut with the Magic on November 5, 2003, as a reserve player in a game against the Chicago Bulls. He played for just over sixteen minutes of the game, scoring seven points and claiming six rebounds. Over the course of the 2003–04 season Pachulia played in 59 games, averaging 3.3 points, 2.9 rebounds, 0.4 steals, and 0.2 assists per game. Following his season with the Magic, Pachulia became eligible for the 2004 NBA expansion draft and was selected by the Charlotte Bobcats, who then promptly traded him to the Milwaukee Bucks. He spent 2004–05 season with the Bucks, averaging 6.2 points, 5.1 rebounds, and 0.8 assists despite limited playing time across 74 games.

ATLANTA AND BEYOND

Pachulia entered free agency prior to the 2005–06 season and in August 2005 signed with the Atlanta Hawks, where he would spend the next eight seasons. Although he was a starter his first year with the team, averaging 11.7 points per game, he soon established a role as a solid backup center coming off the bench. He made his first postseason appearance in 2008, as the Hawks reached the first round of the play-offs but were defeated by the eventual NBA champions, the Boston Celtics. Atlanta proved to be a consistent play-off team, advancing past the first round the next three years but losing in the conference semifinals each year.

After again entering free agency in 2013 Pachulia returned to the Milwaukee Bucks, playing with the team for an additional two seasons. In 2013–14, the team won only fifteen games, but in 2014–15 they went 41–41 and secured a spot in the postseason, where they were eliminated by the Chicago Bulls in the first round. In the 2015 offseason Pachulia was traded to the Dallas Mavericks. He had one of the best performances of his career in 2015–16, averaging 8.6 points and a career-high 9.4 rebounds in 26.4 minutes per game and almost earning enough votes to start in the All-Star Game. He again reached the play-offs, but the Mavericks were eliminated in the first round.

In addition to his NBA career, Pachulia was also active on the international level, playing for (and captaining) Georgia's national team in events such as the EuroBasket competition. He particularly appreciated having the opportunity to play in his native country, where many of his friends and relatives still lived. "It's a great feeling in front of your fans, [in] the place where you were born and raised, and the friends come and see your game," he told Mark Tutton for *CNN* (19 Apr. 2010).

NBA CHAMPION

In 2016, Pachulia signed with the Golden State Warriors for what would become a two-season stint as a frequent starter. His debut season with the Warriors proved to be a strong one for the team, which finished the regular season with an NBA-best 67–15 record. The 2017 playoffs represented a turning point in Pachulia's postseason career, as he reached the conference finals for the first time after Golden State defeated the Portland Trail Blazers and the Utah Jazz. In the subsequent matchup against the San Antonio Spurs, Pachulia stirred some controversy when he slid into and injured opposing star Kawhi Leonard, though he denied accusations that he had done so intentionally. The incident generated considerable online abuse against Pachulia, who already had a reputation as an often physical player. Regardless, the Warriors defeated the Spurs, earning Pachulia his first trip to the NBA Finals.

In the 2017 championship series the Warriors faced off against the Cleveland Cavaliers, winning four games to one. Pachulia started all five games, though he averaged just 13.2 minutes played per game. The victory made him the first player from the nation of Georgia ever to win an NBA championship. "The love of this game has been with me since I heard the word basketball itself," he told Medina following the victory. "The love is even deeper right now."

The 2017–18 season was also successful for the Warriors, which finished the season ranked second in the Western Conference and third in the NBA with a 58–24 record. Once again competing in the play-offs, the team beat the Spurs, the New Orleans Pelicans, and the Houston Rockets before progressing to the championship round. In the finals Pachulia and the Warriors again faced the Cavaliers, and this time swept the series in four games to claim their second consecutive championship. Pachulia had less of a role than the previous year, playing in just two games off the bench.

After again hitting free agency, Pachulia joined the Detroit Pistons in 2018. During the 2018–19 season his playing time and his statistical performance declined considerably. Though the Pistons reached the play-offs, they were eliminated by the Bucks in the first round. This proved to be Pachulia's last season as a player, and in August 2019 he officially announced his retirement.

BUSINESS AND BASKETBALL OUTREACH

In addition to playing basketball, Pachulia was active in a variety of business initiatives, including unsuccessful attempts to operate restaurants in Atlanta begun during his time with the Hawks. "I learned that a business like that is difficult to make work as an investor unless you actually work there," he recalled to Jacob Forchheimer for *ONE37PM* (22 Oct. 2019). "It takes all of your time, it's a 24-hour job, literally." Pachulia experienced greater success in the Republic of Georgia, with investments in real estate as well as in businesses such as gyms and hotels. He also served as a brand ambassador for the Georgian sneaker brand Crosty, one of few footwear brands to have been created in his home country.

Perhaps Pachulia's most significant initiative was the creation of the Zaza Pachulia Basketball Academy, a youth program in Tbilisi. Opened in November 2015, the academy was based in a facility that had previously hosted the 2015 European Youth Summer Olympic Festival. In addition to training young athletes in basketball, the academy held English classes with the goal of preparing players for potential careers in the United States. "They have all the tools that they need, and then it's up to them how much time and effort they're gonna put in," Pachulia told Davies about the academy's students. The program quickly proved popular, growing from about 250 participants to nearly 1,000 in just a few years.

RETURN TO THE WARRIORS

During his final seasons as a basketball player, Pachulia had begun to consider pursuing a career on the business side of his sport following his eventual retirement. He worked to expand his knowledge of team and league operations by sitting in on meetings, particularly those held by Warriors leadership, and shadowing employees at the NBA's head office. His efforts paid off shortly after his retirement, as he almost immediately returned to the Warriors as a team consultant. "I'm so thankful for this opportunity, especially being able to jump right in without any time off from playing," he told Letourneau in late 2019. "I'm surrounded every day by people who are really important to me."

As a consultant, Pachulia took on a wide variety of duties, including attending meetings and participating in televised content with the team. "My role is not anything specific, to be honest. I'm all over the place," he explained to DiFilippo. "I want to learn as much as possible and see this business from different angles and know this business from different angles."

PERSONAL LIFE

Pachulia and his wife, Tika, married in 2008. They have three children. In recognition of Pachulia's contributions to the sport of basketball and representation of Georgia abroad, the government of Georgia presented him with the Order of Honor in August 2017.

SUGGESTED READING

Davies, Spencer. "Pistons' Zaza Pachulia Pays It Forward with European Basketball Academy." *CloseUp360*, 25 Oct. 2018, closeup360.com/global/zaza-pachulia-detroit-pistons-nba-basketball-academy/. Accessed 17 Jan. 2020.

Letourneau, Connor. "Zaza Pachulia Relishes Return to Warriors as Team Consultant." *San Francisco Chronicle*, 6 Oct. 2019, www.sfchronicle.com/warriors/article/Zaza-Pachulia-relishes-return-to-Warriors-as-team-14496728.php. Accessed 17 Jan. 2020.

Medina, Mark. "How Zaza Pachulia's Upbringing in Georgia Shaped NBA Journey." *AJC*, 25 Dec. 2017, www.ajc.com/sports/how-zaza-pachulia-upbringing-georgia-shaped-nba-journey/jgBE5INuCjzYcuK5rPOC7J/. Accessed 17 Jan. 2019.

Pachulia, Zaza. "Zaza Pachulia Is All Business." Interview by Jaco Forchheimer. *ONE37PM*, 22 Oct. 2019, www.one37pm.com/strength/sports/zaza-pachulia-crosty-interview. Accessed 17 Jan. 2019.

——. "Zaza Pachulia Is Getting Used to Life after Basketball in the Warriors Front Office." Interview by Bill DiFilippo. *Dime*, Uproxx, 5 Nov. 2019, uproxx.com/dimemag/zaza-pachulia-interview-warriors-crosty/. Accessed 17 Jan. 2019.

Tutton, Mark. "Zaza Pachulia: Georgia's Basketball Giant." *CNN*, 19 Apr. 2010, www.cnn.com/2010/WORLD/europe/04/19/basketball.zaza.pachulia.georgia/index.html. Accessed 17 Jan. 2019.

"Zaza Pachulia Becomes Georgia's First NBA Champion." *Agenda.ge*, 13 June 2017, agenda.ge/en/news/2017/1202. Accessed 17 Jan. 2020.

—*Joy Crelin*

Winifred Phillips

Occupation: Composer

For composer Winifred Phillips, the turning point in her career came not while creating music but while playing the video game *Tomb Raider*. Struck by the power of the game's musical score, she abruptly realized that every video game with an original score needed a composer and that she was amply prepared to fill that role. "I'd been a gamer from way, way back, but for some reason, it had never occurred to me that I could write music for games," she told Sam Hughes for *Sound Architect* (1 Mar. 2014). "Once the idea got into my head, I never looked back." A working composer since the early 1990s, Phillips began her career creating music for radio adaptations of classic literary works, contributing to more than one hundred episodes broadcast on National Public Radio (NPR) and satellite radio. Having proven herself in radio, she made a relatively seamless transition into video games, contributing to projects such as *God of War* (2005)

and the *Charlie and the Chocolate Factory* game (2005). Later works, including contributions to the *LittleBigPlanet* franchise and a turn as the sole composer for *Assassin's Creed III: Liberation* (2012), solidified her place as one of the major contributors to video game music. She has won numerous awards and received widespread recognition for her work. With each project, however, Phillips prefers to focus on the tasks set before her rather than on the potential recognition that awaits her. "Whether I'm hired as the sole composer or as part of a team, the business is pretty similar," she explained to Neely Tucker for the *Library of Congress Blog* (4 Apr. 2019). "I'm contracted to create a certain amount of music. The game's development team briefs me on the technical specs. We discuss ideas for musical style. Then I get to work."

EARLY LIFE AND EDUCATION

Drawn to music since childhood, Phillips began playing piano when she was five years old and decided that she wanted to become a composer while still a child. Over the course of her early life, she pursued classical training in piano and also trained as a vocalist. She later learned to play a variety of additional instruments, although she has noted in interviews that she is truly proficient only in voice and piano. Alongside her interest in music, Phillips was an avid fan of video games and enjoyed playing games in a wide variety of genres throughout her childhood and early adulthood. "I was a huge fan of the *Final Fantasy* series. Played those games endlessly!" she recalled to Tucker. "I remember spending tons of time with *Crash Bandicoot*. Loved *Prince of Persia*. Sunk huge chunks of playtime into the *Civilization* games. And of course, the *Tomb Raider* games hold a special place in my heart, for a lot of reasons."

EARLY CAREER

Phillips began her composing career with NPR, contributing to the science-fiction radio series *Generations Radio Theater Presents: Radio Tales* in 1992. Working alongside the show's producer Winnie Waldron, Phillips helped narrate and composed music for more than one hundred episodes of the series, which presented adaptations of well-known literary works, fairytales, and similar content, including a radio adaptation of the Edgar Allan Poe story "The Masque of the Red Death." The series moved to XM Satellite Radio in 2002, at which point it was shorted to *Radio Tales*. Over the course of Phillips's involvement with *Radio Tales*, the program received numerous awards, including multiple Gracie Awards for Best National Network Drama. The experience drew substantial attention to her talents and capabilities as a composer, with the many episodes of *Radio Tales* serving as an impressive demo reel as she sought out new opportunities.

For Phillips, who left the show in 2003, new opportunities emerged in an unexpected place. "I never stopped playing video games," she told Tucker about her time with *Radio Tales*. "And then one day, I was playing *Tomb Raider*, and the music suddenly grabbed my attention. I remember the light bulb going off in my head." Having realized that composing music for video games could be a viable career path, she began to plan a move into that industry alongside Waldron, her longtime producer and creative partner. "I convinced Winnie to make the big leap into the game industry with me, and it's been a grand adventure ever since," she told Tucker. Following a period of extensive research into video game composition, Phillips began her entry into the industry by sending copies of her demo reel to video game production companies as well as by pursuing in-person networking opportunities at industry events such as the Electronic Entertainment Expo, or E3.

COMPOSING FOR VIDEO GAMES

Among Phillips's earliest video game projects was the 2005 PlayStation 2 game *God of War*. One of several composers tasked with creating music for the game, she found the process of composing for a new medium to be relatively simple thanks to her extensive experience with *Radio Tales*. "When I crossed over into video games with my first project, *God of War*, the transition was a fairly smooth one," she explained to Koda Kazar for the *Freakin' Awesome Network* (3 Dec. 2012). "I'd been creating music for epic stories, and *God of War* was certainly epic." Upon the game's release, its soundtrack won numerous awards from industry groups and publications. In addition to *God of War*, Phillips worked on a variety of projects during her first several years in video games, including *Charlie and the Chocolate Factory* (2005), *The Da Vinci Code* (2006), and *SimAnimals* (2009).

Phillips's next big project was *LittleBigPlanet 2*, which was released in 2011. The soundtrack to the game included both licensed songs by popular musicians and original music created by a group of composers. Phillips particularly appreciated creating music for the *LittleBigPlanet* games due to the creative approach taken by the game developers and exemplified by the game's style of play. "In the *LittleBigPlanet* franchise, the audio team encourages all of the composers to be unique and step out-of-the-box, because that's what *LittleBigPlanet* is all about—eclectic artistry, visual and aural mashups of unexpected elements, all designed to provoke creativity from the players," she explained to Marcos Gaspar and Stephen Meyerink for *RPG Fan* (4 Apr. 2015). In addition to contributing to *LittleBigPlanet 2*,

Phillips composed music for bonus downloadable *LittleBigPlanet 2* content, before returning again to the world of that series with 2014's *LittleBigPlanet 3*, for which she again served as one of several composers. Following the release of *LittleBigPlanet 3*, Phillips received particular notice for one of her pieces featured in the game, "Ziggurat Theme," which incorporated vocals performed by Phillips and was composed to take advantage of the unique interactivity of the game. Phillips received a Global Music Award and a Hollywood Music in Media Award in recognition of her work on "Ziggurat Theme."

COMPOSING FOR FRANCHISE GAMES

While many of Phillips's earliest video game projects were licensed games based on film or television properties, many others—including the *LittleBigPlanet* games—were new installments in existing franchises that already had dedicated fans. As a composer, Phillips sought to remain cognizant of those fans' expectations while also working to meet the needs of each particular game. "I try to honor the musical style that fans of the franchise would naturally expect from another installment in their favorite game series," she explained to Gaspar and Meyerink. "However, most of the franchise games I've worked on have required a new musical approach be adopted for that particular installment in the series."

The need for a new musical approach was particularly clear during Phillips's time working on the 2012 game *Assassin's Creed III: Liberation*, for which she served as the sole credited composer. Designed for the handheld PlayStation Vita system, *Assassin's Creed III: Liberation* was an installment in a series of video games about the adventures of individual assassins, each operating within a specific geographical and temporal setting. The bulk of *Assassin's Creed III: Liberation* takes place in the mid-eighteenth century and focuses on New Orleans–based assassin Aveline de Grandpré. In composing the score for the game, Phillips sought to create music that reflected not only the events taking place but also the complex setting. "The music definitely needed to simultaneously reflect the past and the present, with both a feeling of authentic antiquity and hi-tech touches. This presented a constant challenge, evaluating each track for opportunities to display both historical and contemporary elements," she explained to Kazar. To address that challenge, Phillips drew from myriad influences to create music that would be suitable for the game and reflect the cultural background of its protagonist, who has French and African ancestry. "I implemented modern rhythms, synths and sound-design textures, combining these with period instruments from both the French and African cultures that were such a part of Aveline's character and daily life," she told Kazar. Received well by fans of the *Assassin's Creed* series and video game critics, the music composed for the game was featured in the 2019–2020 Assassin's Creed Symphony concert tour, a series of live orchestral performances of music from the franchise.

OTHER WORK

In addition to her extensive work as a composer, Phillips is the author of *A Composer's Guide to Game Music*, published in 2014. Written over the course of several years, the book features numerous insights gleaned from Phillips's years of experience and sets out to address the needs of those working in or seeking to enter the field of video game composition. For Phillips, the book specifically filled gaps in the existing body of work dealing with her field. "A lot of the books at that time focused on game audio as a whole, and they were written purely from a technical perspective. They didn't broach the creative issues and aspects that face game composers," she told Amalia Morris and Sylvain Pinot for *Score It* (14 Apr. 2017). "As a new game composer coming into the game industry, that was something that I had really wanted." Well received upon its publication, *A Composer's Guide to Game Music* was reprinted in 2017.

While Phillips continues to compose music for traditional video-game projects, she is particularly intrigued by the subgenre of virtual reality (VR) games, which gained popularity during the second decade of the twenty-first century thanks to the development of VR devices such as Oculus Rift. "We're in the early, wild-west days of virtual reality's development," she told Morris and Pinot about that field. "There aren't any universal tools that everyone is using yet, nor are there any standards in terms of what its music and sound should accomplish." Phillips has delved into the world of VR on several occasions, contributing music to projects such as the VR collectible card game *Dragon Front* (2016) and the VR horror experience *The Haunted Graveyard* (2018).

PERSONAL LIFE

Phillips works in the New York City area.

SUGGESTED READING

Huxtable, Nora. "Top Score: Composer Winifred Phillips." *Classical MPR*, 19 Feb. 2015, www.classicalmpr.org/story/2015/02/19/top-score-composer-winifred-phillips. Accessed 13 Dec. 2019.

Phillips, Winifred. "Interview with Professional Composer Winifred Phillips, Author of *A Composer's Guide to Game Music*." Interview by Sam Hughes. *Sound Architect*, 1 Mar. 2014, www.thesoundarchitect.co.uk/interviews/winifredphilips/. Accessed 13 Dec. 2019.

———. "Interview with Winifred Phillips, Composer and Author of *A Composer's Guide to Game Music*." Interview by Marcos Gaspar and Stephen Meyerink. *RPGFan*, 4 Apr. 2015, www.rpgfan.com/features/Music_of_the_Year_2014/Interview_Winifred_Phillips.html. Accessed 13 Dec. 2019.

———. "A Symphony of Death: Interview with Winifred Phillips." Interview by Koda Kazar. *Freakin' Awesome Network*, 3 Dec. 2012, www.freakinawesomenetwork.net/2012/12/a-symphony-of-death-interview-with-winifred-phillips/. Accessed 13 Dec. 2019.

———. "Winifred Phillips: Composing for Virtual Reality and Interactive Video Game." Interview by Amalia Morris and Sylvain Pinot. *Score It*, 14 Apr. 2017, magazine.scoreit.org/interview-winifred-phillips-game-composer/. Accessed 13 Dec. 2019.

———. "Winifred Phillips: The Music of the Game." Interview by Neely Tucker. *Library of Congress*, 4 Apr. 2019, blogs.loc.gov/loc/2019/04/winifred-phillips-the-music-of-the-game/. Accessed 13 Dec. 2019.

SELECTED WORKS

Generations Radio Theater Presents: Radio Tales, 1992–2003; *God of War*, 2005; *LittleBigPlanet 2*, 2011; *Assassin's Creed III: Liberation*, 2012; *LittleBigPlanet 3*, 2014; *Dragon Front*, 2016; *The Haunted Graveyard*, 2018

—*Joy Crelin*

Joaquin Phoenix

Date of birth: October 28, 1974
Occupation: Actor

Award-winning actor Joaquin Phoenix is best known for his roles in such varied films as *Gladiator* (2000), *Walk the Line* (2005), *The Master* (2012), and *Her* (2013). His star rose still further with his lead role in *Joker* (2019), a reimagined origin story for the famous DC Comics villain shot in the mode of a gritty crime drama from the 1970s. Phoenix's performance in *Joker*, characteristic of his best work, is largely physical. While the film itself divided critics, Anthony Lane, echoing others, concentrated his praise on Phoenix, arguing for the *New Yorker* (27 Sept. 2019) that Phoenix's "prowess . . . holds it all together. His face may get the greasepaint"—a reference to the Joker's iconic painted face—"but it's his whole body, coiled upon itself like a spring of flesh, from which the movie's energy is released."

For his physicality and unsettling interiority, Phoenix is considered among the best actors of

Photo by David Livingston/Getty Images

his generation, but his mercurial public persona gives few hints about what the actor is really like. (The enigma was compounded in 2009 and 2010, when Phoenix tried to convince people that he was retiring from acting to become a rapper, a prank captured in the 2010 mockumentary *I'm Still Here*.) Phoenix has an unusual backstory. His parents were traveling missionaries for a Christian cult. His older brother, River Phoenix, became a famous actor as a teenager, thrusting his large family into the spotlight before his tragic death at the age of twenty-three in 1993. But Phoenix is guarded about these aspects of his biography, and himself in general, preferring in interviews to speak about his animal rights activism—or more commonly, avoiding interviews at all.

EARLY LIFE

Joaquin Rafael Bottom was born in San Juan, Puerto Rico, on October 28, 1974. He had four siblings: River, Rain, Liberty, and Summer. Their parents, as Lena Corner described them for the *Guardian* (8 July 2011), were "bona fide, flowers-in-their-hair hippies." Their mother, Arlyn Dunetz (who later changed her given name to Heart), was hitchhiking across Northern California in the late 1960s, when she met John Bottom, a songwriter. The two married in 1969. In 1973, after the birth of the couple's first two children, River and Rain, they joined a religious group called the Children of God and traveled as missionaries in the southern United States, Puerto Rico, and Venezuela, where they were named "archbishops." By 1977 the group's

problematic sexual practices—which included using sex to lure potential converts as well as alleged child sexual abuse—drove the Phoenix family out; the group was later identified as a cult and is now known as The Family International. Speaking of his parents, Phoenix later told Joe Hagan for *Vanity Fair* (1 Oct. 2019), "They were idealists, and believed that they were with a group who shared their beliefs, and their values. I think they probably were looking for safety, and family."

Phoenix also told Hagan that on the ocean voyage from Venezuela back to the United States—during which Phoenix turned three—he and his family witnessed crew members killing fish by smashing their heads into nails. Shocked by the violence, within a few weeks, the family embraced veganism and later became animal rights activists.

CHILDHOOD ACTING CAREER

The family eventually settled in Los Angeles, California, dropping the surname Bottom in 1979 and adopting Phoenix, after the mythical bird reborn from its own ashes. Heart Phoenix became a secretary at NBC. They met a child agent, who won the children, including Joaquin, parts in commercials and bit work on television. To supplement their income, the Phoenix children busked on the street. Joaquin got into break dancing.

Joaquin, still a child, changed his name to Leaf Phoenix; his earliest roles are attributed to that name. He appeared alongside River in a 1984 episode of *ABC Afterschool Special* called "Backwards: The Riddle of Dyslexia." He also appeared in episodes of *Murder, She Wrote*, *Alfred Hitchcock Presents*, and *Hill Street Blues*. River's career took off after he appeared in the hit 1986 film *Stand by Me* at fifteen. He was soon a major star, and the whole family attracted attention. Joaquin appeared in the Ron Howard film *Parenthood* in 1989 but, as a teenager, took a break from acting and quit his long-distance studies after he was asked to dissect a dead frog. Meanwhile, River introduced him to classic films and convinced him to change his name back to Joaquin. The family moved to Gainesville, Florida, in hopes of protecting themselves from the media attention brought on by River's fame. River also bought them a ranch in Costa Rica.

In 1993 River, then twenty-three, died of a drug overdose that Joaquin and Rain witnessed outside the Viper Room, a Los Angeles nightclub. Joaquin's anguished emergency call was played on the news.

RETURN TO FILM

After River's death, the Phoenix family moved to their ranch in Costa Rica. Two years later Joaquin Phoenix won a role in Gus Van Sant's film adaptation of the Joyce Maynard novel *To Die For*. In the film, loosely based on an actual 1990 murder in New Hampshire, Nicole Kidman's character seduces Phoenix's character, a high school student, and convinces him to kill her husband. Critics were impressed by his performance—Janet Maslin wrote in the *New York Times* (27 Sept. 1995) that his "raw, anguished expressiveness . . . makes him an actor to watch for"—but invariably introduced him as River's brother. It took a number of years for him to be considered an actor in his own right. Meanwhile, his parents divorced.

Phoenix went on to appear in a slew of films, including *Inventing the Abbotts* (1997), Oliver Stone's *U Turn* (1997), *Return to Paradise* (1998), *Clay Pigeons* (1998), *8MM* (1999), and *The Yards* (2000). In 2000, he played the Roman emperor Commodus, son of Marcus Aurelius, in the film *Gladiator*. *Gladiator*, as novelist Bret Easton Ellis argued in his profile of Phoenix for the *New York Times* (6 Sept. 2017), "made him a star." Phoenix was nominated for an Academy Award for Best Supporting Actor for *Gladiator*, and the film won Best Picture.

Phoenix went on to appear in the drama *Quills* (2000) and the comedy *Buffalo Soldiers* (2001). In 2002, he acted alongside Mel Gibson in the M. Night Shyamalan alien invasion film *Signs*. He appeared in Shyamalan's *The Village* in 2004, followed by *Hotel Rwanda* (2004) and *Ladder 49* (2004). In 2005, Phoenix starred as country music superstar Johnny Cash in the biopic *Walk the Line*. Phoenix and costar Reese Witherspoon as June Carter performed their own vocals for the film. He was nominated for an Academy Award for Best Lead Actor, his first nomination in that category, and won his first Golden Globe Award in 2006. Playing Cash, who died in 2003, was another benchmark in his artistic evolution, Phoenix told Hagan. "I had this realization that the experiences I was having as an actor were deepening, becoming more profound to me," he said. "There is this revelatory feeling, and it feels like every step you're dancing closer and closer to the thing."

I'M STILL HERE AND *THE MASTER*
After *Walk the Line*, Phoenix appeared in the dramas *We Own the Night* (2007), *Reservation Road* (2007), and *Two Lovers* (2008). In 2010, he starred in a purported documentary called *I'm Still Here*, directed by Casey Affleck, who was then married to Phoenix's youngest sister, Summer. In it, Phoenix plays a caricature of himself as a Hollywood celebrity who gives up his acting career to become a rapper. *I'm Still Here* was poorly received and marred by lawsuits filed against Affleck by two female staff who charged sexual harassment and breach of contract; Ellis, who himself liked the film, called it "critically

reviled." Phoenix and Affleck insisted that the film was a real chronicle of Phoenix's retirement and transformation. Phoenix kept up the ruse—wearing a scraggly beard and dark sunglasses and otherwise embodying his insufferable alter ego—for nearly two years.

Many speculated that Affleck's poorly executed satire would sink Phoenix's career, but in 2012 Phoenix emerged from his faux retirement to perform one of his most celebrated roles to date. In Paul Thomas Anderson's *The Master*, Phoenix plays Freddie Quell, an alcoholic veteran who finds purpose in a Scientology-esque cult led by Lancaster Dodd (Philip Seymour Hoffman) in 1950s California. The film focuses on the relationship between the two men, demonstrating, Richard Brody wrote for the *New Yorker* (10 Sept. 2012), a riveting "grudge match between two styles of performance." Hoffman was a technician, Brody wrote, while Phoenix is "an actor of furious natural emotion, of inner violence with which his very being trembles as he struggles to keep it in check and to channel it." *The Master* earned Phoenix his third Oscar nomination.

HER AND *JOKER*
In 2013, Phoenix appeared alongside French actress Marion Cotillard in *The Immigrant*, about a young Polish immigrant forced into prostitution in Prohibition-era New York City. The same year, he starred in *Her*, a film by Spike Jonze about a man who falls in love with the voice of the operating system on his cell phone, played by Scarlett Johansson. *Her* received mostly positive reviews and was nominated for an Academy Award for Best Picture. Manohla Dargis drew comparisons between Phoenix's role in *Her* and his role in *The Master*. Phoenix is "an actor who excels at exquisite isolation," Dargis observed in the *New York Times* (17 Dec. 2013). "At his most memorable, Mr. Phoenix plays wounded, stunted souls whose agonies are expressed almost reluctantly." In *Her*, especially, Dargis wrote, "it feels as if his character's solitude had been drawn from some deep, unarticulated place in Mr. Phoenix's own being."

In 2014, Phoenix appeared in *Inherent Vice*, Paul Thomas Anderson's film adaptation of the Thomas Pynchon novel of the same name, and in 2015 he starred in the Woody Allen comedy *Irrational Man*. Phoenix won the award for best actor at the Cannes Film Festival for his starring role in Lynne Ramsay's gruesome drama *You Were Really Never Here* (2017), about a hammer-wielding contract killer. In 2018, Phoenix took on a slew of diverse roles: as cartoonist John Callahan in the Van Sant–directed biopic *Don't Worry, He Won't Get Far on Foot*; as an assassin cowboy in the western *The Sisters Brothers*;

and as Jesus Christ in *Mary Magdalene*, starring Rooney Mara.

In 2019, Phoenix was nominated for an Academy Award and won a second Golden Globe for his role in *Joker*, a film controversial with Batman fans for, among other things, eschewing any comic book fantasy elements in favor of simply exploring the torments of a mentally ill man who turns to crime. Phoenix approached the role with characteristic intensity, losing weight and painfully contorting his body on camera, after also studying narcissism and criminology. He also got to work with Robert De Niro, whom he says is his favorite American actor. Director Todd Phillips, who cowrote the film, conceived the character with Phoenix in mind, though much of the character's strange and beguiling physicality is improvised by Phoenix. "For me, I always thought that acting should be like a documentary," Phoenix told Hagan. "That you should just feel whatever it is that you're feeling, what you think the character is going through at that moment."

PERSONAL LIFE

Phoenix met his partner, Rooney Mara, while making the film *Her*. The couple began dating in 2017 and became engaged in 2019. They live in Los Angeles.

SUGGESTED READING

Brody, Richard. "The Astonishing Power of 'The Master.'" Review of *The Master*, directed by Paul Thomas Anderson. *The New Yorker*, 10 Sept. 2012, www.newyorker.com/culture/richard-brody/the-astonishing-power-of-the-master. Accessed 17 Jan. 2020.

Corner, Lena. "Rain Phoenix's Unusual Childhood." *The Guardian*, 8 July 2011, www.theguardian.com/lifeandstyle/2011/jul/09/rain-phoenix-river-joaquin-family. Accessed 15 Jan. 2020.

Dargis, Manohla. "Disembodied, but, Oh, What a Voice." Review of *Her*, directed by Spike Jonze. *The New York Times*, 17 Dec. 2013, www.nytimes.com/2013/12/18/movies/her-directed-by-spike-jonze.html. Accessed 17 Jan. 2020.

Ellis, Bret Easton. "The Weird Brilliance of Joaquin Phoenix." *The New York Times*, 6 Sept. 2017, www.nytimes.com/2017/09/06/t-magazine/joaquin-phoenix.html. Accessed 16 Jan. 2020.

Hagan, Joe. "'I F—king Love My Life': Joaquin Phoenix on Joker, Why River Is His Rosebud, His Rooney Research, and His 'Prenatal' Gift for Dark Characters." *Vanity Fair*, 1 Oct. 2019, www.vanityfair.com/hollywood/2019/10/joaquin-phoenix-cover-story. Accessed 15 Jan. 2020.

Lane, Anthony. "Todd Phillips's 'Joker' Is No Laughing Matter." Review of *Joker*, directed by Todd Phillips. *The New Yorker*, 27 Sept. 2019, www.newyorker.com/magazine/2019/10/07/todd-phillips-joker-is-no-laughing-matter. Accessed 17 Jan. 2020.

Maslin, Janet. "She Trusts in TV's Redeeming Power." Review of *To Die For*, directed by Gus Van Sant. *The New York Times*, 27 Sept. 1995, www.nytimes.com/1995/09/27/movies/film-review-she-trusts-in-tv-s-redeeming-power.html. Accessed 15 Jan. 2020.

SELECTED WORKS

Gladiator, 2000; *Walk the Line*, 2005; *The Master*, 2012; *Her*, 2013; *You Were Really Never Here*, 2017; *Joker*, 2019

—Molly Hagan

Crystal Pite

Born: December 15, 1970
Occupation: Choreographer

Olivier Award–winning choreographer Crystal Pite is a former ballet dancer known for pushing the boundary between classical and contemporary dance. "Right from the early days my choreography tended to push against ballet, as much as I could while still immersed in it," Pite told Roslyn Sulcas for the *New York Times* (19 Nov. 2015). Though Pite is more likely to characterize herself as a contemporary choreographer—she founded a successful contemporary dance company called Kidd Pivot in 2002—she is one of only a few high-profile female choreographers working in ballet. From *Emergence* (2009) and *The Seasons' Canon* (2016), both commissioned by ballet companies, to *Polaris* (2014), Pite is, in part, known for creating intricate, large-scale works that tap into the energy of an ensemble. Her more intimate, experimental pieces like the short duet "A Picture of You Falling," the show *The You Show* (2010), the searing collaborative performance piece *Betroffenheit* (2015), and the resonant *Flight Pattern* (2017), reveal Pite's strength for conveying emotion through individual movement. "Her work feels undeniably human," Lyndsey Winship wrote for the *Guardian* (18 Sept. 2019), "even when it veers into experimental territory."

EARLY LIFE AND DANCE TRAINING

Pite was born in Terrace, British Columbia, Canada, on December 15, 1970. Growing up in Victoria, she began taking dance classes when she was four at the Pacific Dance Centre, a private studio, under the tutelage of Maureen

Photo by Kat Baulu via Wikimedia Commons

Eastick and Wendy Green, where she remained throughout high school. She began working for a semiprofessional theater, performing musical theater and pantomime, when she was a preteen. "Ballet, tap, jazz, drama, played in the school band, sang in choir, made up dances for high school musicals," she told Sulcas. "I always knew I wanted to be a dancer and I always choreographed." In 1983, at age thirteen, her first choreographed piece, "Bug Dance," was performed at the Greater Victoria Music Festival. She credited Eastick for pushing her to explore her abilities, writing for her blog, *Crystal Pite* (7 July 2000), that both teachers "were amazing mentors," who pushed her to find her individual voice as an artist. They "added a personal element to my training which could not be received from the 'bun heads' of the major ballet schools who produce made to order dancers for their parent companies."

After graduating from high school at age seventeen in 1988, Pite joined a small ensemble called Ballet British Columbia (BC), which focused on new work and contemporary ballet. Two years later, she choreographed her first professional piece, a duet called *Between the Bliss and Me* (1990). It became a part of Ballet BC's repertoire for a United States tour and earned her commissions from other Canadian companies. Pite spent eight years with Ballet BC, during which time she earned the 1995 Banff Centre's Clifford E. Lee Award for choreography. The following year, artistic director John Alleyne commissioned her to choreograph a piece called

Moving Day (1996), about household appliances and chores.

WILLIAM FORSYTHE'S FRANKFURT BALLET

In 1996, Pite, then twenty-five, left Ballet BC to join master choreographer William Forsythe's Frankfurt Ballet in Germany. Forsythe, who works in contemporary and neoclassical modes, is known for fostering dance luminaries like Richard Siegal, Helen Pickett, and Jacopo Godani. "Bill [Forsythe] was attracted to people that were creative to begin with, people that were willing to take risks, and there was this incredible creative spirit at work there," Pite told Laura Cappelle for *Dance Magazine* (16 Mar. 2017). During her time in Frankfurt, Pite was primarily a dancer, though she choreographed some new work, including *Excerpts from a Future Work* (2000), and a duet inspired by Annie Dillard's 1989 book *The Writing Life*. After five years, she left the company and settled in Vancouver in 2001.

KIDD PIVOT

In 2002, Pite and her life partner, dancer and set designer Jay Gowen Taylor, founded a contemporary dance company called Kidd Pivot. The first productions performed by her new company were Pite's *Uncollected Work* (2002), *Double Story* (2004), and *Lost Action* (2006). For the rest of the decade, she worked as both a dancer and a choreographer. "I think those two sides of myself, being a dancer and a choreographer, have always fed each other, and at that point I felt this great synthesis within myself," she told Cappelle. During this time, Pite also served as the resident choreographer at Nederlands Dans Theater and Les Ballets Jazz de Montréal. For her works, she was awarded the Bonnie Bird North American Choreography Award in 2004, the Isadora Award in 2005, the Jessie Richardson Theatre Award in 2006, and the Governor General of Canada's Performing Arts Award in 2008.

In 2009, she received a commission from the National Ballet of Canada. After nearly a decade away from ballet, her project, called *Emergence* (2009), served as a kind of homecoming. In creating the piece, Pite was inspired by the hierarchical structure of a ballet company, and its likeness to the structure of a beehive. She researched the intelligence inherent in a swarm and explored how individual movements can create more complex systems. Reviewers wrote that Pite's work is often in conversation, its creation feeding off something else. In a blog post for the *Pacific Northwest Ballet* (17 Oct. 2013), Pite wrote that she aimed to create a series of self-generating movement parameters that would effectively "help to make the piece make itself." *Emergence* was a notable, and unusual, example of this concept. In 2009, Kidd Pivot premiered Pite's work *Dark Matters*. The next year, Pite accepted a three-year residency with Künstlerhaus Mousonturm in Frankfurt, where she created, among other works, *The You Show* (2010) and *The Tempest Replica* (2011). The latter was based on William Shakespeare's *The Tempest* (ca. 1611) and won Pite international acclaim.

"POLARIS" AND "A PICTURE OF YOU FALLING"

Pite officially retired from dancing in 2011, after the birth of her son, Niko, the previous year. "I always imagined that my dance career would end when I either got injured or had a baby," she told Cappelle. "Fortunately, it ended up being the latter, but the decline was exponential. The aging, the child, the challenges of trying to juggle everything! It was a new beginning and an ending all at once." In 2013, Pite became an associate artist at Sadler's Wells in London, one of the world's most prestigious contemporary dance venues. In 2014, she created a piece called "Polaris" as a part of *Thomas Adès: Concentric Paths—Movement in Music*, a tribute to the contemporary British composer. Utilizing over sixty dancers—and recalling the swarms in *Emergence*—the piece was praised for both its intricacy and its boldness. "Pite rides the music with a reckless choreographic variety," Judith Mackrell wrote for the *Guardian* (2 Nov. 2014). "Her black-costumed dancers appear first as a dark shifting mass, individuals discernible only as a pale pattern of faces and outspread hands. Peeled into lines, they are galvanized into great roiling waves of movement, or shattered into groups that feel like the aftermath of some monumental catastrophe."

The same year, Sadler's Wells mounted a new production of Pite's *The Tempest Replica*. In 2015, as part of a program featuring three choreographers called *The Associates*, the theater produced Pite's duet, "A Picture of You Falling," which was originally presented as part of Pite's 2010 *The You Show*. The piece depicts the end of a love affair. Fragments of speech are accompanied by fragmented movements and interactions. "Each dancer appears in turn, is briefly illuminated, and vanishes. . . . These are moments trapped outside time, endlessly repeating," Luke Jennings wrote in his euphoric review for the *Guardian* (8 Feb. 2015). For the three works presented at Sadler's Wells—"Polaris," *The Tempest Replica*, and "A Picture of You Falling"—Pite won the 2015 Olivier Award for Outstanding Achievement in Dance.

BETROFFENHEIT AND OTHER WORKS

In 2015, Pite partnered with actor and playwright Jonathan Young to create a work called *Betroffenheit*. A German word that describes the shock that comes before grief, *Betroffenheit* tells the story of Young's personal tragedy, when his teenage daughter, niece, and nephew died in a house fire in 2009. Starring Young, a supporting cast of dancers portray the central character's inner demons; the story avoids the specificity of Young's story, focusing on the character's struggles with grief, guilt, and the welcome oblivion of addiction. In her five-star review for the *Guardian* (1 June 2016)—*Betroffenheit* played at Sadler's Wells after premiering in Toronto—Mackrell wrote, "Pite's special genius is in choreographing the body language of emotion in the distorted, lifting, folding shapes of her dancers' bodies. In the sharply specific rhythms of trauma and comfort we can read whole narratives of suffering and recovery." In 2017, *Betroffenheit* won an Olivier Award for Best New Dance Production, and in 2019, the *Guardian* named it the best dance show of the twenty-first century.

In 2016, Pite created a piece for the Paris Opera Ballet called *The Seasons' Canon*, set to Max Richter's version of Antonio Vivaldi's *The Four Seasons*. Like *Emergence* and "Polaris," the piece relies on the creation of large-scale patterns. Pite revisited this concept for a different purpose in 2017 with *Flight Pattern*, a commission from the Royal Ballet in London. *Flight Pattern* explores the refugee crisis, and the terror, uncertainty, and hope of "flight." While Pite is often interested in the movement of masses, *Flight Pattern* utilizes a large cast but also focuses on the story of one character. About the work, Pite told Cappelle, "When there is tension, something flourishes and becomes alive, complex. I want dancing that looks like it's being discovered in the very moment it's being danced. I want it to look like it's reckless, dangerous and also delightful." The show earned Pite her second Olivier Award for Best New Dance Production in 2018.

Pite again collaborated with Young on a production called *Revisor*—based on Nikolai Gogol's 1836 play *The Government Inspector*—which was premiered by Kidd Pivot in February 2019. The same year, she was commissioned by the Paris Opera Ballet to create the production *Body and Soul* (2019).

PERSONAL LIFE

As of 2020, Pite remains based in Vancouver.

SUGGESTED READING

Cappelle, Laura. "Why Crystal Pite Still Feels Like an Outsider in Ballet." *Dance Magazine*, 16 Mar. 2017, www.dancemagazine.com/why-crystal-pite-still-feels-like-an-outsider-in-ballet-2316854067.html. Accessed 14 Aug. 2020.

Mackrell, Judith. "*Betroffenheit* Review—Human Suffering Transformed into Heroic

Brilliance." Review of *Betroffenheit*, choreographed by Crystal Pite. *The Guardian*, 1 June 2016, www.theguardian.com/stage/2016/jun/01/betroffenheit-review-human-suffering-transformed-into-heroic-brilliance. Accessed 14 Aug. 2020.

———. "See the Music, Hear the Dance Review—Adès Provides Exhilarating Inspiration." Review of *See the Music, Hear the Dance*, choreographed by Crystal Pite. *The Guardian*, 2 Nov. 2014, www.theguardian.com/stage/2014/nov/02/see-the-music-hear-the-dance-sadlers-wells-thomas-ades-review. Accessed 14 Aug. 2020.

Pite, Crystal. "Choreographer's Notebook: Crystal Pite on Creating Emergence." *Pacific Northwest Ballet*, 17 Oct. 2013, blogpnborg.wordpress.com/2013/10/17/choreographers-notebook-crystal-pite-on-creating-emergence. Accessed 14 Aug. 2020.

———. "In the Beginning." *Crystal Pite*, 7 July 2000, chrissyrockbottom.wordpress.com/2000/07/07/in-the-beginning. Accessed 14 Aug. 2020.

Sulcas, Roslyn. "The Choreographer Crystal Pite Pushes against Ballet." *The New York Times*, 19 Nov. 2015, www.nytimes.com/2015/11/20/arts/dance/the-choreographer-crystal-pite-pushes-against-ballet.html. Accessed 14 Aug. 2020.

Winship, Lyndsey. "Crystal Pite: The Dance Genius Who Stages the Impossible." *The Guardian*, 18 Sept. 2019, www.theguardian.com/stage/2019/sep/18/crystal-pite-betroffenheit-best-dance-21st-century. Accessed 14 Aug. 2020.

SELECTED WORKS

Uncollected Work, 2002; *Double Story*, 2004; *Lost Action*, 2006; *Emergence*, 2009; *The You Show*, 2010; *The Tempest Replica*, 2011; *Betroffenheit*, 2015; *The Seasons' Canon*, 2016; *Flight Pattern*, 2017; *Revisor*, 2019

—*Molly Hagan*

Kelsey Ramsden

Date of birth: July 12, 1976
Occupation: Entrepreneur

For Canadian entrepreneur Kelsey Ramsden, a certain degree of flexibility is essential when setting goals. Over the course of her career, that ability to pivot has proven deeply important, enabling her to forge a new career path, weather a global recession, and establish herself as a resource for up-and-coming entrepreneurs. Born into a family that was deeply engaged in the construction industry, Ramsden developed a love for that industry during childhood and returned to it in her twenties, seeking to establish a business with a tangible product after a brief and unappealing career in management consulting. The construction company she founded in 2005, Belvedere Place Development, evolved from a focus on building roads to a highly profitable developer of bridges, dams, and airports, among other infrastructure projects. She also served as head of the residential development company Tallus Ridge Development and the subscription-box company SparkPlay, and she went on to launch a new career as a public speaker, writer, and mentor dedicated to helping fellow entrepreneurs improve their businesses and navigate their successes, all the while remaining prepared to pivot and to diverge from established paths. "I am not a huge fan of rules, and this helps when one is an entrepreneur," she told *Lioness* magazine (30 Apr. 2015). "I think that there is a place for the tried and tested methods, but that creating something new—whether it be in product or process—is what separates the great from the exceptional."

EARLY LIFE AND EDUCATION

Ramsden was born Kelsey Kitsch in Kelowna, British Columbia, Canada, on July 12, 1976. Her mother, Esther, was an entrepreneur, and her father, Bruce, owned a civil construction company. Thanks in part to the examples set by their parents, she and her younger brother, Trent, became interested in entrepreneurship from early in life and worked together to devise a variety of informal—and not always

Photo by Klahaie via Wikimedia Commons

aboveboard—business ventures as children. In addition to demonstrating that going into business for oneself was an option, the careers and experiences of their parents taught both her and her brother numerous valuable lessons about business and perseverance. "Growing up in an entrepreneurial family, odds are you probably saw high times and low times," she explained to Margaret Mulligan for the *Globe and Mail* (27 Oct. 2015). "I know we certainly did. I think it's a benefit for the next generation of entrepreneur because you understand that getting low doesn't mean you're out, whereas a first generation entrepreneur can really get knocked out of the game when things get tricky." In addition to Ramsden herself, her brother would also go on to become an entrepreneur as an adult, founding companies such as the underwear brand SAXX and the winery Kitsch Wines.

Throughout her early life, Ramsden was particularly drawn to and inspired by the construction business in which her father worked. "There is actually a product, and the people you work with are amazing, real salt-of-the-earth types," she told *Intouch* (2004), the alumni magazine of the University of Western Ontario's Richard Ivey School of Business. "It's very intense—if something goes wrong, you have to stay and you could be at work for two days straight. When your contract is finished you could be out of work until the next project comes along, so it's exciting." Exposed to various aspects of the construction industry thanks to her father's career, she also held a summer job stopping and directing traffic around construction on the Alaska Highway as a teenager.

After graduating from high school, Ramsden enrolled in the University of Victoria. Although she initially planned to study biology, she failed a required course for that major and went on to switch her focus to economics, in which she earned her bachelor's degree in 2000. Unsure of her ideal career trajectory, she returned to the construction business, working in that industry during the summers and in coffee shops during the winters. She eventually decided to return to school and pursue a master's degree in business administration at the University of Western Ontario's Ivey School of Business, which her brother would also go on to attend (the University of Western Ontario was later rebranded as Western University). Earning her MBA from the Ivey School of Business in 2004, she would go on to join the Advisory Council of the school's Pierre L. Morrissette Institute for Entrepreneurship in 2012.

Following her time in business school, Ramsden began her career as a management consultant in Toronto but soon found that she disliked the work, particularly in comparison to her previous work in construction. "You make a recommendation and nothing happens," she said of her brief period in that role, as quoted by *Canadian Business* (12 Aug. 2011). "I like making things happen. I like seeing dirt move." After working in management consulting for only six months, she quit her job and returned to British Columbia with the goal of starting a business in which her work would have tangible results.

CONSTRUCTION AND DEVELOPMENT

Settling once more in her home city of Kelowna in 2005, Ramsden founded a construction company with the goal of pursuing contracts in a variety of areas, including government contracts. Known as Belvedere Place Development, the company found lucrative work early in its existence, taking on projects such as a government contract to rebuild a portion of the Alaska Highway. Although the global economic downturn that began in 2007 threatened construction businesses in Canada and elsewhere, her company weathered the period well, which she would later attribute to the company's dedication to infrastructure projects, its geographic focus on the northern regions of British Columbia, its ability to build and maintain strong relationships in the business, and its strategic expansion into the private sector. Working in Canada as well as in the Caribbean, where her parents had begun overseeing construction work during the late 1990s, her company took on a wide range of projects over its years of operation, building infrastructure such as roads, bridges, and dams as well as structures such as mines, airports, and piers.

In addition to working widely in the development of infrastructure, Ramsden was active in residential land development through her company Tallus Ridge Development. Also based in Kelowna, Tallus Ridge Development was known primarily for developing the project Tallus Ridge, a residential community located in West Kelowna. Such projects, as well as the work of Belvedere Place Development, proved financially successful and established Ramsden as a significant force within Canada's construction and development industries. In recognition of her work, she was named the number-one female entrepreneur in Canada by *PROFIT* magazine and *Chatelaine* magazine in 2012 and again in 2013. For Ramsden, however, that recognition was not entirely a positive phenomenon. "I guess in some ways, it was the best thing that ever happened to me, and the worst thing that ever happened to me," she explained to Jaime Masters for the podcast *Eventual Millionaire*. "I think a lot of people strive for this sense of accomplishment and success, and potentially notoriety, and that comes with a lot of unintended consequences that a lot of us don't understand until we arrive at that place, and find out that success is a fickle friend." The complex nature of success and the need to find a new purpose after achieving it would become major focuses for Ramsden over the next years, particularly through her work as a writer and mentor.

A YEAR OF CHANGES
Although long involved in the day-to-day operations of her companies in her role as president, Ramsden took a necessary step back from that work in 2012, when she was diagnosed with cervical cancer. Although that period was a difficult one for Ramsden, who underwent surgery and completed treatments to address the cancer, she would later explain in interviews that the experience brought about a significant shift in her outlooks on business and her personal life. "It was one of the greatest opportunities of my life, absolutely," she told Kelly Pedro for the *London Free Press* (6 Apr. 2014). "My surgeon said, 'If you could do it all again, would you do it?' I said, 'Absolutely I would do it again.' The things that were deep, it made them that much deeper and the good times, it made them that much higher."

Declared cancer-free by the end of 2012, Ramsden nevertheless remained committed to those new outlooks, which prompted her to continue to reduce her involvement in her companies' business operations in favor of new pursuits. One such pursuit was a new company, SparkPlay, a relatively small-scale operation that offered subscription boxes of toys and other children's activities. Although she enjoyed running that business, she ultimately shut it down due to its lack of profitability. "It's an awesome idea, but I am here to make money. So I'd rather spend time with my kids than help you spend time with your kids and lose money," she explained to Mulligan.

SPEAKER, MENTOR, WRITER
Having established herself as a successful entrepreneur during the first decades of the twenty-first century, Ramsden next focused on sharing the knowledge she gained during that period with others, inspiring newer entrepreneurs and passing along the ideas essential to her success. In addition to opening a consulting business, she began to work as a public speaker, appearing at events such as the 2013 conference TEDxKelowna. During that conference, she delivered a short talk on the importance of play and creativity, which she identified as essential not only in the personal lives of children but also in the business lives of adults. "When I say play I don't mean go play a round of golf—it could be if that's your thing—I more so mean exposure," she explained to Pedro. She would go on to make numerous speaking engagements in Canada and elsewhere and would also be featured on several podcasts dedicated to business and entrepreneurship.

In addition to speaking and consulting, Ramsden worked to assist other entrepreneurs through various mentorship initiatives and has credited much of her own success to her experiences with mentorship. "This showed me how important it was learning through experience from those willing to share," she told Geoff Dale for the *Londoner* (25 Apr. 2017). "I want to share with others [what I learned] from these great people." To that end, she developed her Manifesto mentorship program, through which she sought to help entrepreneurs develop action plans and better understand the motivations underlying their goals. In 2018, she published the book *Success Hangover*, a work dedicated to helping successful individuals determine their next steps after meeting major career milestones.

PERSONAL LIFE
Ramsden met her future husband, Andrew Ramsden, who began heading Ramsden Industries in 2009, while attending the Ivey School of Business. After living for a time in British Columbia, the couple moved to London, Ontario, around 2009. They have three children.

SUGGESTED READING
Dale, Geoff. "Winning Ways." *The Londoner*, 25 Apr. 2017, www.thelondoner.ca/2017/04/25/winning-ways/wcm/2db06bf3-b8a4-6c96-a8b6-87e4bc759d4d. Accessed 8 Mar. 2020.

"Kelsey Ramsden." *Canadian Business*, 12 Aug. 2011, www.canadianbusiness.com/business-news/kelsey-ramsden/. Accessed 8 Mar. 2020.

Mulligan, Margaret. "Can't Stop, Won't Stop." *The Globe and Mail*, 27 Oct. 2015, www.theglobeandmail.com/partners/advdoorshsbc1015/cant-stop-wont-stop/article26870557/. Accessed 8 Mar. 2020.

Pedro, Kelly. "And You Are? Balancing Immensely Busy Work Life with Love of Family." *London Free*, 6 Apr. 2014, lfpress.com/2014/04/06/and-you-are-balancing-immensely-busy-work-life-with-love-of-family/wcm/a28bf9b0-119a-2f9f-3850-bf0cf234812d. Accessed 8 Mar. 2020.

Ramsden, Kelsey. "The Discomfort of Pursuit with Kelsey Ramsden." Interview by Jaime Masters. *Eventual Millionaire*, eventualmillionaire.com/kelseyramsden/. Accessed 8 Mar. 2020.

——. "Kelsey Kitsch." *Intouch*, 2004, p. 32, www.ivey.uwo.ca/cmsmedia/1002411/2004-summer.pdf. Accessed 11 Mar. 2020.

——. "What $50 Million Mom Entrepreneur Kelsey Ramsden Can Teach You." *Lioness*, 30 Apr. 2015, lionessmagazine.com/what-50-million-mom-entrepreneur-kelsey-ramsden-can-teach-you/. Accessed 8 Mar. 2020.

—Joy Crelin

Peter J. Ratcliffe

Date of birth: May 14, 1954
Occupation: Biologist

Sir Peter J. Radcliffe reached a pinnacle of scientific achievement when he shared in the 2019 Nobel Prize in Physiology or Medicine for his groundbreaking work into how cells regulate oxygen. The honor capped an already decorated career, much of it spent at the University of Oxford as both a researcher and a practicing physician. "Making accurate diagnoses in the clinic and accurate interpretation of laboratory results are not dissimilar processes," Ratcliffe told João Monteiro for the journal *Cell* (Sept. 2016). "They both require considering all manner of possibilities and then great care in coming to a conclusion." Ratcliffe's open-minded and detailed approach helped him earn fellowships with prestigious organizations such as the European Molecular Biology Organization (EMBO) and the Royal Society, and he was elected a foreign member of the American Academy of Arts and Sciences in 2007. He was knighted in 2014 and shared the Albert Lasker Basic Medical Research Award in 2016, the same year he became director of clinical research at the Francis Crick Institute.

EARLY LIFE AND EDUCATION

Peter John Ratcliffe was born in Lancashire, England, on May 14, 1954. From 1965 until 1971 he attended the Lancaster Royal Grammar School. Originally, he had no plans to study medicine, but this changed rather suddenly. In a 2016 speech, as quoted by Gina Kolata and Megan Specia for the *New York Times* (19 Oct. 2019), Ratcliffe noted, "I was a tolerable schoolboy chemist and intent on a career in industrial chemistry. The ethereal but formidable headmaster appeared one morning in the chemistry classroom. 'Peter,' he said with unnerving serenity, 'I think you should study medicine.' And without further thought, my university application forms were changed." Ratcliffe later took this event as a confirmation of the role of serendipity in life, though he reflected that he never knew if his headmaster thought he would excel as a doctor or fail as a chemist.

Ratcliffe won an open scholarship to attend Gonville and Caius College at the University of Cambridge. He also studied at St. Bartholomew's Hospital, earning degrees in surgery and medicine in 1978. He completed his medical degree at Cambridge in 1987. Ratcliffe then moved to the University of Oxford, where he began to focus on renal medicine, or nephrology. He would go on to maintain parallel careers treating patients clinically and pursuing research projects.

Photo by Casa Rosada (Argentina Presidency of the Nation)

Ratcliffe considered his practical medical training very helpful to his work in the laboratory. "As a physician, you get more confident about dealing with unknowns," he told Monteiro. "I always found it helpful not to be too shy to ring up for advice and push until you've got the advice you needed." However, he noted one crucial difference between the two facets of his career: "In the clinic, if you don't know what to do, do nothing. In the lab, if you don't know what to do, do something."

RESEARCH BEGINNINGS

Beginning in the 1980s Ratcliffe became curious about the way that kidneys are susceptible to shock. This led him to consider the kidneys' role in regulating oxygen. Scientists had noted that the kidneys were often harmed in patients with low blood pressure. Ratcliffe began wondering about the ways in which kidneys sense and respond to oxygen levels. As he told Jillian H. Hurst for the *Journal of Clinical Investigation* (Oct. 2016), "Somewhat surprisingly, the kidney is able to distinguish changes in blood oxygen content and the numbers of red blood cells in circulation from changes in renal blood flow. Consideration of this remarkable oxygen-sensing capacity was what initially led me into the field."

In 1989, Ratcliffe set up a laboratory at Oxford's Weatherall Institute of Molecular Medicine to study hypoxia—the state in which all or part of the body receives insufficient oxygen at the tissue level. While too much oxygen can poison the body, too little oxygen harms metabolic function. Many diseases and conditions, including cancer, heart disease, anemia, and stroke, involve hypoxia. In support of his research Ratcliffe was named a senior fellow of the Wellcome Trust in 1990. He was appointed a lecturer at Oxford in 1992 and became a full professor of nephrology in 1996.

Ratcliffe spent much of his time looking at the regulating work of the hormone erythropoietin (EPO), which had only recently been identified when he began his research. EPO responds to low blood oxygen levels by stimulating the production of red blood cells. It was known that kidney cells create EPO when blood oxygen levels drop, but few scientists saw value in deeper research into the phenomenon. Ratcliffe eventually discovered that cells in other organs, such as the liver and the brain, can also sense oxygen levels. Moreover, the sensing process is crucial to a wide range of cell functions. His research led him to identify the prolyl hydroxylation of hypoxia-inducible factor (HIF) molecules as the mechanism behind cells' responses to changing oxygen levels.

To Ratcliffe, the importance later attached to his work highlighted the value of pure research that does not at first appear to have any practical application. As he told Nobel Prize interviewer Adam Smith (7 Oct. 2019), "We make knowledge, that's what I do as a publicly funded scientist," even though he might begin "without a clear understanding of the value of that knowledge."

RECOGNITION AND AWARDS

By the twenty-first century, Ratcliffe's research on HIF molecules was drawing increasing attention in the scientific community. Around 2000 Ratcliffe met William Kaelin, a Harvard Medical School researcher involved in similar and complementary work. The two would subsequently collaborate extensively and coauthor several important papers furthering scientific understanding of cellular oxygen sensing.

In 2002, Ratcliffe was elected to the Academy of Medical Sciences and the Royal Society for his pioneering work. In 2004, he was named the Nuffield Professor of Medicine at Oxford, becoming head of the school's Nuffield Department of Medicine. His deep connection to Oxford as both a teacher and researcher earned considerable praise. Vice Chancellor Louise Richardson told the university's news website (7 Oct. 2019), "While making an immense contribution at the forefront of medical research, [Ratcliffe] has also provided inspirational teaching for our medical students and supported countless patients."

Ratcliffe continued to earn other honors, including election as an EMBO fellow in 2006 and as an honorary foreign member of the American Academy of Arts and Sciences in 2007. In 2010, he received the Canada Gairdner International Award for his work on oxygen sensing. In 2012, he was invited to become a member of the Ludwig Institute for Cancer Research. In a November 2012 news release for that organization, Xin Lu, director of the Ludwig Institute's Oxford Branch, highlighted Ratcliffe's "stellar accomplishments, his renowned international reputation and his ongoing commitment to excellence," noting that his hypoxia research "is simply exceptional and has significant relevance to human cancer."

In 2014, Ratcliffe was knighted for services to clinical medicine, further solidifying his position as a leader in his field. In May 2016, he became clinical research director at the Francis Crick Institute, a renowned biomedical research organization. "His discoveries are based on innovative experiments, highly imaginative mechanisms, and a total dedication to absolute rigour," the institute's director, Paul Nurse, told the *University of Oxford News & Events* site (7 Oct. 2019). "Peter is an exemplary clinician scientist. We are proud to have him." Ratcliffe subsequently stepped down as head of the Oxford medical department, though he remained director of the school's Target Discovery Institute.

Also in 2016 Ratcliffe, along with Kaelin and Gregg Semenza of the Johns Hopkins University School of Medicine, received the Albert Lasker Basic Medical Research Award. The three were credited for discovering the pathway for cellular sensing of and adaptation to oxygen availability. They were similarly recognized in 2018 with the 2018 Massry Prize from the University of Southern California's Keck School of Medicine. Meanwhile, Ratcliffe was also awarded the Royal Society's 2017 Buchanan Medal for distinguished contributions to the biomedical sciences.

WINNING THE NOBEL PRIZE

Ratcliffe added yet another award to his résumé in 2019, one that would bring him attention even beyond the scientific community. He was working on a grant proposal that October when he received the call that he, Kaelin, and Semenza had won the Nobel Prize in Physiology or Medicine, one of the highest-profile awards in all of science. Summoned from a meeting to take the call, he at first thought it was a hoax. After confirming the news and briefly speaking to the media, he reportedly returned to the task at hand. Of the award, Ratcliffe told Oxford University News & Events site (7 Oct. 2019), "I'm honoured and delighted at the news. . . . It's a tribute to the lab, to those who helped me set it up and worked with me on the project over the years, to many others in the field, and not least to my family for their forbearance of all the up and downs."

Many of Ratcliffe's colleagues suggested he well-deserved the Nobel honor, lauding the importance of his contribution to the discovery of oxygen sensing. Media coverage of the award also focused on the many potential applications his research held for disease treatment. Ratcliffe himself acknowledged how his work fell in the bigger picture. "We didn't really foresee the broad reach of this system when we started the work," he told Smith. He went on to note, "History of science tells us over and over again that the value of knowledge can increase with the impact on other people's research, other circumstances, all sorts of random and unpredictable issues brought to bear."

Known for being relatively soft-spoken and content working out of the spotlight, Ratcliffe nevertheless resolved to use the publicity generated by the Nobel Prize to draw attention to important issues, such as Great Britain's intended exit from the European Union (EU). He told Smith, "I think there is a responsibility and a platform to make one's views known. And I do have views on this, and I think they are important for science and for society."

Ratcliffe and his wife, Fiona, married in 1983. The couple have four children.

SUGGESTED READING

Hurst, Jillian H. "William Kaelin, Peter Ratcliffe, and Gregg Semenza Receive the 2016 Albert Lasker Basic Medical Research Award." *The Journal of Clinical Investigation*, vol. 126, no. 10, Oct. 2016, doi:10.1172/JCI90055. Accessed 21 Jan. 2020.

Kolata, Gina, and Megan Specia. "Nobel Prize in Medicine Awarded for Research on How Cells Manage Oxygen." *The New York Times*, 7 Oct. 2019, www.nytimes.com/2019/10/07/health/nobel-prize-medicine.html. Accessed 21 Jan. 2020.

Lewis, Tanya. "Discovery of Molecular Switch for How Cells Use Oxygen Wins 2019 Nobel Prize in Medicine." *Scientific American*, 7 Oct. 2019, www.scientificamerican.com/article/discovery-of-molecular-switch-for-how-cells-use-oxygen-wins-2019-nobel-prize-in-medicine1. Accessed 21 Jan. 2020.

"Peter Ratcliffe." *The Francis Crick Institute*, www.crick.ac.uk/research/find-a-researcher/peter-ratcliffe. Accessed 21 Jan. 2020.

Ratcliffe, Peter, and William Kaelin. "Making Sense of the Unexpected." Interview by João Monteiro. *Cell*, vol. 167, no. 1, Sept. 2016, doi.org/10.1016/j.cell.2016.08.048. Accessed 21 Jan. 2020.

Ratcliffe, Peter J. Interview by Adam Smith. *The Nobel Prize*, 7 Oct. 2019, www.nobelprize.org/prizes/medicine/2019/ratcliffe/interview. Accessed 21 Jan. 2020.

"Sir Peter J. Ratcliffe Wins the Nobel Prize in Medicine 2019." *University of Oxford News & Events*, 7 Oct. 2019, www.ox.ac.uk/news/2019-10-07-sir-peter-j-ratcliffe-wins-nobel-prize-medicine-2019. Accessed 21 Jan. 2020.

—*Judy Johnson*

Nathaniel Rateliff

Born: October 7, 1978
Occupation: Singer and songwriter

"For all of the effusive chatter and ink that's been spilled recently over a revival of classic soul, one thing hadn't yet emerged: a bona fide hit song," Matt Hendrickson wrote for *Garden & Gun* (Feb./Mar. 2016). "That the breakthrough would come from this burly singer who looks like he could either make a mean craft cocktail or chop off your head with an ax makes it even more bizarre." Hendrickson was referring to singer and songwriter Nathaniel Rateliff and his song "S.O.B." Rateliff and his band, the Night Sweats, recorded the song for their 2015 eponymous debut album, but it was after they performed it on *The Tonight Show*, hosted by Jimmy Fallon, in the summer of that year that it took off. The "bawdy, knee-slapping soul anthem," as Hendrickson described it, quickly went viral, hitting the top of the Billboard Adult Alternative Songs chart and crossing over to the top ten in multiple

Photo by Andy Witchger via Wikimedia Commons

other genres. The album eventually went gold, and the band's subsequent tour found them playing almost 250 shows in sixteen countries. "It may be the most improbable breakout of this viral-pop-star decade: a white classic-soul band led by a burly middle-aged singer," David Fricke later wrote for *Rolling Stone* (5 Apr. 2018).

Rateliff went on to put out a well-received follow-up record, *Tearing at the Seams*, with the Night Sweats in 2018 before taking a further leap and releasing a raw solo album, titled *And It's Still Alright*, to high-profile acclaim in 2020. Yet, while seeming to be an overnight sensation, he had been dedicated to making music and performing for years. Determined to identify and remain true to the kind of sound and style he wanted to write and sing, he spent time in Colorado finding his way outside of the mainstream music industry, playing alternative rock with the local band Born in the Flood, performing more stripped-down and folksy music supported by the band the Wheel, and working on his own. After teaming with the Night Sweats to play vintage soul around 2013, he realized he had found his niche. "I always knew I had a strong voice," he explained to Fricke. "Now what I'm doing is actually me."

EARLY YEARS

Nathaniel Rateliff was born on October 7, 1978, in St. Louis, Missouri, and raised, along with his sister, in Hermann, Missouri, which he described to Laura Barton for the *Guardian* (1 Oct. 2015) as "small, rural America." His father, Cecil, who was always known as Bud, worked as a carpenter, never making more than $8,000 or so a year, and hunted for much of the meat the family ate. His mother, Sandy, worked a variety of jobs to contribute to their finances.

The family was deeply religious, and they formed a band that performed at their church each Sunday, with Sandy singing and playing guitar and Bud playing the harmonica and providing harmonies. When Rateliff was seven, he joined them on the drums and also lent his voice. As there was not much to do in his hometown and he was not athletic, he typically spent time swimming and both listening to and playing music.

A few years later, when Rateliff was thirteen, his father was killed in a car accident on the way to church. As his son later discovered, Bud had possessed a more eclectic taste in music in his earlier years, and he had stashed an extensive record collection away in the garage. Listening to his father's albums helped Rateliff to not only further expand his own tastes but to stay connected to his father in a way. Even before this point, despite his parents' wishes, he had begun to think more seriously about secular music. "When I was a kid, we weren't really

supposed to listen to secular music," he recalled to Barton. "But one day, I found a *Led Zeppelin IV* cassette tape in the garage, and it was just amazing-sounding music, not like anything I'd heard before. I remember thinking: 'Well, if God created music, why is his music in church not as good as this?'"

BREAKING WITH RELIGION AND LEAVING MISSOURI

Rateliff soon took up guitar and began learning songs by artists like Duane Allman and Jimi Hendrix. Having stopped attending school at age fourteen, by the time he was sixteen he had begun to support himself and had taken on a series of odd jobs at a grocery store and other places. (At one point he worked as a janitor at his own former high school.) When his mother ultimately remarried and moved to Texas, Rateliff remained in Missouri, crashing with his close friend and fellow musician Joseph Pope, with whom he performed.

At eighteen, seeking opportunities outside of Missouri, Rateliff went to Denver, Colorado, as part of a missionary trip. He quickly realized during the group's intensive Bible study, however, that he was not truly a believer. He broke with the group after a week-long program in which the group evangelized on a Hopi Reservation, when it dawned on him that the Hopi had no interest in being preached to. Returning to Missouri, his passion for music did not fade as he found work at a plastics factory. "Our joke was that, if you worked there long enough, you had to lose a tooth or lose an eye. Or a limb," he told Barton.

After some time, Rateliff joined forces with Pope and moved in 1998 to Colorado, where he worked in the dock and yard of a trucking company. He, Pope, and Pope's girlfriend were living together in a cramped apartment at a time when Pope had been diagnosed with testicular cancer at around age twenty-two. Rateliff worked all day—which he would later state in interviews he did not mind as he enjoyed physical labor, and the work often helped his creative process. He would then come home at night to help care for his friend. "A friend shows his true worth when he helps another to the toilet," he told Hendrickson. "But when things are hard, you have to find something that brings you joy."

That something turned out to be forming a band.

LAUNCHING A MUSIC CAREER

Rateliff and Pope, whose cancer ultimately went into remission, formed the alternative rock band Born in the Flood, playing everything from classic rock covers to original songs. In 2005, they recorded the six-song album *The Fear That We May Not Be*. Yet, although an occasional critic commented favorably on Rateliff's distinctive delivery, it went, for the most part, unnoticed by those outside the Denver club scene.

Rateliff continued to hone his singing skills by studying the work of country and R&B singers he admired. Wanting to move in a different direction, he gradually disbanded Born in the Flood after recording the full-length album *If This Thing Should Spill* (2007) and turning down a record deal with the Nickelback label Roadrunner in favor of continuing with a new backup band, the Wheel, that he had formed, to play softer, folksier music. He released a debut album with the Wheel, *Desire and Dissolving Men*, in 2007. Increasingly comfortable singing and playing in front of larger crowds, Rateliff also performed solo shows. During an industry showcase, he caught the eye of a representative of Rounder Records, a roots-based music label known for overseeing legendary folk musician Woody Guthrie's archives, who signed him to a record deal in 2009.

Though reportedly suffering from narcolepsy and thyroid problems, Rateliff then released his solo debut, *In Memory of Loss*, on the Rounder label in 2010. Most of the spare tracks feature just acoustic guitar, bass, and piano backing his vocals. "His signature sound is warm, intimate and soulful, sparsely decorated with remedial harmonies and threadbare layering," Tom Wooldridge wrote for *Port* (20 June 2011). "Rateliff's compositions exude a euphoria through slow burning tracks that build to a crescendo of sheer volume, masterfully injected with fury, desire and relief."

THE NIGHT SWEATS

Rateliff released a sophomore full-length solo album, *Falling Faster Than You Can Run*, in 2013. However, for a time he considered giving up and returning to his latest day job of gardening, as he had been dropped by Rounder amid creative differences and struggled to get the album out. He then realized he missed performing with a band and that the music he had been creating would work best with a group. He formed the soul-centered Night Sweats, a group that quickly gained a reputation on the Denver bar scene for rowdy, high-energy shows, that same year. The party atmosphere generally continued long after the shows wrapped up, and Rateliff would later discuss in interviews that he got caught up in—but eventually came out of—that kind of music industry lifestyle, including drinking and using drugs. "That's the sort of persona that everyone's supposed to have, just kind of stumbling through, stumbling to the show, falling offstage," he recalled to Madison Vain for *Esquire* (17 Mar. 2020). "And people love the idea of that person, and I don't know why."

Signed to the legendary Stax Records and spurred in part by an impressive appearance on Jimmy Fallon's late-night talk show, Rateliff released *Nathaniel Rateliff & the Night Sweats* in August 2015 and got his first taste of truly international success. "You could argue that the particular allure of Nathaniel Rateliff & the Night Sweats' debut album—not to mention their extraordinary live shows—lies in the pull between the sacred and the secular; the melding of rasping southern soul in the style of Sam & Dave or Otis Redding, with just enough of the Baptist sermon to give Rateliff's performance a touch of fire and brimstone," Barton opined.

As songs such as "S.O.B." garnered mainstream attention, Rateliff and the Night Sweats' first record sold well and was largely positively reviewed, and they toured widely. The band's profile remained relatively high over the next few years, during which they released *Live at Red Rocks* (2017) and a second successful studio album, *Tearing at the Seams* (2018). During live shows and interviews, the band—which included Pope on bass, drummer Patrick Meese, guitarist Luke Mossman, keyboard player Mark Shusterman, trumpeter Scott Frock, and saxophonists Jeff Dazey and Andreas Wild—exhibited a sense of close friendship and togetherness that attracted fans and critics alike.

GOING SOLO AGAIN

Despite the fun of working with his bandmates, Rateliff gradually began realizing that his hard-partying lifestyle needed to change. He started writing more somber, introspective songs meant to be performed solo.

Rateliff had previously approached veteran music producer and friend Richard Swift about making an album distinct from those he had done with the Night Sweats in a style similar to singer-songwriter Harry Nilsson. Swift, however, had been battling hepatitis, and he died in 2018. Grief-stricken and determined to create a tribute to his creative collaborator, Rateliff (who at that time was also reeling from a recent divorce) decamped to Swift's Oregon studio and made *And It's Still Alright*. Released in early 2020, the album won praise for its intimate sound and emotive lyrics. "In the end, what could be an album of well-earned indulgence ends up being as much about reaching outward than burrowing inward, rendering deep personal suffering with a humane light touch," Jon Dolan wrote for *Rolling Stone* (13 Feb. 2020).

Rateliff had to postpone a solo tour scheduled to support *And It's Still Alright* due to the coronavirus 2019 (COVID-19) pandemic. Meanwhile, he also assured fans that the Night Sweats had not disbanded.

PERSONAL LIFE

Nathaniel Rateliff and his wife, Jules Bethea, filed for divorce in 2018. Having rented and lived in the same house for several years, by 2020 he had purchased a new house and about five acres of land outside Denver. He also bought a home back in Hermann for his mother. In 2017, he launched a philanthropic foundation, the Marigold Project, which focuses on issues of social justice and economic reform.

SUGGESTED READING

Barton, Laura. "How Nathaniel Rateliff Grew Up Believing in God and Wound Up Believing in Soul." *The Guardian*, 1 Oct. 2015, www.theguardian.com/music/2015/oct/01/nathaniel-rateliff-god-blues-soul-led-zeppelin. Accessed 22 July 2020.

Dolan, Jon. "Nathaniel Rateliff Warmly Processes Pain on *And It's Still Alright*." Review of *And It's Still Alright*, by Nathaniel Rateliff. *Rolling Stone*, 13 Feb. 2020, www.rollingstone.com/music/music-album-reviews/nathaniel-rateliff-ts-still-alright-950839/. Accessed 22 July 2020.

Fricke, David. "The Long Shot: Nathaniel Rateliff's Hard, Booze-Soaked Road to Rock-Soul Stardom." *Rolling Stone*, 5 Apr. 2018, www.rollingstone.com/music/music-features/the-long-shot-nathaniel-rateliffs-hard-booze-soaked-road-to-rock-soul-stardom-629451/. Accessed 22 July 2020.

Hendrickson, Matt. "Nathaniel Rateliff: Soul Searcher." *Garden & Gun*, Feb./Mar. 2016, gardenandgun.com/feature/nathaniel-rateliff-soul-searcher/. Accessed 22 July 2020.

Martins, Chris. "How Nathaniel Rateliff & The Night Sweats Became the Darlings of Rock Radio." *Billboard*, 1 Mar. 2018, www.billboard.com/articles/columns/rock/8221378/nathaniel-rateliff-night-sweats-interview-rock-radio. Accessed 22 July 2020.

Rateliff, Nathaniel. "Nathaniel Rateliff Is Waiting for a Time When He Can Write a Happy Song Again." Interview by Madison Vain. *Esquire*, 17 Mar. 2020, www.esquire.com/entertainment/music/a31668206/nathaniel-rateliff-interview-and-its-still-alright-night-sweats/. Accessed 22 July 2020.

Wooldridge, Tom. "Nathaniel Rateliff: In Memory of Loss." *Port*, 20 June 2011, www.port-magazine.com/music/nathaniel-rateliff-in-memory-of-loss/. Accessed 22 July 2020.

SELECTED WORKS

Desire and Dissolving Men, 2007; *In Memory of Loss*, 2010; *Falling Faster Than You Can Run*, 2013; *Nathaniel Rateliff & the Night Sweats*, 2015; *Tearing at the Seams*, 2018; *And It's Still Alright*, 2020

—Mari Rich

John W. Raymond
Date of birth: 1962
Occupation: Chief of Space Operations

On January 14, 2020, General John W. "Jay" Raymond became the inaugural chief of Space Operations for the US Space Force, the first separate service branch of the US military to be created since 1947, when the US Air Force was established. Space Force joined the US Army, Navy, Air Force, Marine Corps, and Coast Guard as the sixth service branch.

Raymond had served in the US Air Force for more than thirty-four years before heading Space Force and is seen by Pentagon insiders as the leader who can use his extensive organizational experience and expertise to bring Space Force into shape within its first year. The new branch is tasked with defending US interests in space at a time when Russia and China are becoming more competitive, as well as protecting the planet from existential threats like meteor strikes.

By March 2020 Space Force had two hundred staff members at the Pentagon, the headquarters of the Department of Defense (DOD). Thousands of air force personnel who worked at the air force's Space Command will eventually be transferred to Space Force. Additionally, the new service branch will recruit personnel from other service branches and take over a number of air force bases and focus them on space programs. Space Force will also partner with private space companies like SpaceX and Blue

Photo by U.S. Department of Defense via Wikimedia Commons

Origin to modernize US space capabilities. "We used to operate in a benign domain," Raymond said, as quoted by Sandra Erwin for *Space News* (26 Mar. 2019). "Now we are operating in a contested domain."

EARLY LIFE AND EDUCATION

John W. Raymond was born in 1962 and raised in Alexandria, Virginia. Little has been published about his early life. It is known that he goes by the nickname Jay and that he graduated in 1984 with a BS in administrative management from Clemson University in Clemson, South Carolina. During his undergraduate years, he was in the Reserve Officers' Training Corps (ROTC) and entered the US Air Force as a commissioned lieutenant on July 20, 1984.

While serving in the air force, Raymond continued his formal education. In 1990, he attended Squadron Officer School at Maxwell Air Force Base (AFB) in Alabama and earned his MS in administrative management at Central Michigan University in Mount Pleasant. He earned another graduate degree, a master's degree in national security and strategic studies, at the Naval War College (NWC) in Newport, Rhode Island, in 2003. Raymond studied at the Joint Forces Staff College (JFSC) in Norfolk, Virginia, in 2007. In 2011 he completed the Combined Force Air Component Commander course and, in 2012, the Joint Flag Officer Warfighting course, both also at Maxwell AFB.

EARLY MILITARY CAREER

Raymond began his military career in 1985 at Grand Forks AFB in North Dakota. There he served as a Minuteman intercontinental ballistic missile crew commander, flight commander, instructor crew commander, and missile procedures trainer operator for the 321st Strategic Missile Wing, among other duties. During that assignment, he was promoted to first lieutenant on July 20, 1986, and then to captain on July 20, 1988.

In October 1989, Raymond began serving as operations center officer controller for the First Strategic Aerospace Division and as executive officer for the Thirtieth Space Wing, which operated out of Vandenberg AFB in California. In August 1993, he became the chief of Commercial Space Lift Operations and assistant chief of the Current Operations Branch at the Headquarters of the Air Force Space Command (AFSPC) at Peterson AFB in Colorado. From February to August 1996 he was deputy director of the Commander in Chief's Action Group at Peterson AFB. On July 1 of that year he was promoted to major.

From August 1996 to June 1997, Raymond took a break from his active military career to study at the Air Command and Staff College at

Maxwell AFB. When he returned to active duty, he served as a space and missile force programmer at US Air Force headquarters at the Pentagon in Arlington, Virginia. In September 1998 he became chief of expeditionary aerospace force space and program integration for the Expeditionary Aerospace Force Implementation Division, at Air Force Headquarters. On July 1, 1999, he was promoted to lieutenant colonel.

OVERSEAS ASSIGNMENTS AND WARTIME SERVICE

Raymond moved overseas in April 2000, when he became the commander of the Fifth Space Surveillance Squadron at the Royal Air Force Base in Feltwell, England. He served in this capacity for more than a year before returning to the United States to serve his next assignment as deputy commander of the Twenty-First Operations Group, at Peterson AFB, from June 2001 to July 2002. He then studied for a year at the Naval War College.

During his next assignment, from June 2003 to June 2005, he was a transformation strategist at the Office of Force Transformation, part of the Office of the Secretary of Defense. While on that assignment, he was elevated to colonel on July 1, 2004.

His next three assignments were as commander of the Thirtieth Operations Group at Vandenberg AFB from June 2005 to June 2007; as director of space forces at the Combined Air Operations Center, in Southwest Asia from September 2006 to January 2007; and as commander of the Twenty-First Space Wing at Peterson AFB from June 2007 to August 2009. While he was serving in Southwest Asia, he worked in support of operations for the Afghan and Iraq Wars.

BECOMING A GENERAL

On August 1, 2009, Raymond was named a brigadier general. At that rank he served as director of plans, programs, and analyses at Peterson AFB, from August 2009 to December 2010. He then served as vice commander of the Fifth Air Force and deputy commander of the Thirteenth Air Force, stationed at Yokota Air Base in Japan, from December 2010 to July 2012.

Toward the end of the latter assignment, on May 4, 2012, Raymond was appointed a major general. He was then assigned to be director of plans and policy for the US Strategic Command at Offutt AFB, Nebraska, from July 2012 to January 2014. On January 31, 2014, he was again promoted, this time to lieutenant general. From there he assumed command of the Fourteenth Air Force (Air Forces Strategic) and the Joint Functional Component Command for Space at US Strategic Command at Vandenberg AFB. From August 2015 to October 2016 he was deputy chief of staff, operations, at Air Force Headquarters.

Raymond was made a full general on October 25, 2016. He initially served as commander, AFSPC at Peterson AFB, from October 2016 to December 2019. Beginning in August 2019 he served as commander of US Space Command, at Peterson. Space Command is a unified combat command designed to maintain the peaceful use of outer space, which has proved increasingly challenging. In an interview with *Popular Science* (31 Dec. 2015), Raymond noted that space has "become much more contested. So we talk about congested and contested; it's become much more congested with 23,000 objects that we're tracking each and every day and probably a half a million objects that are too small for us to track. In the past, with that benign domain, we haven't really needed the partnerships that we seek today, both with commercial partners and with international partners."

HEAD OF US SPACE FORCE

In March 2019, President Donald Trump announced Raymond's nomination to serve as the first chief of space operations for the US Space Force, the first new service branch since the US Air Force was established in 1947. Following congressional approval of his nomination, Raymond assumed his position as head of Space Force in December 2019. He would continue to head US Space Command, also out of Peterson, concurrently, until Space Force becomes fully operational.

Prior to the establishment of Space Force, the DOD had ten combat commands spanning the globe. Space Force is the eleventh. It is responsible for US military operations in outer space, beginning with low Earth orbit (LOE), where most satellites are launched. A debate in the Pentagon over the creation of a separate branch had existed for some time. Some believed that Space Command would be sufficient to counter the growing threat from Russia and China over dominance in space. Others, like Raymond, believed that that a separate branch was necessary in a new era of global competition. In an interview with Kathleen H. Hicks for the Center for Strategic and International Studies (CSIS) (18 Nov. 2019), Raymond noted: "Space is a warfighting domain, just like air, land and sea. You know, it used to be you couldn't say that in public—space and warfighting in the same sentence. The U.S. wants to keep the space domain safe. And that's still our goal, is to deter any conflict from beginning or extending into space."

INITIAL CHALLENGES

For the 2020 fiscal year, the DOD requested $83.4 million for Space Force. Roughly six hundred personnel would establish the branch, with more being added from all branches of the military. Air force bases at Shriever, Peterson, Vandenberg, and Offutt are being transferred to Space Force. Critics believe that the relatively small budgetary request masks the branch's true expenses. "The initial costs of setting up the Space Force are likely a small down payment on an undertaking that could cost tens of billions of dollars in the years to come," William D. Hartung, director of the arms and security project at the Center for International Policy (CIP), said to W. J. Hennigan for *Time* (10 Feb. 2020). "The last thing we need is more bureaucracy at the Pentagon, but that's exactly what the Space Force is likely to give us. Creating a separate branch of the armed forces for space also risks militarizing US space policy and promoting ill-advised and dangerous projects that could involve deploying weapons in space."

Raymond and other supporters of Space Force, however, counter those arguments by pointing to threats the US already faces in space. In February 2020 it was reported that a pair of Russian satellites had begun stalking a high-tech US spy satellite. The Russian orbiter was initially a single unit, then split in two, with a smaller satellite emerging from a larger one so they could better study the US spy satellite, which is part of a group of satellites code-named Keyhole/CRYSTAL. "We view this behavior as unusual and disturbing," Raymond said of the Russian satellites' actions, as quoted by Hennigan. "It has the potential to create a dangerous situation in space."

ACCOLADES AND HONORS

Throughout his military career, Raymond has received several accolades and honors, including the Distinguished Service Medal with oak leaf cluster; the Defense Superior Service Medal with oak leaf cluster; the Legion of Merit with oak leaf cluster; the Meritorious Service Medal (MSM) with four oak leaf clusters; the Air Force Commendation Medal (AFCM); and the French Order of Merit. In 2007, he was honored with the General Jerome F. O'Malley Distinguished Space Leadership Award from the Air Force Association. His later accolades include the Air Force Association's 2015 Thomas D. White Space Award and the National Defense Industrial Association's 2016 Peter B. Teets Government Award and 2017 James V. Hartinger Award.

PERSONAL LIFE

Raymond met his future wife, Mollie, in Grand Forks, North Dakota. The couple married after her college graduation, around 1987. They have three children together and moved sixteen times.

SUGGESTED READING

Erwin, Sandra. "Trump Nominates Raymond to Be Commander of U.S. Space Command."

SpaceNews, 26 Mar. 2019, spacenews.com/trump-nominates-raymond-as-the-next-commander-of-u-s-space-command. Accessed 22 June 2020.

———. "U.S. Space Force Begins to Organize Pentagon Staff and Field Operations." *SpaceNews*, 16 Jan. 2020, spacenews.com/u-s-space-force-begins-to-organize-pentagon-staff-and-field-operations. Accessed June 22, 2020.

"General John W. 'Jay' Raymond." *U.S. Air Force*, 20 Dec. 2019, www.af.mil/About-Us/Biographies/Display/Article/108479/lieutenant-general-john-w-jay-raymond/. Accessed 22 June 2020.

"Gen. John W. Raymond Holds a Press Briefing on U.S. Space Force and U.S. Space Command Efforts During the COVID-19 Outbreak." *U.S. Department of Defense*, 27 Mar. 2020, www.defense.gov/Newsroom/Transcripts/Transcript/Article/2131732/gen-john-w-raymond-holds-a-press-briefing-on-us-space-force-and-us-space-comman/. Accessed 22 June 2020.

Henningan, W. J. "Exclusive: Strange Russian Spacecraft Shadowing U.S. Spy Satellite, General Says." *Time*, 10 Feb. 2020, time.com/5779315/russian-spacecraft-spy-satellite-space-force/. Accessed 22 June 2020.

Raymond, John W. "A Conversation with General Raymond." Interview by Kathleen H. Hicks. *CSIS, Center for Strategic and International Studies*, 18 Nov. 2019, www.csis.org/analysis/conversation-general-raymond. Accessed 22 June 2020.

Raymond, John W. "Space Defender: Interview with Air Force Lt. Gen. John W. Raymond." *Popular Science*, 31 Dec. 2015, www.popsci.com/space-defender-interview-with-air-force-lt-gen-john-w-raymond. Accessed 22 June 2020.

—*Christopher Mari*

Jason Reynolds

Date of birth: December 6, 1983
Occupation: Author

Award-winning young-adult (YA) author Jason Reynolds made a point of telling student audiences that he did not read an entire book until he was seventeen years old. "It's not something I'm proud of. It's not cool," he admitted to seventh-graders in Stafford, Virginia, as quoted by Nora Krug for the *Washington Post* (23 Oct. 2017). "The truth is, my life was made infinitely more difficult because I didn't read any books. But I didn't read any books. That's my story. That's my truth." Reynolds's candor—about his early reading experiences, but also about the joy and pain of growing up black in America—is a huge part of his appeal as a best-selling author and a speaker.

Reynolds originally aspired to be a poet, and as a teenager found a home in the thriving spoken-word community in Washington, DC. He never saw himself as a novelist until, as an adult, he revisited the work of Walter Dean Myers, the beloved YA author who wrote about the lives of black teenagers throughout the 1970s to mid-2010s. Reynolds published his first solo book, *When I Was the Greatest*, in 2014. Within the next five years he wrote over a dozen books, sold millions of copies, and amassed numerous accolades, including two nominations for the National Book Award for Young People's Literature and several prestigious awards from the American Library Association (ALA).

EARLY LIFE AND EDUCATION

Jason Reynolds was born on December 6, 1983, the second youngest of his parents' four children. He grew up in Oxon Hill, Maryland, just outside of Washington, DC. His parents divorced when he was about ten, and he was mostly raised by his mother, a teacher.

As his favorite anecdote demonstrates, Reynolds was not an avid reader, a fact he attributed to the gulf between his own life experiences and the subjects of the books he was assigned to read in school. Instead, inspired by the fortuitous purchase of Queen Latifah's album *Black Reign* (1993), he developed an interest in poetry

Photo by Shawn Miller/Library of Congress via Wikimedia Commons

through hip hop. At age ten he read a poem he had written for his grandmother's funeral. "That was the first time I witnessed the power of language, and I decided right then that I would do something with it," he recalled to Lesley-Ann Brown for *NBC News* (22 Aug. 2015). As he got older, he began attending and performing at spoken-word events in Washington, DC. At seventeen he read his first book cover-to-cover: Richard Wright's novel *Black Boy* (1945). He then discovered works by other major African American authors, such as Toni Morrison.

Reynolds graduated from Bishop McNamara High School, where he excelled at running track, in 2000. He enrolled as an English student at the University of Maryland, College Park. There he teamed up with his roommate, artist Jason Douglas Griffin, to publish a coffee-table book called *Self*. The two poured some thirty thousand dollars into the project, racking up enormous debt to print their five-hundred copy run. They graduated in 2005 and relocated to New York City, where they distributed copies of their book to security guards at publishing houses, hoping it would find its way to an influential editor.

Their methods were unsuccessful in landing a publishing deal. However, they did find an agent, who helped them craft an illustrated YA book, about a white artist and a black writer struggling to make it in New York City, called *My Name Is Jason. Mine Too: Our Story, Our Way*. Pieces from the book were exhibited in several galleries. The book was published in 2009 but sold poorly. Nevertheless, the friends continued to collaborate on various artistic projects in the years that followed.

WHEN I WAS THE GREATEST

Reynolds briefly returned to Washington, DC and worked for his father, the director of a mental health clinic, for about a year. His experiences as a caseworker would inform his later writing. "I learned just how interesting stories can be, how complex humanity really is, how necessary it is sometimes to humanize those who have been vilified," he told Krug.

Settling in New York again, Reynolds found a managerial job in retail. He continued to write, but after rejections from three MFA programs, he grew discouraged. His friend Christopher Myers, the son of the legendary YA author Walter Dean Myers, pushed him to continue. As Reynolds recalled to Brown, Myers said that "his father was getting older and that at some point, when Walter was gone, someone was going to have to write the stories of black kids, especially black boys." Reynolds picked up *The Young Landlords*, Myers's 1989 classic about six teenagers who buy a rundown Harlem building for a dollar. Reynolds hoped to find inspiration;

instead, he told Concepción de León for the *New York Times* (29 Oct. 2019), "It chemically changed me."

Myers's work, Reynolds later said, gave him permission to write about his own experiences in his own voice. Reynolds began writing what would become his first novel, *When I Was the Greatest*, published in 2014, the year of the elder Myers's death. The novel follows teenaged Ali, who lives in the Bedford-Stuyvesant neighborhood of Brooklyn. A reviewer for *Kirkus* (20 Oct. 2013), described the critically acclaimed book as a character study of Ali and his family and friends. "Even though Reynolds . . . depicts the neighborhood as one where guns and drug transactions are seen regularly, readers don't necessarily feel the danger due to the tender and deeply protective relationships of the characters, who are realistically if not exquisitely drawn," the reviewer wrote, concluding that Reynolds was an "author worth watching." *When I Was the Greatest* won the ALA's Coretta Scott King/John Steptoe Award for New Talent in 2015.

EARLY WORK

With renewed confidence, Reynolds continued writing fiction in a similar vein. His next novel, *The Boy in the Black Suit* (2015), tells the story of teenaged Matthew, who, grieving the death of his mother, takes a job in a funeral home.

The same year Reynolds teamed up with author Brendan Kiely to write the novel *All American Boys*. Told in alternating chapters, the book concerns a brutal police beating. Reynolds wrote his chapters from the perspective of Rashad, a black teenager savagely beaten by a police officer who accuses him of shoplifting, while Kiely, who is white, wrote his chapters from the perspective of Quinn, a white friend of the officer's younger brother. *All American Boys* was inspired by the acquittal of George Zimmerman, who murdered seventeen-year-old Trayvon Martin in 2012. When news of the acquittal broke in 2013, Reynolds and Kiely, then strangers rooming together on a book tour, unpacked fraught emotions and developed a tentative friendship. After another brutal killing of a black teenager, Michael Brown, in Ferguson, Missouri, in 2014, Reynolds and Kiely decided to collaborate on a book that would give voice to their fury. *All American Boys* won the inaugural Walter Dean Myers Award for Outstanding Children's Literature from We Need Diverse Books.

In 2016 Reynolds published his first middle-grade novel, *As Brave as You*, about two brothers from Brooklyn who visit their grandparents in rural Virginia for the summer. *Kirkus* (30 Mar. 2016) gave it a starred review, concluding, "This pitch-perfect contemporary novel gently explores the past's repercussions on the present." A Kirkus Prize winner, it also won the National

Association for the Advancement of Colored People (NAACP) Image Award for Outstanding Literary Work for Youth/Teen for 2017.

TRACK SERIES AND *LONG WAY DOWN*
In 2016 Reynolds also published *Ghost*, the first novel of his four-book Track series and a modern classic of children's literature. The book, inspired by the experiences of Reynolds's friend Matthew Carter, follows Castle Crenshaw, nicknamed Ghost. Ghost is spectacularly fast but burdened with the memory of the first time he discovered his talent: when he and his mother had to run from his father, who was firing a gun at them. Ghost joins the track team, where he befriends Patina, Sunny, and Lu. In *Ghost*, "Reynolds has created a character whose journey is so genuine that he's worthy of a place alongside Ramona and Joey Pigza on the bookshelves where our most beloved, imperfect characters live," author Kate Messner wrote in her review for the *New York Times* (26 Aug. 2016). The series continued with a full novel about each runner: *Patina*, the first book Reynolds wrote from a female point of view, in 2017 and *Sunny* and *Lu* in 2018.

In 2017, Reynolds published *Miles Morales: Spider-Man*. His novel adaptation of the Marvel Universe series features the titular Morales, an Afro-Puerto Rican teenager from Brooklyn who becomes the famous superhero.

That same year Reynolds published *Long Way Down*, a novel in free verse about a teenager who contemplates avenging his brother's murder. The book takes place over the course of an elevator ride. At each floor he is visited by a different ghost who complicates his decision. The book was inspired by Reynolds's own desire for immediate vengeance at the murder of a close friend when he was nineteen. "I'll never forget the next day, being at his mom's house, overrun with anger and having to admit to myself that in that moment, I was fully aware that we could all leave that house, go in search for whoever we *think* may have done this, and end their lives," he told David Greene for National Public Radio's *Morning Edition* (30 Oct. 2017). He added, "Because what happens is when you feel that kind of pain, time suspends itself, and you believe that . . . the way you feel in this moment will last forever."

The ALA named *Long Way Down* a 2018 Newbery Honor Book and a 2018 Michael L. Printz Honor Book. It also earned Reynolds a second Walter Award.

LOOK BOTH WAYS AND *STAMPED*
In 2018, Reynolds published a book-length poem about aspirations titled *For Every One*. The following year he released a novel of interconnected stories called *Look Both Ways: A Tale Told in Ten Blocks*. *Look Both Ways* interweaves a host of perspectives from different characters as sixth graders make their way home from school. It, too, was a finalist for the National Book Award and a frequent recommendation on best-of lists.

In 2020, Reynolds collaborated with National Book Award–winning historian Ibram X. Kendi to create *Stamped: Racism, Antiracism and You*, a YA adaptation of Kendi's influential six-hundred-page history, *Stamped from the Beginning: The Definitive History of Racist Ideas in America* (2016). Their collaboration earned Reynolds a place on the *Time* 100 Next list for 2019. He was also designated the National Ambassador for Young People's Literature for 2020–21 by the Library of Congress, the Children's Book Council, and the Every Child a Reader organization. In that role he was to give talks around the country and work with the nonprofit StoryCorps to record and archive the stories of children he met.

In addition to his writing, Reynolds taught creative writing in the MFA program at Lesley University in Cambridge, Massachusetts.

PERSONAL LIFE
Reynolds currently lives in Washington, DC.

SUGGESTED READING
Brown, Lesley-Ann. "The Graceful Power of Jason Reynolds." *NBC News*, 22 Aug. 2015, www.nbcnews.com/news/nbcblk/graceful-power-novelist-jason-reynolds-n399721. Accessed 6 June 2020.

De León, Concepción. "Jason Reynolds Is on a Mission." *The New York Times*, 29 Oct. 2019, www.nytimes.com/2019/10/28/books/jason-reynolds-look-both-ways.html. Accessed 6 June 2020.

Greene, David. "In 'Long Way Down,' The Ghosts of Gun Violence Chill a Plan for Revenge." *Morning Edition*, National Public Radio, 30 Oct. 2017, www.npr.org/2017/10/30/560286304/in-long-way-down-the-ghosts-of-gun-violence-chill-a-plan-for-revenge. Accessed 7 June 2020.

Krug, Nora. "How a Kid Who Didn't Read a Book until He Was 17 Grew Up to Become a Literary Star." *The Washington Post*, 23 Oct. 2017, www.washingtonpost.com/entertainment/books/he-didnt-read-books-as-a-kid-but-jason-reynolds-wants-to-make-sure-your-kids-do/2017/10/23/ed4b55da-9d4c-11e7-9083-fbfddf6804c2_story.html. Accessed 6 June 2020.

Messner, Kate. "A Young Sprinter Finds His Team in 'Ghost.'" Review of *Ghost*, by Jason Reynolds. *The New York Times*, 26 Aug. 2016, www.nytimes.com/2016/08/28/books/review/jason-reynolds-ghost.html. Accessed 6 June 2020.

"Review of *As Brave as You*, by Jason Reynolds." *Kirkus*, 30 Mar. 2016, www.kirkusreviews.

com/book-reviews/jason-reynolds/as-brave-as-you/. Accessed 6 June 2020.

"Review of *When I Was the Greatest*, by Jason Reynolds." *Kirkus*, 20 Oct. 2013, www.kirkus-reviews.com/book-reviews/jason-reynolds/when-i-was-the-greatest. Accessed 6 June 2020.

SELECTED WORKS

When I Was the Greatest, 2014; *All American Boys* (with Brendan Kiely), 2015; *The Boy in the Black Suit*, 2015; *As Brave as You*, 2016; *Ghost*, 2016; *Long Way Down*, 2017; *Look Both Ways*, 2020; *Stamped: Racism, Antiracism and You* (with Ibram X. Kendi), 2020

—*Molly Hagan*

Robin Rhode

Born: 1976
Occupation: Artist

Photo by Armchaired via Wikimedia Commons

Photography, sculpture, drawing, animation, film, and performance art all have places within Robin Rhode's artistic repertoire—and often with the same pieces. He is best known for creating series of photographs in which actors pose in front of murals drawn by Rhode, seeming to interact with the two-dimensional drawing. His work is varied but almost always includes a human figure of some kind for the audience to relate to. "I always want to have the audience project themselves into the work of art," he explained in an interview for the Swedish museum Kulturhuset Stadsteatern in 2015.

Rhode's work is heavily influenced by street art and graffiti, reflecting his desire to bring modern art, often considered esoteric and hard to appreciate, into the wider community. "I wanted to bring the art museum to the street as a means to allow art to become accessible to a greater public," he told Courtney Willis Blair for *Forbes* (10 Sept. 2015). However, his art also draws on works found in galleries and museums, he told Kulturhuset Stadsteatern, saying, "Many see me as a street artist, but I reinterpret and filter my art through art history in the same sense that a DJ makes remixes of existing tracks." His influences include American minimalists Donald Judd, Carl Andre, and Sol LeWitt, who was particularly known for his large-scale wall drawings.

Since entering the art scene in the late 1990s, Rhode has won a number of awards, including the 2007 Illy Prize and the 2011 Young Artist Award. In 2018 he won the prestigious Zürich Art Prize, which came with a financial award of 100,000 Swiss francs (slightly more than US$100,000) for a solo exhibition and cash purse.

EARLY LIFE AND EDUCATION

Rhode was born in 1976 in Cape Town, South Africa, and was raised in Johannesburg. He grew up toward the end of the era of apartheid, or racial segregation, and attended poorly funded schools for mixed-race children. Although he discovered a love of drawing at a young age, he had little opportunity to explore that passion in school—officially, at least. "In school, we didn't have art education or any facilities, and chalk was the cheapest mode of expression," he told Antwaun Sargent for *W* magazine (1 July 2015). "We channeled our creativity onto the concrete walls." In particular, his art was heavily influenced by an odd hazing ritual he encountered in high school, in which older students would draw an object of desire—often a bicycle—on the wall in chalk and force younger students to pretend to interact with it.

Following high school, Rhode attended the Technikon Witwatersrand (now part of the University of Johannesburg), from which he graduated with a bachelor of fine arts degree in 1998. He then completed postgraduate studies at the South African School of Film, Television, and Dramatic Art in 2000.

THE ART OF MOVEMENT

In 1997, while still a student, Rhode began doing street performances in which he would draw an image in chalk on a wall and then interact with the drawn object. "I was so anti-studio at art school, so I went to the streets," he told Sargent. "I wanted the people to be my audience and witness the process of contemporary art, so I started to do these fast drawing performances." These early performances included works such as *Classic Bike* (1998), in which Rhode tries to ride a drawing of a bike, and *Car Theft* (1998), in which he attempts to break into a two-dimensional car.

He then began taking sequences of photos showing himself interacting with the drawings, which allowed him to create the illusion of movements that would not be possible in real life. There were also benefits to working in a more permanent medium: in 2000 Rhode sold his first work, a photograph series titled *He Got Game* showing him executing an impossibly high jump and flip to throw a basketball into a drawing of a hoop. Although he continued to do performances occasionally over the following decade, the photographs soon became his focus.

Rhode moved to Berlin, Germany, in 2001 for a three-month artist residency and ultimately decided to make it his home. He felt that living in Germany "allowed [him] to step back from the South African context and to consider [himself] a global player," he told Carol Kino for the *New York Times* (13 May 2007). Nevertheless, he continued to engage artistically with issues facing his native South Africa through such works as *Gun Drawings* (2004), which deals with gun violence in cities such as Cape Town, and *Color Chart* (2004–06), which addresses racial inequity. During this period, he began to use actors in his photographs at times, rather than always appearing in them himself.

GLOBAL STAGE

Rhode came to the attention of the international art scene in 2003, when several of his works, including *Car Theft*, were included in *How Latitudes Become Forms*, a group show about globalization that debuted at the Walker Art Center in Minneapolis, Minnesota, and went on to tour worldwide. That same year he began to have solo exhibits domestically and, the following year, internationally, showing work at the Rose Art Museum in Waltham, Massachusetts, and the Perry Rubenstein Gallery in New York City. He was then invited to take part in the prestigious Venice Biennale in 2005; over the next fifteen years, he would participate in a handful of other biennial and triennial art festivals held in Japan, Australia, New York, Italy, and South Korea.

In 2009 he collaborated with Norwegian pianist Leif Ove Andsnes on *Pictures Reframed*, a performance inspired by Russian composer Modest Mussorgsky's 1874 piano suite *Pictures at an Exhibition*. Rhode created videos to accompany the music for the performance, which had been commissioned by the Lincoln Center in New York and premiered there.

In 2011 Rhode created the installation *Paries Pictus* (Wall drawing), in which visitors to the gallery were encouraged to use giant crayons to color in outlines applied to the wall by Rhode, for the Castello di Rivoli in Italy. He went on to restage this exhibition in New York, Cape Town, and Melbourne, Australia.

Rhode's artwork was exhibited in galleries and museums not only in Europe and North America but also in Israel, Hong Kong, and South Korea in the late 2010s. It has also displayed in the permanent collections of dozens of art institutions around the world, including the South African National Gallery, the Guggenheim Museum, the Museum of Modern Art in New York, and the Centre Pompidou in Paris, France.

BRANCHING OUT

Around 2006 Rhode began to tire of performing in museums and wanted to explore new directions for his art. This led him to dabble in sculpture with pieces such as *Soap & Water* (2007), which consisted of a sculpture of a bicycle carved out of soap and placed next to a bucket of water. He also made the film *Candle* (2007), in which he draws a candle on a piece of paper that he then lights on fire. However, photographs continued to make up the bulk of his work until the mid-2010s.

During that time, he began to apply his interest in interactions between 2-D and 3-D objects to gallery installations, creating hybrids of mural and sculpture. *Chalk Bicycle* (2011–15), for example, gives the impression of an urban alleyway by combining several chalk drawings of bicycles on the gallery walls with a single sculpture of a bicycle, while a discarded spray can and scattered newspaper pages lie on the floor. *The Moon Is Asleep* (2016), meanwhile, features a more abstract painting with a live human figure appearing prone against it with a 3-D pillow.

Rhode also explored other new avenues of artistic expression. In 2014 he directed a music video for the song "Every Breaking Wave" by the Irish rock band U2. The following year he served as artistic director for a production of Arnold Schönberg's 1909 opera *Erwartung* that was commissioned for the Performa 15 biennial and was performed on an outdoor stage in New York's Times Square. Rhode's production used the opera, a solo piece in which a woman known only as Die Frau searches with increasing agitation for her missing lover, as a framework to explore issues relating to migrant labor in South Africa. Working-class South African men are often required to spend large portions of the year working in remote mines, leaving their wives behind. Rhode also compared Die Frau to Winnie

Mandela—who was separated from her then husband, Nelson Mandela, by his long imprisonment—and sought to juxtapose their narratives.

SPIRITUAL WORK

Rhode went on to create the photo series *Under the Sun*, which was exhibited in Israel in 2017. Though it still featured an actor interacting with various murals, the murals themselves differed from Rhode's previous work, featuring shifting combinations of cubes in shades of red, yellow, and orange, rather than depictions of everyday objects. "I felt like I needed a new method, something that rejected chaos. I was looking for a spiritual calmness," Rhode explained to Margaret Carrigan in an interview for *Elephant* magazine (31 Jan. 2018) regarding this decision. "The cube is a massively symbolic geometric shape."

Rhode often works in poor, crime-ridden areas of Johannesburg where he hires local youth to assist him with his murals, such as the backdrops in *Under the Sun*. They prepare and guard the wall, which Rhode remakes daily or every other day, and sometimes appear in his videos or photographs. He has told interviewers that he considers it his duty to help bring discipline and hope for a positive future to young people there.

In 2019 Rhode made a number of pieces in the historical city of Jericho in the West Bank, including *Phantom Rain* and *Tree of Life*. Those series of photographed murals allude to geopolitical tensions, like many of his earlier works, as well as religious or spiritual themes through their form.

PERSONAL LIFE

Rhode divides his time between Berlin and Johannesburg. He married the German artist and writer Sabinah Odumosu; they have two sons, born around 2002 and 2010. Odumosu is the photographer for many of Rhode's projects.

SUGGESTED READING

Carrigan, Margaret. "Robin Rhode: Under the Sun." *Elephant*, 31 Jan. 2018, elephant.art/robin-rhode-under-the-sun. Accessed 13 Apr. 2020.

Forbes, Alexander. "In Times Square, Robin Rhode Stages an Anxious Call to Address Racial Disparities." Review of *Erwartung*, by Arnold Schönberg, directed by Robin Rhode. *Artsy*, 9 Nov. 2015, www.artsy.net/article/artsy-editorial-robin-rhode-stages-an-anxiety-attack-in-times-square. Accessed 13 Apr. 2020.

Kino, Carol. "Something There Is That Loves a Wall." *The New York Times*, 13 May 2007, www.nytimes.com/2007/05/13/arts/design/13kino.html. Accessed 13 Apr. 2020.

Rhode, Robin. "4 Questions with South African Artist Robin Rhode." Interview by Courtney Willis Blair. *Forbes*, 10 Sept. 2015, www.forbes.com/sites/courtneywillisblair/2015/09/10/4-questions-robin-rhode. Accessed 13 Apr. 2020.

———. "An Artist Who Pushes the Borders of His Studio into the Streets." Interview by Osman Can Yerebakan. *T: The New York Times Style Magazine*, 3 Oct. 2019, www.nytimes.com/2019/10/03/t-magazine/robin-rhode-artist.html. Accessed 13 Apr. 2020.

———. "Robin Rhode Draws on Everything." Interview by Antwaun Sargent. *W Magazine*, 1 July 2015, www.wmagazine.com/gallery/robin-rhode-drawings/all. Accessed 13 Apr. 2020.

"Robin Rhode—The Sudden Walk." *Kulturhuset Stadsteatern*, 2015, kulturhusetstadsteatern.se/English/Events/2015/Robin-Rhode. Accessed 13 Apr. 2020.

SELECTED WORKS

Classic Bike, 1998; *Car Theft*, 1998; *He Got Game*, 2000; *Gun Drawings*, 2004; *Color Chart*, 2004–6; *Soap & Water*, 2007; *Paries Pictus*, 2011; *Chalk Bicycle*, 2011–15; *The Moon Is Asleep*, 2016; *Under the Sun*, 2017; *Phantom Rain*, 2019

—*Emma Joyce*

Yoruba Richen

Date of birth: ca. 1972
Occupation: Documentary filmmaker

Filmmaker Yoruba Richen has been widely celebrated for her eye-opening documentaries. These include *Promised Land* (2010), which looks at land reform and racial reconciliation in South Africa after apartheid; *The New Black* (2013), which uncovers the complicated histories of the African American and LGBTQ rights movements; and *The Green Book: Guide to Freedom* (2019), which evocatively uses archival footage to revisit the iconic travel guide created by and for African Americans in an era during which many establishments were closed to them. Of her dedication to this medium, she told Toni Fitzgerald for *Forbes* (22 Feb. 2019), "I've always wanted to give voice to the stories that were not told in the mainstream media, and documentaries are a great way to do that."

Richen, who as of 2019 also served as a distinguished lecturer and the head of the documentary program at the Craig Newmark Graduate School of Journalism at the City University of New York (CUNY), became well known for her efforts to draw attention to the lack of diversity evident in the world of contemporary nonfiction cinema. "There is an amazing group

Photo by Jennifer Lourie/Getty Images

of filmmakers, and amazing filmmakers of color, in particular, who I admire. However, there's still not enough of us telling our own stories, especially as black women," she asserted to Alicia Maule for *MSNBC* (25 Feb. 2015). "There has to be some real pointed strategies around increasing the number of filmmakers of color."

EARLY LIFE AND EDUCATION

Richen was raised in the historically black New York City neighborhood of Harlem. She attended school on Manhattan's Upper East Side, a predominately wealthy, white neighborhood. She would later tell interviewers that commuting by bus each day and seeing the obvious disparities between those two milieus strongly impacted her worldview—and, subsequently, her work.

Richen's mother was the acclaimed playwright Aishah Rahman, who, along with such writers as Amiri Baraka and Sonia Sanchez, was active in the African American art and culture movement of the 1960s and early 1970s. Therefore, Richen's childhood memories were set against the backdrop of her mother steadily typing. Rahman, who was known for plays that melded the personal and political, ensured that her daughter traveled widely during her formative years. On that subject, Richen recalled to Maule that her mother "had a belief that she wanted to show me that the world was bigger than just the United States. And that we, people of color, are the majority in the world, not the minority."

At one point Richen briefly considered the idea of becoming a lawyer, thinking she might

work in the arena of social justice. Given how deeply immersed she was in the theater world, she also contemplated acting or directing. Ultimately, however, she entered Brown University, where her mother became a literary arts professor. There, Richen studied political science, graduating with a bachelor's degree in 1994. She next attended the University of California, Berkeley, earning a master's degree in urban planning in 1998.

EARLY FILMMAKING CAREER

The world of filmmaking was changing by the 1990s, as camera equipment got smaller and less expensive. Seeking a creative outlet while still studying urban planning, Richen partnered with a friend who had a video camera and editing gear. The two collaborated on a film about welfare reform and how it was impacting one African American community on the West Coast. "While making it I had an 'Ah ha!' moment, 'oh, okay, this is how I can combine my creative work with my social justice self,' and this all came together," she told Craig Phillips for the website of the PBS series *Independent Lens* (12 June 2014).

With a new path now in mind, Richen abandoned thoughts of a career in urban planning and moved back to New York after graduation. There she was hired by the late documentary filmmaker St. Clair Bourne to serve as the production coordinator on *Half Past Autumn: The Life and Works of Gordon Parks*, an HBO documentary released in 2000 about the first full-time African American staff photographer ever hired by *Life* magazine. Following this formative experience, she found a series of other production jobs. In 2001, the documentary *Take It from Me*, which she coproduced, premiered on PBS's program *POV*. From 2000 to 2004 she served as an associate producer for an investigative unit of ABC News, and between 2005 to 2007 she worked as a producer for *Democracy Now!*, an independent, nonprofit daily news program. Around 2007, Richen won a Fulbright award for filmmaking. This allowed her to travel to northeastern Brazil to make *Sisters of the Good Death*, a short documentary about the African women's organization founded in the country in the early nineteenth century and its annual religious festival celebrating Afro-Brazilian culture and the end of slavery.

While that short documentary was little seen outside of academic circles, Richen garnered more attention for her work *Promised Land*, which was broadcast nationally by PBS in 2010 as part of its *POV* series. In this documentary film, Richen focuses on two legal cases in which black South Africans, the Mekgareng community and the Molamu family, had fought to reclaim land after the end of apartheid in South Africa (under which white South Africans, despite comprising only 10 percent of the population, owned almost 90 percent of the land). The film was lauded for covering the agonizingly slow pace of land reform and for including a wide range of voices, such as those of white farmers forced to contend with the effects of colonialism.

THE NEW BLACK AND SHORT FILMS

In 2013, Richen released *The New Black*, which attracted viewers through its provocative look at the complex attitudes toward gay rights within the African American community and the overlap between various rights struggles. For Richen, the film was particularly important to make as she considered herself part of both the African American and LGBTQ communities. "President Obama said it at his inauguration, putting the gay rights struggle in the context of Selma and Seneca, that great American march towards fairness and equality," she explained to Beth Schwartzapfel for the *Brown Alumni Magazine* (9 Sept. 2013). "The way I look at it is that we are now seeing the struggles for gay rights as part of the American struggle to expand fairness and equality for all." Considered a balanced look at an emotionally and politically fraught topic, *The New Black* was nominated for a National Association for the Advancement of Colored People (NAACP) Image Award.

Richen followed that effort with *Reconception* (2016), a short film backed by the Economic Hardship Reporting Project, which is dedicated to funding high-quality journalism about inequality and justice. The documentary gives viewers a peek inside Indiana's All-Options Pregnancy Resource Center, which was then developing an "abortion doula" program to offer support and counseling to women ending their pregnancies. Next, in 2018 Richen teamed with codirectors Monica Berra and Jacqueline Olive to make *Crooked Lines*, a short about how the Republican legislature in North Carolina was employing racial gerrymandering for political gain.

Up until that point, it was arguably *The New Black* that had won Richen the most mainstream attention and the largest audiences; the film had had its world premiere at the Los Angeles Film Festival, aired on PBS's *Independent Lens* program in 2014, and earned a nod at the Gay & Lesbian Alliance Against Defamation (GLAAD) Media Awards. Bigger things were on the horizon, however.

THE GREEN BOOK: GUIDE TO FREEDOM

In 2017, a television production company based in the United Kingdom, Impossible Factual Limited, had gotten in touch with Richen about making a documentary on the *Negro Motorist Green Book*, a travel guide first printed in 1936. During the era of segregation, the guide listed restaurants, hotels, gas stations, and other establishments that would serve African American motorists and be safe havens for them when travel was a sometimes-dangerous undertaking. Richen agreed to make the film, not realizing that a major Hollywood production starring Mahershala Ali and Viggo Mortensen that touched upon the same theme was in production.

Fortuitously, the films were released not far apart, with the big-budget drama *Green Book* premiering in September 2018 and Richen's documentary, *The Green Book: Guide to Freedom*, shown on the Smithsonian Channel in February 2019. Although the Hollywood picture, which imagines a budding friendship between Don Shirley (Ali), a real-life American musician who was of Jamaican descent, and his white driver, Tony Lip (Mortensen), won the 2019 Academy Award for Best Picture, it sparked a backlash when critics—who notably included surviving members of Shirley's own family—pointed out its many inaccuracies and outright falsehoods. Chief among these, as Richen herself often discussed with journalists, was the misconception that African American travelers were in danger only in the South; in reality, the documentary shows that almost half of the counties along Route 66 contained so-called "sundown towns," where African Americans were supposed to leave by nightfall. Furthermore, Richen was dismayed that the establishments that welcome Shirley in the dramatization are depicted as squalid and run-down, when most of the places listed in the actual guide were, in fact, fine examples of African American entrepreneurship and initiative. (Richen cites as particular examples the A. G. Gaston Motel in Birmingham, Alabama, and Idlewild, a resort destination in Michigan that attracted generations of middle-class African Americans.)

The commercial success of *Green Book* brought widespread attention to Richen's documentary, and she was invited to discuss the topic with such high-profile media outlets as National Public Radio (NPR). In the *Daily Princetonian* (10 Apr. 2019), Noa Wollstein echoed a general consensus regarding the documentary, writing, "Richen's work is informative, personal, and poignant. . . . And maybe it doesn't have an Oscar, but it preserves a history that the actual award winner uses as little more than a title and a decoration in the passenger seat."

TEACHING CAREER

Richen, who received grants from such organizations as the Sundance Documentary Fund and the Ford Foundation, joined the faculty of CUNY in 2009. Initially, she taught courses in broadcast news, and in 2013 she began teaching documentary filmmaking. A TED speaker and former Guggenheim Fellow, as of 2019 she held the positions of distinguished lecturer and director of the documentary program at the Craig Newmark Graduate School of Journalism at CUNY. "I think what we offer is a real nexus between the art of filmmaking and the rigor of reporting," Richen said, as quoted by the *CUNY* website (21 Mar. 2019). "We were born in the multimedia age, and I think that puts us a step ahead in terms of incorporating multimedia into all of our classes."

There has been little readily available information on Richen's personal life. She has said that among her personal favorite films are *All That Jazz* (1979), directed by Bob Fosse, and *The Landlord* (1970), directed by Hal Ashby.

SUGGESTED READING

"CUNY Newmark Journalism Teacher Yoruba Richen Tells 'Real Story' of the Green Book." *CUNY: The City University of New York*, 21 Mar. 2019, https://www1.cuny.edu/mu/forum/2019/03/21/cuny-newmark-journalism-teacher-yoruba-richentells-real-story-of-the-green-book/. Accessed 21 Nov. 2019.

Fitzgerald, Toni. "New Documentary Explores the Real 'Green Book' behind Oscar-Nominated Film." *Forbes*, 22 Feb. 2019, www.forbes.com/sites/tonifitzgerald/2019/02/22/new-documentary-explores-the-real-green-book-behind-oscar-nominated-film/#5da3cbe2599a. Accessed 21 Nov. 2019.

Richen, Yoruba. "Director Yoruba Richen: 'Not Enough of Us Telling Our Stories.'" Interview by Alicia Maule. *MSNBC*, 25 Feb. 2015, www.msnbc.com/msnbc/yoruba-richen-not-enough-us-telling-our-stories. Accessed 21 Nov. 2019.

——. "Expanding Civil Rights." Interview by Beth Schwartzapfel. *Brown Alumni Magazine*, Sept./Oct. 2013, www.brownalumnimagazine.com/articles/2013-09-09/expanding-civil-rights. Accessed 21 Nov. 2019.

——. "'Guide to Freedom' Documentary Chronicles the Real Life 'Green Book.'" Interview by Dave Davies. *NPR*, 25 Feb. 2019, www.npr.org/2019/02/25/697667279/guide-to-freedom-documentary-chronicles-the-real-life-green-book. Accessed 21 Nov. 2019.

——. "The New Black: Yoruba Richen Expands the Conversation on Marriage Equality." Interview by Craig Phillips. *Independent Lens*, PBS, 12 June 2014, www.pbs.org/independentlens/blog/richen-new-black/. Accessed 21 Nov. 2019.

Wollstein, Noa. "Yoruba Richen's 'The Green Book: Guide to Freedom' Lacks an Oscar but Preserves a History." *The Daily Princetonian*, 10 Apr. 2019, www.dailyprincetonian.com/article/2019/04/yoruba-richens-the-green-book-guide-to-freedom-lacks-an-oscar-but-preserves-a-history. Accessed 21 Nov. 2019.

SELECTED WORKS
Promised Land, 2010; *The New Black*, 2013; *The Green Book: Guide to Freedom*, 2019

—*Mari Rich*

Patrice Roberts

Born: April 11, 1985
Occupation: Musician

Trinidadian singer Patrice Roberts sought to take a new approach to her longtime genre of soca music after striking out on her own as a solo artist in 2015. "I just wanted people to see a different side of me. . . To stray away from the traditional," she told A. C. Christie for *I Love Carnivall* (17 Nov. 2019). "I wanted people to see soca music in an international way." With songs such as "Big Girl Now" (2017), "Sweet Fuh Days" (2017), and "Carry On" (2019), Roberts established herself as a major force in the genre, a dance-oriented form of music that arose out of calypso and became closely associated with events such as the Trinidadian Carnival. Soca artists vie for recognition as the best in the genre through a number of high-profile singing competitions.

A competitive vocalist since childhood, Roberts began her career as a calypso singer and won a Junior Calypso Monarch competition in 1995. Additional accolades followed, including the 2001 National Junior Soca Monarch and Junior Calypso Monarch titles and especially a victory at the Carnival Road March competition in 2006 in collaboration with longtime performer Machel Montano. She then spent nearly a decade as a member of Montano's soca group, Xtatik—also known as the HD Band—during which she continued to elevate her name within the genre that had become her primary musical home. Even after leaving the group in 2015, Roberts remained deeply committed to soca music, continuing to release songs in that genre and perform at soca-oriented events, including her own annual Strength of a Woman concerts. "Soca kind of . . . does that to you," she explained to Anika Klimke for *Carnevale Network* (9 Jan. 2016) of her genre's lasting pull. "From the time you hear a soca music, it's like no other and I feel like I could do this until I'm old and grey, because soca music gives me that energy to go."

EARLY LIFE AND EDUCATION
Roberts was born in the Republic of Trinidad and Tobago on April 11, 1985. She grew up in Toco,

a coastal village on the island of Trinidad. Roberts attended Toco Composite School, where she studied music and drama under vocalist Beulah Bobb (also known as Lady B), a veteran performer of calypso music. Although Roberts had multiple career aspirations as a child and at times hoped to become a flight attendant, as she was drawn to the highly social nature of that job, she developed a love of singing at a young age and began singing extensively by the age of seven. "I always loved to entertain and when you love something, you show more passion and the drive is there, so I guess the drive is just naturally there, for me. It is something I love to do," she told Klimke.

Drawn to the genre of calypso music, Roberts began singing in calypso competitions while still in school. In 1995 she claimed first place at the Sangre Grande Junior Calypso Monarch competition.

SOCA CAREER

In addition to singing calypso, Roberts soon became interested in the similar, yet distinct genre known as soca. A genre native to Trinidad and Tobago, soca music evolved out of calypso but incorporates aspects of other genres, including soul, dance music, and musical styles from elsewhere in the Caribbean. The genre is associated with Trinidad and Tobago's annual Carnival celebration, held each year in February or March, during which soca music is played and danced to in the streets. Much like calypso artists, soca vocalists in Trinidad and Tobago can compete in a variety of high-profile annual competitions, often held in conjunction with Carnival season. Roberts competed as a singer of both calypso and soca throughout her early career, and in 2001 won both the National Junior Soca Monarch and Junior Calypso Monarch titles with her performances of songs written by Bobb.

Although Roberts remained active in the calypso genre throughout her early years as a singer, she switched primarily to soca as a young adult, in part due to the influence of soca musicians such as Kernal Roberts and Machel Montano. The transition was initially a difficult one for Roberts, who found that the overall tone and style of soca music necessitated a shift in her approach as a performer. "Soca music is more energetic, upbeat," she told Christie when explaining the differences between soca and calypso. "You have to learn how to command the crowd. It was difficult for me because I was a really shy person. It took me a while and people like Machel and other big veterans showed me what to do." Roberts began to experience success within her new genre in 2005, when she collaborated with artist Bunji Garlin to record the hit song "The Islands."

POPULAR PERFORMER

In 2006 Roberts began what would become nearly a decade of collaborations with Montano, a longtime soca performer who was the leader of the band Xtatik, later known by names such as the HD Band and HD Family. In addition to joining Xtatik as a vocalist that year, Roberts gained further attention for her contributions to the song "Band of D Year," a collaboration with Montano that became one of the best-known songs of the 2006 Carnival season. "Band of D Year" ultimately won the 2006 Trinidad and Tobago Carnival Road March, a competition determining the most popular song played at Carnival, thus solidifying Roberts's reputation as a promising up-and-coming singer within the soca genre. Over the subsequent years, Roberts continued to record and perform with the band, releasing multiple songs that met with a strong reception during each year's Carnival season. She also continued to compete in major soca competitions, including International Soca Monarch.

A turning point in Roberts's career came in 2015, when she decided to leave the HD Band to focus on a career as a solo soca performer. "I always wanted to branch off on my own and 2015 was the ideal opportunity, because not just me, but also Machel himself wanted to branch off and do his thing," she told Klimke about her decision. "I was able to travel the world and explore many options." Although Roberts had at times recorded solo songs or collaborations with artists other than Montano and his colleagues during her years as a member of Xtatik and the HD Band, striking out on her own provided her with opportunities to explore her own musical interests and give listeners a greater sense of her individual identity as a performer through her songs, videos, and live shows. Hits such as "Big Girl Now" (2017) emphasized a more mature, outgoing, and international side of her personality, "to come out of the box," as she explained to Christie. "I think sometimes you have to set the bar a little higher, a little different. If we stay in a box, then we will not move forward, so I always like to come out of the box a little."

In addition to "Big Girl Now," Roberts's popular releases around this time included "Sweet Fuh Days" (2017); "Like It Like This" (2017), a collaboration with the band Kes; and "This Is De Place" (2018).

SOLO SUCCESS

Roberts experienced considerable success as a solo artist, including with the 2019 track "Carry On," which became one of her biggest hits. However, she began to move away from her longtime presence in traditional soca competitions, for example announcing in January 2018 that she would no longer compete in the International Soca Monarch competition. "I don't compete well; last year was my breaking point. I can't do it anymore," she told Laura Dowrich-Phillips for *Loop* (10 Jan. 2018). "I think it is an opportunity for someone else who never did it before. It has done so much for soca, it put us on the map, gave us an opportunity to be seen on so many levels but that competition does make me question myself."

Nevertheless, Roberts remained a Trinidad Carnival Road March contender during the next several years. In 2019 she released a career-high fourteen songs in conjunction with the Carnival season and the competition, with "Judgement Stage" drawing particular attention. "It was all about pleasing the fans and satisfying their musical appetite. Road March is for the masquerader, and there is always that one song or some songs that add to their overall experience," she told the *Jamaica Gleaner* (26 Apr. 2019), while downplaying the competitive aspect of the event. "I do not ever take Road March personally, to be honest. . . . I am always just happy when the music is accepted and appreciated, not only in Trinidad and Tobago, but throughout the diaspora and wherever else it reaches."

Indeed, as her popularity grew Roberts found appreciative audiences in other countries with soca-loving populations, including Jamaica and the United Kingdom. She performed internationally, including at events such as the Bacchanal Jamaica Carnival. However, it was in Port of Spain, Trinidad, that she held her first headlining concert, Strength of a Woman, in February 2019. A celebration of women in soca, the event featured performances not only by Roberts herself but also by soca artists such as Destra Garcia and Nadia Batson. "The women who were showcased in my first concert were all there for a reason," she later told the *Jamaica Gleaner*. "As women, we have to work ten times harder to be taken seriously, and the public is more critical of us."

Continuing to highlight the work of women in soca, Roberts held a second Strength of a Woman concert in February 2020 and announced plans to continue it as an annual concert series. That same year she had a hit with "Splash," a collaboration with fellow vocalist Nessa Preppy.

PERSONAL LIFE

Roberts and fellow soca performer Ricardo Drue had a daughter, Lily, in 2016. In 2018 Roberts announced plans to establish a line of girls' clothing named after her daughter as a well as a charitable foundation named in her honor. "I want to instill in her the importance of giving back," she explained to Dowrich-Phillips about her plans. "I want her to be a businesswoman from young and to have that mindset."

SUGGESTED READING

Doodnath, Alina. "Watch: Patrice Roberts Shows Strength in Emotional Debut Concert." *Loop*, 1 Mar. 2019, www.loopjamaica.com/content/watch-patrice-roberts-shows-strength-emotional-debut-concert-7. Accessed 12 Apr. 2020.

Dowrich-Phillips, Laura. "Patrice Roberts Moving on from Soca Monarch, Launching Clothing Line." *Loop*, 10 Jan. 2018, www.looptt.com/content/patrice-roberts-moving-soca-monarch-launching-clothing-line. Accessed 12 Apr. 2020.

Moe, Cherisse. "Patrice Chose Music over Flying." *Trinidad & Tobago Guardian*, 3 Feb. 2012, www.guardian.co.tt/article-6.2.415413.0da1ce9dfe. Accessed 12 Apr. 2020.

Roberts, Patrice. "Christina Mais Interviews Patrice Roberts in Jamaica." Interview by Christina Mais. *UK Soca Scene*, 17 Jan. 2017, www.uksocascene.com/she-soca/interviews-patrice-roberts-jamaica/. Accessed 12 Apr. 2020.

———. "5 Questions with Patrice Roberts." *The Gleaner*, 26 Apr. 2019, jamaica-gleaner.com/article/entertainment/20190426/5-questions-patrice-roberts. Accessed 12 Apr. 2020.

———. "Patrice Roberts—Tapping Her Hands into New Waters." Interview by Anika Klimke. *Carnevale Network*, 9 Jan. 2016, www.carnevalenetwork.co.uk/index.php/en/2017-01-31-15-57-06/interviews/1045-patrice-roberts-tapping-her-hands-into-new-waters. Accessed 12 Apr. 2020.

———. "Patrice Roberts: Woman of Soca." Interview by A. C. Christie. *I Love Carnivall*, 17 Nov. 2019, ilovecarnivall.co.uk/patrice-roberts-woman-of-soca/. Accessed 12 Apr. 2020.

SELECTED WORKS

"The Islands" (with Bunji Garlin), 2005; "Band of D Year (with Machel Montano), 2006; "Sweet Fuh Days," 2017; "Big Girl Now," 2017; "Like It Like This" (with Kes), 2017; "This Is De Place," 2018; "Carry On," 2019; "Splash" (with Nessa Preppy and Travis World), 2020

—Joy Crelin

Joan Roca

Born: February 11, 1964
Occupation: Chef and restaurateur

"Dining is often about the memories of food, the sensory experience and how you will remember it," chef and restaurateur Joan Roca told Antoinette Bruno for *StarChefs* magazine (June 2006).

Indeed, the food served at Roca's restaurant—El Celler de Can Roca in Catalonia—is undoubtedly memorable. Combining traditional Catalan cuisine, local or unusual ingredients, and deftly crafted fragrances and smokes, with innovative techniques, such as sous-vide cooking, El Celler de Can Roca's offerings have earned the restaurant a host of major accolades, including the rare rating of three stars from the prestigious Michelin restaurant guide.

More important to Roca than such honors, however, is his restaurant's place within the Catalonian culinary community and within the context of his own family. Both born into restaurant-industry families, his parents founded the original Can Roca restaurant in the late 1960s, and Roca and his two younger brothers grew up immersed in the culinary world thanks to their influence. El Celler de Can Roca is likewise a family business, employing Roca as chef and brothers Josep and Jordi as sommelier and pastry chef, respectively.

For Roca, his family's lifelong passion for food has been key to the restaurant's success and remains central to the guiding ethos of El Celler de Can Roca. "If you're going to pursue this career, do so because you actually love what you do," he told Kristin Tablang for *Forbes* (27 Sept. 2018) about his perspective. "Don't become too obsessed with accolades, recognitions, or Michelin stars. The main reward is to do what you most enjoy, and everything else will follow."

Photo by Vadorgarbos via Wikimedia Commons

EARLY LIFE AND EDUCATION

Joan Roca i Fontané was born on February 11, 1964, in Girona, in Catalonia, a culturally distinct, semiautonomous region in part of present-day northeastern Spain. He was the first of three sons born to Josep Roca i Pont and Montserrat "Montse" Fontané i Serra. His brother Josep was born when Roca was two, while the youngest, Jordi, was born when Roca was fourteen. In 1967 their parents opened their own homestyle restaurant and bar, Can Roca, in the Taialà-Germans Sàbat neighborhood of Girona, Catalonia. Roca's mother cooked for Can Roca, while his father, a former bus driver, worked in the front of the restaurant. Additionally, Roca was influenced significantly by his paternal grandmother, Angeleta, who ran a bistro.

Roca began working in his parents' restaurant as a child. At first, he helped in the dining room and also learned to cook from his mother. As his brothers grew older, they likewise worked in the restaurant, and all three siblings were exposed to the culinary world throughout their childhoods. "We lived alongside our customers as though they were our friends—part of the family," Roca told María García for an online exhibition on the brothers created by the Spanish Royal Academy of Gastronomy and Google Arts & Culture. "We saw our parents working happily and making the people who came to our place happy too. It was the same as it is now: a community bar for hardworking people, with a good, honest menu."

By the time he was ten Roca had decided that he wanted to become a chef and pursued a formal culinary education as a young adult, attending the Institut Escola d'Hostaleria i Turisme de Girona (the School of Hospitality and Tourism of Girona). While his early experiences at Can Roca had granted him a great deal of hands-on experience, he found a more traditional educational experience to be valuable as well. He told Bruno, "You learn faster if you have an academic base." After completing his program in 1983, Roca taught there for a time. He would go on to be awarded an honorary doctorate from the University of Girona in 2010.

EL CELLER DE CAN ROCA

In the mid-1980s Roca and his brother Josep, who had also studied at the Girona hospitality school, set out to open their own restaurant in a space next to their parents' Can Roca. Named El Celler de Can Roca, the restaurant opened in August 1986 with Roca as the chef and Josep as head of the dining room, a position that would evolve into that of sommelier. Their younger brother, Jordi, joined the business around 1998, ultimately becoming the restaurant's pastry chef. Much like the restaurants operated by Roca's parents and grandparents, El Celler de Can Roca was at heart a family business that derived its success in large part from the collaborations among the three brothers, or the "commitment to creativity and innovation—to turning our passion into our profession, which joins us three," as Roca told Tablang.

Though business was slow at first, El Celler de Can Roca became a successful part of Girona's culinary scene in the late 1980s. Roca himself spent a brief period training under acclaimed chefs such as Georges Blanc and Ferran Adrià in France and Spain, respectively, bringing new ideas back to El Celler. El Celler went on to gain international renown in 1995, when the restaurant was featured in the prestigious Michelin restaurant guide for Spain and awarded the rating of one star—indicating gastronomic excellence—for the first time.

El Celler evolved significantly over the 1990s, during which time Roca and his colleagues bought an additional building, a former country home, that they named Torre de Can Sunyer, which they ran as a banquet hall for a time. They undertook significant renovations, and in 2007 the main restaurant moved into the former Sunyer building—which now encompassed a sizeable kitchen, a forty-five-seat dining room, and a wine cellar capable of housing sixty thousand bottles.

In addition to expanding its facilities, the restaurant increased its worldwide recognition during the first decade of the twenty-first century. It earned two Michelin stars for the first time in 2002 and its first three-star rating, the highest possible, in 2009. Among other honors, El Celler was named the best restaurant in the world by the World's 50 Best Restaurant awards program in both 2013 and 2015.

Though pleased with his international reception of the restaurant, Roca typically prefers to highlight the business's food and culinary point of view rather than its accolades. "I'm more focused on the sustainability of the restaurant than achievements," he explained to Lauren Hill for the magazine *Elite Traveler* (15 May 2019). "I'm proud that El Celler de Can Roca is still family-run and that we are able to share our passion."

CULINARY APPROACH

Over more than three decades of operation, El Celler has developed a unique culinary point of view that reflects Roca and his brothers' childhood influences as well as Roca's formal culinary training and interest in innovative culinary techniques. The menu has incorporated dishes inspired by traditional Catalan cuisine, such as those served by Roca's mother at Can Roca over four decades, as well as items emphasizing local ingredients, such as locally produced olive oil. Roca is also known for his use of the sous-vide technique, a slow-cooking method in which ingredients are vacuum-sealed, often using plastic,

and then cooked by being immersed in water that is kept at a consistent temperature.

Some dishes devised by Roca and dessert items created by pastry chef Jordi fall within the domain of molecular gastronomy, incorporating elements such as fragrances and smokes. The process of creating such menu items is intensely collaborative, reflecting the spirit of collaboration that pervades the operations of El Celler. "We bring people together from different disciplines to create thorough research and experiments," Roca explained to Hill. "Sometimes a botanist will show us a new plant; sometimes we succeed in distilling a new essence. The team brings us these ideas, sparking our creativity."

EL CELLER ON TOUR

In 2014, Roca and his brothers began the ambitious endeavor of taking El Celler on an international tour. "We'd received a lot of interesting offers to open restaurants at various latitudes and while it was very tempting to think about being in the world like that, to us, it didn't mean much to open a restaurant that we couldn't actually be at. The restaurant is located where the team is located, and that's when the idea of a travelling Celler came about," he explained to Sorrel Moseley-Williams for *Departures* magazine (July 2015). In partnership with the banking company BBVA, Roca, his brothers, and nearly forty staff members traveled to the United States, Mexico, Colombia, and Peru in the attempt to bring the experience of dining at El Celler to new diners. In addition to showcasing the restaurant's culinary point of view, Roca and his colleagues sought to highlight local ingredients and cuisines while on tour, a goal that at times required additional research and travel prior to arriving in a country.

Traveling in a large group and to multiple countries over more than a month proved challenging for Roca and his colleagues, as did the process of adjusting to working in new locales. He told Moseley-Williams, "At home, we're used to having a kitchen that suits our needs. On tour we have to adapt to the kitchen, the culture, to schedules . . . but it means we've developed a vast capacity to adapt."

Roca, his brothers, and their staff returned to that rewarding challenge twice more. In 2015, they took the touring restaurant to cities in the United States, Argentina, and Turkey. El Celler went on a third tour in 2016, visiting the United States, Hong Kong, the United Kingdom, and Chile. Portions of the restaurant's tours went on to be chronicled in the documentary *Cooking Up a Tribute*, which premiered at the Berlin International Film Festival in 2015.

OTHER VENTURES

In addition to El Celler, Roca for a time oversaw the restaurant Roca Moo at Barcelona's Hotel Omm. "I consulted on the whole thing, from design to dishes," he told Bruno in 2006. He explained that he visited the restaurant intermittently during its years of operation and trained the teams of employees sent to that location, although he did not serve as its chef.

The Roca restaurant business has also expanded to encompass other ventures, including the catering service and banquet space Mas Marroch, the artisanal ice cream parlor Rocambolesc, and a sous-vide home-cooking project called Rocook. In January 2020, Roca and his brothers announced plans to open a tapas bar called Boca Seca in Girona. Then in February, they established the chocolate-themed project Casa Cacao, encompassing a chocolate café as well as a boutique hotel run by Roca's wife. That June, the brothers also launched a Sustainable Gastronomy project with BBVA, for which they would select local, seasonal ingredients and create a recipe for monthly subscribers to receive, along with fresh produce, to make their own two-person meals at home.

Alongside his culinary work, Roca has published several books. Among them were *La Cocina al Vacio* (*The Vacuum Kitchen*) (2003), a text on sous-vide cooking coauthored with chef Salvador Brugués, and *El Celler de Can Roca* (2013), a cookbook cowritten with his brothers.

PERSONAL LIFE

Roca is married to Anna Payet, a hospitality professional who has worked for El Celler and partnered with his brother Jordi on Casa Cacao. Roca and Payet have a son, Marc (b. ca. 1997), and a daughter, Marina (b. ca. 2003). In his spare time, he enjoys eating at his parents' restaurant, biking with his daughter, and playing tennis with his son.

SUGGESTED READING

García, María. "The Roca Brothers: Cooking as the Language of Storytelling." *Google Arts & Culture*, artsandculture.google.com/exhibit/the-roca-brothers-cooking-as-the-language-of-storytelling-real-academia-de-gastronomia-espa%C3%B1ola/0QKSu74hxfYxLQ?hl=en. Accessed 9 Aug. 2020.

Hill, Lauren. "Joan Roca on Keeping El Celler de Can Roca at the Top." *Elite Traveler*, 15 May 2019, www.elitetraveler.com/finest-dining/top-100-restaurants-in-the-world-old/joan-roca-el-celler-de-can-roca. Accessed 9 Aug. 2020.

Jenkins, Allan. "Joan Roca: The No 1 Chef in the World." *The Guardian*, 19 Oct. 2013, www.theguardian.com/lifeandstyle/2013/oct/19/joan-roca-number-one-chef-in-world. Accessed 10 Aug. 2020.

Roca, Joan. "Eating Off Duty with Chef Joan Roca." Interview with Marisel Salazar. *Michelin Guide*, 26 Mar. 2019, guide.michelin.com/us/en/washington/washington-dc/article/dining-out/chef-joan-roca-favorite-food-restaurants. Accessed 9 Aug. 2020.

———. "Interview with Chef Joan Roca of El Celler de Can Roca—Girona, Spain." Interview by Antoinette Bruno. *StarChefs*, June 2006, www.starchefs.com/cook/interview/interview-chef-joan-roca-el-celler-de-can-roca-%E2%80%93-girona-spain. Accessed 9 Aug. 2020.

———. "The Rocas World Tour." Interview by Sorrel Moseley-Williams. *Departures*, July 2015, departures-international.com/food-drink/personalities/chef-roca-brothers-tour-2015-interview. Accessed 9 Aug. 2020.

Tablang, Kristin. "How Michelin-Starred Chef Joan Roca Continues to Elevate Fine Dining." *Forbes*, 27 Sept. 2018, www.forbes.com/sites/kristintablang/2018/09/27/how-el-celler-de-can-rocas-head-chef-joan-roca-continues-to-elevate-fine-dining/#66f495841733. Accessed 9 Aug. 2020.

—Joy Crelin

Joe Rogan

Date of birth: August 11, 1967
Occupation: Comedian and commentator

Joe Rogan is a comedian and Ultimate Fighting Championship (UFC) color commentator who rose to prominence in the 1990s and early 2000s. He has become best known as the host of *The Joe Rogan Experience*, one of the most popular podcasts in the world. Rogan launched the podcast, the second-most downloaded show on Apple Podcasts in 2017 and 2018, as a free-flowing conversation with fellow comedian Brian Redban in 2009. Early guests were representative of some of Rogan's pet interests, including comedy, self-improvement, cage-fighting, and the science of psychedelic drugs. He has since gained a cult-like following, eager for Rogan's blend of comedic commentary and quasi-intellectualizing. Despite his roster of impressive guests—among them astrophysicist Neil DeGrasse Tyson, Democratic presidential candidate Bernie Sanders, Twitter founder Jack Dorsey, and National Security Agency (NSA) whistleblower Edward Snowden—Rogan, a friendly, regular guy, has been the real draw. Happy to oblige his fans, Rogan has put out as many as five episodes a week, many nearly three hours long. Rogan's influence has been real: In 2019 alone, he single-handedly jump-started the presidential campaign of outlier Democratic

Photo by Michael S. Schwartz/Getty Images

EARLY LIFE AND FIGHTING CAREER

Joseph James Rogan was born in Newark, New Jersey, on August 11, 1967. His father, Joseph, was a cop who was abusive. When Rogan was five years old, his parents divorced, and he moved with his free-living mother to San Francisco when he was seven. She remarried a man with a similarly open lifestyle; Rogan recalls that he first smoked pot with his stepfather when he was eight. Later, the family moved to Newton Upper Falls, Massachusetts, a small village outside of Boston. Describing his young self to Erik Hedegaard for *Rolling Stone* (22 Oct. 2015), Rogan said, "I was terrified of being a loser. Super-terrified of being someone who people just go, 'Oh, look at that f—ing loser.' You know? I was always thinking that the other kids were going to turn on me at any moment." After a bully humiliated him in a fight, Rogan took up karate at age fourteen. He progressed quickly, winning the US Open Taekwondo Championships five years later. It was a significant accomplishment, meaning that he claimed the lightweight title and went on to beat the middle and heavyweight titleholders as well. He was also the Massachusetts full-contact taekwondo champion for four consecutive years. Rogan suggests that were it not for taekwondo, his life, given the violent inclinations fostered by his father, could have followed a darker path. "Martial arts was definitely the best vehicle for me to develop my human potential," he told Ryan Schneider for *Black Belt* magazine (Dec. 2002). Rogan continues to practice martial arts, but he quit competing when he was twenty-one because he was concerned about sustaining serious head injuries.

EARLY COMEDY CAREER AND *NEWSRADIO*

Rogan briefly attended the University of Massachusetts in Boston but dropped out before graduating. He worked a number of odd jobs, teaching martial arts and delivering newspapers. He was also hired to drive a private investigator, unable to drive because of a DUI, to stakeouts. Rogan took up comedy in 1988, after performing at an open-mic night on a dare. He started out gigging at bachelor parties and strip clubs, working his way up to comedy clubs. He relocated to New York City and landed a spot on MTV's *Half-Hour Comedy Hour*, which led to a role on a Fox sitcom in 1994 called *Hardball*, about a baseball team. Rogan had never acted before but approached the task with the same attitude with which he had approached stand-up: the pressure of performing was nothing compared to the life-or-death stakes of fighting. *Hardball* was canceled before the end of its first season. Rogan then moved to Los Angeles, and in 1995 he was cast in *NewsRadio*, a successful NBC comedy series about a news radio station starring Dave Foley, Stephen Root, and Phil Hartman. Rogan played Joe Garrelli, the station's electrician and

candidate Andrew Yang and sent stocks for the electric car company Tesla tumbling after CEO Elon Musk smoked a joint on the show. (Rogan and his guests often smoke marijuana during interviews; the show is taped in California, where pot is legal.)

Rogan has the ear of millions, which makes his willingness to entertain a very wide spectrum of guests—including controversial figures like conspiracy theorist Alex Jones and anti-vaccine fitness guru Ben Greenfield—troubling to some. Rogan is known for his libertarian leanings and for siding with those who say political correctness in the United States has gone too far in terms of curbing free speech. In a critical article about Rogan for *Slate* (21 Mar. 2019), Justin Peters wrote that Rogan's "personal politics are a bit hard to nail down." His views tend to be left of center, though he dislikes identity politics (a theme he has returned to again and again), and he appeals to many on the libertarian right. Peters went on to describe Rogan, a teen taekwondo champion-turned-comedian, as the "Larry King of the Intellectual Dark Web," referring to the veteran CNN interviewer and a recent term coined to describe a group of public personalities formed in opposition to political correctness—many of whom, such as conservative commentator Ben Shapiro and Canadian psychologist and antifeminist Jordan Peterson, have appeared on Rogan's show. Rogan seems surprised by this transformation and his podcast's astounding success. "It's an accident," Rogan told author Sam Harris, as quoted by Peters. "I just stuck with it. Stumbled upon it. And kept going. I'm good at that."

handyman. He was a series regular until the show ended in 1999.

FEAR FACTOR AND UFC

In 2001, Rogan became the host of the new NBC reality television show *Fear Factor*, in which contestants completed gross or dangerous challenges to win money. The show, which ended in 2006, became a queasy cultural touchstone as millions tuned in to watch contestants submerge themselves in a pit of live rats, or eat raw sheep's eyes. The show was canceled after its ratings began to dip; Rogan returned to host the reboot in 2011, though the show was quickly canceled again after blowback from an episode in which contestants were asked to drink donkey semen. Meanwhile, Rogan continued to pursue his passion for martial arts. In 1997, he became a backstage interviewer for the Ultimate Fighting Championship (UFC), a mixed martial arts promotion company. At the time, the UFC was still a small-time operation. "I was talking to people at work and they would act like I was doing porn," Rogan recalled to a reporter for *Sports Illustrated* (21 Apr. 2012). "I was on a sitcom and flying all over the country on the weekends doing these cage shows." (Mixed martial arts (MMA) fights take place in an octagonal ring that looks like a cage.) Rogan quit after a couple of years because his pay was not enough to cover the cost of his travel to fights.

In 2002, the UFC's new president, Dana White, convinced Rogan to serve as a cage-side commentator in exchange for free tickets to fights. Soon, he was on the payroll. "The thing about Rogan is, when you watch him call a fight, you know he knows what he's talking about and loves what he's talking about," White told Hedegaard. "The man is passionate." In addition to his job with the UFC, Rogan continues to perform stand-up. In 2007, he famously accused fellow comic Carlos Mencia of plagiarism, winning support from other comics. He also appeared in two Kevin James–helmed comedies: *Zookeeper* (2011) and *Here Comes the Boom* (2012), about cage-fighting. In 2016, he released his first Netflix comedy special, *Triggered*. In 2018, he released his second, called *Strange Times*.

THE JOE ROGAN EXPERIENCE

Rogan and fellow comedian Redban recorded their first episode of *The Joe Rogan Experience* on December 24, 2009. It was charmingly low tech. Rogan and Redban struggled with their audio equipment and how to maintain a clear picture on their video stream. Rogan answered real-time feedback from fans. In many ways, it set the tone for what the podcast would become: friendly, candid, an open forum for regular people—most of them male. Though the production has improved, the *Joe Rogan Experience* remains, in spirit, the opposite of slick. Guests sit at Rogan's table smoking pot and sipping whiskey, holding forth on a variety of subjects.

Rogan has always seen himself as a truth-teller. In a 2002 profile of Rogan for *Black Belt* magazine, journalist Schneider wrote that Rogan, in a set at the famed Comedy Store in Hollywood, criticized the Bush administration for using the terrorist attacks in 2001 as an excuse to crack down on the rights of US citizens. "There's so many things I talk about in stand-up comedy that most people wouldn't," he told Schneider. "I'm not afraid of reality or pointing out things that people normally put in the dark closets of their minds." Rogan does not always differentiate, ethically or empirically, among the items found in this dark closet of the mind. Early in the show's run he expressed support for conspiracy theories involving the US moon landings and the collapse of a particular World Trade Center building on September 11, 2001. He has since walked back some of these opinions, but his feeling about expressing them remains the same: "What I'm willing to do is look stupid," he said in one 2014 episode, as quoted by Peters. "And by talking about things and saying, 'That'"—World Trade Center building 7—"'looks like a controlled demolition,' I know that puts you in the nutter camp. But I'm not saying it's a controlled demolition." He instead advocated "being willing to debate it."

The quote illustrates why Rogan's podcast is so controversial: he is willing to entertain all views, no matter how ridiculous or even dangerous they may be in the view of observers such as *Slate*'s Peters. Further, as he is not a journalist, Rogan feels no particular responsibility to challenge guests like Alex Jones, who is known for trafficking in disinformation, such as the idea that the US government was behind the 9/11 attacks, or that vaccines cause autism. Although he has hosted prominent Democrats and people from across the political and cultural spectrum, Rogan's willingness to give a platform to people like Jones and far-right commentator Gavin McInnes has colored Rogan's reputation as a public figure.

PERSONAL LIFE

Rogan married his longtime girlfriend, Jessica Ditzel, in 2009. Together they have two daughters; Rogan is the stepfather to Ditzel's older daughter from a previous relationship. They live in Los Angeles.

SUGGESTED READING

"Comedian Rogan the Perfect, and Unlikely, Voice for UFC's Broadcasts." *Sports Illustrated*, 21 Apr. 2012, www.si.com/mma/2012/04/21/joe-roganufc. Accessed 11 Nov. 2019.

Hedegaard, Erik. "How Joe Rogan Went from UFC Announcer to 21st-Century Timothy Leary." *Rolling Stone*, 22 Oct. 2015, www.

rollingstone.com/culture/culture-features/
how-joe-rogan-went-from-ufc-announcer-
to-21st-century-timothy-leary-182319/.   Accessed 10 Nov. 2019.

Peters, Justin. "Joe Rogan's Galaxy Brain." *Slate*,
21 Mar. 2019, slate.com/culture/2019/03/
joe-rogans-podcast-is-an-essential-platform-
for-freethinkers-who-hate-the-left.html.   Accessed 10 Nov. 2019.

Schneider, Ryan. "Joe Rogan Owes His Success
to Taekwondo, Thai Boxing and Brazilian Jiu
Jitsu." *Black Belt*, Dec. 2002, blackbeltmag.
com/arts/grappling-mma/joe-rogan-owes-his-
success-to-taekwondo-thai-boxing-and-brazil-
ian-jiu-jitsu. Accessed 10 Nov. 2019.
—*Molly Hagan*

Photo by Austin Miller via Wikimedia Commons

Matt Ross-Spang

Date of birth: January 14, 1987
Occupation: Record producer

When recording engineer and record producer Matt Ross-Spang turned fourteen years old, his parents gave him a gift that dramatically altered the course of his life and career: two hours of recording time at the famed Sun Studio in Memphis, Tennessee. Although the guitar and drum recording Ross-Spang and a friend made during their visit proved largely unsalvageable, the young musician was drawn to the work being performed by the studio's engineer, James Lott. "A lot of people get captured by sound. I wasn't captured by sound at that point, but when I watched him manipulate the sound, I was like 'You can do all of that?'" Ross-Spang recalled to Joe Boone for the *Memphis Flyer* (29 May 2014). Upon returning to the studio as an intern two years later, he began what became a more than a decade-long career at the legendary studio, eventually taking on the roles of lead engineer and operations manager during his time there. Although Ross-Spang left Sun Studio in 2015 to work independently, he remained deeply tied to his home city's music industry, engineering and producing numerous acclaimed albums out of Sam Phillips Recording in Memphis. "Memphis, in general, is the place that people are coming to do the one 'funky' track that ends up being the best track on the record," he explained to Larry Crane for *Tape Op* (Jan./Feb. 2017). For many artists, Ross-Spang played an essential role in giving their work that character, a role for which he received widespread recognition, as well as two Grammy Awards.

EARLY LIFE AND EDUCATION

Matthew R. Ross-Spang was born in Memphis, Tennessee, on January 14, 1987. One of two children born to Carol and Mike Ross-Spang, he has a sister named Allison. His mother worked in human resources, and his father worked as a personal trainer. Ross-Spang grew up near Memphis, Tennessee, and attended Germantown High School. Having developed an interest in music at a young age, he learned to play guitar and formed a music duo with a friend while in his early teens, although he had little confidence in his ability to build a career in the music industry. "I loved playing guitar, but I always knew, deep down, that I'd never be a great guitar player," he told Crane. "I just like being a good rhythm guy."

Ross-Spang's interest in music ran in the family: during his teen years, his cousin served as president of Sun Studio, a recording venue renowned among both musicians and Memphis's music-focused tourists. Founded in 1950 by record producer and engineer Sam Phillips, the studio gained significant fame in the 1950s and 1960s for recording many of the era's pioneering country, blues, and rock and roll artists, including Johnny Cash, B. B. King, Elvis Presley, and Jerry Lee Lewis. Phillips later sold the studio and departed to found Sam Phillips Recording Service. Sun Studio eventually shut down before being reopened in the 1980s. By the beginning of the twenty-first century, Sun Studio was functioning as both an active recording studio and a tourist attraction, hosting tours during the day and recording sessions in the evening.

For Ross-Spang's fourteenth birthday, his parents gave him the gift of two hours of recording time at Sun Studio, during which the young guitarist and his musical collaborator made a recording that Ross-Spang would later describe to Boone as "god awful." Although the experience further solidified his belief that he was not cut out to be a professional performer, he found himself intrigued and inspired by studio recording engineer James Lott. "He had a beret, cussed and smoked like a sailor," Ross-Spang told Marissa R. Moss for *Rolling Stone* (17 Dec. 2018). "He was this cartoon character, and treated us like we deserved to be there when we totally didn't. I never saw myself as a hotshot guitar player, but when I saw him working the board I thought, 'Holy s——, I want to do that.'" Drawn to a career in music engineering, Ross-Spang hoped to return to Sun Studio in a professional capacity later in life, a goal he was able to meet only two years later.

WORKING AT SUN STUDIO

Ross-Spang returned to Sun Studio as an intern at the age of sixteen. In that role, he was responsible for contributing to multiple aspects of the studio's operations, including both its functions as a tourist attraction and its recording business. The studio's unique dual purpose presented a host of challenges to its employees: for instance, the daily tours required regular movement of instruments and equipment and necessitated frequent tuning of instruments such as the studio's piano. "It would be tuned for a session, but the constant flow of fifty or so tourists every hour would swing the temperature in the room and the piano would go out of tune before the session started!" he explained to Crane. Ross-Spang learned a great deal during his early days at the recording studio, which at the time was home largely to equipment brought in upon the studio's reopening in the 1980s. "They had a lot of 80s kinds of equipment; like an 80s home studio with a really big Soundcraft board. . . . There was a big two-inch machine that was basically an ashtray, and not a lot of great mics. But we had a great room," he told Crane. "I didn't know anything about gear when I started. I feel very fortunate to have learned on something like that."

After serving as an intern for several years, learning skills in both customer service and music production, Ross-Spang officially joined Sun Studio as the studio's main engineer in 2010. He also served as operations manager for the Memphis institution. In his role as engineer, Ross-Spang worked on albums by numerous artists, including David Brookings, Chris Isaak, Grace Potter & the Nocturnals, Grand Marquis, and the Howlin' Brothers. He also assisted lesser-known and even amateur musicians who came to Sun Studio specifically to fulfill their dreams of recording at the studio that had once recorded some of American music's mid-twentieth century greats.

In addition to working with recording artists, Ross-Spang dedicated himself to stocking the studio with equipment similar to the pieces that had been present during Phillips's day, including a 1930s mixing console, a 1940s lathe for cutting records, and period-appropriate microphones. That task was a difficult one, as few photographs had been taken of the interior of the studio during its 1950s heyday. Nevertheless, Ross-Spang researched the original studio extensively and sought out appropriate pieces of equipment on the online auction site eBay after consulting with music professionals who had visited the studio decades before. "To this day, I think my X-Men ability is that if I need something and I think about it hard enough, it pops up on eBay," he joked to Boone.

SOMETHING MORE THAN FREE

In 2015, music producer Dave Cobb contacted Ross-Spang with an opportunity. Planning to produce musician Jason Isbell's upcoming album *Something More Than Free*, Cobb asked Ross-Spang to travel to Nashville, Tennessee, for a month and serve as the album's engineer. Ross-Spang hoped to take a monthlong absence from Sun Studio to take that opportunity, but the studio's management was unwilling to allow him to take that time off. Determined to work on the album, Ross-Spang quit his job, leaving Sun Studio to begin his career as an independent engineer and producer.

The move proved to be a beneficial one for Ross-Spang, who enjoyed himself and built multiple strong working relationships during his time in Nashville. "Dave is from Georgia, Jason is from Alabama, and I'm from Memphis," he explained to Moss. "We all come from the same musical place, and we all have the same heroes. It was a magical month." For his work on *Something More Than Free*, Ross-Spang shared the 2015 Grammy Award for Best Americana Album. After the album's success, he continued to collaborate extensively with Cobb, who hired Ross-Spang to engineer many of the albums he produced.

INDEPENDENT CAREER

After leaving Sun Studio, Ross-Spang established himself as an independent engineer who worked primarily out of Studio B at Sam Phillips Recording, another twenty-first-century incarnation of a studio founded by Phillips decades before. Also serving at times as a producer, he opened the production company Southern Grooves. Having demonstrated his abilities as an engineer with the critically acclaimed *Something More Than Free*, Ross-Spang gained further attention for his work as engineer, mixer, and producer for the 2016 album *Midwest Farmer's Daughter*, the solo debut of country musician Margo Price, which had been recorded prior to his departure from Sun Studio. He then worked on Price's second album, *All American Made* (2017).

In addition to his work with Price, Ross-Spang made a name for himself with a number of other major projects after launching his independent career. Prominent among these was *Way Down in the Jungle Room* (2016), a collection of previously unreleased Elvis Presley recordings for which Ross-Spang served as mixer. "I never imagined I'd ever get to work with Elvis," he said in an interview for the Elvis-focused website the *Memphis Flash* (30 Sept. 2016). "It was really great surprise and a dream come true . . . not to mention very heavy."

Ross-Spang then collaborated with Isbell and his band, the 400 Unit, on the album *The Nashville Sound* (2017), for which he served as engineer. The project earned Ross-Spang a second Grammy Award for Best America Album, an honor that he appreciated but considered far less significant than the strength of the work itself. "Obviously the Grammy is an amazing award and doesn't hurt, but I think what people are more drawn to are the records," he told Bob Mehr for *Memphis Commercial Appeal* (31 Jan. 2018). "I've gotten a lot of work based on the Isbell records and especially the Margo (Price) records. People are big fans of that stuff and the sound, and so they call me."

Ross-Spang continued to produce and engineer various records, working with artists such as the Mountain Goats and Eli "Paperboy" Reed. He received particular attention for his work with legendary singer-songwriter John Prine, for whom he engineered the 2018 album *The Tree of Forgiveness*.

PERSONAL LIFE

Ross-Spang credited his hometown of Memphis with inspiring his music career. "If I had been born anywhere else I wouldn't be doing this," he said in an interview, as quoted by Jennifer Velez for the website of the Grammy Awards (22 Mar. 2019). "Memphis has kind of left a big mark on me."

SUGGESTED READING

Boone, Joe. "Sun Studio Makes a Comeback." *Memphis Flyer*, 29 May 2014, www.memphisflyer.com/memphis/sun-studio-makes-a-comeback/Content?oid=3678431. Accessed 9 Feb. 2020.

Mehr, Bob. "Memphian Matt Ross-Spang Nets Second Grammy Award for His Work with Americana Star Jason Isbell." *Memphis Commercial Appeal*, 31 Jan. 2018, www.commercialappeal.com/story/entertainment/music/memphis-music-beat/2018/01/31/grammy-awards-matt-ross-spang-jason-isbell-memphis-nashville-sound/1079159001/. Accessed 9 Feb. 2020.

Moss, Marissa R. "How a Memphis Engineer Became the Secret Weapon for John Prine, Margo Price." *Rolling Stone*, 17 Dec. 2018, www.rollingstone.com/music/music-country/matt-ross-spang-engineer-margo-price-john-prine-769952/. Accessed 9 Feb. 2020.

Ross-Spang, Matt. "Interview with Matt Ross-Spang, Engineer at the Legendary Sun Studio." Interview by Björgvin Benediktsson. *Audio Issues*, www.audio-issues.com/intervews/interview-with-matt-ross-spang-engineer-at-the-legendary-sun-studio/. Accessed 9 Feb. 2020.

——. "Matt Ross-Spang: Eyeing the Future Through the Past." Interview by Larry Crane. *Tape Op*, Jan./Feb. 2017, tapeop.com/interviews/117/matt-ross-spang/. Accessed 9 Feb. 2020.

——. "Way Down in the Jungle Room: Interview with Matt Ross-Spang." *The Memphis Flash*, 30 Sept. 2016, www.memphisflash.de/2016/09/way-down-in-the-jungle-room-interview-with-matt-ross-spang/. Accessed 9 Feb. 2020.

Velez, Jennifer. "Behind the Board: Matt Ross-Spang on Why Memphis Is the Reason He Produces." *Grammy Awards*, 22 Mar. 2019, www.grammy.com/grammys/news/behind-board-matt-ross-spang-why-memphis-reason-he-produces. Accessed 9 Feb. 2020.

—*Joy Crelin*

Maya Rudolph

Date of birth: July 27, 1972
Occupation: Actor and comedian

"I like comedy as a group sport," actor and comedian Maya Rudolph told Terry Gross for the National Public Radio (NPR) program *Fresh Air* (8 Mar. 2012). Indeed, Rudolph's career as a whole reflects her collaborative spirit, first honed at the prestigious Groundlings Theater in Los Angeles and further developed on *Saturday Night Live*. Over the course of her seven-year tenure as a regular cast member, she showcased her strengths, including performing impressions and embodying original characters, and built creative relationships that would remain highly productive in the years following her departure from the show. She went on to costar in films such as *Bridesmaids* (2011) and *Wine Country* (2019), as well as a host of television projects that often featured former SNL colleagues. "I'm used to working with people, great people. And when you know their voices, you have so much fun writing for their voices," Rudolph told Gross. "I personally think it's a more enjoyable way to play."

professionals. There she was friends with Jack Black and Gwyneth Paltrow, who would both go on to their own successful acting careers. As a child and teenager, Rudolph developed a passion for comedy and dreamed of being hired as a cast member on *SNL*, hoping to follow in the footsteps of her personal hero, the comedian Gilda Radner. In addition to comedy, she was also interested in music.

After graduating from high school in 1990, Rudolph enrolled in Porter College, part of the University of California at Santa Cruz, to study photography. She earned her bachelor's degree from the institution in 1995.

MUSIC AND COMEDY

Having played in a band called Supersauce while in college, Rudolph continued to work in music following her graduation. "Music is such a natural part of me, it was something that I always did. So a gig came up, and then it became a job, and the next thing I knew I was just out of college and I thought, All right, I'll do music, because it's the one thing I can do easily without ever worrying about it," she explained to Sischy and Versace. Rudolph joined the band the Rentals as a keyboardist and background vocalist and accompanied the band on tour, during which they served as an opening act for several prominent music groups.

Still drawn to the world of comedy, Rudolph also began to study improvisational (improv) comedy at the Groundlings Theater. One of the United States' most prominent improv organizations, the Los Angeles–based Groundlings had produced numerous *SNL* performers and other famed comedians and comedic actors. In light of her demonstrated musical talents and with the encouragement of her teachers at the theater, Rudolph at times incorporated singing into her work. That skill would remain a key comedic tool for Rudolph during her years on *SNL*. She also pursued acting work during the late 1990s, appearing in television series such as *Chicago Hope* and *City of Angels* as well as in minor parts in films such as *Gattaca* (1997) and *As Good as It Gets* (1997).

SATURDAY NIGHT LIVE

During her time in Los Angeles, Rudolph was scouted by *SNL* writers, including Tina Fey, who invited her to audition for the show. Although she did not attend an in-person audition, her impressive demo reel secured her a spot as a featured player. Over the subsequent years, Rudolph established herself as a full member of the sketch show's repertory ensemble and a key contributor to the high-profile program, which was notorious for its challenging schedule and the demands it placed on its cast members and writing staff. "It was literally my everything," she recalled to Weaver. "My baby and my husband

Photo by Amy Sussman/Getty Images

EARLY LIFE AND EDUCATION

Maya Khabira Rudolph was born on July 27, 1972, in Gainesville, Florida. She and her older brother were the children of Richard Rudolph, a songwriter and music producer, and Minnie Riperton, a singer who would become best known for her song "Lovin' You," a number-one hit single in 1975. For Rudolph, the experience of having well-known parents was at times a challenging one. "When I was a kid, and people would come up to me or stare at me because of my mom, I didn't like it. I really didn't like it," she told Caity Weaver for the *New York Times Magazine* (14 Sept. 2018). "I used to think, Oh, they're staring at my hair, because it's so big and ugly. Because I didn't realize people were just staring at my mother, like, 'Wow, that's her daughter!' I didn't know; I was a kid. And kids always personalize things." As young children, Rudolph and her brother traveled with their parents while they toured the United States. The family eventually settled in Los Angeles, California, where the children continued to live with their father following Riperton's death from cancer in 1979.

"Growing up in LA, you're a city kid, but it's a company town," Rudolph told Ingrid Sischy and Donatella Versace—the latter of whom she portrayed in various *SNL* sketches—in a 2002 interview for *Interview* magazine (20 Feb. 2013). "It's like living in the town where there's a steel mill and everybody works for the mill. It becomes part of your consciousness, whether you realize it or not." Rudolph attended the Crossroads School for Arts and Sciences, a private college prep school in Santa Monica, California, attended by many children of entertainment all at once. I cared about it more than my laundry or my food, which—neither were being well taken care of. I gave all my energy to that show. Plus you're creating a new show every week, so it was just really intense—in a good way. In a way that I liked."

Rudolph played a host of original characters to meet the needs of the show's sketches, and many became very popular with fans. However, she also became particularly known for her spot-on impressions of a wide variety of celebrities, including singer Whitney Houston, television personality Oprah Winfrey, reality-television star Paris Hilton, and poet Maya Angelou. At times, the experience of portraying a real person was an awkward one. As Rudolph recalled to Carrie Clifford in an interview for *Believer* (1 Nov. 2015), one particular show required her to reprise her recurring impression of the singer Beyoncé while her group Destiny's Child was itself making a guest appearance. Although the initial idea for the sketch called for Beyoncé to appear in the sketch alongside Rudolph's version, that plan did not come to fruition. "She was sick apparently and said, [slipping into Beyoncé] "No, I'm not coming," Rudolph told Clifford. "So I was doing Beyoncé while Beyoncé was backstage, watching the show. It was very uncomfortable."

Although she enjoyed her time on *SNL* and considered extending her contract to remain with the show, Rudolph left to focus on other priorities in 2007. She would later make numerous guest appearances in sketches over the years. In addition, she hosted an episode of *SNL* in 2012, for which she was later nominated for the Emmy Award for outstanding guest actress in a comedy series.

BRIDESMAIDS

Throughout her years at *SNL* Rudolph continued to work in film, appearing in projects such as *50 First Dates* (2004) and *A Prairie Home Companion* (2006). Following her departure from the show she remained active in both movies and television, with roles in films such as *Away We Go* (2009), the SNL sketch–based *MacGruber* (2010), and *Grown Ups* (2010). A key point in Rudolph's career came in 2011, when she costarred in the comedy film *Bridesmaids* as part of an ensemble cast that also included fellow *SNL* cast member Kristen Wiig. Due to the film's largely female cast and use of forms of comedy more stereotypically associated with male comedians, *Bridesmaids* became the focus of a widespread media discussion regarding women in comedy. However, Rudolph and her colleagues objected to this to some degree. "We weren't making a 'women's movie.' We were making a story, and we're all women in it," she told Kate Erbland for *IndieWire* (8 May 2019).

Bridesmaids proved extremely popular among viewers and was also a critical success, earning a nomination for the Academy Award for best original screenplay. In some ways it signaled the start of a new era for Rudolph, who would go on to appear in numerous films over the subsequent years. She also had television roles in shows such as the comedy series *Up All Night* and the 2016 variety series *Maya & Marty*, which also starred former *SNL* performer Martin Short.

SCRIPTED PROJECTS

Alongside her appearances on screen, Rudolph became a prolific voice actor. She contributed to animated series such as *The Simpsons* and films like *Turbo* (2013), *Strange Magic* (2015), and *The Emoji Movie* (2017). A supporting voice actor for the 2014 animated Disney film *Big Hero Six*, she reprised her role in episodes of the television spinoff *Big Hero 6: The Series* beginning in 2017. That year also saw the debut of the streaming service Netflix's original series *Big Mouth*, an animated sitcom focusing on a group of middle schoolers and the so-called hormone monsters—one voiced by Rudolph—who pester them.

In 2018, Rudolph debuted another Netflix project, the live-action series *Forever*. She also returned to broadcast television as a guest star in the sitcom *The Good Place*. Rudolph went on to be nominated for two consecutive Emmy Awards for outstanding guest actress for her work in *The Good Place*, in which she plays an immortal judge tasked with determining the fate of the series' protagonists.

In 2019 Rudolph costarred in *Wine Country*, the feature-length directorial debut of fellow actor, comedian, and former *SNL* cast member Amy Poehler. Released on Netflix, *Wine Country* is an ensemble comedy about a group of women who spend a weekend in northern California's Napa Valley. Much like *Bridesmaids*, the release of *Wine Country* stoked media discussion that Rudolph largely disregarded, focusing instead on the opportunity to work with a group of talented and likeminded friends. "Why not make projects with people that are the funniest people you know, and the people that you love, and tell the stories that are funny to you?" she explained to Erbland. "I think when you find the funniest story that you want to tell, that's what makes it funny, other than anything else."

PERSONAL LIFE

Rudolph began dating her longtime partner, director Paul Thomas Anderson, in 2001. They have four children together, and she appeared in his 2014 film *Inherent Vice*. When not filming elsewhere, Rudolph lives in California. She often identifies herself as an avid fan of the Los Angeles Lakers basketball team.

SUGGESTED READING

Erbland, Kate. "Maya Rudolph Reflects on 'Bridesmaids': Why Female-Centric Comedy Became a Surprise Wakeup Call to Hollywood." *IndieWire*, 8 May 2019, www.indiewire.com/2019/05/maya-rudolph-reflects-bridesmaids-female-comedy-1202131970/. Accessed 13 Dec. 2019.

Marine, Brooke. "Maya Rudolph Reveals Why She Calls Paul Thomas Anderson Her 'Husband' Even Though They Are Not Married." *W*, 14 Sept. 2018, www.wmagazine.com/story/maya-rudolph-paul-thomas-anderson-married. Accessed 13 Dec. 2019.

Rudolph, Maya. "An Interview with Maya Rudolph." Interview by Carrie Clifford. *The Believer*, 1 Nov. 2005, believermag.com/an-interview-with-maya-rudolph/. Accessed 13 Dec. 2019.

———. "Interview by Novid Parsi." *Time Out Chicago*, 3 June 2009, www.timeout.com/chicago/film/maya-rudolph-interview. Accessed 13 Dec. 2019.

———. "Maya Rudolph: The *Fresh Air* Interview." Interview by Terry Gross. *NPR*, 8 Mar. 2012, www.npr.org/transcripts/148157572. Accessed 13 Dec. 2019.

———. "New Again: Maya Rudolph." Interview with Ingrid Sischy and Donatella Versace. *Interview*, 20 Feb. 2013, www.interviewmagazine.com/culture/new-again-maya-rudolph. Accessed 13 Dec. 2019.

Weaver, Caity. "How Maya Rudolph Became the Master of Impressions." *The New York Times Magazine*, 14 Sept. 2018, www.nytimes.com/2018/09/14/magazine/maya-rudolph-snl-amazon-forever.html. Accessed 13 Dec. 2019.

SELECTED WORKS

Saturday Night Live, 2000–2007; *Bridesmaids*, 2011; *Friends with Kids*, 2011; *Up All Night*, 2011–12; *Maya & Marty*, 2016; *Big Mouth*, 2017– ; *Forever*, 2018; *The Good Place*, 2018– ; *Wine Country*, 2019

—Joy Crelin

Daniele Rustioni

Born: 1983
Occupation: Conductor

Although those unfamiliar with classical music may believe that a conductor's role is merely to mark the beat for the musicians of an orchestra, conductor Daniele Rustioni refuted that notion to Samantha Janazzo for the Italian American publication *i-Italy* (12 Apr. 2017). "A conductor changes the sound of an orchestra," he noted, citing what he called the "maestro's aura," a method of communicating desired effects to the musicians through body movement, facial expression, and other cues. "Music is a way of transmitting our feelings." It is not even necessary for a conductor to speak the same language as the orchestra, asserted Rustioni, whose work has taken him around the world. In 2017 he became the principal conductor of France's Opéra National de Lyon, and in September 2019 also became chief conductor of the Ulster Orchestra, the only full-time professional symphony orchestra in Northern Ireland. Ultimately, he saw his job as striving "to create a good professional environment, so the orchestra can express themselves," as he explained to Michael Dervan for the *Irish Times* (24 Sept. 2019). "The important realisation is that you need to work with what they offer. You can't be like a teacher in front of a class, I want this, this and this. Of course you need to have your vision and be a leader. But you also need to work with your ear open."

Rising to fame in the classical music world at a relatively young age, over the years Rustioni conducted at such iconic international venues as La Scala, Teatro Regio Torino, London's Royal Opera House, Opernhaus Zürich, Oper Stuttgart, Opéra Bastille in Paris, and New York City's Metropolitan Opera House. His discography includes albums recorded for Sony Classical, Deutsche Grammophon, Opera Rara, and Naxos. Although this meant he often directed musicians far more seasoned than himself, he remained undaunted. "I'm less concerned, even when I go in front of a new and fantastic orchestra, about whether they will like me or not," he told Dervan. "I'm focused more on whether I will serve the music well or not."

EARLY LIFE AND EDUCATION

Daniele Rustioni was born in 1983 in Milan, Italy. His father was a successful businessman with a deep interest in the arts. Rustioni later recalled to interviewers that he frequently woke up to the sounds of his father playing vinyl LPs of Rossini, Beethoven, and Mozart. "I still have a big collection of vinyl, especially historical performances of Italian opera, but I don't often have the chance to listen to them because I am rarely at home," he told an interviewer for the *Guardian*'s Facing the Music column. (13 Feb. 2017). "But I consider these recordings to be some of the most precious things I own."

Rustioni's mother sang in a professional choir, and rather than paying a babysitter when she went to rehearsals, she often took him with her to the church. There, he delighted in sitting near the feet of the organist, quietly listening. "I have all this Bach and church music inside of me," he told Dervan. When he was about five years old, his parents enrolled him at a local Yamaha School, where he studied singing, and by age eight he had joined the boys' choir at Milan's La Scala, a venerable opera house founded in 1778.

Rustioni was active in the choir for almost a decade and would fondly remember performing in the Italian composer's Arrigo Boito's *Mefistofele* (based on the Faust legend). The boys' choir sang in the prologue and epilogue of the piece, and most members left the theater during the two-and-a-half hours in between. By contrast, Rustioni, fascinated by all of the elements that went into mounting a lavish production, perched the whole time on a chair in the wings, where crew members sometimes brought him ice cream to snack on as he watched.

Another highlight of Rustioni's time with the choir came during a production of Mozart's *Die Zauberflöte* (*The Magic Flute*), conducted by the famed Riccardo Muti. Cast as one of the child-spirits in the opera, Rustioni was approached during a rehearsal by Muti, who asked what he wanted to do when he grew up. With little understanding of what being a conductor actually entailed, he blurted out that he was going to conduct one day. Charmed, Muti cautioned him that it was not as easy as it might look and that he would have to seriously study piano and composition for years, at the least.

Taking the advice to heart, Rustioni embarked on a grueling fifteen-year course of study at the Milan Conservatory, where he learned to play organ, piano, violin, and cello (a favorite instrument that he has likened to the human voice). He also took classes in band instrumentation, choral conducting, Gregorian chant, composition, and other such topics. At fourteen he became enamored of Wagner's *Ring Cycle*. He purchased a recording by the New York Metropolitan Opera Orchestra, conducted by James Levine, and his piano teacher lent him the scores, which he dragged home in a large suitcase. He listened to the complete cycle twice in a single week—an intensive experience he later remembered warmly but doubted he would have the stamina or time to repeat as an adult.

FURTHER TRAINING AND EARLY CAREER
Rustioni soon found himself in demand as a pianist in various chamber ensembles, and he was later hired as a *répétiteur* (music tutor) at La Scala. He ultimately decided to focus on orchestral conducting. "It seemed the right continuation of a long musical journey," he told Brittany Lesavoy for the *Glimmerglass Festival* website (6 May 2011). "Breathing together with many talented musicians: that's what inspired me to become a conductor."

Rustioni studied for a time at Accademia Musicale Chigiana, in Siena, Italy, and later decided to continue his education at the Royal Academy of Music, in London. Although he shared a six-person apartment with ten roommates, he considered his two years in England a special time, filled with many opportunities to hone his conducting skills. Thanks to meeting Gianandrea Noseda, then the conductor of the BBC Philharmonic in Manchester, England, he traveled regularly to that city to absorb the older conductor's repertoire. Noseda was at that time also working as the music director at Teatro Regio di Torino (Turin) and he arranged for Rustioni to make his symphonic conducting debut there in 2007, with an all-Mozart program that included Symphonies No. 1 and No. 39. The following year, also in Turin, Rustioni made his operatic debut, conducting Puccini's *La bohème*.

During the 2008–9 season Rustioni was accepted into the Royal Opera House's Jette Parker Young Artist Programme, which supports the development of talented newcomers, who earn salaries and are immersed in the life of the storied venue. He was soon made an assistant conductor under Antonio Pappano and remained in that role for three years, starting in 2009.

Rustioni admitted that being a neophyte conductor had its challenges. "Many conductors at the beginning try to look older. They even speak in front of the orchestra with an artificial voice," he told Dervan. "You just need to be yourself on the podium, and to be honest about what you know and what you don't know. What you can hear with your inner ear. How much music you are able to digest. . . . Then you'll get respect."

DEBUTS AROUND THE WORLD
In 2011 Rustioni worked in the United States for the first time, conducting Luigi Cherubini's *Medea* at the popular Glimmerglass opera festival, held each year in Cooperstown, New York. Praising the production as a "standout," Anthony Tommasini opined for the *New York Times* (2 Aug. 2011) that the "fast-rising Italian conductor" had "led a lean, bracing and elegant performance of this elevated tragic opera."

That same year, Rustioni also became the principal guest conductor of Florence, Italy's Orchestra della Toscana, and he stepped into a permanent role as principal conductor there in 2014. In the interim, in 2013 he was the recipient of the International Opera Award for Best Newcomer of the Year, and, in 2014, he made his Japanese debut, conducting *Madama Butterfly* at the Nikikai Opera. Japanese audiences quickly took to Rustioni, and he would return there to work with such groups as the Osaka Philharmonic, the Kyushu Symphony Orchestra, and the Tokyo Metropolitan Symphony Orchestra.

In 2017 Rustioni made his long-awaited debut at the Metropolitan Opera House. There he conducted a production of Verdi's *Aida*, which David Salazar, in a review for *Opera Wire* (2 Apr. 2017), described as "the best I have heard the

Met Opera Orchestra in 'Aida' in years." Salazar praised Rustioni for "carrying the listener through a truly dramatic adventure that really brought Verdi's detail to life" and wrote, "Perhaps Rustioni's greatest accomplishment on the night was to draw out such wondrous depth from the orchestra without every stealing the spotlight from his cast. If anything, his attention to their subtle gestures was so dedicated that he seemed to push them to another level, offering them exquisite support." Rustioni told Maria Mazzaro for *Opera News* (Sept. 2017) that it was a pleasure to conduct any of Verdi's works. "The connection of words and music reached its highest point with Verdi," he said. "I think, if you love the voice as a conductor, then you can find the colors. . . . It's like finding gold, you know?"

PRINCIPAL CONDUCTOR

Rustioni began his tenure as principal conductor of Opéra National de Lyon during the 2017–18 season, when he conducted Verdi's *Macbeth* and an innovative new staging of Britten's *War Requiem*, among other productions. While at the helm in Lyon, he also appeared in numerous other locales, including Switzerland, England, Scotland, the Netherlands, Austria, Germany, Spain, and Northern Ireland. He told his *Guardian* interviewer that among the most memorable venues in which he worked was the Arena in Verona, Italy, where he conducted such works as *Aida*, *Falstaff*, and Handel's *Messiah*. "The sheer weight of history surrounding us and the audience holding small white candles evoking thousands of fireflies made it magical," he recalled. "There is also a naturally perfect acoustic notwithstanding its majestic vastness."

In September 2019, Rustioni concurrently began serving as chief conductor of the Belfast-based Ulster Orchestra, the only full-time professional symphony orchestra in Northern Ireland. He announced he would step down from the Orchestra della Toscana after the 2019–20 season, making some space in his schedule.

PERSONAL LIFE

Rustioni married the American violinist Francesca Dego in 2015. The two met as students at the Milan Conservatory and sometimes performed and recorded together.

Rustioni has told interviewers that he listens to Bach on a daily basis and that if he could go back in time to any place and moment in musical history, he would choose Vienna in the era of Haydn, Mozart, Beethoven, and Schubert.

SUGGESTED READING

Dervan, Michael. "Ulster Orchestra's New Principal Conductor: 'Opera Was in My DNA.'" *The Irish Times*, 24 Sept. 2019, www.irishtimes.com/culture/music/ulster-orchestra-s-new-principal-conductor-opera-was-in-my-dna-1.4027300. Accessed 13 Apr. 2020.

"Facing the Music: Conductor Daniele Rustioni." *The Guardian*, 13 Feb. 2017, www.theguardian.com/music/2017/feb/13/facing-the-music-conductor-daniele-rustioni. Accessed 13 Apr. 2020.

Lesavoy, Brittany. "Quick Q&A: Daniele Rustioni." *Glimmerglass Festival*, 6 May 2011, glimmerglass.org/2011/05/quick-qa-daniele-rustioni/. Accessed 13 Apr. 2020.

Mazzaro, Maria. "Sound Bites: Daniele Rustioni." *Opera News*, Sept. 2017, www.operanews.com/Opera_News_Magazine/2017/9/Departments/Sound_Bites_%E2%80%94%C2%A0Daniele_Rustioni.html. Accessed 13 Apr. 2020.

Rustioni, Daniele. "Inspiring Interview with 34-year-old Met Maestro Daniele Rustioni." Interview by Samantha Janazzo. *i-Italy*, 12 Apr. 2017, www.iitaly.org/magazine/focus/art-culture/article/inspiring-interview-34-year-old-met-maestro-daniele-rustioni. Accessed 13 Apr. 2020.

Salazar, David. "Aida: Conductor Daniele Rustioni Dominates, Leads Riveting Cast in Memorable Performance." *Opera Wire*, 2 Apr. 2017, operawire.com/metropolitan-opera-2016-17-review-aida-conductor-daniele-rustioni-dominates-leads-riveting-cast-in-memorable-performance/. Accessed 13 Apr. 2020.

Tommasini, Anthony. "A Summer Blizzard at Glimmerglass." *The New York Times*, 2 Aug. 2011, www.nytimes.com/2011/08/03/arts/music/a-new-opera-at-the-glimmerglass-festival.html. Accessed 13 Apr. 2020.

SELECTED WORKS

Daniele Rustioni Conducts Giorgio Federico Ghedini: Orchestral Works, 2016; *Bellini: Adelson e Salvini*, 2017; *Violin Concertos: Paganini 1, Wolf-Ferrari*, 2017; *Goffredo Petrassi: Ouverture da Concerto; Ritratto di Don Chisciotte; Etc.*, 2018; *Alfredo Casella: Concerto per Archi, Pianoforte, Timpani e Batteria; Paganiniana; Scarlattiana*, 2019

—Mari Rich

Marina Rustow

Date of birth: November 11, 1968
Occupation: Historian

Marina Rustow is a social historian of Jewish life during the medieval period, a professor of history and Near Eastern studies at Princeton

University, and the director of the Princeton Geniza Lab. She was awarded a MacArthur Foundation Fellowship in 2015.

EARLY LIFE AND EDUCATION

Born on November 11, 1968, in New York, Marina Rustow grew up on Manhattan's Upper West Side. Her father, Dankwart Rustow, was a university professor and renowned academic specializing in the Middle East.

Rustow obtained a Bachelor of Arts in literature from Yale University in 1990 before earning two master's degrees—in religion and history—from Columbia University in 1998. She then earned an MPhil in history in 1999 and a PhD in history in 2004, both from Columbia.

ACADEMIC CAREER

Rustow began her postdoctoral academic career as a Hazel D. Cook Fellow in the Jewish studies program at the University of Washington, where she was an instructor of history for the winter 2003 term. Later that year, she joined Emory University in Atlanta, Georgia, as an assistant history professor with a dual appointment in the Middle East and South Asian studies department at the school's Tam Institute for Jewish Studies. In 2009, she was promoted to associate professor. The following year, she joined the faculty of Johns Hopkins University, in Baltimore, Maryland. There she held the Charlotte Bloomberg Professorship in the Humanities until July 2015, when she took a position at Princeton University in Princeton, New Jersey. At Princeton, Rustow is the Khedouri A. Zilkha Professor of Jewish Civilization in the Near East as well as the director of the Princeton Geniza Lab.

Rustow's early research focused on understanding the relationship between Jewish communities and the state during the medieval period, especially during the Fatimid Caliphate in North Africa between the tenth and twelfth centuries. In 2008, she published *Heresy and the Politics of Community: The Jews of the Fatimid Caliphate*, which provided a new interpretation of the political and social interactions of two Jewish communities in the Middle East between 909 and 1171 CE. In 2011, she was the coeditor of *Jewish Studies at the Crossroads of Anthropology and History: Authority, Diaspora, Tradition*, a book of essays about Jewish culture and traditions across a span of historical periods and geographical locations.

Rustow has expanded her research to study the social and political relationships between Jews, Muslims, and Christians in the Near East. Today, much of her research focuses on the Jewish and Arab communities in present-day Syria and Egypt during the tenth to fifteenth centuries. For source material, she uses manuscripts stored for over a thousand years in a disused text storage area called a *geniza* in the Ben Ezra Synagogue in what is now Cairo, Egypt. In Jewish tradition, any scrap of text with the name of God written on it was considered sacred and was thus supposed to be deposited in a *geniza* rather than thrown out. The Cairo Geniza is a well-known *geniza*, and the manuscripts it contains are mostly literary texts, but also include personal letters, grocery lists, legal documents, copies of extracts from biblical and rabbinical texts, government and administrative records and decrees, and other personal and state materials written in Hebrew between about 1000 and 1250. Although documents in a *geniza* are expected to decompose, the dry air in the Cairo Geniza preserved its documents, though many are in fragments. Some Hebrew manuscripts were written on repurposed documents, such as government decrees, that were originally written in Arabic script. Such materials raise questions for Rustow about how and why the Jewish community possessed Arabic documents, and her research includes both the Arabic and Hebrew content. She has also used manuscripts written on papyrus for her research. Proficient in numerous languages, including Hebrew, Arabic, Judeo-Arabic, and Aramaic, Rustow is able to decipher the manuscripts and collaborates with other researchers to interpret them.

A prolific writer, Rustow has written numerous articles for peer-reviewed journals such as the *Bulletin of the School of Oriental and African Studies*, *Mamlūk Studies Review*, *Past and Present*, and *Jewish Quarterly Review*, as well as book chapters and articles in encyclopedias such as *The Oxford Dictionary of the Middle Ages* and *The Encyclopedia of Jews in the Islamic World*. She also has been a speaker at numerous conferences, lectures, and seminars.

In 2014, Rustow was awarded a Guggenheim Fellowship in the Humanities. In 2015, she was named a MacArthur Fellow for her scholarship in working with the Geniza source material. After receiving the award, Rustow said she planned to use the $625,000 award money to examine the manuscripts in the Geniza cache in a more leisurely way, saying that "wandering" through material allowed for deeper study and often resulted in the greatest discoveries. She also planned to expand collaboration of the Geniza manuscripts by academic scholars and professionals to increase the cataloging, transcription, translation, and digitization of the documents to make more of them accessible to the public—and other scholars—online.

As 2016, Rustow was working on two books. One is a handbook of previously unpublished Fatimid legal and state documents from the Geniza storeroom. The other is an examination of the Fatimid caliphate from the perspectives of Jewish, Christian, and Muslim subjects. It, too, uses the Geniza documents, especially those written in Arabic.

IMPACT

Rustow has furthered scholarship of Jewish and other Mediterranean communities during the Middle Ages and has put forth new interpretations of how rival communities interacted during the Fatimid period. Her work with the Geniza documents is bringing to life the daily lives of residents of Cairo and their interactions with each other and the state during an important period in the city's history as a center of culture and trade. Her examination of the Geniza's overlooked Arabic texts is making information about the Fatimid empire more accessible and opening new avenues of historical research.

PERSONAL LIFE

Rustow lives in Philadelphia, Pennsylvania. She enjoys Middle Eastern music and plays the *buzuq*, oud, and piano.

SUGGESTED READING

"Meet the 2015 MacArthur Fellows: Marina Rustow." *MacArthur Fellows Program.* MacArthur Foundation, 28 Sept. 2015. www.macfound.org/fellows/class/2015/. Accessed 5 Dec. 2019.

Nathan-Kazis, Josh. "Meet the 4 Jewish Winners of MacArthur 'Genius' Grants." *Forward,* 1 Oct. 2015. forward.com/news/321817/meet-the-4-jewish-winners-of-the-macarthur-genius-grant/. Accessed 5 Dec. 2019.

Rustow, Marina. "Marina Rustow." *Department of Near Eastern Studies, Princeton University,* 29 Oct. 2015.nes.princeton.edu/people/marina-rustow. Accessed 5 Dec. 2019.

———. "Out of Cairo Trove, 'Genius Grant' Winner Mines Details of Ancient Life." Interview by Robert Siegal. *NPR,* 29 Sept. 2015. www.npr.org/2015/09/29/444527433/out-of-cairo-trove-genius-grant-winner-mines-details-of-ancient-life. Accessed 5 Dec. 2019.

———. "Teasing Out the Secrets of Medieval Jewish Life." Interview by Sandee Brawarsky. *Jewish Week,* 6 Oct. 2015. jewishweek.timesofisrael.com/teasing-out-the-secrets-of-medieval-jewish-life/. Accessed 5 Dec. 2019.

—*Barb Lightner*

Alejandro Sanz

Date of birth: December 18, 1968
Occupation: Singer-songwriter

Alejandro Sanz has established himself as one of the best-selling Latin music artists by combining his trademark flamenco sound with mainstream pop and tropical rhythms. Since launching his recording career in 1991, the Spanish singer-songwriter has increasingly experimented with a wide range of musical genres, including rock, R&B, funk, hip-hop, electronica, and jazz. This formula has not only helped him sell millions of albums worldwide but also win twenty-one Latin Grammy Awards and four Grammys within thirty years.

Despite his many accolades, Sanz is not content to rest on his laurels. "I realized that, like it or not, winning brings a responsibility that you must assume," he shared with Agustin Garza for the *Los Angeles Times* (19 Oct. 2003). "The responsibility to not let people down, to keep growing and to show that you deserve all those awards."

A SENSATION IN SPAIN

Alejandro Sanz was born Alejandro Sánchez Pizarro on December 18, 1968, in Madrid, Spain. He grew up alongside older brother Jesús in Cádiz. Sanz seemed destined for a career in music. His father, Jesús Sánchez Madero, was a professional musician who performed with the groups El Trio Juventud and Los Tres de la Bahía; he also presented Sanz with his first guitar at the age of seven. Sanz's mother, Maria Pizarro, signed him for lessons, after discovering the karate school next door had closed.

While learning guitar, Sanz drew inspiration from the summers he spent in his parents' native Andalusia. "When I was very little, I would listen to Paco de Lucía," a legendary flamenco

Photo by Cristina Ruiz/Unnika via Wikimedia Commons

artist, Sanz told Mike Keefe-Feldman during a clinic at Berklee College of Music (8 Nov. 2013). "His guitar sounds like it is singing, and very few people have this ability." As a teenager, Sanz embraced heavy metal music and briefly fronted the group Jinete Inmortal. By age twenty Sanz had returned to his musical roots, recording the solo disc *Los chulos son pa' cuidarlos* (Pimps are for nurturing, 1989), a fusion of flamenco and techno that he released on Spanish EMI subsidiary Hispavox under the name Alejandro Magno.

Although Sanz's debut album fizzled, Iñigo Zabala, Warner Music Latin America's head of A&R, signed the talented newcomer to the record label in 1990. That decision paid off, with the 1991 release of the Latin pop-infused *Viviendo deprisa* (Living in a hurry), Sanz's first album with Warner. It notched three number-one singles ("Pisando fuerte, (Stepping Strong)" "Se le apagó la luz (The Light Went Out)," and "Lo que fui es lo que soy (What I Was Is What I Am)" and sold more than a million copies domestically, becoming the year's top-selling record in Spain. Sanz followed with a successful sophomore effort and first headlining tour with 1993's *Si tú me miras (If You Look at Me)*, which he recorded in London and featured the tracks "El escaparate (The Showcase)" and "Mi primera cancion (My First Song)." Sanz collaborated on both tracks with his idol Paco de Lucía. Sanz's accompanying tour included an acoustic concert at Madrid's Cinearte Studios, a performance that became the basis of *Básico (Basic)* (1993), his first live record.

INDUSTRY RECOGNITION
The singer achieved another milestone with "La fuerza del corazón (The Heart's Power)," the lead single from his fourth album, 3 (1995). It became Sanz's first major international hit, reaching the top ten of the Billboard Latin Pop Airplay chart. Within a year Sanz had released Italian and Portuguese versions of the disc and embarked on his third concert tour.

However, it was his follow-up record, *Más (More)*, released in September 1997, that earned him greater worldwide attention. By the following July, *Más*, a fusion of flamenco, pop, and tropical rhythms, had sold over a million copies domestically and included three top-ten ballads on the Billboard Latin Pop Airplay and Tropical Airplay charts: "Y, ¿Si fuera ella? (And What If It Was Her)," "Amiga mia, (My Friend)" and "Corazón partío (Broken Heart)."

With his sixth studio album, 2000's *El alma al aire (The Soul on Air)*, Sanz incorporated his signature flamenco-infused pop with elements of jazz, R&B, soul, and tango. "It's a complex album . . . but I want to give something to music," Sanz said to Leila Cobo for *Billboard* (10 May 2003). "I don't want to only sell many albums at any price." This approach worked. Hitting shelves in late September, *El alma al aire* sold a million copies in its first week and took less than one month to crack the top five of three Billboard charts: Top Latin Albums, Latin Pop Albums, and Heatseekers Albums. After earning a 2000 Grammy Award nomination for best Latin pop or urban album, Sanz, who had already embarked on his next tour, swept four major Latin Grammy categories: best male pop vocal album honors, as well as album, record, and song of the year (for the titular track). A special edition of the album, released in 2001, boasted the top-ten hits "Quisiera ser (I Would Like to Be)" and "Cuando nadie me ve (When Nobody Sees Me)," as well as three new tracks with Irish folk-rock group the Corrs.

GOES *UNPLUGGED* . . . AND POLITICAL
That fall Sanz made history, as the first Spanish musician to perform an acoustic MTV concert special and release an *Unplugged* album—a career-changing experience. "It was a rediscovery of how to perform, and also how to record, music with musicians," he told Richard Harrington for the *Washington Post* (23 Apr. 2004). "That was the spirit of the music in its pure form." Sanz's second live disc topped the Billboard Top Latin Albums and Latin Pop Albums charts while earning him album, song, and record of the year honors at the Latin Grammys. Other 2002 highlights included a Grammy Award performance with Destiny's Child and his collaboration on the Spanish version of Michael Jackson's September 11 tribute single, "What More Can I Give."

With his seventh studio album, *No es lo mismo (It's Not the Same Thing*, 2003), Sanz tackled various social and political issues, including Spain's 2002 Prestige oil spill with "Sandy a orilla do mundo" (Sandy at the Edge of the earth) and the plight of Cuban refugees with "Labana," a slang term for Havana. *No es lo mismo*, a blend of hip-hop and electronica for a more urban sound, ruled the Billboard top five in three categories: Latin Pop Albums, Top Latin Albums, and Top Heatseekers. The album's title song reached number four on Hot Latin Songs and number three on Latin Pop Airplay.

In 2004, after kicking off a worldwide tour, Sanz claimed his first career Grammy, for best Latin pop album of 2003, and added four more Latin Grammys to his collection, winning best male pop vocal album, along with album, record, and song of the year. He also made headlines for his rebuke of Venezuelan leader Hugo Chávez, following Chávez's disregard of a 2003 referendum by opposition groups requesting a presidential recall vote.

CROSSOVER WITH "LA TORTURA"

Sanz created an even bigger stir in April 2005, when Latin superstar Shakira released their Spanish-language reggaetón-flavored duet, "La tortura (Torture)," on her album *Fijación (Fixation) Oral, Vol. 1*. The lead single from Shakira's sixth album eventually became Sanz's biggest crossover hit. By June "La tortura" had topped the Billboard Hot Latin Songs, Latin Pop, and Tropical Airplay charts. By September it had cracked the Hot 100's top twenty-five. Sanz costarred in the steamy accompanying video, which received heavy rotation on MTV and was the first Spanish-language music video to do so. He also joined Shakira to perform the song at the 2005 MTV Video Music Awards and 2006 Latin Grammys.

The duo reunited to record "Te lo agradezco, pero no" (I Appreciate It, but No), a track on Sanz's eighth studio album, the introspective *El tren de los momentos* (The Train of Moments, 2006). That fusion of pop, hip-hop, funk, rock, and jazz reached the top-five on the Billboard Latin Pop and Top Latin Albums charts. Sanz scored chart-toppers on Hot Latin Track and Latin Pop Airplay with the Shakira duet as well as with the romantic ballad "A la primera persona" (The First Person). In May 2007, two months into his tour, Sanz followed his doctor's orders and took a two-month hiatus, citing exhaustion and stress after his father's death in 2005 and a December 2006 blackmail attempt by two former employees.

After resuming his tour in August, Sanz spent the next six months performing in Europe, Latin America, and North America. His November concert in Caracas was canceled, however, due to his Chávez remarks. Sanz sparked further controversy in December, showing a T-shirt mocking Chávez during his Miami, Florida, concert.

Yet Sanz remained a music industry darling. *El tren de los momentos* snagged the 2007 Grammy Award for best Latin pop album and an album of the year nod at the Latin Grammys.

NEW DUET PARTNER AND LABEL

Sanz's ninth studio album, *Paraiso Express* (*Paradise Express*), hit the shelves in November 2009 and represented a departure from his earlier material. "It is more of a rock album than my past releases, with more elegant and positive lyrics and a happier and more rhythmic spirit," Sanz told Monica Herrera for *Billboard* (22 Sept. 2009).

A prime example is the upbeat lead single: "Looking for Paradise," a bilingual duet featuring R&B artist Alicia Keys singing in English and Sanz responding in Spanish. This collaboration proved successful, topping the Billboard Hot Latin Songs, Latin Pop Songs, and Tropical Songs charts. *Paraiso Express* yielded two more top-ten hits on the Latin Pop Songs chart: "Desde cuándo (Since When)" and "Nuestro amor será leyenda (Our Love Will Be Legend)," helping Sanz claim his third Grammy—his second for best pop Latin album—in February 2011.

That same month, Sanz signed with Universal Music Group, after two decades with Warner. His first record on the new label, *La música no se toca* (*The Music Is Not to Be Touched*, 2012), was a return to familiar territory. "I wanted to do an album like before; an album that sounded big . . . a monumental album of symphonic pop," he recalled in an interview for *Billboard* (25 Sept. 2012). The album's lead single—the classic romantic ballad "No me compares" (Don't Compare Me)—became his first number-one hit with Universal, spending twenty weeks atop both the Hot Latin Songs and Latin Pop Airplay charts. It also earned song and record of the year nominations for the 2012 Latin Grammys.

EXPERIMENTS WITH *SIROPE* AND *#ELDISCO*

However, Sanz had not abandoned his penchant for musical experimentation, melding flamenco with styles ranging from rock, soul, and funk to reggae and cumbia on *Sirope* (*Syrup*) (2015), which topped the Latin Pop Albums and Top Album charts. His eleventh studio album also included the top-ten hit "Un zombie a la intemperie (A Zombie Out in the Open)" while earning the best contemporary pop vocal album prize at the Latin Grammys and a Grammy nomination for best Latin pop album.

For his twelfth record, *#ElDisco* (*#The Disc*) (2019), Sanz collaborated with reggaetón star Nicky Jam, Catalan singer-songwriter Judit Neddermann, and pop artist Camila Cabello. "Mi persona favorita (My Favorite Person)," his flamenco-pop ballad with Cabello, won the 2019 Latin Grammy for record of the year and best pop song while *#ElDisco* won the 2019 Grammy Award for best Latin pop album. Sanz's accompanying tour was canceled due to the novel coronavirus (COVID-19) pandemic. In June 2019 the Hollywood Chamber of Commerce announced that Sanz would receive a star on the Hollywood Walk of Fame in 2020.

PERSONAL LIFE

Sanz lives in Miami. In his free time, he enjoys painting, which helps him push musical boundaries. "Painting teaches you that taking risks rarely leads to failure," he told Garza. "I don't want to be identified with a standard way of making music. . . . I want to create a style that carries my own name."

Sanz became involved with Cuban model and contemporary artist Rachel Valdés following his July 2019 separation from his second wife and former assistant Raquel Perera, with whom he had two children, Dylan and Alma. The singer also had a daughter, Manuela, with his first wife, model Jaydy Michel, and a son, Alexander, with his former girlfriend Valeria Rivera.

SUGGESTED READING

"Alejandro Sanz Q&A: On 'Big' New Album, Reality TV & Surrounding Himself with Women on Tour." *Billboard*, 25 Sept. 2012, www.billboard.com/articles/news/474936/alejandro-sanz-qa-on-big-new-album-reality-tv-surrounding-himself-with-women-on. Accessed 13 July 2020.

Cobo, Leila. "Alejandro Sanz: Special Q&A Session." *Billboard*, Prometheus Global Media, LLC, 10 May 2003, p. LM-12.

Garza, Agustin. "Not Content to Be Stuck in Success." *The Los Angeles Times*, 19 Oct. 2003, www.latimes.com/archives/la-xpm-2003-oct-19-ca-gurza19-story.html. Accessed 20 July 2020.

Harrington, Richard. "Alejandro Sanz Finds His Voice." *The Washington Post*, 23 Apr. 2004, www.washingtonpost.com/archive/lifestyle/2004/04/23/alejandro-sanz-finds-his-voice/9f306283-adeb-4ceb-bdad-a428766a2de4/. Accessed 13 July 2020.

Herrera, Monica. "Alejandro Sanz Recruits Alicia Keys, Sets Date for *Paradise*." *Billboard*, 22 Sept. 2009, www.billboard.com/articles/news/267313/alejandro-sanz-recruits-alicia-keys-sets-date-for-paradise. Accessed 13 July 2020.

Keefe-Feldman, Mike. "Latin Superstar Alejandro Sanz Stresses Passion, Honesty in Music at Berklee Clinic." *Berklee.edu*, 8 Nov. 2013, www.berklee.edu/news/latin-superstar-alejandro-sanz-stresses-passion-honesty-music-berklee-clinic. Accessed 13 July 2020.

SELECTED WORKS

Más, 1997; *MTV Unplugged*, 2001; *No es lo mismo*, 2003; *El tren de los momentos*, 2006; *Paraiso Express*, 2009; *La música no se toca*, 2012; *Sirope*, 2015; *#ElDisco*, 2019

—Bertha Muteba

Ted Sarandos

Born: July 30, 1964
Occupation: Business executive

For Netflix executive Ted Sarandos, the traditional television business, with its set episode lengths and weekly airing schedules, "is based on managed dissatisfaction," he told Stuart Jeffries for the *Guardian* (30 Dec. 2013). "You're watching a great television show you're really wrapped up in? You might get 50 minutes of watching a week and then 18,000 minutes of waiting until the next episode comes along. I'd rather make it all about the joy." Indeed, following the launch of the first Netflix original television series in 2012, the streaming content provider worked to offer subscribers a more personalized viewing experience in which users can choose to watch individual episodes of a series or "binge watch" an entire season in one go. That approach, as well as Netflix's longstanding dedication to licensing and developing a diverse array of film and television content, made the company one of the most powerful forces in the global entertainment industry, operating in nearly two hundred countries by 2017.

A longtime lover of television and film, Sarandos began his career in the video-store industry and spent time working in video distribution during the end of the VHS era. After meeting with one of Netflix's founders in 1999, he joined the company, then a DVD-rental service, early the following year and took on the position of chief content officer. In that role, Sarandos was responsible for overseeing the acquisition and development of content for the company, including original streaming content that would go on to resonate with viewers, win prestigious awards, and dominate popular culture. Yet while Sarandos undoubtedly became an influential figure within his industry, he preferred not to be considered a media tastemaker. "I don't want it to reflect my taste," he explained to Ramin Setoodeh for *Variety* (15 Aug. 2017) about his approach to

Photo by Daniel Benavides via Wikimedia Commons

content. "I want it to reflect your taste. Netflix has to be great for you."

EARLY LIFE AND EDUCATION

Theodore Anthony Sarandos Jr. was born on July 30, 1964, in Phoenix, Arizona. He was the fourth of five children born to Susan Sarandos, a homemaker, and Theodore Sarandos Sr., an electrician. Sarandos was drawn to the world of film and television from a young age and would go on to credit his mother with laying the groundwork for his later career. An avid television watcher, his mother was also an early adopter of new technology, most notably home-video technology. "My parents were young, and generally struggled all the time, and we always joked about my house because we never had all the utilities at the same time. But in this weird, reckless, beautiful thing, my mom bought a VCR. Before I knew anyone who had one, we had a VCR," Sarandos recounted in his acceptance speech for the Producer's Guild's 2020 Milestone Award, as quoted by Matt Grobar for *Deadline* (18 Jan. 2020). "It was almost like she had a vision for me and my future that I didn't know about." However, while Sarandos's upbringing granted him the opportunity to watch a great deal of television and film, his further development as a film buff was limited by the dearth of cinemas showing independent or art films in Arizona during the late 1970s and early 1980s.

Sarandos attended Alhambra High School in Phoenix, where he contributed to extracurricular activities such as the school newspaper. After graduating from high school in 1982, he enrolled in Glendale Community College, located in the nearby city of Glendale. Still interested in journalism, he served for a time as editor of the college newspaper, the *Voice*. He went on to study journalism at Arizona State University (ASU) but soon decided against pursuing a career in that industry, as he believed himself to be a poor writer. Sarandos left ASU without completing a degree, choosing instead to devote his time to his developing career in the video-store business.

EARLY CAREER

In the early 1980s, a new video store opened in Sarandos's area. "Literally only the second video store in the state," as he later told Tina Daunt for the *Hollywood Reporter* (24 Apr. 2012), the store appealed to the young cinema fan, who first visited it in 1983. "There were all these movies I had been reading about," he recalled to Daunt. "That's when I started to learn. I met the owner and started working there part time." In addition to providing Sarandos with income, his job at the video store enabled him to watch many of the films available to customers, giving him a broad knowledge of individual films and genres. He continued to work for that business after leaving

college, becoming general manager of the video store chain.

After working in the video-store business for many years, Sarandos next moved into the distribution side of the industry. He took a position with the video-distribution company East Texas Distributors. Serving as the company's director of sales and operations for the western region by the 1990s, he spearheaded efforts to move into offering DVDs following the introduction of that format late in the decade. Following his time with East Texas Distributors, Sarandos joined the video-store chain Video City/West Coast Video as an executive.

NETFLIX

A turning point in Sarandos's career came in 1999, when he met with Reed Hastings, the CEO and cofounder of the DVD-rental business Netflix. Founded in 1997, Netflix then offered monthly subscriptions that enabled customers to rent DVDs of a wide range of films and television shows, which would be delivered to the customers via mail and later returned via mail at the customers' convenience, without risk of late fees. Although the company experienced significant success with that business model, Hastings envisioned a future in which the company offered video-streaming services that would enable subscribers to watch film and television content online. Due to the state of internet infrastructure in the late 1990s, that theoretical future seemed a long way off to Sarandos, who was skeptical of Hastings's idea. "Reed was a genius engineer and programmer but didn't know about entertainment distribution," he later explained to Charlotte Edwardes for the *Evening Standard* (9 May 2019). "He described Netflix almost exactly how it is now and he sounded like a crazy person." Nevertheless, Sarandos was intrigued by Hastings's vision for the company and eventually decided to join its ranks. He officially took a position with the company in early 2000.

As the chief content officer for Netflix, Sarandos was charged with overseeing the acquisition of content for the service. The company was already known for offering not only the most popular Hollywood films and major television series but also lesser-known works, including those from independent production companies and those appealing specifically to niche audiences. Sarandos was greatly interested in the data Netflix gathered about subscribers' viewing choices and rental habits, which the company used to tailor recommendations to its customers and guide its content-acquisition efforts. As his time with the company progressed, he was intrigued by the habits of customers who rented DVDs of television series, each of which typically contained only several episodes due to the storage limitations of the DVD format. "We saw that people would return those discs for TV series very quickly, given they had three hours of programming on them—more quickly than they would a movie. They wanted the next hit," Sarandos told Jeffries. Netflix's observations of its users' television-watching habits would fuel the company's later decision to make full seasons of its original television programming available for streaming all at once, thus facilitating the so-called binge watching that appeared to be popular among its users.

As internet and streaming-video technology improved, Netflix began to expand into offering streaming services, launching such an initiative in 2007. The company's streaming component existed alongside its DVDs-by-mail service for some time. In the fall of 2011 Netflix briefly split off the DVD component of the business as Qwikster, before bringing it back into the Netflix portfolio as *DVD.com*: A Netflix Company.

ORIGINAL CONTENT

As Netflix continued to expand and offer a broad range of content to its subscribers in the years following the launch of the company's streaming service, the company began to explore the idea of developing or licensing original content for streaming purposes. That initiative took on particular importance due to the at-times contentious relationship between Netflix and existing film studios and television networks, which executives such as Sarandos feared could jeopardize the company's ability to offer the content its users were seeking. "I would say that the relationship between studios and networks has always been that of a frenemy," he told Setoodeh. He went on to explain, "The more successful we get, the more anxious I get about the willingness of the networks to license their stuff to us."

In light of such concerns, Netflix began an aggressive push toward developing original streaming content. This officially launched in 2012 with the debut of *Lilyhammer*, a crime series about a New York mobster, played by Steve Van Zandt, living in Norway. The move into original content took off further following the 2013 debut of *House of Cards*, a critically acclaimed political drama that proved popular among Netflix's subscribers and was credited with drawing new customers to the service. The show's success prompted widespread discussion about Netflix's role in the film and television industries and the increasingly popular phenomenon of binge watching.

For Sarandos, the shift to creating original streaming content was a valuable one for both Netflix and the creators who developed new projects with the company. "It was a start of something entirely new for us, and as it turned out, something entirely new for the whole business," he said, as quoted by Grobar.

"The explosion of production that followed has blown the doors open for new voices, has given a platform for seasoned professionals to practice their craft." In addition to its early series such as *Lilyhammer* and *House of Cards*, major projects produced or distributed by Netflix over the next years included scripted television series such as *Orange Is the New Black* (2013–19), *Stranger Things* (2016–), and *The Crown* (2016–); documentary series such as *Making a Murderer* (2015–18), *Wild Wild Country* (2018), and *Tiger King* (2020); feature-length documentaries such as *13th* (2016) and *American Factory* (2019); documentary shorts such as the Academy Award–winning *The White Helmets* (2016); and critically acclaimed feature films such as *Beasts of No Nation* (2015), *Roma* (2018), and *The Irishman* (2019).

In addition to operating within the United States, Netflix expanded its services into additional countries over the years and by 2017 was active in 190 countries throughout the world. In conjunction with that effort, the company sought to offer original and licensed content from multiple countries and in a variety of languages, expanding the library of film and television available to its users even further. "It opened a world of possibilities—mainstream viewing of subtitled programming in the US and releasing in every language and every territory at the exact same moment," Sarandos told Jeffries about Netflix's worldwide digital push. "To me, that's what the future will be like."

The company's continuing expansion efforts further proved essential as competing services—including Hulu, Amazon Prime Video, and Disney+—broadened their own content offerings and competed for market share. Nevertheless, Sarandos remained adamant that Netflix's primary focus was on providing high-quality content. "We have one product," he told Dominic Patten for *Deadline* (23 Oct. 2019). "We make great television and films for our customers . . . and we have to keep doing that."

PERSONAL LIFE

Sarandos and his first wife, Michelle, had two children together prior to their divorce. He met his second wife, Nicole Avant, a music executive who would later serve as US ambassador to the Bahamas, at a political fundraiser for Barack Obama in 2008. Sarandos lives in Los Angeles, California.

SUGGESTED READING

Edwardes, Charlotte. "Netflix's Ted Sarandos: The Most Powerful Person in Hollywood?" *Evening Standard*, 9 May 2019, www.standard.co.uk/tech/netflix-ted-sarandos-interview-the-crown-a4138071.html. Accessed 10 May 2020.

Grobar, Matt. "PGA's Milestone Honoree Ted Sarandos Pays Tribute to 'Early Adopter' Who Raised Him." *Deadline*, 18 Jan. 2020, deadline.com/2020/01/ted-sarandos-pga-awards-milestone-speech-producers-guild-1202834966/. Accessed 10 May 2020.

Jeffries, Stuart. "Netflix's Ted Sarandos: The 'Evil Genius' behind a TV Revolution." *The Guardian*, 30 Dec. 2013, www.theguardian.com/media/2013/dec/30/netflix-evil-genius-tv-revolution-ted-sarandos. Accessed 10 May 2020.

Martinson, Jane. "Netflix's Ted Sarandos: 'We Like Giving Great Storytellers Big Canvases.'" *The Guardian*, 15 Mar. 2015, www.theguardian.com/media/2015/mar/15/netflix-ted-sarandos-house-of-cards. Accessed 10 May 2020.

Patten, Dominic. "Netflix Has 'No Plans' to Sell, Ted Sarandos Says as Streaming Wars Loom—Vanity Fair Summit." *Deadline*, 23 Oct. 2019, deadline.com/2019/10/netflix-sale-ted-sarandos-streaming-wars-interview-katie-couric-disney-apple-succession-1202767040/. Accessed 10 May 2020.

Setoodeh, Ramin. "Has Netflix's Ted Sarandos Rescued (or Ruined) Hollywood?" *Variety*, 15 Aug. 2017, variety.com/2017/digital/features/ted-sarandos-netflix-original-movies-shonda-rhimes-1202527321/. Accessed 10 May 2020.

Weprin, Alex. "Ted Sarandos Talks Disney+ Launch and a Netflix Future Focused on Original Content." *The Hollywood Reporter*, 14 Nov. 2019, www.hollywoodreporter.com/amp/news/netflixs-ted-sarandos-talks-disney-original-content-1254766. Accessed 10 May 2020.

—*Joy Crelin*

Peter Scholze

Born: December 11, 1987
Occupation: Mathematician

"Peter Scholze possesses a type of mathematical talent that emerges only rarely," Allyn Jackson wrote in a 2018 paper posted on the website of the *International Mathematical Union* (IMU). "He has the capacity to absorb and digest the entire frontier of a broad swath of mathematical research ranging over many diverse and often inchoate developments. What is more, he sees how to integrate these developments through stunning new syntheses. . . . His unifying vision is transforming mathematics." Jackson was hardly alone in bestowing such high praise on Scholze, who earned an array of remarkable appointments and honors extremely early in his career. At age twenty-four he became the youngest person ever to attain the title of professor at a German university when he joined the faculty of the University of Bonn. In 2016, he set another record as the youngest recipient of the Leibniz Prize, a prestigious German award for scientific research. In 2018, he was named director of the Max Planck Institute of Mathematics and won a Fields Medal—considered equivalent in significance to the Nobel Prize—further cementing his reputation as one of the most influential mathematicians in the world.

Scholze became particularly known for his work with p-adic fields, extensions of the ordinary number system used in the study of prime numbers. Employing them, he developed structures known as perfectoid spaces, enabling solutions to intractable problems in geometry, topology, and other areas of mathematics. However, he did not limit himself to any one specialty. "There are many problems that I think about from time to time, anything that I feel is interesting," he explained in an interview for the *2012 Clay Mathematics Institute (CMI) Annual Report*. "In many cases, my desire is just to thoroughly understand some difficult theory. Sometimes I have some vague intuitive idea on how things should work, and I try to reconcile this with the known theory. In some cases, the new perspective leads to new insights, simplifying or clarifying old material and maybe implying new results."

Photo by George M. Bergman via Wikimedia Commons

EARLY LIFE AND EDUCATION

Peter Scholze was born on December 11, 1987, in Dresden, then part of the German Democratic Republic or East Germany. When he was an infant, his family relocated to the city of Berlin, where he was raised. His father was a physicist, and his mother a computer scientist. His sister would also become involved in science, studying chemistry.

Scholze became interested in mathematics at a young age. One of his earliest encounters with the field was through the book *Fregatten-kapitän Eins* (*Frigate Captain One*), a collection of children's stories by Wladimir Ljowschin in which mathematical phenomena figure in the plots. One tale, for example, discusses how to capture a lion by repeatedly bisecting the land on which he is roaming. Scholze later attended Heinrich-Hertz Gymnasium, a Berlin high school specializing in mathematics and science. There he became even more fascinated by high-level mathematics. "Contrary to most schools, being good at math was not something one was mocked for," he recalled to the CMI interviewer. He would later credit one of his instructors there, Klaus Altmann, who taught him algebraic geometry, as being an especially important mentor.

At age sixteen Scholze became fascinated by mathematician Andrew Wiles, who had, a decade before, proved the famous problem known as Fermat's Last Theorem. He initially understood little of the math involved in the groundbreaking proof, but by working backward he gradually made sense of the complex ideas involved. "To this day, that's to a large extent how I learn," he admitted to Erica Klarreich for *Quanta Magazine* (28 June 2016). "I never really learned the basic things like linear algebra, actually—I only assimilated it through learning some other stuff."

As he independently studied Wiles's work, Scholze grew increasingly fascinated by the way disparate areas of number theory, algebra, geometry, and analysis could be unified by means of mathematical structures called modular forms and elliptic curves. This interest would become the foundation for much of his later work. He would continue to gravitate "toward problems that have their roots in basic equations about whole numbers," Klarreich wrote, noting that he felt happiest "when his abstract constructions lead him back around to small discoveries about ordinary whole numbers."

EARLY RECOGNITION

Scholze earned several medals from the International Mathematical Olympiad as a teen before graduating from Heinrich-Hertz Gymnasium in 2007. He then followed Altmann's advice and enrolled at the University of Bonn to study under Austrian mathematician Michael Rapoport. There he amazed his classmates by never taking notes, seemingly able to absorb the material in real time as it was presented. He completed his bachelor's degree in just three semesters and his master's degree in two more. In addition to Rapoport, who served as his adviser, Scholze learned from other eminent names in mathematics. One notable influence was Gerd Faltings, an expert in arithmetic geometry and at the time the only German ever to have won a Fields Medal.

Scholze achieved a measure of renown as a doctoral student, when he distilled a 288-page book dedicated to a famously complex proof (*The Geometry and Cohomology of Some Simple Shimura Varieties*, by Michael Harris and Richard Taylor) into a 37-page paper. He earned the respect of much more experienced researchers for finding an elegant way to circumvent the most complex part of the proof, which dealt with connections between geometry and number theory. In 2011 he became a fellow at the Clay Mathematics Institute, a position he would hold until 2016.

In 2012, Scholze completed his doctoral degree from the University of Bonn. His thesis, which established the idea of perfectoid spaces, was considered so groundbreaking that it caused major buzz in math departments around the world. "Formulating the concept of perfectoid spaces required a new kind of thinking," Jackson explained. "One reason is simply that these spaces are huge. They transcend the usual finiteness conditions that researchers rely on to make mathematical objects tractable." Yet, Scholze saw the potential to use the complexity of perfectoid spaces as a way to simplify and unify other theories. According to Jackson, "The concept was quickly embraced by researchers the world over as just the right notion to clarify a wide variety of phenomena and shed new light on problems that had evaded solution for decades."

PROFESSOR AND RESEARCHER

Immediately upon graduating, Scholze accepted a professorship at the Hausdorff Center for Mathematics (HCM), a Cluster of Excellence at the University of Bonn. (In Germany, Clusters of Excellence are research initiatives funded by the government at individual universities or university alliances.) Just twenty-four years old at the time, he was the youngest person ever to serve as a full professor at a German university.

In addition to his teaching duties, Scholze—who quickly gained a reputation among his students for his down-to-earth nature and approachability—continued his own research, which focused largely on arithmetic geometry. The field uses geometric tools to unpack polynomial equations, which involve only numbers, variables, and exponents. One line of inquiry involves investigating solutions to such equations using p-adic numbers, "which, like the real numbers, are built by filling in the gaps between whole numbers and fractions," as Klarreich explained. "But these systems are based on a nonstandard notion of where the gaps lie, and which numbers are close to each other: In a p-adic number system, two numbers are considered close not if the difference between them is small, but if that difference is divisible many times by p. It's a strange criterion, but a useful one." Scholze's concept of perfectoid spaces allows mathematicians to bridge the gap between p-adic arithmetic and geometry, and its development was hailed as a key innovation in mathematics.

Scholze was also celebrated for expanding the scope of "reciprocity laws," which in mathematical terms state that given two prime numbers, p and q, generally p is a perfect square on a clock with q hours just as q is a perfect square on a clock with p hours. There is a link between reciprocity laws and so-called hyperbolic geometry (as exhibited in some patterns, including in the work of artist M. C. Escher), which, in turn, is a key aspect of the influential group of conjectures known as the Langlands program. Scholze's construction of a perfectoid version of hyperbolic three-dimensional space led to the discovery of a whole new set of reciprocity laws—a result that many of his colleagues characterized as transformational.

Scholze earned a variety of awards and honors in recognition of his important mathematical work. In 2015, he was presented with the Frank Nelson Cole Prize in Algebra from the American Mathematical Society (AMS) as well as the Ostrowski Prize. In 2016, he received the Gottfried Wilhelm Leibniz Prize, the most important research award in Germany and among the most respected in the world.

FIELDS MEDAL

In 2018, Scholze became director of the Max Planck Institute for Mathematics, a research institute focused on pure mathematics headquartered in Bonn, Germany. Aimed at encouraging the exchange of ideas within the international mathematics community, it is one of the more than eighty research institutes that make up the Max Planck Society, named for pioneering German theoretical physicist Max Planck.

Scholze also continued to earn recognition as one of the leading minds in mathematics. Most notably, at the 2018 International Congress of Mathematicians he was named a recipient of the Fields Medal. That highly prestigious prize is awarded every four years by the International Mathematical Union to up to four recipients age forty or younger. Recipients are chosen based on major early-career contributions and potential for future achievements. Scholze's award citation mentioned "the revolution that he launched in arithmetic geometry," and former professor and mentor Michael Rapoport delivered the lecture in his honor at the event. The other medalists that year included Caucher Birkar of the University of Cambridge, Alessio Figalli of the Swiss Federal Institute of Technology, and Akshay Venkatesh of the Institute for Advanced Study in Princeton and Stanford University in California.

Throughout his career Scholze often fielded questions about how his field of extraordinarily complex mathematics benefits society. "Many say that mathematics is important because it is used to build computers, say. I wouldn't agree with that view and would argue that its real value is more indirect and hidden," he said in the CMI interview. "After all, people working in the most abstract mathematical fields, devoid of any practical applications, are still sought after for the skills they developed in thinking about these questions. In a sense, mathematicians are constantly testing the boundaries of what one can meaningfully think about."

PERSONAL LIFE

Peter Scholze is often described as modest and unassuming, never intimidating colleagues despite his exceptional intellect. He married a fellow mathematician, and the couple have a daughter together. Scholze enjoys activities such as cross-country skiing and hiking, and as a teenager he played bass guitar in a rock band.

SUGGESTED READING

Chang, Kenneth. "Fields Medals Awarded to 4 Mathematicians." *The New York Times*, 1 Aug. 2018, www.nytimes.com/2018/08/01/science/fields-medals-mathematics.html. Accessed 1 Sept. 2020.

Jackson, Allyn. "The Work of Peter Scholze." *International Mathematical Union*, 2018, www.mathunion.org/fileadmin/IMU/Prizes/Fields/2018/scholze-final.pdf. Accessed 1 Sept. 2020.

Klarreich, Erica. "A Master of Numbers and Shapes Who Is Rewriting Arithmetic." *Quanta Magazine*, 1 Aug. 2018, www.quantamagazine.org/peter-scholze-becomes-one-of-the-youngest-fields-medalists-ever-20180801/. Accessed 1 Sept. 2020.

———. "The Oracle of Arithmetic." *Quanta Magazine*, 28 June 2016, www.quantamagazine.org/peter-scholze-and-the-future-of-arithmetic-geometry-20160628/. Accessed 1 Sept. 2020.

Scholze, Peter. Interview. *2012 Clay Mathematics Institute Annual Report*, 2012, pp. 12–14, www.claymath.org/library/annual_report/ar2012/ar2012.pdf. Accessed 1 Sept. 2020.

Solly, Meilan. "This Year's Fields Medal Winners Include a Kurdish Refugee and a 30-Year-Old Professor." *Smithsonian Magazine*, 1 Aug. 2018, www.smithsonianmag.com/smart-news/years-fields-medal-winners-include-kurdish-refugee-and-30-year-old-professor-180969810/. Accessed 1 Sept. 2020.

—*Mari Rich*

Naomi Scott

Date of birth: May 6, 1993
Occupation: Actor and singer

Naomi Scott's first love has always been music. Having felt a profound connection with melodies, sounds, and lyrics from a young age, and without limiting herself to a specific genre, she kept her ears open throughout the years to any musical style and the emotions being conveyed. This diversity eventually extended to her own songwriting and recording efforts, as she experimented with different methods and techniques as a singer. She released her first EPs, *Invisible Division* and *Promises*, in 2014 and 2016, respectively.

Yet even as Scott pursued her interest in music, she also began a parallel career as an actor. This side of her life began to take off in the late 2010s, as she was cast in iconic roles in several high-profile projects. She portrayed Kimberly Hart, the Pink Ranger, in the 2017 *Power Rangers* movie and costarred in the reboot of *Charlie's Angels* released in November 2019. But it was arguably her appearance as Princess Jasmine in the 2019 live-action remake of Disney's *Aladdin* that brought her a whole new level of recognition. The musical film merged her acting and singing talents, and the soundtrack album topped the charts while two numbers featuring her vocals also became hit singles.

As her fame grew, Scott sought to balance the two sides of her career to remain creative and, most importantly, true to herself. "I guess I want to do both [acting and music] and I think at the end of the day, if you put good stuff out there . . . then it's fine," she told Mufsin Mahbub for *HuffPost* (28 Mar. 2017), "I'm just taking it one step at a time and just letting it happen organically."

EARLY LIFE AND EDUCATION
Naomi Scott was born on May 6, 1993, in Hounslow, a borough of West London, England. Her father, Christopher, is English, while her mother, Usha, is a Gujarati Indian who was born in Uganda and immigrated with her family to England when she was young. Scott's parents—both devout Christians and pastors—instilled in her and her older brother, Joshua, a deep religious faith from an early age. However, they were neither strict nor stern; quite the contrary, they encouraged their children to be open, ask questions, and discover religion on their own.

When Scott was eight years old, she and her family moved from Hounslow to Woodford, a suburb in East London. Growing up multiracial was, at times, confusing for Scott, who did not see many people who looked like her represented onscreen—that is, until the film *Bend It Like Beckham* came out in 2002. A coming-of-age story about an Indian girl whose desire to play professional soccer challenges the traditional gender views of her parents, the movie was important for Scott, who found a role model in the main character. As she told Hannah Lack for *AnOther Magazine* (10 Sept. 2019), "I'd never seen a movie about an Indian-British girl, from this not-very-glamorous place that I was from."

At the Davenant Foundation School in Essex, Scott often felt she did not fit in. Although she had friends, she was not part of any social clique. However, she found her place doing activities that connected her with the world of the arts. "Where I found my home was more like swing band practice. Or in drama. Those were the places where I felt comfortable," Scott told Zing Tsjeng for *Teen Vogue* (4 Sept. 2019). At home, she would spend hours listening to a wide range of artists and genres. From gospel to R&B to pop, she was always on the lookout for anything emotive.

Photo by iDominick via Wikimedia Commons

MUSIC AND ACTING BEGINNINGS

Figuring out early that music was her calling, Scott began to sing in her local church. Her first solo performance there—a cover of the song "Don't Speak" by the American band No Doubt—was a thrilling, enjoyable experience and one that sparked her craving for more live shows. From her early teens on, Scott sang regularly and wrote songs, determined to commence her career in music.

As luck would have it, one day, when Scott was performing "If I Ain't Got You" by Alicia Keys at church, Kéllé Bryan, a former member of the British girl group Eternal, happened to see her. Impressed by her performance, Bryan immediately signed the fifteen-year-old Scott to her talent agency—and soon, auditions began to come her way. Often Scott tried out for things regardless of her chance of landing the part. "It was when record labels were auditioning people to be in girl bands or boy bands, and I was always the youngest one there," Scott explained to Lack. "There'd be these women in heels, and I'd come in, in a big, baggy T-shirt and my little boots, singing a soul song."

While she kept busy going from audition to audition, it was around this time when she had her first encounter with the world of acting. After a few parts in advertisements, her first notable role came in the Disney Channel's *Life Bites* (2008–09), a sitcom aimed at a teenage audience about the adventures of siblings Chloe and Harvey (played by Amy Wren and Benedict Smith, respectively) and their relationships with family and friends. Scott portrayed Megan, a high school student and one of Chloe's closest friends.

In 2011, continuing her association with Disney, Scott was cast in the made-for-television film *Lemonade Mouth*. The movie follows the lives of five high school students who, after meeting in detention, decide to form a band. Scott played Mohini "Mo" Banjaree, the group's bass player, and the role allowed her to demonstrate her vocal prowess. However, she felt a clear distinction between that kind of performance and her own ongoing development as a musician. "The difficulty with that is playing a character," she told Mahbub of *Lemonade Mouth*. "I sing in it, but it has no connection to me as Naomi Scott and my music. So, the difficulty with that is I don't necessarily see a connection between the two apart from the fact that obviously I'm lending my vocals to a song that doesn't have anything to do with me as an artist."

TERRA NOVA AND EPS

In 2011 Scott was also part of the science-fiction drama series *Terra Nova*, which aired for a single season on the Fox network. Created by British writer Kelly Marcel and executive produced by famed filmmaker Steven Spielberg, the show centers on the Shannon family as they escape the dystopian vanishing world of 2149 and travel back in time to a prehistoric era in which dinosaurs roam free. In *Terra Nova*, Scott portrayed sixteen-year-old Maddy, a student and a member of the Shannon clan.

After *Terra Nova* was canceled, Scott faced a difficult period in which she auditioned for many roles only to watch them ultimately go to someone else. According to the actor, many casting directors often seemed confused about her multiracial background. "There's a thing of someone (being) like, 'She's not white, she's not black, she's not Latina, what is she?'" Scott told Tsjeng. "There were definitely a few leads that I went for where I think, ultimately, I was maybe the other choice, the 'exotic' choice, or the 'other.'" While she persevered in her attempts to get more acting work, she also dedicated more of her time to music.

In 2014 Scott released her first EP, which she called *Invisible Division*. Without binding herself to a specific genre, theme, or technique or method, she went through the songwriting process with total creative autonomy. As she told Mahbub, "I have different processes for different songs. . . . what I usually do is build the track up myself, then I'll come up with a bunch of melodies, and then lyric the melody." In many cases she developed songs on the piano, an instrument she had studied for years to help her general musicianship.

The idea behind Scott's second EP, *Promises* (2016), was that every track on the record would explore a unique perspective of what it is like to be in a relationship for different people. From living a romantic connection in a free-spirited way, to living it with distrust and cynicism, to not living it at all and being closed off to love, tunes such as "Fool" and "Lover's Lies" are meant to depict the ups and downs of an intimate relationship.

HOLLYWOOD BREAKTHROUGH

Scott appeared in a variety of minor acting roles before landing the part of Kimberly Hart, the Pink Ranger, in the 2017 reboot of the popular *Power Rangers* franchise. The big-budget movie production was by far her highest-profile project to that point. Her character, a student attending Angel Grove High School, becomes one of the superheroes—alongside four other rangers—who must defend the earth from villain Rita Repulsa, a humanoid alien played by actor Elizabeth Banks. Although *Power Rangers* received mixed reviews from critics and did not live up to expectations at the box office, the film introduced Scott to a global audience, opening doors for future roles in Hollywood.

Indeed, Scott quickly built on her breakthrough appearance with two blockbuster films in 2019. That May saw the release of Disney's live-action remake of *Aladdin*, in which she starred as Princess Jasmine. Set in the fictitious Arabian city of Agrabah, the story follows a charming street thief named Aladdin (Mena Massoud), who, with the help of a genie (Will Smith) trapped inside a magic lamp, transforms into a prince with the hope of marrying Princess Jasmine. The film received overall mixed reviews but earned over $1 billion, making it one of the highest-grossing films of the year. Critics and viewers alike lauded Scott's performance as a highlight. Her work ethic and positive attitude on set did not go unnoticed, either. As director Guy Ritchie told Christopher Bagley for *W Magazine* (1 May 2019), "Naomi is something of a nuclear reactor when it comes to radiating generosity and talent."

As a musical, *Aladdin* also showcased Scott's singing talents for a global audience. The film's soundtrack became a success in its own right, topping the Billboard soundtracks chart and reaching sixth on the Billboard 200 album chart. Scott's key song as Jasmine, "Speechless," and her duet with Massoud on the signature song "A Whole New World" both also reached the charts as singles.

After the success of *Aladdin*, Scott starred as Elena Houghlin, one of three secret agents in the reboot of *Charlie's Angels*, an action-comedy film released in November 2019. Written and directed by Scott's *Power Rangers* costar Banks, the film sought to put a more feminist spin on the longstanding franchise. Once again, the film received underwhelming reviews (and, in this case, flopped at the box office), but many critics praised the performances of Scott and her co-leads. Banks also praised Scott highly, emphasizing her professionalism. However, the actor remarked that she still considered herself "a work in progress," as she told Bagley. "I'm just trying this approach of being honest, of being myself, and seeing how it goes."

PERSONAL LIFE

Scott met Jordan Spence, who would eventually become a professional soccer player, in church when they were both teenagers. After becoming friends and then dating for several years, they were married in 2014, when she was twenty-one. The two became active supporters of Compassion UK, a Christian humanitarian organization offering support to children around the world who live in poverty.

Scott is vocal about her struggles with eczema and how this condition affects her life and work. In her interview with Tsjeng she noted, "I think it's kind of important to just not hide all the imperfections. You know, it's part of who I am."

SUGGESTED READING

Bagley, Christopher. "Wishing for Naomi Scott, *Aladdin*'s New Princess Jasmine and Hollywood's Next Movie Star." *W Magazine*, 1 May 2019, www.wmagazine.com/story/w-cover-naomi-scott-aladdin-princess-jasmine-charlies-angels-movie. Accessed 25 June 2020.

Lack, Hannah. "Cover Story: Naomi Scott, from Normal Girl to New Superhero." *AnOther Magazine*, 10 Sept. 2019, www.anothermag.com/fashion-beauty/11878/naomi-scott-interview-aladdin-power-rangers-charlies-angels-parents-religion. Accessed 25 June 2020.

Mahbub, Mufsin. "Actress Naomi Scott Explains Her Deep Connection with Music." *HuffPost*, 28 Mar. 2017, www.huffpost.com/entry/actress-naomi-scott-explains-her-deep-connection-with_b_58dabc64e4b07f61a2bb8935. Accessed 25 June 2020.

Tsjeng, Zing. "Naomi Scott on *Charlie's Angels* and Navigating Hollywood." *Teen Vogue*, 4 Sept. 2019, www.teenvogue.com/story/naomi-scott-september-2019. Accessed 25 June 2020.

"Who Is Naomi Scott? 11 Things You Need to Know about the Actress Playing Jasmine in *Aladdin*." *Elle*, 22 May 2019, www.elle.com/culture/celebrities/news/a46649/naomi-scott-facts-jasmine-aladdin. Accessed 25 June 2020.

SELECTED WORKS

Life Bites, 2009; *Lemonade Mouth*, 2011; *Terra Nova*, 2011; *Power Rangers*, 2017; *Aladdin*, 2019; *Charlie's Angels*, 2019

—*Maria del Pilar Guzman*

Travis Scott

Date of birth: April 30, 1992
Occupation: Rapper

Although most often described as a rapper, hip-hop artist Travis Scott has expressed his belief that such a descriptor fails to capture the true breadth of his capabilities as an artist. "What the f—— is a rapper? I dunno," he told Olivier Joyard for *Numéro Homme* (6 Mar. 2017). "Me, I sing, I rap, I do beats, I sometimes make videos." Indeed, Scott's opposition to easy categorization has long made its way into his music, which blends a variety of genres and influences as well as the distinctive contributions of his many guest artists and frequent collaborators. The positive critical and commercial reception of his records, including the Grammy Award–nominated 2018 album *Astroworld*, further signaled his audience's interest in music bound neither by genre

Photo by Frank Schwichtenberg via Wikimedia Commons

conventions nor the dictates of record executives. "I see hip-hop as going in a self-managing place," Scott explained to Dan Hyman for *Billboard* (17 Sept. 2015). "It's very culturally controlled and artist-controlled. It's not really based on a label anymore. Everything is pretty much in the control of the artist. Which is amazing."

EARLY LIFE AND EDUCATION

Scott was born Jacques Webster Jr. on April 30, 1992 in Houston, Texas. He has an older brother as well as two younger siblings. His father was an entrepreneur who later pursued a career in music, while his mother worked in electronics sales. After spending the first years of his life living in Houston with his grandmother, he moved with his immediate family to the suburb of Missouri City, where he would spend the remainder of his childhood and teen years.

The son of a drummer father and the grandson of a jazz composer, Scott was drawn to music from a young age and began playing the drums at the age of three. He later studied piano but eventually quit playing the instrument because, as he would explain in interviews, playing piano did not help him get the attention of girls. As a teenager, Scott had wide-ranging musical tastes that included artists and groups such as Kanye West, Kid Cudi, Portishead, and the Sex Pistols. By the time he was about sixteen, he had developed an interest in hip-hop producing and had begun making beats for use by rappers, a category of performer that soon included Scott himself. "I always wanted to know how to rap. I was just trying to tell my life story, trying to explain who I

am," he recalled to Insanul Ahmed for *Complex* (3 Oct. 2012). "I would make the beats and write the hooks. I was like, 'I got to get better.'"

As a student at Elkins High School, a public high school in Missouri City, Scott participated in theater but focused primarily on his musical aspirations and received encouragement from his guidance counselor, whom he would credit in the 2019 documentary *Travis Scott: Look Mom I Can Fly* with having "saved my life in high school," as quoted by Joey Guerra in the *Houston Chronicle* (8 Sept. 2019). After graduating from high school, Scott enrolled at the University of Texas at San Antonio, where he completed his freshman year of college. He ultimately left the university during his sophomore year and, with money his parents had given him for school, moved to New York to pursue musical opportunities, initially without informing his parents of his departure.

EARLY CAREER

Scott began releasing music while still in high school, working on a variety of projects with friends. Perhaps his most productive collaboration during that period was with Jason Eric, a performer who would later rap under the name OG Che$$. As the duo the Classmates, Scott and Eric released several extended-play (EP) records, including the 2011 mixtape *Cruis'n USA*. As independent artists, the Classmates worked to build a following locally and made their work freely available online through social-networking sites such as MySpace.

After dropping out of college and living in New York for several months, Scott moved to Los Angeles, California, and worked to establish himself there while staying with various friends. His decision to move to California began to pay off almost immediately. "When I got off the plane in LA, I had fourteen text messages from [rapper and record executive] T.I. and his camp," Scott recalled to Ahmed. "They were like, 'Yo, can you come by the studio?' And I was like, 'Yo, this is like nuts man.'" In addition to working with T.I., Scott soon made perhaps the most significant professional connection of his early career when he traveled to New York to meet with rapper and producer Kanye West, one of hip-hop's most popular artists during that period. After playing his music for West, Scott joined the established artist and his numerous collaborators in their work on the compilation album *Cruel Summer* (2012). Scott served as a producer for several tracks on *Cruel Summer*, and his vocals were featured on the song "Sin City."

Remaining closely tied to West over the next several years, Scott formed a strong working relationship with the artist, who became a mentor of sorts. "He's like my stepdad," he told Hyman. "We always had that relationship where we cook up ideas. We [talk] all the time about . . . life and how we can do better as people and as rock stars. Our goal is to help people figure out who they want to be." Scott would later coproduce West's song "New Slaves" from the 2013 album *Yeezus*, which was nominated for the 2014 Grammy Award for Best Rap Song.

SOLO CAREER

In 2013, Scott released his first solo mixtape EP, *Owl Pharaoh*, which features a title derived in part from the artist's own largely nocturnal work schedule. Recalling long nights at the studio during his time in New York, often beginning work at ten at night, he told Ahmed, "I would not see the day until like I woke up in the studio. From my time in Houston, that's when I could just get everything done, in the night." He followed that release with the 2014 mixtape *Days before Rodeo* and in 2015 made his full-length debut with the album *Rodeo*. A popular work among listeners, *Rodeo* reached the number-one spot on the Billboard Top Rap Albums chart and peaked at number three on the Billboard 200. Among other songs, the album produced the single "Antidote," which peaked at number four on the Billboard rap singles chart and number sixteen on the Billboard Hot 100.

Scott went on to release his second album, *Birds in the Trap Sing McKnight*, in 2016. Featuring appearances by artists such as Kendrick Lamar, Quavo, and Young Thug, the album reached the number-one spot on Billboard's rap and R&B and hip-hop album charts as well as on the Billboard 200. In addition to his albums, Scott made numerous appearances as a featured artist, collaborating on songs with artists such as Wiz Khalifa, SZA, Drake, Kodak Black, and others. Scott notably worked with pop singer Justin Bieber and commented in interviews that while such partnerships might have been surprising for some of his fans, he did not shy away from working with pop artists. "I wouldn't make music with you if I didn't know you. If you're a good artist and if you know it as well, I'm down," he explained to Paul Flynn for a 2017 interview for the British edition of *GQ Style*. "So I don't look at it as pop. I also look at the artist, for their voice or influence, their style of music."

ASTROWORLD

In 2017, Scott further asserted himself as a major force in the hip-hop music industry through the establishment of the record label Cactus Jack Records, which would release not only Scott's upcoming music but also records from other artists. "I'm not doing it to have financial control over my music," he told Joyard. "I want first and foremost to help other artists, launch new names, to provide opportunities. I want to do for them what happened to me, but better."

Scott's first album released through Cactus Jack Records was *Huncho Jack, Jack Huncho* (2017), a side project created in collaboration with Quavo, a member of the rap group Migos.

The following year saw the release of Scott's third album, his most successful work up to that point. Titled *Astroworld* after a Houston-area amusement park he had visited as a child, the album claimed the number-one spot on several Billboard charts, including the rap albums chart and the Billboard 200, and likewise reached high positions on several international charts. "It might be the best music that I made. I have two records on the album that are like, man, they are the best," Scott told Flynn about *Astroworld*. In addition to the album as a whole, Scott received extensive attention for the work's single "Sicko Mode," which features a guest appearance by the popular rapper and singer Drake. As well as claiming the top spot on Billboard's rap, R&B/hip-hop, and Hot 100 charts, "Sicko Mode" went on to be nominated for two Grammy Awards, in the categories of Best Rap Performance and Best Rap Song. *Astroworld* in its entirety was nominated for the Grammy for Best Rap Album. Scott followed *Astroworld*, which had further increased his profile to the point where he had the opportunity to serve as the musical guest on *Saturday Night Live* in 2018, with *JackBoys* (2019), a collaboration with various artists signed to Cactus Jack Records as well as numerous guest artists. Meanwhile, a documentary about his career and rise to fame, *Travis Scott: Look Mom I Can Fly*, debuted on Netflix in 2019, and he performed as a guest at the Super Bowl halftime show that same year.

In addition to earning Grammy nominations for his own work, Scott received similar recognition for his work with other artists. Having been nominated for a Grammy for Best Rap/Sung Performance for his work with SZA on the song "Love Galore," from her 2017 album *Ctrl*, in 2020 he was nominated for Best Rap/Sung Performance for the song "The London" with Young Thug and J. Cole, from the Young Thug album *So Much Fun*.

PERSONAL LIFE

Scott was in a relationship with television personality and entrepreneur Kylie Jenner, a younger half-sister of celebrity Kim Kardashian (who married early Scott collaborator Kanye West), between 2017 and 2019. Scott and Jenner had a daughter, Stormi, in 2018. In addition to music, Scott maintains an interest in fashion and collaborated with brands such as Helmut Lang.

SUGGESTED READING

Flynn, Paul. "Travis Scott Interview: 'Astroworld Sounds Like Taking an Amusement Park Away from Kids.'" *British GQ Style*, Spring/Summer

2017. *GQ*, 17 Aug. 2018, www.gq-magazine. co.uk/article/travis-scott-astroworld-tour. Accessed 9 Feb. 2020.

Guerra, Joey. "Meet the High School Counselor Who Rapper Travis Scott Says Saved His Life." *Houston Chronicle*, 8 Sept. 2019, www.houstonchronicle.com/entertainment/movies_tv/article/Meet-the-high-school-counselor-who-rapper-Travis-14420339.php. Accessed 9 Feb. 2020.

Scott, Travis. "Travis Scott Dishes on 'Stepdad' Kanye West and Being Misunderstood." Interview by Dan Hyman. *Billboard*, 17 Sept. 2015, www.billboard.com/articles/news/magazine-feature/6700345/travis-scott-rodeo-rihanna-kanye-west-justin-bieber. Accessed 9 Feb. 2020.

——. "Travis Scott Launches His Label Cactus Jack Records and Other Revelations." Interview by Olivier Joyard. *Numéro Homme*, 6 Mar. 2017, www.numero.com/en/men/travis-scott-interview-nick-knight-numero-music-kany-west#_. Accessed 9 Feb. 2020.

——. "Who Is Travi$ Scott?" Interview by Insanul Ahmed. *Complex*, 3 Oct. 2012, www.complex.com/music/2012/10/who-is-travis-scott/. Accessed 9 Feb. 2020.

Weiner, Jonah. "Travis Scott: In Orbit with Rap's Newest Superstar." *Rolling Stone*, 20 Dec. 2018, www.rollingstone.com/music/music-features/travis-scott-rap-superstar-cover-story-767906/. Accessed 9 Feb. 2020.

SELECTED WORKS
Rodeo, 2015; *Birds in the Trap Sing McKnight*, 2016; *Huncho Jack, Jack Huncho* (with Quavo), 2017; *Astroworld*, 2018; *JackBoys* (with various artists), 2019

—*Joy Crelin*

Stuart Semple
Date of birth: September 12, 1980
Occupation: Artist and curator

Artist Stuart Semple's work as both an artist and an activist focuses on equality and accessibility. He has been called a post-Pop art painter, with clear roots in the work of artists such as Andy Warhol, Jean-Michel Basquiat, and Jeff Koons. As Nathalie Olah wrote for the *Guardian* (30 Aug. 2019), "Semple is best in his childlike work, where his sense of psychological distress is conveyed through the sheer desperation for something more light-hearted and fun." He has curated exhibits for galleries in both London, England, and Milan, Italy, and his works are collected by such celebrities as singer Lady Gaga

and actor Sienna Miller. The popularity of his work made him a millionaire by age twenty-eight. He has also worked with bands like the Futureheads, using their song lyrics in his paintings. Semple has compared his own process to the way musicians work in first composing and then recording their music.

EARLY LIFE AND EDUCATION
Semple was born in Bournemouth, England. He knew from early childhood that he wanted to be an artist, as he told the editors of *Soundsphere Magazine* (16 July 2011), "My mum had taken me to the national gallery and there was a Van Gogh there, it was the sunflowers it hit me like nothing I'd seen before that." Semple expanded on the impact the painting had on him, stating, "I didn't really know what being an artist was, I just knew I wanted to try and make stuff. I went home and I copied every Van Gogh picture I could find with oil paints that my nana let me use." He later attended art school at West Yorkshire's Bretton Hall. When he left home for college, his grandmother bought him a pair of paint coveralls that he cherished.

Semple has numerous allergies, including a nut allergy that nearly killed him when he was a teenager. After unknowingly eating an allergen, Semple had difficulty breathing because of the swelling of his tongue. He expected to die after further complications from a plasma infusion meant to help, in fact, briefly caused him to flatline. As he told Liz Hoggard for *Evening Standard* (28 Apr. 2010), "The doctors told me there was not very much they could do." He

Photo by David M. Benett/Dave Benett/Getty Images for Moncler

spent months in the hospital, but finally his body healed; doctors gave him a list of more than fifty items to which he is allergic, and he developed a fear of swallowing.

EARLY CAREER
Despite his health issues, Semple followed through on his determination to become an artist, exhibiting in clubs and bars and selling his art on eBay. Around 2001, when he was twenty-one, Semple had his first solo show in London. In 2004, the Momart warehouse art storage facility in east London caught fire. The fire caused more than ten million pounds of damage and devoured many noted works of art. The following year, Semple used the remains of British art from the Momart to create a memorial artwork entitled *Burn Baby Burn: RIP YBA* (Young British Artists).

Semple was later part of a 2005 protest at the Saatchi Gallery in London. The exhibit, entitled *The Triumph of Painting: Part Two*, featured several German artists but did not include work from a single English artist. In response, Semple sneaked a twenty-nine-square-inch canvas with the words "British Painting Still Rocks" painted on it into the gallery to protest the omission. In 2007, Semple displayed the exhibit *Fake Plastic Love*—a show featuring billboard-sized paintings—at the Truman Brewery during the Frieze Art Fair. More than ten thousand people visited the exhibit and Semple sold more than one million dollars' worth of artwork in the first five minutes of the show.

Two years later, Semple decided to spread some cheer during the recession in London by releasing more than two thousand pink, smiling cloud sculptures over the Tate Modern Museum as part of an art installation *Happy Clouds*. Semple made the biodegradable clouds out of vegetable dye, soap bubbles, and helium, and released them every seven seconds. As he later told Stephanie Wolf for *Colorado Public Radio* (17 May 2018), "I really believe that creativity, community, mindfulness and self-expression are the ways that we achieve the lasting happiness. And that's just as effective if you're depressed or anxious as it is if you aren't."

A VARIETY OF EXHIBITS
In 2013, Semple created the outdoor art installation titled *JUMP*, a one-hundred-square-meter inflatable sculpture that children could bounce on. The work was first installed in Federation Square in Melbourne, Australia, before moving to various locations around the world. Semple's next exhibit, *Anxiety Generation*, premiered in London in 2014. The exhibit featured a series of paintings that overlaid paint on still images from movies—particularly violent thriller or horror films—and printed lyrics from popular songs.

Jonathan R. Jones wrote in review of the exhibit for *Modern Painters* (Feb. 2015): "To cut through our cynicism and give images again the power to disturb is quite a feat; that Semple manages it via the medium of paint is even more impressive." In 2016, the city of London invited artists to display their work in public spaces to celebrate the new web domain *Dot London*. Semple created the digital design *Happy Dot*, a bright yellow circle featuring all the components of a smiley face.

From April to June 2018, Semple created the city-wide art exhibition *Happy City: Art for the People* in Denver, Colorado. The six-week exhibit featured several different instillations around the city, including new versions of *Happy Clouds* and *JUMP*. Influenced by Semple's time attending Catholic schools and participating in the sacrament of reconciliation, one piece of artwork called *Emotional Baggage Drop* resembled a confessional. The interactive instillation let two visitors enter a booth constructed so that they remained invisible to each other except for their eyes. They could then let go of some emotional weight by telling it to an anonymous stranger. As Semple told Wolf (17 May 2018), "Although I'm not a religious person, there was no denying there's a huge sense of relief after you get something off your chest."

COLOR FEUD
In the mid-2010s, the industrial engineering company Surrey NanoSystems created Vantablack, a color originally developed for aerospace projects. After the company found a simpler and more cost-effective way to produce the color as a spray-on, they saw its potential as the blackest synthetic color in the art world. In 2016, they signed over exclusive rights to the material to sculptor Anish Kapoor. The decision brought many negative comments from other artists.

To counter Kapoor's monopoly, Semple—who had begun making his own pigments during college—created the pigment Pinkest Pink. He made the ultra-fluorescent pink available to everyone except Kapoor. When he offered it for sale on his website, he did so with an explicit signed agreement that the buyer could not sell or give the color to Kapoor. Although the color was intended to be more of a performance piece than for profit, Semple soon sold more than five thousand jars of Pinkest Pink.

Inevitably, Kapoor obtained a jar of the color and posted a photo of his middle finger dipped in the color. In retaliation, Semple began working on a blacker black, with suggestions from artist friends. Black 2.0, similar to Vantablack, was released in 2017. Like Pinkest Pink, it was not to be sold to or purchased for Anish Kapoor, who, having made his point, did not further engage with the debate. Semple, too, was done, as he told Adam Rogers for *Wired* (22 June 2017), "I haven't really had much time to paint. There's nowhere else for me to go as a paintmaker, unless there's a new development in technology. If there's a Black 3.0, that's fine, but that's the end for me. I have to get back to work." Ultimately, he did create Black 3.0 in 2019, with the expense covered by crowdfunding site *Kickstarter*. Semple has developed other colors and pigments as well, including Diamond Dust, described as the world's most glittery glitter, and Lit, the brightest glow pigment.

In a similar display of social commentary, in 2017, Semple began selling bags of pure English soil labeled "England" with the caveat that buyers could not sell or give the dirt to former British prime minister Theresa May. In 2019, Semple made an installation in central London he called a *Kapoor Katcher*, featuring a block of work resembling cheddar cheese; it was a nod to Kapoor's well-known love of cheese.

TWO DECADES OF WORK

In 2018, Semple launched *Hostiledesign.org* to help raise awareness about public spaces that have been designed to be unwelcoming. Semple was particularly outraged by the metal bars that his hometown of Bournemouth attached to public benches to prevent homeless people from sleeping on them. After Semple posted comments about the hostile design on his *Facebook* account, many people responded by tying balloons or yarn-bombing the bench bars; within a day, the town council removed the bars. In 2019, he worked with the British Broadcasting Corporation (BBC) to create a documentary, *Hostile Design*, to further advance awareness.

In 2019, Semple's twenty-year retrospective, *Dancing on My Own, Selected Works 1999–2019*, was shown at Bermondsey Project Space in London. The exhibit included not only paintings but also sculptures, moving images, and digital work; many of the works had never before been exhibited. The works demonstrated Semple's move from anxiety and depression over the near-death experiences his allergies had created to a happier frame of mind. His so-called un-hostile bench is home to a collection of stuffed animals, perhaps a reference to his activism.

Lee Cavaliere, who curated the exhibit, commented on *Bermondsey Project Space*'s website (Aug./Sept. 2019) about the show, "Stuart Semple's work straddles the line between art and activism. A champion of causes from mental health to social justice to homelessness to copyright law, his work draws on personal trauma to challenge, help and speak to our society and its deficiencies."

PERSONAL LIFE

On March 20, 2013, the first International Day of Happiness, the United Nations (UN) awarded Semple a Happiness Hero medal, recognizing his commitment to happiness. He is also a representative for the mental health charity Mind. Semple has a long-term partner, a former model, with whom he has a son.

SUGGESTED READING

Hoggard, Liz. "With My 53 Allergies, I'm Afraid to Swallow." *Evening Standard*, 28 Apr. 2010, p. 29. *Stuart Semple*, stuartsemple.com/evening-standard-wednesday-28th-april-2010/. Accessed 14 Nov. 2019.

Jones, Jonathan R. "Stuart Semple." *Modern Painters*, vol. 27, no. 2, Feb. 2015, p. 74. *Stuart Semple*, stuartsemple.com/wp-content/uploads/2015/01/jonathan-r-jones-stuart-semple-modern-painters_crop.jpg. Accessed 14 Nov. 2019.

Olah, Nathalie. "Fighting for Life and Feuding with Anish Kapoor: The Art of Stuart Semple." *The Guardian*, 30 Aug. 2019, www.theguardian.com/artanddesign/2019/aug/30/art-stuart-semple-feud-anish-kapoor-blacker-than-black-paint. Accessed 20 Nov. 2019.

Rogers, Adam. "Art Fight! The Pinkest Pink Versus the Blackest Black." *Wired*, 22 June 2017, www.wired.com/story/vantablack-anish-kapoor-stuart-semple/. Accessed 20 Nov. 2019.

Semple, Stuart. "Interview: Stuart Semple." *Sound Sphere*, 16 July 2011, www.soundspheremag.com/features/interview-stuart-semple 0. Accessed 15 Nov. 2019.

"Stuart Semple: Dancing on My Own: Selected Works 1999–2019." *Bermondsey Project Space*, Aug./Sept. 2019, project-space.london/stuart-semple-dancing-on-my-own. Accessed 15 Nov. 2019.

Wolf, Stephanie. "Get Ready to Smile: New Downtown Art Will Give Denver A 'Happy City' Makeover." *Colorado Public Radio*, 17 May 2018, www.cpr.org/2018/05/17/get-ready-to-smile-new-downtown-art-will-give-denver-a-happy-city-makeover/. Accessed 15 Nov. 2019.

SELECTED WORKS

Fake Plastic Love, 2007; *Happy Clouds*, 2009; *Anxiety Generation*, 2014; *Happy City: Art for the People*, 2018; *Dancing on My Own, Selected Works 1999–2019*, 2019

—*Judy Johnson*

Namwali Serpell

Born: 1980
Occupation: Writer

Namwali Serpell, a Zambian American novelist, critical theorist, and essayist, is the author of the celebrated 2019 novel *The Old Drift*. Developed over nearly two decades, the book follows three families over four generations. While writing it, Serpell and her friends jokingly referred to it as the "Great Zambian Novel," and in many ways, that is exactly what it is. Mark Athitakis for the *Washington Post* (26 Mar. 2019) described it as a "brilliant literary response" to "generations of colonialism, violence and bad politics." Dwight Garner of the *New York Times* (25 Mar. 2019), described the book as "dazzling" and "audacious." *The Old Drift* begins in what is now Zambia during the colonial era and stretches into the near future. The nearly 600-page novel, named for a colonial settlement on the banks of the Zambezi River, draws on elements of multiple genres including historical fiction, science fiction, and magical realism, and explores themes such as race, colonialism, freedom, and fate. "Serpell carefully husbands her resources," Garner wrote in his review. "She unspools her intricate and overlapping stories calmly. Small narrative hunches pay off big later, like cherries coming up on a slot machine."

The Old Drift won the Windham-Campbell Prize for fiction in March 2020. Although it was Serpell's first novel, she was no stranger to critical acclaim. She earned numerous awards for her early efforts, including the Caine Prize for her 2015 short story "The Sack." She also authored her own book of literary criticism, *Seven Modes of Uncertainty* (2014). In addition to her writing, Serpell held a position as an associate professor of English at the University of California, Berkeley, where she began teaching literature in 2008. She enjoyed the challenge of that work, as she told Isaac Chotiner for the *New Yorker* (3 Apr. 2019): "I think teaching literature courses makes you feel like you're in conversation with the great writers that you're teaching."

EARLY LIFE

Serpell was born Carla Namwali Serpell in 1980 in Lusaka, the capital city of Zambia, a landlocked country in south-central Africa. Serpell's mother, Namposya Nampanya-Serpell, was an economist; she grew up on the border of Zambia and Tanzania, and her own parents were from two different tribes. She died of ovarian cancer in 2016. Serpell's father, Robert Serpell, was a psychology professor. A white man born in London, he became a naturalized Zambian citizen in 1978. He taught at the University of Zambia (UNZA) for forty-two years before retiring

Photo by Slowking via Wikimedia Commons

in 2019. Serpell grew up with her step-brother, Derek, from her father's first marriage; her sisters Zewelanji and Chisha; and her cousins Mwila and Suwilanji.

Serpell's family lived briefly in Hull, England, where her mother was completing her master's degree. In 1989, they moved to Baltimore, Maryland, where her father took a position with the University of Maryland at Baltimore County. She struggled to navigate American conceptions of race. "In Zambia, the category for people like me has its own word, which is 'coloured,'" she explained to Richard Lea for the *Guardian* (30 Apr. 2019). "Obviously it has different connotations in the west, but at home that's just what you're called. It's a third term. . . So when I came to the States and I was asked, 'Well, what are you?', it was very difficult for me to negotiate the binary logic of you're either black or you're white." In the United States, she added, she identified as black. "Partly because I'm perceived as black," she said, but also because "the idea I could look at my mother and say to her that I'm not black makes no sense. To me, blackness is just part of what the family is."

Serpell's family returned to Lusaka for a year when she was fifteen. The time would prove formative. "Without that year spent at home—my mother was doing research for her dissertation, my father was taking a sabbatical—I don't think I would have the same kind of relationship with Zambia that I do," she told Chotiner.

EDUCATION AND EARLY WRITING CAREER

As a teenager, Serpell was an avid reader. She discovered her love for the classic English novel *Jane Eyre*, but also relished science fiction novels by authors like Michael Crichton and Ray Bradbury. She enrolled at Yale University to study biology, but an encounter with John Milton's seventeenth-century epic poem *Paradise Lost* convinced her to switch her major to English. Serpell graduated from Yale in 2001 and enrolled at Harvard University to pursue a master's degree, which she earned in 2004. She received her PhD in 2008. In 2009, her story titled "Muzungu"—later to become a chapter in *The Old Drift*—was selected for publication in the annual *Best American Short Stories* anthology. In 2010, the piece was short-listed for the Caine Prize for African Writing.

In 2014, Harvard University Press published Serpell's debut book of literary criticism, *Seven Modes of Uncertainty*, which was inspired by her doctoral thesis. The book engages with William Empson's foundational critical text, *Seven Types of Ambiguity* (1930). Serpell's book explores the relationship between literature's capacity to "unsettle, perplex, and bewilder us" as she puts it, and its ethical value. As case studies, Serpell uses experimental novels by Nobel Prize–winning novelist Toni Morrison, Thomas Pynchon, and Bret Easton Ellis, among others. Naomi Mandel, who reviewed *Seven Modes of Uncertainty* for the journal *Studies in the Novel* (Summer 2015), described it as an "ambitious and engaging study." Though its subject is unsettling material, Mandel wrote, "this is a fun book to read."

In 2015 Serpell won the Caine Prize for a short story called "The Sack," an enigmatic tale about two men, Jacob and Joseph, both referred to in the text as J, a woman named Naila, and a boy. (The story was originally intended to be the epilogue to *The Old Drift*.) Aaron Bady, who wrote about "The Sack" for the *New Inquiry* (7 July 2015), compared it to a Möbius strip, a loop with a single side that ends where it begins, but on the underside. The story can be understood as an allegory about reading or about race, but Bady also noted that it performs an observation from Serpell's book of criticism. "Literature produces free choice because the reader must decide what something means, and yet it's a free choice *which the text forces on us*," Bady wrote. "That's an uncomfortable place to find yourself, as a reader, to be forced to take responsibility for what you chose to put in the sack."

THE OLD DRIFT

Serpell's first novel, *The Old Drift* (2019) was a book eighteen years in the making. She began writing it while she was still in college. Set in what is now Zambia, *The Old Drift* spans four generations, stretching from the colonial era to the near future. The three families in the book are connected by a chance incident involving the British photographer Percy M. Clark (a real historical figure); an Italian hotelier; and a young African boy named N'gulubu. The lives of their descendants—including Sibilla, who was born with a rare condition that causes hair to grow from every surface of her body, and Matha Mwamba, who cries literal rivers of tears—intersect and ultimately intertwine. Serpell combines elements of magical realism, a nod to one of her guiding influences, Gabriel García Márquez, and reimagines the lives of real figures, like Clark. The character Matha was inspired by a real woman of the same name, who Serpell discovered while writing an article for the *New Yorker* in 2017. (That article—"The Zambian 'Afronaut' Who Wanted to Join the Space Race"—recalls the story of Edward Mukuka Nkoloso, an ambitious schoolteacher who oversaw a half-cocked training program aimed at launching Zambian astronauts, who he called "Afronauts," into space.)

In *The Old Drift*, Matha, the Afronaut, gives birth to Sylvia, a hair stylist, who gives birth to Jacob, who builds a fleet of microdrones the size of mosquitoes. Those pesky, occasionally malarial insects unite the disparate stories in the novel, which focuses on chance and error. "When Serpell daringly pushes past the present day to take us into a technologically advanced future and a climax that combines revolution and catastrophe, the mosquito trope is cleverly transformed and begins to make sense," novelist Salman Rushdie wrote in his review of the novel for the *New York Times* (28 Mar. 2019). "'The Old Drift' is an impressive book," he concluded, "ranging skillfully between historical and science fiction, shifting gears between political argument, psychological realism and rich fabulism."

Serpell later described *The Old Drift* as a product of the late twentieth century, a literary period "marked by those big postmodern, postcolonial, postimperial book[s]," she told novelist Lydia Kiesling for *The Cut* (29 Mar. 2019). Her list of inspirations includes Rushdie's *Midnight's Children* (1981) as well as Zadie Smith's kaleidoscopic, multigenerational tale of multicultural London, *White Teeth* (2000). Like Smith's book, *The Old Drift* engages with racism and Britain's colonial history. (Zambia, a former British colony, declared its independence in 1964.) To adequately capture this history, Serpell told Kiesling, she felt the need to explore various genres. "To me, genre is a kind of lens," she said. "If you look at an African country through lenses other than social realism, anthropology, sociology and so on, you see different things or you see the same things anew. I was keen to maintain the tropes of the genres I was exploring. . .

.That might sound strange, but I'm at a stage in my writing that I feel like the best way for me to critique and ironize something is to use and exaggerate it."

Serpell's next book, *Stranger Faces*, was scheduled for release in 2020. According to her website, the book comprises essays exploring the human face "as a mediated sign or *thing* that we delight in playing with." She also continued to experiment, telling interviewers of her efforts to blend literary criticism and autofiction. For Serpell, the urge to engage with the work of others could not be separated from her own fiction. "I have a lineage in my head of people like [Vladimir] Nabokov, Virginia Woolf, Zadie Smith, who do nonfiction essays and fiction," she told Chotiner. "On Twitter, my quote is from Toni Morrison, and I feel like that's the only way to really describe it, which is I read books, I teach books, I write books, I think about books. It's one job. I'm a book person."

SUGGESTED READING

Athitakis, Mark. "'The Old Drift' Is a Brilliant Literary Response to Generations of Bad Politics." Review of *The Old Drift*, by Namwali Serpell. *The Washington Post*, 26 Mar. 2019, www.washingtonpost.com/entertainment/books/the-old-drift-is-a-brilliant-literary-response-to-generations-of-bad-politics/2019/03/25/dcc678f2-472d-11e9-90f0-0ccfeec87a61_story.html. Accessed 12 May 2020.

Bady, Aaron. "Inside Out, Namwali Serpell's 'The Sack.'" *The New Inquiry*, 7 July 2015, thenewinquiry.com/blog/inside-out-namwali-serpells-the-sack/. Accessed 12 May 2020.

Chotiner, Isaac. "A Novelist and Critic on Fictionalizing Zambian History." *The New Yorker*, 3 Apr. 2019, www.newyorker.com/news/q-and-a/a-novelist-and-critic-on-fictionalizing-zambian-history. Accessed 11 May 2020.

Garner, Dwight. "'The Old Drift' Is a Dazzling Debut Spanning Four Generations." Review of *The Old Drift*, by Namwali Serpell. *The New York Times*, 25 Mar. 2019, www.nytimes.com/2019/03/25/books/review-old-drift-namwali-serpell.html. Accessed 12 May 2020.

Kiesling, Lydia. "She Joked about Writing the Great Zambian Novel. Then She Did It." *The Cut*, 29 Mar. 2019, www.thecut.com/2019/03/namwali-serpell-new-book-the-old-drift.html. Accessed 11 May 2020.

Mandel, Naomi. Review of *Seven Modes of Uncertainty*, by C. Namwali Serpell. *Studies of the Novel*, vol. 47, no. 2, 2015, pp. 279–80, doi:10.1353/sdn.2015.0019. Accessed 12 May 2020.

Rushdie, Salman. "Salman Rushdie Reviews a Sweeping Debut about the Roots of Modern Zambia." Review of *The Old Drift*, by Namwali Serpell. *The New York Times*, 28 Mar. 2019, www.nytimes.com/2019/03/28/books/review/old-drift-salman-rushdie.html. Accessed 13 May 2020.

—*Molly Hagan*

Léa Seydoux

Born: July 1, 1985
Occupation: Actor

It may seem like Léa Seydoux was destined for a career in film, given her impressive lineage. Her grandfather Jérôme Seydoux served as chair of the major film studio Pathé, while her granduncles included Nicolas Seydoux, head of Gaumont, the world's oldest film company, and Michel Seydoux, a prominent producer. However, Seydoux's decision to pursue acting drew little family support. "When I said, 'I want to be an actress,' my parents were like, 'Bullsh——t. Try if you want, but it's never going to work,'" she said during an interview with Alex Morris for *Rolling Stone* (17 Nov. 2015).

Despite her parents' discouragement, Seydoux exceeded expectations. After debuting as a teenager desperate to win a dance contest in *Mes Copines* (2006; *Girlfriends*), she made a name for herself in her native France, playing everything from a teen vixen in *La Belle Personne* (2008; *The Beautiful Person*) to Marie Antoinette's reader in *Les adieu à la reine* (2012; *Farewell, My Queen*) and an impoverished, irresponsible

Photo by Georges Biard via Wikimedia Commons

young woman in *L'enfant d'en haut* (2012; *Sister*). Seydoux's star status in her home country reached new heights with her award-winning portrayal of an alluring blue-haired art student in the controversial same-sex love story *La vie d'Adele* (2013; *Blue Is the Warmest Colour*). But it was her role as psychiatrist Madeleine Swann in the 2015 James Bond film *Spectre* that garnered her worldwide acclaim. Seydoux reprised her role in the next installment, *No Time to Die*, making her the first so-called Bond girl in franchise history to do so.

Seydoux's success has been attributed to her chameleon-like ability to play a wide variety of characters—a notion that she disputed. "I never act. I don't think that I inhabit someone else. I always act myself in all the films," she shared with Chloe Malle for *Town and Country* (3 Mar. 2020). "It's always the same character but molded in a different way. I don't become the character. I feel that I am the character."

EARLY LIFE AND INTRODUCTION TO ACTING

Léa Seydoux was born Léa Hélène Seydoux-Fornier de Clausonne on July 1, 1985, in Paris, France, to philanthropist Valérie Schlumberger and telecommunications magnate Henri Seydoux. Despite a seemingly idyllic childhood spent in the upscale, bohemian district of Saint-Germain-des-Près, Seydoux, whose parents divorced when she was three, grew up alongside her three older siblings in a strict Protestant household with little parental influence. Seydoux's mother often traveled to Senegal for Compagnie du Sénégal et de l'Afrique de l'Ouest (CSAO), her nonprofit promoting the works of West African artists, while Seydoux's father had launched his own 3-D imaging firm in 1986 before cofounding the luxury shoe firm Christian Louboutin in 1991. "I had a big family but I felt lost in the crowd," Seydoux told Hermione Eyre for the *Evening Standard* (31 Jan. 2014). "I always had the feeling I was an orphan."

Seydoux also struggled with shyness. Nevertheless, she aspired to become an opera singer, attending the world-renowned Conservatoire de Paris. She was equally drawn to classic French and American films; Charlie Chaplin's *The Kid* (1921), Disney's *Fantasia* (1940), and Jean Cocteau's *La Belle et la Bête* (1946; *Beauty and the Beast*) were among her childhood favorites. Seydoux's early fascination with American culture began at age seven, when her father enrolled her at Camp Timber Ridge in Maryland, where she spent six successive summers learning English.

It was a chance encounter that ultimately changed the course of the eighteen-year-old's life. "I met [an actor] who was just a friend and I found his life wonderful," Seydoux confided to Vanessa Lawrence for *W Magazine* (4 Oct. 2012). "I thought, Oh my god, you can travel, you're free, you can do what you want,

you're the boss." Against her parents' wishes, Seydoux successfully auditioned for acclaimed theater company *Les Enfants Terribles* (*The Terrible Children*). Within two years (2004–06), not only had she made her acting debut in the dramedy *Père et Maire* (*Father and Mayor*) and appeared in the music video for Raphaël's 2005 single "Ne partons pas fâchés, (Let's Not Leave Upset)" but she also had landed her first major role in Sylvie Ayme's teen flick *Mes Copines* (*My Friends*).

MAKING A SPLASH AT CANNES AND IN HOLLYWOOD

Seydoux's profile was significantly raised in 2007 with her red carpet debut at the Cannes Film Festival. Two of her movies were screened at the event: Nicolas Klotz's dramatic short *La consolation* and the French-Italian costume drama *Une vieille maitresse* (*The Last Mistress*). The same year well-respected French independent filmmaker Jean-Pierre Mocky directed Seydoux in the big-screen crime drama *13 French Street*. Another highlight included her Cannes Lions-winning commercial for Levis jeans, "Dangerous Liaison," chronicling an amorous denim-clad couple removing layers of clothing—each time revealing fashion trends (clothing and hairstyles) spanning the 1870s to 2007.

Seydoux had a further breakthrough in 2008. Following minor roles in the telefilm *Les vacances de Clémence* (*Clémence's Vacation*) and Nora Hamdi's feature directorial debut, *Des poupées et des anges* (*Dolls and Angels*), she costarred in *De la guerre* (*On War*), which premiered at Cannes. But it was her turn as a teen temptress in the coming-of-age drama *La belle personne* that earned her a most promising actress nomination at the Thirty Fourth César Awards. Hollywood quickly took notice, as Seydoux was handpicked to join the cast of two blockbuster films: Quentin Tarantino's World War II drama *Inglourious Basterds* (2009) and Ridley Scott's *Robin Hood* (2010). She also became a festival circuit mainstay, appearing in several French arthouse films, most notably as a nun in the religious drama *Lourdes* (2009), a sexy hitchhiker in the road movie *Plein sud* (2009, *Going South*); and a materialistic bride in the post-WWII flick *Roses à Crédit* (2010; *Roses on Credit*). Her portrayal of a rebellious teenager in *Belle Épine* (2010; *Dear Prudence*) nabbed Seydoux her second nod as most promising actress at the 2011 César Awards. Equally noteworthy was *Time Doesn't Stand Still*, her 2011 short-film collaboration with French dancer/choreographer Benjamin Millepied.

Although she narrowly missed out on the role of the titular protagonist in David Fincher's 2011 adaptation of *The Girl with the Dragon Tattoo* (a part that ultimately went to Rooney Mara), Seydoux remained a rising young talent.

She landed small but memorable roles in two top-grossing Hollywood films—without ever auditioning. After seeing her photograph, famed director Woody Allen cast Seydoux in *Midnight in Paris* (2011) as Gabrielle, a captivating French antique dealer who connects with a vacationing older American writer (Owen Wilson) over their shared love of Cole Porter and walking in the rain. Action star Tom Cruise tapped her to portray Sabine Moreau, a ruthless assassin in *Mission Impossible: Ghost Protocol* (2011). For her first-ever action role, Seydoux performed her own stunts, including an unforgettable fight-to-the-death sequence with costar Paula Patton.

BLUE IS THE WARMEST COLOUR

Seydoux's acting chops were increasingly on full display in 2012. As fictional character Agathe-Sidonie Laborde, a loyal servant to spoiled Marie Antoinette, in Benoît Jacquot's French Revolution drama *Farewell, My Queen*, she received her third César nomination—her first in the best actress category. She followed up that period piece with the modern-day *Sister*, in which she played a feckless twenty-something supported financially by her twelve-year-old brother, a robber of tourists at a nearby lavish Swiss ski resort. Along with earning a best film nod at the 2012 Berlin International Film Festival, the movie was nominated for best international film at the 2013 Independent Spirit Awards.

Building on those successes, Seydoux's portrayal of a free-spirited college art student romantically involved with a younger, inexperienced teenager (played by Adèle Exarchopoulos) in the coming-of-age drama *Blue Is the Warmest Colour* (2013) garnered her far greater recognition than her previous roles. The film's world premiere at Cannes not only earned rapturous applause from the audience but also made history, with the jury jointly awarding the Palme d'Or, the festival's highest prize, to leads Seydoux and Exarchopoulos as well as director Abdellatif Kechiche. The visibly emotional trio embraced onstage while accepting the coveted award.

Despite its critical acclaim, there was also significant controversy surrounding *Blue Is the Warmest Colour*'s graphic depictions of sexual acts and nudity, specifically a seven-minute simulated sex scene that took ten days to shoot and caused some outraged Cannes audience members to abruptly leave the screening. When the film made its US debut at the 2013 Telluride Film Festival in August, Seydoux criticized Kechiche's filming technique. "Of course it was kind of humiliating sometimes, I was feeling like a prostitute," she told Kaleem Aftab for the *Independent* (4 Oct. 2013). "He was using three cameras, and when you have to fake your orgasm for six hours . . . I can't say that it was nothing." Kechiche dismissed Seydoux as a privileged and

pampered heiress. In the wake of their public falling-out, Seydoux, who vowed never to work with Kechiche again, was honored with her second consecutive César nomination for best actress (2014), as well as the Best Actress Lumières Award (2014) for her performances in *Blue Is the Warmest Colour* and the romantic drama *Grand Central* (2013), in which she starred as a married power plant worker caught in a love triangle.

SPECTRE AND INTERNATIONAL STARDOM

Seydoux shifted gears with her next project, tackling the role of Belle (opposite Vincent Cassel's Beast) in *La Belle et La Bête*, Christophe Gans's 2014 version of *Beauty and the Beast*. The project was close to Seydoux's heart, as she was a self-professed huge fan of the timeless classic, viewing Jean Cocteau's 1946 film of the same name more than three hundred times. "For a long time I was obsessed with fairy tales, so this is a dream. . . . I wanted to be a princess," she confided to Jessica Kiang for *Indiewire* (11 Feb. 2012). Seydoux also had a cameo in another high-profile 2014 movie: Wes Anderson's ensemble *The Grand Budapest Hotel*. She then reunited with Jacquot for *Journal d'une femme de chambre* (2015; *Diary of a Chambermaid*) and costarred in the dystopian comedy *The Lobster* (2015), which won the jury prize at Cannes.

Seydoux's next role was her highest-profile yet: playing the love interest/leading lady in the twenty-fourth James Bond film, *Spectre*. However, she nearly lost the part during the first audition, when she struggled to remember her lines after attempting to overcome her nervousness by secretly consuming a beer before her meeting with producers. After convincing them to give her another shot, Seydoux nailed her second audition and was offered the role of Dr. Madeleine Swann, psychiatrist and daughter of recurring villain Mr. White. When *Spectre* premiered in the United States in November 2015, the spy thriller drew about $73 million during its opening weekend—the franchise's second-largest debut (behind 2012's *Skyfall*). With a worldwide gross of over $880 million, *Spectre* became the sixth-highest grossing film of 2015 and raised Seydoux's profile considerably.

The following year Seydoux was back at Cannes, appearing in the French Canadian drama *Juste la fin du monde* (*It's Only the End of the World*), another Cassel collaboration, which won the Grand Prix. After a brief hiatus she returned to the big screen in 2018, with the real-life submarine disaster movie *Kursk* (*The Command*) and the sci-fi romance *Zoe*. She also returned to Cannes—this time, as a jury member. After playing a murder suspect in the 2019 crime drama and Palme d'Or finalist *Roubaix, une lumière* (*Oh Mercy!*), Seydoux completed filming her role as Swann in the next Bond installment, *No Time to Die*. The film was due to be released in November 2020, but its premier was indefinitely postponed due to the coronavirus pandemic.

PERSONAL LIFE

Seydoux had a son, George Meyer, in 2017 with her partner, André Meyer. The notoriously private Seydoux made headlines with an exclusive 2017 piece she wrote for the *Guardian*, in which she detailed film producer Harvey Weinstein's sexual harassment and attempt to sexually assault her, at a time when other actors were coming forward with similar accusations.

SUGGESTED READING

Aftab, Kaleem. "The Many Layers of Léa Seydoux," *Independent*, 20 Oct. 2012, www.independent.co.uk/arts-entertainment/films/features/the-many-layers-of-l-a-seydoux-8216807.html. Accessed 10 May 2020.

Eyre, Hermione. "L'Agent Provocateur: Meet Léa Seydoux, Star of Blue Is the Warmest Colour." *Evening Standard*, 31 Jan. 2014, www.standard.co.uk/lifestyle/esmagazine/lagent-provocateur-meet-l-a-seydoux-star-of-blue-is-the-warmest-colour-9094136.html. Accessed 10 May 2020.

Kiang, Jessica. "Berlinale 2012: Léa Seydoux on 'Farewell, My Queen,' American Filmmaking & the Classic French Cinema She Loves." *IndieWire*, 11 Feb. 2012, www.indiewire.com/2012/02/berlinale-2012-lea-seydoux-on-farewell-my-queen-american-filmmaking-the-classic-french-cinema-she-loves-253740/. Accessed 10 May 2020.

Lawrence, Vanessa. "Five Minutes with Lea Seydoux." *W*, 4 Oct. 2012, www.wmagazine.com/story/lea-seydoux-french-actress-interview/. Accessed 10 May 2020.

Malle, Chloe. "Léa Seydoux and the Last Temptation of James Bond." *Town & Country*, 3 Mar. 2020, www.townandcountrymag.com/leisure/arts-and-culture/a30899223/lea-seydoux-james-bond-girl-no-time-to-die-cover-story/. Accessed 10 May 2020.

Morris, Alex. "Léa Seydoux: Meet the Chic 'Spectre' Bond Girl," *Rolling Stone*, 17 Nov. 2015, www.rollingstone.com/movies/movie-news/lea-seydoux-meet-the-chic-spectre-bond-girl-74042/. Accessed 10 May 2020.

SELECTED WORKS

Inglourious Basterds, 2009; *Mission: Impossible: Ghost Protocol*, 2011; *Midnight in Paris*, 2011; *Farewell, My Queen*, 2012; *Sister*, 2012; *Blue Is the Warmest Colour*, 2013; *Beauty and the Beast*, 2014; *Spectre*, 2015

—Bertha Muteba

Elif Shafak

Date of birth: October 25, 1971
Occupation: Novelist

British Turkish writer Elif Shafak has written more than a dozen books and earned multiple awards. Writing in both English and Turkish, she has had works translated into more than forty languages. After winning the Great Rumi Award from her native Turkey for her debut novel, *Pinhan* (1997), Shafak's body of work—including the memoir *Black Milk* (2007) and the novels *The Bastard of Istanbul* (2006) and *Honour* (2011)—made her an international best seller. Her 2019 English novel, *10 Minutes 38 Seconds in this Strange World*, was longlisted for the 2019 Booker Prize.

Shafak began reading and writing as a child. As she wrote for *World Literature Today* (Jan. 2015), "Books saved me. Books held my pieces together. Books loved me. And I loved them in return. I loved them with my entire soul." Of the work of the novelist, she told Shrestha Saha for the *Telegraph* (20 July 2019), "I don't think fiction writers should ever preach. Or try to teach. Not at all. Our job is not to try to give the answers. Our job is to ask the questions. I will always leave the answers to the readers and respect their diversity." Interested in politics and world issues, Shafak was also a founding member of the European Council on Foreign Relations (ECFR), a member of the World Economic Forum Global Agenda Council on creative economy in Davos and gave several TED Talks.

Photo by Zeynel Abidin via Wikimedia Commons

EARLY LIFE AND EDUCATION

Elif Shafak was born on October 25, 1971, in Strasbourg, France, where her father was then studying, but moved to Ankara, Turkey, with her mother after her parents separated. Her grandmother raised her while her mother went to college. Her grandmother's Middle Eastern influence is clear in Shafak's writing. As she told Saha, "Grandma was not a very educated woman but she was very wise and she would tell me stories of the Middle East. And the technique in these oral stories is always layered—stories within stories. You open a door and there is another door inside."

Because of the violent political demonstrations in Turkey, it was dangerous to play outside during Shafak's early childhood. She instead spent her time reading classic literature. After her mother graduated college, she began working for the Turkish Embassy, spending time in Spain, Jordan, and Germany. An only child who moved frequently, Shafak was often lonely. Her mother gave her a diary and encouraged her to write. Feeling that her own life was boring, at eight years old, Shafak began to write of imaginary people and their doings.

By the time she was ten, Shafak was bilingual. While still in school she read Virginia Woolf's novel *Orlando* (1928), which she found life changing. As she told the *Guardian* (29 Nov. 2019), "Daring to go beyond all boundaries—culture, geography, time, gender, east/west, past/future—*Orlando* gave me what only good literature is capable of providing: a true sense of freedom."

Shafak earned a master's degree in gender and women's studies and a doctorate in political science from the Middle East Technical University. She later taught these subjects as a visiting educator at a number of universities around the world, including at the University of Michigan in the United States and at St. Anne's College, Oxford University, in England.

EARLY TURKISH NOVELS

After traveling extensively, Shafak decided to settle in Istanbul, Turkey, in her early twenties. She also began focusing on her writing career. Shafak published her debut novel, *Pinhan*, in 1997. Written in Turkish, the novel became an instant best seller and won Turkey's 1998 Great Rumi Award, given to the best work of mystical literature. Shafak followed her debut with the novels *Şehrin Aynalari*, in 1998, and *The Gaze*, in 1999. The latter won the Turkish Writers Best Novel Award. Of her popularity in Turkey and quick rise to become one of the best-known writers in the country, she told John Timpane for *Philadelphia Inquirer* (24 Jan. 2018), "most women readers, if they like a book, they share it with their best friends, their aunts, their friends

in foreign countries. My guess would be that each individual copy of a book will be read by five to six readers."

ARRESTED FOR WRITING

While spending time as a teaching fellow in the United States, Shafak released her first English language novel, *The Saint of Incipient Insanities*, in 2004. Her next several books were also written in English, including the novel *The Bastard of Istanbul* (2006) and the memoir *Black Milk* (2007), in which Shafak discusses her struggle with postpartum depression after the birth of her first child. The former, which was longlisted for England's 2008 Orange Prize for Fiction, relates the stories of two families—one living in Turkey and one in San Francisco—and how they are connected through the 1915 Armenian Genocide by the Ottoman Empire.

After *The Bastard of Istanbul* was published in Turkey, Shafak was placed on trial for "insulting Turkishness" by the Turkish government. Authorities objected to her writing about the Armenian genocide of the early twentieth century, preferring not to admit to the massacre of an estimated million and a half Armenians in the final days of the Ottoman Empire or the legacy of that time. A second taboo that Shafak broke was writing about incest. She faced imprisonment of up to three years if convicted. More than sixty other writers and intellectuals had also been charged with the crime in the twenty-first century. Judges decided they lacked enough information to convict Shafak of any crime and granted her an acquittal. Some saw this act as an attempt to pacify European Union (EU) concerns about freedom of expression, as Turkey was being considered for membership in that body.

FURTHER NOVELS

Following her brush with the Turkish government, Shafak relocated to England and continued to write in both English and Turkish. She noted that she found writing about humor easier in English and writing about sorrow easier in Turkish. When she writes in English, she has someone else translate her work into Turkish, then polishes and shapes it based on her own knowledge of the language.

In 2010, Shafak published the English language novel *The Forty Rules of Love*, which was longlisted for the International IMPAC Dublin Literary Award. Her next novel, *Honour* (2011)—about the impact of an honor killing on the lives of Turkish immigrants in London—was also longlisted for the award, as well as for the UK's Women's Prize for Fiction, the Man Asian Literary Prize, and several French awards. Shafak next published the historical fiction *The Architect's Apprentice* (2013), which was longlisted for the 2015 Walter Scott Historical Novel Prize.

Shafak released *Three Daughters of Eve* in 2017. The novel takes place at Oxford University, where three young women nicknamed the Believer, the Confused, and the Sinner become friends and wrestle with their world. The story is told in flashbacks during a dinner party that takes place fifteen years after their years at Oxford. The novel gave her a chance to explore themes that very much concern her: religion, politics, and feminism. Shafak wanted to write a novel with women at the center, trying to bring what in Turkey must be private conversation into public space. *Three Daughters of Eve* "reveals such a timely confluence of today's issues that it seems almost clairvoyant," Ron Charles wrote in a review for the *Washington Post* (11 Dec. 2017). "That hyper-relevance is one of the reasons Shafak is so popular in her native Turkey and around the world. The author . . . speaks in a multivalent voice that captures the roiling tides of diverse cultures."

A POLITICAL TARGET

As the Turkish government persistently attacked her writing, Shafak became more careful when developing nonfiction works. She noted, however, that she was concerned with the potential for eroding democracies in a time of political polarization and rising nationalism. As she told Saha, "The trouble starts the moment we divide humanity into 'us versus them' and start to believe that 'us' is better than 'them.'"

Shafak was also vocal in her criticism of increasing attacks on journalists and artists as characteristic of an authoritarian populism. As a writer, she spoke out when Turkey began restricting the social media platform Twitter, stating that when information is not available through the usual media channels, social media becomes an important tool. It also allows women in conservative Middle Eastern nations access to the world that is forbidden to them.

In 2019, Shafak was again investigated by the Turkish government, not for her political ideas, but for her inclusion of women's issues—such as rape, child brides, and sexual harassment—in her fiction. The investigation followed the publication of her 2019 novel *10 Minutes 38 Seconds in this Strange World*, which focuses on the brutal murder of a prostitute in Istanbul. The title refers to the length of time it takes for the woman's brain to die; during that time, the main character tells her story. The novel was longlisted for the Booker Prize the same year.

PERSONAL LIFE

Shafak married newspaper editor Eyüp Can in 2005. The couple have two children, a daughter and a son. Shafak and Can maintain a long-distance marriage; Shafak and their children live in London, England, while Can lives in Turkey.

SUGGESTED READING

Charles, Ron. "Elif Shafak's New Novel Is So Timely that It Seems almost Clairvoyant." Review of *Three Daughters of Eve*, by Elif Shafak. *The Washington Post*, 11 Dec. 2017, www.washingtonpost.com/entertainment/books/elif-shafaks-new-novel-is-so-timely-that-it-seems-almost-clairvoyant/2017/12/11/f0887b58-ddff-11e7-bbd0-9dfb2e37492a_story.html. Accessed 23 Jan. 2020.

Saha, Shrestha. "In Elif Shafak's World." *The Telegraph*, 20 July 2019, www.telegraphindia.com/culture/books/in-elif-shafak-s-world/cid/1694868. Accessed 29 Jan. 2020.

Shafak, Elif. "Elif Shafak: A New Novel, a Divided Turkey, and Women Power." Interview by John Timpane. *The Philadelphia Inquirer*, www.inquirer.com/philly/entertainment/arts/elif-shafak-a-new-novel-a-divided-turkey-and-woman-power-20180124.html. Accessed 29 Jan. 2020.

——. "No One Does Sisterhood and Resilience Like Audre Lorde." Interview. *The Guardian*, 29 Nov. 2019, www.theguardian.com/books/2019/nov/29/elif-shafak-david-sedaris-makes-me-laugh. Accessed 29 Jan. 2020.

——. "Storytelling, Fake Worlds, and the Internet." *World Literature Today*, vol. 89, no. 1, Jan. 2015, pp. 39–41. *Elif Shafak*, www.elifsafak.com.tr/files/urun_urunler/21/dosya/01.01.2015.pdf. Accessed 23 Jan. 2020.

——. "Q&A: "If I Weren't a Writer I Might Be a Happier Person." *New Statesman*, 18 Dec. 2019, www.newstatesman.com/culture/qa/2019/12/elif-shafak-qa-if-i-weren-t-writer-i-might-be-happier-person. Accessed 23 Jan. 2020.

——. "Why the Novel Matters in the Age of Anger." *New Statesman*, 3 Oct. 2018, www.newstatesman.com/culture/books/2018/10/why-novel-matters-age-anger. Accessed 23 Jan. 2020.

SELECTED WORKS

Pinhan, 1997; *The Bastard of Istanbul*, 2006; *Black Milk*, 2007; *Forty Rules of Love*, 2010; *Honour*, 2011; *The Architect's Apprentice*, 2013; *Three Daughters of Eve*, 2017; *10 Minutes 38 Seconds in This Strange World*, 2019

—*Judy Johnson*

Tiger Shroff

Born: March 2, 1990
Occupation: Actor

Since his debut in the film *Heropanti* in 2014, Tiger Shroff, son of 1980s Bollywood superstar Jackie Shroff, has forged his own path to become one of the most sought-after action stars working in Hindi cinema. "The challenge has been to carve out my own niche," he told Omkar Khandekar for *GQ India* (4 Sept. 2019). "I think I've done a fairly decent job so far." Known for his martial artistry and acrobatic dance skills, Shroff is the star of the blockbuster Baaghi franchise, a series of films thematically linked by Shroff's ability to level bad guys with balletic flips and spins. Although Shroff is often criticized for his acting, his athletic skill is celebrated in films like *Munna Michael* (2017), *Student of the Year 2* (2019), and *War* (2019). Though his career is still quite new, Shroff is shrewd about the roles he chooses for himself, understanding that his audience wants to see him play strong, masculine characters performing tasks that highlight his physical prowess. "I love being typecast because it gives me an identity," he told Khandekar. "That's important in an industry that has so much competition."

EARLY LIFE

Jai Hemant "Tiger" Shroff was born on March 2, 1990. His father is well-known Bollywood actor Jackie Shroff. His mother, Ayesha (Dutt) Shroff, is a film producer and former model. He has a younger sister named Krishna. Shroff told Suhani Singh of *India Today* (8 May 2014) that he credits his career to martial artist and movie star Bruce Lee. "The reason I am here is because of Bruce Lee," Shroff said. "When I was four years old, I saw [Lee's 1973 classic] *Enter the Dragon*. When you are that young, you really don't grasp what's happening. But that man had an aura, which I was drawn to. I knew, right then, that that's what I want to be when I grow up." Shroff began studying martial arts at four, though he added that pop star Michael Jackson—to whom he would later be compared—inspired his interest in dance.

Despite having famous parents, Shroff described his childhood to Singh as mostly normal. He attended the Besant Montessori School in the Juhu neighborhood of Mumbai, though he preferred sports to academics. As a child, he spent time on the sets of his father's films, including the popular romantic comedy *Rangeela* (1995), in which the elder Shroff plays a famous movie star. "I didn't really understand much what was happening but I loved the attention and star treatment that my father got," Shroff recalled to Singh. "Every son's first hero is his father and

Photo by Bollywood Hungama

when you see him in this larger-than-life persona and getting all the adulation, you are amazed."

But as Shroff concedes, life at the whim of the fickle film industry was not always easy. When Shroff was eleven, his mother produced a film, her first, called *Boom* (2003). In it, three supermodels—including actor, chef, and television host Padma Lakshmi—become involved in a diamond heist. In 2002 *Boom* was leaked on the internet before its release, and its financial backers pulled funding, leaving Shroff's family to foot the bill for the film's official release. The film performed poorly at the box office, putting the Shroffs further into debt and forcing them to sell their home. "I remember how our furniture and stuff was sold off, one by one," Shroff recalled to Khandekar. "Things I'd grown up seeing around us started disappearing. Then my bed went. I started to sleep on the floor. It was the worst feeling of my life. I wanted to work at that age but I knew I could do nothing to help." Later, when Shroff started working, he promised his parents that he would earn enough money to buy back their old house. In 2017, he tried to, but his parents declined.

HEROPANTI

After he finished grade twelve in secondary school, Shroff dreamed of becoming a professional soccer player. At about the same time, film producer Sajid Nadiadwala saw Shroff's picture in the newspaper and was struck by his unconventional appearance. When Nadiadwala offered to cast Shroff as a film actor, Shroff initially turned him down before changing his mind, months later. When Nadiadwala called again, Shroff took the offer. Shroff told Khandekar that Nadiadwala was "instrumental" in guiding his career: "The route I should take, the heroes I should look up to, the films I should be doing. [He said] it's important to work with the best makers, that I should work on my craft every day," said Shroff, who trains several hours each day, lifting weights and practicing martial arts, dance, and gymnastics.

In *Heropanti*, his first film, Shroff plays a young hero who falls in love but must contend with his paramour's villainous father. Full of acrobatic fight sequences, songs, and dancing, *Heropanti* was popular with audiences, but fell flat with critics. Faheem Ruhani, writing for *India Today* (23 May 2014), described the film as "insipid," "asinine," and "cheesy." Criticizing the plot, the dialogue, and the "badly choreographed" dance sequences, "Heropanti is nothing but zeropanti," Ruhani concluded. On all of these points, Anupama Chopra of the *Hindustan Times* (24 May 2014) seemed to agree, though she appreciated one aspect of the film. "*Heropanti* is designed to do exactly one thing—make us like Tiger Shroff," Chopra wrote, "and that it does exceedingly well."

Indeed, Bollywood has a colorful history of nepotism, with producers routinely seeking out and casting the kin of popular film stars. Take Prithviraj Kapoor, a Bollywood pioneer, who began his career in the 1920s. Like the Barrymore family in the United States, subsequent generations of Kapoors have been entertaining audiences ever since. But the practice has begun to draw ire. Bhaskar Chawla, writing for the Indian news website *First Post* (29 Mar. 2019), called nepotism "Bollywood's version of casteism," writing: "Star kids are always fast-tracked to lead roles in big productions without any prior work to show and, in most cases, without auditioning for their debut roles." Shroff told Khandekar that he was not asked to audition for his starring role in *Heropanti*. "Had there been one, I wouldn't have got it anyway," he said. In this tradition, *Heropanti* capitalized on Shroff's background in various ways. Filmmakers planted riffs from his father's films in the background music, though the title remains their most obvious ploy—the elder Shroff's famous debut was called *Hero*.

BAAGHI FRANCHISE

In 2016, Shroff starred in the action film *Baaghi*. In it, Shroff's character, Ranveer "Ronny" Pratap Singh, trains at a martial arts school in Kerala, where he becomes a formidable fighter. The story alludes to the ancient Indian epic, the *Ramayana*, which follows the exploits of a prince called Rama. Rachel Saltz of the *New York Times* (1 May 2016) complained that the film's epic aspirations were introduced too late to fully develop, and described the plot as muddy and emotionally "hollow." Still, Saltz offered Shroff a bit of praise. "Mr. Shroff moves well," she wrote. "He bounces balletically off walls to deliver knockout kicks and dances with loose-hipped grace."

Despite reservations from critics, *Baaghi* was a huge hit with audiences, though the filmmakers ran into legal trouble for the film's striking similarities to a 2011 Indonesian film called *The Raid: Redemption*. Shroff starred in two subsequent films in the franchise. *Baaghi 2*, released in 2018, follows Singh, now called "Ronnie," on his search for his ex-lover's kidnapped child. Critics, perhaps predictably, were unenthused—Rohit Vats of the *Hindustan Times* (31 Mar. 2018) described it as a "mere show-reel for Tiger Shroff"—but *Baaghi 2* was a blockbuster hit, far and away the franchise's most popular installment and one of the highest-grossing Bollywood films that year.

Baaghi 3 was released in 2020. In it, Shroff, returning as Ronnie, must rescue his brother, Vikram, who has been kidnapped by a terrorist group in Syria. (Shroff's father, Jackie, plays the boys' abusive dad.) Critics complained about the film's confounding plot, but audiences flocked to the theater in the film's opening week in early March 2020, just as the spread of the coronavirus began to accelerate in India. A nationwide lockdown that started on March 25 cut off dwindling ticket sales altogether.

STUDENT OF THE YEAR 2 AND OTHER FILMS

While appearing in the Baaghi films, Shroff took on other acting roles. In 2016, he starred as a reluctant superhero in the film *A Flying Jatt*. Shroff plays Aman Dhillon, a martial arts instructor turned superhero, Flying Jatt, who is afraid of heights. The film was a flop, which Shroff thinks is because his audience was uncomfortable seeing him play a bumbling character. He made a similar comment about the teen film *Student of the Year 2* (2019), in which he plays a star athlete who is bullied by fellow students. "It didn't go down too well with my audience," he told Khandekar. "I don't think they could digest me coming from *Baaghi 2* to being beaten up by college students." Though teens and children are among Shroff's biggest fans, *Student of the Year 2* was also a flop. Shroff absorbed the blows as a lesson about the value of sticking with what works.

In 2017, Shroff starred in a film called *Munna Michael*, about a dancer named Munna who grows up as an orphan who idolizes Michael Jackson, and agrees to tutor a gangster in dance. The film gave Shroff ample opportunities to show off his two strongest skills sets, with lots of Jackson-inspired choreography, and fight scenes. "In what seems like an encore of his previous work, Tiger dances like a dream and breaks bones with the grace of a ballerina," Meena Iyer wrote for the *Times of India* (25 July 2017). "You can only tell that this is a different film only because he mouths a different dialogue here." In *War* (2019), Shroff stars alongside another formidable Bollywood dancer, superstar Hrithik Roshan. The two men play soldiers in the Indian army. Roshan's character, Kabir, has gone rogue, and Shroff's character, Khalid, is charged with tracking him down. *War* was the highest-grossing Bollywood film of 2019. Roshan told Khandekar that it was a challenge keeping up with his co-star on set. "He's so hardworking," Roshan said of Shroff. "He's going to be untouchable for the next 50 years."

SUGGESTED READING

Chawla, Bhaskar. "Nepotism Debate: It's All about Relative Merit in Bollywood." *First Post*, 29 Mar. 2019, www.firstpost.com/entertainment/nepotism-debate-its-all-about-relative-merit-in-bollywood-6351331.html. Accessed 15 Apr. 2020.

Chopra, Anupama. "Movie Review by Anupama Chopra: Tiger Shroff Starrer *Heropanti* Is Comically Bad." Review of *Heropanti*, directed by Sabbir Khan. *Hindustan Times*, 24 May 2014, www.hindustantimes.com/movie-reviews/movie-review-by-anupama-chopra-tiger-shroff-starrer-heropanti-is-comically-bad/story-uihB0LJC9fbOlHWCL5WUbL.html. Accessed 15 Apr. 2020.

Iyer, Meena. "*Munna Michael* Movie Review." Review of *Munna Michael*, directed by Sabbir Khan. *Times of India*, 25 July 2017, timesofindia.indiatimes.com/entertainment/hindi/movie-reviews/munna-michael/movie-review/59690060.cms. Accessed 15 Apr. 2020.

Khandekar, Omkar. "GQ Exclusive: Tiger Shroff on Dancing and Kicking His Way to the Top of Bollywood." *GQ India*, 4 Sept. 2019, www.gqindia.com/entertainment/content/gq-exclusive-tiger-shroff-on-dancing-and-kicking-his-way-to-the-top-of-bollywood. Accessed 15 Apr. 2020.

Ruhani, Faheem. "Movie Review: *Heropanti* Is Nothing but Zeropanti." Review of *Heropanti*, directed by Sabbir Khan. *India Today*, 23 May 2014, www.indiatoday.in/movies/reviews/story/heropanti-review-tiger-shroff-kriti-sanon-194135-2014-05-23. Accessed 15 Apr. 2020.

Saltz, Rachel. "Review: 'Baaghi,' a Bollywood Rebel Tale in Search of a Cause." Review of *Baaghi*, directed by Sabbir Khan. *The New York Times*, 1 May 2016, www.nytimes.com/2016/05/02/movies/baaghi-review.html. Accessed 15 Apr. 2020.

Shroff, Tiger. "In Conversation with Tiger Shroff." Interview by Suhani Singh. *India Today*, 8 May 2014, www.indiatoday.in/movies/bollywood/story/in-covasation-with-tiger-shroff-192096-2014-05-08. Accessed 15 Apr. 2020.

SELECTED WORKS

Heropanti, 2014; *A Flying Jatt*, 2016; Baaghi franchise, 2016–20; *Munna Michael*, 2017; *Student of the Year 2*, 2019; *War*, 2019

—*Molly Hagan*

Danez Smith

Date of birth: ca. 1990
Occupation: Poet

Danez Smith is an award-winning poet, best known for the 2017 collection *Don't Call Us Dead*, which was a finalist for the National Book Award for Poetry. Smith won fellowships from the McKnight Foundation, the Poetry Foundation, and the National Endowment for the Arts. In 2018, they won the prestigious Forward Prize, becoming the youngest-ever recipient of the British poetry honor. Smith got started as a slam and spoken word poet, and became known for their ability to incorporate the vitality of spoken word poetry into their written work. As Dan Chiasson wrote in a review of *Don't Call Us Dead* for the *New Yorker* (25 Sept. 2017), Smith knows "the magic trick of making writing on the page operate like the most ecstatic speech. And they are, in their cadences and management of lines, deeply literary."

Smith's work often explores various facets of their gay, black, gender-queer, and HIV-positive identity, also drawing inspiration from Smith's beloved Midwestern community. To describe Smith's writing as merely about their own identity, however, undercuts the breadth of their work. Though they often write about oppression—racism, homophobia, or illness—a common word associated with their work is joy. For example, Smith finds joy in the Cheeto-dusted fingers of the boys they grew up with in the poem "summer, somewhere" and in the beauty of poetry itself in the poem "tonight, in Oakland." "I want to move past grief. I want to move past shame," Smith told Lauren K. Alleyne for the literary magazine the *Fight and the Fiddle* (13 Oct. 2017), "I think that grief is definitely a useful emotion and a necessary one, but I am really interested in trying to find the poetics of joy right now, in trying to find those more nuanced and quiet places that I can look. I think for a long time I have looked to the loudest thing in the room, and written about it, and I'm trying to see what I've left unnoticed."

EARLY LIFE AND EDUCATION

Smith was born in St. Paul, Minnesota, around 1990. They grew up as an only child in St. Paul's Selby-Dale neighborhood with their mother, a writer who worked as a secretary in a law office, and their grandparents. "I loved it," Smith told Laurie Hertzel for the *Star Tribune* (15 Sept. 2017). "I feel like a very St. Paul kid; I feel like I had a very typical black St. Paul experience." Growing up, Smith struggled to learn to read until the third grade. As they got older, books by Toni Morrison, James Baldwin, and Mark Twain helped them develop a deeper love of reading and words.

Smith attended Central High School in St. Paul. As a teenager, they worked at a local hardware store during the summer. In school, they studied theater with well-known local educator Jan Mandell, who ran a social justice theater program based on the teachings of Augusto Boal—a Brazilian theater artist and activist who founded the Theatre of the Oppressed, a theatrical form in which actors enact scenes of injustice and then invite spectators to participate. "I came to poetry through acting," Smith told Brandon Stosuy for the *Creative Independent* (7 Feb. 2017). "We were teenagers, high schoolers, really figuring out what was important enough for us to say on a stage. Really some of the first poems I wrote were these things that I thought were monologues."

Photo by Justin Baker/Getty Images

After realizing that the monologues they had been writing in class were akin to spoken word poetry, Smith began performing at slam poetry events with several classmates. In 2005, at age fifteen, Smith competed at the Brave New Voices International Teen Poetry Slam in San Francisco, California, with a group of other youth poets. There they learned "that poetry wasn't just some weird thing a couple of us did—there was a world," as Smith recalled to Dara Moskowitz Grumdahl for *Mpls.St.Paul* (11 Sept. 2017).

After graduating from high school, Smith attended the University of Wisconsin, Madison. They originally majored in education, but were disturbed by the impression that aspiring teachers were subtly trained to view young black students as problems to solve, rather than as people. Smith quit the program, and looking back, considered just how serendipitous that decision ended up being. "It would have been a different life," they told Solomon Gustavo of the *Minnesota Spokesman-Recorder* (28 Nov. 2018). "So, thank you, racists."

After leaving the education program, Smith became a First Wave Urban Arts Scholar. That innovative program combined hip hop, poetry, and spoken word performance. In 2011, Smith was a finalist for the Individual World Poetry Slam. They graduated with a BA in 2012, and earned an MFA from the University of Michigan in 2017.

SLAM POETRY AND *[INSERT] BOY*

Smith found early success as a slam poet, though they would eventually chafe at the term. "I think a slam poet is a stupid term because slam is an event that happens," they told Stosuy. "Do I consider myself a spoken word artist? Yeah, that's part of my practice. A slam poet? No, I always reject that term because a slam is an event." Their accomplishments in slam poetry included three Rust Belt Poetry Slam Championships and a National Underground Poetry Individual Championship. In 2011 and 2014, Smith was an Individual World Poetry Slam finalist.

In 2012, Smith helped cofound the Dark Noise Collective, a group of poets who collaborate on different genres of spoken word poetry. Smith published their first chapbook, *hands on ya knees*, in 2013. The following year, they served as the festival director for the Brave New Voices International Youth Poetry Slam. Also in 2014, a video of Smith performing their poem "dear white america" appeared on *PBS News Hour* and went viral, racking up more than 300,000 views online.

Smith published their first poetry book, *[insert] Boy*, in 2014. *[insert] Boy* won the Kate Tufts Discovery Award and the Lambda Literary Award for Gay Poetry. It was also named one of the *Boston Globe*'s Best Poetry Books of 2014.

The collection is structured to capture the various facets of Smith's identity. In an interview with Isaac Ginsberg Miller for *Public Books* (12 Jan. 2016), Smith described it as "a miraculous book of little failures," in their attempt to segregate different aspects of themselves, including their relationship to masculinity and growing up as a boy. Smith expanded on this idea, stating "There are too many ideas going on in here. These poems are also in conversation with all the poems that didn't make the book, or that will be in the books to come, or the poems that I was too scared to write when I was writing this book." Smith's next chapbook, *black movie*, won the 2014 Button Poetry Prize and was published in 2015. It explores Smith's response to the birth of the Black Lives Matter movement.

Don't Call Us Dead

In 2015, Jeff Shotts, an editor at the prestigious Graywolf Press, reached out to Smith. For the next two years, Smith worked with Shotts, combining poems from two different projects—including "dear white America"—to create their next book. The result, *Don't Call Us Dead*, was published in 2017. A long-form poem in the book called "summer, somewhere" earned Smith the inaugural T. S. Eliot Foundation and Poetry Society of America's Four Quartets Prize for a unified, complete sequence of poems. The poem resurrects the black victims of police shootings and gives the collection its title: "please, don't call/us dead, call us alive someplace better." In *Don't Call Us Dead*, Smith also writes about being diagnosed with HIV. In the poem "it won't be a bullet" they describe HIV as another kind of violence, comparable to the police violence depicted in "summer, somewhere."

Don't Call Us Dead was a finalist for the National Book Award for Poetry and won enthusiastic reviews from critics. Both Chiasson and Sandeep Parmar for the *Guardian* (9 Feb. 2018) compared Smith to Allen Ginsberg, an acclaimed gay poet of the 1950s Beat generation famous for his epic work "Howl." Chiasson went on to note of Smith's work: "I hear Gerard Manley Hopkins, the Jesuit priest who jury-rigged his verse to express personal turmoil, and Hart Crane, whose gentleness was expressed in an American idiom full of thunderclap." Taken alongside these writers and Ginsberg, Chiasson wrote, "The addition of Smith's star turns a random cluster of points into a constellation, the way new work of this calibre always does." In 2018, *Don't Call Us Dead* also earned Smith the Forward Prize for Best Collection, making them, at age twenty-eight, the youngest person to win the prestigious award.

PERSONAL LIFE

Smith lives in St. Paul. They were diagnosed with HIV at the age of twenty-four. In 2019, Smith was named to *Forbes'* 30 Under 30 in Media list.

SUGGESTED READING

Chiasson, Dan. "Danez Smith's Ecstatic Body Language." Review of *Don't Call Us Dead*, by Danez Smith. *The New Yorker*, 25 Sept. 2017, www.newyorker.com/magazine/2017/10/02/danez-smiths-ecstatic-body-language. Accessed 15 Dec. 2019.

Grumdahl, Dara Moskowitz. "Meet Danez Smith, Our Homegrown Poet on the Rise." *Mpls.St.Paul*, 11 Sept. 2017, mspmag.com/arts-and-culture/meet-danez-smith-our-homegrown-poet-on-the-rise/. Accessed 13 Dec. 2019.

Gustavo, Solomon. "Local Poet Takes National Acclaim in Stride." *Minnesota Spokesman-Recorder*, 28 Nov. 2018, spokesman-recorder.com/2018/11/28/local-poet-takes-national-acclaim-in-stride/. Accessed 12 Dec. 2019.

Hertzel, Laurie. "Impassioned Twin Cities Poet Danez Smith Is a Troubadour for Our Turbulent Times." *Star Tribune*, 15 Sept. 2017, www.startribune.com/impassioned-twin-cities-poet-danez-smith-is-a-troubadour-for-our-turbulent-times/444227783/. Accessed 12 Dec. 2019.

Parmar, Sandeep. "*Don't Call Us Dead* by Danez Smith Review—Hope in Resistance and Rebirth." Review of *Don't Call Us Dead*, by Danez Smith. *The Guardian*, 9 Feb. 2018, www.theguardian.com/books/2018/feb/09/dont-call-us-dead-danez-smith-review. Accessed 15 Dec. 2019.

Smith, Danez. "'beautiful & lovable & black & enough': An Interview with Danez Smith." By Lauren K. Alleyne. *The Fight and the Fiddle*, 13 Oct. 2017, fightandfiddle.com/2017/10/13/title-an-interview-with-danez-smith/. Accessed 15 Dec. 2019.

———. "Danez Smith on Poems as Conversations." Interview by Brandon Stosuy. *Creative Independent*, 7 Feb. 2017, thecreativeindependent.com/people/danez-smith-on-poems-as-conversations/. Accessed 12 Dec. 2019.

———. "Imagining Better Gods: An Interview with Danez Smith." By Isaac Ginsberg Miller. *Public Books*, 12 Jan. 2016, www.publicbooks.org/imagining-better-gods-an-interview-with-danez-smith/. Accessed 15 Dec. 2019.

SELECTED WORKS

hands on ya knees, 2013; *[insert] Boy*, 2014; *black movie*, 2015; *Don't Call Us Dead*, 2017

—*Molly Hagan*

Phyllis Smith

Date of birth: July 10, 1951
Occupation: Actor

EARLY LIFE AND EDUCATION

Phyllis Smith was born in St. Louis, Missouri, on July 10, 1951. She was raised in St. Louis, where she lived until her thirties, before relocating to Los Angeles. Throughout her career, she has moved between St. Louis and Los Angeles.

As a child, Smith loved dancing. She began studying ballet, tap, jazz, and modern dancing at age seven. She danced with the San Carlo Opera Company, the St. Louis Dance Theater, and the St. Louis Civic Ballet. Smith attended the University of Missouri–St. Louis, where she earned a degree in elementary education.

Prior to her acting career, Smith worked for seven years as a professional dancer. Dance auditions led to her also audition as a cheerleader for the former St. Louis Cardinals football team. After a year, she moved on to dancing in burlesque performances with the dance troupe Will B. Able and His Baggy Pants Revue, which toured dinner theaters throughout the United States. Smith also performed with the Mercer Brothers' Giggles Galore show as a dancer and comedy actor in the group's skits. Smith's dancing jobs left her with a knee injury, which ended her dancing career. She then worked for several years as a receptionist.

Eager to resume working in entertainment, Smith auditioned for a role in a commercial. During the interview process, she befriended the casting director. Though Smith did not get the part, the casting director later offered her a position in casting. Smith spent the next nineteen years working as a casting director and was eventually asked to work in the casting department on the new NBC sitcom *The Office*.

ACTOR

While working on casting *The Office*, a US sitcom adapted from a UK sitcom of the same name, Smith participated in many script readings. The show's producers, impressed with her readings, eventually created the character Phyllis Lapin-Vance for Smith. She first appeared in the series beginning in its 2005 pilot and remained as a regular cast member until the conclusion of the series in 2013.

An international hit, *The Office* received critical acclaim and several awards during its run. As part of the cast, Smith won two Screen Actors Guild (SAG) Awards (2007 and 2008) along with her *Office* costars for outstanding performance by an ensemble in a comedy series. Smith's television roles have also included

appearances in *Arrested Development, Trophy Wife,* and *The Middle*.

Prior to landing the role of Phyllis on *The Office*, she was cast in the film *The 40-Year-Old Virgin* (2005) in the role of the lead character's mother. The movie was her *Office* costar Steve Carrell's breakout role. It did not bring the same success for Smith, however, as her scenes were edited out of the final cut of the film. Her first appearance in a feature film was in 2006's *I Want Someone to Eat Cheese With*.

Smith's first role in a major film was in the 2011 comedy *Bad Teacher,* in which she played a downtrodden middle school teacher and colleague of Cameron Diaz's lead character. The same year, she appeared in *Butter* with Jennifer Garner and Ty Burrell, about a young girl competing in a local butter-carving contest. After performing in the 2011 animated feature *Alvin and the Chipmunks: Chipwrecked,* Smith earned her second voice-over role with the character Sadness in the 2015 Pixar film *Inside Out*. Smith was offered the role after the film's producer, Jonas Rivera, watched *Bad Teacher* and enjoyed Smith's performance as the morose Lynn Davies.

The opportunity to act in a Pixar feature marked a step up for Smith in her film acting career, which had earlier included mostly small roles in comedies. Her performance in *Inside Out,* a hit children's film, won her a 2015 Annie Award for voice acting in a feature production.

Despite being one of the major characters in the film, Smith claims she did not know her role as Sadness was a prominent part of the film until the final edit was made. Smith reprised the role of Sadness in the 2015 video game *Disney Infinity 3.0*. She has been a regular on the Netflix series *The OA* since 2016.

IMPACT

Smith is best known for her work on *The Office* and for her Annie Award–winning voice acting for the Sadness character in the Pixar film *Inside Out*.

PERSONAL LIFE

Although she has not worked as a professional dancer since the 1970s, Smith has said she still enjoys dancing and will often break out in dance while in public. She has said that one of the most rewarding experiences associated with playing Sadness in *Inside Out* was being asked by a young girl at a Target store to sign her Sadness doll.

SUGGESTED READING

Byrne, Suzy. "Exclusive: 'The Office' Star Phyllis Smith Sets Us Straight about Her NFL Cheerleader and Burlesque-Dancer Past." *Yahoo! TV.* Yahoo!, 17 Sept. 2012, www.yahoo.com/entertainment/bp/

office-star-phyllis-smith-sets-us-straight-her-210308189.html. Accessed 23, Dec. 2019.

Fallon, Kevin. "'Inside Out' Star Phyllis Smith's Journey from G-Stringed Dancer to 'The Office' and Pixar." *Daily Beast*, 19 June 2015, www.thedailybeast.com/inside-out-star-phyllis-smiths-journey-from-g-stringed-dancer-to-the-office-and-pixar. Accessed 23 Dec. 2019.

Hill, Jim. "Phyllis Smith Talks about the Joys of Voicing Sadness for Pixar's *Inside Out*." *Huffington Post*. TheHuffingtonPost.com, 15 Nov. 2015, http://jimhillmedia.com/editor_in_chief1/b/jim_hill/archive/2015/11/15/phyllis-smith-talks-about-the-joys-of-voicing-sadness-for-pixar-s-quot-inside-out-quot.aspx. Accessed 23 Dec. 2019.

Smith, Phyllis. Interview by Jessica Grose. "Questions for Phyllis Smith." *Slate*. Slate Group, 23 June 2011, slate.com/news-and-politics/2011/06/bad-teacher-co-star-phyllis-smith-interview.html. Accessed 23 Dec. 2019.

Terrero, Nina. "*Inside Out*: Phyllis Smith Had No Clue Sadness Would Be Prominent Character." *Entertainment Weekly*, 12 Oct. 2015, ew.com/article/2015/10/12/phyllis-smith-inside-out-sadness/. Accessed 23 Dec. 2019.

SELECTED WORKS

The Office, 2005–2013; *Bad Teacher*, 2011; *Butter*, 2011; *Alvin and the Chipmunks: Chipwrecked*, 2011; *Inside Out*, 2015; *The OA*, 2016–.

—*Richard Means*

Clare Smyth

Date of birth: ca. 1978
Occupation: Chef

When chef Clare Smyth first entered the kitchen at London's Restaurant Gordon Ramsay in 2002, she faced a daunting challenge. "Everyone, including Gordon, said I wouldn't last a week," she recalled in an interview for the *Telegraph* (20 Jan. 2008). "It was full of testosterone and lots of the guys said I didn't belong here." Smyth, however, has never been one to let anything—let alone an unwelcoming workplace—prevent her from reaching her true potential.

Born and raised in Northern Ireland, she moved to England without her parents' permission at the age of sixteen to enroll in a culinary course and work toward her goal of becoming a chef. Stints at major restaurants in the United Kingdom and abroad followed, and in 2007, she claimed the title of head chef at Restaurant

Gordon Ramsay. Smyth excelled throughout her tenure as head chef and chef patron, maintaining the restaurant's rating of three Michelin stars and becoming deeply familiar with the skills needed to run a successful restaurant. After announcing that she was leaving Restaurant Gordon Ramsay in 2015, Smyth put her hard-earned skills to work for a new venture, debut restaurant Core by Clare Smyth. A popular and critically acclaimed establishment, Core received widespread attention following its opening in August 2017 and in late 2018 was awarded two Michelin stars in recognition of its overall excellence. For Smyth, however, such recognition was only the beginning. "It's great that we've had an amazing year but there has to be a longevity to that," she explained to Ben McCormack for the website *SquareMeal* (8 Jan. 2019). "We've got to keep building on what we've achieved and keep our customers coming back. Great restaurants are around for a long time."

EARLY LIFE AND EDUCATION

Smyth was born around 1978 and raised in County Antrim, Northern Ireland. Along with her older brother and sister, she grew up on a farm in that region. Her mother waitressed, often in hotels, during her early life, while her father trained horses. Because of their father's career, the Smyth children grew up riding horses and practicing show jumping. Smyth would later note in interviews that she would likely have pursued a career in show jumping if she had not decided to become a chef. Additionally, living on a farm meant that she developed a strong work

Photo by Miles Willis/Bloomberg via Getty Images

ethic and was exposed to fresh ingredients and rustic food preparation that included butchering, cooking, and eating whole animals.

Having developed a passion for cooking early in life, Smyth developed her culinary knowledge further by reading cookbooks and, after experiencing the front of the house at various establishments on weekends and school breaks, at the age of fifteen obtained a part-time kitchen job at a local restaurant. Almost immediately following the completion of her education, the sixteen-year-old Smyth left Northern Ireland for England, ostensibly for a brief vacation. "I was meant to be going on a two-week holiday," she recalled to Elizabeth Day for the *Observer* (16 Dec. 2007). "At the end, I called up my parents and said, 'You know what? I'm not coming back.'" Intent upon continuing her culinary education despite doubts and concerns expressed by her family and friends, Smyth believed that she would be unable to do so back home and instead needed to remain in England to pursue the opportunities available there. She enrolled in a catering course at Highbury College in Portsmouth, England, and secured an apprenticeship at a spa hotel in Surrey that provided its apprentices with housing.

EARLY CULINARY CAREER

Following her time at Highbury College, Smyth gained hands-on experience as a cook working for a variety of restaurants, including the London restaurant Bibendum. Like many developing cooks, Smyth was interested in honing her skills further under the supervision of some of the industry's most successful established chefs. As such, she sought out opportunities at the restaurants established by chefs such as Heston Blumenthal, owner of the bistro the Fat Duck, and Albert and Michel Roux, French-born brothers who operated a variety of major restaurants throughout the United Kingdom. Seeking further experience abroad, she also traveled to Australia and spent several months working for a catering company there.

A key moment in Smyth's culinary career came in 2002, when, having spent time further improving her craft at a hotel in Cornwall, she took a position at Restaurant Gordon Ramsay, located on Royal Hospital Road in the Chelsea area of London. The first restaurant solely owned by Ramsay, Restaurant Gordon Ramsay had opened in 1998 and in 2001 had received a rating of three stars from the Michelin restaurant guide. Among the most prestigious honors awarded within the culinary world, a rating of three Michelin stars identified a restaurant as one of the best in the world, a status that Ramsay was intent upon maintaining. Considering Ramsay's focus on perfection and his public reputation as an explosive personality, Restaurant Gordon Ramsay's kitchen had an atmosphere that presented a daunting challenge for any young cook. Smyth faced a particularly difficult challenge, as the male-dominated kitchen staff were reluctant to accept a woman into their ranks. "Even though they were often in tears from stress, cutting their fingers or burning themselves, I had to cover anything like that up as it would have been seen as a sign of weakness because I was a woman," she recalled for the *Telegraph* (20 Jan. 2008). After working at Restaurant Gordon Ramsay for a time, ultimately being promoted to senior sous chef, Smyth left the United Kingdom to work and learn even more abroad, including at Le Louis XV, acclaimed chef Alain Ducasse's Monaco restaurant.

HEAD CHEF

Having proven her skills at Restaurant Gordan Ramsay at the beginning of the first decade of the twenty-first century, Smyth returned to that restaurant later in the decade and in 2007 was named the establishment's head chef. Under her leadership, Restaurant Gordon Ramsay retained its three Michelin stars and its reputation for excellence, and Smyth became the first female chef in the United Kingdom to operate a three-Michelin-star restaurant. For Smyth, the success of Restaurant Gordon Ramsay was attributable both to the talents of the professionals working there and to the exacting attention to detail that the establishment required. "I get here at 7 am and I taste everything, all the produce that comes through the door from the mushrooms to the bread to the tomato mix for the bloody Mary," she told Day about her process. "That way I know if something isn't right; it can be fixed early and I'm in control." In recognition of her contributions to the United Kingdom's culinary community, she was made a member of the Order of the British Empire in 2013.

Smyth remained in the position of head chef and chef patron until October 2015, when she announced that she was leaving Restaurant Gordon Ramsay to pursue new opportunities. "I have a great fondness for the restaurant and the team, it has formed me into the chef that I am today and I am grateful for the opportunities it has given me," she explained, as quoted by Jonathan Prynn in the *Evening Standard* (2 Oct. 2015). "I also remain ambitious and want to build on my success. The natural way to do that is by opening my own restaurant." Although Smyth left the Restaurant Gordon Ramsay kitchen behind her, she continued to serve as a consultant for Ramsay's restaurant group, which at that time operated numerous restaurants in the United Kingdom, the United States, continental Europe, and Asia.

CORE BY CLARE SMYTH

Although Smyth initially announced plans to open her first restaurant in the fall of 2016, the launch was delayed until August 2017, when she opened the doors of Core by Clare Smyth. The restaurant proved to be worth the wait: located in the Notting Hill area of west London, Core received highly positive reviews from critics following its opening and quickly gained a following within the UK culinary community. Calling further attention to the quality of Smyth's work, Michelin reviewers awarded Core two stars in the 2019 guide following the restaurant's first full year of eligibility. Smyth's cooking also captured the attention of British royalty, and in May 2018, she provided the food for the wedding reception of the Duke and Duchess of Sussex, also known as Prince Harry and Meghan Markle.

As products of Smyth's culinary experience and training, the dishes served at Core blend British and French cuisines but have a strong emphasis on local ingredients, particularly produce. "The produce in Britain is incredible," she stated in an interview for the website *RTÉ* (30 Nov. 2018). "Obviously, it always has been, but now we're working with so many different producers that are farming everything—people will pretty much grow anything for you now; here, bespoke in the UK, which is phenomenal." In addition to cooking with local produce, Smyth makes a point of visiting local producers with her cooks to learn about the history of the ingredients she uses and the procedures for cultivating them. Her commitment to furthering the education of her cooks is tied deeply to her approach for managing the restaurant's staff, which diverges significantly from some of the management approaches she experienced earlier in her career. "Rather than screaming and shouting at someone who is not capable of doing something, we will just very gently coach them into another role. We may even help them find a job somewhere else," she told Decca Aitkenhead for the *Guardian* (3 Aug. 2018). "But I'm not going to stand and shout and abuse someone because that's not what I'm there for."

Although Smyth at times made small appearances in Ramsay's television programs during her tenure at Restaurant Gordon Ramsay, she has noted in interviews that despite her increased international recognition, she has no desire to follow in her former employer and mentor's footsteps and become a television personality. "That isn't something that inspires me, certainly not at this point in my career," she told Aitkenhead. "Working with food, produce, nature—that's what gets me excited. I'm not a television-studio kind of person." Nevertheless, Smyth has, at times, accepted television opportunities that tie into her interests, including a guest appearance as a judge in a 2018 episode of the Netflix cooking program *The Final Table*. In that role, Smyth challenged the show's contestants to make creative use of English peas, thus calling attention to some of the humble local ingredients the food at Core seeks to celebrate.

PERSONAL LIFE

Smyth married Grant Heath, a financier, around 2015. They live in the Wandsworth borough of London. In interviews, she has mentioned walking her dog as an activity that she enjoys as a form of release in her downtime away from the restaurant.

SUGGESTED READING

Aitkenhead, Decca. "Clare Smyth, World's Best Female Chef: 'I'm Not Going to Stand and Shout at Someone. It's Just Not Nice.'" *The Guardian*, 3 Aug. 2018, www.theguardian. com/lifeandstyle/2018/aug/03/clare-smyth-worlds-best-female-chef-im-not-going-to-stand-and-shout-at-someone-its-just-not-nice. Accessed 17 Jan. 2020.

Burton, Monica. "Core by Clare Smyth Debuts with Two Michelin Stars in 2019 UK Guide." *Eater*, 1 Oct. 2018, www.eater. com/2018/10/1/17924224/core-by-clare-smyth-two-stars-michelin-guide-uk-2019. Accessed 17 Jan. 2020.

Day, Elizabeth. "'She Dresses Food Like Picasso.'" *The Observer*, Guardian News & Media, 16 Dec. 2007, www.theguardian.com/lifeand-style/2007/dec/16/foodanddrink.features10. Accessed 17 Jan. 2020.

"Gordon Ramsay Eats His Own Words." *The Telegraph*, 20 Jan. 2008, www.telegraph. co.uk/news/uknews/1576029/Gordon-Ramsay-eats-his-own-words.html. Accessed 17 Jan. 2020.

McCormack, Ben. "Clare Smyth Interview: 'Thinking about Food Is All-Consuming for Me.'" *SquareMeal*, 8 Jan. 2019, www.squaremeal.co.uk/restaurants/interviews-and-profiles/clare-smyth-interview_8903. Accessed 17 Jan. 2020.

Prynn, Jonathan. "Gordon Ramsay Protegee Clare Smyth Sets Out on Her Own." *Evening Standard*, 2 Oct. 2015, www.standard.co.uk/news/london/ramsay-protegee-clare-smyth-sets-out-on-her-own-a3071676.html. Accessed 17 Jan. 2020.

Smyth, Clare. "Meet Clare Smyth, Star of Netflix's *The Final Table*." *RTÉ*, 30 Nov. 2018, www. rte.ie/lifestyle/food/2018/1130/1014323-meet-clare-smyth-star-of-netflixs-the-final-table/. Accessed 17 Jan. 2020.

—*Joy Crelin*

Erna Solberg

Born: February 24, 1961
Occupation: Prime minister of Norway

Erna Solberg is a Norwegian politician and leader of the Conservative Party. After winning the September 9, 2013, elections, Solberg became the first Conservative prime minister of Norway since 1990.

EARLY LIFE AND EDUCATION

Erna Solberg was born on February 24, 1961, in the city of Bergen, Norway, to Inger Wenche Torgersen and Asbjørn Solberg. Solberg's mother worked as an office clerk, and her father worked as a consultant to the city's municipal transportation company, Bergen Sporvei.

Solberg and her two sisters were raised in Bergen. The middle child, Solberg played piano and was a leader in the Girl Scouts. Despite being a highly motivated student, Solberg struggled in school and was diagnosed with dyslexia at the age of sixteen.

Solberg was a student politician and a member of the Young Conservatives. She went on to become chair of the Bergen Young Conservatives and vice chair of the Hordaland Young Conservatives in 1980. After graduating from high school, Solberg went on to earn her *candidata magisterii* (cand. mag), a five-year Master of Arts degree, in sociology, comparative politics, statistics, and economics from the University of Bergen in 1986.

EARLY CAREER

Solberg was first elected into public office in 1979 at the age of eighteen when she became a deputy member of the Bergen City Council. In 1987, she became a permanent member of the city council, a position she would hold until 1999. In 1989, Solberg was elected to represent her home county of Hordaland in the Storting (the Norwegian parliament). She was twenty-eight years old. As of late 2015, Solberg had been reelected to the Storting five times and was the incumbent representative of Hordaland.

In 2001, Solberg became minister of local government and modernization under the Christian Democratic Party government of Prime Minister Kjell Magne Bondevik. As government minister, Solberg improved the efficiency of Norway's immigration process by streamlining the country's existing refugee and immigration policies and developing an asylum application review process that quickly weeded out ineligible candidates. Her work earned her a reputation for being tough on immigration, which resulted in the nickname of "Jern-Erna" or "Iron Erna."

Additionally, Solberg spent her time as government minister improving Norway's municipal structure. After concluding that there were too many small, disconnected municipalities, Solberg encouraged politicians to merge districts and create broader cooperation across the counties. Her efforts resulted in new guidelines for a better functioning welfare system managed by fewer, stronger communities.

In 2004, she became the head of the Conservative Party. Her term as government minister concluded in 2005. During her first years as chair, the Conservative Party had a reputation of being the party of the elite and wealthy. This designation of being out of touch with ordinary Norwegian citizens came to a head on September 14, 2009, when the Conservatives placed third within the Storting. Many party members held Solberg responsible and called for her resignation.

Instead of resigning, however, Solberg worked to redirect the focus of the Conservative Party away from tax breaks for businesses and wealthy Norwegians to the welfare of ordinary citizens. This transformation was marked by her 2011 book, *Mennesker, ikke milliarder* (People, Not Billions). The book softened her Iron Erna image and broadened the Conservative Party's voter appeal. "People, not Billions" subsequently became the motto of the Conservative Party's 2013 election campaign, which focused on the four main issues of jobs, healthcare, education, and better roads across the fjords. Additionally, Solberg pledged to lower taxes and diversify the economy by mitigating Norway's dependence on oil revenue.

PRIME MINISTER

On September 9, 2013, a center-right coalition made up of the Conservative Party, the Progress Party, and two other parties took control of the Storting by winning a total of 96 out of 169 seats. The coalition's victory ousted incumbent Prime Minister Jens Stoltenberg of the Labour Party. As head of the Conservative Party, which had won the most seats of the center-right coalition, Solberg became the head of the government. On October 16, 2013, King Harald V officially appointed Solberg as prime minister of Norway. Her victory marked the first time there had been a Conservative Party prime minister since 1990.

Since assuming office, the Solberg cabinet has worked to improve public education, decrease the waiting time for health care, and invest in the country's public transit system. As prime minister, Solberg has taken a vocal, world leadership position on the issue of childhood education in developing nations. Solberg, who has stated that education is the key to solving the issue of poverty, announced in June 2014 that Norway would double its development assistance to countries affected by extreme poverty around the world. In 2015, Solberg was vocal in her support of assisting Syrian refugees in Europe misplaced by the ongoing Syrian civil war and called for all European countries to work together to curb the crisis. At the same time, she warned her own parliament of the drain on public funds that a large asylum program would bring and tasked them with finding ways to reduce costs.

IMPACT

From her time as a student politician to her ascent through the Storting, Solberg has worked to make Norway a leader in international humanitarianism. In her time as leader of the Conservative Party, she transformed it from a party interested in the elite to a party of the people, a significant change that brought her party back into power.

PERSONAL LIFE

Erna Solberg is married to Sindre Finnes. The couple have a son, Erik, and a daughter, Ingrid.

SUGGESTED READING

Hipp, Van. "Conservatives, If You Want to Win Look at How Norway's 'Iron Lady' Did It." *Fox News.* FOX News Network, 13 Sept. 2013, www.foxnews.com/opinion/conservatives-if-you-want-to-win-look-at-how-erna-solberg-norways-iron-lady-did-it. Accessed 9 June 2020.

Hovland, Kjetil Malkenes. "Norwegians Vote in a Conservative Prime Minister." *The Wall Street Journal.* Dow Jones, 9 Sept. 2013, www.wsj.com/articles/norway-exit-polls-show-conservative-victory-1378758544?tesla=y. Accessed 9 June 2020.

Koranyi, Balazs, and Gwladys Fouche. "Conservative Leader Solberg Sweeps into Power in Norwegian Election." *Reuters.* 9 Sept. 2013, www.reuters.com/article/us-norway-election/conservative-leader-solberg-sweeps-into-power-in-norwegian-election-idUS-BRE9880Y820130910. Accessed 9 June 2020.

Milne, Richard. "Erna Solberg Eyes Victory in Norway Elections." *Financial Times.* 5 Sept. 2013, www.ft.com/content/e2a7f4ec-155d-11e3-b519-00144feabdc0. Accessed 9 June 2020.

Solsvik, Terje, and Alister Doyle. "NEWS-MAKER—After Softening, 'Iron Erna' Set to Become Norway's PM." *Reuters.* Thomson Reuters, 10 Sept. 2013, news.trust.org/item/20130909222016-e9m6g. Accessed 9 June 2020.

—*Emily E. Turner*

Daniela Soto-Innes

Date of birth: August 26, 1990
Occupation: Chef and restaurateur

The James Beard Award–winning Mexican-born chef and restaurateur Daniela Soto-Innes "pairs genre-bending food with an insistence that fine dining should be enjoyable for everyone involved," as Dan F. Stapleton wrote for the *Australian Financial Review* (19 Aug. 2019). A protégé of the world-renowned Mexican chef Enrique Olvera, Soto-Innes overcame age and gender boundaries to become one of the culinary world's brightest talents. After becoming the head chef and co-owner of Cosme, a restaurant in New York City that she helped Olvera launch in 2014, she was credited with elevating modern Mexican haute cuisine. Creating one-of-a-kind dishes drawing on her cultural experiences growing up in both Mexico and Texas, Soto-Innes helped Cosme become one of the most acclaimed restaurants in the world. She did so while creating a positive and empowering environment for her kitchen staff, an approach that also earned her praise from many culinary observers. In 2017, she and Olvera opened a second New York eatery, Atla, serving more traditional Mexican fare.

EARLY LIFE AND EDUCATION

The youngest of three daughters, Daniela Soto-Innes was born on August 26, 1990, in Mexico City, Mexico. She was raised in the city's bohemian Coyoacán neighborhood, which is known for being the home of the iconic Mexican painter Frida Kahlo. Though both of her parents were lawyers, Soto-Innes grew up surrounded by food. Her grandmother managed a bakery, and from the age of three, she would accompany her to work. As Soto-Innes recalled in an interview with the fashion company M.M.LaFleur (28 May 2017), "I wasn't even big enough to see over the counter, but I would smell bread baking, and make cakes and play with dough."

As a young girl, Soto-Innes also attended cooking classes and farmer's markets with her mother, who initially aspired to become a professional chef. Early on, her grandmother and mother instilled in her the importance of cooking food with joy, love, and passion—an ethos that would later ground her work as a chef. She further cultivated her passion for food through cooking lessons at the Montessori school she attended and through regular walks down Mexico City streets, which were always redolent with the pungent aromas of street vendors and bakeries.

When Soto-Innes was twelve years old, her family moved to Houston, Texas, after her mother accepted a job offer there. At her mother's prompting, she enrolled at a career-centric technical academy where she studied culinary arts. At around age fifteen, she landed her first restaurant job in the kitchen of a Marriott hotel after being inspired by its head chef, who was among a number of culinary professionals to speak at her school; she reportedly showed up at the chef's hotel every day after school until he agreed to take her on as an intern. Working at the hotel several hours a week, she learned the basics of cooking while performing such menial tasks as chopping strawberries and washing lettuce.

One summer during high school, Soto-Innes did a stage, or unpaid apprenticeship, at a restaurant in New York to gain more culinary experience. It was in this high-powered, male-dominated environment where she encountered egregious sexism for the first time; the New York chef who hired her made it a point to inform her that he normally never hired women. Undaunted, she proceeded to run a cooking line of forty-year-old men at the age of sixteen. She has credited her father, a former basketball player, for teaching her that talent is not defined by age or gender. In an interview for the World's 50 Best Restaurants website (24 Apr. 2019), Soto-Innes told Laura Price, "What drew me to cooking was personalities and people and the story behind why they were cooking what they were cooking, more than the actual environment of the kitchen, which I didn't like."

RISE UP THE CULINARY LADDER
After graduating from high school early, Soto-Innes, who was a standout competitive swimmer in her teens, moved to Austin, Texas's capital city, to attend the culinary school Le Cordon Bleu. She attended the school for three years, during which time she worked at restaurants all over Austin. Before her afternoon classes each day, she would work from early in the morning, and she would then return to work after class ended. "I wasn't a rich kid that didn't have to work, so going to school really helped me focus on what I really wanted to do with my life," she noted in an interview with the *Lifestyle Edit* (3 Oct. 2016) about the potential values of structured culinary education.

Upon completing her formal training at Le Cordon Bleu at age nineteen, Soto-Innes spent time living abroad in Europe, where she did stages at a series of restaurants. Eventually, she returned to Houston, where she quickly moved up the culinary ladder at some of the city's top restaurants, most notably James Beard Award–winning chef Chris Shepherd's Underbelly. She agreed to work for Shepherd following a mentally and physically draining sous-chef job—her first—at another restaurant, in which she got burned out after working some eighteen hours per day. Shepherd took Soto-Innes under his wing, teaching her, among other things, how to

delegate responsibility to others. "You have to treat each person as an individual, not as a machine," she explained to Price. "It is important for people with different personalities to follow the same path for a restaurant to work."

Following a year at Underbelly, Soto-Innes, wanting to grow as a chef, travel, and go back to her Mexican roots, wrote a feeler letter to Enrique Olvera, the owner and head chef of Pujol, an internationally renowned Mexican haute cuisine restaurant in Mexico City. Olvera, widely credited with reinventing modern Mexican cuisine, responded to Soto-Innes the next day. Over the next year and a half, Soto-Innes worked two separate months-long stints at Pujol, which has been frequently referred to as the best Mexican restaurant in the world. As a member of Olvera's kitchen staff, she made pastries and performed other tasks, such as butchering animals, a skill she first learned while working at Underbelly.

COSME AND ATLA
In 2014, after her six-month visa expired, Soto-Innes was presented with the opportunity to help Olvera launch his first New York City restaurant, Cosme. Despite not knowing much about opening a restaurant aside from planning menus, she took on the challenge, moving to New York on three days' notice and then spending roughly nine months working out logistics with Cosme's investors. "I was 23 years old, starting a restaurant from zero. I Googled everything," she noted to Rachel Tepper Paley for the James Beard Foundation website (1 Nov. 2018).

Situated in a former strip club space in the Flatiron district, Cosme opened in October 2014 with Soto-Innes as its chef de cuisine. Not long afterward, the restaurant received rave reviews from critics for its innovative Mexican cuisine, which Soto-Innes defined as "another state of Mexico," as she put it to Price. Though ever-changing, the restaurant's menu featured dishes drawing on her combined Mexican and Texan upbringing, highlighting authentic Mexican flavors with either local or southern ingredients. Two menu mainstays included the duck carnitas, which are braised in Mexican-made Coca Cola, and the corn-husk meringue, a signature dessert inspired by a childhood memory of her father.

Soto-Innes's cooking eventually won notice from the food world cognoscenti, and in 2016, at age twenty-five, she won the coveted Rising Star Chef of the Year Award from the James Beard Foundation. The following year, she and Olvera opened Atla, a casual, all-day Mexican café located in New York's NoHo district. Serving such classic Mexican staples as enchiladas and chilaquiles, the café quickly developed a cult following and earned positive critical notices. In a review for the *New York Times* (25 July 2017), critic Pete Wells called Atla "one of the least divisive restaurants Manhattan has seen in some time," commenting that its simple, light, and health-conscious menu distinguished it from the more complex dishes served at Cosme.

WORLD'S 50 BEST RESTAURANTS LIST AND BEYOND

While Soto-Innes established Atla to realize a more modest and straightforward food vision, Cosme enabled her to take Mexican cuisine to new levels of sophistication. Consequently, Cosme built a reputation among food critics, chefs, and restaurateurs as one of the best restaurants in the world. In 2017, it debuted at number forty on *Restaurant* Magazine's popular, if controversial, annual World's 50 Best Restaurants list. Then, after placing twenty-fifth on that list in 2018, Cosme rose to number twenty-three in 2019, making it the highest-rated American restaurant on the list; it was one of only five restaurants included that had a female head chef or cohead chef. Also in 2019, in addition to having been included on the Forbes 30 Under 30 2017 list in the food and drink category, Soto-Innes became, at age twenty-eight, the youngest recipient of the award for the World's Best Female Chef, presented annually by the World's 50 Best Restaurants.

Though grateful, Soto-Innes gave little thought or concern to such recognition, instead focusing on being an inspiring and encouraging leader for her kitchen staffs. At Cosme, which had become equally known for its unpretentious, laidback atmosphere, she continued to run a kitchen predominantly comprised of women and immigrants, each of whom was embraced as a unique and distinct personality. Soto-Innes regularly consulted her staff for their creative input and led them in daily pre-service workout routines to boost energy and morale. "Cosme is not just a restaurant, it's more of a cultural institution, a lot of different cultures coming together," she explained to Price. "We might not know everything about cooking but we all strive to do the best we can, using the most knowledge we can collect between all of us."

Soto-Innes had become a full business partner in Olvera's American restaurant operations in 2017. In addition to Cosme and Atla, by early 2019 it had been announced that she was partnering with Olvera to launch two side-by-side ventures in Los Angeles, California: a Japanese-influenced Mexican restaurant and a traditional taqueria. The pair also set in motion plans to open a third West Coast eatery, Elio, at the Wynn hotel in Las Vegas, Nevada. "We're making our own vista," Soto-Innes told Stapleton.

PERSONAL LIFE

Soto-Innes became engaged to the James Beard Award–winning chef Blaine Wetzel, head chef of the restaurant Willows Inn, located on Lummi Island in Washington State, in early 2019. The two met while in Spain to attend the 2018 World's 50 Best Restaurants ceremony in Bilbao.

SUGGESTED READING

Paley, Rachel Tepper. "Inside Daniela Soto-Innes's Kitchen." *James Beard Foundation*, 1 Nov. 2018, www.jamesbeard.org/blog/inside-daniela-soto-inness-kitchen. Accessed 16 Mar. 2020.

Price, Laura. "Cosme's Daniela Soto-Innes on Corn Husk Meringues, Immigrant Culture and Dancing in the Kitchen." *The World's 50 Best Restaurants*, 24 Apr. 2019, www.theworlds50best.com/stories/News/daniela-soto-innes-worlds-best-female-chef-2019.html. Accessed 24 Feb. 2020.

Soto-Innes, Daniela. "The Most Vivacious Woman in the World." *M.M.LaFleur*, 28 May 2017, mmlafleur.com/most-remarkable-women/daniela-soto-innes. Accessed 24 Feb. 2020.

——. "New York City: Daniela Soto-Innes." *Bird*, www.wearebird.co/daniela-sotoinnes. Accessed 24 Feb. 2020.

——. "This Woman Just Might Be the Most Talked About Chef in New York Right Now." *The Lifestyle Edit*, 3 Oct. 2016, www.thelifestyle-edit.com/daniela-soto-innes-cosme-nyc/. Accessed 24 Feb. 2020.

Stapleton, Dan F. "Meet the World's Best Female Chef (Only Don't Call Her That)." *Australian Financial Review*, 19 Aug. 2019, www.afr.com/life-and-luxury/food-and-wine/meet-the-world-s-best-female-chef-only-don-t-call-her-that-20190815-p52heq. Accessed 24 Feb. 2020.

Wells, Pete. "At Atla, Mexican for Every Moment of the Day." Review of Atla. *The New York Times*, 25 July 2017, www.nytimes.com/2017/07/25/dining/atla-review-mexican-restaurant-noho.html. Accessed 24 Feb. 2020.

—*Chris Cullen*

Sebastian Stan

Date of birth: August 13, 1982
Occupation: Actor

Sebastian Stan is a Romanian American actor best known for his star-making turn as Bucky Barnes in a series of hugely popular films in the Marvel Cinematic Universe (MCU) based on Marvel Comics superheroes. He first appeared

Photo by Jon Kopaloff/Getty Images

as Barnes in *Captain America: The First Avenger* (2011). Across subsequent appearances he portrayed the complex character's evolution from Captain America's lifelong friend and staunchest ally during World War II to a brainwashed assassin known as the Winter Solider, and then a redeemed ally of the superhero team known as the Avengers seeking to find his place in the modern world. Building on his work with Marvel as well as his roles on small screen and the stage, Stan began to make a name for himself in other films, costarring alongside noted actors such as Margot Robbie in *I, Tonya* (2017) and Nicole Kidman in *Destroyer* (2018).

Although he quickly became a recognizable figure in Hollywood, Stan admitted in interviews he was rather unprepared for the kind of attention that came with his involvement in the blockbuster Marvel franchise. He sought to remain humble and dedicated to his craft, with an eye toward expanding his range as an actor further throughout his career. He reflected on his profession in his interview with Cezar Greif for the Malaysian edition of *August Man* (18 Apr. 2018): "Acting, to me, is an amazing experience. For me, personally, it's gratifying. There's a sense of release, a peace I get. But in the end, it's a way to communicate something with somebody."

EARLY LIFE AND EDUCATION

An only child, Sebastian Stan was born on August 13, 1982, in Romania. When he was eight years old, he moved with his mother to Vienna, Austria, where she worked as a pianist. During this time, his mother began suggesting that he

consider becoming an actor. She even brought him to some open calls, though he did not immediately take to the craft.

In 1995, when Stan was twelve, he and his mother moved again, this time to New York. He was raised in Rockland County by his mother and stepfather, who served as the headmaster of a private school, Rockland County Day School, where Stan was educated. As a teenager Stan began developing his own interest in acting, performing in school productions of *Harvey*, *Little Shop of Horrors*, and *West Side Story*, among others. He also began doing productions at the prestigious Stagedoor Manor summer camp program, an experience that he later described as particularly formative. "It was a magical, magical place," he told Max Berlinger for *GQ* (16 May 2016). "There were no distractions. You were forced to embrace your environment. It breaks you out of your shell, and I ended up with some amazing friendships from there."

With this experience under his belt, Stan began to recognize acting as his true calling. Having secured a manager while at Stagedoor, he applied to the acting programs of several colleges, ultimately accepting the opportunity to study at Rutgers University's Mason Gross School of the Arts in New Brunswick, New Jersey. During his undergraduate days he spent a year studying acting at Shakespeare's Globe in London, England. It was also during this period that he began winning parts in Hollywood on television shows and in films, including roles in *Law & Order* (2003), *Tony 'n' Tina's Wedding* (2004), and *Red Doors* (2005). He earned his bachelor of fine arts degree in 2005.

EARLY CAREER AND BECOMING THE WINTER SOLDIER

Stan remained based out of New York City in the early days of his professional career, earning parts in the films *The Architect* (2006), *The Covenant* (2006), and *The Education of Charlie Banks* (2007). His first major break came when he landed the recurring role of Carter Baizen on the CW network's series *Gossip Girl*, appearing in several episodes between 2007 and 2010. Recalling to Greif that appearing on the popular show was an "amazing opportunity," he added, "I guess that was the first time that, here and there, someone was recognising me. I don't think in the industry I was recognised for anything." Further proving the versatility of his talents from an early stage, he also made his Broadway debut in 2007, acting alongside Liev Schreiber as Kent in a revival of *Talk Radio*.

After a brief starring role in the NBC series *Kings* ended after one season in 2009 due to the show's poor ratings, Stan was featured in a pair of notable films, the ballet drama *Black Swan* and the comedy *Hot Tub Time Machine*, in

2010. But the film that would truly cement his reputation as an up-and-coming actor appeared the next year. *Captain America: The First Avenger* was released to rave reviews and became a major box-office hit. The film was also a cornerstone of the Marvel Cinematic Universe (MCU), an interlinked series of movies bringing Marvel Comics characters to life on the big screen that had begun with *Iron Man*, starring Robert Downey Jr., in 2008. Virtually every MCU entry proved financially successful and many won critical acclaim as well, making the superhero franchise a titan in both Hollywood and broader popular culture.

Captain America: The First Avenger describes the initial adventures of Steve Rogers (played by Chris Evans), a strong-willed and brave but physically scrappy young man who becomes a genetically enhanced "super soldier" known as Captain America to fight the Nazis during World War II. In the film, Stan (who originally auditioned for the Captain America role) portrays Bucky Barnes, a sergeant in the US Army and Rogers's childhood friend and comrade-in-arms. The events of the film set off a transformation of Stan's Barnes that plays out over later MCU installments. The character reemerges in the second Captain America film, *Captain America: The Winter Soldier* (2014), as the titular character, having been turned into a super soldier himself, brainwashed, and used by nefarious forces for decades to conduct covert operations and assassinations. Anthony Russo, one of the directors of *The Winter Soldier*, praised Stan's portrayal of Barnes in an interview with Steven Zeitchik for the *Los Angeles Times* (5 May 2016): "He did things in 'Winter Soldier' that blew us away, finding a way to put forth a complex character even though he didn't have many opportunities to speak."

I, TONYA AND DESTROYER

Even as Stan continued to develop his MCU character, he also maintained a presence outside of the superhero world. He held roles on the series *Political Animals* and *Once Upon a Time* (2012), and appeared on stage in a Broadway production of *Picnic* (2013). Especially after the success of *The Winter Soldier*, however, his turn as Bucky Barnes enabled him to take on increasingly higher-profile and challenging roles. He appeared as Lance Tucker in the comedy *The Bronze* (2015), about a former Olympic bronze medalist living in small-town Ohio. In *The Martian* (2015), an adaptation of Andy Weir's 2011 best-selling sci-fi novel of the same name, he portrayed Dr. Chris Beck. Stan then reprised his role as Barnes in an even more prominent and nuanced form in *Captain America: Civil War* (2016), in which Captain America defends Barnes against his brainwashed past. He

followed that up by playing a race car driver in the heist film *Logan Lucky* (2017), by noted director Steven Soderbergh.

Stan's next most influential role, both personally and critically, came with his casting in *I, Tonya* (2017), a film based on real people and events. He appeared as Jeff Gillooly, the scheming ex-husband of figure skater Tonya Harding (played by Margot Robbie) who orchestrated an attack that injured the leg of Harding's rival Nancy Kerrigan (played by Caitlin Carver) just prior to the 1994 Winter Olympics. Critics largely cheered Stan's performance. Writing for *Men's Health* (29 Aug. 2018), Evan Romano declared, "It's *wildly* different from anything else he's done; if this was his first movie you ever saw, you'd never in a million years suspect his *Captain America* history. Part *Fargo*, part *Catch Me If You Can*, this movie is a really well-done take on a story that most people don't know completely."

In 2018, Stan appeared in the independent film *Destroyer* alongside acclaimed actor Nicole Kidman as an agent with the Federal Bureau of Investigation (FBI). In the film, which received mostly positive reviews, the pair go undercover to infiltrate a dangerous gang.

MORE MARVEL AND OTHER ROLES

Also in 2018 Stan had an uncredited cameo in the MCU film *Black Panther*, setting up the character to join the fold of the superhero team known as the Avengers. He subsequently had supporting appearances in the third and fourth films of the Avengers franchise, *Avengers: Infinity War* (2018) and *Avengers: Endgame* (2019), both of which broke box-office records. Stan did seek out other roles—such as that of Charles Blackwood in the 2018 film adaptation of the 1962 Shirley Jackson novel *We Have Always Lived in the Castle*—in part to separate himself somewhat from the more commercial, big-budget MCU. However, he remained appreciative of the opportunity to play Barnes and be part of a pop culture phenomenon. "It changed my life in many ways," he told Greif of his best-known role. "It really catapulted me into the public eye, in a different way than I was used to. But in a nice way. I've been really grateful and lucky to come back and revisit that character over time."

In April 2019, Marvel Studios president Kevin Feige confirmed that Stan would once again reprise his role as Barnes in a series that would be housed on Disney's new streaming platform Disney+. Titled *The Falcon and Winter Soldier*, the show would costar another of Captain America's crime-fighting partners who had appeared in several MCU films: Sam Wilson, also known as the Falcon (played by Anthony Mackie). "This will be a much deeper dive on both of their pasts and both of their presents, post-*Endgame*, in a way that is cool," Feige stated about the series, as quoted by Devan Coggan in *Entertainment Weekly* (23 Aug. 2019).

It was also reported that Stan would lend his voice to the animated series *What If. . .?*, another MCU-related property on Disney+ meant to explore alternate realities. Meanwhile, Stan's film *Endings, Beginnings* premiered at the Toronto International Film Festival in September 2019.

PERSONAL LIFE

Stan, who began living in New York City after his graduation from college, largely keeps his personal life private.

SUGGESTED READING

Coggan, Devan. "Anthony Mackie, Sebastian Stan, and More Tease New *Falcon and the Winter Soldier* Details." *Entertainment Weekly*, 23 Aug. 2019, ew.com/tv/2019/08/23/anthony-mackie-sebastian-stan-falcon-winter-soldier-disney-plus-series-d23/. Accessed 11 Oct. 2019.

Emmrich, Stuart. "Sebastian Stan Just Likes to Watch." *The New York Times*, 1 Dec. 2017, www.nytimes.com/2017/12/01/style/sebastian-stan-tonya-harding-movie.html. Accessed 18 Nov. 2019.

Romano, Evan. "8 Sebastian Stan Movies Worth Watching That We Promise Don't Include Superheroes." *Men's Health*, 29 Aug. 2019, www.menshealth.com/entertainment/g28832170/sebastian-stan-movies-list/. Accessed 11 Oct. 2019.

Stan, Sebastian. "Sebastian Stan on Social Media, Style, and Life after *Captain America*." Interview by Max Berlinger. *GQ*, 16 May 2016, www.gq.com/story/sebastian-stan-style-interview. Accessed 18 Nov. 2019.

———. "Sebastian Stan's Musings on Life in *August Man* Malaysia Issue 115." Interview by Cezar Greif. *August Man*, 18 Apr. 2018, www.augustman.com/my/culture/film-tv/sebastian-stans-musings-life-august-man-malaysia-issue-115/. Accessed 15 Oct. 2019.

Zeitchik, Steven. "With 'Captain America: Civil War,' Sebastian Stan Crosses Over from Parts Unknown." *Los Angeles Times*, 5 May 2016, www.latimes.com/entertainment/movies/la-et-mn-0506-sebastian-stan-captain-america-civil-war-20160504-snap-story.html. Accessed 18 Nov. 2019.

SELECTED WORKS

Gossip Girl, 2007–10; *Captain America: The First Avenger*, 2011; *Captain America: The Winter Soldier*, 2014; *The Bronze*, 2015; *Captain America: Civil War*, 2016; *I, Tonya*, 2017; *Avengers: Infinity War*, 2018; *Destroyer*, 2018; *Avengers: Endgame*, 2019; *Endings, Beginnings*, 2019

—*Christopher Mari*

Lakeith Stanfield

Date of birth: August 12, 1991
Occupation: Actor

After making his feature-film debut as an angry, troubled teen in *Short Term 12* (2013), Lakeith Stanfield emerged as one of Hollywood's most impressive and versatile actors. He soon became known for his ability to tackle a wide variety of movie roles, ranging from an armed, masked bandit in *The Purge: Anarchy* (2014), to a bullying gang member in *Dope* (2015), as well as civil-rights activist Jimmie Lee Jackson in *Selma* (2014) and rap icon Snoop Dogg in *Straight Outta Compton* (2015). However, it was his scene-stealing role as a zombie-like party guest in the thriller *Get Out* (2017) that catapulted him into the mainstream.

Stanfield also carved out a niche for himself in the television landscape and won legions of fans with the role of Darius opposite actor and musician Donald Glover in the quirky FX comedy *Atlanta* (2016–18). On the big screen, he has shown himself to be capable of holding his own in leading roles, playing a wrongfully convicted murderer in *Crown Heights* (2017), and a telemarketer whose success at his white firm comes at a price in *Sorry to Bother You* (2018), as well as in an all-star ensemble cast, in such films as *Knives Out* (2019) and *Uncut Gems* (2019). In 2020, Stanfield starred as a love-struck photojournalist in *The Photograph*. Stanfield's chameleon-like skill to embody diverse characters is something he continually embraces. "I'm trying

Photo by Gage Skidmore via Wikimedia Commons

to reach out and experience as much as I can," he told Tasbeeh Herwees for the *Face* (21 Feb. 2020). "I like to jump around, whatever I haven't touched before, a new experience."

EARLY LIFE

Lakeith Lee Stanfield, also known as Keith Stanfield, was born on August 12, 1991, in San Bernardino, California, where his love for film first surfaced. "My earliest memories are when I was two to four years old and I was watching movies," he told Scott Feinberg for the *Hollywood Reporter* (7 Jan. 2014). "I was just really fixated on this little glowing box. All of the images that were coming out of there were very influential on the way I interacted, the things I did and really kind of influenced me to be who I am." Stanfield grew up with his mother and five siblings. While in San Bernardino, his home life was rather tumultuous, in large part due to his mother's abusive boyfriend. Along with being a first-hand witness, Stanfield was a target of the domestic violence, often while protecting his family, including his two autistic brothers. Despite this, he kept the truth from Child Protective Services (CPS), for fear of the siblings being separated. Stanfield was not immune to trouble himself, often stealing sandwiches from Subway and beer from Stater Bros supermarkets.

When Stanfield was around eleven, he and his family moved away from the boyfriend, settling in the quiet desert town of Victorville, California. Stanfield developed an early fondness for performing, putting on sock puppet shows and staging skits, often while wearing his aunt's wigs and feigning a British accent. Stanfield also discovered another passion: recording rap music in his bedroom, where he would also scrawl poetry and doodle on the walls.

FROM VICTORVILLE TO *SHORT TERM 12*

Acting, however, remained Stanfield's first priority. He honed his performance skills as a member of the high school drama club, which provided a welcome escape from his crime-ridden neighborhood. "I didn't have many friends in my age group because all they wanted to do was fight and have riots," Stanfield recalled to Hugh Hart for *Fast Company* (28 Feb. 2014). "That was like my safe place with great teachers where everyone could let down their guard and not feel judged." Stanfield's decision to pursue acting seriously came after appearing as a frog in his high school musical production. At age fifteen, Stanfield was admitted to the John Casablancas Modeling and Acting Center in Orange County, where he spent two years auditioning for commercials. In 2008, he landed his first-ever part, playing Marcus, an at-risk orphaned teen struggling with his impending group home departure, in writer/director Destin Daniel Cretton's

twenty-two-minute college thesis, *Short Term 12* (2008). The short film captured the 2009 Sundance Film Festival Jury Prize in Short Filmmaking. Stanfield followed this with a lead role in another short film, Anthony Onah's *Gimme Grace* (2010).

Over the next two years, Stanfield hit a dry spell, during which he worked several odd jobs, which included roofing work, landscaping, and door-to-door sales of AT&T cable contracts. When Cretton decided to adapt *Short Term 12* into a full-length feature, he tracked Stanfield to a legal marijuana factory and invited him to audition again. After a heartrending tryout, Stanfield was asked to reprise his role. As the sole returning cast member from the original short, he adopted a specific approach during filming, which took place over twenty days in September 2012. "I already knew this character intimately, and I knew to play this character I had to detach myself completely from everyone in the cast," he told Anna Silman for *The Cut* (11 Nov. 2016). "I made an effort to isolate myself because that's what the character's life was." Stanfield also had creative input, helping rewrite the lyrics to the rap song "So You Know What It's Like" that his character performs in the film.

Shot entirely in Los Angeles, the feature-length version of *Short Term 12* premiered on March 10, 2013, at the South by Southwest (SXSW) film festival, where it received the Grand Jury and Audience Award prizes in the Narrative Feature category. Within three weeks, Cinedigm had obtained distribution rights for the film, which opened in limited release on August 23 and wider release on September 13. For his performance, Stanfield earned his first-ever nomination, for best supporting male actor, at the Independent Spirit Awards.

ATLANTA AND *GET OUT*

Stanfield's successes started to attract the attention of Hollywood. After portraying a creepy, mask-wearing villain in the summer blockbuster horror sequel *The Purge: Anarchy* (2014), he was cast in the historical drama *Selma* (2014) as slain civil-rights activist Jimmie Lee Jackson. He earned the latter role after an impromptu photo-op with the movie's director, Ava DuVernay, at the Independent Spirit Awards. In 2015, Stanfield appeared in several dramatic shorts—including the postapocalyptic *King Ripple* and director Logan Sandler's graduate thesis *Tracks*—while continuing to amass small, yet memorable feature-film parts, like his standout cameo as rapper Snoop Dogg in hip-hop group N.W.A.'s biopic *Straight Outta Compton* (2015) and his turn as a high-school bully in the indie coming-of-age comedy *Dope* (2015). He ended the year appearing alongside Hollywood heavyweights in the biographical dramas *Miles Ahead*, with Don Cheadle, and *Memoria*, alongside James Franco.

Stanfield enjoyed an increasingly visible profile in 2016, starting with his attendance at Sundance, where two of his films were screened: the live-action virtual reality short *Hard World for Small Things* and *Live Cargo*, his second collaboration with Sandler. That same year, he made his television debut with his role as the charmingly eccentric, gun-loving, and pot-smoking philosopher Darius in Donald Glover's critically acclaimed FX comedy *Atlanta*, about the friendship between a budding rapper, his cousin/manager, and their best friend as they navigate the city's hip-hop scene. The show's second season appeared in 2018, and it was subsequently renewed for a third and fourth season. Also in 2016, Stanfield made his big-screen return in Oliver Stone's biopic *Snowden*, playing Patrick Haynes, a computer expert and colleague of CIA whistleblower Edward Snowden.

In 2017, Stanfield gave a chilling performance in Jordan Peele's directorial debut, *Get Out*, that left a lasting impression on the audience; after being abducted from a suburban neighborhood in the film's opening scene, his character resurfaces, glassy-eyed, at a party, issuing a dire warning to the protagonist by shouting the movie's title. He later reprised the character for a 2018 Oscars' opening sketch. For his next feature film, *Crown Heights* (2017), Stanfield starred as Colin Warner, a Trinidadian inmate who is unjustly convicted of a 1980 murder and sentenced to life in prison before being freed two decades later. Released in late August, the biographical drama claimed the US Dramatic Audience Award at the 2017 Sundance Film Festival. The festival also screened *The Incredible Jessica James* (2017), another Stanfield movie that aired on Netflix in July. His other Netflix releases that year included the Brad Pitt comedy *War Machine* and the supernatural thriller *Death Note*.

FURTHER ACCLAIM

Stanfield experienced his first major starring vehicle with Boots Riley's directorial debut *Sorry to Bother You* (2018). In the farcical dark comedy, Stanfield tackled the role of Cassius Green, a financially struggling telemarketer who is promoted from his low-paying job only after successfully adopting a so-called white voice to peddle encyclopedias and finds himself conflicted with his racial identity as he climbs up the corporate ladder.

Sorry to Bother You was widely released in July 2018 to critical praise. In her review for the *Associated Press* (2 July 2018), Lindsey Bahr deemed Stanfield "brilliant" while also remarking that he "delivers a powerful performance as Cassius in his oppression, his empowerment and eventual enlightenment." The film's accolades included the 2019 National Board of Review Award for Top Independent Films and the 2019 Independent Spirit Award for Best First Feature. Stanfield's lesser-known 2018 film credits included the big-screen adaptation of *The Girl in the Spider's Web*, based on the novel by David Lagercrantz; the biographical drama *Come Sunday*, which premiered at Sundance alongside *Sorry to Bother You*; and the shorts *Time of Day* and *Let's Dance*.

Stanfield gave a more restrained performance in his next film, 2019's *Knives Out*, a murder-mystery set against the backdrop of a mansion. As a detective investigating a wealthy patriarch's death and the long list of eccentric suspects, Stanfield held his own amid an all-star ensemble that included Daniel Craig, Chris Evans, Jamie Lee Curtis, Michael Shannon, and Toni Collette. He next appeared in the crime drama *Uncut Gems* (2019), in which he costarred as the street-smart, smooth liaison to a New York City jeweler and compulsive gambler played by Adam Sandler. After playing a music journalist's ex-boyfriend in Netflix's *Someone Great* (2019), Stanfield graduated to romantic leading-man status with *The Photograph* (2020), costarring opposite Issa Rae as a photojournalist who falls in love with an assistant curator while doing research on her mother. Stanfield also lent his voice to the animated adult series *Bojack Horseman* (2019–20).

In addition to his music video appearances for Jay-Z ("Moonlight") and Michael Kiwanuka ("Cold Little Heart") Stanfield writes and performs hip-hop music as part of the duo MOORS, his collaboration with Los Angeles producer HH (Hrishikesh Hirway).

PERSONAL LIFE

The notoriously private actor, Stanfield, lives in Los Angeles with his girlfriend, actor Xosha Roquemore, and their child, who was born in June 2017.

SUGGESTED READING

Bahr, Lindsey. "Review: A Wild, Provocative Vision in *Sorry to Bother You*." Rev. of *Sorry to Bother You*, directed by Boots Riley. *Associated Press*, 2 July 2018, apnews.com/b39baba7c7384a808e2cbadc3c83e933/Review:-A-wild,-provocative-vision-in-'Sorry-to-Bother-You'. Accessed 10 June 2020.

Hart, Hugh. "Behind the Breakout Role: How Spirit Award Nominee Keith Stanfield Dug Deep for his *Short Term 12* Performance," *Fast Company*, 28 Feb. 2014, www.fastcompany.com/3026953/behind-the-breakout-role-how-spirit-award-nominee-keith-stanfield-dug-deep-for-his-big-short. Accessed 5 June 2020.

Herwees, Tasbeeh. "Lakeith Stanfield Is One of Hollywood's Most Stunningly Diverse Actors."

The Face, 21 Feb. 2020, theface.com/culture/lakeith-stanfield-interview-atlanta-get-out-uncut-gems-knives-out-volume-4-issue-003. Accessed 5 June 2020.

Silman, Anna. "Getting Real with Lakeith Stanfield, Atlanta's Pothead Philosopher-Poet." *The Cut*, 11 Nov. 2016, www.thecut.com/2016/11/talking-to-lakeith-stanfield-atlantas-pothead-philosopher.html. Accessed 5 June 2020.

Stanfield, Lakeith. "Will Keith Stanfield Score an Oscar Nom for His Heartbreaking *Short Term 12 Rap Song*? (Q&A)." Interview by Scott Feinberg. *Hollywood Reporter*, 7 Jan. 2014, www.hollywoodreporter.com/race/will-keith-stanfield-score-an-668662. Accessed 10 June 2020.

SELECTED WORKS

Straight Outta Compton, 2015; *Snowden*, 2016; *Get Out*, 2017; *Crown Heights*, 2017; *Sorry to Bother You*, 2018; *Knives Out*, 2019; *Uncut Gems*, 2019; *The Photograph*, 2020

—Bertha Muteba

Elise Stefanik

Date of birth: July 2, 1984
Occupation: Politician

Elise M. Stefanik, a Republican representative for New York's Twenty-First Congressional District, was touted as a rising political star during the impeachment hearings of President Donald Trump in November 2019. A former policy aide to President George W. Bush, Stefanik emerged as a fierce defender of Trump, a shift in tone and ideology that surprised many colleagues.

Stefanik first won office in 2014; at thirty, she was then the youngest woman ever elected to Congress. She campaigned as the new face of the GOP: young, moderate, and female. Her rural New York district lies in a Canadian border region known as the North Country, and many of its residents are blue-collar workers, avid hunters, and veterans. The district leans Republican but had elected a Democrat, Stefanik's predecessor, in 2012 and twice voted for President Barack Obama. Residents value gun rights but also environmental issues, such as protecting the Adirondack Forest, which covers a broad swath of the district. Indeed, Stefanik opposed funding cuts to the Environmental Protection Agency (EPA) in 2017.

Her sharp conservative turn during the impeachment hearings mirrored the political shift underway in her own district. Politics in the Twenty-First District were becoming more reflective of the national partisan divide. For some, Stefanik's political evolution proved controversial. "We saw her as what we thought the future of the Republican Party was and that really has been disproven," Phillip Paige, a college student and former Stefanik backer, told Anna Gronewold for *Politico* (14 Dec. 2019). "Unless, maybe the future of the Republican Party is Donald Trump."

EARLY LIFE AND EDUCATION

Elise Stefanik was born on July 2, 1984, in Albany, New York. She grew up in the town of New Scotland, outside of Albany. Her father, Ken, was a forklift operator and plywood salesman who founded Premium Plywood Products, a wholesale distributor of plywood, hardwood, and laminated products, when Stefanik was about eight years old. Her mother, Melanie, became the venture's chief financial officer. Her younger brother, Matt, also eventually worked for the company.

Growing up, Stefanik initially attended Catholic school, but was bullied for being too studious. She transferred to the Albany Academy for Girls, a prestigious preparatory school, when she was in the fourth grade. There, she won her first political campaign—for the secretary of the student council in the sixth grade, promising to lobby for a snack machine. In eighth grade, after hearing a radio interview with Rick Lazio, a Republican Senate candidate, Stefanik volunteered for his campaign, making posters by hand. Stefanik cultivated other interests, too. In high school, she joined the lacrosse team and played

Photo by the United States House of Representatives

Gretel in a school production of *The Sound of Music*.

Stefanik graduated in 2002 and enrolled as a student at Harvard University, making her the first person in her immediate family to attend college. She studied government and served as an editor and staff writer for the student newspaper, the *Harvard Crimson*. In addition to short pieces about love and friendship, she also wrote about the under-representation of women in academic and political leadership roles.

Stefanik also served as the vice president of Harvard's Institute of Politics and, as a senior, became a student fellow with a conservative think tank, the Foundation for Defense of Democracies. During that time, Stefanik wrote a letter to the editor rebuking historian Joseph Ellis's *New York Times* article that had cautioned against the September 11, 2001, terrorist attacks defining foreign and domestic policy. She characterized the event as one among many and described terrorism as a global, not national, threat. Stefanik graduated with honors in 2006.

EARLY CAREER IN WASHINGTON

After graduation, Stefanik was hired as a staff assistant for President George W. Bush's Domestic Policy Council. On her first day she introduced herself to Karl Zinsmeister, the newly appointed director of domestic policy. The former editor of the *American Enterprise* magazine and conservative think tank fellow hired her immediately as his special assistant. "It was kind of a shock to my colleagues," she recalled to her the Glens Falls, New York, *Post Star* (4 May 2014). "The fact that I was promoted to the White House on my first day was a real privilege." During the next couple of years, Stefanik would work on domestic policy matters in the West Wing, first for Joel Kaplan, then deputy chief of staff of policy, and later as executive assistant to Joshua Bolten, after he became chief of staff.

After Bush left office, Stefanik launched the political magazine *American Maggie*. Named for the former British prime minister Margaret Thatcher, it aimed to publish the work of conservative female writers. It folded within a couple years, however.

In 2011 Stefanik served as the new-media and policy director for the Freedom First political action committee (PAC), which supported Minnesota governor Tim Pawlenty's brief presidential campaign. That same year she filled the role of the director of communications and external affairs for the Foreign Policy Initiative, a think tank founded by the neoconservative political commentator Bill Kristol. During her time there, Stefanik urged more aggressive measures against Syrian dictator Bashar al Assad.

In 2012 Stefanik was hired as policy director for the Republican National Convention (RNC)

Committee on Resolutions, helping develop the platform, which included proposals for the partial privatization of Social Security and Medicare and a total ban on abortion. After the convention, Stefanik joined Mitt Romney's presidential campaign, where she oversaw preparations for Representative Paul Ryan's vice-presidential debate against incumbent vice president Joe Biden. After Romney and Ryan were defeated in the general election, Stefanik moved back to New York State and joined her family's company. She became its director of North Country sales, marketing, and management.

FIRST CONGRESSIONAL CAMPAIGN

In 2013 Stefanik settled in her family's vacation home in Willsboro on Lake Champlain, in New York's Twenty-First District. She made her intention to run for office immediately clear, driving across the massive rural district to introduce herself to local Republican leaders in her spare time. "I was blown away by her," Mark Westcott, a local official, recalled to Brett LoGiurato for *Business Insider* (3 Nov. 2014). "And then to think she has the courage to just show up . . . call me out of the blue, ask to meet with me, talking about running against a popular incumbent. He added, "These are the types of people you don't usually come across. These are innate qualities in a person." At the time Stefanik aimed to challenge Bill Owens, the district's Democratic incumbent. Instead, Owens announced his retirement, a decision that played heavily in Stefanik's favor.

Declaring her candidacy that August, Stefanik presented herself as a fresh—and, notably, female—face in the Republican Party. "I don't look like a typical candidate," she told Tamara Keith for the National Public Radio (NPR) program *Morning Edition* (1 Oct. 2014). "But what I've realized is people have been really looking for someone who isn't necessarily the status quo in Washington." Her claim of being a Washington outsider was dubious, particularly when she won an early endorsement from Romney and enjoyed significant financial support from American Crossroads, a super PAC funded by the once-powerful Republican operative Karl Rove. Her Washington connections helped her fend off challenger Matthew A. Doheny, whom Owens had defeated in 2012, in the competitive GOP primary.

Facing Democrat Aaron G. Woolf in the general election, Stefanik moderated her views, perhaps to reflect the desires of the idiosyncratic district. She advocated repealing the Affordable Care Act, touted her support for the Violence Against Women Act and for equal pay for women, and said she would support abortion in rare cases. Stefanik appealed not only to women but also to younger voters, both demographics that tend to lean left.

Her ties to the Washington establishment continued to give her an edge—John Boehner, then Speaker of the House, appeared at a fundraiser for her just before the election—but Stefanik brushed off accusations of being an insider. "I've been able to outwork other candidates," she told Jesse McKinley for the *New York Times* (28 Oct. 2014). "So I really only think national folks are paying attention to this race because of the hard work on the ground."

CONGRESSIONAL CAREER

Stefanik handily won the 2014 race, becoming the youngest woman elected to Congress up to that point. Her victory was part of a larger midterm sweep in which the GOP won its largest share of House seats since 1928. Stefanik seemed poised to become a star, and she swept her district in her 2016 reelection bid. However, she passed her first two terms in relative obscurity.

After Trump was elected in 2016—he won her district by 14 percentage points—Stefanik won praise from her colleagues across the aisle. In an era of hyperpartisanship, one unnamed Democratic aide described her to Alexander Nazaryan for *Yahoo News* (26 Nov. 2019), as a "sensible moderate, someone we wanted to work with." Stefanik spoke about the threat of climate change, was skeptical of Trump's border wall on the US–Mexico border, and opposed his 2017 tax cuts and troop withdrawal from Syria. She even criticized Trump outright, calling his behavior inappropriate and "contrary to our American ideals," as quoted by Brian Mann for NPR's *Weekend Edition Sunday* (17 Nov. 2019).

Stefanik remained relatively popular among constituents, defeating Democratic challenger Tedra L. Cobb by about thirty thousand votes to win a third term in 2018.

IMPEACHMENT HEARINGS

In the fall of 2019, when Congress began investigating evidence that the president had withheld aid from Ukraine in exchange for political favors, Stefanik was rumored to be among a few Republicans who might favor impeachment. Ultimately, however, Stefanik, like all her Republican colleagues in the House, voted against impeachment. In fact, she became a vocal defender of the president.

Many political observers were surprised by Stefanik's change in tone. As a member of the House Intelligence Committee—notably, the lone Republican woman—Stefanik participated in both closed-door and open impeachment hearings, led by Democrat Adam Schiff. In the first public hearing, she interrogated the deputy assistant secretary of state for European and Eurasian affairs, George Kent, and the top US diplomat in Ukraine, William B. Taylor Jr., who conceded that Ukraine struggled with corruption and that the Ukrainian government ultimately received the aid it was promised—a key parts of Trump's defense. Later, she confronted Schiff over procedural issues and accused him of trying to silence her. During the second hearing, her profile grew further with her questioning of Maria Yovanovich, the former US ambassador to Ukraine.

Stefanik's combative display drew both positive and negative attention. It won a congratulatory tweet from the president, who wrote on Twitter, "A new Republican Star is born. Great going." Her reelection campaign also raised over $3 million in the last months of 2019, but her main 2020 challenger, Cobb, took in over $2 million from Democrats and Stefanik critics. One prominent critic was George Conway, a political commentator married to Trump adviser Kellyanne Conway; he drew criticism for describing Stefanik as "lying trash" on Twitter. Months later, celebrating his acquittal with a speech at the White House in February 2020, Trump praised Stefanik, solidifying her position as a favored acolyte.

Stefanik denied that her support for Trump was born of opportunism. "I ask good questions with every hearing for every committee on which I serve," Stefanik told Gronewold. "And this just happened to be a committee that had bright spotlights at the national level." For her role in the impeachment hearings, *Time* magazine named Stefanik among its inaugural *Time* 100 Next list of the world's emerging influencers in 2019.

PERSONAL LIFE

Stefanik met and began dating Matthew Manda, then a marketing and communications director for Representative Kevin Yoder (R-KS), in 2012. The couple married on August 19, 2017, and divided their time between Washington, DC, and Schuylerville, New York. Stefanik enjoys theater, skeet shooting, and watching television.

SUGGESTED READING

Gronewold, Anna. "A Trumpist Star Is Born." *Politico*, 14 Dec. 2019, www.politico.com/news/magazine/2019/12/14/elise-stefanik-new-york-district-084853. Accessed 14 Apr. 2020.

Keith, Tamara. "In New York's North Country, the Republican Party's New Poster Candidate." *Morning Edition*, NPR, 1 Oct. 2014, www.npr.org/2014/10/01/352925448/30-year-old-congressional-candidate-embraces-her-youth. Accessed 14 Apr. 2020.

LoGiurato, Brett. "This 30-Year-Old Rising Star Is Already Being Touted as the Future of the GOP." *Business Insider*, 3 Nov. 2014, www.

businessinsider.com/elise-stefanik-future-of-the-gop-ny-21-district-positions-2014-11. Accessed 14 Apr. 2020.

McKinley, Jesse. "In Upstate New York House Race, Republican Makes Her Youth a Selling Point." *The New York Times*, 28 Oct. 2014, www.nytimes.com/2014/10/29/nyregion/in-upstate-new-york-house-race-republican-makes-her-youth-a-selling-point.html. Accessed 14 Apr. 2020.

Nazaryan, Alexander. "The Birth of a Trumpist: How Elise Stefanik Became One of the President's Most Ferocious Supporters." *Yahoo News*, 26 Nov. 2019, news.yahoo.com/the-birth-of-a-trumpist-how-elise-stefanik-became-one-of-the-presidents-most-ferocious-supporters-100046537.html. Accessed 14 Apr. 2020.

"Stefanik's Campaign Ramping Up." *The Post Star*, 4 May 2014, poststar.com/news/local/stefanik-s-campaign-ramping-up/article_d2154512-d3b7-11e3-9a69-0019bb2963f4.html. Accessed 14 Apr. 2020.

Zengerle, Patricia. "Republican Elise Stefanik Tangles with Schiff to Defend Trump during Hearings." *Reuters*, 15 Nov. 2019, www.reuters.com/article/us-usa-trump-impeachment-stefanik/republican-elise-stefanik-tangles-with-schiff-to-defend-trump-during-hearings-idUSKBN1XP26I. Accessed 16 Apr. 2020.

—*Molly Hagan*

Stephen Strasburg

Date of birth: July 20, 1988
Occupation: Baseball player

From the time that he made his Major League Baseball (MLB) debut in 2010, pitcher Stephen Strasburg faced tremendous expectations. After being arguably the most highly touted draft prospect in baseball history, the right-hander was selected by the Washington Nationals with the first pick in the 2009 MLB Draft. Hailed as "a once-in-a-generation phenomenon," as Kyle Glaser wrote for *Baseball America* (23 Oct. 2019), Strasburg entered the league with a devastating pitching arsenal—highlighted by a fastball that at times reached a speed in the triple digits—and was poised to become the Nationals' incumbent ace and a perennial Cy Young Award contender. Injuries and other circumstances interfered with those hopes, however, and Strasburg, though putting up largely solid numbers, showed only occasional flashes of brilliance in his first nine years in the league, during which

he was named to three All-Star teams (2012, 2016, and 2017).

Nevertheless, Strasburg elevated his game to elite status in 2019, when he led the National League (NL) in wins (eighteen) and innings pitched (209) during the regular season. Finally settling into his role as a top-of-the-rotation starter, he anchored the Nationals throughout that year's playoffs, posting a perfect 5–0 record to help the team capture their first World Series title. For his performance, he was named the World Series Most Valuable Player (MVP).

EARLY LIFE AND EDUCATION

Strasburg was born on July 20, 1988, in San Diego, California. His father, Jim, worked as a real estate developer, and his mother, Kathy, as a dietitian; they divorced when Strasburg was around six years old. From a young age, he developed a love of baseball and fostered dreams of playing in the major leagues. He first learned how to play the sport from his grandmother, who would play catch with him in the backyard.

Growing up a fan of the hometown San Diego Padres, Strasburg idolized the team's star right-fielder Tony Gwynn, a perennial All-Star and Hall of Famer widely regarded as one of the greatest hitters in MLB history. Instead of following in Gwynn's footsteps, however, Strasburg gravitated toward pitching. Throughout his youth, he pitched for a series of elite travel baseball teams. One of his teammates during this time was Brett Bochy, son of Bruce Bochy, who was the manager of the Padres at that point. During off days in town, Bruce Bochy invited

Photo by Keith Allison via Wikimedia Commons

his son's travel squad to practice at the Padres' former home, Qualcomm Stadium, where Strasburg frequently encountered Gwynn.

When Strasburg entered West Hills High School in Santee, California, he was seemingly on a fast track to MLB stardom. By his sophomore year, he had earned a spot on West Hills' starting pitcher rotation. Control problems and difficulty keeping his emotions in check on the mound led to a disastrous junior season, however. Compounding matters was the six-foot-four player's weight, which reached 250 pounds. "I was a chubby kid," he said to Kirk Kenney for ESPN (4 Feb. 2009), "with a poor mental game out there." Although he recovered his senior year to post a 1.68 earned run average (ERA) and seventy-four strikeouts, he ultimately went undrafted coming out of high school.

TRANSFORMATION INTO AN ELITE PITCHER

Also an academic standout, Strasburg enrolled at his parents' alma mater, San Diego State University (SDSU), in 2006. Gwynn served as its head baseball coach, and though initially unimpressed by Strasburg because of his poor conditioning and work ethic, Gwynn quickly took Strasburg under his wing and became a father figure. Still, Strasburg almost left the school following his preseason workouts with the Aztecs that first fall. "The high school I went to, you just showed up, played the game and went home," he recalled to Scott Miller for *Bleacher Report* (12 July 2016). "Once I got to SDSU, that first week of conditioning, I could barely get through the stretches or the warm-up. I really, really struggled."

Strasburg persevered, however, and lost thirty pounds his first semester, building both his strength and flexibility for the first time. Thanks to his physical transformation, the velocity on his fastball increased, reaching the triple digits at times. After being used as a middle reliever and closer his first year, he was moved to the Aztecs' starting rotation his sophomore season, in which he was named a consensus first team All-American after winning 8–3 with a 1.57 ERA and 133 strikeouts. That season was highlighted by a twenty-three-strikeout performance against the University of Utah.

Strasburg's dominant numbers landed him a spot on the US Olympic team for the 2008 Summer Games in Beijing, China. He was the sole collegiate player selected to the team, which earned a bronze medal at the games. Despite entering his junior season with much fanfare and anticipation, Strasburg remained unfazed, with a 13–1 win-loss record, a 1.32 ERA, and 195 strikeouts in 109 innings pitched, helping the Aztecs secure their first National Collegiate Athletic Association (NCAA) regional playoff berth since 1991.

NATIONALS' NUMBER-ONE PICK

Throughout Strasburg's junior season, professional scouts and media were a ubiquitous presence at his games. Considered a generational talent and surefire number-one draft pick, he drew comparisons to Roger Clemens for his at-times unhittable arsenal of pitches, which, besides fastballs, included a sweeping slider. Following a months long media frenzy, he was drafted number one overall by the Washington Nationals, who signed him to a then record-breaking four-year, $15.1 million contract.

Prior to his reaching the majors, Strasburg's lone scouting report concluded, as noted by Glaser, "He projects as a true No. 1 starter and a Cy Young Award winner, and anything less will be a disappointment." Strasburg seemed destined to fulfill those lofty expectations when, after spending less than one full year in the Nationals' farm system, he turned in an electrifying performance in his major-league debut, which came on June 8, 2010. Facing the Pittsburgh Pirates in one of the most-hyped pitching debuts in baseball history, he struck out fourteen batters and issued no walks over seven innings in a 5–2 win.

Strasburg pitched impressively in eleven more starts for the Nationals as a rookie before being shut down with a tear of his right elbow's ulnar collateral ligament. The injury required him to undergo Tommy John surgery and then about a year of rehabilitation. During the final month of the 2011 season, he made his long-awaited return to the Nationals, striking out twenty-four batters and compiling a 1.50 ERA in five starts.

Returning to full health and form in 2012, Strasburg enjoyed a 15–6 win-loss record with a 3.16 ERA and 197 strikeouts in twenty-eight starts for the upstart Nationals, who won their first NL East Division title and secured a spot in the playoffs for the first time. The team found themselves at the center of controversy, however, after they opted to shut down Strasburg for the postseason in order to protect his arm; they ultimately lost to the St. Louis Cardinals in the NL Division Series (NLDS). Strasburg, nevertheless, was named to his first All-Star team that season and given a Silver Slugger Award.

FLASHES OF BRILLIANCE

Following his first three MLB seasons, Strasburg proceeded to "become a superlative finished product of a pitcher" over the ensuing years, as Tom Verducci wrote for *Sports Illustrated* (30 Oct. 2019). He reached the thirty-start threshold for the first time in his career in 2013 and then led the NL in strikeouts (242) in 2014. During the latter season, he also posted career highs in starts (thirty-four) and innings pitched (215).

Following an injury-plagued 2015 season, in which he was limited to twenty-three starts, Strasburg bounced back in historic fashion in 2016. He opened that year by winning his first thirteen decisions, becoming the first NL starter since 1912 to accomplish such a feat. During that streak, he was awarded a seven-year, $175 million contract extension from the Nationals. He was named to his second All-Star team, and despite being hampered by injuries during the second half of the season, he finished with a 15–4 record. He then duplicated that record in 2017, during which he posted a 2.52 ERA in twenty-eight games and earned his third career All-Star selection. The following season was marked by several stints on the disabled list, which restricted him to twenty-two starts, but he nevertheless racked up four ten-plus strikeout games, fanning a total of 156 batters in 130 innings.

Throughout the 2019 offseason, Strasburg intensified his conditioning program and changed his pitching approach. In the preceding years, he often still relied on his hundred-mile-per-hour fastball to finish hitters off, a strategy that met with mixed results. Instead, Strasburg, who eliminated his slider from his repertoire due to the strain it put on his elbow, started focusing more on his two-seam fastball, his curveball, and a devastating changeup to outwit batters. "It's pretty obvious that the expectations that people had for me from early on were a little insane," he explained to Glaser, commenting on his career trajectory. "And I think you just become more comfortable with yourself, more comfortable with the results, and you set yourself to your own standards."

WORLD SERIES MVP

Strasburg's pitching reinvention resulted in a career season in 2019. Staying healthy all year, he made thirty-three starts and achieved career highs in wins (eighteen) and strikeouts (251), posting a 3.32 ERA in 209 innings. He led the NL in both wins and innings pitched and finished second in the league in strikeouts. During the second month of the season, he set a record for the fastest player in major league history to record 1,500 career strikeouts, doing so in a game against the Cardinals.

Led by a stalwart pitching rotation, the Nationals finished second in the NL East and returned to the postseason after a one-year absence. In the postseason, Strasburg helped anchor the Nationals, winning a series of decisive games in the first three playoff rounds before turning in "a World Series performance for the ages," as Tyler Kepner wrote for the *New York Times* (30 Oct. 2019). He won the second and sixth games of the series, in which he struck out fourteen batters and gave up only twelve hits in

14.1 innings. The Nationals ultimately defeated the Houston Astros in seven games to capture their first World Series title.

Strasburg was named the World Series MVP for his performance, becoming the first former number-one draft pick to accomplish the feat. He finished the 2019 postseason with a perfect 5–0 record, a 1.98 ERA, forty-seven strikeouts, and only four walks in 36.1 innings. In the process, he matched the record for most victories in one postseason and became the first to do so without suffering a loss. "The ups, the downs, it only makes you stronger mentally," Strasburg said after the sixth game, as quoted by Kepner. "I think, without those things, it would have been a lot harder to focus on what I can control out there."

In December 2019, about one month after having opted out of his previous contract, Strasburg agreed to a seven-year contract with the Nationals worth $245 million. Upon announcing the deal, Nationals general manager Mike Rizzo called Strasburg "one of the premier pitching talents of this generation," as quoted by Bob Nightengale in *USA Today* (9 Dec. 2019). "His body of work this season and throughout his career proves that and the way he performed this postseason was nothing short of brilliant."

PERSONAL LIFE

Strasburg married Rachel Lackey, whom he met at San Diego State, in 2010. The couple have two daughters. Strasburg's home in the Washington, DC area is reportedly located only a short drive from the Nationals' home stadium, Nationals Park, where he prefers to work out during the offseason.

SUGGESTED READING

Glaser, Kyle. "'Set Your Own Standards': Stephen Strasburg Embraces Path to World Series." *Baseball America*, 23 Oct. 2019, www.baseballamerica.com/stories/set-your-own-standards-stephen-strasburg-embraces-path-to-world-series. Accessed 17 Jan. 2020.

Jenkins, Lee. "Stephen Strasburg Is Ready to Bring It." *Sports Illustrated*, 25 Mar. 2009, www.si.com/more-sports/2009/03/25/stephen-strasburg. Accessed 17 Jan. 2020.

Kenney, Kirk. "San Diego State's Strasburg Works His Way Up to Becoming 'Next Big Thing.'" *ESPN*, 4 Feb. 2009, www.espn.com/college-sports/news/story?id=3884236. Accessed 17 Jan. 2020.

Kepner, Tyler. "Stephen Strasburg Rewards Nationals for Their Trust." *The New York Times*, 30 Oct. 2019, www.nytimes.com/2019/10/30/sports/baseball/stephen-strasburg-world-series.html. Accessed 13 Feb. 2020.

Miller, Scott. "Stephen Strasburg's Father-Son Bond with Tony Gwynn Made Him an MLB

Star." *Bleacher Report*, 12 July 2016, bleach-erreport.com/articles/2650764-stephen-strasburgs-father-son-bond-with-tony-gwynn-made-him-an-mlb-star. Accessed 17 Jan. 2020.

Nightengale, Bob. "Stephen Strasburg Has Agreed to Seven-Year, $245M Deal to Stay with Washington Nationals." *USA Today*, 9 Dec. 2019, www.usatoday.com/story/sports/mlb/nationals/2019/12/09/stephen-strasburg-agrees-deal-stay-washington-nationals/2633376001/. Accessed 17 Jan. 2020.

Verducci, Tom. "How the Nationals Fixed Stephen Strasburg and Saved Their Season." *Sports Illustrated*, 30 Oct. 2019, www.si.com/mlb/2019/10/30/stephen-strasburg-nationals-saved-season-world-series-game-6. Accessed 17 Jan. 2020.

—*Chris Cullen*

Billy Strings

Born: October 3, 1992
Occupation: Bluegrass musician

Bluegrass music essentially emerged from the United States' Appalachian region, particularly in states such as Tennessee and Kentucky, around the 1940s, combining blues and jazz with traditional country as well as English, Scottish, and Irish folk and dance tunes. It is an energetic style of music steeped in tradition that witnessed more of a resurgence beginning in the early decades of the twenty-first century, due in part to the prowess of young performers like Billy Strings, who has sought to bring bluegrass into the future by combining it with rock and psychedelia. After starting out as a combined act based in Michigan with his mentor, mandolin player Don Julin, putting out two albums and performing live, he relocated to Nashville and released a pair of critically acclaimed solo albums, *Turmoil & Tinfoil* (2017) and *Home* (2019), that wowed bluegrass lovers everywhere. In 2019, the International Bluegrass Music Association (IBMA) named him its New Artist of the Year and Guitar Player of the Year.

Like fellow artists David Grisman and Sam Bush, Strings has aimed to both capture the core of bluegrass in his playing while also trying to expand its reach. "There's people out there that think what I do is absolutely insane or the opposite of bluegrass. And they're not necessarily wrong, we do a lot of psychedelic, crazy stuff," he admitted to Garret K. Woodward for *Rolling Stone* (2 Jan. 2019). "But if you come and talk to me or sit down and pick with me, you won't find somebody who's more into the history of bluegrass or the fathers of bluegrass."

EARLY LIFE

Billy Strings was born William Apostol in Lansing, Michigan, on October 3, 1992. According to a 2012 interview he did for the *Northern Express*, his mother's water broke at a birthday party attended by a large collection of musicians. In the same interview, he explained how he got his stage name. "I was born on my grandpa's birthday, so they named me after Grandpa Bill," he recalled for the *Northern Express* (18 Nov. 2012). "I got the name Billy Strings from my Aunt Mondi. . . . She's the first person who called me that—she said, 'look at little Billy Strings play' when I was a child."

Music was a central part of young Strings's life from an early age, due to the influence of his stepfather, Terry Barber, an amateur musician who loved bluegrass. In addition to demonstrating the power of his music to make people happy, Barber introduced his stepson to some of the genre's greats: Bill Monroe, Doc Watson, Lester Flatt and Earl Scruggs, Jimmy Martin, and Larry Sparks. In an interview for the website *The Bluegrass Situation* (18 Oct. 2017), Strings recalled of his stepfather (whom he calls his dad) to Amanda Wicks, "My dad is a seriously heartfelt musician. When he plays a song, he really means it. He's not just saying the words."

During Strings's childhood, his family moved briefly from Lansing to Morehead, Kentucky, before settling in a small town in Michigan's Ionia County. He got his first guitar at age four—a

Photo by Forrest L. Smith, III

secondhand instrument he begged his stepfather for. At age six he got a better guitar and the opportunity to play alongside his stepfather at bluegrass picking parties. One of his favorite memories from his childhood was attempting to learn how to play "Beaumont Rag" with his stepfather. He tripped over it a pair of times, then watched it being played through before playing it perfectly himself. The sense of pride his stepfather felt in him was something he has never forgotten.

Beginning in middle school, he became more interested in playing electric guitar, first with heavy metal bands and later with more pop-oriented ones, and being able to play with his peers rather than his stepfather's older friends as he had been accustomed to. Although the opportunities to play in these bands taught him more about performing with some energy and expanded his musical repertoire, which now included legends like Jimi Hendrix and Black Sabbath, he also began to get in closer contact with friends who were abusing drugs. By the time he graduated from high school around 2011, despite having struggled and even dropped out, he had returned to bluegrass and decided to put Ionia behind him. "Ionia is a really small town and there's not much to do there, so people resort to drugs and getting in trouble," he told the *Northern Express*. "I wanted to get away from all that and get a fresh start."

BREAKING INTO BLUEGRASS

Strings settled in Traverse City, Michigan, a city that is highly regarded for its music and arts community. There, as a nineteen-year-old bluegrass player, he began impressing locals at open mic competitions, including one at the Hayloft. His guitar skills ultimately impressed Don Julin, a mandolin player who took Strings under his wing and invited him to perform and record with him. Much of what Strings was then playing consisted of very old American bluegrass standards like "The Preacher and the Bear," "The Cuckoo," "Soldier's Joy," and "Red-Haired Boy." As he began earning more money from their gigs together, he was able to focus solely on his music and leave the job that he had secured when he had first moved: "It got to the point where I'm looking at the hotel pay stub and the pile of cash from the week of gigs and it's the same thing," he explained to Brian Baker for the Cincinnati *CityBeat* (3 July 2017). "That's when I quit my little job—the only real day job I ever had." With Julin, he would record the duo albums *Rock of Ages* (2013) and *Fiddle Tune X* (2014). He also performed with a bluegrass group, M-23 Strings.

To further his musical career, Strings moved in 2016 to Nashville, Tennessee, the country and bluegrass music capital of America, and released a six-track EP. Despite his youth, his work and talent impressed veteran bluegrass players

considerably. In 2016, the IBMA presented him with its Momentum Award for Instrumentalist of the Year. In 2017, *Acoustic Guitar* magazine named him as one of its six emerging bluegrass stars of that year. That same year, *Rolling Stone* named him one of the magazine's ten new country artists that audiences needed to know. The recognition was due to incredible playing, as well as his ability to perform classics of the genre alongside his own rock-tinged compositions.

FIRST SOLO ALBUM AND TOURING ARTIST

Strings next put out his first solo full-length album, *Turmoil & Tinfoil*, which was released in September 2017 and reached number three on the Billboard Bluegrass Albums chart. In addition to performing on the record, he also wrote all of the songs. Initially, he was reluctant to show his musical compositions to anyone, but as the years progressed and his confidence increased, he felt more at ease with writing and sharing his own music. He tends to compose by ear, strumming bits out on his guitar and writing down lyrics in notebooks.

Turmoil & Tinfoil was largely well received by critics upon its release. Wicks declared, "As much as he nods to tradition on *Turmoil & Tinfoil*, he also playfully stretches the bounds of bluegrass via face-melting guitar phrasing . . . and socially conscious songs." He has cited Woody Guthrie and Bob Dylan as musicians whose political and social songs have inspired his own songwriting.

To promote the album, Strings toured the country relentlessly, wowing audiences with his guitar skills. Included in his touring band were Billy Failing on banjo, Royal Masat on bass, and Jarrod Walker on mandolin. Of his playing, Jedd Ferris noted for the *Washington Post* (14 Sept. 2017), "Billy Strings is a fiery flat-picking guitarist with virtuosic chops and a penchant for delivering twangy, front-porch tunes with raucous energy and extended instrumental passages."

SIGNING WITH ROUNDER RECORDS AND WINNING AWARDS

Strings and his touring band recorded his second LP, *Home* (2019), over two weeks in January 2019. Guest musicians on *Home* include such noted bluegrass players as Molly Tuttle, Jerry Douglas, and John Mailander. As he had continued to tour and gain additional attention in the world of bluegrass, executives at Rounder Records approached him to sign with their label. Based in Nashville, Rounder is an independent record label founded in 1970, noted for its attention to American roots music. Upon the official announcement that Strings had indeed signed with Rounder in June 2019, label president John Strohm said, as quoted by John Lawless for the website *Bluegrass Today* (25 June 2019), "Billy is not only an instrumentalist to rival the finest talents on Rounder's historic roster, but he's also a phenomenal singer, writer, collaborator, and live performer. It is our great honor and privilege to have the opportunity to work with such a brilliant, innovative young artist to complement Rounder's outstanding musical tradition."

Following the album's release in September 2019, it moved up the Billboard charts, reaching number forty-one on the Top Country Albums chart, number eleven on the Americana/Folk Albums chart, and number one on both the Bluegrass Albums chart and the Heatseekers Albums chart. Many of the songs on the album were inspired by his memories of his hometown in Ionia County, and how his life has changed since then.

As Strings continued to build acclaim, he found his musicianship earning more recognition from the bluegrass community. In 2019, the IBMA named him its New Artist of the Year and Guitar Player of the Year. In an interview with Woodward for *Rolling Stone* (2 Oct. 2019), Strings said, "When I get recognized, that really makes me feel good, because I love traditional bluegrass. I'm passionate about it and it's in my heart and soul forever. I'm just glad to still be accepted into that community, as well as being allowed to express myself in an original way, and in ways that are not so traditional."

Strings was continuing to barnstorm the country in early 2020 to promote *Home*, but he was forced to postpone much of his touring due to the global coronavirus pandemic, which sent much of the world into self-quarantine beginning in mid-March.

PERSONAL LIFE

Living in Nashville as of early 2020, Strings, who additionally enjoys skateboarding, was in a relationship with Ally Dale, who was also cited as his tour manager.

SUGGESTED READING

"The Amazing Billy Strings." *Northern Express*, 18 Nov. 2012, www.northernexpress.com/news/feature/article-5963-the-amazing-billy-strings/. Accessed 17 Apr. 2020.

Baker, Brian. "Youth Is Not Wasted on Bluegrass-and-Beyond Wunderkind Billy Strings." *CityBeat*, 3 July 2017, www.citybeat.com/music/music-feature/article/20866543/youth-is-not-wasted-on-bluegrassandbeyond-wunderkind-billy-strings. Accessed 17 Apr. 2020.

Ferris, Jedd. "Guitar Virtuoso Billy Strings Comes to the Black Cat." *The Washington Post*, 14 Sept. 2017, www.washingtonpost.com/goingoutguide/music/guitar-virtuoso-billy-strings-comes-to-the-black-cat/2017/09/13/0869673e-9420-11e7-89fa-bb822a46da5b_story.html. Accessed 17 Apr. 2020.

Lawless, John. "Billy Strings to Rounder Records." *Bluegrass Today*, 25 June 2019, bluegrasstoday.com/billy-strings-to-rounder-records/. Accessed 17 Apr. 2020.

Strings, Billy. "Billy Strings Talks His Brand of Bluegrass, New Album 'Home.'" Interview by Garret K. Woodward. *Rolling Stone*, 2 Oct. 2019, www.rollingstone.com/music/music-country/billy-strings-home-bluegrass-893800/. Accessed 17 Apr. 2020.

———. "Jumping into the Deep End: A Conversation with Billy Strings." Interview by Amanda Wicks. *The Bluegrass Situation*, 18 Oct. 2017, thebluegrasssituation.com/read/jumping-into-the-deep-end-a-conversation-with-billy-strings/. Accessed 17 Apr. 2020.

Woodward, Garret K. "Why Guitarist Billy Strings Is the Bluegrass Star You Don't Want to Miss." *Rolling Stone*, 2 Jan. 2019, www.rollingstone.com/music/music-country/billy-strings-bluegrass-must-see-774144/. Accessed 17 Apr. 2020.

SELECTED WORKS

Rock of Ages (with Don Julin), 2013; *Turmoil & Tinfoil*, 2017; *Home*, 2019

—*Christopher Mari*

Jason Sudeikis

Born: September 18, 1975
Occupation: Actor

Jason Sudeikis is an American actor and sketch comedian best known as a performer on *Saturday Night Live*.

EARLY LIFE AND EDUCATION

Jason Sudeikis was born in Fairfax, Virginia, on September 18, 1975. His family moved to Kansas when he was a child. He has two sisters, who influenced Sudeikis's love for dancing. As a child, he learned to perform magic tricks and was drawn to comedy performance and playing sports. He began playing basketball in fourth grade. He transferred to a Catholic school and helped his team win a Catholic Youth Organization (CYO) championship when he was in fifth grade. The program in which he played basketball included some future National Basketball Association (NBA) players, such as Kareem Rush and Brandon Rush. Although sports were his primary focus in his youth, he credits seeing Eddie Murphy perform in *Beverly Hills Cop* with his decision to pursue a career in comedy acting. Sudeikis considers Murphy and the television programs *In Living Color* and *The Arsenio Hall Show* as major influences on his comedy.

In high school Sudeikis played point guard for the school's basketball team. He also began acting with ComedySportz (CSz), an improv comedy program for youths in Kansas City.

Sudeikis was recruited by several small colleges for their basketball programs and attended Fort Scott Community College (FSCC). However, college sports proved much more competitive, and Sudeikis was removed from the team in his second year. To get over this disappointment, he immersed himself in theater, scoring a lead role in the school's production of the musical *The Fantasticks*.

Sudeikis's uncle, actor George Wendt, brought Sudeikis to see Chicago's Second City comedy theater, giving Sudeikis his first exposure to live sketch comedy. Sudeikis relocated to Chicago in 1997.

ACTING CAREER

Sudeikis left Chicago to live in Las Vegas in the early 2000s. There he performed sketch comedy and took comedy classes at the Las Vegas branch of Second City where he befriended members of the Blue Man Group. He avidly pursued a job with the Blue Man Group, tirelessly practicing drumming and shaving his head for auditions. He ultimately did not pass auditions and instead sought a job with *Saturday Night Live (SNL)*.

In 2003, Sudeikis was hired as a sketch writer on *Saturday Night Live*. He was given his first opportunity to perform in a small role with the show's cast in 2005 and officially joined the performing cast in 2006. He initially took on "straight man" roles and was often used as a foil to primary characters in his scenes. Sudeikis ultimately became a more established feature actor on the show, portraying recurring characters and impersonating many famous and iconic figures, including politicians Mitt Romney and Joe Biden, the Devil, and Jesus Christ. During his tenure Sudeikis played recurring roles on other comedy shows including *30 Rock*, *Children's Hospital*, and *Eastbound and Down*.

He also appeared in many comedy films while acting on *SNL*. He first played minor roles in comedy films such as *The Ten* (2007) and *Semi-Pro* (2008) before landing a feature role in the 2011 comedy *Hall Pass*. Having established himself as a comedy film actor, Sudeikis starred in *Horrible Bosses* (2011) and *We're the Millers* (2013), both of which were major commercial successes.

Sudeikis left *SNL* in 2013. His departure, which coincided with the departures of fellow cast members Kristen Wiig and Andy Samberg, marked a turnover in the show's cast. Sudeikis took several dramatic film roles in the years following.

Also in 2013, Sudeikis appeared in a television commercial series promoting NBC Sports' coverage of English Premier League soccer. The commercials became viral online hits with millions of views.

His first major dramatic role was as the track coach of legendary Olympian Jesse Owens in *Race* (2016).

IMPACT

Sudeikis was a cast member on *SNL* for seven seasons. Despite acting in his first film at the relatively late age of thirty-two, between 2008 and 2014, Sudeikis was a featured actor in four films that each grossed more than $200 million worldwide.

PERSONAL LIFE

Jason Sudeikis married writer, producer, and actor Kay Cannon in 2004. The couple divorced in 2010. In 2013, Sudeikis became engaged to actor Olivia Wilde. Their son, named Otis after soul singer Otis Redding, was born in 2014. Sudeikis is a personal friend of musician Ben Folds, whom he considers one of his favorite artists.

Sudeikis is a fan of the Kansas University Jayhawks basketball team and sometimes attends their games. He also enjoys photography and has archived thousands of photos from behind the scenes at *SNL*.

SUGGESTED READING

Curtis, Charles. "How Good Was Jason Sudeikis at Hoops?" *ESPN*. ESPN Internet Ventures, 15 Feb. 2013, www.espn.com/blog/playbook/fandom/post/_/id/18254/how-good-was-jason-sudeikis-at-hoops. Accessed 2 Oct. 2020.

Raftery, Brian. "Jason Sudeikis Envisions Life after 'Saturday Night Live.'" *Rolling Stone*. 6 June 2012, www.rollingstone.com/movies/movie-news/jason-sudeikis-envisions-life-after-saturday-night-live-87866/. Accessed 2 Oct. 2020.

Sudeikis, Jason. "GQ&A: Jason Sudeikis on Jennifer Aniston's Striptease, His High-Tops Obsession and That Mumford & Sons Video." Interview by Oliver Franklin-Wallis. *GQ*. Condé Nast, 16 Sept. 2013, www.gq-magazine.co.uk/article/jason-sudeikis-film-style-interview. Accessed 2 Oct. 2020.

———. "#ManCrushMonday: Jason Sudeikis." Interview by Romy Oltuski. *Harper's Bazaar*. Hearst Digital Media, www.harpersbazaar.com/culture/features/a14409/jason-sudeikis-interview/. Accessed 2 Oct. 2020.

———. "A Mighty Heart: Jason Sudeikis Dishes on Love." Interview by Mickey Rapkin. *Elle*. Hearst Digital Media, 17 July 2013, www.elle.com/culture/celebrities/a26306/jason-sudeikis-interview/. Accessed 2 Oct. 2020.

Teodorczuk, Tom. "Hollywood Star Jason Sudeikis Interview: 'I'm Not Very Funny.'" *Independent*. Independent Digital News and Media,

28 Nov. 2014, www.independent.co.uk/arts-entertainment/films/features/hollywood-star-jason-sudeikis-interview-i-m-not-very-funny-9889936.html. Accessed 2 Oct. 2020.

Watson, Sheridan. "Jason Sudeikis' Five Best 'SNL' Characters." *EW.com*. Entertainment Weekly, 4 Aug. 2017, ew.com/article/2013/07/25/jason-sudeikis-best-snl-characters/. Accessed 2 Oct. 2020.

SELECTED WORKS

Hall Pass, 2011; *Horrible Bosses*, 2011; *We're the Millers*, 2013; *Tumbledown*, 2015; *Race*, 2016; *Saturday Night Live*, 2003–13; *30 Rock*, 2007–10; *The Cleveland Show*, 2009–13; *Eastbound and Down*, 2012; *The Last Man on Earth*, 2015

—*Richard Means*

Rishi Sunak

Born: May 12, 1980
Occupation: Politician

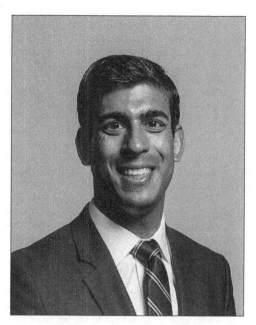

Photo by Chris McAndrew via Wikimedia Commons

On February 13, 2020, Rishi Sunak was named chancellor of the Exchequer, the top finance officer of the United Kingdom and a powerful political post second only to the prime minister. Sunak, a Member of Parliament (MP) representing Richmond in North Yorkshire, has enjoyed a meteoric rise through the ranks of the Conservative and Unionist Party, commonly called the Tories. A former hedge funder, he was elected to his first term in 2015. He was an early supporter of Brexit and provided a crucial endorsement of Prime Minister Boris Johnson, who took office in 2019. But it was his handling of the coronavirus 2019 (COVID-19) pandemic, which began seriously spreading through the United Kingdom in early March, that has come to define his nascent political career.

Sunak assumed his post in mid-February, after the abrupt resignation of his predecessor and former boss, Sajid Javid. Within weeks, his sole objective was to stem the financial fallout from the economic shutdown necessitated by the virus. Sunak, a staunch Conservative, surprised Britons with his willingness to embrace radical measures to keep workers and businesses afloat. His solutions were imperfect, but his sincerity and decisiveness—which came across particularly vividly alongside Johnson's bumbling response—earned him the admiration of Britons across the political spectrum.

EARLY LIFE AND EDUCATION

Rishi Sunak was born in Southampton, Hampshire, on May 12, 1980. He has a younger brother and a younger sister. All four of his grandparents, originally from the Punjab region of India, immigrated to England by way of British East Africa in the 1960s. His father, Yashvir, served as a general practitioner for the National Health Service (NHS), and his mother, Usha, ran a pharmacy. Sunak often helped her with bookkeeping.

Though he missed out on earning a full scholarship to the prestigious boys' boarding school Winchester College, Sunak's family found a way to send him there anyway. The experience, he told Anjali Puri for the Indian finance newspaper *Business Standard* (15 Aug. 2015), was "intellectually transforming." He added, "It put me on a different trajectory." He became the school's head boy, the first of Indian descent.

Sunak completed a degree in politics, philosophy, and economics at Lincoln College, Oxford University. There, he was a member, and eventually president, of the investment society. Later, a fellow minister told George Parker and Sebastian Payne for the *Financial Times* (2 Apr. 2020) that Sunak approaches politics with an analytical eye. "He doesn't have an agenda, he's a problem solver," the minister said. "He's more of a businessman than a politician in that respect."

Sunak professes a love for finance. "You are highly accountable. That's what I like about it," he said, as quoted by Simon Goodley for the *Guardian* (8 Mar. 2020). "You are responsible for your investments and either they're good or they're bad. . . . There are not many other people to blame, there's nowhere to hide."

EARLY CAREER IN FINANCE

After graduating from Oxford, Sunak spent three years as a junior analyst in the merchant banking division of Goldman Sachs. In 2005, he attended Stanford University as a Fulbright Scholar and earned an MBA degree the following year.

Sunak soon began working for the Children's Investment (TCI) Fund Management, a hedge fund founded by billionaire Sir Christopher Hohn. TCI is an activist investor, meaning that it uses its financial authority to influence a company's decisions. The hedge fund came under fire for pressuring the Dutch bank ABN Amro to sell itself to the Royal Bank of Scotland (RBS), which became saddled with massive debts and required a bailout during the global financial crisis in 2008. Although Sunak reportedly had nothing to do with the deal, he was party to another activist campaign against the US rail freight company CSX that resulted in legal action for a conflict-of-interest violation. Still, Hohn praised Sunak to Parker and Payne for his "strong analytical skills, high integrity and low ego."

Around 2009 Sunak left TCI and joined Patrick Degroce, a former TCI cofounder, at his new firm, Thélème Partners. That fund backed companies like the media giant News Corp and the US hospital group Community Health Systems (CHS).

EARLY POLITICAL CAREER

In July 2014 William Hague, the popular MP for Richmond in North Yorkshire, announced his retirement. Sunak was tapped as the Conservative nominee for the seat. It was an unlikely match. The bucolic parish is populated by well-to-do farmers, an overwhelming number of whom are white. In 2015 just 122 Britons of South Asian descent lived in Richmond. The Conservative Party had a history of overt racism and xenophobia and low support among ethnic minorities. Finally, party members had earlier decided to choose a candidate who, like Hague, was from Yorkshire, but Sunak won them over. As Hague recalled to Parker and Payne: "They had in their minds the sort of person they wanted and then this totally different person walked in. To their credit, they did a total U-turn. The key thing is he was obviously very intelligent without any trace of arrogance. That's a very unusual combination in politics."

Sunak won the reliably Conservative seat—some call Richmond as the safest seat in the country—by a 36-point margin. Local papers nicknamed him the Maharajah of the Yorkshire Dales. In his interview with Puri, Sunak dismissed the suggestion made in various media outlets that he was installed in the seat by party leaders eager to improve the party's image and win over England's growing South Asian middle class. Nevertheless, Sunak maintains he won the seat after a competitive vetting process, saying, "It is a huge cause of celebration, that you don't have to fix things, that good people are competing and winning."

BREXIT AND THE ELECTION OF BORIS JOHNSON

In 2016 Sunak aligned himself with Brexit, the campaign for the United Kingdom to leave the European Union (EU). His decision came after then prime minister David Cameron made a personal appeal to Sunak to vote Remain. After the two met to discuss the referendum, Cameron was reported to have said, according to Parker and Payne, "If we've lost Rishi, we've lost the future of the party." Sunak argued that he voted for Brexit for economic reasons—he "went through the numbers," he explained, as quoted by Parker and Payne. Some say his decision was inevitable, though, considering its support in Richmond: his constituents voted Leave by 56 percent. After being reelected in 2017, Sunak worked in the Department for Business, Energy, and Industrial Strategy and, the following year, was named undersecretary for the local government department.

In 2019, he supported Boris Johnson in the general election for prime minister. Sunak knew that Johnson was likely to win the election but briefly considered endorsing Conservative MP Michael Gove. He told colleagues, as quoted by Parker and Payne: "My heart says Gove, my head says Boris." As it had during the Brexit referendum campaign in 2016, Sunak's endorsement meant a great deal. Alongside Robert Jenrick and Oliver Dowden, fellow rising Conservative stars, Sunak announced his support for Johnson in an opinion piece on the front page of the *Times of London* (5 June 2019). "The Tories Are in Deep Peril," the headline read. "Only Boris Johnson Can Save Us."

After Johnson assumed office in July 2019, Sunak was named chief secretary to the Treasury. He served under then chancellor of the Exchequer Sajid Javid. In February 2020, Javid abruptly resigned his post after Johnson pressed Javid to fire his own advisers and instead use staff that ultimately reports to the prime minister. Javid's departure was ill-timed; he was meant to have delivered a budget in March. The task quickly fell to Sunak, who was named Javid's successor—notably, at Javid's urging—the same day.

Javid's resignation, while unexpected, was part of a larger exodus of government ministers, all occurring within the same week. In what has been widely described as a "Valentine's Day massacre" for its proximity to the holiday, Johnson sought to fill important government roles with his own allies, significantly bolstering his power.

According to observers like *Times* of London columnist Jenni Russell, Sunak's competency and leadership provided a marked contrast to his less-able colleagues when they were tasked with running the government while Johnson was hospitalized for COVID-19 in early April 2020.

Indeed, when Johnson was hospitalized, there was significant enthusiasm for Sunak to be named successor in the event of his death. Johnson survived, but Sunak's time in the spotlight has made him a party favorite for the job in the future.

CORONAVIRUS RESPONSE

In February, Sunak sought to boost spending proposals in the northern regions that helped deliver Johnson to office. He also hoped to include in the March budget a £12 billion package to address coronavirus. Within weeks, this vision would radically change. The coronavirus outbreak that began in the United Kingdom in late January escalated through early and mid-March. As Johnson hesitated to encourage social distancing and limit large gatherings, Sunak announced a business bailout worth £350 billion. On March 20, Sunak made an unprecedented announcement: the British government would pay companies up to 80 percent of worker salaries for at least three months if they would keep employees on the payroll; a week later, he announced similar grants available to self-employed workers with earnings up to 50,000 pounds. "We are starting a great national effort to protect jobs," he said, as quoted by Richard Partington for the *Guardian* (20 Mar. 2020). "We want to look back on this time and remember how in the face of a generation-defining moment we undertook a collective national effort and we stood together. It's on all of us."

The wage payment was part of a larger package of economic relief that won Sunak praise. Suggesting widespread frustration with Johnson's failure to act swiftly and decisively, Tom Kibasi wrote in the *Guardian* (20 Mar. 2020): "At last, Rishi Sunak has delivered a fitting response to coronavirus." Some critics expressed concern that the measures did not go far enough, particularly for renters and the self-employed, while others foresaw difficulties ahead with having to raise taxes to cover the tab. But while the response was imperfect, Sunak demonstrated that he grasped both the seriousness of the virus and the economic crater it could create.

Britons were impressed that he would go against his own ideology when the historical moment called for him to do so. "Sunak's response to the stranglehold of coronavirus has been to spend, spend, spend—not very Conservative," as Phoebe Luckhurst wrote for British *Vogue* (6 Apr. 2020). Even Conservatives like Javid and Hague conceded he could not have acted differently given the circumstances.

In early May, as the United Kingdom was poised to begin loosening COVID-19 restrictions, Sunak extended the government-sponsored furlough program through the end of October. Along with the announcement came concerns regarding when and how to phase out the furlough program, which was then supporting a quarter of the workforce, to avoid triggering massive unemployment or propping up businesses that could not survive.

PERSONAL LIFE

Sunak met Akshata Murthy, a financier turned fashion designer, at Stanford. Murthy's father is N. R. Narayana Murthy, a founder of the information technology corporation Infosys and a multibillionaire. She and Sunak married in Bangalore in 2009. The couple's combined wealth makes Sunak one of the richest MPs in Parliament. Sunak and his wife have two daughters: Krishna and Anoushka. The family divides their time between their homes in southwest London and Kirby Sigston, Yorkshire.

An observant Hindu, Sunak abstains from alcohol and beef. In his leisure time, he enjoys cricket, soccer, and films.

SUGGESTED READING

Goodley, Simon. "Rishi Sunak: The Bit-Part Hedge Fund Partner Now Managing the Economy." *The Guardian*, 8 Mar. 2020, www.theguardian.com/politics/2020/mar/08/chancellor-rishi-sunak-the-bit-part-hedge-fund-partner-now-managing-the-whole-economy. Accessed 8 May 2020.

Judah, Ben. "Maharajah of the Yorkshire Dales." *Politico*, 5 May 2015, www.politico.eu/article/maharajah-of-the-yorkshire-dales. Accessed 13 May 2020.

Luckhurst, Phoebe. "Admit It: You Fancy Rishi Sunak." *Vogue*, Britain ed., 6 Apr. 2020, www.vogue.co.uk/arts-and-lifestyle/article/who-is-rishi-sunak-chancellor. Accessed 10 May 2020.

Parker, George, and Sebastian Payne. "The Coronavirus Chancellor: How Rishi Sunak Took Centre Stage." *Financial Times*, 2 Apr. 2020, www.ft.com/content/b465a3fe-73b1-11ea-ad98-044200cb277f. Accessed 8 May 2020.

Partington, Richard. "UK Government to Pay 80% of Wages for Those Not Working in Coronavirus Crisis." *The Guardian*, 20 Mar. 2020, www.theguardian.com/uk-news/2020/mar/20/government-pay-wages-jobs-coronavirus-rishi-sunak. Accessed 10 May 2020.

Puri, Anjali. "UK Cabinet Member Rishi Sunak on Being British, Indian and Hindu at the Same Time." 15 Aug. 2015, *Business*

Standard, 13 Feb. 2020, www.business-standard.com/article/opinion/lunch-with-bs-rishi-sunak-115080601060_1.html. Accessed 8 May 2020.

—*Molly Hagan*

Yuan Yuan Tan

Date of birth: February 14, 1977
Occupation: Dancer

Photo by Wander around via Wikimedia Commons

Yuan Yuan Tan, whose many honors include the 2014 Critics' Circle National Dance Award and the 2016 Isadora Duncan Award, is often referred to as the best Chinese-born ballerina in the world. She made her debut with the renowned San Francisco Ballet (SFB) in 1995, dancing the role of the Sugar Plum Fairy in a midweek matinee of the holiday classic *The Nutcracker*—a performance that caused "those of us who were present [to rub] our critical eyes in disbelief," as critic Allan Ulrich wrote for the *San Francisco Chronicle* (24 Feb. 2015). Her repertoire subsequently expanded to include major roles in such productions as *Giselle, Romeo & Juliet, The Sleeping Beauty, Swan Lake, Don Quixote*, and *The Little Mermaid*, among many others. When she became a principal dancer with the SFB in 1997, at the age of twenty, she was the youngest person to achieve that rank in the company's long and storied history—and the first Chinese dancer to do so. She was named the Richard C. Barker Principal Dancer in 2012.

Achievement of that caliber in the ballet world takes seemingly superhuman dedication, and many dancers hang up their toe shoes when they reach their thirties. Tan, however, remains at the pinnacle of her profession after more than two decades. "I can be very hard on myself, very demanding," she had explained to Jenny Hu for *SFGate* (20 Sept. 2009), as she prepared to headline the first SFB tour through China. "I focus on things I think I should, like dancing, because it takes 100 percent concentration on every step."

EARLY LIFE AND EDUCATION

Yuan Yuan Tan was born on February 14, 1977, in Shanghai, China. She is the only child of Su Zhang and KeQin Tan, whom she has described as traditional and loving Buddhist parents. Her father worked as a semiconductor engineer and harbored ambitions for his daughter to pursue either engineering, like him, or medicine. Her mother noticed that as a child Tan danced whenever music was played, however, and wondered whether her slightly built but naturally athletic daughter might have a future in the ballet world. When Tan undertook a grueling round of auditions for the Shanghai Dance School, beating out almost one thousand other aspiring dancers to gain admission, squabbles ensued. Her father argued that ballet was a Western art form, rather than Chinese, making it a less-than-desirable pursuit—and that even if Tan were successful professionally, a ballerina's career was always destined to be short. Furthermore, he asserted, it was unseemly for a nice Chinese girl to come into physical contact with so many male dancers.

Finally, deciding to trust to fate, Tan's parents tossed a coin. When it landed on heads, it was determined that she would enter the school. At eleven, she was somewhat older than other students, but she soon caught up and began winning international student competitions. Despite her success, the competition circuit was emotionally draining. "This was the first time I saw contemporary ballet and the first time I saw what dancers from all over the world were trying to achieve," Tan told Allan Ulrich for a profile in *Dance Magazine* (24 Nov. 2009). "The bad part was that I was always close to a nervous breakdown when I competed. If I let myself down, I let my country down."

In 1992, Tan won the gold medal in the junior female division at the Fifth International Ballet Competition in Paris, France, where she first caught the attention of SFB artistic director Helgi Tomasson, who vowed to keep an eye on her. She next won the 1993 Nijinsky Award at the First Japan International Ballet and Modern Dance Competition, and she had already accepted a scholarship to the prestigious John Cranko School in Stuttgart, Germany, when Tomasson approached her in 1995 to come dance in San Francisco as a guest artist.

Nervous but excited, Tan arrived with one suitcase and absolutely no English-language skills. "Coming to San Francisco for the first time was overwhelming—total culture shock!" she recalled to Jessie Bryson for the *Beijinger* blog (19 Oct. 2015). "There was a huge language barrier and the style of dancing here . . . was completely different from how I was trained."

A CAREER IN PROGRESS

Within two weeks of arriving in San Francisco, Tan was performing in *The Nutcracker*. After she was featured at the troupe's 1995 fund-raising gala, doing a pas de deux from *La Esmeralda* that left attendees breathless, Tomasson hired her as a soloist, on the condition that she gain some weight and musculature. She did so and, in two short years, was promoted to principal dancer.

Choreographers, as Ulrich wrote for *Dance Magazine*, "rushed to capitalize on Tan's willowy extremities, her long torso, her refined port de bras, her ample jump, and her manner of devouring space without shifting gears." While many of those attributes, such as the length of her torso, owed to genetics, others were the result of long days of sweat and effort. Tan typically began warm-up exercises by nine o'clock in the morning with classes starting at ten and rehearsals lasting until seven thirty in the evening. On days when performances were scheduled, she sometimes did not arrive home until midnight. Ulrich acknowledged as much, writing for *Dance Magazine*, "Tan might have relied on her architecture and ravishing looks, but she has not ceased to investigate the possibilities of her craft. Every choreographer offers a challenge, another step in her continuing education."

Among her earliest challenges were mastering pieces by George Balanchine, the legendary founder of the New York City Ballet, whose famed *Violin Concerto* and *Bugaku* she was asked to perform during her first season, despite never having seen his work before or heard the scores. Counting out the musical phrases, as dancers must do to hit their cues, was a challenge in Chinese, she told interviewers.

As well-known and beloved works like *Swan Lake* and *Paquita* were added to her repertory, contemporary choreographers such as Tomasson and Christopher Wheeldon were also creating new ballets specifically for her. In 2019 Tan, then forty-two, received a coveted Benois de la Danse nomination for her performance of Wheeldon's duet *Take a Deep Breath*.

SIGNATURE ROLES

While Tan has danced dozens of roles throughout her career, a handful have become known as her signatures. She has been celebrated, for example, for her performances as the title character in *Giselle*, the ever-popular tragedy of a beautiful peasant girl who falls in love with a deceitful nobleman. "The character of Giselle possesses a vulnerability and an ethereal essence that comes completely naturally to Yuan Yuan Tan," Joseph Carman wrote for *Dance Magazine* (29 Dec. 2016). She had first danced the second-act pas de deux at the age of sixteen, when she was still a student in Shanghai, and the piece became a staple of her international ballet competition performances. She performed the whole ballet for the first time at the age of twenty-three, under Tomasson's tutelage. "You are human in the first act, with a mad scene that is a test for your ability to act," Tan explained to Carman. "Then in the second act, you transform yourself into a Wili [the ghostly spirit of a betrayed maiden], which is technically very demanding because your dancing has to be as weightless as possible. It's hard to do, but this ballet gives me such joy."

Tan has also become inextricably linked to the title role in John Neumeier's *The Little Mermaid*, which she debuted in 2010 to great acclaim. When the work became a centerpiece of the 2019 SFB season, reviewer Steven Winn wrote for the *Datebook*, an arts news site from the *San Francisco Chronicle* (20 Apr. 2019): "In an absolutely astonishing, emotionally fearless performance, Tan leaves everything on the stage." Describing the scene in which Tan's mermaid gives up her tail to become human, he called it "both an embodiment and metaphor for disfiguring sacrifice, for the daring, doomed flight, across species, into the unknown. For Tan . . . it's also a metaphor for grueling, transforming rigors of ballet itself."

CULTURAL AMBASSADOR

In 2003, when the Shanghai Grand Theater marked its fifth anniversary as a brick-and-mortar symbol of the country's cultural revival, Tan was among a roster of performers invited back to serve as an ambassador of sorts. The weeklong celebration during which she performed "offered dramatic evidence of how far Chinese art and culture have progressed in the two decades since China opened its doors to the outside world," as Kai-Yin Lo wrote for the *New York Times* (8 Oct. 2003).

Tan has taken the role of cultural ambassador seriously. In 2009, she spearheaded the SFB's historic tour to China, and in 2015 the company returned there to great fanfare, with Tan lecturing at Fudan University, giving press conferences and television interviews, and participating in fashion shoots. She now performs regularly in her native country and judges ballet competitions there. She particularly enjoys introducing audiences to the work of Western choreographers like Balanchine and hopes that she is expanding the possibilities for a new generation of Chinese dancers.

Even those who do not follow ballet closely might have seen Tan, as she has appeared in the pages of high-fashion magazines like *Vogue* and *W*, thanks to her beauty and sense of style—attributes that have also led luxury brands such as Van Cleef & Arpels and Rolex to sign her as a spokesmodel. *Time Asia* once named her a hero for her cultural contributions, and in 2018, when Mattel released a new line of Global Role Model Barbie dolls, the company created one in Tan's likeness, clad in a shimmering version of her iconic White Swan tutu from *Swan Lake*.

PERSONAL LIFE

Tan maintains a strict regime of diet, exercise, and meditation. She lives with her parents in San Francisco, not far from the SFB's headquarters at the War Memorial Opera House. When she travels to perform, she enjoys purchasing clothes and accessories rather than conventional souvenirs, and she says that had she not pursued ballet, she might have chosen a career in fashion design.

SUGGESTED READING

Carman, Joseph. "How Three Star Ballerinas Developed Their Signature Roles." *Dance Magazine*, 29 Dec. 2016, www.dancemagazine.com/the-arc-of-artistry-2307053132.html. Accessed 23 Nov. 2019.

Hu, Jenny. "Sunday Profile: Yuan Yuan Tan." *SFGate*, 20 Sept. 2009, www.sfgate.com/news/article/Sunday-Profile-Yuan-Yuan-Tan-3217847.php. Accessed 23 Nov. 2019.

Lo, Kai-Yin. "Chinese Artists Look Homeward." *The New York Times*, 8 Oct. 2003, www.nytimes.com/2003/10/08/style/IHT-chinese-artists-look-homeward.html. Accessed 23 Nov. 2019.

Tan, Yuan Yuan. "Interview with Yuan Yuan Tan, Principal Dancer for the San Francisco Ballet." Interview by Jessie Bryson. *The Beijinger*, 19 Oct. 2015, www.thebeijinger.com/blog/2015/10/19/interview-yuan-yuan-tan-principal-dancer-san-francisco-ballet. Accessed 23 Nov. 2019.

Ulrich, Allan. "Haunting Beauty." *Dance Magazine*, 24 Nov. 2009, www.dancemagazine.com/haunting-beauty-2306898523.html. Accessed 23 Nov. 2019.

——. "Yuan Yuan Tan's 20 Stellar Years at S.F. Ballet." *San Francisco Chronicle*, 24 Feb. 2015, www.sfchronicle.com/performance/article/S-F-Ballet-gains-much-from-Yuan-Yuan-Tan-in-20-6098879.php. Accessed 23 Nov. 2019.

Winn, Steven. "Yuan Yuan Tan Is the Masterpiece in SF Ballet's Overstuffed *Mermaid*." Review of *The Little Mermaid*, performed by the San Francisco Ballet. *Datebook*, San Francisco Chronicle, 20 Apr. 2019, datebook.sfchronicle.com/dance/review-yuan-yuan-tan-is-the-masterpiece-in-sf-ballets-over-stuffed-mermaid. Accessed 23 Nov. 2019.

—*Mari Rich*

Zephyr Teachout

Date of birth: October 24, 1971
Occupation: Academic and Politician

Author, activist, and one-time gubernatorial candidate Zephyr Teachout is a constitutional law professor who revolutionized political organizing as a staffer on former Vermont governor Howard Dean's presidential campaign in 2004. In 2014, she published a book called *Corruption in America: From Benjamin Franklin's Snuff Box to Citizens* and ran a quixotic campaign against New York Governor Andrew Cuomo in the state's Democratic primary in an effort to illustrate the need for campaign finance reforms.

EARLY LIFE AND EDUCATION

Zephyr Rain Teachout was born on October 24, 1971, and grew up in Norwich, Vermont. Her father, Peter Teachout, is also a constitutional law professor and teaches at Vermont Law School. Her mother, Mary Miles Teachout, serves as a state court judge. In high school, Teachout was a star student and a champion cross-country

Photo by Michael Johnson via Wikimedia Commons

runner. In 1993, she received her bachelor's degree from Yale University, where she was editor-in-chief of the *Yale Daily News Magazine*. After graduation she held a series of odd jobs, and in 1994 she serendipitously met the chief of staff of the then-governor of Vermont, Howard Dean, in an elevator. Teachout joined Dean's reelection campaign as his operations director; she was one of only three hired staff members on the campaign. After Dean won the election, Teachout traveled to Morocco where she worked on a database of English textbooks. When she returned to the United States, she worked as an assistant to a writer named George Shreve before enrolling at Duke University, where she earned both her law degree and a degree in political science in 1999. (During her time there she served as editor-in-chief of the Duke law journal.)

Teachout clerked for Chief Judge Edward R. Becker in the US Court of Appeals for the Third Circuit in Philadelphia for one year and then moved back to Durham, North Carolina (where Duke is located), to launch the Fair Trial Initiative, a nonprofit legal center devoted to providing representation for people accused of capital crimes. In 2004, Dean decided to run for president, and Teachout moved back to Vermont to work on his campaign. She became the director of online organizing. Her ideas about organizing supporters through social media was the most successful aspect of Dean's ill-fated campaign; Teachout's methods, which were later adopted by Barack Obama's presidential campaign in 2008, revolutionized grassroots organizing.

POLITICAL AND TEACHING CAREER

After Dean's campaign, Teachout served as the national director for the Sunlight Foundation, a nonprofit organization in Washington, DC, devoted to government transparency. She briefly considered running for the US House of Representatives in Vermont in 2005 but ultimately accepted a fellowship at the Berkman Center for Internet and Society at Harvard University. She began her position as a constitutional law professor at Fordham University in New York City in 2009. (The length of her residence in New York provided fodder for Teachout's political opposition in 2014.) A year after Teachout began teaching at Fordham, the US Supreme Court decided a case called *Citizens United v. Federal Election Commission*. In a 5–4 ruling, the Court decided that political spending was a form of political speech, thereby dismantling a slew of laws governing who could contribute to political campaigns and how much they could give. Constitutional law professor Lawrence Lessig condemned the ruling in his 2011 book *Republic, Lost*. In the book, he argued that money in politics was creating a complex and corrupt "economy of influence." Technically speaking, giving

money to a politician in the hopes of influencing him or her is illegal only if the money is given in exchange for a specific favor—this type of exchange is known as "quid pro quo," or "something for something" in Latin—but Lessig argued that this definition is inadequate. Teachout began working on a book called *Corruption in America: From Benjamin Franklin's Snuff Box to Citizens United* (2014), which expands on the definition of corruption forwarded by Lessig using historical arguments. The book was slated for release on September 8, 2014—one day before the Democratic primaries in New York. To give her views a larger platform, Teachout decided to run against sitting governor Andrew Cuomo in the primary election in 2014.

Teachout's decision to run against Cuomo specifically was not arbitrary; in 2013 the governor came under fire when he abruptly shut down the Moreland Commission, a panel he had formed to investigate corruption in New York State government. Before the panel was disbanded, it issued a preliminary report that echoed Lessig and Teachout's arguments, describing an "epidemic" of public corruption, much of it falling outside the narrow bounds of what is considered illegal. No one expected Teachout to win the primary, but no one expected her to perform as well as she did, either. She entered the race with virtually no name recognition and ended up winning 33.5 percent of the vote. Her running mate, Columbia law professor Tim Wu, won 40 percent of the vote against Kathy Hochul for lieutenant governor. In 2015 Teachout announced that she was taking over Lessig's Mayday PAC, a political action committee that raises money to fund candidates who support taking money out of politics. (The PAC's slogan is "Embrace the irony.")

IMPACT

Teachout may have lost her bid for governor, but her campaign united activists who sought to reform campaign finance laws. Though many thought of her candidacy as an elaborate publicity stunt, her presence in the election forced the governor to address an issue that would have otherwise been ignored.

PERSONAL LIFE

Teachout lives in the Fort Greene neighborhood of Brooklyn.

SUGGESTED READING

Brown, Malina. "Zephyr Rain Teachout J.D. '99, A.M. '99, Accidental Internet Guru." *Duke Magazine*. Duke U, 30 Dec. 2007, alumni. duke.edu/magazine/articles/zephyr-rain-teachout-jd-99-am-99-accidental-internet-guru. Accessed 26 Feb. 2020.

Cole, David. "How Corrupt Are Our Politics?" Rev. of *Corruption in America: From Benjamin Franklin's Snuff Box to Citizens United*, by Zephyr Teachout. *New York Review of Books*. NYREV, 25 Sept. 2014, www.nybooks.com/articles/2014/09/25/how-corrupt-are-our-politics/. Accessed 26 Feb. 2020.

Jaffe, Sarah. "How Zephyr Teachout Became a Contender." *Nation*. Nation, 15 Aug. 2014, www.thenation.com/article/archive/how-zephyr-teachout-became-contender/. Accessed 26 Feb. 2020.

Lepore, Jill. "The Crooked and the Dead." *The New Yorker*. Condé Nast, 25 Aug. 2014, www.newyorker.com/magazine/2014/08/25/crooked-dead. Accessed 26 Feb. 2020.

Lerner, Adam B. "Zephyr Teachout Takes Over Larry Lessig's PAC." *Politico*. Politico, 27 July 2015, www.politico.com/story/2015/07/zephyr-teachout-larry-lessig-mayday-pac-2016-120660. Accessed 26 Feb. 2020.

Teachout, Zephyr. "The Contender." Interview by Andrew Rose. *Guernica*. Guernica, 2 Mar. 2015, www.guernicamag.com/the-contender/. Accessed 26 Feb. 2020.

—*Molly Hagan*

Tedros Adhanom Ghebreyesus

Date of birth: March 3, 1965
Occupation: Director-General of the World Health Organization

Dr. Tedros Adhanom Ghebreyesus was elected director-general of the World Health Organization (WHO), the agency of the United Nations (UN) tasked with establishing guidelines for international public health, in May 2017. A former Ethiopian government official, he had been widely praised for revamping his home country's health care system. His political skills helped make him the first WHO director-general without a background as a physician. Tedros also earned media attention as the first African to lead the WHO, a distinction seen as particularly relevant given the WHO's mixed history in Africa. He took the helm of an organization facing financial challenges and calls for reform along with daunting missions such as extending access to basic health care to all people and countering the rise of the anti-vaccination movement. Yet, it was another crisis that brought Tedros and the WHO a new level of attention: the novel coronavirus disease (COVID-19) that spread from Wuhan, China, beginning in late 2019 and became a global pandemic.

Under Tedros's leadership the WHO led the charge in urging governments to take the

Photo by M. Jacobson - Gonzalez - ITU Pictures via Wikimedia Commons

pandemic seriously, with recommendations including travel restrictions, quarantines and social distancing, and widespread testing. Nevertheless, by mid-2020 the organization reported more than seven million confirmed cases of COVID-19 and more than 404,000 deaths due to the disease. Currently, these numbers appear to be spiraling upward worldwide. Although some praised Tedros's efforts, others sharply criticized his handling of the crisis. Specifically, his praise of the Chinese government's response to the pandemic generated considerable controversy, as China's lack of transparency about details of the virus outbreak was widely seen as problematic. One highly vocal critic of the WHO was US President Donald Trump, who cut US funding and then withdrew the United States from the international organization altogether. For his part, Tedros sought to downplay doubts about his leadership and focus on public health goals. "I don't have extra energy for that," Tedros said when asked about personal criticisms, as quoted by Imogen Foulkes for *BBC News* (7 May 2020). "My focus is on saving lives."

EARLY LIFE AND EDUCATION

Tedros Adhanom Ghebreyesus was born on March 3, 1965, in the city of Asmara, then in Ethiopia but later part of Eritrea. He was raised in the Tigray region of northern Ethiopia. A formative experience of his early life came with the death of his younger brother, who was then just three or four years old. Tedros would come to believe that the cause was measles, a disease easily preventable with a vaccination. "I didn't accept it; I don't accept it now," he told Jamie Ducharme for *Time* (21 Nov. 2019). "Why do people die when we have the means? That motivates me."

Wanting to help prevent needless deaths, Tedros decided to study biology. He received his bachelor's degree from Asmara University in 1986. He then studied in Denmark for several months, where he first saw the benefits of universal health care. Support for such policies became one of his foundational beliefs: "It's when we have strong health systems in each and every country that the world becomes safe. We're as strong as the weakest link," he told Ducharme.

Tedros earned his Master of Science (MS) degree in immunology of infectious diseases from the University of London in the United Kingdom in 1992. By that time, he was a member of the Tigray People's Liberation Front (TPLF), a political party that helped to overthrow Ethiopian dictator Mengistu Haile Mariam in 1991. He also studied at Sweden's Umeå University, and in 2000 he completed his PhD in community health at the UK's University of Nottingham.

ETHIOPIAN GOVERNMENT ROLES

Tedros distinguished himself as a researcher on malaria, authoring scientific papers on the disease and control efforts in Ethiopia in the late 1990s. Building on his success, in 2005 he became Ethiopia's minister of health. In that position he led a major overhaul of the country's health care system. This work included the creation of 3,500 health care centers and 16,000 health care posts, along with training and deploying 38,000 workers in a community-based system that focused on the importance of women in the health workforce. Tedros helped increase the overall number of health care professionals in the country from 16,500 to 115,000 and expand the number of medical schools from just three schools to thirty-three. According to his Curriculum Vitae posted on the WHO's website, these reform efforts helped reduce Ethiopia's number of HIV infections by 90 percent, malaria mortality by 75 percent, and tuberculosis mortality by 64 percent. Child mortality and maternal mortality were also each reduced by about two-thirds.

From 2012 to 2016, Tedros served as the Ethiopian minister of foreign affairs. During this time he took on many duties, including working with the African Union (AU) to deal with the Ebola epidemic. In 2013 he served as chair of the Executive Council of the AU, championing a regional approach to speeding up the continent's political, economic, and social development. In 2015 he served as chair of the International Conference on Financing for Development, a meeting of all UN member nations. However, he did draw criticism from some observers for being part of a government with a poor record on human rights.

In addition to his work with the Ethiopian government, Tedros chaired or co-chaired various regional and international organizations. These included the Roll Back Malaria (RBM) Partnership (2007–09); the Programme Co-ordinating Board (PCB) for the Joint United Nations Programme on HIV/AIDS (UNAIDS) (2009–10); the Global Fund to Fight AIDS, Tuberculosis and Malaria (2009–11); and the Child Survival Conference (2012–13). For his efforts in the public health field, Tedros received the Jimmy and Rosalynn Carter Humanitarian Award in 2011, among other honors.

DIRECTOR-GENERAL OF THE WHO

Tedros, who earned a reputation as a skilled politician, campaigned to succeed Margaret Chan as director-general of the WHO in the organization's May 2017 election. At the time the WHO was facing heavy criticism and calls for reform, many stemming from its handling of the 2014 West African Ebola outbreak. Tedros's supporters suggested he was well suited to turning around the organization, citing his history of successful reforms. The election proved tense, but Tedros prevailed over runner-up David Nabarro of the United Kingdom and Sania Nishtar of Pakistan, winning the final ballot with 133 votes.

Upon officially taking office in July 2017 Tedros set five priorities for the WHO: encouraging basic universal health coverage; providing leadership in health emergencies; prioritizing the health of women, children, and adolescents; better understanding the role of climate change on health; and transforming the organization to provide more inclusivity and diversity. The first priority remained foremost in his mind. "Half of the world's population doesn't have access to essential health services," he told Kai Kupferschmidt for *Science* magazine (10 Feb. 2020). "I just refuse to accept that."

Tedros was applauded by many for his commitment to focusing the WHO on serving vulnerable populations. "He will bring great insight and the political leadership necessary to restore trust in the WHO at a critical moment in its history," Dr. Jeremy Farrar, director of the Wellcome Trust, told Helen Branswell for *STAT* (23 May 2017). However, Tedros stirred controversy several months into his term when he favored bestowing the title of goodwill ambassador upon the former dictator of Zimbabwe, Robert Mugabe. (The recommendation was withdrawn after numerous world leaders condemned it.) Tedros also faced ongoing scrutiny for allegedly attempting to cover up cholera outbreaks in Ethiopia while he was serving as health minister. He strongly denied that charge, suggesting that the accusations were simply an attempt to derail his election campaign.

One major challenge Tedros faced as WHO director-general was a growing trend of misinformation spread online through social media outlets. The rise of the anti-vaccination movement and other misleading medical information was recognized as a significant public health issue in the late 2010s. For example, the WHO reported that there was a 14 percent increase in deaths from measles from 2017 to 2018—to more than 144,000 people worldwide—largely because people were sharing false anti-vaccination information. "This is crisis level already, and Facebook and Twitter or other social media groups should really understand this," Tedros told Kupferschmidt, while urging social media giants to do more about misinformation.

BATTLING THE CORONAVIRUS PANDEMIC

While Tedros in many ways took over an embattled WHO, the organization faced an even more daunting challenge with the breakout of the COVID-19 pandemic in late 2019. The crisis brought about major economic and social disruption worldwide. In order to prevent the spread of the disease, many governments told their citizens to shelter in place, stay home from work, wear masks when they go outside, and maintain social distancing by keeping six feet from other people. Many schools and businesses were closed, and travel was severely restricted. These factors and the resulting massive worldwide recession were also seen as exacerbating many other public health problems around the world as agencies struggled to provide care.

A debate soon raged about whether the WHO did enough in the early days of the outbreak, when the virus was confined primarily to China, to keep it from spreading. Notably, some observers argued that Tedros was too accommodating of the Chinese government, which many suggested suppressed information about the disease. In early January 2020, the WHO advised against travel or trade restrictions. On January 23 Tedros remarked, as quoted by Tamara Keith for *NPR* (15 Apr. 2020), "Make no mistake. This is an emergency in China, but it has not yet become a global health emergency. It may yet become one." On January 30 Tedros declared the novel coronavirus was an international public health emergency, but he continued to recommend against travel bans into February. In March Tedros and the WHO declared COVID-19 had reached pandemic status.

As COVID-19 continued to spread, Tedros and the WHO became more strident in their appeals to contain the virus, urging governments to enact policies for isolating the infected and testing every suspected case. However, by April 2020 the WHO was facing high-profile attacks

from President Trump criticizing the organization's handling of the pandemic. (These attacks came despite Trump's own frequent efforts to downplay the virus.) On April 14 Trump cut US funding to the WHO, and on May 29 he announced that he would withdraw the United States from membership in the organization altogether. The move was widely criticized both in the United States and abroad. The United States had been the WHO's main source of funds, providing roughly $450 million annually. "The US government's and its people's contribution and generosity toward global health over many decades has been immense, and it has made a great difference in public health all around the world," Tedros said at a press conference, as quoted by Pien Huang for *NPR* (1 June 2020). "It is WHO's wish for this collaboration to continue."

Despite the setbacks the WHO experienced under his watch, Tedros vowed to continue the fight against both COVID-19 and other health issues facing the world.

PERSONAL LIFE

Tedros and his wife have five children together. He noted that while his work with the WHO keeps him busy, he enjoys spending any free time with his family. His other hobbies include traveling and reading, especially books on leadership, management, and world history. He is fluent in English, Amharic, and Tigrigna.

SUGGESTED READING

"Biography of Dr Tedros Adhanom Ghebreyesus, Director-General, World Health Organization (WHO)." *World Health Organization*, www.who.int/antimicrobial-resistance/interagency-coordination-group/dg_who_bio/en/. Accessed 1 June 2020.

Branswell, Helen. "WHO Elects Ethiopia's Tedros Adhanom Ghebreyesus as Its New Director General." *STAT*, 23 May 2017, www.statnews.com/2017/05/23/who-director-general-tedros/. Accessed 9 June 2020.

"Curriculum Vitae: Dr Tedros Adhanom Ghebreyesus." *World Health Organization*, www.who.int/dg/election/cv-tedros-en.pdf. Accessed 2 June 2020.

Ducharme, Jamie. "World Health Organization Chief Tedros Adhanom Ghebreyesus Never Stops Worrying." *Time*, 21 Nov. 2019, time.com/5735544/world-health-organization-chief-tedros-adhanom-ghebreyesus-interview/. Accessed 1 June 2020.

Foulkes, Imogen. "Tedros Adhanom Ghebreyesus: The Ethiopian at the Heart of the Coronavirus Fight." *BBC News*, 7 May 2020, www.bbc.com/news/world-africa-51720184. Accessed 1 June 2020.

Huang, Pien. "WHO's Measured Reaction to Trump's Pledge to Cut US Ties to the Agency." *NPR*, 1 June 2020, www.npr.org/sections/goatsandsoda/2020/05/29/865816855/whos-muted-reaction-to-trumps-pledge-to-withdraw-u-s-from-the-u-n-agency. Accessed 9 June 2020.

Keith, Tamara. "A Timeline of Coronavirus Comments from President Trump and WHO." *NPR*, 15 Apr. 2020, www.npr.org/sections/goatsandsoda/2020/04/15/835011346/a-timeline-of-coronavirus-comments-from-president-trump-and-who. Accessed 1 June 2020.

Kupferschmidt, Kai. "Mission Impossible? WHO Director Fights to Prevent a Pandemic without Offending China." *Science*, 10 Feb. 2020, www.sciencemag.org/news/2020/02/mission-impossible-who-director-fights-prevent-pandemic-without-offending-china. Accessed 1 June 2020.

—*Christopher Mari*

Mickalene Thomas

Date of birth: January 28, 1971
Occupation: Visual artist

Mickalene Thomas is an artist best known for her work in mixed media collage, painting, and photography. Using black women as subjects—including, for many years, her mother, Sandra Bush—Thomas's work incorporates the aesthetic of 1970s blaxploitation films, a nod to the era in which she grew up. In the photograph *La Leçon d'amour [The Love Lesson]* (2008), one woman holds another woman in the classical pose of the Pietà. They wear colorful patterned dresses in a wood-paneled room full of various colors, patterns, and textures. Another work, a collage called *Le Déjeuner sur l'Herbe: Les Trois Femmes Noires [The Luncheon on the Grass: The Three Black Women]]* (2010), was inspired by Édouard Manet's 1863 painting, *Le Déjeuner sur l'herbe [The Luncheon on the Grass]*. Instead of two white men and a naked white woman, Thomas imagines three clothed black women in a fractured landscape, embedded with rhinestones. Thomas's work often combines pop culture and European art. It is both conceptual—actively in conversation with various styles and movements—and accessible to a larger audience. "Art is still very much about this elitist way of thinking and being," she told Carol Vogel for *Town & Country* magazine (3 Dec. 2019). "I'm interested in breaking some of those barriers down to allow the opportunity for different demographics to engage with my work. I'm asking the museum to step out of its comfort zone. It's about building bridges and stepping onto the other side."

EARLY LIFE AND EDUCATION

Mickalene Thomas was born in Camden, New Jersey, on January 28, 1971. She and her older brother, Paul, were raised by their mother, Sandra Bush, in Hillside and East Orange, New Jersey. Bush was an aspiring fashion model who encouraged her children's creativity, signing them up for extracurricular programs at the Newark Museum and the Henry Street Settlement in New York City. As Thomas got older, Bush met a man that Thomas considers her stepfather. He was a drug dealer, and Bush developed a drug addiction. When her stepfather was sent to prison, Thomas and her brother moved in with their grandmother, who, Thomas remembered, used secondhand clothes to patch furniture—a memory that would later inform her art. Family life was difficult for Thomas, who had yet to come out as a lesbian because she feared being shunned by homophobic relatives. "I had a gay uncle who was treated so horribly," Thomas told Julie L. Belcove for the London *Financial Times* (31 Aug. 2018). After graduating from high school, she followed a girlfriend to Portland, Oregon. "To leave was effortless," she told Belcove. "There was no anchor holding me there."

Thomas enrolled as a student at Portland State University, studying pre-law with a minor in theater arts while working for the law firm Davis Wright Tremaine. She also did some acting and modeling. Socially, she was surrounded by artists, including indie musicians like the Dandy Warhols and Pink Martini. A friend took her to see an exhibit at the Portland Art Museum featuring lauded artist and photographer Carrie Mae Weems, whom Thomas would photograph for the *New York Times* in 2018. "It was a small retrospective of [Weems's] photographs"—including the iconic Kitchen Table Series—"and it was one of the first times I'd seen contemporary work by an African American woman," Thomas recalled to artist Sean Landers for *BOMB* magazine (1 July 2011). Thomas was particularly struck by a captioned photograph called "Mirror, Mirror," in which a black woman asks a mirror, "Mirror, Mirror, on the wall? Who's the finest of them all?" A white woman stares back at her, and answers: "Snow White, you Black b——, and don't you forget it!!" The Weems show inspired Thomas to take an art therapy workshop, where she began to make her own work.

Thomas applied for admission and was accepted at both the San Francisco Art Institute and the Pratt Institute in Brooklyn. She chose Pratt and moved to New York to begin her art studies in 1995. That October, her mother's friend and Weems collector Rahima Lateef invited her to a showing of Weems's work at the

Museum of Modern Art (MoMA), and introduced her to Weems. The show itself was another formative experience. "Watching [Weems] across the room I thought, I want to be that woman," Thomas recalled to Landers. As a student, Thomas interned with Cristinerose Gallery in SoHo. The job introduced her to other artists and gallerists, including the abstract expressionist Cy Twombly. She studied abroad in Australia and graduated with a BFA degree in 2000.

STUDIES AT YALE

Thomas told Landers that her decision to pursue a graduate degree was a "fluke." In 1999, she had studied with the Yale Norfolk School of Art, a six-week summer residency for undergraduates. The artists she met there encouraged her to apply to Yale University's graduate program; she did, and she got in. According to her professors, including Landers, Thomas showed a willingness to explore various mediums and ideas. "Every time I'd walk into your studio at Yale there'd be something new," Landers told her. "You really were using your time there, I think, as best as anyone I've ever seen." Most significantly, Thomas, who was at that point an abstract painter, began to incorporate figures in her work. An early glitter painting of a rooster and a pit bull called *Black Cock Black Bitch*, (2000) demonstrates this shift. Meanwhile, photographer David Hilliard encouraged Thomas to pick up a camera and use it to explore painful subjects. Hilliard's photography class "was the best thing that could've happened to me," Thomas told Margo Vansynghel for Seattle's *City Arts* magazine (13 July 2018). Hilliard, who had photographed his father, "encouraged us to photograph whoever it was in our life that we had difficulty talking to, had issues about or were estranged from," Thomas told Vansynghel. "That happened to be my mother at that time."

Thomas began photographing her mother, who was in recovery, with a disposable camera because she could not afford a regular one. These early images provide the basis for Thomas's body of work. "The moment I started photographing my mother was the moment my work completely changed," she told Jennifer Blessing for the *New Yorker* (16 Jan. 2016). Thomas began photographing other black women and herself as an alter ego named Quanikah, a childhood nickname. For a performance art class at Yale, Thomas, inspired by artist Cindy Sherman, decided to embody Quanikah, imagining her as a sexy, ultrafeminine black woman and a New Haven local. As Quanikah, Thomas was frequently stopped by campus security, and many classmates failed to recognize her. She began a series of photographs as Quanikah called *Negress* in 2001.

SHE'S COME UNDONE!

Thomas graduated from Yale with an MFA degree in 2002. She moved to Brooklyn and began working retail jobs and cleaning houses. She won a yearlong residency at the Studio Museum in Harlem. She was also selected to appear in *Greater New York 2005*, a high-profile survey of up-and-coming artists at MoMA PS1. The exposure earned her a number of gallery shows, including her first solo showing in Chicago in 2006. In 2008, she made a print of First Lady Michelle Obama called *Michelle O* that was added to the collection of the National Portrait Gallery at the Smithsonian Institute in Washington, DC. In 2009, Thomas presented a solo show called *She's Come UnDone!* at the Lehmann Maupin gallery in New York. Among the artworks on display were paintings, photographs and collages, including the portrait *Don't Forget about Me (Keri)*, a series of portrait prints called *A-E-I-O-U and Sometimes Y*, and *Mama Bush: One of a Kind Two*, all from 2009. Kimberly Lamm, writing for the *Brooklyn Rail* (1 May 2009), reserved particular praise for the show's videos, *Ain't I a Woman (Sandra)*, which offered glimpses of Mickalene's models preparing for their photoshoots. The title of the piece is taken from an 1851 speech by Sojourner Truth. Even with all of their "vibrancy and glamor," Lamm wrote, "Thomas's work argues that the way in which African American women adorn and display themselves is serious business, dense with tales of survival and self-invention worthy of our attention."

MICKALENE THOMAS: ORIGIN OF THE UNIVERSE

In 2012, Thomas's first solo museum exhibition, *Mickalene Thomas: Origin of the Universe* opened at the Santa Monica Museum of Art before moving to the Brooklyn Museum, where it was expanded from fifteen works on display to ninety. The title of the show itself was a reference to Gustave Courbet's 1866 painting, *L'Origine du monde (The Origin of the World)*, a painting of a woman's vulva. *Le Déjeuner sur l'Herbe: Les Trois Femmes Noires* was a centerpiece of *Origin of the Universe*, as well the painting *Sleep: Deux Femmes Noires [Sleep: Two Black Women]* (2012), which reimagined Courbet's *Sleep* (1866). There was also a twenty-three-minute video called *Happy Birthday to a Beautiful Woman: A Portrait of My Mother*, featuring Bush, who had been diagnosed with kidney disease in 2010 and who died the same year that Thomas mounted the show. In the video taken during her illness, Bush appears small and frail. "One of the reasons I used my mother is because of her charisma, her beauty," Thomas told Karen Rosenberg for the *New York Times* (27 Sept. 2012). "And I thought about how I wasn't [using her] because she was sick. And how a different type of beauty, a different type of aging, a different type of portraiture could come across on film." Though Thomas was well known in the art world, *Origin of the Universe* effectively made her career. Roberta Smith gave the show an enthusiastic review for the *New York Times* (27 Sept. 2012). "Through the scale and material capaciousness of painting, [Thomas] celebrates, decorates and really venerates the black female body by making it and its lavish surroundings bracingly tangible," she wrote. "She doesn't so much depict a universal humanity as practically force it into the viewer's place, where it implicates, illuminates and bedazzles."

BETTER DAYS, A MOMENT'S PLEASURE, AND OTHER SHOWS

In 2013, Thomas created an installation art bar called *Better Days*, modeled after her signature 1970s-inspired interiors, at Art Basel in Switzerland. Musical artist Solange performed in the space. In 2018, Thomas continued her foray into the larger culture, creating a Lady Dior handbag for Dior. Her first collaboration with Dior was such a success that she designed a second bag, worth $16,000. She also presented a solo show called *I Can't See You without Me* at the Wexner Center for the Arts in Columbus, Ohio. Much of the work featured Racquel Chevremont, an art consultant and former model, who is Thomas's partner and muse. In 2019, Thomas's 2013 painting, *Naomi Looking Forward*, featuring model Naomi Campbell, sold for $700,000 at a London auction—a career record. In November 2019, Thomas opened a show called *Mickalene Thomas: A Moment's Pleasure* at the Baltimore Museum of Art. The show includes the work of eight other Baltimore-affiliated black artists, including the painter and collage artist Derrick Adams, who was a student with Thomas at Pratt.

PERSONAL LIFE

Thomas has a daughter named Junya Rei, after Japanese designers Junya Watanabe and Rei Kawakubo, from her previous marriage to the artist Carmen McLeod. Thomas and Chevremont live in New York City and Connecticut.

SUGGESTED READING

Belcove, Julie L. "Artist Mickalene Thomas: 'It Was Always a Political Statement.'" *Financial Times*, 31 Aug. 2018, www.ft.com/content/40f8bd16-ab1c-11e8-89a1-e5de165fa619. Accessed 11 Mar. 2020.

Blessing, Jennifer. "Mother, Muse, Mirror." *The New Yorker*, 16 Jan. 2016, www.newyorker.com/culture/photo-booth/mother-muse-mirror. Accessed 11 Mar. 2020.

Lamm, Kimberly. "Mickalene Thomas, She's Come Undone!" *Brooklyn Rail*, 1 May 2009, brooklynrail.org/2009/05/artseen/mickalene-thomas-shes-come-undone. Accessed 12 Mar. 2020.

Landers, Sean. "Mickalene Thomas by Sean Landers." *BOMB*, 1 July 2011, bombmagazine.org/articles/mickalene-thomas-1/. Accessed 11 Mar. 2020.

Rosenberg, Karen. "Mickalene Thomas Rediscovers Her Mother—And Her Muse." *The New York Times*, 27 Sept. 2012, www.nytimes.com/2012/09/30/magazine/mickalene-thomas-rediscovers-her-mother-and-her-muse.html. Accessed 12 Mar. 2020.

Smith, Roberta. "Loud, Proud and Painted." *The New York Times*, 27 Sept. 2012, www.nytimes.com/2012/09/28/arts/design/mickalene-thomas-origin-of-the-universe-at-brooklyn-museum.html. Accessed 12 Mar. 2020.

Vansynghel, Margo. "Up Close and Personal with Mickalene Thomas." *City Arts*, 13 July 2018, www.cityartsmagazine.com/up-close-and-personal-with-mickalene-thomas/. Accessed 11 Mar. 2020.

Vogel, Carol. "The Rise and Rise of Mickalene Thomas." *Town & Country*, 3 Dec. 2019, www.townandcountrymag.com/leisure/arts-and-culture/a29762435/mickalene-thomas-artist-interview/. Accessed 12 Mar. 2020.

SELECTED WORKS

Michelle O, 2008; *La Leçon d'amour*, 2008; *Le Déjeuner sur l'Herbe: Les Trois Femmes Noires*, 2010; *Happy Birthday to a Beautiful Woman: A Portrait of My Mother*, 2012

—Molly Hagan

Kim Thúy

Date of birth: September 19, 1968
Occupation: Writer

Kim Thúy is a best-selling Vietnamese Canadian author. Her debut novel, *Ru* (2009), won Canada's Governor General's Award for French-language fiction in 2010. (It was published in English in 2012.) Her next novels, *Mãn* (2014) and *Vi* (2016), which like *Ru* draw heavily from aspects of her own biography, also earned considerable critical acclaim. Yet Thúy originally had no plans to become a writer; her life story followed an unusual arc, one that in her telling recalls elements of a tall tale. "Writing was all accidental. My whole life in general is accidental," she told Terry Hong for the writing-focused website *Bloom* (18 Sept. 2013). Thúy was born to a wealthy family in Saigon, then the capital of

Photo by G.Garitan via Wikimedia Commons

South Vietnam, but her family fled the country during the Vietnam War when she was ten years old. They settled in Montreal, in the French-speaking province of Quebec, where Thúy became a lawyer and—despite allegedly not knowing how to cook—a restaurateur. She began composing her first novel to help her stay awake while driving home from her restaurant.

Thúy would go on to become a literary celebrity in Quebec. She published an award-winning cookbook, and often appeared on the popular morning television talk show *Tout le monde en parle* [Everybody Talks About It]. Though her prose is restrained, Thúy herself earned a reputation as gregarious and self-effacing. She noted her enjoyment of creating works that resonate in different ways with different people. As she told Hong, "what you say in your book is nothing compared to what happens to it in the reader's imagination!"

EARLY LIFE

Kim Thúy Ly Thanh was born in Saigon, then the Capital of South Vietnam, on September 19, 1968. Saigon fell to North Vietnamese forces in 1975, precipitating a mass exodus of people fleeing the country by boat. Thúy's family left a few years later in 1978, when she was ten years old. They were lucky, Thúy would later contend. The family endured an overcrowded but fortunately uneventful four-day journey by sea to a refugee camp in Malaysia. (Other refugees often experienced bad weather, or theft or assault at the hands of pirates.) By her own account, Thúy was a small, weak child with allergies to fish, milk,

and eggs. When they landed in Malaysia, the family was offered sardines. "That was our first food after four days of hunger. That was it, so I ate it," she recalled to Hong. "Somehow, I lost all my allergies on that boat; I have not reacted to any fish in thirty-five years. I really was granted a second life. My whole body reprogrammed itself before I could react."

Thúy would soon experience more luck: her family spent only four months in the camp, when other refugees waited years to find a permanent home. A Canadian delegation quickly chose the family for relocation because they spoke French. The family had no desire to go to Canada, where Thúy's mother was convinced people lived in igloos, but they were desperate to leave the camp. They ultimately settled in Montreal but felt their refugee status acutely. "Refugee and immigrant are very different," she told Brian Bethune for the Canadian news magazine *Maclean's* (11 Apr. 2018). "A refugee is someone ejected from his or her past, who has no future, whose present is totally empty of meaning. . . . The first time that we got an official piece of paper from Canada, my whole family stared at it—until then, we were stateless, part of nothing."

EDUCATION AND LAW CAREER

Thúy fell in love with literature after reading *The Lover* (*L'amant*, 1984), by French writer Marguerite Duras, when she was fourteen. She and her uncle, only seven years her senior, guiltily spent $15 on the book—a fortune had they still been in Vietnam—so they could absorb Duras's brooding vision of 1920s Saigon. Thúy memorized the book, and later recalled parroting its sensual prose to her friends in high school. "Instead of saying, 'Why are you so bummed out?' I was like, 'But your face is devastated!'" she told Jennifer Warren for CBC (29 Aug. 2017). She also improved her colloquial French by reading Harlequin romance novels.

Despite her love of literature, Thúy chose to study translation as a student at the University of Montreal. "I didn't know then that I could be professor, or a journalist, or a writer," she told Hong. "So I chose to become a translator because I could still work with the language." As she had not yet mastered French, she struggled in her classes. Still, unable to face the humiliation of giving up, she finished her degree in linguistics and translation in 1990.

On the suggestion of her brother, Thúy decided to stay at the school and pursue a law degree. She graduated again in 1993, and was soon recruited by Stikeman Elliott, one of the largest law firms in Canada. According to Thúy she only chose to take the job because the man who interviewed her was handsome—yet another accident of fate. The firm sent her to work on a project in Vietnam, where she lived for several years. Her Quebec-born husband, also a lawyer, worked in Vietnam as well, but was then posted in Thailand. The family—Thúy had two sons while in Southeast Asia—lived in Bangkok, Thailand, for more than two years before returning to Montreal.

RU DE NAM AND COOKBOOK

After returning to Canada, Thúy opened a boutique and Vietnamese restaurant called Ru de Nam in Montreal. She envisioned an art boutique that sold contemporary Asian art, with a kitchen that served real Vietnamese food. Though the restaurant was wildly successful, Thúy quickly realized she was in over her head. "I didn't know a restaurant could be so time-consuming!" she told Hong. Despite the limited menu—she offered only one dish per day—she found herself working sixteen-hour days while raising two young children.

Thúy's youngest son was diagnosed with autism shortly after the restaurant opened. "I had to learn about the autism, how to help him with it, how to deal with it myself," she recalled to Hong. Thúy kept the restaurant open for the duration of its five-year lease, and then moved on, exhausted. However, she would return to the culinary world after her career as a writer had taken off. In 2017, Thúy published her first cookbook, *Le secret des Vietnamiennes* (translated into English in 2019 as *Secrets from My Vietnamese Kitchen: Simple Recipes from My Many Mothers*). It features sections devoted to her mother and aunts.

RU (2009)

Long days at Ru de Nam left Thúy exhausted driving home at night. She noted to interviewers that she would occasionally nod off at red lights and got into a handful of minor car accidents. She began composing grocery lists, and one day, instead of a list, she began to write notes for a story that would become her first novel, *Ru*. Thúy kept writing after she closed the restaurant, putting off her return to work-a-day life month by month. After less than a year of writing each day, a former customer called and asked her what she was doing, looked at what she had written, and sent it to a friend in publishing. The friend agreed to buy the work, and Thúy went on to write a full manuscript. Of the book, Thúy later told John Barber for Canada's *Globe and Mail* (5 Feb. 2012): "I didn't choose to write it or not to write it, or to structure it in any specific way. I just wrote, and I followed its internal rhythm. For me it's one breath."

Ru was published in French in 2009. (The publisher decided to shorten Thúy's name—Kim Thúy Ly Thanh—to Kim Thúy to match the book's short title. Thúy has complained that people think her last name is Thúy, when it is really the second part of her first name.) *Ru* won Canada's Governor General's Award for French-language fiction in 2010. The book's English translation, by Sheila Fischman, was published in 2012; it was shortlisted for the Scotiabank Giller Prize in 2012 and won CBC Radio's Canada Reads debates in 2015.

The book's title plays on two languages. In French, the word means a small stream. In Vietnamese, it means a lullaby. *Ru*'s protagonist, An Tinh, recalls her childhood in Saigon. Her family was wealthy, but war eventually drove them out of the country, first to a refugee camp in Malaysia and then to Canada. In his enthusiastic review for the *Globe and Mail* (10 Feb. 2012), Jim Bartley wrote, "Thúy eschews modes of reminiscence and emotion in favor of recall and assessment." Thúy's prose is poetic but terse, as exemplified by the book's first sentence: "I came into the world during the Tet Offensive, in the early days of the Year of the Monkey, when the long chains of firecrackers draped in front of houses exploded polyphonically along with the sound of machine guns."

In 2011, Thúy partnered with author Pascal Janovjak to write a book called *À toi*. Half-French and half-Slovak, Janovjak lived with his family in Ramallah, Palestine. The book explores the authors' relationships with dominant cultures and colonial powers. It takes the form of a conversation between the two writers, who met while receiving a book prize in Monaco.

MÃN (2014) AND VI (2016)

Thúy published her second novel, *Mãn*, in 2014. (It was translated into English in 2015.) That book follows a Vietnamese woman, Mãn, who enters an arranged marriage with another Vietnamese refugee. She opens a restaurant, and later embarks on a love affair with a Parisian chef named Luc. It drew praise for its mixture of realism and fable-like qualities.

Thúy's third novel, published in French in 2016 and in English in 2018, is called *Vi*. Like Thúy's other books, it incorporates elements of her own life. The main character escapes Vietnam as a refugee and settles in Canada; she becomes a lawyer and returns to Vietnam for her work. Thúy told Robert Everett-Green of the *Globe and Mail* (19 May 2018) that *Vi* was about "the invisible strength of women," a theme that runs through all her work. "We often misinterpret Asian women as kind, submissive and obedient," she said. "On the contrary, that quietness is their way of being strong. They control from under the water, and that is where the current is, under the surface."

PERSONAL LIFE

Thúy and her husband Francis had two sons, Justin and Valmond. They live in Montreal.

SUGGESTED READING

Barber, John. "Thúy's River of Life." *The Globe and Mail*, 5 Feb. 2012, www.theglobeandmail.com/arts/books-and-media/kim-thuys-river-of-life/article545170/. Accessed 14 Jan. 2020.

Bartley, Jim. Review of *Ru*, by Kim Thúy. *The Globe and Mail*, 10 Feb. 2012, www.theglobeandmail.com/arts/books-and-media/ru-by-kim-thuy/article545169/. Accessed 14 Jan. 2020.

Bethune, Brian. "Kim Thúy on How 'Refugee Literature' Differs from Immigrant Literature." *Maclean's*, 11 Apr. 2018, www.macleans.ca/culture/books/kim-thuy-on-how-refugee-literature-differs-from-immigrant-literature/. Accessed 13 Jan. 2020.

Everett-Green, Robert. "How Novelist Kim Thúy Focuses on the 'Invisible Strength of Women.'" *The Globe and Mail*, 19 May 2018, www.theglobeandmail.com/arts/books/article-vietnamese-canadian-novelist-kim-thuys-latest-book-vi-focuses-on-the/. Accessed 14 Jan. 2020.

Thúy, Kim. "Q&A with Kim Thúy." Interview by Terry Hong. *Bloom*, 18 Sept. 2013, bloomsite.com/2013/09/18/qa-with-kim-thuy/. Accessed 13 Jan. 2020.

Warren, Jennifer. "Kim Thúy's Life in Books." *CBC*, 29 Aug. 2017, www.cbc.ca/books/kim-thuy-s-life-in-books-1.4203178. Accessed 13 Jan. 2020.

SELECTED WORKS

Ru (2009); *Mãn* (2014); *Vi* (2016)

—*Molly Hagan*

Bonnie Timmermann

Occupation: Casting director

Bonnie Timmermann is considered one of the most influential casting directors working in Hollywood. Born and raised in New York City, she got her start casting Off-Broadway plays in the 1970s, where she is credited for discovering actors like Glenn Close and Swoosie Kurtz. After casting a young Meryl Streep in a PBS broadcast of Wendy Wasserstein's *Uncommon Women and Others* in 1978, Timmermann began working in television and film. In the early 1980s, she cast a virtually unknown Sean Penn in *Fast Times at Ridgemont High* (1982). Her early high-profile successes led to a lifelong artistic partnership with director Michael Mann. Working for his popular crime show *Miami Vice* in the 1980s, Timmermann brought in a slew of guest actors who would shape the future of Hollywood,

including Bruce Willis, Julia Roberts, Liam Neeson, John Turturro, John Leguizamo, Steve Buscemi, Annette Bening, and Chris Rock. For Timmermann, who is also a producer, casting is a quasi-mystical endeavor that transcends appearance. "As a casting director, if I'm going to put my camera on you, I'm going to look to see what is inside the person as opposed to the physical," Timmermann told Jeryl Brunner for *Forbes* (28 Jan. 2018). "The camera reads what we go through in our lives. And I hope that I am like a camera, that I can read the interior."

EARLY LIFE

Bonnie Timmermann was born in Manhattan and raised near Rockaway Beach in the Brooklyn borough of New York City. Her father, Joseph Golub, was a Russian immigrant and Golden Gloves boxer. Her mother, Shirley Golub, was an opera singer. She has a sister, actor June Gable, and a brother, Michael Golub. In interviews, Timmermann has been vague about her early years, saying only that she did not finish school and left home at the age of sixteen. "Let's just say I learned from the streets," she told Monique P. Yazigi for the *New York Times* (22 Jan. 1995). In the 1970s, Timmermann got a job with the Off-Broadway Phoenix Theater in Times Square. She started out doing odd jobs, but the owner of the theater soon asked her to work for him as a casting director. Timmermann enthusiastically accepted the job. Unsure about what a casting director actually did, she researched how to fulfill the position by reading books and going to plays to study actors.

Timmermann also took a job with National Public Radio (NPR) casting radio plays. She credits this experience for honing her skills. While searching for voice actors, when she went to the theater or to the movies, Timmermann would close her eyes for the first fifteen to twenty minutes to listen to the actors' voices "and hear them, and hear what they looked like, as opposed to seeing what they looked like," she explained to Matthew Steigbigel for the Motion Picture Association (26 Jan. 2015).

EARLY FILM WORK

In 1977, Timmermann cast *Uncommon Women and Others*—the debut play of the late, Pulitzer Prize–winning Wendy Wasserstein—for the Phoenix Theater. The play centers on a reunion of seven female college graduates; Timmermann cast a handful of then relatively unknown actors, including Glenn Close, Jill Eikenberry, and Swoosie Kurtz. In 1978, Timmermann cast a production of *Uncommon Women* that was filmed for PBS, adding Meryl Streep to the ensemble.

The PBS broadcast of *Uncommon Women* brought Timmermann to the attention of

Academy Award–winning director Francis Ford Coppola, who hired her to work for his production company Zoetrope. She also met and worked with other production companies and directors. After serving as the casting director for the television movie *The House of Mirth* (1981), Timmermann cast Sean Penn in Cameron Crowe's teen comedy *Fast Times at Ridgemont High*. Released in 1982, the film helped launch the Academy Award–winning actor's career. She next worked on the comedy *Trading Places* (1983) with Dan Akroyd and Eddie Murphy, and cast Ralph Macchio, based on the strength of his performance in Coppola's 1983 adaptation *The Outsiders*, in his iconic role in *The Karate Kid* (1984). She could also be credited for discovering actor Elisabeth Shue, who played Macchio's love interest in the film.

MIAMI VICE

In 1983, Timmermann began her decades-long partnership with director Michael Mann when she joined the casting department for Mann's horror-fantasy *The Keep* (1983). But Timmermann balked when Mann asked her to work as the casting director for his new television show *Miami Vice*. "I thought whoa, I don't think I'd be very good with TV, and he said 'why is that?' and I said well, I roam the streets, I go on the subway, on buses, I search for people I think are fat, skinny, who've got good skin, bad skin, I don't look for all blonde and blue eyed types," she recalled to Steigbigel. "So he said 'What? that's perfect, that's just what I'm looking for!"

The NBC crime show was shot in Miami and produced in Los Angeles, but Timmermann continued to work out of New York City. "I was really able to really learn about my work because I was on my own," she told Steigbigel. "I began this process of talking to actors like my own little talk show, because no one was there [to tell me not to do it that way]. Sometimes in casting, if you know somebody, you understand more about what they can do." Mann encouraged this approach and was open to Timmermann's occasionally unorthodox casting ideas. Later, Thom Mount, the former head of Universal Pictures, told Yazigi of Timmermann, "She's into voodoo casting—casting without paying too much attention to the preconceived notion of the producer and director. She may say, 'I know this character is Irish and a guy, but if this was a black woman, I think we'd make this picture sing.'"

Miami Vice, which premiered in 1984, ran for five seasons, ending in January 1990. Timmermann cast a slew of virtually unknown actors in guest roles who would later go on to find incredible Hollywood success, including John Turturro in 1985; John Leguizamo and Steve Buscemi in 1986; Annette Bening and Chris Rock in 1987; and Julia Roberts in 1988. In 1984, she cast action movie icon Bruce Willis, in his first credited role. Timmermann also cast music stars like Willie Nelson, Leonard Cohen, Phil Collins, James Brown, and Little Richard. Irish-born actor Liam Neeson recalled to Brunner how Timmermann's decision to cast him in the show in 1986 changed the course of his career. Neeson had just finished a small part in the film *The Mission* (1986), with Robert De Niro. De Niro invited him to New York, and suggested he contact Timmermann. "I couldn't afford a taxi or anything and walked from Tribeca to Bonnie's office in the East 50s," Neeson told Brunner. Timmermann was taken with the young actor. "Bonnie said to me, 'If you don't get this job, I'm quitting,'" he said. She managed to secure him a work visa and he won the part.

FILMS OF THE '80S AND EARLY '90S

Timmermann cast a number of iconic films during her tenure with *Miami Vice*, including *Dirty Dancing* (1987) and *Bull Durham* (1988). But Timmermann did not deal exclusively with actors actively seeking roles. Part of her allure involved her ability to pick faces from a crowd. A frequent diner at the New York City restaurant Rao's, Timmermann cast the iconic restaurant's bartender as a thug in the 1990 film *State of Grace*. Fated interactions such as these are why Timmermann continued to work out of New York. "New Yorkers have so much pain in their faces," she told Yazigi. "People here have been through so much. Their faces tell the story."

In 1992, Timmermann worked on Mann's historical epic *The Last of the Mohicans*. The film famously stars Daniel Day-Lewis, though Timmermann first offered the role to actor Alec Baldwin. The same year, Timmermann cast Baldwin in *Glengarry Glen Ross* (1992), the star-studded film adaptation of David Mamet's Pulitzer Prize–winning play of the same name. Though he was only on screen for seven minutes, Baldwin's character delivers one of the film's most memorable monologues. "He's the one people remember from the film," Timmermann told Holly Millea for *Elle* (2 Nov. 2009). "Actors today come in to audition and repeat his lines to me!"

DEATH AND THE MAIDEN AND THE SHATTERED LENS

While working on *Glengarry Glen Ross*, Timmermann encountered the script for Chilean writer Ariel Dorfman's 1990 play *Death and the Maiden*. In it, a former political prisoner confronts a man she believes to have been her torturer. The story is an allegory about the military dictatorship of Augusto Pinochet in Chile. Timmermann was captivated by the script and wanted to produce it. Around the same time, she met the late Gladys Nederlander—she claimed that she tried to cast Nederlander as a hat check girl in *Glengarry Glen Ross* after seeing her photograph in the newspaper. Nederlander, a theater producer and the wife of the minority owner of the New York Yankees, agreed to contribute funds to produce *Death and the Maiden* on Broadway. The production, which opened in 1992, was directed by the Academy Award–winning film director Mike Nichols, and starred Glenn Close, Gene Hackman, and Richard Dreyfuss. Timmermann later served as a producer for the 1994 film version, directed by Roman Polanski and starring Sigourney Weaver, Ben Kingsley, and Stuart Wilson.

Timmermann next cast such films as Brian De Palma's *Carlito's Way* (1993), the biographical drama *Quiz Show* (1994), and Mann's crimedrama *Heat* (1995), starring Al Pacino and De Niro. In 1998, Timmermann cast Michael Bay's blockbuster *Armageddon*, starring Willis, Ben Affleck, and Liv Tyler. Other action films like *Pearl Harbor* (2001), *Spy Game* (2001), *Black Hawk Down* (2001), and *The Great Raid* (2005) followed as well as the crime-drama *Public Enemies* (2009). Timmermann also coproduced a number of films, including the drama *American Rhapsody* (2001), in which she cast a young Scarlett Johansson on the strength of her performance in *The Horse Whisperer* (1998). Timmermann additionally produced the action-comedy *Violet & Daisy* (2011), casting a young Saoirse Ronan in the lead role, and cast the crime-thriller *Blackhat* (2015), starring Chris Hemsworth and Viola Davis.

In the mid-2010s, Timmermann's affinity for meeting people led her to photojournalist Jonathan Alpeyrie. Timmermann spotted Alpeyrie, who had just returned from Syria where he had been held prisoner, while dining in a New York restaurant. "From across the room, I saw a side to this person and wanted to meet him," she recalled to Brunner. "I asked the maître d' who he was." By the end of their first meeting, Timmermann had the rights to Alpeyrie's harrowing tale. She was instrumental in helping him publish his 2017 book *The Shattered Lens: A War Photographer's True Story of Captivity and Survival in Syria*. They also announced plans to adapt the book for film. Still working, by the end of the 2010s, Timmermann had additionally been involved in the casting of the romantic comedy *Remember Me* (2019).

PERSONAL LIFE

Bonnie Timmermann married John Connor in the early 1980s. She lives in New York.

SUGGESTED READING

Brunner, Jeryl. "How Casting Director/Producer Bonnie Timmermann Nurtured the Careers of Saoirse Ronan and Many More." *Forbes*, 28 Jan. 2018, www.forbes.com/sites/jerylbrunner/2018/01/28/how-casting-directorproducer-bonnie-timmermann-nurtured-the-careers-of-saoirse-ronan-and-many-more/#14721bed1609. Accessed 2 Sept. 2020.

Millea, Holly. "Hollywood Icon: Bonnie Timmermann." *Elle*, 2 Nov. 2009, www.elle.com/culture/movies-tv/a9051/hollywood-icon-bonnie-timmermann-383721. Accessed 6 Sept. 2020.

Steigbigel, Matthew. "Legendary Casting Director Bonnie Timmermann on *Blackhat* and More." *Motion Picture Association*, 26 Jan. 2015, www.motionpictures.org/2015/01/legendary-casting-director-bonnie-timmermann-on-blackhat-more. Accessed 4 Sept. 2020.

Yazigi, Monique P. "Making It Work: Angel to the Unknown, Link to the Mighty." *The New York Times*, 22 Jan. 1995, www.nytimes.com/1995/01/22/nyregion/making-it-work-angel-to-the-unknown-link-to-the-mighty.html. Accessed 3 Sept. 2020.

SELECTED WORKS

Miami Vice, 1984–89; *The Karate Kid*, 1984; *Bull Durham*, 1988; *The Last of the Mohicans*, 1992; *Death and the Maiden*, 1994; *Armageddon*, 1998; *Pearl Harbor*, 2001; *Public Enemies*, 2009; *Blackhat*, 2015; *Remember Me*, 2019

—*Molly Hagan*

Gleyber Torres

Date of birth: December 13, 1996
Occupation: Baseball player

Some professional baseball players take an analytical approach to their sport. The talented infielder Gleyber Torres, by contrast, has tried his best not to overthink it. "The key is not to do too much," he told David Waldstein for the *New York Times* (19 Mar. 2017) through an interpreter. "Have a good at-bat and go with it. The results will come." In Torres's case, the results speak for themselves. A lifelong athlete who first demonstrated his skills as a member of youth baseball teams in Venezuela, he captured the attention of major-league scouts as a young teenager and signed a contract with the Chicago Cubs at sixteen. While working his way through the minor leagues, he was sent to the New York Yankees as part of a blockbuster trade. He made his major-league debut with his new team in April 2018. His first two seasons brought a host of milestones, including back-to-back All-Star selections and postseason competitions. Yet despite his rapid rise to stardom, Torres has remained focused on progressing as a player and

Photo by DR. Buddie via Wikimedia Commons

supporting his teammates. "I want to get better every day. I want to make a play on every ground ball that's hit to me," he told Alfred Santasiere III for *Yankees Magazine* (30 Apr. 2020). "I want to enjoy the game, and I want to help my team every chance I get."

EARLY LIFE AND EDUCATION

Gleyber David Torres was born on December 13, 1996, in Caracas, Venezuela. He spent his childhood in the San Bernardino neighborhood of Caracas. Torres had a close relationship with his parents, Eusebio Torres and Ibelise Castro, who encouraged his athletic pursuits. As Torres would later explain in interviews, they greatly influenced his personal development. "They always gave me all the support that I needed. They taught me how to treat a person, whether the person is older or younger. Everything that they taught me helped me very much," he told Nathan Maciborski for *Yankees Magazine* (30 May 2018). "Everything that I am now and what I will be, I'm really grateful to them for." Torres's parents introduced him to the sport of baseball, taking their son to a stadium for the first time when he was four years old.

Torres began playing baseball as a young child, initially as an outfielder. He later transitioned to shortstop, considered the most demanding defensive position on the field. Torres enjoyed his years playing with youth leagues, which he described to Maciborski as "some of the best years" in which he played. "I always had a lot of fun with my teammates, and those moments were my first steps as a baseball player."

In addition to baseball, Torres played basketball as a young teen and enjoyed riding bicycles and playing games with his friends. Baseball, however, remained his focus—one that he and his family took very seriously. As a teenager he enrolled in a baseball academy in the city of Maracay to develop his skills with the goal of becoming a professional player.

MINOR LEAGUES

Though still a young teenager, Torres received extensive attention from Major League Baseball (MLB) scouts as his skill and potential became apparent. As early as 2012, big-market MLB franchises such as the New York Yankees and the Chicago Cubs began efforts to recruit the young player. Representatives from the Cubs ultimately won him over, and the team was able to sign him officially following his sixteenth birthday, in accordance with MLB regulations governing international amateur free agents. Torres signed with the Cubs on July 2, 2013, for a $1.7 million bonus.

Torres entered the Cubs' farm system for the 2014 season, joining the rookie-level Arizona League Cubs. After several months with that team, he moved to the Class A Short Season Boise Hawks in August of that year. He went on to play with the Class A South Bend Cubs and Class A Advanced Myrtle Beach Pelicans in 2015 and returned to the Pelicans for the start of the 2016 season. At every level he continued to excite observers with both his defensive and offensive play.

A turning point in Torres's baseball career came on July 25, 2016, when the Cubs traded him to the New York Yankees as the key asset in a multiplayer deal in exchange for elite pitcher Aroldis Chapman. Although that trade represented a significant change for the up-and-comer, he soon found it to be a positive one. "I made a lot of friends with the Cubs, but I understand that it is a business," he told Nicholas Cortese, Andrew Galligan, Matthew Gavagan, and Marcus Lester for *Newsday* (6 Sept. 2019). "It ended up being a great opportunity for me."

After moving to the Class A Advanced Tampa Yankees for the remainder of the 2016 season, Torres went on to play for the Double A Trenton Thunder and the Triple A Scranton/Wilkes-Barre RailRiders over the course of 2017. His 2017 season ended early after a torn ligament in his elbow forced him to undergo surgery, but he returned to action the following year, rejoining the RailRiders for the start of the 2018 season. By then he was widely recognized as one of the top prospects in baseball.

NEW YORK YANKEES

Another key milestone in Torres's career came just over two weeks into the 2018 season, when

Yankees leadership called him up to the major-league club. Torres was thrilled with that news, which aligned with his own personal expectations. "My goal was to play fifteen days in the minor leagues and then come up to the team," he told Cortese, Galligan, Gavagan, and Lester. "I played well in those fifteen and they called me and I was really excited." He made his debut with the Yankees on April 22, 2018, in a victory against the Toronto Blue Jays. With Didi Gregorius already established as the team's everyday shortstop, Torres was moved to second base.

As a rookie, Torres soon established himself as a key contributor on a powerful Yankees team. Serving as the primary second baseman and playing occasionally at shortstop, he appeared in 123 games throughout the regular season and was a member of the starting lineup for 119 of them. He compiled a solid .271 batting average, tallying 117 hits in 431 at bats and scoring fifty-four runs. But it was his twenty-four home runs that stood out, particularly as second basemen are not generally known for power hitting. Torres also performed well defensively, with a .970 fielding percentage at second base. His strong all-around play led him to be named American League (AL) Rookie of the Month honors for May 2018 as well as AL Player of the Week in May and again in early September. He was also included on the AL's reserve roster for the 2018 MLB All-Star Game, although he was unable to play in the game due to an injury. Following the season, he finished third in AL Rookie of the Year Award voting.

A FORMATIVE POSTSEASON

The 2018 MLB season was a strong one for the Yankees, as the team finished second in the AL East division with a 100–62 win-loss record. The team earned a wild-card berth and defeated the Oakland Athletics in the AL Wild Card Game. They then advanced to the AL Division Series (ALDS), where Torres and his teammates faced off against the Yankees' traditional archrivals, the Boston Red Sox. Torres played relatively well in the series, hitting .308 across four games. However, the Yankees were unable to overcome the Red Sox, losing three games to one to end their play-off run. (Boston would go on to become the 2018 World Series champions.)

Torres was excited to have the opportunity to compete in the postseason during his first year in the major leagues. However, he also had the unfortunate distinction of hitting into the final out of Game 4 of the ALDS and thus securing Boston's victory. The loss of that game, and the ALDS overall, was tough for the rookie. "I felt really bad. After that season, I went home and I never forgot that moment. I feel bad; I feel frustration," he later said, as quoted by Bryan Hoch for the official *MLB* website (7 Nov. 2019). Yet,

while Torres dwelled on the Yankees' postseason defeat and his own role in it, he treated that incident largely as a source of motivation. "I just took that moment personally and just take advantage of that. During my offseason, I prepared really, really, really good to help my team," he explained, as quoted by Hoch. In addition to developing his baseball skills further, Torres dedicated the period between the 2018 and 2019 seasons to working on preventing injuries.

2019 AND 2020 SEASONS

During the 2019 season Torres further solidified his role as a key member of the Yankees as the team overall struggled with injuries. Splitting time relatively evenly between second base and shortstop, he played in 144 out of 162 regular-season games and started all but two of them. His batting average improved slightly, to .278, while his impressive thirty-eight home runs led the Yankees and ranked sixth in the league. He also had twenty-six doubles, ninety runs batted in (RBIs), and forty-eight walks, helping him to one of the most productive campaigns ever by a Yankees player under age twenty-three. In recognition of his performance, Torres was once again selected as a reserve team member for the All-Star Game and, this time, was able to play in the game, in which the AL team claimed victory.

In addition to being a strong season for Torres, the 2019 season was successful for the Yankees as well. With a 103–59 win-loss record, the team finished first in the AL East and earned the second seed in the playoffs, which got off to a promising start with a three-game sweep in the ALDS against the Minnesota Twins. Torres found his second postseason to be far less daunting than his first. "I felt more relaxed," he recalled to Santasiere. "I was just as excited as I was in 2018, but I felt like I had been there before and that I would be there again. I really enjoyed that whole series against the Twins. It was loud in Yankee Stadium, and I really enjoyed the support we got from our fans in those games." Torres performed well in the ALDS, hitting .417 and scoring five runs in three games. He also stood out in the AL Championship Series (ALCS) against the Houston Astros, batting .280 with two home runs and six RBIs in six games. However, the Astros prevailed in the series four games to two, ending the Yankees' push to reach the World Series.

Torres entered the 2020 season as one of MLB's brightest young stars. He was also poised to return to shortstop full-time, as Gregorius had left the Yankees in free agency. Yet expectations for the season were put on hold due to the onset of the novel coronavirus (COVID-19) pandemic early that year. The Yankees and all other MLB teams were forced to end spring training early, and the start of the season was delayed indefinitely. After several months of planning, schedules for a shortened baseball season were finally announced, with games set to begin in late July 2020 with a few special rules in place. The MLB also planned to hold the World Series in the fall, though things remained somewhat in flux due to the continually evolving public health crisis. Yet even before these unique circumstances, Torres kept his goals for the 2020 season clear: "The first is the same one I had last year: to stay healthy," he told Santasiere. "The second one is simple: to win the World Series."

PERSONAL LIFE

Torres met his future wife, Elizabeth, as a teenager living in Venezuela. They married in 2017. Torres developed a fondness for New York City after moving there following his assignment to the Yankees. "Whenever I get the opportunity, I walk around the city and try to experience as much of it as I can," he told Santasiere. "I'm living in the greatest city in the world, and I'm trying to enjoy it all the time."

SUGGESTED READING

Barker, Barbara. "Unrest in Venezuela a Constant for Yankees Prospect Gleyber Torres." *Newsday*, 3 June 2017, www.newsday.com/sports/baseball/yankees/unrest-in-venezuela-a-constant-for-yankees-prospect-gleyber-torres-1.13706481. Accessed 13 July 2020.

Hoch, Bryan. "Torres' 2019 Trend Points toward Torrid '20." *MLB News*, 7 Nov. 2019, www.mlb.com/news/gleyber-torres-2019-exit-interview. Accessed 13 July 2020.

Maciborski, Nathan. "Yankees Magazine: Memories and Dreams." *Yankees Magazine*, 30 May 2018, www.mlb.com/yankees/news/gleyber-torres-opens-up-about-his-past-c278983286. Accessed 13 July 2020.

Miller, Randy. "Yankees' Gleyber Torres Fueled in October by Unforgettable Past Failure." *NJ.com*, 5 Oct. 2019, www.nj.com/yankees/2019/10/gleyber-torres-fuel-for-yankees-postseason-run-is-an-unforgettable-past-failure.html. Accessed 13 July 2020.

Torres, Gleyber. "Talking with Gleyber Torres." Interview by Nicholas Cortese, Andrew Galligan, Matthew Gavagan, and Marcus Lester. *Newsday*, 6 Sept. 2019, www.newsday.com/lifestyle/family/kidsday/yankees-baseball-kidsday-gleyber-torres-1.35890801. Accessed 13 July 2020.

———. "Yankees Magazine: Gleyber Torres Good to Go." Interview by Alfred Santasiere III. *Yankees Magazine*, 30 Apr. 2020, www.mlb.com/news/gleyber-torres-q-and-a-2020. Accessed 13 July 2020.

Waldstein, David. "Yankees Capitalize on 2nd Chance with Young Star Who Got Away." *The New York Times*, 19 Mar. 2017, www.nytimes.com/2017/03/19/sports/baseball/yankees-gleyber-torres-prospect.html. Accessed 13 July 2020.

—*Joy Crelin*

Kelly Marie Tran

Date of birth: January 17, 1989
Occupation: Actor

Kelly Marie Tran became an overnight star when she was cast in *Star Wars: Episode VIII— The Last Jedi* (2017), which grossed more than $220 million in box-office revenue on its opening night. She also became a lightning rod for the issue of racial representation in Hollywood, as the first woman of color to have a major role in a Star Wars film, and became the first Asian American woman to appear on a cover of *Vanity Fair* magazine. The change from her struggles as a relatively unknown actor to Star Wars fame and fortune was huge, as she told Amy Robach for ABC's *Good Morning America* (9 Dec. 2019), "Whenever there's something that feels so heavy and scary, you can sort of clam up and close up, and I think that's the most dangerous thing. The best thing for me was looking outward and remembering that the world is bigger than myself and that experience."

Photo by MTV International via Wikimedia Commons

EARLY LIFE AND EDUCATION

Kelly Marie Tran was born Loan Tran on January 17, 1989, in San Diego, California, where she grew up with her two sisters and parents, who worked in the funeral and fast-food industries. She later adopted the name Kelly to better fit into mainstream American culture. Her parents also adopted English names after they emigrated from Vietnam, where her father had been homeless for seven years.

Tran felt her family's difference acutely. Because other children made fun of her, Tran stopped speaking Vietnamese at age nine. She told Kimberly Yam for *Huffington Post* (30 Nov. 2017), "Growing up, I've always felt I was from two different worlds. . . . [My parents] raised my sisters and I with the parenting methods of the Vietnamese culture." She told Patrick May for the San Jose *Mercury News* (16 Dec. 2017), about her response while watching television as a young child: "I felt like I needed to see someone that looked like me do something impossible. I wanted to look like everyone else in movies and books and TV shows, and because no one looked like me, I wanted to change."

While still at Westview High School, Tran began searching for an agent. She worked in a yogurt shop to earn money for headshots but received many rejection letters in response. After graduation, Tran attended the University of California, Los Angeles, earning a Bachelor of Arts degree in communications in 2011. While there, she sang in choirs and a cappella groups and acted whenever possible.

EARLY CAREER

Tran initially trained for a career in comedy. At the suggestion of her first commercial agent, in 2011 she joined a well-known improv troupe, the Upright Citizens Brigade in Los Angeles. She also worked with iO West and Second City. As she told Keely Flaherty for *BuzzFeed News* (14 Nov. 2017), "I love the ideals of improv: supporting each other and never being sort of judgmental of other people's ideas. I think they're great rules for life: You get a piece of information, you're like, 'OK, how do I work with that and how do I add to that?'" She joined with other Asian improv artists to form the all-female group "Number One Son."

Tran appeared in several short films in 2011, episodes of various television series in 2012 and 2014, and *Ladies Like Us*, a 2013–15 web series about friends trying to survive romance, career challenges, and other crises. She was also featured in several videos made for CollegeHumor, a sketch-comedy website; Tran drew on her Asian background in a 2015 satirical video "Are You Asian Enough?" to play a judge who determines if someone of mixed Asian ancestry could tell certain jokes or offer Korean restaurant recommendations. She went on to being cast as Butterfly Rave Girl in *XOXO* (2016), a romantic comedy from Netflix that starred Sarah Hyland of *Modern Family* and Graham Phillips of *The Good Wife*.

Tran did improv and wrote comedy sketches afterhours. She went to auditions around her day job as an assistant at a temp agency and recruitment firm, Syndicatebleu. She explained to Anthony Breznican for *Entertainment Weekly* (20 Nov. 2017), "I worked with amazing people, but obviously whenever you are doing something that's not your dream, you kind of feel like, 'Oh, I'm on this grind.'"

THE LAST JEDI

Alongside more seasoned actors such as Benicio del Toro and Laura Dern, Tran was cast in *Star Wars: Episode VIII—The Last Jedi* as Rose Tico, a Resistance mechanic who becomes involved in an unexpected adventure with the character Finn (John Boyega). Vietnamese-born actor Ngô Thanh Vân also joined the cast, playing Rose's sister, Paige.

The audition process required five auditions over as many months and travel to London, England, for the final one, with full makeup, hair, and costumes. A fan of speculative fiction by writers such as J. R. R. Tolkien, J. K. Rowling, and George R. R. Martin, Tran wore a Ravenclaw tie (from the Harry Potter series) to the first Star Wars audition for luck. Committed to being present and simply enjoying herself at the fifth, she relaxed into her character. As director Rian Johnson told May, Tran struck him as just the right fit for the character, explaining, "I wanted someone who—thinking back to me as a kid being a genuine nerd you could relate to—someone who didn't feel like they belong; someone you wouldn't necessarily imagine as a big 'Star Wars' hero. Let's throw them in the mix and see the world through their eyes."

Johnson met with Tran during her day job to offer her the role, emphasizing that she could not yet make the news public. Even after filming began, secrecy remained imperative, so Tran told her family she was on location in Canada for an independent film. To support her tale, she even bought maple syrup to give to family. The film was shot at Pinewood Studios outside London, in 2016. Rose Tico was finally introduced to fans at a Star Wars Celebration in April 2017.

Before being cast, Tran had never watched a Star Wars film, but afterward, she binge-watched the franchise and began appreciating it even more. Tran considered the filming process to be the equivalent of acting school and learned a great deal from her costars. Carrie Fisher, who played Leia Organa, was Tran's example of how to be herself and honest in the process.

For her work on *Last Jedi*, in 2018 Tran was nominated for the Empire Award for Best Female Newcomer and Teen Choice Award for Choice Breakout Movie Star and won the Saturn Award for Best Supporting Actress. After the film was released, she and costar Ngô Thanh Vân promoted it in Vietnam.

HIATUS

After the filming for *The Last Jedi* ended, Tran paid off her student loans and then took time off from acting. She explained to Flaherty, "I also spent a year traveling and a year trying to figure myself out and reminding myself why I got into this." Going on to characterize her hiatus from Hollywood as running away, she added, "I wanted to center myself and remember who I was. My life had just changed so much, and I needed that time to reflect."

Tran spent two months working on a South African reserve for endangered wildlife without running water, electricity, or internet access. Information about Rose Tico had not yet been released. To preserve her anonymity, Tran told her twelve roommates that she was an office temp worker.

Her next stop was Vietnam, to work with orphans there. She also took her parents for their first visit in decades. She saw where her father had lived and met cousins who had been unable to leave the country.

BACKLASH

Some Star Wars fans objected to having a person of Asian descent added to the franchise and made racist and sexist remarks about Tran online. By June 2018, because of that harassment, she had decided to delete all the images from her Instagram account, leaving only the phrase "Afraid, but doing it anyway" in her bio. As she wrote for the *New York Times* (21 Aug. 2018), "Their words reinforced a narrative I had heard my whole life: that I was 'other,' that I didn't belong, that I wasn't good enough, simply because I wasn't like them." In her opinion piece, she expressed her frustration at the sexist and racist stereotypes that remain prevalent in American society and the feelings of shame that she thought she had overcome.

Several of the Star Wars cast and many fans supported Tran and spoke out against the ugly fan reactions. For example, Star Wars novelist Chuck Wendig wrote on Twitter (5 June 2018): "She is a force for light and joy and unabashed engagement with the things you love, and to think of the harassment she's received is infuriating." African American costar John Boyega also gave her advice on coping with the hateful comments.

THE RISE OF SKYWALKER

After Tran returned to Hollywood, she joined the cast of the television dramedy *Sorry for Your Loss* as Jules Shaw, the sister of the main character, a new widow named Leigh (Elizabeth Olsen). She returned for its second season in 2019 as well.

Tran reprised the role of Rose in episodes of Star Wars animated television shows in 2018 and again in *Star Wars: Episode IX—The Rise of Skywalker* (2019), the final film of the Skywalker trilogy and the final entry in the franchise. During filming, she mentored newcomer Naomi Ackie, who played the franchise's first black female character, and shot a number of scenes with Rey (Daisy Ridley) and others. However, Tran had less than ninety seconds of screen time in the final cut. Director-screenwriter J. J. Abrams and screenwriter Chris Terrio were contending with the need to include Leia's scenes in the final film despite Carrie Fisher's untimely death in 2016. Terrio initially explained to *Awards Daily* that their idea was to leave Leia at the base with Rose and that some of their scenes "turned out to not meet the standard of photorealism that we'd hoped for," as quoted by Marissa Martinelli for *Slate* (2 Jan. 2020). He added, "The last thing we were doing was deliberately trying to sideline Rose." Terrio later clarified that at least one Leia-Rose scene, where the emotional dynamic no longer worked, was cut for narrative reasons. When asked whether she felt any disappointment with the result, Tran told Josh Horowitz for *MTV News* (10 Feb. 2020), "I'm really just amazed at the way that J. J. was able to sort of wrap up all these incredible stories. There were so many characters, you know? And at the end of the day, I got to be part of something bigger than me and that's really special."

Many fans of Tran remained convinced that the cuts were an attempt to mollify those who were unhappy with the Rose Tico arc and were dismayed that Rose's story was unresolved. Filmmaker John M. Chu tweeted with the hashtag #RoseTicoDeservedBetter and offered to create and direct a show about Rose for Disney+, which owns the franchise.

Tran was listed among the *Forbes* 30 Under 30 for 2019 and served as a presenter at the 2020 Academy Awards, along with stars such as Julia Louis-Dreyfus, Kristen Wiig, Mindy Kaling, and Lin-Manuel Miranda.

PERSONAL LIFE

Having a family far removed from the film industry proved helpful for Tran amid the surrealness of her big break. She has credited them with keeping her grounded. She also spoke publicly about how therapy helped her to deal both with the online harassment and the sudden life transformation she experienced after her casting in *Last Jedi*.

SUGGESTED READING

Breznican, Anthony. "Kelly Marie Tran Thought She'd Quit Acting—Then *The Last Jedi* Put Her Dream into Hyperdrive." *Entertainment Weekly*, 20 Nov. 2017, ew.com/movies/2017/11/20/kelly-marie-tran-star-wars-the-last-jedi. Accessed 12 Feb. 2020.

Flaherty, Keely. "The Rise of Rose." *BuzzFeed News*, 14 Nov. 2017, www.buzzfeednews.com/article/keelyflaherty/the-rise-of-rose. Accessed 4 Feb. 2020.

Guglielmi, Jodi. "*Star Wars: The Last Jedi*'s Kelly Marie Tran Opens Up about Her Overnight Fame." *People*, 14 Dec. 2017, people.com/movies/kelly-marie-tran-star-wars-fame. Accessed 12 Feb. 2020.

Martinelli, Marissa. "No Explanation Can Justify Kelly Marie Tran's Tiny Role in *The Rise of Skywalker*." *Slate*, 2 Jan. 2020, slate.com/culture/2020/01/rise-of-skywalker-kelly-marie-tran-rose-chris-terrio-explanation.html. Accessed 13 Feb. 2020.

May, Patrick. "Star Wars Star Kelly Marie Tran Is Living Her 'Impossible' Dream." *Mercury News*, 15 Dec. 2017, www.mercurynews.com/2017/12/15/the-world-is-agog-over-star-wars-star-kelly-marie-tran. Accessed 22 Jan. 2020.

Tran, Kelly Marie. "Kelly Marie Tran: I Won't Be Marginalized by Online Harassment." *The New York Times*, 21 Aug. 2018, www.nytimes.com/2018/08/21/movies/kelly-marie-tran.html. Accessed 3 Feb. 2020.

——. "Kelly Marie Tran on the Force of Women in 'Star Wars: The Rise of Skywalker.'" Interview by Amy Robach. *Good Morning America*, 9 Dec. 2019. *YouTube*, youtu.be/Gimp4YZQlh0. Accessed 22 Jan. 2020.

SELECTED WORKS

XOXO, 2016; *Star Wars: The Last Jedi*, 2017; *Star Wars: The Rise of Skywalker*, 2019

—Judy Johnson

Joseph C. Tsai

Date of birth: January 1964
Occupation: Business executive

Joseph C. Tsai first came to the attention of many Americans in the fall of 2019, after he became the owner of the Brooklyn Nets National Basketball Association (NBA) team. In Asia, however, Tsai had long been known as the cofounder and executive vice chair of the online retail giant Alibaba and a key dealmaker in the company's early days. Although Alibaba has remained largely unknown in the West, it thoroughly dominates the Chinese market: in mid-2018, more than 90 percent of its revenue came from within China, and 80 percent of retail sales in the country reportedly went through the company's various platforms in 2019.

The company's initial public offering in 2014 made Tsai one of the wealthiest people in the world; in December 2019, *Forbes* ranked him as the 147th richest person, with an estimated net worth at $11.2 billion. After reaching billionaire status, Tsai has become increasingly involved in funding various forms of athletics, founding the sports investment company J Tsai Sports and purchasing ownership of several professional basketball and lacrosse teams.

EARLY LIFE AND EDUCATION

Joseph "Joe" Tsai Chung-hsin was born in January 1964 in Taipei, Taiwan, to Dr. Paul C. Tsai, a civil servant and lawyer, and Ruby Tsai. Tsai is the oldest of their four children; he has two sisters, Eva and Vivian, and a brother, Benjamin. His parents were active in charitable and educational organizations and raised their children in Taiwan's Christian community.

At the age of thirteen, Tsai was sent to New Jersey to attend a boys' college preparatory boarding school, the Lawrenceville School. He showed an early interest in sports, playing both lacrosse and football at Lawrenceville, as well as playing on an intramural basketball team.

After his high school graduation in 1982, Tsai enrolled in Yale University, his father's alma mater, where he joined the lacrosse team and continued to play basketball recreationally. He

Photo by Yanshan Zhang/Getty Images

earned a bachelor's degree in East Asian studies and economics in 1986 and went on to complete a juris doctorate from Yale Law School, as his father also had, in 1990.

CAREER BEGINNINGS

Shortly after his graduation from Yale Law School, Tsai took an associate-level position at the law firm of Sullivan & Cromwell in New York. In 1993, he joined management buyout firm Rosecliff Inc. as vice president and general counsel. He remained in this position for two years, leaving in 1995 to work for the investment firm Investor AB in Hong Kong.

While managing Investor Asia Limited's private equity investments, Tsai met teacher-turned-internet entrepreneur Jack Ma. Though Ma's first project, an online business directory called China Pages, had failed, Tsai was impressed by Ma's idea for an international business-to-business e-commerce platform but even more taken by his leadership ability. Ma later recalled that, when he proposed in 1999 that Tsai leave his job and join Ma as one of eighteen cofounders of Alibaba, he could only offer Tsai fifty dollars a month in pay. Tsai, however, still believed that the project was worth it. "When he said he wanted to join us, I was very surprised," Ma commented to Andrew Ross Sorkin for the *New York Times* (13 Jan. 2014).

The company's first platform, business-to-business sales platform *Alibaba.com*, launched in 1999, shortly after Tsai joined the team. Ma wanted the platform to be used by businesses around the world. For this reason, the Alibaba site originally launched in English, making it one of the first Chinese internet companies to do so. However, as it became clear that most of the company's business came from within China, Alibaba soon shifted its focus to the Chinese market.

FINDING SUCCESS WITH ALIBABA

Because of his background in law and venture capital, Tsai proved instrumental in creating the new company's financial and legal structure. He briefly served as its chief operating officer (COO) and then became chief financial officer (CFO), a position he held until May 2013. He was also the only cofounder from outside of mainland China and the only one to have been educated in the West, which gave him an advantage in communicating with international investors. "I knew I had a knowledge that nobody else had, so people could trust that aspect to me," Tsai explained to Russell Flannery for *Forbes* (8 Jan. 2014). "So I felt very confident of that and very comfortable in my world. I don't pretend to do everything. I knew what my role was."

Among Tsai's contributions to Alibaba was structuring the financing of Taobao Marketplace, the company's direct-to-consumer auction platform, which launched in 2003. Tsai knew that the platform would not be profitable in the beginning, so he made it a joint venture with Japanese telecommunications company Softbank to minimize the impact of losses on the rest of Alibaba. He also helped secure investment from US tech giant Yahoo! in 2005. Although Taobao did not break even for about six years, it eventually eclipsed eBay in China and became an important revenue source for Alibaba.

Over the course of the first decade of the twenty-first century, Alibaba continued its rapid ascent. In 2004 it launched Alipay, an online and mobile payment platform that became one of the most-used payment services in China, and in 2008 it introduced Taobao Mall (later renamed Tmall), a business-to-consumer retail platform where Chinese and international brands could sell their products.

GOING PUBLIC

By 2012 Alibaba's revenues had vastly surpassed those of US online retailer Amazon—Alibaba made $160 million in sales that year to Amazon's $86 million. Its initial public offering (IPO) on the New York Stock Exchange (NYSE) was much anticipated in the business world, and Tsai was the main decision-maker on the IPO, garnering him some attention from the Western business press. "Well, it always feels very good when people say that they love you and they want to talk to you," Tsai told Sorkin, but added, "The I.P.O. is just one milestone and the company continues. There's a lot of life after an I.P.O." At the time of the New York IPO on September 19, 2014, the Alibaba Group Holding Limited's market capitalization was $231 billion, larger than those of Amazon and eBay combined, and the IPO was the largest to date, raising $25 billion within two days. Tsai himself reportedly owned about $2 billion in company shares at the time.

Tsai became executive vice chair of Alibaba in 2013, and in 2015 he was named non-executive director of Ali Health, a health information-technology business that operates an online pharmacy. Despite no longer being the CFO, he remained responsible for running global mergers and acquisitions for the company, including its expansion into countries such as India.

In 2019 Tsai was the second-largest shareholder in Alibaba, after Ma, with about 8 percent of its stock. He remains a board member as well.

SPORTS INVESTMENTS AND PHILANTHROPY

Tsai's first foray into the world of professional sports came in 2014, when he sponsored the Hong Kong Men's Lacrosse Team trip to Denver,

Colorado, to participate in the World Lacrosse Championships. "I told them, look, I'm going to be your full financial sponsor. I'm going to support you. No strings attached. I just love the sport," he told Flannery.

In 2017, Tsai began exploring sports team ownership. In August of that year, Tsai, through his sports investment firm J Tsai Sports, founded the San Diego Seals professional indoor lacrosse team, and in October J Tsai Sports bought a 49 percent stake in the struggling NBA team the Brooklyn Nets, with an option to purchase the remaining stake no later than 2021. In a press release quoted by Nick Atkin for the *South China Morning Post* (28 Oct. 2017), Tsai said that he felt that Chinese people could become "healthier and happier" by becoming involved in basketball and that he was pleased that Alibaba had given him an opportunity to give back to both the sport and the people who made Alibaba successful. "No other things can make my life happier than this kind of positive circle," Tsai said. As his statement implied, he went on to focus on promoting the NBA in China and even became a board member for NBA China.

Two years later Tsai exercised his purchase option, taking over ownership of the team from Russian financier Mikhail Prokhorov in September 2019. Tsai also purchased the Nets' arena, Barclays Center, in a separate transaction. Speaking of the record-high $2.35 billion Nets deal, he stated, "I've had the opportunity to witness up close the Brooklyn Nets rebuild that Mikhail started a few years ago. . . . I will be the beneficiary of Mikhail's vision, which put the Nets in a great position to compete, and for which I am incredibly grateful," as quoted by Taylor Nicole Rogers for *Business Insider* (13 Nov. 2019). That same year J Tsai Sports had purchased the New York Liberty, a Women's National Basketball Association (WNBA) team for an undisclosed sum. Through J Tsai Sports, he has also invested in the Premier Lacrosse League, Los Angeles FC of Major League Soccer, and G2 Esports.

Tsai has engaged in major philanthropic endeavors as well. He and his wife operate the charitable Joe and Clara Tsai Foundation, through which they have donated millions to Yale University and the Lawrenceville School. Along with his siblings and mother, Tsai has also contributed to an endowment at the Mayo Clinic, which performed life-saving heart surgery on his sister Vivian.

PERSONAL LIFE AND POLITICAL VIEWS

In 1996 Tsai married Clara Ming-Hua Wu, a finance executive. The couple have three children—daughter Alex and sons Dash and Jacob—and live in La Jolla, California. His children play lacrosse, and Alex has even played for the Hong Kong national team.

Tsai strongly supports the government of the People's Republic of China. He made headlines in October 2019 when he criticized Daryl Morey, the general manager of the Houston Rockets NBA team, for expressing support for pro-democracy protesters in Hong Kong, a semiautonomous region of China. In a *Facebook* statement, Tsai said, "Supporting a separatist movement in a Chinese territory is one of those third-rail issues, not only for the Chinese government, but also for citizens of China . . . 1.4 billion Chinese citizens stand united when it comes to the territorial integrity of China and the country's sovereignty over her homeland. This issue is non-negotiable."

SUGGESTED READING

Atkin, Nick. "Alibaba Co-founder Joseph Tsai to Buy 49 Per Cent of Brooklyn Nets." *South China Morning Post*, 28 Oct. 2017, www.scmp.com/sport/china/article/2117398/alibaba-co-founder-joseph-tsai-buy-49-cent-brooklyn-nets-record-nba-deal. Accessed 17 Dec. 2019.

Horwitz, Josh. "Brooklyn Nets Owner, Alibaba Co-founder Tsai Decries Houston Rockets GM's Hong Kong Tweet." *Reuters*, 7 Oct. 2019, www.reuters.com/article/us-china-basketball-nba-tsai/brooklyn-nets-owner-alibaba-co-founder-tsai-decries-houston-rockets-gms-hong-kong-tweet-idUSKBN1WM0C8. Accessed 13 Dec. 2019.

Rogers, Taylor Nicole. "The CEO of the Brooklyn Nets and Barclays Center Is Resigning—and the News Comes Less Than 2 Months after Alibaba Billionaire Joseph Tsai Bought Both in a Record $2.35 Billion Deal." *Business Insider*, 13 Nov. 2019, www.businessinsider.com/alibaba-billionaire-joseph-tsai-buying-out-brooklyn-nets-2019-8. Accessed 12 Dec. 2019.

Sorkin, Andrew Ross. "The Man behind Alibaba's Eventual I.P.O." *The New York Times*, 13 Jan. 2014, dealbook.nytimes.com/2014/01/13/the-man-behind-alibabas-eventual-i-p-o. Accessed 13 Dec. 2019.

Tsai, Joseph. "Full Video and Transcript: Alibaba Executive Vice Chairman Joe Tsai at Code 2018." Interview by Jason Del Rey. *Recode*, Vox, 31 May 2018, www.vox.com/2018/5/31/17397180/full-transcript-alibaba-executive-vice-chairman-joe-tsai-code-2018. Accessed 17 Dec. 2019.

———. "Inside Alibaba: Vice Chairman Joe Tsai Opens Up about Working with Jack Ma and Jonathan Lu." Interview by Russell Flannery. *Forbes*, 8 Jan. 2014, www.forbes.com/sites/russellflannery/2014/01/08/inside-alibaba-vice-chairman-joe-tsai-opens-up-about-working-with-jack-ma-and-jonathan-lu. Accessed 12 Dec. 2019.

—*Emma Joyce*

Mashudu Tshifularo

Born: June 18, 1964
Occupation: Surgeon and educator

The word "ossicle" is derived from the Latin *ossiculum*, meaning "small bone," and the three ossicles in the middle ear are, indeed, among the tiniest and most fragile bones in the human body. Because of the integral role the auditory ossicles play in the hearing process, any damage to them can cause profound deafness. In March 2019, Mashudu Tshifularo, a South African ear, nose, and throat (ENT) specialist, made history by becoming the first surgeon in the world ever to replace damaged ossicles with 3D-printed parts, thereby restoring most of his patient's hearing. The revolutionary technique showed the potential to transform the treatment of middle-ear problems caused by trauma, infection, metabolic diseases, or congenital birth defects.

Tshifularo rose from poverty to become one of the top doctors in South Africa. He was the first Black professor of ENT medicine in the country and was named head of the otorhinolaryngology department at the University of Pretoria. Given his work's enormous promise, he often expressed frustration at the state of research funding in South Africa and the pace of clinical trials, however. "I receive at least 10 emails a day from patients around the world who desperately need my help," he told Sameer Naik for South Africa's *Saturday Star* (3 Mar. 2020). "We have so many problems as a country but we cannot stay behind because advances are coming. When we have a spark of innovation and new ideas, we need to run with it."

EARLY LIFE AND EDUCATION

Mashudu Tshifularo was born on June 18, 1964, in the town of Thohoyandou in Limpopo Province, South Africa. (The area was for several decades considered part of Venda, one of the "Bantustan" territories denoted for Black citizens by the White-dominated government during apartheid.) Tshifularo spent his childhood in the nearby village of Mbahela, growing up with a sister and four brothers. His family was poor, and homes in the village were fashioned from mud and lacked electricity and running water.

As a child Tshifularo worked with his family as a herder, raising goats, donkeys, and cattle for subsistence. He walked barefoot for three miles each day to attend the nearest school, where classes were conducted under a tree. With no textbooks or notebooks, teachers etched lessons on the ground with sticks, as he later recalled. Yet even in the face of daunting circumstances that might have discouraged someone else, Tshifularo knew from a young age that he wanted to become a physician. One day, when he was about thirteen years old, his teacher asked the class to list their goals, and as fellow students answered with a variety of possible careers, Tshifularo stood up and firmly announced that he was going to become a doctor. "From that time I never changed my mind and worked hard to achieve my dream," he told Meta Mphahlele for the *Sunday World* (24 Mar. 2019).

Despite their humble upbringing, Tshifularo noted that all his siblings went on to distinguished careers. His eldest brother earned a PhD, his next oldest became a high school science teacher, one younger brother became a medical doctor, his sister became a school principal, and his youngest brother became an accountant. For his part, once Tshifularo had earned a National Senior Certificate (commonly known as the matriculation or matric certificate and generally considered the equivalent of a high school diploma in the United States), he embarked on his quest for a higher degree. As with most Black students in apartheid-era South Africa, he was forced to overcome numerous systemic and financial hurdles, but he remained determined and within just five years had earned a medical degree in 1989 from the University of Natal (later the University of KwaZulu-Natal). "I passed all my degrees within five years because I was focused," he asserted to Mphahlele. "People like me never arrive. After climbing one mountain we want to climb another one. If I was easily satisfied, I would have never achieved all the breakthroughs in my life."

MEDICAL CAREER

Upon earning his degree and completing a required period of community service, Tshifularo realized that there were few doctors in South Africa specializing in otorhinolaryngology, which deals with diseases of the ears, nose, and throat (ENT). "The reason why these three are grouped together is because they are related," he explained to Xolani Mathibela during an interview posted on the *University of Pretoria* website (17 July 2019). "A patient may complain about an ear ache but the nerve supply and some developmental muscles and vessels are interrelated. So this means that one might think the problem is with the ear only to find that the problem is actually with the sinus or throat." With his specialty decided upon, he began working in 1990 at Tshilidzini Hospital in Thohoyandou.

In 1995 Tshifularo became a chief specialist at the Sefako Makgatho Health Sciences

University (formerly known as the Medical University of South Africa or MEDUNSA). He also began teaching at the University of Pretoria, where he was eventually appointed head of the department of otorhinolaryngology. Many sources refer to him as the first Black ENT professor in South Africa, as well as one of the youngest people to achieve that position. He attained a small measure of renown in 2008, when he developed a surgical technique that employed an endoscope and allowed for a bloodless tonsillectomy.

In the 2010s Tshifularo began researching the possibility of middle-ear replacement surgery. He met with widespread skepticism initially. "Many medical and research companies did not believe in my research, including those in the UK, Germany and China," he recalled to Mathibela. "However, while presenting to them I had to be cautious that they do not steal my work." Eventually, he hit upon the idea of using a 3D printer to create the replacement parts and read several books about what was then still a relatively new technology. "It took me long because nobody believed in what I was doing," he explained to Mathibela. "Even medical companies turned me down. This period has really humbled me. Never expect anything to reach its full maturity within a short period of time."

GROUNDBREAKING SURGERY

Scientists have a good understanding of how we hear. When a sound is made, sound waves travel down the auditory canal and strike the tympanic membrane (known in layperson's terms as the eardrum). The eardrum vibrates, and those vibrations, in turn, are sent to three small bones in the middle ear, called ossicles, which amplify the sound. (The individual ossicles are the malleus, incus, and stapes, also known, respectively, as the hammer, anvil, and stirrup, because of their shapes.) The ossicles transmit the sound waves to the inner ear and into the fluid-filled structure known as the cochlea, where they are converted into electrical impulses, sent to the brain, and recognized as sound.

In early 2019, at the Steve Biko Academic Hospital (a facility attached to the University of Pretoria's Faculty of Health Sciences), Tshifularo was presented with a middle-aged patient who was suffering from total hearing loss as a result of trauma that had damaged his middle ear. In enormous pain, the man agreed to allow Tshifularo to perform a 3D scan of his head and create custom titanium replacement ossicles the same size, weight, length, and shape as his original, undamaged bones. On March 13, 2019, Tshifularo and his team performed the 90-minute endoscopic surgery, and the patient quickly recovered more than three-quarters of his hearing. While waiting for approval of more formal

clinical trials, they performed a second replacement surgery, this time on a man with a congenital middle-ear condition as well as occupational hearing loss. Results were similarly good, and Tshifularo began fielding requests from patients around the world.

Tshifularo's groundbreaking technique required replacing only the ossicles not working properly, thereby posing significantly less risk than other prostheses and surgical replacement procedures. His studies also predicted that it could be used on patients of all ages and conditions. However, it proved difficult for Tshifularo to carry out necessary clinical trials, mainly because of budget constraints. (He received some limited funding from a private foundation and from South Africa's National Research Foundation.) "I sit down with many children who cannot hear and whose families cannot afford operations to fix the problems, and it breaks my heart and I cry for them," he told Naik. "I can't wait to do clinical trials, because that will lead to helping improve millions of people's lives. Once we finish that, and scientifically analyse and fine-tune the whole procedure, we can go to commercialising it all over the world."

Despite those frustrations, Tshifularo, who filed numerous medical patents, remained enthusiastic about the possibilities presented by 3D printing and other high-tech innovations. He hoped, for example, to one day use bone dust or other biological material from the patient instead of titanium, to lessen the chance of rejection. "The Fourth Industrial Revolution (4IR) is changing the world," he asserted to Mathibela. "South Africa needs to jump in otherwise we will be left behind. The entire medical innovation treatment and research sector is changing completely. . . . Soon we are going to have tailormade medicine for patients by taking their blood and DNA and whatever machine we will be using by then will let us know which medication will work better for that specific patient. . . . This means that people are going to live longer and chronic diseases will be a thing of the past. The future is bright."

In addition to his work at the University of Pretoria, Tshifularo studied there for a second doctoral degree while making his important advances in middle ear transplantation. He told interviewers of his dream to one day build his own hospital dedicated to hearing research and rehabilitation.

PERSONAL LIFE

Tshifularo and his wife have six children, two of whom are adopted. Although known to have several hobbies, he has devoted most of his time outside of work to the Christ Revealed Fellowship Church, which he founded under the Mashudu Tshifularo Ministries name and where he serves as senior pastor. Besides publishing numerous articles in peer-reviewed medical journals, Tshifularo has penned multiple books in his capacity as a minister on social and spiritual subjects.

SUGGESTED READING

Gonzalez, Melisa. "South African Surgeons Perform a Successful Middle Ear Transplant Using 3D Printing Technology." *3DPrint.com*, 29 May 2019, 3dprint.com/245318/south-african-surgeons-perform-a-successful-middle-ear-transplant-using-3d-printing-technology/. Accessed 10 July 2020.

"How 3D Printing Enabled the World's First Middle Ear Transplant." *Fast Company*, digimag.fastcompany.co.za/magazine/fast-company/wci-2-3d-ear-transplant-health/. Accessed 13 Aug. 2020.

Mphahlele, Meta. "Prof Mashudu Tshifularo: Breaking New Ground." *Sunday World*, Sowetan Live, 24 Mar. 2019, www.sowetanlive.co.za/sundayworld/news/2019-03-24-prof-mashudu-tshifularo-nbreaking-new-ground/. Accessed 10 July 2020.

Naik, Sameer. "Despite Performing Groundbreaking Transplant, SA Doctor Still Lacks Funding." *The Saturday Star*, Independent Online, 3 Mar. 2020, www.iol.co.za/saturday-star/news/watch-despite-performing-ground-breaking-transplant-sa-doctor-still-lacks-funding-43999874. Accessed 10 July 2020.

Tshifularo, Mashudu. "Editor's Special Award: Dr. Mashudu Tshifularo." Interview. *GQ South Africa*, 16 Feb. 2020, www.gq.co.za/more/gq-men-of-the-year/editors-special-award-dr-mashudu-tshifularo-42840463. Accessed 13 Aug. 2020.

___, and Thabo Molishiwa. "What's Next? Q&A with UP's 3D-Printing Transplant Pioneer Professor Mashudu Tshifularo." Interview by Xolani Mathibela. *University of Pretoria*, 17 July 2019, www.up.ac.za/news/post_2825221-whats-next-qa-with-ups-3d-printing-transplant-pioneer-professor-mashudu-tshifularo. Accessed 10 July 2020.

Wabai, Yvonne. "Black South African Professor, Mashudu Tshifularo, Performs World's First 3D Middle-Ear Surgery." *African Exponent*, 28 Mar. 2019, www.africanexponent.com/post/9963-south-african-professor-who-is-also-a-pastor-performed-the-first-ever-3d-middle-ear-surgery. Accessed 10 July 2020.

—*Mari Rich*

Brendon Urie

Date of birth: April 12, 1987
Occupation: Singer-songwriter

Brendon Urie rose to international stardom as the front man of Panic! at the Disco, the emo-pop rock band he formed in high school with several friends. He also remained the band's one constant as other members came and went and its sound evolved, serving as the primary singer, songwriter, and musician. The changes in lineup did little to dent Panic!'s success, which included a pair of chart-topping studio albums, *Death of a Bachelor* (2016) and *Pray for the Wicked* (2018), on which Urie was the only official member.

Urie earned considerable acclaim for his abilities as a singer and showman, which was inspired by his love of a wide range of artists such as Frank Sinatra, Freddie Mercury of Queen, Led Zeppelin, Weezer, Sublime, A Tribe Called Quest, and Pearl Jam. The diversity of these influences greatly contributed to the eclectic musical style of Panic!, as did Urie's natural inclination as a performer. As he told Peter Robinson for the *Guardian* (28 July 2016), "I've always been comfortable in my own skin—sometimes a little too comfortable, which in turn makes other people uncomfortable. I have no qualms: no shame, no guilt, no embarrassment. I tend to act out a lot."

EARLY LIFE

Brendon Urie was born in St. George, Utah, on April 12, 1987. His family belonged to the Church of Jesus Christ of Latter-day Saints, also known as the Mormons. When he was about two years old, the family moved to Las Vegas, Nevada, an experience that would ultimately help define his musical career. "I can't give enough

Photo by Mauricio Santana/Getty Images

credit to Vegas," Urie recalled to Elisabeth Vincentelli for the *New York Times* (18 May 2017). "I was an eight-minute drive from the Strip, which is an interesting place, especially for me in a religious household. It wasn't a wholesome place. We'd go and see Cirque du Soleil and Blue Man Group. . . . There was an attraction to the theatricality of it. That was Panic! from the get-go: I wanted to dress up."

A love of music came to Urie early. There were always a number of instruments in his house, and he further experimented by building makeshift drum sets out of household items. "I always had something to jump to, to expel all of my nervous energy that I always had and still do to this day," he told Brittany Spanos for *Rolling Stone* (15 Jan. 2016). "It was just a way of trying to be creative and trying to let loose all this pent-up energy that I had." That energy would ultimately prove so disruptive in school that his parents took him to a child psychologist who diagnosed him with ADHD, depression, and anxiety. Urie was given medication to help control his symptoms, but during his last few years of high school he stopped taking it as he felt the drugs hampered his creativity. (A few years later, as he felt the pressures of his growing fame, he would return to taking his medication.)

When he was seventeen Urie declared to his parents that he did not believe in God and would not continue to attend their church. He was later kicked out of the family home, although he would eventually reconcile with his parents. Meanwhile, he had a different life planned out for himself.

FORMING PANIC! AT THE DISCO

In high school, where he was often bullied, Urie experimented with drugs, alcohol, and sex, while also continuing to explore his musical interests. In 2004 he formed a band with friends Spencer Smith on drums, Ryan Ross on guitar, and Brent Wilson on bass guitar. With Urie taking lead vocals as well as some guitar parts, they named themselves Panic! at the Disco. The group began posting songs online, crafted in an emo-pop style with a theatrical splash. Even before they had played a single show they drew the attention of Pete Wentz, a member of the popular emo band Fall Out Boy. Wentz signed Panic! as the first act on his Decaydance Records label.

Urie graduated from high school in 2005 and Panic! soon set out to record their first album. That summer the group had its first live performances and then began touring with Fall Out Boy and other bands on the Nintendo Fusion Tour. The tour proved immensely popular and continued through early 2006. The national exposure helped Panic!'s debut record, *A Fever You Can't Sweat Out* (2005), perform well. After a slow start, it hit number thirteen on the Billboard 200 US chart and would eventually sell more than two million copies. It also spawned a top-ten single, "I Write Sins Not Tragedies." However, the band proved somewhat polarizing, building a dedicated fanbase but also facing criticism for their theatrical sound and image as well as their internet-fueled rise to fame.

Almost as soon as they found success, Panic! began to evolve. In mid-2006 Wilson was fired from the group and replaced with Jon Walker. In 2008 the band released their second LP, *Pretty. Odd.*, which infused their emo-rock stylings with shades of psychedelic pop. Their sophomore record hit number two on the Billboard charts, but it also brought about further changes. In an interview with Lavanya Ramanathan for the *Washington Post* (23 Jan. 2014), Urie recalled, "When we started, we all wrote as a four-piece. By our second record there was a little bit of animosity, honestly. We all wanted to go in different directions, and no one could really compromise. It was a turning point." Urie recognized that while the group's lineup would likely change, he was invested in the band and wanted to step up his level of creative input.

Walker and Ross left the band in June 2009 to form their own group, the Young Veins. Urie and Smith then continued to perform as Panic! as a duo, with Dallon Weekes and Ian Crawford added as touring members. *Vices & Virtues*, the group's third studio album, was released in March 2011 and climbed to number seven in the United States. By the time their fourth record, *Too Weird to Live, Too Rare to Die!*, came out in 2011, Urie's influence over the songwriting had increased considerably, demonstrating his love of electronic music and hip-hop. Although Weekes was now a featured player in the studio, Panic! had really become more of Urie's project.

The rotation of band members continued. Dealing with substance abuse, Smith announced he was leaving the group's touring schedule in 2013; in 2015, he made his departure official and permanent. At the same time, Weekes returned to being a touring member only, leaving Urie as the sole full member of Panic! at the Disco.

SOLO EFFORTS

Urie's first record as the one and only member of Panic! came in 2016, with *Death of a Bachelor*. The record topped the charts in the United States and later earned a Grammy Award nomination for best rock album as well as double platinum certification. In a review of the album for the *New York Times* (13 Jan. 2016), Nate Chinen called Urie "a firecracker of a frontman, unafraid of strident commitment to a garish conceit."

Urie toured relentlessly to promote Panic!'s first number one record, supported by various musicians. He told Ramanathan that touring "brings me immense amounts of joy. I love performing for people. I love traveling, I love waking up in a new city every day. I love sleeping on a bus. I love being able to meet fans. To see fans singing your songs back to you is an indescribable thing." The 2017 tour also resulted in the release of the live album *All My Friends We're Glorious: Death of a Bachelor Tour Live* late that year.

Urie soon returned to the studio to compose Panic!'s next record, *Pray for the Wicked*, which came out in June 2018. Like its immediate predecessor, the album topped the US charts. It featured several singles, including "Say Amen (Saturday Night)," which was the band's first song to reach number one. *Pray for the Wicked* received mainly positive reviews, though like most of Panic!'s efforts it saw a fair amount of criticism as well. Many reviewers praised the theatrical elements of the music but some considered it ultimately lacking in depth. Despite often facing such critiques, Urie often declared his belief in following his creative impulses. "I think bands need to figure out what they want to do and wholeheartedly chase that dream," he told Beatrice Hazelhurst for *Paper* (6 July 2018). "Don't listen to other people: if you have a vision, do your vision."

BROADWAY AND OTHER PROJECTS

In addition to his work with Panic!, Urie also collaborated musically with artists such as Fall Out Boy, Travie McCoy, Dillon Francis, and Every Time I Die, among other performers. In 2019 he had a high-profile collaboration with pop superstar Taylor Swift, cowriting and contributing vocals to her single "ME!"

Urie also pushed his love of theater beyond its influence on his own music. In 2015 he penned a song, "Not a Simple Sponge," for the SpongeBob SquarePants musical. This foreshadowed his Broadway theatrical debut in 2017, playing the starring role of Charlie Price in *Kinky Boots*, the Tony Award–winning show with music and lyrics by Cyndi Lauper and a book by Harvey Fierstein. Urie portrayed Price for several months, an experience he found to be tremendously joyful. "Everybody is unnaturally kind," Urie noted at the time to Haley Weiss for *Interview* (12 June 2017). "Everybody is so happy to actually be there and make people feel a part of it."

Urie's other activities also included philanthropy. In 2018 he founded the Highest Hopes Foundation, a nonprofit aimed at helping marginalized communities and supporting causes dedicated to the protection of human rights.

PERSONAL LIFE

On April 27, 2013, Urie married Sarah Orzechowski, to whom he had been engaged since September 2011. The pair had met at a Panic! concert, and Orzechowski inspired the song "Sarah Smiles" on *Vices & Virtues*. Although he noted he was primarily attracted to women, Urie stated that he had had sexual experiences with men, and he earned much media and fan attention regarding his sexuality. He at times described himself as pansexual, and was seen as an inspirational figure by many in the LGBTQ community.

Urie also made a point of being open about his struggles with mental health. He told interviewers that he often struggled with anxiety and did not enjoy being in large crowds. He told Spanos that he also has a form of synesthesia, sometimes associating sounds with certain colors, words, shapes, or other concepts.

SUGGESTED READING

Chinen, Nate. Review of *Death of a Bachelor*, by Panic! at the Disco. *The New York Times*, 13 Jan. 2016, www.nytimes.com/2016/01/14/arts/music/review-death-of-a-bachelor-from-panic-at-the-disco.html. Accessed 13 Dec. 2019.

Urie, Brendon. "Brendon Urie: 'Everybody Wanted Out from Panic! at the Disco.'" Interview by Peter Robinson. *The Guardian*, 28 July 2016, www.theguardian.com/culture/2016/jul/28/brendon-urie-panic-at-the-disco-home-naked-a-lot. Accessed 13 Dec. 2019.

———. "Brendon Urie Lays It All Out." Interview by Beatrice Hazelhurst. *Paper*, 6 July 2018, www.papermag.com/brendon-urie-lays-it-all-out-2584081623.html. Accessed 17 Dec. 2019.

———. "Brendon Urie and Panic! at the Disco's Cool, Calm, Reinvention." Interview by Lavanya Ramanathan. *The Washington Post*, 23 Jan. 2014, www.washingtonpost.com/going-outguide/music/brendon-urie-and-panic-at-the-discos-cool-calm-reinvention/2014/01/22/673b82f2-82b2-11e3-9dd4-e7278db80d86_story.html. Accessed 11 Dec. 2019.

———. "Brendon Urie Steps Away from the Disco and into 'Kinky Boots.'" Interview by Elisabeth Vincentelli. *The New York Times*, 18 May 2017, www.nytimes.com/2017/05/18/theater/brendon-urie-steps-away-from-the-disco-and-into-kinky-boots.html. Accessed 17 Dec. 2019.

———. "Panic! at the Disco's Brendon Urie: Band Is 'Outlet for Nonchalant Chaos.'" Interview by Brittany Spanos. *Rolling Stone*, 15 Jan. 2016, www.rollingstone.com/music/music-features/

panic-at-the-discos-brendon-urie-band-is-outlet-for-nonchalant-chaos-188429/. Accessed 11 Dec. 2019.

Weiss, Haley. "Brendon Urie." *Interview*, 12 June 2017, www.interviewmagazine.com/music/brendon-urie-kinky-boots. Accessed 11 Dec. 2019.

SELECTED WORKS
A Fever You Can't Sweat Out, 2005; *Pretty. Odd.*, 2008; *Vices & Virtues*, 2011; *Too Weird to Live, Too Rare to Die!*, 2013; *Death of a Bachelor*, 2016; *Pray for the Wicked*, 2018

—*Christopher Mari*

Mirna Valerio

Date of birth: October 15, 1975
Occupation: Runner and activist

Mirna Valerio made a name for herself as a distance runner while challenging preconceived notions of what an athlete looks like. At a weight of about 250 pounds, her body type is not what most expect a runner's to be, but she became a prolific and dedicated participant in marathons and ultramarathons. (The latter refer to any race longer than the approximately twenty-six miles of a standard marathon). Valerio told John Brant for *Runner's World* (20 June 2018) that she ran twenty-five miles a week when she was not training for an event and thirty-five miles when she was training.

In 2011 Valerio started a blog, *Fat Girl Running*, to document her experiences. The blog acquired a devoted following and eventually garnered mainstream media attention, which led her to a career as a writer and speaker advocating for the world of sports to be more inclusive of people with diverse body types. In recognition of these efforts, *National Geographic* named her one of its Adventurers of the Year in 2018.

EARLY LIFE AND EDUCATION
Mirna Valerio was born on October 15, 1975. She was one of four children and grew up in the Bushwick neighborhood of Brooklyn in New York City. She was raised by her mother and stepfather; her father, a merchant seaman from Honduras, was away for long periods due to his job but wrote letters regularly.

Valerio's family took education seriously. Her mother strictly enforced homework time every evening, and her stepfather brought home medical textbooks from the hospital where he worked as part of the cleaning staff. Inspired by these textbooks as well as her mother's struggles with type 2 diabetes, Valerio dreamt of becoming a

doctor. She spent her elementary school years in her public school's classes for gifted and talented students and, upon entering middle school, was selected for a program called Prep 9. Prep 9 was designed to help exceptional students from low-income backgrounds gain admission to prestigious private high schools.

With the support of the teachers in the Prep 9 program, Valerio earned a spot at the all-girls' Masters School in Westchester, New York. There she discovered two new passions. First, she joined the field hockey team. Never having played sports before, she struggled at first, but motivated by her enjoyment of the game, she was determined to improve. Though she was young, she already possessed the dedication and discipline that marked her later career as a runner, deciding to rise at dawn every day to run extra laps around campus. "Though she liked team sports, these runs," she told Gulnaz Khan for *National Geographic* (1 Mar. 2018), "held a special appeal. I'm an introvert by nature, so it was a way for me to start the day on my own using my body and just get my blood flowing."

Then, Valerio, who had never had formal music training, auditioned for the school's glee club and discovered that she possessed a gift for singing. She told Brant that, as she recalled it, the director stopped the audition after two minutes and said, "In 25 years of teaching, I have never heard a soprano voice like that." Teachers encouraged her to audition for the Juilliard School's precollege program, which prepared students to enter the prestigious performing arts academy once they graduated high school. She succeeded and, for the next several years, took the train back into New York City—a two-hour journey—every weekend to attend classes at Juilliard.

However, after high school, Valerio decided not to attend Juilliard. "I had a lot of interests besides music," she told Brant. "If I had just pursued singing, I wouldn't have been happy." Instead she accepted a scholarship to Oberlin College. There she could study liberal arts along with music. Though she remained active, she could not participate in sports at Oberlin because the practices conflicted with her commitment to the college choir.

EARLY CAREER
After graduating from Oberlin, Valerio went to work for the audit, tax, and consulting firm KPMG in New York City. In her spare time she continued to perform in choirs and took up running road races, enrolling in an eight-week running course to hone her skills. "I wasn't doing it to lose weight or anything, at that point anyway," she told Krista Soriano for *Elle* magazine (18 Oct. 2017). "My goal was only to run, and it just became part of my existence."

Valerio ultimately found she did not enjoy working in the corporate world and began to look for an opportunity to change careers. She found that opportunity at the Masters School, her old high school, which was in need of a music teacher. Valerio took the position and soon found that she enjoyed teaching. "After my third day I was hooked," she told Brant. She went on to hold teaching positions at private schools in Maryland, New Jersey, and Georgia.

REDISCOVERING RUNNING

Though she loved teaching, Valerio found that it left her with little time to herself, especially as she often needed to supplement her salary by giving private music lessons on weekends. Her involvement in athletics thus fell by the wayside. She could tell that her health was worsening as a result but lacked the energy to try to address the problem.

In 2008, she learned that she had developed extensive arterial inflammation. "Combined with my weight, it wasn't a question of if I'd have a coronary or stroke, but when," she told Brant. Realizing that she had to make a drastic change in her life, Valerio got in touch with a coworker, Nikki Bucello, who also wanted to lose weight. The two embarked on an intense program of daily exercise over the school's summer vacation.

One day during that summer, Valerio, remembering the road races that she had enjoyed in New York, signed herself and Bucello up for a local 5K race taking place later that evening—much to Bucello's surprise. The race went reasonably well, and the two began running at least one 5K every week. This, however, was not enough for Valerio. "Mirna has a gift for running long distances," Bucello told Brant. "She doesn't start to feel good until she's covered five or ten miles." Valerio began running 10K races, then signed up for her longest run yet, a fifteen-mile trail race. To her disappointment, however, the race was canceled due to inclement weather. Undaunted, she convinced Bucello to meet her the next morning so the two could run fifteen miles on their own. "She was so excited about getting that run in that I did my best to suffer in silence," Bucello told Brant.

LONGER DISTANCES

In 2011 Valerio started training for her first marathon, the Marine Corps Marathon in Washington, DC. During this training period, she started her blog, *Fat Girl Running*, and regularly documented her progress—which, after months of effort, hit an unexpected snag. Two months before the race date, Valerio fractured her ankle. She was determined to keep at it, however. With the help of an orthopedist, she developed a training regimen that would not exacerbate her injury,

and two months later she did indeed complete the marathon.

Valerio enjoyed the marathon, but she wanted to push the limits of her endurance even further. To this end, she became involved in ultramarathons and in trail running, which involves running on trails through the mountains. By 2018, she had completed nine ultramarathons and ten marathons.

Valerio's times were not especially fast. She finished most races squarely in the middle of the pack. However, she was at peace with the likelihood of never being one of the faster people in the race. In her memoir, *A Beautiful Work in Progress* (2017), she wrote, "There is still a beauty about simply doing the difficult thing that I will never be good at, for the pure pleasure of having engaged in the process."

FAME AND ACTIVISM

Valerio's rise to celebrity status was as gradual and steady as her running style. Over the course of about four years, her blog and associated Instagram account built up a big enough following that mainstream outlets began to take notice. In 2015, she was profiled in *Runner's World*. By 2016, it was clear that she had arrived. That year she was profiled on CNN, became a brand ambassador for the high-end sportswear brand Merrell, and secured a book deal for her memoir. The following year she was the subject of a documentary short film, *The Mirnavator*, sponsored by the outfitter REI, and appeared on the cover of the September issue of *Women's Running*.

Being in the spotlight brought Valerio many admirers, but also insults and mockery regarding her weight. "People are really having trouble grappling with the idea that fit comes in many forms and that people can still participate in athletics no matter what kind of body they have," she told Khan. She also told Khan that she thought there was "some inherent racism and sexism going on"—her detractors, she felt, had particular trouble accepting a plus-sized athlete who was a Black woman. Rather than being discouraged, however, Valerio used her newfound platform to promote inclusivity in running and other sports, writing articles for a variety of outlets and traveling the country to offer workshops and presentations on diversity, equity, and inclusion. "This is really an extension of what I do as a teacher, which is demonstrating and being a role model," she told Mason Adams for *Blue Ridge Outdoors* (19 July 2017). Many articles about Valerio note her enthusiasm in trying to convince people that she knows personally—students, coworkers, friends, neighbors, and even strangers she encounters while training—to try running.

In 2018, Valerio was invited to run the Boston Marathon as part of a team of teachers from around the country. She accepted, partly because it was a good opportunity to promote her message that athletics are for everyone, and partly because the prestigious race usually requires runners to have exceptionally fast times in order to qualify. "I don't know that I'll have the opportunity again," she joked to Kelly O'Mara for *ESPN* (12 Apr. 2018). "I'm slow as h——."

Ultimately, throughout her career, Valerio has focused on one consistent, simple message: "Everyone, regardless of their body type, age, race, gender, ability level, or any other characteristics, can benefit from exercise, and everyone deserves to be able to exercise in the way they enjoy most without censure." "I wanted to show people that if you want to run in whatever body you have, you can do it," she told Adams. "And you are entitled to exercise out in public as you are." Or, as she put it more succinctly to Soriano: "If you have two legs, and they work, you can run!"

PERSONAL LIFE

Valerio met her husband, Cito Nikiema, while working for KPMG in New York. They had a son, Rashid, and settled in Georgia.

SUGGESTED READING

Adams, Mason. "Fat Girl Running: Mirna Valerio Is Out with a New Book." *Blue Ridge Outdoors*, 19 July 2017, www.blueridgeoutdoors.com/go-outside/fat-girl-running. Accessed 8 July 2020.

Brant, John. "Ultra: Mirna Valerio." *Runner's World*, 20 June 2018, www.runnersworld.com/runners-stories/a21070665/ultra. Accessed 8 July 2020.

Khan, Gulnaz. "This Ultramarathon Runner Is Redefining What an Athlete Looks Like." *National Geographic*, 1 Mar. 2018, www.nationalgeographic.com/adventure/features/adventurers-of-the-year/2018/mirna-valerio-ultramarathon-runner/. Accessed 8 July 2020.

O'Mara, Kelly. "Mirna Valerio Redefines What a Distance Runner 'Should' Look Like." *ESPN*, 12 Apr. 2018, www.espn.com/espnw/life-style/story/_/id/23137173/mirna-valerio-redefines-distance-runner-look-like. Accessed 8 July 2020.

Valerio, Mirna. *A Beautiful Work in Progress.* Grand Harbor P, 2017.

———. "Mirna Valerio Is Not Here to Be Your Before-and-After Inspiration." Interview by Krista Soriano. *Elle*, 18 Oct. 2017, www.elle.com/life-love/a12837615/mirna-valerio-interview. Accessed 8 July 2020.

Valerio, Mirna. "REI Presents: The Mirnavator." *REI Co-op*, Sept. 2017, www.rei.com/blog/run/rei-presents-the-mirnavator. Accessed 8 July 2020.

—*Emma Joyce*

Ivo van Hove

Date of birth: October 28, 1958
Occupation: Theater director

Ivo van Hove is a Tony Award–winning Belgian theater director best known for his avant-garde interpretations of classic plays. He is also a rare experimental theater director who has found mainstream success both in Europe and the United States. One of his earliest New York productions, Tennessee Williams's *A Streetcar Named Desire* in 1999, was staged around an enormous claw foot bathtub, while his 2015 Broadway debut, Arthur Miller's kitchen-sink drama *A View from the Bridge*, was set in a stylized boxing ring devoid of props. As the longtime artistic director of the Toneelgroep Amsterdam, van Hove has also produced plays like *Roman Tragedies* (2007) and *Kings of War* (2015) that condense and combine various Shakespearean plays in contemporary settings. His more recent works, like *Network* (2017), based on the 1976 film, utilize cameras and screens in an effort to capture modern life on the stage. Van Hove's consistently bold choices—some celebrated, other fiercely derided—are aimed at emphasizing a given play's most elemental themes. Though he often works with twentieth-century

Photo by Michiel Hendryckx via Wikimedia Commons

material, his sensibilities lie with the ancient Greeks.

EARLY LIFE AND EDUCATION

Van Hove was born on October 28, 1958, in Heist-op-den-Berg, Belgium. Growing up in a rural village, his neighbors were farmers and coal miners, but van Hove's father was the village's pharmacist. "In such a small community, that is considered as being of the higher class," van Hove told Rebecca Mead for the *New Yorker* (19 Oct. 2015). Van Hove began attending boarding school when he was eleven. After three weeks of intense homesickness, the experience became, he told Mead, "the best time of my life." He discovered theater. "We would work on a play that we would present at the end of the year," he told Mead. "It felt like the boarding school was a walled world within the world, and the theatre was another walled world within it. That felt so warm, so good."

After boarding school, van Hove, in accordance with his parents' wishes, attended law school. For two years, he took introductory classes in philosophy, psychology, and American law. To his parents' chagrin, he quit in his third year, transferring to an Antwerp arts school where he studied directing.

In Antwerp, van Hove began to develop his own theatrical philosophy, inspired by Antonin Artaud, a drama theorist and major figure of the early European avant garde, and the pioneering US experimental theater company the Wooster Group. "There was video, there was dancing," van Hove told Mead of the Wooster Group's production of *Point Judith*, a performance based on Eugene O'Neill's *Long Day's Journey into Night*, in 1981. "It was a totally new attitude toward theatre." Around the same time, van Hove met set and lighting designer Jan Versweyveld in a modern dance class; the two would become longtime artistic collaborators and romantic partners.

EARLY WORKS

In 1981 van Hove and Versweyveld produced his own play, *Geruchten* (*Rumors*). Based in part on his own family's experience with his younger brother, who as a teen had been diagnosed with schizophrenia, the piece follows a man who might have schizophrenia interacting with doctors and other characters. The play was staged in an abandoned laundry facility. David Willinger, a theater instructor at New York's City College, recalled to Mead: "I didn't know Flemish, but it didn't matter—I walked out saying, 'This is one of the best things I've ever seen.'" In 1982 van Hove wrote and produced another play, titled *Disease Germs*.

Despite the underground success of these plays, van Hove made a fortuitous decision. He stopped writing plays and turned to the work of other, often much older, playwrights. "I discovered I could make much more personal work through the filter of a text by Shakespeare that was four hundred years old—that it was much more directly about me, and about my life," he told Mead. In 1987 he directed his first Shakespearean play, *Macbeth*, as well as a memorable production of Euripides's *The Bacchae*, in which Dionysius, the god of wine and pleasure, appears completely nude. At one performance, van Hove's parents approached a well-known Dutch critic at intermission, expressing embarrassment at their son's outlandish vision. The critic, as quoted by Mead, said, "There was no need to be ashamed. . . . They could be proud of what their son was doing, because he was a little genius." In 1990 van Hove was named the director of Het Zuidelijk Toneel.

NEW YORK THEATRE WORKSHOP

In the mid-1990s Jim Nicola, the artistic director of the Off-Broadway New York Theatre Workshop (NYTW), heard about van Hove's work. Nicola later told Howard Sherman for *The Stage* (24 June 2019) that videos of van Hove's productions of American classics like O'Neill's *Mourning Becomes Electra* and *Desire under the Elms* "knocked me out." Nicola invited van Hove to mount his productions in New York with American actors. In 1997 van Hove made his New York debut with a production of O'Neill's unfinished drama *More Stately Mansions*. Critics struggled with the dense, three-hour performance. Ben Brantley for the *New York Times* (8 Oct. 1997) wrote that van Hove's attempt to stage the unwieldy, naturalistic piece as a "formal tone poem" fell disappointingly flat. Still, van Hove received a 1998 Obie Award for best Off-Broadway director for his work on the production.

In 1998 van Hove returned to NYTW to direct Tennessee Williams's classic *A Streetcar Named Desire*. He staged the play around a clawfoot tub full of water, which appeared in nearly every scene. Critics from the *New York Times* and *Variety* derisively dubbed the production "A Bathtub Named Desire," but it left an indelible impression on New York audiences. The piece was criticized for its crude overemphasis of Williams's script, though actor Elizabeth Marvel, who played Blanche DuBois, was universally praised for her performance. Marvel became a favored member of van Hove's New York–based productions.

In 2000 van Hove directed writer Susan Sontag's fantastical play, *Alice in Bed*, for NYTW. He staged it so that the title character, Alice James (played by Joan McIntosh), spent most of the play uncomfortably contorted on a specially built chaise longue. In 2004 he directed the NYTW production of Henrik Ibsen's *Hedda Gabler*.

Unlike *Streetcar*, critics eagerly embraced van Hove's stylized deconstruction of the realist classic. Charles Isherwood described it in the *New York Times* (22 Sept. 2004) as a "refreshingly daring revival" in which van Hove used "Ibsen's text as a mirror to reflect a contemporary culture in which isolation, self-absorption and a need to instantly satisfy emotional whims are the norm." NYTW's *Hedda Gabler* earned four Obie Awards, including van Hove's second Obie, for best direction.

TONEELGROEP AMSTERDAM

In 2001 van Hove was named director of the Toneelgroep Amsterdam, the largest repertory theater in the Netherlands. During the company's 2006–07 season, van Hove staged *Roman Tragedies*, a six-hour, Dutch-language performance by van Hove and Versweyveld that condensed and combined Shakespeare's plays *Coriolanus*, *Julius Caesar*, and *Antony and Cleopatra*. The production went on to travel all over the world. In 2008 van Hove staged *Angels in America*, Tony Kushner's sprawling epic set during the height of the AIDs epidemic in New York. The play calls for a number of set pieces, and its climax features an angel breaking through the ceiling and descending to the stage; van Hove, by contrast, staged the production with only a record player, an intravenous drip, and a soft-spoken nurse wearing scrubs as the angel.

Van Hove has also adapted a number of films and television productions for the stage, including Ingmar Bergman's *Cries and Whispers* in 2009. In one scene, van Hove directed actor Chris Nietvelt to portray a dying character by flinging herself across the stage and smearing her body with blue paint. Nietvelt, a longtime member of van Hove's ensemble, told Mead: "We go very far, physically, mentally. But that is the way we want to make theatre. It is what we call, in Dutch, *waarachtig*. It means something that's not true but feels so true that you believe it. And that truthfulness can also be conveyed by your body." She added, "I never fall on my knees in normal life. I fell on my knees, I think, five hundred times for Ivo."

BROADWAY DEBUT

In 2014 the Young Vic theater in London, England, asked van Hove to stage a production of Arthur Miller's *A View from the Bridge* (1956), a tragedy about a Brooklyn longshoreman in the 1950s. Van Hove was hesitant. The play was meticulously structured, leaving little room for him to play. He ultimately accepted the job, recognizing elements of his own village upbringing in the struggles of Italian immigrants in the play. Van Hove staged the production in an enclosed space meant to serve as the footprint of the family's row house, though it more closely resembled

a boxing ring. Critics praised van Hove's choice to emphasize the play's moments of intense physicality. In 2015 the production moved to the West End, where it received rapturous reviews and earned three Laurence Olivier Awards, including a best-director award for van Hove.

Van Hove's production opened as his Broadway debut in November 2015. In an effusive review for the *New York Times* (12 Nov. 2015), Brantley wrote that van Hove's staging evokes classical Greek tragedy. "This must be what Greek tragedy once felt like, when people went to the theater in search of catharsis," he wrote. "At the end of its uninterrupted two hours, you are wrung out, scooped out and so exhausted that you're wide awake. You also feel ridiculously blessed to have been a witness to the terrible events you just saw." Van Hove won a Tony Award, an Outer Critics Circle Award, and a Drama Desk Award for his directing.

LAZARUS, THE CRUCIBLE, AND *NETWORK*

It is rare for van Hove to stage new work, but he directed *Lazarus*, a play by Irish playwright Enda Walsh and rock-and-roll superstar David Bowie, which opened in New York in late 2015. The NYTW show included songs from Bowie's final album, *Blackstar*, which was released on his next birthday, January 8, 2016; the iconic singer died of cancer two days later.

Later in 2016 van Hove directed a Broadway revival of Miller's *The Crucible* (1953), a parable set during the Salem witch trials. "I want to make you *believe*" that the young girls in the play are possessed by witches, van Hove told Mead before rehearsals began. Indeed, when the play premiered in March 2016, Brantley wrote that the oft-revived drama felt "like the freshest, scariest play in town."

In 2017 van Hove directed the play *Network* at the Royal National Theatre in London. Adapted from Paddy Chayefsky's 1976 film by Lee Hall, *Network* satirizes the American culture of corporate greed and news as entertainment. Van Hove's production starred Emmy Award–winning actor Bryan Cranston and transferred to Broadway in 2018. *Network* was an unusually immersive production, with multiple cameras projecting various angles of the stage action on screens—an exaggeration of the television studio set. A select few audience members paid for the privilege of dining at the onstage restaurant—while the play went on around them. Van Hove was nominated for a 2019 Tony Award for best director for his production of *Network*.

SUGGESTED READING

Brantley, Ben. "Review: 'A View from the Bridge' Bears Witness to the Pain of Fate." Review of *A View from the Bridge*, directed by Ivo van Hove. *The New York Times*, 12

Nov. 2015, www.nytimes.com/2015/11/13/theater/review-a-view-from-the-bridge-bears-witness-to-the-pain-of-fate.html. Accessed 7 Feb. 2020.

——. "Review: In Arthur Miller's 'Crucible,' First They Came for the Witches." Review of *The Crucible*, directed by Ivo van Hove. *The New York Times*, 31 Mar. 2016, www.nytimes.com/2016/04/01/theater/review-in-arthur-millers-crucible-first-they-came-for-the-witches.html. Accessed 7 Feb. 2020.

——. "Talk, Talk, Talk: O'Neill in the Raw." Review of *More Stately Mansions*, directed by Ivo van Hove. *The New York Times*, 8 Oct. 1997, www.nytimes.com/1997/10/08/theater/theater-review-talk-talk-talk-o-neill-in-the-raw.html. Accessed 6 Feb. 2020.

Isherwood, Charles. "A Hedda for Self-Absorbed Modern Times." Review of *Hedda Gabler*, directed by Ivo van Hove. *The New York Times*, 22 Sept. 2004, www.nytimes.com/2004/09/22/theater/reviews/a-hedda-for-selfabsorbed-modern-times.html. Accessed 6 Feb. 2020.

"Ivo van Hove." *Toneelgroep Amsterdam*, 2020, tga.nl/en/employees/ivo-van-hove. Accessed 17 Feb. 2020.

Mead, Rebecca. "Theatre Laid Bare." *The New Yorker*, 19 Oct. 2015, www.newyorker.com/magazine/2015/10/26/theatre-laid-bare. Accessed 6 Feb. 2020.

Sherman, Howard. "New York Theatre Workshop Artistic Director James Nicola: 'The Stakes Are Higher Than Ever for the Artistic Community.'" *The Stage*, 24 June 2019, www.thestage.co.uk/features/interviews/2019/new-york-theatre-workshop-artistic-director-james-nicola-the-stakes-are-higher-than-ever-for-the-artistic-community/. Accessed 6 Feb. 2020.

SELECTED WORKS

Geruchten (*Rumors*), 1981; *A Streetcar Named Desire*, 1998; *Hedda Gabler*, 2004; *Roman Tragedies*, 2006; *A View from the Bridge*, 2014; *Network*, 2017

—*Molly Hagan*

Victor Vescovo

Born: February 10, 1966
Occupation: Investor and undersea explorer

By early 2020, Victor Vescovo could check off a list of several career and personal accomplishments he had achieved in his life. He had served for approximately twenty years as an intelligence officer in the US Navy Reserve, made a fortune

Photo by Richard Varcoe on behalf of Caladan Oceanic LLC

in private equity, climbed the highest mountains in each of the seven continents, skied at least one hundred kilometers (about sixty-two miles) to both the North Pole and the South Pole and had become the first person to reach the deepest known points in the Earth's five named oceans. Many people might be able to check off some of these categories. However, while numerous individuals had served with distinction in the armed forces or had acquired fortunes by that point, fewer had scaled the seven continents' highest mountains or traveled to the poles, and far fewer had done both. As of early 2020, only one person, Vescovo, had done all of these things *and* plumbed the greatest depths of all of the planet's oceans.

To make his record-setting diving dreams possible, Vescovo dedicated millions of dollars of his personal fortune to commissioning a cutting-edge submersible, the *Limiting Factor*; retrofitting a ship, the *Pressure Drop*, to ferry the sub, himself, and his crew around the world; and buying state-of-the-art sonar to chart the depths. When he completed his goal to reach the deepest parts of the five oceans in 2019, he offered to contribute charting data he and his team had amassed to ongoing efforts to map the Earth's entire underwater terrain. When considering the increased fame that this project resulted in and his motivation behind his adventures, Vescovo has often explained that he particularly considered the ocean exploration important work in advancing human life and knowledge and was not concerned about notoriety. "I'm not on Facebook or Instagram. I really do not care about celebrity," he said to Matt Goodman for the Dallas, Texas, magazine *D* (Feb. 2020). "I do this to do the thing. It's almost like people don't understand that anymore."

EARLY LIFE AND EDUCATION

Victor Lance Vescovo was born on February 10, 1966, and raised in Dallas, Texas. His father, who worked in commercial real estate, and his mother, who was a nurse, divorced when he was about sixteen. Later, he would indicate that if he could point to a single instance that formed the basis of his daredevil lifestyle and philosophy of living life to the fullest, it came early on, at age three, when he got into the family car, shifted it into neutral, and crashed it into a tree. The accident left him with lasting physical damage in his hand after he had spent time in the hospital recovering from injuries such as a fractured skull and some broken ribs. He told Susan Casey for *Outside* (22 Oct. 2019), "I realized that every day is precious, and you may not get another one—best make full use of them." A sense of exploration also came to Vescovo early, in part through the science fiction he devoured growing up. Particularly loving Jules Verne's books, including the nineteenth-century classic novel *20,000 Leagues Under the Sea*, he was also fond of any reading or activity that involved maps.

After graduating from St. Mark's School of Texas in 1984, and having had to give up on the idea of flying fighter jets as his vision had not measured up (though he still learned to fly), Vescovo earned a bachelor's degree as a double major in political science and economics from Stanford University, which he attended from 1984 to 1987. He then studied defense and arms control at the Massachusetts Institute of Technology (MIT) from 1987 to 1988, where he received a master's degree. During this late period of the Cold War (1947–91), he focused on military history and modern methods of ground and aerial combat as well as how to mathematically model armed conflict. Following two years at the institution, Vescovo completed his formal education at Harvard Business School in 1994, leaving with a master of business administration (MBA).

CONCURRENT NAVAL AND BUSINESS CAREERS

Beginning in 1993, Vescovo served in the US Navy Reserve as an intelligence officer, sparking a lingering fascination with the sea. Before retiring as a commander in 2013, he served in various capacities across the world and made use of his proficiency in multiple languages such as Arabic. In 1997, he was an assistant targeting officer, creating strategies for Carrier Air Wing Nine. From 1998 to 2000, he was an intelligence instructor at the Naval Strike and Air Warfare Center. Meanwhile, he worked at the staff level

in combat operations for Operation Allied Force in Kosovo and Serbia in 1999. He participated in a similar capacity regarding counterterrorism from 2001 to 2002 during the US–led invasion of Afghanistan following the terrorist attacks on September 11, 2001. Additionally, he took part in military exercises along the Pacific Rim.

While serving in the Navy Reserve, Vescovo was also building a successful career in business. In the beginning of the 1990s he was involved in mergers and acquisitions with the company Lehman Brothers. From June 1994 to September 1999, he worked his way up to become a manager of Bain & Company at the consulting firm's Dallas office, where he specialized in operational improvements and merger integration with such clients as Continental Airlines and Lockheed Martin. Between January 2000 and October 2001, he was the vice president of product management and development for Military Advantage, overseeing the digital products and interfaces of its website *Military.com*. Finding a particular strength in private equity, he became a managing partner and cofounder in 2002 of Insight Equity, a company dedicated to investing in operational improvements to create value for and turn around underperforming companies in a variety of industries. It has been through his role at this private equity investment firm that he has made most of his fortune.

LAND ADVENTURES AND BEGINNING THE FIVE DEEPS EXPEDITION

When he had time, Vescovo found himself more passionately drawn to adventure, earning a piloting license and laying the foundation for a serious climbing passion starting around 1988. It was in that year, by summiting Africa's Mount Kilimanjaro, that he made the first big step in completing the vaunted "Explorers Grand Slam," which includes climbing the highest mountain on every continent and skiing at least one hundred kilometers (about sixty-two miles) to both the North and South poles. He completed this ambitious project in April 2017, which included climbing to the top of Asia's Mount Everest, the tallest mountain above sea level in the world, in 2010. In doing so, he became only the twelfth American in recorded history as of 2017 to accomplish the grand slam.

Despite finishing such a massive achievement, Vescovo had been seeking to do something no one had ever done before. Switching gears to focus on exploring the lower regions of the Earth, an idea had already been forming in his mind—to dive to the deepest known point in each of the Earth's five named oceans: the Atlantic, the Pacific, the Indian, the Southern, and the Artic. Furthermore, he planned to make each of the deepest dives solo.

To do that, however, he needed to commission the construction of a technologically advanced submersible capable of traveling up to nearly seven miles below the surface. Eventually, he found the right builders in Triton Submarines, whose team, over a period of several years, planned, built, and tested the *Limiting Factor*, a two-person sub with a titanium pressure hull nine centimeters (approximately three inches) thick. It is capable of withstanding crushing ocean depths of up to one thousand bars and was designed to be reused. In discussing the importance of *Limiting Factor*, Vescovo explained to David Biello in an interview conducted at TED2019 (Apr. 2019): "This tool is a door, because with this tool, we'll be able to make more of them potentially and take scientists down to do thousands of dives, to open that door to exploration and find things that we had no idea even existed." He additionally refitted a ship called the *Pressure Drop* that could ferry the sub and his hired crew to various points around the globe as part of what was called the Five Deeps Expedition. To take full advantage of these dives, he also purchased a highly sophisticated sonar system capable of mapping any undersea terrain he chose to visit. For the purposes of preparation, he practiced dives using a simulator installed in his garage at home.

ACCOMPLISHING A GOAL AND ADVANCING OCEAN EXPLORATION

Vescovo completed the first leg of the Five Deeps Expedition in December 2018, when he reached the deepest point of the Atlantic Ocean in the Puerto Rico Trench. The second phase saw him diving into the South Sandwich Trench in February 2019, at the bottom of the Southern Ocean. Then, in April 2019, he piloted his sub to the bottom of the Indian Ocean's Java Trench.

Vescovo's next and fourth dive, to the bottom of the Challenger Deep in the Pacific Ocean's Mariana Trench, completed in late April 2019, was his deepest and most ambitious. The Challenger Deep had been explored just twice before, in 1960, by Lt. Don Walsh of the US Navy and Swiss engineer Jacques Piccard, then again in 2012, by filmmaker James Cameron. Vescovo and his team then made historic additional dives to the Challenger Deep as well as one to the Sirena Deep into the first week of May, which resulted in the observance of a potentially new species of amphipod, a spoon worm, and a snailfish. They also reported finding indications that what seemed to be human-made waste, possibly plastic, had reached the depths. "It is almost indescribable how excited all of us are about achieving what we just did," Vescovo declared after his dives to the Challenger Deep, as quoted by Rebecca Morelle for *BBC News* (13 May 2019). "This submarine and its mother ship, along with its extraordinarily talented expedition team, took marine technology to a ridiculously higher new level by diving—rapidly and repeatedly—into the deepest, harshest, area of the ocean."

In August 2019, Vescovo completed the fifth and final dive of the expedition, when he reached the bottom of the Arctic Ocean's Molloy Deep. Upon this successful conclusion, in which he became the first person to have reached the lowest point in each of the five oceans, he expressed pride at what he and his team had accomplished as well as hopes that it had paved a path for further ocean exploration, science, and technology.

FURTHER EXPEDITIONS

Following the end of Five Deeps, Vescovo continued to voice his belief that a more detailed exploration of the oceans—with a complete mapping of its underwater terrain, an endeavor that he hoped sonar data collected from his dives could help with—would provide unparalleled insights into the planet, its natural phenomena, and the origins of life. "Many scientists believe that the oceans can show us new species of life with unique biochemistries that could unlock new materials or medicines," Vescovo said to Hannah Osborne for *Newsweek* (13 May 2019). "Understanding how life exists in these extreme depths can also help us understand how life originated on Earth and how it could develop on other planets."

In addition to spurring scientific study, Vescovo sought to continue his own personal explorations as well, even mentioning a desire to travel into space one day. By March 2020, he had made dives to explore the depths of the Mediterranean Sea and the Red Sea. Having visited the remains of the *Titanic* in 2019, his plans involved visiting other famous shipwrecks, including those dating back to World War II, such as the USS *Indianapolis* and the USS *Johnston*.

PERSONAL LIFE

When not out on explorative expeditions, Vescovo resides in Dallas with his partner of many years.

SUGGESTED READING

Casey, Susan. "One Man's Wild Quest to Reach the Bottom of Every Ocean." *Outside*, 22 Oct. 2019, www.outsideonline.com/2403988/victor-vescovo-five-deeps. Accessed 30 Apr. 2020.

Goodman, Matt. "Into the Deep." *D* [Dallas, TX], Feb. 2020, www.dmagazine.com/publications/d-magazine/2020/february/victor-vescovo-five-deeps-expedition-dallas-mariana-trench/. Accessed 28 Apr. 2020.

Morelle, Rebecca. "Mariana Trench: Deepest-Ever Sub Dive Finds Plastic Bag." *BBC News*, 13 May 2019, www.bbc.com/news/

science-environment-48230157. Accessed 30 Apr. 2020.

Osborne, Hannah. "Meet Victor Vescovo, Who Just Broke the World Record by Diving 35,853 Feet into the Deepest Part of the Ocean." *Newsweek*, 13 May 2019, www.newsweek.com/victor-vescovo-record-deepest-dive-mariana-trench-1423586. Accessed 30 Apr. 2020.

Vescovo, Victor. "What's at the Bottom of the Ocean—and How We're Getting There." Interview by David Biello. *TED*, Apr. 2019, www.ted.com/talks/victor_vescovo_what_s_at_the_bottom_of_the_ocean_and_how_we_re_getting_there/transcript. Transcript. Accessed 14 May 2020.

"Victor L. Vescovo." *Insight Equity*, www.insight-equity.com/team/victor-l-vescovo/. Accessed 30 Apr. 2020.

—*Christopher Mari*

Magali Villeneuve

Date of birth: 1980
Occupation: Illustrator and artist

"Every current Magic player, whether they realized it at the time or not, has probably taken a moment to admire the art of Magali Villeneuve during a game," Nicholas Wolfram wrote in a piece for the official website of the fantasy-based card game Magic: The Gathering (29 Aug. 2017). "Magali's art [has] made an immediate and noticeable impact within the community. Her strong sense of portraiture combined with a deliberate, dramatic use of lighting and striking poses makes for iconic art." Indeed, Villeneuve's artistic skill made her a highly popular illustrator not only for the Magic brand, but also across broader fantasy and science fiction circles. Along with other trading card games, she provided acclaimed art for books, calendars, and other items from such licensed franchises as *The Lord of the Rings*, *A Song of Ice and Fire* (the basis for the hit television show *Game of Thrones*), and *Star Wars*.

Villeneuve has been especially lauded for her portrayal of strong female characters. "To me it's still very important nowadays to be careful about depicting sci-fi/fantasy women in a modern, evolved way," Villeneuve explained to M. J. Scott for website *Cool Stuff Inc.* (21 Jan. 2016), noting the longstanding tendency toward highly sexualized portrayals in a genre traditionally dominated by males. "It's not about feminism. I'm just as sick and tired of overly muscular, barbarian-types of hero guys. I think it's time we go a step forward in human representation in sci-fi and fantasy."

EARLY LIFE AND EDUCATION

Magali Villeneuve was born in 1980 in Bordeaux, a port city in southwestern France. Although little has been written about her early life, she told several interviewers that her interest in illustration stemmed directly from watching the animated Disney film *Beauty and the Beast* at age twelve, when it appeared in French movie theaters. Entranced, in particular, by the powerful depiction of the Beast, she became enamored of American animation and began dreaming of working in the field one day. In high school, however, few art classes were made available to her, and a correspondence course she took via mail turned out to be relatively useless.

Meanwhile Villeneuve, who enjoyed her literature courses, began to gravitate toward fantasy fiction. Especially influential was Robert Jordan's series *The Wheel of Time*, which she found revelatory. "It was a whole new world and I started to understand that I wanted to draw from books," she told Andrew Burmon for *Inverse* (1 Nov. 2016). "My goals changed." She reasoned that she could blend her love of words with her desire to give life to characters visually by becoming an illustrator.

Unable to afford formal training, Villeneuve embarked upon a project to teach herself to illustrate—a process she later admitted took her at least twice as long as it might have to earn an actual degree. She began by working with traditional techniques such as pencil and oil painting before making the leap to digital painting, which would become a key element of her style. Eventually she developed a general process of beginning a project with a freehand pencil sketch, often using friends or family members as models, and then laboriously adding layers of color, contrast, and texture using digital tools like Adobe Photoshop. (Later she would note that a commission would typically take about ten hours to sketch and thirty or more hours to color.)

Performing a succession of menial food-service jobs by day, at night Villeneuve submitted her work to various amateur fanzines and websites. Finally, in 2006 she decided she was skilled enough to approach professional publishing houses. "Before I started as a pro, I didn't even dare to imagine I would be given such opportunities," she told Scott. "Even today, I still feel incredulous more often than not. As a consequence, whenever I receive new assignments, it still is the very same exhilaration as the first time."

ENTERING GEORGE R. R. MARTIN'S WORLD

Most of Villeneuve's early assignments came from small publishers needing covers for their fantasy novels. Although not exceptionally lucrative, they allowed her to hone her technique and build her portfolio. Then in 2010 she came across a book containing artwork from games based on George R. R. Martin's popular fantasy series A Song of Ice and Fire. She was impressed by the fictional world of Westeros and memorable characters such as members of the Targaryen and Lannister dynasties, which would soon be greatly popularized by the HBO television adaptation Game of Thrones (2011–19). Excited by the prospect of working with the material herself, she sent her portfolio to Fantasy Flight Games, and just a few days later she received an assignment.

Villeneuve went on to create several works for the franchise, effectively setting her career on track. She later noted that one of her most treasured memories was receiving a note from an art director at Fantasy Flight Games informing her that Martin had written "WOW" in capital letters on a proof of her depiction of his heroine Daenerys Targaryen. In 2014, Villeneuve was one of almost thirty artists who contributed pieces to Martin's The World of Ice & Fire: The Untold History of Westeros and the Game of Thrones, an exhaustive companion volume that delved into the minutiae of the saga. Martin later specifically tapped her to create the 2016 Game of Thrones calendar, and she also contributed that year to the gilt-decorated hardcover volume that was published to celebrate the twentieth anniversary of the first novel in the series.

OTHER FANTASY FLIGHT GAMES PROJECTS
Through her association with Fantasy Flight Games, Villeneuve began to regularly contribute to other card games and board games. Many of these were based on popular existing fantasy or science fiction franchises. For example, she did hundreds of illustrations based on J. R. R. Tolkien's iconic Lord of the Rings trilogy. She would later characterize some of these as among the best work of her career.

Villeneuve also worked on Arkham Horror, based upon the works of H. P. Lovecraft. Like Fantasy Flight's Lord of the Rings offering, Arkham Horror is a cooperative card game, meaning that players join forces to achieve a goal, rather than competing against one another. The game's plot, set in the 1920s, concerns defeating alien entities known as Ancient Ones before they wreak havoc on a populace still reeling from World War I.

Villeneuve initially felt somewhat out of her comfort zone when Fantasy Flight tapped her to create illustrations for their products based on the famous Star Wars franchise. Still, she stepped in to work on the Star Wars Living Card Game (a Fantasy Flight trademarked game style in which the company sells a core set of cards and then adds to that pool with frequent expansion packs, ostensibly offering less expensive,

more accessible gameplay than traditional collectible card games). She later worked on the Edge of Empire role-playing game as well. To depict the franchise's beloved science fiction characters, Villeneuve intently watched the Star Wars films and attempted to understand their attitudes and motivations. Her works were widely considered successful, and she was later hired to illustrate an officially licensed short story about the character Princess Leia.

Working across so many different properties, Villeneuve avoided choosing favorites. "I'm lucky enough to be working on all of my dream universes," she told Patrick Scalisi for the website Art of Magic: The Gathering (7 Apr. 2015). "When I started as an illustrator, I would never have believed it if someone told me what would be keeping me busy a few years later. All universes have a special place in my heart."

MAGIC: THE GATHERING
As Villeneuve built her reputation as an illustrator, she continued to draw inspiration from other artists. Notably, she became a fan of the dark fantasy artwork of the popular collectible card game Magic: The Gathering (informally known as Magic), though she did not initially play the game herself. Launched in 1993 by the company called Wizards of the Coast (which would later become a subsidiary of the toy giant Hasbro), Magic features thousands of characters, creatures, artifacts, and spells that players use to defeat their opponents in battle. The game grew steadily in popularity, reaching an estimated 20 million players around the world by 2015 and spawning a dedicated community as well as lucrative merchandise.

Villeneuve particularly admired cards by such artists as Aleksi Briclot, Michael Komarck, and Terese Nielsen. Though she found it intimidating to think of ever counting herself among that group, she eventually sent her growing portfolio to Wizards of the Coast. "I was really drawn to Magic as, in my opinion, they always tend toward a very modern and unique version of fantasy illustration," she explained to Wolfram. "That's why the game's look never grew old through the years and has its own very powerful personality. I wanted to be part of that."

Villeneuve's first Magic illustrations appeared in 2012. Soon after her depiction of the character Narset—an Asian woman with martial arts ability—hit store shelves and became an instant hit among many Magic fans. Scott called the "Narset Transcendent" card an "instant classic" and described it as "strong without being harsh, sensual yet barely showing any skin, packed to the edges of the frame with flavor. . . . simply an iconic image of what modern fantasy illustration can (and should) push itself to be." Villeneuve herself enjoyed a sense of freedom in her work for Magic, despite the need to conform somewhat to the game's established universe and extensive legacy. As she told Scott, "once you've 'assimilated' what it's all about, you can just have fun and be imaginative."

INSPIRATIONS AND WRITING

Villeneuve has often expressed happiness with her career track. "I first wanted to become an illustrator because I kept drawing the characters and scenes from my favorite books, trying to show on paper what I could see in my imagination," she told B. J. Priester in an undated interview for the *FanGirl* blog. "Lucky me, now my real adult job is to do that!" She often discussed both the inspirations and the challenges that informed her career. For example, she noted that living in France proved something of a mixed blessing in her line of work. She sometimes struggled to be taken seriously there as an artist, yet also enjoyed being surrounded by so much classical art and architecture, unconfined to museums and easily accessible to anyone simply strolling the streets. She called the Italian painter Caravaggio (1571–1610) and his followers a particular inspiration, especially their dramatic use of shadow and light. Similarly, she drew on the work of the pre-Raphaelites for their detailed approach to depicting the human figure.

Villeneuve often acknowledged a degree of controversy surrounding consideration of digital painting as the equal of traditional techniques. However, she suggested that digital tools had become not only necessary in the field of illustration but could indeed reach the same level of artistry as physical paint. In her opinion, the only true difference between the two is that digital painting is more accessible and democratized, since once aspiring artists acquire the needed software they are freed from the constraints of costly supplies and preparations. Digital artists, she asserted, can move and delight viewers every bit as much as traditional artists and can possess the same sensitivity and skill. "The techniques are actually very close, which is why I'm a slow painter," she told Burmon.

In addition to her illustration work, Villeneuve has explored writing as well. The first book of her dark-fantasy series *La Dernière Terre* was published in France in 2012.

PERSONAL LIFE

Villeneuve is married to fellow illustrator Alexandre Dainche. They collaborated on *La Dernière Terre*, and Villeneuve once hid a depiction of him in a *Game of Thrones* card for Fantasy Flight Games as a treat for their fans. They have often appeared together at fan festivals and conventions.

SUGGESTED READING

"About." *Magali Villeneuve*, www.magali-ville-neuve.com/. Accessed 5 Nov. 2019.

Villeneuve, Magali. "Artist Interview: Magali Villeneuve." Interview by Patrick Scalisi. *Art of Magic: The Gathering*, 7 Apr. 2015, www.artofmtg.com/artist-interview-magali-ville-neuve/. Accessed 5 Nov. 2019.

———. "The Artists of Magic: Magali Villeneuve." Interview by Nicholas Wolfram. *Magic: The Gathering*. Wizards of the Coast, 29 Aug. 2017, magic.wizards.com/en/articles/archive/feature/artists-magic-magali-ville-neuve-2017-08-29. Accessed 5 Nov. 2019.

———. "How Painting 'A Game of Thrones' Taught an Artist to Love the Lannisters." Interview by Andrew Burmon. *Inverse*, 1 Nov. 2016, www.inverse.com/article/22926-game-of-thrones-illustrations-magali-ville-neuve-westeros-lannisters. Accessed 5 Nov. 2019.

———. Interview. *FanGirl*, fangirlblog.com/in-terviews/magali-villeneuve/. Accessed 5 Nov. 2019.

———. "7 Questions: Magali Villeneuve." Interview by M. J. Scott. *CoolStuffInc.com*, 21 Jan. 2016, www.coolstuffinc.com/a/mjscott-012116-7-questions-magali-villeneuve. Accessed 5 Nov. 2019.

—*Mari Rich*

Hida Viloria

Date of birth: May 29, 1968
Occupation: Writer and activist

In the late 1990s, Hida Viloria emerged as a leading activist and educator for people who identify as intersex. Intersex people are born with sex characteristics that do not fit typical, socially constructed definitions of male or female. Viloria has pointed out that the intersex population is more sizable than many realize, constituting 1.7 percent of the population, which makes them as common as redheads.

Former chairperson of the Organization Intersex International (OII) and founding director of the group's US affiliate, the Intersex Campaign for Equality, Viloria uses the pronouns "s/he" and "he/r" (pronounced "she" and "her") for official purposes and in print, believing that option acknowledges both he/r upbringing as a woman and he/r genderfluid identity. "I think that language is a lot more important than people really give it credit for," s/he explained to Larissa Pham for *Rolling Stone* (20 Mar. 2017). "We've gotten into a position where there's so much division in our culture and our society, and I think that a lot of that could be avoided if people were more careful and precise with their language and really kept in mind what they're trying to say when they say things."

Viloria's activism extends well beyond issues of proper terminology. Although he/r own parents did not instruct doctors to surgically intervene after s/he was born with a large, penis-like clitoris—a decision for which s/he feels grateful—many parents feel pressured by doctors to "correct" their children's "malformed" anatomy. In he/r 2017 memoir, *Born Both: An Intersex Life*, Viloria writes: "One of my dreams is that the institutionalized 'medicalization' of intersex people will one day be deemed the human rights violation that it is by everyone involved." S/he hopes that in the future being intersex will be seen as normal being labeled male or female. "Being intersex hasn't always been easy, but it's been my greatest teacher, and the lessons have been worth every tortured moment," s/he writes. "Now, for me, being intersex is the fusion, the effortless union, of yin and yang. It is a space all its own, where something revolutionarily loving, balanced, and harmonious is created. It actually exists, and it's where I live."

EARLY LIFE AND EDUCATION

Hida Viloria was born on May 29, 1968, in New York. He/r mother, Doris, was Venezuelan, and he/r father, Hugo, was Colombian; the couple had moved from South America to the New York City borough of Queens in 1965. He/r father was a physician in Colombia, and soon earned his medical license to practice in the United States. Viloria has an older brother, Hugo—generally known as Hugh—who was born in Colombia, and a younger sister, Eden. Viloria's father was an overbearing and volatile man, and while Viloria admitted that those traits made life traumatic for the family, s/he credits them for his refusal to allow doctors to perform corrective surgery on he/r genitalia. The family simply treated he/r as a girl and expected he/r to act in traditionally feminine ways. For the most part s/he complied, and s/he has fond memories of the frilly clothes s/he wore on special occasions.

As an elementary school student, Viloria attended St. Andrew Avellino Catholic Academy, where teachers made little attempt to pronounce he/r name correctly (with some settling on "Heidi"). S/he was also subject to extreme bullying from racist classmates. Although s/he was relatively pale, as s/he recalled to Pham, "I grew up with a family with really thick accents; we were obviously not American and we weren't white in the way that the people in our neighborhood were white, and I learned very early on that you can't try to escape discrimination by pretending you're something that you're not."

Viloria then attended St. Francis Preparatory School in Queens, among the largest Catholic high schools in the nation. There, s/he became known for he/r academic achievement, performance as an all-star basketball player, and role on the cheerleading squad. Although s/he developed crushes on other girls from a young age, s/he never admitted those feelings, sensing that he/r parents would not approve. S/he also developed a love for the androgynous musician Prince, finding his nonbinary appearance compelling and acknowledging that s/he, he/rself, was also different. "Despite my budding attraction to androgyny, however, I'm perceived as a girl, and a straight one, in the eyes of all my teachers and classmates," s/he writes of this period in he/r memoir. "Unbeknownst to them, I am actually a lesbian, albeit a nonpracticing one as of yet. Unbeknownst to *me*, as well as them, I am not only a lesbian but an intersex one."

After graduating from high school in 1986, Viloria began attending Wesleyan University in Connecticut. During he/r first year at the school, however, Viloria's life changed dramatically. In 1987, he/r father was accused of sexually assaulting a fourteen-year-old patient at gunpoint. Hugo's family had little doubt that he was capable of such violence; he had once pulled a gun on Hugh upon figuring out that his son was gay. Although the criminal charges were ultimately dropped, Hugo lost his license to practice medicine. In the wake of those events, the year featured even further upheaval for Viloria. During a vicious argument between father and son, Hugo bemoaned the fact that Hugh was not more like his sister; in response, Hugh angrily revealed that s/he was gay too. He/r father immediately withdrew all support and Viloria was forced to drop out of college.

Shortly after, Viloria was raped and hospitalized for an ectopic pregnancy. After surviving surgery for a burst fallopian tube, the doctor requested further testing after noticing he/r enlarged clitoris. S/he denied the tests as this was the first time s/he had been told that he/r genitalia were considered atypical. It was not until 1995, when s/he read a newspaper story about intersexuality headlined "Both and Neither," that s/he had an epiphany. "You could have put an article in front of me about aliens being discovered working in the White House and it would have been less shocking to me than this information," s/he writes in *Born Both*. "I mean I've known that my body is different for a while, but to possibly be a hermaphrodite? And to learn there is a worldwide medical effort to eliminate intersex people? It sounds like a frightening science-fiction movie." The article showed Viloria that there was a label that applied to he/r; s/he also learned that most intersex people had been subject to surgery as infants.

Viloria eventually won a scholarship to the University of California, Berkeley, where s/he created he/r own interdisciplinary major in gender and sexuality and wrote a thesis on the medical mismanagement of intersex people. S/he graduated from the school in 1996.

ACTIVISM

In 1996, Viloria attended a conference in Sonoma County, California, for people identifying as intersex. It was organized by the Intersex Society of North America—a group mentioned in the eye-opening news article s/he had read—and it drew eleven attendees in total, some from as far away as New Zealand. S/he was horrified to discover that the others had all undergone surgical interventions at birth, leading to lack of full sexual function and other physical effects, as well as deep emotional distress. Viloria became determined to get involved in activism.

Viloria turned out to be a compelling spokesperson and soon found he/rself on such popular shows as *Inside Edition, Montel Williams, 20/20,* and *Oprah Winfrey.* "The people that I was trying to appeal to were conservative parents, especially in those early appearances," s/he explained to Pham. "My goal was that a parent who might have recently had an intersex child or have one in the future would see my interview and think, 'Oh, being intersex is fine and this person has been able to grow up happy and successful and feel good about themselves." S/he specifically advocated against the cosmetic surgery done on infants to make their genitalia resemble more traditional male or female characteristics. As s/he told Pham, Viloria hoped to lead parents to think, "There's no reason I have to cut up my child's body in this non-consensual, irreversible way. I'll just let them grow up and decide later on if they want to change anything about their body, the way most people get to decide." Despite some stage fright, s/he realized s/he was doing valuable work thanks to the deluge of letters and emails s/he received after each appearance.

Viloria also became involved in several high-profile initiatives and campaigns. In 2010, for example, after South African track star Caster Semenya was banned from competition because observers speculated that she was male, Viloria was invited to sit in on the International Olympic Committee's meeting of experts, where s/he lobbied for the interests of intersex female athletes. In 2011, s/he became a leader of the OII—a position s/he held until 2017—and founded Intersex Campaign for Equality, the US branch of the organization. S/he later penned an open letter to the United Nations High Commissioner for Human Rights, demanding that the concerns of intersex people be addressed. Human Rights Day in 2013, s/he was given the honor of being the first openly intersex person to speak by invitation at the United Nations Headquarters in New York. S/he later helped members of the UN Free & Equal Campaign prepare a groundbreaking Intersex Fact Sheet and successfully argued against the use of pathologizing term disorders of sex development (DSD), which even some fellow activists had accepted.

In the late 2010s, Viloria advocated the integration of a third sex marker in addition to male and female, stating that the addition would help end the practice of infant surgery to conform to traditional male or female sex characteristics. S/he told Chris O'Donnell for the *Irish Times* (13 Nov. 2019) that a third sex marker would mean that intersex people "do exist, legally. So it's clear that changing who we are is committing an erasive act against an entire group of people." Viloria noted that after the first US intersex birth certificate was issued in 2017, three former US surgeon generals called for doctors to stop performing medically unnecessary surgeries on intersex infants.

PUBLICATIONS AND DOCUMENTARY APPEARANCES

Although s/he had written a number of articles for various publications, Viloria's first major work, *Your Beautiful Child: Information for Parents,* a resource that rejects the stigmatizing language and alarmist tone of most literature given to new parents of intersex infants, came in 2013. He/r work later appeared in such volumes as *The Human Agenda: Conversations about Sexual Orientation & Gender Identity* (2015) and the Oxford University Press textbook *Queer: A Reader for Writers* (2016). In 2017, Viloria published the memoir *Born Both: An Intersex Life,* which was a finalist for a Lambda Literary Award.

Viloria appeared in a 2019 Smithsonian Channel documentary *The General Was Female?* about Casimir Pulaski. An American Revolutionary War hero who helped save George Washington's life in the Battle of Brandywine, Pulaski was identified as intersex thanks to modern DNA evidence. In early 2020, along with biology professor Maria Nieto, s/he published *The Spectrum of Sex: The Science of Male, Female and Intersex,* which explains human sexual development in an inclusive, neutral way and explores issues of gender diversity through a reasoned and accepting lens.

PERSONAL LIFE

Viloria holds the United States' second intersex birth certificate, which was issued to he/r in 2017. S/he lives in Santa Fe with he/r partner and stepson.

SUGGESTED READING

"About." *Hilda Viloria,* 2020, hidaviloria.com/about/. Accessed 12 Feb. 2020.

Jacques, Juliet. "Overcoming Trauma and Intolerance as an Intersex Activist." Review of *Born Both: An Intersex Life,* by Hida Viloria. *The Washington Post,* 24 Mar. 2017, www.washingtonpost.com/opinions/overcoming-trauma-and-intolerance-as-an-intersex-activist/2017/03/24/a586555e-f222-11e6-a9b0-ecee7ce475fc_story.html. Accessed 4 Mar. 2020.

Viloria, Hida. *Born Both: An Intersex Life.* Hachette Books, 2017.

——. "Intersex Activist and Writer Hida Viloria on Being 'Born Both.'" Interview by Larissa Pham. *Rolling Stone,* 20 Mar. 2017, www.rollingstone.com/culture/culture-features/intersex-activist-and-writer-hida-viloria-on-being-born-both-123818. Accessed 12 Feb. 2020.

——. "'It's Hard to Come out as Intersex . . . People Still Don't Know What It Means," Interview by Chris O'Donnell. *The Irish Times,* 13 Nov. 2019, www.irishtimes.com/life-and-style/health-family/it-s-hard-to-come-out-as-intersex-people-still-don-t-know-what-it-means-1.4073377. Accessed 12 Feb. 2020.

——. "Q & A: Hida Viloria, Intersex Activist." Interview by Rachel Glenn. *Daily Princetonian,* 21 Apr. 2016, www.dailyprincetonian.com/article/2016/04/q-a-hida-viloria-intersex-activist. Accessed 12 Feb. 2020.

——. "What's in a Name: Intersex and Identity." *Advocate,* 14 May 2014, www.advocate.com/commentary/2014/05/14/op-ed-whats-name-intersex-and-identity. Accessed 12 Feb. 2020.

SELECTED WORKS

Your Beautiful Child: Information for Parents, 2013; *Born Both: An Intersex Life,* 2017; *The Spectrum of Sex: The Science of Male, Female and Intersex* (with Maria Nieto), 2020

—*Mari Rich*

Emma Walmsley

Date of birth: June 1969
Occupation: Pharmaceutical executive

In April 2017 Emma Walmsley became the chief executive officer of GlaxoSmithKline (GSK), the British-based global pharmaceutical conglomerate. The appointment drew considerable attention, as it made her the first female CEO in the history of Big Pharma, the group of drug companies so massive that they collectively constitute a formidable economic and political force. Media observers were quick to tout the glass ceiling–shattering accomplishment, especially as at the time GSK was the third-largest company in the United Kingdom's Financial Times Stock Exchange (FTSE) 100. For her part, however, Walmsley did not dwell on how being a woman affected her career. "I've never primarily defined myself by my gender," she asserted in a video posted on the GSK website after her appointment was announced, as quoted by Ketaki Gokhale and Kristen Hallam for *Bloomberg* (20 Sept. 2016). "I've been lucky enough to always work for companies or in countries where being female hasn't limited or restricted me."

Walmsley had a long tenure with the cosmetics company L'Oréal before unexpectedly joining GSK in 2010 and quickly rising to lead its consumer health division. Although her lack of experience in medicine led to some investor anxiety when she took over as overall CEO, she quickly found success—including through some major changes. Overhauling GSK's management and culture, she refocused the company on blockbuster drugs such as cancer therapies. "At the heart of pharma is R&D," she said, as quoted by Erika Fry and Claire Zillman for *Fortune* (26 Sept. 2018). "I want us to get back to our mojo around science and discovery and development again."

EARLY LIFE AND EDUCATION

Emma Walmsley was born in 1969 in Barrow-in-Furness, a center of industry located in the northwest British county of Cumbria. Her father, Sir Robert Walmsley, served in the Royal Navy, retiring with the rank of vice admiral. He later worked in the civil service as a chief of military procurement and served on many corporate boards. Walmsley, along with her brother and sister, had a relatively peripatetic childhood because of their father's naval career, at one point moving four times in just six years.

Walmsley was reportedly ambitious and determined even as a child. Family lore has it that each summer her parents would stage a debate about where to spend their vacation, and Walmsley prepared her arguments so methodically that her choice always won out. She went on to attend St. Swithun's, a prestigious all-girls boarding school in Winchester, England. There she excelled in the academically rigorous atmosphere; both classmates and teachers later remembered her as a fiercely intelligent pupil. She also proved to be a gifted amateur performer, adept at public speaking and singing in the choir and memorably playing Prince Charming in a school operetta.

After graduating from St. Swithun's, Walmsley entered Christ Church, a college of Oxford University. There she earned a degree in modern languages and classics.

BEGINNINGS IN BUSINESS

Walmsley began her professional career with the Coba Group, a boutique consulting firm. In

1994 she joined the French-based global cosmetics giant L'Oréal, where she would spend the next seventeen years in a variety of marketing and management jobs. She gradually climbed the corporate ladder with positions that took her all over the world, including stints in New York and Paris. During this time she built a reputation as a strong leader with a strict work ethic and high standards. By the time she became a top executive with the Maybelline brand in the United States, she was widely admired by both the company's higher leadership and her own employees.

In 2007 Walmsley moved to Shanghai to serve as general manager of consumer products for L'Oréal China, overseeing such popular brands as Maybelline and Garnier. It was an adventure that she savored, as she wrote in an undated essay for the website *Lean In*: "Life was a constant juggling act, with never enough sleep but a huge sense of fulfilment. . . . Our business was accelerating fast but there was so much more opportunity to grow."

Walmsley lived and worked in China until 2010. That year she was invited to a casual networking luncheon with Andrew Witty, then CEO of GlaxoSmithKline (GSK). Witty was widely recognized for his emphasis on corporate values while leading a major multinational pharmaceutical company, one with a portfolio of products ranging from cutting-edge drugs to everyday household products as Sensodyne toothpaste and Tums indigestion tablets. Walmsley had admired Witty's management style from afar, and the two connected immediately. After an "inspiring conversation" she wrote for *Lean In*, Witty offered her the "opportunity of a lifetime": an executive position in GSK's global consumer health care business.

JOINING GSK

Walmsley ultimately agreed to take on the challenge—a move she likened to bungee jumping off a cliff. "People regret far more what they don't do rather than what they do," she noted in her *Lean In* piece. In 2010 she officially joined GSK as head of the European division of consumer health care. She quickly set about enacting the kind of deep-rooted changes she had been brought in for. "Walmsley brought her marketing chops and inherent ambition to the role," wrote Fry and Zillman. "GSK's brands . . . improved lives but didn't exactly inspire the consumers who used them. Over-the-counter brands, in fact, polled among the least popular brands on the planet. Walmsley asked, Why shouldn't they be as beloved as Apple or Nike or Coca-Cola?, and set out on a campaign to make them so."

In 2011 Walmsley was named head of GSK's worldwide consumer health care efforts, a division encompassing some 21,000 employees. Among her many accomplishments in that role

were doubling sales of Sensodyne. She also played a key role in a successful 2014 joint venture with fellow pharmaceutical company Novartis, heading up what became one of the largest global businesses for over-the-counter products. Overall, during her leadership of GSK's consumer division Walmsley oversaw sales growth of 38 percent.

MOVING UP THE LADDER

Walmsley's success in the consumer realm marked her as a potential candidate for an even higher position within GSK. Still, many business insiders were surprised when she was placed on the shortlist of possible candidates to replace Witty, who in early 2016 announced he would be stepping down as CEO. Critics noted that Walmsley had no science background or pharmaceutical training, things the company had long emphasized over its consumer ventures. She faced stiff competition, as the other contenders included prominent figures such as GSK's pharma chief Abbas Hussain.

Despite these obstacles, it was announced in September 2016 that Walmsley would succeed Witty as CEO of GSK. She officially took over the role on April 1, 2017, thus becoming arguably the most powerful businesswoman in the United Kingdom, and one of the most powerful business leaders in the entire world. As the seventh woman to head a FTSE 100 company, she was hailed as a pioneer by many advocates of diversity in corporate leadership.

Coverage of Walmsley's appointment also revealed ongoing challenges in the push for gender equality, however. Many outlets focused on Walmsley's personal life, such as her status as a wife and mother, even as they praised her professionalism and intelligence. Controversy also arose over the fact that her starting salary as CEO was significantly lower than that of her predecessor. And even though her pay quickly rose—by 2019 her total compensation of almost £6 million made her the highest-paid woman on the FTSE 100 list—she was still making less than many of Big Pharma's male CEOs. Although she generally downplayed questions about her experience as a woman in the workplace, Walmsley did not ignore issues of gender equality. For example, in 2019 she backed an initiative dubbed #MeTooPay, aimed at closing the wage gap for women in every strata and industry.

BIG PHARMA CEO

Not all stakeholders were initially pleased with the selection of Walmsley as GSK's CEO, and the company's share price dropped slightly when the news was first announced. Many business experts also pointed out that Walmsley was facing a set of challenges that would be daunting for even a more seasoned pharmaceutical executive, including poor returns on research and development, pressure from health care providers, and increased competition from manufacturers of generic drugs.

Such negative views were soon proven misplaced, however. After assuming leadership of the company Walmsley quickly set to work on improving both company culture and performance. She brought in many new managers and ended or sold various experimental programs and less-successful brands, all with an eye to refocusing the company on its core: pharmaceuticals. She led a global restructuring program intended to save hundreds of millions of dollars per year—funds that could then be devoted to research and development. "The way I define the job is, firstly, in setting strategy for the company, and then leading the allocation of capital to that strategy," she said, as quoted by Fry and Zillman. "Until you put the money where you say your strategy is, it's not your strategy."

Among Walmsley's early accomplishments were a series of acquisitions and partnerships. These included an ambitious joint venture with rival Pfizer; acquiring Tesaro, makers of a promising treatment for ovarian cancer; and forging a $300 million deal with the genetics company 23andMe to develop new medications and treatments. In 2019 she spearheaded a $13 billion dollar buyout of Novartis's large stake in GSK Consumer Health, strengthening GSK's organization into pharmaceuticals, vaccines, and consumer health care divisions.

As GSK CEO Walmsley was frequently included on *Fortune* magazine's rankings of the most powerful international women in business, topping the list in 2018 and placing second in both 2017 and 2019. She also appeared at number seventeen on *Forbes* magazine's "Power Women 2019" list. That same year she was elected to the board of directors of technology giant Microsoft, further indicating her status as a major player in the global business world.

PERSONAL LIFE

Walmsley is married to David Owen, an entrepreneur she met at a party when she was in her twenties. The couple have four children together: three sons and a daughter. "I know my kids are fine with us doing our best as parents," Walmsley wrote for *Lean In*. "They are proud of their mum and though she is on a plane a lot, she makes as many school plays, matches and parent evenings as she can."

SUGGESTED READING

Fry, Erika, and Claire Zillman. "Science 'Mojo' and an Executive Dream Team: CEO Emma Walmsley's Bold Prescription for Reviving GlaxoSmithKline." *Fortune*, 26 Sept. 2018, fortune.com/longform/gsk-glaxosmithkline-ceo-emma-walmsley/. Accessed 28 Dec. 2019.

Gokhale, Ketaki, and Kristen Hallam. "Big Pharma's Latest Breakthrough: Choosing Its First Female CEO." *Bloomberg*, 20 Sept. 2016, www.bloomberg.com/news/articles/2016-09-20/big-pharma-s-latest-breakthrough-choosing-its-first-female-ceo. Accessed 28 Dec. 2019.

Kollewe, Julia. "GSK's Emma Walmsley Becomes Highest-Paid Female FTSE 100 Chief." *The Guardian*, 12 Mar. 2019, www.theguardian.com/business/2019/mar/12/glaxosmithkline-gsk-emma-walmsley-highest-paid-female-ftse-100-chief-executive. Accessed 28 Dec. 2019.

Monaghan, Angela. "Emma Walmsley Profile: From Marketing at L'Oréal to GSK Chief." *The Guardian*, 20 Sept. 2016, www.theguardian.com/business/2016/sep/20/emma-walmsley-profile-loreal-gsk-chief-designate-glaxosmithkline. Accessed 28 Dec. 2019.

Neville, Sarah. "Emma Walmsley, A Fast-Talker Shaking Up GSK." *Financial Times*, 21 Dec. 2018, www.ft.com/content/d5385f40-0481-11e9-99df-6183d3002ee1. Accessed 28 Dec. 2019.

Preston, Juliet. "Emma Walmsley Makes History as Big Pharma's First Female CEO." *MedCityNews*, 31 Mar. 2017, medcitynews.com/2017/03/emma-walmsely-big-pharma-first-female-ceo/?rf=1. Accessed 28 Dec. 2019.

Walmsley, Emma. "People Regret Far More What They Don't Do Than What They Do." *Lean In*, leanin.org/stories/emma-walmsley. Accessed 28 Dec. 2019.

—*Mari Rich*

Lulu Wang

Date of birth: February 25, 1983
Occupation: Filmmaker

Filmmaker Lulu Wang had a breakthrough with *The Farewell*, her 2019 comedy drama that was, as the opening title card reads: "Based on an actual lie." In 2013, Wang's eighty-year-old grandmother, Nai Nai, was diagnosed with stage IV lung cancer and given three months to live. Rather than give Nai Nai the terrible diagnosis, Wang's family arranged an elaborate ruse, planning a wedding banquet for Wang's cousin in Nai Nai's hometown, Changchun, China, so that they might see her one last time before she died. Wang, who was born in Beijing and moved with her family to Miami when she was six years old, was deeply conflicted about the undertaking. In 2016, Wang told the story on the National Public Radio (NPR) program *This American Life*. The episode's popularity earned her a production deal, resulting in the creation of *The Farewell*, which she both wrote and directed. The film follows a young Chinese American woman named Billi, played by rapper and actor Awkwafina (Nora Lum). Billi, like Wang, is tasked with navigating cultural and familial boundaries as she decides whether or not to tell her grandmother (Shuzhen Zhou) the truth.

The Farewell met with instant critical acclaim. "Lulu Wang's second feature conjures a premise so rich with potential comedy, heartbreak and family weirdness that it can only have come from real life," A.O. Scott wrote in his review for the *New York Times* (11 July 2019). Among many honors, *The Farewell* was nominated for a Golden Globe Award for best foreign language film—it has dialogue in both English and Mandarin—while Awkwafina won a Golden Globe Award for best actress in a musical or comedy. Wang leveraged this success into other high-profile projects, including an Amazon series based on Janice Y. K. Lee's 2016 novel *The Expatriates*, about a close-knit group of expatriates living in Hong Kong.

EARLY LIFE AND EDUCATION

Lulu Wang was born in Beijing on February 25, 1983. She lived briefly with her grandmother, whom she called Nai Nai, Mandarin for "grandma," in Changchun, China, before emigrating to United States, where her father was pursuing a doctorate at the University of Miami, when she was six years old. Her mother, Jian Yu, was a cultural critic and editor for a prestigious magazine in Beijing before meeting Wang's father, Haiyan Wang, then a Chinese diplomat to the Soviet Union. Wang has a younger brother named Anthony. Wang's mother chose to give up her career to have a family, a decision that Wang grappled with growing up. "We've chosen very different paths, and she says that I have a lot more courage and a lot less fear. She'd always been a very fearful child, and ever since I was little I've always been fearless," Wang told E. Alex Jung for *Vulture* (1 July 2019) of her mother. "Growing up, she would always say, 'As a man you can have it all, but as a woman you have to choose.' I didn't want to believe in her reality."

As a child in the United States, Wang was hyper-aware of being different from others. "[There] wasn't a large Chinese American population, so I didn't grow up having a community of Asian friends," she told Chris Gayomali for *GQ* (11 July 2019). "Even when there were Asian people, we sort of existed on our own." Wang began studying piano at four. In Miami, she was given the key to a local church so she could practice. She continued her studies at an arts conservatory for high school but had doubts about becoming a classical pianist. "I just didn't really want to practice seven hours a day in a room by myself," Wang told Gayomali. Her parents "were just constantly disappointed in me, because they were like, 'But you have a gift and if you don't use it, you're wasting it,'" she recalled. "I was like, 'Is it really a gift if it doesn't make me happy?'"

Wang attended Boston College, where she was double-majored in music and literature, and planned to become a lawyer. She fell in love with filmmaking during her senior year, after watching Steven Shainberg's 2002 drama *Secretary* on a computer in the school's video library. She took a Film 101 class, for which she shot her own films on a Super 8 camera and edited them by hand. "The physicality of that experience of seeing frame by frame, and working with my friends made me fall in love with it," she recalled to Gayomali. She went on to take classes in world cinema and feminist film theory.

EARLY CAREER

Wang graduated from Boston College in 2005. In 2006, after a serendipitous meeting at a bar in Boston, she was commissioned to make a thirty-minute documentary about overfishing in Panama called *Fishing the Gulf*. It was screened at festivals all over the world. Wang moved to Los Angeles in 2007. She took a job as a production assistant on the set of the stoner comedy *Pineapple Express* (2008) but was fired for trying to give a copy of one of her short films to the director, David Gordon Green. Later, Green met her

Photo by MiamiFilmFestival via Wikimedia Commons

for coffee and advised her to find ways to fund her creative projects, instead of trying to climb the ladder of the film industry from the inside.

In 2008, Wang founded a company called LegalREEL Productions, which made videos for plaintiffs' attorneys. This venture allowed her time and money to focus on her own work.

POSTHUMOUS

The idea for Wang's first feature film, *Posthumous*, was born on a trip to the Swedish furniture store IKEA with Swiss producer Bernadette Bürgi. The two bonded over their love for romantic comedies. Neither Wang nor Bürgi had ever made a feature film, or had Hollywood connections, but their naiveté, as Wang later put it, and grit paid off. Wang convinced English actor Jack Huston to star in the film by sending him an impassioned letter. "She's like a firecracker," Huston's costar Brit Marling later told Jung of Wang. "She has an internal source of light and energy. It's not a phony optimism. It's a hard-won optimism."

Posthumous premiered at the Zurich International Film Festival in 2014. Set in Berlin, it tells the story of an artist named Liam Price (Huston) who is mistakenly reported as dead. As his fame soars, he seeks to maintain the ruse, posing as his own twin brother. The plot, part screwball comedy, part art-world satire, is complicated by Liam's romance with expatriate reporter McKenzie Grain (Marling). Alluding to Liam's maxim that great artists are never appreciated when they are alive, *Variety* critic Guy Lodge (31 Mar. 2015) gave the film tempered praise, concluding, "This bright if uneven debut suggests [Wang's] future work may well be recognized in its time" (31 Mar. 2015).

"BASED ON AN ACTUAL LIE"

In 2015, Wang released a short film called *Touch*, about an elderly Chinese man who mistakenly but inappropriately touches a child. The film follows the man as he navigates the American legal system, trying to explain the cultural context for his actions. The film was a finalist in the NBCUniversal Short Film Festival and won an award for best drama at the 2016 Asians On Film Festival.

Wang began pitching an idea for her next feature film, based on her family and their well-intended conspiracy to keep her grandmother in the dark about her serious cancer diagnosis. Producers were skeptical. American producers "wanted it to be my big, fat Chinese wedding. A very broad, ethnic comedy," Wang recalled to Nicole Sperling for the *Vanity Fair* (3 July 2019), referencing the hit 2002 romantic comedy *My Big Fat Greek Wedding*. Chinese producers were baffled by Wang's character's dilemma. "They were like, 'Why is this dramatic? Everybody in China does this,'" Wang told Robert Ito for the *New York Times* (5 July 2019).

In April 2016, Wang shared her family's story on the popular NPR program *This American Life*. The episode, called "In Defense of Ignorance," proved popular with listeners. For Wang, the experience of recording was "so amazing and so pure," as she told Sperling. It renewed her confidence in telling her story the way she wanted it to be told. "That immediacy of storytelling reminded me why I became a storyteller in the first place," she told Sperling. "That direct connection. Films take so long to make. They take so much money, and I don't fit in. Nobody wants to tell my story. They just want to put me in this box, and . . . unless I can do this kind of storytelling, it's not worth it for me to do all that."

THE FAREWELL

Producer Chris Weitz, who wrote and directed the 2002 film *About A Boy*, heard the *This American Life* episode and contacted Wang. Within two weeks, they had teamed up with the production company Big Beach and secured funding for a feature film. Wang began writing a script. She cast Lum, known professionally as actor and rapper Awkwafina, as Billi, the film's lead character and a stand-in for Wang. Awkwafina would become famous for her roles in the 2018 films *Crazy Rich Asians* and *Ocean's 8*, but Wang cast her before that, on the strength of her music videos. Wang took a similar leap of faith casting her own grandaunt (Nai Nai's sister), Hong Lu, to play herself. "The movie made me experience the sadness and the grief again," Lu later admitted to Ito. "I still sometimes question myself, did I make the right decision, even in my dreams. But I had a lot of fun also, to be honest with you. Especially working with Lulu."

But Wang's most brazen decision was to shoot the film on location at her grandmother's house in Changchun. The real-life Nai Nai had outlived her original diagnosis—and remained completely in the dark about both the premise of the film and the lie that it depicted. Wang told Nai Nai the film was about a wedding celebration, and loosely based on their family.

The Farewell premiered at the Sundance Film Festival in January 2019, receiving rave reviews from critics. Emily Yoshida for *Vulture* (11 July 2019) wrote that Wang transcends the film's "hooky premise with confidence and subtlety. The little dramas and themes that emerge during the reunion of the film's far-flung brood become, like a family, more than the sum of its individual parts, and an incredibly satisfying meal of a film." She concluded that *The Farewell* "feels both like the work of a seasoned auteur some 40 films into her career, and a very exciting arrival."

PERSONAL LIFE

Wang had a relationship with Academy Award–winning filmmaker Barry Jenkins, best known for *Moonlight*, which won the Oscar for best adapted screen play in 2017.

SUGGESTED READING

Gayomali, Chris. "How *The Farewell* Director Lulu Wang Stayed True to Herself." *GQ*, 11 July 2019, www.gq.com/story/lulu-wang-the-farewell-interview. Accessed 7 June 2020.

Ito, Robert. "A Family's Real-Life Lie and the Movie That Complicated It." *The New York Times*, 5 July 2019, www.nytimes.com/2019/07/05/movies/farewell-wang-awkwafina.html. Accessed 8 June 2020.

Jung, E. Alex. "Lulu Wang Spots the Lie." *Vulture*, 1 July 2019, www.vulture.com/2019/07/lulu-wang-the-farewell-profile.html. Accessed 7 June 2020.

Lodge, Guy. Review of *Posthumous*, directed by Lulu Wang. *Variety*, 31 Mar. 2015, variety.com/2015/film/festivals/film-review-posthumous-1201460779/. Accessed 8 June 2020.

Scott, A. O. "Review: In 'The Farewell,' a Wedding Is Really a Premature Funeral." Rev. of *The Farewell*, directed by Lulu Wang. *The New York Times*, 11 July 2019, www.nytimes.com/2019/07/11/movies/the-farewell-review.html. Accessed 9 June 2020.

Sperling, Nicole. "Why Lulu Wang Almost Said Farewell to Hollywood." *Vanity Fair*, 3 July 2019, www.vanityfair.com/hollywood/2019/07/why-lulu-wang-almost-said-farewell-to-hollywood. Accessed 8 June 2020.

Yoshida, Emily. "*The Farewell* Is a Big Arrival for Director Lulu Wang." Rev. of *The Farewell*, directed by Lulu Wang. *Vulture*, 11 July 2019, www.vulture.com/2019/07/the-farewell-awkwafina-sundance-movie-review.html. Accessed 9 June 2020.

SELECTED WORKS

Fishing the Gulf, 2005; *Posthumous*, 2014; *Touch*, 2015; The *Farewell*, 2019

—*Molly Hagan*

John David Washington

Date of birth: July 28, 1984
Occupation: Actor

From the time John David Washington, the son of popular veteran actor Denzel Washington, had a one-line speaking role in Spike Lee's 1992 film *Malcolm X* when he was just around seven years old, it was inevitable that any pursuit of a career in the entertainment industry would invite comparisons and discussions of their relationship. Even after his star turn in the Academy Award–winning 2018 film *BlacKkKlansman*, which also won the Grand Prix jury prize at the Cannes Film Festival and proved to most critics that the younger Washington had serious acting chops of his own, that did not change. Few interviews concluded without a journalist asking him how it felt to be in his father's shadow or what career advice the older man had given him. "Who would I be if I complained about having a father that provided for me? Who would I be if I was complaining about having a father who loved me?" Washington said to Chris Wasser for Independent.ie (24 Aug. 2018) when the topic came up. "So, I don't mind the questions—I'm used to the questions. And all I gotta do is be honest about it. So, yeah, it's happening a lot, but it's happened my whole life."

He pointed out to interviewers that his mother, Pauletta, was an esteemed pianist and performer in her own right and had also been a great influence on him. Washington did not initially strive to become an actor partially in the hopes of being able to make a name for himself on his own terms. However, after he had spent several years as a professional football player, a career-ending injury ignited a determination to break into a profession and practice a craft that he had always been drawn to. Applying the same work ethic as he had to football, he landed a memorable role in the hit HBO series *Ballers*, which premiered in 2015, and never looked back.

Photo by CELINA Youtube via Wikimedia Commons

EARLY LIFE AND EDUCATION

John David Washington was born on July 28, 1984, to Pauletta Washington (née Pearson), a Juilliard-trained pianist who also worked as an actor, and Denzel Washington, famed for acting in such films as *Mo' Better Blues* (1990), *Malcolm X* (1992), *Training Day* (2001), *The Book of Eli* (2010), and *Fences* (2016). Washington would later emphasize that both of his parents played important roles in his raising. As quoted by Madeleine Aggeler for *The Cut* (20 Aug. 2018), he asserted during an interview for the program *Today*, "My father taught me how to hunt. My mother taught me how to love."

Washington grew up with three younger siblings: Katia, who also got into acting, and twins Olivia and Malcolm, who became involved in various aspects of the entertainment industry. He was around five years old when one of his father's performances had a particularly affecting impact on him. That occurred during New York's annual Shakespeare in the Park season, where Denzel was appearing in a production of *Richard III*. Amazed and impressed, Washington eventually told journalists that he realized that day that he wanted to make a similar type of impact on an audience. He had his chance a couple of years later, when director Spike Lee asked him to portray a schoolchild in *Malcolm X* (1992), which starred Denzel in the title role. However, even at that young age it began dawning on Washington that if he pursued professional acting, he would perpetually be compared to his father. Despite secretly wearing out VHS tapes watching Denzel's films, he distanced himself from the idea.

A skilled athlete, Washington decided to differentiate himself by focusing on sports and began dreaming of one day joining a National Football League (NFL) team. At Campbell Hall, the exclusive private school he attended in Los Angeles's Studio City neighborhood, he was active in football, track, and basketball. After graduating in 2002 and earning an athletic scholarship, he entered Morehouse College, where he studied sociology and continued to excel on the football field, setting several school records, including single-game and career rushing yards.

FOOTBALL CAREER

When Washington graduated from Morehouse in 2006, he signed with the St. Louis Rams as an undrafted free agent. He failed, however, to make the opening-day roster and instead spent two seasons as part of the team's practice squad. "I felt like Rudy in a way," Washington told Matthew Kredell in an undated interview for *Men's Journal*, referring to Notre Dame walk-on football player Rudy Ruettiger, who gained notoriety for overcoming adversity to attend the school and achieve his dream after participating in a single game. "I wasn't the team mascot, but I was, like, that try-hard guy who was willing to do anything to play because he genuinely and purely loved the game."

Determined to prove himself, Washington briefly joined the NFL's European league before beginning a stint with the fledgling United Football League in 2009, playing for the California Redwoods (renamed the Sacramento Mountain Lions in 2010) until 2012, when the small, second-tier league folded. The highlight of his time with the team had come during a game, his first as a starter in a professional league, in which he had scored a touchdown on fourteen carries. Although he had hoped that his performance might be good enough to try to get back into the NFL, those hopes were dashed during a training exercise, when he severely damaged his Achilles tendon. "A 28-year-old running back that was out of the league, trying to get back in, is not going to be first on the boards," he admitted to Mia Galuppo for the *Hollywood Reporter* (18 Jan. 2018). He added that while sitting in the doctor's office and receiving the news, he was "bawling because you have all of these flashbacks and emotions from when you were playing as a kid, and I knew I was done then."

GETTING A START IN TELEVISION AND EARNING FILM ROLES

Forced into an early retirement from football, a more mature Washington reconsidered his early acting ambitions. Still recovering from surgery and walking with the help of crutches, he set out to audition for the new HBO sports comedy series *Ballers*, starring Dwayne Johnson as a retired NFL player who forges a new career as a financial manager for other NFL players. After approximately ten auditions, he was cast as egotistical but charming receiver Ricky Jerret. The show premiered in 2015 and ran for five seasons, with its final episode airing in 2019. Throughout, Washington, who had made a concerted effort to keep his pedigree under wraps as much as possible, won plaudits for his nuanced portrayal of what might otherwise have been a one-note character. Even after his first real foray into the profession, he knew that he had made the right choice. "The work and the craft. That's what I connect to and love. It's part of me. It's like breathing," he told Ben Baskin for *Sports Illustrated* (31 July 2018).

Meanwhile, in 2017, Washington played the love interest of an aspiring rapper in the little-noticed *Love Beats Rhymes*, and he was somewhat surprised to receive a text that same year from Spike Lee, asking the actor to contact him. Lee was making a film based on a 2014 memoir by black Colorado police detective Ron Stallworth, who in the late 1970s infiltrated the Ku Klux Klan by posing as a white supremacist on the phone, and he had Washington in mind to play Stallworth.

In an interview with Eric Kohn for *IndieWire* (14 Aug. 2018), Washington explained how his own experiences with racism had informed how he approached the part and cemented his interest in being involved in such an important film. He had been visiting family in North Carolina as a ten-year-old, he recalled, when an older white man approached him in public and casually referred to him using a highly offensive slur. "To me, the big takeaway from this film was, this is what hate sounds like," he told Kohn. "What that dude did to me was making it part of the regular vernacular, like this is how to communicate: 'I'm not saying it because I hate you, I'm saying it because it's a fact.' That's dangerous, and that's what this film displays."

BREAKING THROUGH IN FILM

BlacKkKlansman took home the noteworthy Grand Prix jury prize following its premiere at the 2018 Cannes Film Festival. The film, which grossed some $50 million domestically, hit theaters in the United States in August 2018—a date chosen because of its proximity to the one-year anniversary of the infamous white supremacist and neo-Nazi rally in Charlottesville, Virginia, where activist Heather Heyer was killed. Lee had included footage of the rally in *BlacKkKlansman* in to display the parallels in the racist rhetoric used in both the twentieth and twenty-first centuries. Washington's portrayal of Stallworth earned him nominations for a Golden Globe Award, NAACP Image Award, and Screen Actors Guild (SAG) Award, as well as a Hollywood Film Award in the category of Hollywood Breakout Performance Actor and an African American Film Critics Association Award for Best Actor.

Washington's other 2018 credits included the film *Monster* (later sold to a new distribution company and retitled *All Rise*), which premiered at the Sundance Film Festival that year and tells the story of a high school honors student whose world is upended when he is charged with murder, and *The Old Man & the Gun*, a Robert Redford vehicle about an elderly prison escapee. A particularly busy year for the actor who felt he still had a lot more to learn and offer viewers, 2018 also saw him star in the Sundance Film Festival premiere *Monsters and Men* as a conflicted Brooklyn cop who must deal with the aftermath when a fellow officer kills an unarmed black man. (The film was partly inspired by the 2014 death of Eric Garner at the hands of a New York Police Department officer.) "John David Washington offers an insider's viewpoint as a cop caught between bonds of loyalty to fellow officers and a simmering disgust for their barely disguised racism," Phil de Semlyen wrote for *Time Out* (15 Jan. 2019). "His role is more muted than in *BlacKkKlansman*, but he shows tantalising glimpses of dad Denzel's effortless charisma." Such critically appraised performances continued to support his independent reputation in the industry and garner him further attention from filmmakers.

SUGGESTED READING

Aggeler, Madeleine. "John David Washington Interrupts Reporter to Praise His Mom." *The Cut*, Vox Media, 20 Aug. 2018, www.thecut.com/2018/08/john-david-washington-son-pauletta-denzel-washington.html. Accessed 3 Mar. 2020.

Baskin, Ben. "John David Washington: From NFL Practice Squad to Spike Lee's Leading Man." *Sports Illustrated*, 31 July 2018, www.si.com/nfl/2018/07/31/john-david-washington-blackkklansman-spike-lee-ballers-denzel. Accessed 3 Mar. 2020.

Kohn, Eric. "John David Washington on Getting Called the N-Word and Moving beyond the Shadow of Denzel." *IndieWire*, 14 Aug. 2018, www.indiewire.com/2018/08/john-david-washington-interview-blackkklansman-1201994018/. Accessed 30 Jan. 2020.

Kredell, Matthew. "How Denzel's Son Became the Best Thing on HBO's 'Ballers.'" *Men's Journal*, www.mensjournal.com/entertainment/how-denzels-son-john-david-washington-became-the-best-thing-on-hbos-ballers-w431693/. Accessed 30 Jan. 2020.

Semlyen, Phil de. Review of *Monsters and Men*, directed by Reinaldo Marcus Green. *Time Out*, 15 Jan. 2019, www.timeout.com/london/film/monsters-and-men. Accessed 30 Jan. 2020.

Washington, John David. "'I Don't Mind the Questions—I'm Used to the Questions'—John David Washington Talks Being the Son of Denzel and Forging His Own Path in Spike Lee's *BlacKkKlansman*." Interview by Chris Wasser. *Independent.ie*, 24 Aug. 2018, www.independent.ie/entertainment/movies/i-dont-mind-the-questions-im-used-to-the-questions-john-david-washington-talks-being-the-son-of-denzel-and-forging-his-own-path-in-spike-lees-blackkklansman-37241676.html. Accessed 30 Jan. 2020.

——. "John David Washington on Dad Denzel, Spike Lee's 'Black Klansman' and His Sundance Debut." Interview by Mia Galuppo. *The Hollywood Reporter*, 18 Jan. 2018, www.hollywoodreporter.com/news/john-david-washington-dad-denzel-spike-lees-black-klansman-his-sundance-debut-1075103. Accessed 30 Jan. 2020.

SELECTED WORKS

Ballers, 2015–19; *Love Beats Rhymes*, 2017; *Monsters and Men*, 2018; *All Rise*, 2018; *BlacKkKlansman*, 2018; *The Old Man & the Gun*, 2018

—Mari Rich

George Watsky

Date of birth: September 15, 1986
Occupation: Musician and poet

George Watsky can be a difficult artist to characterize. Fans of spoken word, a genre of poetry meant to be performed, know him as the winner of the 2006 Brave New Voices National Poetry Slam and from his subsequent appearance on season six of HBO's *Russell Simmons Presents Def Poetry*. Others know him from the viral video titled "Pale Kid Raps Fast" that he posted on YouTube in early 2011 and quickly garnered millions of views. "It's no wonder now that [Watsky] has become a favorite on YouTube, the place his mind-numbing intellectual hypnotics were made for," Marc Hustvedt wrote for *Tubefilter* (26 Apr. 2011), explaining that "a global network like YouTube could transform slightly offbeat talents into independent stars."

The video, as Watsky told Vanessa Haughton for *Observer* (11 July 2014), "changed the landscape of everything. Suddenly I had this big online following and I was able to get the people who found the fast rap to go back and watch my old stuff. I've just been trying to hammer it home that . . . poetry is still a big part of what I do." Asked by Hustvedt whether he considered himself a rapper or a poet, the artist replied, "I am both, but I also don't really see them as different things. I write lyrics, and sometimes they're in 4/4 time with end rhymes and sometimes they're not. Sometimes they have choruses, sometimes they're more conversational and have themes and messages. . . . All rappers are poets, although not all poets are rappers, because rap is a specific form of poetry with the added element of music." Following his YouTube success, Watsky published *How to Ruin Everything* (2016), a collection of essays, and released several well-received albums, including *All You Can Do* (2014), *Complaint* (2019), and *Placement* (2020).

EARLY LIFE

George Watsky was born on September 15, 1986, and grew up in San Francisco, California. He has a twin brother, Simon, who became a pilot as an adult. His mother, Clare (née Miller), was a librarian, while his father, Paul, was a psychotherapist. Watsky attended Buena Vista Elementary School in the Potrero Hill District of San Francisco, where he participated in a Spanish-language immersion program. When he was in second grade, his parents, worried about the violence that plagued the area surrounding Buena Vista Elementary, transferred him to a different school, where the only cultural immersion

program available was Chinese. In between classes on the Cantonese language and Chinese calligraphy, Watsky was bullied mercilessly, due, in some part, to the orthodontic neckgear he was forced to wear.

Watsky reasoned that if he never stopped talking, no one would have the opportunity to fill the silence with teasing. "I had a seemingly unlimited wealth of annoying insights, and as elementary school dragged on, I was powerless to stop them escaping the dungeon of my mouth, its orthodontic shackles and oppressive Lunchables breath," he wrote in his 2016 book of essays, *How to Ruin Everything*. Of middle school, he wrote, "The system functions through discipline, Ritalin, and respect for authority—anything to keep the school from descending into anarchy. But I always had to know why: *why* can't we be on the yard during free period? *Why* can't I chew gum? *Why* do I have to sing the National Anthem?"

Despite his travails, Watsky's early years were not totally devoid of pleasure. His father passed down his fervent love of sports, and Watsky played on a Little League team for several years, collecting a string of participation trophies along the way. A highlight of his adolescence was the summer he got a job selling concessions at Giants Stadium. He also played percussion in the school orchestra and found a way to bond with his classmates through music. "If there was one bit of glue that held the fractured social world together," he wrote in his book, "it was hip-hop. We had other cultural bonds—Gap, the mall at Stonestown, the Giants and Niners, Pokémon, Hello Kitty—but no common language was more widely spoken than rap."

As a teenager, Watsky watched Black Entertainment Television (BET) and was inspired by such artists as Nelly, Eminem, and OutKast. "I loved the wordplay, the underdogs, and the fact that you could stand up to your enemies by the power of wit," he wrote. He found, unfortunately, that using wit did not always work in the real world; at fourteen, he was expelled from school for directing an obscenity-laden rap at a teacher. He also frequently attended concerts at the Fillmore, an iconic San Francisco music venue, where he saw the Roots and Gnarls Barkley, among other acts.

SLAM POETRY, MYSTERY QUARTET, AND INVISIBLE, INC.

While attending San Francisco University High School, Watsky began competing in poetry slams around the Bay area. (A slam is a competition at which poets read original pieces for an audience, who judges their work on not just content but performance style.) He won numerous local competitions, and in 2005 he traveled to New York City, where he participated as a member of a San Francisco team that competed in the five-day Youth Speaks Teen Poetry Slam.

The following year, as an individual performer at the 2006 Brave New Voices National Poetry Slam, he garnered the championship, impressing judges with his poem "Pickup Line Protest." In the wake of that victory, he was featured on an episode of *Russell Simmons Presents Def Poetry*, an HBO show hosted by Mos Def and featuring a mix of established poets like Nikki Giovanni and Amiri Baraka, as well as up-and-coming figures like Watsky, who recited his poem "V for Virgin" during his segment.

After graduating from high school, Watsky took a year off to form a band with his cousin and a few friends. Calling themselves the Mystery Funk Quartet, they played a hybrid of jazz and hip-hop at any basement party or art-gallery event that would have them. He then entered Emerson College, in Boston, where he designed his own interdisciplinary major, Writing and Acting for the Screen and Stage.

As an Emerson student, he regularly traveled to slams across the country, and in 2007 he formed a poetry-rap group he dubbed Invisible, Inc., which released an eponymous album that same year. He also toured widely to other college campuses, performing at an estimated two hundred schools during his college years.

Despite sometimes-dismal turnouts, Watsky, who billed himself by just his last name, began gaining increased attention. In 2010, he released a self-titled solo album and was profiled in that year in the arts section of the *Boston Globe*. In that piece, from December 4, 2009, Joel Brown wrote, "On stage, Watsky offers the clean-cut Gen-Y angst of Michael Cera channeled through the rapid-fire flow of the poetry-slam star that he is."

YOUTUBE FAME

After graduating from Emerson in 2010, Watsky settled in Los Angeles, hoping to begin a career as an actor. Although he was almost cast in a big-budget project early on, the role fell through, leading him to audition for more commercial roles. In one particularly demoralizing week, however, he auditioned for both a KFC and a People for the Ethical Treatment of Animals spot and got neither.

His big break came in January 2011, when Watsky posted a video of himself rapping titled "Pale Kid Raps Fast" on his YouTube channel. "I think the way that video was titled people clicked on it with a morbid curiosity," he explained to David Ertischek for *Emerson Today* (3 July 2019). "Just the thumbnail and title [drew people in] and not knowing if it'd be good or terrible—and they were willing to watch it either way. Then people were pleasantly surprised I

was rapping well." The ninety-second video was ultimately shared more than twenty-five million times.

His YouTube success helped further launch his music career. Watsky subsequently released several albums, including *Cardboard Castles* (2013), *All You Can Do* (2014), × *Infinity* (2016), and *Complaint* (2019), touring widely in support of each. In 2013, he appeared in a minor role in a single episode of the hit sitcom *Arrested Development*. YouTube continued to be a major forum for him, and his channel attracted almost a million followers. "YouTube is an unparalleled opportunity to get material to a lot of people all over the world. I'm not interested in writing in obscurity for the rest of my life. As technology changes and opens new platforms, I think it's important for an artist who wants to reach a wide audience to embrace the medium of their time," Watsky asserted to Hustvedt. "I believe the medium of our era is becoming the web video, and more and more, people are going to be turning that way for their entertainment."

In addition to his own videos, Watsky appeared in a handful of episodes of the web series *Epic Rap Battles of History*, which satirically pits historical and pop culture figures against one another. In one episode, for example, he portrays Edgar Allan Poe (battling a rapping Stephen King), and in another he plays William Shakespeare (who goes head to head with Dr. Seuss). He has also created multiple web series documenting the making of his albums. In 2020, Watsky released the album *Placement*, which was accompanied by music videos for several of the songs released on YouTube.

Watsky made headlines in May 2020 when he set a new world record for longest freestyle rap. Live streaming the feat from his home in Los Angeles, he rapped continuously—even while using the bathroom—for thirty-three hours, thirty-three minutes, and thirty-three seconds. The previous record had been twenty-five hours and fifty-six minutes, set in 2017. Over the course of his live stream, he raised almost $150,000 for the Sweet Relief Musicians Fund, which aids fans, performers, and crew members affected by the COVID-19 crisis.

PERSONAL LIFE

Watsky, a longtime vegetarian, suffered from juvenile epilepsy, an experience he details in his rap "Seizure Boy." He has been linked romantically to the actor and vlogger Anna Kay Akana.

SUGGESTED READING

Brown, Joel. "Plugging into Poetry as a Media Platform." *The Boston Globe*, 4 Dec. 2009, archive.boston.com/ae/theater_arts/articles/2009/12/04/

slam_artist_george_watsky_plugs_into_po-etry_as_a_media_platform. Accessed 18 May 2020.

Della Cava, Marco. "Watsky to Aspiring Rappers: You Can Do This, Too." *USA Today*, 24 May 2013, www.usatoday.com/story/life/music/2013/05/24/watsky-rapper-cardboard-castles-arrested-development/2116145. Accessed 18 May 2020.

Haughton, Vanessa. "Pale Kid Raps Fast: The Rise of Watsky." *Observer*, 11 July 2014, observer.com/2014/11/watsky. Accessed 18 May 2020.

Watsky, George. "George Watsky: Rapper, Poet, Author and Emerson Alum." Interview by David Ertischek'01. *Emerson Today*, 3 July 2019, today.emerson.edu/2019/07/03/george-watsky-rapper-poet-author-and-emerson-alum. Accessed 18 May 2020.

———. "George Watsky: Rapper and Slam Poet." Interview by Advik Shreekumar. *Harvard Political Review*, 27 Apr. 2014, harvard-politics.com/interviews/george-watsky-rapper-slam-poet. Accessed 18 May 2020.

———. "George Watsky: YouTube's Poet Rapper Breaks Out." Interview by Marc Hustvedt. *Tubefilter*, 26 Apr. 2011, www.tubefilter.com/2011/04/26/george-watsky-youtube/. Accessed 18 May 2020.

———. *How to Ruin Everything*. Plume, 2016.

SELECTED WORKS

Cardboard Castles, 2013; *All You Can Do*, 2014; × *Infinity*, 2016; *Complaint*, 2019; *Placement*, 2020

—Mari Rich

Lynda Weinman

Date of birth: January 24, 1955
Occupation: Business owner and author

In April 2015 the social networking company *LinkedIn* acquired the subscription-based education business *Lynda.com* for $1.5 billion. While that substantial price received widespread attention within the media, the potential for a billion-dollar payout had never been *Lynda.com* founder Lynda Weinman's guiding focus. Rather, she preferred to concentrate on her ability "to build something that is so much bigger than me," she explained to Elisa Balabram for *WomenandBiz.com* magazine (16 Sept. 2008). "To think that what I started feeds the mouths of so many employees, and royalties for so many trainers, and that customers get so much benefit from what we produce." Founded in 1996 by Weinman, a Californian graphic artist and teacher, *Lynda.com* offers subscribers a vast array of instructional videos and other educational resources in a variety of computer-related fields, including graphic design and web design. Although the company's business model originally relied on in-person classes and the sales of instructional books, videotapes, and CD-ROMs, a strategic pivot to a subscription model in the early 2000s transformed *Lynda.com* into both a highly profitable venture and a trailblazer among subscription-based online businesses, qualities that factored into the company's acquisition by LinkedIn in 2015. For the largely self-taught Weinman, the sale of *Lynda.com* was in many ways the culmination of two decades of unexpected success. "I was not techy or geeky, and I figured a lot of things out on my own," she told Jane Porter for *Fast Company* (27 Apr. 2015). "A lot of people came to me to ask, 'How you do this and that?' I didn't realize sharing your enthusiasm about something was teaching."

EARLY LIFE AND EDUCATION

Lynda Susan Weinman was born in Hollywood, California, on January 24, 1955. The oldest child, she has two younger siblings. Weinman's parents divorced when she was three, and Weinman and her siblings spent portions of their childhoods living with their grandparents. They later moved in with their father and stepmother, whom she found unsupportive.

Despite being inquisitive, Weinman struggled with traditional schooling as she got older. Her experience prompted her to seek out Sherwood Oaks Experimental High School (now

Photo by Matt Winkelmeyer/Getty Images for SBIFF

Oaks Film School), a private school that provided what she described to Balabram as "an unorthodox and alternative education." Weinman paid for her tuition with earnings from a part-time job at a food stand. As she later noted in interviews, changing schools dramatically improved her academic performance and reshaped her view of education. "There wasn't a lot of structure or forced prerequisites, and students had a lot of choice," she explained to Balabram. "What this encouraged me to do was to identify what really interested me and learn that it was up to me to find internal motivation to pursue my interests." In addition, the experience likewise brought to life the independent and entrepreneurial spirit that would fuel many of Weinman's later ventures. "I was willing to work hard for something, willing to create my own path and was sort of a self-starter," she explained in an interview for the *New Individualist* magazine, later republished by the *Atlas Society* (26 Oct. 2011).

After graduating from high school, Weinman enrolled at Evergreen State College, an institution with an emphasis on interdisciplinary education, in Washington State. Unsure of her preferred career path, she pursued studies in a variety of areas, including ceramics and museum studies, and ran the school's art gallery for a time. Weinman earned her bachelor's degree in humanities in 1976.

For a time Weinman managed a gift shop. She soon returned to California, however, and in 1978 opened a retail store, Vertigo, in Los Angeles, with a loan from her grandfather. Although Weinman soon opened another Vertigo store, both ultimately failed, and she shut down both locations by the early 1980s.

EARLY CAREER

After her stores closed, Weinman explored work in the film industry with the encouragement of a boyfriend who already worked in that field. Still intrigued by visual arts, she began to learn some of the techniques and processes in use in film and television at that time. "I learned how to create special effects animation and photography, which was still all drawn by hand and shot on analog cameras back then," she recalled to Balabram. Eventually finding work in animation and special effects, Weinman served as an effects animator for the films *Bill & Ted's Excellent Adventure* (1989) and *Waxwork II: Lost in Time* (1992) and as a rotoscope artist for episodes of the television series *McGee and Me!*, among other projects.

A turning point in Weinman's career came in 1982, when she received her first personal computer. She was quickly drawn to the burgeoning field of computer graphics, a technological innovation that appealed to Weinman on multiple levels. "To me, it was a fascinating new discipline

that I found really interesting," she told Nathan Chan for *Foundr* magazine (5 July 2018). "And I found a lot of connections between animation and the computer." Initially using the Apple II and the earliest Macintosh computers, Weinman taught herself to create computer graphics and soon learned that her uncommon level of expertise in that area made her a sought-after teacher and consultant.

Largely leaving film behind, Weinman instead began to work as a computer graphics and animation consultant by the late 1980s. In 1989, she was hired to teach digital media and graphics at the prestigious Art Center College of Design (now the ArtCenter) in Pasadena, California, which she has described as the Ivy League of art institutions. To Weinman's delight, the role allowed her to teach "at the infancy of the computer age" and "to see the industry unfold," as she explained to Benjamin F. Kuo for *socalTECH* (28 Oct. 2010). In addition to the Art Center College of Design, where she continued to teach into the mid-1990s, Weinman went on to teach classes at the American Film Institute, San Francisco State University, and the University of California, Los Angeles Extension School.

LYNDA.COM

Hoping to learn more and teach about designing web graphics in the early 1990s, Weinman was surprised to find that she could not locate any books on that topic in a bookstore. "I remember thinking, Maybe this book doesn't exist yet," she recalled to Porter. "I went home from the bookstore and wrote the book proposal." That proposal eventually became Weinman's first book, *Designing Web Graphics* (1996). A unique work for that period, *Designing Web Graphics* became a hit, and Weinman went on to author and coauthor additional books on designing, coloring, and preparing web graphics as well as designing websites.

Despite the international popularity of *Designing Web Graphics*, Weinman found that publishers were reluctant to publish some of her later offerings. Still hoping to share her knowledge of computer technology with those seeking to learn, she decided to strike out on her own, offering in-person classes that she advertised—alongside books and instructional videos—through her personal website, which had been titled "Lynda's Homegurrrl Page" and registered as *Lynda.com* in 1995. Beginning in 1996, Weinman and illustrator Bruce Heavin rented out classroom space in a Southern California high school to hold weeklong boot camps on web design. The courses attracted students not only from California but also from elsewhere within the United States and even from other countries. They founded the Ojai Digital Arts Center with $20,000, and within a year of operation, the venture earned them $1.7 million. As the business—known as *Lynda.com* after Weinman's web address—continued to grow, Weinman and Heavin opened a dedicated facility in Carpinteria, near Santa Barbara, California, that became the company's headquarters.

BOOMING BUSINESS

Like many businesses related to web technology, *Lynda.com* struggled during the first years of the twenty-first century as the dot-com crash, the economic recession, and post–September 11 fears that characterized those years reduced consumer spending and led businesses to lay off workers or even shutter entirely. Although Weinman and Heavin laid off three-quarters of their employees during that period, the company survived thanks in large part to a risky change in business model in 2002. Rather than offering in-person classes, the company began to operate under a subscription model in which users could access the site's library of resource materials and educational videos for a monthly fee of twenty-five dollars. Although that fee was one-sixtieth the cost of a weeklong in-person class, the web-only model allowed Weinman and her colleagues to reach a far wider audience. Over the next several years, the company foundered but then began to thrive as users the world over increasingly paid to gain access to the resources available on the site; within four years, it gained ten times as many subscribers. "Around the 2006, 2008 timeframe was where we were just growing like a freight train, and we knew we had a tiger by the tail," Weinman recalled to Chan. Around that time, Weinman and Heavin employed a C-suite for the first time.

The open-ended nature of *Lynda.com* fit a different niche than the more traditionally structured massively open online classes (MOOCs) and for-profit online universities that were also enjoying popularity at the time; Weinman has attributed much of the company's success to that flexibility. She also emphasized the importance of customer satisfaction over the churn rate, or number of suspended subscriptions. She also focused on delivering quality content. The platform attracted subscribers from the entertainment industry, businesses, institutions of higher education, and government groups.

By the 2010s *Lynda.com* had an annual revenue in the tens of millions and had attracted the attention of investors intrigued by the company's financial success and business model. "We had people ravenous to invest in us the entire time because we were the only people in our space who were making money," Weinman told Kerry A. Dolan for *Forbes* (18 May 2017). "Eventually we chose to take the VC money as a desire to have an exit. I decided when I turned 59 [that] by the time I'm 65 I'd like to have another chapter." The company received $103 million in venture capital in 2013 and another $186 million in 2015, which drew notice from prospective buyers.

ANOTHER CHAPTER

Weinman's desired exit came in May 2015, shortly after the business-networking platform LinkedIn purchased *Lynda.com* for $1.5 billion, a price that surprised some observers. Weinman's motivation lay elsewhere, however. "[The price] surprised a lot of people who are not in our industry," she explained to Porter. "For me, I'm focused on the impact. The first words out of my mouth were: 'Wow, that will have a big impact.'" By that point, the platform featured thousands of courses and had millions of users. After acquiring *Lynda.com*, LinkedIn was in turn acquired by Microsoft in December 2016.

Advised to take a year off before deciding her future, Weinman did take some time for herself following the sale of *Lynda.com* but soon returned to the film industry to fund the work of filmmakers. She contributed to grants and founded Another Chapter Productions. Particularly dedicated to documentary filmmaking, Weinman is credited as a producer or executive producer for more than a dozen documentaries, including *Unrest* (2017), *This Changes Everything* (2018), and *Better Together* (2019). She has also served as a producer for scripted projects, such as the acclaimed biographical drama *The Tale* (2018), which was nominated for the Emmy Award for Outstanding Television Movie. In addition, Weinman became president of the board of directors for the Santa Barbara International Film Festival, which she had joined around 2009.

PERSONAL LIFE

Weinman married Bruce Heavin, an illustrator and an ArtCenter alumnus, around 1996. The two were business partners at *Lynda.com* and have collaborated on various books, including *Coloring Web Graphics* (1996). Weinman has an adult daughter named Jamie Kirkland, from her previous marriage to Marc Kirkland.

SUGGESTED READING

Chan, Nathan. "206: From Animator to Tech Educator, Lynda Weinman Reflects on a $1.5B Exit and Her New Career." *Foundr*, 5 July 2018, foundr.com/business-exit-lynda-weinman-lynda. Accessed 17 Jan. 2020.

Dolan, Kerry A. "Tips from Lynda Weinman on How She Built and Sold Lynda.com to LinkedIn for $1.5 Billion." *Forbes*, 18 May 2017, www.forbes.com/sites/kerryadolan/2017/05/18/lynda-weinman-advice-she-sold-lynda-com-to-linkedin-for-1-5-billion-dollars/#5aa30b3e68a7. Accessed 17 Jan. 2020.

"Lynda Weinman: Queen of the Triple Win." *The Atlas Society*, 26 Oct. 2011, atlassociety.org/commentary/commentary-blog/4863-lynda-weinman-queen-of-the-triple-win. Accessed 17 Jan. 2020.

Palladino, D. J. "Who in the World Is Lynda. com?" *The Santa Barbara Independent*, 21 July 2011, www.independent.com/2011/07/21/who-world-is-lynda-com. Accessed 22 Jan. 2020.

Porter, Jane. "From Near Failure to a $1.5 Billion Sale: The Epic Story of Lynda.com." *Fast Company*, 27 Apr. 2015, www.fastcompany.com/3045404/from-near-failure-to-a-15-billion-sale-the-epic-story-of-lyndacom. Accessed 17 Jan. 2020.

Weinman, Lynda. "Interview with Lynda Weinman, Founder of Lynda.com." By Elisa Balabram. *WomenandBiz.com*, 16 Sept. 2008, www.womenandbiz.com/2008/09/16/interview-lynda-weinman-founder-lyndacom. Accessed 17 Jan. 2020.

Weinman, Lynda, and Bruce Heavin. "Interview with Lynda Weinman and Bruce Heavin, Lynda.com." By Benjamin F. Kuo. *socalTECH*, 28 Oct. 2010, www.socaltech.com/interview_with_lynda_weinman_and_bruce_heavin_lynda_com/s-0031860.html. Accessed 17 Jan. 2020.

—*Joy Crelin*

Tara Westover

Born: September 27, 1986
Occupation: Memoirist and historian

Writer and historian Tara Westover burst onto the literary scene with her 2018 memoir *Educated*, a best seller that became one of the most talked-about books of the year. As the title suggests, the book describes Westover's education, which followed a highly unusual path. The daughter of fundamentalist Mormons and survivalists, Westover grew up on a remote homestead in Idaho and had a difficult upbringing marked by social isolation and abuse. Her father forbade her and her siblings from attending school, convinced that the government would poison their minds. Yet, a growing desire to learn drove her to break with the teachings of her family and attend Brigham Young University (BYU) in Utah. There, her curiosity about the world drew her to history and politics, and she went on to win a prestigious Gates Cambridge Scholarship to pursue graduate studies at Cambridge

University in England, where she earned her doctorate in 2014.

When Westover published *Educated* four years later it was immediately hailed as "a rare memoir blockbuster," as David Canfield wrote for *Entertainment Weekly* (27 Feb. 2020), on par with other smash hits in the genre such as Jeannette Walls's *The Glass Castle* (2005) and Cheryl Strayed's *Wild* (2012). The book won several awards and was a finalist for many others, and it appeared on numerous best-of lists from prominent publications and celebrities. It also launched Westover's career as a public figure, and she was named on *Time* magazine's list of the one hundred most influential people in 2019. She subsequently traveled widely to speak about her life, which resonated with a wider audience than she had expected. "Maybe they don't have family situations that are quite as dramatic as mine, but a lot of people are trying to answer that basic question about what are the obligations they have to their families, and what do they owe themselves, and what do they do when those two things are in conflict or in tension," she explained to Canfield. "I think stories are part of how people work out how they feel about their own lives."

EARLY LIFE IN BUCK'S PEAK

Tara Westover was born in rural Idaho on September 27, 1986, but her parents originally did not procure a birth certificate. Later, her mother registered her official birthday as September 27, though relatives had different memories of the actual date. Her family made their home on Buck's Peak, a remote mountain in Franklin County, Idaho, where her father's relatives had lived for generations. Her parents, Val and LaRee Westover—she gives them the pseudonyms Gene and Faye in *Educated*—were fundamentalist Mormons with an extremist, survivalist outlook. In particular, her father's religious convictions and fears about the government and modern medicine shaped the family's life. From her earliest days, Westover and her six older siblings were trained to prepare for a coming apocalypse, in whatever form it might take. She helped her family stockpile food, but she also slept with a bag of clothes and a knife at the ready in case the "Feds" came to take them away.

Westover's father ran a junkyard, while her mother, an herbalist, became a midwife. (Later, her mother launched a highly successful business selling herbs and tinctures.) Growing up, Westover and her siblings never saw a doctor or attended school. This last point was crucial to Westover's understanding of herself, and how she and her brothers and sisters were different from other children they encountered through the local church. According to her memoir, when she was seven her paternal grandmother tried to convince her to escape her oppressive father and attend school in Arizona. She ultimately refused, fearing the government would find out about her family and kill them.

Westover was homeschooled to a degree by her mother and learned to read, but, like the rest of her siblings, she was primarily expected to help care for the farm and work in the junkyard. Her memoir describes her siblings suffering various injuries scavenging for scrap metal. None were taken to a doctor. Westover also suggests her mother suffered a serious brain injury that went untreated and that her father may have had schizophrenia, though some of her family members challenged that account. Meanwhile, according to Westover, as she grew older, she suffered physical and emotional abuse from one of her older brothers. Overcoming the many traumas of her upbringing would become a key part of her eventual broader education. "All abuse is foremost an assault on the mind," Westover told Hadley Freeman for *Vogue* (15 Feb. 2018). "When you abuse someone, you limit their perspective and you trap them in your view of them or your view of the world."

UNDERGRADUATE EDUCATION AT BYU

Inspired in part by another older brother, Tyler, who had left the family to attend college, Westover began to take an interest in reading and books, pouring over the Bible and the Book of Mormon. She showed a talent for singing, and she sang the lead in a local production of *Annie*. Still, she did not consider leaving home until Tyler convinced her to apply to Brigham Young University, a college in Provo, Utah, affiliated with the Mormon church. Westover then bought textbooks and taught herself enough mathematics to pass the ACT test necessary for college admission. Tyler helped her fill out an application, and she was accepted. Her father was furious about her decision to attend college, but her mother offered surprising, and secret, encouragement.

Westover moved to Provo and began her studies at age seventeen. Nearly every aspect of her new life, from the behaviors of her roommates to the rituals of classroom behavior, confounded her. Her lack of any previous formal schooling meant she struggled to keep up in many areas, and at first this led her to renew her belief in her father's worldview. In her memoir and in later interviews, Westover noted one particularly uncomfortable moment in a class that emphasized just how disconnected she had been from mainstream society: She raised her hand to ask what the Holocaust was, earning angry silence as the class thought she was making a cruel joke. That embarrassment, however, helped her realize how much she had been missing and sparked a hunger for knowledge. "I felt

like the only dancer who had missed rehearsal," she told Lisa O'Kelly for the *Guardian* (17 Feb. 2018). "But then again, after years of knowing virtually nothing at all I found learning so exciting. I piled up books and read late into the night. Sometimes I barely slept."

Over time Westover came to enjoy her studies. She had enrolled as a music student, but by her junior year found herself dropping music theory classes in favor of courses on history and politics. She took a Jewish history class, and her professor encouraged her to apply for a study-abroad program at the University of Cambridge in England. (The fact that, just two years before, Westover thought Europe was a country, not a continent, demonstrates how rapidly her relationship to the world had changed.) She was accepted to the program in 2007, though she almost was not able to get a passport due to her lack of a traditional birth certificate.

STUDIES AT CAMBRIDGE UNIVERSITY

At Cambridge, Westover focused on historiography—not the study of history, but the study of historians' methods. Her interest stemmed from her own experience of learning of major world events late in life. "I needed to understand how the great gatekeepers of history had come to terms with their own ignorance and partiality," she stated in her memoir. Westover's time studying abroad further developed her expanding perspective and intellectual identity. As Paul Kerry, her BYU history professor, told Chris Giovarelli for *BYU News* (27 Feb. 2008), "The Cambridge experience released Tara's potential. She would often write much more than was required and would discuss her ideas regularly with classmates and faculty."

Westover graduated from BYU with a history degree in 2008. She was then one of just forty-five US students to win a prestigious Gates Cambridge Scholarship to attend graduate school at Cambridge. She studied at Trinity College at Cambridge and received her master's degree in 2009. Meanwhile, she finally told her parents about her brother's abusive behavior, but they refused to believe her, leading to an estrangement. "My parents couldn't deal with that so they turned the other way and made me look like the bad person. In families like mine there is no crime worse than telling the truth," she told O'Kelly.

Westover was a visiting fellow at Harvard University in 2010. She then returned to Cambridge to pursue her PhD. Inspired by her own experiences, her dissertation explores philosophies of family obligation within four different nineteenth-century movements, including Mormonism. It was called "The Family, Morality, and Social Science in Anglo-American Cooperative

Thought, 1813–1890." She earned her doctorate in history in 2014.

EDUCATED

Westover's split with much of her family and her developing academic career came together when, with the encouragement of her thesis adviser, David Runciman, she began writing a memoir chronicling her childhood experiences. However, as with all her other accomplishments in the wider world, the undertaking required learning a completely new skill. She compared the daunting task of writing a memoir to entering a classroom for the first time at seventeen, and to prepare she listened to the *New Yorker* fiction podcast and read other memoirs. "I needed to learn the fundamentals of the craft," she told Tina Jordan for the *New York Times* (2 Mar. 2018). "I had never written a word of narrative. What is a tense shift, what is point of view? I didn't know any of it." Her former professor had more faith. "Tara always wrote in this completely fresh way," Runciman told Freeman. "Most of us mimic how other people write, but maybe because Tara didn't grow up reading what we all did, there was an originality to it."

Westover completed a draft of *Educated* in 2016. As the manuscript was shown to publishers it quickly caused a stir in the industry, sparking a bidding war in the United States and selling within its first day on the market in the United Kingdom. Hype continued to build around the book, and when it was released in 2018 it debuted at number one on the New York Times Best Sellers list and went on to top several other lists as well. *Educated* was nominated for the Carnegie Medal for Excellence and was a finalist for the LA Times Book Prize, the PEN/Jean Stein Book Award, and the National Book Critics Circle's John Leonard Prize, among other honors. It was named one of the best books of the year by the *New York Times*, the *Washington Post*, the *San Francisco Chronicle*, the *Guardian*, *Publishers Weekly*, and many other outlets. In addition, figures ranging from talk show hosts such as Oprah Winfrey to former US President Barack Obama praised the book as a favorite.

Westover was shocked by the book's success and the way so many readers related to her life story. "When I started to write about it, I thought, 'Oh, maybe it will be for the people who have struggled with certain kinds of difficult families or extreme ideologies or things like that,'" she recalled to Canfield. "I really didn't expect that it would be something that a lot of people en masse would identify with or want to read. I'm grateful so many people have taken time out of their own lives to spend it on mine."

PERSONAL LIFE

Tara Westover settled in New York City after the release of *Educated*. She admitted that, for a time, the success of her memoir overwhelmed her personal life. "I'm going to try to get my life back from the book," she told Canfield. "Let the book keep doing its thing, but I'm going to go try to get a little bit of my life back the way it was."

SUGGESTED READING

Freeman, Hadley. "Tara Westover on Turning Her Off-the-Grid Life into a Remarkable Memoir." *Vogue*, 15 Feb. 2018, www.vogue.com/article/tara-westover-memoir-educated-vogue-march-2018-issue. Accessed 8 Sept. 2020.

Giovarelli, Chris. "Third BYU Student in 5 Years Wins Prestigious Gates Scholarship." *BYU News*, 27 Feb. 2008, news.byu.edu/news/third-byu-student-5-years-wins-prestigious-gates-scholarship. Accessed 8 Sept. 2020.

Jordan, Tina. "Spinning a Brutal, Off-the-Grid Childhood into a Gripping Memoir." *The New York Times*, 2 Mar. 2018, www.nytimes.com/2018/03/02/books/review/westover-educated-best-seller.html. Accessed 8 Sept. 2020.

Westover, Tara. *Educated*. Random House, 2018.

———. "Tara Westover: 'In Families Like Mine There Is No Crime Worse Than Telling the Truth.'" Interview by Lisa O'Kelly. *The Guardian*, 17 Feb. 2018, www.theguardian.com/books/2018/feb/17/tara-westover-education-interview-i-was-13-when-i-first-went-to-another-childs-house. Accessed 10 Sept. 2020.

———. "Tara Westover's *Educated* Has Sold 4 Million Copies. She's Ready to Get Her Life Back." Interview by David Canfield. *Entertainment Weekly*, 27 Feb. 2020, ew.com/books/author-interviews/tara-westover-educated-success-future/. Accessed 8 Sept. 2020.

—Molly Hagan

Gretchen Whitmer

Born: August 23, 1971
Occupation: Politician

Gretchen Esther Whitmer became the forty-ninth governor of Michigan when she won the 2018 election. She is seen as a rising star in the Democratic Party, as Aaron Kall, University of Michigan's debate director, told Tara Law for *Time* (4 Feb. 2020): "If not this [election] cycle, certainly in the future, I think there will definitely be talk about her as a vice presidential or

Photo by Julia Pickett via Wikimedia Commons

presidential candidate, given [her] age, [and] the electoral significance of Michigan."

EARLY LIFE AND EDUCATION

Gretchen Whitmer was born on August 23, 1971, and raised in Michigan. Her happy childhood memories include fishing for perch with her sister and brother off a dock in Onekama, a small town in upper Michigan. Whitmer related a childhood mishap for Jo Mathis for *Oakland Legal News* (11 Apr. 2016): "My father nicknamed me 'Gravity Gretchen' when I knocked out my front teeth at church camp, right after the braces he paid for to correct the gap in those teeth were removed. That's the worst chapter in a lengthy book of klutziness."

Her parents, both of whom were lawyers, taught her the value of hard work. She began her first job at fourteen, working for a lumber company. While her mother, Sherry, was a Democrat, her father, Richard, was a Republican; therefore, Whitmer also learned compromise and respect for others' opinions.

She graduated from the East Lansing public school system before going on to earn her bachelor's degree in communications in 1993 and a law degree in 1998, both from Michigan State University. Prior to attending law school, she considered a career in broadcasting, wanting to be the first female sportscaster for ESPN.

STATE LAWMAKER

Whitmer was elected to the Michigan House of Representatives in 2000. During her first term, her eldest daughter was born. At the same time,

she cared for her mother at the end of her life. These activities led to her support for paid family leave for workers to care for a newborn or an ill family member. She served six years in that body, becoming vice-chair of the House Democratic Women's Leadership Caucus.

In 2006 she became a Michigan state senator and later became the first woman to lead a caucus in that body. She also served as the minority leader of the Senate from 2011 until 2014. In that role, she worked with Republicans to pass Healthy Michigan, which expanded health coverage for more than 680,000 Michigan residents. In addition, she worked to raise the minimum wage.

As state senator, Whitmer voted for expanding Medicare; the success of her efforts in this area was her major accomplishment during her tenure. In addition, she supported a fifteen-dollar minimum wage, the use of recreational marijuana, the rights of same-sex adoptive parents, and universal preschool.

Whitmer also championed abortion rights. She was open about her experience of sexual assault, even before the beginning of the #MeToo movement. She did so in support of women's rights; she also supported gay marriage.

As the senate's minority leader, Whitmer pushed for a greater emphasis on higher education, including grants for Michigan high school students to offset higher tuition rates, linked to a decline in state funding. As Tim Martin reported for the Associated Press (run in *Crain's Detroit Business*, 12 Feb. 2012), Whitmer at the time said, "We've got to do something bold to say Michigan believes in education and this is a great place to come and locate your business because we've got the work force you need."

Whitmer also taught a course in gender and law at Michigan State University in 2015. She was the Towsley Policymaker in Residence from 2015 to 2016 in the Gerald R. Ford School of Public Policy at the University of Michigan, where she taught a course of her own design.

After eight years in the state senate, in 2016 Whitmer became Ingham County prosecutor after a scandal forced the incumbent to resign. In that role, she created a new Domestic Violence and Sexual Assault Unit to pursue sex offenders and abusers. Whitmer returned to practicing law as a corporate litigator at Dickinson Wright in Lansing.

MICHIGAN GOVERNOR

In the 2018 Michigan Democratic gubernatorial primary, Whitmer won all eighty-three counties; she then went on to win the general election against Republican state attorney general Bill Schuette with 53 percent of the vote. She ran as the more moderate Democrat in the primary, rejecting the idea of Medicare-for-all, which her opponents and more progressive Democrats favored. She rejected the moderate label, however, insisting she was also a progressive, but likewise claiming the mantle of pragmatist, advertising her record of bipartisanship and compromise in government.

For a campaign slogan she chose a simple, forceful message: "Fix the damn roads." As she told Karen Tumulty for the *Washington Post* (28 July 2019), "I stayed focused on things like fixing the roads, education, ensuring our kids are prepared to have the skills they need and connecting adults with good-paying jobs through skills opportunities as well. And water—cleaning up the drinking water, protecting the Great Lakes." She then continued, "At the end of the day, people want leaders who they respect and who they believe in and who can get things done."

In early September 2019, Whitmer became the first governor to ban flavored e-cigarettes, because vaping was associated with respiratory illnesses. Leaders were especially concerned with marketing that targeted young people and subsequent increased usage by that population. As Mitch Smith reported for the *New York Times* (4 Sept. 2019), Whitmer issued a statement, saying, "Companies selling vaping products are using candy flavors to hook children on nicotine and misleading claims to promote the belief that these products are safe. That ends today." Her directive banned the sale, both online and in stores, of flavored nicotine products. It also called for an end to advertising that used terms such as "natural," "healthy," or "safe."

In addition, Whitmer created a new office of climate and energy and joined the US Climate Alliance, which commits individual states to the principles of the Paris Agreement, following the US withdrawal from the international climate change mitigation agreement under President Donald Trump. Michigan was the twentieth state to join the alliance.

GAINING A NATIONAL PROFILE

Whitmer's profile rose still further when Speaker of the House Nancy Pelosi called on her to give the Democratic response to President Trump's 2020 State of the Union address, delivered on February 4. At the time, she was being touted as a potential vice-presidential running mate in the 2020 election. Given her potential ability to deliver votes in a key Midwestern swing state, she was a logical choice. In the 2016 presidential election, Michigan departed from decades of solid Democrat support to elect Trump by a narrow margin; the state was seen as key to succeeding in the 2020 presidential election.

In addition to giving Whitmer a turn on the national stage, as Law wrote, "For the Democratic Party more broadly, it's an opportunity to contrast their views with those of the President—and to signal their intended vision for the future of the party."

Whitmer spoke from the stage at East Lansing High School, which her daughters attended, to an audience of families and teachers. Some saw the choice as demonstrating support for public education.

In her speech, just over ten minutes in length, Whitmer critiqued the president for his behavior and language, particularly on social media; alluded to his impeachment, which she and others correctly expected to end in acquittal by the Republican-led Senate the following day; and excoriated him over the economy. As Emily Cochrane reported for the *New York Times* (4 Feb. 2020), the governor took issue with Trump's claims on the economy, saying, "It doesn't matter what the president says about the stock market. What matters is that millions of people struggle to get by or don't have enough money at the end of the month after paying for transportation, student loans or prescription drugs." She also appealed to young voters, alluding to the fact that one of her daughters would graduate in 2020 and be eligible to vote in November.

FACING CRITICISM

Not long after the State of the Union speech, the United States and the rest of the world faced the coronavirus pandemic, in which Michigan was one of the US states most negatively affected. Whitmer, who issued a stay-at-home order in March, criticized the federal response as inadequate. She cited a shipment from the national stockpile of personal protective equipment, which was enough for only a single shift at a southeast Michigan hospital. Her critique earned her disdain from President Trump, but praise from Joe Biden, the presumptive 2020 Democratic presidential nominee. Biden said, as quoted by Karen Tumulty for the *Washington Post* (28 Mar. 2020), "Donald Trump could learn a thing or two from Governor Whitmer—speed matters, details matter, and people matter. She's secured more than 10 million N95 masks, more than 4 million gloves, thousands of gallons of hand sanitizer, and critical equipment for health-care providers."

Whitmer faced pushback from some of her constituents for her more restrictive stay-at-home orders issued on April 9, 2020, at the height of the pandemic. Michigan was one of the states where conservative protestors, some armed, occupied the state capitol building in mid-April, blocking roadways and demanding the right to return to work. Some legislators began wearing bulletproof vests to work. At the time of the protest, Michigan had the third-highest number of deaths from the virus of any state.

In the aftermath of the protests, some legislators discussed banning weapons in the state capitol, while others downplayed the event. Other observers noted that the protesters were predominately white and suggested the treatment and outcome might have been different if the protesters had been African Americans.

When the Republican-led state legislature refused to extend the original state of emergency order on April 30, the day it was set to expire, Whitmer reinstated it until May 28. As Jacey Fortin reported for the *New York Times* (2 May 2020), Whitmer issued a statement saying, "By refusing to extend the emergency and disaster declaration, Republican lawmakers are putting their heads in the sand and putting more lives and livelihoods at risk. I'm not going to let that happen."

PERSONAL LIFE

Whitmer married Dr. Marc Mallory. They live in Lansing with her two daughters from a previous marriage. Mallory's three sons also live in Michigan.

SUGGESTED READING

Fortin, Jacey. "Michigan Governor Reinstates State of Emergency as Protests Ramp Up." *The New York Times*, 2 May 2020, www.nytimes.com/2020/05/01/us/michigan-protests-capitol-virus-armed.html. Accessed 2 May 2020.

Law, Tara. "Gretchen Whitmer Is Giving the Democrats' State of the Union Response. Here's What to Know." *Time*, 4 Feb. 2020, time.com/5777872/gretchen-whitmer-democratic-response-state-of-the-union/. Accessed 22 Apr. 2020.

Martin, Tim. "Michigan Senate Democrats Developing College Grant Plan." *Crain's Detroit Business*, 12 Jan. 2012, www.crainsdetroit.com/article/20120112/FREE/120119954/michigan-senate-democrats-developing-college-grant-plan. Accessed 22 Apr. 2020.

Smith, Mitch. "Amid Vaping Crackdown, Michigan to Ban Sale of Flavored E-Cigarettes." *The New York Times*, 4 Sept. 2019, www.nytimes.com/2019/09/04/us/michigan-vaping.html. Accessed 22 Apr. 2020.

———. "Democrats Turn to Gov. Gretchen Whitmer of Michigan for Trump State of the Union Response." *The New York Times*, 5 Feb. 2020, www.nytimes.com/2020/02/04/us/politics/gretchen-whitmer-state-of-the-union.html. Accessed 22 Apr. 2020.

Tumulty, Karen. "Democrats Will Have Better Chances If They Take Page from Michigan's Gretchen Whitmer." *The Washington Post*, 28 July 2019, www.washingtonpost.com/opinions/democrats-will-have-a-better-chance-if-they-take-a-page-from-michigans-gretchen-whitmer/2019/07/28/

d18bcb5a-af0a-11e9-a0c9-6d2d7818f3da_story.html. Accessed 22 Apr. 2020.

———. "Why Joe Biden Should Pick 'That Governor' to Be His Running Mate." *The Washington Post*, 28 Mar. 2020, www.washingtonpost.com/opinions/2020/03/28/why-joe-biden-should-pick-that-governor-be-his-running-mate/. Accessed 22 Apr. 2020.

—Judy Johnson

Heidi Williams

Date of birth: ca. 1981
Occupation: Economist

Heidi Williams is an American economist known for her work regarding the relationship between private investment and patent regulation in health care research and the subsequent distorting effects on technological innovation and health care research.

EARLY LIFE AND EDUCATION

Heidi Williams was born circa 1981 in North Dakota. As a young student, Williams was interested in German cryptography during World War II and would drive two hours with her father to obtain books on the subject. Williams began volunteering to help at-risk teenagers when she was in sixth grade. She later attended Williston Senior High School, where she took advanced mathematics and was a member of the National Honor Society. She was named a US Presidential Scholar in 1999.

Williams attended Dartmouth College, where she majored in mathematics and published papers on cryptology. While in college, she worked as a writing tutor and studied ballet and modern dance. She earned an AB in mathematics in 2003.

In 2002, Williams earned a Truman Scholarship from the Harry S. Truman Scholarship Foundation. The same year, *Glamour* magazine named her in its "Top 10 College Women" list. She earned a Rhodes Scholarship in 2003, and studied development economics at Oxford University, where she earned an MS in 2004.

Williams worked as the research assistant for Harvard economist Michael Kremer, whose work similarly studies the relationship between policy and health care research. Williams earned a PhD in economics from Harvard in 2010. Her doctoral dissertation was the first empirical study to show that scientific development had been impeded by a company's rights to gene data.

Williams has been a faculty research fellow at the National Bureau of Economic Research since 2010. She began teaching as an associate professor at the Massachusetts Institute of Technology (MIT) in 2011.

ECONOMIST AND MACARTHUR FELLOW
Williams has sought to prove the direct causal relationship between patent regulation for health care technology and downstream innovation and development efforts. Additionally, in Williams's research, she has found that private investment in health care intellectual property has a direct distorting effect on later advancements in a particular area of research and development.

The Human Genome Project was completed in 2003, but Williams says health care advancements purported to be accelerated by genome sequencing have lagged behind expectations in the years since. Williams believes economic incentives have not been properly aligned to bolster scientific research into finding cures for common human diseases, such as cancer.

Drugs that target early-stage cancer treatment are underdeveloped and underfunded because of the imbalanced economic incentives created by the patent policy climate, according to Williams's work. Due to the long period of clinical trials required to prove the efficacy of an early-stage treatment drug, corporations are more likely to invest in drugs that treat late-stage cancer, which has a faster return on investment for private funders than early-stage drugs that have a longer path to market.

The lack of incentives is worsened by the policy environment around technical patents in health care research, her findings suggest. As one example, in her dissertation study Williams found that as of 2009, the parts of the human genome data owned by Celera Corporation were the subjects of 20 to 30 percent fewer research studies and medical discoveries than openly accessible parts of the genome data. Celera's patent has a dissuasive effect on scientific research, potentially hampering scientific breakthroughs in researching diseases such as cancer. The research Williams' team conducted does not allege that private corporations are willfully ignoring opportunities to invest in early-stage treatment drugs, but that the economic incentives have led corporations away from such investments.

Williams' research shows the impact of the policy and economics of disease treatment drugs is potentially enormous for both health care innovation and for humans suffering from incurable diseases. A study that she, Eric Budish, and Benjamin N. Roin published in 2015 estimates an impact of 890,000 collective lost life-years among American cancer patients diagnosed in 2003, when human genome sequencing was completed.

IMPACT
Williams' research has been lauded for its relevancy to modern debates surrounding health care privatization in the United States. The MacArthur Foundation said Williams' insights are "informing institutional practice and public policy and sparking new lines of inquiry about innovation more broadly." Her doctoral research was referred to in several briefs submitted by groups such as Yale Law School's Information Society Project for a 2013 gene patents case before the US Supreme Court in which the court ruled that although human genes could not be patented, synthetic genetic material may be legally protected.

Her articles have been published in the *Quarterly Journal of Economics, American Economic Review,* and the *Journal of Political Economy.* For her research into the topic of the causal relationship between health care intellectual property and research, Williams was awarded a 2015 MacArthur Fellowship.

PERSONAL LIFE
Williams married Wellesley College economic historian and applied microeconomist Dan Fetter in 2010.

SUGGESTED READING
Dizikes, Peter. "Heidi Williams Wins MacArthur." *MIT News.* Massachusetts Institute of Technology, 29 Sept. 2015. news.mit. edu/2015/heidi-williams-wins-macarthur-genius-grant-0929. Accessed 5 Dec. 2019.

Donnelly, James. "Dartmouth Senior Named 2003 Rhodes Scholar." *Dartmouth College.* Trustees of Dartmouth College, 9 Dec. 2002. Web. 29 Mar. 2016.

Frakt, Austin. "Why Preventing Cancer Is Not the Priority in Drug Development." *The New York Times,* 28 Dec. 2015. www.nytimes. com/2015/12/29/upshot/why-preventing-cancer-is-not-the-priority-in-drug-development. html. Accessed 5 Dec. 2019.

Gans, Joshua. "Heidi Williams, Macarthur Genius." *Digitopoly,* 29 Sept. 2015. digitopoly. org/2015/09/29/heidi-williams-macarthur-genius/. Accessed 5 Dec. 2019.

"Heidi Williams—MacArthur Fellows Program." *MacArthur Foundation.* MacArthur Foundation, 28 Sept. 2015. Web. 29 Mar. 2016.

"Heidi Williams." *MIT Economics.* Massachusetts Institute of Technology, n.d. Web. 29 Mar. 2016.

O'Keefe, Caitlin. "Economist Heidi Williams, Genius Award Winner, On Invisible Drug Industry Incentives." *WBUR's CommonHealth.* Trustees of Boston University, 7 Oct. 2015. www.wbur.org/commonhealth/2015/10/07/ mit-economist-genius-award-winner-heidi-williams. Accessed 5 Dec. 2019.

Smialek, Jeanna. "MIT's Williams Decodes Economics of Gene Sequencing." *Bloomberg.com*. Bloomberg, 12 Sept. 2013. www.bloomberg.com/news/articles/2013-09-12/mit-s-williams-decodes-economics-of-gene-sequencing. Accessed 5 Dec. 2019.

—*Richard Means*

Ian Williams

Born: June 17, 1979
Occupation: Writer

Canadian novelist and poet Ian Williams won the Scotiabank Giller Prize, one of Canada's highest literary honors, for his debut novel, *Reproduction*, in 2019. The book is a multigenerational love story, but Williams has attributed its inspiration in part to his biological clock, an overwhelming urge to nurture. Williams nurtured his novel like a child, tending to its needs for the seven years it took him to write it. But Williams took his theme further, embedding into the book's structure—or "biology," as he described it to Adina Bresge for Canada's *National Post* (21 Jan. 2019)—the means for its own reproduction, allowing the story to sprawl outward and into the future. Williams, who was born in Trinidad and raised outside of Toronto, made his literary debut with a poetry collection titled *You Know Who You Are* in 2010.

EARLY LIFE AND EDUCATION

Ian Williams was born on June 17, 1979, in Trinidad, where his father, Vincent Williams, worked in the oil sector. As a child, he dreamed of becoming a pilot, but his aspirations changed when his family moved to Canada, settling in the Toronto suburb of Brampton, Ontario, in the mid-1980s. Williams's mother, Judy Williams, worked as a primary school teacher while pursuing a degree at York University. After thumbing through the books on his mother's shelf, Williams was inspired to buy Margaret Atwood's 1964 poetry collection *The Circle Game*. It was the first book he ever bought with his own money. Williams attended Sir John A. MacDonald Sr. Public School, where a teacher named Peter Lucic encouraged his love of poetry and talent for writing. "It didn't take long for us to identify his talents and his abilities," Lucic recalled to Ben Spurr and May Warren for the *Hamilton Spectator* in Ontario (26 Nov. 2019). "He was good at pretty much everything he took his mind to." Williams graduated from Mayfield Secondary School in Caledon and enrolled as a human biology student at the University of Toronto.

Williams set out to study psychiatry, he told Mark Medley for Canada's *National Post* (7 June 2013). "From a young age I knew the most important things to me were people and communication," he said. He saw psychiatry as a way to connect with people using language, but a first-year English elective changed his perspective about his path. "We simply read poems," he told Medley of the class, taught by Julia Reibetanz. "She'd bring out Wordsworth, she'd bring out Keats, and she would read very steadily, and not dramatically. I would take my notes on what she was [reading] and I would sort of write marginalia right next to it. And those things eventually became poems. My conversation with her and these poets eventually turned into writing."

By the end of his first year, Williams was an English student with serious plans of becoming a writer. He earned his undergraduate degree in 2000 and a master's degree, also from the University of Toronto, in 2001. After spending seven months teaching English in South Korea, he went on to pursue a PhD at the University of Toronto as well. His doctoral supervisor was the Canadian poet Dr. George Elliott Clarke.

NOT ANYONE'S ANYTHING

Williams earned his doctorate in 2005, and he accepted a tenure-track position at Fitchburg State University in Fitchburg, Massachusetts. He published his first poetry collection, 2010's *You Know Who You Are*. In it, he explores identity and Black masculinity. The following year he published his debut collection of short stories, *Not Anyone's Anything*. Robyn Read, the former acquiring editor at Freehand Books, pulled the book from the publisher's slush pile on her first day on the job. "I just knew this guy's going to be one of the next big things in Canadian literature," Read recalled to Medley. The book won the Danuta Gleed Literary Award for best debut English-language collection of short stories in Canada in 2012.

Like a lot of Williams's work, *Not Anyone's Anything* has a precise, mathematical arrangement: three sets of three stories, with three of those stories being further divided into thirds. Williams described it to Suzanne Alyssa Andrew for the Canadian magazine *Quill & Quire* (Jan. 2019) as a book "about being alone." Despite the book's success, 2011 was a difficult year for Williams. In June, his apartment building in Fitchburg caught fire, and he lost everything. It was particularly traumatic for Williams, who, since the age of nine, had been obsessively recording his life in a daily journal. The fire, he told Medley, "became a turning point, where I just had to re-evaluate everything. So, now that I have nothing, and now that I'm really starting over again, what do I do, and what's important to me?"

PERSONALS

Williams quit his job at Fitchburg and moved back to Brampton, where he taught English at Sheridan College. He published another book of poems, *Personals*, in 2012. The book explores connection and technology. For research, Williams combed ads on *Craigslist*, pondering the ways in which people seek connection across the Internet. He told Medley that he longed for poetry that grappled with the way people live now. "People feel like poems somehow can't contain this present world," he said. "As if you put technology into it . . . and that robs poetry of its power, or its seriousness, or its import. I'm the complete opposite. Whatever you throw at this, it can absorb and handle and spit back something even better." *Personals* was short-listed for the Robert Kroetsch Poetry Award as well as for the 2013 Griffin Poetry Prize. In the "Judges' Citation" for the Griffin Prize, poet Wang Ping wrote, "The moment I opened *Personals*, I was smitten. . . . When [Williams] pulls the strings of contradictions: light and heavy, hilarious and serious, I can't help but dance like a happy puppet in the masterful hands."

REPRODUCTION

Williams was named the writer-in-residence for the University of Calgary for 2014–15. During his year-long tenure, he toiled on an untitled novel he had begun in 2012. "I don't have any kids, but you know when kids are in their first three months and they give no love back and you're always doing things for them?" he joked to Eric Volmers for the *Calgary Herald* (10 Sept. 2014). "They barely smile at you. They just need and need and need and that's kind of what it feels like now. It takes everything and doesn't have much payoff." Williams was referring to what would become his debut novel, *Reproduction*. Seven years and twelve drafts later, *Reproduction* was published in 2019.

Reproduction's structure is complex, but the story is straightforward. The book begins in Brampton in the 1970s. Felicia Shaw, a teenaged Caribbean woman, and Edgar Gross, a middle-aged German man, meet in a Toronto hospital where both of their mothers are dying. The book quickly moves forward in time, spanning fifty years and encompassing multiple perspectives, including Felicia and Edgar's son Armistice, as characters couple and reproduce.

Reproduction won positive reviews. Stephen Kearse, who reviewed it for the *New York Times* (21 Apr. 2020), praised "its multitude of forms," including "annotated sheet music, simulations of the *Maury* show, equations, Bible verses, numbered lists [and] lyrics from Rihanna and the Wu-Tang Clan," though he also offered criticism for the plot, which, he wrote, felt "narrow and deterministic" at times. A reviewer for *Kirkus* (27

Jan. 2020) offered a similar assessment, calling *Reproduction* "witty" and "formally thrilling," if ultimately too neatly concluded.

Reproduction won the Scotiabank Giller Prize, worth $100,000, in 2019. In an emotional acceptance speech, Williams thanked Lucic, his middle school English teacher, as well as his fellow nominee, Margaret Atwood, best known for her 1985 novel *The Handmaid's Tale*. He told the crowd how he had bought her book of poems as a child. "How do you tell a writer that I feel like I've known you and you've been like my literary mother and you've been here for me this whole time?" Williams said of her in an interview after the ceremony, as quoted by Bresge for the *Global News* (19 Nov. 2019).

NEW WORKS

Williams's next book of poems, *Word Problems*, was slated for release in October 2020. By that time, he had been at work on a novel titled "Disappointment." If *Reproduction* was the book of his thirties, Williams told Andrew, then "Disappointment" would be the book of his forties.

SUGGESTED READING

Andrew, Suzanne Alyssa. "Poet Ian Williams Experiments with Structure to Tell a Classic Love Story." *Quill & Quire*, Jan. 2019, quillandquire.com/authors/poet-ian-williams-experiments-with-structure-to-tell-a-classic-love-story/. Accessed 10 Sept. 2020.

Bresge, Adina. "Acclaimed Poet Ian Williams Says First Novel 'Reproduction' Is Like a Child." *National Post*, 21 Jan. 2019, nationalpost.com/pmn/entertainment-pmn/books-entertainment-pmn/acclaimed-poet-ian-williams-says-first-novel-reproduction-is-like-a-child. Accessed 10 Sept. 2020.

———. "First-Time Novelist Ian Williams Honored with $100K Scotiabank Giller Prize." *Global News*, 19 Nov. 2019, globalnews.ca/news/6187087/ian-williams-scotiabank-giller-prize-reproduction/. Accessed 10 Sept. 2020.

Medley, Mark. "Ian Williams: Poet Seeking Reader." *National Post*, 7 June 2013, nationalpost.com/entertainment/books/ian-williams-poet-seeking-reader. Accessed 10 Sept. 2020.

Spurr, Ben, and May Warren. "Author Never Forgot His Favorite Teacher. Now They've Reconnected Decades Later after a Shoutout from the Giller Stage." *The Hamilton Spectator*, 26 Nov. 2019, www.thespec.com/news/hamilton-region/2019/11/25/author-never-forgot-his-favourite-teacher-now-they-ve-reconnected-decades-later-after-a-shoutout-from-the-giller-stage.html. Accessed 10 Sept. 2020.

Volmers, Eric. "Griffin Nominee Wants Poetry to Be Relevant." *Calgary Herald*, 10 Sept. 2014, calgaryherald.com/entertainment/books/

griffin-nominee-wants-poetry-to-be-relevant.
Accessed 11 Sept. 2020.

Wang Ping. "Judges' Citation." *Griffin Trust*, 2013, www.griffinpoetryprize.com/awards-and-poets/shortlists/2013-shortlist/ian-williams/. Accessed 10 Sept. 2020.

SELECTED WORKS

You Know Who You Are, 2010; *Not Anyone's Anything*, 2011; *Personals*, 2012; *Reproduction* 2019

—*Molly Hagan*

Jumaane Williams

Date of birth: May 11, 1976
Occupation: Politician

Jumaane Williams was elected New York City's public advocate in 2019, first in a February special election and again in the November general election. The public advocate is a nonvoting member of the New York City Council that can introduce legislation, but mainly acts as the city's ombudsman, investigating complaints about city government. The position is also notable for being first in the line of succession if the mayor should suddenly leave office; political insiders view it as a springboard for those hoping to run for mayor. Williams, a former three-term city councilor and longtime activist, hoped to use the office's bully pulpit to raise important issues. Among his chief concerns was affordable housing. At the time of his election almost half of New Yorkers were rent burdened, meaning they paid more than 30 percent of their income toward rent, and one in ten children in New York City's public-school system was homeless. Williams, a former tenants' rights organizer, pushed for universal rent control, revisions to zoning laws that allow public land to be sold to private companies, and the right to sue the city's public housing administration for criminal negligence. Williams won the special election for public advocate in part because of the name recognition he garnered when he ran for lieutenant governor in 2018. Though he lost that race, he won the support of thousands of New Yorkers and a surprise endorsement from the *New York Times*, who touted the fifty pieces of legislation Williams managed to push through the City Council during his tenure.

EARLY LIFE AND EDUCATION

Williams was born in Manhattan on May 11, 1976, and raised in Brooklyn. His parents immigrated to the United States from Grenada in the late 1960s. Williams's father, Gregory, was an obstetrician and gynecologist and then a

Photo by Bauzen/GC Images

Christian minister. His mother, Patricia, worked for many years as a pharmacist. Williams's parents divorced when he was a child.

Williams and his sister, Jeanine, grew up in the federally funded Starrett City housing development in the East New York neighborhood of Brooklyn. He struggled in school and manifested a number of physical and verbal tics. At fourteen, after his mother saw a segment of the television news program *20/20* devoted to Tourette's syndrome, he was diagnosed with that neurological condition; he was also diagnosed with attention deficit hyperactivity disorder (ADHD). Growing up, Williams recalled to Azi Paybarah for the New York *Observer* (30 Aug. 2011), many people did not notice his condition: "People just chalked it up to my personality or me acting a fool, because I was usually the class clown. So, a lot of people didn't even recognize it." Later, he would credit his fifth-grade teacher for taking him under her wing when his perceived unruly behavior nearly got him kicked out of school. As he got older, his tics became more pronounced. He took up singing with the All City High Chorus and acting in an after-school program with the Harlem School of the Arts—activities that helped him control his tics. "When I'm acting, it kind of goes away," Williams told Paybarah. "I do tic when I'm speaking publicly, but I never tic'ed when I was acting."

Williams attended Philippa Schuyler Middle School for the Gifted and Talented, and graduated from Brooklyn Technical High School in 1994. He hoped to win a place in the acting program at New York University's Tisch School of the Arts, but his grades were not good enough for admission. He enrolled instead at Brooklyn College. He continued to do some acting work, appearing in a handful of hip hop music videos in the late 1990s, but he also began taking an interest in campus politics. He joined the Black Student Union and ran for student body president but lost by 95 votes. Williams earned his bachelor's degree in political science from Brooklyn College in 2001, and a master's degree in urban policy and administration in 2005.

EARLY POLITICAL CAREER

After college, Williams worked as the assistant director for the Greater Flatbush Beacon School, and then as the director at the East Flatbush Community Development Corporation. He later served as housing director of the Flatbush Development Corporation and became the executive director of New York State Tenants & Neighbors group, a tenants' rights organization. Williams was a committed activist, but he also briefly dabbled in business. He opened a vegan sandwich shop called Earth Tonez; it closed in 2008, saddling him with thousands of dollars of debt.

When he was still in college, a colleague introduced Williams to Lew Fidler, a Brooklyn politician running for a position on a local school board. (Fidler would later serve as a City Council member for New York City's Forty-Sixth District.) Fidler became a mentor, and introduced Williams to the Thomas Jefferson Democratic Club, one of the oldest and most influential political clubs in New York City. Fidler later appointed Williams to Community Board 18, Williams's first formal civic position. "In Lew, I found someone who I didn't agree with on some things, but . . . there was genuine respect," Williams told Nelson A. King for *Caribbean Life* (8 May 2019). Lew Fidler died in 2019.

NEW YORK CITY COUNCIL

In 2009, with Fidler's encouragement, Williams ran for City Council in New York City's Forty-Fifth District. Incumbent Kendall Stewart was embroiled in controversy after two of his staffers were convicted of stealing thousands of taxpayer dollars. Williams faced four other primary candidates but earned the support of the progressive Working Families Party. He won the six-way race with 37 percent of the vote. In the overwhelmingly Democratic district, his win in the primary all but ensured his ultimate victory. He was sworn to office in 2010.

As a city councilor, Williams supported the burgeoning Occupy Wall Street movement, and condemned Mayor Michael Bloomberg's decision to raid the group's encampment in Manhattan's Zuccotti Park in 2011. He was arrested as an act of civil disobedience—not for the first

or last time—while protesting the eviction. In 2018, Williams was arrested after he and several other protestors blocked an ambulance carrying immigration activist Ravi Ragbir, who was threatened with deportation. Talking about it later, Williams told Meagan Day for *Jacobin* magazine (15 Aug. 2018): "Usually when I participate in civil disobedience . . . there isn't such a sense of urgency. This one was about stopping an immediate act being done to someone I've known for so long. I always say do what you can, with what you have, where you are. I'm a cisgender male, a citizen, and an elected official, which means I have a responsibility to take more risks."

Williams was also an early and outspoken critic of Mayor Bloomberg's stop-and-frisk policy, which allowed police officers to stop, question, and frisk people on a reasonable suspicion of criminal activity—though in practice it was often done based on racial profiling. A federal judge ruled the practice as it was used in New York unconstitutional in 2013. Williams was one of the architects of a successful bill, called the Community Safety Act, to change the policy. The act, which was signed into law in 2014, also created an independent inspector general to serve as a police watchdog. Williams also sponsored the Fair Chance Act, which made it illegal for employers to ask about a potential employee's criminal record before making a job offer. The Fair Chance Act was signed into law in 2015.

Meanwhile, Williams became cochair of the New York City Council's Gun Violence Task Force. He helped create the NYC Crisis Management System, a network of mediators, counselors, and mentors that sought to reduce gun violence by addressing its underlying causes. "Public safety isn't just about law enforcement," he told Paula Katinas for the *Brooklyn Daily Eagle* (4 Dec. 2015). "You have to take a holistic approach." Williams became known for attending vigils and memorials for shooting victims. In 2014, he launched the National Network to Combat Gun Violence to connect local officials all over the country to share and develop ideas to reduce gun violence. Another feature of his tenure on the City Council was an effort to create summer jobs for the city's youth.

CANDIDATE FOR LIEUTENANT GOVERNOR AND PUBLIC ADVOCATE

In 2018, Williams announced his candidacy for the office of lieutenant governor of New York. That year, a slew of progressives mounted campaigns against established Democratic officeholders in the state. (Most famous among them was Alexandria Ocasio-Cortez, who successfully challenged longtime congressman Joe Crowley.) Williams sought to unseat Lieutenant Governor Kathy Hochul in the Democratic primary. Though the job of lieutenant governor is largely ceremonial, Williams sought to use it to hold the governor accountable. The *New York Times*'s editorial board liked that idea and gave Williams their endorsement on September 6, 2018. The newspaper criticized Hochul, writing that she "has served as little more than an echo" for Governor Andrew Cuomo. "We have endorsed Mr. Cuomo for governor in the Democratic primary, while arguing that he is likely to act aggressively against systemic corruption in Albany only if reformers continue to pressure him," they wrote. "Mr. Williams has vowed, if elected, to do what he can to add to that pressure."

Despite a groundswell of support, Williams lost the race to Hochul by six percentage points. In New York City, though, he bested her by 60,000 votes. Bronx borough president Rubén Díaz Jr. encouraged Williams to capitalize on that support and run for New York City public advocate. The former holder of that position, Letitia James, had won the Democratic nomination for state attorney general. She ultimately beat her Republican opponent, triggering a special election in February 2019 to fill her vacated seat.

Seventeen candidates ran to replace James as the city's public advocate. The *New York Times* endorsed Williams again, arguing that he had shown a willingness to hold Mayor Bill de Blasio accountable and push for reforms to the city's housing policies and police department. He won the race several days later, delivering a rousing victory speech that ended, memorably, with an emotional admission that he regularly saw a therapist. He encouraged at-risk populations such as black men and boys to talk about mental health—a subject, Williams later told Jennifer Gonnerman for the *New Yorker* (12 Mar. 2019), that is "still very taboo in certain communities—and communities that I think really need it because of the trauma of daily life. People will talk about visiting the doctor or visiting the dentist, but they can't talk about therapy, they can't talk about mental health. And I want to break down that stigma."

In November 2019, Williams was reelected, easily defeating Republican challenger Joseph Borelli, a city councilor from Staten Island.

SUGGESTED READING

Gonnerman, Jennifer. "Jumaane Williams's Breakthrough Victory Speech." *The New Yorker*, 12 Mar. 2019, www.newyorker.com/news/news-desk/jumaane-williamss-breakthrough-victory-speech. Accessed 13 Jan. 2020.

Katinas, Paula. "In Public Service: Williams Pushes for a New New Deal in NYC." *Brooklyn Daily Eagle*, 4 Dec. 2015, brooklyneagle.com/articles/2015/12/04/in-public-service-williams-pushes-for-a-new-new-deal-in-nyc/. Accessed 12 Jan. 2020.

King, Nelson A. "Adams, Williams Saddened by Passing of Former Brooklyn Councilman." *Caribbean Life*, 8 May 2019, www.caribbeanlifenews.com/stories/2019/5/2019-05-10-nk-lew-fidler-dead-cl.html. Accessed 12 Jan. 2020.

"The New York Times Endorses Jumaane Williams for Lieutenant Governor in Thursday's Primary." *The New York Times*, 6 Sept. 2018, www.nytimes.com/2018/09/06/opinion/editorials/jumaane-williams-democrats-lieutenant-governor.html. Accessed 13 Jan. 2020.

Paybarah, Azi. "Councilman with Tourette's Is a Spokesman for Reform." *Observer*, 30 Aug. 2011, observer.com/2011/08/councilman-with-tourettes-is-a-spokesman-for-reform/. Accessed 12 Jan. 2020.

Williams, Jumaane. "I Have No Problem Saying I'm a Democratic Socialist." Interview by Meagan Day. *Jacobin*, 15 Aug. 2018, jacobinmag.com/2018/08/jumaane-williams-lieutenant-governor-new-york. Accessed 12 Jan. 2020.

—*Molly Hagan*

Chip Wilson

Date of birth: March 3, 1956
Occupation: Businessman and philanthropist

Chip Wilson found worldwide fame with his athletic apparel company Lululemon. The

Photo by Jim Bennett/Getty Images

company, which originally focused on yoga apparel for women, is widely credited with kicking off the so-called athleisure trend—in other words, treating athleticwear as fashion rather than something purely functional. By the time Wilson left the company in 2015, its range had expanded to cover a variety of athletics, such as running, cycling, and exercise, for both women and men. Wilson's work with Lululemon earned him various accolades, including being named professional services firm Ernst & Young's Canadian Entrepreneur of the Year. In January 2020, his net worth was estimated at $4.7 billion, and he was the ninth-richest person in Canada.

Wilson has drawn media attention as much for controversies—such as wanting to have quotes from controversial author Ayn Rand printed on Lululemon shopping bags—as he has for his successes. He told Amy Wallace for the *New York Times* (2 Feb. 2015), however, that he was not concerned about the criticism he received. "If you are doing a brand well, you need to offend somebody, or you're not standing for anything," he told Wallace. "My background has always been people telling me my ideas are crazy. And I've noticed that 90 percent of them have come true."

EARLY LIFE AND EDUCATION
Dennis "Chip" Wilson was born in 1956 to Dennis Wilson and Mary Ruth Noel. His father was a physical education teacher and his mother enjoyed making clothes; Wilson has cited these two influences as the source of his interest in athletic clothing. He spent his early childhood in California, before the family moved to Calgary, Canada, when he was five. His parents later divorced. As a teenager, Wilson was a competitive swimmer. According to his memoir, *Little Black Stretchy Pants: The Unauthorized Story of Lululemon* (2018), this led to his first foray into sports apparel entrepreneurship: he noticed at the time that there was a demand among his fellow swimmers for a greater variety of swimsuit options, so he imported Speedo swimsuits into Canada and resold them, turning a profit.

After graduating from high school in 1972, Wilson began attending the University of Alberta. He was disillusioned with college, however, so at the end of his second year he withdrew from school to work on the Trans-Alaska Pipeline. After two years, Wilson returned to Canada, where he attended the University of Calgary. He graduated with a bachelor's degree in economics in 1980.

CAREER BEGINNINGS
Wilson founded his first company, Westbeach Snowboard Ltd., in 1979. The company marketed clothing to surfers, snowboarders, and skateboarders. It garnered some popularity internationally, with one Westbeach brand, the Homeless line of skateboarding apparel, selling particularly well in Japan. Wilson, along with his two partners, sold the company in 1997.

Shortly after selling Westbeach, Wilson enrolled in a yoga class in the hope that it would help with back issues caused by participating in triathlons. The idea for Lululemon came when he realized that most of his classmates were wearing clothing that was not ideal for the activity. "At that time, everyone wore their worst clothing to the gym," he said in an interview quoted by Nathaniel Meyersohn for *CNN Business* (20 Dec. 2018). "Yoga is about sweating. As the cotton got wet, it started to bind. On top of that, the instructor couldn't really align the body very well." He realized that the stretch fabric he had developed to make long underwear for snowboarders could also be used for yoga pants, so he began making prototypes of the pants and giving them to his yoga teacher to test. Positive feedback from the yoga teacher confirmed Wilson's plan to make the pants the cornerstone of his next company.

LULULEMON
In 1998, Wilson founded Lululemon. Discussing his inspiration for the name, Wilson attributed the success of Homeless in Japan to the fact that the name contained the letter "l." As the sound does not exist in the Japanese language, Wilson felt that this marked the brand as authentically Western. Thus, for his next company, Wilson chose a name with multiple instances of the letter, hoping to capture the international popularity Homeless had enjoyed.

The first few years were difficult. Wilson wrote for the blog of bookkeeping service *Bench* (3 Dec. 2018) that he almost went bankrupt twice. He was undaunted, however. "What made me a good entrepreneur is that I would have worked for no money. I had passion: I was an athlete and no athletic clothes were working for me," he wrote for *Bench*. "It's like when somebody in the tech industry sees something that the world is missing—they know it's possible, but nobody is doing it yet." His perseverance soon paid off as the company gained traction in the athleticwear market. By 2005, the company was valued at $225 million. That year, Wilson left his position as CEO, selling a 48 percent stake in the company to private equity firms Advent International and Highland Capital Partners. The company went public in 2007, selling 18.2 million shares for $327.6 million during its initial public offering. Its ascent only became faster from there: in 2008, the company had $350 million in sales, while in 2011 sales totaled $1 billion. Wilson retained an executive role as chief innovation and branding officer after his time as CEO.

Despite the company's success, Wilson himself attracted increasing controversy in the 2010s. Wilson's desire to feature quotes from Ayn Rand's novel *Atlas Shrugged* (1957) on Lululemon's reusable shopping bags led to conflict with the board in 2011. While the bags were ultimately made despite the board's objections, customers did not respond well. Following this clash, Wilson took a year off from active involvement with the company. He also stepped down from his executive role, though he remained chair of the board of directors.

A much more public conflict occurred in 2013, when the company had to recall 17 percent of its black yoga pants because the material was too sheer. Wilson made a televised statement in which he said, as quoted by Wallace, that "some women's bodies don't work for the pants" and attributed the fabric's transparency to excessive rubbing in the thighs. Wilson was widely condemned for his statement, which was seen as both denying the company's responsibility for the issue and insulting the customers. Within two months of the incident, the company's stock had dropped by almost one-third. Wilson stepped down from his position as chair of the board in December of that year. In 2014, he sold half his shares in the company to Advent International.

LATER VENTURES

Wilson's wife, Shannon Wilson, one of Lululemon's original designers, left the company in 2014 to found the streetwear brand Kit and Ace with Wilson's son (and her stepson), J. J. Wilson. Chip Wilson remained on Lululemon's board and not officially involved with Kit and Ace at first, but in February 2015, Wilson resigned from Lululemon because he felt the companies would inevitably come into competition with one another. Although the brands technically occupied different niches, Wilson felt that the rise of the athleisure trend had blurred the lines between streetwear and athletic clothing to the extent that the two categories would eventually merge completely. Wilson told Jan Crawford for *CBS This Morning* (8 Dec. 2015) that he enjoyed being able to work with his family on Kit and Ace. "I can't think of anything more rewarding at the end of my life [than] having been with family, and being able to . . . mentor and trade ideas and feed off each other." Wilson founded the holding company Hold It All Inc. in 2016 to maintain his family's various business interests. Hold It All's divisions include the real estate company Low Tide Properties and the private equity firm Wilson Capital.

In 2018, Wilson self-published the book *Little Black Stretchy Pants*. (An updated version, titled *Story of Lululemon by the Founder: Chip Wilson*, was published the following year.)

To promote the book, he set up a one-day pop-up shop near a Lululemon store in New York where he sold and signed copies of the book. The book was critical of the direction the company had taken since Wilson's departure, arguing that the company became more inclined to play it safe and avoid trying anything risky or innovative. Wilson expressed similar sentiments in interviews. "The [Lululemon] board has done an incredible job at setting the company from a metrics point of view. But once the process is taken care of, it needs to focus on the soft side of things. . . . Innovation and brand can't be measured," he told Andria Cheng for *Forbes* (29 Oct. 2018). "Soon, there'll be another movement. Lululemon needs to be in front of that." In 2019, Lululemon stripped Wilson of the ability to designate a board nominee, saying that he had violated the terms of an agreement that allowed him to do so as long as he owned at least 8 percent of the company's stock.

Along with the Chinese company Anta, Wilson bought the sporting goods conglomerate Amer in 2019. Amer's brands include the running and hiking gear brand Salomon and Arc'teryx, which is known for its jackets. In September 2019, it was reported that as a result of the deal, Wilson had made $32.3 million in three months.

PERSONAL LIFE AND PHILANTHROPY

Wilson has two sons, J. J. and Brett, from his first marriage, which ended in divorce. J. J. is also an entrepreneur and clothing designer. Wilson married Lululemon designer Shannon (Grey) Wilson in 2002. The couple have three sons: Duke, Tag, and Tor.

Wilson launched the charity imagine1day, dedicated to improving educational opportunities in Ethiopia, in 2008. He sponsors the annual Child Run in Vancouver, a five-kilometer run whose proceeds support the British Columbia Children's Hospital, and donated $12 million to Kwantlen Polytechnic University, a public university in British Columbia, to create the Wilson School of Design. He has also donated money to save public art pieces in Vancouver from removal, including the Amazing Laughter statues and the Trans Am Totem.

SUGGESTED READING

Cheng, Andria. "Founder Chip Wilson Takes Aim at Lululemon: 'I Want the Brand to Stand for Something.'" *Forbes*, 29 Oct. 2018, www.forbes.com/sites/andriacheng/2018/10/29/lululemon-chip-wilson/. Accessed 18 Jan. 2020.

"Lululemon Founder on Past Controversy, New Family Business." *CBS This Morning*, 8 Dec. 2015, www.cbsnews.com/news/kit-and-ace-lululemon-founder-chip-wilson-apology-shannon-jj-retail-revolution-technical-cash-mere/. Accessed 18 Jan. 2020.

Meyersohn, Nathaniel. "Lululemon's Controversial Founder: The Company Is Worse Off without Me." *CNN Business*, 20 Dec. 2018, www.cnn.com/2018/12/20/business/lululemon-founder-chip-wilson/index.html. Accessed 18 Jan. 2020.

Wallace, Amy. "Chip Wilson, Lululemon Guru, Is Moving On." *The New York Times*, 2 Feb. 2015, www.nytimes.com/2015/02/08/magazine/lululemons-guru-is-moving-on.html. Accessed 18 Jan. 2020.

Wilson, Chip, and Amanda Smith. "Lululemon Founder Chip Wilson on Why the Best Entrepreneurs Would Work for No Money." *Bench*, 3 Dec. 2018, bench.co/blog/small-business-stories/chip-wilson/. Accessed 18 Jan. 2020.

Woodin, Hayley. "Lululemon Founder Chip Wilson's Next Apparel Play." *BIV*, 22 Jan. 2020, biv.com/article/2020/01/lululemon-founder-chip-wilsons-next-apparel-play. Accessed 22 Jan. 2020.

—*Emma Joyce*

Daniela Witten

Born: ca. 1984
Occupation: Biostatistician

"I figured out pretty early on in college that I wanted to become a scientist, but I had a lot of trouble deciding what area of science to pursue," biostatistician Daniela Witten told *Amstat News* (1 Sept. 2014), the magazine of the American Statistical Association. "I didn't want to be pigeonholed into a particular research area. Instead, I wanted to be able to work on different types of problems at different points in my career (or even at a single point in my career)." Eventually, her diverse array of research interests, and in particular her developing engagement in fields such as mathematics and biology, led her naturally to biostatistics, an interdisciplinary field that blends statistics research with elements of biology and medicine. She completed her bachelor's, master's, and doctoral degrees at Stanford University with that specialty in mind, and in 2010 joined the faculty at the University of Washington, where she would remain for the subsequent decade.

As a researcher and prolific contributor to journals in her field, Witten specialized in the application of statistical machine learning to the area of public health. Perhaps most notable, she worked to develop methods of handling large sets of data derived from processes such as the sequencing of the human genome. It was her hope, and that of other researchers working with the field, that developing such methods will better enable medical researchers to study the data in question and make significant strides in combating some of humankind's most challenging public-health issues. In recognition of her work as a statistician—a job she identified to Izzy Aguiar, in an article posted to the website *Medium* (1 Feb. 2018), as "a great career choice for a natural skeptic who is also extremely argumentative"—Witten received numerous awards and was included on *Forbes* magazine's 30 Under 30 list of influential scientists three years in a row. Promoted to full professor at the University of Washington in 2018, she also became the inaugural holder of the Dorothy Morrow Gilford Endowed Chair in Mathematical Statistics at the university.

EARLY LIFE AND EDUCATION

Daniela Mottel Witten was born around the mid-1980s and grew up in New Jersey. She was one of three children born to Chiara Nappi and Edward Witten, accomplished physicists affiliated with the Institute for Advanced Study in Princeton. In light of her parents' long-standing careers in science, which included research in major fields of study such as string theory, academic pursuits were a prominent focus in Witten's childhood household. Both she and her older sister Ilana, a future professor of psychology and neuroscience at Princeton University, would go on to enter academia.

As a teenager, Witten attended Princeton High School for two years before moving to California with her parents, who had taken positions as visiting professors at the California Institute of Technology (Caltech, her father) and the University of Southern California (USC, her mother). She completed her junior and senior years of high school at the Polytechnic School, a preparatory school in Pasadena. She graduated from high school in 2001.

Deciding to remain in California after high school, Witten enrolled at Stanford University, where she initially planned to study foreign languages. She later considered studying experimental biology but found that she was poorly suited to working in a laboratory environment. After eventually pursuing a degree in mathematics and biological sciences and taking her first course in statistics as a junior, she decided to focus her further levels of education on statistics, the field of study to which she would devote the next decades of her life. "Statistics appealed to me because it was a good way to combine my interests in math and biology from the safety of a computer terminal instead of a lab bench," she explained in an interview for the blog *Simply Statistics* (14 Oct. 2011). "After spending more time in the department, I realized that if I studied statistics, I could develop a broad skill set that could be applied to a variety of areas, from cancer research to movie recommendations to the stock market."

A strong student during her early years at Stanford, Witten was a Presidential Scholar as an undergraduate, received a research fellowship from the university in 2004, and was awarded the Firestone Medal for Excellence in Research in 2005. She earned her bachelor's degree in mathematics and biological sciences in 2005 and received a master's degree in statistics the following year, having completed portions of her undergraduate and graduate coursework simultaneously. Witten remained at Stanford for her doctoral studies and completed a dissertation titled "A Penalized Matrix Decomposition, and Its Applications" under the supervision of adviser Robert Tibshirani, a mentor whom she later credited with providing valuable guidance about choosing and pursuing research projects. She earned her PhD in statistics from Stanford in 2010.

CAREER IN ACADEMIA

Not long after completing her doctorate, Witten joined the faculty of the University of Washington's Department of Biostatistics as an assistant professor. For Witten, part of the draw of working at the Seattle institution, aside from its own reputation for the strength of its statistics and genomics programs, was the city itself, which she considered beautiful and a leader in technology. She held the Genentech Endowed Professorship in Biostatistics in 2010 and 2011, and in September of the latter year received an Early Independence Award from the National Institutes of Health (NIH), a five-year grant designed to help researchers at the beginning of their careers enter immediately into full-fledged research careers rather than postdoctoral positions. The year 2011 also saw Witten receive the David P. Byar Young Investigator Award from the American Statistical Association. She was promoted to the position of associate professor in 2014.

In her role as a professor of statistics and biostatistics, Witten took on a wide range of career responsibilities, including teaching, mentoring graduate students, and conducting research. "There's no such thing as a typical day!" she told *Amstat News* of her experiences at the University of Washington. "On a given day, I might spend the morning meeting with my PhD students about their statistical methods research projects, the early afternoon working on revisions for a journal submission, and the late afternoon meeting with a genomics researcher about a collaborative project."

RESEARCH AND FULL PROFESSORSHIP

Witten's research primarily concerned statistical machine learning, a field that combines elements of traditional statistics and computer science and makes substantial use of algorithms to sort through data and find data relevant to a certain problem or phenomenon being studied. As her emphasis on the field of biostatistics might suggest, she was particularly intrigued by the intersections between statistics and biology and the ways in which statistical techniques can be used to translate and make sense of information for medical purposes, including the analysis of genetic data. "Incredible scientific breakthroughs in the last decade make it possible to sequence an entire human genome for a relatively low cost," she said, as quoted in a profile posted on the Department of Biostatistics page on the *University of Washington*'s website (6 Feb. 2017). "This means that we should be able to identify the genetic underpinnings of a lot of human diseases and obtain a much better understanding of the science than was ever possible before." Among the many stumbling points for researchers seeking to use such data has been the sheer size of the data sets involved and the presence of irrelevant data, which statisticians often refer to as "noise," as opposed to the "signal" represented by relevant data. "It's really important that we get these things right and figure out best practices for how to deal with these very large data sets," Witten said, as quoted in the University of Washington profile.

In light of the complexity of the data being gathered, Witten hoped to develop means for machines to read and sort such data. This would better enable medical researchers to analyze and understand the factors underlying diseases such as cancer, which represents a particular challenge due to the presence of mutations and the genetic differences that exist between individual cancer cells. She published widely on her research, contributing papers to journals such as *Biostatistics*, the *Journal of the American Statistical Association*, and the *Journal of Computational and Graphical Statistics*.

At the same time as she conducted her own research, Witten continued advancing in her teaching career. Named a full professor at the university in 2018, she was also named to the newly established position of Dorothy Morrow Gilford Endowed Chair in Mathematical Statistics that year. In addition to her work within the Department of Biostatistics, she served as a faculty member for University of Washington bodies such as the eScience Institute and as an affiliate investigator in biostatistics and biomathematics for the Fred Hutchinson Cancer Research Center, based in Seattle.

COMMUNICATING STATISTICS

Along with her research and teaching work, Witten sought to expand the public's awareness of statistics and biostatistics and knowledge of the concepts crucial to those fields. She emphasized the need for statisticians to foster communication both within and outside of their realm of study. "We have a responsibility to clearly communicate what we do, and why it is important, so that we can have a seat at the table," she explained, as quoted by Aguiar. Aware of the need for clear and comprehensive texts for students of statistics, Witten—along with professors Gareth James, Trevor Hastie, and Tibshirani—coauthored the text *An Introduction to Statistical Learning*, first published in 2013.

As a prominent researcher within her field, Witten received extensive public recognition over the course of her career, including from publications outside of her own scientific sphere. Beginning in 2012, she spent three consecutive years on *Forbes* magazine's 30 Under 30 list of important young professionals, initially in the category of science and innovation and later for the category of science and health care. The publicity offered her an uncommon opportunity to bring national attention to her work and that of colleagues in her field. Emphasizing that it had been great to receive such recognition from *Forbes* three times, she told *Amstat News*, "It's really exciting to be a statistician at a time when the scientific community and broader public are becoming increasingly aware of the important role statisticians do and should continue to play in scientific research, public policy, and industry."

Acknowledging the often lackluster reputation of the field of statistics, Witten told *Simply Statistics* that she sometimes surprised people at parties in revealing her profession. Nevertheless, she identified herself as a statistician "with pride," she explained. "It means that I have been rigorously trained, that I have a broadly applicable skill set, and that I'm always open to new and interesting problems." In 2019, she received the American Public Health Association's Mortimer Spiegelman Award, which recognizes the contributions of statisticians under the age of forty to the field of public health.

PERSONAL LIFE

Witten met Ari Steinberg, a tech industry manager and entrepreneur, while they were both attending Stanford University, and they married in 2008. Witten and Steinberg settled in Washington with their children. When not teaching or conducting research, Witten enjoys participating in outdoor sports such as hiking and paddle boarding.

SUGGESTED READING

Aguiar, Izzy. "Getting to Know the Women in Data Science: Daniela Witten." *Medium*, 1 Feb. 2018, medium.com/@izabel.p.aguiar/getting-to-know-the-women-in-data-science-daniela-witten-5b1ac8846c6f. Accessed 10 May 2020.

"Faculty Profile: Daniela Witten." *Department of Biostatistics*, University of Washington, 6 Feb. 2017, www.biostat.washington.edu/news-events/faculty-profile-daniela-witten. Accessed 10 May 2020.

Witten, Daniela. "Interview with Daniela Witten." *Simply Statistics*, 14 Oct. 2011, simplys-tatistics.org/2011/10/14/interview-with-daniela-witten/. Accessed 10 May 2020.

Witten, Daniela, et al. "Which Career Path Will You Follow?" *Amstat News*, 1 Sept. 2014, magazine.amstat.org/blog/2014/09/01/career-path/. Accessed 10 May 2020.

—Joy Crelin

Joshua Wong

Date of birth: October 13, 1996
Occupation: Activist

Joshua Wong, one of the most recognizable faces of Hong Kong's democracy movement, first came to widespread international attention as one of the seminal figures in the Umbrella Movement, a series of public protests that took place

Photo by Studio Incendo via Wikimedia Commons

in 2014, when tens of thousands of Hong Kong residents took to the streets to demand the right to vote in elections without interference from officials in Beijing. Named one of *Time* magazine's Most Influential Teens of 2014, Wong became the subject of a Netflix documentary, *Joshua: Teenager vs. Superpower*, released in 2017, and the following year he was nominated for a Nobel Peace Prize. More recently, he has been involved in the massive protests that broke out in Hong Kong in 2019. That ongoing movement has brought hundreds of thousands of people out to demonstrate for civil liberties and regional autonomy, many wearing masks to combat the tear gas regularly lobbed by police.

Pointing out that the young activist was born in 1996, just a year before Hong Kong, a former British colony, was handed back to China, Megan K. Stack wrote for the *New Yorker* (23 Oct. 2019), "Wong's evolution from defiant teenage protester to international lobbyist and emerging politician is more than an interesting biography. The struggle over Hong Kong's fate runs through Wong's life, and Wong's life runs through the struggle."

When the United Kingdom ceded control, a deal was struck in which Hong Kong would be considered a special administrative region and would be granted fifty years of semiautonomy, based on a framework popularly known as "one country, two systems." By that time, Wong will be fifty. "Nobody knows whether, come 2047, Hong Kong will maintain its unique freedoms or be forced into closer alignment with mainland rules," wrote Stack. "This year's demonstrations are the latest outbreak of a fundamental clash that will keep flaring in different forms, shaping the lives and possibilities of Wong's generation into old age." Wong, she concluded, "is the child of past spasms of unrest and a likely architect of those to come."

The activist claims to be undaunted about continuing his battle into middle age. "If we do nothing, things will be even worse," he asserted to Stack. "They're already winning, so we have nothing to lose." Calling upon a line from the popular Hunger Games series of books and movies, he defiantly declared, "If we burn, they'll burn with us."

CHILDHOOD, EDUCATION, AND EARLY ACTIVISM

Joshua Wong Chi-fung was born in Hong Kong on October 13, 1996, into a middle-class and devoutly Protestant Christian family. His mother, Grace, was a homemaker, and his father, Roger, was an information-technology professional. During Wong's youth, his parents made a point of taking him to visit poor areas of Hong Kong to impress on him the importance of helping the less fortunate.

Though Wong got a large measure of his sense of social responsibility from his parents and his Christian upbringing, and his parents support his pro-democracy activism, they have parted ways at times, as for example regarding LGBT rights, which Wong supports and his father does not. Wong's activism, he told Sue-Lin Wong for the *Financial Times* (8 Nov. 2019), emerged when he realized that prayer did not really work to change society. "The gift from God is to have independence of mind and critical thinking; to have our own will and to make our own personal judgments," he asserted. "I don't link my religious beliefs with my political judgments."

Wong's first foray into protesting came in 2010, when he joined a small group that was speaking out against a proposed high-speed rail line. A more major issue emerged soon after, in 2012, when the Hong Kong government sought to implement mandatory national-education classes deeply influenced by the Communist Party of China. Wong saw the move as a blatant attempt at brainwashing and enlisted a few fellow students to hand out pamphlets decrying the proposal. Their small movement, which was dubbed "Scholarism," quickly spread throughout the region, culminating with the students staging a ten-day sit-in at government offices in Hong Kong. Eventually, officials caved in and shelved the curriculum.

The success of that campaign made Wong, who attended United Christian College, a private secondary school in the Kowloon section of Hong Kong, something of a national celebrity, and he has joked that he was the first student ever to have called a press conference to announce the results of his Diploma of Secondary Education exams due to media interest. Although far from a stellar student—Wong has struggled with dyslexia—he met the basic requirements for admission to a university, and opted to study political science at the Open University of Hong Kong. He remained devoted to social protest movements, however, and told Tania Branigan for the *Guardian* (14 May 2017), "Sometimes it feels as if I major in activism and minor in university."

THE UMBRELLA MOVEMENT

In mid-2014, a time when he was still a high school student with a fondness for video games and laser tag, Wong and his fellow activists in the Scholarism movement were angered by attempts on the part of the National People's Congress, the Chinese legislature, to place restrictions on Hong Kong's electoral system. The proposed changes would, according to critics, effectively allow the Chinese Communist Party to prescreen the candidates for the post of chief executive, the highest office in the Hong Kong

Special Administrative Region—an action directly contrary to the universal suffrage that had been promised to Hong Kong's citizens.

Accordingly, Wong helped organize a massive student strike the last week in September, and, along with a group known as Occupy Central, he helped mobilize tens of thousands of protestors to stage sit-ins. For seventy-nine days the protesters, who set up encampments throughout the region, braved the pepper spray and tear gas deployed by police forces; common umbrellas proved to be a surprisingly effective shield against those tactics, lending the movement its name. By mid-December, however, even the hardiest activists had been forced to disband in the face of mounting aggression on the part of police and injunctions from bus companies and other businesses that had been disrupted. In the end, the movement was not successful: the next chief executive was chosen by the same committee of 1,200 people (mainly wealthy elites with ties to Beijing) as in past contests, rather than by universal suffrage. Furthermore, many of the movement's leaders were arrested and jailed for varying periods.

SERIES OF ARRESTS

On September 27, 2014, Wong was one of some eighty people arrested by the police while occupying an area near the Central Government Complex. Although he was released after less than two days in custody, he was charged in late November with obstructing a bailiff and banned from returning to the protest site where he was arrested. He was next arrested in mid-January 2015 for allegedly inciting another unauthorized assembly, and in August of that year he and other activists were formally charged by the Hong Kong Department of Justice and eventually made to stand trial.

In 2017, Wong, who had in the meantime founded a new pro-democracy political party called Demosistō, was sentenced to six months in prison, along with fellow student protest leaders Nathan Law and Alex Chow. While in prison, he began writing a series of columns for the UK–based *Guardian*. In a column dated September 27, 2017 (the third anniversary of the start of the Umbrella Movement protests), he wrote: "Being locked up is an inevitable part of our long, exhausting path to democracy. Our bodies are held captive, but our pursuit of freedom cannot be contained."

Released on bail after two months, thanks in some part to an international outcry, he was brought before a court again later that year on additional charges of contempt of court. He was later sentenced to an additional two months of imprisonment, and he quipped to interviewers that he was most worried about missing the superhero film *Avengers: Endgame*. He finished

serving the jail term in June 2019—just in time to immerse himself in what has been called the biggest wave of social protest in Asia since the 1989 Tiananmen Square massacre.

2019 PROTESTS

After leaving prison, Wong, who was also detained briefly during past visits to Thailand and Malaysia because of his activities, immediately joined the public unrest again roiling Hong Kong. This time, the issue was a proposed bill that would have allowed fugitives to be extradited from Hong Kong to mainland China for certain crimes, exposing Hongkongers to the mainland's more arbitrary and repressive court system.

Spurred by that issue—but also motivated by instances of police brutality and a desire to see Chief Executive Carrie Lam resign, among other dissatisfactions—tens of thousands of Hong Kong residents poured into the streets, transportation hubs, and public plazas of the region. Although they were met by tear gas, rubber bullets, and water cannons, they persevered, and the protests continued for months, with younger people on the frontlines and older citizens supplying them with funds and other material support. (Although Lam withdrew the extradition bill in September 2019, it was considered too little, too late, to mollify the demonstrators.)

Wong, acting largely as a spokesman thanks to his ability to command attention in the Western press, wrote for the *New York Times* (31 Aug. 2019) along with fellow activist Alex Chow: "The ongoing mass movement in Hong Kong is civil unrest all right—but civil unrest that is the doing of the C.C.P. [Chinese Communist Party]. The protesters are only defending their beloved city, a beacon of liberty, equality and human dignity."

Although the Chinese state-run media often portray him as a puppet of the West, Wong—who is known among compatriots for his almost robotic focus and determination—continues to communicate with international leaders in an effort to bolster support. He has met, for example, with US House Speaker Nancy Pelosi in Washington, DC, and it was a bipartisan group of US congressional representatives who nominated Wong, along with Law and Chow, for the Nobel Peace Prize. "Righting the wrong that is being done in Hong Kong is also the business of the outside world," he and Chow wrote. "World leaders cannot keep mistaking their wish for the peaceful rise of China (and one that perhaps will eventually become democratic) with the reality of the Chinese Communist dictatorship today."

THE FUTURE

Although Wong is banned from running for public office, and Beijing's grip on his region seems only to be tightening, he remains hopeful and currently works for a pro-democracy lawmaker. "Don't be afraid or scared for the future of Hong Kong," he told Branigan. "My starting point was founding Scholarism: at that moment, I couldn't expect 100,000 people in the streets. I couldn't imagine the umbrella movement when it began. I couldn't imagine Demosistō. It's always about turning things that are impossible into the possible."

SUGGESTED READING

Branigan, Tania. "Joshua Wong, the Student Who Risked the Wrath of Beijing: 'It's about Turning the Impossible into the Possible.'" *The Guardian*, 14 May 2017, www.theguardian. com/world/2017/may/14/joshua-wong-the-student-who-risked-the-wrath-of-beijing-its-about-turning-the-impossible-into-the-possible. Accessed 11 Jan. 2020.

Feng, Emily, and Scott Neuman. "Joshua Wong Disqualified from Running in Hong Kong Council Elections." *NPR*, 29 Oct. 2019, www.npr.org/2019/10/29/774298107/joshua-wong-disqualified-from-running-in-hong-kong-council-elections. Accessed 11 Jan. 2020.

Solomon, Feliz. "Facing Jail, Democracy Activist Joshua Wong Says 'Hong Kong Is under Threat.'" *Time*, 17 Aug. 2017, time. com/4902751/hong-kong-joshua-wong-interview-sentencing-democracy/. Accessed 11 Jan. 2020.

Stack, Megan K. "Joshua Wong's Long Campaign for the Future of Hong Kong." *The New Yorker*, 23 Oct. 2019, www.newyorker.com/news/dispatch/joshua-wongs-long-campaign-for-the-future-of-hong-kong. Accessed 11 Jan. 2020.

Wong, Joshua, and Alex Chow. "The People of Hong Kong Will Not Be Cowed by China." *The New York Times*, 31 Aug. 2019, www. nytimes.com/2019/08/31/opinion/hong-kong-protest-joshua-wong.html. Accessed 11 Jan. 2020.

Wong, Sue-Lin. "Joshua Wong: 'We Used to Play Laser Tag. Now We Face Bullets.'" *Financial Times*, 8 Nov. 2019, www.ft.com/content/11b3cfba-f70a-11e9-a79c-bc9a-cae3b654. Accessed 11 Jan. 2020.

—*Mari Rich*

Constance Wu

Date of birth: March 22, 1982
Occupation: Actor

Though actor Constance Wu had been making an impression in a regular role on network television for several years, her star rose even higher following her memorable turn as Rachel Chu in the film *Crazy Rich Asians* in 2018. Recognized as the first studio film produced in the United States with a predominantly Asian cast since *The Joy Luck Club* hit theaters in 1993, *Crazy Rich Asians* was considered culturally significant and proved tremendously popular, particularly with domestic audiences. According to Jiayang Fan for the *New Yorker* (16 Sept. 2019), it "outgrossed every romantic comedy released in the past decade" in the United States. Wu was nominated for a Golden Globe Award for Best Performance by an Actress in a Motion Picture—Musical or Comedy for her role in the film, and in 2017 she had been included on *Time*'s annual list of the one hundred most influential people.

This rise to fame was a remarkable achievement for Wu, a former waitress who had earned her first major role in 2015 on the ABC sitcom *Fresh Off the Boat*, about a Taiwanese American family living in Orlando, Florida. (Like *Crazy Rich Asians*, part of the conversation surrounding the show focused on its significance as one of the few Asian American–focused works to appear in mainstream media.) Seeking to further challenge herself, Wu subsequently starred in the ensemble comedy-drama *Hustlers* (2019), based on a true story about strippers who defraud their Wall Street clients. In discussing her thought process behind picking roles, she told Jen Yamato for the *Los Angeles Times* (29 Aug. 2019), "In every project I choose, I want a character that gets to run the gamut of a full

Photo by Dan MacMedan/Getty Images

spectrum of an arc." Offscreen, Wu became known as an outspoken advocate for women's rights and female and Asian representation in Hollywood.

EARLY LIFE AND EDUCATION

Constance Wu was born in Richmond, Virginia, on March 22, 1982. Her parents, both Taiwanese immigrants, came to the United States in the 1970s. Her father, a science professor at Virginia Commonwealth University, and her mother, a computer programmer, divorced when she was around eighteen. Wu, whose family included three sisters, grew up doing activities such as gymnastics and taking piano lessons.

An avid reader, Wu considered becoming a writer before discovering her love of theater. She would later often credit her passion for literature with her ability to understand character as an actor. Participating in community theater from a young age, she appeared in her first play, an adaptation of Kenneth Grahame's 1908 children's book *The Wind in the Willows*, when she was in about the sixth grade. In interviews she explained that from that point acting just felt like her natural calling. "It was what I was obsessed with and it was the place that I felt the most at home," she told Walter Scott for *Parade* (10 Aug. 2018). As a student at Douglas S. Freeman High School, Wu cheered and sang in the choir. During this time, she also spent six months studying acting at the Lee Strasberg Theatre & Film Institute in New York.

Wu studied acting at Purchase College, State University of New York (SUNY). She was serious about her craft. "It took me a long time to marry that seriousness with the playfulness and the freedom that I had to give," she told Fan. By the time she graduated with a Bachelor of Fine Arts degree in 2005 she had amassed student loans but was determined to live her dream.

EARLY CAREER

Living in New York, Wu endured through a lengthy period of working as a waitress in the evenings to supplement rounds of auditioning during the day. She landed a few small television roles—on shows like *Law & Order: Special Victims Unit* in 2006 and the soap opera *One Life to Live* in 2007—and appeared Off-Off-Broadway. As a big break continued to elude her, she briefly considered ending her nascent acting career and spent time studying psycholinguistics because of her interest in how the brain processes language.

After further personal challenges Wu gave up her acceptance to a graduate program at Columbia University and moved to Los Angeles in 2010. Struggling with credit card and student loan debt, she told Nicole Chung for the *New York Times* (17 Sept. 2015) that, in many ways, "it was the dumbest move I could have made. .

. . But I did it." In Los Angeles she continued to work as a waitress while auditioning for roles. "At one point, I asked myself if I would be O.K. waitressing at forty-five as long as I got to do acting," she told Fan. "My answer was a firm yes."

In 2011 Wu landed a role in a film called *Sound of My Voice*, about documentary filmmakers who set out to expose a cult leader. It premiered at the Sundance Film Festival. After that, she appeared in the first season of *EastSiders*, an independently produced web series that started on *YouTube* in 2012 (she would take part in select episodes of subsequent seasons as well). She landed more small television roles on *Covert Affairs* (2013) and *Franklin & Bash* (2014).

FRESH OFF THE BOAT

Though not primarily a comedic actor up to that point, when the opportunity to audition for a new sitcom called *Fresh Off the Boat* arose, Wu jumped at it. "I was looking for a great job and it was a lead," she recalled to Diane Haithman for *Deadline* (11 June 2015). "If I [audition] for a series regular it's usually the best friend of the lead, or the assistant to the lead, or the secretary to the lead." Though some of the producers expressed initial concern over her suitability to play the character, her talent won them over in the end. The show was inspired by a 2013 memoir of the same name by food personality and restaurateur Eddie Huang. Wu played Huang's mother, Jessica Huang. According to Eddie Huang, it was an appropriate pairing of personalities. "They're both just super-alpha, super-diva, super-unstoppable forces. Constance shows up anywhere, and it's a hurricane," he told Fan.

Fresh Off the Boat follows Eddie Huang's coming-of-age experience in Orlando in the mid-1990s. When the series premiered on ABC in 2015, Neil Genzlinger wrote for the *New York Times* (3 Feb. 2015) that while it showed real promise, it also neutralized much of the voice that had made Huang's grittier memoir so enjoyable. Though Huang was a producer on the show, he voiced similar criticism in an essay that was published on *Vulture* (Jan. 2015). He described being sidelined in the making of the show and claimed that it bore little resemblance to his actual lived experience; Wu supported him. Despite the controversy, the show was a hit overall with audiences, and Wu became its breakout star.

CRAZY RICH ASIANS

Wu was cast in the romantic comedy *Crazy Rich Asians* early in the film's development. Director Jon M. Chu pushed production back about four or five months so that it would not conflict with Wu's shooting schedule for *Fresh Off the Boat*. Based on a best-selling 2013 novel by Kevin Kwan, *Crazy Rich Asians* follows the story of Rachel Chu (Wu), an economics professor teaching in New York. Rachel falls in love with Nick Young (Henry Golding), the heir to a real estate fortune in Singapore. When the couple visit Singapore to attend a lavish wedding, Rachel must prove herself to his wealthy, powerful, and ultra-traditional clan, including Nick's glamorous mother, played by legendary actor Michelle Yeoh.

The film received generally positive reviews from critics—Richard Lawson, writing for *Vanity Fair* (9 Aug. 2018), described it as "breathless fun" if "rather weightless, too." Crucially, however, it was a smash success with audiences, especially in the United States. The film grossed more than $238 million worldwide and was reportedly the highest-grossing romantic comedy of the decade in the United States. Some critics even suggested it helped revitalize interest in the entire romantic comedy genre.

Wu's portrayal of Chu earned her a nomination for a Golden Globe Award for Best Performance by an Actress in a Motion Picture—Musical or Comedy at the seventy-sixth ceremony held in January 2019. In the spring of 2019, ABC announced that it was renewing *Fresh Off the Boat* for a sixth season. Wu voiced her disappointment on the social media platform *Twitter*, writing that the show's renewal prevented her from pursuing a different project, later revealed to reportedly have been a play. The blowback to her profane, off-the-cuff tweets was fierce. "I don't regret being messy and imperfect in public," she told Martha Hayes for the *Guardian* (10 Sept. 2019) later, "but I do regret not taking into account how it might have affected people I care about, like the kids on the show."

HUSTLERS

Also in 2019, Wu starred in a film called *Hustlers*, about a group of strippers who conspire to steal from their Wall Street clients after the 2008 financial crisis. *Hustlers* was based on a true story, and the film was adapted from a 2015 *New York* magazine article about the ill-fated scheme. Wu was keenly interested in appearing in the film, and sent an audition tape to writer-director Lorene Scafaria. "I was looking for a movie with a character that was deeply lonely," she explained to Yamato. She played Destiny, a woman living in New York who struggles to support her grandmother and daughter. The depth of the role offered her the opportunity to continue challenging herself, a luxury she could more easily afford after the success of *Fresh Off the Boat* and *Crazy Rich Asians*. "That complexity is what I seek in any role, and this script really afforded her that journey," she added to Yamato.

Critics complained that *Hustlers* did not quite live up to the performances of its stars, Wu and Jennifer Lopez. Still, the film performed well at the box office, exceeding projected earnings. Meanwhile, by November, ABC had announced that the sixth season of *Fresh Off the Boat* would be its last.

SUGGESTED READING

Fan, Jiayang. "Constance Wu's Hollywood Destiny." *The New Yorker*, 16 Sept. 2019, www.newyorker.com/magazine/2019/09/23/constance-wus-hollywood-destiny. Accessed 17 Nov. 2019.

Hayes, Martha. "'I Don't Regret Being Messy and Imperfect'—Constance Wu on Crazy Rich Asians, Twitter Storms and Acting with J-Lo." *The Guardian*, 10 Sept. 2019, www.theguardian.com/film/2019/sep/10/constance-wu-interview-hustlers. Accessed 18 Nov. 2019.

Lawson, Richard. "*Crazy Rich Asians* Isn't Quite Crazy Enough." Review of *Crazy Rich Asians*, directed by Jon M. Chu. *Vanity Fair*, 9 Aug. 2018, www.vanityfair.com/hollywood/2018/08/crazy-rich-asians-movie-review. Accessed 18 Nov. 2019.

Wu, Constance. "Constance Wu Is Making Her Way in Hollywood." Interview by Nicole Chung. *The New York Times*, 17 Sept. 2015, www.nytimes.com/2015/09/17/magazine/constance-wu-is-making-her-way-in-hollywood.html. Accessed 18 Nov. 2019.

———. "Constance Wu Talks *Crazy Rich Asians, Fresh Off the Boat* and Diversity in Hollywood." Interview by Walter Scott. *Parade*, 10 Aug. 2018, parade.com/690599/walterscott/constance-wu-talks-crazy-rich-asians-fresh-off-the-boat-and-diversity-in-hollywood/. Accessed 18 Nov. 2019.

———. "*Fresh Off the Boat*'s Constance Wu on the Appeal of Her Tiger Mom Role and Embracing Her Roots." Interview by Diane Haithman. *Deadline*, 11 June 2015, deadline.com/2015/06/fresh-off-the-boat-constance-wu-interview-1201441324/. Accessed 18 Nov. 2019.

Yamato, Jen. "Constance Wu Fought for 'Hustlers.' But the Spotlight Is the Real Challenge." *Los Angeles Times*, 29 Aug. 2019, www.latimes.com/entertainment-arts/movies/story/2019-08-29/constance-wu-hustlers-social-media-2019. Accessed 18 Nov. 2019.

SELECTED WORKS
Fresh Off the Boat, 2015–20; *Crazy Rich Asians*, 2018; *Hustlers*, 2019

—Molly Hagan

Xu Zhiyong

Born: March 2, 1973

Photo by Shizhao via Wikimedia Commons

Occupation: Civil rights activist

Xu Zhiyong is an activist who has worked as a lawyer, a university lecturer, and even, briefly, a politician in pursuit of his goal of stronger civil rights protections for Chinese citizens. He was a cofounder of the Open Constitution Initiative, which called for greater transparency from the government and more constitutional protections; after the government shut down the initiative in 2009, Xu founded the New Citizens' Movement in 2010. As governmental restrictions on speech tightened over the early decades of the twenty-first century, Xu increasingly came into conflict with the government and was arrested and charged twice—in 2014 and 2020—on charges related to his political dissidence. Following his second arrest, PEN America honored him with its 2020 PEN/Barbey Freedom to Write Award, which recognizes dissidents who have been jailed for their writings.

EARLY LIFE AND EDUCATION
Xu Zhiyong was born on March 2, 1973, in Minquan County in Henan Province. He earned a bachelor's degree in law from Lanzhou University in 1994, before attending Peking University to study for his PhD. While in law school, Xu met fellow students Teng Biao and Yu Jiang, and the three became close friends. Over shared meals, they often discussed "constitutionalism, democracy, and China's political transformation," Teng told Yaxue Cao for *China Change* (10 Apr. 2014).

During this time, Xu also became an activist—helping organize a campus protest after the 2000 murder of student Qui Qingfeng—and

intervened in several conflicts between citizens and local authorities, including an instance in 2001 in Tieling, Liaoning, where he was briefly detained by the local government. After receiving his doctorate in law in 2002, Xu became a lecturer at the Beijing University of Posts and Telecommunications (BUPT).

OPEN CONSTITUTION INITIATIVE
Xu, Teng, and Yu came to national attention in June 2003, when they became involved in the case of Sun Zhigang. Sun, a twenty-seven-year-old migrant worker, had been beaten to death by police after being arrested for not carrying his residence permit. Under a policy known as Custody and Repatriation, people were required to apply for permits to live and work in specific areas of the country and could be arrested for not having these permits on hand. "When China established the household registration system, or hukou, in 1958, it created two separate worlds: one rural, one urban," Xu later wrote, in a statement translated and published in English by *China Change* (22 Jan. 2014). Following the establishment of Custody and Repatriation in 1961, he continued, "anyone born in a rural area who wanted to find work and try a new life in the city could be arrested and forcibly returned home at any time."

Xu provided legal advice to Sun's family while also petitioning the government to abolish the Custody and Repatriation policy, stating that it was unconstitutional. While the policy was abolished weeks later, the government did not acknowledge Xu's argument about the constitutionality of the procedure. This, Susan Jakes wrote for the *China Beat* (6 Aug. 2009), was characteristic of Xu's approach to activism at the time. "Xu has made a point of investigating and trying to improve troubled political institutions from the inside," Jakes explained.

Following their work on the Sun case, Xu and his former classmates received a number of letters from people who had also experienced poor treatment by police or other government officials. This led them to found the Open Constitution Initiative, a human rights non-governmental organization (NGO) that provided legal aid to victims of social injustice, in October 2003. The organization aimed to challenge abuses of power by the government, dealing with issues such as eviction, forced abortions, torture, and the sovereignty of Tibet. They also continued to campaign for the rights of migrant workers whose issues had not been fully resolved by the abolition of Custody and Repatriation—for example, their children were only allowed to attend school in the district of their parents' officially registered residence, rather than where their parents actually lived.

POLITICAL CAREER

Also in 2003, Xu successfully ran for a seat in the Haidian District People's Congress, a local arm of the Chinese legislature for the Haidian district of Beijing. This was a noteworthy success for a politician running as an independent without the approval of the Communist Party, the country's single political party. Explaining his decision to run, he was quoted by Liu Li for the *China Daily* (17 Dec. 2003) as saying, "I hope my participation will help enhance democratic awareness among intellectuals and help make elections more competitive." The People's Congress was widely seen as unable to do very much in a country where power was increasingly consolidated in the president, but Xu disagreed. "The People's Congress has real power," he told Jakes. "It's just that people don't take it seriously."

Xu won reelection in 2006; this, along with the success of other independent candidates, was hailed as a possible sign of political change in the country. Xu hoped his endeavors would inspire others to work for change within the system as well. "I strive to be a worthy citizen, a member of a group of people who promote the progress of the nation," he told a reporter for a local newspaper, as quoted by Jakes. "I want to make people believe in ideals and in justice and help them see that there is hope for change."

Xu's success, however, led to backlash from the political establishment. In 2011—the next election year after 2006, as the Chinese legislature moved from three-year to five-year terms—the Chinese government banned independent candidates and Xu's name was removed from the candidate list accordingly. He garnered 3,500 write-in votes in a district of approximately 22,000 voters, but this was not enough to maintain his seat in the People's Congress.

NEW CITIZENS' MOVEMENT

In 2009, the government shut down the Open Constitution Initiative, claiming it had dodged taxes. Xu and a colleague, Zhuang Lu, were arrested in connection with this alleged tax evasion, but were released a month later. Their release was partly attributed to pressure from the administration of US President Barack Obama. Xu officially founded the New Citizens' Movement the following year, publishing a manifesto that was quickly censored by officials. The movement, a loose association of activists, called for a peaceful transition to a constitutional society. When speaking about the movement, Xu emphasized the peaceful nature that it shared with the Open Constitution Initiative, but in other ways, his approach had changed. His relationship to the government had become more adversarial; rather than trying to work within the system, he attempted to apply external pressure through organizing protests and writing articles posted on his blog that criticized the government.

In July 2013, Xu was arrested on charges of "gathering crowds to disrupt public order" for a series of small protests in which protesters called for government officials to disclose their assets. To protest the unfairness of the charges, Xu and his lawyer remained silent throughout the trial, except for a closing statement. The court allowed Xu only about ten minutes to read the speech he had prepared, although the full speech was later posted online. The statement promoted the New Citizens' Movement, which the prosecution had avoided any mention of during the trial. In the end, Xu was sentenced to four years in prison; his appeal was denied.

That year, *Foreign Policy* magazine named Xu one of its Global Thinkers "for promoting people power as an antidote to corruption." *Foreign Policy* quoted Xu as saying, in a video released from a detention center earlier that year, "I'm very proud to put the word 'citizen' before my name, and I hope everyone does the same." Xu was released from prison in July 2017.

PEN/BARBEY FREEDOM TO WRITE AWARD

After his release, Xu continued to criticize the government on his blog and Twitter account, despite President Xi's increasing restrictions on speech. In December 2019, Xu went into hiding after learning that four of his fellow activists had been detained following a meeting Xu had attended earlier that month. Several other attendees later told the media that the meeting was simply a gathering of friends and not an attempt to plan action against the government like officials had claimed.

In February 2020, Xu wrote an open letter decrying Xi's responses to the coronavirus 2019 (COVID-19) pandemic and to the pro-democracy protests in Hong Kong, encouraging Xi to resign. The letter was scathing regarding Xi's failings, calling him, among other things, "a big nothing," "lacking confidence," "a befuddled ruler," and "feckless in the face of every major crisis," according to a translation published in *ChinaFile* (26 Feb. 2020). After excoriating Xi's incompetence, indecision, and hunger for power, Xu concluded, "I'm like that kid who blurted out the truth—the Emperor has no clothes!"

Shortly after publishing the letter, Xu was detained, and in June of that year, he was officially arrested on the charge of inciting subversion of state power, which carries a maximum fifteen-year prison sentence. Following the official confirmation of his arrest, PEN America announced that Xu was the winner of the 2020 PEN/Barbey Freedom to Write Award. The announcement came on June 4, the anniversary of the Tiananmen Square massacre.

"In his writings," PEN America's CEO Suzanne Nossel was quoted as saying in a press release on the organization's website (4 June 2020), "Xu has been a persistent voice calling out Beijing's intolerance for dissent—and campaigning for social equity, rule of law, and a joyful vision for his country's future." Xu had previously been made an honorary member of the Independent Chinese PEN Center (ICPC) in 2013.

PERSONAL LIFE

Xu was married to journalist Cui Zheng, with whom he had a daughter in 2014. They later separated. At the time of his arrest in 2020, Xu was living in Beijing with his partner Li Qiaochu, a labor and women's rights activist. Li was detained along with Xu in February 2020 and released on bail in June of that year.

SUGGESTED READING

Jakes, Susan. "China Behind the Headlines: Xu Zhiyong." *The China Beat*, 6 Aug. 2009, thechinabeat.blogspot.com/2009/08/china-behind-headlines-xu-zhiyong.html. Accessed 14 Aug. 2020.

Liu Li. "Independent Candidate Elected." *China Daily*, 17 Dec. 2003, www.chinadaily.com.cn/en/doc/2003-12/17/content_291055.htm. Accessed 14 Aug. 2020.

"PEN America Announces Detained Chinese Essayist Xu Zhiyong as 2020 Pen/Barbey Freedom to Write Award Honoree." *PEN America*, 4 June 2020, pen.org/press-release/pen-america-announces-detained-chinese-essayist-xu-zhiyong-as-2020-pen-barbey-freedom-to-write-award-honoree. Accessed 14 Aug. 2020.

Teng Biao. "Who Is Xu Zhiyong?" Interview by Yaxue Cao. *China Change*, 10 Apr. 2014, chinachange.org/2014/04/10/who-is-xu-zhiyong. Accessed 14 Aug. 2020.

Xu Zhiyong. "Dear Chairman Xi, It's Time for You to Go." Translated by Geremie R. Barmé. *ChinaFile*, 26 Feb. 2020, www.chinafile.com/reporting-opinion/viewpoint/dear-chairman-xi-its-time-you-go. Accessed 14 Aug. 2020.

———. "For Freedom, Justice and Love—My Closing Statement to the Court." *China Change*, 22 Jan. 2014, chinachange.org/2014/01/23/for-freedom-justice-and-love-my-closing-statement-to-the-court. Accessed 14 Aug. 2020.

"Xu Zhiyong." *Foreign Policy*, 2013, 2013-global-thinkers.foreignpolicy.com/zhiyong. Accessed 14 Aug. 2020.

—*Emma Joyce*

Salomé Zourabichvili

Date of birth: March 18, 1952
Occupation: Politician

Salomé Zourabichvili (also spelled Zurabichvili) became the president of Georgia, a former Soviet republic located in the Caucasus region of Eurasia, bordering the Black Sea, in 2018. After declaring its independence in 1991, Georgia clashed frequently with Russia—which it blames for the loss of a substantial portion of the country's territory to separatists—and Zourabichvili has had to contend with that volatile relationship while dealing with infighting and advocating for Georgia's long-awaited admission into the European Union (EU) and the North Atlantic Treaty Organization (NATO).

A longtime diplomat, Zourabichvili first came to widespread attention within Georgia when President Mikheil Saakashvili appointed her foreign minister at the end of 2003. Many Americans first learned of her when she published an op-ed in the *New York Times* (3 Apr. 2009), denouncing the "increasingly authoritarian tendencies" of Saakashvili's government. "What we need," she wrote, "is uncompromising international commitment to the basic institutions of democracy, not simply foreign support for individual leaders. Democracy must have a fresh start in Georgia—and a fresh stance from our genuine friends abroad."

An independent, Zourabichvili ran for the presidency in the October 2018 elections with the support of the coalition party Georgian Dream, beating Saakashvili-backed challenger Grigol Vashadze in a runoff. She was inaugurated on December 16, 2018, to a six-year term as the last Georgian president to be elected by direct ballot. Among other changes, it was outlined in the nation's 2017 Constitution that at the end of her term in 2024, Georgia would transition to an electoral college system.

In her second annual address to the Parliament of Georgia, reprinted in the *Georgian Journal* (4 Mar. 2020), Zourabichvili acknowledged that there was much work to do in the interim. "Instead of being united, mobilizing all our strength and resources to think about the future of the country and how to answer its major issues, instead of looking for audacious solutions, new initiatives and ideas, we are somehow unable to move and we go round and round in circles," she said, asserting that Russia's presence in the disputed territories of Abkhazia and South Ossetia was polarizing the nation and hindering its progress. "Our future resides in building a strong, peaceful, democratic and united Georgia. That means in turn that we have to overcome the social and economic problems of today."

EARLY LIFE AND EDUCATION

Salomé Zourabichvili was born on March 18, 1952, in Paris, France, into a prominent family of the Georgian expatriate community. Her father, Levan Zourabichvili, an engineer, and her mother, Zeinab Kedia, had been driven out of their native Georgia by Soviet occupiers and fled to France in 1921. Some of Zourabichvili's other forebears were Georgian politicians. Her paternal great-grandfather, Niko Nikoladze was a well-known Social Democrat in the late nineteenth century, and her mother was related to Noe Ramishvili, the Democratic Republic of Georgia's first prime minister. Her parents instilled in her a firm belief that Georgia would one day regain its independence: "The question indeed was 'when' and not 'if,'" as she explained to Jim Gibbons for *Europe Diplomatic Magazine* (9 Mar. 2020).

At home in Paris, Zourabichvili was immersed in Georgian culture, with traditional Georgian dishes served on the weekends and Georgian poetry and songs performed around the table. Still, until the Iron Curtain fell in 1989–90, the family had no access to Georgian newspapers. Zourabichvili did not meet anyone who truly lived in Georgia until she was eight, when a Georgian ballet troupe performed in Paris and clandestinely visited expatriate homes.

In her youth, Zourabichvili did not consider diplomacy or politics as a possible career path. "I did not have an early vocation," she explained to Gibbons, "though when the time to choose the orientation of my studies came, I was thinking both in terms of which fields were attractive to me —history, journalism, writing—and what would be useful to the country which my family had left."

As a teen she scored high marks on the French Baccalaureate exam and, in 1969, was granted admission to the highly competitive Institut d'Études Politiques de Paris (Paris Institute of Political Studies, generally known as Sciences Po) Preparatory Year, a foundation program. At the end of the grueling program, only half of the students who went through it were admitted to Sciences Po, and she was one of them, thanks in some part to her final project, for which she chose as a topic "Revolution and Counter-Revolution in Europe between 1917 and 1923" (1970).

Zourabichvili graduated from Sciences Po in July 1972. She then traveled to New York City to attend Columbia University's School of International and Public Affairs. There, she studied under future US National Security Advisor Zbigniew Brzezinski and had the opportunity to complete an internship at the United Nations (UN), where she met members of France's diplomatic corps. Informed that careers in French diplomacy were then being opened to women for the first time, she started to consider it as a possible career direction. She was compelled, as well, by her dawning realization, as she told Gibbons, "that diplomacy was the answer to what would be the most immediate need for a country [like Georgia] in order to reoccupy its place in the world community." Zourabichvili left Columbia in 1973 to embark on what would be a decades-long diplomatic career.

DIPLOMATIC CAREER

Zourabichvili was a member of the French diplomatic service from 1974 to 2004. She began her tenure at the French Embassy in Rome, where she was posted as third secretary until 1977. She next became France's representative to the UN, returning to New York City, which she had come to love during her year of graduate studies. From 1984 to 1988 she was posted to the French Embassy in Washington, DC, where she was assigned to the political and military section, focusing on US–Russian affairs. It was during this period that she visited Georgia for the first time in her life, on a 1986 vacation with her mother. From 1988 to 1989, Zourabichvili was the French representative for the Organization for Security and Cooperation in Europe (OSCE). She then took posts as the French envoy to Chad (1990–93), the representative to North Atlantic Treaty Organization (NATO)–Western European Union (WEU) (1993–96), and an official of the Division of International and Strategic Issues (1996–2003).

Although Zourabichvili had long harbored ambitions to aid Georgia, and her attachment to the country was widely known, she did not work in Georgia until November 2003, when she was assigned to serve as extraordinary and plenipotentiary ambassador of France to Georgia. Just days after she arrived, Georgian President Eduard Shevardnadze was ousted in the peaceful Rose Revolution. A short while later, Saakashvili, a lawyer educated in the United States, was elected in a landslide to replace him.

As president, Saakashvili tapped Zourabichvili to serve in his cabinet as minister of foreign affairs. With the approval of French president Jacques Chirac and the Parliament of Georgia, Zourabichvili agreed. "This was not a defection, it was the marriage of both my parts, not a divorce," she explained to Nora Boustany for the *Washington Post* (4 June 2004) of her unusual appointment, which required her to be named a Georgian citizen by decree. Zourabichvili accepted this requirement and became a dual citizen of France and Georgia—and remained a paid member of the French diplomatic service.

A LEAP INTO POLITICS

Saakashvili was forming a cabinet of people who were mostly under the age of thirty-five, internationally educated, and without ties to Georgia's former regime. For her part, Zourabichvili saw her mission as "a very well-defined task to help in the rebuilding of the county by reforming the Foreign Ministry and developing a diplomatic corps and coming to that country's assistance at the most difficult phase of its history," as she explained to Boustany.

Zourabichvili hoped that during her tenure, the country might reconcile with Russia, affirm its European identity, and strengthen its ties to the United States. Although she was instrumental in negotiating a treaty that led to the withdrawal of Russia from areas other than Abkhazia and South Ossetia, she had little time to further other goals. Not long after her appointment, she fell out with President Saakashvili, and several ambassadors accused her of ordering them to report directly to her rather than to Parliament, ignoring their attempts to contact her, and other forms of administrative misconduct. There were also questions about why she continued to receive a salary from the French Foreign Affairs Office while serving as a Georgian member of Saakashvili's cabinet. Zourabichvili subsequently left the French diplomatic corps, but in October 2005, Prime Minister Zurab Nogaideli ousted her as Georgia's foreign minister.

In 2006, Zourabichvili entered politics by founding a new political party, The Way of Georgia, which she led until 2010. She also began teaching at Sciences Po as an associate professor of international relations, a post she held from 2006 to 2015. Between 2010 and 2015, she led the UN Security Council group that monitored sanctions against Iran.

During this time, Zourabichvili grew increasingly disenchanted with Saakashvili, asserting, as she wrote in the *New York Times* in 2009, that under his rule, "Georgia has become an authoritarian state, buoyed by unbalanced power and millions of dollars in aid," and warning, "Our Parliament, with a two-thirds majority for Saakashvili's party, is unable to provide checks and balances." Saakashvili left office in 2013 and later faced criminal charges of abuse of power.

In the 2016 parliamentary elections, Zourabichvili ran as an independent and won a seat representing the Mtatsminda region of the Georgian capital of Tbilisi, an important steppingstone on her way to the presidency.

THE PRESIDENCY

In 2018, Zourabichvili announced her candidacy for Georgia's presidency. Although she ran as an independent, she had the support of the large coalition party Georgian Dream. It was a grueling and negative campaign, and although international observers deemed that the election was free and competitive, they noted that both sides tried to undermine the process. When polling was done, Zourabichvili received 38.7 percent of the vote in the first round of direct balloting and did not win outright. She then triumphed with 59.52 percent of the vote in a runoff against Grigol Vashadze, who was backed by Saakashvili, by then living in exile.

Zourabichvili became Georgia's fifth president and the first woman to hold the office. She was inaugurated on December 16, 2018, choosing to hold the ceremony in Telavi, a town whose inhabitants had voted overwhelmingly against her, as proof that she was determined to represent all Georgians. Rather than take up residence in the Avlabari Presidential Palace, she chose more modest accommodations in Central Tbilisi.

Zourabichvili has been working under the strictures of a new constitution that had been adopted in 2017 and went into effect on the day of her inauguration. It removed several powers from the presidency, moving them instead to Parliament and the prime minister's office. Significantly, because of further constitutional changes set to take effect in 2024, Zourabichvili would be Georgia's last popularly elected president; thereafter, presidents would instead be elected indirectly by an electoral college.

In a conversation at the Council on Foreign Relations on September 27, 2019, Zourabichvili told Alexander Vershbow, "It's a miracle that Georgia has managed over the years, and despite, again, the frozen conflicts, then the war, then the occupation, that Georgia has managed to . . . become a very stable country that is attracting investment. . . . And that's the Georgian miracle that we have to preserve." She quipped to Vershbow that Georgia's "soft power" resided in its "cuisine, wine, landscapes, hospitality of the Georgians, and their immense tolerance." She continued, "Everybody's ready to come to Georgia."

PERSONAL LIFE

Zourabichvili has two children from her first marriage, to the Iranian American economist Nicolas Gorjestani. Her daughter, Ketevan Gorjestani, is a broadcast journalist, and her son, Teimuraz Gorjestani, is a diplomat and international advisor at the Élysée Palace, the official residence of the French president. Zourabichvili's second husband, the Georgian journalist Janri Kashia, died in 2012.

Zourabichvili speaks Georgian, French, and English fluently and is conversant in Italian.

SUGGESTED READING

Boustany, Nora. "A Georgian Reborn, Still Straddling Two Cultures." *The Washington Post*, 4 June 2004, www.washingtonpost.com/archive/politics/2004/06/04/a-georgian-reborn-still-straddling-two-cultures/a5d37ba3-3c97-463d-9d56-c939107d3d14/. Accessed 4 June 2020.

Keaten, Jamey. "Georgian Leader Sees NATO Future, Seeks Tough Line on Russia." *The Seattle Times*, 10 June 2019, www.seattletimes.com/nation-world/nation/georgian-leader-sees-nato-future-seeks-tough-line-on-russia/. Accessed 4 June 2020.

"Salomé Zourabichvili: Alumna and President." *SciencesPo*, 2 Feb. 2019, www.sciencespo.fr/en/news/news/salom%C3%A9-zourabichvili-alumna-and-president/3971. Accessed 4 June 2020.

Zourabichvili, Salomé. "Annual Address by H.E. Salome Zourabichvili, President of Georgia, to the Parliament of Georgia." *Georgian Journal*, 4 Mar. 2020, www.georgianjournal.ge/politics/36321-annual-address-by-he-salome-zourabichvili-president-of-georgia-to-the-parliament-of-georgia.html. Accessed 4 June 2020.

———. "Salomé Zourabichvili: A Portrait and Exclusive Interview." Interview by Jim Gibbons. *Europe Diplomatic Magazine*, 9 Mar. 2020, europe-diplomatic.eu/salome-zourabichvili-a-portrait-and-exclusive-interview/. Accessed 4 June 2020.

———. "A Conversation with President Salome Zourabichvili of Georgia." Interview by Alexander Vershbow. *Council on Foreign Relations*, 27 Sept. 2019, www.cfr.org/event/conversation-president-salome-zourabichvili-georgia. Accessed 4 June 2020.

———. "A Fresh Start in Georgia." *The New York Times*, 3 Apr. 2009, www.nytimes.com/2009/04/04/opinion/04iht-edzourabichvili.html. Accessed 4 June 2020.

—*Mari Rich*

OBITUARIES

Richard Anuszkiewicz

Born: Erie, Pennsylvania; May 23, 1930
Died: Englewood, New Jersey; May 19, 2020
Occupation: Artist

Having begun in 1960 to "dazzle," as the critics said, New York gallery-goers with his paintings of geometric shapes in compositions scientifically determined by the interaction of complementary colors, Richard Anuszkiewicz was in line a few years later to be dubbed an old master of the perception-altering style known as Op Art.

Richard Joseph Anuszkiewicz was born in Erie, Pennsylvania on May 23, 1930, to Adam Jacob and Victoria Ann (Jankowski) Anuszkiewicz, natives of Poland who grew up there in villages not far apart, but did not meet until both had settled in Pennsylvania. His father was employed in an Erie paper mill. By an earlier marriage of his mother, Anuszkiewicz had a half-sister and four half-brothers.

"I wanted to be an artist from the first," Anuszkiewicz told the art scholar and critic Gene Baro in a conversation that was printed in the catalog of the painter's 1975 exhibition at the Andrew Crispo Gallery. His formal training began at a vocational high school in Erie, where he began capturing, in realistic paintings, atmospheric details and moods reminiscent of the work of the Ashcan School and the WPA (Works Progress Administration) representational artists. He later trained at the Cleveland Institute of Art and the Yale University School of Art and Architecture. At the latter, he studied with Josef Albers, a painter whose explorations of optical phenomena in geometric color configurations made him an important progenitor of the Op Art movement.

When Anuszkiewicz left Yale with his MFA degree in 1955, he enrolled in Kent State University. While at Kent he had his first one-man show, at the Butler Institute of American Art in Youngstown, Ohio. He received his BS degree in Education from Kent in 1956.

Moving to New York City in 1957, he got a job at the Junior Museum of the Metropolitan Museum of Art (the Met). He tried to find a gallery but was repeatedly told his work was too difficult to look at. Some gallery owners claimed it actually hurt their eyes. Finally, in 1960, one well-known gallery agreed to show his pieces, and two were purchased by the director of the Museum of Modern Art (MoMA), launching his career.

Anuszkiewicz was soon being shown in major museum exhibits and featured in national magazines. Although Op Art's heyday was short, he continued to exhibit regularly in galleries and museums, and some 75 institutions around the world now own his work. Anuszkiewicz received a Lee Krasner Award for lifetime achievement in 2000, and in 2013, at age 82, he had his first exhibition of new work in New York in over a decade.

He is survived by his wife, Sarah, along with their children (Adam, Stephanie, and Christine) and six grandchildren.

See *Current Biography 1978*

Peter Beard

Born: New York, New York; January 22, 1938
Died: Montauk, New York; April 19, 2020
Occupation: Photographer

Peter Beard was known as much for his hard-partying persona as for his often provocative and heart-wrenching pictures of African wildlife. That dichotomy often caused journalists to assert that the description "wild" could be applied to him in multiple ways.

Peter Beard was born in New York City on January 22, 1938. He is the great-grandson of J. J. Hill, who founded the Great Northern Railway, and the grandson of the tobacco heir Pierre Lorillard IV, who is credited with designing the first tuxedo. Beard's father, Anson Mc-Cook Beard, a stockbroker, and mother, Rosanne Hoar, raised Peter and his two brothers, Anson Jr. and Samuel, in a nine-room apartment on the Upper East Side of Manhattan, in New York City. Though he has been an avid diarist since the age of 14, Beard has revealed little about his childhood. As a teenager, he attended boarding schools, and then went on to study art at Yale University, in New Haven, Connecticut, where he was a member of the fraternal organization Scroll and Key. He earned a bachelor's degree in 1961.

Beard's enthusiasm for Africa, and particularly Kenya, was sparked in 1954, when he read Isak Dinesen's celebrated 1937 memoir *Out of Africa*. He made his first trip to the continent during his college years. He eventually developed a friendship with Dinesen (whose real name was Karen Blixen) and bought a 45-acre ranch adjoining property she owned in the Ngong Hills, just outside of Nairobi, the capital of Kenya.

His work was the subject of solo exhibitions at such prestigious venues as the International Center of Photography in Manhattan and the Centre National de la Photographie in Paris, and his books of photography include *The End of the Game* (1965), *Longing for Darkness: Kamante's Tales from Out of Africa* (1975), and *The Art of* the Maasai: 300 Newly Discovered Objects and Works of Art, 1992.

Besides documenting Africa's animals, he photographed fashion shoots for Vogue, Elle, and other glossy magazines. He dated actress Candice Bergen and Lee Radziwill, the sister of Jacqueline Kennedy Onassis, and for a time he was married to the supermodel Cheryl Tiegs. He counted among his friends the artists Andy Warhol and Salvador Dalí, the writer Truman Capote, and the members of the Rolling Stones. Even as he aged, he maintained his bacchanalian lifestyle, and one interviewer referred to him as a "hard-partying septuagenarian shutterbug."

In 1996, the Centre International de la Photographie mounted a retrospective exhibition of Beard's work. That same year he was nearly killed by a charging elephant, who almost severed a femoral artery with a tusk and crushed his pelvis and numerous ribs.

In his final years he suffered from dementia, and on March 31, 2020, he disappeared from his home on the East End of Long Island. After an extensive search, his body was found three weeks later in a nearby state park.

He is survived by his wife, Nejma; a daughter, Zara; a granddaughter; and his brothers.

See *Current Biography 1997*

Alan S. Boyd

Born: Jacksonville, Florida; July 20, 1922
Died: Seattle, Washington; October 18, 2020
Occupation: U.S. Government Official

In 1966 Alan S. Boyd was charged with integrating the country's highways, rails, airlines, and shipping concerns under one umbrella, thus becoming the first United States secretary of transportation.

Alan Stephenson Boyd was born in Jacksonville, Florida, on July 20, 1922, to Clarence and Elizabeth (Stephenson) Boyd. Transportation was something of a family tradition: his great-grandfather invented the country's first horse-drawn streetcar on rails, his father was a transportation engineer, and his stepfather was an attorney for a railroad company.

Boyd studied at the University of Florida from 1939 to 1941. From 1942 to 1945 he was a pilot with the Troop Transport Command of the U.S. Army, attaining the rank of major. (His total flying time, including the hours he later accumulated in the Korean conflict, amounted to over 3,000 hours.) After World War II, he completed work for his LL.B. degree at the University of Virginia, earning it in 1948.

In 1954 Governor Leroy Collins appointed him chairman of a civilian committee for the development of aviation in Florida, and he served as general counsel for the Florida State Turnpike Authority in 1955, when he was also appointed a member of the Florida Railroad and Public Utilities Commission in Tallahassee. He was elected to a full term on the commission in 1956 and served as its chairman in 1957–58. Dwight D. Eisenhower appointed Boyd to the Civil Aeronautics Board (CAB) in 1959, and John F. Kennedy named Boyd to the chairmanship in February 1961.

Four years later, Boyd was named undersecretary of commerce for transportation by Lyndon B. Johnson. Johnson soon charged him with streamlining the nation's fragmented transportation systems, then encompassing thirty-five agencies with overlapping responsibilities. On Boyd's recommendation, Johnson signed a bill to create the U.S. Department of Transportation (DOT) on October 15, 1966, and the new department began operating on April 1, 1967, with Boyd as its head. He became known for appointing both Democrats and Republicans to the department, on the grounds that transportation was nonpartisan, and he oversaw a fruitful period of airport modernization, improved auto safety standards, and highway beautification projects.

When Richard M. Nixon took office, Boyd left government service to take on a variety of transportation-related roles, including president of the Illinois Central Railroad, president of Amtrak, and president of the North American arm of Airbus Industrie.

Boyd died on October 18, 2020, at a Seattle nursing home. He was predeceased by his wife, Flavil, a high school teacher, in 2007. He is survived by his son, Mark; two grandchildren; and one great-grandchild. The department he helped found now has a budget of more than $76 billion and employs almost 55,000 people.

See *Current Biography 1965*

Julian Bream

Born: London, England; July 15, 1933
Died: Wiltshire, England; August 14, 2020
Occupation: Guitarist; lutenist; musicologist

Julian Bream's virtuosity on the classical Spanish guitar made him, in the opinion of most critics, the heir apparent to Andrés Segovia, and by his mastery of the lute he almost single-handedly effected a revival of interest in that sixteenth-century ancestor of the guitar.

Julian Bream was born on July 15, 1933, in the London borough of Battersea. His mother, Violet, was a homemaker, and his father, Henry G. Bream, was a commercial artist and book illustrator who loved music and could play the piano, banjo, and guitar.

Disrupted in his formal education by wartime evacuations from London, Bream had little interest in studies other than music and quit school when he was 14. In 1943 he began to take piano lessons, but he also picked up the elder Bream's guitar, plucking the strings in accompaniment to any music that happened to be on the radio. When Henry Bream discovered his son's enthusiasm for the instrument, he helped him to master the basic techniques of the jazz guitar, and within a few months Bream played well enough to sit in with the local dance band his father had formed. For Bream's eleventh birthday, he received an old Spanish guitar, and when he heard an old 78 rpm recording by Andrés Segovia he decided to focus on classical instead of jazz guitar. Concurrently, he began to study the cello, believing it would be easier to earn a living that way.

In 1946, Bream was heard in the first of a series of programs on the BBC, and the following year he made his first public appearance as a recitalist. Later in 1947, he became a full-time student at the Royal College of Music. There was no professor of guitar at the college—or at any college in England, for that matter—so Bream studied the piano and composition. He earned a subsistence living by teaching the guitar, giving occasional concerts, and playing for film soundtracks. In 1950, he began a serious study of the Elizabethan lute and was soon being credited with its renewed popularity.

Bream made his London debut at Wigmore Hall in 1951; and after serving in the British Army from 1952 to 1955, he toured widely, performing at international festivals and giving recitals. He made his American debut in 1958, at Town Hall in New York and continued to mount annual tours for the next four decades. Bream gave his final formal recital in 2002, but he continued to play occasionally at churches near his home until 2011.

He is particularly celebrated in the music world for the number of pieces he commissioned, many of which became staples of the guitar literature, including Benjamin Britten's "Nocturnal" and William Walton's "Five Bagatelles." His honors included the Order of the British Empire in 1964 and Commander of the British Empire in 1985.

Twice divorced, Julian Bream died on August 14, 2020. He was predeceased by his youngest brother, Paul. He is survived by his other brother, Anthony, and his sister, Janice.

See *Current Biography 1968*

Lou Brock

Born: El Dorado, Arkansas; July 18, 1939
Died: Saint Louis, Missouri; September 3, 2020
Occupation: Baseball player

Lou Brock, a left fielder for the St. Louis Cardinals, has been called the greatest base-stealer the major leagues had ever known.

Lou Brock was born on July 18, 1939 in El Dorado, Arkansas, and grew up in Collinston, Louisiana, where his mother moved to be near her extended family after his father abandoned her. Brock explained to interviewers that his mother was married three times and had a total of nine children; he was the youngest of the second group. Some sources refer to his extended family as cotton sharecroppers.

Growing up in the Jim Crow South, Brock attended a one-room schoolhouse. One day, he heard a radio broadcast of a game between the Cardinals and the Brooklyn Dodgers, whose player Jackie Robinson had just broken the major leagues' color barrier. Excited about baseball, Brock began practicing with the equipment available to him: swatting rocks with tree branches. The summer before he entered high school, he joined a sandlot team as a substitute right fielder. When the team's manager saw his arm in action, he was moved to the mound, first for batting practices and later for games; and he continued to pitch, as well as to play outfield, at Union High School in Mer Rouge. With the Union High team, he never batted under .350; and, normally left-handed, he became a .535 switch hitter in his senior year.

After high school Brock entered all-black Southern University in Baton Rouge, Louisiana, to study math on an academic scholarship. He did poorly in his classes and lost the scholarship after his first year, however. With no money for food or a room, he knew his best hope was an athletic scholarship, so he concentrated on improving his performance on the university's baseball team and succeeded in raising his batting average from .186—his freshman tally—to a phenomenal .542. The improvement brought him not only the scholarship but also the attention of major league scouts; and in 1961, he made his major league debut with the Chicago Cubs.

He was traded to the Cardinals in 1964, and that season he played in 103 games, hit .348, stole 33 bases, and scored 81 runs, and ultimately helped his team defeat the Yankees in the World Series.

In all, before his retirement from pro ball in 1979, he helped the Cardinals take home three pennants and two World Series championships. Over the course of his career he led the National

League in steals eight times, and his 938 career steals broke Ty Cobb's mark of 892.

Later in life Brock, who was elected to the Baseball Hall of Fame in 1985, pursued various business ventures and worked as an instructor for the Cardinals. In 2015 the complications of diabetes necessitated the amputation of his leg, and two years later he was diagnosed with multiple myeloma. He died on September 3, 2020.

Twice divorced, Lou Brock is survived by his third wife, Jacqueline; his son, Lou Jr., and daughter, Wanda, from his first marriage; three stepchildren; and two granddaughters.

See *Current Biography 1975*

E. Margaret Burbidge

Born: Davenport, England; August 12, 1919
Died: San Francisco, California; April 5, 2020
Occupation: Astronomer; astrophysicist

E. Margaret Burbidge devoted her life to increasing our understanding of the universe, while at the same time overcoming sexual discrimination in what was traditionally a male-dominated field.

She was born Eleanor Margaret Peachey on August 12, 1919, to Stanley Peachey, a research chemist and teacher, and Marjorie Peachey. She graduated from the Francis Holland School, a private school for girls, and then enrolled at University College, London, which—unlike most other colleges at the time—offered a major in astronomy. She was one of only four University College students, and the only woman, who majored in that field. In 1939, after earning a BS degree, with first-class honors, she enrolled in the graduate program at the University of London Observatory. Thanks to the blackouts enforced in London during World War II, the sky was dark enough for stargazing, and she became skilled at operating the observatory's one functional telescope. She was awarded a PhD degree in 1943.

In 1946, on the strength of her facility with the telescope, she had secured a job as an assistant to the director of the University of London Observatory. By the time she left, in 1951, she had become the observatory's acting director.

She was denied a fellowship that would have let her work at Mount Wilson Observatory, near Pasadena, California, because women were not permitted to use the telescopes there. Later, she gained access only by posing as her husband's assistant. (She had married fellow scientist Geoffrey Burbidge in 1948.)

Burbidge was the co-author of the 1957 paper "Synthesis of the Elements in Stars," which was published in the journal *Reviews of Modern Physics*, and which is still considered among the most influential scientific works of its era. It has been said that she and her co-authors—who included her husband, as well as future Nobel laureate William Fowler—laid the foundations for modern nuclear astrophysics.

Burbidge joined the faculty of the University of California, San Diego, in the early 1960s and went on to become the founding director of its Center for Astrophysics and Space Sciences. From 1972 to 1973 she served as the director of the Royal Observatory—the first woman to do so—and she was also the first woman to serve as president of the American Astronomical Society (AAS), a post she held from 1976 to 1978.

Her honors include the Helen B. Warner Prize from the AAS, shared with her husband, and the Catherine Wolfe Bruce Gold Medal from the Astronomical Society of the Pacific. (She turned down the Annie Jump Cannon Award from the AAS, however, because it was earmarked for women, and she did not agree with the practice of giving gender-specific prizes.) The asteroid known as Minor Planet 5490 Burbidge is named for her.

At the time of her death Burbidge was a university professor emeritus at the University of California, San Diego. She is survived by her daughter, Sarah, and a grandson.

See *Current Biography 2000*

Herman Cain

Born: Memphis, Tennessee; December 13, 1945
Died: Atlanta, Georgia; July 30, 2020
Occupation: Businessman; radio host; writer; politician

Herman Cain rose from poverty to become a millionaire businessman before unsuccessfully seeking the 2012 Republican presidential nomination, and he remained in the political spotlight until his death, as a conservative commentator and staunch ally of Donald Trump.

Herman Cain was born on December 13, 1945, in Memphis, Tennessee, and was raised in Atlanta, Georgia. His mother, Lenora, was a domestic worker, and his father, Luther, worked various jobs as a barber, janitor, and the chauffeur to the president of Coca-Cola.

Cain—the first in his family to graduate college—earned a bachelor's degree in math from Morehouse in 1967 and a master's degree in computer science from Purdue University in 1971. Returning to Atlanta, he began working for Coca-Cola as a computer-systems analyst; and in 1977 he joined Pillsbury, where within five years he had risen through the ranks to become vice president of corporate systems and services. He later joined Pillsbury's Burger King division, successfully increasing the profitability of the 400 restaurants under his charge.

Cain was still with Burger King when, in 1986, Pillsbury purchased Diversifoods Inc. That conglomerate included hundreds of Godfather's pizza restaurants. Cain served as chairman and CEO of that chain from 1986 to 1996. Concurrently, he was becoming a vocal political advocate for business owners. He was elected to the board of directors of the National Restaurant Association in 1988 and became president and CEO of the group in 1996, overseeing its development into a powerful lobbying group.

Cain attracted widespread attention in 1994, during a televised town-hall meeting at which he famously challenged President Bill Clinton on his proposal for health-care reform, and he soon found himself among the ranks of Washington insiders. In 2000 he co-chaired publishing executive Steve Forbes's failed presidential campaign, and in 2004 he made an unsuccessful run for a US Senate seat.

His political aspirations reached a peak in 2011, when he announced his bid for the Republican presidential nomination. Although popular with members of the right-wing Tea Party, Cain drew ire for declaring that he would never appoint a Muslim to his administration and for his proposed tax plan, which economists pointed out would disproportionally target the poor. His candidacy fell apart altogether after reports surfaced that he had been accused by multiple women of sexual harassment.

After his run for president, Cain (who had hosted an eponymous talk radio show from 2008 to 2011) became a Fox News contributor, signed on to a new radio show, and penned columns for conservative news outlets. In the final years of his life he was a vocal booster of Donald Trump; and in June 2020, in the midst of the coronavirus pandemic, he attended a packed indoor rally for the president, where he was photographed with no mask, in defiance of public-health guidelines.

Herman Cain died July 30, 2020, in Atlanta, from the effects of the virus. He is survived by his wife of more than four decades, Gloria; their children, Melanie and Vincent; and four grandchildren.

See *Current Biography 2011*

Lewis John Carlino

Born: New York, New York; January 1, 1932
Died: Whidbey Island, Washington; June 17, 2020
Occupation: Dramatist; filmmaker

Lewis John Carlino was perhaps best known for writing the screenplay for the 1977 hit *I Never Promised You a Rose Garden*, about a schizophrenic teenage girl, and for both adapting and directing 1979's *The Great Santini*, based on an autobiographical novel by Pat Conroy. His other screenwriting credits included the Kris Kristofferson vehicle *The Sailor Who Fell from Grace with the Sea* (1976), which he also directed; the Kirk Douglas mafia film *The Brotherhood* (1968); and *Resurrection* (1980), which starred Ellen Burstyn.

The youngest of three children of a Sicilian immigrant tailor, Lewis John Carlino was born in New York City on January 1, 1932. When he was 12 years old, he moved with his family to California. In about 1951, he enlisted in the United States Air Force, and after his discharge four years later, he enrolled under the GI Bill at the University of Southern California, where he majored in film. To help defray the cost of his education, he worked summers as a day camp counselor and as a hospital surgical technician. He earned his BA degree, Phi Beta Kappa and magna cum laude, in 1959 and his MA degree a year later.

While an undergraduate at the University of Southern California, Carlino indulged his interest in the theater by writing a number of one-act plays, including *The Brick and the Rose: A Collage for Voices, Used Car for Sale*, and *Junk Yard. The Brick and the Rose*, a somewhat conventional study of narcotics addiction, was produced by the Los Angeles chapter of the American National Theatre and Academy in 1957, and in 1960 it was the first presentation of the *CBS Television Workshop*. One of Carlino's early works won him the 1960 British Drama League Prize in international playwriting.

After receiving his MA degree, Carlino traveled around the world for a few years "to let the ideas cook," as he once put it. On his return to the United States, he settled in New York City, where he found a job teaching at Columbia University. Still interested in a career in the theatre, he joined the New Dramatists Committee, an organization devoted to the development of talented young playwrights, and in his spare time, he continued to write. Carlino made his New York debut in 1963, with the Off-Broadway production of *Cages*, which ran for 176 performances at the York Playhouse.

Although his work was sometimes accused of being mawkish, he eventually caught the eye of Edward Lewis, a motion picture producer, and John Frankenheimer, a director, who helped him launch his screenwriting and directing career.

Carlino, whose first marriage ended in divorce, died of the complications of myelodysplastic syndrome, a blood disease, and is survived by his daughter, Alessa; a grandson; and a great-granddaughter. He was predeceased by his two other children (Voné Natelle and Lewis John II), as well as by his second wife, Jilly.

See *Current Biography 1983*

Marge Champion

Born: September 2, 1919, Los Angeles, California
Died: October 21, 2020, Los Angeles, California
Occupation: Dancer

Marge Champion won renown as one-half of a dancing duo: she and her husband, Gower—the first dance team to achieve fame through the then-new medium of television—were considered worthy successors to Fred Astaire and Ginger Rogers.

The dancer was born Marjorie Celeste Belcher in Los Angeles on September 2, 1919, to Ernest and Gladys (Basquette) Belcher. Her father was a Hollywood ballet master who taught many well-known movie stars, and he coached Marge in acrobatic, tap, ballet, and Spanish dancing, beginning when she was three years old. Changing her name to Marjorie Bell, she made her movie debut in 1938 in a small part in the Astaire-Rogers film, *The Castles*. The same year she modeled for Walt Disney's cartoon heroines in *Snow White* and *Pinocchio* (posing as the blue fairy). Her moves were also copied by animators for the graceful dancing hippos in *Fantasia*.

While attending Hollywood High School, she appeared in local Civic Opera musical productions, making her stage debut at the age of thirteen before an audience of 23,000 in the Hollywood Bowl.

An early marriage to Art Babbitt, a commercial artist, ended in divorce after two years, and in 1947 the young dancer went to New York to appear in the Broadway musicals, *Dark of the Moon* and Duke Ellington's *Beggar's Holiday*.

At about that time, Gower Champion, a former student of her father's, was looking for a dancing partner and asked her to team up with him. She agreed, and in 1949, they became fixtures on the weekly *Admiral Broadway Revue*, which aired on NBC. Their brand of engaging, pantomime-filled dancing attracted millions of fans each week, and they soon began appearing on the big screen, in such films as *Mr. Music*

(1950), which starred Bing Crosby; *Show Boat* (1951); *Lovely to Look At* (1952); and *Everything I Have Is Yours* (1952).

In 1957 they were given their own eponymous sitcom, but three years later they split professionally; Gower began directing Broadway productions, and Marge threw herself in a succession of television roles and choreographing gigs. (In 1975, she won an Emmy for choreographing the television movie *Queen of the Stardust Ballroom*.)

In later years, she taught dance and choreography in New York, lectured, sat on the boards of several arts organizations, and was a member of the Tony Awards nominating committee. She also continued to perform on occasion, and her last Broadway appearance came when she was eighty-two years old, in Stephen Sondheim's *Follies*.

Marge Champion died on October 21, 2020, in Los Angeles, at the age of 101. She and Gower had divorced in 1972 but remained close friends. He died in 1980. She was also predeceased by her third husband, the director Boris Sagal, in 1981, and by one of her sons, Blake, in 1987. She is survived by her other son, Gregg, and three grandchildren.

See *Current Biography 1953*

Christo

Born: Gabrovo, Bulgaria; June 13, 1935
Died: New York, New York; May 31, 2020
Occupation: Artist

Urban buildings wrapped in fabric and rope, large "air packages" suspended over city streets, a rocky chunk of Australian seacoast shrouded in fabric, a Paris street blocked with oil drums, a Rocky Mountain valley gapped by a quarter-mile-wide nylon curtain, and a 24-mile-long fabric fence following the contours of the rolling northern California coastal hills—these are among the art works of the artist known as Christo. His huge, often bizarre monuments force the viewer to reexamine the nature of art, because he is not primarily interested in creating permanent art objects for display in museums. He prefers instead to go out into the world and create temporary monuments that involve many people in their construction and are seen by people who would never enter a museum.

Christo Vladimirov Javacheff was born on June 13, 1935, in Gabrovo, Bulgaria, the second son of Ivan Vladimir Javacheff, a chemist and businessman, and the former Tzveta Dimitrova, who was active in politics during her youth. He had two brothers, Anani and Stefan.

As a student at the National Academy of Arts in Sofia (1952–56), Christo learned to paint according to the dictates of the Socialist Realist school. In 1956, he went to Prague, Czechoslovakia, to study and work at the Burian Theatre, but three months later the Hungarian Revolution broke out, and the Bulgarian artist fled to the West. In Vienna he trained at the Fine Arts Academy and, after a sojourn in Switzerland, arrived in Paris in 1958. In Paris he was included in three of the exhibitions organized by the *nouveau réalisme* movement, creating sculptures that consisted of collections of bottles and cans, some of which were left unmodified whereas others were wrapped or painted. During the early 1960s Christo made large monuments with barrels, including "Iron Curtain—Wall of Oil Drums," which temporarily blocked traffic on the Rue Visconti in Paris, in June 1962.

He moved to the United States in 1964 and approached several art museums, hoping to wrap them entirely in fabric. The Chicago Museum of Contemporary Art agreed in 1969. That year he also wrapped a million square feet of Australian coastline in erosion-control fabric.

The 1980s and '90s found his stature increasing, as he was given permission for many dramatic urban projects, including wrapping the Pont Neuf in Paris in honey-colored fabric in 1985 and fully encasing the Reichstag in Berlin, in 1995. Among his most famed works in later years was "The Gates," (2005) for which he installed more than 7,500 steel frames supporting panels of saffron-colored fabric along 23 miles of pathways in Central Park.

Christo was predeceased in 2009 by his wife and artistic collaborator, Jeanne-Claude. He is survived by his son, Cyril Christo, a wildlife photographer; his brothers; a grandson; and two nephews. At the time of his death, he was planning to wrap Paris's Arc de Triomphe in silver-blue fabric and red rope.

See *Current Biography 1977*

Ben Cross

Born: London, England; December 16, 1947
Died: Vienna, Austria; July 10, 2020
Occupation: Actor

Ben Cross was virtually unknown before *Chariots of Fire*, a dramatic account of the victories of two British runners at the 1924 Olympics, won the 1981 Academy Award for best picture over several more elaborate Hollywood films. His face subsequently became familiar to audiences on both sides of the Atlantic, and he reached a new level of renown when he appeared in a 2009 *Star Trek* reboot playing Spock's father.

Ben Cross was born Harry Bernard Cross on December 16, 1947, in Paddington, a working-class section of London. He had two older sisters. His father, a doorman, died when Cross was eight of tuberculosis contracted in Burma during World War II. Cross's mother worked from dawn to dusk as a cook and cleaning woman.

Hoping to help his family make ends meet, he quit school at age 15 and worked as a window washer, dishwasher, butcher's helper, and, eventually, a stagehand. He had loved performing in school plays and watching the actors from the wings inspired him to apply to the Royal Academy of Dramatic Art (RADA). After graduating in 1972 from RADA, Cross steadily won roles in regional theater productions and had a small part in the 1977 war film *A Bridge Too Far*. He received his big break in 1977, when he was hired for a West End production of the American musical, *I Love My Wife*, remaining with the show for a year. Then, in 1979, he took on the role of Billy Flynn, the male lead in Bob Fosse's *Chicago*, during its London run.

When his agent suggested that he try out for the part of Harold Abrahams, the 100-meter running champion of the 1924 Olympics in the forthcoming *Chariots of Fire*, Cross thought he was joking. The part would require him to be in stellar physical shape; and as he later told journalists, his only exercise since leaving school had come from "running to pubs late at night." Still, intrigued by the prospect of starring in a film, he began training and ultimately won the role of the wealthy, Jewish, Cambridge-educated athlete.

The film, which co-starred Ian Charleson as a Scottish Presbyterian missionary who refuses to take part in the Games on the Sabbath, and Ian Holm as a coach, won almost universally positive reviews; and in addition to its best-picture Oscar, it garnered awards for its screenplay, costume design, and original score.

Cross went on to be featured in numerous other films and television series—always with an eye to not being typecast—and he drew particular attention for his role in the popular 2009 film *Star Trek*, directed by J. J. Abrams.

At the time of his death, from unspecified causes on July 10, 2020, he had several screen projects in various stages of completion. Twice divorced, Ben Cross is survived by his third wife, Deyana Boneva; a son (Theo) and daughter (Laura) from his first marriage; and three grandchildren.

See *Current Biography 1984*

Stanley Crouch

Born: Los Angeles, California; December 14, 1945
Died: Bronx, New York; September 16, 2020
Occupation: Essayist; critic

During the late 1970s and 1980s, Stanley Crouch built a reputation as both a jazz critic and a pundit with his eye on American society in general and African American culture and politics in particular. He has been widely celebrated for helping to found Jazz at Lincoln Center, in New York City, which has grown into one of the most prestigious showcases in the world for the genre.

The oldest of three children, Stanley Crouch was born on December 14, 1945, in Los Angeles, California. His mother, Emma Bea, was a domestic who worked six days a week and earned $11 a day; his father, James, a drug addict and petty criminal, was reportedly serving time for drug possession in a San Francisco jail when Stanley was born. Father and son did not meet until 12 years later, and then saw each other only occasionally. Crouch has credited his mother, who exposed him to cultural events and taught him to read before he started school, with helping to counter the negative influences of his surroundings.

Crouch attended East Los Angeles Junior College and Southwest Junior College. He did not receive a degree from either institution, perhaps because he was more interested in the arts than in his studies. Following the 1965 riots in the Watts area of Los Angeles, he became fascinated by the militant, separatist rhetoric of the black nationalists, although he later drifted away from that movement. From 1965 to 1967 he was a member of Studio Watts, a guerilla theater company, where he worked as an actor and writer. After a stint teaching at the associated Claremont Colleges, in California, in 1975 he moved to New York City, where he contributed articles to a variety of alternative periodicals and helped book jazz acts at a downtown club.

He was hired as a staff writer at the *Village Voice* in 1979 but was fired in 1988 after engaging in a physical altercation with another writer. He later became a syndicated columnist at the *Daily News*.

Among his many books were *Notes of a Hanging Judge: Essays and Reviews, 1979–1989* (1990); *The All-American Skin Game, or, The Decoy of Race: The Long and the Short of It, 1990–1994* (1995); *Don't the Moon Look Lonesome: A Novel in Blues and Swing* (2000); *Considering Genius: Writings on Jazz* (2006); and the biography *Kansas City Lightning: The Rise and Times of Charlie Parker* (2013).

Among his many honors were a 1991 Whiting Foundation Award for nonfiction, a 1993 MacArthur Foundation fellowship, and designation in 2019 as a Jazz Master by the National Endowment for the Arts, in recognition of his advocacy for the artform.

Crouch died at a hospital in the New York City borough of the Bronx following a long, unspecified illness. He is survived by his second wife, the sculptor Gloria Nixon Crouch; his daughter, Gaia Scott-Crouch; and a granddaughter.

See *Current Biography 1994*

Mac Davis

Born: Lubbock, Texas; January 21, 1942
Died: Nashville, Tennessee; September 29, 2020
Occupation: Singer; songwriter

Mac Davis penned hits for such artists as Elvis Presley and Kenny Rogers before becoming a star in his own right with the 1972 hit single "Baby, Don't Get Hooked on Me."

Scott Mac Davis was born on January 21, 1942, in Lubbock, Texas, the second of the three children of T.J. Davis, a builder, and Edith Irene (Lankford) Davis. Following his parents' divorce, when he was nine, Davis remained in Lubbock with his father. He also spent much of his boyhood at an uncle's nearby ranch.

Davis's earliest musical roots were in the country tunes that blared from every West Texas radio station when he was a youngster. But then, in the mid-1950's, the music changed. Rock 'n' roll hit the airwaves, and Davis bought his first guitar at fifteen. His main inspiration was Presley, for whom he dreamed of writing songs one day.

On graduating from high school, Davis set out on his own for Atlanta, Georgia, where his mother had remarried. There he found work as a probation officer with the Georgia State Board of Probation and formed a band that played local venues. The Zots, as the band was known, released a pair of singles on a small label, and Davis subsequently made a move into the business side of the industry, becoming regional manager for the independent Vee-Jay Records. He later signed on with Boots Enterprises, a production company owned by Nancy Sinatra, and during that time he played on her studio recordings and in live shows. He also began publishing his own songs, including "In the Ghetto" and "Don't Cry Daddy," which Presley and other artists recorded.

In 1970 Davis signed his own contract with Columbia Records, and he had his first major pop hit, "Baby Don't Get Hooked on Me," two years later; among his other pop hits were "Stop and Smell the Roses" and "One Hell of a Woman," both from 1974. He made an even bigger splash on the country charts, recording sixteen Top-40 singles between 1972 and 1985.

From 1974 to 1976 Davis hosted an eponymous variety show on NBC, and he made his acting debut in the 1979 football movie *North Dallas Forty*.

Davis, who was honored with a star on the Hollywood Walk of Fame in 1998 and was inducted into the Songwriters Hall of Fame in 2006, experienced something of a revival in the 2010s, collaborating with such artists as Avicii and Bruno Mars. He died on September 29, 2020, in Nashville, following heart surgery. He is survived by his wife of almost forty years, Lise; their two sons, Noah and Cody; another son, Joel, from his first marriage; a sister, Linda; his mother; and a granddaughter.

See *Current Biography 1980*

Olivia de Havilland

Born: Tokyo, Japan; July 1, 1916
Died: Paris, France; July 26, 2020
Occupation: Actress

Olivia de Havilland earned fame for her role in the 1939 Civil War epic *Gone with the Wind*, holding her own against scene-stealing co-stars Clark Gable and Vivien Leigh. Over the course of her career, she earned five Academy Award nominations, winning two of the coveted statuettes: one for *To Each His Own* (1946) and a second for *The Heiress* (1949).

Born to English parents in Tokyo, Japan, on July 1, 1916, Olivia de Havilland is the older of two daughters of Lilian Augusta (Ruse) de Havilland and Walter Augustus de Havilland, who headed a firm of patent attorneys in that city. Her sister was the motion-picture actress Joan Fontaine.

When de Havilland was about three years old, her parents separated, and they were later divorced. Her mother took the two girls to California and eventually married a department store owner, George M. Fontaine.

In 1933, de Havilland made her stage debut in an amateur production of *Alice in Wonderland*. She abandoned her plans to enter college when Max Reinhardt gave her the opportunity to play Hermia in his production of *A Midsummer Night's Dream* at the Hollywood Bowl in 1934, and the following year she appeared in his film version, signing a contract with Warner Brothers, the producer.

She quickly established herself as a fixture at Warner Bros., where she frequently appeared in costume dramas opposite Errol Flynn, including *Captain Blood* (1935), *The Charge of the Light Brigade* (1936), and *The Adventures of Robin Hood* (1938). The studio only reluctantly agreed to allow her to appear as the kindhearted Melanie Wilkes in David O. Selznick's *Gone with the Wind*, released by rival Metro Goldwyn Meyer (MGM), and that battle made her a key player in the successful movement to weaken the major studios' grip on their contract actors,

Although directors still tended to typecast her for her delicate beauty and graceful demeanor, de Havilland's career also included many show-stopping, intense roles, including an unwed mother forced to give up her baby in *To Each His Own*, a mental patient in 1948's *Snake Pit*, and a repressed spinster in *The Heiress*;

In the 1950s, tired of Hollywood, she settled in Paris, returning only sporadically to appear in a play or film. Among the most notable of these was 1964's *Hush . . . Hush, Sweet Charlotte*, in which she co-starred alongside fellow legend Bette Davis.

Later in life she took on an occasional television role, including guest spots on shows like *The Love Boat* and mini-series like *Roots: The Next Generation* (1979) and *Anastasia: The Mystery of Anna* (1986), the latter of which earned her a Golden Globe Award and an Emmy nomination.

In her youth, de Havilland was linked romantically to James Stewart, Howard Hughes, and John Huston. The actress's two marriages (the first to a Texas-born novelist and the second to an editor of *Paris Match*) ended in divorce. Olivia de Havilland was predeceased by her son in 1991 and her sister in 2013. She is survived by her daughter, Gisele.

See *Current Biography 1966*

Brian Dennehy

Born: Bridgeport, Connecticut; July 9, 1938
Died: New Haven, Connecticut; April 15, 2020
Occupation: Actor

For most of the 1980s, Brian Dennehy was one of those indispensable actors whose faces are better known than their names, but he later came to be regarded as a member of the upper tier of American character actors, in a class with Gene Hackman and Robert Duvall. Artistically ambitious, he also developed a powerful stage presence and won Tony Awards for his memorable performances in the 1998 Broadway production of *Death of a Salesman* and the 2003 production of *Long Day's Journey into Night*. An acclaimed performer in small-screen dramas, he was nominated for multiple Emmy Awards as well.

The oldest in a family of three boys, Brian Manion Dennehy was born on July 9, 1938, in Bridgeport, Connecticut, where his father, Ed, the son of an Irish immigrant, worked as a reporter for a local newspaper. The family later settled in the Long Island town of Mineola.

Dennehy appeared in a production of *Macbeth* while in high school, and he fell in love with the theater. It was, however, his athletic prowess that gained him a scholarship to Columbia University, where he majored in history, played on the football team, and left without earning a degree. In about 1960 he joined the Marine Corps, serving for five years in the United States, South Korea, and Japan.

Returning to New York City in 1965, Dennehy supported himself with odd jobs and auditioned for acting roles. He won parts in Off-Off-Broadway plays and appeared in dinner theater on Long Island, and in 1977 he appeared for the first time in a film, as a football player in *Semi-Tough* (1977), starring Burt Reynolds. (He was amazed to be paid $10,000 a week for ten weeks for his performance.)

He soon found himself in great demand as a character actor, appearing in such films as *F.I.S.T.* (1978), *Foul Play* (1978), *First Blood* (1982), *Gorky Park* (1983), *Cocoon* (1985), and *F/X* (1986). Most often he was called upon to play either a gruff everyman or a law-enforcement official, and in the 1980s alone he garnered more than 45 screen credits. The 1990s were equally busy; he starred that decade as a Chicago police investigator in a series of six television movies, directing some of them himself, and he was introduced to a new generation of fans when he played Chris Farley's father in the hit 1995 comedy *Tommy Boy*.

Dennehy never abandoned his love of stage acting, and his final Broadway appearance came in 2014, in a production of *Love Letters*. In more recent years he took on recurring roles in such television series as *Public Morals* and *The Blacklist*.

Dennehy, whose first marriage ended in divorce, is survived by his second wife, Jennifer Arnott; three children from his first marriage, Elizabeth, Kathleen, and Deirdre; two children from his second marriage, Cormac and Sarah; and several grandchildren.

See *Current Biography 1991*

Hugh Downs

Born: Akron, Ohio; February 14, 1921
Died: Scottsdale, Arizona; July 1, 2020
Occupation: Broadcaster

For several decades, the low-keyed, unhurried, and cerebral Hugh Downs was one of the most watched and loved television personalities in the country. The longtime host of such mainstay programs as *Today* on NBC and *20/20* on ABC, he wrote a 1986 memoir titled *On Camera: My 10,000 Hours on Television*, and for years he held the Guinness world record for most total hours on commercial networks.

Hugh Malcolm Downs was born in Akron, Ohio, on February 14, 1921, the son of Milton Downs, a dealer in auto accessories, and Edith (Hick) Downs. He had two younger brothers, Paul and Wallace. When he was ten his father rented a small farm three miles from Lima, and there the family remained for the next eight years. When Milton Downs's business failed during the Depression, the family turned to raising chickens, which also provided a staple of food for the growing Downs brothers. Meanwhile, they obtained their primary education in a one-room schoolhouse.

After graduating from Shawnee High School in 1938, Downs entered Bluffton (Ohio) College. Family finances were low, however, and after completing his freshman year, he returned from school with instructions from his father to find a job. After a long job hunt, he wandered into Lima's 100-watt radio station WLOK and landed a job beginning the following Monday for $7.50 a week. It was May 18, 1939, and Downs was 18 years old.

Downs worked as an announcer and conducted a man-on-the-street interview show, and when WLOK became a 250-watt station, he was promoted to program director at $25 a week. When the United States entered World War II, Downs was drafted into the Army and assigned to the 123rd Infantry.

Returning to civilian life after a medical discharge in 1943, Downs joined WMAQ in Chicago, an NBC-owned station, where he served as radio announcer, disc jockey, interviewer, and master of ceremonies. In 1956–57 he was the announcer for *Caesar's Hour*, starring Sid Caesar, and in July 1957 he joined Jack Paar's *Tonight* show on NBC. It was on the popular Paar show that Downs first emerged as a personality in his own right, an ideal foil for the temperamental and volatile Paar.

In September 1962, Downs took over as anchor on the *Today* show, NBC's two-hour morning television program, which then aired to an estimated audience of 12,000,000. In June

1978 he was invited by ABC executives to take over the newsmagazine *20/20*, which had just launched. He served as sole host of that trusted and popular show until 1984, when he was joined by Barbara Walters, and he ultimately remained there until his retirement in 1999. In his later years he worked occasionally as a spokesman for products aimed at senior citizens.

Downs was predeceased in 2017 by his wife, Ruth, to whom he had been married since 1944. He is survived by their children, Hugh and Deirdre; a brother, Wallace; two grandchildren; and four great-grandchildren.

See *Current Biography 1965*

Rosalind Elias

Born: Lowell, Massachusetts; March 13, 1930
Died: New York, New York; May 3, 2020
Occupation: Opera singer

One problem sometimes faced by the opera realm is the fact that some of its brightest stars, although vocally superb, lack acting ability. That was not, however, the case with Rosalind Elias, who possessed a beautiful mezzo-soprano voice, an innate and highly developed musicality, and dramatic sensitivity and capability.

Rosalind Elias was born on March 13, 1930, in Lowell, Massachusetts. She was the youngest of thirteen children of Salem and Shelahuy Rose (Namay) Elias, who had immigrated to the United States from Lebanon. Arabic was her first language. Ambitious to become an opera star since her early teens, she began to take singing lessons, at her own insistence, with a local music teacher while attending high school in Lowell, and she appeared in featured roles in school musicals and revues.

After graduating from high school, she entered the New England Conservatory of Music in Boston. While a student at the conservatory she also appeared with the Boston Symphony Orchestra. She soon became a member of the New England Opera and secured the first of three summer scholarships at Tanglewood. She made her debut with the New England Opera in 1948 as Maddalena in Verdi's *Rigoletto*.

In 1952, chaperoned by an older sister, Elias went to Italy to study with Maestro Luigi Ricci of the Rome Opera. Her talents quickly came to the attention of impresarios from La Scala in Milan and the San Carlo Opera in Naples, and she was offered two contracts. She sang in Italy for a year, and not long after her return to the United States, she made her Metropolitan Opera debut on February 23, 1954, in the supporting role of Grimgerde, one of the Valkyrs, in a performance of Wagner's *Die Walküre*.

During her first Metropolitan season she gave 55 performances, and her early roles included those of Siebel in *Faust*, the musician in Puccini's *Manon Lescaut*, the second squire in *Parsifal*, a genie in *The Magic Flute*, and the off-stage priestess in *Aida*. Within a few seasons, critics began to notice her. Something of a turning point came in 1958, when she sang the role of the meek, young Erika in the world premiere of Samuel Barber's *Vanessa*. She was widely lauded for her vocal richness and musical acumen, and over the next decades, she became a mainstay at the Met, appearing in almost 700 performances of more than 50 roles. Her last came in 1996 as Háta in Smetana's *The Bartered Bride*.

In 2007, at age 77, she sang in two world premieres: Ricky Ian Gordon's *The Grapes of Wrath* at the Minnesota Opera and David Carlson's *Anna Karenina* at the Florida Grand Opera. In 2011, at age 82, Elias made her Broadway debut in a highly regarded revival of Stephen Sondheim's *Follies*.

Her death, at age 90, was announced by her manager. She was predeceased by her husband, law professor Zuhayr Moghrabi (2015) and has no immediate survivors.

See *Current Biography 1967*

Jean Erdman

Born: Honolulu, Hawaii; February 20, 1916
Died: Kailua, Hawaii; May 4, 2020
Occupation: Dancer and choreographer

For decades Jean Erdman, a former member of the Martha Graham Dance Company who later won renown as a choreographer, enriched modern dance with her intellectual breadth, wit, and passion for experimentation.

Jean Erdman was born in Honolulu, Hawaii, on February 20, 1916. Her mother, the former Marion Dillingham, was a singer whose parents had emigrated from New England to Hawaii in the 1820s. Her father, John Pinney Erdman, was a nondenominational Protestant minister who settled in Hawaii as a missionary after earning a doctoral degree in divinity.

In addition to early exposure to the native dancing of Hawaii, Erdman was introduced to the dance technique of Isadora Duncan by a gym teacher. Her parents sent her to the mainland to complete her secondary education, and she graduated from Miss Hall's School in Pittsfield, Massachusetts, in 1934. She then entered Sarah Lawrence College in Bronxville, New York, where she studied contemporary dance and the theatre. By the time she graduated in 1938 she had decided to become a professional dancer, but before launching her career she went on a round-the-world tour with her parents and sister that enabled her to see dance in such places as Bali, Java, Cambodia, India, and Spain.

Returning to the United States, she joined the Martha Graham Dance Company and made her professional debut in New York City at Carnegie Hall. Among her solo roles over the next five years with the Graham group were the Ideal Spectator in *Every Soul Is a Circus* and the dancing-speaking parts in *Letter to the World*, Graham's take on the life of Emily Dickinson. During the summers she studied dancing and composition at the Bennington College modern dance school, and in 1942 she made her debut as a choreographer at the Bennington Summer Festival.

In the mid-1940s, tired of Graham's autocracy, she founded her own eponymous company. She forged collaborations with several leading contemporary composers, including John Cage and Alan Hovhaness, and among her best-known choreographed works were *The Coach with the Six Insides*, a comic adaptation of James Joyce's *Finnegans Wake*; the New York Shakespeare Festival's 1971 adaptation of *Two Gentlemen of Verona*; *Creature on a Journey*, inspired by Balinese dance; and *The Transformations of Medusa*, which later became the basis for a film.

Erdman founded the dance theater program at New York University's Tisch School of the Arts in 1966, and over the years she also held teaching posts at Columbia University, Bard College, and the University of Colorado.

She was married to renowned scholar Joseph Campbell, with whom she founded the avant-garde New York-based Theater of the Open Eye, and not long after he died in 1987, she moved back permanently to her native Hawaii. At the time of her death, at age 104, she was in a nursing facility there. She has no immediate survivors.

See *Current Biography 1971*

Harold Evans

Born: Manchester, England; June 28, 1928
Died: New York, New York; September 23, 2020
Occupation: Writer; editor

In 2002 Harold Evans was named the greatest newspaper editor of all time by the *British Journalism Review*, and two years later he was knighted by the Queen for his service to journalism. He also made a mark in the United States serving as the highly admired head of Random House for almost a decade.

Harold Matthew Evans was born on June 28, 1928, in Manchester, England, the oldest of four sons of Frederick Albert Evans and his wife, Mary. Determined to obtain for her children the formal education that she and her husband did not have an opportunity to pursue, Mary opened a small grocery shop in their front room in the late 1930s. The business prospered, providing a supplement to Frederick Evans's steady salary as a railroad engineer.

After his graduation in 1943 from St. Mary's Road Central School, Evans signed up for shorthand and typing courses, hoping that those skills would give him a head start in his chosen career of journalism. His resolve paid off the following year when he landed a job as a general assignment reporter for the *Tameside Reporter* in Ashton-under-Lyne.

From 1946 to 1949 Evans served in the Royal Air Force, and upon his discharge, he enrolled at the University of Durham on a government veteran's grant. Shortly after earning a BA degree with honors in 1952, Evans secured a position as copy desk editor with the daily *Manchester Evening News*. By 1954 he had advanced to covering regional politics and to writing daily editorials.

In 1966 he was hired by the London *Sunday Times*, where he rose to the post of managing editor within weeks, He took over as editor of Britain's most prestigious weekly newspaper the following year. He remained in that capacity until 1981, revolutionizing the look of the paper with eye-catching graphics, ordering hard-hitting investigative reports on hot-button issues, and substantially increasing readership. He then began editing the venerable daily *London Times*, but his stormy, short-lived tenure culminated in a dispute with the newspaper's owner, the Australian media magnate Rupert Murdoch, over editorial independence that resulted in Evans's forced resignation in March 1982. In 1984 Evans moved to the United States where he took posts at such publications as *U.S. News & World Report* and *Condé Nast Traveler* and served, from 1990 to 1997, as president and publisher of Random House.

The author of several well-received books, including *The American Century* (1998), *War Stories: Reporting in the Time of Conflict from the Crimea to Iraq* (2003), and the memoir *My Paper Chase: True Stories of Vanished Times* (2009), Evans died on September 23, 2020, of congestive heart failure.

He is survived by his second wife, the well-known editor Tina Brown, to whom he had been married since 1981. He is also survived by the three children from his first marriage: Ruth, Katherine, and Michael.

See *Current Biography 1985*

Charles Evers

Born: Decatur, Mississippi; September 11, 1922
Died: Brandon, Mississippi; July 22, 2020
Occupation: Civil rights leader; politician

While the name Medgar Evers may be better known, his older brother, Charles, who took over as Mississippi field director for the National Association for the Advancement of Colored People (NAACP) after Medgar was assassinated in 1963, was an influential figure in his own right.

James Charles Evers was born in the rural town of Decatur, Mississippi, on September 11, 1922. (Some reputable sources instead list September 14, 1923.) The Evers brothers differed radically in their personalities: Medgar was gentle and easy going, whereas Charles was blunt and strong willed.

Dropping out of school upon completion of the eleventh grade, Evers enlisted in the US Army and served in the Pacific during World War II. After the war he finished high school and went on to study social science at Alcorn A. and M. College in Mississippi, graduating in 1950. Following a year's duty with his Army Reserve unit in Korea, he settled in Philadelphia, Mississippi, and opened a restaurant, hotel, taxi service, and gas station. He was known to engage, as well, in running numbers, bootlegging, and procuring prostitutes.

Clandestinely, the brothers began enrolling members in the NAACP, then a wildly radical organization by local standards. In 1954 Medgar became the NAACP's first Mississippi field director, at a salary of $3,000 a year. Remaining in Philadelphia, Charles became Mississippi's first black disc jockey, but in 1950, facing pressure from business rivals and a group called the White Citizens Council, he moved to Chicago, where he ultimately opened a series of cocktail lounges,

After Medgar was killed by a sniper, Charles asked to assume his post in the NAACP. Over the next several years, he became a nationally known civil rights figure; and in 1968, he served as a leader of Mississippi's first racially integrated delegation to the Democratic National Convention (DNC). The following year he was elected mayor of Fayette, Mississippi, the first Black man in a century to lead that town, where Black citizens had long had their votes suppressed by threats and violence. He famously said of his victory, "Hands that picked cotton can now pick the mayor."

In 1971 he became the first Black candidate for governor of Mississippi, although he was defeated in the end by William Waller. In 1978 he ran as an independent for a US Senate seat; and while he was again unsuccessful, he made a strong showing. After four nonconsecutive terms as the mayor of Fayette, Evers lost the 1989 Democratic primary for a fifth term and retired from politics. He spent the latter part of his life as a businessman, overseeing his real estate holdings, supermarkets, and liquor stores. He also became a right-leaning conservative who often railed against Black-on-Black crime.

Accounts of his personal life conflict. He was reportedly married and divorced at least twice. After his death, from undisclosed causes on July 22, 2020, Charles Evers's survivors were said to include ten children; three sisters; two brothers; and twenty-four grandchildren.

See *Current Biography 1969*

Ludwig Finscher

Born: Kassel, Germany; March 14, 1930
Died: Wolfenbüttel, Germany; June 30, 2020
Occupation: Musicologist

One of the most eminent musicologists in the world, Ludwig Finscher conducted seminal research into the history of Western music. He was the editor of the second edition of the massive music encyclopedia *Die Musik in Geschichte und Gegenwart* (which can be translated as "music in the past and present"), a German-language reference work referred to by its devotees as MGG. The multi-volume work has been compared in scope and importance to the English-language *New Grove Dictionary of Music and Musicians*.

Ludwig Finscher was born on March 14, 1930, in Kassel, Germany, to a family of music lovers. Although he could not play a musical instrument, he was an avid listener, and in 1949, intending to pursue a career in music journalism, he enrolled at Göttingen University, where he took courses in musicology with professor Rudolf Gerber. In 1954, he graduated after completing a doctoral dissertation on the work of Loyset Compère, a French composer of the Renaissance period. Although candidates for doctoral degrees in Germany were not required to publish their dissertations, Finscher wanted to do so, and in 1964 the 262-page work was published as a volume of the English-language series *Musicological Studies and Documents*.

Finscher next worked at the Deutsches Volksliedarchiv (now known as Zentrum für Populäre Kultur und Musik (Centre of Popular Culture and Music), a research institute devoted to folk music, and in 1967, at the Saarland University, Saarbrücken, he earned his habilitation, an academic qualification required in some countries to become a professor. In his dissertation, he probed the origins of string quartets and the role of the composer Franz Joseph Haydn in popularizing them.

In 1968, Finscher became a professor of music at the Goethe University in Frankfurt am Main, where he expanded his study to include other musical genres, which, he postulated, developed over long periods of time and cannot easily be traced back to particular composers. In 1981, Finscher began teaching at the Heidelberg University, a position he held until his retirement, in 1995. At the end of the 1980s he was invited to edit the second edition of the MMG, which ultimately consisted of more than 25 volumes. (He himself wrote dozens of the included articles.)

On November 24, 2006, Finscher was presented with the Balzan Prize, an honor given to those who have made significant contributions in the areas of the humanities, social sciences, physics, mathematics, natural sciences, and medicine. He was the first musicologist to win the award since its inception, in 1961.

Finscher served as the president of the International Society of Musicology from 1977 to 1982 (some sources say 1981), and throughout his life he was a member of several international academies, including the Royal Music Association and the Academia Europaea. He held the Ordre pour le Mérite, originally a Prussian military honor, now given to civilians in the arts and sciences.

His death, at age 90, was mourned on several websites devoted to classical music.

See *Current Biography 2007*

Leon Fleisher

Born: San Francisco, California; July 23, 1928
Died: Baltimore, Maryland; August 2, 2020
Occupation: Pianist

Leon Fleisher was one of the most highly regarded pianists of his generation, and that was despite being stricken by a mysterious disability that paralyzed his right hand and limited his playing to the specialized repertoire of one-handed piano music at the peak of his career.

Leon Fleisher was born in San Francisco on July 23, 1928 to Isidor and Bertha (Mittelman) Fleisher, who had emigrated to the United States from Eastern Europe and opened a hat shop. Fleisher began to study the piano at an early age, pressured by his parents to excel, and because his musical studies took up much of his time, he was privately educated.

In 1935 he gave his first public recital, and when he was nine, the great pianist Artur Schnabel took him on as a student. (After a year,

Schnabel decreed that he had taught his protégé all he could.) In 1943, Fleisher made his concert debut with the San Francisco Orchestra under Pierre Benjamin Monteux. He first performed in New York City on November 4, 1944, as a soloist with the New York Philharmonic, again under the baton of Monteux, who called the 16-year-old "the pianistic find of the century."

Fleisher gained international stature as an artist in 1952, when he became the first American to win a major European music competition, the Concours International Reine Élisabeth de Belgique, whose judges deemed him "the best young pianist in the world." After that triumph, he embarked on a series of acclaimed concert appearances throughout the world.

In the mid-1960s, Fleisher started to suffer a paralysis of his right hand that threatened to bring his career to an end. Determined not to give up playing the piano completely, he began to specialize in the limited repertoire of music written for the left hand alone—mainly concertos commissioned by the pianist Paul Wittgenstein, who lost his right arm in World War I, from such composers as Ravel, Prokofiev, Richard Strauss, and Benjamin Britten.

In 1968 he helped co-found the Theater Chamber Players, a Washington, DC.–based ensemble that provided him the chance to both play and conduct. He later began guest-conducting around the country, and in 1973 he became associate conductor of the Baltimore Symphony Orchestra.

By the time that orchestra was preparing to open a new Symphony Hall in 1982, Fleisher had undergone surgery that allowed him to regain some use of his right hand, and on the occasion of the venue's televised opening, he staged a comeback, playing Franck's Symphonic Variations. In the 1990s he discovered that Botox injections improved his ability even further, and he gradually began performing his old repertoire.

Fleisher was teaching master classes online almost up until the time of his death, on August 2, 2020, at the age of 92. Leon Fleisher is survived by his third wife, Katherine, a fellow pianist; his children from his first marriage, Deborah, Richard, and Leah; his children from his second marriage, Julian and Paula; and two grandchildren.

See *Current Biography 1971*

Whitey Ford

Born: New York, New York; October 21, 1928
Died: Lake Success, New York; October 8, 2020
Occupation: Baseball player

Yankees' Hall of Fame southpaw Whitey Ford was christened the Chairman of the Board for his style and winning record. Over the course of his career, he won 236 games, the most of any Yankee, and had a career-winning percentage of .690.

Edward Charles Ford was born on October 21, 1928, in a tenement district in midtown Manhattan to James Ford, a bartender, and his wife, Edith. As a child, he moved with his family to the Astoria section of Queens. Although he was an undersized left-hander, he began to play first base with the Thirty-fourth Avenue Boys Club of Astoria, the most successful of the neighborhood's many sandlot teams. As William Cullen Bryant High School in Long Island City near his home had no baseball team, he traveled two hours a day on the subway to attend Manhattan High School of Aviation Trades, which did field a team. From 1944 through 1946 he alternated between first base and the pitcher's mound.

Not long after he graduated from high school in 1946 Ford attracted modest offers from the New York Yankees, the Brooklyn Dodgers, and the Boston Red Sox. He ultimately signed with the Yankees for $7,000.

After three and a half years in the minors, Ford made his Yankee debut on July 1, 1950, and subsequently won nine straight games. Although he missed the 1951 and 1952 seasons while in the Army, he returned strong, winning 53 games from 1954 to 1956. Ford's best season was undeniably 1961, when he posted a 25–4 record and garnered the Cy Young Award.

Ford ultimately helped the Yankees win 11 pennants and holds World Series records for most games won (10), innings pitched (146), strikeouts (94) and most consecutive scoreless innings (33). The only two losing seasons of his career came in 1966 and 1967, when he posted a combined 4–9 record while battling injuries. Plagued by circulatory problems and a bad elbow, Ford retired in May 1967.

Ford was elected to the Baseball Hall of Fame in 1974, and sports historians have since asserted that he embodied the iconic New York Yankees team that so captivated the postwar generation. He holds a revered place in Yankee history along with famed players like Joe DiMaggio, Mickey Mantle, Yogi Berra, and Phil Rizzuto.

Ford died on October 8, 2020, at the age of 91. He was surrounded by family members and watching the Yankees' Division Series game against the Tampa Bay Rays. He is survived by his wife, Joan; their son Eddie; their daughter, Sally Ann Clancy; and his grandchildren. He was predeceased by another son, Tommy, in 1999.

Ford was the second-oldest surviving Hall of Famer, behind the former Dodger manager Tommy Lasorda. In the announcement of his death, Yankees managing general partner Hal Steinbrenner called him "one of the greatest Yankees to ever wear the pinstripes."

See *Current Biography 1962*

Bruce Jay Friedman

Born: Bronx, New York; April 26, 1930
Died: Brooklyn, New York; June 3, 2020
Occupation: Novelist and playwright

Bruce Jay Friedman was renowned as a pioneer in the art of modern black (dark) humor; his protagonists were generally deeply insecure, white, male, middle-class, and (often) Jewish—and much of his work contained mildly autobiographical elements.

Friedman was born in the Bronx on April 26, 1930, to Irving Friedman, a garment company manager, and Molly (Liebowitz) Friedman. The Friedmans had show business connections, of sorts: the father had been a silent-movie accompanist; the mother was a part-time ticket seller in Broadway box offices.

With his older sister, Dolly, Friedman grew up on Sheridan Avenue at 163d Street, and much of his childhood was spent in the neighborhood movie house, the Earl, near Yankee Stadium. After graduating from DeWitt Clinton High School, he entered the University of Missouri, where he majored in journalism and reviewed plays for the campus daily. After earning his bachelor's degree, in 1951, Friedman served in the US Air Force, assigned to the staff of the magazine *Air Training*.

After his discharge he found a job at a publisher of men's adventure magazines, and during his tenure there he sold a small number of vaguely autobiographical stories to such publications as *Commentary*, *Mademoiselle*, and *Playboy*.

Friedman's first novel was *Stern* (1962), whose protagonist is a city-bred Jewish Air Force veteran. New to suburbia, he allows an ostensibly anti-Semitic incident to drive him to a nervous breakdown and ulcers. The novel sold only 4,000 copies, but it won rave notices from influential critics.

His subsequent works included *Far from the City of Class* (1963), a collection of short stories; the highly acclaimed *A Mother's Kisses* (1964), the story of a 17-year-old boy's love-hate relationship with his outrageously possessive mother; the short-story collection *Black Angels*

(1966); *The Dick* (1970), a farce about a detective agency that was sold to Hollywood even before publication; and *About Harry Towns* (1974), whose main character is a cocaine-using screenwriter. His later novels, which enjoyed less critical success, included *Tokyo Woes* (1985), about an American's adventures in Japan; *The Current Climate* (1989), which featured Harry Towns; and *A Father's Kisses* (1996), about a down-on-his luck poultry distributor who becomes a hit man.

Called "The Hottest Writer of the Year" by the *New York Times Magazine* in 1968, Friedman also wrote a handful of plays, including the 1967 Off-Broadway hit *Scuba Duba* and *Steambath*, which appeared Off-Broadway in 1970 and imagined God in the guise of a Puerto Rican towel attendant. (*A Mother's Kisses* was adapted into a stage musical but closed out of town before it made it to New York.)

Friedman, known for his wide circle of celebrity friends from both the literary world and Hollywood, also wrote screenplays for such films as *Stir Crazy* (1980) and *Splash* (1984) and on occasion took on small roles himself, most often in movies directed by Woody Allen.

Friedman, who suffered from neuropathy, is survived by his second wife, Patricia O'Donohue; their daughter, Molly Stout; three sons from his first marriage, Josh, Kipp, and Drew; and three grandchildren.

See *Current Biography 1972*

Bob Gibson

Born: Omaha, Nebraska; November 9, 1935
Died: Omaha, Nebraska; October 2, 2020
Occupation: Baseball player

As a member of the St. Louis Cardinals, Bob Gibson was one of baseball's most feared and respected pitchers, winning 251 games in 17 seasons with his daunting fastball.

Robert Gibson was born in Omaha, Nebraska, on November 9, 1935. He was the seventh child of Pack Gibson, a mill worker who died of pneumonia a month before his son's birth, and Victoria Gibson, who worked in a laundry to support her family. In infancy Gibson was afflicted with rickets, and he later suffered from asthma, hay fever, and a rheumatic heart.

Gibson was encouraged to pursue sports by his brother Leroy, and at Omaha Technical High School, where he was considered too skinny for football, he starred in baseball, basketball, and track. After graduating, he entered Creighton University on a basketball scholarship. There he majored in sociology and became the first

Black athlete to play basketball and baseball at the school. He was then known less as a pitcher than as a shortstop and hard-hitting outfielder who batted .340 in his senior year. He knew, however, that pitching was the surest route to the top—because good pitchers are scarcer than good fielders among major-league aspirants—and he decided to take that route.

During summer vacation Gibson pitched semi-pro ball, and in 1957, when he signed a contract with the St. Louis Cardinals, he left school without a degree. He pitched in the minors that year, played basketball for the Harlem Globetrotters in the off-season, and made his debut with the Cardinals in 1959.

With his star on the rise and his reputation for no-holds-barred pitching cemented, in 1968 he won both the National League's Most Valuable Player (MVP) Award and the Cy Young Award (the first of two he would garner) by winning 22 games, striking out 268 batters, pitching 13 shutouts, and posting an earned run average of 1.12, that season. Over the course of his career, Gibson won at least 20 games five times and struck out 3,117 batters, thanks to a formidable fastball and slider. He threw 56 career shutouts, was an eight-time All-Star, and won nine Gold Glove awards for his fielding. He ultimately won seven World Series games in a row and holds the records for most strikeouts in a World Series game (17) and in a single World Series (35), both set in 1968. He retired after the 1975 season and spent time as a coach, broadcaster, and businessman.

Gibson, who was voted into the Baseball Hall of Fame in 1981, died of pancreatic cancer on October 2, 2020, in Omaha. He is survived by his wife, Wendy (Nelson) Gibson, and their son, Christopher, as well as by two daughters, Renee and Annette, from his marriage to Charline Johnson, which ended in divorce.

See *Current Biography 1968*

Ruth Bader Ginsburg

Born: Brooklyn, New York; March 15, 1933
Died: Washington, DC; September 18, 2020
Occupation: Supreme Court Justice

Ruth Bader Ginsburg was a pioneering advocate for women's rights and only the second woman ever to serve on the Supreme Court of the United States.

The Supreme Court Justice was born Ruth Bader in the New York City borough of Brooklyn on March 15, 1933. Her father, Nathan Bader, had immigrated to New York as a teen. The family owned small retail stores, including a fur store and a hat shop, but money was always tight. Her mother, Celia, died of cancer the day before Ginsburg's graduation from high school.

Ginsburg attended Cornell University and later entered Harvard Law School, where she was one of few women in her class. She subsequently transferred to Columbia University Law School, graduating in 1959, tied for first in her class. After clerking for two years she began teaching at Rutgers University Law School, where she first became interested in gender discrimination law and co-wrote the first casebook in that field. In 1972, she joined the faculty of Columbia Law School and became head of the Women's Rights Project, which had been launched by the American Civil Liberties Union (ACLU).

As head of the Women's Rights Project, Ginsburg presented six cases before the Supreme Court from 1973 to 1978, winning five of them and persuading the all-male body that the Fourteenth Amendment's guarantee of equal protection applied not just to racial discrimination but to sex discrimination too.

In 1980, Ginsburg was appointed to the Federal Court of Appeals for Washington, DC, by President Jimmy Carter, and in 1993, when Supreme Court Justice Byron R. White retired, President Bill Clinton nominated her. She was overwhelmingly confirmed by the U.S. Senate, 96 to 3. A staunch member of the Court's liberal bloc, she became famed for her pointed dissents (and for the special collar she always wore while dissenting).

One of the most consequential decisions of her Supreme Court career came in a 1996 case involving the Virginia Military Institute, which had argued that its tough, physically demanding curriculum was unsuitable for young women. In the 7–1 majority opinion, which ruled that an all-male admissions policy of a state-supported military college was unconstitutional, Ginsburg wrote, "Generalizations about 'the way women are,' estimates of what is appropriate for most women, no longer justify denying opportunity to women whose talent and capacity place them outside the average description."

In her final years Ginsburg became a pop culture icon, dubbed the Notorious R.B.G. (a nod to the late rapper Notorious B.I.G.); women of all ages began getting tattoos of her likeness, dressing up like her for Halloween, and flocking to movies based on her life.

Ginsburg died at her home in Washington, DC, on September 18, 2020, of metastatic pancreatic cancer. She was predeceased by her famously devoted and supportive husband, Martin Ginsburg, in 2010. Her survivors include her children, Jane and James; four grandchildren; two step-grandchildren; and a great-granddaughter. She was the first woman and the first Jewish American to lie in state in the U.S. Capitol.

See *Current Biography 1994*

Milton Glaser

Born: New York, New York; June 26, 1929
Died: New York, New York; June 26, 2020
Occupation: Illustrator and designer

Book jackets, record album covers, posters, magazines, restaurants, a toy store, and even a 600-foot mural for the Federal Office Building in Indianapolis are all creations of the graphic designer Milton Glaser, who has said that the most significant thing about his work is its range. He will perhaps be most remembered, however, for the iconic "I ♥ NY" logo to promote tourism in his home state.

Milton Glaser was born on June 26, 1929, in New York City to Eugene and Eleanor (Bergman) Glaser, both Hungarian Jews. During Glaser's childhood, which was spent in the Bronx, an illness at the age of ten forced on him a prolonged confinement that had much to do with his becoming an artist. Encouraged in his pursuit of art by his family, which included his sister, Estelle, he qualified for admission to the High School of Music and Art in Manhattan. He then attended Cooper Union, graduating in 1951 and then headed to Italy to study at the Academy of Fine Arts in Bologna during the next two years.

In 1954, after he had returned to New York City, Glaser set up his own shop, Art & Design Studio, and then joined another designer, Seymour Chwast, in establishing Push Pin Studios, which Glaser headed as president until 1974. The studio was marked by a remarkable variety not only in style but also in product: book jackets, magazine illustrations, record album covers, television commercials, typography, and other areas of graphics. Push Pin artists also undertook such unorthodox assignments as a one-ton prototype of a Christmas tree for Macy's department store and a trailer for Stanley Kubrick's film *2001: A Space Odyssey* (1968). Among his most widely seen works of this era was a 1967 poster of Bob Dylan, sketched in silhouette with wildly colored bands of hair; some six million of the posters were distributed in the singer's greatest hits album.

In 1968, Glaser and editor Clay Felker founded *New York* magazine, where he was president and design director until 1977. He also wrote a dining column, "The Underground Gourmet," for the magazine, and it later inspired a cookbook.

Glaser started his own eponymous design firm in 1974, right before leaving Push Pin and just as he was being honored with his own show at the Museum of Modern Art (MoMA). He created the beloved "I ♥ NY" logo in 1977, sketching it on the back of an envelope with a red crayon during a taxi ride. He often expressed amazement that the simple work was so fully embraced and widely recognized as a symbol of New York City.

Among his later well-known works were a late-1980s AIDS logo for the World Health Organization (WHO), the retro-looking packaging for Brooklyn Brewery, and a poster for the final season of the television series *Mad Men* in 2014.

Glaser, who suffered renal failure and a stroke, is survived by his wife, Shirley.

See *Current Biography 1980*

Slade Gorton

Born: Chicago, Illinois; January 8, 1928
Died: Seattle, Washington; August 19, 2020
Occupation: Politician

During his multiple terms in the US Senate, Slade Gorton was known as a firmly moderate Republican and staunch champion of Washington State's timber, aviation, and technology industries.

The oldest of four children, Thomas Slade Gorton III was born on January 8, 1928, in Chicago, the son of Thomas Slade Gorton Jr. and Ruth (Israel) Gorton. After his father sold the family business, Gorton's of Gloucester, a fish-processing company, to General Mills, the family settled in Evanston, Illinois, where Gorton grew up and attended public schools. After a stint in the US Army, he enrolled at Dartmouth College, earning his A.B. degree in international relations in 1950. Three years later he received his law degree from Columbia University and reenlisted in the armed forces, this time as an officer in the Air Force, rising over the next three years from first lieutenant to colonel.

Having adopted his father's moderate conservative ideals, in 1956 Gorton decided to move to a city in which an ambitious Republican was likely to excel. He settled upon Seattle, established a law practice there, and became active in the local Young Republicans organization.

In 1958, he was elected to the Washington legislature on a platform of reduced spending and lower taxes. He was returned to office in each of the four subsequent elections, which were held biennially. After leaving the legislature, he served as state attorney general, a post to which he was reelected in 1972 and again in 1976.

On capturing the US Senate seat held by Warren G. Magnuson, Washington State's septuagenarian, six-termer, in 1980, Gorton became one of the so-called giant-killers—Republicans who ousted senior Democratic senators in that year's congressional elections. (Their victories enabled the Republicans to win control of the Senate for the first time since 1954.)

Calling himself a "passionate moderate," Gorton won a seat on the Budget Committee and backed Ronald Reagan's tax cuts, slashes to social-welfare programming, and military buildup. He broke ranks with the president, however, by endorsing the Equal Rights Amendment (ERA) and supporting federal funding for abortion.

Gorton served until 1987 before being ousted by constituents angered by some of his political missteps, including his vote against a rise in Social Security benefits. After losing his reelection bid to Brock Adams, he resumed practicing law, but he threw his hat back into the ring again in 1988, when Washington State's other senator decided to retire. Admitting his past mistakes, he was returned to the Senate by voters and served from 1989 to 2001. Back in the Senate for a second time, Gorton became known as a strong booster of the Seattle-based technology giant Microsoft, and he also vociferously advocated for his state's aviation and logging industries.

Slade Gorton died from the effects of Parkinson's disease on August 19, 2020. Predeceased in 2013 by Sally, his wife of more than five decades, he was survived by their three children, Thomas, Sarah, and Rebecca; his three siblings; and seven grandchildren.

See *Current Biography 1993*

David Graeber

Born: New York, New York; February 12, 1961
Died: Venice, Italy; September 2, 2020
Occupation: Activist; professor

David Graeber forged a dual career, publishing academic works on sociology in peer-reviewed journals while working as a political activist and writing about that aspect of his life as well.

Born on February 12, 1961, David Graeber was raised in Manhattan's Chelsea neighborhood. His mother was a garment worker who once starred in an all-women musical revue put on by the International Ladies' Garment Workers' Union (ILGWU); his father was a plate stripper of offset printers who had fought in the Spanish Civil War with the Republicans, who included anarchists among their number. Graeber and his older brother grew up surrounded by radicals in a cooperative apartment building sponsored by a trade union. By sixteen, he was self-identifying as an anarchist.

Meanwhile, as a preteenager, Graeber became obsessed with Mayan hieroglyphics, and within a few years his original translations earned him a scholarship to the private Phillips Academy, Andover, MA. He studied anthropology as an undergraduate at the State University of New York at Purchase; as a graduate student at the University of Chicago, he did field research in Madagascar and was awarded his doctoral degree in 1998.

Graeber taught at Yale University from 1998 to 2005, becoming known there for his fiery denunciations of capitalism. He was never a candidate for tenure, and his contract was not renewed in 2005, leading thousands of supporters to sign petitions calling (unsuccessfully) for his reinstatement.

Meanwhile, he was not remaining in an ivory tower: He was part of the massive 1999 protests against global free trade in Seattle, where the World Trade Organization (WTO) was meeting, and he later got involved with other protests as well, including demonstrations at the Republican National Conventions (RNC) in 2000 and 2004; the Group of Eight Summit protest in Genoa, Italy, in 2001; the Summit of the Americas protest in Quebec City in 2001; and the 2010 tuition protests in London. He played a major role in the Occupy Wall Street demonstrations in Lower Manhattan in 2011 and is widely credited with coming up with the slogan, "We are the 99 percent."

Although no universities in North America were amenable to hiring him, in 2008, Graeber became a lecturer and then a reader at Goldsmiths College at the University of London. He accepted a position in 2013 at the London School of Economics, where he was teaching at the time of his death, on September 2, 2020. (He had admitted to feeling ill during an online lecture the week before.)

David Graeber is survived by his wife, Nika Dubrovsky, an artist. He leaves a body of work that includes such influential books as *Debt: The First 5000 Years* (2011), *The Democracy Project: A History, a Crisis, a Movement* (2013), and *The Utopia of Rules* (2015).

See *Current Biography 2015*

Shirley Ann Grau

Born: New Orleans, Louisiana; July 8, 1929
Died: Kenner, Louisiana; August 3, 2020
Occupation: Writer

Pulitzer Prize-winning Southern author Shirley Ann Grau wrote so unflinchingly about race relations that the Klu Klux Klan once attempted to burn a cross on her lawn.

Shirley Ann Grau—one of the two daughters of Adolph Grau (a dentist) and his wife, the former Katherine Onions (a homemaker)—was born in New Orleans, Louisiana. She was educated at the Booth School in Montgomery, Alabama, and at Tulane University, in her native city. She earned a B.A. in 1950 with honors in English, and after a year's graduate work at Tulane, she settled down to writing. (She had reportedly dropped out after hearing that the chair of the school's Department of English refused to hire female teaching assistants.) Soon, her short stories were appearing in such national publications as the *New Yorker*, the *Saturday Evening Post*, *Vogue*, and *Cosmopolitan*.

Her first book was a 1955 collection of stories about bayou people called *The Black Prince*. It was greeted by one reviewer as "the most impressive US short story debut between hard covers since J. D. Salinger's *Nine Stories*" and was a finalist for a National Book Award. Other collections followed, including *The Wind Shifting West* (1973), *Nine Women* (1985), and *Selected Stories* (2003).

She penned several novels, as well. The first, *The Hard Blue Sky* (1958), about a Franco-Spanish island community at the mouth of the Mississippi, was not well-reviewed, but while many critics advised her to stick with short stories, she was undaunted, and she next published *The House on Coliseum Street* (1961), about a young New Orleans woman who undergoes a clandestine abortion. This novel, too, was met with poor reviews, but Grau's persistence was rewarded in 1965, when *The Keepers of the House* garnered a Pulitzer Prize for Fiction. (So unexpected was the honor that when Grau received the phone call informing her, she thought it was a prank.)

It was *The Keepers of the House* that attracted the attention of the Klan, thanks to its description of a wealthy white man who has a decades-long relationship with his Black housekeeper and fathers three children with her. In addition to the attempted cross-burning (which fizzled out on her lawn when no one was even home to see it), she regularly received threatening phone calls. These did not bother her, she told journalists, because she had hunted in her youth and remained an excellent shot.

Grau's later novels included *The Condor Passes* (1971), *Evidence of Love* (1977), and *Roadwalkers* (1994), the last-named title referring to the homeless wanderers who roamed the South during the Great Depression.

Shirley Ann Grau died from the complications of a stroke on August 3, 2020 and is survived by two daughters, Katherine and Nora; two sons, Ian and William; and six grandchildren. She was predeceased in 1987 by her husband, James Kern Feibleman, a philosophy professor at Tulane, to whom she had been married since 1955.

See *Current Biography 1959*

Juliette Gréco

Born: Montpellier, France; February 7, 1927
Died: Saint-Tropez, France; September 23, 2020
Occupation: Singer; actress

For decades, Juliette Gréco toured the world as an ambassador of French song, captivating audiences with her aura of elegance, nostalgia, and seduction. In France, she was widely considered a musical institution whose repertoire of finely tuned texts seemed impervious to popular fashion and fads.

Juliette Gréco was born on February 7, 1927, in the Mediterranean city of Montpellier, France, the younger daughter of Louis Gérard Gréco, a police officer from Corsica, and the former Juliette Lafeychine, an aspiring artist some thirty years his junior. After her parents split, she was brought up for a time by her grandmother.

Gréco was thirteen when Hitler's troops occupied Paris. Both her mother and her sister were active in the Resistance and were deported; because of that family association, Gréco spent a short time in a French prison. After the war, her mother joined the women's naval service, and Gréco lived in a small, rented room in Paris. She found work as a hostess at Le Tabou, a jazz club in the heart of Saint-Germain-des-Prés, a bohemian Left Bank neighborhood whose denizens included Jean-Paul Sartre, Simone de Beauvoir, Albert Camus, and Maurice Merleau-Ponty, and she, herself, became a familiar figure thanks to her signature dark hair and slim-fitting, black clothing.

When the Right Bank cabaret Le Boeuf sur le Toit reopened in 1949, Gréco was offered a job helping to organize the first show, and she cast herself, effectively launching her decades-long singing career. Her first hit single, "Je Suis Comme Je Suis,"(I Am What I Am) was released in 1951, and her first album, *Juliette Gréco: Chante Ses Derniers Succès (Sings His Latest*

Hits), came out the following year. Her 1954 concert at Olympia Hall in Paris is now considered among the defining events of her singing career. Known as a master of chanson française, a storytelling genre of popular French music, she recorded her final album, *Gréco Chante Brel*, in 2013 and toured until 2017.

Gréco also appeared on the big screen in some thirty films, including Jean Cocteau's *Orphée* (Orpheus; 1950), *The Sun Also Rises* (1957), and the Orson Welles vehicle *Crack in the Mirror* (1960), Her final acting role came in the 2002 drama *Jedermann's Fest (Everyone's Party)*.

Gréco's love life was complex. From 1953 to 1956 she was married to the actor Philippe Lemaire, and her union with the actor Michel Piccoli lasted from 1966 until their divorce in 1976. She and the pianist and composer Gérard Jouannest, her third husband, were together from 1988 until his death in 2018. She was also romantically involved with the filmmaker Darryl Zanuck and with jazz trumpeter Miles Davis, whom she met in 1949. Davis reportedly declined to marry her because of the racism she was certain to face in the United States as the white wife of a Black man, but they remained close nonetheless until his death in 1991.

Gréco was predeceased in 2016 by her daughter from her first marriage, Laurence-Marie Lemaire.

See *Current Biography 1992*

Winston Groom

Born: Washington, DC; March 23, 1943
Died: Fairhope, Alabama; September 17, 2020
Occupation: Writer

Winston Groom is the author of *Forrest Gump*—the 1986 novel that was adapted to the screen in 1994 by the director Robert Zemeckis, with Tom Hanks playing the lovable protagonist. A modest seller before the movie was released, it was purchased by millions of readers after Hanks brought the titular character to life.

Groom was born on March 23, 1943, in Washington, DC, to Winston Francis Groom, a Pentagon lawyer who later practiced in Alabama, and his wife, Ruth, a teacher. Groom attended a military prep school and had aspirations of following in his father's footsteps as a lawyer. After graduating with an English degree in 1965 from the University of Alabama, however, he found himself in Vietnam as a second lieutenant in the infantry; he eventually became a captain. He returned from Vietnam disillusioned by his thirteen months in the military and carrying twenty notebooks in which he had documented his experiences. Groom then began working at the (now defunct) *The Washington Star*, where he spent a decade before quitting to focus on fiction.

His debut novel, *Better Times Than These*, about the Vietnam War, was published in 1978 to some acclaim, and he followed that up with *As Summers Die* (1980), which was set in Alabama and followed the travails of a white small-town lawyer who is confronted with the quagmire of southern politics in the 1950s when he defends a poor Black family's property rights. He pivoted to nonfiction in 1983 for *Conversations with the Enemy*, an account of a Vietnam-era prisoner of war co-written with Duncan Spencer. The volume was a finalist for a Pulitzer Prize. The following year Groom's next book, *Only*, a memoir about his beloved dog, *Fenwick*, hit bookstore shelves.

When *Forrest Gump* was published in 1986, critics praised the adventures of its kind-hearted Southern protagonist, who appears at pivotal moments in contemporary American history to dispense wisdom. It was not until the film was released that it became a cultural phenomenon, and Forrest's aphorisms ("Life is like a box of chocolates; you never know what you might get") entered the popular lexicon. The film grossed more than $670 million at the box office and won six Oscars, including best picture. The attention made the novel a bestseller long after it had first appeared, and it led Groom to write a sequel, *Gump & Co.*, published the following year.

Groom's other books include *Shrouds of Glory* (1995), about the Civil War; *Patriotic Fire* (2006), about the Battle of New Orleans; and *The Patriots* (2020), about Alexander Hamilton, Thomas Jefferson, and John Adams.

Groom was married three times. (He and his first wife, Baba, whom he met when they were college students, remained close after their divorce in 1984.) He died in his sleep of a probable heart attack on September 16, 2020, at his home in Fairhope, Alabama, and is survived by his third wife, Susan; a daughter, Carolina; and three stepchildren, Guy, Margaret, and Frederick.

See *Current Biography* 1997

Pete Hamill

Born: Brooklyn, New York; June 24, 1935
Died: Brooklyn, New York; August 5, 2020
Occupation: Newspaper columnist; novelist; memoirist

For decades, Pete Hamill was widely considered one of the finest print journalists in the country.

The writer was born William Hamill, Jr. on June 24, 1935, in the New York City borough of Brooklyn. His parents, William (Billy) Hamill and the former Anne Devlin, were both Irish immigrants. After breaking his leg in a soccer game, doctors were forced to amputate Billy Hamill's left leg above the knee to save him from gangrene. He held a few different jobs during Pete's childhood, but also went through periods of unemployment and heavy drinking. (In his 1994 memoir, Hamill revealed that he drank too heavily for decades but quit in 1972.)

Hamill, who had five younger brothers and one sister, attended Catholic school and became a comic book fanatic during World War II, when many of the most popular titles featured a mix of superhero fantasy and wartime reality. At age ten, to help his struggling family, he took a job as a delivery boy for the *Brooklyn Eagle*, and he began reading that paper each day.

In 1949, Hamill won a scholarship to Regis High School, a Manhattan college-prep school run by Jesuit priests. Unhappy with the elitism he found there, he dropped out and took a job in the Brooklyn Navy Yard. At 17 he joined the Navy, but by the mid-1950s, Hamill was back in Brooklyn, drinking and fighting by night, and working by day as an assistant to a graphic designer. Inspired by the writings of Ernest Hemingway and Jack Kerouac, he tried his hand at writing, and in 1960, he was hired by the *New York Post*.

It was the start of a storied career: within two years he had won the Meyer Berger Award for Distinguished Journalism, given by the Columbia University Graduate School of Journalism, and a special award from the Newspaper Reporters Association. Over the ensuing decades, he wrote thousands of columns for the *New York Post*, *Daily News*, and *Newsday*, and his articles appeared in such high-toned magazines as *Vanity Fair* and *Esquire*—despite his characteristic blunt, everyman style.

Hamill covered conflicts in Vietnam, Nicaragua, Northern Ireland, and Lebanon, among other hotspots, but he was equally comfortable in the wealthy environs of Manhattan, where he befriended figures like Jacqueline Kennedy Onassis, Shirley MacLaine, Norman Mailer, and Jack Lemmon.

In addition to his work in periodicals, he published numerous novels and short stories, as well as biographies, collections of essays, and screenplays. (He won a Grammy Award in 1976 for a project of a different type: liner notes for Bob Dylan's album *Blood on the Tracks*.)

Hamill, who won a 2014 George Polk Career Award for his lifetime contributions to journalism, died of kidney and heart failure at a Brooklyn hospital on August 5, 2020. Pete Hamill is survived by his second wife, Fukiko Aoki, a journalist; his daughters, Adrienne and Deirdre, from his first marriage, to Ramona Negron; four siblings; and a grandson.

See *Current Biography 1998*

Andre Harrell

Born: Lynchburg, South Carolina; September 26, 1960
Died: West Hollywood, California; May 7, 2020
Occupation: Music executive

A rapper at the age of 15, Andre Harrell worked his way up to the presidency of both Motown Records and Bad Boy Entertainment, the enormously successful record label created by Sean "Puffy" Combs. He was widely considered one of the most influential figures in the music scene of the 1980s and 1990s.

Andre O'Neal Harrell was born on September 26, 1960, in Lynchburg, South Carolina, after which his family moved to the New York City borough of the Bronx. Harrell grew up in the Bronxdale housing project in the Soundview section of the borough. His mother worked as a nurse's aide, while his father worked as a foreman at a produce market; they divorced when Harrell was 16. Just a year before that, Harrell and his friend Alonzo Brown founded the rap group Dr. Jeckyll and Mr. Hyde.

Harrell attended New York City's Lehman College, where he studied business management, but he dropped out before the end of his senior year to sell radio advertising. In 1983, he joined Russell Simmons's Rush Communications, which owned Def Jam Records, making $200 a week as the company's vice president. Supplementing his low salary with rap performances and royalties from his record sales, Harrell continued to learn about the record business, and in 1986 he left to found Uptown Records, which became known as the source of the music style "New Jack Swing," a smooth blend of rhythm and blues (R&B) and hip hop. Two years later, Uptown, whose artists included hitmakers like Jodeci and Mary J. Blige, began its partnership with major label MCA, and in 1992 Harrell

inked a $50 million deal with MCA's Universal Pictures and Universal Television divisions to produce screen projects with a new company, Uptown Entertainment.

In 1995, Harrell became head of the legendary label Motown, which was then ailing, and set about trying to turn the company around. After a series of disputes, he left in 1997, and his next job came from an unlikely quarter: In the early 1990s, he had served as a mentor to Sean "Puffy" Combs, but the two had suffered a bitter and public falling-out. Combs had been exceptionally successful since then, launching Bad Boy Entertainment, signing iconic rapper Notorious B.I.G., and racking up hundreds of millions of dollars in record sales. To the surprise of many, when Harrell left Motown, Combs hired him to lead Bad Boy.

Despite naysayers, the two enjoyed a solid working relationship, and in 2013 Harrell was appointed vice chairman of Combs's Revolt TV.

Harrell, whose marriage to entertainment lawyer and producer Wendy Credle ended in divorce, had long suffered from heart problems. He is survived by his son, Gianni Credle-Harrell; a brother, Greg; and his father.

See *Current Biography 2000*

Lynn Harrell

Born: New York, New York; January 30, 1944
Died: West Hollywood, California; April 27, 2020
Occupation: Cellist

Over the course of his career cellist Lynn Harrell performed with the world's leading symphony orchestras in concert halls and at music festivals at home and abroad, and he made some 50 highly acclaimed recordings—always intent on showing, as he believed, that the cello has more direct audience appeal than any other musical instrument.

Lynn Morris Harrell was born in New York City on January 30, 1944, to Mack Harrell, the distinguished Texas-born baritone who specialized in cantatas and oratorios, and the former Marjorie Fulton, a professional violinist.

While growing up in Dallas, Texas, Harrell was mainly interested in sports—especially baseball—and managed to be on some of the best school teams in the city. In junior high school he played on the basketball team that won the city championship. Meanwhile, he was also developing his interest in music. After a few weeks of studying the piano, which failed to inspire him, Harrell became attracted to the cello at the age of nine, when his parents invited friends, one of them a cellist, to their home to play string quartets. Harrell's musical studies after he left Texas included classes at the Juilliard School in New York City and the Curtis Institute in Philadelphia, as well as summer sessions at the Meadowmount School in upstate New York, a center renowned for training young string players.

Harrell first attracted nationwide attention in the spring of 1960, when he shared top honors in the Merriweather Post Contest in Washington, DC. As part of his award, he was booked for four performances with the National Symphony Orchestra in the nation's capital later that year.

At eighteen Harrell was hired to play in the string section of the Cleveland Orchestra, and at 21, he was promoted to the position of principal cellist, becoming the youngest principal player in the history of the Cleveland Orchestra to that date.

After his mentor and conductor George Szell died in 1970, Harrell decided to leave the orchestra to pursue a solo career. From 1971 on, Harrell's new career as a solo cellist in recitals and guest engagements with leading orchestras took him across the United States, to the concert halls of such cities as New York, Boston, Philadelphia, Cleveland, Atlanta, St. Louis, Chicago, Washington, and Los Angeles, and abroad, to Canada, England, France, Belgium, Germany, Austria, and Israel. He became a favorite at such music festivals as those at Stratford, Aspen, Marlboro, and Ravinia, and at the Casals Festival in Puerto Rico.

In the 1980s he garnered two Grammy Awards (along with the violinist Itzhak Perlman and the pianist Vladimir Ashkenazy), for recordings of Beethoven's Complete Piano Trios and Tchaikovsky's Trio in A Minor.

Before the coronavirus pandemic forced the cancellation of his scheduled performances in 2020, Harrell had planned to announce his retirement at the end of the season. He is survived by his wife, Helen Nightengale, a violinist.

See *Current Biography 1983*

Shere Hite

Born: Saint Joseph, Missouri; November 2, 1942
Died: Tottenham, London, England; September 9, 2020
Occupation: Cultural researcher; historian

Shere Hite's groundbreaking reports on female sexuality, which drew upon anonymized primary data from thousands of women, caused a major stir when they were released in the 1970s.

Hite was born Shirley Diana Gregory on November 2, 1942, in Saint Joseph, Missouri, the daughter of Paul Gregory, a flight controller for the military, and his wife, Shirley. Her parents later divorced, and her mother married Raymond Hite, a truck driver, who legally adopted her. That marriage, too, ended in divorce. Hite spent most of her childhood in the care of her conservative-minded maternal grandparents. When her grandparents' thirty-year marriage ended in divorce in the mid-1950s, she went to live with an aunt and uncle in Daytona Beach, Florida. A bright and diligent student, she shone academically at Seabreeze High School and demonstrated considerable musical talent as a pianist and clarinetist. Following her graduation in 1960, she enrolled at the University of Florida, where she majored in history. She received her BA degree, cum laude, in 1964, and her MA degree four years later.

Hite next moved to New York City to begin work on a PhD degree in history at Columbia University, where she found herself one of only a few women in the department. Short of funds and disappointed with the doctoral program, she dropped out of school after two semesters and signed on with Wilhelmina Models.

Hite, tired of appearing in ads that demeaned women, joined the National Organization for Women (NOW) in the 1970s. At one point she developed an open-ended questionnaire about women's sexual practices and preferences for a NOW "speak-out." Intrigued by the responses, she decided to extend the project, mailing out thousands of questionnaires throughout the country. In 1976 she published *The Hite Report: A Nationwide Study on Female Sexuality.* It's central findings (that for most women conventional sexual intercourse was an ineffective method of achieving orgasm) shocked many readers, but her work was compared in professional literature and in the popular press to earlier research by Alfred C. Kinsey and by William H. Masters and Virginia E. Johnson.

Hite later published *The Hite Report on Men and Male Sexuality* (1981) and *Women and Love: A Cultural Revolution in Progress* (1987), and although they didn't cause quite the buzz of her 1976 book, they kept Hite in the public eye. That was often an uncomfortable place, as she was regularly denounced as an angry, man-bashing feminist and subjected to vitriolic personal attacks.

She renounced her US citizenship in 1995 and settled in Europe, where she lectured at various universities and wrote additional books, including *The Hite Report on Hite: A Sexual and Political Autobiography* (2000).

Hite was married for fourteen years to the German pianist Friedrich Höricke; they divorced in 1999. Suffering from Alzheimer's and Parkinson's diseases during her final years, she died in

London on September 9, 2020, and is survived by her second husband, Paul Sullivan.

See *Current Biography 1997*

Stanley Ho

Born: Hong Kong, China; November 25, 1921
Died: Hong Kong, China; May 26, 2020
Occupation: Businessman

Casino magnate Stanley Ho was credited for turning Macau, a tiny former Portuguese colony off the coast of China, into one of the world's premier gambling destinations.

Stanley Ho Hung-sun was born in Hong Kong on November 25, 1921. His mother was Portuguese, and his father, Ho Sai-Kwong, came from Hong Kong's Hotung family, famous for its relationship with foreign merchants based in Hong Kong. The Ho family had a comfortable middle-class lifestyle during the 1920s and early 1930s, but Ho Sai-Kwong lost all of his money in the stock market in 1934. He fled in disgrace to Saigon, Vietnam, leaving his wife and their 13 children, including 13-year-old Stanley, destitute.

Despite his poverty, Ho excelled academically, and his achievements entitled him to scholarships for high school and, later, Hong Kong University, where he studied science. His schooling was interrupted, however, by World War II, and Ho left Hong Kong for Macau, where he had an uncle.

After working briefly for his uncle, Ho landed a secretarial job in a large trading firm, and a year after he started, he became a partner in the company. Using his newfound wealth, he subsequently established his own companies that traded gold, toys, and textiles, and also bought and developed real estate in Hong Kong after the war.

In 1961, the Portuguese-appointed Macanese government decided to auction off exclusive gambling rights for the territory, and Ho and a consortium of business partners put in a successful bid. Over the course of his career Ho operated or owned 20 casinos and their related businesses, including a ferry service that brought gamblers from Hong Kong; he employed a quarter of the small nation's labor force, and some years his enterprises were responsible for almost three-quarters of Macau's tax revenues.

Much of his success was due to his ability to negotiate and collaborate with a wide variety of entities, including the Japanese, who occupied Hong Kong during World War II; the Communist government of mainland China; American-based casino entrepreneurs who envisioned establishing an Asian foothold; and even the Chinese crime syndicates called triads.

Although some observers speculated about the possibly illicit nature of his activities, others lauded his philanthropy. He was known for funding educational and cultural causes, and he was once honored for his community work by Pope John Paul II.

Ho's personal life was as colorful and complex as his business dealings. Ho had 17 children by Clementina Leitão (whom he legally married in 1948), Lucina Laam (whom he legally married in 1971), Ina Chan, and Angela Leong. (Hong Kong outlawed multiple marriages in 1972 but honored those that existed before that; Ho considered all four women to be his wives.)

Ho was predeceased by his eldest son, Robert, in 1981, and by his first wife, Clementina, in 2004. *Forbes* magazine estimated that at his death, after bitter squabbling among family members, his fortune had fallen to $3.7 billion from a high of more than $12 billion.

See *Current Biography 2003*

Rolf Hochhuth

Born: Eschwege, Germany; April 1, 1931
Died: Berlin, Germany; May 13, 2020
Occupation: Dramatist

There have arguably been few plays in the history of the theater that have done more to trouble the conscience of the Western world than Rolf Hochhuth's widely translated *The Deputy*, a scathing indictment of Pope Pius XII's failure to protest the Nazi massacre of the Jews. Following its world premiere in West Berlin in 1963, it touched off a debate on guilt and moral responsibility comparable in its impact to that produced by Zola's *J'Accuse* and Remarque's *All Quiet on the Western Front*. The extraordinary publicity surrounding the play instantly catapulted its author from obscurity to international fame. Condemned by some as a sensationalist, Hochhuth was hailed by others as a zealous and courageous idealist who dared to bring vital issues back into the theater.

Rolf Hochhuth was born on April 1, 1931, in Eschwege on the Werra River, in northeastern Hesse, five miles west of what later became the East German frontier. His parents, Walter and Ilse (Holzapfel) Hochhuth were members of the German Evangelical Church. His father, an officer in both world wars, worked as an accountant after his shoe factory went bankrupt in the Depression. Hochhuth attended the local Realgymnasium and in 1941 joined the Deutsches Jungvolk, a Hitler youth organization. He readily admits that fact as evidence that he had an "ordinary" German upbringing, even though his parents risked their lives to help Jews, including some distant relatives by marriage, escape Nazi persecution. After the war he held his first and only political job—as a city hall runner for his uncle, a retired army officer, whom the American occupation authorities had appointed as the first post-Nazi mayor of Eschwege. In 1948, he left school and took bookkeeping courses at a vocational college. Later he entered into apprenticeship as a bookseller. A neurological ailment compelled him to delay his university education, but he eventually studied history and philosophy at the universities of Marburg, Heidelberg, and Munich, from 1952 to 1955. During that time, he read extensively and began to write poetry and short stories.

In 1955, Hochhuth took a job as a reader and editor with the publishing house Verlag C. Bertelsmann, and while there he began researching and writing *The Deputy,* subtitled *A Christian Tragedy.* Published by the Rowohlt Verlag of Hamburg as Der Stellvertreter on February 20, 1963, the play opened that same day under the direction of the celebrated avant-gardist Erwin Piscator at the Freie Volksbühne in West Berlin and was met with stunned, painful silence from the audience.

Hochhuth's later works include *Soldiers: An Obituary for Geneva,* was censored in Britain for presenting Winston Churchill in an unfavorable light, and *Guerrillas: Tragedy in Five Acts,* which is set in the United States and Guatemala toward the end of the Presidency of Lyndon B. Johnson.

Hochhuth's first two marriages ended in divorce; his third wife died in 2004. He is survived by his fourth wife, Johanna Binger, a bookseller; two sons, Martin and Friedrich; and two grandsons.

See *Current Biography 1976*

Ian Holm

Born: Goodmayes, England; September 12, 1931
Died: London, England; June 19, 2020
Occupation: Actor

Ian Holm was known for his extreme versatility as both a character actor and in leading roles, and his work ranged from plays by Shakespeare and Harold Pinter to popular movies like the "Lord of the Rings" trilogy.

The son of James Harvey Cuthbert and Jean Wilson Cuthbert, he was born Ian Holm Cuthbert on September 12, 1931, in Goodmayes, England, at the mental asylum where his father worked as a psychiatrist and superintendent. He had an older brother, Eric, who died of cancer when Holm was a teen.

As a seven-year-old, Holm had seen Charles Laughton perform in a stage version of *Les Misérables* and decided that he, too, would become an actor. In 1950, he enrolled at the Royal Academy of Dramatic Arts (RADA) in London. Before he graduated from the academy, in 1953, he spent a year in the British military, to fulfill his National Service requirement. In 1954, he became a member of the famed Royal Shakespeare Company (RSC) in Stratford-upon-Avon, where, that same year, he made his stage debut as a sword carrier in William Shakespeare's *Othello.*

Over the ensuing years, Holm gained a reputation as one of the leading young lights in British theater. In 1965 and 1967, he received Evening Standard Actor of the Year Awards for his work in Shakespeare's *Henry V* and Pinter's *The Homecoming,* respectively. The 1967 Broadway production of the latter play brought him a Tony Award. He remained closely associated with Pinter throughout his career.

Holm made his film debut in 1968, in the military drama *The Bofors Gun,* winning a British Academy Television Award (BAFTA) as best supporting actor. Thereafter, he found steady screen work, and in 1974 he starred as Napoleon in the television miniseries *Napoleon and Love.* His performance in the film *Chariots of Fire* (1981) brought Holm an Oscar nomination and BAFTA and Cannes Film Festival awards for best supporting actor.

Among his most popular roles in the 1990s were the tough cop Liam Casey in Sidney Lumet's police melodrama *Night Falls on Manhattan* (1997); Vito Cornelius, a priest, in Luc Besson's science-fiction film *The Fifth Element* (1997); and the main character in the Russell Banks adaptation *The Sweet Hereafter* (1997). Later that decade he appeared in the title role of Shakespeare's *King Lear* at London's National Theater in 1998. The first actor in recent memory to strip completely naked during the storm scene in Act III, he garnered an Evening Standard Award, an Olivier Award, and the Critics Circle Theatre Award.

Holm was discovered by a new generation of fans when he played the hobbit Bilbo Baggins in *The Fellowship of the Ring* (2001) and *The Return of the King* (2003), from Peter Jackson's "Lord of the Rings" trilogy, and Jackson's subsequent prequel "Hobbit" films. (At just 5 feet 5 inches, as critics pointed out, he was the perfect height for a hobbit.)

Holm, who was knighted in 1998, is survived by his fourth wife, the artist Sophie de Stempel; five children; and several grandchildren.

See *Current Biography 2002*

Roy Horn

Born: Nordenham, Germany; October 3, 1944
Died: Las Vegas, Nevada; May 8, 2020
Occupation: Magician

Roy Horn dazzled Las Vegas audiences for decades as part of the duo Siegfried and Roy, widely known for their feats of magic, elaborate costumes, and willingness to perform with exotic wild animals—until after Horn was mauled onstage by a 400-pound white tiger in 2003.

Born Uwe Ludwig Horn in 1944, in the town of Nordenham, Germany, Horn was raised by his mother and an abusive stepfather, and spent much of his time roaming the fields with his wolf-dog, Hexe. He also enjoyed visiting the local zoo, where he developed a special friendship with a cheetah named Chico.

While working as a bellboy on a German luxury liner in 1957, he met Siegfried Fischbacher, a steward who earned additional tips by performing magic tricks for passengers. Convincing the older boy that he could wow his audience more with a cheetah than the rabbit he was then using, Horn smuggled Chico onto the ship in a laundry bag, and a partnership was born.

In 1964, Siegfried and Roy went on the road as partners, performing with Chico in small cabarets and theaters throughout Germany and Switzerland. After they earned the acclaim of Princess Grace of Monaco at a 1966 Red Cross gala, their career took off, and they were soon able to expand their repertoire by adding additional exotic animals to their show.

Coming to the United States in 1970, they worked mainly at clubs in Las Vegas, and by 1981, having achieved considerable renown, the magicians had established themselves as the main act at Las Vegas's Frontier Hotel. During their seven years there, they performed before a total of more than three million people, and they broke the record for the longest-running show in Las Vegas.

In 1987, they signed a contract with Steve Wynn, the owner of the not-yet-opened $640 million Mirage Hotel, that guaranteed the pair a minimum salary of $57.5 million over a five-year period. They began performing there in 1990, with their opening night marking the show's 10,000th performance in Las Vegas. In 2001, after two decades of sold-out performances that had brought in hundreds of millions of dollars, they signed lifetime contracts to work at the Mirage.

That changed on October 3, 2003, when, in front of 1,500 horrified audience members, Horn was inexplicably attacked and dragged offstage by one of the performing tigers. With his windpipe crushed and a vital artery severely damaged, he underwent two operations and was placed on life support. After weeks in critical condition, Horn began a long process of recovery, first at a rehabilitation facility and later at his palatial home in Las Vegas.

The duo, who were also domestic partners, made one final appearance, at a 2009 benefit for the Lou Ruvo Center for Brain Health in Las Vegas, and officially retired from show business the following year.

In addition to Siegfried Fischbacher, Roy Horn is survived by a brother, Werner.

See *Current Biography 1998*

Zizi Jeanmaire

Born: Paris, France; April 29, 1924
Died: Tolochenaz, Switzerland; July 17, 2020
Occupation: Dancer

Zizi Jeanmaire enjoyed a six-decade career as a ballerina, cabaret singer, and actress, and while she often reinvented herself, she was known in all of those milieus for her gamine beauty, grace, and charisma.

She was born Renée Jeanmaire, in Paris, on April 29, 1924. Her father, Marcel, owned a chromium factory. When she was nine years old, she entered the Paris Opera Ballet School and while there appeared with the children's ballet corps from the school in the French film *La Mort du Cygne (Death of the Swan)*. At the school she also met Roland Petit and when she left the Paris Opera Ballet at the age of seventeen, she appeared in some of the young choreographer's early ballets. After spending several seasons with the de Basil and de Cuevas Russian ballets, she became an original member of Les Ballets de Champs-Élysées, a company formed in October 1945 by Petit and other young dancers. She left this group in early 1948 to join Petit's newly organized company known as Les Ballets de Paris de Roland Petit. As part of the troupe, Jeanmaire starred in *Carmen*, a choreographic version of Bizet's opera, which played to full houses for a record three months in Paris and made a similar splash when it opened in New York on October 6, 1949, at the Winter Garden Theater.

After she proved she could also sing in Petit's *La Croqueuse de Diamants (The Diamond Crusher)*, the Hollywood producer Howard Hughes offered Jeanmaire a movie contract. Samuel Goldwyn produced her first film, *Hans Christian Andersen*, and he suggested that she change her professional name from Renée to "Zizi," a childhood nickname.

She later danced with Bing Crosby in the film *Anything Goes*; on Broadway in *The Girl* in *Pink Tights* and *Can-Can*; and in several French films. Notably, she starred in a 1966 film of Petit's *Le Jeune homme et la mort* (*The Young Man and Death*) alongside famed dancer Rudolf Nureyev, as well as in a 1980 television film of *Carmen*, alongside equally iconic dance star Mikhail Baryshnikov.

Jeanmaire also maintained a thriving cabaret career—her signature number involved several male performers fanning her with large feathers—and Serge Gainsbourg once wrote an entire revue for her, *Zizi, Je t'aime* (*Zizi, I Love You*). Over the course of her career she made more than two-dozen albums.

She continued to perform well into her seventies, often in revues created for her by Petit. She performed for the final time in 2000, in the amphitheater of the Opéra Bastille in Paris.

British singer-songwriter Peter Sarstedt introduced her name to pop fans who might never have been aware of her in a 1969 song, "Where Do You Go to My Lovely," whose lyrics included the line: "You talk like Marlene Dietrich, and you dance like Zizi Jeanmaire."

Jeanmaire was predeceased in 2011 by Petit, to whom she had been married since 1954. She is survived by their daughter, Valentine, a singer and songwriter.

See *Current Biography 1952*

Larry Kramer

Born: Bridgeport, Connecticut; June 25, 1935
Died: New York, New York; May 27, 2020
Occupation: Writer and AIDS activist

"I don't consider myself an artist," Larry Kramer once said. "I consider myself a very opinionated man who uses words as fighting tools. I perceive certain wrongs that make me very angry, and somehow I hope that if I string my words together with enough skill, people will hear them and respond. I am under no delusion that this will necessarily be the case, but I seem to have no choice but to try."

Larry Kramer was born on June 25, 1935, in Bridgeport, Connecticut. He was the second of two children of George L. Kramer and Rea (Wishengrad) Kramer. Kramer characterized his childhood as extremely unhappy: He felt fear and guilt about being gay, and by his own account, he hated his father.

In 1953, Kramer enrolled at Yale, and the process of accepting his sexual identity began when he had an affair with one of his professors. Kramer graduated from Yale with a BA degree in 1957, and later the same year he began serving in the Army. After his discharge he got a job

in the mailroom of the William Morris Agency in New York, and he next worked for Columbia Pictures, first as a telex operator and then as an assistant story editor.

While living as a member of New York City's gay community in the mid-1970s, during what proved to be the heyday of the sexual revolution, Kramer had difficulty forming a lasting love relationship. Inspired by his experiences, he wrote *Faggots* (1978), a controversial novel about a gay man's futile search for love.

In July 1981, Kramer read about the appearance of Kaposi's sarcoma, a rare form of skin cancer that up to that time had afflicted primarily older men, in 41, mostly young, gay men, eight of whom had died of the disease. Alarmed, he and a few compatriots formed the Gay Men's Health Crisis (GMHC), the first organization established to gather and disseminate information on the disease that would eventually come to be known as AIDS.

Kramer worked tirelessly to convey to people the latest medical news about the disease that was killing gay men, giving speeches and writing articles criticizing not only the gay community but also the administration of President Ronald Reagan, the medical profession, and the press for failing to act. In 1987, he helped form ACT UP, a radical activist group that drew attention to AIDS-related issues through demonstrations and confrontational meetings with government officials and people in the medical professions; the organization was instrumental in establishing testing programs for experimental treatments and getting new drugs on the market.

The author of the popular play *The Normal Heart* and the mammoth (and less-popular) two-volume historical novel *The American People*, Kramer suffered from ill health for years: he had been infected with HIV, later contracted liver disease, and ultimately required a liver transplant. He died of pneumonia and is survived by his husband, architect David Webster, whom he married in 2013 after living together for years.

See *Current Biography 1994*

Norman Lamm

Born: Brooklyn, New York; December 19, 1927
Died: Englewood, New Jersey; May 31, 2020
Occupation: Rabbi and university administrator

As the president of Yeshiva University, Rabbi Norman Lamm stood at the helm of America's oldest and largest university under Jewish auspices, a school whose commitment to two often opposed spheres of learning is reflected in its motto, *Torah Umadda* ("Torah and worldly knowledge"). A creative and independent thinker whose academic training, appropriately, encompassed both rabbinic studies and organic chemistry, Lamm was especially well known for his interest in the problems of religious doubt engendered in modern society.

Norman Lamm, the son of Samuel Lamm, a civil servant, and Pearl (Baumol) Lamm, was born on December 19, 1927, in Brooklyn, New York. He had two sisters, Sondra and Miriam, and a younger brother, Maurice, who also became an esteemed rabbi. Raised in the Williamsburg section of Brooklyn, a neighborhood then heavily populated by traditionally observant Jews, Lamm attended the Yeshiva Torah Vodaath, an Orthodox parochial institution, for his primary schooling, and then went on to the Mesivta Torah Vodaath, where he was the editor of his class yearbook, for his secondary education. In 1945, he matriculated at Yeshiva College, majoring in chemistry but also taking a required course of studies in traditional religious subjects.

While still a student at Yeshiva during the Israeli War of Independence in 1947–48, Lamm was recruited by Israel's Atomic Energy Commission to work on a secret munitions project at a laboratory sequestered in upstate New York.

In 1949, after compiling a brilliant academic record that won him prizes in both Talmud and general scholarship as well as the honor of being chosen class valedictorian, Lamm received his BA degree summa cum laude. While continuing his Jewish studies at Yeshiva, Lamm also did graduate work in organic chemistry at the Brooklyn Polytechnic Institute (now part of NYU).

At that juncture Lamm won a four-year medical school scholarship, and he was forced to make a long-deferred decision—whether to enter the rabbinate or pursue a secular career. He chose rabbinics and was ordained in 1950. After working at a variety of synagogues, in 1958 he joined the Jewish Center on West 86th Street in Manhattan, one of New York City's most prestigious Orthodox synagogues, where he remained until September 1976.

Concurrently, he forged an academic career, and became a professor of Jewish Philosophy at Yeshiva University in 1966, the same year he received his PhD degree there. On November 7, 1976, he was formally invested as president of the university, which was then facing bankruptcy because of a national recession. He was widely credited with rescuing the institution, considered foundational to the modern Orthodox movement, from the precipice of financial ruin.

By 2001, when he stepped down as president and became chancellor, a largely ceremonial post, Yeshiva's endowment was $875 million. He retired fully in 2013.

He was predeceased by his wife of 66 years, Mindella, in April 2020, after she contracted coronavirus. A daughter, Sara, died in 2013. He is survived by two sons, Joshua and Shalom; a daughter, Chaye; and 17 grandchildren.

See *Current Biography 1978*

Lee Kun-hee

Born: Ŭiryŏng, Korea; January 9, 1942
Died: Seoul, South Korea; October 25, 2020
Occupation: Businessman

Lee Kun-hee built Samsung into a respected global tech giant, and while his career included twice being pardoned for white collar crimes, he was widely credited with changing the perception of Korean products.

Born on January 9, 1942, Lee Kun-hee (in the press his name is often written Kun-hee Lee, in accordance with the Western model of given name followed by family name) was the third son of Lee Byung-Chull. The Lees had a long history of producing writers and teachers, genteel professions they could afford to pursue because their forebears had been adept in land acquisition. It was unexpected, then, when twenty-five-year-old Lee Byung-Chull founded a small business to export fruit and dried fish in 1938. He called it the Samsung Store and based it in the southeastern city of Taegu. (Samsung means "three stars" in Korean, and three is considered a lucky number.) Samsung later took part in the government's industrial development drive, delving into areas such as electronics, shipbuilding, petrochemicals, heavy machinery, and construction and steadily established itself as a producer of cheap electronic goods.

Lee, although considered something of a playboy, earned a degree in economics from Waseda University, in Tokyo, in 1965, and an MBA degree from George Washington University in 1966. He had also worked in the employ of his father his entire adult life, joining *Joong-Ang Daily News* and Tongyang Broadcasting Corporation (divisions of the Samsung Group), in 1966, and becoming, in 1968, their executive director, a position he kept until 1978, when he became vice chairman of the Samsung Group.

Upon assuming the post of chairman in 1987, Lee buckled down and set out to redefine the Samsung brand. (The company had been profitable, but its products, like many from Korea, were often regarded as second rate.) He invested heavily in research and development, and by the early 1990s, under his leadership, Samsung had surged past Japanese and American rivals to dominate the computer memory chip market; it soon became a big name in flat-screen televisions and cell phones, as well, and today it is a major driver of the South Korean economy.

Lee chaired the Samsung Group until 1998 and later headed Samsung Electronics, becoming South Korea's richest man in the process.

His tenure was tarred by two incidents: in 1996, he was convicted of bribing the country's president, and in 2009, he was found guilty of tax evasion. He was pardoned both times, and many observers simply dismissed the crimes as being emblematic of how South Korea's family business empires, known as chaebol, operate.

Lee was severely affected by a heart attack in 2014, and his son, Lee Jae-yong, took over as the company's public face.

Lee died on October 25, 2020, in Seoul. Besides Lee Jae-yong, he is survived by his wife, Hong Ra-hee; his daughters, Boo-jin and Seo-hyun; four sisters; and seven grandchildren.

See *Current Biography 2005*

Ming Cho Lee

Born: Shanghai, China; October 3, 1930
Died: New York, New York; October 23, 2020
Occupation: Set Designer

The Chinese-born Ming Cho Lee is credited with inventing the spare, sculptural unit set that revolutionized theatrical design in the 1960s and was referred to as the dean of American set designers.

Ming Cho Lee was born in Shanghai, China, on October 3, 1930, the only child of Tsu Fa Lee, a Yale graduate who worked as a representative for an international insurance company, and his wife, the former Ing Tang. When Lee was six years old, his parents divorced. The boy remained in the custody of his father and, for many years, saw his mother only on weekends. On those weekend visits, his mother often took him to see Western films, operas, and plays. During the Japanese occupation of Shanghai in World War II, the theater became an even more important outlet for the somewhat withdrawn adolescent. To complement his cultural education, he also studied ink drawing and landscape painting.

Following the Communist takeover in 1949, the Lees fled to the British colony of Hong Kong, where Lee completed his high school education. Lee had intended to continue his studies at the University of Hong Kong, but, because his knowledge of English was limited, he failed the matriculation exam. Instead, he enrolled at Occidental College in Los Angeles as an art major.

Although he later switched his major to speech, Lee designed sets for several campus theatrical productions, and after receiving his BA degree from Occidental in 1953, he continued his training as a graduate student in theater arts at the University of California at Los Angeles (UCLA). In 1954 he was hired as an apprentice to Jo Mielziner, then Broadway's premier scenic designer, and within five years he had risen to assistant designer.

Lee made his New York debut in 1958, as the set and lighting designer for a staging of *The Infernal Machine*. Although critics found the production, lackluster, they singled out Lee for praise. Later the same year, he designed costumes for the Metropolitan Opera's production of *Madama Butterfly* and the sets for several Off-Broadway shows, including a highly praised revival of Arthur Miller's *Crucible*.

Lee was the principal designer for the New York Shakespeare Festival from 1962 to 1973, and during this period he largely revolutionized the American approach to stage design, employing pipes or wooden scaffolding, rough textures, and unusual industrial materials. He won a Tony Award for the 1983 play *K2*, about two climbers scaling a Himalayan peak: The centerpiece of his design was an awe-inspiring Styrofoam-and-wood mountain. His sets were often considered the most noteworthy part of productions.

Lee was equally celebrated for his teaching: He taught at Yale from 1969 to 2017, chairing the design department for much of his tenure, and many of his students went on to become renowned set designers themselves.

Lee, a 2002 recipient of the National Medal of Arts, died in New York City on October 23, 2020, at the age of 90. He is survived by his wife of more than six decades, Elizabeth (Rapport); three sons, Richard, Christopher, and David; and three grandchildren.

See *Current Biography 1989*

John Lewis

Born: Troy, Alabama; February 21, 1940
Died: Atlanta, Georgia; July 17, 2020
Occupation: US congressman and civil rights activist

John Robert Lewis was a towering figure in both the Civil Rights movement and in the US Congress, where he served for more than three decades.

Lewis was born on February 21, 1940, in the rural town of Troy, Alabama. He was one of ten children born to Eddie and Willie Mae Carter Lewis, poor sharecroppers. As a child, he aspired to become a minister and was known to preach to the family's chickens.

Inspired by radio broadcasts by Martin Luther King, Jr., he embraced the concept of nonviolent protest, and as a student at American Baptist College, he participated in his first sit-in. In 1960, he helped form a new civil rights group, the Student Nonviolent Coordinating Committee (SNCC). The following year he became one of the original Freedom Riders, activists who challenged southern laws that segregated interstate bus travel and bus stations. Lewis and the others faced angry mobs and violent beatings, but the Freedom Riders were ultimately successful.

In 1963, Lewis was elected chairman of the SNCC, and in that capacity he helped organize the March on Washington for Jobs and Freedom, which featured King as the main speaker. At age 23, Lewis was the youngest speaker at the march's rally at the Lincoln Memorial.

In 1964, Lewis helped organize one of the most well-known marches in US history. During that event some 600 protesters marched from Selma, Alabama, to Montgomery, the state capital, to advocate for voting rights. On Sunday, March 7, 1965, the marchers were met on the Edmund Pettus Bridge by state police in riot gear who attacked them with tear gas, dogs, and nightsticks. The attack became known as Bloody Sunday. Lewis sustained a fractured skull when a trooper beat him. The march spurred public sympathy for the Civil Rights movement and prompted President Lyndon B. Johnson to introduce the Voting Rights Act, which passed Congress and was signed into law on August 6. Lewis remained active in civil rights over the next several years, and in 1977, he was named by President Jimmy Carter to head ACTION, a federal agency that coordinated volunteer work.

In 1981, Lewis won a seat on the Atlanta City Council, and in 1986 he was elected to represent Georgia's Fifth Congressional District. In Congress, Lewis focused on civil rights, women's rights, and peace, and during his decades of service, he became known as the "conscience of the Congress." Among his many laurels as a public servant were the John F. Kennedy Profile in Courage Award, the Spingarn Medal of the National Association for the Advancement of Colored People (NAACP), and the Martin Luther King, Jr. Nonviolent Peace Prize. In 2011, Barack Obama awarded him the Presidential Medal of Freedom.

In late 2019, Lewis announced that he had late-stage pancreatic cancer. He died still holding the congressional seat he had won in 1986. He was predeceased in 2012 by his wife, Lillian, to whom he was married since 1968. He is survived by their son, John-Miles.

See *Current Biography 1980*

Little Richard

Born: Macon, Georgia; December 5, 1932
Died: Tullahoma, Tennessee; May 9, 2020
Occupation: Singer

Known for his flamboyant persona and bravura performances, Little Richard drew upon gospel, rhythm and blues, and other traditionally Black forms of music to create a sound all his own. An inaugural member of the Rock and Roll Hall of Fame, he was a strong influence on such artists as the Beatles, the Rolling Stones, David Bowie, Prince, and Michael Jackson.

Richard Wayne Penniman was one of twelve children born to Charles "Bud" and Leva Mae Penniman. Part of a poor, but deeply religious family, he began performing at church at an early age. As a teenager, he learned to play piano and went on the road to perform with various traveling shows, sometimes in gender-bending attire.

In 1951, Little Richard, as he was by then known, won an Atlanta talent contest that landed him a recording contract with RCA, but the following year, his father was murdered, and he returned home to help support his family, working as a dishwasher and occasional nightclub performer.

In 1955, Little Richard earned a recording contract in New Orleans, where he cut his first hit, the rollicking "Tutti Frutti," which rocketed to the top of the charts and was covered by such artists as Elvis Presley and Pat Boone. He followed with a string of hits—including "Lucille," "Good Golly, Miss Molly," "Keep A-Knockin'," and "Long Tall Sally." Although his records were popular, it was his concert performances—which involved sequined capes, heavy makeup, a greased pompadour, and plenty of pounding on the piano—that cemented his reputation.

Late in 1957, he gave up performing to enroll in a Seventh-day Adventist college in Alabama. He became an ordained minister but by the early 1960s, he had begun touring again, performing alongside the newly formed Beatles and a young Jimi Hendrix. He quickly succumbed to the lure of drugs and alcohol during this period, and he once again turned to religion for succor, recording gospel music and preaching.

It was not until the mid-1980s that Little Richard found a peaceful balance between his faith and rock-and-roll. He continued to evangelize but also performed popular songs and occasionally took on small roles on the screen. In the 1990s he branched into making music for children, still maintaining his distinctive sound even as he recorded such perennial favorites as "Itsy Bitsy Spider."

A film based on his life was released in 2000, and a decade later, "Tutti Frutti" was inducted into the National Recording Registry of the Library of Congress. (By then, he had already won lifetime achievement awards from the National Academy of Recording Arts and Sciences and the Rhythm and Blues Foundation, among numerous other laurels.)

While he still continued to perform until 2013, it became apparent that his health was deteriorating. In October 2019 he was presented with a Distinguished Artist Award from the governor of Tennessee, in recognition of his status as one of the early pioneers of rock-and-roll. Months later he died from bone cancer. His survivors include a son, Danny Jones Penniman.

See *Current Biography 1986*

Trini Lopez

Born: Dallas, Texas; May 15, 1937
Died: Rancho Mirage, California; August 11, 2020
Occupation: Singer

During his heyday in the 1960s, Trini Lopez's unique blend of rockabilly, folk, and Latin music landed him regularly on the pop charts.

One of six children, Trinidad Lopez III was born to impoverished Mexican parents in Dallas on May 15, 1937. His father eventually became superintendent of maintenance at Southern Methodist University, but for many years he eked out a bare subsistence for his family at a variety of common laboring jobs. The family lived in a one-room house in Dallas's Spanish-American slum ghetto, and Lopez spoke mostly Spanish until he entered high school.

Lopez was only eleven when he made up his mind to become a musical star. His father, himself an amateur guitarist and singer, bought him a $12 guitar, and Lopez taught himself to play and sing by listening to Frank Sinatra and Ray Charles records. In adolescence he formed his own combo, which at first worked for a pittance in a Mexican restaurant and eventually won engagements at nightclubs throughout the Southwest. In 1960 Lopez took his combo to Los Angeles, but the only booking he could get was a single for himself; while he had never worked alone, he needed the money, and that job led to a string of others, drawing the attention of record executives and of Frank Sinatra, who became an avid fan.

Lopez signed with Reprise Records and in 1963 released his debut album, *Trini Lopez: Live at P.J. 's*, which was recorded at a popular nightclub and sold 1,000,000 copies; one of its tracks, "If I Had a Hammer," released as a single, reached international sales of 4,500,000. It had been a solid hit for the folk trio Peter, Paul, and Mary several years earlier, but Lopez's version shot to number-one on the charts thanks to a catchy, danceable arrangement. Coincidentally, another of his major hits, "Lemon Tree," was also a Peter, Paul, and Mary remake that reached a higher chart position than its predecessor.

In all, he made Billboard's top-40 chart fifteen times. Although early in his career Lopez had been advised to change his name and hide his Mexican heritage, he always refused, insisting on recording traditional songs and punctuating his arrangements with the yelps and trills often heard in Mexican folk music.(*Live at P.J. 's* included versions of "La Bamba" and "Cielito Lindo," a Mexican classic often performed by Mariachi bands.)

In 1969 Lopez starred in an NBC variety special, and he also took on small roles in a handful of movies. While he enjoyed his greatest popularity in the 1960s, he remained active as a performer in Las Vegas and at clubs around the world, and he continued to record albums until 2011, when he released *Into the Future*, a collection that included multiple Sinatra covers.

Trini Lopez, who never married or had children, died on August 11, 2020, from the complications of Covid-19.

See *Current Biography 1968*

Iris Love

Born: New York, New York; August 1, 1933
Died: New York, New York; April 17, 2020
Occupation: Archaeologist

The discovery by Iris Love, in 1969, of the great circular temple of Aphrodite in the ruins of the ancient Greek port of Cnidus (in what is now Turkey) was one of the most spectacular modern finds in classical archeology, and it typified the professional style of a woman considered that field's controversial enfant terrible. Her claim, a year later, to have located the head of Praxiteles' statue of Aphrodite in a storeroom at the British Museum only further heightened her visibility in a profession whose heroic days were generally considered to be past. (One source called her "Indiana Jones in a miniskirt.")

Iris Cornelia Love was born on August 1, 1933 to Cornelius Ruxton Love Jr., a diplomat, collector, and descendant of Alexander Hamilton; and Audrey B. (Josephthal) Love, an heiress and arts patron. Her parents were remote figures, as was the custom of the time for her demographic, but luckily, she had a British governess, Katie Wray, who happened to be a classicist. Love learned Latin before first grade and would grow up to speak Greek, French, German, Italian, Turkish, Mandarin, Russian, and Arabic.

She majored in art and archeology at Smith College, earning her BA degree, in 1955. (She later did graduate work in art history at New York University (NYU), fulfilling the course requirements for a PhD degree but never completing her dissertation; she made waves while studying there, however, for her discovery that a group of sculpted Etruscan warriors at the Metropolitan Museum of Art (MMA) was a forgery.) Her Smith advisor, Phyllis Williams Lehmann, spent summers directing archeological excavations on the Aegean island of Samothrace, and Love participated almost every year from 1955 to 1965.

With extensive excavations already completed or underway at Grecian and Roman sites, when it was time to lead her own expedition in 1967, Love turned her attention to Turkey, focusing on the ruins at Cnidus, an ancient harbor city. By 1969 she had identified several Byzantine churches, a council house, a cemetery, a theater, a large Doric portico, and three temples, including the great circular temple of Aphrodite.

Missing from the great circular temple in Cnidus was Praxiteles' statue of Aphrodite, the most-copied statue in antiquity. In 1970, in the basement of London's British Museum, Love was picking through artifacts when she came across a severely damaged sculptured head, which she identified as a fragment of the statue. Museum officials resented the international publicity given to her, and its scholars disputed her stylistic analysis. (Some observers attributed the vitriol leveled against her to be a product of sexism.)

In later years, Love, the longtime partner of newspaper columnist Liz Smith, became a champion breeder of dachshunds, many of which she gave names derived from Greek mythology.

She died of the novel coronavirus. Predeceased by Smith in 2017, she left no immediate survivors.

See *Current Biography 1982*

Sirio Maccioni

Born: Montecatini Terme, Italy; April 5, 1932
Died: Montecatini Terme, Italy; April 20, 2020
Occupation: Restaurateur

After restaurateur Sirio Maccioni introduced such previously unheard-of dishes like pasta primavera and crème brûlée to the rich and powerful at his Manhattan hotspot Le Cirque, they eventually became fixtures on America's culinary map. It was Maccioni, himself, rather than his restaurant or any specific recipe, however, who earned the respect and love of so many that the New York Landmarks Conservancy once named him a "living landmark."

Sirio Maccioni was born on April 5, 1932, on a farm just outside the spa town of Montecantini-Terme, in Tuscany, Italy. His father, Eugenio, was a hotel concierge, and his mother, Sylvia, a homemaker. Sylvia died in 1940, after suffering a pulmonary infection, and Eugenio was killed in 1944, amid World War II. Maccioni was raised by his paternal grandmother. Although both of his parents had urged him to become a farmer, Maccioni decided to accept a scholarship to a local hotel-and-restaurant school, and after graduating, in 1950, he moved to Paris and took a job as a waiter at the world-famous Plaza Athénée restaurant. After earning a reputation as an excellent server there, Maccioni worked in such celebrated Paris dining rooms as Maxim's and the Kempinski Hotel.

In 1956, Maccioni relocated to New York, where he worked at some of that city's finest restaurants, among them Delmonico's and the Colony, where he charmed high-profile, demanding guests such as Frank Sinatra and the Duke and Duchess of Windsor. By 1974, he had saved enough money to open the restaurant he had been dreaming of since his earliest days in the business. The original Le Cirque, which was located in the Mayfair Hotel, achieved instant acclaim and attracted a regular celebrity clientele that included Henry Kissinger, Diana Ross, and Woody Allen with its lobster risotto, black sea bass, and the famed pasta primavera.

Maccioni won the prestigious James Beard Award for Outstanding Restaurant for Le Cirque in 1995, received multiple four-star reviews from the *New York Times*, and retained the Wine Spectator Grand Award for nearly two decades. The restaurant was later renamed Le Cirque 2000 and relocated to the Palace Hotel, located on Madison Avenue and 50th Street. That iteration closed its doors on New Year's Eve 2004, marking what some Manhattan insiders saw as the end of an era, but Maccioni opened a new Le Cirque in 2006 on the Upper East Side.

In addition to Le Cirque, Maccioni oversaw such New York City restaurants as Circo and Sirio Ristorante. Among the chefs who went on to fame after working in his kitchens are David Bouley, Jacques Torres, and Daniel Boulud.

Maccioni, who published an autobiography, *Sirio: The Story of My Life and Le Cirque*, in 2004, is survived by his wife, Egidiana; three sons, Marco, Mauro, and Mario; five grandchildren; and a sister, Clara.

See *Current Biography 1998*

Madeline H. McWhinney

Born: Denver, Colorado; March 11, 1922
Died: Red Bank, New Jersey; June 19, 2020
Occupation: Economist

Throughout her career, Madeline H. McWhinney, the first-ever female officer of the Federal Reserve Bank, smashed glass ceilings and counteracted the effects of years of sexism on the financial community.

Born on March 11, 1922 in Denver, Colorado, Madeline Houston McWhinney was the oldest of the seven children of Leroy and Alice Barse (Houston) McWhinney. Her father was the vice-president of the International Trust Company of Denver, and he often discussed his work with her.

During her summer vacations from her private girls' prep school, she worked at the International Trust Company, and when she entered Smith College in 1939, she chose economics as her major. Because of her father's death in a car accident the previous year, the family found itself in financial straits, but McWhinney won several scholarships and supplemented her income by working part-time in the college bookstore and by selling cigarettes and candy bars in her dormitory. After receiving her BA degree magna cum laude in 1943, she moved to New York City and opted for a job as a research assistant at the New York branch of the Federal Reserve System. In the evenings she worked on her master's degree at the New York University Graduate School of Business, earning an MBA in 1947.

Advanced by the Fed to the rank of staff economist, she handled special assignments for the Securities Department, chaired research and statistics committees, and assisted the manager of the System Open Market Account. In 1955, she was named chief of the Fed's Financial and Trade Statistics Division, and five years later she became the first woman officer of the Federal Reserve Bank of New York as chief of the newly established Market Statistics Department, which had been set up to monitor the government securities market. A decade later she ascended to a vice presidency, another first for a woman.

As the women's liberation movement gained strength in the early 1970s, feminist leaders became more concerned about the widespread discrimination against women by banks, credit card companies, and department stores. They concluded that women must organize their own financial institutions, and in 1974, McWhinney became president of the First Women's Bank, which was, as the name implied, the first full-service commercial bank in the United States that was majority owned and operated by women.

McWhinney resigned in 1976, frustrated that feminist politics on the part of the organization's board interfered with her agenda of creating a financial institution just as successful as its male-run counterparts. (The First Women's Bank folded in 1992, having never become profitable.)

In 1980, McWhinney began serving on the first New Jersey Casino Control Commission, and in 1983, she became Chief Financial Officer (CFO) of the Whitney Museum of American Art. She spent later years sitting on various corporate and foundation boards.

Madeline McWhinney's husband, John Dale, a management consultant, died in 1993. She is survived by her son, Tom; stepson, John Jr.; three of her siblings; and four grandchildren.

See *Current Biography 1976*

Joe Morgan

Born: Bonham, Texas; September 19, 1943
Died: Danville, California; October 11, 2020
Occupation: Baseball player

In the 1970s, Hall of Fame second baseman Joe Morgan was widely considered the "engine" of the Big Red Machine, as the Cincinnati Reds were then known.

Joseph Leonard Morgan was born on September 19, 1943, in Bonham, Texas. In the late 1940s the Morgans moved to Oakland, California, where his father nurtured his interest in baseball, taking him to Pacific Coast League games, giving him his first lessons in batting and fielding, and encouraging his aspiration to play in the major leagues. Jackie Robinson, the second baseman who broke the major-league color barrier, was his first hero. In his early days on the sandlots, Morgan had trouble hitting, because he was smaller than the other boys, but he swung as if he had their heft, gripping the bat at the end of the handle. When he learned to choke up, his batting improved.

He began trying out for the major leagues while playing for Castlemont High School in Oakland. Because of his slight physique, scouts were unimpressed, and after graduating, Morgan enrolled in Oakland City College. In the spring of his freshman year, however, a scout for the National League's Houston Astros (then called the Houston Colt .45's) noticed him.

Signed by the Astros, Morgan began his professional career with the team's California League Class A farm club. Later the same season he was transferred to Durham in the North

Carolina League but quickly returned the next year for further experience with the Astros' farm club at San Antonio, Texas. The statistics he racked up there—a league-leading 106 double plays, a .967 fielding percentage, a .323 batting average, 90 runs batted in, and 42 double-base hits that tied for league lead—earned him the Texas League's Most Valuable Player (MVP) award. Once again, he was summoned to Houston toward season's end, and this time he remained.

Over the course of his career, Morgan, who was traded to the Reds after the 1971 season, won five consecutive Gold Gloves and led National League second basemen in fielding percentage three times. He was considered among the most accomplished base-stealers in Major League history, stealing 689 bases in 851 attempts, for an 81 percent success rate. Because of his relatively small size (5-foot-7 and 160 pounds), observers were sometimes surprised by his batting power: He hit at least 22 home runs in four seasons and had a record of 268 overall.

Morgan became a free agent in 1979 and retired at the end of the 1984 season. In 1990 he became a first-ballot inductee into the Hall of Fame. After his playing career, Morgan began working as a broadcaster on a variety of local and national stations. From 1990 to 2010 he appeared on ESPN's *Sunday Night Baseball*.

Morgan had a bone-marrow transplant in 2016 and died on October 11, 2020, in Danville, California. He is survived by his wife of 30 years, Theresa; their twin daughters, Kelly and Ashley; and two daughters, Lisa and Angela, from his first marriage, which ended in divorce.

See *Current Biography 1984*

Ennio Morricone

Born: Rome, Italy; November 10, 1928
Died: Rome, Italy; July 6, 2020
Occupation: Film composer

Ennio Morricone provided the scores for some 500 films, many by such esteemed directors as Bernardo Bertolucci, Brian De Palma, Mike Nichols, Barry Levinson, John Carpenter, Quentin Tarantino, and horror maven Dario Argento. He is perhaps best known for the theme to the spaghetti Western *The Good, the Bad, and the Ugly*, starring Clint Eastwood, which remains one of the most frequently played, honored, and spoofed pieces of cinematic music.

Morricone was born on November 10, 1928, in Rome, to Libera Ridolfi and Mario Morricone, a trumpeter who played jazz and opera and lent his talents to several movie scores. He had four siblings: Adriana, Aldo, Maria, and Franca. When he was six years old, Morricone began writing his own compositions, and at the age of 12, he enrolled at the Santa Cecilia Conservatory to study trumpet. There he met classmate Sergio Leone, with whom he would become famously linked in later years.

Morricone received a diploma in instrumentation in 1952 and a diploma in composition in 1954. He began composing and arranging pieces for radio dramas, and in 1955 he started ghostwriting scores for films. A few years later, after completing his military service, he also began writing music for television shows. In 1964, he supplied the music for the Sergio Leone film *Per un Pugno di Dollari*, released in the United States as *A Fistful of Dollars*. Starring a then-unknown actor named Clint Eastwood, *A Fistful of Dollars* revived the Western genre and made Eastwood a star. Morricone's inspiration for the theme came from a lullaby he had composed years earlier. Morricone worked with Leone on the two sequels: *For a Few Dollars More* (1965) and *The Good, The Bad and The Ugly* (1968), the latter of which featured an instantly memorable whistling piccolo and ominous drumbeat in its theme.

In 1969, he re-teamed with Leone for his operatic masterpiece *Once Upon a Time in the West*. By then Morricone's music had attracted a number of Hollywood directors, and he composed the score for such high-profile pictures as the Clint Eastwood film *Two Mules for Sister Sara* (1970); the horror sequel *The Exorcist II: The Heretic* (1977); the Jaws-inspired *Orca* (1977); Terrence Malick's saga *Days of Heaven* (1978)—the last of which earned him his first Oscar nomination. Although he did not win the award, the nomination served to raise his profile even further, and he continued to find steady work both in Italy and Hollywood.

Morricone was given an Oscar for lifetime achievement in 2007 and won his first competitive Academy Award for Tarantino's *The Hateful Eight* (2015), a Western mystery thriller. He also garnered multiple Golden Globes, four Grammys, and dozens of international awards during his long career.

He died while trying to recuperate from falling and fracturing his femur. He is survived by his wife, Maria Travia, to whom he was married since 1956; four children, Marco, Alessandra, Andrea (a composer and conductor) and Giovanni; and four grandchildren.

See *Current Biography 2000*

Alan Parker

Born: London, England; February 14, 1944
Died: London, England; July 31, 2020
Occupation: Filmmaker; screenwriter

Considered one of the motion picture industry's most gifted storytellers, Alan Parker was also among the more controversial contemporary filmmakers. Out of a desire "to say something different with each film," as he put it, he tackled projects of notable diversity, including *Midnight Express* (1978), which, with its disturbing images, throbbing soundtrack, and sensationalized treatment of powerful subject matter, embodied the essential elements of the style for which he is perhaps best known; *Fame* (1980) and *Birdy* (1984), works that reinforced his reputation for creating narratives of absorbing interest; *Angel Heart* (1987), which made headlines when Parker challenged the decision of the Motion Picture Association of America's ratings board to tag the film with an X rating; and *Mississippi Burning* (1988), which generated heated debate about its interpretation of history.

An only child, Alan William Parker was born on February 14, 1944 in Islington, a working-class borough of London. His father, William, was a house painter; his mother, Elsie, worked as a dressmaker. At the age of eleven, Parker won a scholarship to the Owen's School, an elite private institution, but during his years there, the working-class boys from his neighborhood remained his closest friends.

After his graduation from Owen's, Parker got a job in the mailroom of a London advertising agency. Within a short time, he was writing ad copy, and by 1968 Parker's employer had promoted him from copywriter to director of television commercials. In 1970, he founded his own production company, which won virtually every major national and international prize in the field over the next decade and significantly influenced the development of advertising in Great Britain.

With hundreds of commercials to his credit, he made a move into feature films, writing the screenplay for the little-seen teen drama *Melody* (1971), directing a BBC Television movie about Jewish children in World War II called *The Evacuees* (1974), and then turning his attention to American settings and subjects in such films as *Bugsy Malone* (1976), a gangster spoof, 1978's *Midnight Express*, a harrowing look at a young US citizen's time in a Turkish prison; the rousing 1980 musical *Fame*, about a New York City performing-arts high school; and *Mississippi Burning*, his 1988 fictionalized version of the murder of three civil rights workers in Mississippi during the Civil Rights era.

Parker earned Oscar nods for both *Midnight Express* and *Mississippi Burning*, and his collection of statuettes includes the British Academy Film Awards (BAFTA) for best director and best picture for *The Commitments*, his 1991 film about an Irish band inspired by Motown music and a Cannes Grand Jury Prize for *Birdy*.

Parker, whose last film was the 2003 drama *The Life of David Gale*, garnered a lifetime achievement award from the Directors Guild of Great Britain in 1998 and was knighted in 2002. Alan Parker died on July 31, 2020, and is survived by his second wife, Lisa Moran-Parker; a son from their marriage, Henry; four children (Lucy, Alexander, Jake, and Nathan) from his first marriage, to Annie Inglis; and seven grandchildren.

See *Current Biography 1994*

Regis Philbin

Born: New York, New York; August 25, 1931
Died: Greenwich, Connecticut; July 24, 2020
Occupation: Television personality

Talk- and game-show host Regis Philbin charmed audiences for decades with his everyman persona and mock (but relatable) irascibility.

Regis Francis Xavier Philbin was born in New York City on August 25, 1931 to Frank Philbin, a personnel director, and his wife, Florence. He was named Regis after his father's alma mater, Regis High School, a Jesuit boy's school in Manhattan. As a skinny teenager growing up in the borough of the Bronx, Philbin took up weightlifting. Following his graduation from Cardinal Hayes High School, he entered the University of Notre Dame, where he majored in sociology and participated in intramural boxing.

After earning his B.A. degree in 1953, Philbin did a tour of duty in the U S Navy. Upon his return to civilian life, he began his television career as a stagehand and delivery boy at KCOP-TV in Los Angeles, where he soon rose to the position of news writer. He then worked at various stations as a news anchor and sportscaster, and in 1961 at KOGO he launched the late-night program *The Regis Philbin Show*, which was later syndicated.

For two and a half years ending in 1969, Philbin was the announcer and sidekick to Joey Bishop on his late-night ABC network variety program (an unhappy time, he has recalled, because of Bishop's caustic humor), and he then hosted a succession of his own television programs.

From 1975 to 1981 he co-hosted the top-rated *A.M. Los Angeles*, and in 1983 he reunited with his co-host, Cyndy Garvey, on ABC's *The Morning Show*. In 1985 Garvey was replaced by Kathie Lee Gifford, and after the show went into syndication in 1988, it became *Live! With Regis and Kathie Lee*. Later, Kelly Ripa stepped into the co-hosting spot, and from 2001 to 2011 the show was known as *Live! With Regis and Kelly*.

Over the decades, Philbin became an almost ubiquitous presence on television, thanks not only to that popular morning show but to his appearances on sitcoms, variety shows, Miss America pageants, and holiday specials. From 1999 to 2002, he hosted a game show, *Who Wants to Be a Millionaire*, which aired several nights a week, regularly drew 30 million viewers to each episode, and was largely credited with reviving the game show genre in the United States. (It has since aired in different iterations with various hosts, with Philbin reprising his role from time to time on special editions of the show.)

Philbin died on July 24, 2020 at the age of 88. He is survived by his second wife, Joy (whom he often mentioned on his morning shows); his daughter Amy, from his first marriage to Catherine Faylen, which ended in divorce; his daughters with Joy (Joanna and Jennifer); and four grandchildren. He was predeceased by his and Faylen's son, Danny.

At the time of his death, Regis Philbin reportedly held the record as the most-watched person in television history, with more than 17,000 hours of airtime.

See *Current Biography 1994*

Michel Piccoli

Born: Paris, France; December 27, 1925
Died: Saint-Philbert-sur-Risle, France; May 12, 2020
Occupation: Actor

Michel Piccoli, who appeared alongside such actresses as Brigitte Bardot and Catherine Deneuve, was a fixture of French cinema for more than five decades.

Jacques Daniel Michel Piccoli was born on December 27, 1925, in Paris. His parents, who were musicians, instilled in their only child a love of the arts, and he began acting professionally when he was twenty. He spent the next decade working in the theater, first at the Renauld-Barrault Company, under the direction of the innovative actor and mime Jean-Louis Barrault, and later at the famous Théâtre de Babylone.

Piccoli also found work in film, starting with a small part in the 1945 film *Sortilèges* (*The Bellman*). Over the next sixteen years he acted in more than 30 films, gradually working his way up

to more substantial roles. In 1961, Piccoli's role as Nuttbeccio in Jean-Pierre Melville's film noir classic *Le Doulos* (*The Finger Man*) was widely acclaimed by the French film community, and two years later he received international acclaim for his role in Jean-Luc Godard's *Contempt*, which also starred Bardot. The film, widely considered a masterpiece of modern cinema, brought Piccoli much attention in France, and he seemed to be on the brink of stardom.

Yet he undercut his chance to become a major film star by continually choosing small, controversial roles in small, provocative films. This was particularly true of his association with the Spanish surrealist director Luis Buñuel, with whom he made multiple films, including *Belle de Jour* (1967) [Beautiful Day], in which he played an glib aristocrat who encourages Catherine Deneuve's character to go into prostitution; *Diary of a Chambermaid* (1964); and *The Discreet Charm of the Bourgeoisie* (1972).

In the 1980s, he made almost forty films, most of which were never released in America, and he continued that pattern throughout the majority of his career—working prolifically and earning a dedicated fan base in Europe. He did appear occasionally in American films, most notably playing a Soviet spy in France in Alfred Hitchcock's *Topaz* (1969), and an urbane croupier in Louis Malle's *Atlantic City* (1980).

Before the widespread use of home VCRs, American moviegoers could watch his work mainly at festivals and in small art cinemas, and among his most popular film in that milieu was 1973's *La Grande Bouffe* (*The Big Feast*), a dark satire about four hedonistic friends spending an indulgent weekend at a villa in the French countryside.

Piccoli was nominated four times for the César Award, the French equivalent of the Oscars: for *Strange Affair* (1981), *Dangerous Moves* (1984), *May Fools* (1990), and *La Belle Noiseuse* [The Beautiful Troublemaker] (1991), and in 2012, when he was 86, he was named best actor at the 2012 David di Donatello awards, the Italian equivalent of the Oscars, for the film *We Have a Pope*. His final film, *Le Goût des Myrtilles* (*The Taste of Blueberries*), was released in 2014.

Piccoli's first two marriages ended in divorce. He is survived by his third wife, Ludivine Clerc; a son, Inor; and two daughters, Anne-Cordélia and Missia.

See *Current Biography 2002*

Joaquín Salvador Lavado (Quino)

Born: Guaymallén, Argentina; July 17, 1932
Died: Luján de Cuyo, Argentina; September 30, 2020
Occupation: Cartoonist

Joaquín Salvador Lavado was known throughout the Spanish-speaking world for his cartoon strip *Mafalda*, whose six-year-old protagonist dared to utter sometimes-uncomfortable truths about life and politics.

Joaquín Salvador Lavado Tejón, known since childhood as Quino, was born on July 17, 1932, in Guaymallén, Argentina, two years after the country's government had been overthrown in a military coup. At an early age, he had decided he wanted to draw for a living. In addition to cultivating his artistic skills, Quino became very political at a young age. Living under the yoke of a military dictatorship in Argentina gave him an early awareness of local politics as well as the turbulent situation in the rest of the world, where Italian fascism and German Nazism were both on the rise. Quino's political consciousness was further nourished by a highly politicized household; his parents were Spanish citizens, who believed in the Republican cause, and his grandmother was a communist. The mix inspired constant political debate.

In 1954 Quino moved to Buenos Aires, where he struggled to find work and pay the rent on a cramped studio apartment that he shared with four other people. One day he sold a set of cartoons to the weekly magazine *Esto Es* (This Is) and always recalled that as the single greatest day of his life.

On September 29, 1964 Quino published his first strip featuring Mafalda, who eventually brought him worldwide attention. Mafalda pondered the social and political bleakness of the world, especially the evils of fascism and oppression. She often critiqued society through playful symbolism—her pet turtle was named "Bureaucracy," and the bane of her existence was soup, which was a metaphor for the military dictatorships Argentineans were forced to swallow.

On June 25, 1973, Quino published an original Mafalda cartoon for the last time. The strip's popularity and merchandising potential was skyrocketing, but it was becoming increasingly risky to publish an overtly political cartoon during an era of political terror that left legions dead or missing. In 1976 a military coup led by Jorge Rafael Videla took power, and writers, artists, and anyone else who might be critical of the new regime found themselves in danger. Quino, fearful of persecution, fled to Italy, where he continued to draw darkly humorous cartoons.

New generations have been introduced to Mafalda through compilation books, and statues of the character were erected in Buenos Aires and Spain. In 2001, the first English-language Mafalda book was published.

Quino, who has won such major prizes as Spain's Príncipe de Asturias Prize and France's Legion of Honor, divided his time between Buenos Aires (after democracy returned to Argentina), Madrid, Milan, and Paris.

In his final years he suffered from glaucoma, and he died of a stroke on September 30, 2020. He was predeceased in 2017 by his wife of more than five decades, Alicia, a chemist. He is survived by a niece and five nephews.

See *Current Biography 2004*

James Randi

Born: Toronto, Canada; August 7, 1928
Died: Plantation, Florida; October 20, 2020
Occupation: Magician and scientific skeptic

Known professionally as the Amazing Randi, the magician James Randi spent much of his career investigating the claims of some of his colleagues, incisively debunking practices like spoon bending and mind reading and warning the credulous about faith healers and others he characterized as charlatans.

James Randi was born Randall James Hamilton Zwinge on August 7, 1928, in Toronto, Ontario, Canada, one of the three children of George Randall and Marie Alice (Paradis) Zwinge. His father was a telephone company executive and his mother a housewife. A child prodigy with an I.Q. of 168, he was too small for boyhood sports and was bored and disruptive in school.

At the age of twelve, after being mesmerized by a performance of the magician Harry Blackstone, Randi began to frequent Toronto's Arcade Novelty and Magic Shop. His knowledge of magic progressed to the point where he quickly recognized its use when at fifteen he visited a local spiritualist church whose pastor specialized in reading the contents of sealed envelopes. Rushing on stage, the incensed adolescent demonstrated how the trick worked and was arrested for disrupting a religious meeting.

After attending the Oakwood Collegiate Institute in Toronto from 1940 to 1945, Randi was offered college scholarships in chemistry, physics, and mathematics. Despite that, he abandoned his formal education just a few days short of his high school graduation to join a traveling carnival as a magician. Now billing himself as "the Amazing Randi," he worked up a nightclub act in Montreal. In the manner of Harry Houdini, his idol, he drummed up audiences by escaping from the local jail. His career moved forward full tilt in the 1950s after he appeared on American television, and by the mid-1960s, he had performed all over the world.

Randi's interest in exposing parapsychological fakery had its origins in a radio show on Manhattan's WOR that he hosted for two years beginning in 1964. Alarmed by the numbers who phoned in with reports of self-declared clairvoyants and faith healers and by the fact that the press was publishing such claims, Randi began speaking out against such fakery.

On the college and university circuit during the 1970s he discovered that his debunking of paranormal phenomena by duplicating "psychic" marvels like spoon-bending, telepathy, and clairvoyance was beginning to draw bigger audiences than his magic act.

The recipient of a 1986 MacArthur "genius" grant and the co-founder (along with such noted figures as Carl Sagan and Isaac Asimov) of the Committee for Skeptical Inquiry, Randi wrote numerous books, including, *Flim-Flam! The Truth About Unicorns, Parapsychology, and Other Delusions* (1980) and *An Encyclopedia of Claims, Frauds, and Hoaxes of the Occult and Supernatural* (1995).

Randi died on October 20, 2020, at his home in Florida. His death was announced by the James Randi Educational Foundation, a group that once offered a prize of $1 million to anyone who could scientifically demonstrate evidence of a paranormal or supernatural phenomenon. He is survived by his husband, the artist Deyvi Peña.

See *Current Biography 1987*

Helen Reddy

Born: Melbourne, Australia; October 25, 1941
Died: Los Angeles, California; September 29, 2020
Occupation: Singer

Helen Reddy is perhaps best remembered for her 1972 hit song, "I Am Woman," which became a feminist anthem and radio staple, propelling her to stardom in the process.

Helen Reddy was born in Melbourne, Australia, on October 25, 1941, (some sources give her date of birth as 1942) to Max Reddy, a producer, writer, and actor, and Stella (Lamond) Reddy, an actress who for many years played a leading character in one of Australia's most popular soap operas. At the age of four, Reddy made her stage debut at the Tivoli Theatre in Perth, as the youngest member of her family's vaudeville troupe. For the next decade she performed with her family in theaters throughout Australia and on the radio, and by the time she was fifteen she was an established professional.

In the late 1950s, Reddy became a regular on *In Melbourne Tonight*, a popular late-night variety and talk show. She also appeared in the long-running television series *Sunnyside Up*, and in 1960 she moved to Sydney as the star of her own weekly television show, *Helen Reddy Sings*. In 1966 she entered a talent contest and won a trip to New York City, an audition with Mercury Records, and $400 in cash. When she arrived in New York several months later, however, she was denied an audition by the recording company, which was not in the market for female vocalists. To remain in the country, she took whatever singing jobs she could get: in Irish bars in Greenwich Village; at weddings on Long Island; at private clubs in Connecticut; at resorts in the Catskills; and at a veterans' hospital in New Jersey.

Her recording career took off in 1971, when she released a hit cover of "I Don't Know How to Love Him" from the musical *Jesus Christ Superstar*. "I Am Woman" followed a year later.

"I Am Woman" reached number one on the Billboard chart, thanks in part to radio call-in requests, and earned her the Grammy Award for best female pop vocal performance. Later that decade "Delta Dawn" and "Angie Baby" went to number one, and three other singles—"You and Me Against the World," "Leave Me Alone (Ruby Red Dress)" and "Ain't No Way to Treat a Lady"—made the top 10.

Reddy made her big-screen debut in the 1974 comedy *Airport*, playing a guitar-playing nun, and in 1977 she had a starring role in the Disney movie *Pete's Dragon*. She also became a popular guest star on primetime television shows like *Love Boat* and *Fantasy Island*.

Reddy, who released music until the 1980s, died on September 29, 2020, in Los Angeles. She had lived with Addison's disease for decades and developed dementia during her last few years.

Reddy was married and divorced three times. Her survivors include her two children, Traci Wald Donat, a daughter from her first marriage; and Jordan Sommers, a son from her second marriage; and a grandchild. She is also survived by her half-sister, Toni Lamond, a singer and actress.

See *Current Biography 1975*

Sumner Redstone

Born: Boston, Massachusetts; May 27, 1923
Died: Los Angeles, California; August 11, 2020
Occupation: Media executive

Sumner Redstone ran his media empire, which encompassed CBS and Viacom, well into his 80s, making billions of dollars in the process.

Born Sumner Murray Rothstein on May 27, 1923 in Boston, he was the older of the two sons of Michael and Belle (Ostrovsky) Rothstein. (The family later changed the surname). Redstone was raised in the predominantly Jewish West End section of Boston. During the Depression, his father sold linoleum out of his truck and worked as a liquor wholesaler; in the 1940s he came to own two prominent Boston nightclubs.

Redstone attended the prestigious Boston Latin School, where he headed the debate team and won numerous academic prizes; he graduated at the top of his class in 1940, with the highest grade-point average in the school's history. At the age of seventeen, he entered Harvard, where he studied foreign languages, including Japanese, French, and German.

After graduating with a Bachelor of Arts degree in only two and a half years, he was selected to join an elite U S Army group of cryptographers who decoded Japanese military and diplomatic messages. After the war ended in 1945, he returned to Harvard to earn a law degree and used his GI Bill discount to purchase large quantities of surplus military merchandise, including office supplies and tools, which he sold for a hefty profit at local department stores.

Upon earning his LL.B. degree in 1947, Redstone began a clerkship with the United States Court of Appeals and worked as a law instructor at the University of San Francisco. He later entered private law practice.

In 1954 Redstone joined the family business, Redstone Management, which operated a dozen drive-in theaters. The name was later changed to National Amusements, which pioneered the idea of housing multiple small theaters in a single building: the now-common multiplex.

Redstone acquired Viacom and its cable channels in 1987 by using the thriving family movie-chain business as collateral. He expanded Viacom exponentially in 1994, when he gained control of Paramount. Then 70, he showed no sign of slowing down, and in 1999 he merged Viacom with CBS in a $37.3 billion deal.

By 2006 he had split CBS into a separate business, naming Leslie Moonves to lead that entity, and he stepped down as Viacom's chief executive, settling into semi-retirement. In 2016, Redstone—in failing health and engaged in bitter business disputes with his own children—stepped down for good, amidst the ascendancy of video streaming, which was decimating advertising revenues from traditional television and cable.

Redstone's personal life was as complex as his business dealings. In 1999 his wife of 52 years, Phyllis, filed for divorce, and he married 40-year-old Paula Fortunato in 2003. They divorced six years later. Subsequently, he had other relationships, some of which ended in contention and lawsuits.

Sumner Redstone died on August 11, 2020, at the age of 97. He was survived by his daughter, Shari, who had seized the reins of the company in 2016; his son, Brent, and five grandchildren.

See *Current Biography 1996*

Carolyn Reidy

Born: Washington, DC; May 2, 1949
Died: Southampton, New York; May 12, 2020
Occupation: Editor and publishing executive

As one of the few women ever to helm a major American publishing house, Carolyn Reidy led Simon & Schuster through numerous turbulent shifts, including an economic recession and a digital-book revolution.

One of four children of Henry August Kroll and Mildred Josephine Kroll, Reidy was born Carolyn Kroll in Washington, DC, on May 2, 1949. She attended Middlebury College, where she received a bachelor's degree in 1971. In 1974, she received her master's degree from Indiana University and completed her PhD from Indiana University in 1982.

Reidy began her career in publishing in 1975 at Random House in New York City, working in various capacities until 1983, when she left to join William Morrow & Co. as subsidiary-rights director. Two years later, however, she returned to Random House to become vice president and associate publisher of Vintage Books. In 1987, she made a move to Avon Books, a mass-marketing division of Hearst.

In 1992, she made yet another move, this one to Simon & Schuster, where she would become president and publisher of its trade division; in the new position Reidy supervised editorial operations, marketing, sales, and distribution. During her eight years in that role, the division led the way in the company's large-type publishing endeavors. By 2001, the trade division had more than doubled its sales volume and published 194 *New York Times* best-sellers and six Pulitzer Prize winners.

In 1999, Simon & Schuster announced its intention to allow customers to download chapters of books by such best-selling authors as Stephen King and Mary Higgins Clark. The company also began exploring the possibility of digitally distributing and promoting books. In 2001, Simon & Schuster made Reidy head of the newly created Adult Publishing Group, which combined the company's trade division with all domestic adult imprints to form a massive entity.

In January 2008, she rose to president and Chief Executive Officer (CEO) of the entire publishing giant, becoming the first woman to hold that position. As CEO, Reidy had charge over not only adult publishing but also the audiobook, children's publishing, digital, and international divisions. Months after she assumed the position, the global economic recession of the late 2000s struck. Around that time Reidy accurately assessed the emerging competitive challenge from e-books, aiding the company in embracing digital innovations and enhanced direct-to-consumer marketing, and helped navigate a period of slowing book sales overall.

Reidy was known for attending personally to many aspects of the business and for her connections with both employees and authors. She served on the boards of Literacy Partners, the Association of American Publishers (AAP), and the National Book Foundation (NBF), and her honors included being designated one of 50 Women to Watch by the *Wall Street Journal* in 2007, *Publishers Weekly*'s Person of the Year in 2017, and a PEN America Publisher Honoree in 2018.

Reidy, who died from a heart attack as she helped steer her company through the COVID-19 pandemic, is survived by her husband, Stephen; siblings; and a number of nieces and nephews.

See *Current Biography 2002*

Carl Reiner

Born: Bronx, New York; March 20, 1922
Died: Beverly Hills, California; June 29, 2020
Occupation: Writer; director; actor

Carl Reiner entertained audiences for almost seven decades, earning an exalted place in comedy history in the process.

Reiner was born on March 20, 1922 in the New York City borough of the Bronx, to Bessie (Mathias) and Irving Reiner, a watchmaker. After graduating high school at the age of 16, Reiner worked in a shop that made millinery equipment, concurrently attending drama school, and after eight months of study he joined a small theater group. During that period Reiner also acted in local summer-stock productions and at Catskill Mountains resorts.

With America's entrance into World War II, Reiner joined the Army, and when his acting ability was noticed by superiors, he was assigned to tour South Pacific bases in GI revues. Returning to civilian life in 1946, he haunted Broadway casting offices for comedy roles, successfully winning a handful.

Reiner first came to widespread public attention in 1950, when he was contracted to appear on NBC's popular *Your Show of Shows* alongside comedian Sid Caesar, with whom he subsequently enjoyed a long working relationship. While he was still working with Caesar, Reiner sat in on writers' conferences, and that experience, coupled with watching some poor television dramas, led the comedian to try his own hand at writing. In July 1959, he left for California to accept a long-term assignment, becoming a regular writer for Dinah Shore's eponymous show and acting in some of his own routines.

In the early 1960s Reiner and fellow comedian Mel Brooks began performing their "2,000 Year Old Man" sketch. In the bit, Brooks, adopting a broad Yiddish accent, played the oldest man alive, while Reiner, playing the straight man, interviewed him. The sketch, widely considered among the most influential in comedy history, ultimately spawned several albums.

In 1961, Reiner began producing the popular series *The Dick Van Dyke Show*, writing scripts and appearing in the role of Alan Brady, the self-centered head of a team of TV writers, who was loosely based on Caesar. It ran until 1966 and is said to have ushered in the golden age of the sitcom. During its run the show won more than a dozen Emmy Awards, several of which went to Reiner for his writing.

Reiner remained busy thereafter, writing, directing, and sometimes taking on character roles in a steady stream of films, including 1977's *Oh, God!*, which starred comedy legend George Burns, and several starring Steve Martin.

Even into the new millennium, Reiner, who won the Mark Twain Prize for American humor in 2000, remained a familiar face to audiences, guesting on such popular shows as *Frasier, Mad About You, Boston Legal, Two and a Half Men,* and *Parks and Recreation.* In his final years he maintained an active Twitter account, which he used for political commentary and issues of social justice.

Reiner's wife, Estelle, died in 2008. He is survived by his daughter, Annie, a psychoanalyst; his son, Lucas, an artist; his son, Rob, a well-known director and actor; and five grandchildren.

See *Current Biography 1961*

Diana Rigg

Born: Doncaster, Yorkshire; July 20, 1938
Died: London, England; September 10, 2020
Occupation: Actress

Diana Rigg was perhaps best-known to a previous generation as the stylish and sexy crime-fighter Emma Peel in the 1960s television hit *The Avengers* but in the years before her death she was introduced to a younger cadre of fans in the blockbuster series *Game of Thrones.*

Diana Rigg was born on July 20, 1938 in Doncaster, an industrial city in Yorkshire. She had a younger brother, Hugh. When she was two months old, her family moved to Jodhpur, in northwest India, where her father, a civil engineer, became manager of the state railroad. She lived there until the age of eight, when she was sent home to England to go to boarding school.

At seventeen she successfully auditioned for the Royal Academy of Dramatic Art (RADA) and made her professional debut in 1957 in *The Caucasian Chalk Circle.* Two years later she was accepted by the Royal Shakespeare Company in Stratford-on-Avon, and after a period as an understudy and bit player, she was deemed one of the company's most promising newcomers.

She never abandoned the theater, appearing on the stage well into her seventh decade in such works as *The Cherry Orchard* in 2008 and *Pygmalion* in 2011. Her many laurels included the Evening Standard Theater Award for her parts in *Medea, Who's Afraid of Virginia Woolf,* and *Mother Courage,* and *Medea* also brought her a 1994 Tony.

Despite the scope of her theater work, American audiences always identified her most closely with the character of Emma Peel. *The Avengers* premiered in the United States in March 1966 after first airing on British television, and the tongue-in-cheek espionage-adventure about a pair of undercover agents proved to have appeal on both sides of the Atlantic. (Some of that appeal was due to seeing Rigg's character cavort in tight leather outfits.) Rigg was nominated for Emmy awards as best actress in a dramatic series in 1967 and 1968. Emma Peel fan clubs were formed, and eventually the actress became known worldwide.

Never wanting to be typecast as Peel, Rigg took on a variety of big-screen roles throughout her career. Among her most popular was *On Her Majesty's Secret Service* (1969), in which she became the only love interest in a James Bond picture to marry the secret agent. (She was killed off in the final scene, so that future plot lines could still include "Bond girls.")

Her small-scale work involved serious roles in teleplays like *Hedda Gabler, King Lear,* and *Bleak House,* and from 1989 to 2003 she hosted the PBS series *Mystery!* It was her turn as the sharp-tongued Lady Olenna Tyrell on HBO's juggernaut costume drama *Game of Thrones* from 2013 to 2016 that won her an entirely new set of fans late in life.

She was made a Commander of the Order of the British Empire in 1988 and a Dame Commander in 1994. She was divorced twice. Diana Rigg died on September 10, 2020, of cancer and was survived by a daughter, Rachel, from her second marriage, and a grandson.

See *Current Biography 1974*

Susan Rothenberg

Born: Buffalo, New York; January 20, 1945
Died: Galisteo, New Mexico; May 18, 2020
Occupation: Artist

Painter and printmaker Susan Rothenberg was widely considered one of the most talented and original artists of her generation.

She was born on January 20, 1945, in Buffalo, New York, where she was raised by parents who strongly supported her early interest in painting and drawing. She took art classes in high school, then studied sculpture at Cornell until, after two years, the department head deemed her untalented. She was devastated by the criticism. A five-month interval in Greece followed, after which Rothenberg returned to Cornell and concentrated on painting. After graduating in 1967, she entered a somewhat aimless period. She began a master's degree at the Corcoran School of Art in Washington, DC, but soon left the program. On her own she did some painting, but spent much of her time in a jazz bar. By the fall of 1969, she found herself back in Buffalo. From there she boarded a train to Nova Scotia, planning to find a teaching post. But at Montreal she impulsively boarded a train to New York City, where her artistic career was to begin.

In New York, Rothenberg settled in a downtown studio and became part of a community of interdisciplinary artists that included painters, musicians, composers, and dancers. Her art during that period ranged from punching holes in plastic to geometric pattern painting. Minimalism was still the dominant mode, but Rothenberg found it uncongenial and tedious. By 1973, four years after her arrival in the city, she grew bored with the geometric pattern painting she had been doing. The only good thing about her pattern paintings, she decided, was the simple pencil line she drew down the middle. Drawing a horse one day, she bisected it with a thick line.

Over the next six years Rothenberg completed a series of about forty horse paintings, and her first exhibited work, "Triphammer Bridge" (1974), depicted the attenuated silhouette of a stationary black horse, poised on a rich brown background, bisected by a vertical line. Critics were startled and beguiled by Rothenberg's stark, formalist treatment of such a conventional and culturally resonant image. Within a year of that show, she was being represented by the prestigious Willard Gallery, and the Museum of Modern Art (MoMA) purchased a painting for its collection.

In the 1980s, she abandoned the horse motif in favor of human anatomy, boats, bones, birds, and goats, still using the heavy, raw brushwork that had gained her attention. In addition to MoMA, her paintings are included in museum collections around the globe, and major retrospectives have been held at the Albright-Knox Art Gallery in Buffalo and the Modern Art Museum of Fort Worth.

Rothenberg's marriage to sculptor George Trakas ended in divorce in 1979. She is survived by their daughter, Maggie, and by her second husband, fellow artist Bruce Nauman, with whom she moved to New Mexico in the late 1980s.

See *Current Biography 1985*

Murray Schisgal

Born: Brooklyn, New York; November 25, 1926
Died: Port Chester, New York; October 1, 2020
Occupation: Playwright

"Murray Schisgal . . . has not only made his vision—that of Everyman wrapped in a cloak of borrowed pain—coherent, he has made it hilarious," Walter Kerr wrote when Schisgal's highly successful farce *Luv* opened on Broadway in November 1964. The avant-garde playwright's dramas were compared to those of Ionesco and Beckett, but his work most familiar to the general public was the gender-bending hit film *Tootsie* (1982).

Murray Joseph Schisgal was born on November 25, 1926, and raised (along with his sister, Diane) in Brooklyn, New York, to Abraham and Irene (Sperling) Schisgal. His father, an immigrant from Vilnius, Lithuania, was a tailor and a steam presser in a clothing factory. At age seventeenth Schisgal quit high school to join the navy. During World War II he served in the Atlantic and the Pacific theatres, and he was discharged in 1946 with the rank of radioman third class.

Back in civilian life, Schisgal wrote fiction while supporting himself by a long and varied succession of odd jobs, including pinsetter in a bowling alley, hand trucker in the garment district, dress racker in Klein's Department Store, and saxophonist-clarinetist in a small wedding band. In the meantime, he went to school at night, earned his high school diploma, took classes at Long Island University, and studied law at Brooklyn Law School.

After receiving his LL.B. degree, in 1953, Schisgal went into law practice but found that the profession took too much time and attention away from his writing; he quit after two years and began teaching in New York City's public-school system.

By 1959 Schisgal had written sixty short stories and three novels, none of which had been published. Frustrated, he decided to try another literary form, and chose drama. He had his first major success with *The Typists* and *The Tiger*, a double bill of plays that appeared Off-Broadway in 1963 and won Schisgal the Vernon Rice Award for outstanding achievement and the Outer Critics Circle (OCC) award for best new playwright.

His first Broadway success came in 1964 with *Luv*, a three-character tour de force about love and marriage that ran for 902 performances, won three Tony Awards, and earned Schisgal nominations for best play and best author.

Outside of theater circles, Schisgal was best known for his part in writing the movie *Tootsie*, which starred Dustin Hoffman as a struggling actor who gets a role by auditioning as a woman. Hoffman and Schisgal had met while working in regional theater in the mid-1960s, and the two had a solid professional relationship, as well as a friendship. That, however, did not stop studio executives from replacing Schisgal midway through the project, asserting that they wanted a different comedic voice.

Schisgal died on October 1, 2020, at the age of 93. He was predeceased by his wife in 2017 and is survived by a son, Zach; a daughter, Jane; his sister, Diane Troy; and four grandchildren.

See *Current Biography 1968*

Joel Schumacher

Born: New York, New York; August 29, 1939
Died: New York, New York; June 22, 2020
Occupation: Filmmaker

"I'm a pop-culture sponge," Joel Schumacher told an interviewer in 1993. Indeed, several of his films, which included *Flatliners* (1990), the blockbuster *Batman Forever* (1995), *Batman and Robin* (1997), *Phone Booth* (2002), and *Trespass* (2011), were noted for being, as one writer put it, "more flashy than substantive." Schumacher was typically nonplussed by such implicit criticism of his work. "If you ask people to leave their homes, spend a lot of money on a movie, buy that terrible popcorn, and those diluted sodas, you'd better tell them a story and entertain them," he told Bernard Weinraub of the *New York Times* (June 11, 1995). "There's absolutely nothing wrong with that."

Schumacher was born on August 29, 1939, in Long Island City, a blue-collar neighborhood in Queens. After his father, Francis, died, when Joel was four years old, he was raised by his mother, Marian, who worked in a dress store.

Schumacher worked odd jobs until he was 15, when he lied about his age to get a steady position working on window designs at Macy's department store. In the late 1950s, he moved to Miami, where he developed a drug habit. He ultimately returned to New York City and enrolled at the Parsons School of Design, and after graduating, with honors, in 1965, he became a fashion designer.

Devastated by his mother's death, however, he became even more dependent on drugs, and eventually he could no longer function at work. In 1970, Schumacher summoned the courage to quit cold turkey and returned to designing department store windows. Some of those windows caught the eye of television producers, leading him to costume design jobs in Hollywood. During his spare time, he began to write scripts, including those for *Car Wash* (1976), *Sparkle* (1976), and *The Wiz* (1978).

He parlayed that experience into a motion-picture directorial debut with *The Incredible Shrinking Woman* (1981), which starred Lily Tomlin. His next big break came with *St. Elmo's Fire* (1985), which received a lot of media attention because it featured seven of Hollywood's hottest young stars, collectively known as the "brat pack."

He soon developed a reputation for directing slick, entertaining, and "commercial" films featuring young, good-looking actors, and his career took another turn when he was hired by Warner Bros. to helm the "Batman" series, following the departure of Tim Burton.

While his heyday was considered the 1980s and 1990s, Schumacher continued to work well into the new millennium, directing such features as *Tigerland* (2000), the comedic thriller *Bad Company* (2002), and the Cate Blanchett–led drama *Veronica Guerin* (2003). Further proving his versatility, he took on directing and co-writing the 2004 film *The Phantom of the Opera*, returned to the thriller genre with 2007's *The Number 23*, directed the horror film *Blood Creek* (2009), and branched into television to direct part of the 2013 season of the Netflix series *House of Cards* and executive produce the 2015 documentary series *Do Not Disturb: Hotel Horrors*.

Joel Schumacher died following a long battle with cancer.

See *Current Biography 1997*

Gil Schwartz

Born: New York, New York; May 20, 1951
Died: Santa Monica, California; May 2, 2020
Occupation: Humorist and television executive

While working by day as the CBS network's long-time chief communications officer, Gil Schwartz was concurrently, under the pen name Stanley Bing, lambasting corporate culture in columns for *Esquire* and *Fortune*.

Schwartz attended Brandeis University, earning a BA degree in theater arts and English. Following graduation, he worked as a humor writer for the *Boston Phoenix* and as a theater-company manager, among other jobs. At age 28 Schwartz moved to New York, with the ambition of acting. He had some luck finding parts, usually as henchmen or criminals, and he next turned to writing plays, two of which were mounted Off-Broadway.

In 1981, to support his writing, Schwartz found work in the public-relations department of the TelePrompter Corp., then among the largest cable-systems operators in the United States. His responsibilities included speechwriting. Through a series of corporate acquisitions and promotions, he became director of communications for Group W Cable in 1984, and when Group W merged with CBS, in 1996, Schwartz was made CBS Television's senior vice president for communications.

In February 1985, *Esquire* had published the first of Stanley Bing's (really Schwartz's) essays on corporate strategies for men in their 30s, "How to Draw the Line." "Bing's" first book, *Biz Words: Power Talk for Fun and Profit* (1989), was an amalgam of humor and advice for those aspiring to climb the corporate ladder, and he later wrote several more tongue-in-cheek advice books (like 2000's *What Would Machiavelli Do? The Ends Justify the Meanness*, and novels, such as 2003's *You Look Nice Today*, which involves a sexual harassment lawsuit.) His last column for *Esquire* appeared in that magazine's July 1995 issue; his first for *Fortune* was published in its August 7, 1995 edition. Five months later Bing's identity was revealed in the *New York Times*. Network officials did not seem to care, asserting that CBS had a sense of humor about itself.

In 2004, Schwartz was named executive vice president of the newly created CBS Communications Group, responsible for public relations, media relations, and corporate and internal communications for all the divisions directed by

Leslie Moonves, the president and Chief Executive Officer (CEO) of the CBS Corp.

Schwartz was sorely tested in 2018, when accusations of sexual misconduct against Moonves emerged. At Schwartz's urging, Moonves finally stepped down, in September 2018, and Schwartz announced his retirement later that month, hoping to continue writing in a less-stressful milieu.

Schwartz died of cardiac arrest and is survived by his wife, Laura Svienty; daughter, Nina Pajak; son, Will; stepdaughter, Rachel Bender; stepson, Kyle Bender; and two grandchildren. He is also survived by his brother, Michael, a law professor.

See *Current Biography 2007*

Brent Scowcroft

Born: Ogden, Utah; March 19, 1925
Died: Falls Church, Virginia; August 6, 2020
Occupation: Business executive; policy consultant

Brent Scowcroft had a hand in shaping American policy for decades as an adviser to several presidential administrations.

Brent Scowcroft was born in Ogden, Utah, on March 19, 1925. He obtained his elementary and secondary education in the local public schools, then enrolled in the United States Military Academy at West Point. After receiving his B.S. degree from the academy in 1947, he was commissioned as a second lieutenant in the U S Air Force. He earned his fighter pilot wings the following year. Several months later, Scowcroft, who had hoped to become a career military pilot, was seriously injured when his disabled plane crashed.

Between 1948 and 1953 Scowcroft held a succession of operational and administrative Air Force staff positions. At some point during this period, he resumed his education as a graduate student in international relations at Columbia University. Upon receiving his M.A. in 1953, he taught Russian history for four years at West Point. After studying Slavic languages at Georgetown University, he employed that knowledge as an assistant air attaché at the American Embassy in Belgrade for two years.

Returning to the United States, he taught political science at the Air Force Academy in Colorado until 1963 and then joined the Air Force planning division in Washington. Concurrently, he studied for a doctoral degree in international relations at Columbia University, which he earned in 1967. He then took on a variety of Pentagon posts, including military aide to President Richard Nixon, whom he accompanied on

an historic trip to China to establish diplomatic relations.

In 1973 he became a deputy to Henry A. Kissinger, then head of national security, and after Nixon left office, President Gerald Ford tapped Scowcroft to succeed Kissinger as the national security adviser.

Scowcroft, a moderate Republican, left the White House in 1977, when Jimmy Carter was elected, but after Ronald Reagan took office, Scowcroft was appointed to a commission to investigate the so-called Iran-Contra scandal, which involved the covert sale of weapons to Iran and the secret diversion of some of the profits from that sale to the Nicaraguan rebels, or Contras. (The commission ultimately found no evidence that Reagan had known of the sales.)

Under President George H.W. Bush, Scowcroft was once again named national security adviser, and in that post he helped develop cautious policies regarding US involvement in post-communist Russia. He was also instrumental in planning Operation Desert Storm, the 1991 mobilization of an international coalition to oust dictator Saddam Hussein from Kuwait.

Scowcroft, who holds the Presidential Medal of Freedom, the nation's highest civilian honor, left formal government service in 1993 and launched the Washington-based Scowcroft Group, a consulting firm.

Brent Scowcroft died on August 6, 2020 at the age of 95. He was predeceased by his wife of more than four decades, Marian, and survived by their daughter, Karen, as well as by a granddaughter.

See *Current Biography 1987*

Tom Seaver

Born: Fresno, California; November 17, 1944
Died: Calistoga, California; August 31, 2020
Occupation: Baseball player

Tom Seaver is considered one of pro baseball's greatest right-handed pitchers. Although he played in the latter part of his career for the Cincinnati Reds, the Chicago White Sox, and the Boston Red Sox, he is most celebrated by baseball historians for his time as a young player with the "Miracle Mets."

The youngest of four children in a sports-oriented family, Tom Seaver was born in Fresno, California, on November 17, 1944. He began playing Little League baseball when he was nine, and in his senior year at Fresno High School he made the varsity team as a pitcher, although he did not attract any professional offers at that time.

After a six-month tour of duty with the Marines, Seaver entered Fresno City College, and in 1964 he transferred to the University of Southern California at Los Angeles on a baseball scholarship. His pitching attracted the notice of scouts for the Los Angeles Dodgers, who selected him in the free agent draft in June 1965 but never came through with a contract.

The Atlanta Braves signed Seaver to a contract carrying a reported $40,000 bonus in February 1966, but the Commissioner of Baseball nullified the deal, on the grounds that the Braves had violated the so-called college rule (which prohibits the professional drafting of a college player while the college season is in progress). At the same time the National Collegiate Athletic Association (NCAA) stripped Seaver of his amateur eligibility. When the latter fact was brought to William Eckert's attention, the Commissioner declared Seaver eligible for draft by any team other than the Braves willing to match the Braves' bonus offer. The Philadelphia Phillies, the New York Mets, and the Cleveland Indians asked for Seaver, and the Mets's name was drawn in a lottery held in the Commissioner's office on April 3, 1966.

The Mets, established five years before he arrived, had never finished higher than ninth in the ten-team National League. He was named the league's rookie of the year in 1967, and in 1969 he was instrumental in earning the team the name "Miracle Mets." That season, the seemingly hapless team rocketed from ten games behind in mid-August to capture the National League's East Division crown. The Mets then swept the Atlanta Braves in the National League Championship Series and ultimately defeated the Baltimore Orioles, winners of 109 regular-season games, for the World Series title.

With the advent of the free-agency system in the mid-1970s, Seaver engaged in bitter salary negotiations with the Mets that ended with him being traded to Cincinnati. He spent his final season with the Sox in Boston, and after retiring, in 1986, he worked as a sports announcer and later opened an eponymous vineyard.

The Mets retired Seaver's number, 41, in 1988, and in 1992 he was elected to the Hall of Fame. Tom Seaver died on August 31, 2020, due to the complications of Lewy body dementia and Covid-19. He is survived by his wife, Nancy; daughters Sarah and Anne; and four grandsons.

See Current Biography 1970

William Steele Sessions

Born: Fort Smith, Arkansas; May 27, 1930
Died: San Antonio, Texas; June 12, 2020
Occupation: FBI director

The director of the Federal Bureau of Investigation (FBI) from 1987 to 1993, William S. Sessions was an experienced jurist who had established a reputation for being tough but fair. Although he was credited with making positive changes at the bureau, he was also accused of ethical violations and held responsible for the FBI's handling of fatal standoffs at Ruby Ridge, Idaho, and near Waco, Texas. Fired by Bill Clinton, Sessions became the first director in the bureau's history to be dismissed before completing a ten-year term.

Sessions was born on May 27, 1930 in Fort Smith, Arkansas, a former United States Army post, to Will Anderson Sessions Jr. and his wife, the former Edith Steele. The father, a minister in the Disciples of Christ denomination, wrote the handbook used by the Boy Scouts of America for their "God and Country" Award. After Sessions graduated from high school in 1948, he entered college, but in 1951, during the Korean War, he interrupted his education to join the US Air Force. He served as an airborne radar intercept instructor and rose to the rank of captain before receiving his discharge in 1955. Thanks to the GI Bill, Sessions earned a BA degree from Baylor University in 1956. He then graduated from Baylor's Law School in 1958, whereupon he entered private practice.

In 1968, Sessions won election to a term on the Waco City Council, and the following year he was appointed chief of the government operations section of the United States Department of Justice. In 1971, he was appointed the United States attorney for the western district of Texas—a vast jurisdiction covering the geographic triangle anchored by Austin, El Paso, and San Antonio and including 650 miles on the Texas–Mexico border, Three years later he was named United States district judge, and in early 1980, he assumed the responsibilities of chief judge for the district. In those capacities his stiff courtroom demeanor and rigid sense of propriety became almost legendary.

In 1987, President Ronald Reagan nominated Sessions as the new director of the FBI. Sessions was confirmed by the Senate, 90-0, to oversee 10,000 agents and 56 field offices. Although he was expected to complete a ten-year term—and despite his successes in making the bureau more diverse—his tenure was marred by publicly botched deadly sieges with extremists at Ruby Ridge, Idaho, and Waco, Texas, as well as by accusations of ethical lapses, and he was relieved of his post.

In subsequent years, Sessions served on Texas commissions on crime, judicial efficiency, and homeland security, and in 2000, he became a partner in the firm Holland & Knight, where he took on pro bono death row and human rights cases.

Sessions, who retired in 2016, was predeceased by his wife, the former Alice June Lewis. He is survived by their daughter, Sara; three sons, William (who goes by his middle name, Lewis), Mark, and Pete (a former congressman); and numerous grandchildren and great-grandchildren.

See *Current Biography 1988*

Gail Sheehy

Born: Mamaroneck, New York; November 27, 1936
Died: Southampton, New York; August 24, 2020
Occupation: Journalist

Throughout her career, Gail Sheehy examined the lives of presidential candidates, world leaders, Cambodian refugees, and middle-class Americans for clues to their successful navigation of life's challenges. The author of numerous books, she is best known for helping to popularize the concept of the midlife crisis, the parameters of which she delineated in her 1976 bestseller *Passages*.

Gail Henion Sheehy was born on November 27, 1936 in Mamaroneck, New York, to Harold Merritt Henion, an advertising executive, and Lillian Rainey (Paquin) Henion, who had been a beauty consultant before becoming a full-time homemaker when Gail was born. (Gail's sister, Patricia, was born nine years later.)

In 1958 Sheehy graduated from the University of Vermont in Burlington with a bachelor's degree in home economics, which she felt was the closest thing to business school open to her as a woman. After graduating, she took on a series of jobs as a department-store fashion consultant, fashion editor for the *Rochester Democrat and Chronicle*, and feature writer for the *New York Herald Tribune*, then a hub of New Journalism, which called upon the tools of fiction (such as long passages of dialogue and scene-setting) to create evocative stories. Among her well-received work was an exclusive interview with Robert Kennedy right before his assassination and an exposé about public maternity clinics. In 1968, when *New York* magazine was founded, she joined its staff.

Sheehy's books included *Speed Is of the Essence* (1971), a look at counter-cultural lifestyles; *Hustling: Prostitution in Our Wide Open Society* (1973), which was later the basis for a film; *Spirit of Survival* (1986), an account of the life of her adopted Cambodian daughter, who had survived the brutal Pol Pot regime; *The Man Who Changed the World* (1990), about Soviet leader Mikhail S. Gorbachev; *Hillary's Choice* (1999), an examination of the Clinton marriage; and *Middletown, America: One Town's Passage from Trauma to Hope* (2003), about a New Jersey town in the aftermath of 9/11.

She was most widely recognized, however, for *Passages*, subtitled *Predictable Crises of Adult Life*, which propelled her to the forefront of the legion of popular psychology and self-help gurus who emerged during the "me" decade of the 1970s. The book, which sold 10 million copies, spawned several subsequent volumes, including *The Silent Passage* (1992), about menopause; *New Passages: Mapping Your Life Across Time* (1995), about life after 50; *Understanding Men's Passages* (1998); *Passages in Caregiving: Turning Chaos into Confidence* (2010), about coping with an aging loved one. She titled her 2014 memoir *Daring: My Passages*.

Gail Sheehy died from the complications of pneumonia on August 24, 2020 at the home of her companion, Robert Emmett Ginna Jr., a co-founder of *People* magazine. He survives her, as do her daughters—Maura (from her first marriage, which ended in divorce) and Mohm (adopted from Cambodia)—and three grandchildren. She was predeceased in 2008 by her second husband, Clay Felker, the founding editor of *New York* magazine.

See *Current Biography 1993*

Don Shula

Born: Grand River, Ohio; January 4, 1930
Died: Indian Creek, Florida; May 4, 2020
Occupation: Football coach

As the winningest coach in the National Football League (NFL), Don Shula helped shape pro football for a new generation.

Donald Francis Shula, the third of six children of Dan and Mary (Miller) Shula, was born on January 4, 1930, in Grand River, Ohio. His father, a Hungarian immigrant, worked as a nurseryman until the birth of triplets doubled his family, forcing him to take a better job with a Lake Erie fishery. An athletic youngster, Shula began organizing football games while a student at St. Mary's elementary school.

Shula attended John Carroll University, a Jesuit school in Cleveland, where he majored in sociology and racked up an impressive record on the varsity football team. He graduated from college in 1951 with a BS degree and received an MA in physical education from Western Reserve University in 1953.

A ninth-round college draft choice of the Cleveland Browns, he was traded after two seasons to the Baltimore Colts but was released from that team before the beginning of the 1957 season. After a short and disappointing stint with the Washington Redskins, he returned to Ohio to look for a coaching job. In 1960, he joined the Detroit Lions as a defensive backfield coach, and three years later, he was made head coach of the Baltimore Colts. In seven seasons with the Colts, Shula compiled a 71–23–4 record for a remarkable .755 percentage. In Super Bowl III, however, in what has been described as one of the biggest upsets in professional sports, the heavily favored Colts lost to the New York Jets (then part of the American Football League), saddling Shula with a reputation as a coach whose team could not compete on the main stage.

After that ignominious defeat, he eagerly accepted an offer to try to turn around the struggling Miami Dolphins—a task he accomplished brilliantly: Coaching the Dolphins from 1970 to 1995, he took the team to two Super Bowl victories, crowning the 1972 and 1973 seasons.

Fans still discuss the 1972 campaign, during which the Dolphins won all 14 regular-season games and three playoff games, capturing Super Bowl VII and recording a still-unmatched string of victories.

During his 33-year pro coaching career, Shula's teams won 328 regular-season games—still an NFL record. He also holds the records for games coached (526) and total victories (347). He was inducted into the Pro Football Hall of Fame in 1997. An expressway in Miami is named in his honor, as is the stadium at his alma mater.

After retiring from football, Shula played golf, made speaking appearances, and lent his name to a chain of steakhouses.

He was predeceased by his first wife, Dorothy, in 1991 after 32 years of marriage. He is survived by his second wife, Mary Anne; his five children (David Donald, Donna Dorothy, Sharon Lee, Anne Marie, and Michael John); three stepchildren (John Smith, Jimmy Stephens, and Carrie LaNoce); and numerous grandchildren and great-grandchildren. Two of his sons, David and Michael, are football coaches.

See *Current Biography 1974*

Abigail M. Thernstrom

Born: New York, New York; September 14, 1936
Died: Arlington, Virginia; April 10, 2020
Occupation: Social critic and writer

In her body of work, the conservative scholar and social critic Abigail M. Thernstrom underscored the need for racial equality in the United States, at the same time attacking as misguided the various government-sponsored programs aimed at achieving it.

She was born Abigail Mann on September 14, 1936, in New York City to Jewish parents. She grew up on Finney Farm, a commune in Croton-on-Hudson. Her parents, while not members of the Communist Party, shared its beliefs and surrounded themselves with like-minded people. Thernstrom's father, she said in numerous interviews, was a failed businessman. When Thernstrom was a year old, her mother was diagnosed with breast cancer; she died when her daughter was a teenager. Though Thernstrom received her education at communist-leaning schools, she resented her parents' willingness to overlook the Soviet Union's atrocities. She accepted one of their beliefs, however: the equality of all people, regardless of race.

Thernstrom enrolled at a succession of colleges, attending Reed College for a few months, then New York University, before settling on Barnard College. She graduated in 1958 with a bachelor's degree in European history and moved that year to Cambridge, Massachusetts, where she began graduate work in Harvard University's Middle Eastern studies program. After a hiatus to raise her children, she received her PhD from Harvard's Department of Government, in 1975 and was offered a teaching position in the school's social-studies program, where she remained for three years. (She lectured at Harvard again from 1988 to 1989 and also taught at Boston College and Boston University.)

In 1981, Thernstrom received a grant from the Twentieth Century Fund, a New York City–based nonprofit public-policy research institution, to write a book about voting and race in America. In 1987, she published *Whose Votes Count? Affirmative Action and Minority Rights*, in which she set out her arguments against affirmative action and gerrymandering to create minority districts, which she viewed as marginalizing and stigmatizing. If such policies had ever served as a means of reducing disparities, they were no longer necessary, she asserted. Her second book, *America in Black and White: One Nation Indivisible* (1997), amplified those themes. Her overarching point was that fully colorblind policies worked better to ensure equality than preferential treatment, and those views endeared her to neoconservatives. In 2001, President George W. Bush appointed her to the United States Commission on Civil Rights. (She was vice-chair from 2010 to 2012.)

Thernstrom was also the co-author of *No Excuses: Closing the Racial Gap in Learning* (2003), in which she argued for charter schools and vouchers, and she was a member of the Massachusetts State Board of Education for more than a decade.

Thernstrom—whose other posts included senior fellow at the Manhattan Institute in New York and adjunct scholar at the American Enterprise Institute in Washington—often collaborated and co-wrote with her husband, the noted conservative scholar Stephan Thernstrom. He survives her, along with their daughter, Melanie, an author; their son, Samuel, the founder of a nonprofit alternative energy organization; and four grandchildren.

See *Current Biography 2010*

James R. Thompson

Born: Chicago, Illinois; May 8, 1936
Died: Chicago, Illinois; August 14, 2020
Occupation: Politician

James R. Thompson, who was often known as Big Jim, was the longest-serving governor in Illinois history.

James Thompson was born in Chicago on May 8, 1936. His father was a pathologist. Growing up in middle-class Garfield Park on the city's west side, Thompson became interested in politics early on, and at eleven he announced for the first time his intention to become President of the United States. In high school he pinned down the year, writing in his yearbook: "1984–1992, President of the US"

Thompson earned a law degree from Northwestern University in 1959. He served for the next five years as an assistant on the prosecutorial staff of the state attorney for Cook County. In 1970 he became first assistant to the United States Attorney for the Northern District of Illinois.

Appointed United States Attorney for the Illinois Northern District in November 1971, Thompson soon tripled its small prosecutorial staff, long accustomed to handling merely routine legal matters, and turned it into a virtual juggernaut aimed at crooked politicians and police. Of over 300 indictments, Thompson obtained convictions in 90 percent of the cases. He successfully prosecuted hundreds of public employees on charges of corruption, including Mayor Richard J. Daley's press secretary, several Chicago aldermen and state legislators, nineteen employees of the Cook County assessor's office, and over fifty policemen. Thompson's prosecution of one Chicago officer accused of gratuitous brutality against a black youth resulted in the first civil rights conviction against a policeman in the city's history. By far the biggest fish caught in Thompson's net was former Governor Otto Kerner, who, at the time of his 1973 conviction on seventeen counts of income tax evasion,

fraud, perjury, bribery, and conspiracy, had been serving on the United States Circuit Court of Appeals for the seventh district.

In 1975 Thompson left his post as United States attorney and entered private practice. Still, his reputation as a relentless and incorruptible government prosecutor kept him in the public eye, giving him an image of "Mr. Clean" in his home state, at a time when Republicans in Washington were sinking in the mire of Watergate. To a party sorely in need of candidates untainted by scandal, he seemed the perfect candidate for governor in 1976, and he won in a landslide.

A moderate Republican, he remained in office until 1991, beloved by his constituents for his good nature and obvious love for meeting them.

Among his signature accomplishments was "Build Illinois," a $2.3 billion project to rebuild the state's infrastructure. He also created the Illinois Historic Preservation Agency and is widely credited with helping to keep the White Sox in Chicago by arranging for a new stadium.

After Thompson left the governor's office, he returned to private law practice. James Thompson died on August 14, 2020, while recuperating from a long illness. He is survived by his wife, Jayne; his daughter, Samantha; and a granddaughter.

See *Current Biography 1979*

John Thompson

Born: Washington, DC; September 2, 1941
Died: Arlington, Virginia; August 30, 2020
Occupation: Basketball coach

Georgetown University's John Thompson Jr. was the first African American coach to take a team to the National Collegiate Athletic Association (NCAA) basketball championship.

The youngest of four children, Thompson was born on September 2, 1941 in Washington, DC, and was raised in housing projects in the predominantly black Anacostia section of the city. Although illiterate, Thompson's father was a hardworking man who supported his family as a mechanic and laborer. His mother, Anna, had studied to be a teacher but was unable to get a job and instead worked as a maid for five dollars a day.

Devout Roman Catholics, Thompson's parents sent their son to a parochial school, where he was branded a slow learner until it was discovered that it was his poor eyesight, undiagnosed for several years, that made it difficult for him. By the age of thirteen, he had developed into a good student and talented athlete. Recruited by basketball coaches from several local parochial high schools, he decided to attend Archbishop Carroll High, where an alumnus secretly paid his tuition.

Thompson, who had reached his adult height of six feet, ten inches, by his sophomore year, played center on the Archbishop Carroll basketball team, earning high-school all-American honors and leading the team to 55 consecutive victories. Although Washington's Catholic schools had been desegregated by that time, many local summer basketball leagues, to Thompson's dismay, continued to exclude blacks.

As a freshman at Providence College in Rhode Island, Thompson averaged over 32 points per game. He was ballyhooed in the press as "the next Bill Russell," after the great Boston Celtics center, led his school to the National Invitation Tournament (NIT) championship his junior year, and as a senior was named New England College Player of the Year.

After graduating from Providence with a degree in economics, Thompson was selected in the third round of the 1964 National Basketball Association (NBA) draft by the Celtics, but he retired from the NBA after two seasons to become a high school guidance counselor and coach. In 1972 he accepted the position of head basketball coach at Georgetown University, where school officials were trying to reverse the fortunes of the Hoyas, a team that had lost 23 out of 26 games the previous season.

Turning things around, he led the Hoyas to the 1984 NCAA championship, and during his tenure at the school, which lasted until 1999, his teams won 596 games and captured seven Big East titles.

After leaving Georgetown, Thompson coached the US Olympic team to a bronze medal in 1988. He was inducted into the Naismith Memorial Basketball Hall of Fame in late 1999 and worked as a television and radio commentator. In 2000 he started an eponymous foundation that supports children's causes.

Thompson experienced multiple health problems and died on August 30, 2020. John Thompson is survived by his son John, who also coached at Georgetown; another son, Ronny, a former assistant at Georgetown and head coach at Ball State University; and a daughter, Tiffany.

See *Current Biography 1989*

John Turner

Born: Richmond, England; June 7, 1929
Died: Toronto, Canada; September 18, 2020
Occupation: Prime Minister of Canada

Although Canadian politician John Turner served only briefly as prime minister, over the course of his career, he was responsible for sweeping reforms in his country's laws.

John Napier Wyndham Turner was born on June 7, 1929, in Richmond, Surrey, England, to Leonard and Phyllis (Gregory) Turner. His father, a British journalist, died in 1931. His mother, a native of British Columbia, returned to Canada with John and his younger sister, Brenda, in 1932. Although Turner spent his early years in modest circumstances, his mother managed to send him to prestigious private schools, and at sixteen he entered the University of British Columbia, where he studied political science and ran sprints for the track team. Only the physical aftermath of a car accident kept him off the Canadian Olympic team in 1948.

Educated at Oxford University on a Rhodes Scholarship, he was admitted to the Quebec bar in 1954 and joined a Montreal law firm. Turning his attention toward politics, in 1962 he successfully ran for the Canadian House of Commons as a member of the Liberal Party.

In 1965, Prime Minister Lester B. Pearson appointed Turner minister without portfolio, and two years later he became Canada's first minister of consumer and corporate affairs. When Pearson announced his resignation, Turner declared his candidacy for his party's leadership, but he finished third, and Pierre Trudeau was chosen as the new Liberal chief. When Trudeau became prime minister in 1968, he appointed Turner justice minister, and in that capacity, he oversaw sweeping changes that legalized homosexuality and abortion, among other measures. Later, as finance minister, he helped steer the country through a period of high inflation and high unemployment.

In 1975 Turner left government service to practice law, but he returned in 1984 to enter the race to replace Trudeau, who was thinking of stepping down. At the Liberal party's convention in mid-June, Turner scored an easy victory, winning 1,862 votes to his opponent's 1,368. In late June, Trudeau submitted his resignation to Governor General Jeanne Sauvé, who promptly invited Turner to form a new government.

On September 4, 1984, however, the Liberal party suffered its worst defeat in Canada's history, and Turner, who was widely blamed for his less-than-inspired campaign, relinquished the prime ministership on September 17, when Brian Mulroney was sworn in to head the new

Progressive Conservative government. Turner's 79-day tenure as prime minister was the second shortest of any of his predecessors.

After his defeat in 1984, Turner, as the opposition leader, mounted a crusade against Mulroney's embrace of a free trade agreement with the United States, asserting that the lopsided deal would turn Canada into a virtual American colony. Despite his efforts, when he again faced Mulroney in 1988, he lost.

Turner died on September 18, 2020, in Toronto and is survived by his wife of several decades, Geills McCrae Kilgour; a daughter, Elizabeth Turner; three sons, Michael, David and Andrew; and his sister.

See *Current Biography 1984*

Eddie Van Halen

Born: Nijmegen, Netherlands; January 26, 1955
Died: Santa Monica, California; October 6, 2020
Occupation: Musician

Eddie Van Halen was considered one of the most influential and proficient guitarists in rock history.

Edward Lodewijk Van Halen was born in the Netherlands, on January 26, 1955, the son of Jan and Eugenia Van Halen. Jan was a bandleader, saxophonist, and clarinetist. Both Eddie and his older brother, Alex, were taught classical piano at a young age.

In 1962 the Van Halen family immigrated to the United States with the equivalent of only around $15 and a piano in their possession. Settling in Pasadena, California, Jan, who ultimately developed a drinking problem and died fairly young, held several jobs to support his family, including washing dishes and working as a janitor. On weekends he played saxophone and clarinet at various functions.

In 1965 Alex and Eddie formed their first band, the Broken Combs, which featured Eddie on piano and Alex on saxophone. Although Eddie Van Halen was not into rock music while in Holland, in the United States he became a huge fan.

In 1967, Van Halen bought his first guitar and began practicing on it nightly. In 1971 he attended a Led Zeppelin concert where, after watching that band's guitarist, Jimmy Page, perform, he developed his now-famous "finger tapping" guitar technique. He also formed a new band that went through multiple names and personnel changes before settling the name Van Halen and a line-up that consisted of Eddie on guitar, Alex on drums, Michael Anthony on bass, and David Lee Roth as lead vocalist. (During

one long period of estrangement, Sammy Hagar replaced Roth.)

The band went from playing covers at local venues to selling out arenas as one of the most popular rock acts of all time. They ultimately sold more than fifty-six million albums in the United States, and ten of their studio albums went multi-platinum, with two passing the ten million mark (the band's eponymous debut in 1978, and *1984*, released the year of the title).

In the late 1990s the guitarist, then married to the popular actress Valerie Bertinelli, descended into heavy drinking and drug use, and the band lost its recording contract. He had hip replacement surgery in 1999 and, the following year underwent treatment for tongue cancer. Despite those travails, the band continued to record and tour in various iterations including Hagar, Roth, and Van Halen's teenage son, Wolfgang.

In 2007, the group was inducted into the Rock & Roll Hall of Fame, and the following year Van Halen announced that he had been in rehab and was sober. In 2012, the year *Guitar World Magazine* ranked him number one on its list of the "100 Greatest Guitarists of All Time," the band released *A Different Kind of Truth*, their first new album in more than a dozen years.

In 2019, reports emerged that Van Halen was being treated for throat cancer, and he died on October 6, 2020. He was survived by his second wife, Janie, to whom he had been married since 2009; his son, Wolfgang; and his brother, Alex.

See *Current Biography 2001*

Hans-Jochen Vogel

Born: Göttingen, Germany; February 3, 1926
Died: Munich, Germany; July 26, 2020
Occupation: West German political leader

Hans-Jochen Vogel was considered among the most significant postwar figures in Germany's Social Democratic Party (SPD).

Hans-Jochen Vogel was born on February 3, 1926 in the city of Göttingen in Lower Saxony, where his father, Hermann Vogel, was a university lecturer. As was mandatory under the Nazi regime, Vogel joined the Hitler Youth in his teens. Inducted into the German army in 1943, he served as a noncommissioned officer in Italy but was wounded in a battle near Bologna and taken prisoner.

After the war, Vogel was briefly employed as a transport worker until the reopening of the German universities in 1946 enabled him to study law at Marburg and Munich. In 1948 he passed his preliminary law examination, and in January 1949 he became a Referendar, or junior barrister, in the Bavarian town of Miesbach. That year, he heard Social Democratic leaders speak and was so inspired by their ideas of social reform within a democratic framework that in 1950 he became a member of the Social Democratic party.

Vogel qualified, magna cum laude, in 1950 for his Doctor of Jurisprudence degree, and the following year he completed his final Bavarian state law examination, in first place among 374 candidates. He entered government service, and although he was invited by Willy Brandt, then the mayor of West Berlin, to join his administration, Vogel decided instead to run as a candidate for the Munich city council; he was elected in May 1958.

In October 1959 Vogel was chosen by a Social Democratic conference of delegates as candidate in the forthcoming Bavarian local elections for Oberbürgermeister, or chief mayor, of Munich. Elected on March 27, 1960 with 64.3 percent of the vote, he became, at 34, the youngest chief mayor of a major European city at the time. During the second half of his tenure as Munich's chief mayor, Vogel devoted much of his energy to preparations for the 1972 Olympics.

He was elected chairman of the Bavarian Social Democratic party organization for a five-year term in May 1972, and on expiration of his mayoral term that June, he moved to Bonn, where he was named to the party's presidium. Elected to the federal Bundestag in November 1972, he was appointed to Chancellor Willy Brandt's coalition cabinet.

In the 1983 general election, Vogel was the SPD's candidate for chancellor. Considered by some observers as the most crucial in West Germany since the end of World War II, the election campaign was conducted primarily on economic and defense issues. Despite Vogel's efforts, he lost to Helmut Kohl, an experienced center-right politician.

Vogel headed the SPD from 1987 to 1991, and during his tenure the Berlin Wall fell, and Germany was reunified. He retired fully in 1994 and suffered from Parkinson's disease in his final years. Hans-Jochen Vogel died on July 26, 2020, in Munich. He was mourned by politicians of all stripes, with Chancellor Angela Merkel leading the tributes.

See *Current Biography 1984*

Flossie Wong-Staal

Born: Guangzhou, China; August 27, 1946
Died: San Diego, California; July 8, 2020
Occupation: Molecular biologist

Flossie Wong-Staal was renowned for her discovery of HIV, the virus that causes AIDS.

She was born Yee Ching Wong on August 27, 1946, in Guangzhou, China. Her father, Sueh-Fung, was a textile importer-exporter. Her mother, Wei-Chung (Chor), stayed home to raise her. When she was six the family moved to Hong Kong, where she took on an English name at the request of teachers at her Roman Catholic girls' school. (She wanted to avoid a more common name like Mary or Theresa, and her father suggested Flossie, drawing upon the name of a typhoon that had recently fit the region.)

Although no woman in her family had ever before studied science or worked outside the home, her parents encouraged her academic pursuits, and she came to the United States to attend the University of California, Los Angeles (UCLA), earning a BA in bacteriology in 1968 and a PhD in molecular biology in 1972. The following year she became a research investigator at the National Cancer Institute (NCI), part of the National Institutes of Health (NIH). She was ultimately promoted to section chief of tumor cell biology, and in that capacity, she delved deeply into the study of cancer-causing viruses. Several viruses were then known to cause cancer in animals, but none had been discovered to perform similarly in humans. Wong-Staal focused on retroviruses, which replicate by transmitting genetic information from RNA to DNA—the opposite of the usual process. In 1981, she and her colleague Robert Gallo discovered human T-cell leukemia virus, the first virus proven to cause cancer in humans.

As the first cases of what came to be called acquired immunodeficiency syndrome (AIDS) emerged, she and Gallo discovered that HTLV-3, another virus they had uncovered, caused disease. (HTLV-3 was later renamed human immunodeficiency virus or HIV). A French team made the same discovery at about the same time, setting off a bitter dispute over who should be given credit. She avoided the political infighting, opting instead to continue rigorously studying HIV's biochemical properties, Wong-Staal cloned the virus in 1984 and mapped it genetically, gaining new insights into the progression of the disease.

In 1990, Wong-Staal accepted a post as a professor of biology and medicine at the University of California, San Diego (UCSD), and in 1994, she was named director of the university's Center for AIDS Research, where she led efforts to develop a vaccine and new treatments. She retired from the university in 2002 to become chief scientific officer of a now-defunct biotech company she co-founded. (Originally called Immusol, it was later renamed iTherX Pharmaceuticals, after its focus switched from AIDS to hepatitis C.)

A member of the National Academy of Medicine, she was inducted into the National Women's Hall of Fame a year before her death from pneumonia. While in graduate school she wed oncologist Stephen Staal; that marriage ended in divorce in 1986. She later married neurologist Jeffrey McKelvy, who survives her. She is also survived by her two daughters, Stephanie and Caroline.

See *Current Biography 2001*

CLASSIFICATION BY PROFESSION

ACTIVISM
Perry Bellegarde
Mirna Valerio
Hida Viloria
Xu Zhiyong

ART
Vikky Alexander
Sophie Blackall
William Cordova
Teresita Fernández
Junju Ito
Christine Sun Kim
Kent Monkman
Robin Rhode
Stuart Semple
Mickalene Thomas
Magali Villeneuve

BUSINESS
Mike Adenuga
Abhijit Banerjee
Alex Blumberg
Sukhinder Singh Cassidy
Wendy Clark
Channing Dungey
Adena Friedman
Theresia Gouw
Bert and John Jacobs
Tyshawn Jones
Mikyoung Kim
Karlie Kloss
Oliver Luck
Judith McKenna
Arte Moreno
Adam Mosseri
Lisa Nishimura
Zaza Pachulia
Kelsey Ramsden
Joan Roca
Ted Sarandos
Joseph C. Tsai
Victor Vescovo
Emma Walmsley
Lynda Weinman
Chip Wilson

DANCE
Crystal Pite
Yuan Yuan Tan

EDUCATION
Jennifer Aaker
Abhijit Banerjee
Marcelo Gleiser

Eva Illouz
John Johnson
Satoshi Ōmura
Zephyr Teachout
Mashudu Tshifularo

ENTERTAINMENT
Grayson Boucher

FASHION
Ruth Carter
Guo Pei

FICTION
Sophie Blackall
David Chariandy
Alan Gratz
Junju Ito
Caroline Kepnes
Tom King
Ken Liu
Marjorie Liu
Rebecca Makkai
Heather O'Neill
Jason Reynolds
Namwali Serpell
Efif Shafak
Kim Thúy
Ian Williams

FILM
Stephen Amell
Yalitza Aparicio
Awkwafina
Elizabeth Banks
Ruth Carter
Noah Centineo
Gemma Chan
Jodie Comer
Jai Courtney
Ajay Devgn
Alexander Dreymon
Mamoru Hosoda
Jane Levy
Zoë Kravitz
Richard Mofe-Damijo
Joaquin Phoenix
Yoruba Richen
Maya Rudolph
Naomi Scott
Léa Seydoux
Tiger Shroff
Phyllis Smith
Sebastian Stan
Lakeith Stanfield

Jason Sudeikis
Bonnie Timmermann
Kelly Marie Tran
Lulu Wang
John David Washington
Constance Wu

FOOD
Ted Allen
Alain Ducasse
Asma Khan
Samin Nosrat
Joan Roca
Clare Smyth
Daniela Soto-Innes

GOVERNMENT
Steven Dillingham
John W. Raymond

HISTORY
Marina Rustow

JOURNALISM
Hannah Dreier
Hala Gorani
Phoebe Judge
Ari Melber

LAW
Ari Melber

MEDICINE
Satoshi Ōmura
Peter J. Ratcliffe
Mashudu Tshifularo
Emma Walmsley

MILITARY
David Bellavia

MODELING
Adut Akech
Noah Centineo
Karlie Kloss

MUSIC
Awkwafina
Adrienne Bailon
Lewis Capaldi
Christopher Comstock
Alex Cuba
Marina Diamandis
Billie Eilish
Hildur Guðnadóttir
Christone Ingram
Angélique Kidjo
Zoë Kravitz
Ravyn Lenae
Lil Nas X
Lizzo

Natti Natasha
Tove Lo
Winifred Phillips
Nathaniel Rateliff
Patrice Roberts
Matt Ross-Spang
Daniele Rustioni
Alejandro Sanz
Naomi Scott
Travis Scott
Billy Strings
Brendon Urie
George Watsky

NONFICTION
Ted Allen
David Chariandy
Marcelo Gleiser
Eva Illouz
Robert Macfarlane
Samin Nosrat
Hida Viloria
Lynda Weinman
Tara Westover

ONLINE PERSONALITY
Shane Dawson

PLAYWRIGHT
Jackie Sibblies Drury

POETRY
Jericho Brown
Danez Smith
George Watsky
Ian Williams

POLITICS, FOREIGN
Abiy Ahmed Ali
Perry Bellegarde
Xavier Bettel
Zuzana Čaputová
Marie-Louise Coleiro Preca
Giuseppe Conte
Mette Frederiksen
Kersti Kaljulaid
Sebastian Kurz
Sanna Marin
Mikhail Mishustin
George Osborne
Erna Solberg
Rishi Sunak
Joshua Wong
Salomé Zourabichvili

POLITICS, U.S.
Keisha Lance Bottoms
Kate Brown
Pete Buttigieg
Carmen Yulín Cruz
Sharice Davids

Josh Hawley
Ilhan Omar
Peter J. Ratcliffe
Elise Stefanik
Zephyr Teachout
Gretchen Whitmer
Jumaane Williams

SCIENCE
Jennifer Aaker
Sangeeta N. Bhatia
William C. Campbell
Sean Carroll
Kizzmekia Corbett
Brian Cox
Samantha Cristoforetti
Christian Drosten
Jeremy Farrar
Limor Fried
Jeffrey M. Friedman
Tedros Adhanom Ghebreyesus
Marcelo Gleiser
Rachel Haurwitz
John Johnson
Christina Koch
Arthur B. McDonald
Jessica Meir
Adriana Ocampo
Satoshi Ōmura
Peter Scholze
Victor Vescovo
Heidi Williams
Daniela Witten

SPORTS
Ronald Acuña Jr.
Kimia Alizadeh
Bianca Andreescu
Javier Báez
Saquon Barkley
Ashleigh Barty
Kiki Bertens
Grayson Boucher
Mitchie Brusco
Fletcher Cox
Kendall Coyne Schofield
Allyson Felix
Gennady Golovkin
Phil Heath
Ada Hegerberg
Wim Hof
Alex Honnold
Hou Yifan
Jarrod Jablonski
Tyshawn Jones
Eliud Kipchoge
Jürgen Klopp
Fyodor Konyukhov
Rodrigo Koxa

Joey Logano
Oliver Luck
Lieke Martens
Stipe Miocic
Kento Momota
Arte Moreno
Alyssa Nakken
Kia Nurse
Ryan O'Reilly
Zaza Pachulia
Joe Rogan
Stephen Strasburg
Gleyber Torres
Mirna Valerio

TECHNOLOGY
Adam Mosseri
Katie Moussouris
Lynda Weinman

TELEVISION
Ted Allen
Stephen Amell
Awkwafina
Adrienne Bailon
Elizabeth Banks
Samantha Brown
Ruth Carter
Noah Centineo
Gemma Chan
Jodie Comer
Jai Courtney
Alexander Dreymon
Ree Drummond
Channing Dungey
Sutton Foster
Hala Gorani
Zoë Kravitz
Jane Levy
Ari Melber
Richard Mofe-Damijo
John Mulaney
Lisa Nishimura
Samin Nosrat
Joe Rogan
Maya Rudolph
Phyllis Smith
Sebastian Stan
Jason Sudeikis
Bonnie Timmermann
Kelly Marie Tran
John David Washington
Constance Wu

THEATER
Sutton Foster
John Mulaney
Ivo van Hove

LIST OF PROFILES